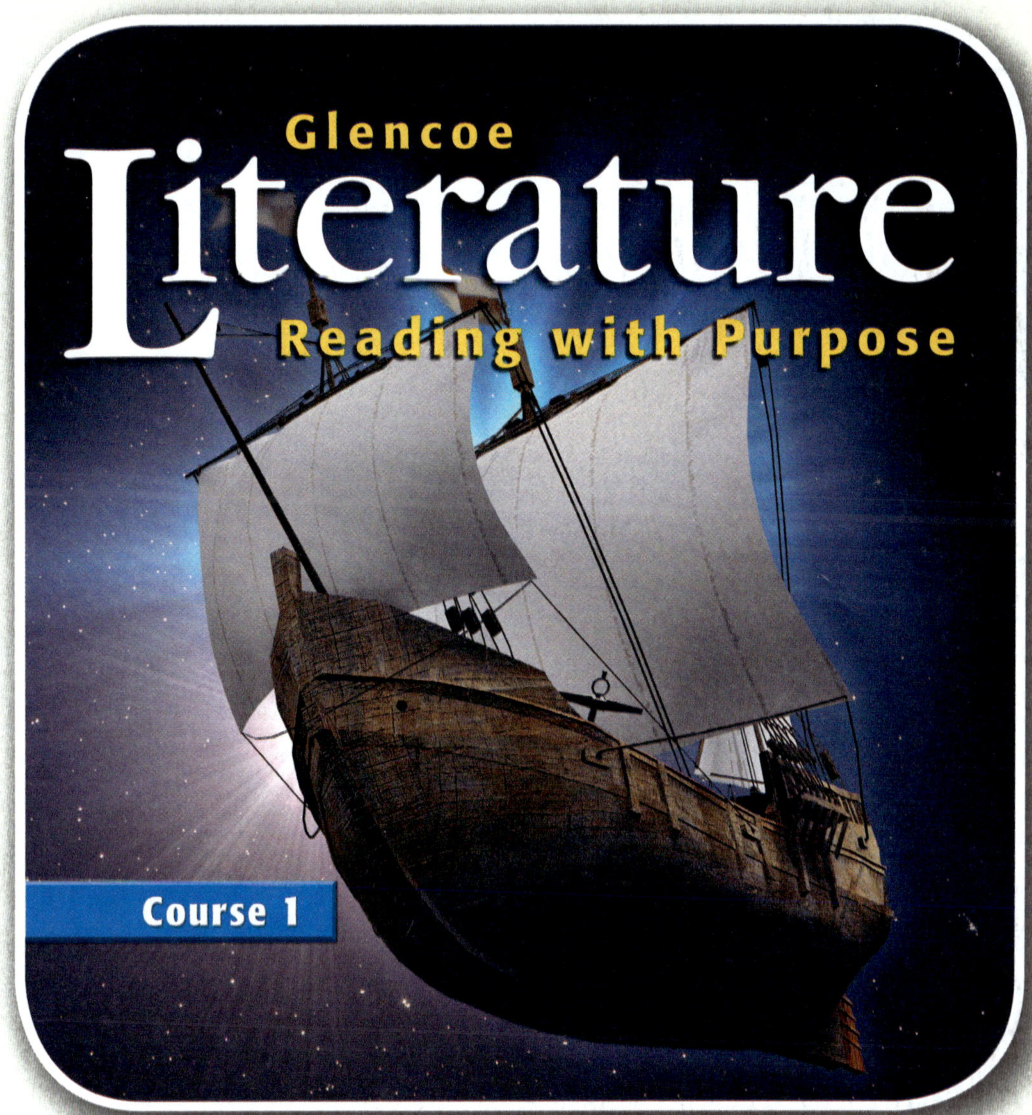

Glencoe Literature
Reading with Purpose

Course 1

Program Consultants

Jeffrey D. Wilhelm, PhD

Douglas Fisher, PhD

Kathleen A. Hinchman, PhD

David O'Brien, PhD

Taffy Raphael, PhD

Cynthia Hynd Shanahan, EdD

New York, New York   Columbus, Ohio   Chicago, Illinois   Peoria, Illinois   Woodland Hills, California

Acknowledgments

Grateful acknowledgment is given authors, publishers, photographers, museums, and agents for permission to reprint the following copyrighted material. Every effort has been made to determine copyright owners. In case of any omissions, the Publisher will be pleased to make suitable acknowledgments in future editions.

Acknowledgments continued on page R83.

Glencoe

The McGraw·Hill Companies

Copyright © 2007 by The McGraw-Hill Companies, Inc. All rights reserved. Except as permitted under the United States Copyright Act of 1976, no part of this publication may be reproduced or distributed in any form or by any means, or stored in a database or retrieval system, without prior permission of the publisher.

TIME © TIME, Inc. TIME and the red border design are trademarks of TIME, Inc. used under license.

Send all inquiries to:
Glencoe/McGraw-Hill
8787 Orion Place
Columbus, OH 43240-4027

ISBN-13 (student edition): 978-0-07-845476-9
ISBN-10 (student edition): 0-07-845476-X
ISBN-13 (teacher wraparound edition): 978-0-07-845487-5
ISBN-10 (teacher wraparound edition): 0-07-845487-5

Printed in the United States of America.

2 3 4 5 6 7 8 9   079/111   12 11 10 09 08 07 06

Program Consultants

Senior Program Consultants

Jeffrey D. Wilhelm, PhD Jeffrey Wilhelm is Professor of English Education at Boise State University and Director of the Boise State Writing Project. He specializes in reading and adolescent literacy and does research on ways to engage readers and writers. A middle and high school teacher for thirteen years, Wilhelm is author or coauthor of eleven books, including the award-winning works *You Gotta BE the Book* and *Reading Don't Fix No Chevys.*

Douglas Fisher, PhD Douglas Fisher is Professor of Language and Literacy Education at San Diego State University. He is also Director of the award-winning City Heights Educational Pilot, a project for improving urban adolescent literacy. Fisher has published many articles on reading and literacy and has coauthored *Improving Adolescent Literacy: Strategies that Work.*

Program Consultants

Kathleen A. Hinchman, PhD Kathleen Hinchman is Professor and Chair, Reading and Language Arts Center, School of Education, Syracuse University. A former middle school English and reading teacher, Hinchman researches social perspectives toward literacy. She is coauthor of three books on reading and literacy, including *Principled Practices of a Literate America: A Framework for Literacy and Learning in the Upper Grades.*

David G. O'Brien, PhD David O'Brien is Professor of Literacy Education at the University of Minnesota and a former classroom teacher. O'Brien's research explores reading in content areas as well as ways to motivate learners to engage in school-based literacy tasks. He is conducting studies on the use of technology-based literacy, using computers and related technology.

Taffy Raphael, PhD Taffy Raphael is Professor of Literacy Education at the University of Illinois at Chicago (UIC). She does literacy research on upper elementary and middle school students and has coauthored several books, including *Book Club: A Literature-Based Curriculum* and *Book Club for Middle School.* She has received the International Reading Association (IRA) Outstanding Educator Award and is in the IRA Hall of Fame.

Cynthia Hynd Shanahan, EdD Cynthia Hynd Shanahan is Professor in the Reading, Writing, and Literacy program at the University of Illinois at Chicago (UIC). She is also a consultant with the Center for Literacy at UIC. Hynd Shanahan has been a classroom teacher and has taught reading instruction to elementary-level through college-level teachers. She has authored a chapter in the book *Engaged Reading,* edited by John T. Guthrie and Donna Alverman.

Advisory Board

Special Consultants

FOLDABLE Dinah Zike, MEd Dinah Zike was a classroom teacher and a consultant for many years before she began to develop Foldables™—a variety of easily created graphic organizers. Zike has written and developed more than 150 supplemental books and materials used in classrooms worldwide. Her *Big Book of Books and Activities* won the Teacher's Choice Award.

Mary A. Avalos, PhD Mary Avalos is Assistant Professor and Director of the TESOL Graduate Program at the University of Miami, Coral Gables, Florida. Her contributions to TESOL books include "No Two Learners Are Alike: Readers with Linguistic and Cultural Differences," in *Reading Assessment and Instruction for All Learners,* by J. S. Schrum (ed.) Avalos is a frequent presenter at reading and TESOL conferences.

Glencoe National Reading and Language Arts Advisory Council

Wanda J. Blanchett, PhD
Associate Dean for Academic Affairs and Associate Professor of Exceptional Education
School of Education
University of Wisconsin-Milwaukee
Milwaukee, Wisconsin

William G. Brozo, PhD
Professor of Literacy
Graduate School of Education, College of Education and Human Development
George Mason University
Fairfax, Virginia

Nancy Drew, EdD
LaPointe Educational Consultants
Corpus Christi, Texas 78411

Susan Floria-Ruane, EdD
Professor, College of Education
Michigan State University
East Lansing, Michigan

Nancy Frey, PhD
Associate Professor of Literacy in Teacher Education
School of Teacher Education
San Diego State University
San Diego, California

Kimberly Lawless, PhD
Associate Professor
Curriculum, Instruction and Evaluation
College of Education
University of Illinois at Chicago
Chicago, Illinois

Sharon Fontenot O'Neal, PhD
Associate Professor
Texas State University
San Marcos, Texas

William Ray, MA
Lincoln-Sudbury Regional High School
Sudbury, Massachusetts

Victoria Gentry Ridgeway, PhD
Associate Professor
Reading Education
Clemson University
Clemson, South Carolina

Janet Saito-Furukawa, MEd
Literacy Coach
Washington Irving Middle School
Los Angeles, California

Bonnie Valdes, MEd
Independent Reading Consultant
CRISS Master Trainer
Largo, Florida

Teacher Reviewers

The following teachers contributed to the review of *Glencoe Literature*.

Bridget M. Agnew
St. Michael School
Chicago, IL

Monica Anzaldua Araiza
Dr. Juliet V. Garcia Middle School
Brownsville, TX

Katherine R. Baer
Howard County Public Schools
Ellicott City, MD

Tanya Baxter
Roald Amundsen High School
Chicago, IL

Danielle R. Brain
Thomas R. Proctor Senior High School
Utica, NY

Yolanda Conder
Owasso Mid-High School
Owasso, OK

Gwenn De Mauriac
The Wiscasset Schools
Wiscasset, ME

Courtney Doan
Bloomington High School
Bloomington, IL

Susan M. Griffin
Edison Preparatory School
Tulsa, OK

Cindi Davis Harris
Helix Charter High School
La Mesa, CA

Joseph F. Hutchinson
Toledo Public Schools
Toledo, OH

Ginger Jordan
Florien High School
Florien, LA

Dianne Konkel
Cypress Lake Middle School
Fort Myers, FL

Melanie A. LaFleur
Many High School
Many, LA

Patricia Lee
Radnor Middle School
Wayne, PA

Linda Copley Lemons
Cleveland High School
Cleveland, TN

Heather S. Lewis
Waverly Middle School
Lansing, MI

Sandra C. Lott
Aiken Optional School
Alexandria, LA

Connie M. Malacarne
O'Fallon Township High School
O'Fallon, IL

Lori Howton Means
Edward A. Fulton Junior High School
O'Fallon, IL

Claire C. Meitl
Howard County Public Schools
Ellicott City, MD

Patricia P. Mitcham
Mohawk High School (Retired)
New Castle, PA

Lisa Morefield
South-Western Career Academy
Grove City, OH

Kevin M. Morrison
Hazelwood East High School
St. Louis, MO

Jenine M. Pokorak
School Without Walls Senior
High School, Washington, D.C.

Susan Winslow Putnam
Butler High School
Matthews, NC

Paul C. Putnoki
Torrington Middle School
Torrington, CT

Stephanie L. Robin
N. P. Moss Middle School
Lafayette, LA

Ann C. Ryan
Lindenwold High School
Lindenwold, NJ

Pamela Schoen
Hopkins High School
Minnetonka, MN

Megan Schumacher
Friends' Central School
Wynnewood, PA

Fareeda J. Shabazz
Paul Revere Elementary School
Chicago, IL

Molly Steinlage
Brookpark Middle School
Grove City, OH

Barry Stevenson
Garnet Valley Middle School
Glen Mills, PA

Paul Stevenson
Edison Preparatory School
Tulsa, OK

Jane Thompson Rae
Cab Calloway High School of the Arts
Wilmington, DE

Kathy Thompson
Owasso Mid-High School
Owasso, OK

Book Overview

How to Use *Reading with Purpose* xxx
Foldables™ xxxvi
Scavenger Hunt xxxvii
Reading Handbook RH1

UNIT 1 — Why Read? . . . 1
- **Genre Focus:** Informational Media
- **Reading Skills:** Setting a Purpose for Reading, Skimming and Scanning, Understanding Graphics, Identifying Main Idea and Supporting Details
- **Text and Literary Elements:** Text Features, Titles and Subheads, Process, Author's Purpose
- **Writing Product:** Summary
- **English Language Coach:** Word References, Multiple-Meaning Words
- **Grammar:** Parts of Speech, Verbs

UNIT 2 — What Brings Out the Best in You? . . . 114
- **Genre Focus:** Biography/Autobiography
- **Reading Skills:** Activating Prior Knowledge, Connecting, Predicting, Questioning
- **Literary Elements:** Narrator, Point of View, Chronological Order, Tone
- **Writing Product:** Autobiographical Narrative
- **English Language Coach:** Synonyms, Antonyms, Negating Prefixes, Word Choice
- **Grammar:** Nouns, Pronouns

UNIT 3 — What's Fair and What's Not? . . . 252
- **Genre Focus:** Persuasive Writing
- **Reading Skills:** Distinguishing Fact and Opinion, Clarifying, Inferring, Identifying Problems and Solutions
- **Literary Elements:** Author's Style, Bias, Argument, Mood
- **Writing Product:** Persuasive Essay
- **English Language Coach:** Denotation/Connotation, Synonyms and Shades of Meaning, Semantic Slanting
- **Grammar:** Adjectives, Adverbs, Other Parts of Speech

UNIT 4 — What Makes You Who You Are? . . . 370
- **Genre Focus:** Poetry
- **Reading Skills:** Visualizing, Responding, Interpreting, Monitoring Comprehension
- **Literary Elements:** Poetic Features, Sound Devices, Rhythm, Rhyme, and Meter, Figurative Language
- **Writing Product:** Poetry
- **English Language Coach:** Context Clues, Definition and Restatement, Comparison and Contrast, Examples
- **Grammar:** Sentences, Fragments, Subject/Predicate, Direct and Indirect Objects

UNIT 5 How Should You Deal with Bullies?..........480
- **Genre Focus:** Short Story
- **Reading Skills:** Drawing Conclusions, Understanding Cause and Effect, Identifying Sequence, Paraphrasing and Summarizing
- **Literary Elements:** Dialogue, Conflict, Plot, Characterization
- **Writing Product:** Short Story
- **English Language Coach:** Base Words, Prefixes, Suffixes, Roots
- **Grammar:** Phrases, Independent and Dependent Clauses, Commas

UNIT 6 What Makes a Hero?..........614
- **Genre Focus:** Folktale, Fantasy, and Myth
- **Reading Skills:** Activating Prior Knowledge, Clarifying, Comparing and Contrasting, Predicting
- **Literary Elements:** Hero, Cultural Context, Theme, Setting
- **Writing Product:** Fable
- **English Language Coach:** Compound Words, Borrowed Words, Word Histories
- **Grammar:** Capitalization, Sentence Combining, Run-on Sentences, Commas in Sentences

UNIT 7 What Can We Learn from Our Mistakes?..........772
- **Genre Focus:** Historical Fiction and Nonfiction
- **Reading Skills:** Synthesizing, Identifying Main Idea and Supporting Details, Evaluating, Inferring
- **Literary Elements:** Symbol, Narrator, Description, Time Order/Sequence
- **Writing Product:** Personal Narrative
- **English Language Coach:** Base Words and Roots, Latin Roots, Greek Roots, Anglo-Saxon Origins
- **Grammar:** Subject-Verb Agreement

UNIT 8 What Makes a Friend?..........926
- **Genre Focus:** Drama
- **Reading Skills:** Visualizing, Clarifying, Skimming and Scanning, Predicting
- **Literary Elements:** Act and Scene, Characterization, Stage Directions, Sensory Imagery
- **Writing Product:** Speech
- **English Language Coach:** Dialect and Slang, Literal/Figurative Meanings, Historical Influences on English, Idioms
- **Grammar:** Hyphens, Colons, Semicolons, Quotation Marks

Reference Section

Author Files R1	Study and Test-Taking Skills Handbook . . . R49
Foldables R8	Glossary/Glosario R54
Literary Terms Handbook R10	Index of Skills R70
Writing Handbook R17	Index of Authors and Titles R79
Language Handbook R28	Index of Art and Artists R81
Listening, Speaking, and Viewing Handbook R45	Acknowledgments R83

Contents

UNIT 1

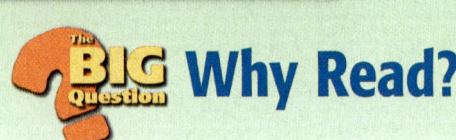 **Why Read?** 1

Genre Focus: Informational Media

Reading Skills Focus
Setting a Purpose for Reading
Skimming and Scanning
Understanding Graphics
Identifying Main Idea and
   Supporting Details

Text Elements
Text and Literary Features
Titles and Subheads
Process
Author's Purpose

Vocabulary Skills
Word References
Multiple-Meaning Words

Grammar
Parts of Speech
Verbs

WARM-UP 2

Genre Focus: Informational Media 4

Sally S. Stich **Animal Attraction** . . . . *Informational Text:* Magazine Article . . . 6

READING WORKSHOP 1

Skill Lesson: Setting a Purpose for Reading 8

Consumer Reports 4 Kids **Ballpark Food** . . . . *Informational Text:* Web Article . . . 12

Amy Bertrand **How He Did It: Health Advice, Kid-to-Kid** . . *Informational Text:* Web Article . . . 20

WRITING WORKSHOP PART 1

Summary 26
Applying Good Writing Traits: Ideas 27
Grammar Link: Verbs 29

viii

Contents

READING WORKSHOP 2
Skill Lesson: Skimming and Scanning 30

Kathryn R. Hoffman	**Messaging Mania**	Informational Text: Magazine Article . . . 34
Nancy Gibbs	**The Real Magic of Harry Potter** . .	Informational Text: TIME Magazine Article . . 42

READING WORKSHOP 3
Skill Lesson: Understanding Graphics 48

Uncredited	**Make Your Own Kite**	Informational Text: Instructions . . . 52
Jeff Smith	**from *The Great Cow Race***	Graphic Story . . . 58

WRITING WORKSHOP PART 2
Summary 64
Listening, Speaking, Viewing: Getting Information from Visuals 67

READING WORKSHOP 4
Skill Lesson: Identifying Main Idea and Supporting Details 68

Gwendolyn Brooks	**To Young Readers**	Poem . . . 72
Neil Gaiman	**Why Books Are Dangerous**	Personal Essay . . . 78

COMPARING LITERATURE WORKSHOP
Comparing Literature: Author's Purpose 84

Judith Viorst	**The Southpaw**	Short Story . . . 88
Mary Helen Ponce	**Concha**	Short Story . . . 93

WRAP-UP
. . . . 100

Your Turn: Read and Apply Skills

Kristin Hunter	**The Scribe**	Short Story . . 102

Reading on Your Own 108
Skills and Strategies Assessment 110

Contents

UNIT 2

 **What Brings Out the Best in You?** 114

Genre Focus: Biography/Autobiography

Reading Skills Focus
Activating Prior Knowledge
Connecting
Predicting
Questioning

Literary Elements
Narrator
Point of View
Tone
Chronological Order

Vocabulary Skills
Synonyms
Antonyms
Negating Prefixes
Word Choice

Grammar
Nouns
Pronouns

WARM-UP		116
Genre Focus: Biography/Autobiography		118
Jim Haskins **Madam C. J. Walker** . . . . Biography . .		119
READING WORKSHOP 1		
Skill Lesson: Activating Prior Knowledge		126
Gary Soto **The Jacket** . . . . Autobiography . .		130
Nikki Giovanni **The World Is Not a Pleasant Place to Be** . . . . Poem . .		139
WRITING WORKSHOP PART 1		
Autobiographical Narrative		142
Applying Good Writing Traits: Conventions		144
Grammar Link: Nouns		145

Contents

READING WORKSHOP 2

Skill Lesson: Connecting 146

Bill Littlefield	**Satchel Paige**	Biography	150
Sara Van Alstyne Allen	**Song for a Surf-Rider**	Poem	161

READING WORKSHOP 3

Skill Lesson: Predicting 164

William Jay Jacobs	**Eleanor Roosevelt**	Biography	168
Uncredited	**In Eleanor Roosevelt's Time**	Informational Text: Timeline	180

WRITING WORKSHOP PART 2

Autobiographical Narrative 184

Listening, Speaking, Viewing: Active Listening in a Group Discussion 187

READING WORKSHOP 4

Skill Lesson: Questioning 188

Alice Park	**Gentleman of the Pool**	Informational Text: TIME Magazine Article	192
Judith Ortiz Cofer	**Primary Lessons**	Autobiography	198

COMPARING LITERATURE WORKSHOP

Comparing Literature: Character 208

Paul Zindel	**from *The Pigman & Me***	Autobiography	211
Avi	**The Goodness of Matt Kaizer**	Short Story	221

WRAP-UP 236

Your Turn: Read and Apply Skills

Mary Whitebird	**Ta-Na-E-Ka**	Short Story	238

Reading on Your Own 246

Skills and Strategies Assessment 248

Contents

UNIT 3

 What's Fair and What's Not? 252

Genre Focus: Persuasive Writing

Reading Skills Focus
Distinguishing Fact and Opinion
Clarifying
Inferring
Identifying Problems and Solutions

Vocabulary Skills
Denotation/Connotation
Synonyms and Shades of Meaning
Semantic Slanting

Literary Elements
Author's Style
Bias
Argument
Mood

Grammar
Adjectives
Adverbs
Other Parts of Speech

WARM-UP 254

Genre Focus: Persuasive Writing 256

Sojourner Truth — **And Ain't I a Woman?** . . . . Speech . . 257

READING WORKSHOP 1

Skill Lesson: Distinguishing Fact and Opinion 260

Richard Durbin — **Preserving a Great American Symbol** . . . . . Speech . . 264
Elizabeth Partridge — **Looking for America** . . . . Essay . . 270

WRITING WORKSHOP PART 1

Persuasive Essay 278
Applying Good Writing Traits: Sentence Fluency 280
Grammar Link: Adjectives and Adverbs 281

xii

Contents

READING WORKSHOP 2

	Skill Lesson: Clarifying		282
Uncredited	**Two Advertisements**	Functional Document: Advertisements	286
Cynthia Rylant	**Stray**	Short Story	292

READING WORKSHOP 3

	Skill Lesson: Inferring		298
Melanie Bertotto	**Dressed for Success?**	Informational Text: TIME Magazine Article	302
Sandra Cisneros	**Eleven**	Short Story	308

WRITING WORKSHOP PART 2

Persuasive Essay		314
Listening, Speaking, Viewing: Effective Speaking		317

READING WORKSHOP 4

	Skill Lesson: Identifying Problems and Solutions		318
The Earth Works Group	**from *50 Simple Things Kids Can Do to Save the Earth***	Informational Text: Book	322
Jane Yolen	**Greyling**	Short Story	328

COMPARING LITERATURE WORKSHOP

	Comparing Literature: Conflict		336
Marta Salinas	**The Scholarship Jacket**	Short Story	339
Francisco Jiménez	**The Circuit**	Short Story	347

WRAP-UP ... 356

Your Turn: Read and Apply Skills

Ray Bradbury	**All Summer in a Day**	Short Story	358
	Reading on Your Own		364
	Skills and Strategies Assessment		366

xiii

Contents

UNIT 4

The BIG Question: What Makes You Who You Are? 370

Genre Focus: Poetry

Reading Skills Focus
Visualizing
Responding
Interpreting
Monitoring Comprehension

Vocabulary Skills
Context Clues
(Definition and Restatement,
   Comparison and Contrast,
   Examples)

Literary Elements
Poetic Features
Sound Devices
Rhythm, Rhyme, and Meter
Figurative Language

Grammar
Sentences
Fragments
Subject/Predicate
Direct and Indirect
   Objects

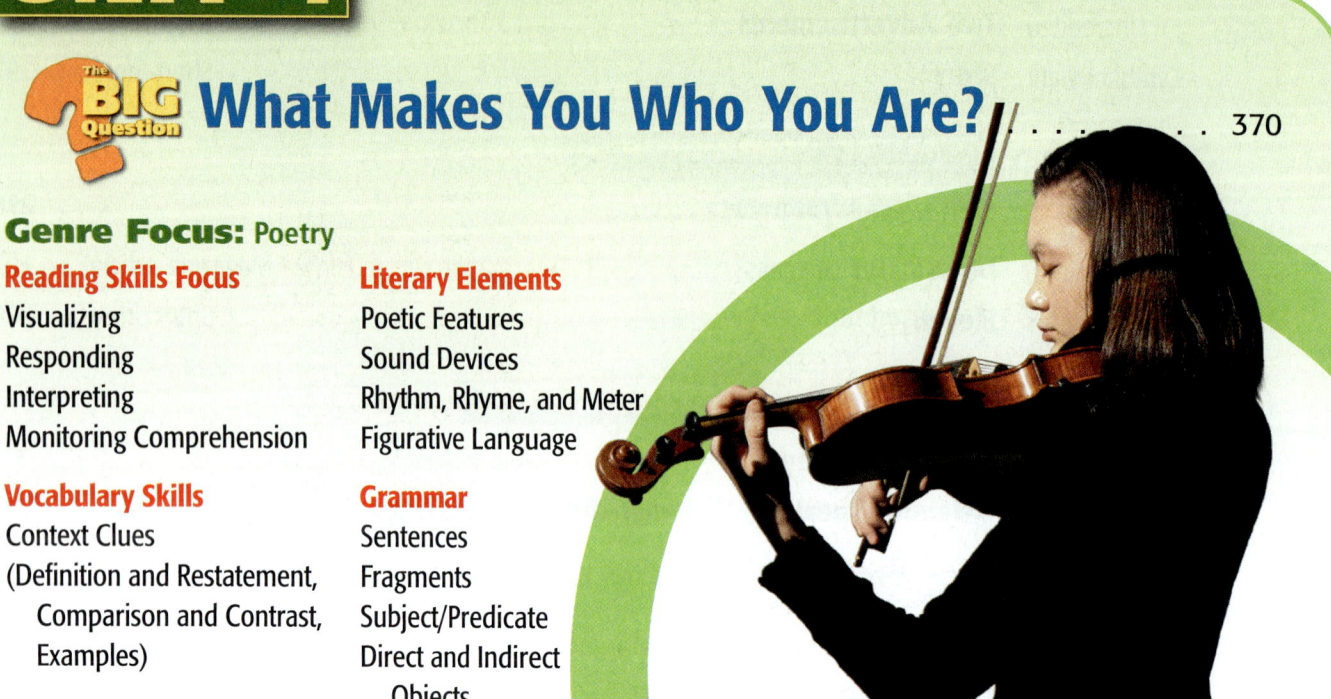

WARM-UP 372

Genre Focus: Poetry 374

Shel Silverstein — **Whatif** .... Poem .. 375

READING WORKSHOP 1

Skill Lesson: Visualizing 376

Luis Omar Salinas — **My Father Is a Simple Man** .... Poem .. 380
Lensey Namioka — **The All-American Slurp** .... Short Story .. 386

WRITING WORKSHOP PART 1

Poetry 398
Applying Good Writing Traits: Word Choice 400
Grammar Link: Complete Sentences 401

xiv

Contents

READING WORKSHOP 2

Skill Lesson: Responding 402

| Maya Angelou | **Life Doesn't Frighten Me** . . . . Poem . . 406 |
| Toni Cade Bambara | **Geraldine Moore the Poet** . . . . Short Story . . 412 |

READING WORKSHOP 3

Skill Lesson: Interpreting 420

| Pat Mora | **Same Song** . . . . Poem . . 424 |
| Elizabeth Ellis | **Flowers and Freckle Cream** . . . . Short Story . . 430 |

WRITING WORKSHOP PART 2

Poetry 436
Listening, Speaking, Viewing: Reading Poetry Aloud 439

READING WORKSHOP 4

Skill Lesson: Monitoring Comprehension 440

| Robert Service | **The March of the Dead** . . . . Poem . . 444 |
| Jordan Brown | **The Gene Scene** . . . . Informational Text: TIME Magazine Article . . 452 |

COMPARING LITERATURE WORKSHOP

Comparing Literature: Figurative Language 458

| e. e. cummings | **maggie and milly and molly and may** . . . . Poem . . 461 |
| Eloise Greenfield | **Daydreamers** . . . . Poem . . 463 |

WRAP-UP 468

Your Turn: Read and Apply Skills

| Lewis Carroll | **The Walrus and the Carpenter** . . . . Poem . . 470 |

Reading on Your Own 474

Skills and Strategies Assessment 476

xv

Contents

UNIT 5

The BIG Question: How Should You Deal with Bullies? 480

Genre Focus: Short Story

Reading Skills Focus
Drawing Conclusions
Understanding Cause and Effect
Identifying Sequence
Paraphrasing and Summarizing

Literary Elements
Dialogue
Conflict
Plot
Characterization

Grammar
Phrases
Independent and Dependent Clauses
Commas

Vocabulary Skills
Base Words   Prefixes
Suffixes   Roots

	WARM-UP	482
	Genre Focus: Short Story	484
Rona Maynard	**The Fan Club** ..... Short Story ..	485
	READING WORKSHOP 1	
	Skill Lesson: Drawing Conclusions	494
Will Eisner	**Street Magic** ..... Graphic Story ..	498
Uncredited	**What Kids Say About Bullying** ..... Informational Text: Web Article ..	510
	WRITING WORKSHOP PART 1	
	Short Story	516
	Applying Good Writing Traits: Organization	517
	Grammar Link: Independent and Dependent Clauses	519

xvi

Contents

READING WORKSHOP 2

Skill Lesson: Understanding Cause and Effect 520

Norma Fox Mazer	**Tuesday of the Other June** .... Short Story	524
Stephen Spender	**My Parents** .... Poem	540

READING WORKSHOP 3

Skill Lesson: Identifying Sequence 544

Richard Peck	**Priscilla and the Wimps** .... Short Story	548
Ritu Upadhyay *and* Andrea DeSimone	**Let the Bullies Beware** .... Informational Text: TIME Magazine Article	556

WRITING WORKSHOP PART 2

Short Story 562

Listening, Speaking, Viewing: Reading Aloud 565

READING WORKSHOP 4

Skill Lesson: Paraphrasing and Summarizing 566

Ellen Conford	**Don't Let the Bedbugs Bite** .... Short Story	570
Jack Prelutsky	**The New Kid on the Block** .... Poem	583

READING ACROSS TEXTS WORKSHOP

Comparing Solutions 586

Jon Swartz	**Bullies in the Park** .... Informational Text: Magazine Article	589
Elizabeth Siris	**The Bully Battle** .... Informational Text: Magazine Article	593

WRAP-UP 598

Your Turn: Read and Apply Skills

Charles J. Finger	**El Enano** .... Short Story	600

Reading on Your Own 608

Skills and Strategies Assessment 610

Contents

UNIT 6

 **What Makes a Hero?** 614

Genre Focus: Folktale, Fantasy, and Myth

Reading Skills Focus
Activating Prior
  Knowledge
Clarifying
Comparing
  and Contrasting
Predicting

Vocabulary Skills
Compound Words
Borrowed Words
Word Histories

Literary Elements
Hero
Cultural Context
Theme
Setting

Grammar
Capitalization
Sentence Combining
Run-on Sentences
Commas in Sentences

	WARM-UP	616
	Genre Focus: Folktale, Fantasy, and Myth	618
Alice Low	**Persephone** .... Myth ..	619
	READING WORKSHOP 1	
	Skill Lesson: Activating Prior Knowledge	624
Thomas Fields-Meyer, Steve Helling, Lori Rozsa	**Hurricane Heroes** .... Informational Text: TIME Magazine Article ..	628
Harold Courlander	**All Stories Are Anansi's** .... Folktale ..	636
	WRITING WORKSHOP PART 1	
	Fable	642
	Applying Good Writing Traits: Voice	644
	Grammar Link: Compound and Complex Sentences	645

xviii

Contents

READING WORKSHOP 2

Skill Lesson: Clarifying 646

Walker Brents	**The Twelve Labors of Hercules**	Myth	650
Mary Pope Osborne	**Pecos Bill**	Folktale	660

READING WORKSHOP 3

Skill Lesson: Comparing and Contrasting 670

John Gardner	**Dragon, Dragon**	Fantasy	674
Jack London	**The King of Mazy May**	Short Story	688

WRITING WORKSHOP PART 2

Fable 702
Listening, Speaking, Viewing: Storytelling 705

READING WORKSHOP 4

Skill Lesson: Predicting 706

Mary Steele	**Aunt Millicent**	Short Story	710
Clifton Davis	**A Mason-Dixon Memory**	Personal Essay	734

COMPARING LITERATURE WORKSHOP

Comparing Heroes 744

Toni Cade Bambara	**The Toad and the Donkey**	Folktale	748
Virginia Hamilton	**Doc Rabbit, Bruh Fox, and Tar Baby**	Folktale	751

WRAP-UP 758

Your Turn: Read and Apply Skills

Alma Luz Villanueva	**The Sand Castle**	Fantasy	760

Reading on Your Own 766
Skills and Strategies Assessment 768

Contents

UNIT 7

 **What Can We Learn from Our Mistakes?** . . 772

Genre Focus: Historical Fiction and Nonfiction

Reading Skills Focus
Synthesizing
Identifying Main Idea and
    Supporting Details
Evaluating
Inferring

Vocabulary Skills
Base Words and Roots
Latin Roots
Greek Roots
Anglo-Saxon Origins

Literary Elements
Symbol
Narrator
Description
Time Order/Sequence

Grammar
Subject-Verb
    Agreement

	WARM-UP 774
	Genre Focus: Historical Fiction and Nonfiction. 776
San Francisco Chronicle	**The Great Radio Scare** . . . . Informational Text: Historical News Article . . 777
	READING WORKSHOP 1
	Skill Lesson: Synthesizing 782
Mildred D. Taylor	**The Gold Cadillac** . . . . Short Story . . 786
Sue Alexander	**Nadia the Willful** . . . . Short Story . . 806
	WRITING WORKSHOP PART 1
	Personal Narrative 814
	Applying Good Writing Traits: Voice 816
	Grammar Link: Subject-Verb Agreement 817

xx

Contents

READING WORKSHOP 2

Skill Lesson: Identifying Main Idea and Supporting Details 818

Yoshiko Uchida	**The Bracelet**	Short Story	822
Dorothy M. Johnson	**Too Soon a Woman**	Historical Fiction	832

READING WORKSHOP 3

Skill Lesson: Evaluating 840

Robert Cormier	**President Cleveland, Where Are You?**	Short Story	844
David Fischer	**Nobody's Perfect**	Informational Text: TIME Magazine Article	860

WRITING WORKSHOP PART 2

Personal Narrative 866
Listening, Speaking, Viewing: News Report 869

READING WORKSHOP 4

Skill Lesson: Inferring 870

Patricia C. McKissack and Frederick McKissack, Jr.	**The Shutout**	Informational Text: Historical Nonfiction	874
Donna L. Washington	**The Talking Skull**	Folktale	884

READING ACROSS TEXTS WORKSHOP

Comparing Author's Credibility 894

Jim Murphy	**from The Great Fire**	Informational Text: Historical Nonfiction	897
Justin and Fannie Belle Becker	**Letters About the Fire**	Historical Document	905

WRAP-UP
. . . . 910

Your Turn: Read and Apply Skills

Stan Sakai	**A Lesson in Courtesy**	Graphic Story	912

Reading on Your Own 920
Skills and Strategies Assessment 922

Contents

UNIT 8

BIG Question: What Makes a Friend? 926

Genre Focus: Drama

Reading Skills Focus
Visualizing
Clarifying
Skimming and Scanning
Predicting

Literary Elements
Act and Scene
Characterization
Stage Directions
Sensory Imagery

Vocabulary Skills
Dialect and Slang
Clipped Words
Literal/Figurative Meanings
Idioms

Grammar
Hyphens
Semicolons
Colons
Quotation Marks

WARM-UP 928

Genre Focus: Drama 930

Gary Soto — **from *Novio Boy*** .... Drama .. 931

READING WORKSHOP 1

Skill Lesson: Visualizing 938

Kenneth Grahame — **The Reluctant Dragon, Scene 1** .... Drama .. 942
Kenneth Grahame — **The Reluctant Dragon, Scene 2** .... Drama .. 954

WRITING WORKSHOP PART 1

Speech 966
Applying Good Writing Traits: Presentation 968
Grammar Link: Apostrophes 969

xxii

Contents

READING WORKSHOP 2

Skill Lesson: Clarifying 970

Fan Kissen	**Damon and Pythias**	Drama ..	974
Joe Smith	**Charlie Johnson**	Short Story ..	988

READING WORKSHOP 3

Skill Lesson: Skimming and Scanning 996

Eric Alter	**The Bully of Barksdale Street**	Drama ..	1000
Christina Hamlett	**Tales of the Tangled Tresses**	Drama ..	1016

WRITING WORKSHOP PART 2

Speech 1032
Listening, Speaking, Viewing: Oral Presentation 1035

READING WORKSHOP 4

Skill Lesson: Predicting 1036

Isaac Bashevis Singer	**Zlateh the Goat**	Short Story ..	1040
Kevin Gray *and* Cindy Dampier	**Best of Buddies**	Informational Text: TIME Magazine Article ..	1052

READING ACROSS TEXTS WORKSHOP

Comparing Primary and Secondary Source Documents 1056

Catherine Clarke Fox	**Baby Hippo Orphan Finds a Friend**	Informational Text: Web Site ..	1059
Stephen Tuei	**from *The Caretaker's Diary***	Informational Text: Web Journal ..	1063

WRAP-UP 1072

Your Turn: Read and Apply Skills

Robert Frost	**A Time to Talk**	Poem ..	1074

Reading on Your Own 1076
Skills and Strategies Assessment 1078

xxiii

Selections by Genre

Fiction

The Southpaw 88
Judith Viorst

Concha 93
Mary Helen Ponce

The Scribe 102
Kristin Hunter

The Goodness of Matt Kaizer 221
Avi

Ta-Na-E-Ka 238
Mary Whitebird

Stray 292
Cynthia Rylant

Eleven 308
Sandra Cisneros

Greyling 328
Jane Yolen

The Scholarship Jacket 339
Marta Salinas

The Circuit 347
Francisco Jiménez

All Summer in a Day 358
Ray Bradbury

The All-American Slurp 386
Lensey Namioka

Geraldine Moore the Poet 412
Toni Cade Bambara

Flowers and Freckle Cream 430
Elizabeth Ellis

The Fan Club 485
Rona Maynard

Tuesday of the Other June 524
Norma Fox Mazer

Priscilla and the Wimps 548
Richard Peck

Don't Let the Bedbugs Bite 570
Ellen Conford

El Enano 600
Charles J. Finger

Dragon, Dragon 674
John Gardner

The King of Mazy May 688
Jack London

Aunt Millicent 710
Mary Steele

The Sand Castle 760
Alma Luz Villanueva

The Gold Cadillac 786
Mildred D. Taylor

Nadia the Willful 806
Sue Alexander

The Bracelet 822
Yoshiko Uchida

Too Soon a Woman 832
Dorothy M. Johnson

President Cleveland, Where Are You? 844
Robert Cormier

Charlie Johnson 988
Joe Smith

Zlateh the Goat 1040
Isaac Bashevis Singer

Poetry

To Young Readers 72
Gwendolyn Brooks

The World Is Not a Pleasant Place to Be 139
Nikki Giovanni

Song for a Surf-Rider 161
Sara Van Alstyne Allen

xxiv

Selections by Genre

Whatif 375
Shel Silverstein

My Father Is a Simple Man 380
Luis Omar Salinas

A Minor Bird 399
Robert Frost

Life Doesn't Frighten Me 406
Maya Angelou

Same Song 424
Pat Mora

The March of the Dead 444
Robert Service

maggie and milly and molly and may 461
e. e. cummings

Daydreamers 463
Eloise Greenfield

The Walrus and the Carpenter 470
Lewis Carroll

My Parents 540
Stephen Spender

The New Kid on the Block 583
Jack Prelutsky

A Time to Talk 1074
Robert Frost

Drama

from Novio Boy 931
Gary Soto

The Reluctant Dragon, Scene 1 942
Kenneth Grahame

The Reluctant Dragon, Scene 2 954
Kenneth Grahame

Damon and Pythias 974
Fan Kissen

The Bully of Barksdale Street 1000
Eric Alter

Tale of the Tangled Tresses 1016
Christina Hamlett

Folktales

Persephone 619
Alice Low

All Stories Are Anansi's 636
Harold Courlander

The Twelve Labors of Hercules 650
Walker Brents

Pecos Bill 660
Mary Pope Osborne

The Toad and the Donkey 748
Toni Cade Bambara

Doc Rabbit, Bruh Fox, and Tar Baby 751
Virginia Hamilton

The Talking Skull 884
Donna L. Washington

Graphic Stories and Cartoons

from The Great Cow Race 58
Jeff Smith

Street Magic 498
Will Eisner

A Lesson in Courtesy 912
Stan Sakai

xxv

Selections by Genre

Personal Essays

Why Books Are Dangerous 78
   Neil Gaiman

Looking for America. 270
   Elizabeth Partridge

A Mason-Dixon Memory 734
   Clifton Davis

Biography, Autobiography, Memoirs, Letters

Madame C. J. Walker 119
   Jim Haskins

The Jacket 130
   Gary Soto

Satchel Paige. 150
   Bill Littlefield

Eleanor Roosevelt 168
   William Jay Jacobs

Primary Lessons 198
   Judith Ortiz Cofer

from The Pigman & Me 211
   Paul Zindel

Informational Texts

Animal Attraction 6
   Sally S. Stich

Ballpark Food 12
   Consumer Reports 4 Kids

How He Did It: Health Advice, Kid-to-Kid 20
   Amy Bertrand

Messaging Mania 34
   Kathryn R. Hoffman

The Real Magic of Harry Potter 42
   Nancy Gibbs

Make Your Own Kite 52

In Eleanor Roosevelt's Time 180

Gentleman of the Pool 192
   Alice Park

Dressed for Success? 302
   Melanie Bertotto

from 50 Simple Things Kids Can Do to Save
   the Earth 322
   The EarthWorks Group

The Gene Scene 452
   Jordan Brown

What Kids Say About Bullying 510

Let the Bullies Beware. 556
   Ritu Upadhyay and Andrea DeSimone

Bullies in the Park 589
   Jon Swartz

The Bully Battle 593
   Elizabeth Siris

Hurricane Heroes 628
   Thomas Fields-Meyer, Steve Helling, and Lori Rosza

The Great Radio Scare. 777

Nobody's Perfect 860
   David Fischer

The Shutout 874
   Patricia C. McKissack and Fredrick McKissack Jr.

from The Great Fire 897
   Jim Murphy

Best of Buddies 1052
   Kevin Gray and Cindy Dampier

Baby Hippo Orphan Finds a Friend 1059
   Catherine Clarke Fox

from The Caretaker's Diary 1063
   Stephen Tuei

Historical Documents

And Ain't I a Woman?. 257
　Sojourner Truth

Preserving a Great American Symbol. 264
　Richard Durbin

Letters About the Great Fire 905
　Justin *and* Fannie Belle Becker

Functional Texts

Advertisements 286

Skills Features

READING SKILLS

Reading Workshops

Setting a Purpose for Reading	8
Skimming and Scanning	30
Understanding Graphics	48
Identifying Main Idea and Supporting Details	68
Activating Prior Knowledge	126
Connecting	146
Predicting	164
Questioning	188
Distinguishing Fact and Opinion	260
Clarifying	282
Inferring	298
Identifying Problems and Solutions	318
Visualizing	376
Responding	402
Interpreting	420
Monitoring Comprehension	440
Drawing Conclusions	494
Understanding Cause and Effect	520
Identifying Sequence	544
Paraphrasing and Summarizing	566
Activating Prior Knowledge	624
Clarifying	646
Comparing and Contrasting	670
Predicting	706
Synthesizing	782
Identifying Main Idea and Supporting Details	818
Evaluating	840
Inferring	870
Visualizing	938
Clarifying	970
Skimming and Scanning	996
Predicting	1036

Reading Across Texts

Read to Compare Solutions	586
Read for Author's Credibility	894
Read to Compare Primary and Secondary Sources	1056

LITERATURE SKILLS

Literary Elements

Text Features	11
Titles and Subheads	33
Process	51
Author's Purpose	71
Narrator	129
Speaker	141
Point of View	149
Chronological Order	167
Tone	191
Style	263
Bias	285
Argument	301
Repetition	307
Mood	321
Poetic Features	379
Rhyme, Rhythm, and Meter	405
Sound Devices	423
Figurative Language	449
Dialogue	497
Conflict	523
Plot	547
Characterization	569
Hero	627
Cultural Context	649
Theme	673
Setting	709
Symbol	785
Description	843
Time Order/Sequence	873
Act and Scene	941
Stage Directions	999
Sensory Imagery	1039

Genre Focus

Informational Media	4
Biography/Autobiography	118
Persuasive Writing	256

Skills Features

Poetry 374
Short Story 484
Folktale, Fantasy, and Myth 618
Historical Fiction and Nonfiction 776
Drama 930

Comparing Literature
Author's Purpose 84
Character 208
Conflict 336
Figurative Language 458
Comparing Heroes 744

VOCABULARY SKILLS

English Language Coach
References and Multiple Meaning Words . . . . . Unit 1
Synonyms and Antonyms . . . . Unit 2
Denotation, Connotation, and Semantic Slanting . . Unit 3
Context Clues . . . . Unit 4
Roots, Prefixes, and Suffixes . . . . Unit 5
Compound Words, Borrowed Words,
    Word Histories . . . . Unit 6
Word Roots (Latin, Greek, and Anglo-Saxon) . . . Unit 7
Dialect and Slang . . . . Unit 8

WRITING SKILLS

Writing Products
Summary 1 26
Summary 2 64
Autobiographical Narrative 1 142
Autobiographical Narrative 2 184
Persuasive Essay 1 278
Persuasive Essay 2 314
Poem 1 398
Poem 2 436
Short Story 1 516
Short Story 2 562
Fable 1 642

Fable 2 702
Personal Narrative 1 814
Personal Narrative 2 866
Speech 1 966
Speech 2 1032

Writing Traits
Ideas 27
Conventions 144
Sentence Fluency 280
Word Choice 400
Organization 517
Voice 644
Voice 816
Presentation 968

GRAMMAR SKILLS
Verbs . . . . Unit 1
Nouns and Pronouns . . . . Unit 2
Adjectives, Adverbs, and Other Parts of Speech . . Unit 3
Sentences . . . . Unit 4
Phrases, Clauses, and Commas . . . . Unit 5
Sentence Combining . . . . Unit 6
Subject-Verb Agreement . . . . Unit 7
Hyphens, Colons, Semicolons,
and Quotation Marks . . . . Unit 8

LISTENING, SPEAKING, AND VIEWING
Getting Information from Visuals 67
Active Listening in a Group Discussion 187
Effective Speaking 317
Reading Poetry Aloud 439
Reading Aloud 565
Storytelling 705
News Report 869
Oral Presentation 1035

How to Use *Reading with Purpose*

Consultant's Note

People read for enjoyment, to help themselves think, to solve problems, and to get work done. Their reading is often organized around "inquiry" questions. These questions help them explore how what they learn can help make a difference in the real world.

—Jeff Wilhelm

Wouldn't you like to read better—and understand more? That's what *Reading with Purpose* is all about. This book will help you bridge the gap between a writer's meaning and your understanding.

The next few pages will show you some of the ways *Reading with Purpose* can help you read, think, and write better.

What's in it for you?

Every unit in *Reading with Purpose* is built around a **Big Question,** a question that you will want to think about, talk about, maybe even argue about, and finally answer. The unit's reading selections will help you come up with your answers.

Organization

Each unit contains:

- A **Unit Warm-Up** that introduces the unit's Big Question
- Four **Reading Workshops,** each one containing reading selections that will help you think about the Big Question
  - **Literature** such as short stories, poems, plays, and biographies
  - **Informational texts** such as nonfiction, newspaper and magazine articles, reference books, and manuals
  - **Functional documents** such as signs, schedules, labels, and instructions
- A two-part **Writing Workshop** to help you put your ideas about the Big Question into writing
- A **Comparing Workshop** that will give you a chance to compare different pieces of writing.
- A **Unit Wrap-Up** where you'll answer the Big Question.

Reading and Thinking

Here are some of the ways *Reading with Purpose* will help you develop your reading and thinking skills.

Skills and Strategies The skills you need to become a better reader are related to the standards that state and local school districts test you on. We call these objectives.

Consultant's Note
Standards tell what you are expected to do or learn—the learning objectives. They help teachers plan lessons and select reading and writing tasks. In addition, standards ensure that the content taught at one school will be similar to the content at other schools in the state. The standards also help you figure out what will be on tests. Standards help you figure out what you need to learn to do well in school!
—Doug Fisher

Margin Notes These notes will help you with a difficult passage, point out an important development, model a skill, or ask a question to get you thinking about what you are reading.

How to Use Reading with Purpose

Question and Answer Relationship

Four types of questions are used on standardized tests:

1. **Right There Questions** The answer is "right there" on the page.

2. **Think and Search Questions** The answers to these questions are on the page (or pages), but you'll need to use information from different parts of the text.

3. **Author and Me Questions** Information from the text may help, but you'll put it together with your own ideas to answer a question.

4. **On My Own Questions** Answers do not come from the text. You'll base your answer on what you know.

Knowing how to deal with such questions can help improve your test scores. At the end of most Workshops is a set of questions. In the first two units, each question is followed by a tip to help you answer. For example:

- What promise does Victor make to himself about this school year?

    TIP **Right There** You will find the answer in the story.

Vocabulary

Vocabulary Words may be difficult or new to you, but they're useful words.

Vocabulary Preview Vocabulary words are introduced on the Before You Read page. Each word is followed by its pronunciation, its part of speech, a definition, and a sample sentence.

xxxii

How to Use Reading with Purpose

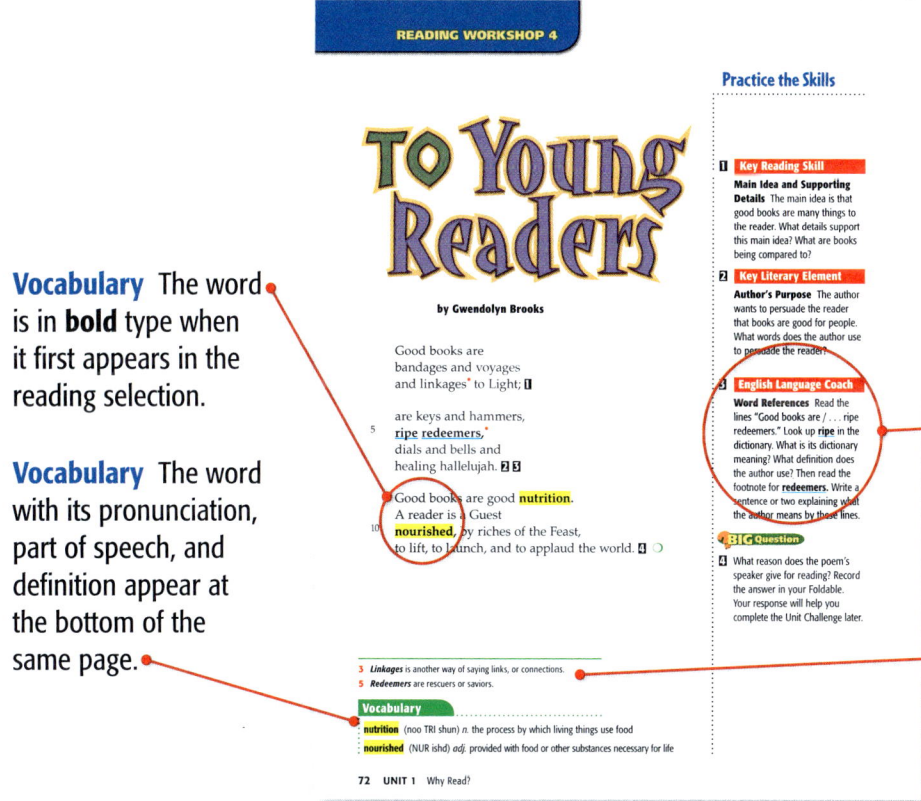

Vocabulary The word is in **bold** type when it first appears in the reading selection.

Vocabulary The word with its pronunciation, part of speech, and definition appear at the bottom of the same page.

English Language Coach These notes help students whose first language is not English. For example, they help explain multiple meaning words and also idioms—phrases that mean something other than what their individual words mean.

Footnotes Selection footnotes explain words or phrases that you may not know to help you understand the story.

Academic Vocabulary These are words you come across in your school work—in science, math, or social studies books as well as this book. The academic words are treated the same as regular vocabulary words.

xxxiii

How to Use *Reading with Purpose*

Organizing Information

Foldables For every unit, you'll be shown how to make a *Foldable* that will help you keep track of your thoughts about the Big Question. See page xxxvi for more about Foldables.

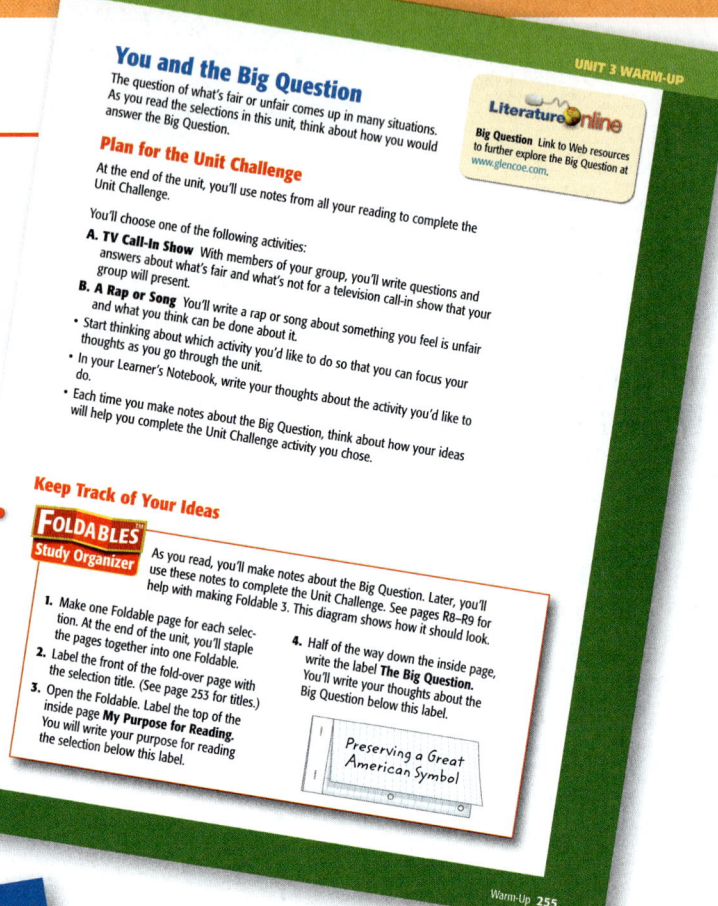

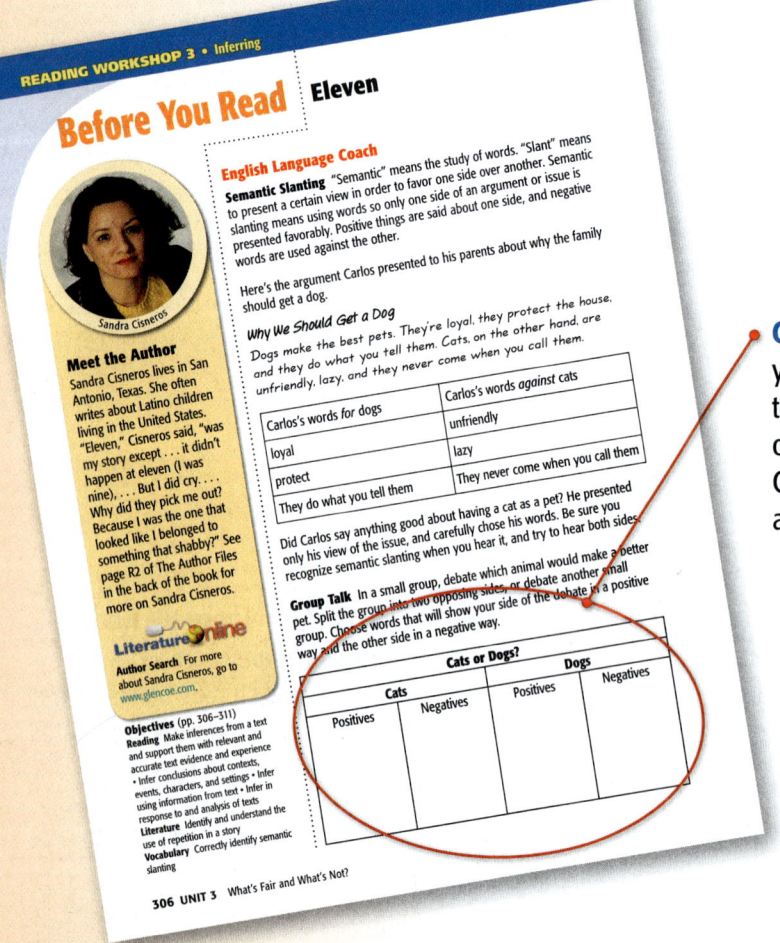

Graphic organizers In *Reading with Purpose*, you will use different kinds of graphic organizers to help you arrange information. These graphic organizers include, among others, Venn Diagrams, Compare and Contrast Charts, Cluster Diagrams, and Chain-of-Events Charts.

xxxiv

How to Use *Reading with Purpose*

Writing

In the selections on *Reading with Purpose,* you'll read many examples of excellent writing. And you'll explore what makes those pieces of writing so good.

Here are some other ways *Reading with Purpose* will help you become a better writer.

Writing to Learn As you learn new skills, you will sometimes complete a short writing assignment that will help you practice or think about your new skill.

Test Preparation and Practice

Following each unit, you will be tested on the literature, reading, and vocabulary skills you learned. This simulated standardized test will give you the practice you need to succeed while providing an assessment of how you have met the unit objectives.

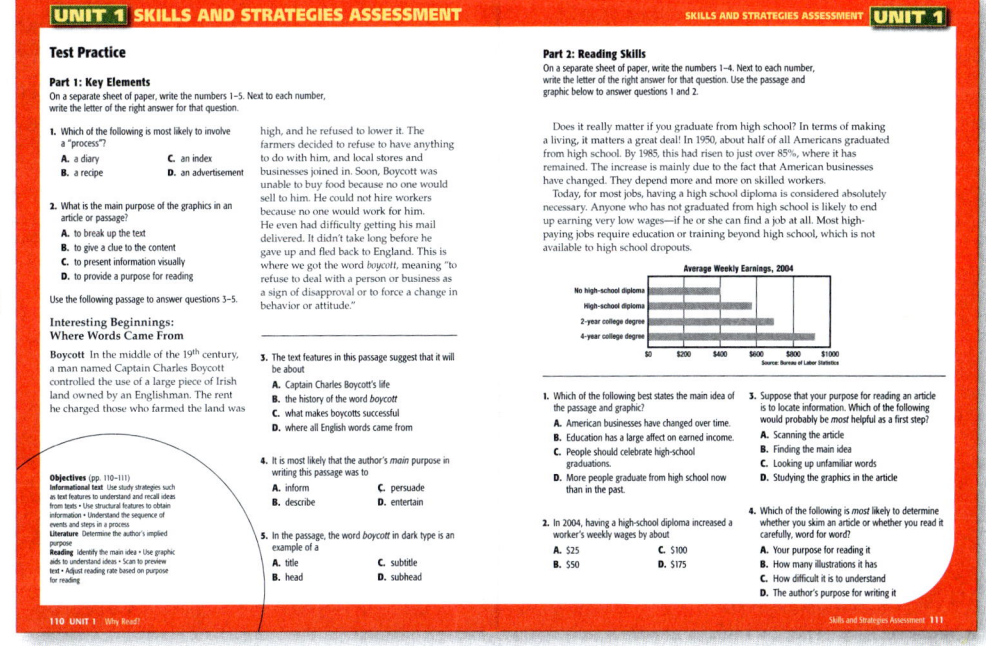

xxxv

Foldables™

by Dinah Zike, M.Ed., Creator of Foldables™

 Foldables™, are three-dimensional interactive graphic organizers for taking notes and organizing your ideas. They're also fun! You will fold paper, cut tabs, write, and manipulate what you have made in order to organize information; review skills, concepts, and strategies; and assess your learning.

Using Dinah Zike's Foldables in Reading and Literature Classes

Use Foldables before, during, and after reading selections in *Glencoe Literature: Reading With Purpose*.

- **Before you read:** Your unit Foldable will help you to focus on your purpose for reading by reminding you about the Big Question.

- **During reading:** Your unit Foldable will help you to stay focused and engaged. You will track key ideas and your thoughts about each selection and how it helps you answer the Big Question. It will also encourage you to use higher level thinking skills in approaching text.

- **After reading:** Your Foldable will help you to review your thoughts from your reading and to analyze, interpret, and evaluate various aspects of the Big Question. Your Foldable notes will also help you with your unit challenge. They also stimulate rich group discussions and inquiry.

 As you read, you'll make notes about the Big Question. Later, you'll use these notes to complete the Unit Challenge. See pages R8–R9 for help with making Foldable 1. This diagram shows how it should look.

1. Make one page for each selection. At the end of the unit, you'll staple the pages together into one Foldable.

2. Label the front of the fold-over page with the selection title. (See page 1 for the titles.)

3. Open the fold-over page. On the right side, write the label **My Purpose for Reading**.

4. Open the Foldable all the way. At the top center, write the label **The Big Question**.

Become an active reader, track and reorganize information so that you can better understand the selection.

Practice reading and following step-by-step directions.

Use the illustrations that make the directions easier to follow.

Scavenger Hunt

Reading with Purpose has a lot of information, excitement, and entertainment. This Scavenger Hunt will help you explore the book. You'll learn how to find what you need quickly. There are ten questions in your scavenger hunt. All the answers are in this book. Write your answers in your Learner's Notebook.

1. How many units are there in the book?

2. How many types of Workshops are in a unit and what are their names?

3. What is the genre focus of Unit 6?

4. How many short stories are in Unit 3?

5. Where can you find a list of all the poems in this book?

6. What's the fastest way to find a particular short story in the book?

7. Where in this book can you quickly find the correct pronunciation of the word *anesthetist*?

8. Where could you most quickly find the difference between a simile and a metaphor?

9. Where can you look for the answer to a question about grammar?

10. Name two places in the book where you can find biographical information about a writer.

 After you answer all the questions, meet with a small group to compare answers.

READING HANDBOOK

Identifying Words and Building Vocabulary RH1

Reading Fluently... RH5

Reading for a Reason... RH6

Becoming Engaged RH8

Understanding What You Read.. RH9

Thinking Critically About Your Reading RH13

Understanding Text Structure RH16

Reading for Research... RH18

You don't read a news article the way you read a novel. You read a news article mainly for information; you read a novel mainly for fun. To get the most out of your reading, you need to choose the right reading strategy to fit the reason you're reading. This handbook focuses on skills and strategies that can help you understand what you read.

Identifying Words and Building Vocabulary

What do you do when you come across a word you don't know as you read? Do you skip over the word and keep reading? If you're reading for fun or entertainment, you might. And that's just fine. But if you're reading for information, an unfamiliar word may get in the way of your understanding. When that happens, try the following strategies to figure out how to say the word and what it means. These strategies will help you better understand what you read. They will also help you increase the vocabulary you use in everyday speaking and reading.

Reading Unfamiliar Words

Sounding the Word Out

One way to figure out how to say a new word is to sound it out, syllable by syllable. Look carefully at the word's beginning, middle, and ending. Inside the new word, do you see a word you already know how to pronounce? What vowels are in the syllables? Use the following tips when sounding out new words.

▶ **Ask Yourself**

- What letters make up the beginning sound or beginning syllable of the word?
  Example: In the word *coagulate*, *co-* rhymes with *so*.

- What sounds do the letters in the middle part of the word make?
  Example: In the word *coagulate*, the syllable *ag* has the same sound as the *ag* in *bag*, and the syllable *u* is pronounced like the letter *u*.

- What letters make up the ending sound or syllable?
  Example: In the word *coagulate*, *late* is a familiar word you already know how to pronounce.

- Now try pronouncing the whole word: *co ag u late*.

Using Word Parts

Looking closely at the parts of a word is another way to learn it. By studying word parts—the root or base word, prefixes, and suffixes—you may discover more than just how to pronounce a word. You may also find clues to the word's meaning.

- **Roots and Base Words** The main part of a word is called its **root.** When the root is a complete word, it may be called the **base word.** Many roots in English come from an old form of English called Anglo-Saxon. You probably know many of these roots already. For example, *endearing* and *remarkable* have the familiar words *dear* and *mark* as their roots. Other roots come from Greek and Latin.

Reading Handbook

You may not be as familiar with them. For example, the word *spectator* contains the Latin root *spec*, which means "to look at." You can see that root in the word *spectator*, "one who looks."

When you come across a new word, check whether you recognize its root or base word. It can help you pronounce the word and figure out its meaning.

- **Prefixes** A prefix is a word part that can be added to the beginning of a root or base word to change the word's meaning. For example,

    the prefix *semi-* means "half" or "partial," so *semicircle* means "half a circle"

    un- means "not," so *unhappy* means "not happy"

- **Suffixes** A suffix is a word part that can be added to the end of a root or base word to change the word's meaning. Adding a suffix to a word can also change that word from one part of speech to another. For example,

    the word *joy* (which is a noun) becomes an adjective when the suffix *-ful* (meaning "full of") is added. *Joyful* means "full of joy."

Determining a Word's Meaning

Using Syntax

Languages have rules and patterns for the way words are arranged in sentences. The way a sentence is organized is called the **syntax** of the sentence. If English is your first language, you have known this pattern since you started talking in sentences. If you're learning English now, you may find the syntax is different from the patterns you know in your first language.

In a simple sentence in English, someone or something (the **subject**) does something (the **predicate** or **verb**) to or with another person or thing (the **object**).

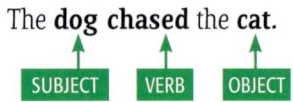

Sometimes adjectives, adverbs, and phrases are added to spice up the sentence.

▶ Check It Out

Knowing about syntax can help you figure out the meaning of an unfamiliar word. Just look at how syntax can help you figure out the following nonsense sentence.

The blizzy kwarkles sminched the flerky broogs.

Your experience with English syntax tells you that the action word, or verb, in this sentence is *sminched.*

Who did the *sminching?* The *kwarkles.*
What kind of *kwarkles* were they? *Blizzy.*
Whom did they *sminch?* The *broogs.*
What kind of *broogs* were they? *Flerky.*

Even though you don't know the meaning of the words in the nonsense sentence, you can make some sense of the entire sentence by studying its syntax.

Using Context Clues

You can often figure out the meaning of an unfamiliar word by looking at its context (the words and sentences that surround it).

▶ Do It!

To learn new words as you read, follow these steps for using context clues.

1. Look before and after the unfamiliar word for
   - a definition or a synonym (another word that means the same as the unfamiliar word)

     Some outdoor plants need to be **insulated,** or shielded, against cold weather.

   - a general topic associated with the word

     The painter brushed **primer** on the walls before the first coat of paint.

   - a clue to what the word is similar to or different from

     Like a spinning top, the dancer **pirouetted** gracefully.

   - an action or a description that has something to do with the word

     The cook used a **spatula** to flip the pancakes.

2. Connect what you already know with what the author has written.

3. Predict a possible meaning.

4. Use the meaning in the sentence.

5. Try again if your guess does not make sense.

Using reference materials

Dictionaries and other reference sources can help you learn new words. Check out these reference sources:

- A **dictionary** gives the pronunciation and the meaning or meanings of a word. Some dictionaries also give other forms of words, their parts of speech, and synonyms. You might also find the historical background of a word, such as its Greek, Latin, or Anglo-Saxon origins.

- A **glossary** is a word list that appears at the end of a book or other written work. It includes only words that are in that work. Like dictionaries, glossaries have the pronunciation and definitions of words. However, the definitions in a glossary give just enough information to help you understand the words as they are used in that work.
- A **thesaurus** lists groups of words that have the same, or almost the same, meaning. Words with similar meanings are called **synonyms.** Seeing the synonyms of words can help you build your vocabulary.

Understanding Denotation and Connotation

Words can have two types of meaning.

Denotation is the literal meaning, the meaning you find in dictionaries.

Connotation is a meaning or feeling that people connect with the word.

For example, you may say that flowers have a *fragrance* but that garbage has a *stench.* Both words mean "smell," but *fragrance* has a pleasant connotation, while *stench* has a very unpleasant one. As you read, it's important to think about the connotation of a word to completely understand what a writer is saying.

Recognizing Word Meanings Across Subjects

Have you ever learned a new word in one class and then noticed it in your reading for other subjects? The word may not mean exactly the same thing in each class. But you can use what you know about the word's meaning to help you understand what it means in a different subject area.

Look at the following example from three subjects:

Social Studies: One major **product** manufactured in the South is cotton cloth. (something manufactured by a company)

Math: After you multiply those two numbers, explain how you arrived at the **product.** (the result of multiplying two numbers)

Science: One **product** of photosynthesis is oxygen. (the result of a chemical reaction)

In all three subject areas, a product is the result of something.

▶ Practice It!

1. Write each word below in your Learner's Notebook. Then underline the familiar word or root inside it. (Notice that the end of the familiar word or root may change in spelling a little when a suffix is added to it.)

Reading Handbook

   a. configuration
   b. contemporary
   c. reformation
   d. perspective
   e. invaluable

2. Try to pronounce each of the words. Then check your pronunciation against the pronunciation given in a dictionary.

3. The following sentences can all be completed by the same word or form of the word. Use context clues to find the missing word. Write the word in your Learner's Notebook.
   a. I took the ___ to the photo shop to have a large print made.
   b. Protons are positive; electrons are ___.
   c. You always think ___; can't you think positively for a change?

Reading Fluently

Reading fluently is reading easily. When you read fluently, your brain recognizes each word so you can read without skipping or tripping over words. If you're a fluent reader, you can concentrate on the ideas in your reading because you don't have to worry about what each word means or how to say it.

To develop reading fluency. . .

- **Read often!** The more, the better. Reading often will help you develop a good sight vocabulary—the ability to quickly recognize words.

- **Practice reading aloud.** Believe it or not, reading aloud does help you become a better silent reader.
   – Begin by reading aloud a short, interesting passage that is easy for you.
   – Reread the same passage aloud at least three times or until your reading sounds smooth. Make your reading sound like you are speaking to a friend.
   – Then move on to a longer passage or a slightly more difficult one.

▶ **Practice It!**
Practice reading the paragraph under the following heading. After you think you can read it fluently—without errors or unnecessary pauses—read it aloud to a partner. Ask your partner to comment on your fluency.

Reading for a Reason

Why are you reading that paperback mystery? What do you hope to get from your science textbook? And are you going to read either of these books in the same way that you read a restaurant menu?

The point is, you read for different reasons. The reason you're reading something helps you decide on the reading strategies you use with a text. In other words, how you read will depend on why you're reading.

Knowing Your Reason for Reading

In school and in life, you'll have many reasons for reading, and those reasons will lead you to a wide range of materials. For example,

- **To learn and understand new information,** you might read news magazines, textbooks, news on the Internet, books about your favorite pastime, encyclopedia articles, primary and secondary sources for a school report, instructions on how to use a calling card, or directions for a standardized test.

- **To find specific information,** you might look at the sports section for the score of last night's game, a notice on where to register for a field trip, weather reports, bank statements, or television listings.

- **To be entertained,** you might read your favorite magazine, e-mails or letters from friends, the Sunday comics, or even novels, short stories, plays, or poems!

Adjusting How Fast You Read

How quickly or how carefully you should read a text depends on your purpose for reading it. Think about your purpose and choose a strategy that works best. Try out these strategies:

- **Scanning** means quickly running your eyes over the material, looking for **key words** or **phrases** that point to the information you're looking for. Scan when you need to find a particular piece or type of information. For example, you might scan a newspaper for movie showtimes or an encyclopedia article for facts to include in a research report.

- **Skimming** means quickly reading a piece of writing **to find its main idea** or to **get a general overview** of it. For example, you might skim the sports section of the daily newspaper to find out how your favorite teams are doing. Or you might skim a chapter in your science book to prepare for a test.

- **Careful reading** involves **reading slowly and paying attention** with a purpose in mind. Read carefully when you're learning new concepts, following complicated directions, or preparing to explain information to someone else. You definitely should read carefully when you're studying a textbook to prepare for class.

Reading Handbook

But you might also use this strategy when you're reading a mystery story and don't want to miss any details. Below are some tips you can use to help you read more carefully.

- **Take breaks** when you need them. There's no point in reading when you're sleepy. And if you're reading on the computer, give your eyes a break about every fifteen minutes by focusing on something more distant than your monitor screen.
- **Take notes** as you read. Write in your book if it's okay or use a notebook or sticky notes on the pages. Your notes may be words or phrases that will jog your memory when you need to review. If you use a notebook, write page numbers from the book in the margin of your notes. That way you can quickly find the original material later if you need it.
- **Make graphic organizers** to help you organize the information from your reading. These can sort out ideas, clear up difficult passages, and help you remember important points. For example, **webs** can show a main idea and supporting details. A **flowchart** can help you keep track of events in a sequence. A **Venn diagram,** made up of overlapping circles, can help you organize how two characters, ideas, or events are alike and different.

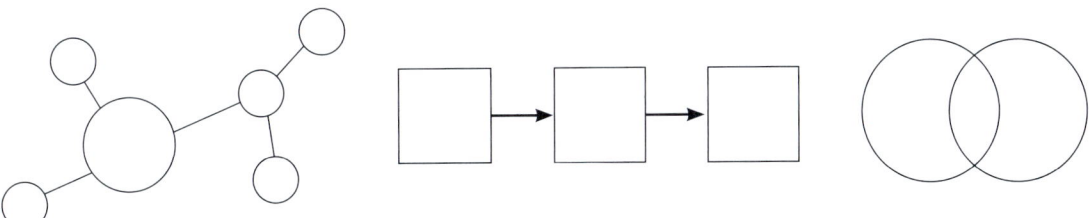

- **Review material** before stopping. Even a short review will help you remember what you've read. Try rereading difficult passages. They will be much easier to understand the second time.

▶ **Practice It!**
1. In your Learner's Notebook, write whether you would **skim, scan,** or **read carefully** in each of the following cases.
   a. a short story for your English class
   b. the school newspaper for your team's score in last week's game
   c. reviewing a chapter for tomorrow's social studies test
   d. a science book to find if it has information about nuclear waste
   e. to decide which stories and articles to read in a magazine

Reading Handbook

Becoming Engaged

In reading, *engagement* means relating to what you're reading in a way that makes it meaningful to you. It means finding links between the text and your own life. As you begin to read something, be ready to become engaged with the text. Then as you read, react to the text and relate it to your own experience. Your reading will be much more interesting, and you'll find it easier to understand and remember what you read.

Connect

You will become more involved with your reading and remember events, characters, and ideas better if you relate what you're reading to your own life. Connecting is finding the links between what you read and your own experience.

▶ **Ask Yourself**

- Have I been to places similar to the **setting** described by this writer?
- What **experiences** have I had that compare or contrast with what I am reading?
- What **opinions** do I already have about this topic?
- What **characters** from life or literature remind me of the characters or narrator in the selection?

Respond

Enjoy what you read and make it your own by responding to what's going on in the text. Think about and express what you like or don't like, what you find boring or interesting. What surprises you, entertains you, scares you, makes you angry, makes you sad, or makes you laugh out loud? The relationship between you and what you're reading is personal, so react in a personal way.

Understanding What You Read

Reading without understanding is like trying to drive a car on an empty gas tank. You can go through all the motions, but you won't get anywhere! Skilled readers adopt a number of strategies before, during, and after reading to make sure they understand what they read.

Previewing

If you were making a preview for a movie, you would want to let your audience know what the movie is like. When you preview a piece of writing, you're treating yourself like that movie audience. You're trying to get an idea about that piece of writing. If you know what to expect before reading, you will have an easier time understanding ideas and relationships. Follow these steps to preview your reading assignments.

▶ **Do It!**
1. **Look** at the title and any illustrations that are included.
2. **Read** the headings, subheadings, and anything in bold letters.
3. **Skim** over the passage to see how it is organized. Is it divided into many parts? Is it a long poem or short story? Don't forget to look at the graphics—pictures, maps, or diagrams.
4. **Set a purpose** for your reading. Are you reading to learn something new? Are you reading to find specific information?

Activating Prior Knowledge

Believe it or not, you already know quite a bit about what you're going to read. You don't know the plot or the information, of course, but keep in mind that you bring knowledge and unique personal experience to a selection. Drawing on your own background is called **activating prior knowledge,** and it can help you create meaning in what you read. Ask yourself, What do I already know about this topic? What do I know about related topics?

Reading Handbook

Predicting

You don't need a crystal ball to make **predictions** when you read. The predictions don't even have to be accurate! What's important is that you get involved in your reading from the moment you turn to page one. Take educated guesses before and during your reading about what might happen in the story. Follow these steps:

1. Use your prior knowledge and the information you gathered in your preview to predict what you will learn or what might happen in a selection. Will the hero ever get home? Did the butler do it?

2. As you read on, you may find that your prediction was way off base. Don't worry. Just adjust your predictions and go on reading.

3. Afterwards, check to see how accurate your predictions were. You don't have to keep score. By getting yourself involved in a narrative, you always end up a winner.

Visualizing

Creating pictures in your mind as you read—called **visualizing**—is a powerful aid to understanding. As you read, set up a movie theater in your imagination.

- Imagine what a character looks like.
- Picture the setting—city streets, the desert, or the surface of the moon.
- Picture the steps in a process or the evidence that an author wants you to consider. If you can visualize what you read, selections will be more vivid and you'll recall them better later on.

Identifying Sequence

When you discover the logical order of events or ideas, you are **identifying sequence**. Look for clues and signal words that will help you find the way information is organized.

Are you reading a story that takes place in chronological, or time, order? Do you need to understand step-by-step directions? Are you reading a persuasive speech with the reasons listed in order of importance? You'll understand and remember the information better when you know the organization the author has used.

Determining the Main Idea

When you look for the **main idea** of a selection, you look for the most important idea. The examples, reasons, or details that further explain the main idea are called supporting details.

Some main ideas are clearly stated within a passage—often in the first sentence of a paragraph, or sometimes in the last sentence of a passage.

Other times, an author doesn't directly state the main idea but provides details that help readers figure out what the main idea is.

▶ Ask Yourself
- What is each sentence about?
- Is there one sentence that tells about the whole passage or that is more important than the others?
- What main idea do the supporting details point out?

Questioning

Keep up a conversation with yourself as you read by **asking questions** about the text. Feel free to question anything!

- Ask about the importance of the information you're reading.
- Ask how one event relates to another or why a character acts a certain way.
- Ask yourself if you understand what you just read.
- As you answer your own questions, you're making sure that you understand what's going on.

Clarifying

Clear up, or **clarify,** confusing or difficult passages as you read. When you realize you don't understand something, try these techniques to help you clarify the ideas.

- Reread the confusing parts slowly and carefully.
- Diagram relationships between ideas.
- Look up unfamiliar words.
- Simply "talk out" the part to yourself.

Then read the passage once more. The second time through is often much easier and more informative.

Reviewing

You probably **review** in school every day in one class or another. You review what you learned the day before so the ideas stick in your mind. Reviewing when you read does the same thing.

Take time now and then to pause and review what you've read. Think about the main ideas and reorganize them for yourself so you can recall them later. Filling in study aids such as graphic organizers, notes, or outlines can help you review.

Monitoring Your Comprehension

Who's checking up on you when you read? You are! There's no teacher standing by to ask questions or to make sure that you're paying attention. As a reader, you are both the teacher and the student. It's up to you to make sure you accomplish a reader's most important task: understanding the material. As you read, check your understanding by using the following strategies.

- **Summarize** what you read by pausing from time to time and telling yourself the main ideas of what you've just read. When you summarize, include only the main ideas of a selection and only the useful supporting details. Answer the questions *Who? What? Where? When? Why?* and *How?* Summarizing tests your comprehension by encouraging you to clarify key points in your own words.

- **Paraphrase** Sometimes you read something that you "sort of" understand, but not quite. Use **paraphrasing** as a test to see whether you really got the point. Paraphrasing is retelling something in your own words. So shut the book and try putting what you've just read into your own words. If you can't explain it clearly, you should probably have another look at the text.

▶ **Practice It!**

Here are some strategies good readers use to understand a text. In your Learner's Notebook, tell which way is shown by each statement below.

connect   respond   predict   monitor comprehension
visualize   question   clarify   preview

1. I'm sure the doctor's going to be the main character in this story.

2. Why would this smart character make a dumb remark like that?

3. This woman reminds me of my mother when she's really mad.

4. This is a difficult passage. I'd better read it again and also look up the word *malefactor* in the dictionary.

5. Let's see if I've got this plot straight. So far, Greg's crazy about Donna, but she's hooked on Jesse, who seems interested in Sheila, who is Greg's date for the dance. And Dana's out to mess up everybody.

Thinking Critically About Your Reading

You've engaged with the text and used helpful reading strategies to understand what you've read. But is that all there is to it? Not always. Sometimes it's important to think more deeply about what you've read so that you can get the most out of what the author says. These critical thinking skills will help you go beyond what the words say and get at the important messages of your reading.

Interpreting

When you listen to your best friend talk, you don't just hear the words he or she says. You also watch your friend, listen to the tone of voice, and use what you already know about that person to put meaning to the words. In doing so, you are making meaning from what your friend says by using what you understand. You are interpreting what your friend says.

Readers do the same thing when they interpret as they read. Interpreting is more than just understanding the facts or story line you read. It's asking yourself, What's the writer really saying here? and then using what you know about the world to help answer that question. When you interpret as you read, you come to a much better understanding of the work.

Inferring

You may not realize it, but you infer, or make inferences, every day. Here's an example:

> You run to the bus stop a little later than usual. There's no one there. "I've missed the bus," you say to yourself. You may be wrong, but that's the way our minds work. We look at the evidence (you're late; no one's there) and come to a conclusion (you've missed the bus).

When you read, you go through exactly the same process because writers don't always directly state what they want you to understand. By providing clues and interesting details, they suggest certain information. Whenever you combine those clues with your own background and knowledge, you are making an inference.

Drawing Conclusions

Skillful readers are always drawing conclusions, or figuring out much more than an author says directly. The process is a little like a detective solving a mystery. You combine information and evidence that the author provides to come up with a statement about the topic, about a character, or about anything else in the work. Drawing conclusions helps you find connections between ideas and events and helps you have a better understanding of what you're reading.

Analyzing

Analyzing, or looking at separate parts of something to understand the entire piece, is a way to think critically about written work.

- In analyzing **fiction,** for example, you might look at the characters' values, events in the plot, and the author's style to figure out the story's theme.
- In analyzing persuasive **nonfiction**, you might look at the writer's reasons to see if they actually support the main point of the argument.
- In analyzing **informational text,** you might look at how the ideas are organized to see what's most important.

Distinguishing Fact from Opinion

Distinguishing between fact and opinion is one of the most important reading skills you can learn.

A **fact** is a statement that can be proved with supporting information.

An **opinion,** on the other hand, is what a writer believes on the basis of his or her personal viewpoint. An opinion is something that cannot be proved.

As you examine information, always ask yourself, Is this a fact or an opinion?

Don't think that opinions are always bad. Very often they are just what you want. You read editorials and essays for their authors' opinions. Reviews of movies and CDs can help you decide whether to spend your time and money on something. It's when opinions are based on faulty reasoning or prejudice or when they are stated as facts that they become troublesome.

For example, look at the following examples of fact and opinion.

Fact: California produces fruits and other agricultural products.

Opinion: California is a wonderful place for a vacation.

You could prove that fruits and other agricultural products are grown in California. It's a fact. However, not everyone might agree that California is a great vacation site. That's someone's opinion.

Evaluating

When you form an opinion or make a judgment about something you're reading, you are **evaluating.**

If you're reading **informational texts** or something on the Internet, it's important to evaluate how qualified the author is to write about the topic and how reliable the information that's presented is. Ask yourself whether

- the author seems biased.
- the information is one-sided.
- the argument presented is logical.

If you're reading **fiction,** evaluate the author's style or ask yourself questions such as

- Is this character interesting or dull?
- Are the events in the plot believable or realistic?
- Does the author's message make sense?

Synthesizing

When you **synthesize,** you combine ideas (maybe even from different sources) to come up with something new. It may be a new understanding of an important idea or a new way of combining and presenting information.

Many readers enjoy taking ideas from their reading and combining them with what they already know to come to new understandings. For example, you might

1. Read a manual on coaching soccer

2. Combine what you learn from that reading with your own experiences playing soccer

3. Add what you know about coaches you've had

4. Come up with a winning plan for coaching your sister's soccer team this spring.

Understanding Text Structure

Writers organize each piece of their writing in a specific way for a specific purpose. That pattern of organization is called **text structure.** When you know the text structure of a selection, you'll find it easier to locate and recall an author's ideas. Here are four ways that writers organize text, along with some signal words and phrases containing clues to help you identify their methods.

Comparison and Contrast

Comparison-and-contrast structure shows the similarities and differences between people, things, and ideas. When writers use comparison-and-contrast structure, often they want to show you how things that seem alike are different or how things that seem different are alike.

- **Signal words and phrases:** similarly, more, less, on the one hand, on the other hand, in contrast to, but, however

    Example: That day had been the best and worst of her life. **On the one hand,** the tornado had destroyed her home. **On the other hand,** she and her family were safe. Her face was full of cuts and bruises, **but** she smiled at the little girl on her lap.

Cause and Effect

Just about everything that happens in life is the cause or the effect of some other event or action. Sometimes what happens is pretty minor: You don't look when you're pouring milk (cause); you spill milk on the table (effect). Sometimes it's a little more serious: You don't look at your math book before the big test (cause); you mess up on the test (effect).

Writers use cause-and-effect structure to explore the reasons for something happening and to examine the results of previous events. A scientist might explain why the rain falls. A sportswriter might explain why a team is doing badly. A historian might tell us why an empire rose and fell. Cause-and-effect structure is all about explaining things.

- **Signal words and phrases:** so, because, as a result, therefore, for the following reasons

    Example: The blizzard raged for twelve hours. **Because** of the heavy snow, the streets were clogged within an hour of being plowed. **As a result,** the city was at a standstill. Of course, we had no school that day, **so** we went sledding!

Reading Handbook

Problem and Solution

How did scientists overcome the difficulty of getting a person to the moon? How can our team win the pennant this year? How will I brush my teeth when I've forgotten my toothpaste? These questions may be very different in importance, but they have one thing in common: each identifies a problem and asks how to solve it. Problems and solutions are part of what makes life interesting.

By organizing their texts around that important question-word *how,* writers state the problem and suggest a solution. Sometimes they suggest many solutions. Of course, it's for you to decide if they're right.

- **Signal words and phrases:** how, help, problem, obstruction, overcome, difficulty, need, attempt, have to, must

    Example: A major **difficulty** in learning to drive a car with a standard shift is starting on hills. Students **need** to practice starting slowly and smoothly on a level surface before they graduate to slopes. Observing an experienced driver perform the maneuver will also **help.**

Sequence

Consider these requests: Tell us what happened at the picnic. Describe your favorite CD cover. Identify the causes of the Civil War. Three very different instructions, aren't they? Well, yes and no. They are certainly about different subjects. But they all involve sequence, the order in which thoughts are arranged. Take a look at three common forms of sequencing.

- **Chronological order** refers to the order in which events take place. First you wake up; next you have breakfast; then you go to school. Those events don't make much sense in any other order. Whether you are explaining how to wash the car, giving directions to a friend's house, or telling your favorite joke, the world would be a confusing place if people didn't organize their ideas in chronological order. Look for signal words such as *first, next, then, later,* and *finally.*

- **Spatial order** describes the order of things in space. For example, take a look at this description of an ice cream sundae:

    At the bottom of the dish are two scoops of vanilla. The scoops are covered with fudge and topped with whipped cream and a cherry.

    Your eyes follow the sundae from the bottom to the top. Spatial order is important in descriptive writing because it helps you as a reader to see an image the way the author does. Signal words include *above, below, behind, left, right,* and *next to.*

- **Order of importance** is going from most important to least important or the other way around. For example, a typical news article has a most-to-least-important structure. Readers who don't have the time to read the entire article can at least learn the main idea by reading the first few paragraphs. Signal words include *principal, central, important,* and *fundamental.*

Reading for Research

An important part of doing research is knowing how to get information from a wide variety of sources. The following skills will help you when you have a research assignment for a class or when you want information about a topic outside of school.

Reading Text Features

Researching a topic is not only about asking questions. It's about finding answers. Textbooks, references, magazines, and other sources provide a variety of text features to help you find those answers quickly and efficiently.

- **Tables of contents** Look at the table of contents first to see whether a resource offers information you need.
- **Indexes** An index is an alphabetical listing of significant topics covered in a book. It is found in the back of a book.
- **Headings and subheadings** Headings often tell you what information is going to follow in the text you're reading. Subheadings allow you to narrow your search for information even further.
- **Graphic features** Photos, diagrams, maps, charts, graphs, and other graphic features can communicate large amounts of information at a glance. They usually include captions that explain what they show.

Interpreting Graphic Aids

When you're researching a topic, be sure to read and interpret the graphic aids you find. **Graphic aids** explain information visually. When reading graphic aids, read the title first to see if you're likely to find information you want.

- **Reading a map** Maps are flat representations of land. A **compass rose** shows you directions—north, south, east, and west. A **legend**, or **key**, explains the map's symbols. A **scale** shows you how distances shown on the map relate to the actual distances.
- **Reading a graph** A graph shows you how two or more things relate. Graphs can use circles, dots, bars, or lines. For example, on the weather part of a TV newscast you might see a weather graph that predicts how the temperatures for the next five days will rise or fall.
- **Reading a table** A table groups numbers or facts and puts them into categories so you can compare what is in each category. The facts are organized in rows and columns. Find the row that has the category you're looking for. Then read across to the column that has the information you need.

Organizing Information

When researching a topic, you can't stop after you've read your sources of information. You also have to make sense of that information, organize it, and put it all together in ways that will help you explain it to someone else. Here are some ways of doing just that.

- **Record** information from your research and keep track of your resources on note cards.

- **Summarize** information before you write it on a note card. That way you'll have the main ideas in your own words.

- **Outline** ideas so you can see how subtopics and supporting information will fit under a main idea.

- **Make a table or graph** to compare items or categories of information.

UNIT 1

The BIG Question: Why Read?

"The only way to do all the things you'd like to do is to read."

—**Tom Clancy**
action and adventure novelist

LOOKING AHEAD

The skill lessons and readings in this unit will help you develop your own answer to the Big Question.

UNIT 1 WARM-UP • Connecting to the Big Question
GENRE FOCUS: Informational Media
Animal Attraction 6
by Sally S. Stich from *TIME*

READING WORKSHOP 1   Skill Lesson: Setting a Purpose for Reading
Ballpark Food 12
by Consumer Reports 4 Kids

How He Did It: Health Advice, Kid-to-Kid 20
by Amy Bertrand

WRITING WORKSHOP PART 1   Summary 26

READING WORKSHOP 2   Skill Lesson: Skimming and Scanning
Messaging Mania 34
by Kathryn R. Hoffman

The Real Magic of Harry Potter 42
by Nancy Gibbs from *TIME*

READING WORKSHOP 3   Skill Lesson: Understanding Graphics
Make Your Own Kite 52
from *The Great Cow Race* 58
by Jeff Smith

WRITING WORKSHOP PART 2   Summary 64

READING WORKSHOP 4   Skill Lesson: Identifying Main Idea and Supporting Details
To Young Readers 72
by Gwendolyn Brooks

Why Books Are Dangerous 78
by Neil Gaiman

COMPARING LITERATURE WORKSHOP
The Southpaw 88
by Judith Viorst

Concha 93
by Mary Helen Ponce

UNIT 1 WRAP-UP • Answering the Big Question

UNIT 1 WARM-UP

Connecting to The BIG Question — Why Read?

Reading helps you learn about the world and your place in it. How do you find out where the bus stops, what time a movie starts, or where the movie is showing? You find out by reading. In this unit, you'll learn how reading can help you get the information you need.

Real Kids and the Big Question

KENNEDY'S best friend, Ashley, is moving to another state next month. They don't want distance to change their friendship. However, Kennedy knows it's going to be hard to keep in touch. She thinks instant messaging and e-mailing will help her stay connected to her friend. How do you think Kennedy might answer the question, "Why read?"

DOMINIC'S aunt and uncle have asked him to babysit for their young twins two days a week. Dominic is used to babysitting, but he has never helped with twins. He is worried about how to keep them entertained, so he checked out some library books to read to the twins before their naps. How do you think Dominic might answer the question, "Why read?"

Warm-Up Activity

Think about the reasons that Kennedy and Dominic read. With a partner, discuss how reading helps Kennedy and Dominic. Write a paragraph telling how each person might answer the Big Question.

You and the Big Question

We read for many reasons. Reading different selections will give you ideas about why people read. You will also think about why *you* read.

Plan for the Unit Challenge

At the end of the unit, you'll use notes from all your reading to complete the Unit Challenge. The Challenge will help you explore your answer to the Big Question!

You'll choose one of the following activities:

A. Comic Strip You'll work with classmates to create a comic strip about a reading superhero who fights illiteracy, which means not knowing how to read.

B. Conduct Interviews You'll interview friends and family members to find out what they read and why they read it.

- Start thinking about which activity you'd like to do so that you can focus your thoughts as you go through the unit.
- In your Learner's Notebook, write about which you like better—working by yourself or working with other students. That may help you decide which activity you'd like to do.
- Remember to take notes about possible answers to the Big Question. Your notes will help you complete the Unit Challenge activity you choose.

Literature Online

Big Question Link to Web resources to further explore the Big Question at www.glencoe.com.

Keep Track of Your Ideas

As you read, you'll make notes about the Big Question. Later, you'll use these notes to complete the Unit Challenge. See pages R8–R9 for help with making Foldable 1. This diagram shows how it should look.

1. Use this Foldable for the selections in this unit. Label each page with a selection title. (See page 1 for titles.) You should be able to see all the titles without opening the Foldable.

2. Below each title, write **My Purpose for Reading.** You'll write your purpose for reading the selection below this label.

3. A third of the way down on the page, write the label **The Big Question.** You'll write your thoughts about the Big Question below this label.

```
from The Great Cow Race
Make Your Own Kite
The Real Magic of Harry Potter
Messaging Mania
How He Did It
Ballpark Food

Unit 1
Why Read?
```

UNIT 1 GENRE FOCUS: INFORMATIONAL MEDIA

The term **informational media** (MEE dee uh) might be new to you. (**Media** is the plural for **medium.**) But you probably use some form of media every day. Media are ways of communicating with large groups. Media that provide information are called **informational media.** The newspaper on your doorstep, the television in your living room, the radio in the car, the Web sites you visit on the computer, and the advertisements you find in magazines, newspapers, and on billboards are forms of media.

- **Television** is the most popular medium. At least ninety-nine percent of households own at least one television set. The average American watches more than four hours of TV each day.

- Before television, **radio** was the most popular medium. Radio was first broadcast in 1920. From its start, radio carried sports, news, and musical programming. This format is still used by most radio stations today.

- The **newspaper** is a form of print media. Besides news, people read the paper for the comics, advice columns, recipes, sports news, and ads.

- **News articles** found in magazines and newspapers provide information about particular topics, issues, or events.

- The **Internet** is a vast system of computer networks connected to one another around the world. The Internet provides a wide variety of information at your fingertips.

- **Web pages** are the basic units of the Internet. The main purpose of Web pages is to provide information, entertainment, or advertising. These electronic pages contain text, pictures, animation, and movies.

- A **Web site** is a collection of pages grouped together to organize the information offered by the person, company, or group that owns it. For example, your favorite musical performer or actor probably has a Web site. Many companies and organizations have Web sites, where you can learn more about them.

- **Advertising** is the use of media—such as television, newspapers, and radio—to promote a product or service. The aim of advertising is to get the reader, viewer, or listener to buy or use a certain product or service.

Skills Focus
- Key skills for reading informational media
- Key text and literary elements of informational media

Skills Model
You will see how to use the key reading skills and text and literary elements as you read
- *"Animal Attraction,"* p. 6

Objectives (pp. 4–7)
Reading Set a purpose for reading • Skim and scan text • Identify main ideas and supporting details • Use graphics
Informational Text Use text features: title, subtitle, deck, subheads • Identify text structure: steps in a process
Literature Identify literary elements: author's purpose

UNIT 1 GENRE FOCUS

Why Read Informational Media?

You need practical information every day. Whether you want to find out about the weather or your favorite team's stats, you can often get the facts through informational media. You can read informational media to
- get the latest news
- learn how to make or do something
- find information for a school report

How to Read Informational Media

Key Reading Skills

These reading skills are especially useful tools for reading and understanding informational media. You'll see these skills modeled in the Active Reading Model on pages 6–7, and you'll learn more about them later in this unit.

- **Setting a purpose for reading** Before you read, decide *why* you are reading. (See Reading Workshop 1.)
- **Skimming and scanning** Get a rough idea of what a selection is about by scanning to look for key words and phrases. To skim, read through something quickly to find its main idea or get a general overview. (See Reading Workshop 2.)
- **Understanding graphics** Use the information from graphics to locate and analyze information. (See Reading Workshop 3.)
- **Identifying main idea and supporting details** As you read, find the most important idea in a paragraph or selection. Also find the details that support the most important idea. (See Reading Workshop 4.)

Key Text and Literary Elements

Recognizing and thinking about the following elements will help you understand the text more fully.

- **Text features:** titles, subtitles, and decks (See "Ball Park Food.")
- **Titles:** large or dark type that introduces text and grabs the reader's attention **Subheads:** smaller titles that introduce parts of the text (See "The Magic of Harry Potter.")
- **Process:** the way things need to happen in order to get a certain result (See "Make Your Own Kite.")
- **Author's purpose:** the writer's goal in a particular work, which may be to entertain, inform, persuade, or express emotions (See "To Young Readers.")

The notes in the side columns model how to use the skills and elements you read about on page 5.

Animal Attraction

Sure, pets provide lots of pleasure. But now scientists think they might help people live longer, too. **1 2 3**

By SALLY S. STICH

Informational Media
ACTIVE READING MODEL

When her father died, Karen Wright was very worried. Her mother, Violet, was 72 years old. "Mom had always been full of energy and enthusiasm," says Wright. "But after Dad died, she didn't take care of herself and got sick a lot." Wright's mother didn't feel that she had much to live for—except a dog named Buddy. "I never paid much attention to Buddy when my husband was alive," says Violet. "But suddenly he depended on me for his survival."

Most people agree that a pet adds joy to a person's life. This can be more true after a loved one dies. Scientists are now finding that having a pet may keep its owner healthy. And good health may add years to a person's life. **4**

Scientists have been looking at the tie between pets and health for years. In 1990, a study was done with people age 65 and older. It showed that pet owners went to the doctor less than people without pets. Do pets make people happier? Do they help people live on their own longer? Are people able to handle their everyday lives better? Alan Beck is the head of the Center for the Human-Animal Bond. Beck says that if the answer to these questions is yes, then having pets may be a good idea.

Can pets also help people live longer? Rebecca Johnson did a study to find out. Johnson teaches nurses how to care for older people. She shared the findings of her study at a meeting about Pets and the Aging. Her study shows that having pets may cause people to age more slowly.

1 Key Text Element
Titles and Decks *The title tells me that the article is going to be about animals. The deck tells that pets might help people live longer.*

2 Key Reading Skill
Setting a Purpose for Reading *How can pets help people live longer? My purpose for reading is to find the answer.*

3 Key Reading Skill
Skimming and Scanning *As I skimmed this article, I saw that it's about how pets add joy and good health to people's lives. I scanned for the word* dog *and learned that some people have robotic dogs!*

4 Key Reading Skill
Identifying Main Idea and Supporting Details *The main idea is that scientists think animals can help people live longer. Let's see what details the article provides to support that idea.*

UNIT 1 GENRE FOCUS

ACTIVE READING MODEL

The human body makes many chemicals. Some of the chemicals make people feel good. Others make people feel bad. In Johnson's study, levels of the "good" chemicals rose when people were around pets. Levels of the "bad" chemicals went down. The good chemicals seemed to slow the aging of cells. If this is true, maybe people should spend more time with their pets. Then the levels of good chemicals will go up. People might feel better and age more slowly. They might even live longer. **5**

Having pets may also be good for people in nursing homes. In a study of five nursing homes with pets, 25% fewer people stayed in bed all day. And sores caused by being in bed were down 57%. Having pets around was good for the workers too. They missed work 48% less than before the pets came.

Of course, you could be allergic to pets. Or you may not want to take care of a pet. Never fear. A robotic, or computer, pet may be just the thing for you. Scientists are testing computer pets, like the robotic dog AIBO.[1] They want to see if computer pets can help people the way real dogs do. **6**

Will a robotic pet take the place of the pet pal snuggling with you on the sofa? Something tells us that the furry couch potato lying next to you has little to worry about.

—Updated 2005, from *Time*, October 20, 2003

---

1. **AIBO** is a robotic dog made by a major electronics company. It is programmed to react to directions from its owner.

Partner Talk With a partner, talk about the different reasons someone may have for reading this article.

5 Key Text Element
Process *If you have a pet, your body makes "good" chemicals. What's the next step? The good chemicals rise, the "bad" chemicals go down, and you age more slowly.*

6 Key Literary Element
Author's Purpose *I think that the author's main purpose is to inform readers about the positive effects of pets on people's health.*

7 Key Reading Skill
Understanding Graphics *The picture is kind of funny. But it also helps me understand the article. The man is relaxing with his cat. He's smiling. I'll bet his "good chemicals" are rising!*

Study Central Visit www.glencoe.com and click on Study Central to review informational text.

Genre Focus: Informational Media

READING WORKSHOP 1

Skills Focus

You will practice using these skills when you read the following selections:
- "Ballpark Food," p. 12
- "How He Did It: Health Advice, Kid-to-Kid," p. 20

Reading
- Setting a purpose for reading

Informational Text
- Understanding text features

Vocabulary
- Understanding and using word references
- Academic Vocabulary: *text*

Writing/Grammar
- Identifying parts of speech

Skill Lesson

Setting a Purpose for Reading

Learn It!

What Is It? When you **set a purpose for reading,** you ask yourself questions about *what* you're reading and *why* you're reading it. This affects *how* you read. For example, your purpose for reading an adventure story may be to find out what happens in the story. You might ask yourself, "How is this going to work out?" If you are reading directions for setting up a new computer, though, your purpose for reading is different. You might ask, "How can I make this computer work?" Many times, your purpose for reading changes as you read.

HEART OF THE CITY © 2004 Mark Tatulli. Dist. By UNIVERSAL PRESS SYNDICATE. Reprinted with permission. All rights reserved.

Analyzing Cartoons
Setting a purpose for reading helps you to figure out what you can get out of a **text**. Does the girl in the cartoon have a purpose for reading? What is it?

Objectives (pp. 8–9)
Reading Set a purpose for reading

Academic Vocabulary

text (tekst) *n.* the printed or written words of a page, book, or another form of communication

8 UNIT 1

READING WORKSHOP 1 • Setting a Purpose for Reading

Why Is It Important? It always helps to know why you're doing something! Also, setting a purpose for reading helps you choose the way to read something. For example, if you have to define certain words for a science worksheet, your purpose for reading a chapter in your science book is to find the meanings of those words. So you look quickly through the chapter, searching for those words. When you find one, you slow down and read carefully to find out what it means.

How Do I Do It? Before you start to read, think about what might be interesting or what you might need to learn from the selection. What questions come into your mind? Write these questions down. They are your purpose for reading. After reading the title and deck of "Animal Attraction," this is how one student set her purpose for reading.

> Animal Attraction
> Sure, pets provide lots of pleasure. But now scientists think they might help people live longer, too.

It looks like this is about pets, but I had no idea pets could help people live longer. I've never heard of anything like that, and it doesn't make sense to me. How can pets do this? I want to find out how a pet can help someone live longer, so I'll read to find out. That's my purpose for reading.

Literature Online

Study Central Visit www.glencoe.com and click on Study Central to review setting a purpose for reading.

Practice It!

The title of the first selection is "Ballpark Food." Look over the headings, questions, and pictures and use them to set a purpose for reading. In your Learner's Notebook, write your purpose for reading.

Use It!

"Ballpark Food" starts with some multiple choice questions. As you read make notes in your Learner's Notebook of what *you* think are the right answers. Does this activity change your purpose for reading? That's okay! It means that you are thinking and learning as you read! Just write any new purpose in your Learner's Notebook.

READING WORKSHOP 1 • Setting a Purpose for Reading

Before You Read : Ballpark Food

Meet the Authors
A group of thirty-six kids, who call themselves the Snack Squad, decided to gather information about foods sold at baseball parks. The Snack Squad wanted to know if it was cheaper and healthier to bring your own food than to eat the food sold at the ballparks. They also wanted to know what effect the advertisements in the ballparks had on food sales. They put all the information into the quiz you are about to read. Find out what they learned as you read and take the quiz.

Objectives (pp. 10–15)
Reading Set a purpose for reading
Informational Text Use text features: title, subtitle, deck
Vocabulary Use word references: dictionary, glossary

Vocabulary Preview

vendors (VEN durz) *n.* people who sell products or services **(p. 14)**
Vendors sell food, clothes, and other items during a game.

ushers (USH urz) *n.* people who help others find their seats in a theater or stadium **(p. 15)** *The ushers took us to our seats in row twelve.*

Partner Talk Discuss the vocabulary words with a partner.
1. **Vendors** Have you ever bought something from a vendor, like food at an amusement park or a t-shirt at a sporting event? Did you pay too much for it, or was the price fair? Talk about what you bought, where you bought it, and why. What are some other items vendors might sell?
2. **Ushers** Talk about three places you might see an usher.

English Language Coach

Word References Sometimes you will see a new word or a word you recognize used in a new way. Don't panic! Use a dictionary or a glossary to help you find the word's meaning.

- A dictionary can show you a word's definition, how to pronounce the word, and its part of speech.

- You can also learn the word's root (the history of where it comes from). Look at this dictionary entry.

> **sale** \sāl\ *n.* [Old English *sala* act of selling.] **1.** transfer of ownership from one party to another in exchange for money: *the sale of a house.* **2.** selling goods at a reduced price: *an end-of-the-season sale.* **3. for sale.** available for purchase. **4. on sale.** offered at a reduced price: *to buy pants on sale.*

- A glossary is similar to a dictionary, but it appears at the back of a book and shows the meanings of words that appear in that book. See the glossary in this book that begins on p. R54.

Write to Learn Look in the glossary on p. R54 and choose a word. Write its meaning and its part of speech. Then write a sentence using the word you chose.

READING WORKSHOP 1 • Setting a Purpose for Reading

Skills Preview

Key Reading Skill: Setting a Purpose for Reading

There are many purposes for reading, and there may be several different reasons for reading one selection. You've already written one purpose for reading "Ballpark Food." It might be to learn

- why ballpark food costs so much
- who gets the money from the food sales

Write to Learn Pick one of these questions and write the answers as you read. The answer won't always be in one place.

- Which is cheaper, food bought from a grocery store or a ballpark? How do you know?
- Why do you think there are so many ads in a ballpark? Explain.

Key Text Element: Text Features

When you're looking at a page of informational text, you hardly ever see a big block of words that all look alike. Instead, you see titles printed big and other words in italics. You may see bullets—those dots like big periods that come before one of a series of things. These are all **text features,** which are special ways of presenting information. They make what you're reading easier to understand.

The title of an article can be important when you are setting a purpose to read. It may give you an idea of what the article is about or just make it sound interesting.

In "Ballpark Food," the text is set as questions and answers, with numbers and boldface (dark) text to make the material look more interesting and make it easier to read. While you're reading, ask yourself whether this text feature works.

Partner Talk With a partner, find text features that appear in "Ballpark Food." How do they hint at what the text is about? Does a graphic make the text more clear?

Get Ready to Read

Connect to the Reading

Have you ever felt as though you paid too much for something? As you read, think about where your money goes when you buy items at a ballpark.

Write to Learn In your Learner's Notebook, write about how you decide which items are worth buying and how you save money for those items.

Build Background

The Snack Squad asked questions about the high price of ballpark food and found some interesting answers.

Set Purposes for Reading

BIG Question One answer to "Why read?" is "To get information." Read "Ballpark Food" to discover where your money goes at the ballpark and how you can save some of it.

Set Your Own Purpose What else would you like to learn from the selection to help you answer the Big Question? Write your own purpose on the "Ballpark Food" page of Foldable 1.

Interactive Literary Elements Handbook
To review or learn more about the literary elements, go to www.glencoe.com.

Keep Moving

Use these skills as you read the following selection.

Ballpark Food 11

READING WORKSHOP 1

INFORMATIONAL TEXT
WEB SITE
zillions.org

Consumer Reports 4 Kids

Do you have major-league complaints about the high price of ballpark food? **1**

Take this quiz to see if you can guess what our 36-kid Snack Squad discovered when they visited baseball parks to buy and test their food.

1. How did the price of hot dogs, soda, and peanuts at the ballpark compare to their price at a food store?
   A. The food cost twice as much at the ballpark.
   B. It cost three to seven times more at the ballpark.
   C. Ballpark and food store prices were the same.

2. Say you paid $2.50 for this hot dog at a ballpark. How much of that covers the cost of the hot dog and bun?
   A. 10¢   D. $1.50
   B. 50¢   E. $2
   C. $1

3. Will most baseball parks let you bring in your own food?
   A. Yes   B. No

4. How many ads do you think our Snack Squad spotted in the ballparks they visited? **2**
   A. None   B. Just a few   C. Dozens

Practice the Skills

1 Key Text Element

Text Features What can you find out about the topic of this selection from the title? Does it help you set your purpose for reading?

2 Key Reading Skill

Setting a Purpose for Reading Look at the questions on this page. What purpose could you set for reading this part of the selection?

12   UNIT 1   Why Read?

READING WORKSHOP 1

ANSWERS 3

1. B! Hot dogs, soda, and peanuts cost three to seven times more at the ballpark than at a store!

You almost need a major-league salary to afford ballpark food! The hot dogs, soda, and peanuts our Snack Squad bought cost three to seven times more than their local food stores charged. In Ohio, for example, $7.50 bought a hot dog, 24-ounce soda, and bag of about 90 peanuts at the Cincinnati Reds stadium. But that same $7.50 would buy five hot dogs, 190 ounces of soda, and about 380 peanuts at a grocery store!

Practice the Skills

3 Key Text Element

Text Features This text feature tells me that this is the answer key. I see that the correct answer to the first question is **B**.

Analyzing the Photo This ballpark vendor is tossing a bag of peanuts to a customer. Look closely. How much do they cost? Is that more or less than at a store?

Ballpark Food

READING WORKSHOP 1

Analyzing the Graphic Complete this sentence to summarize what you learn from the "Food-Price Scorecard": The next time I go to the ballpark, I'll be sure to . . .

2. B! Of the $2.50 you pay for a hot dog at a ballpark, only 50¢ goes for the cost of the hot dog and bun!

If the hot dog and bun and all the fixings only cost the concession companies (food-sellers) 50¢, where does the other $2 go? Wages for **vendors** who sell the hot dogs come to 50¢. The concession **company** takes 25¢ as a profit, and 25¢ covers cleaning, phones, and other costs. The biggest chunk of that hog-dog price ($1.00) goes to the baseball team and stadium owners! 5

Practice the Skills

4 **Key Text Element**

Text Features Do you think the question and answer form of the text helps you understand the material better? Why or why not?

5 **English Language Coach**

Word References Some words have more than one meaning. You can find all the meanings for a word in a dictionary. What are two meanings for the word **company**?

Vocabulary

vendors (VEN durz) *n.* people who sell products or services

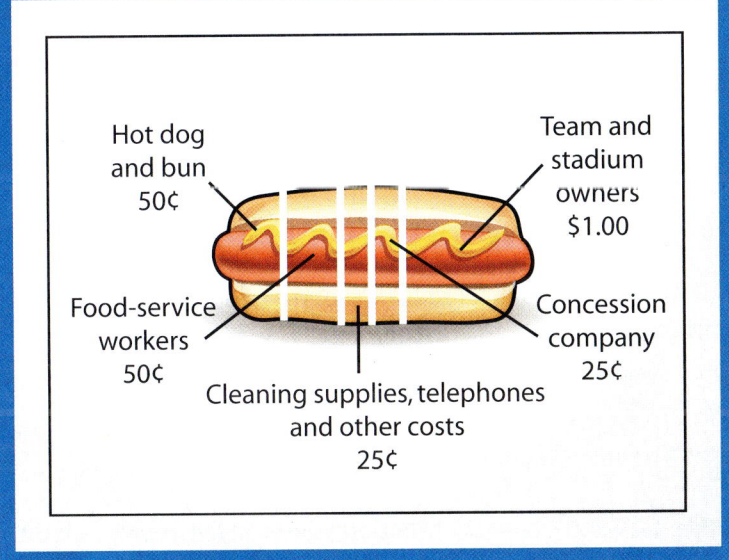

Analyzing the Graphic Who gets the greatest amount of the money you spend on a hot dog at the ballpark? How much do they get for each hot dog?

3. **A! Yes, most ballparks will let you bring in your own food.**

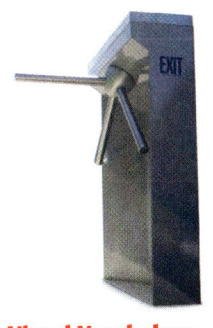

Visual Vocabulary
Turnstiles are posts that allow only one person at a time to pass through an entrance on foot.

Nearly all major-league stadiums say they'll let fans bring food from home. When our Snack Squad brought their own food, some were stopped at the turnstiles and asked to open their packs. "They were just looking for cans," reported Peter, 11. Ushers have the right to inspect bags and take away glass bottles, cans, thermoses, and other items that could be thrown onto the field. Juice boxes and plastic bottles are usually okay. In the end, *none* of our testers had their food taken away.

4. **C! Snack Squad kids spotted dozens of ads in the ballparks they visited.**

Kids spotted ads on their scorecards, ticket stubs, and seatbacks. They saw ads on lighting towers and at the concession stands. According to Tess, the sneakiest ads at the Oakland Coliseum were on the big-screen TV. "Right after replays, when everyone's attention was on the big screen, they showed commercials," she said. 6 7 ○

Vocabulary

ushers (USH urz) *n.* people who help others find their seats in a theater or stadium

Practice the Skills

6 **Key Reading Skill**

Setting a Purpose for Reading Suppose your purpose for reading this article was to answer the question "Can I bring my own food to a ballpark?" How would that change *how* you read the selection? Write your answer in your Learner's Notebook.

BIG Question

7 Why might a baseball fan want to read this selection? How does this help you answer the Big Question? Write your answer on the "Ballpark Food" page of Foldable 1. Your response will help you answer the Unit Challenge later.

READING WORKSHOP 1 • Setting a Purpose for Reading

After You Read | Ballpark Food

Answering the BIG Question

1. Think about the article you just read. Explain why you would—or would not—recommend this article to a friend.
2. **Recall** What problem with ballpark food does the writer mention in the first paragraph?
   TIP Right There You will find the answer in the text.
3. **Recall** At the Oakland Coliseum, what do you see after replays on the big-screen TV?
   TIP Right There You will find the answer in the text.

Critical Thinking

4. **Analyze** Why does food cost so much more at a ballpark than at a store?
   TIP Author and Me You will find clues in the text, but you must also use the information in your head.
5. **Analyze** Why don't stadium owners want people to bring in bottles, cans, or thermoses?
   TIP Author and Me You will find clues in the text, but you must also use the information in your head.
6. **Apply** How might reading this selection be helpful to someone who is going to a ballpark?
   TIP On My Own Answer from your own experiences.

Talk About Your Reading

Discuss this article with a partner. Think about these topics as you discuss "Ballpark Food":

- Which text features did you find the most helpful and why?
- Pick out one passage in the text that is *surprising,* another passage that is *important,* and finally, pick out something you will *remember* from the reading and be able to use outside of class. Discuss these passages with your partner.
- Share your purpose for reading with your partner, and talk about something in "Ballpark Food" that you'd like to learn more about.

Objectives (pp. 16–17)
Reading Set a purpose for reading
Informational Text Use text features: title, subtitle, deck
Vocabulary Use word references: dictionary, glossary
Grammar Identify parts of speech

Skills Review

Key Reading Skill: Setting a Purpose for Reading

7. Look at the purpose (or purposes) for reading that you wrote in your Learner's Notebook. Did your purpose for reading change? Why or why not? Explain your answer in your Learner's Notebook.

Key Text Element: Text Features

8. Do you think it was a good idea for the writers to use a multiple-choice quiz at the beginning of "Ballpark Food?" Explain.
9. Why did the writers use sentences in dark type at the beginning of each answer?
10. Which text feature did you find most helpful? Explain.

Vocabulary Check

In your Learner's Notebook, use your own words to write the meaning of each vocabulary word.

11. **vendors**
12. **ushers**
13. **Academic Vocabulary** Which part of a newspaper article is the text?
14. **English Language Coach** Use a dictionary to find two meanings for the word *bill*. Then write two sentences, each using the word *bill* in a different way.

Web Activities For eFlashcards, Selection Quick Checks, and other Web activities, go to www.glencoe.com.

Grammar Link: Parts of Speech

Words can be organized into eight groups called **parts of speech.** Each part of speech describes what a particular kind of word does. Here's an overview of the eight parts:

What is it?	What does it do?
Noun	names a person, a place, or a thing
Verb	shows action or state of being
Pronoun	takes the place of a noun
Adjective	tells which one, what kind, how many
Adverb	tells how, when, where, how much
Preposition	helps show space, time, position
Conjunction	connects words or groups of words
Interjection	expresses feeling

In many cases you'll need to see a word in a sentence before you can know what part of speech it is.

In the first sentence below, for example, *phone* works as a verb. In the second sentence, *phone* works as a noun. In the third sentence, *phone* works as an adjective.

- **Verb: Phone** Jody and ask if she's coming with us.
  (*Phone* shows action.)
- **Noun:** We bought a new **phone** and gave Max the old one.
  (*Phone* names a thing.)
- **Adjective:** They had a **phone** conversation six days ago.
  (*Phone* describes the conversation.)

Grammar Practice

Write two sentences for each word listed below. In the first sentence, use the word as a verb. In the second sentence, use the word as a noun. Label the word *noun* or *verb*.

show   surprise   roll

READING WORKSHOP 1 • Setting a Purpose for Reading

Before You Read: How He Did It: Health Advice, Kid-to-Kid

Meet the Author
Amy Bertrand is the Health and Fitness Editor for the *St. Louis Post-Dispatch* newspaper.

Author Search For more about Amy Bertrand, go to www.glencoe.com.

Vocabulary Preview

obesity (oh BEE si tee) *n.* condition of being extremely overweight **(p. 20)** *Obesity is a serious health problem.*

advisory (ad VY zuh ree) *adj.* having the power to give advice **(p. 21)** *The school formed an advisory group to recommend a change in the dress code.*

administrator (ad MIN i stray tur) *n.* person who manages or directs **(p. 21)** *The administrator makes sure that all work is done on time.*

calories (KAL uh reez) *n.* units used to measure the energy supplied by food **(p. 22)** *Some foods have more calories than others.*

ultimate (UL tuh mut) *adj.* greatest; most important **(p. 22)** *My ultimate hope is that the Web site helps someone who has questions.*

Partner Talk Give your partner a clue to one of the words above (for example, "it is a health problem"). Have your partner name the vocabulary word without looking at the book. Take turns until you both know the words and their definitions.

English Language Coach

Word References A thesaurus is a dictionary of synonyms, or words with similar meanings. A thesaurus can be helpful when you are unsure of a word's meaning, or if you are looking for words with similar meanings.

Look at this thesaurus entry for the word *lively*.

> **lively** *adjective*
> 1. very brisk, alert, and high-spirited:
> *a lively personality*
> **Syns:** animated, bouncy, peppy

Objectives (pp. 18–23)
Reading Set a purpose for reading
Informational Text Use text features: title, subtitle, deck
Vocabulary Use word references: thesaurus

Partner Talk With a partner, use a thesaurus to find at least two words with similar meanings to each underlined word.
1. She will <u>walk</u> to the store.
2. It was a <u>hot</u> day.
3. I <u>admire</u> that singer.

READING WORKSHOP 1 • Setting a Purpose for Reading

Skills Preview

Key Reading Skill: Setting a Purpose for Reading

"How He Did It: Health Advice, Kid-to-Kid" is about a boy who is concerned about overweight kids and creates a Web site to help them stay fit. Why would you want to read this article? Maybe you have questions about fitness or a healthy diet. Maybe you have a similar idea that might help others.

Write to Learn Write your purpose for reading in your Learner's Notebook.

Key Text Element: Text Features

Titles can have a lot of information in them or just a little. They can catch your attention and make you want to read.

- If You Traveled on the Underground Railroad
- Green Eggs and Ham
- Here, There and Everywhere: My Life Recording the Music of the Beatles

The first title gives you a good idea of what the book is about. The second one suggests that the book will be funny. (You hope!) The last title doesn't tell you much, but it has a **subtitle** that does. A subtitle usually comes after a colon and adds more information to the title.

Another text feature that gives more information is a **deck.** A deck is a sentence or two that tells you about something you are going to read.

Write to Learn Find a text feature that you found helpful. Write a short paragraph telling how it helped you understand what you were reading.

Interactive Literary Elements Handbook
To review or learn more about the literary elements, go to www.glencoe.com.

Get Ready to Read

Connect to the Reading

Name an important project you've done. Maybe you had to do a project for science, math, or language arts class. What kinds of text features did you include in your project? Explain.

Partner Talk With a partner, make a list of projects that you think might be interesting for kids your age to do.

Build Background

In this article you'll learn how a boy named Robert starts a little project that turns into a big help for overweight kids.

- Body fat is important for good health, but too much body fat can lead to health problems.
- When the body stores too much fat, it can result in obesity.
- Obesity can lead to health problems such as high blood pressure and heart disease.
- Health officials are worried that obesity is an epidemic, or a rapidly spreading disease.
- Robert's Web site, which is no longer online, encouraged kids to make good decisions about diet and exercise.

Set Purposes for Reading

BIG Question Read the selection "How He Did It: Health Advice, Kid-to-Kid" to find out about how you can make healthy choices.

Set Your Own Purpose What else would you like to learn from the article to help you answer the Big Question? Remember that you can have more than one purpose. Write your own purpose on the "How He Did It: Health Advice, Kid-to-Kid" page of Foldable 1.

Keep Moving

Use these skills as you read the following selection.

READING WORKSHOP 1

**INFORMATIONAL TEXT
WEB SITE**

How He Did It:
Health Advice, Kid-to-Kid

by Amy Bertrand

Sixth-grader's Web site helps other children stay fit. 1

Ever since Robert Kohn can remember, his parents have stressed the importance of healthy eating and exercise.

"I think I've heard about it forever," he says.

That education led to a remarkable project by Robert, a sixth-grader. For a school project, he wrote a research paper on childhood **obesity**, then created an advisory council on it, which in turn led to a Web site, created especially for use by children.

Robert's not known for being big into team sports at school, says his mom, Dee Dee, but he still values the importance of working out. He plays golf and tennis and works out about two days a week in a gym, lifting weights and "focusing on cardio[1] right now," he says.

He's never had a weight problem, but knows kids who have. "It's a huge problem," he says.

That's why he wanted to **tackle** it for his school project. 2

Practice the Skills

1 Key Text Element

Text Features Read the subtitle and the deck, which is right below the writer's name. Do they give you information that might help you set a purpose for reading?

2 English Language Coach

Word References What does it mean to **tackle** a problem? Use a dictionary to find the meaning of *tackle* that is used here.

---

1. **Cardio** is short for *cardiovascular,* meaning of the heart and blood vessels. Exercise that increases heart rate is often referred to as *cardio.*

Vocabulary

obesity (oh BEE si tee) *n.* condition of being extremely overweight

READING WORKSHOP 1

The project:

In his language arts class, students were required to come up with a topic that would be used in a three-pronged,[2] yearlong project. The first part of the project was to write a research paper; the second part was to come up with an action plan; and the third portion was to get someone to take action.

Robert began by reading books and searching the Web. He found quite a bit of information on the topic, but not much of it was directed at children.

So, he put together an **advisory** council on the subject, which included teachers, a dietitian,[3] a hospital **administrator** and a chef. They met a couple of times and helped Robert cultivate information[4] for his next big project: creating a Web site just for kids. 3

Analyzing the Photo Do you think that this would be a good picture to appear on Robert's Web site? Why or why not?

The Web site:

What resulted was **www.healthychoicesforkids.com.**
Robert gathered all of the information he wanted to include, then sketched out what he wanted each page of the Web site to look like, along with the words to go on it. A professional designed the Web site for him, and the result is a kid-friendly site with kid-friendly graphics. It's easy to navigate and written in a language kids can easily understand.

---

2. **Three-pronged** means that the project has three parts.
3. A **dietitian** is an expert in planning meals or diets.
4. When someone **cultivates information,** he or she prepares and organizes it in a way that is clear and easy to follow.

Vocabulary

advisory (ad VY zuh ree) *adj.* having the power to give advice

administrator (ad MIN i stray tur) *n.* person who manages or directs

Practice the Skills

3 **Key Reading Skill**

Setting a Purpose for Reading Has your purpose for reading changed now that you've started to read the article? Think about your original purpose, and then think of a second purpose for reading.

READING WORKSHOP 1

Topics on the site include:
- How do I know if I'm overweight?
- What are the risks of being overweight?
- Portion sizes.
- Making healthy choices while dining out.
- How many <mark>calories</mark> do I burn during common activities?

"I'm hoping other kids get educated about obesity: What it is, the risks of being obese, how to get in better shape," Robert says. **4**

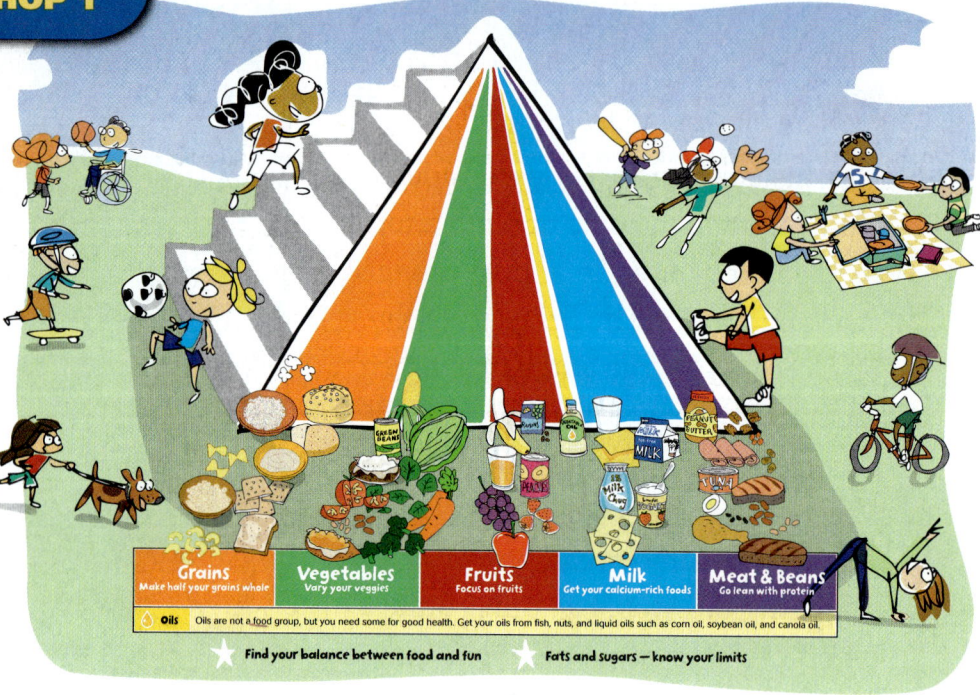

Analyzing the Graphic According to this food pyramid, what is one food *you* should eat more of for better health?

The action plan:

Robert's strong views on the subject took him to his next step: writing lawmakers.

"In my research I found HB 81,⁵ a bill about having exercise and healthy foods at public schools," Robert says.

So he wrote the supporters of that bill, and though he's still waiting for confirmation, he's been asked to speak about his findings.

"I think I'll tell them why I think childhood obesity is such a huge problem, how horrible obesity is and how many people are suffering," he says. "It can cause diseases like cancer, heart disease, high blood pressure."

His <mark>ultimate</mark> goal is to have the lawmakers take over his Web site. "I want to see what they can do." **5**

---

5. **HB 81** means "House Bill 81," a proposed law on which Congress has been asked to vote.

Practice the Skills

4 **BIG Question**
What information could you read on Robert's Web site that might help you or someone you know?

5 **BIG Question**
Write three things that you learned from reading this article. Write your answer on the "How He Did It" page of Foldable 1. Your response will help you complete the Unit Challenge later.

Vocabulary

<mark>calories</mark> (KAL uh reez) *n.* units used to measure the energy supplied by food
<mark>ultimate</mark> (UL tuh mut) *adj.* greatest; most important

22 UNIT 1 Why Read?

The Activity Pyramid

READING WORKSHOP 1

The Peak
Add daily activity to break up periods of sitting. Cut down on
- Watching TV
- Playing computer games
- Sitting for more than 30 minutes at a time

Leisure Activities
Do leisure activities a couple of times each week to add balance to your weekly Activity Pyramid. Leisure activities are low-level activities that don't expend as much energy as recreational activities. Examples include
- Badminton
- Frisbee

Flexibility and Strength
Flexibility exercises help improve or maintain muscle flexibility. Strength exercises help improve muscle strength if they are done two or three times per week. Flexibility examples include
- Gymnastics
- Stretching

Strength examples include
- Weight Machine
- Hand Weights

Aerobic Exercise
Aerobic exercise—best for your heart—means moving continuously for 20 minutes or more. Examples include
- Running/Jogging
- Jumping Rope
- In-Line Skating

The Base
It's important for everyone to add as many steps as possible to each day. The goal is to try to get 30 minutes of activity every day. Activities at this level include
- Taking the stairs
- Walking or Biking

Recreational Activities
Recreational activities will also improve your health. It's fun to try these sports. Examples include
- Volleyball
- Racquetball
- Karate

How He Did It 23

READING WORKSHOP 1 • Setting a Purpose for Reading

After You Read

How He Did It: Health Advice, Kid-to-Kid

Answering the BIG Question

1. Why do people read articles like "How He Did It"?
2. **Recall** How did Robert choose his topic for his school project?
   TIP **Right There** You will find this information in the article.
3. **Recall** According to the food pyramid, what foods should you eat the least?
   TIP **Right There** You will find this information in the article.

Critical Thinking

4. **Apply** Plan a menu for tomorrow's meals that meets the food pyramid guidelines.
   TIP **Author and Me** You will find clues in the article, but you must also use the information in your head.
5. **Infer** Why did Robert ask other people for help to create his Web site?
   TIP **Author and Me** You will find clues in the article, but you must also use the information in your head.
6. **Evaluate** Should the government be involved in helping people decide what to eat? Explain.
   TIP **On Your Own** Answer from your own experiences.

Write About Your Reading

Think about a Web site you'd like to design to help people. The front page, or home page, of a Web site is what you see when you go to the site. Create the home page of your Web site on a blank piece of paper. Your home page should include the answers to these questions:

- What will the site be about; what is your purpose or goal?
- Who will it help?
- How will it help people?
- What will you call your Web site, and where will the title be?
- What kind of graphics will you have, and where will they be?

Think about other Web sites you have seen.

Objectives (pp. 24–25)
Reading Set a purpose for reading
Grammar Identify parts of speech: action verbs

READING WORKSHOP 1 • **Setting a Purpose for Reading**

Skills Review

Key Reading Skill: Setting a Purpose for Reading

7. Review the sentence you wrote about your purpose for reading. Now write why your purpose stayed the same or why it changed as you read "How He Did It."

Key Text Element: Text Features

8. Look again at the Activity Pyramid. Do you think this is a good title for it? Explain your answer.
9. Think about the title and subtitle of this article, "How He Did It: Health Advice, Kid-to-Kid." Which part gives you more information? Explain your answer.

Vocabulary Check

In your Learner's Notebook write the words matched with their correct definition below. Then write a sentence for each word.

administrator   **advisory**
obesity   **calories**
ultimate

10. condition of being overweight
11. given the power to inform or give opinions
12. person who manages or directs
13. units used to measure the energy supplied by food
14. greatest; most important
15. **English Language Coach** What is the meaning of the word *wages*? Use a thesaurus to find two words that have a meaning similar to that of *wages*.

Grammar Link: Action Verbs

A verb is a word that shows an action or a state of being. **Action verbs** show what someone or something does.

Many action verbs are easy to spot, but some are not. To find an action verb, look for what something or someone *does*. In the following paragraph, all of the words in italics are physical or mental actions.

Ginny *walks* to school. Harvey *runs* to catch up. Leo *jumps* onto the sidewalk. Harvey and Ginny *leap* in surprise. At school, Ginny *reads* her textbook, Harvey *writes* a report, and Leo *dreams* about the weekend.

Some action verbs might be less obvious. Some action verbs show what someone or something is *thinking* or *feeling*.

Tania *cares* about all living things, but she really *loves* cats and dogs. She *wants* a kitten, but her mom *dislikes* pets.

Grammar Practice

Underline the action verbs in the following sentences.

16. Aisha and Frank share a seat on the bus.
17. During the game, Lisa twisted her ankle.
18. Grandpa plants a new crop of peppers every year.
19. I respect Quinn's talent as a singer.

Writing Application

Look at your Web site design page and circle all the action verbs you can find.

Web Activities For eFlashcards, Selection Quick Checks, and other Web activities, go to www.glencoe.com.

WRITING WORKSHOP PART 1

Summary
Prewriting and Drafting

ASSIGNMENT Write a summary

Purpose: Summarize main ideas and important details

Audience: You, your teacher, and some classmates

Writing Rubric

As you work through this assignment, you should

- write a summary of a selection you've read
- state the main idea in your own words
- correctly use linking verbs
- include important details
- leave out minor details
- correctly use linking verbs

See page 66 in Part 2 for a model of a summary.

Objectives (pp. 26–29)
Writing Use the writing process: prewriting, drafting • Paraphrase and summarize text: main ideas and supporting details
Grammar Identify parts of speech: linking verbs

Writing a summary of a selection in this unit will help you answer the Unit 1 Big Question: Why Read?

What Is It? A summary is a short piece of writing that retells the main idea and important details of a story or an event in your own words.

Prewriting
Get Ready to Write

In this workshop you'll write a summary about one of these selections:
- "Animal Attraction"
- "How He Did It: Health Advice, Kid-to-Kid"

Gather Ideas

After you choose the selection you want to summarize, read that selection again. As you reread, answer these questions in your Learner's Notebook:
- What is the selection's main, or most important, idea?
- Who or what is this selection about?
- What are the most important details?
- What happens in this selection?

Drafting
Start Writing!

It's time to start your summary. Whether you feel ready or not, get your pencil out and start writing!

Get It on Paper

These tips can help you start your summary:
- Look at the notes you made about the main points of the selection.
- Write the main idea in your own words.
- Write details that will help readers understand the main idea.
- Use your own words—don't copy what the author wrote.

WRITING WORKSHOP PART 1

Applying Good Writing Traits

Ideas

One of the best things about writing is that you get to share your ideas with other people. The ideas you share when you write may be yours, or they may belong to someone else like a friend, a family member, an author, or an expert on the topic you are writing about.

What Are Ideas?

Ideas are the important points a writer or speaker expresses.

- In nonfiction, the most important idea is called the **main idea**. The main idea is what you want readers to remember the most from your writing.
- In fiction, the main idea is called the **theme**.
- An **important detail** explains a lot about the main idea or the theme.
- A less important detail is called a **minor detail**.

Why Are They Important?

- People write for the purpose of sharing ideas.
- The main idea tells the reader what the rest of the writing will be about.

How Do I Do It?

1. **Main Idea** Write the main idea in one simple sentence.
2. **Important Detail** Write another sentence that explains the main idea.
3. **Minor Detail** Include a specific detail that relates to the important detail.

Analyzing Cartoons
Imagine that the person in this cartoon is a writer. What do the light bulbs represent? What size light bulbs does the writer want to catch?

In the example below, Damon writes about his day. Notice that he includes a main idea, an important detail, and a minor detail.

Today I had a really good day (**main idea**). *I got an A on the French quiz* (**important detail**) *that I studied really hard for* (**minor detail**). *After school, my basketball team won our game* (**important detail**). *The team we played was really tough* (**minor detail**).

When you write a summary, find the author's main idea and important details. Include the main idea and the most important details in your summary. Remember that summaries are short retellings of an original work, so don't include the minor details.

Write to Learn Write a paragraph about a good day that you had recently. This will be your main idea. Include important details that tell your

Writing Workshop Part 1   Prewriting and Drafting   27

WRITING WORKSHOP PART 1

Writing Models For models and other writing activities, go to www.glencoe.com.

Writing Tip

Authors write for many reasons:
- to persuade
- to explain
- to inform
- to entertain

Knowing why the author is writing will help you find the main idea to include in your summary.

Writing Tip

Summaries include the main idea and the most important details. Remove any extra or unnecessary information from your summary.

Writing Tip

Paraphrase by briefly retelling what you just read. Paraphrasing helps you understand and remember the selection.

Building Your Draft

Form

Your summary should be written in paragraph form. A paragraph is a series of sentences that are all about the same topic. When you write a summary, the topic of the paragraph is the main idea of the selection that you are summarizing.

Structure

- Begin by writing the main idea in a clear and simple sentence.
- Reread the original selection and then write three sentences that are related to the main idea.
- Put these sentences together to form a paragraph.
- You can begin your paragraph with the main idea, or you can end your paragraph with the main idea.

Main Idea	**OR**	Sentence About Main Idea
↓		↓
Sentence About Main Idea		Sentence About Main Idea
↓		↓
Sentence About Main Idea		Sentence About Main Idea
↓		↓
Sentence About Main Idea		**Main Idea**

Read the summary below. One of the sentences in this summary does not support the main idea. Can you find it?

"How He Did It: Health Advice, Kid-to-Kid" is an informational article about a nutrition Web site. The site was created by a boy named Robert Kohn as part of a school project. Robert's school is in Weston, New Jersey. Robert uses the site to help kids make healthy choices about diet and exercise.

Style

As you write your summary, keep in mind these two tips:

1. Write the main idea and supporting sentences in your own words. Using the author's words is copying, not summarizing. You will remember the selection better if you summarize in your own words.
2. Summaries do not include your own opinions or thoughts. Stick to the important details of the selection when you write a summary.

Go for It! Use the information in this workshop to continue your draft. Don't worry about spelling and grammar for now—just get your draft on paper!

Grammar Link

Linking Verbs

What Are They?

Not every sentence is about doing, thinking, or feeling. Some are just about the way things *are*. So not every verb is an action verb. Some verbs show a **state of being**. These are **linking verbs**.

Why Are They Important?

We use linking verbs all the time. They connect a person, place, or thing with a word that *describes* it or *tells what it is*.

The Linking Verb *To Be* The most common linking verb is the verb *to be*. Here are some forms of the *to be* verb:

is, am, are, was, were, been

- The food **is** spicy.

The verb *is* links *food* to *spicy*. *Spicy* describes *the food*.

- The trees in the park **were** all maples.

The verb *were* links *the trees* to *maples*. *Maples* names the kind of *trees*.

Other Linking Verbs Here are some other common linking verbs:
seem, look, feel, become, appear, grow, turn, taste, feel, smell, sound

- Chandra **turns** thirteen today.

The verb *turns* links *Chandra* and *thirteen*. *Thirteen* describes *Chandra*.

- At her party, Elli **seemed** shy.

The verb *seemed* links *Elli* to *shy*. *Shy* describes *Elli*.

How Do I Use Them?

Warning, Warning, Warning! Some words can be used as either action verbs or linking verbs. The job a verb does in the sentence makes it an action verb or a linking verb.

- Maria **looks** for music on the Internet.

Here the verb *looks* is an action. Maria is doing something.

- Maria **looks** pretty in that picture.

Here the verb *looks* connects *Maria* and *pretty*.

There's an easy test to tell whether a verb is a linking verb. Try replacing the verb with a form of the verb *to be*. If the sentence still makes sense, you're dealing with a linking verb.

- Maria **is** music on the Internet. (No! This use of *looks* is not a linking verb.)
- Maria **is** pretty in that picture. (Yes! This use of *looks* is a linking verb.)

Grammar Practice Copy the following sentences and underline the linking verb (or verbs) in each. If there are no linking verbs in a sentence, write an "N" next to it.

1. They seem serious about their work.
2. Food at ballparks is expensive, but it tastes good.
3. Ferdinand smells the flower.
4. The pitcher on the baseball team looked nervous.

Writing Application Underline all of the linking verbs in your summary.

Looking Ahead

That's all for now! Keep the writing you've done so far to use in Part 2 of this Writing Workshop.

READING WORKSHOP 2

Skills Focus

You will practice using these skills when you read the following selections:
- "Messaging Mania," p. 34
- "The Real Magic of Harry Potter," p. 42

Reading
- Skimming and scanning

Informational Text
- Using titles and subheads

Vocabulary
- Understanding multiple-meaning words in context

Writing/Grammar
- Using main and helping verbs
- Using present and present progressive tenses

Objectives (pp. 30–31)
Reading Skim and scan text

Skill Lesson

Skimming and Scanning

Learn It!

What Are They? To get information fast, try **skimming** and **scanning**. Skimming means quickly reading a piece of writing to get a *general idea* of what it's about. Scanning means looking for *key words* or *phrases,* usually ones you already know. For example, you would skim a newspaper article to find out what it is about. You would scan a newspaper article to see if it mentions your favorite musician.

- Skim to get the general idea of a text.
- Scan to look for specific words and information.
- Skimming and scanning are quick ways to get information, and they save time when you have a lot of reading to do.

"I don't like to give a lot of homework over the weekend, so just read every other word."

1998 Randy Glasbergen

Analyzing Cartoons
Moby Dick is the name of a famous American novel. Why wouldn't reading every other word be a good way to skim the novel?

READING WORKSHOP 2 • Skimming and Scanning

Why Are They Important? Skimming and scanning can help you save time, and who doesn't like to save time? When you skim, you can find out if a text is something you want or need to read without having to read the text carefully. When you scan a text, you can quickly find a section or part of a text that has the information you need.

How Do I Do Them? There are many ways to skim a text. Usually, you read only the title, any subheads, and the beginning of each paragraph. When you scan, you keep in mind the words or phrases you are looking for, then you run your eyes over the text to see if you can see them. Here is what one student noticed when using these skills to research a report on the Cinco de Mayo (SEENK oh day MY oh) celebration in Mexico.

Literature Online

Study Central Visit www.glencoe.com and click on Study Central to review skimming and scanning.

Mexican Culture

Celebrations Throughout the year, Mexicans enjoy several special celebrations called fiestas (fee EHS tuhs). National holidays include Independence Day (September 16) and Cinco de Mayo (May 5). Cinco de Mayo celebrates the day in 1862 that Mexicans defeated an invading French army in battle.

When I skimmed the passage, I saw the words Mexican Culture and Celebrations in dark print; that must be what this section is about. When I scanned the paragraph, I saw the words Cinco de Mayo, so I know this has information I need.

Practice It!

Skim and scan the article "Messaging Mania." Here, *mania* means a feeling of excitement over the trend of instant messaging. Skim the entire selection to find out what the article is about, and then scan for the word *parents*.

Use It!

Copy this list of questions in your Learner's Notebook. Write answers to the questions as you skim and scan "Messaging Mania."
- What do the subheads tell you?
- What does the first paragraph tell you?
- What is the selection about?
- What do some parents think about the subject?

READING WORKSHOP 2 • Skimming and Scanning

Before You Read : Messaging Mania

Meet the Author
Kathryn R. Hoffman enjoys being a writer. She says, "I like the idea of being able to reach out to a lot of people at once." Hoffman has always loved to read. Reading inspired her to start writing. Hoffman writes best in her journal. She says, "It's like talking to a good friend who won't criticize anything I say."

Author Search For more about Kathryn R. Hoffman, go to www.glencoe.com.

Vocabulary Preview

formal (FOR mul) *adj.* proper, following rules **(p. 34)** *Many kids speak formal English at school, but when they're with friends they speak in a more relaxed way.*

monitor (MAHN ih tur) *v.* to check or watch **(p. 36)** *Many parents monitor their children's use of the computer.*

Write to Learn Write the vocabulary word that each clue describes:
- You might do this if you want to follow the wins and losses of your favorite team.
- This describes the clothes you would wear to go to a wedding or some other special occasion.

English Language Coach

Multiple-Meaning Words Many words you already know have more than one meaning. The context, or other words in the sentence and paragraph, can help you find the correct meaning. Look at these two words in dark type and some of their meanings.

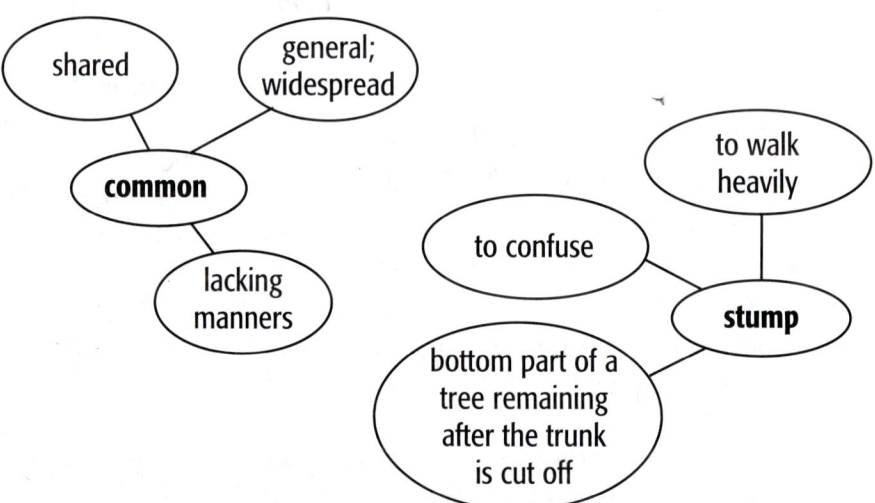

Partner Talk With a partner, read these sentences. Which definition of the underlined word makes sense in each sentence? Which words help you figure out the correct meanings? Talk it over with your partner.

1. His cousin was very <u>common</u>; he talked with food in his mouth.
2. We tried to <u>stump</u> Juan with hard questions, but he always knew the answers.

Objectives (pp. 32–37)
Reading Skim and scan text • Make connections from text to self
Informational Text Use text features: title, subheads
Vocabulary Use context clues: multiple meanings

READING WORKSHOP 2 • Skimming and Scanning

Skills Preview

Key Reading Skill: Skimming and Scanning

Before you read the selection, get a general idea of what it's about by skimming the title, the subheads, and parts of paragraphs and the text. Then, scan the text to find specific information about kinds of instant-messaging software, parents and IM, and IM slang.

Write to Learn After scanning the article, write down two companies that offer instant messaging software. Also, write down three examples of IM slang and their meanings.

Key Text Element: Titles and Subheads

A *title* is the name of a selection. *Subheads* emphasize parts of a selection and spark interest. To grab your attention, subheads are darker or a larger size than the rest of the text. Titles and subheads help you find and use information. Sometimes they show the important points of a selection. Use these tips to help you understand and use titles and subheads:

- Read the title and think about it.

  What does the title tell me about the subject of the selection?

- Read the subheads.

  What do the subheads tell me about the subject of the selection? What do they tell me about how the selection is organized?

- Think about how the title and subheads grab your attention.

  Do the title and subheads make me want to read this selection? Why or why not?

Partner Talk With a partner, talk about types of writing that use titles and subheads. Write at least three of these sources in your Learner's Notebook. Explain how titles and subheads help you find or understand information that you read in these sources.

Get Ready to Read

Connect to the Reading

Think about the ways you stay in touch with friends. Do you get together? Do you call each other? Do you send e-mails or instant messages to one another?

Whole Class Talk about ways to communicate with friends. List different ways you can stay in touch. Find out which ways your classmates use most or like best.

Build Background

Instant messaging is popular, but it's not new.

- Instant messaging is communicating over the Internet by two or more people typing messages that they receive instantly.
- People at colleges and universities started instant messaging in the 1980s and 1990s.
- After a program allowing most computer users to instant message came out in 1996, the Internet became a place for anyone to hold a conversation.

Set Purposes for Reading

BIG Question Read "Messaging Mania" to answer the Big Question "Why read?"

Set Your Own Purpose What else would you like to learn from the selection to help you answer the Big Question? Write your own purpose on the "Messaging Mania" page of Foldable 1.

Interactive Literary Elements Handbook
To review or learn more about the literary elements, go to www.glencoe.com.

Keep Moving

Use these skills as you read the following selection.

READING WORKSHOP 2

Messaging Mania

by Kathryn R. Hoffman

INFORMATIONAL TEXT
MAGAZINE

TIME for Kids

1 **2**

Think fast! Translate this conversation into **formal** English: "Wass^?" "N2M, U?" "JC." "G2G. BFN." Stumped?[1] The dictionary won't help you, but our handy guide will (*see page 37*).

If you figured it out right away, you are probably among the 60% of kids online who use instant messaging, or IM. Yahoo, MSN and AOL offer software that allows users to have real-time[2] conversations in pop-up text windows online. Instant messages are typed so fast that users don't slow down to capitalize, add periods and commas or spell out words. As a result, new word abbreviations and IM slang[3] are being invented faster than a high-speed Internet connection.

KEYBOARD NATION

An instant-messaging "chat" usually lasts more than half an hour, is between three or more people and often includes friends from different areas. More than one in three IM users say they use it every day, according to the Pew Internet and American Life Project. Nearly half of all online teens believe that the Internet has made their friendships better. It's a quick, easy way to keep in touch. **3**

---

1. **Stumped** means confused about something.
2. **Yahoo, MSN** (Microsoft Network), and **AOL** (America Online) are companies that provide **software**, or computer programs, for instant messaging. The programs allow for **real-time** text conversations, or typed messages on a computer screen that show up as the typing comes in.
3. **Abbreviations** (uh bree vee AY shuns) are letters or groups of letters that stand for longer words or phrases, such as ASAP for "as soon as possible." **Slang** is a relaxed language that people use in conversation.

Vocabulary

formal (FOR mul) *adj.* proper, following rules

Practice the Skills

1 **Key Text Element**

Titles and Subheads What does the title tell you about this selection? What do you learn from the subheads?

2 **Key Reading Skill**

Skimming and Scanning Skim the text to get a "big picture" of the selection. What does it look like this article is about?

3 **Key Reading Skill**

Skimming and Scanning Scan the first three paragraphs to find out about teens and instant messaging. How do many teens feel about IM?

READING WORKSHOP 2

Steven Mintz, 13, prefers messaging to the phone "because I can talk to more people at once." Chatting online is also a good way to keep up with friends who live far away. Kids don't have to worry about running up the telephone bill.

WRONG MESSAGE?

Instant messaging is not always a friendship builder. Sometimes, kids use it to air[4] angry or hurt feelings. Such kids aren't necessarily trying to be mean. Often, it's just easier to say something online than in person. Oliver Davies, 11, of Palo Alto, California, says that with IM, "I can express my emotions more easily, without having the guilt of saying it face-to-face."

Many parents and teachers thinks kids' instant messaging habits are taking away from more important things. Julia Long of Bellingham, Washington, says that when her son Taylor, 13, "is waiting for a beep,[5] it's hard (for him) to stay focused on homework or any kind of family activity."

---

4. When you *air* feelings, you express them or make them known to other people.
5. *Waiting for a beep* means waiting for the sound that means you have an instant message.

Analyzing the Graphic The article says, "Instant messaging is not always a friendship builder." Does this graphic support that idea? Explain.

READING WORKSHOP 2

Teachers get upset when Internet slang and emoticons,[6] such as "u" and "r" and "wuz," show up in kids' writing.

Kids' safety is also a concern. Staying connected is fine, but an online friendship with a stranger is not. Many parents **monitor** IM'ing, either by limiting time online or by keeping the computer in a **common** area. 4

I.M. NOT SO BAD

Researchers who study kids and the Internet say instant messaging isn't getting in the way of real life. They note that new technology often triggers[7] old, exaggerated fears. "It's similar to what was said in the 1980s about video games and in the '60s about television," says Nalini Kotamraju, an expert on how kids use technology to communicate. "There was this worry that kids would do nothing else."

Even parents and teachers who don't like IM have to admit that at least kids are writing. And their typing skills are improving. Is it at the expense of[8] proper English? Not so long as kids learn the difference between formal and conversational English,[9] says Naomi Baron, professor of linguistics[10] at American University in Washington, D.C.

"Language has always changed, and it always will," Baron said. "It must change as the things we do and things we encounter change."

Wat a relief! G2G. L8R. 5 ○

EMOTICONS

:-)	happy
:-(	sad
:-|	no feelings
:-D	very happy
:-P	tongue out
:-&	tongue twisted
;-)	wink
:-$	mouth shut, "not tellin'"
:'(	crying
:-O	surprised

Analyzing the Graphic Which emoticon on this graphic best describes how you feel as you read this article? Explain your answer.

Practice the Skills

4 English Language Coach

Multiple-Meaning Words Use the other words in a sentence or paragraph to help you figure out the meaning of a word with more than one meaning. Which meaning for the word **common** makes the most sense here?

5 BIG Question

On the "Messaging Mania" page of Foldable 1, explain how instant messaging relates to the Big Question. Your answer will help you complete the Unit Challenge later.

---

6. **Emoticons** are groups of keyboard characters that are supposed to look like facial expressions. People use them to express feelings when typing.
7. **Trigger** means to start something.
8. When something is done **at the expense of** something else, one thing is given up for the other.
9. **Conversational English** is the relaxed language you speak with friends or family members.
10. **Linguistics** (ling GWIS tiks) is the study of language and how people speak.

Vocabulary

monitor (MAHN ih tur) v. to check or watch

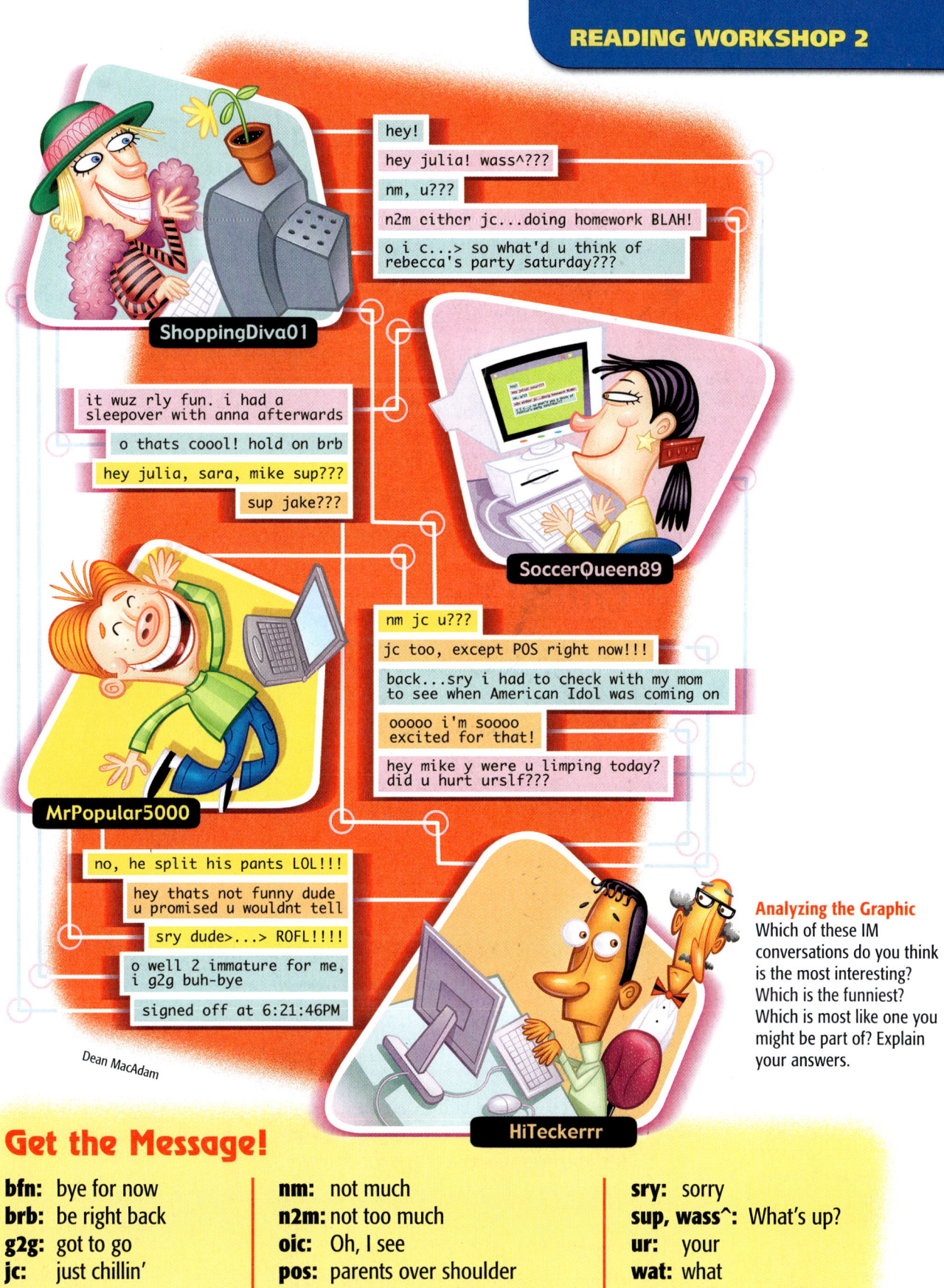

READING WORKSHOP 2 • Skimming and Scanning

After You Read : Messaging Mania

Answering the BIG Question

1. What is the most useful thing you learned from reading "Messaging Mania"? How do you think you will use this information?

2. Recall What are two reasons kids like instant messaging better than talking on the phone?

> **TIP Right There** You will find the answer in the article.

3. Summarize What are some problems with instant messaging?

> **TIP Think and Search** The answer is in the article, but the details are not all in one place.

Critical Thinking

4. Compare and Contrast The article lists two other forms of technology that caused "exaggerated fears" in the past. **(a)** What were they? **(b)** Compare those fears with fears of instant messaging today.

> **TIP Author and Me** You must use information from the article and your own thoughts.

5. Infer What effect do you think instant messaging will have on the English language?

> **TIP Author and Me** You must use information from the article and your own thoughts.

6. Evaluate Does instant messaging help or hurt friendships? Explain.

> **TIP On My Own** Answer from your own experiences.

Talk About Your Reading

Internet slang and abbreviations are common online, but we also use slang in our everyday conversations. With a partner, talk about slang that you use in conversation with friends and family.

- Make a list of three terms or phrases that you use in conversational, or slang, English, and talk about what they mean in formal, or proper, English.
- For example, does *chillin'* mean that you're relaxing?
- Talk about why it is a good idea to separate slang from formal English at school.

Objectives (pp. 38–39)
Reading Skim and scan text
Informational Text Use text features: title, subheads
Vocabulary Use context clues: multiple meanings
Grammar Identify parts of speech: main and helping verbs, present and present progressive tenses

READING WORKSHOP 2 • Skimming and Scanning

Skills Review

Key Reading Skill: Skimming and Scanning

7. How did skimming the article at the beginning help you learn what it was about in general? How did scanning the article help you find specific information about instant messaging?

Key Text Element: Titles and Subheads

8. The title of the selection is "Messaging Mania." What does the title suggest about instant messaging?
9. What did you learn about the main points of the article from the subheads in the selection?
10. Why are titles and subheads helpful in a magazine article?

Vocabulary Check

In the following sentences, fill in the blank with the correct vocabulary word from below.

        formal   monitor

11. Many teachers ___ their classes during tests.
12. Most people wear ___ clothes to the prom.
13. **English Language Coach** In your own words, write a short definition for each multiple-meaning word in bold. Use the context of the sentence for help.
    - He's the **kind** of person who is **kind**.
    - She works at a **bank** on the **bank** of a river.

Web Activities For eFlashcards, Selection Quick Checks, and other Web activities, go to www.glencoe.com.

Grammar Link: Main and Helping Verbs

- A **verb** is a word that shows action or a state of being.
- A **helping verb** is a verb that helps the main verb tell about an action or make a statement.

In these sentences, the verb is bold, and the helping verb or verbs are underlined.

Juan <u>is</u> **acting** in a play tonight.
Our class <u>will</u> **study** global warming.
Emilio <u>had been</u> **yelling** all day.
You <u>should have</u> **tried** harder.
No one <u>could have</u> **been** nicer to me.

- A **verb phrase** is one or more helping verbs followed by a main verb. In each sentence above, the underlined and bold words form a verb phrase.

Grammar Practice

Rewrite each sentence below, circle the main verb, and underline the helping verb or verbs.

14. The Internet club will meet after school.
15. Carol had been watching the basketball game.
16. Tiffany has helped her brother often.
17. Both girls are riding red bicycles.
18. The children should be listening to the story.

Writing Application Look back at the list you made of terms or phrases you use in conversational, or slang, English. Use each one in a sentence with a helping verb and a main verb.

READING WORKSHOP 2 • Skimming and Scanning

Before You Read: The Real Magic of Harry Potter

Meet the Author
Nancy Gibbs has been writing for TIME magazine for twenty years. Almost 100 of her stories have appeared in TIME. Gibbs writes about all types of interesting people, events, and issues. She reported for TIME on the events of September 11, 2001. When writing about heroes, she noted, "On a normal day, we value heroism because it is uncommon. On September 11, we valued heroism because it was everywhere."

Author Search For more about Nancy Gibbs, go to www.glencoe.com.

Vocabulary Preview

brilliant (BRIL yuhnt) *adj.* having or showing great ability or talent **(p. 43)** *He was a brilliant soccer player who always scored goals.*

familiar (FUH mil yur) *adj.* commonly seen, heard, or experienced; well-known **(p. 43)** *The words were familiar, but I couldn't remember the name of the song.*

resourceful (rih SORS ful) *adj.* able to deal with new or difficult situations **(p. 44)** *She is a resourceful artist who could make a work of art out of a pile of junk.*

Write to Learn In your Learner's Notebook, write a description of a person you know. Think of a friend or family member. Use at least two of the vocabulary words in your description.

English Language Coach

Multiple-Meaning Words You know that many words have more than one meaning. You can use other words in the sentence or paragraph to find out which meaning is being used. As you read "The Real Magic of Harry Potter," watch for these words. Use context clues to choose the correct meaning.

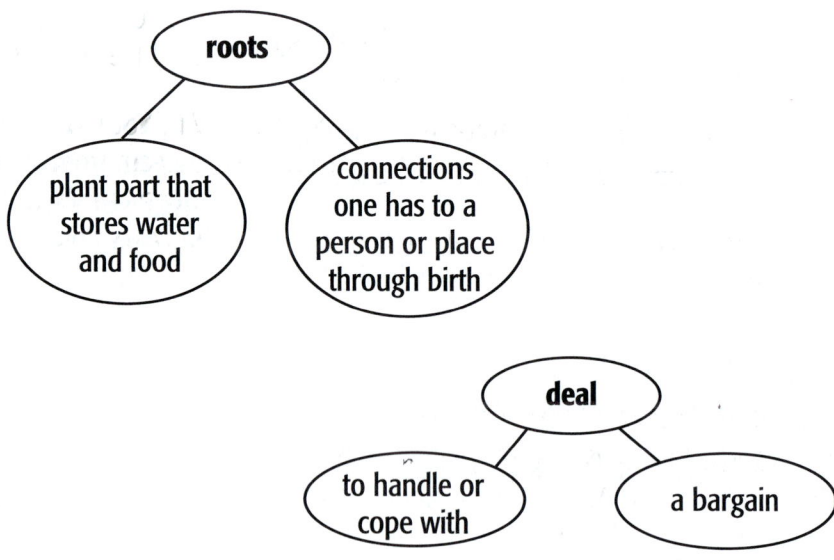

Work with a Partner Work with a partner to write sentences showing the different meanings of *roots* and *deal*. One of you should take the word *roots*; the other should take the word *deal*. Trade work with your partner and identify the meaning in each sentence.

Objectives (pp. 40–45)
Reading Skim and scan text • Make connections from text to self
Informational Text Use text features: title, subheads
Vocabulary Use context clues: multiple meanings

READING WORKSHOP 2 • Skimming and Scanning

Skills Preview

Key Reading Skill: Skimming and Scanning

Skimming and scanning make a good pair. You skim an article to get the big idea. You scan it to find specific information.

- When you skim, look at the title and subheads. Read the beginnings of paragraphs and quickly look over the entire text.
- When you scan, look for key words and phrases that have to do with the information you need.

Whole Class Discussion Point to the title and subheads in the selection. Discuss what the subject of the article might be. Brainstorm a short list of topics connected with the subject that you'd like to know more about. List key words that might lead you to that information in the article.

Key Text Element: Titles and Subheads

Titles and subheads make you curious, help you find information, and hint at what a selection is about. These tips will help you use titles and subheads.

- What hints does the title of the article give you about the subject of the article?
- If the title poses a question, there's a good chance you'll find an answer to the question in the text.
- What do you learn about the article from the deck?
- What do the subheads tell you about the article?

Partner Talk "The Real Magic of Harry Potter" has two subheads.
- Wild About Harry
- Bridging the Gap

With a partner, pick one of the subheads. Talk about what the subhead means and what main points it might touch on, and think of a question it might answer.

Interactive Literary Elements Handbook
To review or learn more about the literary elements, go to www.glencoe.com.

Get Ready to Read

Connect to the Reading

Do you have a favorite video game, TV show, book, or movie? Why do you like it?

Write to Learn If you were going to write a book that most kids could relate to, what would the book be about? Explain.

Build Background

You will learn from the article that people of all ages are fans of the Harry Potter books. There are now six books in the series.

- The author of the books, J. K. Rowling, first thought of the character Harry Potter in 1990 while riding on a train.
- It took Rowling a few years to write the first Harry Potter book. She was busy with a small child and had time to write only while her child slept.
- *Harry Potter and the Half-Blood Prince,* the sixth book in the series, was published July 16, 2005.

Set Purposes for Reading

BIG Question Read the selection the "Real Magic of Harry Potter" to find out why kids like to read the Harry Potter books.

Set Your Own Purpose What else would you like to learn from the article to help you answer the Big Question? Write your own purpose on the "Real Magic of Harry Potter" page of Foldable 1.

Keep Moving

Use these skills as you read the following selection.

READING WORKSHOP 2

TIME

The Real Magic of HARRY POTTER

Why are kids around the world so eager for each installment[1] of a story about a boy wizard? Some kids say it's because they see themselves in him. **1 2**

Glynis Sweeny

By **NANCY GIBBS**

It is hard not to believe in magic when you think about what J. K. Rowling has done. The author of the Harry Potter books has written the most popular children's series ever. Through more than 250 million copies of her books, Rowling speaks to kids in 200 countries—from China to the United States and points in between—in 61 languages and in Braille.[2]

It's probably no surprise to Rowling's fans that many children buy the books with their own money. Or that they wear out flashlight batteries reading the books after lights-out. And, no surprise here, even readers who dislike thick books have read Harry Potter not once or twice but a dozen times. For many fans, the books are far better than watching TV or staring at a computer screen.

When the fifth book in the series, *Harry Potter and the Order of the Phoenix,* was published in June 2003, it created a lot of excitement. There were Potter parties complete with owls,

1 **Key Text Element**

Titles and Subheads Read the title and the deck. Which tells you more about the subject of the article? What does it tell you?

2 **Key Reading Skill**

Skimming and Scanning Skim the entire article to get an idea of what it's about. What questions do you have after skimming? What key words and phrases would you use to scan the article for answers to these questions?

---

1. An ***installment*** is a part of a story that is published separately.
2. ***Braille*** (brayl) is a system of printing for people without sight. It is "read" by running your fingers over raised dots on a page or surface.

42   UNIT 1   Why Read?

cloaks, and butterbeer.[3] Kids wore their Potter pajamas. They even wanted to sleep in a "cupboard under the stairs," as Harry is forced to do by his creepy adopted family on Privet Drive. Some families ordered two or three books so that everyone could read the book at the same time. At close to 900 pages, *Harry Potter and the Order of the Phoenix* is the longest children's book there is. It was the best seller online only two hours after it was possible for computer users to order copies of it.

Other children's authors are fans of Rowling, too. "I think Rowling's a terrific writer," says Maurice Sendak, the award-winning author and illustrator of children's books. "She's a ripper-offer,[4] like me. She has taken from some of the best English literature and cooked up her own stew. It's **brilliant**."

Wild About Harry

So why all the fuss about Harry Potter? There were already lots of books with unicorns and wizards in them before Harry came along. And there were certainly lots of books about orphans searching for their **roots** and young people coming of age. [3]

What makes Rowling's books different? Simply put, readers say, she gets everything right. Rowling writes as though she knows what it's like to be 13 years old. She knows how it feels to be nervous or shocked at discovering what you can do if you try. Through her books, Rowling talks to kids as though they know as much as—or more than—she does about the things that matter. Many readers say they like the characters she has created, Harry above all, not because he is fantastic but because he is **familiar**.

Unlike big and all-powerful superheroes, Harry has the look of an ordinary guy but the heart of a hero. He is small but fast, and his slogan might be "The wand is mightier than the sword."

---

3. ***Butterbeer*** is a fictional drink from the Harry Potter books.
4. When Sendak says that Rowling is a ***ripper-offer***, he means that she borrows ideas from other works of literature.

Vocabulary

brilliant (BRIL yuhnt) *adj.* having or showing ability or talent

familiar (FUH mil yur) *adj.* commonly seen, heard, or experienced; well-known

[3] **English Language Coach**

Multiple-Meaning Words
Review the meanings of the word **roots** on page 40. Use the context around the word *roots* to determine the right definition in this sentence.

GERMANY Children at a Stuttgart library dress up as Harry, his friends, and some dragons.

"He's kind of like me," says Alex Heggen, 12, of Des Moines, Iowa, who sees some of himself in Harry and hopes to find more of Harry in himself. "He's just brave sometimes. . . . I've got black hair, I wear glasses, we're about the same height. . . . Wearing glasses and having braces—getting picked on is just your life. You have to deal with it."

Kids say that the friendship between Harry, Ron, and Hermione shows that Rowling understands how young people deal with one another. "She gets almost everything right," says Ligia Mizhquiri, 12, of Chicago, Illinois. "What happens [at Harry's school] happens to us. Some of us are popular. Some of us are not. Some of us get bullied. Some of us are bullies." 4

Harry's friendship with his buddy Ron is so familiar to kids that when word got out that a character would die in Book 4, children wrote to Rowling and begged her not to kill off Ron. They were afraid it would be the way it often is in the movies—the sweet best friend is the one who dies.

And Hermione is more than "the smart one." She's **resourceful** and at times she can be the toughest of the three. "Hermione ignores a lot," says Ellis O'Connor, 10, of Evanston, Illinois. "Ignoring while people are teasing is very, very important, because if you don't ignore them, they'll get on your nerves more, and it will be worse."

Kids who are teased because they don't have cool clothes can connect with Ron Weasley and his large family. "If you took all three [Harry, Ron, and Hermione] and put them into a blender, you'd get me," says Ryan Gepperth, 12, of Chicago. "I like to try new things, like Harry. I love reading, like Hermione. And I have problems of my own, like Ron. Ron gets made fun of a lot because he has a lot of brothers and sisters and he comes from a poor family. The other kids don't like him because of that."

The Weasleys *are* poor, but they also are hardworking, loving, and generous. Mrs. Weasley can cast a spell to make dirty dishes clean themselves, but she can't create money out of thin air to buy new appliances for the kitchen. That's the kind of family many Potter readers can understand.

SCOTLAND Fans young and old await Rowling's arrival aboard a recreated Hogwarts Express in Edinburgh.

4 Key Reading Skill

Skimming and Scanning Skim the article to find out more information about Hermione and Ron. What did you learn?

Vocabulary

resourceful (rih SORS ful) *adj.* able to deal with new or difficult situations

Bridging the Gap

Rowling creates a bridge for kids that connects Harry's world to their own. And the two worlds are very similar. The author knows the real world is "a bit spooky," she says. "I sleep at the top of the house (like Ron), and when it's stormy, I keep waking up wondering what creaked. . . . You see, I'm not as brave as Harry. If you told me there was a gigantic snake wandering around at night where I was living, I'd hide under the bedclothes and let someone else sort it out."

Rowling has created a world in which a boy can fly on a broom, talk to snakes, and grow gills like a fish. But he also has a hard time dealing with his sadness about his dead parents. "She mixes the real-life struggles in with the imaginary, magic struggles," says Casey Brewer, 15, of Longwood, Florida. "Harry and his friends have to think through [problems] in life the same as they have to think through a [problem] that's a three-headed dog. It's, like, inspirational."[5]

As in real life, Harry's world is exciting but not perfect. Wizards have worries and egos[6] and worn-out robes that they are embarrassed to wear. Even in Harry's magical world, there's no spell that fills a person's head with knowledge. The best Hermione can do in Book 3 is the Time Turner, which gives her more hours to study. Learning takes time for characters in a book as well as for real-life humans.

Harry is capable of jealousy and of not caring for others. He breaks rules and doesn't always tell grown-ups everything they'd like to know. He gets into trouble. ("If he didn't, you wouldn't have all those pages to read," notes Zack Ferleger, 12, of Encino, California.) Hermione may be smart, but she can be stubborn. Ron is loyal but unsure of himself.

Rowling loves her characters and invites her readers to love them, too. But the author doesn't love Harry, Ron, and Hermione only for their good qualities. She also loves them for the mistakes and the blemishes[7] that make them just like real kids—and real adults.

—Updated 2005, from *Time*, June 13, 2003

FRANCE Reading *Harry Potter et la Coupe de Feu* seems like more fun if you have the right accessories.

Key Text Element

Titles and Subheads Subheads divide the text of this article into sections. What is the main idea of each section?

BIG Question

On the "Harry Potter" page of Foldable 1, write three reasons to read a Harry Potter book. Think about why other kids said they enjoyed reading about Harry and his friends. Your response will help you complete the Unit Challenge later.

---

5. *Something **inspirational** (in spuh RAY shun ul) gives you hope.*
6. ***Egos** (EE gohs) are people's sense or feeling of self.*
7. ***Blemishes** (BLEM ish es) are flaws or marks that keep things from being perfect.*

After You Read

The Real Magic of Harry Potter

Answering the BIG Question

1. What did you learn about the Harry Potter books that might make you interested in reading them?
2. **Recall** Who is J. K. Rowling?
   TIP **Right There** You will find the answer in the article.
3. **Summarize** Who reads the Harry Potter books?
   TIP **Author and Me** Answer from the information in the article and from your own experience.

Critical Thinking

4. **Interpret** What does Maurice Sendak mean on page 43 when he calls Rowling a "ripper-offer"? How do you know?
   TIP **Author and Me** Answer using clues from the article and your own thoughts.

5. **Analyze** What makes the Harry Potter books so popular among kids?
   TIP **Author and Me** Answer from the information in the article and from your own thoughts.

6. **Compare and Contrast** (a) How is Harry Potter's world like the real world? (b) How is it different from the real world?
   TIP **Author and Me** Answer using clues from the article and from your own thoughts.

7. **Evaluate** Would you rather read a book about a superhero or about a hero like Harry Potter? Explain.
   TIP **On My Own** Answer from your own experiences.

Write About Your Reading

Imagine that you are going to interview a fan of the Harry Potter books. Write a list of seven questions about the books to ask the reader. Skim the article to get ideas for questions, but also think of questions that weren't covered in the article.

Objectives (pp. 46–47)
Reading Skim and scan text
Informational Text Use text features: title, subheads
Vocabulary Use context clues: multiple meanings
Grammar Identify parts of speech: present and progressive tenses

Skills Review

Key Reading Skill: Skimming and Scanning

8. Think about how skimming and scanning helped you understand and find information in the article. What general idea did you get by skimming the article? What specific information did you find by scanning?

Key Text Element: Titles and Subheads

9. What hints did the title "The Real Magic of Harry Potter" give you about the article?
10. What important information did the subheads give you?
11. Did the subheads tell you much about the sections of the article? Suggest two new subhead titles that would tell more about each section of the article.

Reviewing Skills: Setting a Purpose for Reading

12. What purpose do you think adults might have for reading the Harry Potter books?

Vocabulary Check

Copy the sentences below. Mark each sentence with a T or an F to show whether it is true or false.

13. Izzy can't play a note, so he's a brilliant musician.
14. A resourceful person can often get out of a difficult situation.
15. Icebergs are a familiar sight in Florida.
16. **English Language Coach** Write the word *cool* in the center of a word web. Use a dictionary to find the different meanings of *cool* and add them to your web. On page 44, read the first sentence of paragraph 5. What does *cool* mean here?

Grammar Link: Present and Present Progressive Tenses

Verbs change to tell when an action or state of being occurred. These different forms are called **verb tenses**.

The **present tense** may be used to talk about something that is happening now.

- The bus **is** late.
- We **need** help over here!

More often, the present tense is used to talk about actions that happen regularly, to describe something, or to state a general truth.

- Nate **plays** basketball. (happens regularly)
- Tia **has** long hair. (description)
- French people **speak** French. (general truth)

Usually, to show that something is happening at this very minute, you use the **present progressive tense**. To do so, use a form of the helping verb *be* and add *-ing* to the end of the main verb.

- I **am playing** the violin.
- You **are playing** the violin.

Grammar Practice

Copy each sentence below, filling in the correct verb or verb phrase. Use the verb shown before the sentence. Use the *form* of that verb that will communicate the fact given after the sentence.

17. (ride) Ed and Lily ___ the bus. (They regularly do.)
18. (walk) Joe ___ home. (He's doing this now.)
19. (write) She ___ poetry. (She's doing this now.)
20. (work) He ___ at the park. (He regularly does.)

Web Activities For eFlashcards, Selection Quick Checks, and other Web activities, go to www.glencoe.com.

READING WORKSHOP 3

Skills Focus

You will practice using these skills when you read the following selections:
- "Make Your Own Kite," p. 52
- from *The Great Cow Race*, p. 58

Reading
- Understanding graphics

Informational Text
- Identifying steps in a process

Vocabulary
- Understanding multiple-meaning words in context
- Academic Vocabulary: *process*

Writing/Grammar
- Using verb tenses correctly

Skill Lesson

Understanding Graphics

Learn It!

What Is It? The term **graphics** refers to pictures, drawings, maps, charts, tables, and graphs that present information to readers. Photographs, pictures, and art in books, magazines, and newspapers are graphics.

- Graphics get the reader's attention and direct the reader to particular information.
- Graphics add to the reader's understanding of information in a text.
- Graphics arrange information so that it's easy to read at a glance.

Analyzing Cartoons Look at the graphic on the wall in this cartoon. Who do you think created this graphic? Explain. What information are the children getting from the graphic?

Objectives (pp. 48–49)
Reading Use graphics to understand reading

READING WORKSHOP 3 • Understanding Graphics

Why Is It Important? It's not *always* true that a picture is worth a thousand words. But many things are easier to show than to tell. They may also be easier to understand. Graphics often give a great deal of information at a glance.

Study Central Visit www.glencoe.com and click on Study Central to review graphics.

How Do I Do It? Look at the picture and the words together. On a graphic, the few words are used to explain or label what the picture shows you. Sometimes, there are also lines and arrows that point from the words to the parts of the graphic they explain. Here's how one student used a graphic to learn about the cost of food at a ballpark.

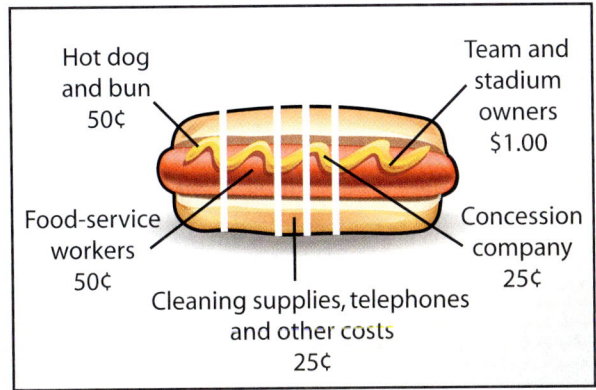

When I buy a hot dog, who gets the money? Where does the money go? This graphic really explains the answer, and it's easy to follow. The lines connecting the picture to the words show me where the money ends up.

Practice It!

Below are some questions you will learn answers to in "Make Your Own Kite." A graphic will help you answer each question. In your Learner's Notebook, try to write answers and draw pictures to answer these questions before you read. You may not know the answer to all these questions yet.

- What does a kite's frame look like?
- How do you make the *bridle* for a kite?
- What is the *tail* of a kite?
- How do you make a kite fly?

Use It!

As you read "Make Your Own Kite," think about the answers you wrote. Rewrite your answers and draw new pictures if necessary.

READING WORKSHOP 3 • Understanding Graphics

Before You Read: Make Your Own Kite

Technical writers write and sometimes design schedules, instructions, manuals, maps, and other important materials. Very few technical writers are famous. You usually don't see their names in print. Yet we all read the work of these specialized writers. They help us learn how to do and to make many things.

Vocabulary Preview

English Language Coach

Multiple-Meaning Words Sometimes you'll see a word you know, but it doesn't make sense in the sentence. That may be because you do not know all the meanings of the word.

Many words have multiple meanings. Often you can figure out the meaning that's being used by using clues from other words in the sentence or paragraph.

Look at the words below and some of their meanings.

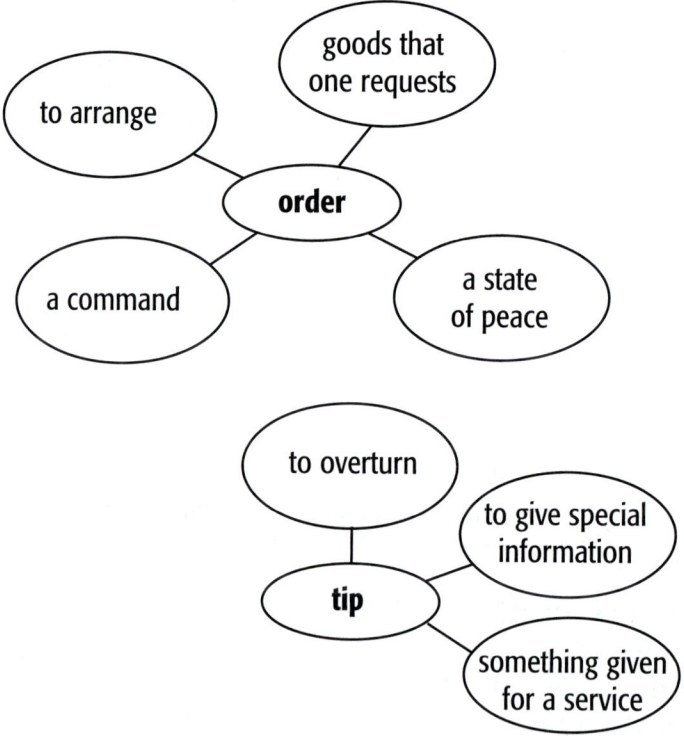

Partner Talk With a partner, discuss the meanings of the words *tip* and *order* in the following sentences.

1. Mr. Jones enjoyed his meal, so he left the waiter a <u>tip</u>.
2. Is your lunch <u>order</u> ready?
3. If you <u>tip</u> the boat, we're going to get wet.
4. The soldiers followed the general's <u>order</u>.
5. After the disaster, the police called for law and <u>order</u>.

Objectives (pp. 50–53)
Reading Use graphics • Make connections from text to self
Informational Text Identify text structure: steps in a process
Vocabulary Use context clues: multiple meanings

50   UNIT 1   Why Read?

READING WORKSHOP 3 • Understanding Graphics

Skills Preview

Key Reading Skill: Understanding Graphics

Before you read, think about the importance of graphics in your life. Have you ever

- followed signs and arrows to go somewhere?
- found information from a graph or chart?

Partner Talk With a partner, discuss two graphics you have each used in the past week. Explain what you learned from each graphic.

Key Text Element: Process

The events in a story are usually told in the order in which they happened. That's called time order. The organization of an article or a set of directions may be the order in which things *need* to happen in order to get a certain result. That's called a **process**. Seeing the structure of a process makes it much easier to understand what you're reading.

As you read, use these tips to help you recognize and understand process.

- Locate what the writer wants you to do or to make.
  Does the writer want you to understand an idea or an object?
- Look for a specific order or organization.
  How does the writer structure information? Does the writer use words such as first, next, now, *and* finally?
- Look for graphic aids, such as pictures, bullets, numbers, or bold type.
  Does the writer use graphics to walk you through a series of steps or groups of information?

Write to Learn Write a step-by-step process of one thing you do every day.

Academic Vocabulary

process (PRAH ses) *n.* a series of steps to follow in making or doing something

Get Ready to Read

Connect to the Reading

Have you ever tried to put something new together? Maybe you bought a game and needed to figure out how to play it. Or maybe you followed the directions for cooking a frozen pizza. You probably use processes to learn how to do things all the time!

Write to Learn Quickwrite for five minutes about a time you used directions. What did you learn? How did the directions help you?

Build Background

The selection you are going to read is about kites.

- There are many different kinds of kites. Most kites are simple wooden frames covered with paper or cloth and attached to a long line.
- Many people believe that a Chinese man named Mo Zi invented the kite more than 2,000 years ago. He got the idea for the kite after watching hawks fly through the sky.

Set Purposes for Reading

BIG Question Read "Make Your Own Kite" to learn how you can use graphics to build something.

Set Your Own Purpose What would you like to learn from the selection to help you answer the Big Question? Write your own purpose on the "Make Your Own Kite" page of Foldable 1.

Interactive Literary Elements Handbook
To review or learn more about the literary elements, go to www.glencoe.com.

Keep Moving

Use these skills as you read the following selection.

Make Your Own Kite **51**

READING WORKSHOP 3

INFORMATIONAL TEXT: WEB SITE

Make Your Own Kite

It's easy to make your own kite! **1**

All you need is:
—2 sticks (one stick should be three feet long, the other two feet long)
—string
—scissors
—glue
—a big sheet of paper

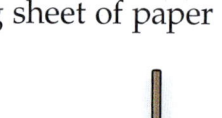

Make the String Frame

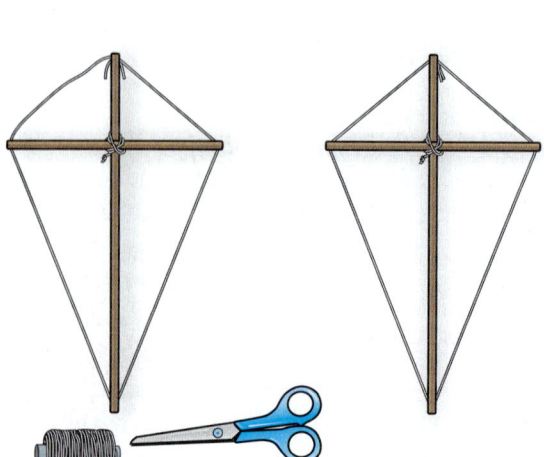

First, make a cross with the sticks, centering the shorter stick one-third of the way down the longer stick. Tie a piece of string to the joint and wrap it around, crossing over and under. Cut it and knot it. Cover the end of the string with glue and let it dry. Have an adult notch the ends of the sticks with a knife. Slot the string into the notches and pull it tight, all the way around. Knot the two ends of string together.

Practice the Skills

1 Key Text Element

Process Before you read on, skim the selection. What clues tell you that the writer is describing a process?

52 UNIT 1 Why Read?

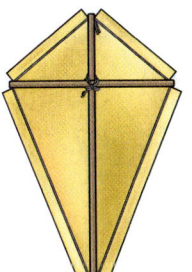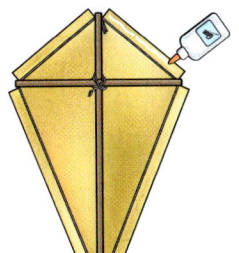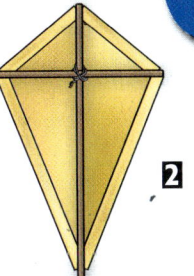

Key Reading Skill

Understanding Graphics How does the graphic help you understand the second step?

Cover the Kite

Lay the kite frame on the paper. Cut all around it, leaving the paper cover a little larger than the frame all the way around. Cut away the corners. Bend the edges of the cover over the string and the frame. Fasten them down with glue. If you haven't decorated your kite yet, now's a good time!

Make the Bridle

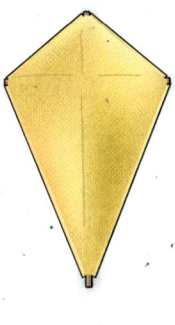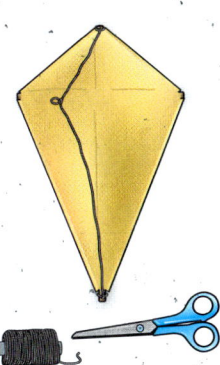

Now cut a piece of string the length of two sides of the kite (that's one short side plus one long side). Tie one end of the string around the top of the spine. Make a loop one-third of the way down the string and knot it. Tie the other end of the string to the bottom of the spine. Cut off any extra string.

English Language Coach

Multiple-Meaning Words Look up the word **bridle** in the dictionary. Which meaning of *bridle* fits best in this selection? How can you tell?

Make the Kite's Tail

Measure and cut a string that is five times as long as the kite. Cut more paper into little strips, measuring 2X3 inches. Tie the strips onto the string, 8 inches apart. Tie one end of the tail to the bottom of the kite. Now tie the kite line to the loop. The kite is ready to fly!

Key Text Element

Process Draw a picture for each step of the process in this paragraph. Number each picture in order. (Stick figures are okay!)

Make It Fly!

If you're by yourself, stand with your back to the wind. With one hand, hold your kite in the air by the lower corner. With your other hand, hold the winder. When the wind blows, let go of the kite, giving it a little push.

If you're with a friend, have your friend hold the kite in the air, with his or her face to the wind. Walk backward into the wind, letting out string as you walk. When the wind tugs at the kite, your friend should let it go. As the kite goes up, keep walking backward, letting out more line.

It's Easy to Bring a Kite Down

Walk toward the kite in the direction the wind is blowing and reel in the kite line as you walk.

BIG Question

What did you learn from this selection? How does the selection help you answer the Big Question? Write your answers on the "Make Your Own Kite" page of Foldable 1. Your response will help you complete the Unit Challenge later.

READING WORKSHOP 3 • Understanding Graphics

After You Read | Make Your Own Kite

Answering the BIG Question

1. Why is it important to read directions? What can they help you do?
2. **Recall** What do you do after you cover the end of the string with glue and let it dry?
   TIP **Right There** You will find the answer in the selection.
3. If you fly your kite by yourself, how should you stand?
   TIP **Right There** You will find the answer in the selection.

Critical Thinking

4. **Infer** Where should you fly a kite? What clues from the selection tell you?
   TIP **Author and Me** You will find clues in the selection, but you must also use the information in your head.
5. **Evaluate** The writer says, "It's easy to make your own kite!" After reading the selection, do you agree with the writer? Use details from the selection to explain your answer.
   TIP **Author and Me** You will find clues in the selection, but you must also use the information in your head.

Write About Your Reading

Write a Letter If you wanted to make a kite, would the selection help you build it successfully? Write a brief letter to the writer about how the directions were helpful or how they could be improved. Remember to include details. Use the following questions to get started.

- Overall, are the directions helpful? Why or why not?
- What is good about the directions?
- Which part of the directions would most help you make your kite?
- Which part of the directions confuse you?
- What would you change about the directions?
- What steps would you add to the directions?

Objectives (pp. 54–55)
Reading Use graphics
Informational Text Identify text structure: steps in a process
Vocabulary Use context clues: multiple meanings
Writing Write a letter to provide information
Grammar Identify parts of speech: past and past progressive tenses

Skills Review

Key Reading Skill: Understanding Graphics

6. How do the graphics in this selection help you better understand the process of building a kite? Do you think you could build a kite if the writer had not included graphics?
7. Which graphic most helps you "see" what to do? Why?

Key Text Element: Process

8. What words in the text help you recognize that the writer is describing a process?
9. Summarize the process of building a kite in five or six steps. Use the subheads if you need help.

Vocabulary Check

10. **Academic Vocabulary** A process is a series of ___ that you follow when you make or do something.

English Language Coach You saw the word *frame* in the selection. Look at the word and some of its meanings below. Then rewrite the sentences and match each meaning of *frame* to a sentence.

frame
- a. the skeleton of a human or animal body
- b. a construction that gives shape or strength
- c. an open structure that holds a picture, mirror, etc.
- d. to create false evidence against someone

11. Before you add walls, you must build the frame of the house.
12. He needs very long pants because of his tall frame.
13. The burglar tried to frame me for his crime.
14. I put the photo in a frame.

Web Activities For eFlashcards, Selection Quick Checks, and other Web activities, go to www.glencoe.com.

Grammar Link: Past and Past Progressive Tenses

The **past tense** of a verb shows an action or state of being that has already happened. Usually, you form the past tense by adding *-ed* to the end of the verb.

- It **rained** hard last night.
- As a child, Mom **played** tennis.

There is more than one way to talk about the past. You may want to talk about continuing action. To show that something was still going on at the time you're talking about, use the **past progressive tense**. To do this, use the helping verb *was* or *were* and add *-ing* to the main verb.

In the sentences below, the helping verb is underlined and the main verb is bold.

- We <u>were</u> **watching** TV together.
- While I <u>was</u> **sleeping**, the rain started.
- Fran <u>was</u> **cooking** dinner, while her brothers <u>were</u> **cleaning** the house.
- They <u>were</u> **eating** when the phone rang.

Grammar Practice

Copy the sentences below on a separate sheet of paper. Underline all the verbs or verb phrases in each sentence. Look for both the past tense and the past progressive!

15. I was practicing all afternoon.
16. Cara was swimming while Marsha was walking on the track.
17. Jon and Milly bought books at the mall while they were shopping.
18. The cookies were baking when Les arrived.

Writing Application Look back over the letter you wrote. Check to make sure that you used the past and past progressive tenses correctly.

READING WORKSHOP 3 • Understanding Graphics

Before You Read : from *The Great Cow Race*

Meet the Author
Jeff Smith was born and raised in the American Midwest. He wrote comic strips for Ohio State University's student newspaper for four years. In 1991 he started his own company, Cartoon Books. Smith's work has been published in thirteen languages, and he received an Eisner Award for *The Great Cow Race* in 1994.

Author Search For more about Jeff Smith, go to www.glencoe.com.

Vocabulary Preview

English Language Coach

Multiple-Meaning Words When you run into a word with more than one meaning, the first step is to look for clues to its meaning in the sentences around it. But sometimes the meaning used may be unfamiliar to you. In that case, you also need to look in a dictionary. Then you can try the different meanings to see which one makes sense in the sentence. Look at the examples in the chart.

Sentence	Multiple Meanings of Word	Context Definition
I took the dog for a walk in the park.	a piece of ground kept in a city for recreation; an enclosed arena or stadium used for games; a space occupied by vehicles	a piece of ground kept in a city for recreation
She delivered the puppies from the thief's clutches.	to send to an intended destination; to set free; to assist in giving birth	to set free
Miles needed a new reed for his saxophone.	tall grasses with slender, jointed stems that grow in wet areas; a person or thing too weak to rely on; a thin wood or plastic tongue that vibrates against the mouthpiece of a wind instrument causing sound when blown upon	a thin wood or plastic tongue that vibrates against the mouthpiece of a wind instrument causing sound when blown upon

Write to Learn Look up the following words in a dictionary. In your Learner's Notebook, write the multiple meanings of the words. Then write a paragraph for one of the words using several of its meanings.

1. cook
2. pass
3. reflect

Objectives (pp. 56–61)
Reading Use graphics • Make connections from text to self
Informational Text Identify text structure: steps in a process
Vocabulary Use context clues: multiple meanings

READING WORKSHOP 3 • Understanding Graphics

Skills Preview

Key Reading Skill: Understanding Graphics

Graphics, such as charts, graphs, time lines, and pictures, give you information at a glance and explain something visually. Graphics are especially important in graphic novels, cartoons, and comic strips. These all have little text, so writers use graphics to share information with readers. Keep the following questions in mind as you read the selection:

- How do the graphics share the characters' emotions?
- What information do the graphics give you that the text does not?

Write to Learn Pick a school subject that you have seen graphics in, and write about how graphics help you to understand that subject (a time line in a history class, for example). How does the graphic help you to understand the subject?

Key Text Element: Process

To understand a **process**, you need to be able to see and follow the steps. Writers use clues to help you, including time words (such as *next* and *finally*), numbers, and graphics. As you read, you can use the tips below to help you recognize the steps in a process and understand what you're reading.

- Sometimes a process will use words like *first, then, after, next,* and *finally* to show when to complete the different steps in the process.

  How do these steps show you the end of one step and the beginning of another?

- Sometimes a process is numbered.

  Do you see numbers indicating the order of the steps?

- Some processes have graphics or pictures to explain the steps visually.

  How can a graphic be helpful when you are learning a process?

Write to Learn Think of a process you go through every day. In your Learner's Notebook, number and list all of the steps. Circle any steps that might be hard for someone else to understand. Make notes next to those steps about ways to explain them clearly.

Get Ready to Read

Connect to the Reading

Have you ever admired someone, but didn't know how to express yourself? Did you call them on the phone, have a friend tell them, write a letter, or say something in person? What kind of advice would you give a friend in that situation?

Write to Learn In your Learner's Notebook, write about how you would approach someone you admire. Would you write a letter or a poem, call the person on the phone, write a song, or draw a picture? Explain why your choice is the best way to impress the person you admire.

Build Background

The selection that you are about to read is a passage from the graphic novel *The Great Cow Race*. *The Great Cow Race* is the second novel in a series called *Bone*. It is about the adventures of the Bone cousins: Fone Bone, Phoney Bone, and Smiley Bone.

- A graphic novel is a long, illustrated story.
- Graphic novels are growing in popularity in the United States. In 2003 graphic novels had more than $120 million in sales.

Set Purposes for Reading

BIG Question Read *The Great Cow Race* to find out why you should read the letters people write you.

Set Your Own Purpose What else would you like to learn from the selection to help you answer the Big Question? Write your own purpose on the "Great Cow Race" page of Foldable 1.

Interactive Literary Elements Handbook
To review or learn more about the literary elements, go to www.glencoe.com.

Keep Moving

Use these skills as you read the following selection.

from *The Great Cow Race*

READING WORKSHOP 3

Practice the Skills

from The Great Cow Race

1 Key Reading Skill

Understanding Graphics Look at the first graphic. One piece of information you learn from the graphic is that Bone is in a forest. What other information does the graphic give you that the text does not?

2 BIG Question

You can see that Bone is in the woods reading. What might be his purpose for reading? Your response will help you complete the Unit Challenge.

3 Key Reading Skill

Understanding Graphics The fourth picture, or frame, contains no words at all. What does the graphic tell you about Bone's thoughts? How do you know this?

From BONE ®: THE GREAT COW RACE by Jeff Smith. Copyright © 2005, 1993, 1992 by Jeff Smith. Published by Graphix, an imprint of Scholastic Inc. Reprinted by permission.

READING WORKSHOP 3

Practice the Skills

4 **English Language Coach**

Multiple-Meaning Words You'd probably say that a joke is <u>funny</u> because it makes you laugh. But notice how *funny* is used here. Can you find the clue to the meaning of *funny* in Ted's reply to Bone? If not, check a dictionary.

from *The Great Cow Race*

READING WORKSHOP 3

Practice the Skills

5 **Key Text Element**

Process Bone is actually going through a *writing process*. Look back through the graphics, and find the beginning of Bone's writing process. How do you know when his process begins; how do you know when it ends? Is most of the process shown with pictures or words? How many steps are in Bone's process?

READING WORKSHOP 3

Practice the Skills

6 **Key Reading Skill**

Understanding Graphics In the last graphic, Bone's letter is sitting on a stump. What do you think that means? Why do you think that graphic is so much larger than all the others?

7 **BIG Question**

What would you do if you were walking through the woods and saw a letter sitting on a stump? What might your reasons be for reading the letter? Write your answer on "The Great Cow Race" page of Foldable 1. Your response will help you complete the Unit Challenge later.

from *The Great Cow Race* 61

READING WORKSHOP 3 • Understanding Graphics

After You Read from *The Great Cow Race*

Answering the BIG Question

1. What are two reasons for reading graphic novels?
2. **Recall** To whom is Bone writing his poem?
   TIP **Right There** You will find the answer in the text.
3. **Recall** Why does Ted suggest that Bone write a poem?
   TIP **Right There** You will find the answer in the text.

Critical Thinking

4. **Infer** Does Ted think Bone has the ability to write a love poem? Use details from the text to support your answer.
   TIP **Author and Me** You will find clues in the story, but you must also use the information in your head.
5. **Draw Conclusions** What do you think happens at the end of the story?
   TIP **Author and Me** You will find clues in the story, but you must also use the information in your head.
6. **Evaluate** Do you think writing a love poem is a good way to show someone that you like him or her?
   TIP **On My Own** You must use the information in your head.

Write About Your Reading

Design your own "graphic novel" explaining a process. Look back at the activity on page 57 in which you explained and numbered a process. Use the process you explained or choose another one. Give each step its own graphic (draw boxes, use text, and maybe even create your own character–like Bone–to help explain the steps). If you have time, add color. You don't have to be a perfect artist–use stick figures or simple shapes if you want.

Objectives (pp. 62–63)
Reading Use graphics • Make connections from text to self
Informational Text Identify text structure: steps in a process
Vocabulary Use context clues: multiple meanings
Writing Design a graphic novel
Grammar Identify parts of speech: present perfect and past perfect verb tenses

Skills Review

Key Reading Skill: Understanding Graphics

7. The graphics show Bone's different expressions. How do these expressions reveal what Bone is thinking or feeling? Give examples from the story.

Key Text Element: Process

8. How many steps are there in Bone's writing process? What is each step?

Vocabulary Check

9. English Language Coach Look back at the word *sweeps* in the tenth frame of the story. In your Learner's Notebook, write two sentences with different meanings for that word. Use a dictionary to look up the meanings of *sweep* if necessary.

Grammar Link: Present Perfect and Past Perfect Tenses

Another tense to use while talking about the past is the **present perfect tense**. To form it, use the helping verb *have* or *has* and what is called the "past participle" of the main verb. (For most verbs, the past participle is the same as the past tense.)

You can use this tense to talk about something that happened but only if *when* it happened isn't important. Don't use it to talk about a specific time.

- Right: I **painted** my house.
- Right: I **have painted** my house.
- Wrong: I **have painted** my house in May.

You can use this tense with *never* or *already*, because they don't refer to a particular time.

- Right: I **have** already **painted** my house.
- Right: I **have** never **painted** my house.

You *must* use this tense to talk about something that happened and is still happening.

- Wrong: I **collected** stamps since last year.
- Right: I **have collected** stamps since last year.

To talk about something that happened (or didn't happen) before something else, you can use the **past perfect tense**. To form it, use the helping verb *had* and the past participle of the main verb.

- Hilda **had mowed** the lawn before the rain started.
- Hilda **had** never **mowed** the lawn until Ruth showed her how.

Don't use this tense to talk about only one event. Use it only if you're talking about something that happened before something else.

- Wrong: This morning, Dad **had poured** my juice.
- Right: Before I got up, Dad **had poured** my juice.

Grammar Practice

Write the numbers from 10 to 15 on a separate sheet of paper. Next to each, write *C* if the sentence is correct. If it's incorrect, write it correctly.

10. I have never missed a day of school.
11. When Martha was six, she has learned to read.
12. Since July, Chaz played better.
13. Every year, tulips have bloomed in our yard.
14. Last summer, we have traveled to Mexico.
15. When we got there, Sam had not arrived.

Writing Application Look back at your writing assignment. Check to see if you wrote correctly about things that happened in the past. If you made any mistakes, correct them.

Web Activities For eFlashcards, Selection Quick Checks, and other Web activities, go to www.glencoe.com.

WRITING WORKSHOP PART 2

Summary
Revising, Editing, and Presenting

ASSIGNMENT Write a summary

Purpose: Summarize main ideas and important details

Audience: You, your teacher, and some classmates

Revising Rubric

Your revised summary should have

- a main idea stated in your own words
- important details from the selection
- no unrelated information
- all words spelled correctly
- verbs used correctly

Objectives (pp. 64–67)
Writing Use the writing process: paraphrasing and summarizing • Revise a draft to include: main ideas and supporting details • Compare summary to original • Edit writing for: grammar, spelling, punctuation • Present writing
Grammar Use verbs
Listening, Speaking, and Viewing Use visuals in presentation • Listen actively

---

In Writing Workshop Part 1, you drafted a summary about one selection from the beginning of the unit. You may not remember what these selections were about, and that's okay. Read the draft of your summary to refresh your memory. Then reread the original selection. Think about how well your summary reflects the original selection.

Revising
Make It Better

In this workshop, you'll work on a few skills to improve your draft. This part of the writing process is called revising, and it is your chance to make your writing look and sound just right. As you revise, you will use the tips in this workshop to turn your draft into a final product.

Check for Main Idea Read your summary again and ask yourself these questions: Have I included the author's main idea? Have I included the most important details?

If you answered *no* to one or both of these questions, go back and correct your summary.

Check for Coherence When all of the sentences in the paragraph fit together just right, the writing is coherent. That means that it holds together and makes sense. Here is one way to make your writing more coherent:

- Write events in the order that they happened: this is called **chronological order.**

Chronological Order	Not Chronological Order
Robert was given a homework assignment.	Robert decided that childhood obesity was a good topic.
He talked about the assignment with his parents.	Robert researched topics for his assignment.
Robert decided that childhood obesity was a good topic.	Robert was given a homework assignment.

- Start your sentences with linking words and phrases. These are called **transitions.** Some transitions can help you write in chronological order. Try using the words *first, in the beginning, next, finally,* or *last.*

64 UNIT 1 Why Read?

WRITING WORKSHOP PART 2

Editing
Finish It Up

After you finish writing, it's time to edit your work for grammar, usage, mechanics, and spelling. Read your summary one sentence at a time and use the **Editing Checklist** to look for errors.

Editing Checklist
- ☑ All words are spelled correctly.
- ☑ Every sentence has a verb.
- ☑ All verbs agree with their subjects.
- ☑ Verb tenses are correct.

Compare Your Summary with the Original

Before you say that your summary is finished, compare it with the original selection. Read the entire selection and ask yourself the following questions about your summary:

- Have I created a shorter version of the original?
- Have I included the author's main idea?
- Have I clearly written what this selection is about?
- Have I left the minor details out of my summary?

You should have answered *yes* to all of the questions, but if you didn't, there is still time to go back and make changes to your summary.

Publishing and Presenting
Show It Off

Now that your summary is finished, print it out or write a new copy that is easy for you to read.

- Find a partner who has summarized a different selection.
- Take turns reading your summaries aloud.
- After your partner reads his or her summary, tell the writer interesting sentences, phrases, or words that you heard in the summary.

Listen for these parts of your classmate's summary:
- Main idea
- Important details
- Extra information

After school, ask a family member to read your summary. See if the person can identify the main idea and topic sentences.

Writing Models For models and other writing activities, go to www.glencoe.com.

> **Writing Tip**
>
> One of the most important parts of editing is making sure that all words are spelled correctly. Even if you use a spellchecker on your computer, look up words you're not sure about in a dictionary.

> **Writing Tip**
>
> If you are handwriting your final draft, try to use your best handwriting. Take your time. Erase your mistakes instead of crossing them out.

WRITING WORKSHOP PART 2

Active Writing Model

Writer's Model

Summary of "Ballpark Food"
By Sharice Johnson

The student wrote the main idea of the original selection in her own words.

Thirty-six kids investigated the high price of food at baseball parks. The kids found that ballpark food costs three to seven times more than the same food at the grocery store. Most of the profits of high-priced stadium food go to the athletes and the stadium owners. The kids concluded, "You almost need a major-league salary to afford ballpark food!"

This is an important detail that supports the main idea.

The writer uses a transition, *the kids concluded,* to begin this sentence.

One way to avoid high prices at the ballpark is to bring your own food. Most stadiums let you do this, but ushers have the right to check inside bags and take away items that could be thrown onto the field.

This paragraph begins with an important detail from the article.

The kids also collected information about advertisements found at ballparks. They found ads on just about everything, including concession stands. One fan named Tess believed that the "sneakiest ads" followed the replays on the big-screen television because everyone in the stadium watches the replays.

This sentence supports the important detail.

Listening, Speaking, and Viewing

Getting Information from Visuals

What Are Visuals?

Visuals are the images or pictures that you see in various forms of mass communication such as television, the Internet, and magazines. When you look at visuals in media, you make a judgment of what you see—either you like it, or you don't. How you respond to a picture of a sleeping kitten is different from how you respond to a picture of a roaring tiger.

Why Are Visuals Important?

Pictures are powerful. They appeal to our minds, our feelings, and our imaginations. Looking at a picture carefully can help you notice more details and get more information. You may also see things that entertain you or make you laugh.

At the same time, learning to look at a picture carefully can help you make up your own mind about things. Otherwise, a picture may make you think things that are not true.

How Do I Do It?

Here are some ways to evaluate visuals:

- Look at all the parts of the picture. If there are people, look at their expressions. Look at how they are standing or sitting. If a picture shows an activity, imagine the movement it shows.
- Look at the colors in a picture. If they are dark, they may make you feel sad, even if what the picture shows is not particularly sad. A dark picture of a person may make you like that person less.
- Think about what the picture suggests. Suppose an article is about crime, and the picture shows a young person. Does that suggest that young people are the worst criminals or that lots of young people are criminals? Do the facts in the article back up what the picture or pictures suggest?

View to Learn Analyze the advertisement on this page. With a partner, answer these questions:

- What is the purpose of this advertisement?
- Does the visual in this advertisement affect the viewers' feelings in a positive or negative way? How?

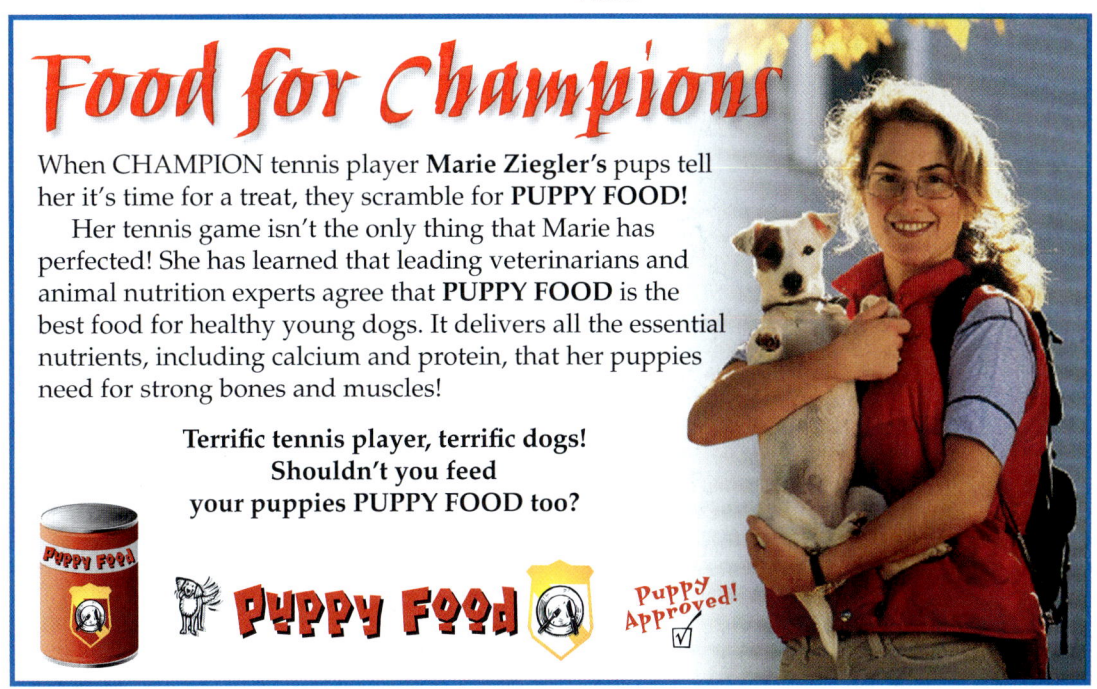

READING WORKSHOP 4

Skills Focus

You will practice using these skills when you read the following selections:
- "To Young Readers," p. 72
- "Why Books Are Dangerous," p. 78

Reading
- Identifying main idea and supporting details

Literature
- Determining the author's purpose

Vocabulary
- Using word references to determine the meaning of unknown or multiple-meaning words

Writing/Grammar
- Identifying and using irregular verbs

Skill Lesson

Identifying Main Idea and Supporting Details

Learn It!

What Is It? The **main idea** is the most important idea in a paragraph or an article. In many paragraphs, a topic sentence states the main idea. The other sentences add **supporting details.** Other times the main idea is not clearly stated, and the reader needs to figure out the main idea that connects the supporting details. If you can't find a topic sentence, try to state the main idea in your own words.

Analyzing Illustrations
What is going on in this picture? Keep in mind that light bulbs stand for ideas.
- What is the man in the middle of the picture doing?
- Who has "the best idea" in this picture? Explain why you think so.

Objectives (pp. 68–69)
Reading Identify main ideas and supporting details

READING WORKSHOP 4 • Identifying Main Idea and Supporting Details

Why Is It Important? Finding the main idea helps you
- understand what the author is trying to say
- understand and recall information better
- form your own opinions and ideas as you read

How Do I Do It? A writer may tell you the main idea at the beginning of an article or paragraph. "People should plant more trees," for example. This idea is followed by details that support it. If the main idea isn't stated, you need to figure out what it is. Look for clues as you read. Does the writer go back to one idea again and again? Do most of the details seem to be about one thing? When you finish reading, try to finish this sentence: "This writer believes . . ." Here's how one student found the main idea in "Animal Attraction."

Study Central Visit www.glencoe.com and click on Study Central to review main idea and supporting details.

> Most people agree that a pet adds joy to its owner's life. A pet can give a person's life meaning. And this can be more true after the death of a loved one. Scientists are now finding that pets may also keep their owners healthy.

This paragraph is about people and pets. I think the main idea is that owning a pet is good because every sentence talks about some way in which pets help people.

Practice It!

In your Learner's Notebook, practice finding the main idea and supporting details for the opening lines of "To Young Readers." You can ask yourself these questions to help find the main idea and supporting details.
- What are these lines about, and what do I already know about this topic?
- Is there one idea that all of the lines in the poem relate to?
- What main idea do the supporting details point out?

Good books are / bandages and voyages / and linkages to Light;

Use It!

As you read "To Young Readers" and "Why Books Are Dangerous," remember to use these questions to help you find the main idea and supporting details of a text. Write the questions out in your Learner's Notebook ahead of time, and answer them as you read the selection.

READING WORKSHOP 4 • Identifying Main Idea and Supporting Details

Before You Read : To Young Readers

Meet the Author

"I loved poetry very early [in life] and began to put rhymes together at about seven," Gwendolyn Brooks said. At the age of 33, she became the first African American to win the Pulitzer Prize in poetry. Brooks says, "Reading is important—read between the lines. Don't swallow everything." For more about Gwendolyn Brooks, see page R1 of the Author Files.

Author Search For more about Gwendolyn Brooks, go to www.glencoe.com.

Objectives (pp. 70–73)
Reading Identify main ideas and supporting details • Make connections from text to self
Literature Identify literary elements: author's purpose
Vocabulary Use word references: dictionary

Vocabulary Preview

nutrition (noo TRI shun) *n.* that which feeds the body **(p. 72)** *Proper nutrition helps you stay healthy.*

nourished (NUR ishd) *adj.* provided with food or other substances necessary for life **(p. 72)** *I feel nourished after I have eaten a hot breakfast.*

Partner Talk With a partner, think of a food. Write a short paragraph describing the food, but don't name it. Include the vocabulary words in your paragraph. Exchange your paragraph with your partner. Guess the food described.

English Language Coach

Word References When you use a reference book to learn the meaning of an unknown word or a word with more than one meaning, consider the way it's used in the text. Read the sentence and the dictionary entries below for the word *address.* Which meaning best fits the word as it is used in this sentence?

Mrs. Woy gave an inspiring graduation address.

> ad•dress (*n.* ə dres′, ad′ res; *v.,* ə dres′) *n.* 1. a formal speech. 2. location of a building or place at which a person or organization can be reached. 3. writing on a letter or other item to be delivered stating its destination.

If you said the first definition, you are correct. The first definition, a formal speech, makes sense.

Write to Learn Look up the underlined words in a dictionary. Then look at how the words are used in the sentences. Which dictionary definition fits each word? Write the word and the correct definition of it in your Learner's Notebook.

1. Jackson made a <u>rash</u> decision when he chose to eat six pieces of cake.
2. Becky could not play in the last inning because of her <u>game</u> leg.
3. My mother wants to use the coupon before it <u>expires</u>.

READING WORKSHOP 4 • Identifying Main Idea and Supporting Details

Skills Preview

Key Reading Skill: Identifying Main Idea and Supporting Details

As you read the poem, look for the main idea. Remember that the main idea in poetry is often not stated directly. To find the main idea

- ask yourself what the poem is about
- use the details to determine the main idea

Write to Learn In your Learner's Notebook, list the things that Brooks compares good books to. What do these items have in common? Use your answer to determine the main idea.

Key Literary Element: Author's Purpose

There are many different purposes for writing. There are, however, four main ones: to entertain, inform, persuade, or express emotions. Of course, most of the time, an author has more than one purpose. To understand the author's purpose, ask yourself some questions as you read.

- What is the genre? This can give you an idea about the author's purpose. For example, short stories are often written to entertain, and editorials are often written to persuade.
- Who is the intended audience? That is, who is supposed to be reading the material?
- What words were chosen? An author who uses a lot of emotional or strong words may be trying to persuade you of something.

Interactive Literary Elements Handbook
To review or learn more about the literary elements, go to www.glencoe.com.

Get Ready to Read

Connect to the Reading

Brooks says, "Good books are good nutrition." She means that books are like healthy food; they strengthen her. What hobby do you have that feeds you? Sports? Dancing? Painting? Video games?

Write to Learn Complete the line *To Young* ____. Finish the line with *Football Players, Dancers, Painters, Gamers,* or some other audience. Then write what you would say to people who are just beginning to enjoy your favorite hobby.

Build Background

Gwendolyn Brooks lived most of her life in Chicago and was Poet Laureate of Illinois. Her poetry often showed the impact of urban, or city, life.

- Brooks taught classes and held poetry contests for young people.
- The classes and contests were ways to help inner-city children see "the poetry" in their lives.
- "To Young Readers" was written for the Chicago Public Library.

Set Purposes for Reading

BIG Question Read "To Young Readers" to discover reasons that people read.

Set Your Own Purpose What else would you like to learn from the poem to help you answer the Big Question? Write your own purpose on the "To Young Readers" page of Foldable 1.

Keep Moving

Use these skills as you read the following selection.

To Young Readers   71

READING WORKSHOP 4

To Young Readers

by Gwendolyn Brooks

Good books are
bandages and voyages
and linkages* to Light; **1**

are keys and hammers,
5　**ripe redeemers**,*
dials and bells and
healing hallelujah. **2 3**

Good books are good **nutrition**.
A reader is a Guest
10　**nourished**, by riches of the Feast,
to lift, to launch, and to applaud the world. **4** ○

3　*Linkages* is another way of saying links, or connections.
5　*Redeemers* are rescuers or saviors.

Vocabulary

nutrition (noo TRI shun) *n.* that which feeds the body

nourished (NUR ishd) *adj.* provided with food or other substances necessary for life

---

Practice the Skills

1 **Key Reading Skill**
Identifying Main Idea and Supporting Details How soon do you begin to get a sense of the main idea of this poem?

2 **Key Literary Element**
Author's Purpose You know the author wrote this poem for the Chicago Public Library. What do you think her purpose is?

3 **English Language Coach**
Word References Read the footnote for **redeemers**. Then look up **ripe** in the dictionary. Read all its meanings. Which one do you think Brooks wanted you to think about? Do you think she might have wanted you to think about more than one meaning?

BIG Question

4 What reasons does the poem's speaker give for reading? Record the answer in your Foldable. Your response will help you complete the Unit Challenge later.

72　UNIT 1　Why Read?

READING WORKSHOP 4

The Library, 1960. Jacob Lawrence. Tempera, 60.9 x 75.8 cm. National Museum of American Art, Washington, DC.

Analyzing the Art Does this painting help you understand Brooks's poem? Explain your answer.

READING WORKSHOP 4 • Identifying Main Idea and Supporting Details

After You Read | To Young Readers

Answering the BIG Question

1. What does this poem tell you about why people read?
2. **Recall** The author compares books to many things. Name five of these things.
   TIP **Right There** You will find the answer in the poem.
3. **Recall** What does the author suggest that a reader should do for the world?
   TIP **Right There** You will find the answer in the poem.

Critical Thinking

4. **Analyze** Why do you think Brooks capitalizes the words *Light, Guest,* and *Feast?*
   TIP **Author and Me** You will find clues in the poem, but you must also use information in your head.

5. **Evaluate** Does the poem leave out anything important about reading? If so, what is it?
   TIP **On My Own** Answer from your own experiences.

6. **Apply** Do you agree with Brooks about the power of reading? Explain.
   TIP **On My Own** Answer from your own experiences.

Write About Your Reading

Choose just one of the things Brooks says a book can be.

bandage   voyage   linkage   key
hammer   redeemer   dial   bell
hallelujah   nutrition

Write a short essay, two or three paragraphs long, about how a book could be one of these things. If you can, use a book you have read as an example. Begin with a sentence that states your main idea. For example, "A book can be a hammer." Then give details that support and explain that idea.

Objectives (pp. 74–75)
Reading Identify main ideas and supporting details
Literature Identify literary elements: author's purpose
Vocabulary Use word references: dictionary
Writing Write a short essay • Respond to literature
Grammar Identify parts of speech: future verb tense

74   UNIT 1   Why Read?

READING WORKSHOP 4 • Identifying Main Idea and Supporting Details

Skills Review

Key Reading Skill: Identifying Main Idea and Supporting Details

7. How well did the poem's details support the main idea? Give examples from the poem to support your answer.

Key Literary Element: Author's Purpose

8. Which of these helped you most in determining the author's purpose—the author's word choices, the audience she was writing for, or the way the poem was organized? Explain.
9. Did the author achieve her purpose? Explain.

Vocabulary Check

Fit each vocabulary word into the correct sentence. Then explain why the word does not fit into the other sentence.

10. **nutrition**

    Proper ___ gives children necessary vitamins and minerals.

    Carlos was worried about the ___ of the painting.

11. **nourished**

    By the time we finally got to the restaurant, I was ___.

    I felt ___ after the large meal.

English Language Coach Match the correct meaning with the underlined word in each group of sentences.

12. Go <u>change</u> for gym.
13. Get the correct <u>change</u> when you pay.
14. My mom suggested a <u>change</u> in attitude.

    a. *n.* coins or money returned
    b. *v.* to put on different clothing
    c. *n.* the act of becoming different

15. <u>Draw</u> a picture of your new bike.
16. When neither team scored, we called it a <u>draw</u>.
17. <u>Draw</u> close to hear his secret.

    a. *n.* undecided game or contest; tie
    b. *v.* make lines with a pencil or pen
    c. *v.* move toward someone or something

Grammar Link: Future Tense

When you want to talk about an action that will happen in the future, there are two ways to do it. You can use the word *will* as a helping verb and the present tense of the main verb.

- I **will wash** the dishes later.

You can also use *going to* with *am*, *is*, or *are* along with the present tense of the main verb.

- I **am going to wash** the dishes later.

You can use *not* or *never* with either of these phrases.

- I **will** never **wash** the dishes.
- I **am** never **going to wash** the dishes.

Grammar Practice

In your Learner's Notebook, write a sentence about a future action you will take. Use *will*. Then rewrite the sentence, using *am going to*.

Writing Application Look back at the essay you wrote about what a book can be. Underline any verb phrases you used to talk about the future.

Web Activities For eFlashcards, Selection Quick Checks, and other Web activities, go to www.glencoe.com.

READING WORKSHOP 4 • Identifying Main Idea and Supporting Details

Before You Read

Why Books Are Dangerous

Neil Gaiman

Meet the Author
Neil Gaiman is best known for his graphic novels, or long-form comic books with high-quality story lines and artwork. As a boy, Gaiman says that he was a "bookie kid . . . one of those kids who had books on them." He admits to becoming "very grumpy at school when they'd tell us that we couldn't read comics, because 'if you read comics, you will not read OTHER THINGS.'" Gaiman proved his teachers wrong. He read comics as well as the entire children's library.

Author Search For more about Neil Gaiman, go to www.glencoe.com.

Objectives (pp. 76–81)
Reading Identify main ideas and supporting details • Make connections from text to self
Literature Identify literary elements: author's purpose
Vocabulary Use word references: dictionary

Vocabulary Preview

confiscated (KAHN fuh skayt id) *v.* took someone's property by authority **(p. 79)** *The headmaster probably confiscated books from other students.*

interrogated (in TAIR uh gayt id) *v.* asked questions harshly or in great detail **(p. 79)** *The spy was nervous when interrogated by the police.*

fragments (FRAG munts) *n.* small pieces that are broken off **(p. 81)** *The glass broke into fragments when it hit the floor.*

sarcastic (sar KAS tik) *adj.* describes sharp or bitter words that are meant to hurt or make fun of someone **(p. 81)** *The bully made sarcastic comments about my clothes.*

Guess What? With a partner, role-play the words *confiscated, interrogated,* and *sarcastic.* Perform one of your role plays for another pair of classmates. Have them guess the vocabulary word you are acting out.

English Language Coach

Word References We speak the same language and use most of the same words as people in England, but some of those words have different meanings. Someone from England would understand the first sentence in each pair of sentences below. You may not. Use a dictionary to look up the words that seem to have a different meaning in England.

The lorry on the side of the road had an open bonnet and boot.
The truck on the side of the road had an open hood and trunk.

The baby in the pram needs a dummy and a clean nappy.
The baby in the buggy needs a pacifier and a clean diaper.

Try to match each term from England in the left column to one of the meanings from the United States in the right column. Use a dictionary to help you.

Word used in England	Word used in U.S.
fringe	french fries
biscuit	bangs
torch	flashlight
chips	cookie

76 UNIT 1 Why Read?

READING WORKSHOP 4 • Identifying Main Idea and Supporting Details

Skills Preview

Key Reading Skill: Identifying Main Idea and Supporting Details

To determine which supporting details are important and which are not, find the main idea of the paragraph or the passage. Then, for each detail, ask yourself this question:

- Does the reader need this detail to understand the main idea?

  If you answer yes, then the detail is important. If the answer is no, then it's a minor detail.

  It may be important to the main idea to know that the character ordered a pizza, but it's probably not really necessary to know that it was a pepperoni pizza.

Write to Learn In your Learner's Notebook, make a two-column chart. When you read "Why Books Are Dangerous," record the main ideas in the first column. Record the supporting details in the second column.

Key Literary Element: Author's Purpose

The author's purpose shows up in many ways, from word choices to how the writing is organized. You decide whether the author is informing the reader, entertaining, expressing an opinion, or trying to convince you, the reader, to agree.

These tips will help you determine the author's purpose when you read the selection:

- Look carefully at what the author is telling you. Decide whether the author really means what he or she says.

  Does Gaiman really believe that books are dangerous? Explain.

- Think about why the author might say the opposite of what he or she means.

  If Gaiman does not believe that books are dangerous, why would he say that they are? How does he really feel about books?

- Consider the reason for the author's writing.

  Why does the author want to share this particular incident from his life? Does he want to teach or entertain the reader?

Get Ready to Read

Connect to the Reading

Have you ever been in trouble in school or at home? Why were you in trouble? Did you learn something, good or bad, from that experience?

Freewrite Write a short paragraph about a time that you were in trouble at home or school. What did you do? What was the consequence? Did you believe that the consequence was fair?

Build Background

This short story takes place at a boys' school in the 1970s in the south of England. Discipline was very tough at such schools.

Set Purposes for Reading

BIG Question Read the selection "Why Books Are Dangerous" to discover reasons why people read.

Set Your Own Purpose What else would you like to learn from the essay to help you answer the Big Question? Write your own purpose on the "Why Books Are Dangerous" page of Foldable 1.

Interactive Literary Elements Handbook
To review or learn more about the literary elements, go to www.glencoe.com.

Keep Moving

Use these skills as you read the following selection.

Why Books Are Dangerous **77**

READING WORKSHOP 4

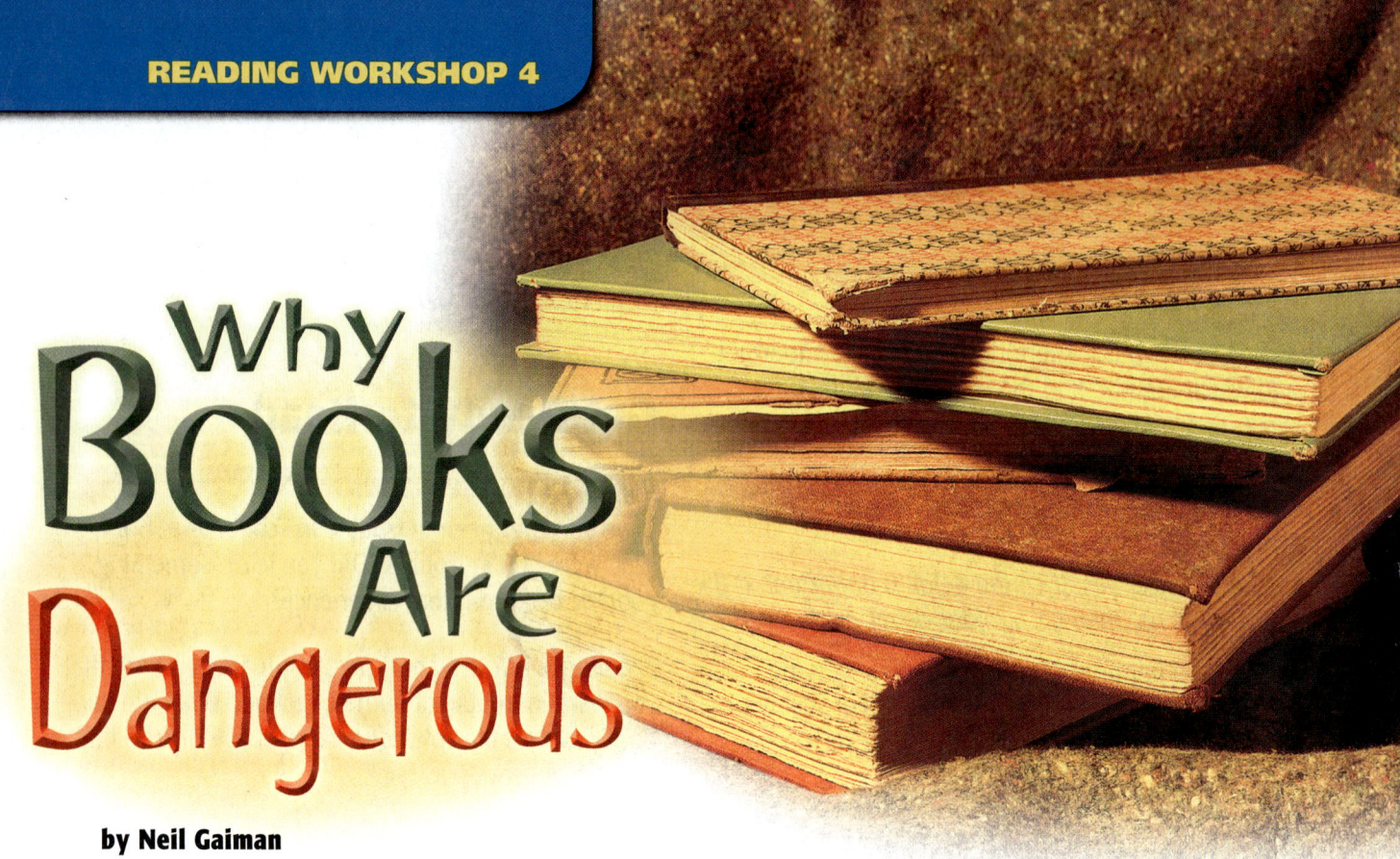

Why Books Are Dangerous

by Neil Gaiman

When I was a boy, I was almost always carrying a book. It might not have been obvious. Paperbacks were fairly easy to slip into pockets, after all. My father would frisk[1] me for books before family weddings or funerals; otherwise he knew that, while other people were being bored, I'd be sitting comfortably, probably under a table, off in my own world, reading.

I liked books. I did not yet suspect that books were dangerous. I didn't care what the books were about, as long as they had a story of some kind—spy stories, horror stories, SF or fantasy, histories, adventures, tales. I'd read true-life stories about people who caught spies or captured rare animals for zoos or people who hunted down man-eating tigers. I also was very fond of detectives and the books they came in. These were, I think, looking back on it, all very sensible things for a boy to like, and not the least bit dangerous. **1**

The headmaster of my school in the south of England, a pipe-smoking, gruff gentleman who was famous for his precise and painful use of the slipper[2] on boys who were sent

---

1. To search for something by running the hands over the clothing and through the pockets is to **frisk** the person.
2. A teacher who is famous for his **use of the slipper** is one well-known for using a slipper or other type of shoe to spank students.

Practice the Skills

1 **Key Reading Skill**

Identifying Main Idea and Supporting Details Reread the second paragraph. What is the main idea of this paragraph? Where in the paragraph do you see the main idea? Name one important detail that supports this main idea.

to him for misbehaving, once **confiscated** a book from me. It was called *And to my nephew Albert I leave the island what I won off Fatty Hagen in a poker game,* and it had a photograph of a naked lady on the cover, which was why it was confiscated. This seemed particularly unfair, as in the early 1970s, most books seemed to have naked ladies on the covers, which, at least in the case of *And to my nephew Albert . . .* political comedy, had little or nothing to do with what was going on inside the book. I was **interrogated** by the **headmaster** and was given the book back at the end of term, with a warning to watch what I read. He didn't use the slipper, though. Not that time. **2**

Vocabulary

confiscated (KAHN fuh skayt id) *v.* took someone's property by authority

interrogated (in TAIR uh gayt id) *v.* asked questions harshly or in great detail

Practice the Skills

2 **English Language Coach**

Word Reference Use a dictionary to find the meaning of the word **headmaster.** What is a more common American word that has the same meaning as *headmaster?*

Neil Gaiman went to a school in the south of England. The school was run by a *headmaster,* and academic standards were very high. Students had to wear uniforms, as the students do in this present-day photo.

Analyzing the Photo Based on the picture, what feelings do you get about the students at this school? Do they seem happy? Explain your answers.

READING WORKSHOP 4

Obviously the headmaster understood the dangers of books. He was trying to tell me something. I didn't listen. Eventually I started to read the dangerous books.

The really dangerous books had titles like *1001 Jolly Interesting Things a Boy Can Do.* You could make dyes from common garden vegetables. It explained it all. 3

Visual Vocabulary
Beetroot is a beet grown for its edible red root.

I read the article on making dyes from common garden vegetables, and then I boiled a beetroot and soaked a white school shirt in the beet water, and turned it a purply sort of red. I decided that I wouldn't be caught dead wearing it. Then I put it in the washing, and it turned all the shirts and socks and underwear it was washed with a rather startling shade of pink.

I had not learned my lesson. The next thing I found was the toffee[3] recipe.

I learned that if I melted some butter in a saucepan, and then added sugar and golden syrup and a tablespoon of water, and I heated it all together and got it very hot (but didn't burn it), and dripped drops of the boiling liquid into a glass of cold water, when the drops went solid, it was done. Then I'd pour it out onto a greased pie-pan, and let it set hard.

I was so proud. I'd made a golden-clear, buttery toffee. Pure sugar, with a little fat. It tasted amazing. Chewing it was a battle between the toffee and my teeth. Sometimes my teeth would win, sometimes the toffee would prove the victor and pull out a filling, or deal with a loose tooth.

This went on for several months.

I was, I think, in a math lesson. I'd put a fist-sized lump of the toffee into my pocket, where it had melted, slowly, to the shape of my leg. And I had forgotten about it. I also had a handkerchief in the pocket.

"You. Boy," said the teacher. "Gaiman. You're sniveling,[4] boy. Blow your nose."

I said, "Yes, sir," and pulled the handkerchief from the pocket. It came out, and as it did so, a large lump of toffee that was stuck to the handkerchief sailed out across the room and hit the tiled floor.

Practice the Skills

3 **Key Literary Element**

Author's Purpose Do you believe that Gaiman really wants to show you that books are dangerous? Or does he have some other purpose? Explain.

---

3. **Toffee** is a kind of hard, caramel candy.
4. Someone who is **sniveling** has a runny nose.

READING WORKSHOP 4

The Scholar, Saturday Evening Post Cover, June 26, 1926. Norman Rockwell.
Analyzing the Art This painting shows an English schoolboy and a headmaster. Do you think the artist meant for this picture to be funny? Do you think the picture *is* funny? Explain your answers.

   It shattered when it hit the floor, like glass, into several hundred sharp-edged **fragments**.
   I spent the rest of the lesson on my knees, picking up the sticky-sharp bits of toffee from the floor, while the teacher, convinced that I had done this on purpose to be funny (as if I'd waste a huge lump of toffee on a joke), made **sarcastic** comments. And, at the end of the lesson, I was sent to the headmaster with a note explaining what I'd done.
   The headmaster read the note, puffed on his pipe, then walked slowly to the cupboard at the back of his study and, opening it, produced a large tartan[5] slipper.
   That was the day I discovered that books were dangerous.
   At least, books that suggested you do something.... 4 5 6

---

5. Tartan refers to a piece of plaid cloth or clothing.

Vocabulary

fragments (FRAG munts) *n.* small pieces that are broken off

sarcastic (sar KAS tik) *adj.* describes sharp or bitter words that are meant to hurt or make fun of someone

Practice the Skills

4 **Key Reading Skill**

Identifying Main Idea and Supporting Details Think of the title and the last two sentences. What did the author do? What happened as a result? What is the main idea of the entire essay?

5 **Key Reading Skill**

Identifying Main Idea and Supporting Details What is one important detail that supports the main idea of the article? What is one unimportant, minor detail?

6 **BIG Question**

How would Gaiman answer the question, "Why read?" Record your answer on the "Why Books Are Dangerous" page of Foldable 1. Your response will help you complete the Unit Challenge later.

Why Books Are Dangerous **81**

READING WORKSHOP 4 • Identifying Main Idea and Supporting Details

After You Read

Why Books Are Dangerous

Answering the BIG Question

1. What have you learned from this essay about why people read?
2. **Recall** How does Gaiman turn his shirt, socks, and underwear pink?
   TIP **Right There** You will find the answer in the essay.
3. **Recall** How does toffee get Gaiman into trouble?
   TIP **Right There** You will find the answer in the essay.

Critical Thinking

4. **Analyze** Would Gaiman's father and headmaster think books are dangerous? Why?
   TIP **Think and Search** You will find this information in the essay, but you will have to look for it.
5. **Infer** Do you think that Gaiman stopped reading after getting into trouble? Explain.
   TIP **Author and Me** Answer using clues from the selection and from your own experiences.
6. **Connect** What is one interesting thing you learned to do from reading a book that you chose to read?
   TIP **On Your Own** Answer from your own experiences.

Write About Your Reading

Suppose that you are Gaiman. If you could speak to the headmaster without fear of punishment, what would you say? Write a letter to the headmaster. Tell him what you think and try to persuade him to agree with your point of view.

- Would you argue that everyone was overreacting? How so?
- Would you feel you were in the wrong and apologize? Why or why not?
- Would you blame the book? What for?
- Would you say that more kids should read books? Why or why not?

Objectives (pp. 82–83)
Reading Identify main ideas and supporting details • Make connections from text to self
Literature Identify literary elements: author's purpose
Vocabulary Use word references: dictionary
Writing Respond to literature
Grammar Identify parts of speech: irregular verbs

READING WORKSHOP 4 • Identifying Main Idea and Supporting Details

Skills Review

Key Reading Skill: Identifying Main Idea and Supporting Details

7. How did sorting important details from less important details help you determine the main idea of the article?

Key Literary Element: Author's Purpose

8. Did determining the main idea of the article help you learn the author's purpose? Explain.
9. Did the title give any clues to the author's purpose? Explain.

Reviewing Skills: Skimming and Scanning

10. Why is it helpful to skim or scan text before reading?

Vocabulary Check

Complete the following sentences with the correct vocabulary word.

    interrogated   confiscated
    fragments   sarcastic

11. The teacher ___ the girl's bubble gum.
12. The guard ___ the prisoner.
13. Her friend's ___ comment made Emily cry.
14. The plate broke into ___ when it hit the floor.
15. **English Language Coach** What word meanings or cultural references from England did you find difficult to understand when you read "Why Books Are Dangerous"? Which new words or references did you most enjoy discovering?

Web Activities For eFlashcards, Selection Quick Checks, and other Web activities, go to www.glencoe.com.

Grammar Link: Irregular Verbs

All verbs have "principal parts" that are used to form the various tenses. Most verbs are **regular**. Their parts look like this:

Regular Verbs			
Base	Present Participle	Past	Past Participle
walk	walking	walked	walked

So you would say, "I walk to school. I am walking today. I walked yesterday. I have walked every day."

Some verbs are **irregular**. The past and past participle are not formed by simply adding -ed to the base form. Also, the past participle for some irregular verbs is different from the past. Here are a few examples:

Irregular Verbs		
Base	Past	Past Participle
bring	brought	brought
leave	left	left
win	won	won
begin	began	begun
go	went	gone
know	knew	known
run	ran	run
see	saw	seen
speak	spoke	spoken

Grammar Practice

Choose three verbs from the chart of irregular verbs. Write three sentences for each one, using the base form, the past form, and the past participle.

Writing Application Look at the letter that you wrote. Do you recognize any irregular verbs in your writing? If so, circle the verbs. If not, add sentences that contain the past or past participle of irregular verbs.

Why Books Are Dangerous **83**

COMPARING LITERATURE WORKSHOP

The Southpaw
by Judith Viorst

& Concha
by Mary Helen Ponce

Skills Focus

You will use these skills as you read and compare the following selections:
- "The Southpaw," p. 88
- "Concha," p. 93

Reading
- Comparing and contrasting

Literature
- Identifying author's purpose

Writing
- Writing to compare and contrast

Objectives (pp. 84–85)
Literature Identify literary elements: author's purpose • Compare and contrast: literature
Writing Write a response to literature: compare and contrast

Comparing is nothing new to you. You compare things every day. When you choose between two jackets, you compare how they look on you and their warmth. When you talk about movies with a friend, you might compare how funny or exciting they are. You compare all kinds of things, including literature. Comparing is thinking about how two things are *alike* and how they are *different*.

How to Compare Literature: Author's Purpose

Before you compare two things, you need to figure out what you're going to base your comparison on. When you compare "The Southpaw" and "Concha" you'll compare the **authors' purposes** for writing the stories. Often, a writer will have more than one purpose. Use the clues below to help you figure out an author's purposes.

If a work	Its purpose is usually
• tells a story or is funny	• to *entertain*
• tells why to do something	• to *persuade*
• gives facts or tells steps	• to *explain*
• describes something the writer cares about	• to *express emotion*

As you read, look for clues that might tell you the *authors' purposes* for these stories.

COMPARING LITERATURE WORKSHOP

Get Ready to Compare

In a short story one of the author's purposes is usually to entertain. While you're reading a story, try to figure out *how* the author is trying to entertain you. Some of the ways an author will entertain readers are through

- Humor—funny stories
- Excitement—adventure, science fiction, horror stories
- Mystery—suspense stories, science fiction stories
- Connection—poems and stories

To figure out an author's purpose, take notes in a chart like the one below. For example, if you read a horror story about how pollution causes house flies to grow very large and attack people, you might make a chart like this:

Author's Purpose

Entertain	Persuade	Inform or Explain	Express Emotion
Excitement: The way the flies attack people is scary.	Pollution causes the problem. The author wants us to do something to stop pollution.	There is a lot of detail about how pollution can ruin our environment.	The author expresses anger and fear about the effects of pollution.

Making Your Comparison

Before you start reading, make a chart like the one below in your Learner's Notebook for each of the stories. Then, as you read each story, fill in the chart with clues you find about the author's purpose. You won't fill in every square for each story.

Author's Purpose—(Name of Story)

Entertain (Humor, Excitement, Mystery, Connection)	Persuade	Inform or Explain	Express Emotion

After you've finished, you'll use your notes to compare the authors' purposes for writing these stories.

COMPARING LITERATURE WORKSHOP

Before You Read: The Southpaw

Judith Viorst

Meet the Author
Born in Newark, New Jersey, in 1931, Judith Viorst (vyorst) knew that she wanted to be a writer in the second grade. Many of her poems, short stories, and novels have presented humorous views of her family life. "The Southpaw" was published in 1974. See page R7 of the Author Files for more on Judith Viorst.

Author Resources For more about Judith Viorst, go to www.glencoe.com.

Objectives (pp. 86–91)
Literature Identify literary elements: author's purpose • Compare and contrast: literature
Vocabulary Use word references: dictionary

Vocabulary Preview

former (FOR mer) *adj.* earlier; coming before in time **(p. 88)** *Mr. Judson, my former baseball coach, sent me a letter.*

cavities (KAV ih teez) *n.* hollow spaces in a tooth caused by decay **(p. 88)** *The dentist found two cavities in my tooth.*

laughingstock (LAF ing stahk) *n.* a person or thing that is made fun of **(p. 89)** *Alphonse became the laughingstock of the class when he almost ate the gerbil's food.*

English Language Coach

Word References Imagine that you've just started reading this selection when you come across a word you've never seen before. Luckily, you don't have to go too far to find its meaning. The bold, or darker, type tells you to look at the bottom of the page for a definition. But what if the word isn't defined on the page? You can look up the word in a dictionary but you will still have a decision to make.

Look at these dictionary entries for the words *formative, former,* and *formerly.*

> **for • ma • tive** (fôr′ mə tiv) *adj.* giving or capable of giving form.
>
> **for • mer** (fôr′ mər) *adj.* 1. being first (of two mentioned or understood). 2. belonging to, being of, or occurring in the past; previous; earlier.
>
> **for • mer • ly** (fôr′ mər lē) *adv.* in time past; once; previously.

As you can see, *former* has two definitions. Which definition you use depends on how the word is used in a sentence.

- As you read "The Southpaw," use a dictionary to look up any words that you don't understand.
- Write the words and their definitions in your Learner's Notebook.

86 UNIT 1 Why Read?

COMPARING LITERATURE WORKSHOP

Get Ready to Read

Connect to the Reading

In "The Southpaw," the story is told in an exchange of notes between two former friends, Richard and Janet. Has a disagreement ever caused you to lose a friend? How did you feel? Were you able to make up?

Partner Talk With a partner, talk about an argument you had with a friend and how you handled it.

Build Background

A story written in the form of an exchange of letters is called an epistolary (ee PIS toh lare ee) story. In "The Southpaw," two friends—a boy and a girl—argue by letter whether or not girls can play on the team.

- *Southpaw* is a baseball term for a left-handed pitcher.
- A batting average indicates how often a batter gets a hit. A batting average higher than .300 is very good.
- The nine positions in baseball are pitcher, catcher, first base, second base, third base, shortstop, left field, center field, and right field.
- Pitcher is a difficult position to play. Often, the best athlete on a team is selected to pitch.
- Vassar College created the first women's baseball team in 1866.
- Early women players wore high-button shoes, high necklines, long skirts, and long sleeves.
- Amelia Bloomer created loose women's pants called "bloomers." The female baseball players who wore these pants were called "Bloomer Girls."
- Women were first paid to play baseball in 1875.
- During World War II, the All-American Girls Baseball League (AAGBL) was formed. The AAGBL continued for twelve years.
- Girls were not allowed to play Little League baseball until 1974. This story was published that year.
- In 1994, a group of women formed a team called the Colorado Silver Bullets.
- The American Women's Baseball Federation (AWBF) was founded to help promote women's baseball teams. Since 1992 the AWBF has organized regional and national tournaments, giving girls and women opportunities to play organized baseball.

Set Purposes for Reading

BIG Question Read the selection to learn how reading helped two friends settle a problem.

Set Your Own Purpose What would you like to learn from this selection to help you answer the Big Question? Write your own purpose on the "Southpaw" page of Foldable 1.

COMPARING LITERATURE WORKSHOP

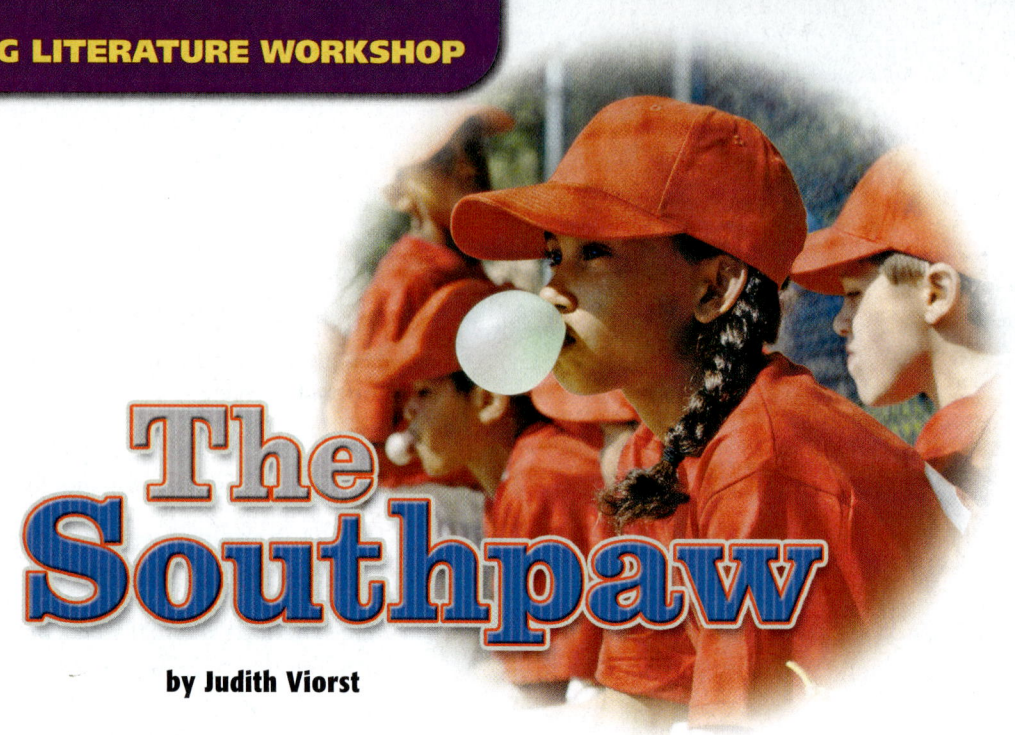

The Southpaw

by Judith Viorst

Dear Richard,

Don't invite me to your birthday party because I'm not coming. And give back the Disneyland sweatshirt I said you could wear. If I'm not good enough to play on your team, I'm not good enough to be friends with.

Your **former** friend,
Janet

P.S. I hope when you go to the dentist he finds twenty **cavities**. **1**

Dear Janet,

Here is your stupid Disneyland sweatshirt, if that's how you're going to be. I want my comic books now—finished or not. No girl has ever played on the Mapes Street baseball team, and as long as I'm captain, no girl ever will.

Your former friend,
Richard

P.S. I hope when you go for your checkup you need a tetanus[1] shot. **2**

---

1. **Tetanus** (TET un us) is a serious disease that people can get when bacteria get into a wound. A doctor gives a person a tetanus shot to keep her from getting tetanus.

Vocabulary

former (FOR mer) *adj.* from the past

cavities (CAV ih teez) *n.* hollow spaces in a tooth caused by decay

Practice the Skills

1 **Comparing Literature**

Author's Purpose In this selection, the author uses letters from Richard and Janet to tell the story. Why do you think the author does this? Does it make the story more entertaining? How do the letters support the author's purpose? In your Author's Purpose chart, write "use of letters" under the author's purpose that you selected.

2 **Comparing Literature**

Author's Purpose This letter shows you how Richard feels about having girls on a baseball team. Do you think the author agrees with Richard? Do you think the author might be trying to persuade or convince readers of something? If so, write a note in the *Persuade* box of the Author's Purpose chart.

COMPARING LITERATURE WORKSHOP

Dear Richard,
   I'm changing my goldfish's name from Richard to Stanley. Don't count on my vote for class president next year. Just because I'm a member of the ballet club doesn't mean I'm not a terrific ballplayer.
   Your former friend,
   Janet

P.S. I see you lost your first game, 28–0.

Dear Janet,
   I'm not saving any more seats for you on the bus. For all I care you can stand the whole way to school. Why don't you forget about baseball and learn something nice like knitting?
   Your former friend,
   Richard

P.S. Wait until Wednesday.

Dear Richard,
   My father said I could call someone to go with us for a ride and hot-fudge sundaes. In case you didn't notice, I didn't call you.
   Your former friend,
   Janet

P.S. I see you lost your second game, 34-0.

Dear Janet,
   Remember when I took the laces out of my blue-and-white sneakers and gave them to you? I want them back.
   Your former friend,
   Richard

P.S. Wait until Friday.

Dear Richard,
   Congratulations on your unbroken record. Eight straight losses, wow! I understand you're the **laughingstock** of New Jersey. 🔳
   Your former friend,
   Janet

P.S. Why don't you and your team forget about baseball and learn something nice like knitting maybe.

Vocabulary

laughingstock (LAF ing STAHK) *n.* a person or thing that is made fun of

Meeting on the Mound, © 1994 Stretar.
Analyzing the Art Do you think the artist meant for this picture to be serious or funny? Explain your answer.

Practice the Skills

🔳 **English Language Coach**

Word References Use a thesaurus or dictionary to find a word or phrase that means about the same as **laughingstock**. Then test the word or phrase by reading it instead of *laughingstock* in Janet's letter.

The Southpaw **89**

COMPARING LITERATURE WORKSHOP

Dear Janet,
   Here's the silver horseback-riding trophy that you gave me. I don't think I want to keep it anymore.
   Your former friend,
   Richard
P.S. I didn't think you'd be the kind who'd kick a man when he's down.[2]

Dear Richard,
   I wasn't kicking exactly. I was kicking back.
   Your former friend,
   Janet
P.S. In case you were wondering, my batting average is .345.

Dear Janet,
   Alfie is having his tonsils[3] out tomorrow. We might be able to let you catch next week. 4
   Richard

Dear Richard,
   I pitch.
   Janet

Dear Janet,
   Joel is moving to Kansas and Danny sprained his wrist. How about a permanent place in the outfield?
   Richard

Dear Richard,
   I pitch.
   Janet

Dear Janet,
   Ronnie caught the chicken pox and Leo broke his toe and Elwood has these stupid violin lessons. I'll give you first base, and that's my final offer.
   Richard

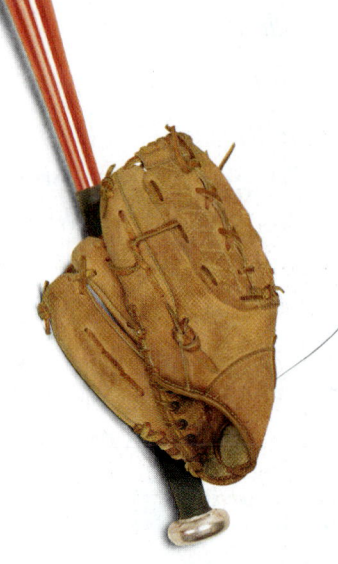

Practice the Skills

4 Comparing Literature

Author's Purpose Richard is starting to change his mind about letting girls play on the team. Why is he changing his mind? Does this tell you anything about one of the author's purposes for this story? If so, write a note in your chart.

---

2. If you **kick a man when he's down,** you are being mean to someone who has already had bad things happen to him.
3. **Tonsils** are small organs in the throat near the back of the mouth. Sometimes doctors perform surgery to remove them.

90 UNIT 1 Why Read?

Dear Richard,
    Susan Reilly plays first base, Marilyn Jackson catches, Ethel Kahn plays center field, I pitch. It's a package deal.[5]
    Janet
P.S. Sorry about your 12-game losing streak.

Dear Janet,
    Please! Not Marilyn Jackson.
    Richard

Dear Richard,
    Nobody ever said that I was unreasonable. How about Lizzie Martindale instead?
    Janet

Dear Janet,
    At least could you call your goldfish Richard again? [5]
Your friend,
    Richard ○

---

5. A ***package deal*** is an offer that includes several items. Whoever agrees to the deal must take all of the items.

Practice the Skills

[5] **BIG Question**
Did you enjoy reading "The Southpaw"? Explain why or why not. Write your answer on the "Southpaw" page of Foldable 1. Your response will help you complete the Unit Challenge later.

Analyzing the Photo Does the story you've just read change your thoughts about this photograph? Why or why not?

COMPARING LITERATURE WORKSHOP

Before You Read : Concha

Meet the Author
Mary Helen Ponce (POHN say) grew up in a Mexican American community in California. She says, "We feared few things in the barrio [*neighborhood*]. We knew everyone; everyone knew us. We belonged." Mary Helen Ponce was born in 1938. "Concha" was published in 1988.

Author Resources For more about Mary Helen Ponce, go to www.glencoe.com.

Objectives (pp. 92–97)
Literature Identify literary elements: author's purpose • Compare and contrast: literature
Vocabulary Use word references: dictionary

Vocabulary Preview

amassed (uh MAST) *v.* piled up, collected, or gathered a great quantity of something **(p. 93)** *Joey amassed a huge pile of berries to shoot.*

pelted (PELT id) *v.* struck over and over again **(p. 94)** *The kids pelted each other with peas from their pea shooters.*

treacherous (TRECH ur us) *adj.* dangerous and unpredictable **(p. 95)** *Ants and bees can be treacherous.*

feat (feet) *n.* an act that shows skill, strength, or courage **(p. 96)** *Standing still while a wasp walks on you is quite a feat.*

incident (IN suh dunt) *n.* an event or situation **(p. 97)** *They all remembered the incident in which Concha got stung.*

English Language Coach

Word References In this book, a lot of words are defined in footnotes. A footnote tells you what a word or phrase means as it's used in the text. You can look up any other confusing words in a dictionary. Another useful word reference is a **thesaurus**. It lists words that mean the same, or almost the same, as the word you have looked up. A thesaurus may also list words that mean the opposite.

Get Ready to Read

Connect to the Reading
What were your favorite outdoor games when you were younger? Did you ever make up games? Were any of them dangerous or risky?

Build Background
- This story takes place in California during the 1940s.
- Stinging red ants are common in some areas of California.
- Kick-the-can, kickball, and red rover are all children's games.

Set Purposes for Reading
BIG Question Read to find out what kinds of games the children played and how Concha became a champion of one game.

Set Your Own Purpose What else would you like to learn from the selection that might help you answer the Big Question? Write your own purpose on the "Concha" page of Foldable 1.

COMPARING LITERATURE WORKSHOP

Concha

by Mary Helen Ponce

While growing up in the small barrio[1] of Pacoima,[2] my younger brother Joey and I were left alone to find ways *para divertirnos,*[3] to keep ourselves busy—and out of our mother's way. One way in which we whiled away long summer days was by making pea shooters. These were made from a hollow reed which we first cleaned with a piece of wire. We then collected berries from *los pirules,*[4] the pepper trees that lined our driveway. Once we **amassed** enough dry berries we put them in our mouths and spat them out at each other through the pea shooter. **1**

---

1. A ***barrio*** is a neighborhood of Spanish-speaking people.
2. ***Pacoima*** (PAW koh EE maw) is a community in Los Angeles, California.
3. ***Para divertirnos*** (PAH rah dee vair TEER nohs) means "to amuse ourselves" in Spanish, or, as the speaker in the story says, "to keep ourselves busy."
4. ***Los pirules*** (lohs pee ROO lays) is Spanish for "the pepper trees."

Vocabulary

amassed (uh MAST) *v.* piled up, collected, or gathered a great quantity of something

Practice the Skills

1 Comparing Literature

Author's Purpose Start taking notes in the "Concha" chart you made in your Learner's Notebook. Does the first paragraph give clues about the author's purpose in writing this story? Does the author seem to want to entertain, persuade, inform, or express her feelings?

COMPARING LITERATURE WORKSHOP

The berries had a terrible taste—they were even said to be poison! I was most careful not to swallow them. We selected only the hard, firm peas. The soft ones, we knew, would get mushy, crumble in our mouths and force us to gag—and lose a fight. During an important battle a short pause could spell defeat.[5] Oftentimes while playing with Joey I watched closely. When he appeared to gag I dashed back to the pepper tree to load up on ammunition. I **pelted** him without mercy until he begged me to stop.

"No more. Ya no," Joey cried as he bent over to spit berries. "No more!"

"Ha, ha I got you now." I spat berries at Joey until, exhausted, we called a **truce** and slumped onto a wooden bench. 2 3

In fall our game came to a halt—the trees dried up; the berries fell to the ground. This was a sign for us to begin other games.

Our games were seasonal. During early spring we made whistles from the long blades of grass that grew in the open field behind our house. In winter we made dams, forts and canals from the soft mud that was our street. We tied burnt matchsticks together with string. These were our men. We positioned them along the forts (camouflaged with small branches). We also played kick the can, but our most challenging game was playing with red ants.

5. When you say something **could spell defeat,** you mean that it could result in defeat.

Vocabulary

pelted (PELT id) *v.* struck over and over again

Practice the Skills

2 Comparing Literature

Author's Purpose These paragraphs tell more about the peashooter fights. What details hint at the author's purpose? Write them in your chart.

3 English Language Coach

Word References Work with a classmate. Use a dictionary to find the meaning of **truce** while your partner uses a thesaurus. Compare your findings.

Red ants are also known as fire ants because their painful stings can cause blisters, and even death.

The ants were of the common variety: red, round and **treacherous**. They invaded our yard and the *llano*[6] every summer. We always knew where ants could be found, *donde habia hormigas*.[7] We liked to build mud and grass forts smack in the middle of ant territory. The ants were the enemy, the matchstickmen the heroes, or good guys.

Playing with ants was a real challenge! While placing our men in battle positions we timed it so as not to get bitten. We delighted in beating the ants at their own game.

Sometimes we got really brave and picked up ants with a stick, then twirled the stick around until the ants got dizzy-drunk (or so we thought)—and fell to the ground. We made ridges of dirt and pushed the ants inside, covered them with dirt and made bets as to how long it would take them to dig their way out.

Concha, my best friend and neighbor, was quite **timid** at school. She avoided all rough games such as kickball and Red Rover. When it came to playing with ants however, Concha held first place for bravery. She could stand with her feet atop an anthill for the longest time! We stood trembling as ants crawled up our shoes, then quickly stomped our feet to scare them off. But Concha never lost her nerve. 4

One time we decided to have an ant contest. The prize was a candy bar—a Sugar Daddy sucker. We first found an anthill, lined up, then took turns standing beside the anthill while the juicy red ants climbed over our shoes. We dared not move— but when the first ant moved towards our ankles we stomped away, our Oxfords making swirls of dust that allowed us to **retreat** to the sidelines. But not Concha. She remained in place as big red ants crept up her shoes. One, five, ten! We stood and counted, holding our breath as the ants continued to climb. Fifteen, twenty! Twenty ants were crawling over Concha! 5

La Nina del Chupetin. Graciela Genoves (b. 1962). Zurbaran Galeria, Buenos Aires, Argentina.

Analyzing the Art What feeling do you get from this picture? Is it similar to the feeling you get from reading the story? Explain.

Practice the Skills

4 English Language Coach

Word References Do you know any other words for **timid**? List them in your Learner's Notebook. Then look up *timid* in a thesaurus. List any new synonyms (words that mean the same thing) you find there.

5 English Language Coach

Word References Look up **retreat** in a dictionary. What did everyone except Concha do?

---

6. **Llano** (YAH noh) is the Spanish word for "flat ground."
7. **Donde habia hormigos** (DOHN day ah BEE ah or MEE gohs) means "where ants lived."

Vocabulary

treacherous (TRECH ur us) *adj.* dangerous and unpredictable

"*Ujule*,[8] she sure ain't scared," cried Mundo in a hushed voice. *"No le tiene miedo a las hormigas."*[9]

"Uhhhhh," answered Beto, his eyes wide.

". . . I mean for a girl," added Mundo as he poked Beto in the ribs. We knew Beto liked Concha—and always came to her rescue.

We stood and counted ants. We were so caught up in this **feat** that we failed to notice the twenty-first ant that climbed up the back of Concha's sock . . . and bit her!

"Ay, ay, ay," screeched Concha.

"Gosh, she's gonna die," cried an alarmed Virgie as she helped stomp out ants. "She's gonna die!"

"She's too stupid to die," laughed Mundo, busy brushing ants off his feet. "She's too stupid."

"But sometimes people die when ants bite them," insisted Virgie, her face pale. "They gets real sick."

"The ants will probably die," Mundo snickered, holding his stomach and laughing loudly. "Ah, ha, ha."

"Gosh you're mean," said a shocked Virgie, hands on hips. "You are so mean."

"Yeah, but I ain't stupid." 6

"Come on you guys, let's get her to the *mangera*,"[10] Beto cried as he reached out to Concha who by now had decided she would live. "Come on, let's take her to the faucet."

We held Concha by the waist as she hobbled[11] to the water faucet. Her cries were now mere[12] whimpers as no grownup had come out to investigate. From experience we knew that if a first cry did not bring someone to our aid we should stop crying—or go home.

Children's Games, 1959. Rufino Tamayo. Oil on canvas. The Metropolitan Museum of Art, New York.

Analyzing the Art Does this picture look to you like children playing games? Explain why or why not.

Practice the Skills

6 **Comparing Literature**

Author's Purpose Reread the page up to this point. What clues do you see about the author's purpose? Look especially at the sentences "She's too stupid to die" and "The ants will probably die." Based on those sentences, is the author trying to entertain, to persuade, to explain, or to express feelings? Explain your answer.

---

8. ***Ujule*** (oo HOO lay) is a Spanish exclamation that means something like "Oh my!" or "Wow!"
9. ***No le tiene miedo*** (noh lay TYEH nay mee AY doh) ***a las hormigas*** means "She's not afraid of the ants."
10. ***Mangera*** (mahn HAY raw) is Spanish for "faucet."
11. ***Hobbled*** means "walked with a limp."
12. ***Mere*** is another word for "only" or "nothing more than."

Vocabulary

feat (feet) *n.* an act that shows skill, strength, or courage

We helped Concha to the faucet, turned it on and began to mix water with dirt. We knew the best remedy for insect bites was *lodo*.[13] We applied mud to all bug stings to stop the swelling. Mud was especially good for wasp stings, the yellowjackets we so feared—and from which we ran away at top speed. Whenever bees came close we stood still until they flew away, but there were no set rules on how to get rid of *avispas*.[14] We hit out at them, and tried to scare them off but the yellowjackets were fierce! In desperation[15] we flung dirt at them, screamed and ran home.

Visual Vocabulary
Jacks is a game in which the object is to pick up a number of small, six-pointed metal pieces while bouncing and catching a small rubber ball with the same hand.

Not long after the ant **incident** Concha decided she was not about to run when a huge wasp broke up our game of jacks. She stood still, so still the wasp remained on her dark head for what seemed like hours. We stood and watched, thinking perhaps the wasp had mistaken Concha's curly hair for a bush! We watched—and waited.

"*Ujule*, she sure is brave," exclaimed Virgie as she sucked on a popsicle. "She sure is brave."

"She's stupid," grunted Mundo, trying to be **indifferent**. "She's just a big show-off who thinks she's so big." 7

"So are you," began Virgie, backing off. "So are you."

"Yeah? Ya wanna make something outta it?"

"Let's go," interrupted Beto in his soft voice.

"*Ya vamonos*."[16] He smiled at Concha—who smiled back.

In time the wasp flew away. Concha immediately began to brag about how a "real big wasp" sat on her hair for hours. She never mentioned the ant contest—nor the twenty-first ant that led her to *el lodo*. 8 9 ○

---

13. **Lodo** (LOH doh) means "mud."
14. **Avispas** (ah VEES pahs) are wasps.
15. When you do something **in desperation**, you have usually run out of ideas about what to do.
16. **Ya vamonos** (yah VAH moh nohs) means "Let's go."

Vocabulary

incident (IN suh dunt) *n.* an event or situation

COMPARING LITERATURE WORKSHOP

Practice the Skills

7 English Language Coach

Word References Do you know what **indifferent** means? Look up this word in a dictionary or thesaurus. Then explain its meaning to a partner.

8 Comparing Literature

Author's Purpose The selection ends with a story about Concha and a huge wasp. Talk with a partner about the story. Discuss its effect on you. Did you enjoy it? In your chart, add any details from the end of the story that give clues about the author's purpose.

BIG Question

9 What kinds of books or magazines do you think the kids in this story might have liked to read? Write your answer on the "Concha" page of Foldable 1. Your response will help you complete the Unit Challenge later.

COMPARING LITERATURE WORKSHOP

After You Read

The Southpaw & Concha

Vocabulary Check

Write the answers to the following twelve questions on a separate sheet of paper. For the first two items below, write the word from the list that best fits each meaning.

The Southpaw
former   cavity

1. a hollow space in a tooth, caused by decay ___
2. something from the past ___

Concha

For items 3–7, write the word from the list that means most nearly the same as the words below.

amassed   pelted   treacherous   feat   incident

3. attacked ___
4. remarkable accomplishment ___
5. unsafe ___
6. gathered together ___
7. event ___

Now complete each sentence with one of the vocabulary words from "Concha."

8. Mary and Joey ___ as many dry berries as they could.
9. The author writes about what she calls "the ant ___."
10. Counting all those ants was quite a ___.
11. Mary feared the ants. They seemed ___.
12. Mary ___ her brother with dry berries.

Objectives (pp. 98–99)
Reading Evaluate text
Literature Identify literary elements: author's purpose • Compare and contrast: literature
Vocabulary Use word references: dictionary
Writing Write a response to literature: compare and contrast

98   UNIT 1   Why Read?

Reading/Critical Thinking

On a separate sheet of paper, answer the following questions.

The Southpaw

13. **Analyze** Richard didn't want Janet to pitch, even after he realized that she could help his team. Why do you think he resisted? Was it only because she was a girl? Explain.

    TIP **On My Own** You must use what you know from your own experience.

14. **Analyze** When do Richard and Janet start trying to understand each other? Which note shows the change?

    TIP **Author and Me** You will find clues in the story, but you'll also need to use information in your head.

Concha

15. **Interpret** Why do you think Concha and her friends find the ants so fascinating?

    TIP **Author and Me** You will find clues in the story, but you'll also need to use information in your head.

16. **Contrast** What does the author show about Concha by contrasting the way she acts at school with the way she deals with ants?

    TIP **Author and Me** You will find clues in the story, but you'll also need to use information in your head.

Writing: Compare the Literature

Use Your Notes

17. Follow these steps to help you compare the author's purposes in "The Southpaw" with the author's purposes in "Concha."

    Step 1: Look at the notes you wrote in your Author's Purpose charts. Based on your notes, write down what you think the *author's purpose* or *purposes* for "The Southpaw" are. Remember, the author might have more than one purpose.

    Step 2: Look at your notes for "Concha." Write down what you think the *author's purpose* or *purposes* were for that story.

Get It on Paper

At the beginning of this lesson, you saw a list of several methods that authors use to entertain readers. These methods included

humor   excitement   mystery   connection

To compare "The Southpaw" and "Concha" and evaluate how well each author carried out her purpose, answer these questions in your Learner's Notebook.

18. For both of these stories, one of the *author's purposes* was to entertain. Which of the above methods did the author of "The Southpaw" use to entertain? Using details from your chart, describe at least one way the author used this method to entertain her readers.

19. What method or methods did the author of "Concha" use to entertain you? Using details from your chart, describe at least one way the author used this method.

20. Look at your charts. Do you feel that either or both of these authors had a second purpose for writing? If so, explain what those purposes were, and why you think that was the author's purpose.

21. Use your author's purpose charts and your answers to questions 17–19 to help you answer this question: Which author, do you think, was more successful in achieving her purposes? Give details from your notes to support your opinion.

BIG Question

22. Why do you think people might want to read stories like "The Southpaw" and "Concha"?

UNIT 1 WRAP-UP

Answering The BIG Question: Why Read?

You've just read several different selections, and you thought about why people read. Now use what you've learned to do the Unit Challenge.

The Unit Challenge

Choose Activity A or Activity B and follow the directions for that activity.

A. Group Activity: Comic Strip

You and three friends have been asked to create a comic strip to tell why reading is important. A comic strip is a short sequence of cartoon drawings that tell a story.

1. **Discuss the Assignment** First brainstorm with your group to come up with a list of answers to the question *Why Read?* Use the notes on your Foldable. Discuss all the reasons why you read. Do you read to be entertained, to pass the time, to visit other worlds, or to learn how to do something?

2. **Get Started** Think about some of the comic strips that you've read. Remember that a comic strip uses a sequence of comic drawings to tell a story. Use the reasons you listed to brainstorm a story line for your comic strip that would fit into four or five frames.

3. **Make a Storyboard** A storyboard is a rough draft of what your comic strip will look like. It shows what the characters will look like and what you think they will say to each other. Keep working on your storyboard until you all agree on the story line.

4. **Create the Comic** Draw your comic strip on a clean sheet of paper. Color in the drawings, and have a group member check all the spelling and grammar.

5. **Present Your Comic Strip** Now it's time to present your comic strip to the class. Choose one member of the group to read your comic strip to the class. Hang it in the classroom.

Storyboard

Description	Description
Description	Description

B. Solo Activity: Conduct Interviews

Why people read does not have to be a mystery. All you need to do is ask! Interview three friends or family members to find out why they read.

1. **Gather Information** Before conducting your interview, use the notes from your Foldable to prepare a list of questions. Also include this question:
   - What have you read lately?

   Use a chart like the one below to record the answers.

2. **Summarize What You Find** Write a paragraph for each person you interviewed. Summarize what each person says. Ask your sources if you may use their names in your report. If not, you might refer to the people you interviewed as Subject A, Subject B, and so on. Write a paragraph drawing a conclusion about all the people you interviewed. You might learn, for example, that older people read more books than magazines. You might also learn that your friends read more magazines than newspapers.

3. **Present Your Findings** Make sure your paragraphs are neat and easy to read. Check your spelling. Then hand in your detective's report.

Question Row	Subject A	Subject B	Subject C
What have you read lately?	a teen magazine	the Sunday comics	school books
How does this help you?	Reading helps me keep up with fashions. I learn what's cool to wear.		

UNIT 1
Your Turn: Read and Apply Skills

Meet the Author
At the age of 14, Kristin Hunter began writing for the *Pittsburgh Courier.* Her writings include novels, short stories, poems, and magazine articles for young adults and children. She has received numerous awards, including the Children's Prize of the Council on Interracial Books for Children, the Lewis Carroll Shelf Award for *Soul Brothers and Sister Lou,* and the *Chicago Tribune* Book World Prize for *Guests in the Promised Land.* See page R3 of the Author Files for more on Kristin Hunter.

Author Search For more about Kristin Hunter, go to www.glencoe.com.

by Kristin Hunter

We been living in the apartment over the Silver Dollar Check Cashing Service five years. But I never had any reason to go in there till two days ago, when Mom had to go to the Wash-a-Mat and asked me to get some change.

And man! Are those people who come in there in some bad shape.

Old man Silver and old man Dollar, who own the place, have signs tacked up everywhere:

NO LOUNGING, NO LOITERING[1]
THIS IS NOT A WAITING ROOM
and
MINIMUM CHECK CASHING FEE, 50¢
and
LETTERS ADDRESSED, 50¢
and
LETTERS READ, 75¢
and
LETTERS WRITTEN, ONE DOLLAR

---
1. **Loitering** (LOY tur ing) is staying around without a purpose.

102 UNIT 1 Why Read?

And everybody who comes in there to cash a check gets their picture taken like they're some kind of criminal.

After I got my change, I stood around for a while digging the action. First comes an old lady with some kind of long form to fill out. The mean old man behind the counter points to the "One Dollar" sign. She nods. So he starts to fill it out for her.

"Name?"

"Muskogee Marie Lawson."

"SPELL it!" he hollers.

"M, m, u, s—well, I don't exactly know, sir."

"I'll put down 'Marie,' then. Age?"

"Sixty-three my last birthday."

"Date of birth?"

"March twenty-third"—a pause—"I think, 1900."

"Look, Marie," he says, which makes me mad, hearing him first-name a dignified old gray-haired lady like that, "if you'd been born in 1900, you'd be seventy-two. Either I put that down, or I put 1910."

"Whatever you think best, sir," she says timidly.

Analyzing the Photo This store might look like the Silver Dollar Check Cashing Service. What words would you use to describe the way the store looks?

He sighs, rolls his eyes to the ceiling, and bangs his fist on the form angrily. Then he fills out the rest.

"One dollar," he says when he's finished. She pays like she's grateful to him for taking the trouble.

Next is a man with a cane, a veteran[2] who has to let the government know he moved. He wants old man Silver to do this for him, but he doesn't want him to know he can't do it himself.

"My eyes are kind of bad, sir. Will you fill this thing out for me? Tell them I moved from 121 South 15th Street to 203 North Decatur Street."

Old man Silver doesn't blink an eye. Just fills out the form, and charges the crippled man a dollar.

And it goes on like that. People who can't read or write or count their change. People who don't know how to pay their gas bills, don't know how to fill out forms, don't know how to address envelopes. And old man Silver and old man Dollar cleaning up on all of them. It's pitiful. It's disgusting. Makes me so mad I want to yell.

And I do, but mostly at Mom. "Mom, did you know there are hundreds of people in this city who can't read and write?"

Mom isn't upset. She's a wise woman. "Of course, James," she says. "A lot of the older people around here haven't had your advantages. They came from down South, and they had to quit school very young to go to work.

"In the old days, nobody cared whether our people got an education. They were only interested in getting the crops in." She sighed. "Sometimes I think they *still* don't

2. A *veteran* (VEH tuh run) is someone who has served in the armed services.

YOUR TURN: READ AND APPLY SKILLS

The Arab Scribe, Cairo. John Frederick Lewis, (1805–1876). Private Collection.

care. If we hadn't gotten you into that good school, you might not be able to read so well either. A lot of boys and girls your age can't, you know."

"But that's awful!" I say. "How do they expect us to make it in a big city? You can't even cross the streets if you can't read the 'Walk' and 'Don't Walk' signs."

"It's hard," Mom says, "but the important thing to remember is it's no disgrace. There was a time in history when nobody could read or write except a special class of people."

And Mom takes down her Bible. She has three Bible study certificates and is always giving me lessons from Bible history. I don't exactly go for all the stuff she believes in, but sometimes it *is* interesting.

"In ancient times," she says, "no one could read or write except a special class of people known as scribes.[3] It was their job to write down the laws given by the rabbis and the judges.[4] No one else could do it.

"Jesus criticized the scribes," she goes on, "because they were so proud of themselves. But he needed them to write down his teachings."

"Man," I said when she finished, "that's something."

My mind was working double time. I'm the best reader and writer in our class. Also it was summertime. I had nothing much to do except go to the park or hang around the library and read till my eyeballs were ready to fall out, and I was tired of doing both.

So the next morning, after my parents went to work, I took Mom's card table and a folding chair down to the sidewalk. I lettered a sign with a Magic Marker, and I was in business. My sign said:

PUBLIC SCRIBE—ALL SERVICES FREE

I set my table up in front of the Silver Dollar and waited for business. Only one thing bothered me. If the people couldn't read, how would they know what I was there for?

But five minutes had hardly passed when an old lady stopped and asked me to read her grandson's letter. She explained that she had just broken her glasses. I knew she was fibbing, but I kept quiet.

I read the grandson's letter. It said he was having a fine time in California but was a

---

3. **Scribes** were educated people who served as copyists, editors, and teachers.

4. **The rabbis and the judges** were the teachers and rulers of the ancient Hebrews.

little short. He would send her some money as soon as he made another payday. I handed the letter back to her.

"Thank you, son," she said, and gave me a quarter.

I handed that back to her too.

The word got around. By noontime I had a whole crowd of customers around my table. I was kept busy writing letters, addressing envelopes, filling out forms, and explaining official-looking letters that scared people half to death.

I didn't blame them. The language in some of those letters—"Establish whether your disability is one-fourth, one-third, one-half, or total, and substantiate[5] in paragraph 3 (b) below"—would upset anybody. I mean, why can't the government write English like everybody else?

Most of my customers were old, but there were a few young ones too. Like the girl who had gotten a letter about her baby from the Health Service and didn't know what "immunization"[6] meant.

At noontime one old lady brought me some iced tea and a peach, and another gave me some fried chicken wings. I was really having a good time when the shade of all the people standing around me suddenly vanished. The sun hit me like a ton of hot bricks.

Only one long shadow fell across my table. The shadow of a tall, heavy, blue-eyed cop. In our neighborhood, when they see a cop, people scatter. That was why the back of my neck was burning.

"What are you trying to do here, sonny?" the cop asks.

"Help people out," I tell him calmly, though my knees are knocking together under the table.

"Well, you know," he says, "Mr. Silver and Mr. Dollar have been in business a long time on this corner. They are very respected men in this neighborhood. Are you trying to run them out of business?"

"I'm not charging anybody," I pointed out.

"That," the cop says, "is exactly what they don't like. Mr. Silver says he is glad to have some help with the letter writing. Mr. Dollar says it's only a nuisance[7] to them anyway and takes up too much time. But if you don't charge for your services, it's unfair competition."

Well, why not? I thought. After all, I could use a little profit.

"All right," I tell him. "I'll charge a quarter."

"Then it is my duty to warn you," the cop says, "that it's against the law to conduct a business without a license. The first time you accept a fee, I'll close you up and run you off this corner."

He really had me there. What did I know about licenses? I'm only thirteen, after all. Suddenly I didn't feel like the big black businessman anymore. I felt like a little kid who wanted to holler for his mother. But she was at work, and so was Daddy.

"I'll leave," I said, and did, with all the cool I could muster. But inside I was burning up, and not from the sun.

One little old lady hollered "You big bully!" and shook her umbrella at the cop. But the rest of those people were so beaten down they didn't say anything. Just

---

5. When you **substantiate** something, you give evidence to prove a claim.
6. An **immunization** (im yuh nuh ZAY shun) is medicine given to protect against disease.
7. A **nuisance** (NOO sunts) is something that is annoying or unpleasant.

YOUR TURN: READ AND APPLY SKILLS

shuffled back on inside to give Mr. Silver and Mr. Dollar their hard-earned money like they always did.

I was so mad I didn't know what to do with myself that afternoon. I couldn't watch TV. It was all soap operas anyway, and they seemed dumber than ever. The library didn't appeal to me either. It's not air-conditioned, and the day was hot and muggy.

Finally I went to the park and threw stones at the swans in the lake. I was careful not to hit them, but they made good targets because they were so fat and white. Then after a while the sun got lower. I kind of cooled off and came to my senses. They were just big, dumb, beautiful birds and not my enemies. I threw them some crumbs from my sandwich and went home.

"Daddy," I asked that night, "how come you and Mom never cash checks downstairs in the Silver Dollar?"

"Because," he said, "we have an account at the bank, where they cash our checks free."

"Well, why doesn't everybody do that?" I wanted to know.

"Because some people want all their money right away," he said. "The bank insists that you leave them a minimum balance."

"How much?" I asked him.

"Only five dollars."

"But that five dollars still belongs to you after you leave it there?"

"Sure," he says. "And if it's in a savings account, it earns interest."

"So why can't people see they lose money when they *pay* to have their checks cashed?"

"A lot of *our* people," Mom said, "are scared of banks, period. Some of them remember the Depression,[8] when all the banks closed and the people couldn't get their money out. And others think banks are only for white people. They think they'll be insulted, or maybe even arrested, if they go in there."

Wow. The more I learned, the more pitiful it was. "Are there any black people working at our bank?"

"There didn't used to be," Mom said, "but now they have Mr. Lovejoy and Mrs. Adams. You know Mrs. Adams, she's nice. She has a daughter your age."

"Hmmm," I said, and shut up before my folks started to wonder why I was asking all those questions.

The next morning, when the Silver Dollar opened, I was right there. I hung around near the door, pretending to read a copy of *Jet* magazine.

"Psst," I said to each person who came in. "I know where you can cash checks *free*."

It wasn't easy convincing them. A man blinked his red eyes at me like he didn't believe he had heard right. A carpenter with tools hanging all around his belt said he was on his lunch hour and didn't have time. And a big fat lady with two shopping bags pushed past me and almost knocked me down, she was in such a hurry to give Mr. Silver and Mr. Dollar her money.

But finally I had a little group who were interested. It wasn't much. Just three people. Two men—one young, one old—and the little old lady who'd asked me to read her the letter from California. Seemed the

---

8. The **Depression**, or Great Depression, was a period of high unemployment from 1929 through the 1930s.

grandson had made his payday and sent her a money order.

"How far is this place?" asked the young man.

"Not far. Just six blocks," I told him.

"Aw shoot. I ain't walking all that way just to save fifty cents."

So then I only had two. I was careful not to tell them where we were going. When we finally got to the Establishment Trust National Bank, I said, "This is the place."

"I ain't goin' in there," said the old man. "No sir. Not me. You ain't gettin' me in *there*." And he walked away quickly, going back in the direction where we had come.

To tell the truth, the bank did look kind of scary. It was a big building with tall white marble pillars. A lot of Brink's armored trucks and Cadillacs were parked out front. Uniformed guards walked back and forth inside with guns. It might as well have a "Colored Keep Out" sign.

Whereas the Silver Dollar is small and dark and funky and dirty. It has trash on the floors and tape across the broken windows.

I looked at the little old lady. She smiled back bravely. "Well, we've come this far, son," she said. "Let's not turn back now."

So I took her inside. Fortunately Mrs. Adams's window was near the front.

"Hi, James," she said.

"I've brought you a customer," I told her.

Mrs. Adams took the old lady to a desk to fill out some forms. They were gone a long time, but finally they came back.

Analyzing the Photo In what way do you think this bank teller might be helping the man in the picture?

"Now, when you have more business with the bank, Mrs. Franklin, just bring it to me," Mrs. Adams said.

"I'll do that," the old lady said. She held out her shiny new bankbook. "Son, do me a favor and read that to me."

"Mrs. Minnie Franklin," I read aloud. "July 9, 1972. Thirty-seven dollars."

"That sounds real nice," Mrs. Franklin said. "I guess now I have a bankbook, I'll have to get me some glasses."

Mrs. Adams winked at me over the old lady's head, and I winked back.

"Do you want me to walk you home?" I asked Mrs. Franklin.

"No thank you, son," she said. "I can cross streets by myself all right. I know red from green."

And then she winked at both of us, letting us know she knew what was happening.

"Son," she went on, "don't ever be afraid to try a thing just because you've never done it before. I took a bus up here from Alabama by myself forty-four years ago. I ain't thought once about going back. But I've stayed too long in one neighborhood since I've been in this city. Now I think I'll go out and take a look at *this* part of town."

Then she was gone. But she had really started me thinking. If an old lady like that wasn't afraid to go in a bank and open an account for the first time in her life, why should I be afraid to go up to City Hall and apply for a license?

Wonder how much they charge you to be a scribe?

UNIT 1

Reading on Your Own

To read more about the Big Question, choose one of these books from your school or local library. Work on your reading skills by choosing books that challenge you.

Fiction

The House of Dies Drear
by Virginia Hamilton

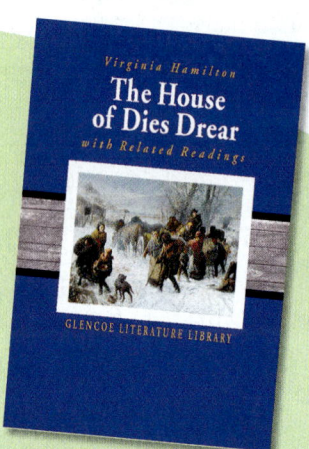

When Thomas moves into a new (haunted?) house, he decides to do some sleuthing. Soon, he discovers that his new home was once a stop on the Underground Railroad. Exploring the dark passageways in and under the building, Thomas moves closer to the truth about his Civil War–era home . . . and into harm's way, as well.

The Firebringer and Other Great Stories: Fifty-five Legends That Live Forever
by Louis Untermeyer

This anthology is packed with retold tales from cultures near and far. Read one or two or ten of the legends in Untermeyer's book—but make sure you're ready to travel. Like all great story collections, *The Firebringer* will transport you to places you've never been!

Letters from Rifka
by Karen Hesse

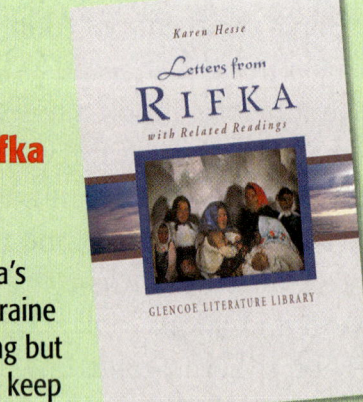

Twelve-year-old Rifka's journey from the Ukraine to the U.S. is anything but easy, and she has to keep her wits about her to survive. Read about how she survives typhus, ringworm, and the high seas in her fearless quest for a new and better life.

I, Juan de Pareja
by Elizabeth Borton de Trevino

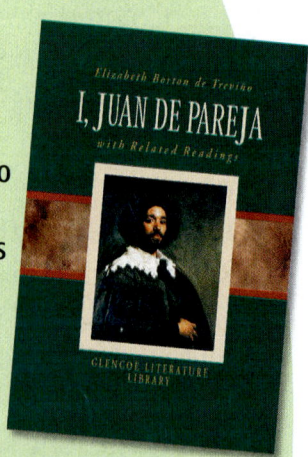

Juan de Pareja was a painter's servant; he was also an artist himself. Despite the fact that sixteenth-century Spanish law prohibited slaves from making art, de Pareja became an accomplished painter.

UNIT 1 READING ON YOUR OWN

Nonfiction

A Strong Right Arm: The Story of Mamie "Peanut" Johnson
by Michelle Y. Green

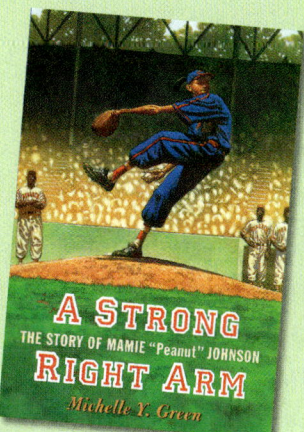

One of the first women to play professional baseball, Mamie "Peanut" Johnson was a pitcher with the Negro League's Indianapolis Clowns from 1953–1955. This biography details the struggles and triumphs that defined her—as a ball player and as a person.

Shipwreck at the Bottom of the World: The Extraordinary True Story of Shackleton and the Endurance
by Jennifer Armstrong

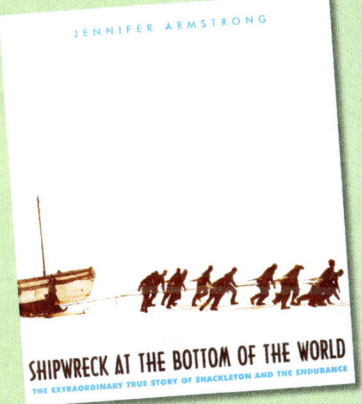

Shipwrecked in Antarctica, Shackleton and his crew of 27 survived a brutal winter and walked over 600 miles to the deserted Elephant Island. Leaving 22 men behind and sailing 800 miles in a tiny open boat, Shackleton and five others made it to civilization . . . then led a rescue party to retrieve those left behind.

Top Secret: A Handbook of Codes, Ciphers, and Secret Writing
by Paul B. Janeczko

Want to learn how to write in code, or how to pen a note in invisible ink? If so, this guide to the secrets of the super-secret is a must-read for you!

The Life and Death of Crazy Horse
by Russell Freedman

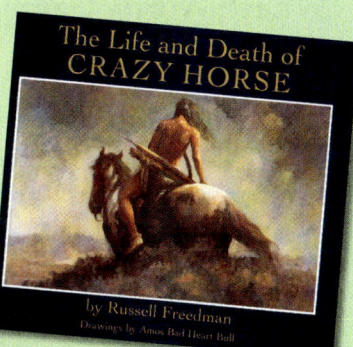

Crazy Horse was a shy young man, but he grew up to be a fierce Sioux warrior. Believing nothing was more important than freedom, he led the fight to save his people's hunting grounds—and their entire way of life.

Reading on Your Own 109

UNIT 1 SKILLS AND STRATEGIES ASSESSMENT

Test Practice

Part 1: Text and Literary Elements

On a separate sheet of paper, write the numbers 1–5. Next to each number, write the letter of the right answer for that question.

1. Which of the following is most likely to involve a "process"?
   A. a diary
   B. a recipe
   C. an index
   D. an advertisement

2. What is the main purpose of the graphics in an article or a passage?
   A. to break up the text
   B. to give a clue to the content
   C. to present information visually
   D. to provide a purpose for reading

Use the following passage to answer questions 3–5.

Interesting Beginnings: Where Words Came From

Boycott In the middle of the 19th century, a man named Captain Charles Boycott controlled the use of a large piece of Irish land owned by an Englishman. The rent he charged those who farmed the land was high, and he refused to lower it. The farmers decided to refuse to have anything to do with him, and stores and other local businesses joined in. Soon, Boycott was unable to buy food because no one would sell to him. He could not hire workers because no one would work for him. He even had difficulty getting his mail delivered. It didn't take long before he gave up and fled back to England. This is where we got the word *boycott,* meaning "to refuse to deal with a person or business as a sign of disapproval or to force a change in behavior or attitude."

---

3. The text features in this passage suggest that it will be about
   A. Captain Charles Boycott's life
   B. the history of the word *boycott*
   C. what makes boycotts successful
   D. where all English words came from

4. It is most likely that the author's *main* purpose in writing this passage was to
   A. inform
   B. entertain
   C. persuade
   D. express emotion

5. In the passage, the phrase "Where Words Came From" is an example of a
   A. deck
   B. head
   C. subtitle
   D. subhead

Objectives (pp. 110–111)
Reading Set a purpose for reading • Identify main ideas and supporting details • Skim and scan text • Use graphics
Informational Text Use text features: title, subtitle, deck, subheads • Identify text structure: steps in a process
Literature Identify literary elements: author's purpose

110 UNIT 1 Why Read?

SKILLS AND STRATEGIES ASSESSMENT UNIT 1

Part 2: Reading Skills

On a separate sheet of paper, write the numbers 1–4. Next to each number, write the letter of the right answer for that question. Use the passage and graphic below to answer questions 1 and 2.

Does it really matter if you graduate from high school? In terms of making a living, it matters a great deal! In 1950, about half of all Americans graduated from high school. By 1985, this had risen to just over 85%, where it has remained. The increase is mainly due to the fact that American businesses have changed. They depend more and more on skilled workers.

Today, for most jobs, having a high school diploma is considered absolutely necessary. Anyone who has not graduated from high school is likely to end up earning very low wages—if he or she can find a job at all. Most high-paying jobs require education or training beyond high school, which is not available to high school dropouts.

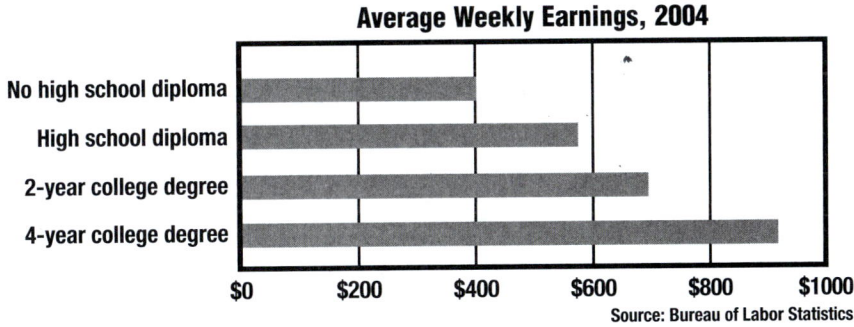

1. Which of the following best states the main idea of the passage and graphic?
   A. American businesses have changed over time.
   B. Education has a large effect on earned income.
   C. People should celebrate high school graduations.
   D. More people graduate from high school now than in the past.

2. In 2004, having a high school diploma increased a worker's weekly wages by about
   A. $25
   B. $50
   C. $100
   D. $175

3. Suppose that your purpose for reading an article is to locate information. Which of the following would probably be *most* helpful as a first step?
   A. scanning the article
   B. finding the main idea
   C. looking up unfamiliar words
   D. studying the graphics in the article

4. Which of the following is *most* likely to determine whether you skim an article or whether you read it carefully, word for word?
   A. your purpose for reading it
   B. how many illustrations it has
   C. how difficult it is to understand
   D. the author's purpose for writing it

UNIT 1 SKILLS AND STRATEGIES ASSESSMENT

Part 3: Vocabulary Skills

On a separate sheet of paper, write the numbers 1–8. Next to each number, write the letter of the right answer for that question.

For questions 1–5, write the letter of the word or phrase that means about the same as the underlined word.

1. to <u>encounter</u> a problem
   - A. avoid
   - B. expect
   - C. run into
   - D. be afraid of

2. a <u>treacherous</u> journey
   - A. long
   - B. risky
   - C. boring
   - D. exciting

3. to <u>monitor</u> an activity
   - A. enjoy
   - B. hear about
   - C. take part in
   - D. keep an eye on

4. was <u>nourished</u> by
   - A. fed
   - B. lit up
   - C. surprised
   - D. entertained

5. had <u>interrogated</u> them
   - A. met
   - B. questioned
   - C. made fun of
   - D. run away from

6. Choose the multiple-meaning word that best fits in both of the sentences.

   Be sure to ___ your answers.
   Dad used a ___ to pay the bill.
   - A. fix
   - B. pen
   - C. check
   - D. change

7. Choose the multiple-meaning word that fits in both of the sentences.

   Turn ___ and then go two blocks.
   Think about what is the ___ thing to do.
   - A. left
   - B. right
   - C. smart
   - D. around

8. "Ballpark Food" says, "The hot dogs, soda, and peanuts our snack squad bought cost three to seven times more than their local food stores <u>charged</u>." In which sentence below does *charged* have the same meaning?
   - A. The babysitter <u>charged</u> $4 an hour.
   - B. I yelled when the bull <u>charged</u> right at me.
   - C. Has anyone been <u>charged</u> with the crime?
   - D. She didn't have enough cash, so she <u>charged</u> her purchase.

Objectives (pp. 112–113)
Vocabulary Use word references: dictionary • Use context clues: multiple meanings
Grammar Identify parts of speech: main, helping, action verbs; verb tenses

Part 4: Writing Skills

On a separate sheet of paper, write the numbers 1–8. Next to each number, write the letter of the right answer for that question.

---

1. In which sentence is *light* used as an adjective?
   - A. Turn on the light.
   - B. Is that package light?
   - C. Let's light the candles.
   - D. The porch light has burned out.

2. In which sentence is *iron* used as a verb?
   - A. The iron is hot!
   - B. We put up an iron railing.
   - C. Hurry up and iron your shirt.
   - D. Did they find iron in the mine?

3. What word in the sentence below is a helping verb?

   I saw Andy and waved while I was looking for Jim.
   - A. saw
   - B. waved
   - C. was
   - D. looking

4. Which of the following verbs is "irregular"?
   - A. see
   - B. watch
   - C. allow
   - D. remember

5. In which sentence is *taste* a linking verb?
   - A. Just taste the soup.
   - B. The potatoes taste good.
   - C. Some people have good taste.
   - D. I just want a little taste of your dessert.

6. Which verb or verb phrase belongs in the blank in the sentence below?

   Next month, we ___ to Ohio.
   - A. travels
   - B. traveled
   - C. traveling
   - D. will travel

7. Which sentence should you use to mean that Lucy's action happens regularly?
   - A. Lucy uses my book.
   - B. Lucy used my book.
   - C. Lucy had used my book.
   - D. Lucy was using my book.

8. Which sentence is written correctly?
   - A. We winned the game.
   - B. They spoken in loud voices.
   - C. She has grown two inches this summer.
   - D. The boys had knew each other for a long time.

UNIT 2

The BIG Question

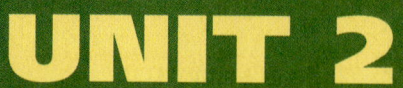

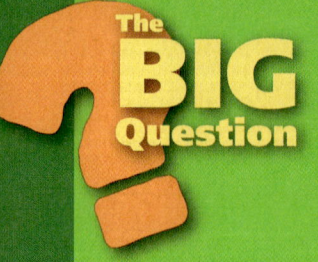

What Brings Out the Best in You?

"Friends laugh at your silliest jokes, put up with your worst moves, go along with your craziest ideas, and always see the best in you."

– Unknown

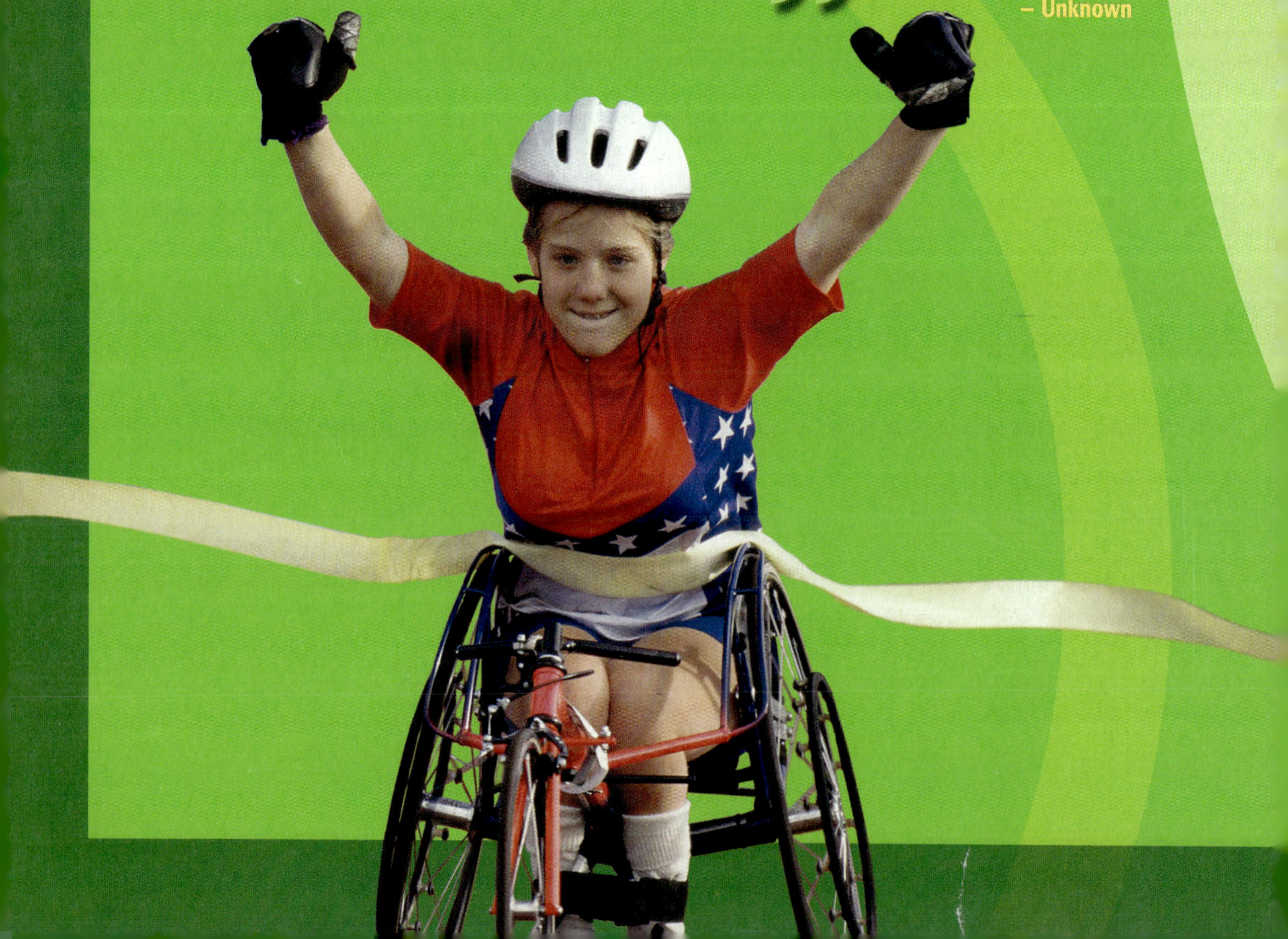

LOOKING AHEAD

The skill lessons and readings in this unit will help you develop your own answer to the Big Question.

UNIT 2 WARM-UP • Connecting to the Big Question
GENRE FOCUS: Biography and Autobiography

Madam C. J. Walker 119
   by Jim Haskins

READING WORKSHOP 1   Skill Lesson: Activating Prior Knowledge

The Jacket 130
   by Gary Soto

The World Is Not a Pleasant Place to Be 139
   by Nikki Giovanni

WRITING WORKSHOP PART 1   Autobiographical Narrative ... 142

READING WORKSHOP 2   Skill Lesson: Connecting

Satchel Paige 150
   by Bill Littlefield

Song for a Surf-Rider 161
   by Sara Van Alstyne Allen

READING WORKSHOP 3   Skill Lesson: Predicting

Eleanor Roosevelt 168
   by William Jay Jacobs

In Eleanor Roosevelt's Time 180

WRITING WORKSHOP PART 2   Autobiographical Narrative ... 184

READING WORKSHOP 4   Skill Lesson: Questioning

Gentleman of the Pool 192
   by Alice Park from *TIME*

Primary Lessons 198
   by Judith Ortiz Cofer

COMPARING LITERATURE WORKSHOP

from *The Pigman & Me* 211
   by Paul Zindel

The Goodness of Matt Kaizer 221
   by Avi

UNIT 2 WRAP-UP • Answering the Big Question

UNIT 2 WARM-UP

Connecting to The BIG Question: What Brings Out the Best in You?

Every day you have different kinds of experiences. How you respond to these experiences shows what type of person you are. Sometimes you might act bravely. Other times you might show kindness. Think about who or what has helped to bring out the best in you.

Real Kids and the Big Question

JORDAN is one of the smartest students at school. Jordan's friend Guy asked Jordan to help him improve his reading skills. Because of Jordan's help, Guy is more confident when he has to read aloud in class. Do you think helping his friend brings out the best in Jordan? Why or why not?

BETTINA sings in a city choir. The choir is planning a trip to Mexico. Bettina's parents told her that she would have to pay for the trip. Bettina has been walking dogs, cutting grass, and babysitting for almost a year to earn enough money. How can working to pay her own way bring out the best in Bettina?

Warm-Up Activity

As a class, discuss the things that you think bring out the best in people. Talk about how helping friends and neighbors can bring out the best in a person. Then tell the class about an experience that brought out your best.

UNIT 2 WARM-UP

You and the Big Question

Reading about experiences that brought out the best in others can help you recognize what might bring out the best in you.

Plan for the Unit Challenge

At the end of the unit, you'll use notes from all your reading to complete the Unit Challenge, which will explore your answer to the Big Question.

You will choose one of the following activities:

A. Magazine Article Work with a group to write an article telling others how they can bring out the best in themselves.

B. Your Interview Prepare for an interview by answering a list of questions.

- Start thinking about which activity you'd like to do so that you can narrow your focus as you read each selection.
- In your Learner's Notebook, write your thoughts about the activity you'd like to do.
- Each time you make notes about the Big Question, think about how your ideas will help you with the Unit Challenge activity you chose.

Big Question Link to Web resources to further explore the Big Question at www.glencoe.com.

As you read, you'll make notes about the Big Question. Later, you'll use these notes to complete the Unit Challenge. See pages R8–R9 for help with making each Unit 2 Foldable. This diagram shows how each should look.

1. Make one Foldable for each workshop. Keep all of your Foldables for the unit in your Foldables folder.
2. On the bottom fold of your Foldable, write the workshop number and the Big Question.
3. Write the titles of the selections in the workshop on the front of the flaps—one title on each flap. (See page 115 for the titles.)
4. Open the flaps. At the very top of each flap, write **My Purpose for Reading.** Below each crease, write **The Big Question.**

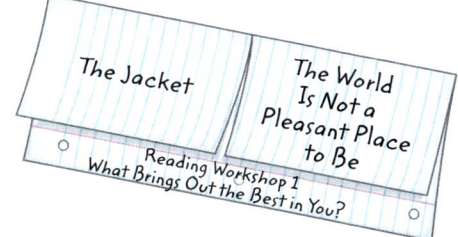

UNIT 2 GENRE FOCUS: BIOGRAPHY AND AUTOBIOGRAPHY

A **biography** is the story of a person's life, written by another person. Biographies tell about real people, real times, and real events. Reading biographies is a great way to find out what brought out the best in a real person. An **autobiography** is a biography in which the author tells his or her own story.

Why Read Biography and Autobiography?

Reading about the lives of real people can be interesting. You'll learn about
- people from other cultures and other times in history
- what happened to bring out the best in other people

How to Read Biography and Autobiography

Key Reading Skills

These key reading skills are especially useful tools for reading and understanding biography and autobiography. You'll see these skills modeled in the Active Reading Model on pages 119–125, and you'll learn more about them later in this unit.

- ■ **Activating prior knowledge** As you read, use what you know to help you understand the subject, the story, the main character, or the setting. (See Reading Workshop 1.)
- ■ **Connecting** Link what you are reading to your own experiences. (See Reading Workshop 2.)
- ■ **Predicting** Based on what you know and have read, guess what will happen next in the selection. (See Reading Workshop 3.)
- ■ **Questioning** Check your understanding as you read by asking yourself questions about the text. (See Reading Workshop 4.)

Key Literary Elements

Recognizing and thinking about the following literary elements will help you understand a text more fully.

- ■ **Narrator:** the voice telling the story (See "The Jacket.")
- ■ **Point of view:** the person through whose eyes you see the story (See "Satchel Paige.")
- ■ **Chronological order:** the order in which events in a story happen (See "Eleanor Roosevelt.")
- ■ **Tone:** the attitude of the author (See "Gentleman of the Pool.")

Skills Focus
- Key skills for reading biography and autobiography
- Key literary elements of biography and autobiography

Skills Model
You will see how to use the key reading skills and elements as you read
- *Madam C. J. Walker,* p. 119

Objectives (pp. 118–125)
Reading Activate prior knowledge • Make connections from text to self • Make predictions • Ask questions
Literature Identify literary elements: narrator, point of view, chronological order, tone

UNIT 2 GENRE FOCUS

The notes in the side columns model how to use the skills and elements you read about on page 118.

Biography

ACTIVE READING MODEL

Madam C.J. Walker

by Jim Haskins

1 Key Reading Skill
Connecting I would like to earn a million dollars! I wonder how Madam C. J. Walker did it!

Madam C. J. Walker was the first American woman to earn a million dollars. There were American women millionaires before her time, but they had inherited their wealth, either from their husbands or from their families. Madam Walker was the first woman to earn her fortune by setting up her own business and proving that women could be financially independent of men. The company she started in the early years of this century is still in operation today. **1**

This photo of Madam Walker was taken around 1914. It was widely used in Walker Company advertisements. This portrait was also used on a 1998 commemorative postage stamp.

Madam C. J. Walker

UNIT 2 GENRE FOCUS

ACTIVE READING MODEL

Madam C. J. Walker was born Sarah Breedlove on December 23, 1867. She grew up in the South under very racist conditions. Her parents, Owen and Minerva Breedlove, had been slaves until President Abraham Lincoln's Emancipation Proclamation and the Union victory in the Civil War had freed the slaves.

After the war, few provisions[1] were made to help former slaves become independent. They did not receive money to help them get started in their new lives. They were uneducated, they had few skills except the ability to grow crops, and many were unaware of what freedom meant. Like the majority of former slaves, the Breedloves remained on the Burney family plantation in Delta, Louisiana. They had little choice but to stay on the same land where they had been slaves, only now they were sharecroppers. 2

The Breedloves sharecropped cotton. Like her brothers and sisters, Sarah was working in the cotton fields by the time she was six. By the time she was eleven, both her parents were dead, and she moved in with her older sister, Louvenia. A few years later, they moved across the river to Vicksburg, Mississippi.

Sarah married a man named McWilliams to get away from her sister's household. At that time, conditions in the South for blacks were actually worse than they had been during slavery. This was the time when Jim Crow laws were passed, segregating[2] southern blacks from whites in nearly every area of life. It was the time when white supremacy groups like the Ku Klux Klan achieved their greatest power, and lynchings[3] of blacks were common.

Sarah and her husband lived with the terror of being black as best they could. In 1885 their daughter, Lelia, was born, and her parents dreamed of making a better life for their little girl. Then, when Lelia was two, McWilliams was killed by a lynch mob.[4]

2 Key Reading Skill
Questioning *What are sharecroppers? I better look up the meaning of the word in a dictionary, in case it appears later in the text.*

1. Here **provisions** (pruh VIZH unz) are arrangements made for the future.
2. **Segregating** means "separating or setting apart."
3. **Lynchings** are acts of killing by a mob, without a trial or other legal action.
4. **McWilliams . . . mob.** No documentation actually proves that he died this way.

120 UNIT 2 What Brings Out the Best in You?

Sarah was a widow at the age of twenty, and the sole support of a two-year-old daughter. She took in laundry to earn a living and was determined to leave the South. With Lelia, she made her way up the Mississippi River and settled in St. Louis, where she worked fourteen hours a day doing other people's laundry. She enrolled Lelia in the St. Louis public schools and was pleased that her daughter would get the education that had been denied to her. But she wanted more for her daughter and for herself. **3**

Not long after they moved to St. Louis, Sarah McWilliams realized that her hair was falling out. She did not know why, but it is likely that the practice of braiding her hair too tightly was part of the cause. At the time, few hair-care products were available for black women. For years she tried every hair-care product available. But nothing worked. **4**

Then one night she had a dream. As she told the story many years later, in her dream "a black man appeared to me and told me what to mix up for my hair. Some of the remedy was grown in Africa, but I sent for it, mixed it, put it on my scalp, and in a few weeks my hair was coming in faster than it had ever fallen out." Sarah never publicly revealed[5] the formula of her mixture.

Sarah's friends remarked on what a full and healthy head of hair she had, and she gave some of her mixture to them. It worked on them, too, so she decided to sell it. She later said that she started her "Hair Grower" business with an investment of $1.50.

She had not been in business long when she received word that a brother who lived in Denver, Colorado, had died, leaving a wife and daughters. Sarah decided to go to Denver to live with her sister-in-law and nieces.

Wonderful Hair Grower was the most popular product made by Madam Walker's Company. It was released in 1906.

3 Key Reading Skill

Activating Prior Knowledge *I know that St. Louis is a big city in the Midwest. It is farther north than Vicksburg, Mississippi. The North was less racist than the South. I bet that's why Sarah moved north.*

4 Key Reading Skill

Predicting *Sarah had a problem. Her hair was falling out! Maybe Sarah will invent her own hair-care product.*

---

5. *Revealed* means "showed or made known."

UNIT 2 GENRE FOCUS

ACTIVE READING MODEL

In Denver, Sarah began to sell her special haircare product and did well. But she realized she needed to advertise to get more customers. Six months after arriving in Denver, she married C. J. Walker, a newspaperman who knew a lot about selling by mail order. With his help, she began to advertise her product, first in black newspapers across the state and later in black newspapers nationwide, and to make more money.

But soon her marriage was in trouble. As Sarah Walker later said of her husband, "I had business disagreements with him, for when we began to make ten dollars a day, he thought that amount was enough and that I should be satisfied. But I was convinced that my hair preparations would fill a longfelt want, and when we found it impossible to agree, due to his narrowness of vision, I embarked in business for myself." 5

5 **Key Reading Skill**
Predicting Based on what I know about Sarah, I predict that her business will be successful because she is smart and works hard.

1939 graduates of the St. Louis Walker Beauty School. "I got my start by giving myself a start." Madam C. J. Walker

122 UNIT 2 What Brings Out the Best in You?

In addition to helping her learn about advertising, her marriage gave Sarah Breedlove McWilliams Walker the name she would use for the rest of her life—Madam C. J. Walker. The "Madam" part was an affectation,[6] but Sarah liked the way it sounded. She thought it would be good for her business. By 1906 her business was so well that she was able to stop doing laundry for a living and devote all her time to her hair-care company.

Madam Walker was very proud of being a woman, and she was convinced that she could make it in the business world without the help of men. Almost from the start she determined that her business would be run by women. In 1906 she put her twenty-one-year-old daughter, Lelia, in charge of her growing mail-order business.

Madam Walker realized that the normal outlets for her products—white department stores and pharmacies—were not open to her. These stores would not stock black products because they did not want black customers. In addition to advertising, mostly in black newspapers, Madam Walker had to depend on the institutions in the black communities, the black churches, and the black women's clubs. [6]

Madam Walker's lectures on hair culture were widely attended. She was an excellent speaker and a commanding woman, nearly six feet tall, who was always beautifully dressed and coiffed.[7] She made a lasting impression wherever she went.

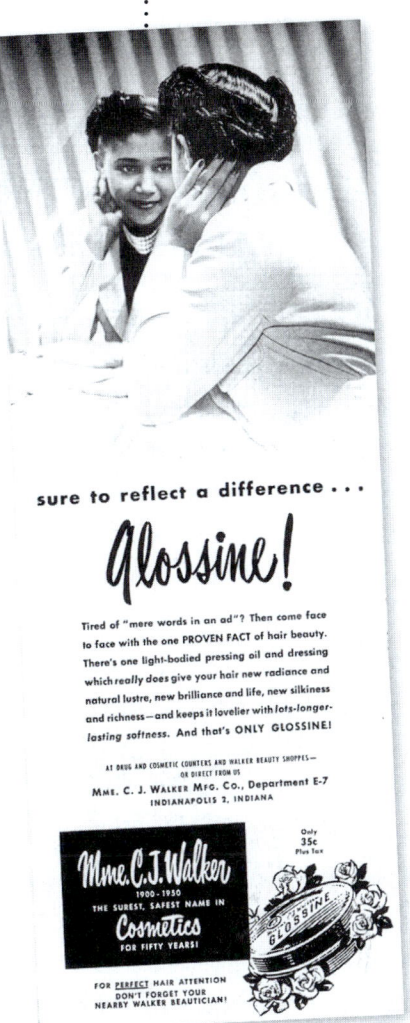

Advertisements like this were placed in newspapers around the country.

[6] Key Literary Element
Narrator *Someone other than Madam Walker is telling this story. The person telling Madam Walker's story seems to admire her.*

---

6. An **affectation** (af ek TAY shun) is a fake way of acting.
7. **Coiffed** (kwafd) means "styled," especially hair.

Although she lacked the formal education that most of these women had, Madam Walker never felt ashamed of her shortcomings[8] in that area. She taught herself as much as she could and was not afraid to ask someone to define a word she did not know or explain something she did not understand.

Madam Walker also wanted black women to go into business. Why should they toil over hot laundry tubs and clean white people's houses when they could be in business for themselves? Helping other black women also helped the Walker Company, and with this goal in mind Madam Walker recruited[9] and trained scores of women to use and sell Walker products. Many of them set up salons in their own homes. Others traveled door-to-door selling Walker products and demonstrating the Walker System. Madam Walker insisted that her agents sign contracts promising to abide by her strict standards of personal hygiene[10]—long before various states passed similar laws for workers in the cosmetics field. By 1910 the Walker Company had trained around 5,000 black female agents, not just in the United States but in England, France, Italy, and the West Indies. The company itself was taking in $1,000 a day, seven days a week. [7] [8]

That same year, Madam Walker's travels took her to Indianapolis, Indiana, a city that impressed her so much that she decided to move her headquarters there.

Madam Walker did not have much of a private life. She spent her time thinking of new ways to increase her business. The friends she had were people who could help her.

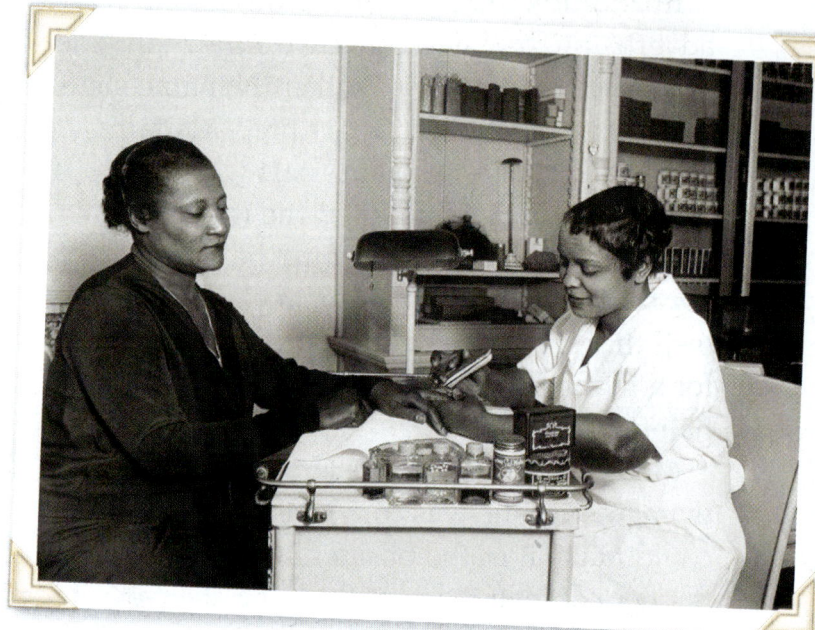

Madam Walker's daughter A'Lelia Walker getting a manicure at the Walker Beauty School in New York City.

ACTIVE READING MODEL

[7] **Key Literary Element**
Point of View The narrator calls Madam Walker by name and uses the pronoun "her." This is third-person point of view.

[8] **Key Literary Element**
Tone The author says a lot of good things about Madam Walker. The tone is admiring.

---

8. **Shortcomings** are weaknesses.
9. **Recruited** means "hired or engaged the services of."
10. **Hygiene** (HI jeen) is cleanliness and sanitary practices.

By 1917 the years of traveling and overwork began to take their toll on her. She developed high blood pressure, and in 1918 her doctors warned her that she had to slow down. She died quietly of kidney failure resulting from hypertension in May 1919. 9

In her will, Madam Walker left the bulk of her estate and the business to her daughter A'Lelia. But she also provided generously for a variety of educational institutions run by black women. She established a trust fund for an industrial and mission school in West Africa and provided bequests[11] to Negro orphanages, old people's homes, and Negro YWCA branches. In addition, she made bequests to many friends and employees.

Also in her will, Madam Walker insisted that the Madam C. J. Walker Company always be headed by a woman, and her wishes were carried out. Her daughter, A'Lelia, became president of the company after her death and presided at the dedication of the new company headquarters in Indianapolis in 1927, fulfilling a long-held dream of her mother's. ○

9 Key Literary Element
Chronological Order
Dates, such as 1917 and 1919, help me know the sequence of events.

11. **Bequests** (bih KWESTS) are things handed down or passed on.

In 1917 Madam Walker moved into this mansion, where she lived until her death in 1919. The house has thirty or more rooms and was decorated with valuable statues, tapestries, and paintings.

READING WORKSHOP 1

Skills Focus

You will practice using these skills when you read the following selections:
- "The Jacket," p. 130
- "The World Is Not a Pleasant Place to Be," p. 139

Reading
- Activating prior knowledge

Literature
- Identifying the narrator in what you read
- Recognizing the effect of the narrator on the story

Vocabulary
- Using synonyms
- Academic Vocabulary: *prior*

Writing/Grammar
- Properly using nouns and pronouns

Skill Lesson

Activating Prior Knowledge

Learn It!

What Is It? Activating **prior** knowledge means using what you already know. You should do this every time you read. It helps you understand what you're reading about. Can you imagine reading a story about a bicycle race if you had never seen or even heard of a bicycle? It would be very hard to understand. But when you read a story about a bicycle race, the image of a bicycle might pop into your head. You have activated your prior knowledge!

Analyzing Cartoons
What prior knowledge should Calvin activate the next time he comes through the door? Why?

Objectives (pp. 126–127)
Reading Activate prior knowledge

Academic Vocabulary

prior (PRY er) *adj.* earlier; coming before

126 UNIT 2

READING WORKSHOP 1 • Activating Prior Knowledge

Why Is It Important? Activating prior knowledge helps you understand what you read and makes reading more useful and more fun. For example, if a story takes place in New York City, you think about everything you have ever heard and learned about the city to help you understand what the author is describing.

How Do I Do It? Before you read, skim the title and text. Look at the pictures. Think about what you already know about the topic. Here's how one student used his prior knowledge when reading an article on downhill mountain bike racing.

Study Central Visit www.glencoe.com and click on Study Central to review activating prior knowledge.

> Thick pads shield their chests, hips, arms, and legs. The special gloves they wear have padding on each finger. On their heads, they display space-age helmets designed to protect the face as well as the head. These are the daredevils known as downhill mountain bike racers.

I've never seen mountain bike helmets, but I have seen bike helmets. The ones I've seen don't cover your face, though. I know some motorcycle helmets do. Maybe mountain bike helmets look more like motorcycle helmets.

Practice It!

Below are some of the feelings that the narrator of "The Jacket" experiences. In your Learner's Notebook, describe a time that you felt these emotions. What caused those feelings? What was it like? What did you do?
- anger
- embarrassment
- sadness
- loneliness

Use It!

As you read "The Jacket," remember what you wrote about the above emotions. Activate your prior knowledge about those feelings to help you understand what you read.

READING WORKSHOP 1 • Activating Prior Knowledge

Before You Read : The Jacket

Gary Soto

Meet the Author
Gary Soto was born in Fresno, California, in 1952. His parents, although born in America, were of Mexican heritage. Soto uses his poems and stories to tell about his experiences as a boy growing up. Many of his stories focus on issues that deal with being Latino in America. See page R6 of the Author Files for more on Gary Soto.

Author Search For more about Gary Soto, go to www.glencoe.com.

Objectives (pp. 128–135)
Reading Activate prior knowledge • Make connections from text to self
Literature Identify literary elements: narrator
Vocabulary Identify synonyms

Vocabulary Preview

vinyl (VY nul) *adj.* made of vinyl, which is a tough, shiny plastic **(p. 130)** *That vinyl chair looks very similar to a leather chair.*

profile (PROH fyl) *n.* a side view **(p. 131)** *You could tell he had a small nose when he stood sideways and you saw his profile.*

mope (mohp) *v.* to be gloomy or in low spirits **(p. 134)** *When it rains I mope around the house and wish the sun would come out.*

Write to Learn Answer each question about the vocabulary words.
1. Would vinyl be more useful for making a belt or for making a shirt? Why?
2. Why would a photograph of someone in profile be a good way to get an idea of their facial features?
3. What is something that might cause you to mope? Write a sentence about a time that you moped.

English Language Coach

Synonyms Synonyms are words that have the same or similar meanings. For example, the words *taunt* and *insult* are synonyms, but they have slightly different meanings. A *taunt* is a kind of *insult* that mocks someone.

- It is rare for synonyms to mean exactly the same thing.
- There are almost always small differences between synonyms. These differences may be important.
- The best way to find a synonym for a word is to use a thesaurus, a dictionary of synonyms.

Write to Learn In your Learner's Notebook, answer each question by thinking about the meanings of the synonyms. If you need help, look up the definitions of the words in a dictionary.
1. Which word best describes a baby's first steps—**walking, tottering,** or **marching**?
2. What word is better for describing loud construction in the street—**racket** or **sound**?
3. If you just scored a 100% on your science test, would you feel **content, satisfied,** or **thrilled**?

128 UNIT 2 What Brings Out the Best in You?

READING WORKSHOP 1 • Activating Prior Knowledge

Skills Preview

Key Reading Skill: Activating Prior Knowledge

Before you read the story, think about what you know about

- being a fifth or sixth grader
- getting new clothes
- feeling like an outsider

Write to Learn Pick one of the topics above and, in your Learner's Notebook, write a brief paragraph about that topic. Why did you choose that topic? What do you already know about the topic? What experiences have you had that come to mind?

Key Literary Element: Narrator

The person telling a story is the **narrator.** When you read a story, you feel the hopes and disappointments with the narrator as he or she describes them. The narrator of a *biography* is someone other than the person being written about. The narrator of an *autobiography* is the author. In this selection from Gary Soto's autobiography, Soto is the narrator. As you read, use these tips to help you learn about the narrator:

- An autobiography gives only one side of what happened—the author's side. Think about the details that the author provides.

  Do you think that being a fifth or sixth grader affected how Soto felt about his new jacket?

- Decide if you trust the narrator as a storyteller.

  Does he exaggerate details? Does he seem honest or dishonest?

Partner Talk How do you know when a narrator is trustworthy? Take turns with your partner telling a story about something that happened to you on your way to school. Keep it short, but exaggerate one detail. Let your partner try to pick out the detail you exaggerated in the story.

Get Ready to Read

Connect to the Reading

As you read "The Jacket," think about how the narrator felt when he wore his new jacket. Compare his feelings to the way you might have felt.

Class Talk Talk about clothes at your school. How are clothing trends started? If you have a dress code at school, do kids ever try to push the limits of the dress code? Explain.

Build Background

"The Jacket" is about the narrator's life as a fifth- and sixth-grader, a time when he didn't quite fit in and was growing out of his clothes fast.

- Soto's family is of Mexican heritage, and he grew up in California.
- Soto often draws upon experiences from his youth in his writing.

Set Purposes for Reading

 Read the "The Jacket" to find out how looking back on an event can bring out the best in you.

Set Your Own Purpose What else would you like to learn from the story to help you answer the Big Question? Write your purpose on "The Jacket" part of the Workshop 1 Foldable.

Literature Online

Interactive Literary Elements Handbook
To review or learn more about the literary elements, go to www.glencoe.com.

Keep Moving

Use these skills as you read the following selection.

READING WORKSHOP 1

The Jacket

by Gary Soto

My clothes have failed me. I remember the green coat that I wore in fifth and sixth grades when you either danced like a champ or pressed yourself against a greasy wall, bitter as a penny toward the happy couples. ◼1

When I needed a new jacket and my mother asked what kind I wanted, I described something like bikers wear: black leather and silver studs with enough belts to hold down a small town. We were in the kitchen, steam on the windows from her cooking. She listened so long while stirring dinner that I thought she understood for sure the kind I wanted. The next day when I got home from school, I discovered draped on my bedpost a jacket the color of day-old guacamole. I threw my books on the bed and approached the jacket slowly, as if it were a stranger whose hand I had to shake. I touched the **vinyl** sleeve, the collar, and peeked at the mustard-colored lining. ◼2

From the kitchen mother yelled that my jacket was in the closet. I closed the door to her voice and pulled at the rack of clothes in the closet, hoping the jacket on the bedpost wasn't

Vocabulary

vinyl (VY nul) *adj.* made of vinyl, which is a tough, shiny plastic

Practice the Skills

1 Reviewing Skills

Setting a Purpose for Reading This story is an autobiography. It's about a boy in sixth grade. What purpose could you set for reading an autobiographical story like "The Jacket"?

2 Key Reading Skill

Activating Prior Knowledge The narrator has mentioned

- a jacket "like bikers wear,"
- "the color of day-old guacamole,"
- "mustard-colored"

Did your prior knowledge help you understand these terms or anything else in the first two paragraphs? Explain.

130 UNIT 2 What Brings Out the Best in You?

READING WORKSHOP 1

for me but my mean brother. No luck. I gave up. From my bed, I stared at the jacket. I wanted to cry because it was so ugly and so big that I knew I'd have to wear it a long time. I was a small kid, thin as a young tree, and it would be years before I'd have a new one. I stared at the jacket, like an enemy, thinking bad things before I took off my old jacket whose sleeves climbed halfway to my elbow. **3**

I put the big jacket on.

I zipped it up and down several times, and rolled the cuffs up so they didn't cover my hands. I put my hands in the pockets and flapped the jacket like a bird's wings. I stood in front of the mirror, full face, then **profile**, and then looked over my shoulder as if someone had called me. I sat on the bed, stood against the bed, and combed my hair to see what I would look like doing something natural. I looked ugly. I threw it on my brother's bed and looked at it for a long time before I slipped it on and went out to the backyard, smiling a "thank you" to my mom as I passed her in the kitchen. With my hands in my pockets I kicked a ball against the fence, and then climbed it to sit looking into the alley. I hurled orange peels at the mouth of an open garbage can and when the peels were gone I watched the white puffs of my breath thin to nothing.

I jumped down, hands in my pockets, and in the backyard on my knees I teased my dog, Brownie, by swooping my arms while making bird calls. He jumped at me and missed.

Practice the Skills

3 **Key Literary Element**

Narrator In the opening paragraphs you can already begin to hear the narrator's "voice." He seems disappointed. What do you think of the narrator at this point? Explain.

Analyzing the Art How does this picture help you understand how the narrator felt about the green jacket? Explain, using details from the story.

Vocabulary

profile (PROH fyl) *n.* a side view

The Jacket

READING WORKSHOP 1

He jumped again and again, until a tooth sunk deep, ripping an L-shaped tear on my left sleeve. I pushed Brownie away to study the tear as I would a cut on my arm. There was no blood, only a few loose pieces of fuzz. Dumb dog, I thought, and pushed him away hard when he tried to bite again. I got up from my knees and went to my bedroom to sit with my jacket on my lap, with the lights out.

That was the first afternoon with my new jacket. The next day I wore it to sixth grade and got a D on a math quiz. During the morning recess Frankie T., the playground terrorist, pushed me to the ground and told me to stay there until recess was over. My best friend, Steve Negrete, ate an apple while looking at me, and the girls turned away to whisper on the monkey bars. The teachers were no help: they looked my way and talked about how foolish I looked in my new jacket. I saw their heads bob with laughter, their hands half-covering their mouths. 4

Even though it was cold, I took off the jacket during lunch and played kickball in a thin shirt, my arms feeling like Braille from goose bumps. But when I returned to class I slipped the jacket on and shivered until I was warm. I sat on my hands, heating them up, while my teeth chattered like a cup of crooked dice. Finally warm, I slid out of the jacket but a few minutes later put it back on when the fire bell rang. We paraded out into the yard where we, the sixth graders, walked past all the other grades to stand against the back fence. Everybody saw me. Although they didn't say out loud, "Man, that's ugly," I heard the buzz-buzz of gossip and even laughter that I knew was meant for me.

And so I went, in my guacamole-colored jacket. So embarrassed, so hurt, I couldn't even do my homework. I received Cs on quizzes, and forgot the state capitals and the rivers of South America, our friendly neighbor. Even the girls who had been **friendly** blew away like loose flowers to follow the boys in neat jackets. 5

I wore that thing for three years until the sleeves grew short and my forearms stuck out like the necks of turtles. All during that time no love came to me—no little dark girl in a Sunday dress she wore on Monday. At lunchtime I stayed with the ugly boys who leaned against the chainlink fence and looked around with propellers of grass spinning in our

Practice the Skills

4 Key Reading Skill

Activating Prior Knowledge
Think about what a teacher's job is all about. Do you think the teachers are really talking about how the narrator looks in his jacket? Why or why not?

5 English Language Coach

Synonyms What are some synonyms for **friendly**? If the author had used the word *helpful* or the word *kind*, would the meaning of the sentence have changed? Why or why not?

mouths. We saw girls walk by alone, saw couples, hand in hand, their heads like bookends pressing air together. We saw them and spun our propellers so fast our faces were blurs. 6

I blame that jacket for those bad years. I blame my mother for her bad taste and her cheap ways. It was a sad time for the heart. With a friend I spent my sixth-grade year in a tree in the alley, waiting for something good to happen to me in that jacket, which had become the ugly brother who tagged along wherever I went. And it was about that time that I began to grow. My chest puffed up with muscle and, strangely, a few more ribs. Even my hands, those fleshy hammers, showed bravely through the cuffs, the fingers already hardening for the coming fights. But that L-shaped rip on the left sleeve got bigger, bits of stuffing coughed out from its wound after a

Practice the Skills

6 Key Literary Element

Narrator Now that you've read more of the story, what do you think of the narrator? Do you trust him? Is he honest? Does he exaggerate?

Analyzing the Art Which boy in this picture is the narrator? How do you know? Where do you think the green jacket might be?

READING WORKSHOP 1

hard day of play. I finally Scotch-taped it closed, but in rain or cold weather the tape peeled off like a scab and more stuffing fell out until that sleeve shriveled into a palsied[1] arm. That winter the elbows began to crack and whole chunks of green began to fall off. I showed the cracks to my mother, who always seemed to be at the stove with steamed-up glasses, and she said that there were children in Mexico who would love that jacket. I told her that this was America and yelled that Debbie, my sister, didn't have a jacket like mine. I ran outside, ready to cry, and climbed the tree by the alley to think bad thoughts and watch my breath puff white and disappear. **7**

But whole pieces still casually flew off my jacket when I played hard, read quietly, or took vicious spelling tests at school. When it became so spotted that my brother began to call me "camouflage," I flung it over the fence into the alley. Later, however, I swiped the jacket off the ground and went inside to drape it across my lap and **mope**.

I was called to dinner: steam silvered my mother's glasses as she said grace; my brother and sister with their heads bowed made ugly faces at their glasses of powdered milk. I gagged too, but eagerly ate big rips of buttered tortilla that held scooped-up beans. Finished, I went outside with my jacket across my arm. It was a cold sky. The faces of clouds were piled up, hurting. I climbed the fence, jumping down with a grunt. I started up the alley and soon slipped into my jacket, that green ugly brother who breathed over my shoulder that day and ever since. **8** ○

Practice the Skills

7 **Key Literary Element**

Narrator Can you "hear" the narrator's voice in this paragraph? Explain. What words would you use to describe the way the narrator is feeling?

8 **BIG Question**

Do clothes bring out the best in people? Think about your own experiences and knowledge. Answer this question on "The Jacket" part of the Workshop 1 Foldable.

---

1. *palsied* (PAWL zeed) means "withered by disease."

Vocabulary

mope (mohp) *v.* to be gloomy or in low spirits

134 UNIT 2 What Brings Out the Best in You?

READING WORKSHOP 1

Analyzing the Art What details from the story's final paragraph do you see in this picture?

READING WORKSHOP 1 • **Activating Prior Knowledge**

After You Read : The Jacket

Answering the BIG Question

1. Do you think the narrator's new coat brings out the best in him? Why or why not?
2. **Recall** Who is this story mostly about?
   TIP **Right There** You will find the answer in the story.
3. **Summarize** What does the narrator's new jacket look like?
   TIP **Think and Search** The answer is in the story, but the details are not in one place.

Critical Thinking

4. **Infer** How does the narrator feel when he sees his new green jacket? Why do you think he feels this way?
   TIP **Author and Me** You will find clues in the story, but you must also use the information in your head.
5. **Conclude** Why does the narrator wear the jacket even though he hates it?
   TIP **Think and Search** The answer is in the story, but the details are not in one place.
6. **Infer** How can you tell the narrator cares about his mother's feelings?
   TIP **Author and Me** You will find clues in the story, but you must also use the information in your head.
7. **Analyze** Do you think the narrator's attitude toward the jacket changes by the end of the story? Explain.
   TIP **Author and Me** You will find clues in the story, but you must also use the information in your head.

Talk About Your Reading

The writer Mark Twain said that "Clothes make the man." What do you think that means? Think about what you just read, and consider the big question. Think about your own experiences and discuss the quote with the class. Answer these questions:

- Do you think the narrator of "The Jacket" would agree that "Clothes make the man" or not?
- Do you ever feel pressure to fit in by dressing a certain way? Explain.
- Do your clothes make you who you are?

Objectives (pp. 136–137)
Reading Activate prior knowledge • Make connections from text to self
Literature Identify literary elements: narrator
Vocabulary Identify synonyms
Grammar Identify parts of speech: common and proper nouns

136 UNIT 2 What Brings Out the Best in You?

Skills Review

Key Reading Skill: Activating Prior Knowledge

8. What prior knowledge did you have that most helped you understand this selection?
9. How did the activities on page 129 help you read and understand this selection? Rank the activities in order of helpfulness, with 1 being the most helpful and 3 the least helpful. Explain your rankings.
   - Talking about clothing trends
   - Previewing the reading skill
   - Reading the facts in Build Background

Key Literary Element: Narrator

10. Describe the narrator. Is he suspenseful, funny, serious? Use a line from the text to back up your opinion.
11. How might the story be different if Soto's mother narrated "The Jacket"?
12. Do you think time has changed the way the narrator feels about his green jacket? Explain.

Reviewing Skills: Setting a Purpose for Reading

13. If you recommended this story to someone, what would you tell them is a good purpose for reading "The Jacket"?

Vocabulary Check

In your own words write a definition for each vocabulary word. Next write a sentence for each word.

14. vinyl
15. profile
16. mope
17. **Academic Vocabulary** What *prior* knowledge would you need to use the Internet?
18. **English Language Coach** What three words would you use to describe the narrator of this story? What are their synonyms?

Grammar Link: Nouns

A **noun** names a person, place, thing, or idea.
- A **common noun** names *any* person, place, thing, or idea.
- A **proper noun** names a *particular* person, place, thing, or idea. Proper nouns always begin with a capital letter.

Common Nouns	Proper Nouns
city	Los Angeles
actor	Johnny Depp
school	Wilson Middle School
baseball team	Chicago White Sox

Grammar Practice

Rewrite each sentence, circle both common and proper nouns, then write a **C** above each *common noun* and a **P** above each *proper noun*.

19. Bart and Trent went to a movie.
20. In Washington D.C., the class visited several monuments.
21. Our family will have a picnic at Lincoln Park this weekend.

Now write three sentences of your own using both common and proper nouns. For each sentence you write, circle the nouns, and write a **C** above each *common noun* and a **P** above each *proper noun*.

Web Activities For eFlashcards, Selection Quick Checks, and other Web activities, go to www.glencoe.com.

READING WORKSHOP 1 • Activating Prior Knowledge

Before You Read

The World Is Not a Pleasant Place to Be

Yolande Cornelia "Nikki" Giovanni, Jr.

Meet the Author
Yolande Cornelia "Nikki" Giovanni, Jr., was born in 1943 in Knoxville, Tennessee. She is a poet, writer, and educator. Giovanni is one of the most widely read American poets. She takes pride in being "a Black American, a daughter, a mother, a professor of English." Giovanni is committed to the fight for civil rights and equality. See page R3 of the Author Files for more on Nikki Giovanni.

Author Search For more about Nikki Giovanni, go to www.glencoe.com.

Objectives (pp. 138–139)
Reading Activate prior knowledge • Make connections from text to self
Literature Identify literary elements: speaker

Skills Preview

Key Reading Skill: Activating Prior Knowledge
Before you read the poem, think about how you feel when you're alone. How do you feel when you're with your family and friends?

Write to Learn Write a short paragraph about what you think makes the world a pleasant place to be.

Literary Element: Speaker
In a poem, the narrator is called the speaker. The **speaker** is the voice that communicates the poem's ideas, actions, descriptions, and feelings. As you read "The World Is Not a Pleasant Place to Be," pay special attention to the thoughts and emotions that the speaker expresses.

- Try to get a feeling for what the speaker is like.
  How would you describe this speaker to a friend?

Get Ready to Read

Connect to the Reading
The speaker in this poem expresses feelings of loneliness through images of a river and the ocean. What everyday objects or scenes in life and nature make you think about loneliness?

Build Background
Nikki Giovanni began writing in the 1960s, a time of great social change. Many of her poems focus on social and political issues. In her later poetry she writes about personal subjects such as family, love, and loneliness. This poem comes from Giovanni's book of poems, *My House*.

Set Purposes for Reading
BIG Question Read the poem "The World Is Not a Pleasant Place to Be" to learn about what the speaker feels brings out the best in people.

Set Your Own Purpose What else would you like to learn from the poem to help you answer the Big Question? Write your own purpose on the "The World" part of the Workshop 1 Foldable.

Keep Moving
Use these skills as you read the following selection.

138 UNIT 2 What Brings Out the Best in You?

The World Is Not a Pleasant Place to Be

by Nikki Giovanni

the world is not a pleasant place
to be without
someone to hold and be held by **1**

a river would stop
5 its flow if only
a stream were there
to receive it

an ocean would never laugh
if clouds weren't there
10 to kiss her tears **2**

the world is not
a pleasant place to be without
someone **3** ○

Practice the Skills

1 **Key Reading Skill**

Activating Prior Knowledge Think about your experiences with family, friends, or even pets. Would the world be less pleasant without them in your life?

2 **Literary Element**

Speaker The speaker has specific ideas about what makes the world "pleasant." Do you agree with the speaker?

3 **BIG Question**

What does the speaker say makes the world a better place? Do you agree or disagree? Write your answer on "The World" part of the Workshop 1 Foldable.

After You Read

The World Is Not a Pleasant Place to Be

Answering the BIG Question

1. Who brings out the best in you? How?

2. **Summarize** What is this poem about?

   TIP **Think and Search** The answer is in the poem, but the details are not in one place.

3. **Identify** Write two lines from the poem that use images from nature.

   TIP **Think and Search** The answer is in the poem, but the details are not in one place.

Critical Thinking

4. **Infer** Think about the feelings expressed in the poem. How do you think the author felt when she wrote this poem?

   TIP **Author and Me** You will find clues in the poem, but you must also use the information in your head.

5. **Evaluate** Do you agree with the speaker about what is important in life, or can you think of more important things in life? Explain.

   TIP **Author and Me** You will find clues in the poem, but you must also use the information in your head.

6. **Analyze** Why do you think the author starts and ends the poem using the phrase "the world is not a pleasant place to be"? That phrase is also the title. Explain why you think the author repeated that phrase so often.

   TIP **Author and Me** You will find clues in the poem, but you must also use the information in your head.

Write About Your Reading

Use the poem "The World Is Not a Pleasant Place to Be" as a model to write your own poem about what makes the world a good and pleasant place.

- Choose a speaker. Will the speaker be you or someone else?
- What feelings do you want to express: happiness, sadness, loneliness, frustration? What words will help you express those feelings?
- Make sure that your poem has four stanzas, like "The World Is Not a Pleasant Place to Be." Stanzas are sections of a poem and are similar to paragraphs.

Objectives (pp. 140–141)
Reading Activate prior knowledge • Make connections from text to self
Literature Identify literary elements: speaker
Grammar Identify parts of speech: subject and object pronouns
Writing Respond to literature: write a poem

Skills Review

Key Reading Skill: Activating Prior Knowledge

7. Do the images from nature in the poem help you understand the speaker's feelings? Why or why not?

Literary Element: Speaker

8. Do the words the speaker uses help you understand the way the speaker feels? Why or why not?
9. Do you think the speaker and author are the same person in this poem? Explain.
10. In what ways do you think the speaker is like you? In what ways do you think the speaker is different?

Vocabulary Check

11. **Academic Vocabulary** What *prior* knowledge do you think the author of this poem had to help her write this poem about the world?
12. **English Language Coach** List three synonyms for the word *pleasant*. If you want to, use a thesaurus. Why do you think the poet chose the word *pleasant* instead of one of its synonyms?
13. **English Language Coach** The words *river* and *stream* are synonyms. Use a dictionary to discover the slightly different meanings of the words.

Grammar Link: Pronouns

A **pronoun** is a word that takes the place of one or more nouns. Pronouns make reading easier. For example, look at the sentence below. It doesn't use any pronouns.

Ben let Ben's sister borrow Ben's bike so Ben's sister could ride to Ben and Ben's sister's school.

Now look at the sentence with pronouns.

Ben let **his** sister borrow **his** bike so **she** could ride to **their** school.

What pronoun you use depends on how and when you use it in a sentence. Some pronouns replace nouns that are the **subject** of a sentence. Other pronouns replace nouns that are the **object** of a sentence. (You will learn more about subjects and objects in Unit 4.)

Subject pronouns: *I, you, he, she, it, we, they*
Object pronouns: *me, you, him, her, us, them*

Grammar Practice

Rewrite each sentence below replacing each underlined word or group of words with the correct **subject pronoun**.

14. <u>Queen Latifah</u> is a movie star.
15. After ice-skating, <u>Jenny and Juan</u> had hot chocolate.
16. The movie was scary, but <u>Sumi and I</u> watched <u>the movie</u> anyway.

Rewrite each sentence below replacing each underlined word or group of words with the correct **object pronoun**.

17. Have you seen <u>Jamal and Derek</u>?
18. Mr. Yoshida drove <u>Alex and Kaori</u> to the dance.
19. Emily told <u>Luz</u> a joke.

Writing Application Choose one stanza in your poem with a noun, or group of nouns, that you could change into a pronoun. Rewrite that stanza with the noun, or group of nouns, changed to a pronoun.

Web Activities For eFlashcards, Selection Quick Checks, and other Web activities, go to www.glencoe.com.

WRITING WORKSHOP PART 1

Autobiographical Narrative
Prewriting and Drafting

ASSIGNMENT Write an autobiographical narrative

Purpose: Share a story about a friend who brought out the best in you

Audience: You, your teacher, and your classmates

Writing an autobiographical narrative will help you think about the Unit 2 Big Question: What brings out the best in you?

Autobiography: When you write about your life or an event in your life, you write autobiography.

\+

Narrative: Any story, real or imagined, is a narrative.

\=

Autobiographical Narrative: When you write or tell a story that is about your life, you are creating an autobiographical narrative.

Writing Rubric

As you work through this Writing Workshop, you will

- write about an important friendship
- tell a story in your own words
- write details and descriptions
- use chronological order
- use nouns correctly

See page 186 in Part 2 for a model of an autobiographical narrative.

Prewriting
Get Ready to Write

In this Writing Workshop you are going to write about a time in your life when a friend helped you do something that you thought was impossible.

Gather Ideas and Choose a Topic

In your Learner's Notebook make a list of important friends in your life. Next to each name on your list, write a memorable experience you shared with that friend that made you better or stronger. Next, choose the friend and the experience you'd like to write an autobiographical narrative about.

Drafting
Start Writing!

For about five or ten minutes, freewrite about your friend and the experience. Try to remember the order in which the events took place. Write descriptions, details, feelings, or whatever else comes to mind.

Objectives (pp. 142–145)
Writing Use the writing process: autobiographical narrative • Use literary elements: details, chronological order, conventions of language
Grammar Use nouns: common, proper, abstract, collective

Get It on Paper

Autobiographical narratives are usually about a special event in the writer's life. In this narrative, the special event is a time when a friend brought out the best in you. Make sure that your draft tells the reader how this event was special to you.

Sort Through the Details

Choose only the details that are important to the story. Do this so your reader won't get confused by unimportant information. Read the example below and pick out the detail that the writer should leave out of this narrative.

> Last year, I ran for fifth grade class president. Fifth grade was really fun because Pablo and I were in the same homeroom and lunch period. Pablo gave me the idea to run for class president. On the day of the election, I had to give a speech in front of the entire grade about why I would make a good class president. As I was waiting for my turn to speak, I became really nervous. My stomach felt like it was tied in knots and my hands got sweaty. I started thinking that I didn't want to be class president anymore.

What detail is not necessary and can be deleted from this narrative?

Put the Story in Order

As you write, you need to make sure that the events of your narrative are in a particular order. Chronological, or time, order is a good way to organize an autobiographical narrative. Just write events in the order that they happened: first, second, third, and so on. Begin some sentences with words like *then* and *next* to help readers follow your story. Read the passage below for an example of chronological order.

> Pablo helped me with all of the election preparations. *First*, we made posters to hang in the fifth grade hallway. *Then*, we made buttons with my name on them for our classmates to wear. *Finally*, on the night before the election, we baked cookies to pass out at school the next day.

Writing Tip
Remember that autobiographical narratives are written in the first-person point of view. That means you should use words like *I* and *me* to refer to yourself.

Writing Tip
Stay focused on the story that you are telling. Make a list of the important events you want to write about and stick to those events in your narrative.

Writing Tip
Keep your readers interested by including details about how you felt at certain points throughout the narrative.

Writing Models For models and other writing activities, go to www.glencoe.com.

WRITING WORKSHOP PART 1

Applying Good Writing Traits

Conventions

Writers have a common set of rules. It's not terrible to break the rules, but you have to know the rules in order to play the game.

What Are Conventions?

Conventions are the rules of language–spelling, capitalization, punctuation, grammar, usage, and paragraphing.

Why Are Conventions Important?

When you follow the rules of language, your writing is easy for others to read. Readers can pay attention to your message and your unique ideas instead of trying to figure out what you meant to say.

You can play around with conventions for a specific effect. For example, you may misspell a word or break a grammar rule to show how a character speaks. However, your writing must show strong control of conventions so readers know you're breaking the rules on purpose and for good reasons.

How Do I Use Conventions in My Writing?

- Read your paper slowly. Focus on seeing the words as they appear on the page.
- Look for one kind of error at a time.

1. Look for grammatical errors. Reading your paper aloud may help you find them.
2. Check to make sure you have punctuation and capital letters in all the right places.
3. Check that your paragraphs begin in the right places and that the first line of each paragraph is indented.
4. Circle any words you need to check for spelling and then look them up in a dictionary. If you use a computer, you can use the spell-check feature, but don't trust it completely. If you accidentally typed *here* but meant to type *hear*, the spell-check feature won't notice the mistake.

Write to Learn Read over your draft carefully. Follow the steps above to find and correct errors in conventions.

ADAM @ 1999 HOME © by UNIVERSAL PRESS SYNDICATE. Reprinted with permission. All rights reserved.

Analyzing Cartoons
Here, *fundamentals* means "the most important skills." What is Clint's problem? How are the fundamentals in a sport like the conventions in writing?

144 UNIT 2 What Brings Out the Best in You?

Grammar Link

Nouns

A **noun** names a person, place, or thing. Using a variety of nouns is an important part of good writing.

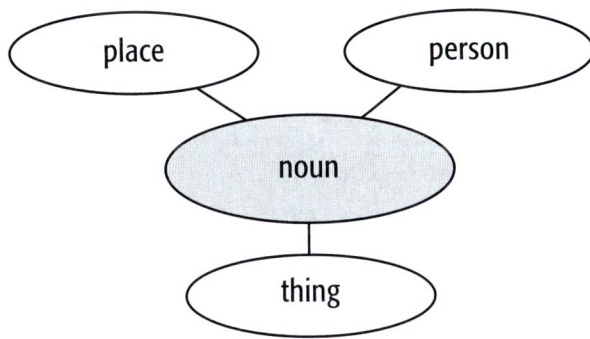

Look at the three underlined nouns in the following sentence.

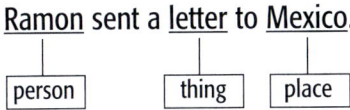

What Are the Different Types of Nouns?

A *common noun* is the name of a general person, place, or thing.
- The boys are playing baseball.

A *proper noun* is the name of a specific person, place, or thing. Proper nouns are capitalized.
- Tom and Jarrod are playing for the Yankees.

An *abstract noun* refers to something that is an idea, emotion, or feeling, rather than something that you can touch.
- The teacher expressed joy when she read the students' reports.

A *collective noun* refers to a group of people or things.
- The family took a walk every Saturday.

How Can I Use Nouns Correctly in My Autobiographical Narrative?

Read your autobiographical narrative. Circle all the nouns you find.

Step 1: Review all sentences that have common nouns that are NOT abstract or collective.
- Is it the right noun for that sentence?
- Should it be singular or plural?

Step 2: Review all sentences that have abstract nouns.
- Is it the right noun for that sentence?
- Should it be singular or plural?

Step 3: Review all sentences that have collective nouns.
- Is it the right noun for that sentence?

Step 4: Review all sentences that have proper nouns.
- Is it the right noun for that sentence?
- Is it capitalized?

Step 5: See if there are any nouns that you have not already fixed.

As you continue writing your autobiographical narrative, correctly use a variety of nouns to keep your reader interested in your story.

Looking Ahead

Keep the writing you did here. In Part 2 you will add the finishing touches.

READING WORKSHOP 2

Skills Focus

You will practice using these skills when you read the following selections:
- "Satchel Paige," p. 150
- "Song for a Surf-Rider," p. 161

Reading
- Connecting to the text

Literature
- Identifying the author's point of view

Vocabulary
- Using antonyms

Writing/Grammar
- Identifying pronouns and their antecedents correctly
- Identifying indefinite pronouns

Skill Lesson

Connecting

Learn It!

What Is It? Connecting means linking what you read to events in your own life or to other selections you've read.

When you connect to what you read, you
- compare the characters to yourself, people you know, and people you have read about.
- compare the setting to places you have been to or places you have learned about.
- relate the events to emotions and events in your own life.

Analyzing the Art
Does this artwork show what it's like to *connect* with another person's (or a writer's) thinking? Explain your answer.

Objectives (pp. 146–147)
Reading Make connections from text to self

146 UNIT 2

READING WORKSHOP 2 • Connecting

Why Is It Important? You'll be more involved in your reading and able to recall information and ideas better by connecting events, emotions, and characters to your own life.

How Do I Do It? Ask yourself:
- Do I know someone like this?
- Have I ever felt this way?
- What else have I read that is like this selection?

Study Central Visit www.glencoe.com and click on Study Central to review connecting.

Here's how one reader connected to a paragraph in Jim Haskins's biography of Madam C. J. Walker.

> Then one night she had a dream. As she told the story many years later, in her dream "a black man appeared to me and told me what to mix up for my hair. Some of the remedy was grown in Africa, but I sent for it, mixed it, put it on my scalp, and in a few weeks my hair was coming in faster than it had ever fallen out."

I once had a dream about a project for a science fair. I did the project I dreamed about and won a ribbon. I know that dreams sometimes help us solve problems that we are thinking about when we are awake. Sarah's dream helped her solve her problem about losing her hair, just like my dream helped me with my science project.

Practice It!

Below are some experiences that happened to Satchel Paige, the main character in the selection you are about to read. Think about how you might connect to each experience.
- being treated unfairly because of his race
- doing what he loved to do, but under very hard circumstances
- being recognized for his talents

Use It!

As you read "Satchel Paige," practice connecting to the text. Compare what you know and have experienced with what you read about in the selection. Write the connections you make in your Learner's Notebook.

READING WORKSHOP 2 • Connecting

Before You Read : Satchel Paige

Bill Littlefield

Meet the Author
Bill Littlefield writes sports stories. His stories show young readers why it is important to focus on goals and work hard to reach them. Littlefield says, "As a writer, I've invented the stories of fictional characters, recounted the tales of old baseball scouts and young ballplayers, and retold for young readers the stories of great athletes."

Author Search For more about Bill Littlefield, go to www.glencoe.com.

Objectives (pp. 148–157)
Reading Make connections from text to self
Literature Identify literary elements: point of view
Vocabulary Identify antonyms

Vocabulary Preview

potential (puh TEN shul) *adj.* capable of being; possible **(p. 152)** *Satchel Paige was a potential superstar in Major League Baseball.*

confrontations (kon frun TAY shunz) *n.* unpleasant face-to-face meetings **(p. 154)** *The new baseball player had some confrontations with the coach.*

prejudice (PREJ uh dis) *n.* an opinion that is formed unfairly **(p. 154)** *When Satchel was on the field people cheered, yet they showed their prejudice against him when he was off the field.*

exploits (EK sploytz) *n.* brave acts or deeds **(p. 156)** *The woman who saved the little boy from drowning in the river did not brag about her exploits.*

Class Talk As a class, take turns defining the words and using them in sentences.

English Language Coach

Antonyms Antonyms are words that have opposite meanings. You can use antonyms to help you tell how two things are different, such as *it's <u>cold</u> outside, but <u>hot</u> inside*. Knowing antonyms can help you understand the meanings of other words and help you increase your vocabulary.

Look at the following chart. In the left-hand column, you will see words from the selection "Satchel Paige." In the right-hand column, you will see the antonyms of those words.

Selection Words	Antonyms
narrow	wide
late	early
triumph	failure

Partner Talk In your Learner's Notebook, rewrite the sentences below using the antonym of each underlined word. With a partner, discuss how the meaning of the sentences changed.

1. Satchel slung a pole across his <u>narrow</u> shoulders to hang the bags.
2. Satchel Paige was inducted into the Baseball Hall of Fame <u>late</u> in his life.
3. Satchel Paige had many baseball <u>triumphs</u>.

148 UNIT 2 What Brings Out the Best in You?

READING WORKSHOP 2 • Connecting

Skills Preview

Key Reading Skill: Connecting

As you read, connect your personal experiences with what you read. Think about

- the ways you are like the people in a selection.
- how the events are like experiences you may have had.

Key Literary Element: Point of View

Point of view is the relationship of the writer or narrator to the story. A story may be told by someone in the story. The storyteller refers to himself or herself as *I*, and the reader sees everything through that person's eyes. This is the *first-person point of view*. All autobiographies are written this way. Many novels and short stories also use first-person point of view.

At other times, a story is told by someone outside the story, someone who is not part of what happens. This is called *third-person point of view*. All biographies are written this way, and most magazine and news articles are, too. Many novels and short stories also use third-person point of view.

As you read, use this tip to help you identify the point of view:

- Pay attention to who is telling the story. Is the storyteller a character or person in the story or not?

Write to Learn In your Learner's Notebook, name a story that uses third-person point of view and one that uses first-person. Explain how you know which point of view is used in each.

Get Ready to Read

Connect to the Reading

Think about how it feels to be treated unfairly. Satchel Paige probably felt that it was unfair that he was not allowed to play in the major leagues because he was African American. As you read Satchel's story, think about how you would feel if you were kept from doing the one thing you love to do, even though you're as good as everyone else—or better.

Freewrite Write about something you love and how you would feel about not being able to participate due to other people's prejudices.

Build Background

This biography of Satchel Paige describes his love and talent for baseball as a child, how he got started playing pro baseball, and the challenges he faced as an African American player.

- Before 1947, African American baseball players were not allowed to play in Major League Baseball. They could only play in the Negro Leagues.
- Jackie Robinson became the first African American Major League Baseball player when he signed with the Brooklyn Dodgers in 1947.

Set Purposes for Reading

Read this selection to find out what brought out the best in Satchel Paige as he faced prejudice.

Set Your Own Purpose What else would you like to learn from the selection to help you answer the Big Question? Write your own purpose on the "Satchel Paige" part of the Workshop 2 Foldable.

Interactive Literary Elements Handbook
To review or learn more about the literary elements, go to www.glencoe.com.

Keep Moving

Use these skills as you read the following selection.

Satchel Paige

READING WORKSHOP 2

Satchel Paige

by Bill Littlefield

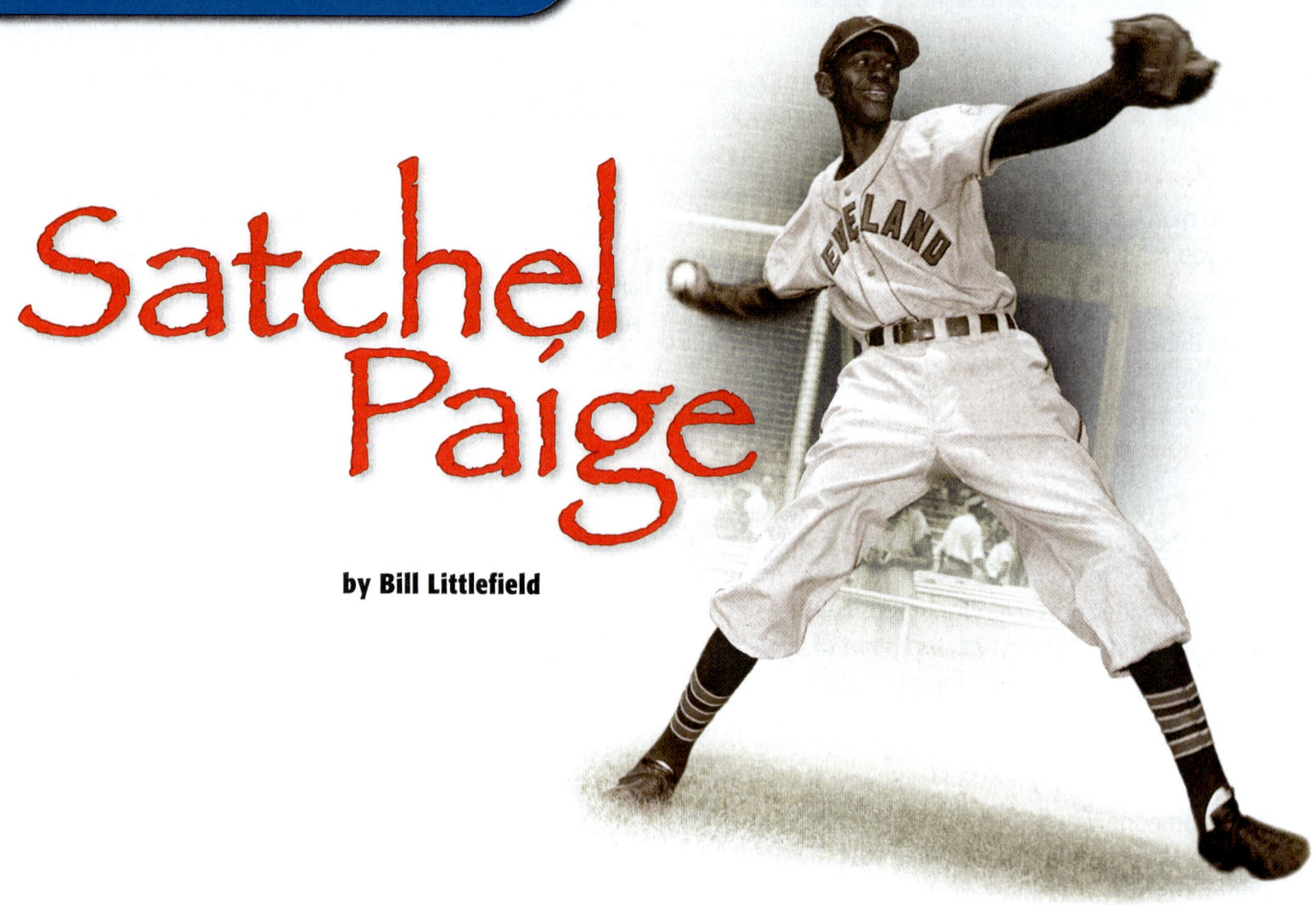

Practice the Skills

Late in the afternoon of July 9, 1948, Leroy "Satchel" Paige began the long walk from the bullpen to the mound at Cleveland's Municipal Stadium. He didn't hurry. He never hurried. As he said himself, he "kept the juices flowing by jangling gently" as he moved. The crowd roared its appreciation. This was the fellow they'd come to see. **1**

When Satchel finally reached the mound, Cleveland manager Lou Boudreau took the ball from starting pitcher Bob Lemon, who would eventually be voted into the Hall of Fame but had tired that day, and gave it to Paige. Probably he said something like, "Shut 'em down, Satchel." Whatever he said, Paige had no doubt heard the words a thousand times. Though he was a rookie with the Indians that year, no pitcher in the history of baseball had ever been more thoroughly prepared for a job. He kicked at the rubber, looked in for the sign, and got set to throw. In a moment, twenty-odd years later than it should have happened, Satchel Paige would deliver his first pitch in the big leagues.

1 **Key Literary Element**

Point of View What point of view is this selection told through? What pronoun gives you a clue?

Visual Vocabulary
A *satchel* is a type of suitcase.

The tall, skinny kid named Leroy Paige became Satchel Paige one day at the railroad station in Mobile, Alabama. He was carrying bags for the folks getting on and off the trains, earning all the nickels and dimes he could to help feed his ten brothers and sisters. Eventually it occurred to him that if he slung a pole across his narrow shoulders and hung the bags, or satchels, on the ends of the pole, he could carry for more people at once and collect more nickels and dimes. It worked, but it looked a little funny. "You look like some kind of ol' satchel tree," one of his friends told him, and the nickname stuck. 2

Even in those days, before he was a teenager, Satchel Paige could throw hard and accurately. Years later, Paige swore that when his mother would send him out into the yard to get a chicken for dinner, he would brain the bird[1] with a rock. "I used to kill *flying* birds with rocks, too," he said. "Most people need shotguns to do what I did with rocks."

It was not a talent that would go unnoticed for long. He was pitching for the semipro[2] Mobile Tigers before he was eighteen . . . or maybe before he was sixteen, or before he was twelve. There is some confusion about exactly when Satchel Paige was born, and Satchel never did much to clarify the matter. But there never has been any confusion about whether he could pitch. His first steady job in baseball was with the Chattanooga Black Lookouts. He was paid fifty dollars a month. In the seasons that followed he would also pitch for the Birmingham Black Barons, the Nashville Elite Giants, the

Practice the Skills

2 Key Reading Skill

Connecting Have you ever had a nickname? Who gave it to you? How did you get it?

Satchel Paige and his teammates on the Pittsburgh Crawfords pose as the champions of the Negro National League in 1935.

---

1. To **brain the bird** means to "hit it in the head."
2. To be **semipro** means the team member is only paid to play part-time and may have another full-time job.

READING WORKSHOP 2

Baltimore Black Sox, the Pittsburgh Crawfords, and the Kansas City Monarchs, among other teams.

If those names are not as familiar sounding as those of the New York Yankees, the Los Angeles Dodgers, or the Boston Red Sox, it's because they were all clubs in the Negro leagues, not the major leagues. Today the presence of black baseball players in the big leagues is taken for granted. Hank Aaron is the greatest of the home run hitters, and Rickey Henderson has stolen more bases than any other big leaguer. But before 1947, neither of them would have had the opportunity to do what they have done. Until Brooklyn Dodger general manager Branch Rickey signed Jackie Robinson, black players had no choice but to play for one of the all-black teams, and making that choice, they faced hardships no major-leaguer today could imagine.

Players in the Negro leagues crowded into broken-down cars and bumped over rutted[3] roads to makeshift[4] ball fields with lights so bad that every pitch was a **potential** weapon. Then they drove all night for an afternoon game three hundred miles away. On good days they played before big, **appreciative** crowds in parks they'd rented from the major league teams in Chicago, New York, or Pittsburgh. On bad days they learned that the team they were playing for was too broke to finish the season, and they would have to look for a **healthier** team that could use them, or else find a factory job. 🔳

It took talent, hard work, and a sense of humor to survive in the Negro leagues, and Satchel Paige had a lot of all three. But he didn't just survive. He prospered. Everybody knows about the fastball, the curve, and the slider. But Satchel threw a "bee" ball, which, he said, "would always *be* where I wanted it to *be*." He featured a trouble ball, which, of course, gave the hitters a lot of trouble. Even the few who could see it couldn't hit it. Sometimes he'd come at them with his hesitation pitch, a delivery so mysterious that the man at the plate would sometimes swing before the ball left Satchel's hand.

---

3. A road that's been well-worn by wheels or travel is **rutted**.
4. **Makeshift** means "a temporary substitute."

Vocabulary

potential (puh TEN shul) *adj*. capable of being; possible

Practice the Skills

🔳 **English Language Coach**

Antonyms Find the words *appreciative* and *healthier* in this paragraph. Do you know what they mean? List these words in your Learner's Notebook. Then write the antonym for each word. Use a dictionary if you need help.

152 UNIT 2 What Brings Out the Best in You?

Nor was pitching his sole triumph. Early in his career Satchel Paige began building a reputation as a storyteller, a spinner of tall tales as well as shutouts. He particularly liked to recall an occasion upon which he was asked to come on in relief of a pitcher who'd left men on first and third with nobody out. "It was a tight situation," Satchel would say.

The first successful Negro Baseball League was started in 1920. The Negro Leagues played eleven World Series and created their own All-Star game that became the biggest black sports attraction in the country. This picture shows players of the Negro Leagues.

We only had a one-run lead, and that was looking mighty slim. But I had an idea. When I left the bench, I stuck a baseball in my pocket, so when the manager gave me the game ball on the mound, I had two. I went into my stretch just like usual. Then I threw one ball to first and the other to third. It was a good pick-off move, you see, and it fooled the batter, too. He swung, even though there was no ball to swing at. Those boys at first and third were both out, of course, and the umpire[5] called strike three on the batter, so that was it for the inning. It's always good to save your strength when you can. ◾

Major-leaguers today make enough money so that they don't have to work over the winter, but it hasn't always been so. Big-leaguers and Negro-leaguers alike used to make extra money after their regular seasons ended by putting together makeshift teams and playing each other wherever they could draw a paying crowd. This practice was called barnstorming, and Satchel Paige was the world champion at it. For thirty years, from 1929 to 1958, he played baseball summer and winter. When it was too cold to play in the Negro league cities, he played in Cuba, Mexico, and the Dominican Republic. In Venezuela he battled a boa constrictor in the outfield, or so he said, and in Ciudad Trujillo[6] he dodged the machine-gun fire of fans who'd bet on the losing team.

Practice the Skills

4 **Key Literary Element**

Point of View Here Satchel Paige is telling a story. Is he the main subject of his own story? How do you know? What point of view is he using? How do you know?

---

5. An *umpire* is the official in a baseball game. The umpire makes sure the players follow the rules.
6. **Cuidad Trujillo** (SEE yoo dahd troo HEE oh) is the Spanish name for a city in northwestern Venezuela.

Throughout the early years of these adventures, the years of Satchel's prime, he often barnstormed against the best white ballplayers of his day. St. Louis Cardinal great Dizzy Dean once told him, "You're a better pitcher than I ever hope to be." Paige beat Bob Feller and struck out Babe Ruth. And when Joe DiMaggio, considered by some the most multi-talented ballplayer ever, beat out an infield hit against Paige in 1936, DiMaggio turned to his teammates and said, "Now I know I can make it with the Yankees. I finally got a hit off of ol' Satch."

Everywhere these **confrontations** took place, Satchel Paige would hear the same thing: "If only you were white, you'd be a star in the big leagues." The fault, of course, was not with Satchel. The fault and the shame were with major league baseball, which stubbornly, stupidly clung to the same **prejudice** that characterized many institutions in the United States besides baseball. Prejudice has not yet disappeared from the game. Black players are far less likely than their white counterparts[7] to be hired as managers or general managers. But today's black players can thank Robinson, Paige, and a handful of other pioneers for the opportunities they enjoy. 5

Though the color line prevented Satchel Paige from pitching in the company his talent and hard work should have earned for him, he was not bitter or defeated. Ignorant white fans would sometimes taunt him, but he kept their insults in perspective. "Some of them would call you names," he said of his early years on the road, "but most of them would cheer you." Years later he worked to shrug off the pain caused by the restaurants that would not serve him, the

Bob Feller (Hall of Fame pitcher for the Cleveland Indians) and Satchel Paige in 1948, the year the Indians won the World Series

Practice the Skills

5 Reviewing Skills

Identifying Main Idea and Supporting Details What is the main idea of this paragraph? What details support the main idea?

---

7. Here, *counterparts* refers to people who hold similar positions.

Vocabulary

confrontations (kon frun TAY shunz) *n.* unpleasant face-to-face meetings

prejudice (PREJ uh dis) *n.* an opinion that is formed unfairly

154 UNIT 2 What Brings Out the Best in You?

hotels that would not rent him a room, the fans who would roar for his bee ball but would not acknowledge him on the street the next day. "Fans all holler the same at a ball game," he would say, as if the racists[8] and the racist system had never touched him at all.

When he finally got the chance to become the first black pitcher in the American League at age forty-two (or forty-six, or forty-eight), he made the most of it. On that first day in Cleveland, Satchel Paige did the job he'd never doubted he could do. First he smiled for all the photographers. Then he told the butterflies in his stomach to leave off their flapping around. Then he shut down the St. Louis Browns for two innings before being lifted for a pinch hitter.

And still there were doubters. "Sure," they said to each other the next day when they read the sports section. "The old man could work two innings against the Browns. Who couldn't?"

But Satchel Paige fooled 'em, as he'd been fooling hitters for twenty-five years and more. He won a game in relief six days later, his first major league win. Then on August 3 he started a game against the Washington Senators before 72,000 people. Paige went seven innings and won. In his next two starts he threw shutouts against the Chicago White Sox, and through the waning[9] months of that summer, his only complaint was that he was "a little tired from underwork." The routine on the major league level must have been pretty leisurely for a fellow who'd previously pitched four or five times a week.

Satchel Paige finished the 1948 season with six wins and only one loss. He'd allowed the opposing teams an average of just over two runs a game. Paige was named Rookie of the Year, an honor he might well have achieved twenty years earlier if he'd had the chance. The sports-writers of the day

Satchel Paige played in his first Major League game on July 9, 1948, at age 42.

---

8. **Racists** are people who believe that one race is better than another.
9. Here, **waning** means "nearing the end of it."

agreed that without Satchel's contribution, the Indians, who won the pennant, would have finished second at best. Many of the writers were dismayed when Satchel appeared for only two-thirds of an inning in the World Series that fall. Paige, too, was disappointed that the manager hadn't chosen to use him more, but he was calm in the face of what others might have considered an insult. The writers told him, "You sure take things good." Satchel smiled and said, "Ain't no other way to take them."

Satchel Paige outlasted the rule that said he couldn't play in the big leagues because he was black. Then he made fools of the people who said he couldn't get major league hitters out because he was too old. But his big league numbers over several years—twenty-eight wins and thirty-two saves—don't begin to tell the story of Paige's unparalleled[10] career. Playing for teams that no longer exist in leagues that came and went with the seasons, Satchel Paige pitched in some 2,500 baseball games. Nobody has ever pitched in more. And he had such fun at it. Sometimes he'd accept offers to pitch in two cities on the same day. He'd strike out the side for three innings in one game, then fold his long legs into his car and race down the road toward the next ballpark. If the police could catch him, they would stop him for speeding. But when they recognized him, as often as not they'd escort him to the second game with sirens howling, well aware that there might be a riot in the park if Satchel Paige didn't show up as advertised. Once he'd arrived, he'd instruct his infielders and outfielders to sit down for an inning, then he'd strike out the side again.

For his talent, his energy, and his showmanship, Satchel Paige was the most famous of the Negro league players, but when he got some measure of recognition in the majors, he urged the writers to remember that there had been lots of other great ballplayers in those Negro league games. He named them, and he told their stories. He made their **exploits** alive and real for generations of fans who'd never have known. 6

---

10. If something is **unparalleled**, nothing is equal to it or better than it.

Vocabulary

exploits (EK sploytz) *n.* brave acts or deeds

Practice the Skills

6 **BIG Question**
In this paragraph, how does Satchel Paige show that he is the best person that he can be? Write your answer on the "Satchel Paige" part of the Workshop 2 Foldable. Your answer will help you with the Unit Challenge later.

156 UNIT 2 What Brings Out the Best in You?

In 1971, the Baseball Hall of Fame in Cooperstown, New York, inducted[11] Satchel Paige. The action was part of the Hall's attempt to remedy baseball's shame, the color line. The idea was to honor Paige and some of the other great Negro league players like Josh Gibson and Cool Papa Bell, however late that honor might come. Satchel Paige could have rejected that gesture. He could have told the baseball establishment that what it was doing was too little, too late. But when the time came for Satchel Paige to speak to the crowd gathered in front of the Hall of Fame to celebrate his triumphs, he told the people, "I am the proudest man on the face of the earth today." **7**

Satchel Paige was the first Negro League star elected to the National Baseball Hall of Fame.

Satchel Paige, whose autobiography was entitled *Maybe I'll Pitch Forever*, died in Kansas City in 1982. He left behind a legend as large as that of anyone who ever played the game, as well as a long list of achievements celebrated in story and song—and in at least one fine poem, by Samuel Allen:

To Satch
Sometimes I feel like I will *never* stop
Just go on forever
Till one fine mornin'
I'm gonna reach up and grab me a handfulla stars
Swing out my long lean leg
And whip three hot strikes burnin' down the heavens
And look over at God and say
How about that!

Practice the Skills

7 Key Reading Skill

Connecting How would you feel if you were finally recognized for your work after years of being snubbed? How would you act?

---

11. When players are ***inducted*** into the Hall of Fame, they are honored by being admitted into this special group.

READING WORKSHOP 2 • Connecting

After You Read | Satchel Paige

Answering the BIG Question

1. **After reading "Satchel Paige," why do you think it is important for people to be the best they can be? Support your answer with details from the selection.

2. **Recall** Why wasn't Satchel Paige allowed to play in the major leagues?
   TIP **Right There** You will find the answer in the text.

3. **Summarize** How much did some players in the Negro Leagues earn per month? What else did they do to make a living?
   TIP **Think and Search** The answers are in the text, but the details are not all in one place.

Critical Thinking

4. **Analyze** Why were the Negro Leagues created?
   TIP **Author and Me** You will find clues in the text, but you must also use the information in your head.

5. **Predict** If Satchel Paige was a young baseball player today, how would his life be different?
   TIP **Author and Me** You will find clues in the text, but you must also use the information in your head.

6. **Evaluate** What kind of person do you think Satchel Paige was? How can you tell? Support your answer with details from the selection.
   TIP **Author and Me** You will find clues in the text, but you must also use the information in your head.

Write About Your Reading

Pretend you are Satchel Paige. Write a letter to the commissioner of baseball telling why you should be allowed in the major leagues. As you write, remember

- your letter should have a salutation, a body, and a closing
- each paragraph in your letter should be indented
- each paragraph should contain a main idea and supporting details

Objectives (pp. 158–159)
Reading Make connections from text to self
Literature Identify literary elements: point of view
Writing Write a letter: persuasive
Grammar Identify parts of speech: pronoun antecedents

158 UNIT 2   What Brings Out the Best in You?

Skills Review

Key Reading Skill: Connecting

7. What would you have done if you wanted to play on a team but were not allowed to because of the color of your skin? What would you do to make the situation better?

8. How did the activities on page 149 help you connect with Satchel Paige and his story? Rank the activities in order of helpfulness, with 1 being the most helpful. Explain your rankings.
   - Using the advice in **Key Reading Skill: Connecting**
   - Doing the **Freewrite** in **Connect to the Reading**
   - Reading the facts in **Build Background**
   - **Set Purposes for Reading**

Key Literary Element: Point of View

9. What is point of view?
10. Is the selection "Satchel Paige" told mostly in first-person or third-person point of view?
11. Who tells the story—the main character, Satchel Paige, or a narrator outside the story?

Reviewing Skills: Identifying Main Idea and Supporting Details

12. In your opinion, what is the main idea of the selection "Satchel Paige"? Support your answer with details from the selection.

Vocabulary Check

Rewrite each sentence below, replacing the underlined word or phrase with the correct vocabulary word.

prejudice   exploits   confrontations   potential

13. Satchel Paige reached his full <u>capability</u>.
14. <u>Unfair opinions</u> kept a lot of talented players out of the major leagues.
15. There were many <u>unpleasant meetings</u> on the ball field between black and white players.
16. Satchel Paige told stories about the <u>brave deeds</u> of other ball players.

17. **English Language Coach** Find and write down an antonym for each of the following words:

throw   hard   triumph   shame   familiar

Grammar Link: Pronoun Antecedents

The noun or group of words that a pronoun refers to is called its *antecedent*.

Satchel Paige showed that **he** was a talented pitcher.

When you use a pronoun, be sure that it refers to its antecedent clearly. Read the following sentence.

Mark competed against David for the starting lineup. He waited to see who won.

The second sentence is not clear because the word *he* could refer to either Mark or David.

Clear pronoun antecedents make sure readers know to whom or what each pronoun refers.

Grammar Practice

Write the antecedent of the underlined pronoun.

18. I brought my baseball cards to school. I wanted to show <u>them</u> to my friends.
19. I also play on a Little League team. <u>It</u> is in first place.

Writing Application Look back at your Write About Your Reading assignment. Make sure your antecedents are clear.

Web Activities For eFlashcards, Selection Quick Checks, and other Web activities, go to www.glencoe.com.

READING WORKSHOP 2 • Connecting

Before You Read: Song for a Surf-Rider

Meet the Author
In the 1930s four of Sara Van Alstyne Allen's poems appeared in *Street & Smith's Love Story* magazine. Her poem "Vine in Early Spring" was published in *Poetry* magazine in 1941. *The Season's Name*, her book of poems, was published by Golden Quill Press in 1968. In the poem "Song for a Surf-Rider," Sara Van Alstyne Allen uses some very striking figurative language when she compares the sea to a horse—and surfing to horseback riding.

Author Search For more about Sara Van Alstyne Allen, go to www.glencoe.com.

Vocabulary Preview

mane (mayn) *n.* the long, thick hair on an animal's neck or head **(p. 161)** *Jewel braided her horse's mane with ribbon.*

emerald (EM ur uld) *adj.* brightly or richly green **(p. 161)** *The emerald ocean was beautiful under the orange sunset.*

quivers (KWIV urz) *v.* to shake or move with a slight trembling motion **(p. 161)** *Knowing we would soon surf on the Pacific Ocean made us quiver with excitement.*

Key Reading Skill: Connecting
Read the poem and connect your personal experiences with those of the speaker. Think about what you know about surfing and horses.

Key Literary Element: Point of View
Point of view is the speaker's relationship to the story or poem. Poets can use the first-person point of view if they are telling about themselves, such as "As I was going to St. Ives I met a man with seven wives." The third-person point of view is used in poems like "Jack and Jill."

Get Ready to Read

Connect to the Reading
The speaker loves surfing and compares it with horse-riding. What do you love to do? What would you compare it to in a poem?

Build Background
Surfing, or surfboarding, is the sport of riding on a wave while standing or lying on a surfboard. It's a popular sport all over the world.

Set Purposes for Reading
Read the poem "Song for a Surf-Rider" to find out if surfing helps the speaker be the best that he or she can be.

Set Your Own Purpose What else would you like to learn from this poem to help you answer the Big Question? Write your own purpose on the "Song for a Surf-Rider" part of the Workshop 2 Foldable.

Keep Moving
Use these skills as you read the following selection.

Objectives (pp. 160–161)
Reading Make connections from text to self
Literature Identify literary elements: point of view

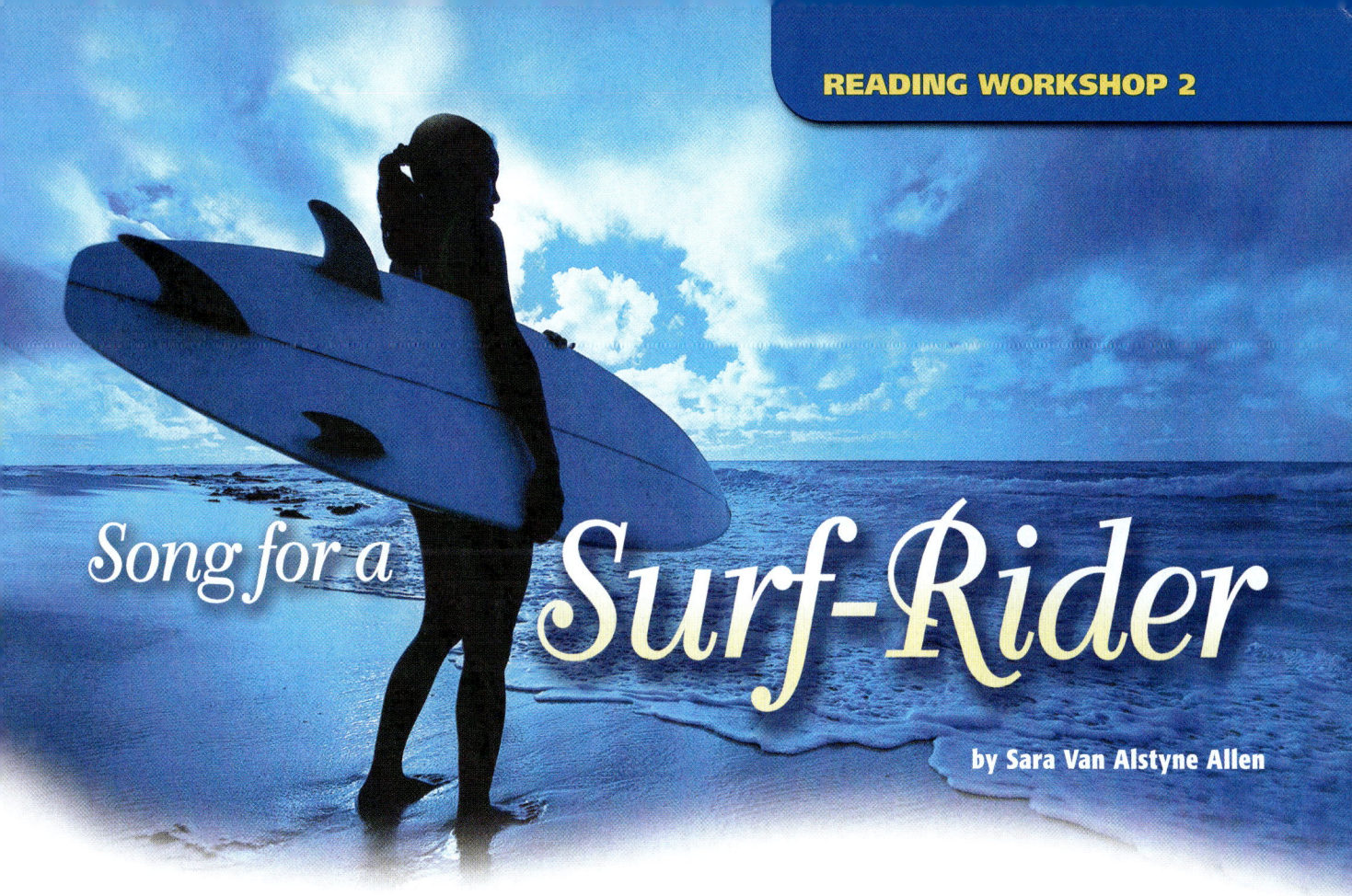

Song for a Surf-Rider

by Sara Van Alstyne Allen

I ride the horse that is the sea.
His **mane** of foam flows wild and free.
His eyes flash with an **emerald** fire.
His mighty heart will never tire.
⁵ His hoofbeats echo on the sand.
He **quivers** as I raise my hand.
We race together, the sea and I,
Under the watching summer sky
To where the magic islands lie. **1 2 3** ○

Practice the Skills

1 Key Reading Skill

Connecting Have you ever gone swimming in an ocean, lake, or at the beach? What was it like?

2 Key Literary Element

Point of View Who or what is the speaker talking about? From what point of view is the poem written?

3 BIG Question

What do you think brings out the best in the speaker? Explain your answer on the "Song for a Surf-Rider" part of the Workshop 2 Foldable.

Vocabulary

mane (mayn) *n.* the long, thick hair on an animal's neck or head

emerald (EM ur uld) *adj.* brightly or richly green

quiver (KWIV urz) *v.* to shake or move with a slight trembling motion

READING WORKSHOP 2 • Connecting

After You Read : Song for a Surf-Rider

Answering the BIG Question

1. The ocean seems to bring out the best in the poem's speaker. Have you ever felt so connected to something that it brought out the best in you? Explain.

2. **Recall** What is the speaker describing?
   TIP Right There You will find the answer in the poem.

3. **Recall** Who or what does the speaker race with?
   TIP Right There You will find the answer in the poem.

Critical Thinking

4. **Infer** What is really making the sound of "hoofbeats"?
   TIP Author and Me You will find clues in the poem, but you must also use the information in your head.

5. **Draw Conclusions** Why will the "horse"—the sea—never tire?
   TIP On My Own Answer from your own experiences.

6. **Evaluate** Do you think the speaker will ever tire of surfing? Explain.
   TIP Author and Me You will find clues in the poem, but you must also use the information in your head.

Write About Your Reading

The speaker helps us understand how free she feels on a surfboard by making it seem like riding a horse. Horses and surfing have little in common, but the poem helps us to link the two.

Think about your favorite activity and something that seems very different from that, such as playing basketball and flying. Write a poem that describes the connection you make between your favorite activity and something different.

What do you see? What do you hear? How do you feel?

Use descriptive words that help your poem's reader to experience the things you are writing about. Your poem does not have to rhyme.

Objectives (pp. 162–163)
Reading Make connections from text to self
Literature Identify literary elements: point of view
Writing Write a poem • Use literary elements: imagery, sensory details
Grammar Identify parts of speech: indefinite pronouns

Skills Review

Key Reading Skill: Connecting

7. Did writing a poem about your favorite activity help you to connect to the selection? Why or why not?

Key Literary Element: Point of View

8. *His* and *he* refer to whom or what in the poem?
9. From what point of view is the poem written?

Vocabulary Check

Copy the sentences onto a separate sheet of paper and complete with the correct vocabulary word below.

mane   emerald   quiver

10. The lion's long and heavy ___ framed its face.
11. To tremble is also to ___.
12. The ___ grass looked beautiful after the rain.
13. **English Language Coach** In your Learner's Notebook, write sentences that correctly use the antonym for each of these words: *wild*, *never*, and *together*.

Grammar Link: Indefinite Pronouns

An *indefinite pronoun* is a pronoun that does not refer to a particular person, place, or thing.

   Does **anyone** know the poem "Song for a Surf-Rider"?

Most indefinite pronouns are either singular or plural.

Singular: another, anybody, anyone, anything, each, either, everybody, everyone, everything, much, neither, nobody, no one, nothing, one, somebody, someone, something

Plural: both, few, many, others, several

Some indefinite pronouns can be singular or plural:

all, any, most, none, some

Often, an indefinite pronoun will be the subject of a sentence. The verb must agree with the indefinite pronoun in number.

   Everyone likes the poem. [singular]

   Many enjoy reading it aloud. [plural]

   All of poetry uses sound to convey a message. [singular]

   We read many poems. **All** are very interesting. [plural]

Grammar Practice

Write each sentence, using the verb in parentheses that correctly agrees with the indefinite pronoun. Underline each indefinite pronoun and write whether it is *singular* or *plural*.

14. Some (have, has) important skills that help them be the best they can be.
15. One of them (is, are) Dwain, who knows how to fix bikes.
16. Others (is, are) very happy for Dwain.
17. Anything (is, are) possible if you have the right attitude.
18. No one (think, thinks) that Dwain will have any trouble finding a summer job.
19. Everyone (want, wants) to do well in life.

Writing Application Look back at the poem you wrote. Check to see if you have used the correct verbs with any indefinite pronouns you used.

Web Activities For eFlashcards, Selection Quick Checks, and other Web activities, go to www.glencoe.com.

READING WORKSHOP 3

Skills Focus

You will practice using these skills when you read the following selections:
- "Eleanor Roosevelt," p. 168
- "In Eleanor Roosevelt's Time," p. 180

Reading
- Making predictions about reading

Literature
- Recognizing and understanding chronological order

Vocabulary
- Using prefixes

Writing/Grammar
- Using reflexive pronouns
- Using intensive pronouns

Skill Lesson

Predicting

Learn It!

What Is It? Predicting means making good guesses about what will happen next. When you predict, you
- are involved in your reading
- think about what you already know
- look for clues from the writer about upcoming events

In a mystery book, you would try to solve the mystery. In a biography, you might use information about the person's childhood to predict what might happen later on in life.

- As you read, you will find more information. Pay attention to details. You will probably need to change your predictions.
- When you have finished reading, see if your predictions were correct.

Analyzing Cartoons
The soccer player predicted where the ball would be kicked. What was wrong with her prediction? Think of a situation where you made a bad prediction because you didn't have enough information.

Objectives (pp. 164–165)
Reading Make predictions

READING WORKSHOP 3 • Predicting

Why Is It Important? Making predictions keeps you thinking while you read so that you become more active as a reader. It gives you a purpose for reading and makes reading more interesting.

How Do I Do It? Before you read, look at the title and any introductions or pictures. Then skim the selection. Use your prior knowledge and what you learned from your preview of the selection to predict the main ideas. While you are reading, continue to make and revise predictions as you gather new information.

Study Central Visit www.glencoe.com and click on Study Central to review predicting.

Here is how one student made predictions as she read the following part of the *Madam C. J. Walker* selection.

> Not long after they moved to St. Louis, Sarah McWilliams realized that her hair was falling out.... At the time, few hair-care products were available for black women. For years she tried every hair-care product available. But nothing worked.... Then one night she had a dream.

I know from the introduction to the selection that Sarah made a million dollars. I also know that people can get rich by starting businesses. I predict that Sarah's dream was about a new hair care product that would become very successful.

Practice It!

Read the title and the first three paragraphs of the selection "Eleanor Roosevelt." In your Learner's Notebook, predict what the selection will be about and what you think you will learn from it.

Look at "In Eleanor Roosevelt's Time." In your Learner's Notebook, predict what kind of additional information you will learn from the time line.

Use It!

After you read the first paragraph of each page of "Eleanor Roosevelt," make a prediction in your Learner's Notebook about what might happen later in the selection. If you learn something that causes you to change your mind about that prediction, write a new one. Continue making and checking predictions throughout the story.

READING WORKSHOP 3 • Predicting

Before You Read : Eleanor Roosevelt

Meet the Author
William Jay Jacobs wrote many biographies of American heroes and stories about American history for children and young adults. His research and writing are very important to him. His parents were immigrants who chose to come to America. Jacobs says, "America to me is more than just a place of residence. It is a passion."

Author Search For more about William Jay Jacobs, go to www.glencoe.com.

Vocabulary Preview

self-discipline (self DIS uh plin) *n.* control over your behavior in order to improve yourself **(p. 170)** *It took self-discipline for Eleanor Roosevelt to do exercises and take cold showers every day.*

prominent (PROM uh nunt) *adj.* well-known **(p. 171)** *Eleanor Roosevelt was a prominent person.*

slums (slumz) *n.* parts of cities where poor people live in crowded, run-down buildings **(p. 173)** *The slums in many large cities are being rebuilt.*

migrant (MY grunt) *adj.* moving from place-to-place **(p. 173)** *Mrs. Roosevelt was concerned about the suffering of migrant farm workers who were poorly paid.*

Partner Talk Choose the vocabulary word that best fits the blank in each sentence below. Then take turns reading the completed sentences with a partner.

1. George Washington, Abraham Lincoln, and Franklin D. Roosevelt were ___ American presidents.

2. Eleanor Roosevelt cared about poor people who lived in ___.

3. The ___ workers worked in the south in the winter and in the north in the summer.

4. It took ___ for Eleanor Roosevelt to do what it took to be successful as a student and athlete.

English Language Coach

Prefixes Prefixes are word parts placed at the beginning of root or base words. Prefixes change the meaning of a word. The prefix *un-* means "not" or "do the opposite of." This prefix changes the meaning of a word to its antonym, a word that means the opposite.

Word	Prefix	Antonym
happy	un-	unhappy
complete	in-	incomplete

Partner Talk Work with a partner to make a list of six words that begin with the prefixes *un-* or *in-*. Take turns telling the meaning of the words. If you get a definition from a dictionary, explain it in your own words.

Objectives (pp. 166–175)
Reading Make predictions • Make connections from text to self
Literature Identify literary elements: chronological order
Vocabulary Use prefixes

166 UNIT 2 What Brings Out the Best in You?

READING WORKSHOP 3 • Predicting

Skills Preview

Key Reading Skill: Predicting
As you read about Eleanor Roosevelt, make predictions about
- how she was affected by the experience of an unhappy childhood.
- how her life changed when her husband became president of the United States.
- what she did after her husband died.

Class Talk Brainstorm a list of predictions about what you will learn about Eleanor Roosevelt as you read this selection. Write the ideas on the board.

Key Literary Element: Chronological Order

Chronological order refers to the time order in which events take place. Whether you are giving instructions on how to bake a cake or giving directions to your school, the information has to be put in a certain order so it will make sense. Some terms most often used to show chronological order are dates and times, such as *December 4, 1921, in the 1950s,* or *Tuesday afternoon,* and signal words, such as *first, next, then, later,* and *finally.*

Write to Learn Make a list of important events that have happened in your own life. Then write a paragraph about them. Put the events in chronological order, using both dates and signal words to show the reader the order in which they happened.

Get Ready to Read

Connect to the Reading
Eleanor Roosevelt enjoyed helping other people. As you read her biography, think about things that you do to help others. Think about the problems in our country that concerned Eleanor and the problems that concern you.

Class Talk Discuss ways in which young people today can volunteer to help other people in your community. (Think about groups and events which help the environment, serve the poor, tutor students, assist the elderly, or welcome newcomers.)

Build Background
Eleanor Roosevelt was a pioneer in many areas. She was the first president's wife to
- speak in front of a national convention.
- write a national newspaper column.
- become a radio commentator.
- hold regular press conferences.

When Eleanor's husband, President Franklin D. Roosevelt, was paralyzed by polio, she traveled around the United States to gather firsthand knowledge and speak for him.

Set Purposes for Reading
BIG Question Read "Eleanor Roosevelt" to find out what brought out the best in her.

Set Your Own Purpose What else would you like to learn from the selection to help you answer the Big Question? Write your own purpose on the "Eleanor Roosevelt" part of the Workshop 3 Foldable.

Interactive Literary Elements Handbook
To review or learn more about the literary elements, go to www.glencoe.com.

Keep Moving
Use these skills as you read the following selection.

Eleanor Roosevelt **167**

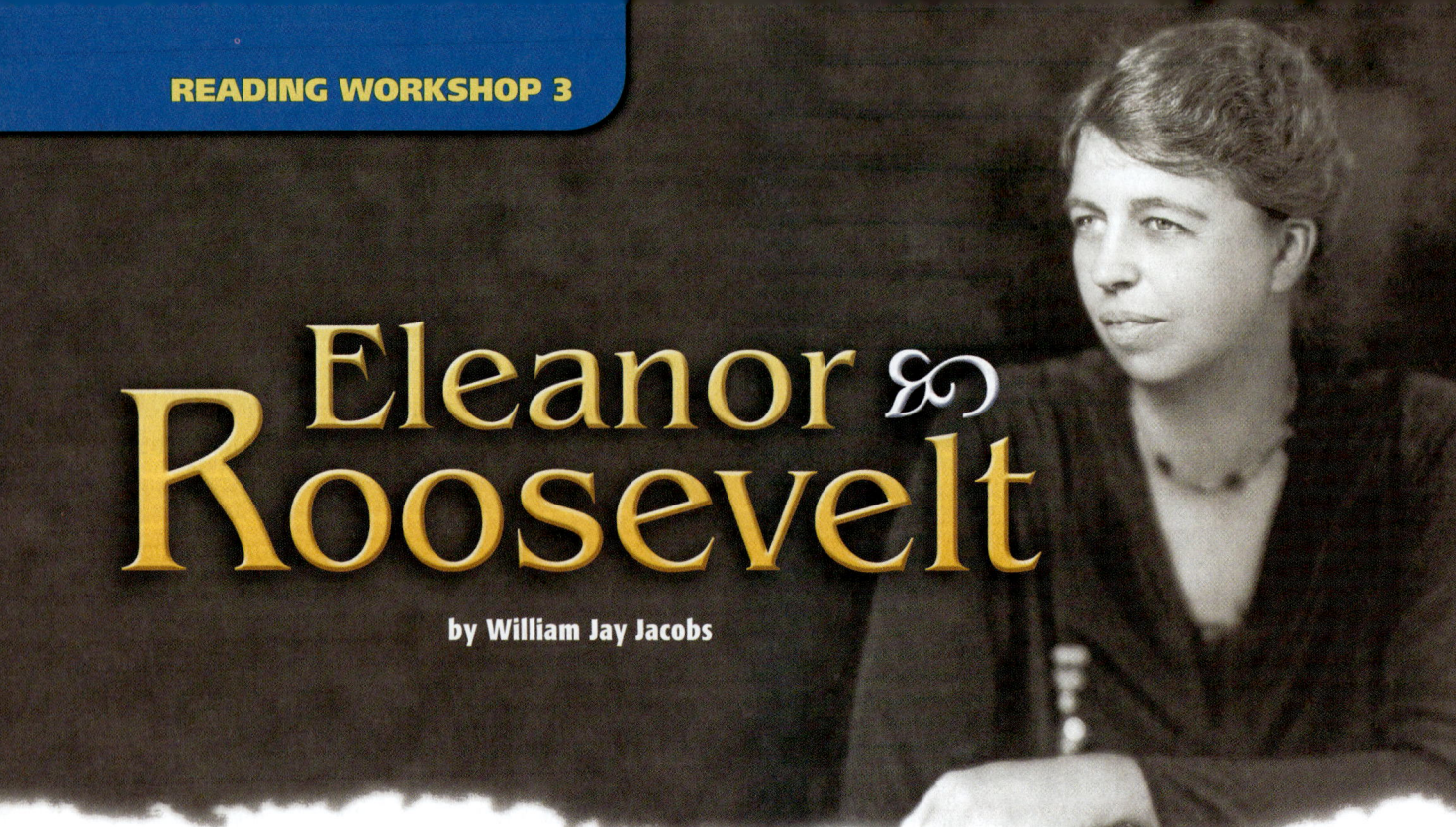

READING WORKSHOP 3

Eleanor Roosevelt

by William Jay Jacobs

Eleanor Roosevelt was the wife of President Franklin Delano Roosevelt. But Eleanor was much more than just a president's wife, an echo of her husband's career.

Sad and lonely as a child, Eleanor was called "Granny" by her mother because of her seriousness. People teased her about her looks and called her the "ugly duckling." . . .

Yet despite all of the disappointments, the bitterness, the misery she experienced, Eleanor Roosevelt refused to give up. Instead she turned her unhappiness and pain to strength. She devoted her life to helping others. Today she is remembered as one of America's greatest women.

Almost from the day of her birth, October 11, 1884, people noticed that she was an unattractive child. As she grew older, she could not help but notice her mother's extraordinary beauty, as well as the beauty of her aunts and cousins. Eleanor was plain looking, ordinary, even, as some called her, homely. For a time she had to wear a bulky brace on her back to straighten her crooked spine. **1**

When Eleanor was born, her parents had wanted a boy. They were scarcely able to hide their disappointment. Later, with the arrival of two boys, Elliott and Hall, Eleanor watched her mother hold the boys on her lap and lovingly stroke their hair, while for Eleanor there seemed only coolness, distance.

Practice the Skills

1 Key Reading Skill

Predicting Based on the information so far, what do you think Eleanor Roosevelt might be like as an adult? Do you predict that she turned out to be a confident person?

168 UNIT 2 What Brings Out the Best in You?

Feeling <u>unwanted</u>, Eleanor became shy and withdrawn. She also developed many fears. She was afraid of the dark, afraid of animals, afraid of other children, afraid of being scolded, afraid of strangers, afraid that people would not like her. She was a frightened, lonely little girl. **2**

The one joy in the early years of her life was her father, who always seemed to care for her, love her. He used to dance with her, to pick her up and throw her into the air while she laughed and laughed. He called her "little golden hair" or "darling little Nell."

The next year, when Eleanor was eight, her mother, the beautiful Anna, died. Afterward her brother Elliott suddenly caught diphtheria[1] and he, too, died. Eleanor and her baby brother, Hall, were taken to live with their grandmother in Manhattan.

A few months later another tragedy struck. Elliott Roosevelt, Eleanor's father, also died. Within eighteen months Eleanor had lost her mother, a brother, and her dear father.

Few things in life came easily for Eleanor, but the first few years after her father's death proved exceptionally hard. Grandmother Hall's dark and gloomy townhouse had no place for children to play. The family ate meals in silence. Every morning Eleanor and Hall were expected to take cold baths for their health. Eleanor had to work at better posture by walking with her arms behind her back, clamped over a walking stick.

Instead of making new friends, Eleanor often sat alone in her room and read. For many months after her father's death she pretended that he was still alive. She made him the hero of stories she wrote for school. Sometimes, alone and unhappy, she just cried.

Just before Eleanor turned fifteen, Grandmother Hall decided to send her to boarding school in England. The school she chose was Allenswood, a private academy[2] for girls located on the outskirts of London.

It was at Allenswood that Eleanor, still thinking of herself as an "ugly duckling," first dared to believe that one day she might be able to become a swan. **3**

---

1. **Diphtheria** is a disease that is easily spread from one person to another.
2. An **academy** is a school.

Practice the Skills

2 **English Language Coach**

Prefixes Use your knowledge of prefixes to understand what <u>unwanted</u> means in this paragraph.

3 **Key Literary Element**

Chronological Order In what order did these events occur?
- Death of Eleanor's father
- Eleanor sent to Allenswood
- Eleanor sent to live with her Grandmother

Eleanor with her father, Elliott Roosevelt April 30, 1889

READING WORKSHOP 3

At Allenswood she worked to toughen herself physically. Every day she did exercises in the morning and took a cold shower. Although she did not like competitive team sports, as a matter of **self-discipline** she tried out for field hockey. Not only did she make the team but, because she played so hard, also won the respect of her teammates. 4

Eleanor was growing up, and the joy of young womanhood had begun to transform her personality.

In 1902, nearly eighteen years old, she left Allenswood, not returning for her fourth year there. Grandmother Hall insisted that, instead, she must be introduced to society as a debutante—to go to dances and parties and begin to take her place in the social world with other wealthy young women.

Eleanor, as always, did as she was told. She went to all of the parties and dances. But she also began working with poor children at the Rivington Street Settlement House on New York's Lower East Side. She taught the girls gymnastic exercises. She took children to museums and to musical performances. She tried to get the parents interested in politics in order to get better schools and cleaner, safer streets.

Meanwhile Eleanor's life reached a turning point. She fell in love! The young man was her fifth cousin, Franklin Delano Roosevelt.

Eleanor and Franklin had known each other since childhood. Shortly after her return from Allenswood, they had met by chance on a train. They talked and almost at once realized how much they liked each other.

For a time they met secretly. Then they attended parties together. Franklin—tall, strong, handsome—saw her as a person he could trust. He knew that she would not try to dominate him.

Practice the Skills

Eleanor as a young girl with her horse. She described her self-conscious age in her autobiography, *This is My Story*: "I was tall, very thin, and very shy."

4 BIG Question
How did getting involved in exercise and sports at Allenswood bring out the best in Eleanor?

Vocabulary

self-discipline (self DIS uh plin) *n.* control over your behavior in order to improve yourself

Unit 2 What Brings Out the Best in You?

On March 17, 1905, Eleanor and Franklin were married. In May 1906 the couple's first child was born. During the next nine years Eleanor gave birth to five more babies, one of whom died in infancy. Still timid, shy, afraid of making mistakes, she found herself so busy that there was little time to think of her own drawbacks.

Meanwhile Franklin's career in politics advanced rapidly. In 1910 he was elected to the New York State Senate. In 1913 President Wilson appointed him Assistant Secretary of the Navy—a powerful position in the national government, which required the Roosevelts to move to Washington, D.C.

In 1917 the United States entered World War I as an active combatant. Like many socially **prominent** women, Eleanor threw herself into the war effort. Sometimes she worked fifteen and sixteen hours a day. She made sandwiches for soldiers passing through the nation's capital. She knitted sweaters. She used Franklin's influence to get the Red Cross to build a recreation room for soldiers who had been shell-shocked in combat. . . .

In the summer of 1921 disaster struck the Roosevelt family. While on vacation Franklin suddenly fell ill with infantile paralysis—polio—the horrible disease that each year used to kill or cripple thousands of children, and many adults as well. When Franklin became a victim of polio, nobody knew what caused the disease or how to cure it.

Franklin lived, but the lower part of his body remained paralyzed. For the rest of his life he never again had the use of his legs. He had to be lifted and carried from place to place. He had to wear heavy steel braces from his waist to the heels of his shoes. 5

His mother, as well as many of his advisers, urged him to give up politics, to live the life of a country gentleman on the Roosevelt estate at Hyde Park, New York. This time, Eleanor, calm and strong, stood up for her ideas. She argued that he should not be treated like a sick person, tucked away in the country, inactive, just waiting for death to come.

Practice the Skills

FDR and Eleanor with their children, Elliot, James, Franklin Jr., John, and Anna, circa 1915

5 Key Reading Skill

Predicting You know that Franklin Roosevelt became president in spite of his paralysis. Predict what this selection will tell you about how that happened. Write your prediction in your Learner's Notebook.

Vocabulary

prominent (PROM uh nunt) *adj.* well-known

READING WORKSHOP 3

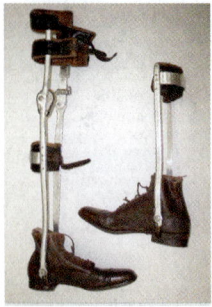

Visual Vocabulary
A *brace* is a device used to support part of the body.

Franklin agreed. Slowly he recovered his health. His energy returned. In 1928 he was elected governor of New York. Then, just four years later, he was elected president of the United States.

Meanwhile Eleanor had changed. To keep Franklin in the public eye while he was recovering, she had gotten involved in politics herself. It was, she thought, her "duty." From childhood she had been taught "to do the thing that has to be done, the way it has to be done, when it has to be done." 6

After becoming interested in the problems of working women, she gave time to the Women's Trade Union League (WTUL). It was through the WTUL that she met a group of remarkable women—women doing exciting work that made a difference in the world. They taught Eleanor about life in the slums. They awakened her hopes that something could be done to improve the condition of the poor. She dropped out of the "fashionable" society of her wealthy friends and joined the world of reform—social change.

For hours at a time Eleanor and her reformer friends talked with Franklin. They showed him the need for new laws: laws to get children out of the factories and into schools; laws to cut down the long hours that women worked; laws to get fair wages for all workers.

By the time that Franklin was sworn in as president, the nation was facing its deepest depression. One out of every four Americans was out of work, out of hope. At mealtimes people stood in lines in front of soup kitchens for something to eat. Mrs. Roosevelt herself knew of once-prosperous families who found themselves reduced to eating stale bread from thrift shops or traveling to parts of town where they were not known to beg for money from house to house.

Practice the Skills

6 Key Literary Element

Chronological Order When did Franklin Roosevelt become ill with polio? Name one important thing that happened *before* he got polio and one important thing that happened *after* he got polio.

Eleanor Roosevelt and FDR on election night, 1932

Eleanor worked in the charity kitchens, ladling out soup. She visited slums. She crisscrossed the country learning about the suffering of coal miners, shipyard workers, migrant farm workers, students, housewives—Americans caught up in the paralysis of the Great Depression. Since Franklin himself remained crippled, she became his eyes and ears, informing him of what the American people were really thinking and feeling. Eleanor also was the president's conscience, personally urging on him some of the most compassionate, forward-looking laws of his presidency.

She lectured widely, wrote a regularly syndicated[3] newspaper column, "My Day," and spoke frequently on the radio. She fought for equal pay for women in industry. Like no other First Lady up to that time, she became a link between the president and the American public.

Above all she fought against racial and religious prejudice. When Eleanor learned that the DAR (Daughters of the American Revolution) would not allow the great black singer Marian Anderson to perform in their auditorium in Washington, D.C., she resigned from the organization. Then she arranged to have Miss Anderson sing in front of the Lincoln Memorial.

Similarly, when she entered a hall where, as often happened in those days, blacks and whites were seated in separate sections, she made it a point to sit with the blacks. Her example marked an important step in making the rights of blacks a matter of national priority.[4] 7

On December 7, 1941, Japanese forces launched a surprise attack on the American naval base at Pearl Harbor, Hawaii. The United States entered World War II, fighting not only against Japan but against the brutal dictators who then controlled Germany and Italy. 8

---

3. When an article is **syndicated**, it is sold to different newspapers to be printed.
4. A **priority** is something that needs to be done first.

Vocabulary

slums (slumz) *n.* parts of cities where poor people live in crowded, run-down buildings

migrant (MY grunt) *adj.* moving from place-to-place

Practice the Skills

First Lady Eleanor Roosevelt, on the cover of *TIME* magazine, April 17, 1939

7 BIG Question
How did fighting against racial prejudice bring out the best in Eleanor Roosevelt?

8 Key Reading Skill
Predicting From everything you have read about Eleanor Roosevelt, what do you think she might have done when America went to war?

Eleanor helped the Red Cross raise money. She gave blood, sold war bonds. But she also did the unexpected. In 1943, for example, she visited barracks and hospitals on islands throughout the South Pacific. When she visited a hospital, she stopped at every bed. To each soldier she said something special, something that a mother might say. Often, after she left, even battle-hardened men had tears in their eyes. Admiral Nimitz, who originally thought such visits would be a nuisance, became one of her strongest admirers. Nobody else, he said, had done so much to help raise the spirits of the men.

By spring 1945 the end of the war in Europe seemed near. Then, on April 12, a phone call brought Eleanor the news that Franklin Roosevelt, who had gone to Warm Springs, Georgia, for a rest, was dead. 9

With Franklin dead, Eleanor Roosevelt might have dropped out of the public eye, might have been remembered in the history books only as a footnote to the president's program of social reforms. Instead she found new strengths within herself, new ways to live a useful, interesting life—and to help others. Now, moreover, her successes were her own, not the result of being the president's wife.

In December 1945 President Harry S. Truman invited her to be one of the American delegates going to London to begin the work of the United Nations. Eleanor hesitated, but the president insisted. He said that the nation needed her; it was her duty. After that Eleanor agreed.

In the beginning some of her fellow delegates from the United States considered her unqualified for the position, but after seeing her in action, they changed their minds.

Mrs. Roosevelt helped draft the United Nations Declaration of Human Rights. The Soviets wanted the declaration to list the duties people owed to their countries. Eleanor insisted that the United Nations should stand for individual freedom—the rights of people to free speech, freedom of religion, and such human needs as health care and education. In December 1948, with the Soviet Union and its allies refusing to vote, the Declaration of Human Rights won approval of the UN General Assembly by a vote of forty-eight to zero.

Practice the Skills

9 Key Reading Skill

Predicting After Franklin Roosevelt died, many people thought that Mrs. Roosevelt would retire from public service. What do you predict she will do? Why?

Eleanor Roosevelt holds a poster of the Universal Declaration of Human Rights. This document was adopted by the United Nations General Assembly on December 10, 1948, in honor of Human Rights Day.

Even after retiring from her post at the UN, Mrs. Roosevelt continued to travel. In places around the world she dined with presidents and kings. But she also visited tenement slums in Bombay, India; factories in Yugoslavia; farms in Lebanon and Israel.

Everywhere she met people who were eager to greet her. Although as a child she had been brought up to be formal and distant, she had grown to feel at ease with people. They wanted to touch her, to hug her, to kiss her.

Eleanor's doctor had been telling her to slow down, but that was hard for her. She continued to write her newspaper column, "My Day," and to appear on television. She still began working at seven-thirty in the morning and often continued until well past midnight. Not only did she write and speak, she taught special needs children and raised money for health care of the poor.

As author Clare Boothe Luce put it, "Mrs. Roosevelt has done more good deeds on a bigger scale for a longer time than any woman who ever appeared on our public scene. No woman has ever so comforted the distressed or so distressed the comfortable."

Gradually, however, she was forced to withdraw from some of her activities, to spend more time at home.

On November 7, 1962, at the age of seventy-eight, Eleanor died in her sleep. She was buried in the rose garden at Hyde Park, alongside her husband.

Adlai Stevenson, the American ambassador to the United Nations, remembered her as "the First Lady of the World," as the person—male or female—most effective in working for the cause of human rights. As Stevenson declared, "She would rather light a candle than curse the darkness."

And perhaps, in sum, that is what the struggle for human rights is all about.

Eleanor Roosevelt, Chair of Human Rights Committee, United Nations, 1950

Eleanor Roosevelt arrives at a U.S. Navy yard in Pearl Harbor, September 22, 1943

Practice the Skills

10 BIG Question

What do you think brought out the best in Eleanor Roosevelt? Name three events in her life that you believe affected her the most. Write your answer on the "Eleanor Roosevelt" part of the Workshop 3 Foldable. Your response will help you answer the Unit Challenge.

READING WORKSHOP 3 • Predicting

After You Read : Eleanor Roosevelt

Answering the BIG Question

1. Do you think that Eleanor Roosevelt's experience at boarding school brought out the best in her? Why or why not?

2. **Summary** In your Learner's Notebook, write a paragraph about Eleanor's unhappy childhood. Explain at least three reasons why her childhood was unhappy.

   TIP **Think and Search** The answer is in the text, but the details are not all in one place.

3. **Recall** What caused Franklin Roosevelt to become paralyzed?

   TIP **Right There** You will find the answer in the text.

Critical Thinking

4. **Infer** How do you think the author feels about Eleanor Roosevelt? How can you tell?

   TIP **Author and Me** Answer from information in the selection and from your own thoughts.

5. **Evaluate** Was Eleanor Roosevelt a good role model for future First Ladies? Why or why not?

   TIP **Author and Me** Answer from information in the selection and from your own thoughts.

6. **Analyze** Eleanor Roosevelt went through many hard times. What did you notice about how she faced the challenges in her life?

   TIP **Author and Me** Answer from information in the selection and from your own thoughts.

Talk About Your Reading

In a group, talk about whether it was harder for Eleanor Roosevelt to overcome her lack of confidence in order to speak in public and help her husband or for Franklin Roosevelt to get elected president in spite of his physical disability. Use information from the story and your own life experience to think of the challenges each of them faced.

Objectives (pp. 176–177)
Reading Make predictions • Make connections from text to self
Literature Identify literary elements: chronological order
Vocabulary Use prefixes
Grammar Identify parts of speech: reflexive pronouns

Skills Review

Key Reading Skill: Predicting

7. What did you predict you would learn about Eleanor Roosevelt from this selection? Explain how you made your predictions and whether your predictions were correct.

Key Literary Element: Chronological Order

8. Did Eleanor go to boarding school before or after her father died?
9. Put the following events in chronological order:
   - The United States entered World War II.
   - The Japanese forces launched a surprise attack at Pearl Harbor.
   - Eleanor Roosevelt visited hospitals in the South Pacific.
10. Did Eleanor become the American delegate to the United Nations before or after Franklin D. Roosevelt died?

Vocabulary Check

self-discipline   prominent   migrant   slum

Answer *true* or *false* to each statement.

11. Eleanor Roosevelt continued to be a **prominent** woman even after the president died.
12. A rich person would probably have lived in a **slum** during Roosevelt's time.
13. Eleanor Roosevelt loved field hockey so much that it did not require any **self-discipline** for her to practice hard.
14. **Migrant** workers had a difficult time during the depression.
15. **English Language Coach** Rewrite the following sentences, replacing the two underlined words with one word beginning with the prefix *-in* or *-un*.

- Why is Chandra <u>not lucky</u> today?
- Cerise didn't apply for the job, because she thought she was <u>not qualified</u>.

Grammar Link: Reflexive Pronouns

You know that a pronoun takes the place of a noun or, sometimes, another pronoun. So every pronoun refers back to another noun or pronoun. But **reflexive pronouns** refer back in a special way. We use reflexive pronouns anytime a pronoun that is *not possessive* refers back to the subject of the sentence. We say "I stopped my swing," but it's wrong to say "I stopped me." Instead, we say "I stopped myself." The stopped one *reflects* the stopper, so we use a reflexive pronoun.

- The cat cleaned itself.
- Juan bought himself a soccer ball.
- Jasmine walked home by herself.

Singular Reflexive Pronouns	Plural Reflexive Pronouns
myself	ourselves
yourself	yourselves
himself, herself, itself	themselves

Grammar Practice

Choose the correct reflexive pronoun to complete each sentence below. Rewrite each sentence with the correct word in place. The subjects *I, We,* and *Jin* will give you clues to help you choose the correct reflexive pronoun.

16. I gave ___ a present for my birthday.
17. We found ___ on the wrong bus.
18. Jin told ___ that he should not eat another donut.

Web Activities For eFlashcards, Selection Quick Checks, and other Web activities, go to www.glencoe.com.

READING WORKSHOP 3 • Predicting

Before You Read: In Eleanor Roosevelt's Time

Meet the Author
Biographers are authors who write the story of another's person life. Many biographers write about the events that happened in a person's life in chronological order. A time line is a great way for a biographer to begin writing about a person's life. The biographer can use the time line to decide which dates and events to highlight in a biography.

Vocabulary Preview

Congress (KONG gris) *n.* the part of the United States government that makes laws **(p. 180)** *Congress passed a new law yesterday.*

seminary (SEM ih nair ee) *n.* a school for advanced education **(p. 180)** *The girls learned about history in the seminary.*

appointed (uh POIN tid) *v.* selected or named for an office or position **(p. 180)** *The president appointed Supreme Court justices.*

morale (muh RAL) *n.* the state of a person's mind and spirit **(p. 181)** *The cheerleaders gave a special cheer to boost the football team's morale.*

Class Talk Discuss the meaning of each vocabulary word. Practice using each word in a sentence.

English Language Coach

Prefixes You already know that a negative prefix can change a word into its antonym. Another important prefix is *re-*. It means "again" or "back," and it is attached to verbs and nouns made from verbs. If you see the word *rebuild,* you can figure out that it means "to build again" or "build back." Look at these other words and see whether you can figure out what they mean.

readjust   reboot   redecorate   reinvest   reorder

Sometimes, to make a word easier to read or to prevent confusion with another word, there may be a hyphen between a prefix and the word it has been added to. For example, we write *re-sort* to mean "to sort again" because there is already an English word spelled *resort,* meaning a place to go for vacation.

Individual Activity Write a short paragraph using all of the words below.
reappear   re-create   rewrite

Objectives (pp. 178–181)
Reading Make predictions • Make connections from text to self
Literature Identify literary elements: chronological order
Vocabulary Use prefixes

178 UNIT 2   What Brings Out the Best in You?

READING WORKSHOP 3 • Predicting

Skills Preview

Key Reading Skill: Predicting

Since you've just read a story about Eleanor Roosevelt, you have a lot of knowledge you can use to make predictions about the selection you are about to read. The following time line gives important events in Eleanor Roosevelt's life and things that were accomplished during her husband's time in office. It also shows some other events that happened in the world during Eleanor's lifetime.

Class Talk Discuss the kind of person Eleanor Roosevelt was and try to predict the kinds of activities she would have been involved in during her life. Make notes in your Learner's Notebook.

Key Literary Element: Chronological Order

Chronological order refers to the order in which events take place. "In Eleanor Roosevelt's Time" shows important dates and events in chronological order.

Write to Learn

- Draw a horizontal line across a new page in your Learner's Notebook.
- Under the line on the left end, write the year you were born.
- Under the line on the right end, write the year it is now.
- *Above* the line, list five important events from your life.
- *Under* the events, write the years when they happened. Keep them in chronological order.

Interactive Literary Elements Handbook
To review or learn more about the literary elements, go to www.glencoe.com.

Get Ready to Read

Connect to the Reading

As a child, Eleanor Roosevelt was very shy. She decided to set some goals to become more confident. Think about goals you have set so you would feel better about yourself. If you have never set any goals to improve your feelings about yourself, set one now.

Freewrite Answer the following questions about one goal:

- Why did I choose that goal?
- What actions would I have to take to reach it?
- How much time should I give myself to reach it?
- Who or what could encourage and help me to reach it?

Build Background

- When Eleanor Roosevelt was born, women did not have the right to vote in the United States.
- During her lifetime, women were fighting for equal rights in the home and in the workplace.
- During her lifetime, there were two world wars and other tragic events.
- During her lifetime, segregation of races was common and organizations were allowed to reject people because of their race.

Set Purposes for Reading

BIG Question Read the time line to better understand the events in Eleanor Roosevelt's life that brought out the best in her.

Set Your Own Purpose What else would you like to learn from the time line to help you answer the Big Question? Write your own purpose on the "In Eleanor Roosevelt's Time" part of the Workshop 3 Foldable.

Keep Moving

Use these skills as you read the following selection.

In Eleanor Roosevelt's Time 179

READING WORKSHOP 3

In Eleanor Roosevelt's Time

1905 March 17: Eleanor marries Franklin D. Roosevelt in New York.

1920 **Congress** passes the Nineteenth Amendment[2] granting women the right to vote.

1917 The United States enters World War I.

1939 DAR denies Marian Anderson the right to sing in their concert hall. Eleanor arranges to hold Anderson's concert on the steps of the Lincoln Memorial.

1932 Franklin D. Roosevelt is elected president of the United States.

1900 1910 1920 1930 1940

1912 Eleanor attends her first Democratic Party Convention.[1]

1926 Eleanor helps purchase Todhunter School, a girls **seminary**, where she teaches history and government.

1928 Eleanor is **appointed** Director of Women's Activities for the Democratic Party; FDR is elected governor of New York.

1933 Frances Perkins becomes Secretary of Labor, the first woman cabinet member in U.S. history.

1936 FDR runs for and wins re-election. With Eleanor's help, African American Mary McLeod Bethune is appointed director of Negro Affairs in the National Youth Administration (NYA).

1938 Congress passes a law banning child labor.

1941 December 7: The U.S. enters the war in Europe.

1. The **Democratic Party Convention** is a meeting for people who are part of the Democratic political party.
2. The **Nineteenth Amendment** is the 19th change to the Constitution of the United States.

Vocabulary

Congress (KONG gris) *n.* the part of the United States government that makes laws

seminary (SEM ih nair ee) *n.* a school for advanced education

appointed (uh POIN tid) *v.* selected or named for an office or position

180 UNIT 2 What Brings Out the Best in You?

READING WORKSHOP 3

Practice the Skills

1 **Key Reading Skill**

Predicting In 1952 Eleanor resigned from the United Nations. Do you predict that she stopped being involved with politics and social issues after that? Why or why not?

2 **English Language Coach**

Prefixes What does the word **reappoints** mean? Use your knowledge of prefixes to help you.

3 **Key Literary Element**

Chronological Order Which of the events happened first?
- The U.S. entered World War II
- Eleanor Roosevelt attended her first Democratic Party Convention
- Eleanor Roosevelt was elected head of the United Nations Human Rights commission

4 **BIG Question**

What is one experience that brought out the best in Eleanor Roosevelt? Write your answer on the "In Eleanor Roosevelt's Time" part of the Workshop 3 Foldable. Your response will help you complete the Unit Challenge later.

1943 Eleanor tours the South Pacific to boost the soldiers' **morale**.

1945 Eleanor influences the Army Nurse Corps to open its membership to black women; she joins the NAACP board of directors.

April 12: Franklin Delano Roosevelt dies.
September 2: Japan surrenders to the Allies, World War II ends.

1957 Congress passes a law making it a federal crime to prevent an African American from voting.

1961 John F. Kennedy **reappoints** Eleanor to the United Nations and appoints her as chair of the President's Commission on the Status of Women.

1948 Eleanor's leadership leads to passage of the Universal Declaration of Human Rights.

1954 The *Brown v. Board of Education* decision outlaws segregation in public schools.

1952 Eleanor resigns from the United Nations. **1**

1962 November 7: Eleanor dies at the age of seventy-eight of tuberculosis.³

2 3 4

1946 Eleanor is elected as head of the United Nations Human Rights commission.

---

3. **Tuberculosis** is a deadly lung disease that is easily spread from one person to another.

Vocabulary

morale (muh RAL) *n.* the state of a person's mind and spirit

In Eleanor Roosevelt's Time **181**

READING WORKSHOP 3 • Predicting

After You Read

In Eleanor Roosevelt's Time

Answering the BIG Question

1. What issue, more than any other, do you believe brought out the best in Eleanor Roosevelt?

2. **Recall** When was Franklin Roosevelt first elected president?
   TIP Right There You will find the answer in the text.

3. **Recall** How long was Franklin Roosevelt president?
   TIP Right There You will find the answer in the text.

Critical Thinking

4. **Analyze** Look closely at the events that occurred during Franklin Roosevelt's time in office. How do you think Eleanor may have influenced him?
   TIP Author and Me You will find information in the text, but you must also use the information in your head.

5. **Draw Conclusions** What kind of person do you think Eleanor Roosevelt was?
   TIP Author and Me You will find information in the text, but you must also use the information in your head.

6. **Interpret** How might Eleanor Roosevelt have affected the future of human rights?
   TIP Author and Me You will find information in the text, but you must also use the information in your head.

Write About Your Reading

The time line tells the important events in Eleanor Roosevelt's life. It also includes some national events that had an impact on her, such as World War II. Think about some of the important things that have happened in the country during your lifetime. Add those events to the time line in your Learner's Notebook. Also add events in your school, community, country, and around the world which have affected your life.

Objectives (pp. 182–183)
Reading Make predictions • Make connections from text to self
Literature Identify literary elements: chronological order
Vocabulary Use prefixes
Writing Respond to literature: time line
Grammar Identify parts of speech: intensive pronouns

Skills Review

Key Reading Skill: Predicting

7. Look back at the predictions you wrote in your Learner's Notebook. Did they help you to stay focused and involved with the text? Why or why not?
8. Were your predictions right about the kinds of activities Eleanor would be involved in?

Key Literary Element: Chronological Order

9. Name one event that happened before Franklin D. Roosevelt became president and one event that happened afterward.
10. How many years did Eleanor spend in the United Nations the first time she served?
11. How many years passed from when Eleanor Roosevelt resigned from the United Nations until she was reappointed by President Kennedy?

Vocabulary Check

seminary   appointed   morale

Write the vocabulary word that each clue describes.

12. It will probably be good if the team wins a lot of games.
13. Students go here to study.
14. One way a person is picked for a position.
15. **English Language Coach** The word *comparable* means *similar to others*. The word *incomparable* means *outstanding* or *beyond comparison*. Name three things Eleanor Roosevelt did that show she was incomparable.

Grammar Link: Intensive Pronouns

A pronoun is a word that takes the place of a noun, a group of words acting as a noun, or another pronoun. **Intensive pronouns** are a lot like reflexive pronouns. They also end with *-self* or *-selves*. They are used to draw special attention to a noun or a pronoun already named. If they are removed, the meaning of the sentence will be the same.

- Yolanda *herself* repaired the engine.
- Yolanda repaired the engine *herself*.

In both sentences, the word *herself* draws special attention back to Yolanda.

Singular Intensive Pronouns	Plural Intensive Pronouns
myself	ourselves
yourself	yourselves
himself, herself, itself	themselves

Grammar Practice

Choose the correct intensive pronoun to complete each sentence below. Rewrite each sentence with the correct word in place.

16. Lakisha designed the computer game ___.
17. The trumpet player ___ wrote his music.
18. James ___ taught the dog to jump through a hoop.

Writing Application Look back at your writing assignment. Add an intensive pronoun to a note on your time line. (*I myself played a solo. I went to New York myself.*) Make sure you use the pronoun correctly.

Web Activities For eFlashcards, Selection Quick Checks, and other Web activities, go to www.glencoe.com.

WRITING WORKSHOP PART 2

Autobiographical Narrative
Revising, Editing, and Presenting

ASSIGNMENT: Write an autobiographical narrative

Purpose: Share a story about a friend who brought out the best in you

Audience: You, your teacher, and your classmates

Revising Rubric

Your revised autobiographical narrative should have
- first-person point of view
- events told in chronological order
- well-chosen details and elaborations
- no spelling or grammatical errors
- nouns and pronouns used correctly

Objectives (pp. 184–187)
Writing Use the writing process: autobiographical narrative • Revise a draft to include: main ideas and supporting details, audience • Edit writing for: grammar, spelling, punctuation • Present writing
Grammar Use nouns and pronouns
Listening, Speaking, and Viewing Participate in a group discussion • Listen actively

In Part 1 of the Writing Workshop, you wrote the first draft of your autobiographical narrative. In Part 2 of the Writing Workshop, you will revise and edit your work and share it with your classmates.

Revising
Make It Better

The best way to start revising is to reread your draft and underline the places where you think your writing sounds awkward. Cross out sentences that you think are unnecessary and write notes about information you'd like to add.

Consider the Audience

Read the questions below and write the answers in your Learner's Notebook.
- What do you want your readers to know about your friend?
- What about this friend brought out the best in you?
- What did you learn about yourself from this experience?

Reread your draft and make sure that the answers you wrote can be found in your narrative. Now is the time to add the information you forgot to include in your first draft.

Check the Details

As you revise, write more details in the places where your autobiography needs further explanation or more details.

One of the most important details in a narrative is the setting, or where the story takes place. Find the setting in your draft and add to the description of that place. Can't find the setting in your draft? Now is the time to add one!

Setting	More Details
Pablo and I ate lunch in the **cafeteria.**	The cafeteria smelled like fish sticks, and I had trouble hearing Pablo over the noise of all the other students.
Lucy and I were at the **shopping mall** after school.	Lucy and I were sitting in the food court at the mall. The neon sign for Pita Palace flashed behind Lucy's head.

184 UNIT 2 What Brings Out the Best in You?

Partner Talk The best way to find out where you should add more details is by asking a friend. Read your story out loud to a partner. Ask these questions when you are finished:

- What parts of my autobiography need more details?
- What else would you like to know about my friend?

Editing
Finish It Up

Writing Models For models and other writing activities, go to www.glencoe.com.

Now it's time to put the finishing touches on your autobiographical narrative. A careful editing job shows your readers that you care about your work and don't want them distracted by any errors. During the editing process you should check spelling and grammar, and follow the Proofreading Checklist that is below.

Proofreading Checklist

- ✔ Proper nouns are capitalized correctly.
- ✔ Pronouns are in the correct form and agree with their antecedents.
- ✔ All words are spelled correctly.
- ✔ All sentences are complete.

Presenting
Show It Off

Write or type a final version of your autobiographical narrative.

Add illustrations or fancy title lettering to make your paper really stand out. You may also cut images from magazines or download images from your computer.

Make a class binder called *How We Became the Best We Can Be* to compile the autobiographies of your entire class. Use a three-hole puncher to punch holes in your paper and then add your work to the class binder.

Read your autobiographical narrative to the class. Listen as everyone reads his or her narrative. Talk about any common experiences that you have with your friends and how they bring out the best in you.

> **Writing Tip**
> Remember that some nouns have different endings when they become plural. Singular nouns that end in a consonant and *y* get an *ies* ending when they become plural (*story/stories*).

> **Writing Tip**
> If your autobiographical narrative is written on a computer, use your spell checker, but also check it manually. Spell checkers only tell you if the word you used is not a word. They won't tell you if you used the wrong form of a word (for example: there, their, and they're). If you're unsure of the spelling, look it up in a dictionary.

> **Writing Tip**
> Don't let messy handwriting get in the way of your story! Make your final draft easy to read by using your best handwriting or a word processor.

WRITING WORKSHOP PART 2

Writer's Model

The Election
By Oscar Mendez

Late last August, I was walking home from playing soccer with my friend Pablo. "Our school needs a fifth grade soccer team," I told Pablo.

"You should run for fifth grade class president," said Pablo. "Then you could set one up."

"Who'd want me for president?" I asked, shocked at the idea.

"You always do your best in sports and in school," said Pablo. "Maybe you're not a big shot, but that means you're not stuck up. You're friendly to everybody. Those are the things we need in a class president."

"I don't know," I stalled. "Running for president will be so much work, and I already have trumpet practice and all the homework we get."

"I'll help you," said Pablo.

I did run, and Pablo helped me. First, we made posters to hang in the fifth grade hallway. Then, we made soccer ball shaped buttons with my name on them. Next, Pablo helped me write a speech about why I'd make a good class president.

On the day of the election, I had to give my speech in front of the whole fifth grade. When I got to the microphone, I promised my classmates that if they elected me, I'd start a fifth grade soccer team and promote any other worthwhile project that anyone suggested to me.

For the rest of the day, Pablo and I nervously waited for the election results. When it was finally announced that I was fifth grade class president, we gave each other high fives.

"Come on over on Saturday," I told Pablo. "My dad'll take us to a soccer game!"

"Sure," said Pablo, "but right now you go ask Coach Simpson how you can start our new fifth grade soccer team!"

The author uses the proper conventions for writing and punctuating dialogue. Dialogue makes the story more interesting to read.

Several events happen in this paragraph. The writer uses chronological order to organize the events.

The author includes the emotions he remembers feeling at the time.

Specific details help the reader visualize the characters and the scene.

Listening, Speaking, and Viewing

Active Listening in a Group Discussion

Just as you need skills to play football or write a story, you also need skills to be a good listener and an effective speaker.

What Is It?

Have you ever sat in a class discussion just thinking about what you're going to say next? Or looking out the window and wondering if practice was going to get rained out? If so, you may have heard what was being said, but you weren't actively listening. Active listening involves paying attention to the person speaking, thinking about what's being said, and asking yourself questions about whether you understand and agree with what's being said. Hearing is something that happens. Listening is something you do.

Why Is It Important?

Group discussions are good ways to learn things you don't know, but they are even better for something else. They help you explore what you think about things. You share your ideas. Then, if you really listen to what others have to say, you may change your ideas or add to them. Your listening can lead you to think about things in different ways.

How Do I Do It?

Follow these tips to be an active listener:

- Clear your mind of other thoughts and distractions.
- Look at the speaker and focus on the words he or she is saying.
- Connect what you hear to your own knowledge and experience.
- Identify the main ideas.
- If you don't understand something, raise your hand and ask a question.
- Let your own ideas grow as you listen to others. Don't only focus on your own point of view.
- Try to be open to different ideas and points of view, even if you don't agree with them at first.

Speak to Learn Follow these tips for participating in a group discussion about the Big Question:

- Form a group of three or more students.
- Discuss activities in your lives that bring out the best in you.
- Ask your group members questions about the activities they mention.
- Be respectful of your group members by not interrupting when they are speaking and responding appropriately to their questions.

READING WORKSHOP 4

Skills Focus

You will practice using these skills when you read the following selections:
- "Gentleman of the Pool," p. 192
- "Primary Lessons," p. 198

Reading
- Asking questions

Literature
- Understanding tone

Vocabulary
- Understanding word choice

Writing/Grammar
- Understanding pronoun case and usage

Skill Lesson
Questioning

Learn It!

What Is It? Reading is like having a conversation between the author and the reader. You don't get to tell the author what you're thinking, but you can ask questions in your head. Then you read to find out the answers. That's the way the best readers always read.

They ask questions that help them
- use their own knowledge.
- make predictions.
- grasp the meaning.
- figure out the author's purpose.
- find specific information.
- understand and remember events and characters.
- wonder about "big" ideas.

Analyzing Cartoons
What did the bird ask itself? Do you think it considered the answer to its own question?

© Patrick McDonnell. Reprinted with permission of King Features Syndicate.

Objectives
(pp. 188–189)
Reading Ask questions

READING WORKSHOP 4 • Questioning

Why Is It Important? Asking questions makes you an active reader. It helps you really think about what you're reading. When you do that, you remember more. You also understand more and get new ideas that will help you in school and in your life.

How Do I Do It? Begin asking questions even before you read. Ask yourself what you already know about the subject. Then ask what you expect or hope to learn from reading. While you're reading, don't let anything slip past you. If the author mentions something you haven't heard of before, ask yourself questions. Then look to see if the author tells you the answers. If there's a word you don't know, ask whether there are any clues that will help you understand it. If there's a mystery, ask how it will be solved. After you've finished, ask what the main idea of the selection was and whether you agree with that idea.

While a student was reading "Madam C. J. Walker," he asked questions:

> Sarah was a widow at the age of twenty, and the sole support of a two-year-old daughter. She took in laundry to earn a living and was determined to leave the South. With Lelia, she made her way up the Mississippi River and settled in St. Louis, where she worked fourteen hours a day doing other people's laundry.

Literature Online

Study Central Visit www.glencoe.com and click on Study Central to review asking questions.

Before I read the paragraph, I asked myself who and what this was about. As I read this paragraph, I asked myself why it was important for Sarah to leave the South. After I read the paragraph, I asked myself why this information was important to the selection.

Practice It!

In your Learner's Notebook, write the following questions. Then write a question of your own.

Who is this selection about? Who else is important?

Use It!

As you read "Gentleman of the Pool" and "Primary Lessons," come up with more questions about the selections. Add them to your Learner's Notebook and answer the questions as you read.

READING WORKSHOP 4 • Questioning

Before You Read : Gentleman of the Pool

Meet the Author
Alice Park is a senior science reporter with *TIME* magazine. Since 1993, she has reported on health and medicine, including articles on AIDS, cancer, and Alzheimer's disease. At Harvard Medical School, Ms. Park designed a program to help doctors understand the latest research on AIDS.

Author Search For more about Alice Park, go to www.glencoe.com.

Vocabulary Preview

goal (gohl) *n.* something that you aim for **(p. 192)** *Michael had a goal to win at least one gold medal.*

ambitions (am BISH unz) *n.* strong desires to succeed **(p. 193)** *The members of the swim team had a lot of different ambitions, but all of them wanted to win.*

victory (VIK tur ee) *n.* the win in a contest or battle **(p. 193)** *The team celebrated their victory after the swimming competition.*

Partner Activity
- Write each vocabulary word on a strip of paper.
- Fold the strips so you cannot see the words.
- Take turns picking a strip.
- Use each word you pick in a sentence.
- Refold the strips, and choose again. This time tell what the word means.

English Language Coach

Word Choice Using just the *right* word is called good **word choice**. Sometimes there are plenty of words you *could* use, but one is often better than the rest. Choosing the right word is important, and a good writer has the ability to strengthen descriptions and give details with this skill. One way to determine which word is the best is to think about synonyms by using a thesaurus. Keep in mind that the best word isn't *always* a synonym. Picking the *best* word is all about understanding what you want to say and making it as clear as possible.

Write to Learn In your Learner's Notebook rewrite each sentence. Pick one of the words in parentheses to replace the word in dark print. You might notice that more than one word will work, but only one word is the *best* word. If you are unsure about the meaning of any words, use a dictionary.

1. Andre has a **large** baseball card collection. (massive, bulky, excessive)
2. Chandra, a **talented** writer, always wins the school poetry slam. (excellent, gifted, genius)
3. It was a close election, but Marq was **defeated** when he ran for student council. (obliterated, unsuccessful, trounced)

Objectives (pp. 190–193)
Reading Ask questions • Make connections from text to self
Literature Identify literary elements: tone
Vocabulary Identify synonyms • Make word choices

READING WORKSHOP 4 • Questioning

Skills Preview

Key Reading Skill: Questioning

As you read "Gentleman of the Pool," have a conversation with yourself by asking and trying to answer questions. You might ask yourself questions like these:
- Why does the author call Michael Phelps a gentleman?
- How is he a winner "out of the pool"?

Write to Learn As you read, write your questions and answers in your Learner's Notebook.

Key Literary Element: Tone

"Don't use that tone of voice with me!" You've probably heard that, particularly if you were being rude or unpleasant. It's easy to pick up on someone's tone of voice. But how do you figure out the tone of someone's writing?

The **tone** of a piece of writing is the attitude of the author. Since the author doesn't have an actual voice, he or she chooses particular words and phrases. They show how the author feels about the subject of the writing. Some words that describe tone are *respectful, admiring, angry, bored, amused,* and *hurt.*
- Carrie had a wide range of knowledge.
- Carrie was a know-it-all.

It's pretty easy to tell what the authors of these sentences think about Carrie, isn't it?

Partner Talk Exchange sentences that have a clear tone. Then rewrite the sentences so that they express a different attitude.

Interactive Literary Elements Handbook
To review or learn more about the literary elements, go to www.glencoe.com.

Get Ready to Read

Connect to the Reading

Michael Phelps loves to swim. Think about sports, games, or other group activities that you like to participate in or watch. Think about the winning teams you know of.

Class Talk Discuss what makes a person a good team player.

Build Background

- The Olympics Games are athletic competitions which began over 2700 years ago and lasted almost 1200 years. They were held in Olympia, Greece, in the summer every four years. Just like today, many of the best athletes became famous and were treated like celebrities for the rest of their lives.
- The modern Olympic Games began in 1896 in Athens, Greece.
- The Games are held in cities around the world. The number of athletes, participating countries, and events has increased over the years.
- All Olympic events are still held every four years. However, since 1996, winter events (like skiing) and summer events (like swimming) are held in different cities two years apart.

Set Purposes for Reading

BIG Question Read the biography "Gentleman of the Pool" to find out what brought out the best in Michael Phelps.

Set Your Own Purpose What else would you like to learn from the story to help you answer the Big Question? Write your own purpose on the "Gentleman of the Pool" part of the Workshop 4 Foldable.

Keep Moving

Use these skills as you read the following selection.

Gentleman of the Pool **191**

READING WORKSHOP 4

TIME

Gentleman of the POOL

Michael Phelps didn't beat the Olympic gold medal record at the 2004 Games. But the young swimmer left no doubt. He is a winner in—and out of—the pool.

By ALICE PARK

OLYMPIC WINNER Michael Phelps is all smiles as he shows off one of the six gold medals he won at the 2004 Olympic Games in Athens, Greece.

During the 2004 Olympics in Athens, Greece, the world expected record-breaking success from swimmer Michael Phelps. The 19-year-old American was favored to win the most gold medals ever at a single Olympics. To reach that **goal**, Phelps would have needed to win 8 gold medals. That number would beat the record held by U.S. swimmer Mark Spitz, who had won 7 gold medals at the 1972 Olympics in Munich, Germany. 🔢

Phelps's swimming meets were the most popular events of the first week of the Games. Fans streamed into the Olympic Aquatic Centre. TV ratings hit the roof.[1] Phelps chose to swim in the 200-meter freestyle on day three. The teenage swimmer knew he was not favored to win. But that didn't keep him from reaching for a personal goal.

🔢 Key Reading Skill

Questioning At this point, you might ask *why* Michael Phelps was favored to win so many medals.

---

1. If the television ratings **hit the roof,** a lot of people watched the Olympics on TV.

Vocabulary

goal (gohl) *n.* something that you aim for

Instead of giving in to doubt and fear, Phelps raced stroke for stroke against Olympic medal winners Ian Thorpe of Australia and Pieter van den Hoogenband of the Netherlands. Phelps came in third place, winning a bronze medal. That third-place win ended the race for the record 8 gold medals that the world had been watching for.

For Phelps, there was more to the Olympics than earning gold medals. The 200-meter bronze medal was proof that he could compete with the world's best—and enjoy it. "Racing the two greatest freestylers of all time in an Olympic final—it's fun," Phelps said after the race. "I had fun out there."

Phelps had gone to Athens as a star attraction. While there, he also became known as a sportsman. After the 200-meter freestyle, the teenage swimmer continued to work toward his goals. But he also cared about the **ambitions** and feelings of his teammates. Phelps wanted to share the fun of the Games. 2 So he gave up his spot in a medley relay[2] to teammate Ian Crocker. Earlier in the week, Crocker had cost the U.S. team the gold medal in another event. "He wasn't feeling too well [then], and I was willing to give him a chance to step up," says Phelps. "It was the right thing to do." 3

By the end of the Games in Athens, Phelps had won 8 medals (6 gold medals and 2 bronze). That matched the record for the most medals earned at an Olympics. Building on Phelps's powerful swimming, the U.S. team had achieved its own **victory**. It swam to a world-record win in the medley relay. Phelps's winning effort had paid off for everyone. The young swimmer was an all-around winner. 4 5

—From *TIME*, August 30, 2004

2. A *medley relay* has four swimmers working together with each athlete swimming a different stroke in his or her part of the competition.

Vocabulary

ambitions (am BISH unz) *n.* strong desires to succeed

victory (VIK tur ee) *n.* the win in a contest or battle

---

2 English Language Coach

Word Choice Michael Phelps cared about the *ambitions* of his teammates. Synonyms for *ambitions* are *aims*, *goals*, and *hopes*. Which of those words would you choose to replace the word *ambitions* here? Why?

3 Key Reading Skill

Questioning Phelps wanted to share the fun of the Olympic Games. What question could you ask about that?

4 Key Literary Element

Tone How would you describe the author's tone in this article? Can you tell what her attitude is toward Michael Phelps?

5 BIG Question

What brought out the best in Phelps as a sportsman? Write your answer on the "Gentleman of the Pool" part of the Workshop 4 Foldable.

READING WORKSHOP 4 • Questioning

After You Read | Gentleman of the Pool

Answering the BIG Question

1. What brought out the best in Michael Phelps at the Olympic Games in Athens?
2. **Recall** What is one of the swimming events in which Michael competed at the Olympics? Which medals did he win?
   TIP **Right There** You will find the answer in the text.
3. **Recall** Whose record did Michael try to beat?
   TIP **Right There** You will find the answer in the text.

Critical Thinking

4. **Infer** Why were the swimming meets in which Michael Phelps competed the most popular events of the first week of the Olympic Games?
   TIP **Author and Me** You will find clues in the text, but you must also use the information in your head.
5. **Infer** Why did Michael choose to swim in the 200-meter freestyle even though he was not favored to win?
   TIP **Author and Me** You will find clues in the text, but you must also use the information in your head.
6. **Support** What fact from this selection supports the conclusion that Michael was not upset when he won the bronze medal for the 200-meter freestyle?
   TIP **Author and Me** You will find clues in the text, but you must also use the information in your head.

Talk About Your Reading

Michael Phelps gave up his place in a medley relay to his teammate Ian Crocker. What if the team had lost with Crocker? Get together with a partner to discuss whether Phelps giving his place to Crocker was a good idea or not. One of you will list reasons why it was a good idea and one of you will list reasons why it was a bad idea. Discuss the ideas on your lists and see if you come to the same conclusion in the end.

Objectives (pp. 194–195)
Reading Ask questions
Literature Identify literary elements: tone
Vocabulary Identify synonyms • Make word choices
Grammar Identify parts of speech: subject pronouns

194 UNIT 2 What Brings Out the Best in You?

Skills Review

Key Reading Skill: Questioning

7. What questions did you ask yourself as you read this selection? How did asking yourself questions help you as a reader?

Key Literary Element: Tone

8. Which of the following words would you choose to describe the tone of this article about Michael Phelps?
   admiring
   playful
   disappointed
   jealous
   sympathetic

9. Do you think a writer could use the same facts and a different tone? Do you think he or she could you make you feel differently about Michael Phelps? Explain your answer.

Vocabulary Check

goal   ambition   victory

10. In your Learner's Notebook, write two to four sentences about Michael Phelps using all three vocabulary words above. (You can use more than one word in a sentence.)

11. **English Language Coach** Pick three sentences from the selection. Copy the sentences in your Learner's Notebook. Choose one word in each sentence to replace with a synonym. Rewrite the sentences with that word.

Grammar Link: Subject Pronouns

You already know that sometimes it is correct to use *she* or *I* and sometimes it is correct to use *her* or *me*. The problem is knowing when to use which.

The subject of a sentence is who or what the sentence is about. A pronoun used as a subject must be one of the "subject pronouns."

Singular subject pronouns: I, you, he, she, it
Plural subject pronouns: We, you, they

It's easy to use subject pronouns correctly when the subject is one person. You would never say "Me ate breakfast" or "Her ran a mile." You must also use subject pronouns when the subject is more than one person.
- Wrong: Him and Joan tied for first place.
- Wrong: Joan and him tied for first place.
- Right: He and Joan tied for first place.

If you wonder what the correct subject is, get rid of the extra person (or people) in your mind.

Grammar Practice

Choose a pronoun to complete each sentence below. Rewrite each sentence with an appropriate pronoun in place. (There might be more than one correct answer.)

12. ___ and Lucy played catch.
13. The director chose Jarrod and ___ to play the lead roles.
14. ___ and Una asked my mother for cookies.

Web Activities For eFlashcards, Selection Quick Checks, and other Web activities, go to www.glencoe.com.

READING WORKSHOP 4 • Questioning

Before You Read : Primary Lessons

Judith Ortiz Cofer

Meet the Author
Judith Ortiz Cofer wrote about things that happened to her when she was a child. Through her writing, she shows her readers ways to adapt to new places and new cultures. She once wrote that memories come into her poems and stories "like time-travelers popping up with a message for me." See page R2 of the Author Files for more on Judith Ortiz Cofer.

Author Search For more about Judith Ortiz Cofer, go to www.glencoe.com.

Objectives (pp. 196–205)
Reading Ask questions • Make connections from text to self
Literature Identify literary elements: tone
Vocabulary Identify synonyms • Make word choices

Vocabulary Preview

emerged (ih MERJD) *v.* came out; past tense of *emerge* **(p. 198)** *The students emerged from their classrooms when the bell rang.*

chaos (KAY ahs) *n.* total confusion and disorder **(p. 198)** *Many children getting ready at the same time resulted in chaos.*

defiance (dih FY uns) *n.* bold resistance to authority **(p. 199)** *She showed defiance when she argued with her mother about going to school.*

indifference (in DIF fur uns) *n.* a lack of feeling or concern **(p. 200)** *Judith showed indifference to her friend's wishes.*

yearning (YUR ning) *n.* wanting something badly; past participle of *yearn* **(p. 201)** *Judith felt a yearning to stay at her grandmother's familiar house.*

unmindful (un MYND ful) *adj.* not aware **(p. 204)** *Judith was unmindful of the prejudice shown toward Lorenzo.*

relish (REL ish) *v.* to enjoy **(p. 204)** *If Lorenzo was asked to host the PTA show, he would relish the opportunity.*

Partner Talk Discuss the meaning of each word. Work together to create a sentence for each word. Write your sentences in your Learner's Notebook.

English Language Coach

Word Choice Good **word choice** is using just the *right* word. Choosing the right word will help you give the best descriptions and details. Sometimes there are plenty of words to choose from, but usually there is one that really stands out. One way to determine which word is the best is to use a thesaurus. To pick the best word, think about what you want to say and make it as clear as possible.

Write to Learn Choose one of the five situations below and think about ways to describe the scene using good word choice. First, make a list of vivid words and phrases that come to mind. Next, use those words and phrases in a paragraph describing the scene.

- a busy playground
- a sinking pirate ship
- harsh weather or environment
- a treasure hunt in the jungle
- an active animal indoors or outdoors

196 UNIT 2 What Brings Out the Best in You?

READING WORKSHOP 4 • Questioning

Skills Preview

Key Reading Skill: Questioning
As you read, it's important to ask yourself questions about the text. Look for the answers as you read. If you have questions that have not been answered when you are done reading, review the text. See if there is information you overlooked that will answer those questions.

Class Talk Brainstorm a list of questions you would ask someone to find out what brings out the best in him or her. Write the questions on the board.

Key Literary Element: Tone
The **tone** of a piece of writing shows you the author's attitude toward the subject. And it can change. It can be different in one part of the article or story than it is in another part. That's one of the ways an author leads readers to change their feelings about something.

It's important to remember, though, that the **tone** is the author's attitude, not the main character's or any other character's attitude. An author could even have an amused tone while one of the characters was very angry.

In an autobiographical story, the author may have a different attitude when writing about an event than he or she did while the event was happening. The author may be angry about something he or she was confused about twenty years before.

Group Discussion Talk in a group about things you feel differently about now than you did when they happened. Try to find examples in your own lives. Then ask why you feel differently. What caused the change in your attitude? What would your tone be now if you were writing about one of those events?

Interactive Literary Elements Handbook
To review or learn more about the literary elements, go to www.glencoe.com.

Get Ready to Read

Connect to the Reading
You learn a lot of different things at school, such as multiplying or writing reports. You also learn more real-life lessons, like how to get along with other people or how to be a dependable person. Think about the real-life lessons you have learned in school.

Write to Learn In your Learner's Notebook, list the three most important life lessons you have learned in school.

Build Background
Puerto Rico is a Caribbean island. The Taíno Indians were the first people to live there. In 1493 the explorer Christopher Columbus claimed the island for Spain. In 1899 America took it over after winning the Spanish-American War.

- Puerto Rico is about the size of the state of Delaware and has a population of about four million people.
- In 1917 Puerto Ricans were granted U.S. citizenship.
- Puerto Rico has two official languages: Spanish and English.

Set Purposes for Reading
BIG Question Read "Primary Lessons" to find out what brought out the best in Judith Ortiz Cofer.

Set Your Own Purpose What else would you like to learn from the story to help you answer the Big Question? Write your own purpose on the "Primary Lessons" part of the Workshop 4 Foldable.

Keep Moving
Use these skills as you read the following selection.

Primary Lessons 197

READING WORKSHOP 4

Primary LESSONS

by Judith Ortiz Cofer

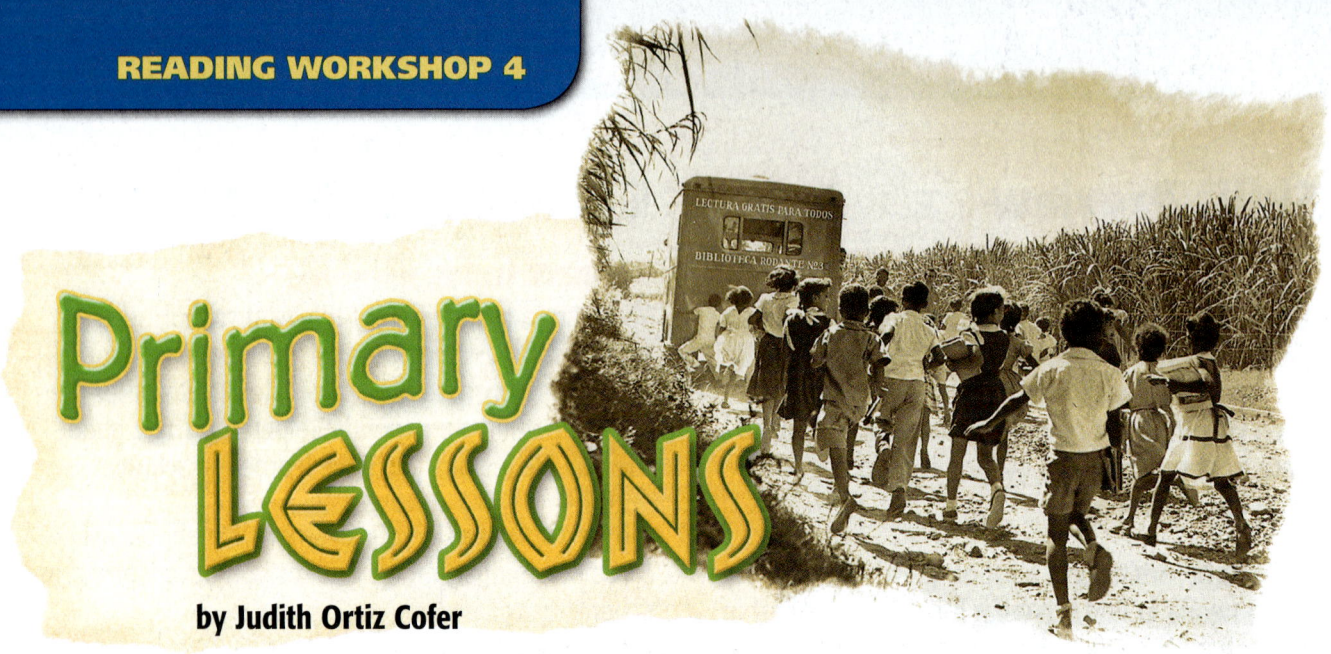

My mother walked me to my first day at school at La Escuela Segundo Ruiz Belvis, named after the Puerto Rican patriot born in our town. I remember yellow cement with green trim. All the classrooms had been painted these colors to identify them as government property. This was true all over the Island.

Everything was color-coded, including the children, who wore uniforms from first through twelfth grade. We were a midget army in white and brown, led by the hand to our battleground. From practically every house in our barrio[1] **emerged** a crisply ironed uniform inhabited by the wild creatures we had become over a summer of running wild in the sun. 1

At my grandmother's house where we were staying until my father returned to Brooklyn Yard in New York and sent for us, it had been complete **chaos**, with several children to get ready for school. My mother had pulled my hair harder than usual while braiding it, and I had dissolved into a pool of total self-pity. I wanted to stay home with her and *Mamà*, to continue listening to stories in the late afternoon, to drink *café con leche*[2] with them, and to play rough games with my many cousins. I wanted to continue living the dream of summer

Practice the Skills

1 Key Reading Skill

Questioning What question could you ask about the color-coding in the school?

---

1. A ***barrio*** (BAH ree oh) is a neighborhood where Hispanic people live.
2. ***Café con leche*** (KAH fay con LAY chay) is coffee with milk in it.

Vocabulary

emerged (ih MERJD) *v.* came out

chaos (KAY ahs) *n.* total confusion and disorder

198 UNIT 2   What Brings Out the Best in You?

afternoons in Puerto Rico, and if I could not have that, then I wanted to go back to Paterson, New Jersey, back to where I imagined our apartment waited, peaceful and cool for the three of us to return to our former lives. Our gypsy lifestyle had convinced me, at age six, that one part of life stops and waits for you while you live another for a while—and if you don't like the present, you can always return to the past. Buttoning me into my stiff blouse while I tried to squirm away from her, my mother tried to explain to me that I was a big girl now and should try to understand that, like all the other children my age, I had to go to school. 2

"What about him?" I yelled pointing at my brother who was lounging on the tile floor of our bedroom in his pajamas, playing quietly with a toy car.

"He's too young to go to school, you know that. Now stay still." My mother pinned me between her thighs to button my skirt, as she had learned to do from *Mamà*, from whose grip it was impossible to escape.

"It's not fair, it's not fair. I can't go to school here. I don't speak Spanish." It was my final argument, and it failed miserably because I was shouting my **defiance** in the language I claimed not to speak. Only I knew what I meant by saying in Spanish that I did not speak Spanish. I had spent my early childhood in the U.S. where I lived in a bubble created by my Puerto Rican parents in a home where two cultures and languages became one. I learned to listen to the English from the television with one ear while I heard my mother and father speaking in Spanish with the other. I thought I was an ordinary American kid—like the children on the shows I watched—and that everyone's parents spoke a secret second language at home. When we came to Puerto Rico right before I started first grade, I switched easily to Spanish. It was the language of fun, of summertime games. But school—that was a different matter.

I made one last desperate attempt to make my mother see reason: "Father will be very angry. You know that he wants us to speak good English." My mother, of course, ignored me as she dressed my little brother in his playclothes. I could not

Practice the Skills

2 **Reviewing Skills**

Connecting Have you ever felt sorry for yourself? Why or why not?

The author, Judith Ortiz Cofer, as a child

Vocabulary

defiance (dih FY uns) *n.* bold resistance to authority

Primary Lessons **199**

believe her **indifference** to my father's wishes. She was usually so careful about our safety and the many other areas that he was forever reminding her about in his letters. But I was right, and she knew it.

Our father spoke to us in English as much as possible, and he corrected my pronunciation constantly—not "jes" but "y-es." Y-es, sir. How could she send me to school to learn Spanish when we would be returning to Paterson in just a few months? **3**

But, of course, what I feared was not language, but loss of freedom. At school there would be no playing, no stories, only lessons. It would not matter if I did not understand a word, and I would not be allowed to make up my own definitions. I would have to learn silence. I would have to keep my wild imagination in check. Feeling locked into my stiffly starched uniform, I only sensed all this. I guess most children can intuit[3] their loss of childhood's freedom on that

3. When you *intuit* (in TOO it) something, no one teaches or explains it to you; you just know it.

Vocabulary

indifference (in DIF fur uns) *n.* a lack of feeling or concern

Practice the Skills

3 **Key Literary Element**

Tone How does the young Judith Ortiz feel in this part of the story? What is her attitude toward going to school? What attitude does the older Judith Ortiz Cofer, the author, have toward her younger self?

El Sol Asombre, 1989. Rafael Ferrer (b. 1933). Puerto Rico (Spanish descent). Oil on canvas, 60 x 72 in. The Butler Institute of American Art, Youngstown, OH.

Analyzing the Art In this painting, Puerto Rican artist Rafael Ferrer shows the brilliant light and striking colors of the Caribbean islands. Does Ortiz Cofer write about Puerto Rico's beautiful scenery in this story? Why or why not?

first day of school. It is separation anxiety[4] too, but mother is just the guardian of the "playground" of our early childhood.

The sight of my cousins in similar straits[5] comforted me. We were marched down the hill of our barrio where *Mamà's* robin-egg-blue house stood at the top. I must have glanced back at it with **yearning**. *Mamà's* house—a place built for children—where anything that could be broken had already been broken by my grandmother's early batch of offspring (they ranged in age from my mother's oldest sisters to my uncle who was six months older than me). Her house had long since been made child-proof. It had been a perfect summer place. And now it was September—the cruelest month for a child.

La Mrs., as all the teachers were called, waited for her class of first-graders at the door of the yellow and green classroom. She too wore a uniform: it was a blue skirt and a white blouse. This teacher wore black high heels with her "standard issue." I remember this detail because when we were all seated in rows she called on one little girl and pointed to the back of the room where there were shelves. She told the girl to bring her a shoebox from the bottom shelf. Then, when the box had been placed in her hands, she did something unusual. She had the little girl kneel at her feet and take the pointy high heels off her feet and replace them with a pair of satin slippers from the shoebox. She told the group that every one of us would have a chance to do this if we behaved in her class. Though confused about the prize, I soon felt caught up in the competition to bring *La Mrs.* her slippers in the morning. Children fought over the privilege. **4**

Our first lesson was English. In Puerto Rico, every child has to take twelve years of English to graduate from school. It is the law. In my parents' schooldays, all subjects were taught in English. The U.S. Department of Education had specified that as U.S. territory, the Island had to be "Americanized," and to accomplish this task, it was necessary for the Spanish

Practice the Skills

4 **Key Reading Skill**

Questioning What question would you ask yourself about the children changing the teacher's shoes?

---

4. **Separation anxiety** is the fear that some people feel when they are away from their loved ones.
5. **Straits** means "difficult positions."

Vocabulary

yearning (YUR ning) *n.* wanting something badly

language to be replaced in one generation through the teaching of English in all schools. My father began his school day by saluting the flag of the United States and singing "America" and "The Star-Spangled Banner" by rote,[6] without understanding a word of what he was saying. The logic behind this system was that, though the children did not understand the English words, they would remember the rhythms. Even the games the teacher's manuals required them to play became absurd adaptations. "Here We Go Round the Mulberry Bush" became "Here We Go Round the Mango Tree." I have heard about the confusion caused by the use of a primer[7] in which the sounds of animals were featured. The children were forced to accept that a rooster says *cockadoodledoo*, when they knew perfectly well from hearing their own roosters each morning that in Puerto Rico a rooster says *cocorocó*. Even the vocabulary of their pets was changed; there are still family stories circulating about the bewilderment of a first-grader coming home to try to teach his dog to speak in English. The policy of assimilation by immersion[8] failed on the Island. Teachers adhered to it on paper, substituting their own materials for the texts, and no one took their English home. In due time, the program was minimized[9] to the one class in English per day that I encountered when I took my seat in *La Mrs.'s* first-grade class. 🔟 6️⃣

Catching us all by surprise, she stood very straight and tall in front of us and began to sing in English: "Pollito—Chicken, Gallina—Hen, Làpiz—Pencil, Y Pluma—Pen."

"Repeat after me, children: Pollito—Chicken," she commanded in her heavily accented English that only I understood, being the only child in the room who had ever been exposed to the language. But I too remained silent. No use making waves, or showing off. Patiently *La Mrs.* sang her song and gestured for us to join in. At some point it must have dawned on the class that this silly routine was likely to

Practice the Skills

5 Key Literary Element

Tone What attitude does the author have toward the attempts to replace Spanish with English? How would you describe the tone of this section?

6 English Language Coach

Word Choice What words in this paragraph help you understand the author's tone?

---

6. If you do a thing by **rote**, you do it from memory without thinking about it.
7. A **primer** is a textbook that children use to learn to read.
8. **The policy of assimilation by immersion** is the method of teaching English by having all school work done in English in the hope that students will start using English as their first language.
9. **Minimized** (MIN ih myzd) means "cut back."

go on all day if we did not "repeat after her." It was not her fault that she had to follow the rule in her teacher's manual stating that she must teach English *in* English, and that she must not translate, but must repeat her lesson in English until the children "begin to respond" more or less "unconsciously." This was one of the vestiges of the regimen followed by her predecessors in the last generation. To this day I can recite "Pollito—Chicken" mindlessly, never once pausing to visualize chicks, hens, pencils, or pens. 7

Analyzing the Photo The author says that she was the "teacher's pet," or the teacher's favorite student. Who do you think might be the "teacher's pet" in this photo? Explain your answer.

I soon found myself crowned "teacher's pet" without much effort on my part. I was a privileged child in her eyes simply because I lived in "Nueva York," and because my father was in the Navy. His name was an old one in our pueblo, associated with once-upon-a-time landed people and long-gone money. Status is judged by unique standards in a culture where, by definition, everyone is a second-class citizen. Remembrance of past glory is as good as titles and money. Old families living in decrepit old houses rank over factory workers living in modern comfort in cement boxes—all the same. The professions raise a person out of the dreaded "sameness" into a niche of status, so that teachers, nurses, and everyone who went to school for a job were given the honorifics of *El Míster* or *La Mrs.* by the common folks, people who were likely to be making more money in American factories than the poorly paid educators and government workers.

My first impression of the hierarchy[10] began with my teacher's shoe-changing ceremony and the exaggerated respect she received from our parents. *La Mrs.* was always right, and adults scrambled to meet her requirements. She wanted all our schoolbooks covered in the brown paper now

Practice the Skills

7 Key Reading Skill

Questioning Ask yourself whether this reciting was a good way to learn. Does the author think it was good?

---

10. A *hierarchy* (HY ur ar kee) is a ranking of people or things based on certain standards.

READING WORKSHOP 4

used for paperbags (used at that time by the grocer to wrap meats and other foods). That first week of school the grocer was swamped with requests for paper which he gave away to the women. That week and the next, he wrapped produce in newspapers. All school projects became family projects. It was considered disrespectful at *Mamà's* house to do homework in privacy. Between the hours when we came home from school and dinner time, the table was shared by all of us working together with the women hovering in the background. The teachers communicated directly with the mothers, and it was a matriarchy[11] of far-reaching power and influence. 8

There was a black boy in my first-grade classroom who was also the teacher's pet but for a different reason than I: I did not have to do anything to win her favor; he would do anything to win a smile. He was as black as the cauldron that *Mamà* used for cooking stew and his hair was curled into tight little balls on his head—*pasitas*, like little raisins glued to his skull, my mother had said. There had been some talk at *Mamà's* house about this boy; Lorenzo was his name. I later gathered that he was the grandson of my father's nanny. Lorenzo lived with Teresa, his grandmother, having been left in her care when his mother took off for "Los Nueva Yores" shortly after his birth. And they were poor. Everyone could see that his pants were too big for him—hand-me-downs—and his shoe soles were as thin as paper. Lorenzo seemed **unmindful** of the giggles he caused when he jumped up to erase the board for *La Mrs.* and his baggy pants rode down to his thin hips as he strained up to get every stray mark. He seemed to **relish** playing the little clown when she asked him to come to the front of the room and sing his phonetic version of "o-bootifool, forpashios-keeis" leading the class in our incomprehensible tribute to the American flag. He was a bright, loving child, with a talent for song and mimicry[12] that

Practice the Skills

8 Key Reading Skill

Questioning What questions would you ask yourself to help understand this paragraph better?

---

11. A ***matriarchy*** (MA tree ar kee) is a form of rule where women have most of the power.
12. ***Mimicry*** (MIH mih kree) is the act of mimicking, or copying, someone.

Vocabulary

unmindful (un MYND ful) *adj.* not aware

relish (REL ish) *v.* to enjoy

UNIT 2 What Brings Out the Best in You?

everyone commented on. He should have been chosen to host the PTA show that year instead of me. **9**

At recess one day, I came back to the empty classroom to get something, my cup? My nickel for a drink from the kioskman? I don't remember. But I remember the conversation my teacher was having with another teacher. I remember because it concerned me, and because I memorized it so that I could ask my mother to explain what it meant.

"He is a funny *negrito*, and, like a parrot, he can repeat anything you teach him. But his *mamà* must not have the money to buy him a suit."

"I kept Rafaelito's First Communion suit; I bet Lorenzo could fit in it. It's white with a bow-tie," the other teacher said.

"But, Marisa," laughed my teacher, "in that suit, Lorenzo would look like a fly drowned in a glass of milk."

Both women laughed. They had not seen me crouched at the back of the room, digging into my schoolbag. My name came up then.

"What about the Ortiz girl? They have money."

"I'll talk to her mother today. The superintendent, *El Americano* from San Juan, is coming down for the show. How about if we have her say her lines in both Spanish and English." **10**

Visual Vocabulary
Women and girls used to wear **crinoline petticoats**, stiff underskirts that made dresses or skirts stand out.

The conversation ends there for me. My mother took me to Mayagüez and bought me a frilly pink dress and two crinoline petticoats to wear underneath so that I looked like a pink and white parachute with toothpick legs sticking out. I learned my lines, "Padres, maestros, Mr. Leonard, bienvenidos/Parents, teachers, Mr. Leonard, welcome . . ." My first public appearance. I took no pleasure in it. The words were formal and empty. I had simply memorized them. My dress pinched me at the neck and arms, and made me itch all over. **11**

I had asked my mother what it meant to be a "mosca en un vaso de leche," a fly in a glass of milk. She had laughed at the image, explaining that it meant being "different," but it wasn't something I needed to worry about. **12** ○

Practice the Skills

9 **Key Reading Skill**

Questioning Ask yourself why Lorenzo was not chosen to host the PTA show. Look for an answer in the rest of the story.

10 **Key Literary Element**

Tone Carefully read the last seven paragraphs again. Can you tell what the author thinks about the teachers and the way they talked about Lorenzo? If you're not sure, keep reading to find out.

11 **Key Reading Skill**

Questioning Did you ask a question about the importance of the lessons Judith learned in school? If you didn't write a question about the importance of what Judith learned, write one in your Learner's Notebook. Be sure to answer your question.

12 **BIG Question**

A struggle often brings out the best in a person. What does Judith struggle with in this story? Do you think it brings out the best in her? Explain your answer on the "Primary Lesson" part of the Workshop 4 Foldable.

Primary Lessons **205**

READING WORKSHOP 4 • Questioning

After You Read : Primary Lessons

Answering the BIG Question

1. Do you think the school brought out the best in either Judith or Lorenzo? Explain.
2. **Recall** How did Judith know the school was government property?
   TIP Right There You will find the answer in the text.
3. **Describe** What did Judith look like when she was ready for school?
   TIP Think and Search The answer is in the text, but the details are not all in one place.

Critical Thinking

4. **Infer** What kind of person was Judith's father? How can you tell?
   TIP Author and Me You will find clues in the text, but you must also use the information in your head.
5. **Explain** Why do you think the children were required to wear uniforms?
   TIP Author and Me You will find clues in the text, but you must also use the information in your head.
6. **Draw Conclusions** Why did the fact that Judith had lived in New York cause her to be considered a privileged child?
   TIP Author and Me You will find clues in the text, but you must also use the information in your head.

Write About Your Reading

Use what you learned from "Primary Lessons" to complete this **RAFT** assignment. Scan the story if you need to find particular details or events you don't remember clearly.

R   Your role is a school inspector.
A   Your audience is the school board.
F   Your form is a three-paragraph report.
T   Your topic is whether the children of Puerto Rico should have been forced to speak only English in school. Give examples to support your position.

Objectives (pp. 206–207)
Reading Ask questions • Make connections from text to self
Literature Identify literary elements: tone
Vocabulary Identify synonyms • Make word choices
Writing Write a response to literature
Grammar Identify parts of speech: object pronouns

206 UNIT 2   What Brings Out the Best in You?

Skills Review

Key Reading Skill: Questioning

7. How did you use questioning to help you understand this story? List the three questions you wrote that most helped you.

Key Literary Element: Tone

8. How would you describe the overall tone of "Primary Lessons"? Look at the words below and see if any of them fit. Or choose your own words.

angry   critical   gentle   heartbroken   anxious

9. What would you write about in an angry tone? Explain your answer.

Reviewing Skills: Connecting

10. Have you ever felt different at school? What was that experience like for you? If you have never felt different at school, why do you think that is?

Vocabulary Check

chaos   yearning   defiance

Write *True* or *False* for each statement below.

11. There was **chaos** in grandmother's house when all the children got ready for school.
12. Judith was **yearning** to go to school in Puerto Rico.
13. Judith showed **defiance** to her teacher, *La Mrs.*
14. **English Language Coach** Copy three sentences from the selection into your Learner's Notebook. Choose one word in each sentence to replace with a synonym. Rewrite the sentences with that word.

Web Activities For eFlashcards, Selection Quick Checks, and other Web activities, go to www.glencoe.com.

Grammar Link: Object Pronouns

You'll learn about objects later on in this book. Then the term *object pronouns* will make more sense. For now, you need to know one thing: object pronouns are the personal pronouns that aren't used as subjects.

Singular object pronouns: me, you, him, her, it
Plural object pronouns: us, you, them

It's easy to use object pronouns correctly when you're talking about one person. You would never say "The ball hit I" or "I really like she." You must also use object pronouns when the object is more than one person.

- Wrong: Keira made Patsy and I lunch.
- Wrong: She argued with he and Greg.
- Right: Jerry laughed at Gary and him.

If you wonder what the correct pronoun is, get rid of the extra person (or people) in your mind.

- Yuri liked Will and (she, her).

You would never say "Yuri liked she," so you would use *her* in this sentence.

Grammar Practice

Choose a pronoun to complete each sentence below. Rewrite each sentence with an appropriate pronoun in place.

15. Lauren took ____ to the store on the island.
16. La Mrs. started singing and asked Judith and ____ to join in.
17. The teachers respected Judith and ____.

Writing Application Look back at your writing assignment. Check to see that you used all pronouns correctly.

COMPARING LITERATURE WORKSHOP

from The Pigman & Me
by Paul Zindel

& The Goodness of Matt Kaizer
by Avi

What You'll Learn
- How to compare two pieces of literature
- How to analyze characters

Skills Focus
You will practice using these skills when you read the following selections:
- from *The Pigman & Me*, p. 211
- "The Goodness of Matt Kaizer," p. 221

Point of Comparison
- Character

Purpose
- To compare characters in two texts

Objectives (pp. 208–209)
Literature Identify literary elements: character • Compare and contrast: literature

---

How is a dinosaur like a bird? How are they different? To answer these questions, you have to compare the characteristics that you know about each. For example, you might compare when they lived, how big they are (or were), and whether they had feathers. Whether you are comparing two animals, two movies, or two books, the skills you use are the same.

How to Compare Literature: Character

You can't compare every single detail in two stories. It would take too much time, and most of the details wouldn't be important. You need to think about the characteristics of the selections that are most important. When you compare the excerpt from *The Pigman & Me* and "The Goodness of Matt Kaizer," you will look closely at the *main character* in each selection. One is a real person and the other is fictional, but you can use the same methods to look at both of them.

As you read, look for details and clues that tell you what the main character is like. Think of words that you might use to describe the character—like *brave, scared, confident, cruel, greedy, thoughtful,* or *funny*. To find details about the character, look at:

- the things a character says and does
- the things that other characters think and say about a particular character
- the way other characters react to a particular character
- the author's description of the character

COMPARING LITERATURE WORKSHOP

Get Ready to Compare

Before you compare the main characters in the excerpt from *The Pigman & Me* and "The Goodness of Matt Kaizer," you need to analyze and understand those characters. One good way to analyze a character is to make notes about the clues you find that reveal things about the character. Then write down what each clue tells you about the character. Sometimes you'll find out that a character changes during the selection. Early in the selection a clue might tell you that a character is mean to other people. Later in the selection, though, you might find clues that tell you the character has changed—he's nice to other people.

Here's how one student filled out a character chart for a story about a boy named Antoine.

Character Chart For Antoine

Clue	What it tells me about Antoine
Antoine looked away when Elise looked at him.	Antoine was either shy or he liked Elise.
Antoine could speak to his friend Jenny but not to Elise.	He wanted Elise to be his girlfriend, but he didn't have confidence.
Antoine hated to look in the mirror.	He thought he was not attractive. He didn't have confidence.
After the contest, he spoke to Elise.	He gained confidence after the contest.

Use Your Comparison

In the excerpt from *The Pigman & Me*, the main character is named Paul. Before you start reading this selection, make a chart like the one above. The columns should have the headings "Clues" and "What it tells me about Paul." Fill in the chart as you read.

After you finish the selection, make a similar chart for the character Matt in "The Goodness of Matt Kaizer." When you've finished both charts, compare the two main characters to see which character changed the most.

COMPARING LITERATURE WORKSHOP

Before You Read *from* The Pigman & Me

Paul Zindel

Meet the Author
Paul Zindel is the author of realistic books for adults, children, and teenagers. His stories teach the lessons that he learned while growing up. Many of his characters and stories are based on his own experiences. One of his most popular novels, *The Pigman & Me,* is an autobiographical book about Zindel's life growing up in Staten Island, New York. See page R7 of the Author Files for more on Paul Zindel.

Author Search For more about Paul Zindel, go to www.glencoe.com.

Objectives (pp. 210–219)
Literature Identify literary elements: character • Make connections from text to self • Compare and contrast: literature

Vocabulary Preview

paranoid (PAIR uh noyd) *adj.* feeling like everyone is against you **(p. 211)** *Grace was so paranoid that we couldn't even joke with her anymore.*

observant (ub ZER vunt) *adj.* good at noticing details **(p. 216)** *I wasn't observant enough to notice the stain on my shirt.*

vicious (VISH us) *adj.* mean and cruel **(p. 216)** *Eldon's vicious dog kept everyone away from his house.*

decent (DEE sunt) *adj.* kind or thoughtful **(p. 219)** *Even though some kids were afraid of her, Mrs. Wren was decent to me.*

Get Ready to Read

Connect to the Reading
Have you ever felt like an outsider? Why? What did you do to make yourself feel better?

Build Background
This excerpt from *The Pigman & Me* takes place during Paul's first week at a new school. Paul lives with his sister Betty and his mother. The other kids mentioned in the selection are friends and neighbors of Paul. Paul's family is of Italian heritage.

- *Nonno* means "grandfather" in Italian.
- Nonno Frankie is an older man who is a friend of Paul's family.
- Nonno Frankie tells Paul about Sicilian combat tactics. Sicily is an island off the coast of Italy.

Set Purposes for Reading
BIG Question Read to find out if anyone in this story has an experience that brings out the best in him or her.

Set Your Own Purpose What else would you like to learn from the story to help you answer the Big Question? Write your own purpose on "The Pigman & Me" part of the Comparing Literature Workshop Foldable.

210 UNIT 2 What Brings Out the Best in You?

COMPARING LITERATURE WORKSHOP

from The Pigman & Me

by Paul Zindel

When trouble came to me, it didn't involve anybody I thought it would. It involved the nice, normal, smart boy by the name of John Quinn. Life does that to us a lot. Just when we think something awful's going to happen one way, it throws you a curve and the something awful happens another way. This happened on the first Friday, during gym period, when we were allowed to play games in the school yard. A boy by the name of Richard Cahill, who lived near an old linoleum factory, asked me if I'd like to play paddle ball with him, and I said, "Yes." Some of the kids played softball, some played warball, and there were a few other games where you could sign out equipment and do what you wanted. What I didn't know was that you were allowed to sign out the paddles for only fifteen minutes per period so more kids could get a chance to use them. I just didn't happen to know that little rule, and Richard Cahill didn't think to tell me about it. Richard was getting a drink from the water fountain when John Quinn came up to me and told me I had to give him my paddle. **1**

"No," I said, being a little **paranoid** about being the new kid and thinking everyone was going to try to take advantage of me.

Vocabulary

paranoid (PAIR uh noyd) *adj.* feeling like everyone is against you

Practice the Skills

1 Comparing Literature

Character This paragraph describes how Paul feels when he starts going to a new school. Think about what it tells you about Paul. Is he nervous or calm? Is he afraid or unafraid? In your Character Chart, write what Paul says or does that gives you a clue to his character. Now write what the clue tells you about Paul in the second column.

from *The Pigman & Me* **211**

COMPARING LITERATURE WORKSHOP

"Look, you have to give it to me," John Quinn insisted. That was when I did something beserk. I was so wound up and frightened that I didn't think, and I struck out at him with my right fist. I had forgotten I was holding the paddle, and it smacked into his face, giving him an instant black eye. John was shocked. I was shocked. Richard Cahill came running back and he was shocked. 2

"What's going on here?" Mr. Trellis, the gym teacher, growled.

"He hit me with the paddle," John moaned, holding his eye. He was red as a beet, as Little Frankfurter, Conehead, Moose, and lots of the others gathered around.

"He tried to take the paddle away from me!" I complained.

"His time was up," John said.

Mr. Trellis set me wise to the rules as he took John over to a supply locker and pulled out a first-aid kit.

"I'm sorry," I said, over and over again.

Then the bell rang, and all John Quinn whispered to me was that he was going to get even. He didn't say it like a nasty rotten kid, just more like an all-American boy who knew he'd have to regain his dignity about having to walk around school with a black eye. Before the end of school, Jennifer came running up to me in the halls and told me John Quinn had announced to everyone he was going to exact revenge on me after school on Monday. That was the note of disaster my first week at school ended on, and I was terrified because I didn't know how to fight. I had never even been in a fight. What had happened was all an accident. It really was.

When Nonno Frankie arrived on Saturday morning, he found me sitting in the apple tree alone. Mom had told him it was O.K. to walk around the whole yard now, as long as he didn't do any diggings or mutilations other than weed-pulling on her side. I was expecting him to notice right off the bat that I was white with fear, but instead he stood looking at the carvings Jennifer and I had made in the trunk of the tree. I thought he was just intensely curious about what "ESCAPE! PAUL & JENNIFER!" meant. Of course, the twins,

Practice the Skills

2 **Comparing Literature**

Character How does Paul feel after he hits Richard? Write your clue in the Clues column on your chart. In the second column, write what the clue tells you about Paul.

Apple Tree, 1912. Gustav Klimt. On deposit at the Oesterreichische Galerie, Vienna, Austria. Private Collection.

212 UNIT 2   What Brings Out the Best in You?

being such copycats, had already added their names so the full carving away of the bark now read, "ESCAPE! PAUL & JENNIFER! & NICKY & JOEY!" And the letters circled halfway around the tree.

"You're killing it," Nonno Frankie said sadly.

"What?" I jumped down to his side.

"The tree will die if you cut any more."

I thought he was kidding, because all we had done was carve off the outer pieces of bark. We hadn't carved deep into the tree, not into the heart of the tree. The tree was too important to us. It was the most crucial place to me and Jennifer, and the last thing we'd want to do was hurt it.

"The heart of a tree isn't deep inside of it. Its heart and blood are on the outside, just under the bark," Nonno Frankie explained. "That's the living part of a tree. If you carve in a circle all around the trunk, it's like slitting its throat. The water and juices and life of the tree can't move up from the roots!" I knew about the living layer of a tree, but I didn't know exposing it would kill the whole tree. I just never thought about it, or I figured trees patched themselves up.

"Now it can feed itself from only half its trunk," Nonno Frankie explained. "You must not cut any more."

"I won't," I promised. Then I felt worse than ever. Not only was I scheduled to get beat up by John Quinn after school on Monday. I was also a near tree-killer. Nonno Frankie finally looked closely at me. **3**

"Your first week at school wasn't all juicy meatballs?" he asked.

That was all he had to say, and I spilled out each and every horrifying detail. Nonno Frankie let me babble on and on. He looked as if he understood exactly how I felt and wasn't going to call me stupid or demented or a big yellow coward. When I didn't have another word left in me, I just shut up and stared down at the ground.

"Stab nail at ill Italian bats!" Nonno Frankie finally said.

"What?"

He repeated the weird sentence and asked me what was special about it. I guessed, "It reads the same backward as forward?"[1]

---

1. Words, phrases, or sentences that are spelled the same way backwards and forwards (not counting spaces and punctuation) are called **palindromes.**

Practice the Skills

3 **Comparing Literature**

Character How does Paul feel after he learns what carving the tree could do to it? What does his reaction tell you about his character? Write this clue and what it tells you in your Character Chart.

COMPARING LITERATURE WORKSHOP

"Right! Ho! Ho! Ho! See, you learn! You remember things I teach you. So today I will teach you how to fight, and you will smack this John Quinn around like floured pizza dough."

"But I can't fight."

"I'll show you Sicilian combat tactics."**2**

"Like what?"

"Everything about Italian fighting. It has to do with your mind and body. Things you have to know so you don't have to be afraid of bullies. Street smarts my father taught me. Like 'Never miss a good chance to shut up!'" **4**

VAROOOOOOOOOOM!

A plane took off over our heads. We walked out beyond the yard to the great field overlooking the airport.

Nonno Frankie suddenly let out a yell.

"Aaeeeeyaaaayeeeeh!" It was so blood-curdlingly weird, I decided to wait until he felt like explaining it.

"Aaeeeeeyaaaayeeeeeh!" he bellowed again. "It's good to be

---

2. The word **Sicilian** refers to Sicily, an island off the coast of Italy. **Sicilian combat tactics** are ways of fighting.

Practice the Skills

4 **Comparing Literature**

Character Nonno Frankie claims that his father taught him street smarts like, "Never miss a good chance to shut up!" What can you guess about Nonno Frankie's father from this advice?

Analyzing the Photo What word does the author use to help readers "hear" the sound that this plane makes?

able to yell like Tarzan!" he said. "This confuses your enemy, and you can also yell it if you have to retreat. You run away roaring and everyone thinks you at least have guts! It confuses everybody!"

"Is that all I need to know?" I asked, now more afraid than ever of facing John Quinn in front of all the kids.

"No. Tonight I will cut your hair."

"Cut it?"

"Yes. It's too long!"

"It is?"

"Ah," Nonno Frankie said, "you'd be surprised how many kids lose fights because of their hair. Alexander the Great always ordered his entire army to shave their heads. Long hair makes it easy for an enemy to grab it and cut off your head."[3]

"John Quinn just wants to beat me up!"

"You can never be too sure. This boy might have the spirit of Genghis Khan!"[4]

"Who was Genghis Khan?"

"Who? He once killed two million enemies in one hour. Some of them he killed with yo-yos." 5

"Yo-yos?"

"See, these are the things you need to know. The yo-yo was first invented as a weapon. Of course, they were as heavy as steel pipes and had long rope cords, but they were still yo-yos!"

"I didn't know that," I admitted. 6

"That's why I'm telling you. You should always ask about the rules when you go to a new place."

"I didn't think there'd be a time limit on handball paddles."

"That's why you must ask."

"I can't ask everything," I complained.

"Then you *read*. You need to know all the rules wherever you go. Did you know it's illegal to hunt camels in Arizona?"

"No."

"See? These are little facts you pick up from books and teachers and parents as you grow older. Some facts and rules

---

3. **Alexander the Great** was a Greek soldier-king who built a huge empire more than 2300 years ago that included parts of three continents.
4. **Genghis Kahn** was an Asian soldier-emperor who conquered much of Asia and built an enormous empire between the years 1185 and 1226.

Practice the Skills

5 Comparing Literature

Character How would you describe Nonno Frankie? List three interesting or unusual things that he says or does. Then explain what these "clues" tell you about Nonno Frankie.

6 Comparing Literature

Character Do you think Paul believes Nonno Frankie's statement that yo-yos were used as weapons by Genghis Khan? Does Paul's response to the statement tell you anything about him? If so, make a note of it in your Character Chart.

COMPARING LITERATURE WORKSHOP

come in handy, some don't. You've got to be **observant**. Did you know that Mickey Mouse has only *four* fingers on each hand?"

"No."

"All you have to do is look. And rules change! You've got to remember that. In ancient Rome, my ancestors worshipped a god who ruled over mildew. Nobody does anymore, but it's an interesting thing to know. You have to be connected to the past and present and future. At NBC, when they put in a new cookie-cutting machine, I had to have an open mind. I had to prepare and draw upon everything I knew so that I didn't get hurt." **7**

Nonno Frankie must have seen my mouth was open so wide a baseball could have flown into my throat and choked me to death. He stopped at the highest point in the rise of land above the airport. "I can see you want some meat and potatoes. You want to know exactly how to beat this **vicious** John Quinn."

"He's not vicious." **8**

"Make believe he is. It'll give you more energy for the fight. When he comes at you, don't underestimate the power of negative thinking! You must have only positive thoughts in your heart that you're going to cripple this monster. Stick a piece of garlic in your pocket for good luck. A woman my mother knew in Palermo did this, and she was able to fight off a dozen three-foot-tall muscular Greeks who landed and tried to eat her. You think this is not true, but half her town saw it. The Greeks all had rough skin and wore backpacks and one-piece clothes. You have to go with what you feel in your heart. One of my teachers in Sicily believed the Portuguese man-of-war jellyfish originally came from England. He felt that in his heart, and he eventually proved it. He later went on to be awarded a government grant to study tourist swooning sickness in Florence."

Visual Vocabulary
A **Portuguese man-of-war** is a jelly-like animal that lives in the ocean and has long, stinging tentacles.

Practice the Skills

7 Comparing Literature

Character Why did Nonno Frankie have to have an open mind when they put in a new machine where he worked? What did his determination to learn to use it safely say about his character?

8 Comparing Literature

Character When Nonno Frankie calls John Quinn "vicious," Paul defends John. What does this tell you about Paul's sense of fairness? Write the clue and what it tells you in your Character Chart.

Vocabulary

observant (ub ZER vunt) *adj.* good at noticing details

vicious (VISH us) *adj.* mean and cruel

216 UNIT 2   What Brings Out the Best in You?

"But how do I hold my hands to fight? How do I hold my fists?" I wanted to know.

"Like *this*!" Nonno Frankie demonstrated, taking a boxing stance with his left foot and fist forward.

"And then I just swing my right fist forward as hard as I can?"

"No. First you curse him."

"*Curse* him?"

"Yes, you curse this John Quinn. You tell him, 'May your left ear wither and fall into your right pocket!' And you tell him he looks like a fugitive from a brain gang! And tell him he has a face like a mattress! And that an espresso coffee cup would fit on his head like a sombrero. And then you just give him the big Sicilian surprise!" 9

"What?"

"You *kick* him in the shins!"

By the time Monday morning came, I was a nervous wreck. Nonno Frankie had gone back to New York the night before, but had left me a special bowl of pasta and steamed octopus that he said I should eat for breakfast so I'd have "gusto" for combat. I had asked him not to discuss my upcoming bout with my mother or sister, and Betty didn't say anything so I assumed she hadn't heard about it.

Jennifer had offered to get one of her older brothers to protect me, and, if I wanted, she was willing to tell Miss Haines so she could stop anything from happening. I told her, "No." I thought there was a chance John Quinn would have even forgotten the whole incident and wouldn't make good on his revenge threat. Nevertheless, my mind was numb with fear all day at school. In every class I went to, it seemed there were a dozen different kids coming over to me and telling me they heard John Quinn was going to beat me up after school.

At 3 P.M. sharp, the bell rang.

All the kids started to leave school.

I dawdled.[5]

Practice the Skills

9 **Comparing Literature**

Character What do you think is the purpose for the curses? What do they tell you about Nonno Frankie's personality? Write this clue and what it tells you in your Character Chart.

Analyzing the Art Does this picture remind you of the advice that Nonno Frankie gives to Paul? Explain why or why not.

---

5. To *dawdle* is to take more time than needed.

from *The Pigman & Me*

COMPARING LITERATURE WORKSHOP

I cleaned my desk and took time packing up my books. Jennifer was at my side as we left the main exit of the building. There, across the street in a field behind Ronkewitz's Candy Store, was a crowd of about 300 kids standing around like a big undulating[6] horseshoe, with John Quinn standing at the center bend glaring at me.

"You could *run*," Jennifer suggested, tossing her hair all to the left side of her face. She looked much more than pretty now. She looked loyal to the bone.

"No," I said. I just walked forward toward my fate, with the blood in my temples pounding so hard I thought I was going to pass out. Moose and Leon and Mike and Conehead and Little Frankfurter were sprinkled out in front of me, goading[7] me forward. I didn't even hear what they said. I saw only their faces distorted in ecstasy and expectation. They looked like the mob I had seen in a sixteenth-century etching where folks in London had bought tickets to watch bulldogs attacking water buffalo. **10**

John stood with his black eye, and his fists up.

I stopped a few feet from him and put my fists up. A lot of kids in the crowd started to shout, "Kill him, Johnny!" but I may have imagined that part.

John came closer. He started to dance on his feet like all father-trained fighters do. I danced, too, as best I could. The crowd began to scream for blood. Jennifer kept shouting, "Hey, there's no need to fight! You don't have to fight, guys!"

But John came in for the kill. He was close enough now so any punch he threw could hit me. All I thought of was Nonno Frankie, but I couldn't remember half of what he told me and I didn't think any of it would work anyway.

"Aaeeeeeyaaaayeeeeeh!" I suddenly screamed at John. He stopped in his tracks and the crowd froze in amazed silence. Instantly, I brought back my right foot, and shot it forward to kick John in his left shin. The crowd was shocked, and booed me with mass condemnation for my Sicilian fighting

Borders & Boundaries, 2002. Diana Ong. Computer graphics.

Practice the Skills

10 **Comparing Literature**

Character Why do you think Paul says "No" when Jennifer suggests that he run? Could he have more than one reason? Does this tell you anything about his character? If so, write your clue and what it tells you in your Character Chart.

---

6. **Undulating** means "moving back and forth or up and down like a wave."
7. If you **goad** someone, you push him or her into doing something they don't want to do.

218 UNIT 2 What Brings Out the Best in You?

technique. I missed John's shin, and kicked vainly again. He threw a punch at me. It barely touched me, but I was so busy kicking, I tripped myself and fell down. The crowd cheered. I realized everyone including John thought his punch had floored me. I decided to go along with it. I groveled in the dirt for a few moments, and then stood up slowly holding my head as though I'd received a death blow. John put his fists down. He was satisfied justice had been done and his black eye had been avenged. He turned to leave, but Moose wasn't happy. **11**

"Hey, ya didn't punch him enough," Moose complained to John.

"It's over," John said, like the **decent** kid he was.

"No, it's not," Moose yelled, and the crowd began to call for more blood. Now it was Moose coming toward me, and I figured I was dead meat. He came closer and closer. Jennifer shouted for him to stop and threatened to pull his eyeballs out, but he kept coming. And that was when something amazing happened. I was aware of a figure taller than me, running, charging. The figure had long blond hair, and it struck Moose from behind. I could see it was a girl and she had her hands right around Moose's neck, choking him. When she let him go, she threw him about ten feet, accidentally tearing off a religious medal from around his neck. Everyone stopped dead in their tracks, and I could see my savior was my sister. **12**

"If any of you tries to hurt my brother again, I'll rip your guts out," she announced.

Moose was not happy. Conehead and Little Frankfurter were not happy. But the crowd broke up fast and everyone headed home. I guess that was the first day everybody learned that if nothing else, the Zindel kids stick together. As for Nonno Frankie's Sicilian fighting technique, I came to realize he was ahead of his time. In fact, these days it's called karate.[8] **13** ○

---

8. **Karate** is a form of self-defense that uses kicks and punches.

Vocabulary

decent (DEE sunt) *adj.* kind or thoughtful

Practice the Skills

11 Comparing Literature

Character Paul acted like he was hurt even though he wasn't. Why did he do that? What do you think was more important to him than winning the fight? Does this add anything to your view of Paul's character? If so, put it in your Character Chart.

12 Comparing Literature

Character This paragraph describes how Paul's sister helps him. What does the description tell you about Paul's relationship with his sister? Make a note of this relationship in your Character Chart.

13 BIG Question

In this story, did anything bring out the best in Paul? Explain. Did the fight bring out the best in anyone else? Explain. Write your answer on "The Pigman & Me" part of the Comparing Literature Workshop Foldable. Your answer will help you complete the Unit Challenge later.

COMPARING LITERATURE WORKSHOP

Before You Read : *The Goodness of* Matt Kaizer

Meet the Author
When Avi was a child in Brooklyn, New York, he had a lot of trouble with writing. He misspelled words and reversed letters. He even failed many of his courses in high school. But he did not give up writing. Today Avi is one of the most popular writers of books for young people. See page R1 of the Author Files for more on Avi.

Author Search For more about Avi, go to www.glencoe.com.

Vocabulary Preview

taunt (tawnt) *v.* to try to anger someone by teasing him or her **(p. 222)** *Don't taunt me about my haircut.*

retreat (rih TREET) *v.* to move backward, away from a situation **(p. 225)** *If it's too dangerous, we'll retreat.*

gloomy (GLOO mee) *adj.* dull, dark, and depressing **(p. 226)** *The closed curtains made the room look really gloomy.*

reputation (rep yuh TAY shun) *n.* character as judged by other people **(p. 230)** *Matt was concerned about his reputation.*

English Language Coach

Synonyms and Antonyms Good writers use a lot of different words in their writing. To practice learning the synonyms and antonyms of a word, create a word web like the one below that has *goodness* in the inner circle. Fill in the synonyms and antonyms in the outer circles.

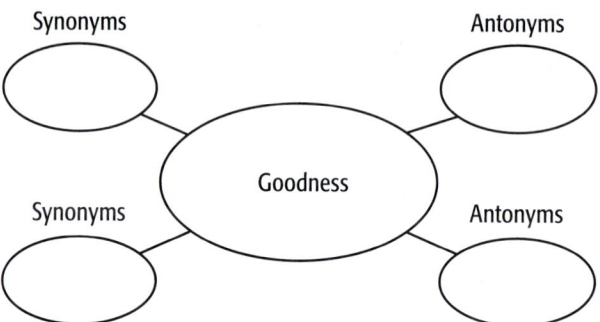

Get Ready to Read

Connect to the Reading
How would you feel if you tried to do something that was bad or cruel, but other people thought that what you did was good or kind?

Set Purposes for Reading
BIG Question Read to find out how Mr. Bataky brings out the best in Matt and how Matt brings out the best in Mr. Bataky.

Set Your Own Purpose What else would you like to learn from the story to help you answer the Big Question? Write your own purpose on "The Goodness of Matt Kaizer" part of the Comparing Literature Workshop Foldable.

Objectives (pp. 220–233)
Literature Identify literary elements: character • Make connections from text to self • Compare and contrast: literature
Vocabulary Identify synonyms and antonyms

220 UNIT 2 What Brings Out the Best in You?

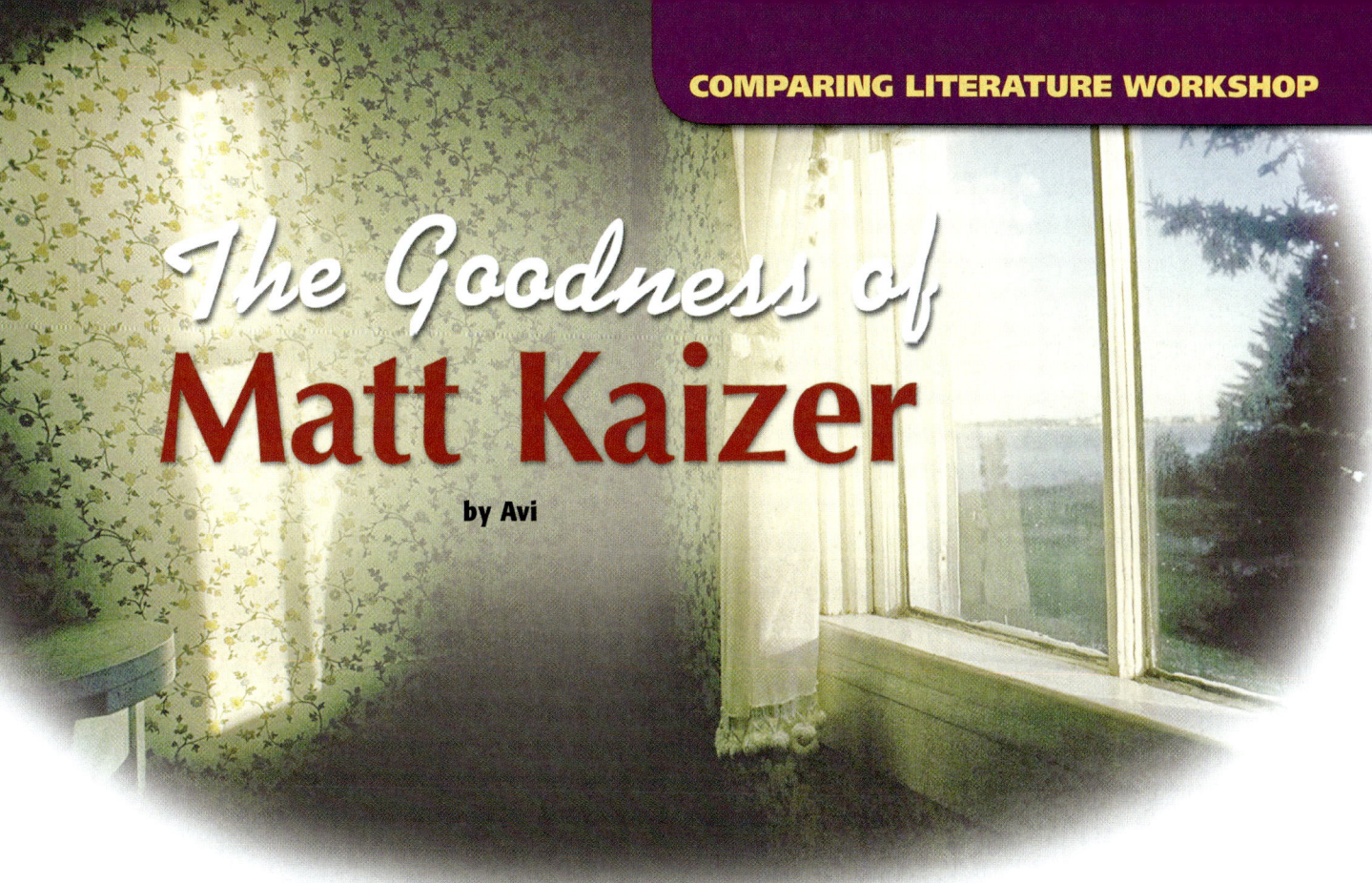

The Goodness of Matt Kaizer

by Avi

People are always saying, "Nothing's worse than when a kid goes bad." Well, let me tell you, going good isn't all that great either. Tell you what I mean.

Back in sixth grade there was a bunch of us who liked nothing better than doing bad stuff. I don't know why. We just liked doing it. And the baddest of the bad was Matt Kaizer. 1

Matt was a tall, thin kid with long, light blond hair that reached his shoulders. He was twelve years old—like I was. His eyes were pale blue and his skin was a vanilla cream that never—no matter the season—seemed to darken, except with dirt. What with the way he looked—so pale and all—plus the fact that he was into wearing extra large blank white T-shirts that reached his knees, we called him "Spirit."

Now, there are two important things you need to know about Matt Kaizer. The first was that as far as he was concerned there was nothing good about him at all. Nothing. The second thing was that his father was a minister.

Our gang—I'm Marley, and then there was Chuck, Todd, and Nick—loved the fact that Matt was so bad and his father a minister. You know, we were always daring him to do bad

Practice the Skills

1 **Comparing Literature**

Character Create a Character Chart for Matt like the one you made for Paul. As you read, fill in clues to Matt's character. Then write a note for each clue that explains what you learned about Matt from that clue.

things. "Hey, minister's kid!" we'd taunt. "Dare you to . . ." and we'd challenge him to do something, you know, really gross. Thing is, we could always count on Matt—who wanted to show he wasn't good—to take a dare.

For instance: Say there was some dead animal out on the road. We'd all run to Matt and say, "Dare you to pick it up."

Matt would look at it—up close and personal—or more than likely poke it with a stick, then pick it up and fling it at one of us.

Disgusting stories? Someone would tell one and then say, "Dare you to tell it to Mary Beth Bataky"—the class slug—and Matt would tell it to her—better than anyone else, too.

TV and movies? The more blood and gore there was, the more Matt ate it up—if you know what I mean. MTV, cop shows, all that bad stuff, nothing was too gross for him.

And it didn't take just dares to get Matt going. No, Matt would do stuff on his own. If anyone blew a toot—even in class—he would bellow, "Who cut the cheese?" He could belch whenever he wanted to, and did, a lot. Spitballs, booger flicking, wedgie yanking, it was all wicked fun for Matt. No way was he going to be good! Not in front of us. 2

Now, his father, the minister, "Rev. Kaizer" we called him, wasn't bad. In fact just the opposite. The guy was easygoing, always dressed decently, and as far as I knew, never raised his voice or acted any way than what he was, a nice man, a good man. Sure, he talked a little funny, like he was reading from a book, but that was all.

Did Matt and his father get along? In a way. For example, once I was with Matt after he did something bad—I think he blew his nose on someone's lunch. Rev. Kaizer had learned about it. Instead of getting mad he just gazed at Matt, shook his head, and said, "Matt, I do believe there's goodness in everyone. That goes for you too. Someday you'll find your own goodness. And when you do you'll be free."

Practice the Skills

2 Comparing Literature

Character These paragraphs give you several clues about Matt's character. For example, they tell you how Matt acted around other people, and how Matt wanted to act. In your Character Chart, write at least two clues you found to Matt's character in these paragraphs. Then write notes about what you learned from these clues.

Analyzing the Photo In what ways does the boy in this photo fit the description of Matt Kaizer?

Vocabulary

taunt (tawnt) v. to try to anger someone by teasing him or her

"I'm not good," Matt insisted.

"Well, I think you are," his father said, patiently.

Matt grinned. "Long as my friends dare me to do bad things, I'll do 'em."

"Never refuse a dare?" his father asked, sadly.

"Never," Matt said with pride.

Rev. Kaizer sighed, pressed his hands together, and looked toward heaven.

So there we were, a bunch of us who knew we were bad and that it was doing bad things that held us together. And the baddest of the bad, like I said, was Matt—the Spirit—Kaizer. But then . . . oh, man, I'll tell you what happened.

One day after school we were hanging out in the playground. The five of us were just sitting around telling disgusting stories, when suddenly Chuck said, "Hey, hear about Mary Beth Bataky?"

"What about her?" Matt asked.

"Her old man's dying."

Right away Matt was interested. "Really?"

"It's true, man," Chuck insisted. "He's just about had it."

"How come?" I asked.

"Don't know," said Chuck. "He's sick. So sick they sent him home from the hospital. That's why Mary Beth is out. She's waiting for him to die."

"Cool," said Matt. 3

Now, Mary Beth was one small straw of a sad slug. She had this bitsy face with pale eyes and two gray lines for lips all framed in a pair of frizzy braids. Her arms were thin and always crossed over her chest, which was usually bundled in a brown sweater. The only bits of color on her were her fingernails, which, though chewed, were spotted with bright red nail polish—chipped.

So when we heard what was going on with Mary Beth and her father, we guys eyed one another, almost knowing what was going to happen next. But, I admit, it was me who said, "Hey, Spirit, I dare you to go and see him."

Matt pushed the blond hair out of his face and looked at us with those pale blue, cool-as-ice eyes of his.

"Or maybe," Todd said, "you're too chicken, being as you're a minister's kid and all."

Practice the Skills

3 **Comparing Literature**

Character Think about how Matt reacts when he learns that the father of one of the kids in his class is dying. Write down how he reacts in the clues column of your Character Chart. Is Matt just being cool? Or is he being cruel? Write down what this clue tells you in your chart.

COMPARING LITERATURE WORKSHOP

That did it. Course it did. No way Matt could resist a dare. He got up, casual like. "I'll do it," he said. "Who's coming with me?" **4**

To my disgust the other guys backed off. But I accepted. Well, actually, I really didn't think he'd do it.

But then, soon as we started off, I began to feel a little nervous. "Matt," I warned. "I think Mary Beth is very religious."

"Don't worry. I know about all that stuff."

"Yeah, but what would your father say?"

"I don't care," he bragged. "Anyway, I'm not going to do anything except look. It'll be neat. Like a horror movie. Maybe I can even touch the guy. A dying body is supposed to be colder than ice."

That was Matt. Always taking up the dare and going you one worse.

The more he talked the sorrier I was we had dared him to go. Made me really uncomfortable. Which I think he noticed, because he said, "What's the matter, Marley? You scared or something?" **5**

"Just seems . . ."

"I know," he taunted, "you're too good!" He belched loudly to make his point that he wasn't. "See you later, dude." He started off.

I ran after him. "Do you know where she lives?"

"Follow me."

"They might not let you see him," I warned.

He pulled out some coins. "I'm going to buy some flowers and bring them to him. That's what my mother did when my aunt was sick." He stuffed his mouth full of bubble gum and began blowing and popping.

Mary Beth's house was a wooden three-decker[1] with a front porch. Next to the front door were three bell buttons with plastic name labels. The Batakys lived on the first floor.

By the time Matt and I got there he had two wilted carnations in his hand. One was dyed blue, the other green. The flower store guy had sold them for ten cents each.

"You know," I said in a whisper, as we stood before the door, "her father might already be dead."

Practice the Skills

4 **Comparing Literature**

Character Think about why people take dares. Is it for the adventure? Are they proving something to themselves or to others? In your chart, write that Matt took the dare to see Mary Beth's father. Then write down what this tells you about Matt.

5 **Comparing Literature**

Character How does the narrator, Marley, feel now that he has to go with Matt to see Mary Beth's father? Does this tell you anything about the character of the narrator? Why do you think he agrees to go?

---

1. A **three-decker** house is a house with three floors, or levels.

COMPARING LITERATURE WORKSHOP

"Cool," Matt replied, blowing another bubble, while cleaning out an ear with a pinky and inspecting the earwax carefully before smearing it on his shirt. "Did you know your fingernails still grow when you're dead? Same for your hair. I mean, how many really dead people can you get to see?" he said and rang the Bataky's bell.

From far off inside there was a buzzing sound.

I was trying to get the nerve to leave when the door opened a crack. Mary Beth—pale eyes rimmed with red—peeked out. There were tears on her cheeks and her lips were crusty. Her small hands—with their spots of red fingernail polish—were trembling.

"Oh, hi," she said, her voice small and tense.

I felt tight with embarrassment.

Matt spoke out loudly. "Hi, Mary Beth. We heard your old man was dying."

"Yes, he is," Mary Beth murmured. With one hand on the doorknob it was pretty clear she wanted to **retreat** as fast as possible. "He's delirious."[2]

"Delirious?" Matt said. "What's that?"

"Sort of . . . crazy."

"Oh . . . wow, sweet!" he said, giving me a nudge of appreciation. Then he held up the blue and green carnations, popped his gum, and said, "I wanted to bring him these." **6**

Mary Beth stared at the flowers, but didn't move to take them. All she said was, "My mother's at St. Mary's, praying."

Now I really wanted to get out of there. But Matt said, "How about if I gave these to your father?" He held up the flowers again. "Personally."

"My mother said he may die any moment," Mary Beth informed us.

"I know," Matt said. "So I'd really like to see him before he does."

Mary Beth gazed at him. "He's so sick," she said, "he's not up to visiting."

"Yeah," Matt pressed, "but, you see, the whole class elected me to come and bring these flowers."

---

2. A *delirious* person is confused, has problems speaking, and sees things that aren't there.

Vocabulary

retreat (rih TREET) *v.* to move backward, away from a situation

Practice the Skills

6 **Comparing Literature**

Character When Matt learns that Mary Beth's father is delirious, he says "Oh. . . wow, sweet!" Do you feel this is the right thing to say to Mary Beth? In your Character Chart, write down what Matt says and what this tells you about him.

The Goodness of Matt Kaizer

COMPARING LITERATURE WORKSHOP

Analyzing the Photo Based on what you know about Mary Beth, does the girl in this photo look like her? Describe the expression on her face.

Practice the Skills

His lie worked. "Oh," Mary Beth murmured, and she pulled the door open. "Well, I suppose . . ." 7

We stepped into a small entrance way. A low-watt bulb dangled over our heads from a wire. Shoes, boots, and broken umbrellas lay in a plastic milk crate.

Mary Beth shut the outside door then pushed open an inner one that led to her apartment. It was **gloomy** and stank of medicine.

Matt bopped me on the arm. "Who cut the cheese!" he said with a grin. I looked around at him. He popped another bubble.

"Down this way," Mary Beth whispered.

We walked down a long hallway. Two pictures were on the walls. They were painted on black velvet. One was a scene of a mountain with snow on it and the sun shining on a stag with antlers. The second picture was of a little girl praying by her bed. Fuzzy gold light streamed in on her from a window.

At the end of the hall was a closed door. Mary Beth halted. "He's in here," she whispered. "He's really sick," she warned

7 Comparing Literature

Character Matt makes up a lie about why he came to see Mary Beth's father. Why doesn't he just tell her the truth? In your chart, write down this clue. Then write down what this tells you about Matt.

Vocabulary

gloomy (GLOO mee) *adj.* dull, dark, and depressing

again. "And he doesn't notice anyone. You really sure you want to see him?"

"You bet," Matt said with enthusiasm. 8

"I mean, he won't say hello or anything," Mary Beth said in her low voice. "He just lies there with his eyes open. I don't even know if he sees anything."

"Does he have running sores?" Matt asked.

I almost gagged.

"Running *what*?" Mary Beth asked.

"You know, wounds."

"It's his liver," Mary Beth explained sadly, while turning the door handle and opening the door. "The doctor said it was all his bad life and drinking."

Dark as the hall had been, her father's room was darker. The air was heavy and really stank. A large bed took up most of the space. On one side of the bed was a small chest of drawers. On top of the chest was a lit candle and a glass of water into which a pair of false teeth had been dropped. On the other side of the bed was a wooden chair. Another burning candle was on that.

On the bed—beneath a brown blanket—lay Mr. Bataky. He was stretched out on his back perfectly straight, like a log. His head and narrow chest were propped up on a pile of four pillows with pictures of flowers on them. At the base of the bed his toes poked up from under the blanket. He was clothed in pajamas dotted with different colored hearts. His hands—looking like a bunch of knuckles—were linked over his chest. His poorly shaven face—yellow in color—was thin. With his cheeks sunken, his nose seemed enormous. His thin hair was uncombed. His breathing was drawn out, almost whistling, and collapsed into throat gargles—as if he were choking.

Worst of all, his eyes were open but he was just staring up, like he was waiting for something to happen in heaven.

Mary Beth stepped to one side of the bed. Matt stood at the foot, with me peering over his shoulder. We stared at the dying man. He really looked bad. Awful.

"I don't think he'll live long," Mary Beth murmured, her sad voice breaking, her tears dripping.

Matt lifted the blue and green carnations. "Mr. Bataky," he shouted, "I brought you some flowers to cheer you up." 9

Practice the Skills

8 English Language Coach

Synonyms and Antonyms
What does the word *enthusiasm* mean in this sentence? Name a word that means about the same as *enthusiasm*. How would the tone of Matt's voice change if he said "You bet" with the opposite of enthusiasm?

9 Comparing Literature

Character Why does Matt speak to Mr. Bataky? Is it just to keep up the lie that he told to Mary Beth? Does Matt's comment tell you anything about how he feels at this point? If so, write down this clue and what it means in your Character Chart.

The Goodness of Matt Kaizer **227**

COMPARING LITERATURE WORKSHOP

"His hearing isn't good," Mary Beth said apologetically.

Matt looked about for a place to put the flowers, saw the glass with the teeth near Mr. Bataky's head, and moved to put them into the water. In the flickering candlelight, Matt's pale skin, his long blond hair, seemed to glow.

Now, just as Matt came up to the head of the bed, Mr. Bataky's eyes shifted. They seemed to fasten on Matt. The old man gave a start, made a convulsive[3] twitch as his eyes positively bulged. Matt, caught in the look, froze.

"It's . . . it's . . . an *angel* . . ." Mr. Bataky said in a low, rasping[4] voice. "An angel . . . from heaven has come to save me."

Matt lifted his hand—the one that held the carnations—and tried to place them in the glass of water. Before he could, Mr. Bataky made an unexpected jerk with one of his knobby hands and took hold of Matt's arm. Matt was so surprised he dropped the flowers.

"Father!" Mary Beth cried.

"Thank . . . you . . . for coming, Angel," Mr. Bataky rasped.

"No . . . really," Matt stammered, "I'm not—"

"Yes, you're an angel," Mr. Bataky whispered. His eyes—full of tears—were hot with joy.

Matt turned red. "No, I'm not . . ."

"Please," Mr. Bataky cried out with amazing energy. "I don't want to die bad." Tears gushed down his hollow cheeks. "You got to help me. Talk to me. Bless me."

Matt, speechless for once, gawked at the man.

With considerable effort he managed to pry Mr. Bataky's fingers from his arm. Soon as he did he bolted from the room.

"Don't abandon me!" Mr. Bataky begged, somehow managing to lift himself up and extend his arms toward the doorway. "Don't!"

Frightened, I hurried out after Matt.

My buddy was waiting outside, breathing hard. His normally pale face was paler than ever. As we walked away he didn't say anything. 🔟

Now, according to Matt—he told us all this later—what happened was that night Rev. Kaizer called him into his study.

---

3. When someone is **convulsive**, the person cannot control his or her muscle movements.
4. A **rasping** voice sounds like someone has almost lost his or her voice.

Practice the Skills

🔟 **Comparing Literature**

Character Why is Matt quiet as he walks away from the Batakys' house? Write this clue in your character chart, then try to figure out what it tells you about Matt.

228 UNIT 2 What Brings Out the Best in You?

"Matt, please sit down."

Matt, thinking he was going to get a lecture about visiting Mary Beth's house, sat.

His father said, "Matt, I think it's quite wonderful what you've done, going to the home of your classmate's dying father to comfort him."

"What do you mean?" Matt asked.

Rev. Kaizer smiled sweetly. "A woman by the name of Mrs. Bataky called me. She said her husband was very ill. Dying. She said you—I gather you go to school with her daughter—came to visit him today. Apparently her husband thought you were an . . . angel. It's the first real sign of life her poor husband has shown in three days. And now, Matt, he's quite desperate to see the angel—you—again."

"It's not true," Matt rapped out.

"Now, Matt," his father said, "I found the woman's story difficult to believe, too. 'Madam,' I said to her, 'are you quite certain you're talking about *my* son? And are you truly saying your husband really thought he was . . . an angel?'

"And she said, 'Rev. Kaizer—you being a minister I can say it—my husband led a bad, sinful life. But there's something about your son that's making him want to talk about it. Sort of like a confession.[5] Know what I'm saying? I mean, it would do him a lot of good. What I'm asking is, could you get your son to come again? I'm really scared my husband will get worse if he doesn't.'

"Matt," said Rev. Kaizer, "I'm proud of you. I think it would be a fine thing if you visited him again."

"I'm not an angel," Matt replied in a sulky[6] voice.

Analyzing the Art Which two characters in the story might this picture show? How do you know?

---

5. In a ***confession***, a person tells the things he or she has done wrong and asks for forgiveness.
6. A ***sulky*** voice sounds moody and unhappy.

The Goodness of Matt Kaizer 229

COMPARING LITERATURE WORKSHOP

"I never said you were an angel," his father said. "But as I've told you many times, there is goodness inside you as there is in everyone. And now you are in the fortunate position of being able to help this sinful man."

"I don't want to."

"Son, here is a sick man who needs to unburden himself of the unhappy things he's done. I know your **reputation**. Are you fearful of hearing what Mr. Bataky has to say for himself?"

"I don't want to."

Rev. Kaizer sat back in his chair, folded his hands over his stomach, smiled gently, and said, "I dare you to go back and listen to Mr. Bataky. I dare you to do goodness."

Alarmed, Matt looked up. "But . . ."

"Or are you, being a minister's son, afraid to?"

Matt shifted uncomfortably in his seat and tried to avoid his father's steady gaze.

Rev. Kaizer offered up a faint smile. "Matt, I thought you never refused a dare."

Matt squirmed. Then he said, "I'll go." 11

Anyway, that's the way Matt explained it all. And as he said to me sadly, "What choice did I have? He dared me."

We all saw then that Matt was in a bad place.

So the next day when Matt went to visit Mr. Bataky, the bunch of us—me, Chuck, Todd, and Nick—tagged along. We all wanted to see what Matt would do. We figured it *had* to be gross.

Mary Beth opened the door. I think she was surprised to see all of us. But she looked at Matt with hope. "Thank you for coming," she said in her tissue paper voice. "He's waiting for you."

Matt gave us an imploring⁷ look. There was nothing we could do. He disappeared inside. We waited outside.

Half an hour later, when he emerged, there was a ton of worry in his eyes. We waited him out, hoping he'd say something ghastly. Didn't say a word.

Carnations and Clematis in a Crystal Vase, 1882. Edouard Manet. Oil on canvas, 56 x 35.5 cm. Musee d'Orsay, Paris.

Practice the Skills

11 Comparing Literature

Character Matt doesn't want to go back to see Mr. Bataky. But when his father dares him to go, he agrees to return. What does this tell you about Matt? In your Character Chart, write this clue and what it means.

---

7. If you give an *imploring* look, you are begging for something.

Vocabulary

reputation (rep yuh TAY shun) *n.* character as judged by other people

230 UNIT 2 What Brings Out the Best in You?

COMPARING LITERATURE WORKSHOP

Two blocks from Mary Beth's house I couldn't hold back. "Okay, Matt," I said. "What's happening?"

Matt stopped walking. "He really thinks I'm a good angel." **12**

"How come?" Nick asked.

"I don't know." There was puzzlement in Matt's voice. "He thinks I'm there to give him a second chance at living."

"I don't get it," Todd said.

Matt said, "He thinks, you know, if he tells me all his bad stuff, he'll get better."

We walked on in silence. Then I said—easy like, "He tell you anything, you know . . . really bad?"

Matt nodded.

"Oooo, that's so cool," Nick crowed, figuring Matt would—as he always did—pass it on. "Like what?"

Instead of answering, Matt remained silent. Finally, he said, "Not good."

"Come on!" we cried. "Tell us!"

"He dared me to forgive him. To give him a second chance."

"Forgive him for what?" I asked.

"All the stuff he's done."

"Like what?"

"He said he was talking to me . . . in confidence."

"What's that mean?"

"Angels can't tell secrets." **13**

"You going to believe that?" Todd asked after a bit of silence.

Matt stopped walking again. "But . . . what," he stammered. "What . . . if it's true?"

"What if *what's* true?" I asked.

"What if I'm really good inside?"

"No way," we all assured him.

"But he thinks so," Matt said with real trouble in his voice. "And my father is always saying that too."

"Do *you* think so?" Chuck asked.

Matt got a flushed look in his eyes. Then he said, "If it is true, it'll be the grossest thing ever."

"Hey, maybe it's just a phase,"[8] I suggested, hopefully. "You know, something you'll grow out of."

---

8. Everyone goes through different **phases**, or stages, in life.

Practice the Skills

12 Comparing Literature

Character Matt is worried because Mr. Bataky thinks he is a "good angel." Why do you think this worries Matt? Doesn't it sound like a joke that Matt would usually enjoy? Write this clue and what it tells you about Matt in your Character Chart.

13 Comparing Literature

Character At the beginning of the story, Matt likes to say and do gross things. But after Mr. Bataky thinks that Matt is an angel, Matt won't tell the boys any of the bad things Mr. Bataky has done. Why not? Write this clue and what you think it means in your Character Chart.

The Goodness of Matt Kaizer

COMPARING LITERATURE WORKSHOP

Matt gave a shake to his head that suggested he was really seriously confused. **14**

Anyway, every afternoon that week, Matt went to see Mr. Bataky. Each time we went with him. For support. We felt we owed him that, though really, we were hoping we'd get to hear some of the bad stuff. But I think we were getting more and more upset, too. See, Matt was changing. Each time he came out of the sick man's room, he looked more and more haggard.**9** And silent.

"What did he say this time?" someone would finally ask.

"Really bad," he'd say.

"Worse than before?"

"Much worse."

We'd go on for a bit, not saying anything. Then the pleading would erupt. "Come on! Tell us! What'd he say?"

"Can't."

"Why?"

"I told you: He thinks I'm an angel," Matt said and visibly shuddered. "Angels can't tell secrets."

As the week progressed, Matt began to look different from before. He wasn't so grubby. His clothes weren't torn. Things went so fast that by Friday morning, when he came to school, he was actually wearing a tie! Even his hair was cut short and combed. It was awful.

"What's the matter with Matt?" we kept asking one another.

"I think he's beginning to think he really is an angel," was the only explanation I could give.

Finally, on Friday afternoon, when Matt came out of Mary Beth's house, he sat on the front steps, utterly beat. By that time he was dressed all in white: white shirt, pale tie, white pants, and even white sneakers. Not one smudge on him. I'm telling you, it was eerie. Nothing missing but wings.

"What's up?" I asked.

"The doctor told Mr. Bataky he's better."

"You cured him!" cried Nick. "Cool! That mean you don't have to visit him again?"

"Right." But Matt just sat there looking as sad as Mary Beth ever did.

14 Comparing Literature

Character At the beginning of the story, Matt believed he was bad. Now what does he believe? Write this clue and what it means in your Character Chart.

---

9. A thin, tired, and worried person looks **haggard**.

"What's the matter?" I asked.

"I've been sitting and listening to that guy talk and talk about all the things he's done. I mean, I used to think I was bad. But, you know what?"

"What?"

"I'm not bad. No way. Not compared to him. I even tried to tell him of some of the things I've done."

"What did he say?"

"He laughed. Said I was only a young angel. Which was the reason I didn't have wings."

Matt stared down at the ground for a long time. We waited patiently. Finally he looked up. There were tears trickling down his pale face.

"I have to face it," he said, turning to look at us, his pals, with real grief[10] in his eyes. "The more I heard that stuff Mr. Bataky did, the more I knew that deep down, inside, I'm just a good kid. I mean, what am I going to do? Don't you see, I'm just like my father said. I'm *good*."

You can't believe how miserable he looked. All we could do was sit there and pity him. I mean, just to look at him we knew there weren't going to be any more wicked grins, belches, leers,[11] sly winks, wedgies, or flying boogers.

Life went on, but with Matt going angel on us, our gang couldn't hold together. We were finished. Busted.

So I'm here to tell you, when a guy turns good, hey, it's rough. 15 ○

The Sick Spaniard. Edvard Munch (1863–1944). National Gallery, Oslo, Norway.

Practice the Skills

15 **BIG Question**

What brings out the goodness in Matt Kaizer? What makes Mr. Bataky get better? Write your answers on the "Goodness of Matt Kaizer" part of the Comparing Literature Workshop Foldable. Your answer will help you answer the Unit Challenge later.

---

10. ***Grief*** is deep sadness.
11. When you give a ***leer,*** you give someone a nasty look as if you know something bad.

COMPARING LITERATURE WORKSHOP

After You Read

from **The Pigman & Me** & **The Goodness of Matt Kaizer**

Vocabulary Check

For items 1 to 8, copy the definitions listed below into your Learner's Notebook. Then write the word next to the correct definition.

from The Pigman & Me

paranoid   observant   vicious   decent

1. kind or thoughtful: ___
2. feeling like everyone is against you: ___
3. mean and cruel: ___
4. good at noticing things: ___

The Goodness of Matt Kaizer

taunt   retreat   gloomy   reputation

5. to move backward, away from a situation: ___
6. your character as judged by other people: ___
7. to try to anger someone by teasing him or her: ___
8. dull, dark, and depressing: ___

Reading/Critical Thinking

On a separate sheet of paper, answer the following questions.

from The Pigman & Me

9. **Infer** What important life lessons do you think Nonno Frankie taught Paul?

   Tip **Author and Me** You will find clues in the text, but you must also use the information in your head.

10. **Infer** What do you think Paul learned from the fight with John Quinn? Do you think he will act differently after the fight? Why or why not?

Objectives (pp. 234–235)
Literature Identify literary elements: character • Compare and contrast: literature
Writing Write a response to literature: character, diagram

234 UNIT 2   What Brings Out the Best in You?

COMPARING LITERATURE WORKSHOP

> **TIP** **Author and Me** You will find clues in the text, but you must also use the information in your head.

The Goodness of Matt Kaizer

11. Analyze Why is Matt's appearance important to the plot of this story?

> **TIP** **Author and Me** You will find clues in the text, but you must also use the information in your head.

12. Describe How does Matt change from the beginning of the story to the end?

> **TIP** **Author and Me** You will find clues in the text, but you must also use the information in your head.

Writing: Compare the Literature

Use Your Notes

13. Follow these steps to use your Character Charts to compare the main characters in these two selections.

Step 1: Review the Character Charts you completed for these two selections.

Step 2: In the two charts, circle ways in which Paul and Matt were completely different at the beginnings of both stories. You'll need to look carefully. You may not have used the exact same words to describe Paul and Matt.

Step 3: Now find ways in which Paul and Matt were similar by the end of the story. Put a star beside those similarities.

Step 4: In your Learner's Notebook, draw a diagram like the one at the top of the next column to show how Paul and Matt were similar and different at the beginning of the story. In the overlapping center section of the circles, list the traits that Paul and Matt have in common **at the beginning of the story.** On the left side list only traits that describe Paul. On the right side list only traits that describe Matt.

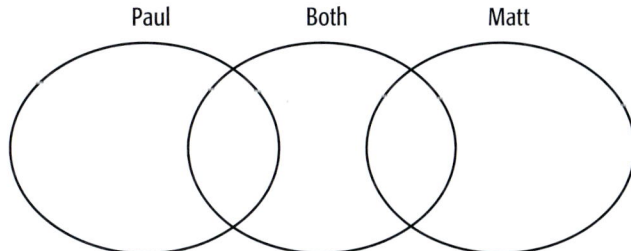

Beginning

Paul — Both — Matt

Step 5: Now draw another diagram to show how Paul and Matt were similar and different **at the end of the story.** Title this diagram **Ending.** In the center circle list the traits that Paul and Matt have in common at the end of the stories. On the left side list only traits that describe Paul. On the right side list only traits that describe Matt.

Step 6: Examine your two diagrams. They show how the boys changed during the course of the stories, and they show how the boys were similar and different at the beginnings and ends of the stories.

Get It on Paper

Answer the following questions on a separate sheet of paper.

14. How were Paul and Matt different at the beginnings of the two stories? Write details from your Character Charts to support your statements.

15. How were Paul and Matt similar at the end of the two stories? Write details from your Character Charts to support your statements.

16. At the end of "The Goodness of Matt Kaizer," how has Matt changed? Give at least one detail that shows what he was like at the beginning of the story and one detail that shows what he was like at the end of the story.

17. At the end of the selection from *The Pigman & Me*, how has Paul changed? Support your statement with two details from the selection. If you don't think he has changed, give two details that show that he is the same.

BIG Question

18. Choose either Paul or Matt and explain why the character became the best that he could be.

Comparing Literature Workshop **235**

UNIT 2 WRAP-UP

Answering the BIG Question: What Brings Out the Best in You?

You have just read about people who answered the Big Question: What brings out the best in you? Now use what you've learned to complete the Unit Challenge.

The Unit Challenge

Choose Activity A or Activity B and follow the directions for that activity.

A. Group Activity: Magazine Article

Look at the notes on your Foldables about what brings out the best in people. Think about what brings out the best in you. It could be music, sports, writing, helping a friend, or even reading. You'll use what you think has brought out your best to advise others.

- You and a group of friends will write an article for a teen magazine called "Bringing Out the Best in Yourself."

1. **Discuss the Assignment** As a group think about and discuss these questions:
   - What is something in which you do your best?
   - What makes you do your best?
   - What advice would you give to someone who wanted to be the best at what you like to do?

   Write down your answers. Then have each group member decide on something that they think brings out their best.

2. **Create Your Article** According to what each group member decides brings out his or her best, each group member will write an article telling other sixth graders how they can also bring out their best in that area.

3. **Write Your Article** As you begin writing your article, these tips may be helpful.
   - Look over the answers to the questions that you wrote.
   - Use key words and phrases from the answers to the questions that you wrote to begin your article.
   - Work together to use the words and phrases in a paragraph that explains what you did to bring out the best in what you like to do.
   - Review the paragraph to make sure it makes sense.

4. **Present Your Article**
   - Make sure the article is clear and has no mistakes, such as misspelled words.
   - With your teacher and the other groups in your class, use the finished articles to create an issue of the "Bringing Out the Best in Yourself" magazine.

B. Solo Activity: Your Interview

You see and hear people being interviewed on the television and radio all the time: now it's your turn to be interviewed.

1. **Think about the Assignment** You are being interviewed to find out what brings out the best in you. Create a web diagram like the one below and include those things that you like to do that you think bring out the best in you.

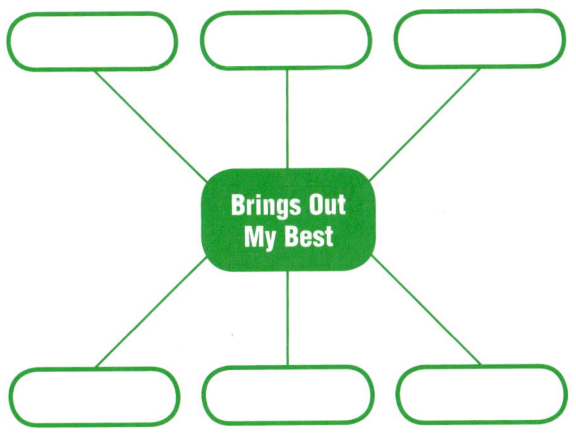

2. **Write Interview Questions** When you decide what brings out your best, write three or four questions that you think an interviewer would ask about what brings out your best. Use the notes on your Foldables.

If you want, make a list like the one below.

INTERVIEW QUESTIONS
1. What qualities do people need to bring out their best?

2. Who has helped bring out the best in you? How did they help?

3. How does what you like to do bring out your best?

4. What advice would you give to people about how to bring out their best?

3. **Answer the Questions** Now that you've written your questions, think of how you would answer them. Jot down some possible answers.

4. **"Publish" Your Interview** Write a final draft of your interview that includes the questions and your answers. Be sure to include details about the people and events that have helped bring out your best. Check your final draft for grammar and spelling, and post your interview in the classroom for other students to read.

UNIT 2
Your Turn: Read and Apply Skills

Meet the Author

Mary Whitebird is a member of the Kaw or Kansa Nation, also known as the "wind people." The names Kaw and Kansa are from early French traders and both were used. The Kaw/Kansa originally lived in central Kansas along the Kansas and Saline Rivers. They hunted buffalo and farmed. They lived in villages consisting of dome-shaped lodges. See page R7 of the Author Files for more on Mary Whitebird.

Author Search For more about Mary Whitebird, go to www.glencoe.com.

by Mary Whitebird

As my birthday drew closer, I had awful nightmares about it. I was reaching the age at which all Kaw Indians had to participate in Ta-Na-E-Ka.

Well, not all Kaws. Many of the younger families on the reservation were beginning to give up the old customs. But my grandfather, Amos Deer Leg, was devoted to tradition. He still wore handmade beaded moccasins instead of shoes and kept his iron-gray hair in tight braids. He could speak English, but he spoke it only with white men. With his family he used a Sioux dialect.[1]

Grandfather was one of the last living Indians (he died in 1953, when he was eighty-one) who actually fought against the U.S. Cavalry. Not only did he fight, he was wounded in a skirmish at Rose Creek—a famous encounter in which the celebrated Kaw chief Flat Nose lost his life. At the time, my grandfather was only eleven years old.

Eleven was a magic word among the Kaws. It was the time of Ta-Na-E-Ka, the "flowering of adulthood." It was the age,

---

1. The **Sioux dialect** is a language spoken by some Native Americans of the Great Plains.

my grandfather informed us hundreds of times, "when a boy could prove himself to be a warrior and a girl took the first steps to womanhood."

"I don't want to be a warrior," my cousin Roger Deer Leg, confided to me. "I'm going to become an accountant."

"None of the other tribes make girls go through the endurance ritual," I complained to my mother.

"It won't be as bad as you think, Mary," my mother said, ignoring my protests. "Once you've gone through it, you'll certainly never forget it. You'll be proud."

I even complained to my teacher, Mrs. Richardson, feeling that, as a white woman, she would side with me.

She didn't. "All of us have rituals of one kind or another," Mrs. Richardson said. "And look at it this way: How many girls have the opportunity to compete on equal terms with boys? Don't look down on your heritage."

Heritage, indeed! I had no intention of living on a reservation for the rest of my life. I was a good student. I loved school. My fantasies were about knights in armor and fair ladies in flowing gowns, being saved from dragons. It never once occurred to me that being an Indian was exciting.

But I've always thought that the Kaw were the originators of the women's liberation movement. No other Indian tribe—and I've spent half a lifetime researching the subject—treated women more "equally" than the Kaw. Unlike most of the sub-tribes of the Sioux Nation, the Kaw allowed men and women to eat together. And hundreds of years before we were "acculturated,"[2] a Kaw woman had the right to refuse a prospective husband even if her father arranged the match.

The wisest women (generally wisdom was equated with age) often sat in tribal councils. Furthermore, most Kaw legends revolve around "Good Woman," a kind of supersquaw, a Joan of Arc[3] of the high plains. Good Woman led Kaw warriors into battle after battle, from which they always seemed to emerge victorious.

And girls as well as boys were required to undergo Ta-Na-E-Ka. The actual ceremony varied from tribe to tribe, but since the Indians' life on the plains was dedicated to survival, Ta-Na-E-Ka was a test of survival.

"Endurance is the loftiest virtue[4] of the Indian," my grandfather explained. "To survive, we must endure. When I was a boy, Ta-Na-E-Ka was more than the mere symbol it is now. We were painted white with the juice of a sacred herb and sent naked into the wilderness without so much as a knife. We couldn't return until the white had worn off. It wouldn't wash off. It took almost 18 days, and during that time we had to stay alive, trapping food, eating insects and roots and berries, and watching out for enemies. And we did have enemies—both the white soldiers and the Omaha warriors, who were always trying to capture Kaw boys and girls undergoing

---

2. A group that is **acculturated** is forced to adopt another people's culture, in this case the culture of the European Americans.
3. **Joan of Arc** was a French heroine in the early 1400s.
4. The **loftiest virtue** is the most noble quality.

Sea-buckthorn berries are nutritious, but very unpleasant to eat raw.

their endurance test. It was an exciting time."

"What happened if you couldn't make it?" Roger asked. He was born only three days after I was, and we were being trained for Ta-Na-E-Ka together. I was happy to know he was frightened, too.

"Many didn't return," Grandfather said. "Only the strongest and shrewdest. Mothers were not allowed to weep over those who didn't return. If a Kaw couldn't survive, he or she wasn't worth weeping over. It was our way."

"What a lot of hooey," Roger whispered. "I'd give anything to get out of it."

"I don't see how we have any choice," I replied.

Roger gave my arm a little squeeze. "Well, it's only five days."

Five days! Maybe it was better than being painted white and sent out naked for eighteen days. But not much better.

We were to be sent, barefoot and in bathing suits, into the woods. Even our very traditional parents put their foot down when Grandfather suggested we go naked. For five days we'd have to live off the land, keeping warm as best we could, getting food where we could. It was May, but on the northernmost reaches of the Missouri River the days were still chilly and the nights were fiercely cold.

Grandfather was in charge of the month's training for Ta-Na-E-Ka. One day he caught a grasshopper and demonstrated how to pull its legs and wings off in one flick of the fingers and how to swallow it.

I felt sick, and Roger turned green. "It's a darn good thing it's 1947," I told Roger teasingly. "You'd make a terrible warrior." Roger just grimaced.

I knew one thing. This particular Kaw Indian girl wasn't going to swallow a grasshopper no matter how hungry she got. And then I had an idea. Why hadn't I thought of it before? It would have saved nights of bad dreams about squooshy grasshoppers.

I headed straight for my teacher's house. "Mrs. Richardson," I said, "would you lend me five dollars?"

"Five dollars!" she exclaimed. "What for?"

"You remember the ceremony I talked about?"

"Ta-Na-E-Ka. Of course. Your parents have written me and asked me to excuse you from school so you can participate in it."

"Well, I need some things for the ceremony," I replied, in a half-truth. "I don't want to ask my parents for the money."

"It's not a crime to borrow money, Mary. But how can you pay it back?"

"I'll baby-sit for you ten times."

"That's more than fair," she said, going to her purse and handing me a crisp, new five-dollar bill. I'd never had that much money at once.

"I'm happy to know the money's going to be put to a good use," Mrs. Richardson said.

A few days later the ritual began with a long speech from my grandfather about how we had reached the age of decision, how we now had to fend for ourselves and prove that we could survive the most horrendous of ordeals.[5] All the friends and relatives who had gathered at our house for dinner made jokes about their own Ta-Na-E-Ka experiences. They all advised us to fill up now, since for the next five days we'd be gorging[6] ourselves on crickets. Neither Roger nor I was very hungry. I'll probably laugh about this when I'm an accountant," Roger said, trembling.

"Are you trembling?" I asked.

"What do you think?"

"I'm happy to know boys tremble, too," I said.

At six the next morning, we kissed our parents and went off to the woods. "Which side do you want?" Roger asked. According to the rules, Roger and I would stake out "territories" in separate areas of the woods, and we weren't to communicate during the entire ordeal. "I'll go toward the river, if it's okay with you," I said.

"Sure," Roger answered. "What difference does it make?"

To me, it made a lot of difference. There was a marina a few miles up the river, and there were boats moored there. At least, I hoped so. I figured that a boat was a better place to sleep than under a pile of leaves.

"Why do you keep holding your head?" Roger asked.

"Oh, nothing. Just nervous," I told him. Actually, I was afraid I'd lose the five-dollar bill, which I had tucked into my hair with a bobby pin. As we came to a fork in the trail, Roger shook my hand. "Good luck, Mary."

"N'ko-n'ta," I said. It was the Kaw word for "courage."

The sun was shining and it was warm, but my bare feet began to hurt immediately. I spied one of the berry bushes Grandfather had told us about. "You're lucky," he had said. "The berries are ripe in the spring, and they are delicious and nourishing." They were orange and fat, and I popped one into my mouth.

Argh! I spat it out. It was awful and bitter, and even grasshoppers were probably better tasting, although I never intended to find out.

I sat down to rest my feet. A rabbit hopped out from under the berry bush. He nuzzled the berry I'd spat out and ate it. He picked another one and ate that, too. He liked them. He looked at me, twitching his nose. I watched a red-headed woodpecker bore into an elm tree, and I caught a glimpse of a civet cat[7] waddling through some twigs. All of a sudden I realized I was

---

5. An **ordeal** is a difficult or painful experience.
6. If you are **gorging** yourself, you are stuffing yourself with food.
7. A **civet cat** is a spotted skunk.

YOUR TURN: READ AND APPLY SKILLS

no longer frightened. Ta-Na-E-Ka might be more fun than I'd anticipated. I got up and headed toward the marina.

"Not one boat," I said to myself dejectedly.[8] But the restaurant on the shore, "Ernie's Riverside," was open. I walked in, feeling silly in my bathing suit. The man at the counter was big and tough-looking. He wore a sweatshirt with the words "Fort Sheridan, 1944," and he had only three fingers on one of his hands. He asked me what I wanted.

"A hamburger and a milkshake," I said, holding the five-dollar bill in my hand so he'd know I had money.

"That's a pretty heavy breakfast, honey," he murmured.

"That's what I always have for breakfast," I lied.

"Forty-five cents," he said, bringing me the food. (Back in 1947, hamburgers were twenty-five cents and milkshakes were twenty cents.) "Delicious," I thought. "Better'n grasshoppers—and Grandfather never once mentioned that I couldn't eat hamburgers."

While I was eating, I had a grand idea. Why not sleep in the restaurant? I went to the ladies room and made sure the window was unlocked. Then I went back outside and played along the riverbank, watching the water birds and trying to identify each one. I planned to look for a beaver dam the next day.

8. To react **dejectedly** is to respond in a depressed manner.

A diner (DY nuhr) is a small restaurant built to look like the dining car of a train.

The restaurant closed at sunset, and I watched the three-fingered man drive away. Then I climbed in the unlocked window. There was a night light on, so I didn't turn on any lights. But there was a radio on the counter. I turned it on to a music program. It was warm in the restaurant, and I was hungry. I helped myself to a glass of milk and a piece of pie, intending to keep a list of what I'd eaten so I could leave money. I also planned to get up early, sneak out through the window, and head for the woods before the three-fingered man returned. I turned off the radio, wrapped myself in the man's apron, and in spite of the hardness of the floor, fell asleep.

"What the heck are you doing here, kid?"

It was the man's voice.

It was morning. I'd overslept. I was scared.

"Hold it, kid. I just wanna know what you're doing here. You lost? You must be from the reservation. Your folks must be worried sick about you. Do they have a phone?"

"Yes, yes," I answered. "But don't call them."

I was shivering. The man, who told me his name was Ernie, made me a cup of hot chocolate while I explained about Ta-Na-E-Ka.

"Darnedest thing I ever heard," he said, when I was through. "Lived next to the reservation all my life and this is the first I've heard of Ta-Na whatever-you-call-it." He looked at me, all goose bumps in my bathing suit. "Pretty silly thing to do to a kid," he muttered.

That was just what I'd been thinking for months, but when Ernie said it, I became

Analyzing the Photo Do you think this is the way Mary's grandfather pictured her surviving Ta-Na-E-Ka? Explain.

YOUR TURN: READ AND APPLY SKILLS

angry. "No, it isn't silly. It's a custom of the Kaw. We've been doing this for hundreds of years. My mother and my grandfather and everybody in my family went through this ceremony. It's why the Kaw are great warriors."

"Okay, great warrior," Ernie chuckled, "suit yourself. And, if you want to stick around, it's okay with me." Ernie went to the broom closet and tossed me a bundle. "That's the lost-and-found closet," he said. "Stuff people left on boats. Maybe there's something to keep you warm."

The sweater fitted loosely, but it felt good. I felt good. And I'd found a new friend. Most important, I was surviving Ta-Na-E-Ka.

My grandfather had said the experience would be filled with adventure, and I was having my fill. And Grandfather had never said we couldn't accept hospitality.[9]

I stayed at Ernie's Riverside for the entire period. In the mornings I went into the woods and watched the animals and picked flowers for each of the tables in Ernie's. I had never felt better. I was up early enough to watch the sun rise on the Missouri, and I went to bed after it set. I ate everything I wanted— insisting that Ernie take all my money for the food. "I'll keep this in trust for you, Mary," Ernie promised, "in case you are ever desperate for five dollars." (He did, too, but that's another story.)

I was sorry when the five days were over. I'd enjoyed every minute with Ernie. He taught me how to make Western omelets and to make Chili Ernie Style (still one of my favorite dishes). And I told Ernie all about the legends of the Kaw. I hadn't realized I knew so much about my people.

But Ta-Na-E-Ka was over, and as I approached my house, at about nine-thirty in the evening, I became nervous all over again. What if Grandfather asked me about the berries and the grasshoppers? And my feet were hardly cut. I hadn't lost a pound and my hair was combed.

"They'll be so happy to see me," I told myself hopefully, "that they won't ask too many questions."

I opened the door. My grandfather was in the front room. He was wearing the ceremonial beaded deerskin shirt which had belonged to *his* grandfather. "N'g'da'ma," he said. "Welcome back."

I embraced my parents warmly, letting go only when I saw my cousin Roger sprawled

Analyzing the Photo Does this grasshopper look delicious to you?

---

9. Hospitality is the kindness that people extend to their guests.

on the couch. His eyes were red and swollen. He'd lost weight. His feet were an unsightly mass of blood and blisters, and he was moaning: "I made it, see. I made it. I'm a warrior. A warrior."

My grandfather looked at me strangely. I was clean, obviously well-fed, and radiantly healthy. My parents got the message. My uncle and aunt gazed at me with hostility.

Finally my grandfather asked, "What did you eat to keep you so well?"

I sucked in my breath and blurted out the truth: "Hamburgers and milkshakes."

"Hamburgers!" my grandfather growled.

"Milkshakes!" Roger moaned.

"You didn't say we had to eat grasshoppers," I said sheepishly.

"Tell us all about your Ta-Na-E-Ka," my grandfather commanded.

I told them everything, from borrowing the five dollars, to Ernie's kindness, to observing the beaver.

"That's not what I trained you for," my grandfather said sadly.

I stood up. "Grandfather, I learned that Ta-Na-E-Ka is important. I didn't think so during training. I was scared stiff of it. I handled it my way. And I learned I had nothing to be afraid of. There's no reason in 1947 to eat grasshoppers when you can eat a hamburger."

I was inwardly shocked at my own audacity.[10] But I liked it. "Grandfather, I'll bet you never ate one of those rotten berries yourself."

Grandfather laughed! He laughed aloud! My mother and father and aunt and uncle were all dumbfounded. Grandfather never laughed. Never.

"Those berries—they are terrible," Grandfather admitted. "I could never swallow them. I found a dead deer on the first day of my Ta-Na-E-Ka—shot by a soldier, probably—and he kept my belly full for the entire period of the test!"

Grandfather stopped laughing. "We should send you out again," he said.

I looked at Roger. "You're pretty smart, Mary," Roger groaned. "I'd never have thought of what you did."

"Accountants just have to be good at arithmetic," I said comfortingly. "I'm terrible at arithmetic."

Roger tried to smile but couldn't. My grandfather called me to him. "You should have done what your cousin did. But I think you are more alert to what is happening to our people today than we are. I think you would have passed the test under any circumstances, in any time. Somehow, you know how to exist in a world that wasn't made for Indians. I don't think you're going to have any trouble surviving."

Grandfather wasn't entirely right. But I'll tell about that another time. ○

---

10. Audacity is the act of being bold.

UNIT 2
Reading on Your Own

To read more about the Big Question, choose one of these books from your school or local library. Work on your reading skills by choosing books that are challenging to you.

Fiction

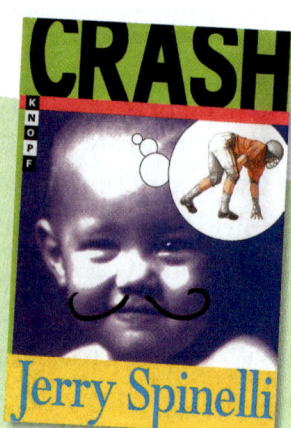

Crash
by Jerry Spinelli

Seventh-grader Crash Coogan is a bully. He's aggressive, mean, and smug . . . until an unlikely friendship makes him realize a thing or two about the way he treats others. Read Crash's story to find out what—and who—he comes to care about, after all.

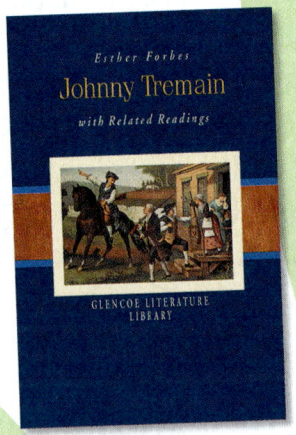

Johnny Tremain
by Esther Forbes

A compelling historical drama, this book chronicles the events leading up to the 1776 signing of the Declaration of Independence. Read this classic story of one young boy's journey to adulthood, and let history come to life.

Cezanne Pinto
by Mary Stolz

This fictional memoir follows Cezanne from Virginia to Canada and back down to Texas. In Texas, Cezanne becomes a cowboy, finds a home, and begins a family of his own. Read this book to learn more about Cezanne's journeys—journeys that take him out on the road and deep inside himself, too.

Flip-Flop Girl
by Katherine Paterson

After her father dies, Vinnie and her family move to a small town to live with Vinnie's grandmother. Things aren't going well when Vinnie makes a new friend at school—someone who is also an outsider. Read to find out how Vinnie's friendship helps her and her family get past their grief and come together again.

Nonfiction

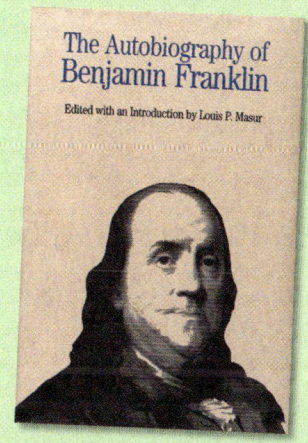

The Autobiography of Benjamin Franklin
by Benjamin Franklin

Originally, Franklin wrote this work, or "family history," as an encouragement for his son. Franklin's account of his own rise from penniless printer's apprentice to a place of world renown, however, is a "rags-to-riches" story everyone can enjoy.

Ellington Is Not a Street
by Ntozake Shange

Told as an illustrated poem, this account brings to life the language and music of a bygone era. Using biographical sketches of men like Paul Robeson and Duke Ellington, *Ellington Is Not a Street* depicts an important part of African American history—and some of the great men who made it.

Basketball Year: What It's Like to Be a Woman Pro
by Robin Roberts

Eight women from the Women's National Basketball Association discuss their jobs, their lives, and the elite level at which they compete. Read to learn more about how these amazing women have turned their passion into a paycheck—and are having a ball, too.

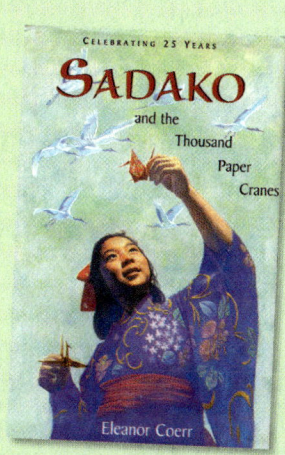

Sadako and the Thousand Paper Cranes
by Eleanor Coerr

Sadako is her school's track star when she is diagnosed with leukemia. Then she remembers a Japanese legend that says the gods will grant the wish of any sick person who folds a thousand paper cranes. Sadako sets to work—folding cranes and searching for the courage to face what lies ahead.

UNIT 2 SKILLS AND STRATEGIES ASSESSMENT

Test Practice

Part 1: Literary Elements

On a separate sheet of paper, write the numbers 1–5. Next to each number, write the letter of the right answer for that question.

Each of the following passages is from a different short story about the same people. Use these passages to answer questions 1–4.

from Story 1: Scotty has called me "Ram Man" instead of Ramon ever since I accidentally knocked him down one day. He thinks it's funny. I don't, but it doesn't upset me. I mean, what difference does it make, really?

from Story 2: Whenever Scotty got angry, the other boys took a step back, as if he had a disease they didn't want to catch. Ramon would try to calm him down because Scotty's temper scared him, scared him down to his bones.

from Story 3: I know I've got a temper. I wish I could control it and be all laid back, but things are always ticking me off, you know? Ramon's always telling me, "Take it easy, Scott, my man!" I wish I could.

from Story 4: My firstborn, Sonya, is always in a sunny mood and has been since the moment she was born. My second, Scotty, has never heard the word *no* without having a tantrum.

1. Which story is written from the third-person point of view?
   - **A.** Story 1
   - **B.** Story 2
   - **C.** Story 3
   - **D.** Story 4

2. Which story is *sure* to reveal Scotty's thoughts and feelings?
   - **A.** Story 1
   - **B.** Story 2
   - **C.** Story 3
   - **D.** Story 4

3. Who is the narrator in Story 4?
   - **A.** Scotty himself
   - **B.** a friend of Scotty's
   - **C.** Scotty's mother or father
   - **D.** someone outside the story

4. Which of the following best describes the tone of Story 2?
   - **A.** angry
   - **B.** serious
   - **C.** proud
   - **D.** playful

Use the following passage to answer question 5.

Before raising her hand, Kavitha checked her notes. After writing Kavitha's answer on the chalkboard, the teacher praised her for getting it right.

5. Which event occurred first?
   - **A.** Kavitha raised her hand.
   - **B.** Kavitha checked her notes.
   - **C.** The teacher wrote down Kavitha's answer.
   - **D.** The teacher praised Kavitha.

Objectives (pp. 248–249)
Reading Ask questions • Make connections from text to self • Make predictions • Activate prior knowledge
Literature Identify literary elements: narrator, point of view, chronological order, tone

SKILLS AND STRATEGIES ASSESSMENT UNIT 2

Part 2: Reading Skills

On a separate sheet of paper, write the numbers 1–4. Next to numbers 1–3, write the letter of the right answer for that question. Next to number 4, write your answer to the final question.

1. As you read, what is the main purpose of asking yourself questions and trying to answer them?
   A. to remain interested in the material
   B. to prove that the material is hard to read
   C. to check your understanding of the material
   D. to remind yourself that you don't know as much as the author

The following passage is from the beginning of a short story. Use it to answer questions 2 and 3.

Erika liked to run whether she was in a hurry to get some place or not. She liked the rhythm of the movement and the sound of her feet hitting the ground. She liked the feel of the wind on her face and the warmth that flowed through her muscles. She just liked running. She was good at it, too.

On the first day of sixth grade, Erika was surprised to see a notice posted in the gym. "Franklin Middle School Track Team Try-Outs," it said. "Wednesday, September 10, immediately after school behind the gym. See the coach, Mr. Seward, for details."

2. After reading this passage, it is **most** reasonable to predict that Erika will
   A. be chosen for the track team.
   B. try out for the team but not make it.
   C. decide she doesn't have time for track.
   D. ask Mr. Seward if she can help coach the team.

3. Which statement might be made by a reader who was "making a connection" to this passage?
   A. I wonder why Erika was surprised to see the notice.
   B. I'll bet Erika is the most important character in this story.
   C. Erika's probably getting faster and stronger as time goes on.
   D. Running makes me feel warm, too, and I know why she likes it.

4. What does it mean to "activate prior knowledge"? Why is it a good idea to do this when you are reading?

UNIT 2 SKILLS AND STRATEGIES ASSESSMENT

Part 3: Vocabulary Skills

On a separate sheet of paper, write the numbers 1–10. Next to each number, write the letter of the right answer for that question.

Write the letter of the word or phrase that means about the same as the underlined word.

1. to quiver with anger
   - A. yell
   - B. shake
   - C. respond
   - D. make a plan

2. to show their indifference
   - A. similarity
   - B. worried feeling
   - C. high hopes
   - D. lack of interest

3. when they emerged
   - A. came out
   - B. joined together
   - C. fell down
   - D. shared ideas

4. a gloomy day
   - A. busy
   - B. surprising
   - C. dull and dark
   - D. extremely hot

5. to mope all day
   - A. try hard
   - B. be foolish
   - C. show fear
   - D. act unhappy

Choose the correct answer for each question.

6. Which pair of words are synonyms?
   - A. no / know
   - B. high / low
   - C. big / large
   - D. penny / dime

7. Which pair of words are antonyms?
   - A. left / right
   - B. begin / start
   - C. small / tiny
   - D. friend / neighbor

8. Which word can be made into its antonym by adding the prefix *in-*?
   - A. door
   - B. crease
   - C. come
   - D. correct

9. Which prefix, when added to all of the words below, would make them into their antonyms?

   happy   broken   cooked
   - A. in-
   - B. un-
   - C. dis-
   - D. non-

10. Which synonym for *hard* could be used to replace it in the following sentence?

    "The test was so hard that most of us failed it."
    - A. firm
    - B. difficult
    - C. powerful
    - D. unbreakable

Objectives (pp. 250–251)
Vocabulary Identify synonyms and antonyms
Grammar Identify parts of speech: nouns, pronouns

250 UNIT 2   What Brings Out the Best in You?

SKILLS AND STRATEGIES ASSESSMENT UNIT 2

Part 4: Writing Skills

On a separate sheet of paper, write the numbers 1–8. Next to each number, write the letter of the right answer for that question.

1. Which of the following words is a common noun?

   A. January
   B. Mary
   C. India
   D. house

2. Which of the following is a collective noun?

   A. herd
   B. meeting
   C. stamp
   D. togetherness

3. Which of the following is an abstract noun?

   A. book
   B. piano
   C. sorrow
   D. raindrop

4. Which noun in the following sentence is a proper noun that should be capitalized?

   When we arrived in the city of denver, we got off the bus and took a cab to my uncle's house.

   A. city
   B. denver
   C. bus
   D. uncle

5. In which sentence is a pronoun used incorrectly?

   A. Chiyo and I are going.
   B. Himself did all the work.
   C. Mike told Dan and me the score.
   D. The teacher gave everyone a paper.

6. In which sentence is the word *run* used as a noun?

   A. Cars won't <u>run</u> without gas.
   B. Laura can <u>run</u> faster than Richard.
   C. Would you <u>run</u> to the store for me?
   D. If we get one more <u>run</u>, we'll win the game.

7. Which pronoun in the following passage has an unclear antecedent?

   Joan called Melissa to talk about <u>her</u> birthday party. After a while, Joan looked at the clock. <u>She</u> could hardly believe what <u>it</u> said. <u>They</u> had been talking for an hour!

   A. her
   B. She
   C. it
   D. They

8. Which of the following sentences uses pronouns correctly?

   A. Both he and his brother were tall.
   B. Both his brother and him were tall.
   C. Both him and his brother were tall.
   D. Both his brother and himself were tall.

Skills and Strategies Assessment 251

UNIT 3

The BIG Question: What's Fair and What's Not?

" It's not fair to ask of others what you are not willing to do yourself. "

—Eleanor Roosevelt, First Lady, human rights activist, and diplomat

LOOKING AHEAD

The skill lessons and readings in this unit will help you develop your own answer to the Big Question.

UNIT 3 WARM-UP • Connecting to the Big Question
GENRE FOCUS: Persuasive Writing

And Ain't I a Woman? 257
   by Sojourner Truth

READING WORKSHOP 1 — Skill Lesson: Distinguishing Fact and Opinion

Preserving a Great American Symbol 264
   by Richard Durbin

Looking for America 270
   by Elizabeth Partridge

WRITING WORKSHOP PART 1 — Persuasive Essay 278

READING WORKSHOP 2 — Skill Lesson: Clarifying

Two Advertisements 286

Stray 292
   by Cynthia Rylant

READING WORKSHOP 3 — Skill Lesson: Inferring

Dressed for Success? from *TIME FOR KIDS* 302
   by Melanie Bertotto

Eleven 308
   by Sandra Cisneros

WRITING WORKSHOP PART 2 — Persuasive Essay 314

READING WORKSHOP 4 — Skill Lesson: Identifying Problems and Solutions

from *50 Simple Things Kids Can Do to Save the Earth* 322
   by The EarthWorks Group

Greyling 328
   by Jane Yolen

COMPARING LITERATURE WORKSHOP

The Scholarship Jacket 339
   by Marta Salinas

The Circuit 347
   by Francisco Jiménez

UNIT 3 WRAP-UP • Answering the Big Question

UNIT 3 WARM-UP

Connecting to The BIG Question: What's Fair and What's Not?

You've seen it happen. Or maybe it has happened to you. Someone is treated differently from others. Somebody gets to do something you don't. A decision or rule doesn't make sense. What do you do when you think something's unfair? In this unit, you'll read about people in various situations that they thought were unfair. You'll learn how they felt and how they reacted.

Real Kids and the Big Question

JODI knows that any player who misses three soccer practices is off the team. Because Jodi has to walk her little brother home after school, she has already missed two practices. If she misses another practice, she can't play on the soccer team. What advice would you give Jodi?

HECTOR heard students laughing in the cafeteria. When he walked into the cafeteria, he realized that they were laughing at his new neighbor, Stella. Whenever she got close to a table, suddenly there was no room to sit there. Hector remembered what it was like to be the new kid. What would you do if you were Hector?

Warm-Up Activity

In a small group, talk about how you would feel and what you would do if you were Jodi or Hector. Then tell about a situation you experienced that was unfair. Describe how you felt and what you did.

UNIT 3 WARM-UP

You and the Big Question

The question of what's fair or unfair comes up in many situations. As you read the selections in this unit, think about how you would answer the Big Question.

Big Question Link to Web resources to further explore the Big Question at www.glencoe.com.

Plan for the Unit Challenge

At the end of the unit, you'll use notes from all your reading to complete the Unit Challenge.

You'll choose one of the following activities:

A. TV Call-In Show With members of your group, you'll write questions and answers about what's fair and what's not for a television call-in show that your group will present.

B. A Rap or Song You'll write a rap or song about something you feel is unfair and what you think can be done about it.

- Start thinking about which activity you'd like to do so that you can focus your thoughts as you go through the unit.
- In your Learner's Notebook, write your thoughts about the activity you'd like to do.
- Each time you make notes about the Big Question, think about how your ideas will help you complete the Unit Challenge activity you chose.

Keep Track of Your Ideas

As you read, you'll make notes about the Big Question. Later, you'll use these notes to complete the Unit Challenge. See pages R8–R9 for help with making Foldable 3. This diagram shows how it should look.

1. Use this Foldable for the selections in this unit. Label the stapled edge with the unit number and the Big Question.
2. Label each flap with a selection title. (See page 253 for titles.)
3. Open each flap. Label the top of the inside page **My Purpose for Reading.** You will write your purpose for reading the selection below this label.
4. Halfway down the inside page, write the label **The Big Question.** You'll write your thoughts about the Big Question below this label.

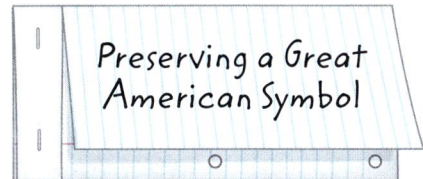

Warm-Up **255**

UNIT 3 GENRE FOCUS: PERSUASIVE WRITING

In **persuasive writing,** a writer tries to persuade the reader to share a certain point of view or take a particular action. Persuasive writing can take many forms, including speeches, editorials, billboards, and advertisements.

Why Read Persuasive Writing?

Discovering what makes effective persuasive writing is a great way to develop your thinking skills. You'll learn how an author feels about a subject, how you feel about a subject, and what you think is fair and what's not fair.

How to Read Persuasive Writing

Key Reading Skills

These key reading skills are useful tools for reading and understanding persuasive writing. You'll see them modeled in the Active Reading Model on pages 257–259, and you'll learn more about them in this unit.

- **Distinguishing fact and opinion** A fact can be proved. An opinion is different; it's what someone thinks or feels about something. Learn to tell them apart. (See Reading Workshop 1.)
- **Clarifying** Figure out confusing words, phrases, or ideas by using the text and other resources. (See Reading Workshop 2.)
- **Inferring** Figure out information the author doesn't give you by using what he or she does give you and your own knowledge and experience. (See Reading Workshop 3.)
- **Identifying problems and solutions** Learn to spot problems and solutions presented by the author. (See Reading Workshop 4.)

Key Literary Elements

Recognizing and thinking about the following literary elements will help you understand more fully what the author is telling you.

- **Style:** a form of expression in writing, just as in music and fashion (See "Preserving a Great American Symbol.")
- **Bias:** being for or against something or a preference for one side of an argument (See "Two Advertisements.")
- **Argument:** the case a writer presents for or against something (See "Dressed for Success?")
- **Mood:** the feeling that writing creates in the reader (See "from *50 Things Kids Can Do to Save the Earth.*")

Skills Focus
- Key skills for reading and persuasive writing
- Key literary elements of persuasive writing

Skills Model
You will see how to use the key reading skills and literary elements as you read
- "And Ain't I a Woman?" p. 257

Objectives (pp. 256–259)
Reading Distinguish fact and opinion • Monitor comprehension: clarify • Make inferences • Identify problems and solutions
Literature Identify literary elements: style, author's bias, argument, mood

And Ain't I a Woman?

by Sojourner Truth

Address to the Ohio Women's Rights Convention, 1851

That man over there says that women need to be helped into carriages, and lifted over ditches, and to have the best place everywhere. Nobody ever helps me into carriages, or over mud-puddles, or gives me any best place! And ain't I a woman? Look at me! Look at my arm. I have ploughed and planted, and gathered into barns, and no man could head[1] me! And ain't I a woman? I could work as much and eat as much as a man—when I could get it—and bear the lash as well! And ain't I a woman? I have borne thirteen children, and seen them most all sold off to slavery, and when I cried out with my mother's grief, none but Jesus heard me! And ain't I a woman?

---

1. In this speech, **head** means "to do something better than someone else."

Personal and Persuasive Text
ACTIVE READING MODEL

The notes in the side columns model how to use the skills and elements you read about on page 256.

1 Key Literary Element
Argument I can see that Truth is giving very effective examples to back up her argument that women are equal to men.

2 Key Reading Skill
Distinguishing Fact and Opinion The number of children that a person has is a matter of fact, not opinion.

3 Key Literary Element
Style Repeating the question "And ain't I a woman?" reminds me of preaching. I think Truth has kind of a "preaching" style.

UNIT 3 GENRE FOCUS

Then they talk about this thing in the head; what's this they call it? [Intellect,[2] someone whispers.] That's it, honey. What's that got to do with women's rights or Negroes rights? If my cup won't hold but a pint, and yours holds a quart, wouldn't you be mean not to let me have my little half-measure full? 4 5

---

2. A person's **intellect** (IN tuh lekt) is his or her intelligence

ACTIVE READING MODEL

4 Key Literary Element
Bias Truth obviously prefers one side of the argument about women's rights. So, her speech is biased in favor of women's rights.

5 Key Reading Skill
Inferring Truth doesn't say it directly, but I think that she means what's in a person's head, or intellect, doesn't have anything to do with having equal rights.

In *Sojourner Truth I Fought for the Rights of Women as Well as Blacks*, 1947. Elizabeth Catlett. Linocut. 15 x 22.5 cm. Private Collection.

Analyzing the Art Sojourner Truth looks very *determined* in this picture. What other qualities does she seem to have, based on this picture? Explain your answer.

258 UNIT 3 What's Fair and What's Not?

This photograph was taken in Belton, South Carolina, in 1899. These women did not have the right to vote, and their husbands and sons were denied their legal rights, too.

Then that little man in black there, he says women can't have as much rights as men, 'cause Christ wasn't a woman! Where did your Christ come from? Where did your Christ come from? From God and a woman! Man had nothing to do with Him. 6

If the first woman God ever made was strong enough to turn the world upside down all alone, these women together ought to be able to turn it back, and get it right side up again! And now they is asking to do it, the men better let them.

Obliged[3] to you for hearing me, and now old Sojourner ain't got nothing more to say. 7 8 ○

---

3. **Obliged** (uh BLYJD) is another word for "grateful."

Whole-Class Discussion Give some examples of common stereotypes. Talk about how bias leads to forming stereotypes about people.

Write to Learn Write in your journal an example of persuasive writing or speaking that you have read or heard recently. Did it persuade you to change your thoughts or to do something? Explain your answer.

Study Central Visit www.glencoe.com and click on Study Central to review persuasive writing.

UNIT 3 GENRE FOCUS

ACTIVE READING MODEL

6 Key Reading Skill
Clarifying I'll have to read this paragraph again more slowly. I didn't get what Truth was saying.

7 Key Reading Skill
Identifying Problems and Solutions According to Truth, the problem is that women don't have the same rights as men. The solution is for men to give women equal rights.

8 Key Literary Element
Mood Reading this makes me feel sad about what Truth went through but also respectful of her. I'll bet the people who heard her give the speech felt like working hard for women's rights.

Genre Focus: Persuasive Writing 259

READING WORKSHOP 1

Skills Focus

You will practice using these skills when you read the following selections:
- "Preserving a Great American Symbol," p. 264
- "Looking for America," p. 270

Reading
- Distinguishing fact and opinion

Literature
- Identifying an author's style
- Explaining how style affects the reader

Vocabulary
- Understanding hyperbole
- Academic Vocabulary: *distinguish*

Writing/Grammar
- Identifying and using adjectives and adverbs

Objectives (pp. 260–261)
Reading Distinguish fact from opinion

Skill Lesson

Distinguishing Fact and Opinion

Learn It!

What Is It? A **fact** is something that can be proved. An **opinion** is what someone believes is true. Opinions are based on feelings and experiences; they cannot be proved. When deciding whether to believe what a writer has written, you'll have to **distinguish** *fact from opinion*. Writers can support their opinions with facts, but an opinion is something that cannot be proved.

Fact: Beijing is the capital of China.

Opinion: China is the best place to vacation.

You could prove that Beijing is the capital of China. It's a fact. But not everyone would agree that China is the best place for a vacation. That's someone's opinion.

POOCH CAFE © 2005. Dist. by UNIVERSAL PRESS SYNDICATE. Reprinted with permission. All rights reserved.

Analyzing Cartoons
Is the larger dog presenting a fact or an opinion? How do you know? How does the smaller dog feel about this bit of information?

Academic Vocabulary

distinguish (dih STING gwish) *v.* to know the difference between, tell apart

READING WORKSHOP 1 • Distinguishing Fact and Opinion

Why Is It Important? As you read, ask yourself, *Is this a fact or an opinion?* Opinions can be useful, but sometimes opinions are based on prejudice or feelings you don't share. Before you accept something as true, you need to find out if it's *fact* or *opinion*.

How Do I Do It? To tell fact from opinion, ask: *Can this be proved?*
- *What is the source of the statement?* The source is where the information came from. An encyclopedia is one trustworthy source.
- *Is the author an expert on the subject?* An expert on that topic would usually know a lot of proven facts about it.
- *Are there numbers or dates with the statement?* Numbers and dates could prove the time, the place, how much, or how many.

Take a look at how one student distinguished between facts and opinions in a newspaper article about a supposed UFO sighting.

Literature Online

Study Central Visit www.glencoe.com and click on Study Central to review distinguishing fact and opinion.

> Recorded calls to the station-house indicate that the policeman radioed in the sighting on April 4, 1997 at 2:48 AM. "You're not going to believe this," he said, "But *I think* I saw a UFO! The engine died on my car, and the radio started going haywire! All of the sudden I saw red, white, and green lights flashing from behind the trees!" Weather reports prove that there were no thunderstorms that evening, but the policeman was near a swamp. Sometimes, people mistake swamp gas for a UFO.

> They have a recording of the policeman with the date and time saying that he saw a UFO, so I know he saw <u>something</u>. It's a fact that he called in on his radio; that can be proven. But I wonder <u>what</u> he saw? He said he <u>thinks</u> he saw a UFO, but that doesn't make it a fact—just an opinion.

Practice It!
Look at articles in a newspaper. Find a sentence that tells a fact and a sentence that tells an opinion. Copy the examples in your Learner's Notebook. Explain why you think the example is a fact or an opinion.

Use It!
Remember what you've learned about facts and opinions as you read "Preserving a Great American Symbol."

READING WORKSHOP 1 • Distinguishing Fact and Opinion

Before You Read : Preserving a Great American Symbol

Meet the Author
Richard Durbin has been a member of Congress since 1983. Today he represents the people of Illinois in the United States Senate. Senator Durbin makes many speeches. Most are about more serious issues than saving the baseball bat. Education, for instance, is an issue Durbin takes very seriously. He sees education as "the key to opportunity."

Author Search For more about Richard Durbin, go to www.glencoe.com.

Vocabulary Preview

condemn (kun DEM) *v.* to express a strong feeling against something **(p. 264)** *Don't condemn a person for making a bad choice.*

endure (en DUR) *v.* to put up with **(p. 264)** *When Emilio moved from Florida to New York he found the winters hard to endure.*

indignities (in DIG nuh teez) *n.* insulting treatment **(p. 264)** *The new members had to suffer many indignities before they were accepted into the club.*

forsake (for SAYK) *v.* to give up something or someone **(p. 265)** *When Y-Ming became famous, she refused to forsake her old friends.*

Fill in the Blank Write a sentence for each word. Put a blank in each sentence where the word should appear. Trade sentences with a partner. Then fill in the blanks in each other's sentences with the correct words.

English Language Coach

Hyperbole "When I lost my new scarf, I almost died!" Have you ever said anything like that? Did you really mean your life was in danger? Of course not. You were exaggerating. That kind of extreme exaggeration is called **hyperbole**. People may use it to express strong feelings or to emphasize a point. Sometimes, people use it to be funny. Hyperbole uses exaggerated words and exaggerated comparisons. As a reader, you're expected to understand that it is not the exact truth.

Partner Work Read the sentences below to each other. Then discuss which ones you think use hyperbole. Talk about what your reasons are.
1. I'm so tired I could sleep for a year.
2. You could put his common sense in a thimble and have room left over for the Great Lakes.
3. When I lost my homework, I was quite worried.
4. Bella has told that same joke a million times.
5. Cafeteria workers faced a tragedy today when they ran out of tortilla chips.

Objectives (pp. 262–265)
Reading Distinguish fact and opinion
• Make connections from text to self
Literature Identify literary elements: style, symbol, hyperbole
Vocabulary Understanding hyperbole

READING WORKSHOP 1 • Distinguishing Fact and Opinion

Skills Preview

Key Reading Skill: Distinguishing Fact and Opinion

Sometimes it's difficult to tell a fact from an opinion, especially when the writer is being funny. After all, most humor is not written for the purpose of giving information. And yet, sometimes a writer uses humor to make a point. Then, facts may be scattered in among the jokes and exaggerations.

As you read "Preserving a Great American Symbol," look for statements that can be proved. Ask yourself whether these facts help support the writer's opinions.

Write to Learn In your Learner's Notebook, write one way in which you can tell facts and opinions apart.

Key Literary Element: Style

You probably know all about **style** when it comes to fashion and music. You might dress in a certain style or like a particular style of music. Style is just a particular way of doing something. A writer's style is his or her own way of putting words and sentences together.

One style of writing is sometimes called "mock seriousness." (*Mock* means "pretend, not real.") The writer chooses a subject that isn't very important and writes about it as if it were. There is usually some hyperbole in the mock serious style. This style can be very funny. It can also help the author make a point.

Partner Talk With a partner choose an unimportant subject. Then work together to make up a mock serious sentence about it.

Get Ready to Read

Connect to the Reading

A symbol is an object that stands for a big idea. For example, a lion is often a symbol for courage. People often have strong feelings about symbols, such as the flag and even wooden baseball bats. What symbol has special meaning for you? Why is it important to you?

Whole-Class Discussion Name a symbol that means something special to you. Explain its meaning, and talk about its importance. How would you feel without it?

Build Background

In this selection, Richard Durbin argues that the wooden baseball bat is a part of the baseball tradition that must be saved.

- Baseball is often called our "national pastime" because so many Americans enjoy the sport.
- Professional baseball players must use wooden bats. Aluminum bats are not allowed.
- Wooden bats are made either from one piece of wood or from layers of wood that are pressed together.

Set Purposes for Reading

BIG Question Read the selection "Preserving a Great American Symbol" to find out why Richard Durbin thinks replacing wooden bats with metal ones would harm the tradition of baseball.

Set Your Own Purpose What else would you like to learn from the reading to help you answer the Big Question? Write your purpose on the "Preserving a Great American Symbol" page of Foldable 3.

Interactive Literary Elements Handbook
To review or learn more about the literary elements, go to www.glencoe.com.

Keep Moving

Use these skills as you read the following selection.

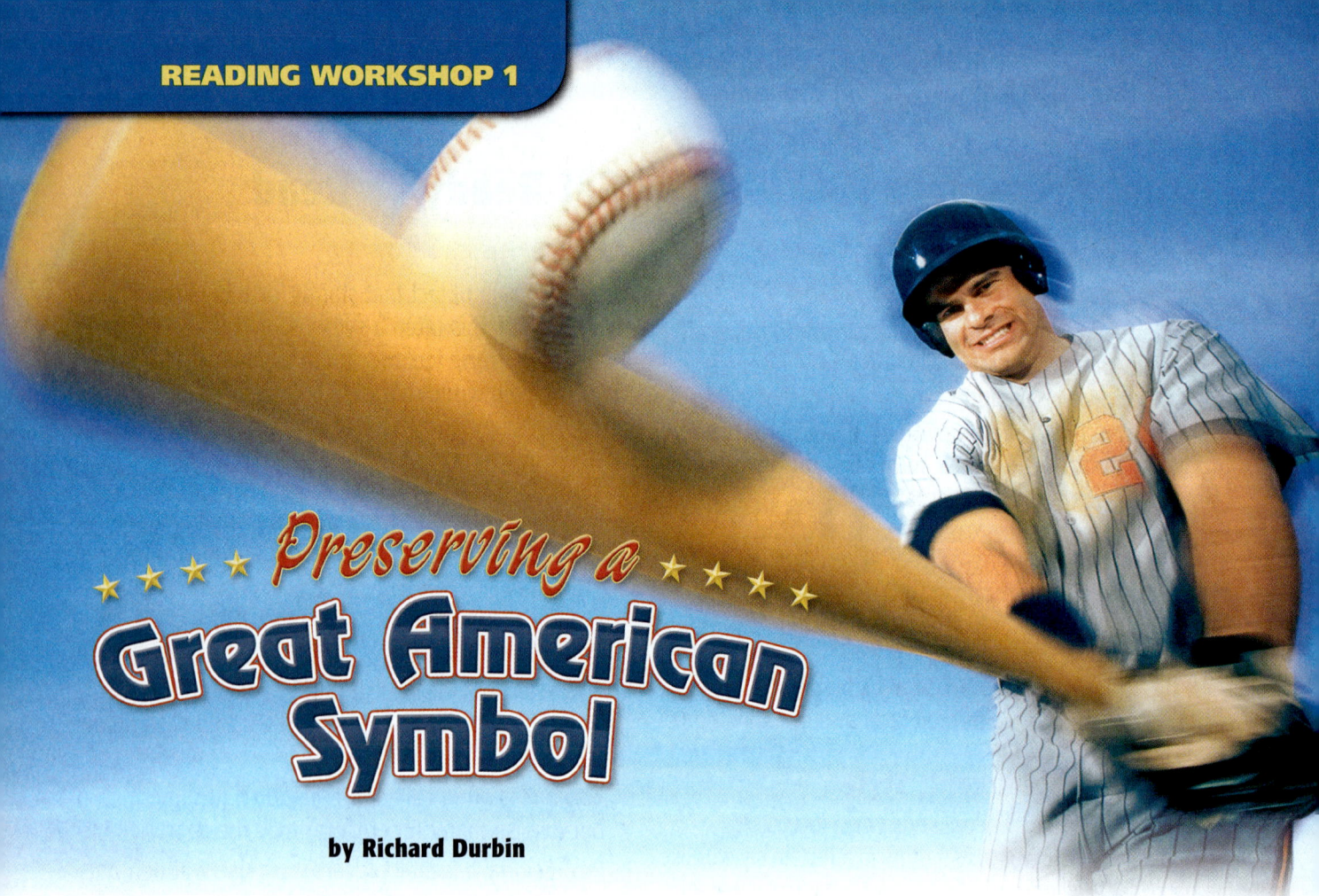

Preserving a Great American Symbol

by Richard Durbin

Mr. Speaker, I rise to **condemn** the desecration[1] of a great American symbol. No, I am not referring to flagburning; I am referring to the baseball bat. 1

Several experts tell us that the wooden baseball bat is doomed to extinction, that major league baseball players will soon be standing at home plate with aluminum bats in their hands.

Baseball fans have been forced to **endure** countless **indignities** by those who just cannot leave well enough alone: designated hitters,[2] plastic grass, uniforms that look like pajamas, chicken clowns dancing on the base lines, and,

Practice the Skills

1 Key Literary Element

Style Look at the footnote for *desecration* at the bottom of the page. Do you think this word is usually used for things a lot more important than a baseball bat? What clue does that give you about the style of this selection?

---

1. A **desecration** is an act that shows disrespect for something sacred.
2. A **designated hitter** bats in place of the pitcher.

Vocabulary

condemn (kun DEM) *v.* to express a strong feeling against something

endure (en DUR) *v.* to put up with

indignities (in DIG nuh teez) *n.* insulting treatment

of course, the most heinous sacrilege,[3] lights in Wrigley Field.[4] 2 3

Are we willing to hear the **crack** of a bat replaced by the dinky **ping**? Are we ready to see the Louisville Slugger[5] replaced by the aluminum ping dinger? Is nothing sacred?

Please do not tell me that wooden bats are too expensive, when players who cannot hit their weight are being paid more money than the President of the United States.

Please do not try to sell me on the notion that these metal clubs will make better hitters.

What will be next? Teflon[6] baseballs? Radar-enhanced gloves? I ask you.

I do not want to hear about saving trees. Any tree in America would gladly give its life for the glory of a day at home plate. 4

I do not know if it will take a constitutional amendment to keep our baseball traditions alive, but if we **forsake** the great Americana of broken-bat singles and pine tar,[7] we will have certainly lost our way as a nation. 5 ○

Practice the Skills

2 Key Reading Skill

Distinguishing Fact and Opinion Is it a fact that fans of baseball have to put up with the things listed in this paragraph? Is it a fact that these things are **indignities**, or insulting treatment? Explain.

3 BIG Question

Durbin thinks that a change from wooden to metal bats would be unfair to baseball fans. What other changes in the sport does he think have been unfair to fans? Record your answers on the "Preserving a Great American Symbol" page of Foldable 3. These notes will help you complete the Unit Challenge later.

4 Key Literary Element

Style What is there about this paragraph that might be thought of as mock serious in style?

5 English Language Coach

Hyperbole What example or examples of hyperbole can you find in this paragraph?

---

3. A **heinous sacrilege** is the act of misusing something that is sacred in an unusually shocking way. Here the statement is meant to be dramatic.
4. Chicago's **Wrigley Field** is one of the oldest baseball fields in the United States. No night games were played there until 1988, when the field finally got lights.
5. The wooden baseball bat known as the **Louisville Slugger** was first made in Louisville, Kentucky, in 1884. Today it is the official bat of major league baseball.
6. **Teflon** is the name for a tough, waxy material that is very hard to damage.
7. **Americana** includes anything that has something to do with American culture. When a batter breaks a bat while hitting but gets safely to first base, the play is called a **broken-bat single**. **Pine tar** is a sticky substance that batters use to get a tight grip on a wooden bat.

Vocabulary

forsake (for SAYK) *v.* to give up something or someone

READING WORKSHOP 1 • Distinguishing Fact and Opinion

After You Read

Preserving a Great American Symbol

Answering the BIG Question

1. Do you agree with the author that changing from wooden bats to metal bats would be unfair to baseball fans? Explain.
2. **Recall** Name three things that the writer says baseball fans have been forced to endure.
   TIP Right There
3. **Recall** What does Durbin call "the most heinous sacrilege"?
   TIP Right There
4. **Summarize** What are some of the reasons Durbin prefers wooden bats to aluminum?
   TIP Think and Search

Critical Thinking

5. **Infer** Do you think Richard Durbin is a baseball fan? Explain.
   TIP Author and Me
6. **Analyze** Which details in the final paragraph show that this speech is not meant to be serious?
   TIP Author and Me
7. **Evaluate** What effect do you think this speech had on its audience?
   TIP On My Own

Talk About Your Reading

Think about these statements in Durbin's speech:

I do not want to hear about saving trees. Any tree in America would gladly give its life for the glory of a day at home plate.

This is Durbin's *opinion.* How would you feel if you were the tree? With a partner, take turns making your own speech, but pretend that you are the tree. Include facts and opinions of your own. Before you begin, take a few moments to jot down at least three points you'd like to make in your speech. Do you think it would be fair to be turned into a baseball bat? Would you favor aluminum bats instead, or is Durbin right? Would you "gladly" give your life "for the glory of a day at home plate"?

Objectives (pp. 266–267)
Reading Distinguish fact and opinion
Literature Identify literary elements: style, hyperbole
Grammar Identify parts of speech: adjectives

266 UNIT 3 What's Fair and What's Not?

Skills Review

Key Reading Skill: Distinguishing Fact and Opinion

8. In your Learner's Notebook, answer the following questions about the selection.
   - What was the subject of the speech?
   - What was the speaker's opinion on the subject?
   - What facts did he use to support his opinion?

Key Literary Element: Style

9. Write down two words or phrases that you think might be "mock serious" in the selection. Explain why you think they are.
10. Do you think the big words in the selection help make it funny? Explain why or why not.
11. Do you think the style of the selection helped the author make his point? Why or why not?

Vocabulary Check

Look over the vocabulary words from the story:

condemn   endure   indignities   forsake

Then come up with as many answers as you can to these questions. Write the questions and the answers on a separate sheet of paper. You may be "mock serious" if you like.

12. What would you **condemn**?
13. What do you have to **endure**?
14. What **indignities** have you suffered in your life?
15. Who or what would you never **forsake**?
16. **Academic Vocabulary** Which pair of things below might be difficult to **distinguish** from each other? Explain the reason for your choice.
    apple and orange
    glass and plate
    moth and butterfly
17. **English Language Coach** What makes the sentence below an example of hyperbole? What point is the writer making?
    The bell rang, shattering our ear drums.

Grammar Link: Adjectives

As you know, different kinds of words do different jobs in a sentence. Words that are used to describe nouns or pronouns are **adjectives**. Adjectives answer these questions:
- What kind?
- Which one?
- How many

The adjectives in the sentences below are in bold type. The nouns they describe are underlined.

Deb found a **young** squirrel under a tree. (*What kind?*)
She fed it with **this** bottle. (*Which one?*)
Careful treatment helped the **lonely** squirrel. (*What kind? What kind?*)
Deb has helped **several** animals. (*How many?*)

Sometimes a word that you think of as a noun does the job of an adjective. Then, the word is an adjective.

Deb found a **baby** squirrel under an **oak** tree.

Most adjectives come right before the noun they describe. Some come after a linking verb. As you learned before, a linking verb shows a condition or state of being.

The tornado was **huge** and **dark**.
Suddenly, the sky looked **green**.

Grammar Practice

Copy the sentences below on another sheet of paper. Underline each adjective.

18. Bees gather a sweet liquid from flowers.
19. One bee may visit five hundred flowers in one trip.
20. Each flower has powder called pollen that is yellow.
21. Pollen gets on the busy bee.
22. She leaves some powder on another flower.

Web Activities For eFlashcards, Selection Quick Checks, and other Web activities, go to www.glencoe.com.

READING WORKSHOP 1 • Distinguishing Fact and Opinion

Before You Read: Looking for America

Meet the Author

Elizabeth Partridge grew up in a large family. During the summers, her family often traveled across the country in an old Cadillac limousine, usually not returning until after school had started. As a writer, Partridge believes that it is important to "offer our young adults examples of critical listeners and critical thinkers. We need . . . to let them know that they, too, can have a voice."

Author Search For more about Elizabeth Partridge, go to www.glencoe.com.

Vocabulary Preview

architect (AR kuh tekt) *n.* a person who designs buildings **(p. 271)** *The architect designed a famous house made of glass.*

cicadas (sih KAY duz) *n.* large insects, also called locusts; males make a shrill buzzing sound **(p. 271)** *You could hear cicadas buzzing in the trees.*

beckoned (BEK und) *v.* moved the head or hand to make a sign to approach or come nearer; form of the verb *beckon* **(p. 272)** *Her mother beckoned her to the table.*

buffet (BUF it) *v.* to strike with force **(p. 275)** *The strong wind will buffet the kids as they walk to school.*

Write to Learn Write the vocabulary word that each clue describes.
- This describes what a storm can do to the branches of a tree.
- If you did this, a waiter would come take your order.
- This person might draw plans for a skyscraper.
- You might see these (and hear them) in the summertime.

English Language Coach

Word Choice You might sometimes wonder why writers use uncommon words instead of the plainest, simplest ones. There's often a good reason. Maybe he or she writes, "Suki ambled by." Why? Well, *ambled* is a really good verb. It doesn't just mean "walked." It means "walked in a slow, easy way, usually without an important goal."

Even if you know the definition of a word a writer chooses to use, sometimes you need to think about it. In "Looking for America," Elizabeth Partridge says, "[In] Yellowstone, we were drenched by Old Faithful." She doesn't say "got wet" because that's not what she means. She means that they were soaked, wet clear through, dripping.

Partner Work With a partner, look up one of the verbs below. If possible, use more than one dictionary. (Make sure you look for the *verb* definition.) Find out all you can. Then talk about why a writer might choose to use it.

sprawl   zigzag   shepherd

Objectives (pp. 268–275)
Reading Distinguish fact and opinion • Make connections from text to self
Literature Identify literary elements: style
Vocabulary Understand word choice

268 UNIT 3   What's Fair and What's Not?

READING WORKSHOP 1 • Distinguishing Fact and Opinion

Skills Preview

Key Reading Skill: Distinguishing Fact and Opinion

As you read "Looking for America," think about facts you already know about segregation, or the separation of races, in America's history. For example, it is a fact that African Americans and whites were separated in the South at the time Partridge had the experience she writes about. Think about the *opinions* that led to racial separation.

Group Talk In a small group, discuss this question: How can unfair opinions lead to the unfair treatment of people?

Key Literary Element: Style

Style is personal. You dress a certain way, and you like certain colors. Style is what makes one writer's work unlike the work of any other. Style is made up of all the ways the writer uses language to express feelings and attitudes. Use these tips to help you learn about Elizabeth Partridge's style in "Looking for America."

- *What kind of language does the author use and how is memory part of the author's style?*
- *What are the sentence patterns? How important are conversations to the selection?*
- *How does the author feel about this subject?*

Write to Learn Authors have their own style; so do you! What kind of style do you have when you tell a story? Do you use humor when you tell a story? Are you serious? Do you use facts or opinions? Are you dramatic? Do you exaggerate details or stretch the truth? In your Learner's Notebook, write about your storytelling style.

Interactive Literary Elements Handbook
To review or learn more about the literary elements, go to www.glencoe.com.

Get Ready to Read

Connect to the Reading

As a little girl, Elizabeth Partridge saw that laws were not the same for everyone. What reasons did people give for making unfair rules and laws? Were those reasons based on facts or opinions? Can you think of any rules or laws we have now that we will say were unfair one day?

Partner Talk With a partner, talk about a time when it seemed as though one set of rules applied to you and another set of rules applied to others. Was this fair treatment? Is it ever fair to have different rules for different people?

Build Background

The events in Elizabeth Partridge's essay take place in the summer of 1963 in Atlanta, Georgia.

- In the American South at that time, laws kept African Americans segregated—or separated—from whites. These laws were known as Jim Crow laws.
- It was against the law for African Americans and whites to eat at the same restaurants, sit together on buses or trains, or go to school together.
- It was also against the law for African Americans to use bathrooms or drinking fountains labeled "Whites Only." Bathrooms or drinking fountains for African Americans were not always available.

Set Purposes for Reading

BIG Question Read the essay "Looking for America" to find out what Elizabeth Partridge learned about fairness.

Set Your Own Purpose What else would you like to learn from the story to help you answer the Big Question? Write your own purpose on the "Looking for America" page of Foldable 3.

Keep Moving

Use these skills as you read the following selection.

Looking for America **269**

READING WORKSHOP 1

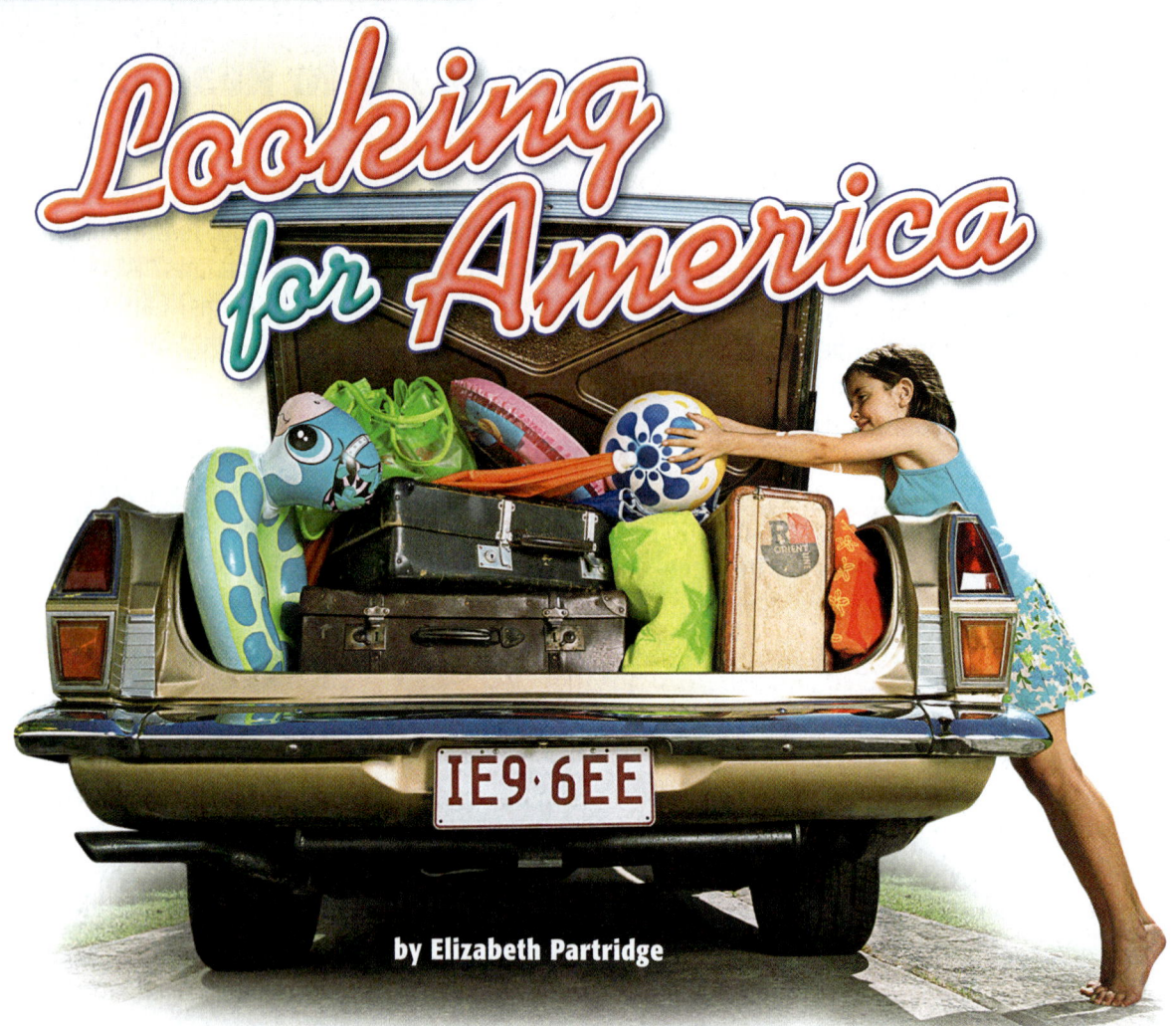

Looking for America

by Elizabeth Partridge

What I hated most was how people stared at us. I didn't mind so much while we were driving, and I would see people's mouths drop open as we flew by. But I hated it when we pulled into a campground or a gas station. As soon as my father rolled down the window, someone would stick his head in, look us over, and ask, "Where're you folks from?"

"California," my dad would say. They'd nod, like that explained it.

But it didn't, of course. It didn't begin to explain why our family was driving across the country in the summer of 1963, in an old Cadillac limousine painted a bright, metallic gold. The five of us kids didn't sit tidily in a row like regular kids but instead were sprawled on a double bed mattress that my dad had spread across the back. My parents called it "looking for America." I thought it was more like being looked *at* by America. **1**

Practice the Skills

1 **Key Literary Element**

Style Do most stories begin like this? Do you feel as though someone just started talking to you? That's a clue to the artist's style.

270 UNIT 3 What's Fair and What's Not?

My dad was a freelance photographer,[1] and to fund our trip he'd arranged to photograph buildings and parks all over the United States. We ranged in age from my seventeen-year-old sister, Joan, to baby Aaron. I was eleven, smack in the middle of the pack, with my brother Josh three years older and my sister Meg two years younger.

We threaded our way through national and state parks, zigzagging toward New York City. In the Southwest we climbed rickety wooden ladders up a cliff into old Pueblo Indian houses; in Yellowstone we were drenched by Old Faithful;[2] in Kansas we rolled out of bed at five A.M. to watch a farmer milk his cows. 🟦

"Look at it!" my father would say, throwing his arms out. "Just look at it all." With off-the-cuff comments[3] by my father, and more thoughtful views from my mother, we took in the rhythms and lives of other Americans. "We're lucky to be alive," my father said. "Right now, right here!"

By late August we had made it to New York, camped our way down the Great Smoky Mountains,[4] and were headed for Atlanta, Georgia.

An **architect** my father knew, Mr. McNeeley, had designed his own house in Atlanta. We were invited to stay while my father photographed the house. I was excited—after weeks of smoky fires and pit toilets, we were going to stay in a real house. Maybe they'd even have a TV in their rumpus room[5] and we could spread out on a comfortable couch and watch something like *The Wonderful World of Disney.*

We hit the Deep South just as a hot spell struck. The air was thick and steamy and smelled like mildew. The buzz of **cicadas** filled my ears.

Analyzing the Photo Read the second paragraph on this page and footnote 2. What place does this photo show? What is a geyser?

Practice the Skills

🟦 **English Language Coach**

Word Choice Think about the verbs the author uses in this paragraph—*threaded, zigzagging, drenched,* and *rolled.* Think about why she chose those particular verbs.

---

1. A *freelance photographer* is a photographer who works on his or her own for many different employers.
2. The *Pueblo Indians* are a group of Native Americans living mainly in New Mexico and Arizona. *Yellowstone* is a park in Wyoming, Idaho, and Montana; it is famous for a hot spring known as *Old Faithful* that sprays water and steam from the ground.
3. To make an *off-the-cuff comment* is to say something without thinking carefully about it.
4. The *Great Smoky Mountains* are mountains on the border between North Carolina and Tennessee.
5. A *rumpus room* is a play room or family room.

Vocabulary

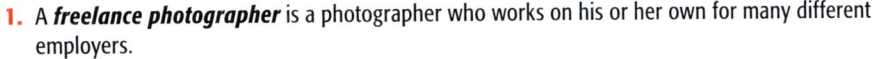

architect (AR kuh tekt) *n.* a person who designs buildings

cicadas (sih KAY duz) *n.* large insects also called locusts; males make a buzzing sound

READING WORKSHOP 1

My mother insisted we stop for the night at a campground outside of Atlanta, so we could clean up. After dinner she handed out towels and shepherded us into the public showers, a squat cement building with huge spiders in the corners and black beetles scuttling across the wet floors. Washing my hair, I discovered a big knotted tangle in the back, but it hurt too much when I tried to brush it out so I just left it. At least my hair was clean.

Late the next morning when we arrived at the McNeeleys', I saw that my mother had been right to tidy us up. Their new house was perfect. Every surface was shiny clean, nothing out of place. Built around a courtyard filled with plants, floor to ceiling glass windows let a dappled[6] green light into every room. Antique Persian rugs[7] covered the smooth cement floors, and modern sculptures made of glass and ceramic perched on back-lit shelves. There wasn't a rumpus room in sight. Mrs. McNeeley wore bright red lipstick and white slacks with a crisp linen blouse. I was painfully aware of the big snarl in my hair.

Mrs. McNeeley showed my sisters and me into a guest room with its own bathroom loaded with huge, fluffy towels and sweet-smelling soap, then left us, saying she needed to speak with the cook about lunch arrangements.

I stood on one foot and stared out into the courtyard. Our mother was right to be concerned: we didn't fit in. "How long do you think we're staying here?" I asked Meg nervously. 3

At lunchtime my mother **beckoned** me to take the chair next to Aaron. A tall black woman wearing a starched apron came in through a swinging door. She carried a casserole with a heavy silver spoon laid across the top.

"Thank you, Annie," said Mrs. McNeeley. I stared at my mother, frozen. What were we supposed to do

Visual Vocabulary
A *casserole* is a baked food with many types of ingredients inside.

---

6. Something *dappled* is marked with spots or patches of color.
7. *Antique Persian rugs* are rugs made in an early period of Iran's history. The rugs are very expensive.

Vocabulary

beckoned (BEK und) *v.* moved the head or hand to make a sign to approach or come nearer

Practice the Skills

3 **Reviewing Skills**

Connecting Have you ever been in a situation in which you weren't sure how to act? In your Learner's Notebook, explain what happened.

now? Did we dip the spoon in the casserole and serve ourselves? Did we get served? Annie stood next to my mother, the casserole in her outstretched arms. My mother looked uncomfortable and busied herself with tucking a napkin into the neck of Aaron's shirt. My stomach twisted. Even my mother wasn't sure what to do. 4

"Please," said Mrs. McNeeley to my mother, "help yourself."

When Annie stood next to me I just looked at her helplessly, afraid I would spill casserole all over my lap from the big silver spoon. She winked at me so quickly I wasn't sure she had, and put a spoonful of casserole on my plate.

After lunch my father started shooting interiors[8] of the house. The rest of us were shepherded to the courtyard. My mother and Mrs. McNeeley sat under a big umbrella, and Annie brought out a pitcher of iced tea and tall glasses full of clinking ice cubes.

Meg and I played hopscotch on the flagstones, while Joan challenged Josh to a game of rummy.[9] Aaron sat and banged on a metal pail. The heat fell down on us, heavy and moist, and the whiny buzz of the cicadas set my teeth on edge. Aaron smashed his hand under the pail and started screaming. Suddenly my head felt like it was exploding with noise and heat and an anxious worry.

I had to get away from my sisters and brothers, away from Mrs. McNeeley sitting stiffly with a tight smile. I slipped inside, crossed the dining room, and bolted through the swinging door, right into the kitchen. Annie stood with her back to me, working at the sink. 5

"Yes, Ma'am?" she said, turning around. "Oh," she said, surprised to see me. I stood awkwardly, ready to dash out again. Maybe I wasn't allowed in the kitchen. The cook tipped her head toward a small pine table.

"Sit, honey," she said. I tried to ease graciously into the chair but managed to knock my funny bone on the edge of the table and let out a yelp.

"You must be growing," the cook said. "Skinny as all get out, and don't know where your body's at."

I didn't want to tell her I was always banging myself on something. She put two sugar cookies and a tall, cold glass

---

Practice the Skills

4 Key Literary Element

Style Here the author asks many questions. How are the questions a part of her style? Do they make you feel as if you know her and what she's feeling?

5 English Language Coach

Word Choice Look at the verbs in the second sentence of this paragraph—*slipped, crossed,* and *bolted.* How do they describe the narrator's trip from the backyard to the kitchen?

---

8. If a photographer is **shooting interiors**, he or she is taking pictures inside.
9. **Flagstones** are paving stones, and **rummy** is a card game for two or more players.

of milk in front of me. As I ate, I watched her wash the lunch dishes. Steam rose from the sink, and moisture beaded up on her forehead. When she finished she filled a quart-size canning jar with cold water and drank. I was grateful for her quiet company.

When Aaron woke up from his nap we walked to a nearby city park. Though the sun was low, the air still felt like we were walking in a huge oven, with more heat radiating[10] up from the cement. My mother sat on a bench next to the sandbox and plunked Aaron down in the sand.

I spotted a drinking fountain and ran over, guzzling the water in great big gulps. Meg thumped into my back.

"My turn!" she said. I clung tight to the faucet and jabbed backward at her with my elbows until my stomach was full.

When I stood up, water slid down my neck and under my shirt. Over the fountain was a sign I hadn't noticed: "Whites Only."

"Mom," I yelled back across the playground. "What does 'Whites Only' mean?"

My mother flung her hand out. "Sh. . . ." she said. "Come over here."

I stood next to my mother, who leaned in close. "Negroes aren't allowed to drink from the same fountains as whites in the South, or use the same bathrooms."

I stared at my mother, disbelieving.

"Are those rules?"

"More than rules," she said sadly. "Laws."

I walked all around the playground, but I didn't see any other drinking fountain. 6

T he next morning as my parents were packing the car, I slipped back into the kitchen.

"We're leaving," I said to Annie.

"I know, honey," she said. "You have a good trip now, you hear?"

The breakfast dishes were sitting in the rack drying, carrots and potatoes lay on the counter, next to her half-full jar of water. I wanted to ask Annie what she did when she got

Practice the Skills

6 **Key Reading Skill**

Distinguishing Fact and Opinion Is what the narrator's mother tells her here a fact or an opinion? Could what she says be proved?

---

10. Here *radiating* means that the heat was coming up from the sidewalk.

thirsty at the park. But it seemed like too big a question. I searched for something I could ask, something that was small and not tangled up.

"Why do you drink from a jar?" I blurted out.

She looked at me, considering. Her eyes were full of a lot of things I couldn't read.

"I get mighty thirsty," she finally said. "Those glasses aren't big enough for me."

I didn't understand. She was by the sink all day where she could easily refill her glass.

I heard my father call out, "Let's go!" and I spun out of the kitchen through the swinging door. We drove away from the house of clean rooms and dappled green light and extra-good behavior. Away from the park and kitchen and rules—laws—I didn't understand.

In no time we were out on the highway, my father whistling with the joy of being back on the open road. I leaned over the front seat and asked my mother, "Why did Annie drink out of a jar?"

My mother didn't look at me but spoke softly to her hands resting in her lap. "She probably wasn't allowed to drink from the glasses the family used."

I lay back on the mattress and thought about that. The cook prepared all their food, washing, peeling, chopping, and serving. She set the table, touching every dish. Why couldn't she drink out of their glasses?

My mother must have felt me thinking behind her, because she turned around and said gently, "Some things just don't make sense." **7**

She turned back, discomfort settling on her shoulders like an old sorrow. It was all too big, too complicated, even for her.

I still didn't understand. Why would everyone go along with something that didn't make any sense? I rolled down my window and let the hot air **buffet** my face, hoping it would blow away some of the helplessness I felt. ○

U.S. Highway 1, Number 5, 1962. Allan D'Arcangelo. Gift of Mr. and Mrs. Herbert Fischbach. The Museum of Modern Art, New York.

Analyzing the Art Study this painting. Does it help you understand why Elizabeth's father was "whistling with the joy of being back on the open road"? Explain your answer.

Practice the Skills

7 🟠 **BIG Question**

Do you agree with the author's mother that "Some things just don't make sense," when it comes to what's fair and what's not? Explain. Are there ways to change things that are unfair? Write your answers on the "Looking for America" page of Foldable 3. Your response will help you complete the Unit Challenge later.

Vocabulary
buffet (BUF it) *v.* to strike with force

READING WORKSHOP 1 • Distinguishing Fact and Opinion

After You Read | Looking for America

Answering the BIG Question

1. If you were the narrator, how would you respond to the unfair situation that Annie faced?
2. **Recall** How does Annie help the narrator at lunch?
   TIP Right There
3. **Recall** List three places the narrator visited that summer.
   TIP Think and Search

Critical Thinking

4. **Infer** Why is the narrator uncomfortable at the McNeeleys' house?
   TIP Author and Me
5. **Infer** a) What question does the narrator want to ask Annie? b) Why doesn't she ask this question?
   TIP Author and Me
6. **Analyze** At the end of the essay, why does the narrator feel helpless?
   TIP Author and Me

Write About Your Reading

Suppose that you are the narrator. Write two postcards. Write the first postcard to a friend. Describe an event from the beginning of the trip, such as the trip through New York City or the scene at Old Faithful. Then write a second postcard to the same person after the visit to the McNeeleys'.

Objectives (pp. 276–277)
Reading Distinguish fact and opinion
• Make connections from text to self
Literature Identify literary elements: style
Vocabulary Understand word choice
Grammar Identify parts of speech: adverbs
Writing Respond to literature: postcard

276 UNIT 3 What's Fair and What's Not?

Skills Review

Key Reading Skill: Distinguishing Fact and Opinion

7. Which of the following statements from the story are statements of opinion?
   - "We're lucky to be alive."
   - "Their new house was perfect."
   - "Aaron smashed his hand under the pail and started screaming."
   - "But it seemed like too big a question."

8. List three things mentioned in the story that are statements of facts.

Key Literary Element: Style

9. How would you describe the author's style in "Looking for America"? You can choose one or more of the words below or use your own.

   formal   chatty   personal   dramatic
   colorful simple   funny   complicated

Reviewing Skills: Connecting

10. The narrator is upset by the way Annie is treated by the McNeeleys. Describe a time when you saw a person being treated unfairly. How did you feel?

Vocabulary Check

Which of these sentences using vocabulary words makes sense? Which do not?

11. We sat in the shade of the **cicada**.
12. She **beckoned** me to come over.
13. The waves began to **buffet** the boat.
14. The bus broke down, so we called an **architect**.
15. **Academic Vocabulary** What are two things that you find it difficult to distinguish between?
16. **English Language Coach** Rewrite the following sentence with a more descriptive verb. Use a thesaurus if necessary.
    - I drove into the door of the garage.

Grammar Link: Adverbs

Adverbs describe verbs by giving information that answers *how, when,* or *where* questions. The adverbs in the sentences below are in bold type. The words they describe are underlined.

- She spoke **quietly**. (*How?*)
- He jogged **yesterday**. (*When?*)
- They danced **there**. (*Where?*)

Another job adverbs have is to describe adjectives.
- She was **very** tired.
- The sky was **pale** blue.

Adverbs also describe other adverbs.
- We'll arrive **late tomorrow**.
- I **absolutely** never do that.

Many adverbs end in *-ly*, especially those that answer the question *How?*

Grammar Practice

Rewrite each sentence. Circle each adverb. (Hint: Look for the types of words adverbs *can* describe, and see if they *are* described.) The number after each sentence tells how many adverbs you should find.

17. Suzanne and Joel danced gracefully. (1)
18. We gradually stopped taking the bus. (1)
19. Geoff reads very quickly. (2)
20. The car is bright red, and it runs well. (2)
21. He was barely awake and yawned deeply. (2)

Writing Application Look back at the postcards you wrote. See if you can add adverbs to describe any of your verbs.

Web Activities For eFlashcards, Selection Quick Checks, and other Web activities, go to www.glencoe.com.

WRITING WORKSHOP PART 1

Persuasive Essay
Prewriting and Drafting

ASSIGNMENT Write a persuasive essay

Purpose: Write an essay that argues either *for* or *against* a specific issue

Audience: You, your teacher, and classmates

Writing Rubric

As you work through this assignment, you should

- write your opinion about a topic
- include evidence to support your opinion
- write a five paragraph essay that includes an introduction, a body, and a conclusion
- address arguments that oppose your own views

See page 316 in Part 2 for a model of a persuasive essay.

Objectives (pp. 278–281)
Reading Use the writing process: prewriting, drafting • Write persuasively • Include main ideas and supporting details • Write with fluency and clarity
Grammar Understand function of modifiers • Identify parts of speech: adjectives, adverbs

An effort to persuade someone usually involves arguing *for* or *against* something. In this workshop, you will identify a problem you think is unfair and persuade your readers to take action.

Prewriting
Get Ready to Write

You should choose a topic that you are already familiar with and have strong feelings about.
- What problem do I care most about?
- Can I think of a possible solution?
- What about this problem is unfair?

Choose a Topic

Explore different topics by making an idea tree like the one below. Choose a problem from your idea tree to be the subject of your persuasive essay.

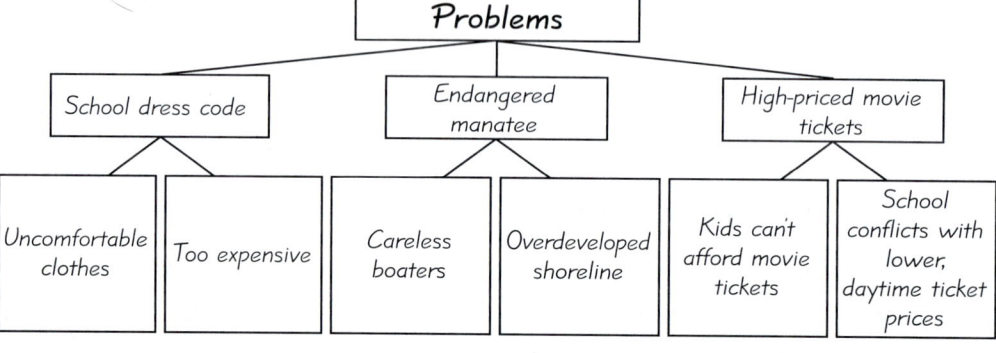

Take a Stand

Now that you have chosen a problem, think about what makes it unfair. In your Learner's Notebook, freewrite a short paragraph describing your problem and why you think it is unfair.

> I think having a dress code at school is unfair. Students should be able to express themselves through the clothes they choose to wear. No two students look alike, so why should we have to dress alike?

278 UNIT 3 What's Fair and What's Not?

Consider Other Views

When you write persuasively, you should be prepared for people who do not agree with you. In your Learner's Notebook, make a pro and con chart to determine how others may argue against your position.

Position: End the school dress code	
Pros + :	**Cons − :**
Jeans and sneakers are more comfortable	Students focus more on school and less on clothing
Dress code clothing is too expensive	Students learn how to dress for a job
Students get to express their individuality	Nice clothing will increase self-esteem

Make a Plan

- Your essay should be divided into five paragraphs: the introduction, three main paragraphs, and the conclusion.
- Pick three reasons from your "pros" list to write about; these are your main points.
- Provide facts, examples, and reasons to support your position.

Introduction: The school dress code is unfair because it requires students to wear clothing that is uncomfortable and expensive.

Main Point I. Dressy clothes are uncomfortable

Evidence A. Girls should be allowed to wear jeans instead of skirts, especially in cold weather

   B. Sneakers are more supportive than dress shoes.

Main Point II. Dress clothes are expensive

Evidence A. Many students have families living on tight budgets

   B. Jeans and sneakers cost less than dress pants and shoes

Main Point III. Increase self esteem

Evidence A. Students should be allowed to express themselves

   B. Students have more self respect when they choose their own clothes

Conclusion: A dress code does not help students focus on learning. Students are capable of choosing both comfortable and appropriate school clothes.

Drafting
Start Writing!

By now your views about this topic are clear and you are ready to start persuading. Begin by stating your topic and why you think it is unfair. Keep your Learner's Notebook nearby and follow your plan.

Writing Tip

Prewriting Each main point should be developed in a separate paragraph. The strongest point of the argument should be either first or last.

Writing Tip

Drafting Get your reader's attention by using a real life example in your introduction, *"Last week Jimmy Albert sprained his ankle during morning recess. The sprain was caused by playing basketball in dress shoes that did not have enough support for such activities . . ."*

Writing Models For models and other writing activities, go to www.glencoe.com.

WRITING WORKSHOP PART 1

Applying Good Writing Traits

Sentence Fluency

Have you ever put on your favorite pants, your favorite shirt, your favorite sweater and your favorites shoes . . . and realized the outfit looked terrible? Each piece was just fine, but they didn't work together. Sentences can be just like that.

What Is Sentence Fluency?

Fluency is a fancy word for flow. When you're writing, your sentences should flow. Your writing should help the reader go from one sentence to the next to the next. Here are some problems to watch out for:

- short, choppy sentences
- long, rambling sentences
- confusing word order
- sentences that don't lead to the next one

Why Is Sentence Fluency Important?

Fluent sentences make your writing easier to understand and more enjoyable to read. Which example below is fluent and which is not?

A. There are lots of holes in my backyard. My dog Skippy likes to dig. Skippy is a terrier. Terriers are known for digging in the ground. My dad gets angry at Skippy for digging holes in the ground.

B. My dog Skippy likes to dig. As a result, there are lots of holes in my backyard. Even though Skippy is a terrier, a type of dog known for digging, my dad gets angry at him.

How Do I Do It?

Transitions help. Transitions are words or phrases that connect ideas from one sentence to another. In the example above, the writer used the transitions *as a result* to link two sentences about the same topic.

Transitions can also link ideas in the same sentence. *Even though* connects the dog to the father's anger.

Use this transition chart to improve sentence fluency.

Sentence Type	Transition Words and Phrases
Locate Students cheered **inside** the gymnasium.	above, below, beside, in the distance, around the corner, underneath, inside
Sequence We waited and waited. **Finally** my sister arrived at the restaurant.	first, next, when, later, finally, meanwhile, then, after
Importance **More importantly,** she brought the birthday cake.	First, most importantly, mainly, primarily, above all
Compare Skippy digs holes **just like** the terrier down the street.	also, like, just as, just like, similarly, similar to
Contrast **However,** Skippy's holes are much deeper.	But, even so, however, unlike

Write to Learn Use transitions to make these sentences more fluent.

1. Sal and I rode our bikes to the park. We played soccer and went home.
2. Marcia plays the harmonica well. Her sister does not.
3. Skippy plays in the yard, runs through the house, jumps on my neighbor, digs a hole, eats dinner, and goes to sleep.

Grammar Link

Adjectives and Adverbs

What Are Adjectives and Adverbs?

Remember, you can tell what part of speech a word is by what it *does* in the sentence. One word can be many different parts of speech.

Adjectives and adverbs do similar things. They are both **modifiers**. They modify, or tell more about, other words. As you know, **adjectives** modify nouns or pronouns. **Adverbs** modify verbs, adjectives, or other adverbs.

Adjectives may come before or after the word they modify. *He's a nice boy, sweet and friendly.* When a linking verb is used, the adjective comes afterwards.
- The music was loud and clear. (*Was* is a linking verb. *Loud* and *clear* describe the music.)
- bullet>This sandwich tastes salty. (*Tastes* is a linking verb. *Salty* describes the sandwich.)

It is easy to tell if a word is acting as an adverb if it comes right after the verb or if it ends in *-ly*.
- The child waited patiently. (*Patiently* tells *how* the child waited. It modifies the verb.)

But not all adverbs are so easy to spot!
- Bob never pets strange dogs. (*Never* tells *when* Bob pets strange dogs. It modifies the verb.)
- I shop here for clothes. (*Here* tells *where* I shop. It modifies the verb.)
- The unusually ugly cat was sleeping. (*Unusually* modifies the adjective *ugly*.)
- She talks too loudly. (*Too* modifies the adverb *loudly*.)

Warning! Warning! Warning! Beware of words that look like verbs! Sometimes a word that you think is a verb might really be a modifier (or even a noun).
- That smiling man is my Uncle Albert. (Even though *smiling* can be a verb, here it is an adjective describing *man*.)

Why Are Adjectives and Adverbs Important?

Adjectives and adverbs combined make your writing more interesting.

How Do I Use Adjectives and Adverbs?

Use an adjective to tell more about a person, a place, a thing, or an idea. Use an adverb to tell how, when, or where things are done.

Grammar Practice

Copy the sentences. Then underline the adjectives and circle the adverbs.

> Every player is waiting eagerly.
>
> The final game will start soon.
>
> The bright red uniforms are very colorful.
>
> Our excellent band will play loudly and well.

Writing Application Review your draft to see if you should add any modifiers to make your writing more clear and interesting.

Looking Ahead

Keeping the writing you did here. In Part 2, you'll learn how to turn it into a solid, persuasive essay.

READING WORKSHOP 2

Skills Focus

You will practice using these skills when you read the following selections:
- "Two Advertisements," p. 286
- "Stray," p. 292

Reading
- Clarifying

Literature
- Identifying author's bias
- Identifying point of view

Vocabulary
- Identifying semantic slanting
- Understanding denotation and connotation

Writing/Grammar
- Comparative and superlative adjectives
- Comparative and superlative adverbs

Skill Lesson
Clarifying

Learn It!

What Is It? As you know by now, you can learn skills that will help you better understand what you read. One of these skills is **clarifying**. That means "making things clear." When you're reading, you sometimes come to a word, a sentence, or a paragraph that you don't really understand. When you stop and try to figure it out, you're clarifying. Not all readers do that, but really good readers do.

Why Is It Important? Authors often build ideas one on another. If you don't clear up a confusing passage, you may not understand main ideas or information that comes later.

© Patrick McDonnell. Reprinted with Permission of King Features Syndicate.

Analyzing Cartoons
When the crab said, "Let's do lunch," what did he mean? How could he *clarify* what he said?

Objectives (pp. 282–283)
Reading Monitor comprehension: clarify

READING WORKSHOP 2 • Clarifying

How Do I Do It? Go back and read a confusing section slowly. Look up words you don't know, and read any footnotes. Ask questions about what you don't understand. Sometimes you may want to read on to see if further information helps you clarify.

Study Central Visit www.glencoe.com and click on Study Central to review clarifying.

Here is how one student clarified a hard section from his science book.

> The earth's surface seems solid and stable. The outer layer of our planet, however, is split into large pieces called *plates.* Plates are like pieces of a puzzle—an enormous jigsaw puzzle in which the pieces slowly move together, apart, and past one another. Where the edges of the plates bump together, as they do in the region around Mexico, earthquakes can occur.

> It looks like the main point of this paragraph is about how the moving plates cause earthquakes in Mexico, but I'm not sure I understand this part about the plates. It's clearer when the author compares the moving plates to moving jigsaw puzzle pieces. That makes more sense to me. I think I'll read it again and look up the word "enormous."

Practice It!

In your Learner's Notebook, write down the point that Richard Durbin is making in this sentence from "Preserving a Great American Symbol."

Please do not tell me that wooden bats are too expensive, when players who cannot hit their weight are being paid more money than the President of the United States.

Use It!

Use the following questions to help you clarify hard sections of a text.
- Do I understand all the words?
- Is there some information missing?
- Is there a chance that this will make more sense to me if I read on further?

READING WORKSHOP 2 • Clarifying

Before You Read : Two Advertisements

Reading an Advertisement

"Buying this product will make you a happier person!" That's the idea behind a lot of advertisements, or ads. This method is called an **emotional appeal**. Advertisers use emotional appeals to persuade you to buy things. Would any of these appeals persuade you to buy a product?

- Your friends will feel jealous.
- You will get a feeling of well-being.
- This product is made better than similar products.
- This product will give you the energy to keep up with your busy schedule.
- This product contributes to better health.

Think about these appeals as you read the two advertisements on pages 286–287.

Vocabulary Preview

envy (EN vee) *n.* jealousy; desire to have something someone else has **(p. 286)** *Kori's new sweater filled Maria with envy.*

well-being (wel BEE ing) *n.* good physical and mental condition **(p. 286)** *Torrance had a feeling of well-being after his workout at the gym.*

nutrition (noo TRISH un) *n.* the food needed for life and health **(p. 287)** *Fresh fruit is a good source of nutrition.*

unique (yoo NEEK) *adj.* having no like or equal **(p. 287)** *You are a unique person.*

Write to Learn Use each vocabulary word in a sentence.

English Language Coach

Semantic Slanting "Semantic" means the study of words. "Slant" means to present a certain view in order to favor one side over another. Semantic slanting means using words so only one side of an argument or issue is presented favorably. Positive things are said about one side, and negative words are used against the other.

Here's Carlos's argument for why the family should get a dog.

Why We Should Get a Dog

Dogs make the best pets. They're loyal, they protect the house, and they do what you tell them. Cats, on the other hand, are unfriendly, lazy, and they never come when you call them.

Carlos's words *for* dogs	Carlos's words *against* cats
loyal	unfriendly
protect	lazy
do what you tell them	never come when you call them

Did Carlos say anything good about having a cat as a pet? He presented only his view of the issue and carefully chose his words. Be sure you recognize semantic slanting when you hear it and try to hear both sides.

Write to Learn Write two short paragraphs about hip hop or rock music. Give one a positive semantic slant and the other a negative slant.

Objectives (pp. 284–287)
Reading Monitor comprehension: clarify • Make connections from text to self
Literature Identify literary elements: author's bias
Vocabulary Identify semantic slanting

READING WORKSHOP 2 • Clarifying

Skills Preview

Key Reading Skill: Clarifying

If you read something that doesn't make sense, take a minute to clarify. Clarifying is clearing up confusing or difficult passages. To clarify an advertisement, make sure you understand not only the words, but also any illustrations and the writer's purpose. Ask yourself these questions.

- What is the purpose of this ad?
- What is the ad trying to persuade me to do, and how is it trying to do that?
- What emotions does the ad appeal to? How are words and images used for that purpose?

Key Literary Element: Bias

A **bias** is a tendency to be in favor of something or against it. Use these tips to find each writer's bias as you read "Two Advertisements."

- Think about the writer's purpose.

  Is the author trying to persuade, entertain, inform?

- Think about the writer's opinions.

  How many sides of the story does the writer give— more than one? Or do you just see the writer's side?

  Does the writer use facts to prove points?

- Pay attention to word choice.

  How do the writer's words make you feel about the subject?

Partner Talk Remember that bias is a tendency for or against something. Think about a conversation you've had recently in which one person showed a bias, or favoritism. Tell your partner about that conversation. What was the person's bias? How were you able to recognize that bias?

Interactive Literary Elements Handbook
To review or learn more about the literary elements, go to www.glencoe.com.

Get Ready to Read

Connect to the Reading

Have you ever wanted people to be jealous of you and wish they had what you have? Have you ever been particularly proud of something you owned? Could someone get you to do something or buy something by telling you it would give you that feeling?

Write to Learn Think about your answers to the questions above. Jot down your thoughts on a separate piece of paper.

Build Background

Advertisers use certain writing "tricks" to get their messages across. Understanding advertisers' tricks helps readers make better choices about what they believe and what they buy.

The car advertisement you will read, uses a "picture of success."

- It shows smiling, well-dressed, successful-looking people using the product.
- The message is that you will also be smiling, well dressed, and successful if you use the product.

Set Purposes for Reading

BIG Question Read "Two Advertisements" to decide whether these ads use fair methods to get readers to buy their products.

Set Your Own Purpose What else would you like to learn from the reading to help you answer the Big Question? Write your purpose on the "Two Advertisements" page of Foldable 3.

Keep Moving

Use these skills as you read the following selections.

READING WORKSHOP 2

Two Advertisements

Practice the Skills

New 1951 Packard Convertible—one of nine all-new models

Pride of Possession[1] is Standard Equipment [1]

How can we put a price tag on your neighbors' look of **envy** . . . or on your own feeling of **well-being** . . . as you drive your new 1951 Packard home for the first time?

We can't, of course. So—*Pride of Possession is Standard Equipment.*

Like the exclusiveness[2] of Packard beauty—and the years–ahead superiority[3] of Packard engineering[4]—you can't buy a new 1951 Packard without it. And you never can match it—no matter how much you may be willing to pay—*in any other car!* [2] [3]

It's more than a car . . . it's a

PACKARD

ASK THE MAN WHO OWNS ONE

1. Here, **possession** (puh ZEH shun) means ownership—the state of having or owning something.
2. **Exclusiveness** (eks KLOO suv niss) is the quality of belonging only to a small group.
3. **Superiority** (suh PEER ee OHR uh tee) is the quality of being better than others.
4. **Engineering** (en juh NEER ing) is the planning, building, and workmanship involved in creating a product.

Vocabulary

envy (EN vee) *n.* jealousy; desire to have something that someone else has

well-being (wel BEE ing) *n.* good physical and mental condition

[1] **Key Literary Element**

Bias Does every advertisement writer have a bias in favor of the product? Do you expect to see all the facts in an advertisement? What words in the ad show the writer's bias? List them in your Learner's Notebook.

[2] **Key Reading Skill**

Clarifying As you read, ask yourself questions to help you clarify the claims made in the ad.

In your Learner's Notebook, write a question of your own about one of the claims in this ad.

[3] **English Language Coach**

Semantic Slanting What examples of semantic slanting can you find in this advertisement? Explain why you think they are semantic slanting.

READING WORKSHOP 2

Classes and tests. 4
Practices and meetings.
Chores and homework. 5

Who has time for nutrition?
YOU DO.

JIFFY JUICE has the vitamins and minerals to help keep up with your busy schedule and a unique shape that makes it easy to take with you. So now you have NO EXCUSES. 6

For nutrition that's ready when you are, drink JIFFY JUICE.

Practice the Skills

4 Key Literary Element

Bias What words or phrases in this ad show the writer's bias? List them in your Learner's Notebook.

5 Key Reading Skill

Clarifying Reread these first three lines. What do the lines tell you about the audience the ad is aimed at? What is the writer saying with these three lines? Why do you think the writer used fragments rather than complete sentences?

6 BIG Question

Each ad uses emotional appeals. The writer of the car ad uses words like *pride of possession, envy,* and *superiority.* The writer of the juice ad says things like, *So now you have no excuses.* Is it fair that writers use emotional appeals to persuade readers to buy products? Why or why not? Write your response on the "Two Advertisements" page of Foldable 3. Your response will help you complete the Unit Challenge later.

Vocabulary

nutrition (noo TRISH un) *n.* the food needed for life and health
unique (yoo NEEK) *adj.* having no like or equal

Two Advertisements **287**

READING WORKSHOP 2 • Clarifying

After You Read Two Advertisements

Answering the BIG Question

1. Do you think it's fair to use emotional appeals to win arguments or sell things? Why or why not?
2. **Recall** What kind of car is the first ad trying to sell?
   TIP Right There
3. **Summarize** According to the Jiffy Juice ad, why should you drink Jiffy Juice?
   TIP Think and Search

Critical Thinking

4. **Draw Conclusions** Would you buy Jiffy Juice? Why or why not?
   TIP Author and Me
5. **Infer** What audience do you think the car ad is aimed at? Explain your answer.
   TIP Author and Me
6. **Evaluate** Which of the two ads works better to make the product seem appealing? Explain.
   TIP On My Own

Write About Your Reading

Think about a product you own or would like to own. Using the ads you've just read as models, write a one-page ad for that product. In your ad, be sure to
- tell what the product is and what it does
- tell readers why they should buy the product
- use emotional appeals to persuade readers to buy the product

If you need help, look through magazines to see some other ads and use those as models.

Objectives (pp. 288–289)
Reading Monitor comprehension: clarify
Literature Identify literary elements: author's bias
Vocabulary Identify semantic slanting
Writing Use persuasive techniques to write an ad
Grammar Identify parts of speech: comparative and superlative adjectives
• Use comparative and superlative adjectives correctly

Skills Review

Key Reading Skill: Clarifying

7. In your Learner's Notebook, write at least one method you used to clarify a section of "Two Advertisements."

Key Literary Element: Bias

8. Give an example of how the writer's word choice reveals bias in favor of the 1951 Packard.
9. Do the writers' emotional appeals make you feel a bias for or against either product? Explain.
10. The Packard ad is more than half a century old. In what ways are today's car ads similar to the 1951 ad?
11. Since you are a kid, do you feel that you relate to the Jiffy Juice ad? Does that mean you have a bias? Explain.

Vocabulary Check

Answer the following questions about the vocabulary words.

envy   well-being   nutrition   unique

12. Would you rather have a feeling of **envy** or of **well-being**?
13. Are things made in a factory usually **unique**?
14. Does good **nutrition** help you have a feeling of **well-being**?
15. **English Language Coach** Both ads put a positive slant on their product. For each ad, list one way it uses semantic slanting.

Web Activities For eFlashcards, Selection Quick Checks, and other Web activities, go to www.glencoe.com.

Grammar Link: Comparative and Superlative Adjectives

Use the **comparative** (kum PAIR uh tiv) form of an adjective to compare two persons, places, things, or ideas.

- Most adjectives of one syllable are made into the comparative by adding *-er* to the adjective.
  *Joan is **older** than Elizabeth.*
- Most adjectives with more than one syllable add *more* or *less* before the word.
  *This week was **less exciting** than last week.*

Use the **superlative** (soo PUR luh tiv) form of an adjective to compare more than two persons, places, things, or ideas.

- Most adjectives of one syllable are made into the superlative by adding *-est* to the adjective.
  *Aaron is the **youngest** of the five children.*
- Most adjectives with more than one syllable add *most* or *least* before the word.
  *Who is the **most helpful** person you know?*
- Do not use both the *-er/-est* ending and *more/less* or *most/least* together in a sentence.
  WRONG: *He was the **most smartest** student in the class.*
  RIGHT: *He was the **smartest** student in the class.*

Grammar Practice

Rewrite each sentence below, choosing the correct form of the adjective in parentheses.

16. The Partridges were the (most unusual/more unusual) of all the families on their street.
17. Hayden was (faster/fastest) than Mitchell.
18. Elizabeth was (more tired/most tired) than Meg.
19. Dawson's car was (more nicer/nicer) than the car we rented.

Two Advertisements 289

READING WORKSHOP 2 • Clarifying

Before You Read: Stray

Cynthia Rylant

Meet the Author
When Cynthia Rylant was four years old, her parents separated. She went to live with her grandparents in West Virginia. She lived with them for nearly four years, and her experiences from that time are an important part of the stories she tells. Rylant writes to make the world a better place, saying, "Every person is able to add beauty." See page R5 of the Author Files in the back of the book for more on Cynthia Rylant.

Author Search For more about Cynthia Rylant, go to www.glencoe.com.

Objectives (pp. 290–295)
Reading Clarify ideas and text • Make connections from text to self
Literature Identify narrator • Understand point of view
Vocabulary Understand denotation and connotation

Vocabulary Preview

abandoned (uh BAN dund) *v.* given up or left behind; form of the verb *abandon* **(p. 292)** *Their plan to go camping was abandoned once it started to rain.*

timidly (TIM ud lee) *adv.* fearfully **(p. 292)** *The child was shy, and she entered the playground timidly.*

grudgingly (GRUJ ing lee) *adv.* unhappily, unwillingly **(p. 293)** *Chloe didn't want to sit beside Amy on the bus, but she did it grudgingly.*

distress (dis TRES) *n.* pain or suffering **(p. 294)** *It caused her distress to see a pet without a home.*

Group Work With a few other students, make up a very short story about an old, empty house. Use all the vocabulary words in it.

English Language Coach

Denotation and Connotation All words have a **denotation** (dee noh TAY shun), a meaning found in the dictionary. Many words also have a **connotation** (kawn noh TAY shun), which is a feeling associated with that word.

Look at the words *house* and *home,* for example. They have the same dictionary meaning, or denotation. But the word *home* also has a connotation.

- **Denotation** for *house* and *home:* A place where people live
- **Connotation** for *home:* A familiar place where people feel safe and comfortable

Think-Pair-Share Each of the words below has a strong connotation. Copy each word and write down some notes about what it suggests to you. Then share the words and connotations with a partner. Do your connotations match?

family   chef   rat

290 UNIT 3 What's Fair and What's Not?

READING WORKSHOP 2 • Clarifying

Skills Preview

Key Reading Skill: Clarifying
Before you read "Stray," plan your strategy for clarifying confusing sections. Be sure to
- reread confusing sections slowly and carefully
- look up unfamiliar words
- ask yourself questions about what you don't understand

Write to Learn As you read "Stray," list any unfamiliar words that make the selection hard to understand. Also, list any questions you ask yourself to help clarify what you read.

Literary Element: Point of View
As you know, in **first-person point of view,** a narrator who is "I" tells the story. The reader knows only what that narrator actually sees, hears, thinks, or feels. In **third-person point of view,** the narrator is not named and is not a character in the story. That narrator is outside the story, not involved in it.

There are two major kinds of third-person point of view.
- Many stories are written from a point of view called **third-person limited.** In this type of narration, the writer doesn't use an "I" narrator, but he or she limits the story to what the main character sees, hears, thinks, and feels.
- A few stories use a point of view called **third-person omniscient.** In these stories, the narrator reveals what many or all of the characters see, hear, think, and feel.

As you read "Stray," notice what the narrator reveals to you, the reader. See if you can tell what point of view the story is being told from.

Think-Pair-Share Think about stories you see on TV and in movies. What point of view is used? What would a movie be like if it showed things from just one character's point of view? Discuss with a classmate how a movie like that might work.

Get Ready to Read

Connect to the Reading
Have you ever deeply wanted something, even though there were plenty of good reasons against it? As you read "Stray," think about what Doris wants. Think about why her parents want something different. What would you do if you were in Doris's situation?

Partner Talk With a partner, talk about a time when you did not get something you wanted. What was it? Why didn't you get it? How did you react?

Build Background
- Animal shelters—often called *pounds*—take in 6 to 8 million dogs and cats each year.
- These shelters try to find new homes for many of the animals, but some cats and dogs cannot be adopted. They may be too sick, they may have behavior problems, or there may just not be enought people willing to adopt them.

Set Purposes for Reading
BIG Question Read "Stray" to find out how one family struggles to make a fair decision about a stray animal.

Set Your Own Purpose What else would you like to learn from the reading to help you answer the Big Question? Write your purpose on the "Stray" page of Foldable 3.

Interactive Literary Elements Handbook
To review or learn more about the literary elements, go to www.glencoe.com.

Keep Moving
Use these skills as you read the following selection.

Stray 291

READING WORKSHOP 2

Stray
by Cynthia Rylant

In January, a puppy **wandered** onto the property of Mr. Amos Lacey and his wife, Maggie and their daughter, Doris. Icicles hung three feet or more from the eaves[1] of houses, snowdrifts swallowed up automobiles, and the birds were so fluffed up they looked comic. **1 2**

The puppy had been **abandoned**, and it made its way down the road toward the Laceys' small house, its tail between its legs, shivering.

Doris, whose school had been called off because of the snow, was out shoveling the cinder-block front steps when she spotted the pup on the road. She set down the shovel.

"Hey! Come on!" she called.

The puppy stopped in the road, wagging its tail **timidly**, trembling with shyness and cold.

Doris trudged through the yard, went up the shoveled drive and met the dog.

"Come on, pooch."

"Where did *that* come from?" Mrs. Lacey asked as soon as Doris put the dog down in the kitchen.

---

1. **Eaves** (eevz) are the lower edges of roofs.

Vocabulary

abandoned (uh BAN dund) *v.* given up or left behind

timidly (TIM ud lee) *adv.* fearfully

Practice the Skills

1 **English Language Coach**

Denotation and Connotation The puppy **wandered** into the Laceys' yard. Why do you suppose the author used the word *wandered* instead of *walked* or *strolled*?

2 **Key Reading Skill**

Clarifying The first paragraph describes a snowy January day. Think about the statement that "snowdrifts swallowed up automobiles, and the birds were so fluffed up they looked comic." What does the author mean? How could you clarify those words?

292 UNIT 3 What's Fair and What's Not?

Mr. Lacey was at the table, cleaning his fingernails with his pocketknife. The snow was keeping him home from his job at the warehouse.

"I don't know where it came from," he said mildly, "but I know for sure where it's going."

Doris hugged the puppy hard against her. She said nothing.

Because the roads would be too bad for travel for many days, Mr. Lacey couldn't get out to take the puppy to the pound in the city right away. He agreed to let it sleep in the basement, while Mrs. Lacey **grudgingly** let Doris feed it table scraps. The woman was sensitive about throwing out food.

By the looks of it, Doris figured the puppy was about six months old and on its way to being a big dog. She thought it might have some shepherd in it.

Four days passed and the puppy did not complain. It never cried in the night or howled at the wind. It didn't tear up everything in the basement. It wouldn't even follow Doris up the basement steps unless it was invited.

It was a good dog.

Several times Doris had opened the door in the kitchen that led to the basement, and the puppy had been there, all stretched out, on the top step. Doris knew it had wanted some company and that it had lain against the door, listening to the talk in the kitchen, smelling the food, being a part of things. It always wagged its tail, eyes all sleepy, when she found it there. **3**

Even after a week had gone by, Doris didn't name the dog. She knew her parents wouldn't let her keep it, that her father made so little money any pets were out of the question, and that the pup would definitely go to the pound when the weather cleared. **4**

Still, she tried talking to them about the dog at dinner one night.

Vocabulary

grudgingly (GRUJ ing lee) *adv.* unhappily, unwillingly

READING WORKSHOP 2

Practice the Skills

3 **Literary Element**

Point of View What do you know about the point of view of the story so far? Is the narrator first-person or third-person? Is the narrator a character in the story?

4 **BIG Question**

Why do Mr. and Mrs. Lacey want to get rid of the dog? Do you think getting rid of the dog is fair? Write your answers on the "Stray" page of Foldable 3. Your response will help you complete the Unit Challenge later.

Analyzing the Photo Would you keep this puppy if you found it abandoned in the snow? Why or why not?

"She's a good dog, isn't she?" Doris said, hoping one of them would agree with her.

Her parents glanced at each other and went on eating.

"She's not much trouble," Doris added. "I like her." She smiled at them, but they continued to ignore her.

"I figure she's real smart," Doris said to her mother. "I could teach her things."

Mrs. Lacey just shook her head and stuffed a forkful of sweet potato in her mouth. Doris fell silent, praying the weather would never clear.

But on Saturday, nine days after the dog had arrived, the sun was shining and the roads were plowed. Mr. Lacey opened up the trunk of his car and came into the house.

Doris was sitting alone in the living room, hugging a pillow and rocking back and forth on the edge of a chair. She was trying not to cry but she was not strong enough. Her face was wet and red, her eyes full of **distress**.

Mrs. Lacey looked into the room from the doorway.

"Mama," Doris said in a small voice. "Please."

Mrs. Lacy shook her head.

"You know we can't afford a dog, Doris. You try to act more grown-up about this." 5

Doris pressed her face into the pillow.

Outside, she heard the trunk of the car slam shut, one of the doors open and close, the old engine cough and choke and finally start up.

"Daddy," she whispered. "Please."

She heard the car travel down the road, and though it was early afternoon, she could do nothing but go to her bed. She cried herself to sleep, and her dreams were full of searching and searching for things lost.

It was nearly night when she finally woke up. Lying there, like stone, still exhausted, she wondered if she would ever in her life have anything. She stared at the wall for a while. 6

But she started feeling hungry, and she knew she'd have to make herself get out of bed and eat some dinner. She wanted not to go into the kitchen, past the basement door. She wanted not to face her parents.

Practice the Skills

5 Literary Element

Point of View Have you noticed more about the narrator? Does the narrator reveal what Doris feels and thinks? Does the narrator reveal what Mr. and Mrs. Lacey feel and think?

6 Reviewing Skills

Connecting How do you think Doris feels about not keeping the puppy? Think of a time you wanted something like a pet, clothes, or a bike, but knew you couldn't have it. Why couldn't you have it? How did you feel?

Vocabulary

distress (dis TRES) *n.* pain or suffering

READING WORKSHOP 2

But she rose up heavily.

Her parents were sitting at the table, dinner over, drinking coffee. They looked at her when she came in, but she kept her head down. No one spoke.

Doris made herself a glass of powdered milk and drank it all down. Then she picked up a cold biscuit and started out of the room.

"You'd better feed that mutt before it dies of starvation," Mr. Lacey said.

Doris turned around.

"What?"

"I said, you'd better feed your dog. I figure it's looking for you."

Doris put her hand to her mouth.

"You didn't take her?" she asked.

"Oh, I took her all right," her father answered. "Worst-looking place I've ever seen. Ten dogs to a cage. Smell was enough to knock you down. And they give an animal six days to live. Then they kill it with some kind of a shot."

Doris stared at her father.

"I wouldn't leave an *ant* in that place," he said. "So I brought the dog back."

Mrs. Lacey was smiling at him and shaking her head as if she would never, ever, understand him.

Mr. Lacey sipped his coffee.

"Well," he said, "are you going to feed it or not?" 7 ○

Practice the Skills

7 **BIG Question**

Do you think Mr. Lacey makes a fair decision in the end? Do you think the reason he gives for keeping the dog is the *only* reason he decides to let the dog stay? Write your response on the "Stray" page of Foldable 3. Your response will help you complete the Unit Challenge later.

Analyzing the Photo Does this picture fit in well with the ending of the story? Why or why not?

Stray **295**

READING WORKSHOP 2 • Clarifying

After You Read   Stray

Answering the BIG Question

1. Do you think people sometimes feel forced to do things that seem unfair because they have no choice? Explain. Use the situation in "Stray" as an example.

2. **Recall** Why did Doris's parents let the dog stay at first?
   TIP Right There

3. **Summarize** How do you know that the stray is a friendly, good dog?
   TIP Think and Search

Critical Thinking

4. **Infer** Do you think the author wants readers to like Mr. and Mrs. Lacey? Explain.
   TIP Author and Me

5. **Infer** a) Why doesn't Doris name the dog when it arrives?
   b) How would naming the dog change Doris's feelings about it?
   TIP Author and Me

6. **Synthesize** At the end of the story, why doesn't Doris want to face her parents?
   TIP Author and Me

Write About Your Reading

Make a comparison chart to show how Mr. Lacey felt at the beginning of the story, and how he felt at the end. Explain his reasons at the beginning, and explain what changed his feelings. Use quotes and examples from the story.

Objectives (pp. 296–297)
Reading Monitor comprehension: clarify • Make connections from text to self
Literature Identify narrator • Understand point of view
Vocabulary Understand denotation and connotation
Writing Make a comparison chart
Grammar Identify parts of speech: comparative and superlative adverbs • Use comparative and superlative adverbs correctly

Mr. Lacey

BEGINNING:	END:
How did he feel about the stray in the beginning?	*How* did he feel about the stray by the end of the story?
Use a quote:	Use a quote:
Why did he feel this way?	*Why* did his feelings change?
Give an example or a quote:	Give an example or a quote:

296 UNIT 3   What's Fair and What's Not?

Skills Review

Key Reading Skill: Clarifying

7. Did you need to use your clarifying strategies to understand any parts of this story? Explain.

Literary Element: Point of View

8. Was the narrator of this story a first-person narrator or a third-person narrator? How could you tell?
9. Was the information you received limited to the experiences of one character? If so, which one?

Reviewing Skills: Connecting

10. When you were reading "Stray," were you able to understand Doris's feelings? Had you ever felt any of the things she felt? Explain.

Vocabulary Check

Write a sentence that answers each of the following questions. Use the vocabulary word in your answer.

11. What is one thing you do **grudgingly**?
12. What is one place you might enter **timidly**?
13. What would you feel like if you were **abandoned** by your friends?
14. What is one thing that might cause you **distress**?
15. **English Language Coach** For each word below write its denotation and its connotation.

    exhausted   trudged   mutt

Web Activities For eFlashcards, Selection Quick Checks, and other Web activities, go to www.glencoe.com.

Grammar Link: Comparative and Superlative Adverbs

- Use the **comparative** form of an adverb to compare **two actions**. For one-syllable adverbs, form the comparative by adding -er to the end of the word. Use the word *more* or *less* before adverbs that end in -*ly*:

The dog ran **faster** than Doris.

The stray dog behaved **more timidly** than the other dog.

- Use the **superlative** form of an adverb to compare **more than** two actions. For short adverbs, form the superlative by adding -*est*. Use the word *most* or *least* for adverbs that end in -*ly*:

Of all the dogs at the pound, the black one barked **loudest**.

The toy varieties of poodles are my **least** favorite.

- Do not use both the -er/-est ending and *more/less* or *most/least*.

Grammar Practice

Rewrite each sentence below, choosing the correct form of the adverb in parentheses.

16. By afternoon, the snow began to pile up (most quickly/more quickly) than it did in the morning.
17. On Saturday, Doris got up (earlier/more earlier) than usual.
18. Mr. Lacey acted (more calmly/most calmly) than Doris.
19. Doris waited (more patiently, most patiently) than her mother.

Writing Application Look back at your comparison chart and make sure you used adverbs correctly. Circle comparative adverbs and underline any superlative adverbs.

READING WORKSHOP 3

Skills Focus

You will practice using these skills when you read the following selections:
- "Dressed for Success?" p. 302
- "Eleven," p. 308

Reading
- Making inferences

Literature
- Understanding elements of argument
- Recognizing repetition

Vocabulary
- Identifying balanced language
- Academic Vocabulary: *infer*

Writing/Grammar
- Identifying demonstratives
- Identifying articles

Skill Lesson

Inferring

Learn It!

What Is It? When you **infer**, you use your knowledge, reasoning, and experiences to guess what a writer does not come right out and say.

Without realizing it, you make inferences every day. For example, you arrive at the bus stop a little later than usual. No one is there. You say to yourself, "I've missed the bus." You may be wrong, but you've used the evidence (you're late; no one's there) to make an inference (you've missed the bus).

Many times in a piece of writing the author does not come right out and say every little thing about every character or event. To really understand what is going on, you have to make inferences.

Calvin and Hobbes © 1990 Watterson. Distributed by UNIVERSAL PRESS SYNDICATE. Reprinted with permission. All rights reserved.

Analyzing Cartoons
What happens in the first two panels of this cartoon? In the next two panels, Calvin makes an inference. Do you agree with his inference? Why or why not?

Objectives (pp. 298–299)
Reading Make inferences

Academic Vocabulary

infer (in FUR) *v.* to use reason and experience to figure out what an author does not say directly

READING WORKSHOP 3 • Inferring

Why Is It Important? Making inferences will help you to find meaning in what you read. Inferring helps you understand characters, find the theme of a selection, and stay involved with what you are reading.

How Do I Do It? Inferring uses many of the skills you have learned in the previous units, such as activating prior knowledge, connecting, and predicting. In order to make inferences, pay attention to details. They give you the clues you need. But be careful. Making inferences does *not* mean guessing without thinking! Here's how one student used inferring to understand the passage below:

Study Central Visit www.glencoe.com and click on Study Central to review inferring.

> Everything was all set—the balloons, the presents and the cake. Darla nervously glanced out the window. Things must go as planned! Darla had worked for weeks on the details for the party, everything from the colors to the strawberry filling in the cake. She hoped her brother would get this one thing right—picking their grandmother up from the station. "Please let him do this!" thought Darla. "I knew I should have gone myself!"

This must be an important party since it's taken Darla weeks to plan it and she's nervous. I think she doesn't trust her brother. He's probably messed up before.

Practice It!

You can often tell when a person is upset by how he or she acts and what he or she says . . . or doesn't say.

> *Grandmother said the taxi driver was very nice. Darla fumed for the rest of the party.*

What can we infer here? Remember who was supposed to pick up Grandmother. What probably happened?

Use It!

As you read "Dressed for Success?" and "Eleven," notice the clues the authors provide. In your Learner's Notebook, use these clues to make inferences.

READING WORKSHOP 3 • Inferring

Before You Read : Dressed for Success?

Meet the Writer

Melanie Bertotto was born in 1992 and is on the 2004–2005 team of kid reporters for *TIME FOR KIDS*. Bertotto's other stories are "Book Review: Wolf Brother Chronicles of Ancient Darkness" and "Meet Ming-Na, Voice of Mulan."

As you read "Dressed for Success?" you'll notice that the writer interviewed several people for the article, including a school principal, a student, a deputy superintendent, and a lawyer. Interviewing different people is one way that journalists present different viewpoints on a topic.

Author Resources For more on Melanie Bertotto, go to www.glencoe.com.

Vocabulary Preview

adopt (uh DOPT) *v.* to accept and put into effect **(p. 303)** *Our middle school will adopt a student dress code for the new school year.*

discipline (DIS uh plin) *n.* self-control; the obeying of rules **(p. 303)** *Supporters claim that uniforms and dress codes improve discipline and increase student achievement.*

individuality (in duh vij oo AL uh tee) *n.* the combined qualities or characteristics that make one person or thing different from another **(p. 303)** *Some people argue that dress codes take away from a student's individuality.*

Write to Learn Write the vocabulary word that each clue describes:
- A strict teacher might believe in this.
- A person might wear unusual clothes to express this.
- Members of a city council would vote to decide whether to do this to a new law.

English Language Coach

Balanced Language In persuasive writing, the way the writer makes his or her argument is very important. You have learned how writers use semantic slanting and hyperbole. In addition, they may make *generalizations*, which are broad statements about a large group. "Snakes are dangerous" and "Big cars use a lot of gas" are both generalizations—true in many, but not all, cases.

However, other writers will be very careful *not* to make generalizations or to exaggerate. They remind the reader that they are simply giving *their* view. These writers try to use **balanced language.** Recognizing the use of balanced language will help you decide if you want to be persuaded, and whether you can believe what the writer is saying. To see if a writer is using balanced language look for words such as *I think, in my opinion, probably, possibly, generally, many, some, often,* and *sometimes*.

Partner Up Together, rewrite the statement below, adding at least two of the words listed above. Then discuss whether this changes your opinion of the statement.

> Individuality is less important than discipline. Dress codes will give students the discipline they need.

Objectives (pp. 300–303)
Reading Make inferences • Make connections from text to self
Literature Understand characteristics of argument
Vocabulary Identify balanced language

300 UNIT 3 What's Fair and What's Not?

READING WORKSHOP 3 • Inferring

Skills Preview

Key Reading Skill: Inferring

Writers don't always say what they want you to know. Sometimes they give clues. Details in a piece of writing can help the reader infer, or figure out, information that is not stated directly. As you read "Dressed for Success?" you will probably need to make inferences. Think about what you know about the writers' arguments and whether they have stated those things directly.

Write to Learn Write down what you are inferring in your Learner's Notebook.

Key Literary Element: Argument

In writing, an **argument** is the reason or reasons a writer uses to support his or her opinion. Let's say your teacher wants you to learn some new spelling tricks, and you ask why. Your teacher might say, "You aren't doing well in spelling. You need to get better. These tricks have helped lots of other students spell better. They're easy to learn and will help you. Then you'll pass the tests and get better grades in English." Those are good reasons, and using them makes a good argument for learning the spelling tricks!

The article "Dressed for Success?" presents the reader with two arguments—one on each side of the issue of dress codes and school uniforms. By doing so, it provides a fair and balanced view of the subject. As you read, look at the arguments presented in favor of and against dress codes and uniforms. Do the deputy superintendent and the lawyer give good reasons for their views?

Write to Learn Imagine that you need to create an argument for or against the use of uniforms at your school. Make a list of reasons that you would use to support your opinion.

Get Ready to Read

Connect to the Reading

This article talks about the pros and cons of uniforms and dress codes in public schools. Does your school have a dress code or require uniforms? What do you think about this? If your school does not have a dress code, do you think it would be a good idea?

Partner Talk With a partner, discuss whether school dress codes or uniforms are a good idea.

Build Background

- Most schools have some type of dress code, and many are now requiring uniforms.
- The American Civil Liberties Union (ACLU) is a group of lawyers who act to protect the rights of people in the United States.
- The ACLU has been involved in a number of famous "test cases," or cases that test whether certain laws are against the Constitution. For example, ACLU lawyers helped end school segregation in the 1950s.

Set Purposes for Reading

BIG Question Read the selection "Dressed for Success?" to think about whether dress codes are fair.

Set Your Own Purpose What else would you like to learn from the article to help you answer the Big Question? Write your own purpose on the "Dressed for Success" page of Foldable 3.

Interactive Literary Elements Handbook
To review or learn more about the literary elements, go to www.glencoe.com.

Keep Moving

Use these skills as you read the following selection.

Dressed for Success? **301**

READING WORKSHOP 3

TIME

Dressed for Success?

What should students wear to class?

By MELANIE BERTOTTO

At my school in Lemoyne, Pennsylvania, Principal Joseph Gargiulo follows the latest styles. But his interest has nothing to do with a love of fashion. He is just trying to back up Lemoyne Middle School's dress code.

Lemoyne does not let students wear flip-flops and pajama pants. "Pajamas are for sleeping in," says Gargiulo. "School is a student's job. You don't go to your job in pajamas."

Seventh-grader Leah Hawthorn disagrees. She says that wearing whatever she likes helps her do good work at school. "You worry less about how you look," she says. "So you are more focused on what you're doing in class."

Pennsylvania is one of 28 states that has given school districts[1] the power to decide what students can wear to class. Many who are in charge of education believe that dress codes are good for students. They point to places such as the Long Beach Unified School District in California to prove it. In 1994, that school district became the first public school system to order elementary and middle school students to wear uniforms. Soon after, the school district found that fewer students had been absent and fewer had been put out of school than before. **1**

1 Key Reading Skill

Inferring Remember that inferring is using reasoning to figure out what a writer doesn't say outright. When this school district made students wear uniforms, fewer students were absent and fewer students were put out of school. What inference can you make from this statement?

1. A **school district** is an area of public schools that are managed together.

READING WORKSHOP 3

Some people say that dress codes and uniforms go against the right of freedom of expression. The American Civil Liberties Union (ACLU) has filed lawsuits for parents and students who say that school dress codes are unfair.

—From TIME FOR KIDS, February 4, 2005

Should schools be able to tell students what to wear?

Dorothy Harper *was the deputy of the Long Beach Unified School District.*

YES! Dress codes can play a major role in helping schools fulfill one of their [main] responsibilities: keeping students safe. Dress codes help schools [set] standards of behavior. This results in safe and orderly classrooms. Most important, dress codes require that all students be held accountable for maintaining a school climate that encourages learning. Schools that successfully **adopt** dress codes are generally safer, have more positive climates, and have a stronger sense of school pride. That's a lot to gain without having to give up much at all. 🢂

Allen Lichtenstein *is an ACLU lawyer in Nevada.*

NO! The Supreme Court has said that students do not leave their constitutional rights at the schoolhouse door. Yet some schools' dress codes restrict students' freedom of expression. Supporters claim that uniforms and dress codes improve **discipline** and increase student achievement. But there is little evidence to support this. Codes stifle **individuality.** While no one supports allowing clothing that is dangerous, disruptive, or too revealing, many codes go too far. America has always prided itself on the individual's right to self-expression. That respect should extend to student clothing. 🢂 🢂

Vocabulary

adopt (uh DOPT) *v.* to accept and put into effect

discipline (DIS uh plin) *n.* self-control; the obeying of rules

individuality (in duh vij oo AL uh tee) *n.* the combined qualities or characteristics that make one person or thing different from another

2 English Language Coach

Balanced Language Why do you think Dorothy Harper uses such words and phrases as "generally" and "more positive"? How would her argument have changed if she used "always" instead of "generally"? What if she had used "most positive" instead of "more positive"? Would that change what you thought of her argument?

3 Key Literary Element

Argument Have the writers stated their arguments? If so, which sentence in each half of the boxed section states that writer's main argument?

4 BIG Question

Is it fair for schools to decide what students wear to school? Record your answer on the "Dressed for Success" page of Foldable 3. Your response will help you complete the Unit Challenge later.

Dressed for Success? **303**

READING WORKSHOP 3 • Inferring

After You Read | Dressed for Success?

Answering the BIG Question

1. After reading this article, are you for or against school dress codes or uniforms? Do you feel dress codes are fair to students?
2. **Recall** What does Leah Hawthorn say about how clothing affects schoolwork?
   TIP Right There
3. **Summarize** What does Dorothy Harper say about dress codes?
   TIP Think and Search

Critical Thinking

4. **Synthesize** Why might a dress code affect school attendance and suspensions?
   TIP On My Own
5. **Infer** Harper says that schools have more to gain than give up in regard to dress codes. What would schools be giving up if they adopted a dress code?
   TIP On My Own
6. **Evaluate** Is student clothing a form of self-expression? Explain.
   TIP On My Own

Talk About Your Reading

Suppose that your local school district is thinking about making students wear uniforms. Based on the arguments in "Dressed for Success?" discuss whether or not you agree or disagree with this decision, and explain your reasoning. For help, use a graphic organizer like the one below.

Should students wear uniforms?	
Agree Reasons:	**Disagree** Reasons:

Objectives (pp. 304–305)
Reading Make inferences
Literature Understand characteristics of argument
Vocabulary Identify balanced language
Grammar Identify parts of speech: demonstrative adjectives, demonstrative pronouns

Skills Review

Key Reading Skill: Inferring

7. When Dorothy Harper writes that a school's major responsibility is keeping students safe, can you infer anything about her experiences with schools?

Key Literary Element: Argument

8. Which writer (Harper or Lichtenstein) do you think makes a better argument? Why?

Vocabulary Check

9. Fill in the blanks with the correct vocabulary words.

   adopt   individuality   discipline

   Our school has strict ___ and rules.

   Last school year, our school decided to ___ a dress code.

   Some kids feel it stifles their ___, but I don't mind the dress code.

10. **Academic Vocabulary** Your friend tells you that the drama club meeting starts at 7:00. When you arrive, no one is there. What can you *infer* from this?

11. **English Language Coach** Review "Dressed for Success?" and find words or phrases that are examples of balanced language. Write down two sentences from the article that contain such words and underline the example or examples of balanced language in each.

Web Activities For eFlashcards, Selection Quick Checks, and other Web activities, go to www.glencoe.com.

Grammar Link: Demonstratives

The words *this, that, these,* and *those* are called **demonstratives.** They "demonstrate," or point out, people, places, or things.

- *This* and *these* point out people or things near to you. *That* and *those* point out people or things at a distance from you.
- *This* and *that* are singular demonstratives. Each refers to one thing. *These* and *those* are plural demonstratives. Each refers to more than one thing.

Demonstrative adjectives *This, that, these,* and *those* are called demonstrative adjectives when they describe nouns. They are followed by nouns.

- **That** bridge is unusual. (*That* describes bridge.)
- Look at **those** DVD players. (*Those* describes DVD players.)

Demonstrative pronouns *This, that, these,* and *those* are called demonstrative pronouns when they take the place of nouns and point out something.

- **This** is a glass dome. (*This* takes the place of the noun *dome* and points it out.)
- **Those** are large windows. (*Those* takes the place of the noun *windows* and points them out.)

Grammar Practice

Identify whether each demonstrative is an adjective or a pronoun.

12. **That** skirt does not follow the dress code.
13. **This** is mine.
14. **These** shirts are acceptable, but **those** are not.

Write the correct demonstrative adjective below.

15. (This, These) coats are the latest style.
16. (This, These) picture shows proper clothes to wear at school.
17. (This, That) girl down the hall wrote an editorial in favor of a dress code.
18. (This, That) leaflet I'm holding tells about the school dress code.

Before You Read: Eleven

Meet the Author

Sandra Cisneros lives in San Antonio, Texas. She often writes about Latino children living in the United States. "Eleven," Cisneros said, "was my story except . . . it didn't happen at eleven (I was nine), . . . But I did cry. . . . Why did they pick me out? Because I was the one that looked like I belonged to something that shabby?" See page R2 of the Author Files in the back of the book for more on Sandra Cisneros.

Author Search For more about Sandra Cisneros, go to www.glencoe.com.

English Language Coach

Denotation and Connotation As you know, some words have a connotation—an extra meaning suggested by a word.

Some words have a positive connotation. For example, *slender* can suggest an appearance that is more attractive than *thin*. Some words have a negative connotation. For example, *cheap* often suggests something more negative than *inexpensive*.

Positive	Negative
young	childish
plump	fat
daring	reckless

Many connotations are neither positive nor negative. They're just feelings or ideas we associate with certain words. For example, the word *warrior* suggests an extra meaning that *soldier* doesn't have. It makes us think of a brave and mighty fighter from the past.

The words in this web are ways of *looking,* but each word has a different connotation. For example, when someone *stares* at you, it can be upsetting.

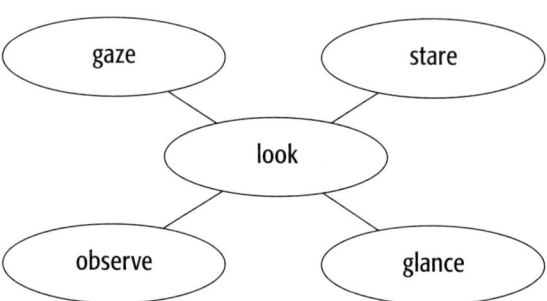

Partner Talk With a partner, talk about what each word says about ways of looking.

Objectives (pp. 306–311)
Reading Make inferences • Make connections from text to self
Literature Identify literary elements: repetition • Understand effects of repetition
Vocabulary Understand denotation and connotation • Identify uses of connotative meaning in semantic slanting

READING WORKSHOP 3 • Inferring

Skills Preview

Key Reading Skill: Inferring

Sometimes people don't always say what they're thinking. It can be the same way in a story. Everything about a character isn't always stated. You'll see this in "Eleven." When you learn to draw inferences, reading becomes more interesting. You're more involved in the story. You will dig deeper into the characters and the plot.

Quick Write In your Learner's Notebook, write about a time—either at school, home, or elsewhere—when you kept your true feelings to yourself. What did you show outwardly and what did you hold inside you?

Literary Element: Repetition

Repetition is the frequent use of words or phrases in a story or poem for emphasis. A writer may use repetition to emphasize an idea or a feeling. For example, in the book "Millions of Cats" by Wanda Gag, the phrase *"hundreds of cats, thousands of cats, millions and billions and trillions of cats"* is repeated throughout the book.

As you read "Eleven," use these tips to help you understand repetition:

- Watch for the words and phrases that are repeated in the story.

  What do these particular words or phrases have to do with the story? What do they mean to the character?

- Pay attention to when repetition shows up in the story.

  What is going on in the story when you see the words and phrases? What is the character going through and feeling at that point?

- Pay attention to the sound or rhythm of the repeated words.

  How do they make you feel? Do they remind you of anything?

Get Ready to Read

Connect to the Reading

Have you ever been afraid to speak up for yourself? Have you ever been embarrassed in front of the whole class? As you read "Eleven," think of what you might do if these things happened to you.

Write to Learn Write about a time when you should have stood up for yourself, but you didn't. To help you organize your thoughts use the bullets below:

- What happened:
- What I did:
- What the result was:
- What I should have done:
- What would have been the result:

Set Purposes for Reading

BIG Question Read "Eleven" to find out if what happens to Rachel is fair or not.

Set Your Own Purpose What else would you like to learn from the selection to help you answer the Big Question? Write your own purpose on the "Eleven" page of Foldable 3.

Interactive Literary Elements Handbook
To review or learn more about the literary elements, go to www.glencoe.com.

Keep Moving

Use these skills as you read the following selection.

Eleven **307**

Eleven

by Sandra Cisneros

What they don't understand about birthdays and what they never tell you is that when you're eleven, you're also ten, and nine, and eight, and seven, and six, and five, and four, and three, and two, and one. And when you wake up on your eleventh birthday you expect to feel eleven, but you don't. You open your eyes and everything's just like yesterday, only it's today. And you don't feel eleven at all. You feel like you're still ten. And you are—underneath the year that makes you eleven. **1**

Like some days you might say something stupid, and that's the part of you that's still ten. Or maybe some days you might need to sit on your mama's lap because you're scared, and that's the part of you that's five. And maybe one day when you're all grown up maybe you will need to cry like if you're three, and that's okay. That's what I tell Mama when she's sad and needs to cry. Maybe she's feeling three. **2**

Because the way you grow old is kind of like an onion or like the rings inside a tree trunk[1] or like my little wooden dolls that fit one inside the other, each year inside the next one. That's how being eleven years old is.

---

1. If something is **like the rings inside a tree trunk,** it has layers that show its age. Each ring in a tree trunk is a layer of wood added during a single growth period.

Practice the Skills

1 **Key Reading Skill**

Inferring The narrator explains that "underneath" eleven you are also ten, nine, eight, and so on. She also says that you expect to feel different when you wake up on your birthday, but you don't. How do you think the narrator feels when she wakes up on her eleventh birthday?

2 **Reviewing Skills**

Connecting Can you think of a time when you were expected to act your age, but you wanted to act as though you were younger? Do you agree or disagree with the narrator's thoughts about age? Explain.

You don't feel eleven. Not right away. It takes a few days, weeks even, sometimes even months before you say Eleven when they ask you. And you don't feel smart eleven, not until you're almost twelve. That's the way it is.

Only today I wish I didn't have only eleven years rattling inside me like pennies in a tin Band-Aid box. Today I wish I was one hundred and two instead of eleven because if I was one hundred and two I'd have known what to say when Mrs. Price put the red sweater on my desk. I would've known how to tell her it wasn't mine instead of just sitting there with that look on my face and nothing coming out of my mouth.

"Whose is this?" Mrs. Price says, and she holds the red sweater up in the air for all the class to see. "Whose? It's been sitting in the coatroom for a month."

"Not mine," says everybody. "Not me." "It has to belong to somebody," Mrs. Price keeps saying, but nobody can remember. It's an ugly sweater with red plastic buttons and a collar and sleeves all stretched out like you could use it for a jump rope. It's maybe a thousand years old and even if it belonged to me I wouldn't say so.

Maybe because I'm **skinny**, maybe because she doesn't like me, that stupid Sylvia Saldívar[2] says, "I think it belongs to Rachel." An ugly sweater like that, all raggedy and old, but Mrs. Price believes her. Mrs. Price takes the sweater and puts it right on my desk, but when I open my mouth nothing comes out. 3 4

"That's not, I don't, you're not . . . Not mine," I finally say in a little voice that was maybe me when I was four.

"Of course it's yours," Mrs. Price says. "I remember you wearing it once." Because she's older and the teacher, she's right and I'm not.

Not mine, not mine, not mine, but Mrs. Price is already turning to page thirty-two, and math problem number four. I don't know why but all of a sudden I'm feeling sick inside, like the part of me that's three wants to come out of my eyes, only I squeeze them shut tight and bite down on my teeth real hard and try to remember today I am eleven, eleven. Mama is making a cake for me for tonight, and when Papa comes home everybody will sing Happy birthday, happy birthday to you. 5

---

2. *Saldívar* (sa DEE var)

Practice the Skills

3 **Key Reading Skill**

Inferring What can you infer from the sentence "An ugly sweater like that . . . but Mrs. Price believes her."

4 **English Language Coach**

Denotation and Connotation The denotation of **skinny** is "very thin." What do you think the connotation of *skinny* is? Do you think that the narrator is suggesting that she likes the way she looks or not?

5 **Literary Element**

Repetition There are three examples of repetition in this paragraph. What are they? Why do you think the author repeated these words and phrases? When you read them does it make you think of anything? Does it remind you of anything?

But when the sick feeling goes away and I open my eyes, the red sweater's still sitting there like a big red mountain. I move the red sweater to the corner of my desk with my ruler. I move my pencil and books and eraser as far from it as possible. I even move my chair a little to the right. Not mine, not mine, not mine.

In my head I'm thinking how long till lunchtime, how long till I can take the red sweater and throw it over the schoolyard fence, or leave it hanging on a parking meter, or bunch it up into a little ball and toss it in the alley. Except when math period ends Mrs. Price says loud and in front of everybody, "Now, Rachel, that's enough," because she sees I've shoved the red sweater to the tippy-tip corner of my desk and it's hanging all over the edge like a waterfall, but I don't care.

"Rachel," Mrs. Price says. She says it like she's getting mad. "You put that sweater on right now and no more nonsense."

"But it's not—"

"Now!" Mrs. Price says.

This is when I wish I wasn't eleven, because all the years inside of me—ten, nine, eight, seven, six, five, four, three, two, and one—are pushing at the back of my eyes when I put one arm through one sleeve of the sweater that smells like cottage cheese, and then the other arm through the other and stand there with my arms apart like if the sweater hurts me and it does, all itchy and full of germs that aren't even mine. 6

That's when everything I've been holding in since this morning, since when Mrs. Price put the sweater on my desk, finally lets go, and all of a sudden I'm crying in front of everybody. I wish I was invisible but I'm not. I'm eleven and it's my birthday today and I'm crying like I'm three in front of everybody. I put my head down on the desk and bury my face in my stupid clown-sweater arms. My face all hot and spit coming out of my mouth because I can't stop the little animal noises from coming out of me, until there aren't any more tears left in my eyes, and it's just my body shaking like when you have the hiccups, and my whole head hurts like when you drink milk too fast.

Practice the Skills

6 **Literary Element**

Repetition What is the repetition here in this paragraph? Why do you think the writer decided to reemphasize the ages again? How is Rachel feeling right now?

I wish I was invisible but I'm not.

But the worst part is right before the bell rings for lunch. That stupid Phyllis Lopez, who is even dumber than Sylvia Saldívar, says she remembers the red sweater is hers! I take it off right away and give it to her, only Mrs. Price pretends like everything's okay.

Today I'm eleven. There's a cake Mama's making for tonight, and when Papa comes home from work we'll eat it. There'll be candles and presents and everybody will sing Happy birthday, happy birthday to you, Rachel, only it's too late.

I'm eleven today. I'm eleven, ten, nine, eight, seven, six, five, four, three, two, and one, but I wish I was one hundred and two. I wish I was anything but eleven, because I want today to be far away already, far away like a runaway balloon, like a tiny *o* in the sky, so tiny-tiny you have to close your eyes to see it. **7** ○

Practice the Skills

7 **BIG Question**

What would Rachel say about what's fair and what's not? Record your response on the "Eleven" page of Foldable 3. Your answer will help you complete the Unit Challenge later.

Analyzing the Art Do you think this painting expresses the narrator's feelings in the story's last sentence? Explain your answer.

READING WORKSHOP 3 • Inferring

After You Read — Eleven

Answering the  BIG Question

1. Do you think that Rachel is treated fairly? Explain.

2. **Recall** Why does the teacher think the red sweater belongs to Rachel?
   TIP Right There

3. **Recall** What does the teacher make Rachel do?
   TIP Right There

Critical Thinking

4. **Infer** Why does Rachel move the sweater to the edge of her desk with a ruler and move her belongings away from the sweater?
   TIP Author and Me

5. **Connect** Early in the story, the narrator says that a birthday party at home later should make her feel better. Do you think it will? Would it make you feel better if you were in her situation?
   TIP Author and Me

Write About Your Reading

Use the RAFT system to write about "Eleven." A RAFT assignment provides four details:

- **R** is for your *role* as a writer—who or what you must pretend to be as you write.
- **A** stands for your *audience*—the person or group who will read what you write.
- **F** means *format*—the form for your writing, such as a letter or a speech.
- **T** means *topic*—what your writing should be about.

Role: Write as if you were Mrs. Price, Sylvia Saldívar, or Phyllis Lopez.

Audience: Write to yourself.

Format: A journal entry

Topic: Rewrite what happened about the sweater from your point of view (first-person). Remember that when you use the first-person point of view, the narrator is speaking and using the pronoun *I*.

Objectives (pp. 312–313)
Reading Make inferences • Make connections from text to self
Literature Identify literary elements: repetition • Understand effects of repetition
Vocabulary Understand denotation and connotation
Writing Use the RAFT system: respond to literature
Grammar Identify parts of speech: definite and indefinite articles

Skills Review

Key Reading Skill: Inferring

6. On page 309 Rachel says "the part of me that's three wants to come out of my eyes . . ." What can you infer is happening to Rachel?

7. At the end of the story Mrs. Price "pretends like everything is okay." What can you infer about what Rachel wanted Mrs. Price to do?

Literary Element: Repetition

8. Rachel believes that people are made up of every age they have ever been. She thinks, "when you're eleven, you're also ten, and nine, and eight, and seven, and six, and five, and four, and three, and two, and one." What does the repetition of ages tell you about Rachel?

9. Find another example of repetition in "Eleven." Tell what that example adds to the story.

Reviewing Skills: Connecting

10. Do you agree that your younger ages still live inside of you? Explain.

Vocabulary Check

11. **Academic Vocabulary** You see your friend after his or her basketball game. He or she looks sad and angry. What can you infer about the results of the game?

12. **English Language Coach** The denotation of *snake* is "a scaly, legless reptile." Its connotation might involve something sneaky or wicked. In your Learner's Notebook write the denotation of *kitten*. Then write its connotation.

Web Activities For eFlashcards, Selection Quick Checks, and other Web activities, go to www.glencoe.com.

Grammar Link: Articles

The words *a, an,* and *the* make up a special group of adjectives called **articles**.

- *A* and *an* are called **indefinite** articles. They refer to any one item of a group of people, places, things, or ideas.

  She bought **a** ticket.

- Use *a* before words that begin with a consonant sound.

  a pilot   **a** space ship

- Use *an* before words that begin with a vowel sound.

  an hour   **an** astronaut

- *The* is a **definite** article. It indicates that the noun is a specific person, place, or thing.

  She liked **the** movie.

  Neil Armstrong was **the** first man to walk on **the** moon.

Grammar Practice

On a separate sheet of paper, tell whether the bolded articles are indefinite or definite.

13. **The** way you grow old is like **an** onion.
14. The hat's been left in **the** coatroom for **a** month.
15. **The** red sweater's still sitting there, like **a** big red mountain.
16. Your smile is **the** part of you that I like best.

Now write each word or group of words with the correct indefinite article–*a* or *an*.

17. birthday
18. onion
19. tree trunk
20. wooden doll
21. ugly sweater
22. eraser

Writing Application Look back at the RAFT assignment you wrote. Make sure that the definite and indefinite articles you used are correct.

WRITING WORKSHOP PART 2

Persuasive Essay
Revising, Editing, and Presenting

ASSIGNMENT Write a persuasive essay

Purpose: Write an essay that argues either for or against a specific issue and persuade others to agree with you

Audience: You, your teacher, and classmates

You've already chosen a topic, organized your ideas, and written the first draft of your essay. Great work! Now it's time to revise your draft and share your work with an audience.

Revising
Make It Better

Revising is your chance to make changes to your writing. You may need to write more in places where your draft seems unclear. Or, you may need to delete parts of your draft that repeat or are unnecessary.

Revising Rubric

Your revised essay should have

- evidence to support your opinion
- responses to possible counterarguments
- five paragraphs that include an introduction, a body, and a conclusion
- transitions to improve sentence fluency
- adjectives and adverbs used correctly

Check Your Draft

Read over your draft and add missing information. The questions below will help you decide what to revise.

- Does the introduction explain the unfair situation?
- Is your position stated clearly?
- Does the body of your essay have three main paragraphs?
- Does each paragraph include a main point about why the topic is unfair?
- Does each paragraph have evidence to support your main points?
- Is your evidence in the best and most persuasive order?

You probably answered "no" to some of the questions. That's okay! Drafts are not supposed to be perfect. You may need to think of more evidence to support your main points or write a stronger introduction to interest readers. Go back and make the necessary improvements to your essay.

Say It Like You Mean It

Your persuasive essay should be about an issue that you feel strongly about. Use words that express your emotions or personal views. Use detailed arguments. If your readers feel that you really know and care about the issue, they will be more willing to listen to your argument. Consider these examples.

Following a dress code makes students feel like robots. After a few weeks we get tired of seeing the same colors and outfits every day.

Objectives (pp. 314–317)
Writing Write persuasively • Revise writing for key elements, style, and word choice • Present writing
Listening, Speaking, and Viewing Speak effectively • Use persuasive techniques

> Students should not have to wear the same clothes. Following a dress code is a bad idea.

The first example is more persuasive because it is more descriptive. It lets the reader know not only that the writer thinks that dress codes are a bad idea but also *why* they are a bad idea. The use of descriptions such as "feel like robots" puts some emotion into the writing as well.

Editing
Finish It Up

Now you are ready to edit your persuasive essay. Read your essay and look for errors in grammar, punctuation, and usage. Follow the editing checklist to spot your errors.

Editing Checklist
- ☑ All sentences end with correct punctuation.
- ☑ Each paragraph begins on a new line.
- ☑ All names are capitalized.
- ☑ Commas and apostrophes are used correctly.
- ☑ Spelling is correct.

Finally, take one last look at the language of your essay. Does the writing sound like you really *mean* what you're saying? Could you add an adjective or adverb to make a sentence stronger? Double check that you used the most persuasive language and chose the most effective words.

Presenting
Show It Off

Read your essay to a small group of classmates. As you read, make sure to vary the volume and pitch of your voice to emphasize the main points of your essay. You have spent a lot of time writing your essay, now is your chance to persuade a real audience. Read with enthusiasm to show your classmates that you really care about this topic.

Literature Online

Writing Models For models and other writing activities, go to www.glencoe.com.

Writing Tip
Proofreading Make sure that you have used the correct forms of superlative and comparative adjectives and adverbs.

Writing Tip
Proofreading The normal way to form an adverb is to add *-ly*, as in *commonly, slowly,* or *nervously.* However, there are exceptions: If the word already ends *-ll*, just add *-y* (for example, *fully*).

Writing Tip
Spelling Break long words into small parts to help you remember how they are spelled. For example, you could break the following words:
busi/ness
to/mor/row

WRITING WORKSHOP PART 2

Active Writing Model

Writer's Model

The introduction grabs the reader's attention.

The writer states the issue and proposes a solution.

The writer responds to counterarguments to help convince readers the dress code is unfair.

The writer provides evidence to support a point.

This transition word increases the fluency of the essay.

This transition phrase links two sentences about the same topic. Transition phrases make writing more fluent.

Ending the essay with an emotional appeal helps persuade readers to agree with the writer's argument.

    The Hope Middle School dress code caused student Jimmy Albert to spend his Friday night at the emergency room. Jimmy sprained his ankle playing basketball during afternoon recess. His sprain was caused because the dress shoes he was wearing did not provide enough support for basic recess activities. Jimmy's injury is one of several reasons why it is unfair for students to have to follow a dress code. I suggest the school dress code be changed to allow jeans and sneakers.

    According to our principal, the dress code prevents distractions and helps students focus on learning. I disagree. Dressy clothes are distracting because the pants are itchy and dress shoes cause our feet to hurt. As a result, uncomfortable clothes actually distract students from schoolwork.

    The second reason the dress code is unfair is because dress clothes are expensive. Many families at our school live on a tight budget and don't have money to invest on clothes that are only worn at school. This expense is unfair to parents who are struggling to make ends meet and students who can't afford to buy other clothes. Blue jeans are a practical alternative because they don't wear out quickly and they are easy to clean.

    Finally, wearing a uniform makes students feel like robots. After a few weeks we get tired of seeing the same outfits and colors every day. Students should be allowed to express themselves through the clothes they choose to wear. In fact, making students conform to a dress code shows disrespect for the student's ability to make decisions.

    A dress code does not help students focus on learning. Students like Jimmy shouldn't have to worry about hurting themselves during recess. I propose allowing jeans and sneakers to be part of the school dress code immediately, before another student gets hurt.

Listening, Speaking, and Viewing

Effective Speaking

You don't always persuade other people in writing. Sometimes you have to persuade using your voice and body language. Effective speaking is an important part of sharing your ideas and opinions with others.

What Is Effective Speaking?

Effective speaking is being able to communicate your thoughts and ideas clearly through the spoken word.

Why Is Effective Speaking Important?

Sometimes you have to speak for more important reasons, like giving directions, explaining a process, or making a speech. In these situations, it is important that you express yourself to your listeners as clearly as possible. Effective speakers use more than just their voice to express themselves—they also use their eyes, arms, hands, and feet.

How Do I Do It?

To practice effective speaking, choose a passage or paragraph from a Unit 3 reading selection and read it aloud to your classmates.

Once you have chosen a passage, read it silently to yourself. Then follow the tips below for reading it aloud to a small group.

1. **Voice**
   - Speak loudly enough to be heard easily by the rest of your group.
   - Speak clearly so that each word you say is distinct.
   - Keep a steady tempo—don't speak too slowly or too fast.
   - Match the tone of your voice to the tone of your passage.

2. **Face**
   - Keep your head up! Look at your audience, and move your eyes from person to person.
   - Use facial expressions. Smile, raise an eyebrow, or roll your eyes to express emotions that are conveyed in your speech.

3. **Body**
   - Make gestures with your hands and arms to help describe what you are saying. Words like *huge* and *tiny,* and phrases like *over there, I have an idea,* and *come here* can easily include a gesture.
   - Keep your audience's attention by standing up and acting out parts of your passage as you speak.

Don't forget to practice your reading a few times before presenting it to your group—the more you practice, the better you will sound!

Analyzing the Photo
What does the "thumbs up" gesture mean? What might you be speaking about when you use this gesture?

READING WORKSHOP 4

Skills Focus

You will practice using these skills when you read the following selections:
- "from *50 Simple Things Kids Can Do to Save the Earth*," p. 322
- "Greyling," p. 328

Reading
- Identifying problems and solutions

Literature
- Understanding mood

Vocabulary
- Understanding synonyms and shades of meaning

Writing/Grammar
- Identifying prepositions
- Identifying interjections

Skill Lesson

Identifying Problems and Solutions

Learn It!

What Is It? What will happen to Richelle who is sick and can't keep up with her homework? How will Safa make friends in a new school where no one speaks her language? How will Sean get home if his bike has a flat tire? What will Dippy, the Talking Dog, do when she is attacked by an angry ostrich? Problems make stories interesting. Some problems are very serious and some may be humorous. When identifying **problems and solutions** in a text, you need to figure out what the obstacles or conflicts are and how they are overcome. Authors may use words such as *need, attempt, help, problem,* or *obstruction* when they write about

- fights, disagreements, or arguments.
- challenges or obstacles.
- questions or mysteries.

CALVIN AND HOBBES © 1993 Watterson. Dist. By UNIVERSAL PRESS SYNDICATE. Reprinted with permission. All rights reserved.

Analyzing Cartoons
Do you think that Calvin has found a good solution to his problem? Explain.

Objectives (pp. 318–319)
Reading Identify problems and solutions

READING WORKSHOP 4 • Identifying Problems and Solutions

Study Central Visit www.glencoe.com and click on Study Central to review identifying problems and solutions.

Why Is It Important? Finding the problems and solutions in a selection will help you understand what's happening and why. If you know that a story is about a girl searching for her missing parents, you'll know which events are key parts of the story. Understanding problems and solutions may even help you solve your own problems.

How Do I Do It? As you read, ask questions to help identify the main problems. For instance, you might ask, "What challenge does the narrator face?" or "What are these characters arguing about?" Then you can pick out the parts of the story that move these problems toward their solutions. Also, notice how story elements such as setting and characters affect problems and their solutions.

Here's how a student looked at the problem/solution structure in "Stray."

> Even after a week had gone by, Doris didn't name the dog. She knew her parents wouldn't let her keep it, that her father made so little money any pets were out of the question, and that the pup would definitely go to the pound when the weather cleared.

I can see the problem. Doris is attached to the stray dog, but she knows that she can't keep it unless she convinces her parents to let it stay. I'll read on to find out what she did. I'll also think about whether her solution could be used for any problems that I have.

Practice It!

As you read "from *50 Simple Things Kids Can Do to Save the Earth*" and "Greyling," look closely to pick out important problems or conflicts. Ask yourself, "What are these problems about? What is causing them?" Then pay attention to the solutions.

Use It!

Make notes as you answer these questions, and refer to them later.
- What is the problem or conflict?
- Who is involved?
- What is the cause of the problem or conflict?
- What solutions are tried?
- What is the final outcome?

READING WORKSHOP 4 • Identifying Problems and Solutions

Before You Read : from *50 Simple Things Kids Can Do to Save the Earth*

The EarthWorks Group is dedicated to helping to save the environment. Here's what one EarthWorks member says about the book *50 Simple Things Kids Can Do to Save the Earth:*

"I guess a lot of kids don't really think they can make a difference in saving the Earth. They think they don't have the power.

"But they're wrong.

"Kids have a lot of power.... This book is full of things you can do to help protect our planet. A lot of them are fun. Some take work. Some give you a chance to teach your parents, instead of the other way around. But all of them will show you that you can make a difference. And that is the power to save the Earth."

English Language Coach

Synonyms and Word Choice As you know, writers carefully choose the words they will use. Sometimes a writer uses a certain word because of its connotation. Sometimes, though, it's a matter of choosing among synonyms to get the exact right word.

Because synonyms rarely mean exactly the same thing, it matters which one a writer chooses. There is a difference between *frightened* and *terrified*. There is a difference between *run* and *scamper*. The differences may be small, but they're important.

Choosing just the right word is especially important in persuasive writing. The following choices all involve the use of synonyms:

- Would you choose a health bar described as *chewy* or one described as *leathery*?
- Would you rather walk on *a gloomy trail* or *a shady path*?
- Would you prefer to be *greeted by a fragrance* or *met by an odor*?

The words below in dark type are all synonyms for *eat.* Although they have similar meanings, the differences are important.

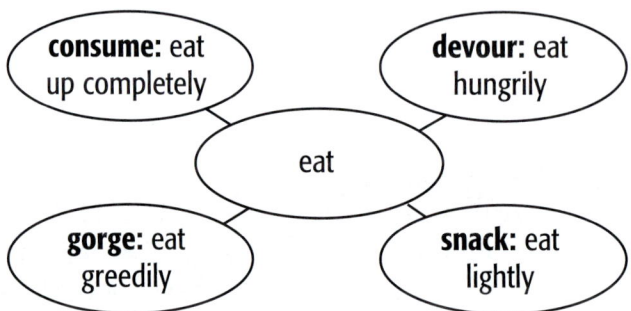

Word Webs Make your own word webs, like the one above, for any two of the following words. (You do not need to include the definitions.) Use a dictionary or thesaurus if you need help.

- fear
- beautiful
- laugh
- difficult
- run
- say

Objectives (pp. 320–323)
Reading Identify problems and solutions
Literature Identify literary elements: mood
Vocabulary Understand synonyms: shades of meaning

READING WORKSHOP 4 • Identifying Problems and Solutions

Skills Preview

Key Reading Skill: Identifying Problems and Solutions

Think about a TV show you've seen in which the main character had a problem. Think about

- what the problem was and what caused it
- what actions were taken to solve it
- what the solution was

Key Literary Element: Mood

The **mood** of a piece of writing is the feeling it creates in the reader. We often talk about the mood created by a story or play, but nonfiction writing can also have a mood. A newspaper article might create a mood of sympathy or anger or even joy. A letter to the editor can make a reader feel determined or, perhaps, amused.

Persuasive writing always involves an attempt to make the reader react. In good persuasive writing, the attempt is often successful, and the reaction may well involve emotions of one sort or another.

As you read, use these tips to help you understand the selection's mood.

- Pay attention to the feelings you get as you read.

  Do you have an emotional reaction to what you're reading? Do you feel, for example, hopeless or encouraged?

- Is the writer trying to make you feel a particular way? Is this successful?

  Does the author try to reach out to you as a reader, to get you to react?

Partner Talk Think about something you've read that excited you, surprised you, made you laugh, or affected you in some other noticeable way. Tell your partner about what you read and how you reacted.

Get Ready to Read

Connect to the Reading

How do you feel about forests and trees? Do they make you feel peaceful and happy? Do you think they are beautiful? Or do you not think about them much at all?

Partner Talk Talk about whether you think it's important to save the trees and forests of the Earth.

Build Background

This selection is from *50 Simple Things Kids Can Do to Save the Earth*.

- The selection is about **recycling** paper products. Recycling is the process of using waste materials, or trash, to make new objects.
- More than 500,000 trees are cut down every year just to create the paper for newspapers.
- Today about half of the used paper in this country is sent for recycling.

Set Purposes for Reading

BIG Question Read "50 Simple Things Kids Can Do to Save the Earth" to find out whether or not it's fair for people to waste paper.

Set Your Own Purpose What else would you like to learn from the reading to help you answer the Big Question? Write your own purpose on the "50 Simple Things" page of Foldable 3.

Interactive Literary Elements Handbook
To review or learn more about the literary elements, go to www.glencoe.com.

Keep Moving

Use these skills as you read the following selection.

from *50 Simple Things Kids Can Do to Save the Earth*

READING WORKSHOP 4

INFORMATIONAL TEXT
BOOK
50 Simple Things Kids Can Do to Save the Earth

50 Simple Things Kids Can Do to Save the Earth
from

by The EarthWorks Group

Take a Guess.
If you stacked up all the paper an average American uses in a year, the pile would be as tall as . . .
A) A car B) An elephant's eye C) A two-story house

It takes years for a tree to grow enough to be made into paper. And it takes many forests to make all the paper we use . . . and throw away.

Wouldn't it be great if old paper could be turned back into new paper? Then we'd have more trees and a greener world.

We can make that happen—there *is* a way. We can recycle our paper.

Does that really work? You bet! **1**

Did You Know?

- Americans use millions of tons of paper every year.
- To make all that paper, we use more than a *billion* trees! **2**
- How much is that? The paper that four people use in a year weighs as much as a big car.
- If everyone in the U.S. recycled their newspapers (including the comics), we'd save hundreds of thousands of trees every week.
- How is paper recycled? It's shredded and mashed into a glop called pulp, which is then turned back into paper.

Answer: C. Believe it or not, as high as a two-story house!

Practice the Skills

1 Key Literary Element

Mood What mood is created by these opening paragraphs?

2 Key Reading Skill

Identifying Problems and Solutions What problem is the writer presenting here? Write the problem on your problem-and-solution chart.

READING WORKSHOP 4

What You Can Do

- You can recycle all kinds of paper—cereal boxes, note paper, bags, newspaper, and so on. **3**
- To start recycling in your house, first find a place where you can put a pile of newspapers and a box for collecting other types of paper.
- Whenever you empty a cereal box, or get ready to toss out a piece of paper, put it in the box instead of the garbage. If you get a newspaper at your house, stack it neatly on the pile every day.
- Don't put shiny paper or paper with plastic attached to it in your box—you can't recycle that stuff.
- Ask a parent to find out where the nearest recycling center is. Maybe your neighborhood has a curbside recycling program. That would really make it easy!
- Every week or two, tie the newspapers into small bundles and take them (and other paper) to the recycling center or put them on the curb for pickup.
- **Extra Tip:** Don't use just one side of a piece of paper—use the other side for scrap paper. That's recycling, too. **4 5** ○

Practice the Skills

3 **Key Reading Skill**

Identifying Problems and Solutions The writer proposes one *big* solution–recycling. Write that on your problem-and-solution chart. Continue reading to find out what *smaller* solutions the writer suggests to help kids recycle paper. Write at least three of those on your chart also.

4 **English Language Coach**

Synonyms and Word Choice The word *recycle* is familiar to most people. What about its synonym, *reuse*? Does it have a different connotation than *recycle*?

5 **BIG Question**

Do you think it's fair to expect people to follow the writer's suggestion and try to save the world's trees? Or do you think it's too much trouble? Explain your answer on the "50 Simple Things" page of Foldable 3. Your answer will help you complete the Unit Challenge later.

Analyzing the Photo Study the photo. What ideas does it give you about ways to conserve paper at home? Explain.

from *50 Simple Things Kids Can Do to Save the Earth*

READING WORKSHOP 4 • Identifying Problems and Solutions

After You Read

from *50 Simple Things Kids Can Do to Save the Earth*

Answering the BIG Question

1. The writer of this selection creates a cheerful, "can-do" mood about recycling, partly by telling only about easy ways to recycle. Do you think this writer is being fair in using these methods to get kids to recycle? Why or why not?

2. **Recall** How many trees does it take to make all the paper that Americans use in a year?
   TIP Right There

3. **Summarize** What does the writer want readers to do, and why?
   TIP Think and Search

Critical Thinking

4. **Infer** Do you think this writer is suggesting that kids should "take charge" of recycling in their families? Explain.
   TIP Author and Me

5. **Draw Conclusions** Imagine that you have decided to ask your family to start recycling paper. Based on this selection, what one main reason would you give them to recycle?
   TIP Author and Me

6. **Evaluate** Does this writer seem qualified to write about this subject? Does the writer show a bias, or favoritism, toward one opinion or another? Explain your answers.
   TIP On My Own

Write About Your Reading

Imagine that you want to start a paper recycling program at your school. Using the selection as a model, create a bulleted list of at least five activities students can do at school as part of the recycling program.

If you need help thinking of activities, review the bulleted list under "What You Can Do" in the selection and write your list so the activities can apply to your school.

Objectives (pp. 324–325)
Reading Identify problems and solutions
Literature Identify literary elements: mood
Vocabulary Understand synonyms: shades of meaning
Writing Write a list
Grammar Identify parts of speech: prepositions, prepositional phrases

Skills Review

Key Reading Skill: Identifying Problems and Solutions

7. Do you think the solutions that the writer suggests can really solve the problem? Explain your answer.

Key Literary Element: Mood

8. Describe the mood of this selection.
9. How does the writer create a mood in the selection?
10. It would certainly be possible to create a mood of hopelessness while writing about the environment. Why do you think this writer might have wanted to avoid creating that mood?
11. **English Language Coach** All the words below are synonyms for the word *walks*. Think about which one best communicates the kind of walking suggested by each sentence. Then copy the sentences and fill in the blanks.

   totters   struts   trudges   strolls   creeps
   - Roger is so stuck-up, he ___ like a rooster!
   - The silent tiger ___ through the jungle.
   - Tired after a hard day, Peter ___ home.
   - I watch the baby as she ___ a few steps before losing her balance.
   - Every summer evening, Mr. Hu ___ around the neighborhood to relax.

Web Activities For eFlashcards, Selection Quick Checks, and other Web activities, go to www.glencoe.com.

Grammar Link: Prepositions

- A **preposition** is a word that shows the relationship of a noun or pronoun to some other word in the sentence.
- Prepositions include the following: *about, above, among, before, behind, below, between, by, in, into, near, of, to, through, under.*

  The troll hid <u>under</u> the bridge.

  The preposition *under* shows the relationship between *troll* and *bridge*.

- A preposition is always part of a **prepositional phrase**. A prepositional phrase begins with a preposition and ends with a noun or pronoun.

Preposition ↓
Ramona left the recycling bag on the sidewalk.
Prepositional phrase

Preposition ↓
The boy with my brother is our new next-door neighbor.
Prepositional phrase

Grammar Practice

Underline the preposition in each of the following sentences.

12. Aggie tucked the coupon into her tablet.
13. The leader of the band waved her baton.
14. Nobody on her street used house numbers.
15. The bat bounced in the dirt.
16. The ball sailed over the fence.

Writing Application Look back at the list of recycling activities you wrote. Add one prepositional phrase to a sentence on your list.

from *50 Simple Things Kids Can Do to Save the Earth*

READING WORKSHOP 4 • Identifying Problems and Solutions

Before You Read: Greyling

Jane Yolen

Meet the Author
Born in 1939, Jane Yolen is an author, songwriter, teacher, and storyteller. She has become well known for her fairy tales and folktales. "I don't care whether the story is real or fantastical. I tell the story that needs to be told," she says. See page R7 of the Author Files for more on Jane Yolen.

Author Search For more about Jane Yolen, go to www.glencoe.com.

Vocabulary Preview

grief (greef) *n.* unhappiness or suffering, often about the loss of something **(p. 329)** *The death of the fisherman would add to his wife's grief.*

stranded (STRAN did) *adj.* left helpless in a difficult place **(p. 329)** *The seal was stranded on a sandbar.*

sheared (sheerd) *v.* cut off sharply; form of the verb *shear* **(p. 329)** *The cliffs sheared off into the sea.*

kin (kin) *n.* family or relatives **(p. 329)** *The seal pup was not old enough to find its kin.*

tended (TEN did) *v.* cared for; kept in working order; form of the verb *tend* **(p. 330)** *Greyling tended his father's boat.*

Write to Learn Write a short paragraph that correctly uses all of the vocabulary words.

English Language Coach

Synonyms and Word Choice Synonyms are words that have the same—or similar *but not the same*—meanings. The right word can help you create a clear picture in your mind. By paying attention to synonyms, you can clearly imagine what a character is like or how an author feels about a topic. Compare these two sentences:

Jamal *hung up* the phone.
Jamal *slammed down* the phone.

- The words *hung up* and *slammed down* describe the same action, but *slammed down* lets you know how Jamal felt.

Synonym Chart Copy the chart in your Learner's Notebook. For each word, write a synonym that has a more precise meaning. Next to each synonym, write the feeling or idea that the word creates.

	Synonym	Feeling or Idea
walk		
huge		
pretty		
difficult		

Objectives (pp. 326–333)
Reading Identify problems and solutions • Make connections from text to self
Literature Identify literary elements: mood
Vocabulary Understand synonyms: shades of meaning

READING WORKSHOP 4 • **Identifying Problems and Solutions**

Skills Preview

Key Reading Skill: Identifying Problems and Solutions

Before you read the story, think about the following:
- Have you ever put off dealing with a problem you knew you'd have to solve eventually?
- Why didn't you want to solve this problem right away?
- How did you feel when you finally solved the problem?

Write to Learn Write your answers to these questions in your Learner's Notebook. Think about these responses as you read the story.

Key Literary Element: Mood

The feeling or atmosphere created in a story is called the **mood**. Word choice, settings, and characters all help create mood. Think about how these different descriptions create different moods:

"It was a dark and stormy night."
"It was a beautiful evening of cool rain."

As you read "Greyling,"
- Think about how the story is making you feel.
- What details in the story are helping to create the mood?
- Does the mood stay the same?

Partner Talk Talk about the scariest or saddest books you ever read. List some ways in which the author set the mood in one of those books.

Interactive Literary Elements Handbook
To review or learn more about the literary elements, go to www.glencoe.com.

Get Ready to Read

Connect to the Reading

You probably have felt at times that it's hard to be fair. Maybe something that you did made one friend happy, but upset another friend. The characters in this story find themselves in a similar situation and have to make tough decisions. As you read "Greyling," think about what you would do in their places.

Small Groups In small groups, talk about fair and unfair solutions to the following problem:

Your parents told you that you can invite two friends to go to a concert for your birthday. Four of your friends have told you that they love the band that is playing and hope you will chose them to go with you.

Build Background

This story tells of a fisherman and his wife who take in a selchie (SELL kee) that the fisherman finds stranded on a sandbar. The selchie grows up to become a young man named Greyling.

- A selchie is an imaginary creature often described in Celtic myths. Selchies live as seals in the ocean and as humans on land.
- Seals are mammals that live in the ocean and have fins or flippers instead of feet.

Set Purposes for Reading

BIG Question Read "Greyling" to find out more about how people respond to situations that seem unfair.

Set Your Own Purpose What else would you like to learn from the story to help you answer the Big Question? Write your own purpose on the "Greyling" page of Foldable 3.

Keep Moving

Use these skills as you read the following selection.

Greyling **327**

READING WORKSHOP 4

GREYLING

by Jane Yolen

Once on a time when wishes were aplenty,[1] a fisherman and his wife lived by the side of the sea. All that they ate came out of the sea. Their **hut** was covered with the finest mosses that kept them cool in the summer and warm in the winter. And there was nothing they needed or wanted except a child. **1 2**

Each morning, when the moon touched down behind the water and the sun rose up behind the plains, the wife would say to the fisherman, "You have your boat and your nets and your lines. But I have no baby to hold in my arms." And again, in the evening, it was the same. She would weep and wail and rock the cradle that stood by the hearth.[2] But year in and year out the cradle stayed empty.

---

1. When something is *aplenty,* a large amount of it can be found.
2. A **hearth** is the area in front of a fireplace.

Practice the Skills

1 **Reviewing Skills**

Activating Prior Knowledge
You have probably read many stories that begin with the similar words "Once upon a time." What do you know about stories that begin with these words?

2 **English Language Coach**

Synonyms and Word Choice
What kind of house is a **hut**? Why might the writer have used this word instead of one of its synonyms, such as *shack* or *cottage*?

328 UNIT 3 What's Fair and What's Not?

Now the fisherman was also sad that they had no child. But he kept his sorrow to himself so that his wife would not know his **grief** and thus double her own. Indeed, he would leave the hut each morning with a breath of song and return each night with a whistle on his lips. His nets were full but his heart was empty, yet he never told his wife. **3**

One sunny day, when the beach was a tan thread spun between sea and plain, the fisherman as usual went down to his boat. But this day he found a small grey seal **stranded** on the sandbar, crying for its own.

The fisherman looked up the beach and down. He looked in front of him and behind. And he looked to the town on the great grey cliffs that **sheared** off into the sea. But there were no other seals in sight.

So he shrugged his shoulders and took off his shirt. Then he dipped it into the water and wrapped the seal pup carefully in its folds.

"You have no father and you have no mother," he said. "And I have no child. So you shall come home with me."

And the fisherman did no fishing that day but brought the seal pup, wrapped in his shirt, straight home to his wife.

When she saw him coming home early with no shirt on, the fisherman's wife ran out of the hut, fear riding in her heart. Then she looked wonderingly at the bundle which he held in his arms.

"It's nothing," he said, "but a seal pup I found stranded in the shallows and longing[3] for its own. I thought we could give it love and care until it is old enough to seek its **kin**."

The fisherman's wife nodded and took the bundle. Then she uncovered the wrapping and gave a loud cry. "Nothing!" she said. "You call this nothing?"

The fisherman looked. Instead of a seal lying in the folds, there was a strange child with great grey eyes and silvery grey hair, smiling up at him.

---

3. **Longing** for something means really wanting it.

Practice the Skills

3 **Key Literary Element**

Mood To figure out the mood, look at the words that the writer uses. In this paragraph, the writer uses the words *sad, sorrow, grief,* and *empty.* What mood do those words create?

Vocabulary

grief (greef) *n.* unhappiness or suffering, often about the loss of something

stranded (STRAN did) *adj.* left helpless in a difficult place

sheared (sheerd) *v.* cut off sharply

kin (kin) *n.* family or relatives

READING WORKSHOP 4

The fisherman wrung his hands. "It is a selchie," he cried. "I have heard of them. They are men upon the land and seals in the sea. I thought it was but a tale."

"Then he shall remain a man upon the land," said the fisherman's wife, clasping the child in her arms, "for I shall never let him return to the sea."

"Never," agreed the fisherman, for he knew how his wife had wanted a child. And in his secret heart, he wanted one, too. Yet he felt, somehow, it was wrong. 4

"We shall call him Greyling," said the fisherman's wife, "for his eyes and hair are the color of a storm-coming sky. Greyling, though he has brought sunlight into our home."

And though they still lived by the side of the water in a hut covered with mosses that kept them warm in the winter and cool in the summer, the boy Greyling was never allowed into the sea.

He grew from a child to a **lad**. 5 He grew from a lad to a young man. He gathered driftwood for his mother's hearth and searched the tide pools for shells for her mantel.[4] He mended his father's nets and **tended** his father's boat. But though he often stood by the shore or high in the town on the great grey cliffs, looking and longing and grieving in his heart for what he did not really know, he never went into the sea. 6

Then one wind-wailing morning just fifteen years from the day that Greyling had been found, a great storm blew up suddenly in the North. It was such a storm as had never been seen before: the sky turned nearly black and even the fish had trouble swimming. The wind pushed huge waves onto the shore. The waters gobbled up the little hut on the beach. And Greyling and the fisherman's wife were forced to flee to the town high on the great grey cliffs. There they looked down at the roiling, boiling,[5] sea. Far from shore they spied the fisherman's boat, its sails flapping like the wings of

Practice the Skills

4 BIG Question
Do you think that keeping the selchie was fair when the fisherman had a feeling that it was wrong? Explain your answer.

5 English Language Coach
Synonyms and Word Choice What does the word **lad** mean or suggest to you? Why do you think the author used that word instead of *boy*?

6 Key Reading Skill
Identifying Problems and Solutions What problem does Greyling face as he grows up? Think about possible solutions.

---

4. A *mantel* is a shelf above a fireplace.
5. *Roiling* and *boiling* mean "bubbling" and "churning."

Vocabulary

tended (TEN did) *v.* cared for; kept in working order

a wounded gull. And clinging to the broken mast[6] was the fisherman himself, sinking deeper with every wave. [7]

The fisherman's wife gave a terrible cry, "Will no one save him?" she called to the people of the town who had gathered on the edge of the cliff. "Will no one save my own dear husband who is all of life to me?"

But the townsmen looked away. There was no man there who dared risk his life in that sea, even to save a drowning soul.

"Will no one at all save him?" she cried out again.

"Let the boy go," said one old man, pointing at Greyling with his stick. "He looks strong enough."

But the fisherman's wife clasped Greyling in her arms and held his ears with her hands. She did not want him to go into the sea. She was afraid he would never return.

"Will no one save my own dear heart?" cried the fisherman's wife for a third and last time.

---

6. The *mast* of a ship is the tall pole to which the sail ties.

Practice the Skills

[7] **Key Literary Element**

Mood A key event such as a storm often adds mood to a story. What mood does the author create with this storm?

Analyzing the Art How does this picture make you feel? Does it create a mood? If it does, does that mood match the mood of the story? Explain your answer.

Sunset Over the Sea, 1887. George Inness. Oil on panel, 22 1/16 x 36 1/8 in. Brooklyn Museum of Art, NY.

READING WORKSHOP 4

But shaking their heads, the people of the town edged to their houses and shut their doors and locked their windows and set their backs to the ocean and their faces to the fires that glowed in every hearth.

"I will save him, Mother," cried Greyling, "or die as I try."

And before she could tell him no, he broke from her grasp and dived from the top of the great cliffs, down, down, down into the tumbling sea.

"He will surely sink," whispered the women as they ran from their warm fires to watch.

"He will certainly drown," called the men as they took down their spyglasses[7] from the shelves.

They gathered on the cliffs and watched the boy dive down into the sea.

As Greyling disappeared beneath the waves, little fingers of foam tore at his clothes. They snatched his shirt and his pants and his shoes and sent them bubbling away to the shore. And as Greyling went deeper beneath the waves, even his skin seemed to slough off[8] till he swam, free at last, in the sleek grey coat of a great grey seal.

The selchie had returned to the sea. 8

---

7. **Spyglasses** are objects that help people see things that are far away.
8. To **slough off** is to shed or get rid of something.

Practice the Skills

8 Key Reading Skill

Identifying Problems and Solutions How is the storm a solution to Greyling's problem?

Analyzing the Photo Do you think this is what Greyling looks like at the end of the story? Explain your answer using details from the selection.

But the people of the town did not see this. All they saw was the diving boy disappearing under the waves and then, farther out, a large seal swimming toward the boat that wallowed⁹ in the sea. The sleek grey seal, with no effort at all, eased the fisherman to the shore though the waves were wild and bright with foam. And then, with a final salute, it turned its back on the land and headed joyously out to sea.

The fisherman's wife hurried down to the sand. And behind her followed the people of the town. They searched up the beach and down, but they did not find the boy.

"A brave son," said the men when they found his shirt, for they thought he was certainly drowned.

"A very brave son," said the women when they found his shoes, for they thought him lost for sure.

"Has he really gone?" asked the fisherman's wife of her husband when at last they were alone.

"Yes, quite gone," the fisherman said to her. "Gone where his heart calls, gone to the great wide sea. And though my heart grieves at his leaving, it tells me this way is best."

The fisherman's wife sighed. And then she cried. But at last she agreed that, perhaps, it was best. "For he is both man and seal," she said. "And though we cared for him for a while, now he must care for himself." And she never cried again. So once more they live alone by the side of the sea in a new little hut which was covered with mosses to keep them warm in the winter and cool in the summer. **9**

Yet, once a year, a great grey seal is seen at night near the fisherman's home. And the people in town talk of it, and wonder. But seals do come to the shore and men do go to the sea; and so the townfolk do not dwell upon it very long.

But it is no ordinary seal. It is Greyling himself come home—come to tell his parents tales of the lands that lie far beyond the waters, and to sing them songs of the wonders that lie far beneath the sea. **10**

---

9. **Wallowed** means "tossed or rolled about in something."

Practice the Skills

9 🎯 **BIG Question**

Was it fair of the fisherman and his wife to keep Greyling from the sea? Why or why not? Write your answer on the "Greyling" page of Foldable 3. Your response will help you answer the Unit Challenge later.

10 **Key Reading Skill**

Identifying Problems and Solutions Not every solution to a problem has a happy ending. How is the main problem in "Greyling" finally solved? Do you think this is the best solution?

READING WORKSHOP 4 • Identifying Problems and Solutions

After You Read | Greyling

Answering the BIG Question

1. Was it fair for Greyling's parents to keep him out of the sea? Explain.
2. **Recall** What did the fisherman think he was bringing home at the beginning of the story?
   TIP Right There
3. **Summarize** What is Greyling's life like as a young boy? Write your answer in your own words.
   TIP Think and Search

Critical Thinking

4. **Contrast** How was Greyling's childhood different from your own?
   TIP Author and Me
5. **Draw Conclusions** After reading about his actions in the story, what kind of person do you think the fisherman is?
   TIP Author and Me
6. **Interpret** What does the author mean by saying that Greyling "grieved in his heart for what he did not really know"?
   TIP Author and Me
7. **Infer** Why do you think the fisherman's wife cried once after losing Greyling and then never cried again?
   TIP Author and Me

Write About Your Reading

What do you think of the author's solution to Greyling's problem? Can you think of a different ending for the story? Write a new ending from the point at which Greyling dives into the sea.

- Include details and description when you tell what happens.
- Include dialogue with quotation marks and characters' names to show who is speaking.

Objectives (pp. 334–335)
Reading Identify problems and solutions
Literature Identify literary elements: mood
Vocabulary Understand synonyms: shades of meaning
Writing Respond to literature: write a story ending
Grammar Identify parts of speech: interjections

READING WORKSHOP 4 • Identifying Problems and Solutions

Skills Review

Key Reading Skill: Identifying Problems and Solutions

8. Think about your own experiences with problems and solutions as you answer the questions below.
   - What is Greyling's main problem?
   - How do Greyling's parents react when his problem is finally solved?

Key Literary Element: Mood

9. How would you describe the overall mood of the story? Explain your answer.
10. Does the mood of the story help you better understand it? Would you have enjoyed the story more if the mood were different?

Reviewing Skills: Activating Prior Knowledge

11. What did you already know about seals before you read the story? How would having seen a live seal help the reader understand Greyling?

Vocabulary Check

Choose the best word from the list to match each definition below. Rewrite the correct words and definitions on a separate sheet of paper.

sheared   grief   stranded   kin   tended

12. ___ left helpless in a difficult place
13. ___ cared for; kept in working order
14. ___ cut off sharply
15. ___ family or relatives
16. ___ unhappiness or suffering, often about the loss of something
17. **English Language Coach** The word *gobble* can mean "eat." It means something a little different than just "eat," however, and it has a strong connotation! Think of three other synonyms for *eat*. Make sure each means or suggests something a little different, and use each in a sentence.

Grammar Link: Interjections

- An **interjection** is a word or phrase that shows feeling, such as surprise, or attracts attention. An interjection often appears before the beginning of a sentence.

  Hooray! We won!

  Oh, thank you.

  Hey, watch it!

- Sometimes an interjection stands by itself.

  Ouch!

  Yikes!

- An exclamation point follows an interjection that shows very strong feeling. A comma appears after an interjection that isn't as strong.

  Wow! You won the spelling bee!

  Yes, you may go to the concert.

Grammar Practice

Rewrite each of the following sentences, using one of these interjections to show your feelings.

hey   wow   uh-oh   oops

18. Watch where you're going.
19. I didn't study enough for the test.
20. You got an A on that test.
21. Maria broke the vase.

Writing Application Add two interjections that show how the characters felt in the new ending you wrote for "Greyling."

Web Activities For eFlashcards, Selection Quick Checks, and other Web activities, go to www.glencoe.com.

Greyling 335

COMPARING LITERATURE WORKSHOP

The Scholarship Jacket
by Marta Salinas

& The Circuit
by Francisco Jiménez

What You'll Learn
- How to compare two pieces of literature
- How to identify external and internal conflict

What You'll Read
- "The Scholarship Jacket," p. 339
- "The Circuit," p. 347

Point of Comparison
- Conflict

Purpose
- To compare conflict in two texts

Objectives (pp. 336–337)
Reading Compare and contrast across texts: conflict
Literature Identify literary elements: external conflict, internal conflict

Whenever you've decided between two outfits or sandwiches or solutions to a problem, you've had to make comparisons. You can make comparisons in literature, too. Comparing the similarities and differences in two stories can help you understand both stories better.

How to Compare Literature: Conflict

In the next two selections you will look at the similarities and differences between the **conflicts** in two stories.

In life or in literature, a **conflict** is a struggle between two people or forces or feelings. Most stories contain a conflict, and usually more than one. Conflict is the gas that keeps the engine of the story running. It makes stories interesting because you ask the question, "Who or what will win?"

There are two main types of conflict:

External conflict
- conflict between two people, such as a race or an election or a difference of opinion
- conflict between a person and nature, in the form of storms or animals and so forth
- conflict between a person and society, such as a struggle to be yourself while fitting in with the community you live in

Internal conflict
- a conflict within a person, such as having to make a difficult choice

Get Ready to Compare

To figure out the **conflicts** in a story, pay attention to whether someone is happy or unhappy. (Happy people generally are not in conflict with something or someone.) Remember that one story can have many conflicts and many different kinds of conflict.

When you think about a story's conflicts, remember these terms:
- **Forces** are not living things, but they create conflicts. They are problems such as poverty or prejudice or the weather.
- **Obstacles** are any problems that make it hard for a person to get what he or she wants. They can be physical, such as a fence or ocean, or not physical, such as fear or ignorance.

Use Your Comparison

To help yourself find and keep track of the conflicts in the two stories you are about to read, use conflict charts like the one below.

Conflict Chart "The Scholarship Jacket"	
Who is the main character?	
Who does he or she have problems (conflicts) with?	
What forces is he or she in conflict with?	
Is there an obstacle to overcome? What is it?	
What internal conflicts does he or she have?	
Do other characters have similar conflicts?	
Is the main character's main conflict resolved? How?	

Now copy and fill in the conflict chart for each story you'll read in this workshop.

COMPARING LITERATURE WORKSHOP

Before You Read : The Scholarship Jacket

Vocabulary Preview

coincidence (koh IN sih dens) *n.* a situation in which two events that seem unrelated accidentally occur at the same time **(p. 341)** *It was a lucky coincidence when we both won tickets for the same show.*

dismay (dis MAY) *n.* a feeling of disappointment or unpleasant surprise **(p. 341)** *She felt dismay that the room was such a mess.*

muster (MUS tur) *v.* to find and gather together; collect **(p. 342)** *We'll need to muster our courage to face the champions in this game.*

withdrawn (with DRAWN) *adj.* shy, quiet, or unsociable **(p. 344)** *He seemed unusually withdrawn at the dance.*

vile (vyl) *adj.* very bad; unpleasant; foul **(p. 344)** *A vile odor leaked from the lunch bag they found in the closet.*

Get Ready to Read

Connect to the Reading
How would you feel if you were in a contest and the rules were changed just so someone else could win? How would you feel if the rules were changed so *you* could win?

Build Background
- This story takes place in a small town in Texas.
- The word *valedictorian* comes from the Latin word *valedicere,* which means "to say farewell." The valedictorian has gotten the highest grades in the class and often gives a speech at the graduation.

Set Purposes for Reading
BIG Question Read to find out how the main character dealt with an unfair situation.

Set Your Own Purpose What else would you like to learn from the story to help you answer the Big Question? Write your own purpose on "The Scholarship Jacket" page of Foldable 3.

Meet the Author
Marta Salinas is the author of many short stories. Her short story "The Scholarship Jacket" was first published in *Cuentos Chicanos: A Short Story Anthology.* "Cuentos Chicanos" means "stories by Americans of Mexican descent." Her work has also appeared in the *Los Angeles Herald Examiner* and in *California Living* magazine.

Author Search For more about Marta Salinas, go to www.glencoe.com.

Objectives (pp. 338–345)
Reading Compare and contrast across texts: conflict • Make connections from text to self
Literature Identify literary elements: external conflict, internal conflict

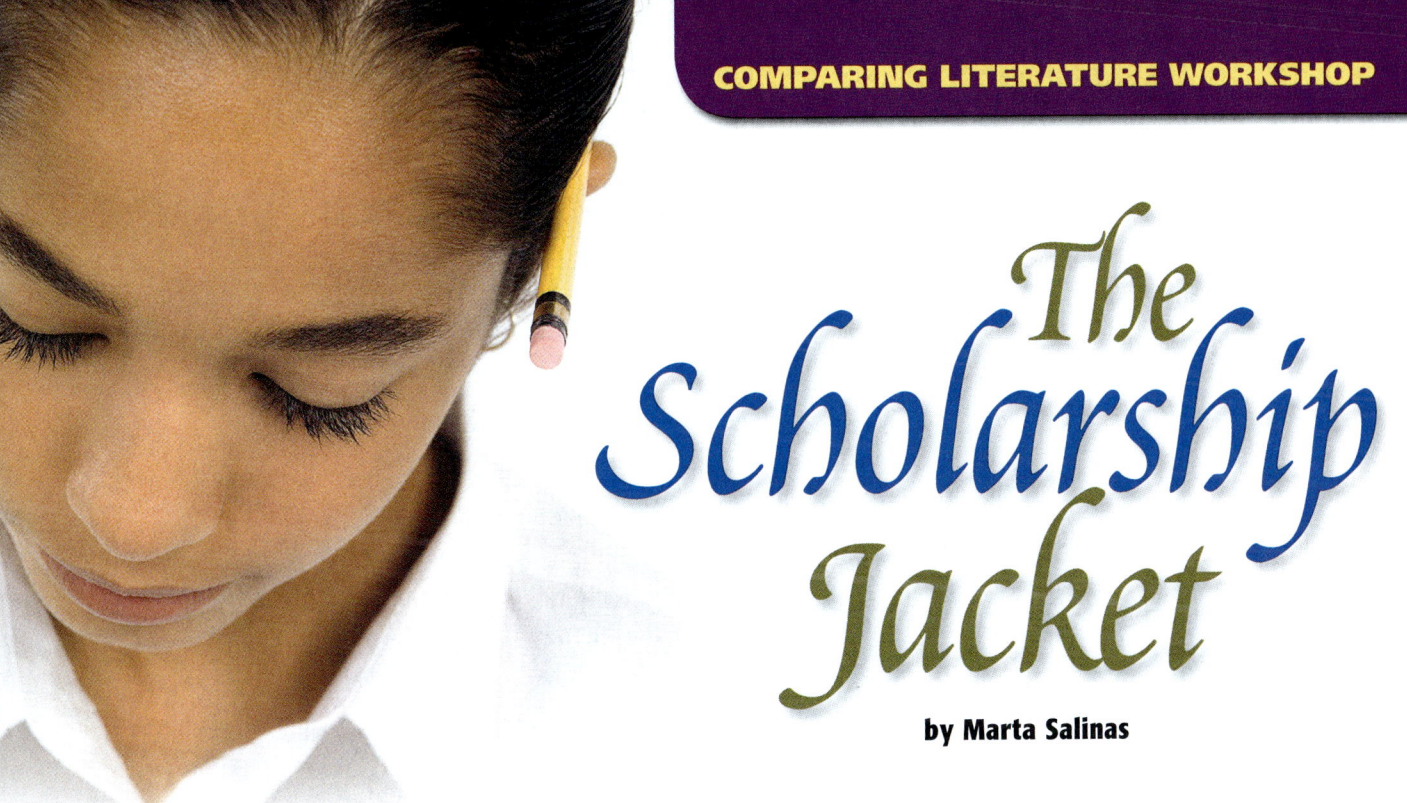

COMPARING LITERATURE WORKSHOP

The Scholarship Jacket

by Marta Salinas

Practice the Skills

The small Texas school that I attended carried out a tradition every year during the eighth grade graduation; a beautiful gold and green jacket, the school colors, was awarded to the class valedictorian, the student who had maintained the highest grades for eight years. The scholarship jacket had a big gold S on the left front side and the winner's name was written in gold letters on the pocket.

My oldest sister Rosie had won the jacket a few years back and I fully expected to win also. I was fourteen and in the eighth grade. I had been a straight A student since the first grade, and the last year I had looked forward to owning that jacket. My father was a farm laborer who couldn't earn enough money to feed eight children, so when I was six I was given to my grandparents to raise. We couldn't participate in sports at school because there were registration fees, uniform costs, and trips out of town; so even though we were quite agile and athletic, there would never be a sports school jacket for us. This one, the scholarship jacket, was our only chance. 1

In May, close to graduation, spring fever struck, and no one paid any attention in class; instead we stared out the windows and at each other, wanting to speed up the last few weeks of school. I despaired every time I looked in the mirror. Pencil

1 🔑 **BIG Question**
Because the narrator's family was poor, she couldn't participate in sports at school. Do you feel this is fair or not? Explain your answer.

The Scholarship Jacket   339

COMPARING LITERATURE WORKSHOP

thin, not a curve anywhere, I was called "Beanpole" and "String Bean" and I knew that's what I looked like.

A flat chest, no hips, and a brain, that's what I had. That really isn't much for a fourteen-year-old to work with, I thought, as I absentmindedly wandered from my history class to the gym. Another hour of sweating in basketball and displaying my toothpick legs was coming up. Then I remembered my P.E. shorts were still in a bag under my desk where I'd forgotten them. I had to walk all the way back and get them. Coach Thompson was a real bear if anyone wasn't dressed for P.E. She had said I was a good forward and once she even tried to talk Grandma into letting me join the team. Grandma, of course, said no. 2

I was almost back at my classroom's door when I heard angry voices and arguing. I stopped. I didn't mean to eavesdrop; I just hesitated, not knowing what to do. I needed those shorts and I was going to be late, but I didn't want to interrupt an argument between my teachers. I recognized the voices: Mr. Schmidt, my history teacher, and Mr. Boone, my math teacher. They seemed to be arguing about me. I couldn't believe it. I still remember the shock that rooted me flat against the wall as if I were trying to blend in with the graffiti written there.

Practice the Skills

2 **Comparing Literature**

Conflict Who is the main character? Are there any forces or people stopping her from doing something? If so, write this down in your conflict chart.

COMPARING LITERATURE WORKSHOP

"I refuse to do it! I don't care who her father is, her grades don't even begin to compare to Martha's. I won't lie or falsify records. Martha[1] has a straight A plus average and you know it." That was Mr. Schmidt and he sounded very angry. Mr. Boone's voice sounded calm and quiet.

"Look, Joann's father is not only on the Board, he owns the only store in town; we could say it was a close tie and—"

The pounding in my ears drowned out the rest of the words, only a word here and there filtered through. ". . . Martha is Mexican. . . . resign. . . . won't do it. . . ." Mr. Schmidt came rushing out, and luckily for me went down the opposite way toward the auditorium, so he didn't see me. Shaking, I waited a few minutes and then went in and grabbed my bag and fled from the room. Mr. Boone looked up when I came in but didn't say anything. To this day I don't remember if I got in trouble in P.E. for being late or how I made it through the rest of the afternoon. I went home very sad and cried into my pillow that night so grandmother wouldn't hear me. It seemed a cruel **coincidence** that I had overheard that conversation. **3**

The next day when the principal called me into his office, I knew what it would be about. He looked uncomfortable and unhappy. I decided I wasn't going to make it any easier for him so I looked him straight in the eye. He looked away and fidgeted with the papers on his desk.

"Martha," he said, "there's been a change in policy this year regarding the scholarship jacket. As you know, it has always been free." He cleared his throat and continued. "This year the Board decided to charge fifteen dollars—which still won't cover the complete cost of the jacket."

I stared at him in shock and a small sound of **dismay** escaped my throat. I hadn't expected this. He still avoided looking in my eyes. **4**

"So if you are unable to pay the fifteen dollars for the jacket, it will be given to the next one in line." **5**

---

1. The main character is called **"Martha"** at school and "Marta" at home. Martha is an English version of the main character's Spanish name.

Vocabulary

coincidence (koh IN sih dens) *n.* a situation in which two events that seem unrelated accidentally occur at the same time

dismay (dis MAY) *n.* a feeling of disappointment or unpleasant surprise

---

Practice the Skills

3 Comparing Literature

Conflict What conflict has been introduced to the story in the last few paragraphs? Add it to your conflict chart.

4 Comparing Literature

Conflict Do you think the principal has an internal conflict? If so, add it to your conflict chart. Is Martha faced with a new conflict? If so, add it to your conflict chart.

5 BIG Question

In your opinion, why did the board change the rules for winning the scholarship jacket? Do you believe that changing the rules was fair? Write your answers in your Learner's Notebook.

COMPARING LITERATURE WORKSHOP

Standing with all the dignity I could **muster**, I said, "I'll speak to my grandfather about it, sir, and let you know tomorrow." I cried on the walk home from the bus stop. The dirt road was a quarter of a mile from the highway, so by the time I got home, my eyes were red and puffy.

"Where's Grandpa?" I asked Grandma, looking down at the floor so she wouldn't ask me why I'd been crying. She was sewing on a quilt and didn't look up.

"I think he's out back working in the bean field."

I went outside and looked out at the fields. There he was. I could see him walking between the rows, his body bent over the little plants, hoe in hand. I walked slowly out to him, trying to think how I could best ask him for the money. There was a cool breeze blowing and a sweet smell of mesquite in the air, but I didn't appreciate it. I kicked at a dirt clod. I wanted that jacket so much. It was more than just being a valedictorian and giving a little thank you speech for the jacket on graduation night. It represented eight years of hard work and expectation. I knew I had to be honest with Grandpa; it was my only chance. He saw me and looked up.

He waited for me to speak. I cleared my throat nervously and clasped my hands behind my back so he wouldn't see them shaking. "Grandpa, I have a big favor to ask you," I said in Spanish, the only language he knew. He still waited silently. I tried again. "Grandpa, this year the principal said the scholarship jacket is not going to be free. It's going to cost fifteen dollars and I have to take the money in tomorrow, otherwise it'll be given to someone else." The last words came out in an eager rush. Grandpa straightened up tiredly and leaned his chin on the hoe handle. He looked out over the field that was filled with the tiny green bean plants. I waited, desperately hoping he'd say I could have the money. 6

He turned to me and asked quietly, "What does a scholarship jacket mean?"

Visual Vocabulary
Mesquite (mes KEET) is a small, thorny tree. Its pleasant-smelling wood is a favorite barbecue fuel in the Southwest.

Practice the Skills

6 Comparing Literature

Conflict Is Martha facing a new conflict now? If so, add it to your conflict chart.

Vocabulary

muster (MUS tur) *v.* to find and gather together; collect

COMPARING LITERATURE WORKSHOP

I answered quickly; maybe there was a chance. "It means you've earned it by having the highest grades for eight years and that's why they're giving it to you." Too late I realized the significance of my words. Grandpa knew that I understood it was not a matter of money. It wasn't that. He went back to hoeing the weeds that sprang up between the delicate little bean plants. It was a time consuming job; sometimes the small shoots were right next to each other. Finally he spoke again.

"Then if you pay for it, Marta, it's not a scholarship jacket, is it? Tell your principal I will not pay the fifteen dollars."

I walked back to the house and locked myself in the bathroom for a long time. I was angry with grandfather even though I knew he was right, and I was angry with the Board, whoever they were. Why did they have to change the rules just when it was my turn to win the jacket? 7

Practice the Skills

7 BIG Question

Martha was angry with her grandfather for refusing to pay the fifteen dollars, but she still believed he was right. Why did she feel he was right? Do you feel he was being fair or unfair to Martha? Explain.

New Mexico Peon, 1942. Ernest L. Blumenschein. Oil on canvas, 40 x 25 in. Gerald Peters Gallery, Santa Fe.

Analyzing the Painting Does the person in the painting remind you of anyone in the story? Explain.

The Scholarship Jacket 343

COMPARING LITERATURE WORKSHOP

It was a very sad and <mark>withdrawn</mark> girl who dragged into the principal's office the next day. This time he did look me in the eyes.

"What did your grandfather say?"

I sat very straight in my chair.

"He said to tell you he won't pay the fifteen dollars."

The principal muttered something I couldn't understand under his breath, and walked over to the window. He stood looking out at something outside. He looked bigger than usual when he stood up; he was a tall gaunt[3] man with gray hair, and I watched the back of his head while I waited for him to speak.

"Why?" he finally asked. "Your grandfather has the money. Doesn't he own a small bean farm?" **8**

I looked at him, forcing my eyes to stay dry. "He said if I had to pay for it, then it wouldn't be a scholarship jacket," I said and stood up to leave. "I guess you'll just have to give it to Joann." I hadn't meant to say that; it had just slipped out. I was almost to the door when he stopped me.

"Martha—wait."

I turned and looked at him, waiting. What did he want now? I could feel my heart pounding. Something bitter and <mark>vile</mark> tasting was coming up in my mouth; I was afraid I was going to be sick. I didn't need any sympathy speeches. He sighed loudly and went back to his big desk. He looked at me, biting his lip, as if thinking.

"Okay. We'll make an exception in your case. I'll tell the Board, you'll get your jacket." **9**

I could hardly believe it. I spoke in a trembling rush. "Oh, thank you sir!" Suddenly I felt great. I didn't know about adrenalin[4] in those days, but I knew something was pumping through me, making me feel as tall as the sky. I wanted to yell, jump, run the mile, do something. I ran out so I could cry in the hall where there was no one to see me. At the end of the day, Mr. Schmidt winked at me and said, "I hear you're getting a scholarship jacket this year."

---

3. A *gaunt* person is thin and bony.
4. *Adrenalin* (uh DREN uh lin) is a chemical released into the blood in times of stress or excitement. It increases the body's energy.

Vocabulary

<mark>withdrawn</mark> (with DRAWN) *adj.* shy, reserved, or unsociable

<mark>vile</mark> (vyl) *adj.* very bad; unpleasant; foul

Practice the Skills

8 🎃 **BIG Question**

How do you think the principal felt when Martha told him her grandfather refused to pay for the jacket? Do you think he wanted the other girl to get the jacket? Do you think the principal felt he was being fair? Explain why or why not.

9 **Comparing Literature**

Conflict Is Martha's conflict resolved? If so, how? Is the principal's conflict resolved? If so, how?

His face looked as happy and innocent as a baby's, but I knew better. Without answering I gave him a quick hug and ran to the bus. I cried on the walk home again, but this time because I was so happy. I couldn't wait to tell Grandpa and ran straight to the field. I joined him in the row where he was working and without saying anything I crouched down and started pulling up the weeds with my hands. Grandpa worked alongside me for a few minutes, but he didn't ask what had happened. After I had a little pile of weeds between the rows, I stood up and faced him.

"The principal said he's making an exception for me, Grandpa, and I'm getting the jacket after all. That's after I told him what you said."

Grandpa didn't say anything, he just gave me a pat on the shoulder and a smile. He pulled out the crumpled red handkerchief that he always carried in his back pocket and wiped the sweat off his forehead.

"Better go see if your grandmother needs any help with supper."

I gave him a big grin. He didn't fool me. I skipped and ran back to the house whistling some silly tune. 10 ○

Practice the Skills

10 BIG Question

For Martha to win the jacket, the principal had to bend or break the new rule that the school board had made. When is it fair to break a rule? Record your answer on "The Scholarship Jacket" page of Foldable 3. Your response will help you complete the Unit Challenge later.

Analyzing the Photo How do you think the girl in this picture is feeling? Explain your answer.

The Scholarship Jacket **345**

COMPARING LITERATURE WORKSHOP

Before You Read : The Circuit

Meet the Author
Born in Mexico, Francisco Jiménez came to the United States when he was four years old. At the age of six, he became a farm laborer like others in his family. Jiménez is now a professor of literature at Santa Clara University in California, and the author of many books and stories. "The Circuit" is based on journal notes that Jiménez wrote while in college. See page R4 of the Author Files for more on Francisco Jiménez.

Author Search For more about Francisco Jiménez, go to www.glencoe.com.

Objectives (pp. 346–353)
Reading Compare and contrast across texts: conflict
Literature Identify literary elements: external conflict, internal conflict

Vocabulary Preview

sharecropper (SHAIR krop ur) *n.* a farmer who works land owned by someone else and shares the crop or the money from its sale with the landowner **(p. 347)** *The sharecropper worked thirteen hours a day during the harvest.*

acquired (uh KWY urd) *v.* obtained, got, received; form of the verb *acquire* **(p. 349)** *He acquired the old car from another farmer.*

drone (drohn) *n.* steady, low, humming sound **(p. 351)** *I could hear the drone of the truck engine across the field.*

instinctively (in STINK tiv lee) *adv.* in a way that comes naturally, without thinking **(p. 351)** *Jerome instinctively ducked as the bee flew toward his face.*

savoring (SAY vur ing) *v.* taking great delight in; form of the verb *savor* **(p. 352)** *We were still savoring the chicken when my father brought in the pie.*

hesitantly (HEZ uh tunt lee) *adv.* in a way that shows uncertainty or fear **(p. 353)** *We boarded the battered old bus hesitantly.*

Get Ready to Read

Connect to the Reading
Think about something that you really want or have wanted. Is anything keeping you from getting this thing? How much control do you have over this obstacle? In "The Circuit," the narrator faces obstacles that keep him from what he wants.

Build Background
Migrant workers travel from farm to farm to pick vegetables and fruit.
- They follow the harvest, moving to another farm after each type of crop is harvested.
- Traveling from farm to farm is sometimes called traveling "the circuit."

Set Purposes for Reading
BIG Question Read to learn about what's fair and what's not.

Set Your Own Purpose What else would you like to learn from the story to help you answer the Big Question? Write your own purpose on "The Circuit" page of Foldable 3.

COMPARING LITERATURE WORKSHOP

The Circuit

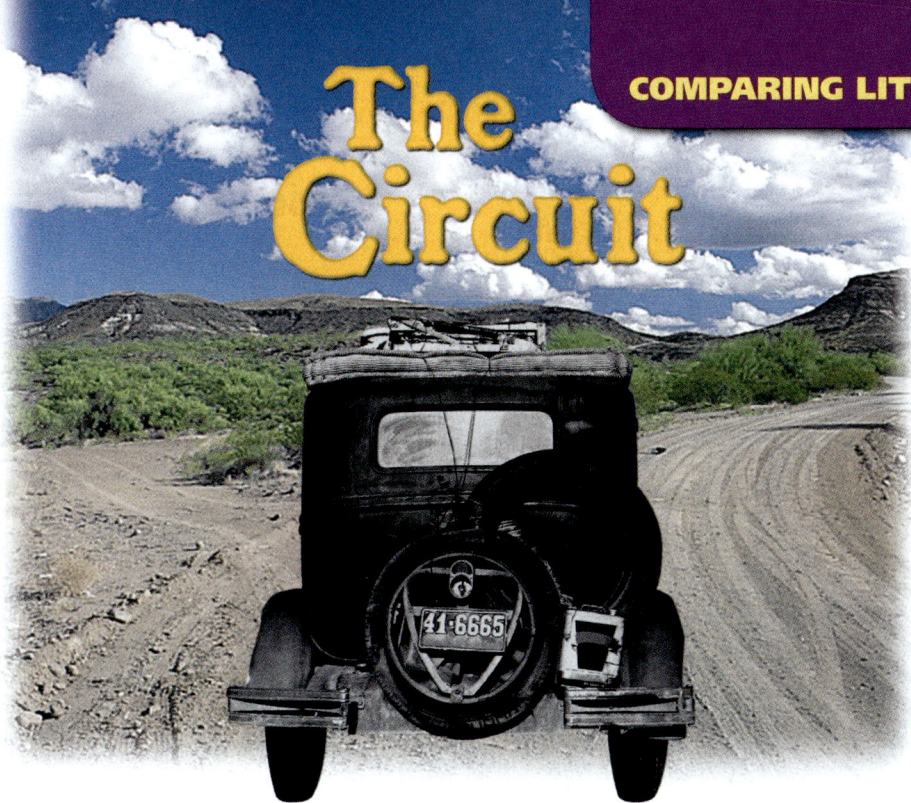

by Francisco Jiménez

Practice the Skills

It was that time of year again. Ito,[1] the strawberry **sharecropper,** did not smile. It was natural. The peak of the strawberry season was over and the last few days the workers, most of them *braceros,*[2] were not picking as many boxes as they had during the months of June and July.

As the last days of August disappeared, so did the number of braceros. Sunday, only one—the best picker—came to work. I liked him. Sometimes we talked during our half-hour lunch break. That is how I found out he was from Jalisco,[3] the same state in Mexico my family was from. That Sunday was the last time I saw him.

When the sun had tired and sunk behind the mountains, Ito signaled us that it was time to go home. *"Ya esora,"*[4] he yelled in his broken Spanish. Those were the words I waited for twelve hours a day, every day, seven days a week, week after week. And the thought of not hearing them again saddened me. **1**

1 Comparing Literature

Conflict Who is the main character? Do you know a name? If not, write "narrator" in your conflict chart.

---

1. *Ito* (EE toh)
2. *Braceros* (brah SAY rohs) are Mexican farm laborers.
3. *Jalisco* (hah LEES koh)
4. *Ya esora* Ito is trying to say *"Ya es hora"* (yah es OH rah), which means "It is time."

Vocabulary

sharecropper (SHAIR krop ur) *n.* a farmer who works land owned by someone else and shares the crop or the money from its sale with the landowner

COMPARING LITERATURE WORKSHOP

As we drove home Papa did not say a word. With both hands on the wheel, he stared at the dirt road. My older brother, Roberto, was also silent. He leaned his head back and closed his eyes. Once in a while he cleared from his throat the dust that blew in from outside.

Yes, it was that time of year. When I opened the front door to the shack, I stopped. Everything we owned was neatly packed in cardboard boxes. Suddenly I felt even more the weight of hours, days, weeks, and months of work. I sat down on a box. The thought of having to move to Fresno[5] and knowing what was in store for me there brought tears to my eyes.

That night I could not sleep. I lay in bed thinking about how much I hated this move. 2

A little before five o'clock in the morning, Papa woke everyone up. A few minutes later, the yelling and screaming of my little brothers and sisters, for whom the move was a great adventure, broke the silence of dawn. Shortly, the barking of the dogs accompanied them.

While we packed the breakfast dishes, Papa went outside to start the "Carcanchita."[6] That was the name Papa gave his old '38 black Plymouth. He bought it in a used-car lot in Santa Rosa in the winter of 1949. Papa was very proud of his little jalopy. He had a right to be proud of it. He spent a lot of time looking at other cars before buying this one. When he finally chose the "Carcanchita," he checked it thoroughly before driving it out of the car lot. He examined every inch of the car. He listened to the motor, tilting his head from side to side like a parrot, trying to detect any noises that spelled car trouble. After being satisfied with the looks and sounds of the car, Papa then insisted on knowing who the original owner was. He never did find out from the car salesman, but he

Practice the Skills

2 **Comparing Literature**

Conflict Has a conflict been introduced to the story yet? If so, enter it into the right place on your conflict chart.

Trabajadores, 1950. Castera Bazile. Oil on canvas, 27 x 19 1/2 in. Private collection.

Analyzing the Art *Trabajadores* (trah hah bah DOHR ays) means "workers" in Spanish. Do you think it is the beginning or the end of the workers' day?

---

5. *Fresno* is a city in one of California's main farming regions.
6. *Carcanchita* (kar kahn CHEE tah)

bought the car anyway. Papa figured the original owner must have been an important man because behind the rear seat of the car he found a blue necktie.

Papa parked the car out in front and left the motor running. *"Listo,"*[7] he yelled. Without saying a word, Roberto and I began to carry the boxes out to the car. Roberto carried the two big boxes and I carried the two smaller ones. Papa then threw the mattress on top of the car roof and tied it with ropes to the front and rear bumpers. 3

Everything was packed except Mama's pot. It was an old large galvanized pot she had picked up at an army surplus store in Santa María the year I was born. The pot had many dents and nicks, and the more dents and nicks it **acquired** the more Mama liked it. *"Mi olla,"*[8] she used to say proudly.

I held the front door open as Mama carefully carried out her pot by both handles, making sure not to spill the cooked beans. When she got to the car, Papa reached out to help her with it. Roberto opened the rear car door and Papa gently placed it on the floor behind the front seat. All of us then climbed in. Papa sighed, wiped the sweat off his forehead with his sleeve, and said wearily: *"Es todo."*[9]

As we drove away, I felt a lump in my throat. I turned around and looked at our little shack for the last time

7. **Listo** (LEES toh) means "Ready."
8. Mama's favorite **olla** (OH yah) is a **galvanized** (GAL vun yzd) **pot**, an iron pot with a thin coat of zinc. She got it at an **army surplus store**, which sells goods no longer needed by the U.S. military.
9. **Es todo** (es TOH doh) means "That's everything."

Vocabulary

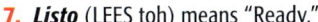

acquired (uh KWY urd) *v.* obtained, got, received

Despedida, 1941. Hector Poleo. Oil on linen, 60 x 50 cm. Private collection.

Analyzing the Art *Despedida* (dehs pay DEE dah) means "departure" in Spanish. Does the mood of the painting remind you of anything in the story? Explain.

Practice the Skills

3 **BIG Question**

Is it fair that the narrator and his family have to move? Is it fair that Roberto had to carry two bigger boxes? Explain why or why not.

The Circuit **349**

COMPARING LITERATURE WORKSHOP

At sunset we drove into a labor camp near Fresno. Since Papa did not speak English, Mama asked the camp foreman if he needed any more workers. "We don't need no more," said the foreman, scratching his head. "Check with Sullivan down the road. Can't miss him. He lives in a big white house with a fence around it."

When we got there, Mama walked up to the house. She went through a white gate, past a row of rose bushes, up the stairs to the front door. She rang the doorbell. The porch light went on and a tall husky man came out. They exchanged a few words. After the man went in, Mama clasped her hands and hurried back to the car. "We have work! Mr. Sullivan said we can stay there the whole season," she said, gasping and pointing to an old garage near the stables. 4

The garage was worn out by the years. It had no windows. The walls, eaten by termites, strained to support the roof full of holes. The dirt floor, populated by earth worms, looked like a gray road map.

Visual Vocabulary
This lamp can burn *kerosene,* a liquid fuel made from petroleum.

That night, by the light of a kerosene lamp, we unpacked and cleaned our new home. Roberto swept away the loose dirt, leaving the hard ground. Papa plugged the holes in the walls with old newspapers and tin can tops. Mama fed my little brothers and sisters. Papa and Roberto then brought in the mattress and placed it on the far corner of the garage. "Mama, you and the little ones sleep on the mattress. Roberto, Panchito, and I will sleep outside under the trees," Papa said.

Early next morning Mr. Sullivan showed us where his crop was, and after breakfast, Papa, Roberto, and I headed for the vineyard to pick.

Around nine o'clock the temperature had risen to almost one hundred degrees.

I was completely soaked in sweat and my mouth felt as if I had been chewing on a handkerchief. I walked over to the end of the row, picked up the jug of water we had brought, and began drinking. "Don't drink too much; you'll get sick," Roberto shouted. No sooner had he said that than I felt sick to my stomach. I dropped to my knees and let the jug roll off my hands. I remained motionless with my eyes glued on the hot

Practice the Skills

4 Comparing Literature
Conflict What conflict was introduced in the first paragraph on this page and resolved in the second? Add this conflict to your conflict chart. What does this tell you about the life of the narrator?

sandy ground. All I could hear was the **drone** of insects. Slowly I began to recover. I poured water over my face and neck and watched the dirty water run down my arms to the ground.

I still felt a little dizzy when we took a break to eat lunch. It was past two o'clock and we sat underneath a large walnut tree that was on the side of the road. While we ate, Papa jotted down the number of boxes we had picked. Roberto drew designs on the ground with a stick. Suddenly I noticed Papa's face turn pale as he looked down the road. "Here comes the school bus," he whispered loudly in alarm. **Instinctively**, Roberto and I ran and hid in the vineyards. We did not want to get in trouble for not going to school. The neatly dressed boys about my age got off. They carried books under their arms. After they crossed the street, the bus drove away. Roberto and I came out from hiding and joined Papa. *"Tienen que tener cuidado,"*[10] he warned us. "You have to be careful." 5 6

After lunch we went back to work. The sun kept beating down. The buzzing insects, the wet sweat, and the hot dry dust made the afternoon seem to last forever. Finally the mountains around the valley reached out and swallowed the sun. Within an hour it was too dark to continue picking. The vines blanketed the grapes, making it difficult to see the bunches. *"Vámonos,"*[11] said Papa, signaling to us that it was time to quit work. Papa then took out a pencil and began to figure out how much we had earned our first day. He wrote down numbers, crossed some out, wrote down some more. *"Quince,"*[12] he murmured.

When we arrived home, we took a cold shower underneath a water-hose. We then sat down to eat dinner around some wooden crates that served as a table. Mama had cooked a special meal for us. We had rice and tortillas with *carne con chile*,[13] my favorite dish.

---

10. ***Tienen que tener cuidado*** (TYEH nen kay tay NAIR kwee DAH doh)
11. ***Vámonos*** (VAh moh nohs) means "Let's go."
12. ***Quince*** (KEEN say) means "fifteen."
13. A ***tortilla*** (tor TEE yuh) is made from corn or wheat meal and baked on a griddle so that it resembles a very flat pancake. ***Carne con chile*** (KAR nay kohn CHEE lay) is meat cooked with red peppers and beans.

Vocabulary

drone (drohn) *n.* steady, low, humming sound

instinctively (in STINK tiv lee) *adv.* in a way that comes naturally, without thinking

Practice the Skills

5 **Comparing Literature**

Conflict What conflict has been introduced in this paragraph? Make a note of it in your conflict chart.

6 **BIG Question**

The boys have to hide so they won't get in trouble for not going to school. Why can't they go to school? Do you think it's fair that they can't go to school? How do you think the boys feel about it? Explain.

COMPARING LITERATURE WORKSHOP

The next morning I could hardly move. My body ached all over. I felt little control over my arms and legs. This feeling went on every morning for days until my muscles finally got used to the work.

It was Monday, the first week of November. The grape season was over and I could now go to school. I woke up early that morning and lay in bed, looking at the stars and **savoring** the thought of not going to work and of starting sixth grade for the first time that year. Since I could not sleep, I decided to get up and join Papa and Roberto at breakfast. I sat at the table across from Roberto, but I kept my head down. I did not want to look up and face him. I knew he was sad. He was not going to school today. He was not going tomorrow, or next week, or next month. He would not go until the cotton season was over, and that was sometime in February. I rubbed my hands together and watched the dry, acid stained[14] skin fall to the floor in little rolls. **7**

When Papa and Roberto left for work, I felt relief. I walked to the top of a small grade next to the shack and watched the "Carcanchita" disappear in the distance in a cloud of dust.

Two hours later, around eight o'clock, I stood by the side of the road waiting for school bus number twenty. When it arrived I climbed in. Everyone was busy either talking or yelling. I sat in an empty seat in the back.

When the bus stopped in front of the school, I felt very nervous. I looked out the bus window and saw boys and girls carrying books under their arms. I put my hands in my pant pockets and walked to the principal's office. When I entered I heard a woman's voice say: "May I help you?" I was startled. I had not heard English for months. For a few seconds I remained speechless. I looked at the lady who waited for an answer. My first instinct was to answer her in Spanish, but I held back. Finally, after struggling for English words, I managed to tell her that I wanted to enroll in the sixth grade. After answering many questions, I was led to the classroom.

Mr. Lema, the sixth grade teacher, greeted me and assigned me a desk. He then introduced me to the class. I was so nervous and scared at that moment when everyone's eyes were on me

Practice the Skills

7 **Comparing Literature**

Conflict What conflict has been solved for the narrator? What new conflict does he have? What about Roberto? Does he have a conflict? If so, what is it? Write your answers in your conflict chart.

---

14. The narrator's hands are *acid stained* by grapes.

Vocabulary

savoring (SAY vur ing) *v.* taking great delight in

that I wished I were with Papa and Roberto picking cotton. After taking roll, Mr. Lema gave the class the assignment for the first hour. "The first thing we have to do this morning is finish reading the story we began yesterday," he said enthusiastically. He walked up to me, handed me an English book, and asked me to read. "We are on page 125," he said politely. When I heard this, I felt my blood rush to my head; I felt dizzy. "Would you like to read?" he asked **hesitantly**. I opened the book to page 125. My mouth was dry. My eyes began to water. I could not begin. "You can read later," Mr. Lema said understandingly.

For the rest of the reading period I kept getting angrier and angrier with myself. I should have read, I thought to myself. 8

During recess I went into the restroom and opened my English book to page 125. I began to read in a low voice, pretending I was in class. There were many words I did not know. I closed the book and headed back to the classroom.

Mr. Lema was sitting at his desk correcting papers. When I entered he looked up at me and smiled. I felt better. I walked up to him and asked if he could help me with the new words. "Gladly," he said.

The rest of the month I spent my lunch hours working on English with Mr. Lema, my best friend at school.

One Friday during lunch hour Mr. Lema asked me to take a walk with him to the music room. "Do you like music?" he asked me as we entered the building.

"Yes, I like *corridos*,"[15] I answered. He then picked up a trumpet, blew on it, and handed it to me. The sound gave me goose bumps. I knew that sound. I had heard it in many *corridos*. "How would you like to learn how to play it?" he asked. He must have read my face because before I could answer, he added: "I'll teach you how to play it during our lunch hours."

That day I could hardly wait to get home to tell Papa and Mama the great news. As I got off the bus, my little brothers and sisters ran up to meet me. They were yelling and screaming. I thought they were happy to see me, but when I opened the door to our shack, I saw that everything we owned was neatly packed in cardboard boxes. 9 10

---

15. ***Corridos*** (koh REE dohs) are songs, especially slow, romantic ones.

Vocabulary

hesitantly (HEZ uh tunt lee) *adv.* in a way that shows uncertainty or fear

Practice the Skills

8 Comparing Literature

Conflict What conflicts does the narrator face when he goes to school? Are they external or internal conflicts, or both? Add them to your conflict chart.

9 Comparing Literature

Conflict When the narrator opens the door to his home at the end of the story, what new conflict does he face? Does that tell you anything about the major conflict of this story? Do you think the conflict will be resolved? At the end of your conflict chart, make a few notes about this.

10 BIG Question

How do you think the main character of "The Circuit" would answer the Big Question about what is fair and what is not? Record your answer on "The Circuit" page of Foldable 3. Your response will help you complete the Unit Challenge later.

The Circuit 353

COMPARING LITERATURE WORKSHOP

After You Read

The Scholarship Jacket & The Circuit

Vocabulary Check

For items 1–11, choose the best vocabulary word from the list to fill each blank. Write your answers on a separate sheet of paper.

The Scholarship Jacket

coincidence   dismay   muster   withdrawn   vile

1. The sticky cough medicine caused me to wrinkle my nose because of its ___ taste.
2. I ran into my cousin twice in one day: once at the grocery store and once at the doctor's office. What a ___!
3. I felt ___ when I saw the amount of work we had to finish before dinner.
4. With all the courage that I could ___, I marched into the store and demanded that my money be returned.
5. On the boy's first day of school, he was shy and ___.

The Circuit

sharecropper   acquired   drone   instinctively   savoring   hesitantly

6. The ___ of the lawnmower woke me.
7. Most mother animals protect their babies ___.
8. I knew that our neighbor wasn't very friendly, so I rang the doorbell ___.
9. The ___ gave the landowner part of the money he earned from crop sales.
10. I ___ some skill in carpentry when I worked in my uncle's shop.
11. I was ___ the taste of hot, cheesy pizza.

Objectives (pp. 354–355)
Reading Compare and contrast across texts: conflict
Literature Identify literary elements: external conflict, internal conflict

Reading/Critical Thinking

On a separate sheet of paper, answer the following questions.

BIG Question

12. Was Grandpa being fair when he said he wouldn't pay the fifteen dollars? Explain.

The Scholarship Jacket

13. **Recall** Why did Martha deserve to receive the scholarship jacket more than Joann?
    TIP Right There

14. **Recall** What were Mr. Boone and Mr. Schmidt arguing about?
    TIP Think and Search

15. **Interpret** What does Grandpa mean when he says, "If you pay for it, Marta, it's not a scholarship jacket, is it?"
    TIP Author and Me

16. **Infer** Did the principal want Martha to receive the jacket?
    TIP Author and Me

17. **Evaluate** Did you find this story realistic and believable? Explain why or why not?
    TIP On My Own

The Circuit

18. **Recall** What does the narrator mean when he says in the first sentence, "It was that time of year again"?
    TIP Right There

19. **Interpret** At the beginning of the story, how did the main character feel about moving to Fresno?
    TIP Author and Me

20. **Interpret** Why do you think the narrator spent recess practicing his reading?
    TIP On My Own

21. **Interpret** At the end of the story, how do you think the boy feels when he sees the packed boxes?
    TIP On My Own

Writing: Compare the Literature

Use Your Notes

22. Follow these steps to use the notes in your Conflict charts to compare the conflicts in "The Scholarship Jacket" and "The Circuit."

    Step 1: Look at your charts and make notes about what you think is the **main conflict** in each story.

    Step 2: Write down the total number of conflicts in each story. Also, make notes about whether only the main character faced conflicts or if other characters in the story had conflicts as well.

    Step 3: Look at the charts and make notes about the different kinds of conflicts in each story. Were there more external or internal conflicts? If there were external conflicts, make notes about what kind they were. Were they between two people? Were they between a person and a force outside the person?

Get It on Paper

To compare the conflicts in "The Scholarship Jacket" and "The Circuit," answer these questions on a separate sheet of paper.

23. Is the main conflict different or the same in the two stories? Explain your answer.

24. How many conflicts did you find in "The Scholarship Jacket"? What kind were they?

25. How many conflicts did you find in "The Circuit"? What kind were they?

26. Was the main conflict resolved in both stories? Did this affect the way you felt about each story?

UNIT 3 WRAP-UP

Answering  What's Fair and What's Not?

You've just read several different selections and you thought about what's fair and what's not. Now use what you've learned to do the Unit Challenge.

The Unit Challenge

Choose Activity A or Activity B and follow the directions for that activity.

A. Group Activity: TV Call-In Show

With five other students, imagine that you produce a TV show in which people call in with questions about a topic. The topic today is "What's fair and what's not?"

1. **Discuss the Assignment** Brainstorm with members of your group to come up with unfair situations. The notes you made on your Foldable will give you some ideas from the selections in the unit. Choose a member of the group to record the group's ideas. You can also share ideas from your own experience.

2. **Plan the Show** Discuss the ideas on the list. Choose three situations to feature on the show. Then decide what each group member will do.
   - Choose one member to act as the host.
   - Choose group members who will call the show with questions.
   - Choose another member to act as the show's expert, or person who answers the callers' questions.

3. **Write a Script** Work together to write a script for the show. When you write a script, you write down what the people who are participating will do and say.
   - Decide what the host will say about the topic at the beginning and end of the show.
   - For each caller, write a description of the situation and finish with a question about what is unfair in that situation.
   - Discuss how each situation should be resolved. Then write an answer for the expert to give to each caller's question.
   - Organize the script in the order in which the different parts will be used in the show. Each member of the group should have a copy of the final script.

4. **Practice the Show** As a group, practice reading your parts. Change the script as needed to clarify questions or answers and to help the show run more smoothly.

5. **Present the Show** Now you're ready to present your show to the class. At the end of the show, ask your audience to share their ideas about what's fair and what's not in the situations you presented.

B. Solo Activity: A Rap or Song

Musicians write raps and songs about things that they think are unfair. Think about a situation or issue that you think is unfair. You'll write a rap or song to get others to see the situation as you do.

1. **Choose Your Topic** Think about possible topics for your rap or song. Look through your Foldable notes for ideas. Think of experiences that you or someone close to you has had that seemed unfair. List all of your ideas in your Learner's Notebook.

2. **Select a Song** Think of a rap or song whose beat, rhyme pattern, or tune you like. You're going to use that rap or song's beat, rhyme pattern, or tune to write lyrics (words to a song) about a topic you think is unfair.

3. **Start Writing** Keep your audience in mind and the message you want them to understand. Write down the topic of your rap or song.
   - Tell the story of the topic you chose. Include your thoughts and feelings about it. Explain what is unfair and what should be done about it.
   - Make your words fit the same beat, rhyme pattern, or tune as the song or rap you chose.
   - If you are having trouble writing the story in song or rap form, don't worry! Just write the story in sentences first.
   - Think of a catchy title for your rap or song. Your title should draw attention to the topic and make people want to hear your message.

Rap or Song	
Topic:	
Title:	
Rap or song to pattern mine after:	
Lyrics:	

4. **Give It Some Shape** Now it's time to go back and revise your rap or song.
   - If you need to, read over your sentences and separate them into "lines." Now look at each line. Does it say what you want it to? Can you make it shorter and clearer? Can you change the last words of lines so that they rhyme?
   - Review your song or rap to make sure it makes sense.

5. **Say It!** When you are ready, present your rap or song to the members of your class. Discuss with your classmates whether or not they got your message about your subject, or if they agree or disagree.

UNIT 3
Your Turn: Read and Apply Skills

Ray Bradbury

Meet the Author
Ray Bradbury was born in Illinois. He is best known for his science fiction and fantasy stories. He has published more than 30 books, including a collection of short stories, poems, essays, and plays. His most popular books include *The Martian Chronicles, Fahrenheit 451,* and *Something Wicked This Way Comes.* In his writing, Bradbury offers warnings against the dangers of uncontrolled technological development. Bradbury has won numerous awards for his science fiction writing. See page R1 of the Author Files for more on Ray Bradbury.

Author Search For more about Ray Bradbury, go to www.glencoe.com.

All Summer in a Day

by Ray Bradbury

"Ready?"
"Ready."
"Now?"
"Soon."
"Do the scientists really know? Will it happen today, will it?"
"Look, look; see for yourself!"

The children pressed to each other like so many roses, so many weeds, intermixed, peering out for a look at the hidden sun.

It rained.

It had been raining for seven years; thousand upon thousands of days compounded and filled from one end to the other with rain, with the drum and gush of water, with the sweet crystal fall of showers and the concussion[1] of

---
1. Here, *concussion* refers to a violent shaking or pounding.

storms so heavy they were tidal waves come over the islands. A thousand forests had been crushed under the rain and grown up a thousand times to be crushed again. And this was the way life was forever on the planet Venus, and this was the schoolroom of the children of the rocket men and women who had come to a raining world to set up civilization and live out their lives.

"It's stopping, it's stopping!"

"Yes, yes!"

Margot stood apart from them, from these children who could never remember a time when there wasn't rain and rain and rain. They were all nine years old, and if there had been a day, seven years ago, when the sun came out for an hour and showed its face to the stunned world, they could not recall. Sometimes, at night, she heard them stir, in remembrance, and she knew they were dreaming and remembering gold or a yellow crayon or a coin large enough to buy the world with. She knew they thought they remembered a warmness, like a blushing in the face, in the body, in the arms and legs and trembling hands. But then they always awoke to the tatting drum, the endless shaking down of clear bead necklaces upon the roof, the walk, the gardens, the forests, and their dreams were gone.

All day yesterday they had read in class about the sun. About how like a lemon it

Analyzing the Photo How would you describe the feeling you get from this photo? Is it similar to the feeling you get from the story? Explain.

was, and how hot. And they had written small stories or essays or poems about it:

> *I think the sun is a flower,*
> *That blooms for just one hour.*

That was Margot's poem, read in a quiet voice in the still classroom while the rain was falling outside.

"Aw, you didn't write that!" protested one of the boys.

"I did," said Margot. "I *did*."

"William!" said the teacher.

But that was yesterday. Now the rain was slackening,[2] and the children were crushed in the great thick windows.

---

2. When the rain was *slackening*, it was beginning to stop.

YOUR TURN: READ AND APPLY SKILLS

"Where's teacher?"

"She'll be back."

"She'd better hurry, we'll miss it!"

They turned on themselves, like a feverish wheel, all tumbling spokes.

Margot stood alone. She was a very frail girl who looked as if she had been lost in the rain for years and the rain had washed out the blue from her eyes and the red from her mouth and the yellow from her hair. She was an old photograph dusted from an album, whitened away, and if she spoke at all her voice would be a ghost. Now she stood, separate, staring at the rain and the loud wet world beyond the huge glass.

"What're *you* looking at?" said William.

Margot said nothing.

"Speak when you're spoken to." He gave her a shove. But she did not move; rather she let herself be moved only by him and nothing else.

They edged away from her, they would not look at her. She felt them go away. And this was because she would play no games with them in the echoing tunnels of the underground city. If they tagged her and ran, she stood blinking after them and did not follow. When the class sang songs about happiness and life and games her lips barely moved. Only when they sang about the sun and the summer did her lips move as she watched the drenched windows.

And then, of course, the biggest crime of all was that she had come here only five years ago from Earth, and she remembered the sun and the way the sun was and the sky was when she was four in Ohio. And they, they had been on Venus all their lives, and they had been only two years old when last the sun came out and had long since forgotten the color and heat of it and the way it really was. But Margot remembered.

"It's like a penny," she said once, eyes closed.

"No it's not!" the children cried.

"It's like a fire," she said, "in the stove."

"You're lying, you don't remember!" cried the children.

But she remembered and stood quietly apart from all of them and watched the patterning windows. And once, a month ago, she had refused to shower in the school shower rooms, had clutched her hands to her ears and over her head, screaming the water mustn't touch her head. So after that, dimly, dimly, she sensed it, she was different and they knew her difference and kept away.

Analyzing the Photo Does the person in this picture remind you of Margot in the story? Why or why not?

There was talk that her father and mother were taking her back to Earth next year; it seemed vital[3] to her that they do so, though it would mean the loss of thousands of dollars to her family. And so, the children hated her for all these reasons of big and little consequence.[4] They hated her pale snow face, her waiting silence, her thinness, and her possible future.

"Get away!" The boy gave her another push. "What're you waiting for?"

Then, for the first time, she turned and looked at him. And what she was waiting for was in her eyes.

"Well, don't wait around here!" cried the boy savagely. "You won't see nothing!"

Her lips moved.

"Nothing!" he cried. "It was all a joke, wasn't it?" He turned to the other children. "Nothing's happening today. *Is* it?"

They all blinked at him and then, understanding, laughed and shook their heads. "Nothing, nothing!"

"Oh, but," Margot whispered, her eyes helpless. "But this is the day, the scientists predict, they say, they *know*, the sun . . ."

"All a joke!" said the boy, and seized her roughly. "Hey, everyone, let's put her in a closet before teacher comes!"

"No," said Margot, falling back.

They surged[5] about her, caught her up and bore her, protesting, and then pleading, and then crying, back into a tunnel, a room, a closet, where they slammed and locked the door. They stood looking at the door and saw it tremble from her beating and throwing herself against it. They heard her muffled cries. Then, smiling, they turned and went out and back down the tunnel, just as the teacher arrived.

"Ready, children?" She glanced at her watch.

"Yes!" said everyone.

"Are we all here?"

"Yes!"

The rain slackened still more.

They crowded to the huge door.

The rain stopped.

It was as if, in the midst of a film concerning an avalanche, a tornado, a hurricane, a volcanic eruption, something had, first, gone wrong with the sound apparatus,[6] thus muffling and finally cutting off all noise, all of the blasts and repercussions[7] and thunders, and then, second, ripped the film from the projector and inserted in its place a peaceful tropical slide which did not move or tremor. The world ground to a standstill. The silence was so immense and unbelievable that you felt your ears had been stuffed or you had lost your hearing altogether. The children put their hands to their ears. They stood apart. The door slid back and the smell of the silent, waiting world came in to them.

The sun came out.

It was the color of flaming bronze and it was very large. And the sky around it was a blazing blue tile color. And the jungle burned with sunlight as the children, released from their spell, rushed out, yelling, into the springtime.

---

3. Something that is **vital** is very important.
4. **Consequence** is importance.
5. When the children **surged**, they pushed or moved forward with a force like a wave.
6. An **apparatus** is something created or invented for a particular purpose.
7. **Repercussions** are echoes or vibrations.

"Now, don't go too far," called the teacher after them. "You've only two hours, you know. You wouldn't want to get caught out!"

But they were running and turning their faces up to the sky and feeling the sun on their cheeks like a warm iron; they were taking off their jackets and letting the sun burn their arms.

"Oh, it's better than the sun lamps, isn't it?"

"Much, much better!"

They stopped running and stood in the great jungle that covered Venus, that grew and never stopped growing, tumultuously,[8] even as you watched it. It was a nest of octopi, clustering up great arms of fleshlike weed, wavering, flowering in this brief spring. It was the color of rubber and ash, this jungle, from the many years without sun. It was the color of stones and white cheeses and ink, and it was the color of the moon.

Visual Vocabulary
Octopi is the plural form of octopus. An octopus is a sea creature that has eight arms.

The children lay out, laughing, on the jungle mattress, and heard it sigh and squeak under them, resilient[9] and alive. They ran among the trees, they slipped and fell, they pushed each other, they played hide-and-seek and tag, but most of all they squinted at the sun until tears ran down their faces, they put their hands up to that yellowness and that amazing blueness and breathed of the fresh, fresh air and listened and listened to the silence which suspended them in a blessed sea of no sound and no motion. They looked at everything and savored everything. Then, wildly, like animals escaped from their caves, they ran and ran in shouting circles. They ran for an hour and did not stop running.

And then—

In the midst of their running one of the girls wailed.

Everyone stopped.

The girl, standing in the open, held out her hand.

"Oh, look, look," she said, trembling.

They came slowly to look at her opened palm.

In the center of it, cupped and huge, was a single raindrop.

She began to cry, looking at it.

They glanced quietly at the sky.

"Oh. Oh."

A few cold drops fell on their noses and their cheeks and their mouths. The sun faded behind a stir of mist. A wind blew cool around them. They turned and started to walk back toward the underground house, their hands at their sides, their smiles vanishing away.

A boom of thunder startled them and like leaves before a new hurricane, they tumbled upon each other and ran. Lightning struck ten miles away, five miles away, a mile, a half mile. The sky darkened into midnight in a flash.

They stood in the doorway of the underground for a moment until it was raining hard. Then they closed the door and heard the gigantic sound of the rain falling in tons and avalanches, everywhere and forever.

8. **Tumultuously** means "in a wildly excited or confused way."
9. Something that is **resilient** is capable of springing back into shape or position after being bent, stretched, or pressed together.

Sunrise, 1887. George Inness.

"Will it be seven more years?"

"Yes. Seven."

Then one of them gave a little cry.

"Margot!"

"What?"

"She's still in the closet where we locked her."

"Margot."

They stood as if someone had driven them, like so many stakes, into the floor. They looked at each other and then looked away. They glanced out at the world that was raining now and raining and raining steadily. They could not meet each other's glances. Their faces were solemn and pale. They looked at their hands and feet, their faces down.

"Margot."

One of the girls said, "Well . . . ?"

No one moved.

"Go on," whispered the girl.

They walked slowly down the hall in the sound of cold rain. They turned through the doorway to the room in the sound of the storm and thunder, lightning on their faces, blue and terrible. They walked over to the closet door slowly and stood by it.

Behind the closet door was only silence.

They unlocked the door, even more slowly, and let Margot out. ◯

UNIT 3
Reading on Your Own

To read more about the Big Question, choose one of these books from your school or local library. Work on your reading skills by choosing books that challenge you.

Fiction

High Elk's Treasure
by Virginia Driving Hawk Sneve

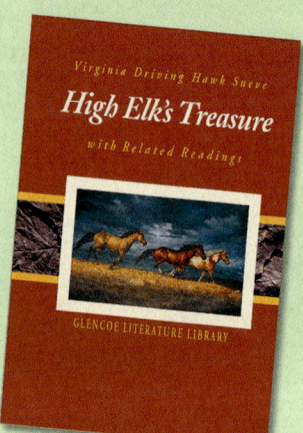

Joe High Elk learns the importance of family and cultural heritage in this tale of exploration and adventure. Read for more details about Joe and the South Dakota reservation on which he lives.

The True Confessions of Charlotte Doyle
by Avi

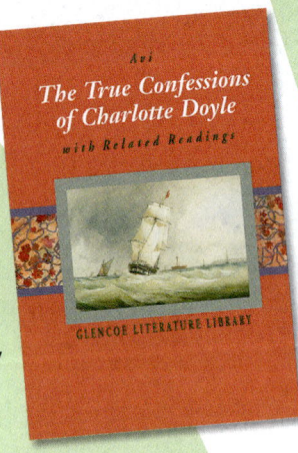

The only passenger aboard an 1832 sailing ship, thirteen-year-old Charlotte must decide whether she will side with a tyrannical captain or a crew ready for mutiny. Dive right in to this tale of adventure on the high seas!

Lucy's Wish
by Joan Lowery Nixon

In 1886, Lucy is a ten-year-old orphan on the streets of New York. She finds hope when the Children's Aid Society sends her to a new home out West…but her new family is far from perfect.

The Cat Ate My Gymsuit
by Paula Danziger

At first, Marcy Lewis just wants to fit in. She is overweight and overlooked—convinced she'll never get asked out. Then Marcy stands up for one of her teachers, a woman whose courage and conviction Marcy admires. Read to find out what Marcy learns afterward about her own convictions.

Nonfiction

Oh, Freedom!: Kids Talk About the Civil Rights Movement with the People Who Made It Happen
by Casey King, Linda Barrett Osborne

This collection of oral histories about the civil rights movement includes 31 interviews, all conducted by students. Don't miss these profiles in courage—read to find out more about real people's lives during and after segregation.

Words That Built a Nation: A Young Person's Collection of Historic American Documents
by Marilyn Miller

Discover for yourself the Declaration of Independence or the beauty of a Chief Joseph speech. Read this collection of 39 original documents and speeches to learn more about history, language, and the force of big ideas.

When I Was Your Age: Original Stories About Growing Up
Edited by Amy Ehrlich

This collection of stories by ten popular writers includes fiction and nonfiction. Read it to yourself, or read it aloud—either way, these short pieces about growing up will give you something to think about.

Beyond the Limits
by Stacy Allison and Peter Carlin

Stacy Allison sets out with three other climbers to scale Mt. Everest—something no other woman had yet succeeded in doing. Read to find out more about her amazing adventure.

UNIT 3 SKILLS AND STRATEGIES ASSESSMENT

Test Practice

Part 1: Literary Elements

On a separate sheet of paper, write the numbers 1–4. For the first three questions, write the letter of the correct answer next to the number for that question. Then, next to number 4, write your answers to the question.

1. What is the most important part of your writing "style"?
   A. whether you spell correctly
   B. whether you print or use cursive writing
   C. how you put words and sentences together
   D. how many reasons you give for your opinions

Use the following passage to answer question 2.

Rena's rowboat moved gently on the lake. The sun was warm on her face, and a slight breeze moved her hair. From the nearby shore came the faint rustle of chipmunks moving among the trees. A single, feathery cloud moved lazily, high in the blue sky.

2. The mood of this passage could best be described as
   A. sad
   B. angry
   C. peaceful
   D. enthusiastic

Use the following passage to answer questions 3 and 4.

The child of today is the adult of tomorrow. What a scary thought! I mean, just think about today's kids! If they're inside, they're watching some junk on TV. They have no interest in the educational shows they could be watching. Or maybe they're "instant messaging" their pals, as if that was the only thing a computer could be used for. If they're outside, are they playing sports or doing something useful? Not a chance! They're spray painting slogans on a garage or crowding old people off the sidewalk. The whole time, of course, they're blasting idiotic pop music at an eardrum-cracking volume. Now, can you imagine what our country will be like when these people are *running* it?

3. Which of the following is something the writer has a negative bias about?
   A. television
   B. computers
   C. pop music
   D. old people

4. What makes the writer's argument a bad one? (Think about what you learned about such things as "support for a view," "generalizations," and "bias.")

Objectives (pp. 366–367)
Literature Identify literary elements: style, bias, mood • Understand characteristics of argument
Reading Distinguish fact and opinion • Monitor comprehension: clarify • Make inferences • Identify problem and solution

SKILLS AND STRATEGIES ASSESSMENT **UNIT 3**

Part 2: Reading Skills

On a separate sheet of paper, write the numbers 1–4. Next to numbers 1–3, write the letter of the right answer. Next to number 4, write your answer to the question.

1. Which of the following is often a helpful way to clarify confusing text?
   A. Reread it more carefully.
   B. Skip the parts that are unclear.
   C. Concentrate on the parts you understand.
   D. Ignore any words that are unfamiliar.

Read the following passage and answer the questions that follow it.

   The bell rang, ending Mr. Wang's class, and the students raced for the door. Three who were trying to get through the doorway at the same time ended up on the floor. One boy hit his head hard enough to raise a large lump.
   Mr. Wang began class the next day with an announcement. "I have new rules for this class," he said. He paused until the sound of groans died down. "The first requires everyone to form a single line in order to leave class. Do you understand?"
   Fritz raised his hand. "Sure," he said. "When we want to leave class, we form a line." He stood up. "OK, everybody, let's line up and get out of here!"
   Mr. Wang had to work hard not to laugh. "That's not funny, Fritz," he said sternly.

2. What can you infer from the students' response to the news that there would be new rules?
   A. They feared Mr. Wang.
   B. They were unhappy about it.
   C. They did not intend to obey the rules.
   D. They understood that rules were necessary.

3. Which of the following is a statement of opinion?
   A. The bell rang, ending Mr. Wang's class.
   B. One boy hit his head hard enough to raise a large lump.
   C. "I have new rules for this class."
   D. "That's not funny, Fritz."

4. What is the problem described in this passage, and what effort is made to solve it?

Unit Assessment To prepare for the Unit test, go to www.glencoe.com.

UNIT 3 SKILLS AND STRATEGIES ASSESSMENT

Part 3: Vocabulary Skills

On a separate sheet of paper, write the numbers 1–10. Next to each number, write the letter of the correct answer for that question.

For questions 1–5, write the letter of the word or phrase that means about the same as the underlined word.

1. feelings of <u>distress</u>
   - A. anger
   - B. misery
   - C. delight
   - D. jealousy

2. to have to <u>endure</u> it
   - A. bear
   - B. finish
   - C. leave
   - D. correct

3. a <u>vile</u> remark
   - A. loud
   - B. funny
   - C. horrible
   - D. embarrassing

4. if we <u>forsake</u> them
   - A. notice
   - B. annoy
   - C. enjoy
   - D. desert

5. the child's <u>individuality</u>
   - A. success
   - B. loneliness
   - C. shyness
   - D. personality

6. Which of the following synonyms best communicates the idea that a wound is a really bad one?
   - A. gash
   - B. scrape
   - C. cut
   - D. scratch

7. Which of the following synonyms best communicates the idea of looking at something quickly and briefly?
   - A. gaze
   - B. watch
   - C. view
   - D. glance

8. Which of the following synonyms has the most negative connotation?
   - A. funny
   - B. amusing
   - C. ridiculous
   - D. humorous

9. Which description is an example of semantic slanting?
   - A. The room was a cluttered mess.
   - B. The room contained many objects.
   - C. A large variety of things filled the entire room.
   - D. There was a lot of furniture as well as other items in the room.

10. Which statement shows an awareness of the connotation of words?
    - A. It's more *rectangular* than *square*.
    - B. Do you call root beer *pop* or *soda*?
    - C. I would say I'm *selective*, not *fussy*.
    - D. That dog is really a *spaniel*, not a *terrier*.

Objectives (pp. 368–369)
Vocabulary Learn and use new vocabulary
• Identify semantic slanting • Understand connotation • Understand synonyms: shades of meaning
Grammar Identify parts of speech: adjectives, adverbs, demonstrative pronouns, prepositions, interjections

SKILLS AND STRATEGIES ASSESSMENT **UNIT 3**

Part 4: Writing Skills

On a separate sheet of paper, write the numbers 1–8. Next to each number, write the letter of the correct answer for that question.

---

1. In the sentence below, which word is an adjective?

   I heard a nervous voice loudly call my name.

   A. nervous
   B. voice
   C. loudly
   D. my

2. In the sentence below, which word is an adverb?

   The whole family often goes to a nearby beach.

   A. whole
   B. often
   C. goes
   D. nearby

3. Which word or phrase best fills in the blank in the sentence below?

   Ray responded ___ than I did.

   A. happier
   B. happily
   C. happilier
   D. more happily

4. In the sentence below, which word is an article?

   Wow, that was such a good movie!

   A. Wow
   B. such
   C. a
   D. movie

5. Which word or phrase best fills in the blank in the sentence below?

   Our pitcher is the ___ player on the team.

   A. taller
   B. tallest
   C. most tall
   D. most tallest

6. In which sentence is the demonstrative *that* used as a pronoun?

   A. That was mean.
   B. That dog is mine.
   C. Is that movie any good?
   D. Could I borrow that jacket?

7. In the sentence below, which word is a preposition?

   If you like lakes, mountains, or both, you will like the view around the bend.

   A. If
   B. or
   C. around
   D. the

8. Which sentence contains an interjection?

   A. Stop right there!
   B. Gee, I thought so.
   C. What a beautiful day!
   D. Remember, Jake said he'd be late.

UNIT 4

The BIG Question: What Makes You Who You Are?

"Make the most of yourself, for that is all there is of you."

—Ralph Waldo Emerson,
American author, poet, and philosopher

LOOKING AHEAD

The skill lessons and readings in this unit will help you develop your own answer to the Big Question.

UNIT 4 WARM-UP • Connecting to the Big Question
GENRE FOCUS: Poetry
Whatif 375
by Shel Silverstein

READING WORKSHOP 1   Skill Lesson: Visualizing
My Father Is a Simple Man 380
by Luis Omar Salinas

The All-American Slurp 386
by Lensey Namioka

WRITING WORKSHOP PART 1   Poetry 398

READING WORKSHOP 2   Skill Lesson: Responding
Life Doesn't Frighten Me 406
by Maya Angelou

Geraldine Moore the Poet 412
by Toni Cade Bambara

READING WORKSHOP 3   Skill Lesson: Interpreting
Same Song 424
by Pat Mora

Flowers and Freckle Cream 430
by Elizabeth Ellis

WRITING WORKSHOP PART 2   Poetry 436

READING WORKSHOP 4   Skill Lesson: Monitoring Comprehension
The March of the Dead 444
by Robert Service

The Gene Scene 452
by Jordan Brown, from TIME FOR KIDS

COMPARING LITERATURE WORKSHOP
maggie and milly and molly and may 461
by e. e. cummings

Daydreamers 463
by Eloise Greenfield

UNIT 4 WRAP-UP • Answering the Big Question

UNIT 4 WARM-UP

Connecting to The BIG Question: What Makes You Who You Are?

If there were another person who looked exactly like you, how would your family and friends know who was the real you? What is it about *you* that they would recognize? What interests do you have? What are your beliefs and values? All of these things—besides your good looks!—help to make you who you are.

Real Kids and the Big Question

MILES had gone away for the summer to visit his grandparents. When he returned home, Miles had grown at least two inches. Miles looked like a different person. Do you think that a summer away from home and growing two inches will change who Miles is? Why or why not?

LAN moved to the United States from Vietnam when she was eight years old. Now she speaks English very well. She loves to cook and often helps her grandmother in the kitchen. Lan's class is having a picnic, and everyone will bring food to share. Lan is worried that the other students will not like the kind of food she and her grandmother prepare. What advice would you give her?

Partner Talk

With a partner, discuss what you would say to Miles or Lan. Then discuss with your partner what you think makes a person who he or she is. Is it interests, beliefs, culture, or a combination of all of these things?

You and the Big Question

Many things go into making you who you are. Reading the selections in this unit will give you a chance to think about some of them.

Plan for the Unit Challenge

At the end of the unit, you'll use notes from all your reading to complete the Unit Challenge.

You'll choose one of the following activities:

A. Who Am I? Play a game to see how much you know about your classmates.

B. Self-Portrait Collage Make a collage showing what helps to make you who you are.

- Start thinking about which activity you'd like to do so that you can focus your thinking as you go through the unit.
- In your Learner's Notebook, write your thoughts about which activity you'd like to do.
- Each time you make notes about the Big Question, think about how your ideas will help you with the Unit Challenge.

Literature Online

Big Question Link to Web resources to further explore the Big Question at www.glencoe.com.

Keep Track of Your Ideas

As you read, you'll make notes about the Big Question. Later, you'll use these notes to complete the Unit Challenge. See pages R8–R9 for help with making Foldable 4. This diagram shows how it should look.

1. Use this Foldable for all selections in this unit.
2. On the front, write **Unit 4** and **What Makes You Who You Are?** Leave the other half of that folded page blank.
3. Across the top of each of the next folded pages, write a selection title. (See page 371 for titles.)
4. To the left of each crease, write **My Purpose for Reading.** Below this heading, you will write your purpose for reading each selection.
5. To the right of each crease, write **The Big Question.** Below this, you will write your thoughts about the Big Question.

UNIT 4 GENRE FOCUS: POETRY

Poetry looks different from other kinds of literature. Poetry is written in **verse**—that is, in lines instead of running text. Many poems may be divided into groups of lines called **stanzas**. Stanzas function like paragraphs in a story. The following are types of poetry:
- **Narrative** poetry tells a story.
- **Lyric** poetry tells about the poet's feelings or emotions.
- **Free verse** has no fixed meter, rhyme, line length, or stanza arrangement.

Why Read Poetry?

A good poem sharpens all of your senses. It helps you see and hear things in a fresh, exciting way. In this unit, you'll learn how to:
- appreciate the use of rhythm and rhyme in poetry
- understand sensory language

How to Read Poetry

Key Reading Skills

These key reading skills are especially useful tools for reading and understanding poetry. You'll see these skills modeled in the Active Reading Model on page 375, and you'll learn more about them later in this unit.

- ■ **Visualizing** As you read, try to picture in your mind what the writer is describing. (See Reading Workshop 1.)
- ■ **Responding** Tell what you like, dislike, or find surprising or interesting about a selection. (See Reading Workshop 2.)
- ■ **Interpreting** Use your own understanding of the world to decide what the events or ideas in a selection mean. (See Reading Workshop 3.)
- ■ **Monitoring comprehension** You may have to reread a passage to fully understand what a writer means (See Reading Workshop 4.)

Key Literary Elements

Recognizing and thinking about the following literary elements will help you understand more fully what the author is telling you.

- ■ **Poetic features:** the characteristics that make poetry different from prose (See "My Father Is a Simple Man.")
- ■ **Rhyme, rhythm, and meter:** the repetition of the end sounds of words and the pattern of beats and stresses (See "Life Doesn't Frighten Me.")
- ■ **Sound devices: Alliteration:** the repetition of the beginning sounds of words (See "Same Song.")
- ■ **Figurative language:** language used for descriptive effect, such as personification, simile, and metaphor (See "March of the Dead.")

Skills Focus
- Key skills for reading poetry
- Key literary elements of poetry

Skills Model
You will see how to use the key reading skills and literary elements as you read
- "Whatif," p. 375

Objectives (pp. 374–375)
Reading Visualize • Respond to literature • Interpret text • Monitor comprehension
Literature Identify features of poetry • Identify sound devices: rhyme, rhythm, meter, alliteration • Identify and interpret figurative language: simile, metaphor, personification

Whatif

by Shel Silverstein

Last night, while I lay thinking here,
Some Whatifs crawled inside my ear
And pranced and partied all night long
And sang their same old Whatif song:
5 Whatif I'm dumb in school?
Whatif they've closed the swimming pool?
Whatif I get beat up?
Whatif there's poison in my cup?
Whatif I start to cry?
10 Whatif I get sick and die?
Whatif I flunk that test?
Whatif green hair grows on my chest?
Whatif nobody likes me?
Whatif a bolt of lightning strikes me?
15 Whatif I don't grow taller?
Whatif my head starts getting smaller?
Whatif the fish won't bite?
Whatif the wind tears up my kite?
Whatif they start a war?
20 Whatif my parents get divorced?
Whatif the bus is late?
Whatif my teeth don't grow in straight?
Whatif I tear my pants?
Whatif I never learn to dance?
25 Everything seems swell, and then
The nightmare Whatifs strike again!

Write to Learn If you wrote a poem about your nighttime thoughts, what exact words might you use to give readers a vivid picture of the thoughts that go through your mind?

ACTIVE READING MODEL

1 Key Literary Element
Poetic Features Even if I didn't know this was a poem, the way the lines look would tell me.

2 Key Literary Element
Sound Devices: Alliteration The repeated p in "pranced and partied" emphasizes these words.

3 Key Reading Skill
Visualizing I can imagine tiny, annoying animals jumping around.

4 Key Literary Element
Figurative Language The speaker describes worries and fears as if they are little creatures having a party in his head.

5 Key Literary Element
Rhyme, Rhythm, and Meter This poem has a regular way of rhyming and a strong rhythm, which make it fun to read.

6 Key Reading Skill
Responding I worry about things at bedtime, too!

7 Key Reading Skill
Monitoring Comprehension At first, I was confused about what Whatifs are. That didn't last long! I might reread this poem for fun, but not because I don't get it.

8 Key Reading Skill
Interpreting I think the poet is saying that everyone has "What if?" worries and that they're no big deal.

Study Central Visit www.glencoe.com and click on Study Central to review poetry.

READING WORKSHOP 1

Skills Focus

You will practice these skills when you read these selections:
- "My Father Is a Simple Man," p. 380
- "The All-American Slurp," p. 386

Reading
- Visualizing

Literature
- Understanding poetic features

Vocabulary
- Using context clues that involve restatement
- Academic Vocabulary: *visualize*

Writing/Grammar
- Identifying and using different sentence types and end punctuation

Skill Lesson

Visualizing

Learn It!

What Is It? When you **visualize**, you form pictures in your mind as you read. Visualizing means using your imagination to "see" the scenes that are described in words in a poem or story. When you read about a blue sky, you should "see" a clear blue sky in your mind. Visualizing helps you connect to what you're reading.

- To *visualize* something is to see it in your mind. The writer uses words that help you create pictures as you read.
- Poems create pictures in your mind that suggest different emotions and moods. Can you think of some words that suggest vivid pictures to you?

CALVIN AND HOBBES © 1988 Watterson. Dist. By UNIVERSAL PRESS SYNDICATE. Reprinted with permission. All rights reserved.

Analyzing Cartoons
What is Hobbes asking Calvin to visualize here? Why is Calvin so frightened?

Objectives (pp. 376–377)
Reading Visualize • Make connections from text to self

Academic Vocabulary

visualize (VIH zhu ul eyez) *v.* to form a mental image or picture of

376 UNIT 4

READING WORKSHOP 1 • Visualizing

Why Is It Important? Visualizing is one of the best ways to understand and remember information in fiction, nonfiction, and informational text. When you read, you try to visualize, or picture, something or someone that is described through words. This helps you to understand what the author is saying.

How Do I Do It? As you read, imagine that you are painting a picture. Read carefully, so that you will be able to include all the details. Imagine what the characters look like. Visualize the setting—a darkened room at night, a small-town street, a family's dinner table. If you are reading a poem or short story, imagine all the details the writer provides.

As you read, jot down notes or make sketches of details that you can "see." Here are the notes that one student jotted down after reading Shel Silverstein's poem "Whatif."

Study Central Visit www.glencoe.com and click on Study Central to review visualizing.

> I could see the boy lying in bed at night thinking about all sorts of horrible stuff. I saw all of his worries—green hair on his chest, his head shrinking, his kite tearing apart. If I had to paint a picture of the scene, I'd do it by showing the little worry monsters going into his ear, filling up his head with awful things. I could make a great drawing of the scene!

Practice It!

Below are some images that are related to the selections that follow this Workshop. As you read each one, what do you see? In your Learner's Notebook, jot down notes or make a sketch about the things you visualize for each phrase.

- a father and son walking together
- a juicy orange cut in half
- a girl munching a stalk of celery
- a fancy restaurant

Use It!

As you read "My Father Is a Simple Man" and "The All-American Slurp," remember the notes you jotted down or the sketches you made to practice visualizing. When you find a detail that you can picture clearly, add it to your notes and sketches.

READING WORKSHOP 1 • Visualizing

Before You Read: My Father Is a Simple Man

Meet the Author

Luis Omar Salinas is one of the founding fathers of Chicano poetry in America. Many of Salinas's poems show how he was shaped by his experiences as a Mexican American. Salinas once said that he deals with the real world by accepting the tragic and painful parts of life in order to "gain a vision that transcends this world in some way."
See page R6 of the Author Files for more on Luis Omar Salinas.

Author Search For more about Luis Omar Salinas, go to www.glencoe.com.

Vocabulary Preview

perpetual (pur PEH choo ul) *adj.* continuing forever (**p. 380**) *The Earth revolves around the sun in a perpetual cycle.*

scholar (SKOL ur) *n.* a person of great learning (**p. 381**) *Mr. Wilson is a great scholar who has earned many degrees.*

pretense (PREE tens) *n.* a false show or appearance, pretending (**p. 381**) *I was terrified, but I grinned with a pretense of bravery.*

fanfare (FAN fair) *n.* a very noticeable public display (**p. 381**) *When the mayor cut the ribbon for the new park, there was a lot of fanfare.*

I Write, You Write In a small group, take turns writing a sentence using the vocabulary words until each word is used. The goal is to write a paragraph that makes sense. Read the paragraph aloud. Were the words used correctly?

English Language Coach

Context Clues When you read a word you don't know, you can figure out its meaning by looking at context clues. **Context clues** are the other words in the sentence or paragraph that help you understand the word you don't know.

*My father walked in an **unhurried** way, moving **slowly** so he could enjoy the outdoors.*

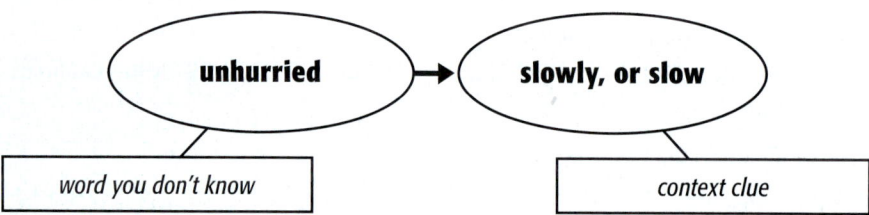

With this context clue, the meaning of *unhurried* is inside the sentence. *Unhurried* means "slow."

On Your Own Using context clues found inside the sentences, write the meaning of the words in dark type on a separate sheet of paper.

1. The Johnsons are a **simple** family; they're honest and ordinary.
2. Although they're quite **affluent,** having a lot of money doesn't change them.
3. The Johnsons are helpful to others. Any one who witnesses the Johnsons' acts of kindness or other good deeds can see how **benevolent** they are.

Objectives (pp. 378–381)
Reading Visualize • Make connections from text to self
Literature Identify features of poetry: narrative and lyric poems, free verse
Vocabulary Use context clues: restatement

READING WORKSHOP 1 • Visualizing

Skills Preview

Key Reading Skill: Visualizing
Words can tell a story or explain an idea. They can also give you the outlines and colors to paint pictures in your mind. But *you* have to supply the attention and the imagination. If a writer says, "The autumn leaves looked like splashes of bright paint," you have to pay attention to the words *splashes* and *bright paint*. Then you have to use your imagination to "see" splashes of bright paint in your mind.

Quickwrite Think about a special time you spent with a family member. In your Learner's Notebook, write about the pictures that form in your mind as you remember that time.

Key Literary Element: Poetic Features
A person who writes stories or essays may use several pages to get an idea across, but a poet might use only a few words. Poets choose words that appeal to the reader's emotions, senses, and imaginations. Poetry looks different from prose. The lines of a poem usually don't run all the way across the page. Instead, poets carefully decide how long each line will be, and each line adds something to the meaning of the poem.

Groups of lines are called **stanzas.** Stanzas are like paragraphs in a story. Each one contains a single idea or helps develop the poem's main idea.

There are many kinds of poems. Two broad categories are *narrative* and *lyric*. **Narrative** poems tell stories. They can be serious, or they can be funny. **Lyric** poems express thoughts and feelings. They present clear images.

Many poems have a regular "beat," or rhythm, and many poems contain rhyme. **Free verse** is poetry that has irregular rhythm and often doesn't rhyme. There's no regular pattern, and the rhythm can be like everyday speech or conversation. "My Father Is a Simple Man" is a poem written in free verse.

Get Ready to Read

Connect to the Reading
Think about the parents you know or have known. Think about your own parents and the parents of your friends. What can a parent do to make a child feel proud or safe? What can a parent do to make a child feel loved and happy? As you read "My Father Is a Simple Man," think about your own experience of what makes a good parent.

Small Group Discussion With a small group of classmates, talk about ways a parent can influence or shape a child. What are some helpful things the parent can do? What are good values—standards and ways of living—for a son or daughter to learn? Make a list of your ideas.

Set Purposes for Reading
BIG Question Read the selection "My Father Is a Simple Man" to find out how the speaker learned some important life lessons from his father—lessons that helped him become the person he is now.

Set Your Own Purpose What else would you like to learn from the selection to help you answer the Big Question? Write your own purpose on the "My Father Is a Simple Man" page of Foldable 4.

Interactive Literary Elements Handbook
To review or learn more about the literary elements, go to www.glencoe.com.

Keep Moving
Use these skills as you read the following selection.

My Father Is a Simple Man 379

READING WORKSHOP 1

My Father Is a Simple Man

by Luis Omar Salinas

I walk to town with my father
to buy a newspaper. He walks slower
than I do so I must slow up.
The street is filled with children. **1**
⁵ We argue about the price
of pomegranates,* I convince
him it is the fruit of scholars.
He has taken me on this journey
and it's been lifelong.
¹⁰ He's sure I'll be healthy
so long as I eat more oranges,
and tells me the orange
has seeds and so is **perpetual**; **2**
and we too will come back
¹⁵ like the orange trees.
I ask him what he thinks
about death and he says
he will gladly face it when
it comes but won't jump
²⁰ out in front of a car.

---

6 A **pomegranate** is a pulpy golden-red fruit with many seeds.

Vocabulary

perpetual (pur PEH choo ul) *adj.* continuing forever

Practice the Skills

1 **Key Reading Skill**

Visualizing Create a picture in your mind of these two men walking down the street. As the poem goes on, add to that picture with details of what they see and what happens on their trip into town.

2 **English Language Coach**

Using context clues Look at the word **perpetual**. How does the next line help you figure out the meaning of *perpetual*?

380 UNIT 4   What Makes You Who You Are?

I'd gladly give my life
for this man with a sixth
grade education, whose kindness
and patience are true . . .
25 The truth of it is, he's the **scholar**,
and when the bitter-hard reality
comes at me like a punishing
evil stranger, I can always
remember that here was a man
30 who was a worker and provider,
who learned the simple facts
in life and lived by them,
who held no **pretense**. 3
And when he leaves without
35 benefit of **fanfare** or applause
I shall have learned what little
there is about greatness. 4

Practice the Skills

3 Key Literary Element

Poetic Features Reread the poem. How would it be different if it were a short story?

4 BIG Question

Who helped the speaker become the person he is? How? Write your answer on the "My Father Is a Simple Man" page of Foldable 4. Your response will help you complete the Unit Challenge later.

Vocabulary

scholar (SKOL ur) *n.* a person of great learning

pretense (PREE tens) *n.* a false show or appearance; pretending

fanfare (FAN fair) *n.* a very noticeable public display

READING WORKSHOP 1 • Visualizing

After You Read

My Father Is a Simple Man

Answering the BIG Question

1. What are your thoughts about what makes you who you are after reading "My Father Is a Simple Man"?
2. **Recall** What kind of education does the speaker's father have?
   TIP Right There

3. **Recall** What qualities does the father have?
   TIP Think and Search

Critical Thinking

4. **Infer** Is the speaker's father a young man or an older man? How do you know?
   TIP Author and Me

5. **Interpret** In what way do you suppose the speaker's father is a scholar? What has his father learned about life?
   TIP Author and Me

6. **Evaluate** In the speaker's eyes, what makes his father great?
   TIP Author and Me

Write About Your Reading

Use the RAFT system to write about "My Father Is a Simple Man." A RAFT assignment provides four details:

Role: Write as if you were a passerby who sees the father and son on the street

Audience: Write to a friend

Format: A paragraph

Topic: Describe the father and son from the poem as you see them, during their walk

Objectives (pp. 382–383)
Reading Visualize
Literature Identify poetic features: free verse
Vocabulary Use context clues: restatement
Writing Use the RAFT system: paragraph
• Respond to literature
Grammar Identify sentence types: declarative, interrogative, exclamatory, imperative

Skills Review

Key Reading Skill: Visualizing

7. How did visualizing help you read and understand the poem "My Father Is a Simple Man"? What pictures did you form in your mind as you read the poem? Which words from the poem created the most vivid pictures for you?

Key Literary Element: Poetic Features

8. When you were reading "My Father Is a Simple Man," did it seem like a poem to you even though it didn't rhyme? Explain your answer.

Vocabulary Check

Use your knowledge of the vocabulary words to decide whether each sentence is true or false.

9. There would probably be a great deal of **fanfare** if the president visited our town.
10. A **scholar** knows very little about any subject.
11. A **perpetual** motion machine would never stop.
12. You expect **pretense** from someone you think is a phony.
13. **Academic Vocabulary** Answer *true* or *false:* When you visualize something, you erase it.
14. **English Language Coach** Using context clues in the following sentence, figure out the meaning of the word *jovial*.
    - Our neighbor is a **jovial** man, always cheerful and smiling.

Grammar Link: Sentence Types

A sentence is a group of words that expresses a complete thought. For example,
This is not a sentence: *The poet each morning.*
This is a sentence: *The poet writes each morning.*

Different types of sentences have different purposes. There are four main types of sentences:

- A **declarative** sentence makes a statement.
  The two men walk through town.
- An **interrogative** sentence asks a question.
  What is the price of pomegranates?
- An **exclamatory** sentence expresses a strong feeling.
  I love oranges!
- An **imperative** sentence gives a command or makes a request.
  Shut the window.

Grammar Practice

For each sentence, write in your Learner's Notebook whether it is declarative, interrogative, exclamatory, or imperative.

15. The children play on the sidewalk.
16. There is no one on earth like my father!
17. Tell me about the orange tree.
18. Are the pomegranates in season?

Writing Application Look back at the RAFT assignment you wrote.

- Make sure all your sentences express complete thoughts.

Web Activities For eFlashcards, Selection Quick Checks, and other Web activities, go to www.glencoe.com.

READING WORKSHOP 1 • Visualizing

Before You Read : The All-American Slurp

Meet the Author
Lensey Namioka was born in China in 1929. Her family moved often. Namioka came to the United States as a young adult and attended Radcliffe College. Namioka has said that her books draw heavily on her Chinese cultural heritage and on her husband's Japanese cultural heritage. See page R5 of the Author Files for more on Lensey Namioka.

Author Search For more about Lensey Namioka, go to www.glencoe.com.

Objectives (pp. 384–395)
Reading Visualize • Make connections from text to self
Literature Identify stereotyping
Vocabulary Use context clues: definition

Vocabulary Preview

disgraced (dis GRAYSD) *v.* brought shame upon; form of the verb *disgrace* **(p. 386)** *The child's rudeness disgraced his parents.*

lavishly (LAV ish lee) *adv.* in a way that provides much more than is needed **(p. 387)** *The bed was lavishly covered with pillows.*

spectacle (SPEK tih kul) *n.* something that attracts too much of the wrong kind of attention **(p. 388)** *He made a spectacle of himself by wearing an orange suit to the funeral.*

consumption (kun SUMP shun) *n.* eating, drinking, or using up **(p. 392)** *Our consumption of too much fast food is causing health problems.*

coping (KOHP ing) *v.* successfully dealing with something difficult; form of the verb *cope* **(p. 395)** *He's coping with having a broken leg.*

Write to Learn Create a sentence for each vocabulary word. Leave a blank where the word should go. Have a partner fill in the blanks.

English Language Coach: Using Context Clues
You can often guess the meaning of an unfamiliar word by looking at **context clues.** These are nearby words and phrases that provide hints to the word's meaning. Sometimes the meaning of an unfamiliar word may be **restated** in different words.

After the flood, we had to **disinfect** the basement. That is, we had to kill the germs.

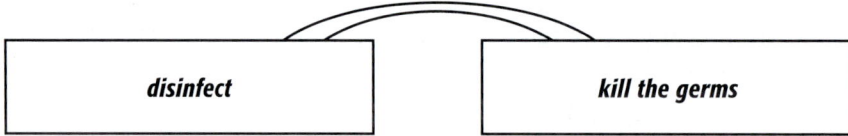

The context tells you that *disinfect* means "to kill the germs."

Get a Clue On a separate sheet of paper, write each word that appars in italic (slanted) type in the sentences below. Next to it, write the context clue that helps you find the meaning. Compare answers with a partner.
- Tony *hoodwinked* me. That is to say, he tricked me completely!
- My brother's behavior *mortified* me. In other words, I was horribly embarrassed.

Skills Preview

Key Reading Skill: Visualizing

Some writers don't give you much help when you visualize. The author of "The All-American Slurp" gives you a lot! In fact, it's the kind of story that a cartoonist would have fun illustrating. Instead, you need to illustrate it yourself—inside your mind. When the author says that her family "packed" themselves into a sofa, imagine four people jammed together on a sofa that barely holds them. Then, if you visualize what happens after that, it will be even funnier.

Literary Element: Stereotyping

This story talks about the customs of people from different backgrounds. It's interesting and funny, but while you're reading any story about different cultures, you should ask yourself: "Is this a real cultural difference or a **stereotype**?" A stereotype is a broad, general idea about a group. It is often an exaggeration. And it is never true of every member of the group. A writer who expresses such an idea is *stereotyping* the people he or she is describing.

You need to recognize stereotypes because they can limit the way you see people. "Boys like sports" might seem like an accurate statement. But if you don't realize it's a stereotype and not true of all boys, you will never understand real life.

Get Ready to Read

Connect to the Reading

Have you ever felt really different from everyone around you? Has your family ever embarrassed you? Think about these things as you read the story.

Small Group Discussion Discuss the good and bad parts of feeling different from other people.

Build Background

In the story "The All-American Slurp," a Chinese family and an American family share a meal at each other's homes. Food, manners, and dining situations cook up very funny scenes. Author Lensey Namioka drew on her Chinese American background to write this amusing story. Keep these facts in mind as you read:

- In traditional Chinese culture, people consider it polite to eat a little bit of everything instead of picking out only one or two favorite foods at a meal.
- Traditional Chinese meals usually offer a number of different dishes, but the foods are not mixed together on a single plate.

Partner Talk With a partner, make a list of some foods you enjoy that are difficult to eat neatly, such as corn on the cob, fried chicken, or spaghetti. How do you manage to eat these foods? What is the polite way to do this? Discuss any funny or embarrassing moments that have to do with handling a tricky food.

Set Purposes for Reading

BIG Question Read "The All-American Slurp" to find out how just being who they are causes funny situations for the narrator's family.

Set Your Own Purpose What else would you like to learn from the selection to help you answer the Big Question? Write your own purpose on the "All-American Slurp" page of Foldable 4.

Interactive Literary Elements Handbook
To review or learn more about the literary elements, go to www.glencoe.com.

Keep Moving

Use these skills as you read the following selection.

READING WORKSHOP 1

The All-American SLURP

by Lensey Namioka

The first time our family was invited out to dinner in America, we **disgraced** ourselves while eating celery. We had emigrated[1] to this country from China, and during our early days here, we had a hard time with American table manners.

In China we never ate celery raw, or any other kind of vegetable raw. We always had to disinfect[2] the vegetables in boiling water first. When we were presented with our first relish tray, the raw celery caught us unprepared.

We had been invited to dinner by our neighbors, the Gleasons. After arriving at the house, we shook hands with our hosts and packed ourselves into a sofa. As our family of four sat stiffly in a row, my younger brother and I stole glances at our parents for a clue as to what to do next.

Mrs. Gleason offered the relish tray to Mother. The tray looked pretty, with its tiny red radishes, curly sticks of carrots, and long, slender stalks of pale green celery. "Do try some of the celery, Mrs. Lin," she said. "It's from a local farmer, and it's sweet."

Mother picked up one of the green stalks, and Father followed suit. Then I picked up a stalk, and my brother did too. So there we sat, each with a stalk of celery in our right hand. **1**

---

1. A family who has **emigrated** has moved from one place or country to settle in another place.
2. When you **disinfect** something, you clean it to kill the germs on it.

Vocabulary

disgraced (dis GRAYSD) *v.* brought shame upon

Practice the Skills

1 **Key Reading Skill**

Visualizing Can you create a picture in your mind of the Lin family at this point?

386 UNIT 4 What Makes You Who You Are?

Mrs. Gleason kept smiling. "Would you like to try some of the dip, Mrs. Lin? It's my own recipe: sour cream and onion flakes, with a dash of Tabasco sauce."

Most Chinese don't care for dairy products, and in those days I wasn't even ready to drink fresh milk. Sour cream sounded perfectly revolting. Our family shook our heads in unison.[3]

Mrs. Gleason went off with the relish tray to the other guests, and we carefully watched to see what they did. Everyone seemed to eat the raw vegetables quite happily.

Mother took a bite of her celery. *Crunch.* "It's not bad!" she whispered.

Father took a bite of his celery. *Crunch.* "Yes, it is good," he said, looking surprised.

I took a bite, and then my brother. *Crunch, crunch.* It was more than good; it was delicious. Raw celery has a slight sparkle, a zingy taste that you don't get in cooked celery. When Mrs. Gleason came around with the relish tray, we each took another stalk of celery, except my brother. He took two.

There was only one problem: long strings ran through the length of the stalk, and they got caught in my teeth. When I help my mother in the kitchen, I always pull the strings out before slicing celery. I pulled the strings out of my stalk. *Z-z-zip, z-z-zip.* My brother followed suit. *Z-z-zip, z-z-zip, z-z-zip.* To my left, my parents were taking care of their own stalks. *Z-z-zip, z-z-zip, z-z-zip.* **2**

Suddenly I realized that there was dead silence except for our zipping. Looking up, I saw that the eyes of everyone in the room were on our family. Mr. and Mrs. Gleason, their daughter Meg, who was my friend, and their neighbors the Badels—they were all staring at us as we busily pulled the strings of our celery.

That wasn't the end of it. Mrs. Gleason announced that dinner was served and invited us to the dining table. It was **lavishly** covered with platters of food, but we couldn't see

---

3. When people speak or act in **unison,** they say or do the thing at the same moment.

Vocabulary

lavishly (LAV ish lee) *adv.* in a way that provides much more than is needed

Practice the Skills

2 **Key Reading Skill**

Visualizing Have you ever had celery stuck in your teeth? If so, maybe you can imagine what this scene must look like. The narrator describes a lot of things to help you visualize: sights, sounds, and even tastes. Visualizing is a good way to understand what is happening. When you think about the dinner, how do you picture it in your mind?

READING WORKSHOP 1

any chairs around the table. So we helpfully carried over some dining chairs and sat down. All the other guests just stood there.

Mrs. Gleason bent down and whispered to us, "This is a **buffet** dinner. You help yourselves to some food and eat it in the living room." 3

Our family beat a retreat back to the sofa as if chased by enemy soldiers. For the rest of the evening, too mortified to go back to the dining table, I nursed[4] a bit of potato salad on my plate.

Next day Meg and I got on the school bus together. I wasn't sure how she would feel about me after the **spectacle** our family made at the party. But she was just the same as usual, and the only reference she made to the party was, "Hope you and your folks got enough to eat last night. You certainly didn't take very much. Mom never tries to figure out how much food to prepare. She just puts everything on the table and hopes for the best."

I began to relax. The Gleasons' dinner party wasn't so different from a Chinese meal after all. My mother also puts everything on the table and hopes for the best.

Meg was the first friend I had made after we came to America. I eventually got acquainted with a few other kids in school, but Meg was still the only real friend I had.

My brother didn't have any problems making friends. He spent all his time with some boys who were teaching him baseball, and in no time he could speak English much faster than I could—not better, but faster.

I worried more about making mistakes, and I spoke carefully, making sure I could say everything right before opening my mouth. At least I had a better accent than my parents, who never really got rid of their Chinese accent, even years later.

---

4. To *nurse* food or drink is to eat or drink it very slowly.

Vocabulary

spectacle (SPEK tih kul) *n.* something that attracts too much of the wrong kind of attention

Practice the Skills

3 **English Language Coach**

Context Clues Look at the word **buffet** (buh FAY). What does it mean? You probably know it has to do with food because the word *dinner* is right next to it. What does the next sentence say you do? So a buffet is a dinner in which you serve yourself the food.

Analyzing the Photo Does this picture seem to reflect the friendship between the narrator and Meg? Why or why not?

388 UNIT 4 What Makes You Who You Are?

My parents had both studied English in school before coming to America, but what they had studied was mostly written English, not spoken.

Father's approach to English was a scientific one. Since Chinese verbs have no tense, he was fascinated by the way English verbs changed form according to whether they were in the present, past imperfect, perfect, pluperfect, future, or future perfect tense. He was always making diagrams of verbs and their inflections,[5] and he looked for opportunities to show off his mastery of the pluperfect and future perfect tenses, his two favorites. "I shall have finished my project by Monday," he would say smugly.

Mother's approach was to memorize lists of polite phrases that would cover all possible social situations. She was constantly muttering things like "I'm fine, thank you. And you?" Once she accidentally stepped on someone's foot, and hurriedly blurted, "Oh, that's quite all right!" Embarrassed by her slip, she resolved to do better next time. So when someone stepped on *her* foot, she cried, "You're welcome!" **4**

In our own different ways, we made progress in learning English. But I had another worry, and that was my appearance. My brother didn't have to worry, since Mother bought him blue jeans for school, and he dressed like all the other boys. But she insisted that girls had to wear skirts. By the time she saw that Meg and the other girls were wearing jeans, it was too late. My school clothes were bought already, and we didn't have money left to buy new outfits for me. We had too many other things to buy first, like furniture, pots, and pans.

The first time I visited Meg's house, she took me upstairs to her room, and I wound up trying on her clothes. We were pretty much the same size, since Meg was shorter and thinner than average. Maybe that's how we became friends in the first place. Wearing Meg's jeans and T-shirt, I looked at myself in the mirror. I could almost pass for an American—from the back, anyway. At least the kids in school wouldn't stop and stare at me in the hallways, which was what they did when they saw me in my white blouse and navy blue skirt that went a couple of inches below the knees. **5**

---

5. A word's *inflection*—or form and tense—changes depending on how it's used in a sentence.

Practice the Skills

4 **Literary Element**

Stereotyping Could either of these approaches to learning English lead someone to form a stereotype of Chinese people? Does getting to know the individuals through this story help keep those stereotypes from forming?

5 **Reviewing Skills**

Connecting The narrator tells about how kids in school stared at her when she wore a certain blouse and skirt. Think about a time when you felt like you weren't wearing the right clothes or shoes. How did you feel?

READING WORKSHOP 1

When Meg came to my house, I invited her to try on my Chinese dresses, the ones with a high collar and slits up the sides. Meg's eyes were bright as she looked at herself in the mirror. She struck several sultry poses, and we nearly fell over laughing.

The dinner party at the Gleasons' didn't stop my growing friendship with Meg. Things were getting better for me in other ways too. Mother finally bought me some jeans at the end of the month, when Father got his paycheck. She wasn't in any hurry about buying them at first, until I worked on her. This is what I did. Since we didn't have a car in those days, I often ran down to the neighborhood store to pick up things for her. The groceries cost less at a big supermarket, but the closest one was many blocks away. One day, when she ran out of flour, I offered to borrow a bike from our neighbor's son and buy a ten-pound bag of flour at the big supermarket. I mounted the boy's bike and waved to Mother. "I'll be back in five minutes!"

Before I started pedaling, I heard her voice behind me. "You can't go out in public like that! People can see all the way up to your thighs!"

"I'm sorry," I said innocently. "I thought you were in a hurry to get the flour." For dinner we were going to have pot-stickers (fried Chinese dumplings), and we needed a lot of flour. **6**

"Couldn't you borrow a girl's bicycle?" complained Mother. "That way your skirt won't be pushed up."

"There aren't too many of those around," I said. "Almost all the girls wear jeans while riding a bike, so they don't see any point buying a girl's bike."

We didn't eat pot-stickers that evening, and Mother was thoughtful. Next day we took the bus downtown and she bought me a pair of jeans. In the same week, my brother made the baseball team of his junior high school, Father started taking driving lessons, and Mother discovered rummage sales. We soon got all the furniture we needed, plus a dart board and a 1,000-piece jigsaw puzzle (fourteen hours later, we discovered that it was a 999-piece jigsaw puzzle). There was hope that the Lins might become a normal American family after all. **7**

Practice the Skills

6 **English Language Coach**

Context Clues What are *pot stickers*? How does the author tell the reader what they are?

7 **Literary Element**

Stereotyping Think about what people mean when they refer to "a normal American family." Where does this kind of family live? How many children do they have? What is the father's job? What does the mother do? Is the idea of "the normal American family" a stereotype?

READING WORKSHOP 1

Visual Vocabulary
The headwaiter is wearing a formal suit with a jacket that has long panels in the back. The jacket is called **tails** because the panels look like the tail of a bird.

Then came our dinner at the Lakeview restaurant.

The Lakeview was an expensive restaurant, one of those places where a headwaiter dressed in tails conducted you to your seat, and the only light came from candles and flaming desserts. In one corner of the room a lady harpist played tinkling melodies. 8

Father wanted to celebrate, because he had just been promoted. He worked for an electronics company, and after his English started improving, his superiors decided to appoint him to a position more suited to his training. The promotion not only brought a higher salary but was also a tremendous boost to his pride.

Up to then we had eaten only in Chinese restaurants. Although my brother and I were becoming fond of hamburgers, my parents didn't care much for western food, other than chow mein.⁶

But this was a special occasion, and Father asked his coworkers to recommend a really elegant restaurant. So there we were at the Lakeview, stumbling after the head-waiter in the murky dining room.

At our table we were handed our menus, and they were so big that to read mine I almost had to stand up again. But why bother? It was mostly in French, anyway.

Father, being an engineer, was always systematic. He took out a pocket French dictionary. "They told me that most of the items would be in French, so I came prepared." He even had a pocket flashlight, the size of a marking pen. While Mother held the flashlight over the menu, he looked up the items that were in French.

"*Pâté en croûte*," he muttered. "Let's see . . . *pâté* is paste . . . *croûte* is crust . . . hmm . . . a paste in crust."

---

6. Chow mein is a Chinese American dish made of shredded fish or meat and vegetables, served with noodles or rice.

Practice the Skills

8 Key Reading Skill

Visualizing Have you ever seen a fancy restaurant on television or in a movie? What did it look like? The narrator has given you details about this restaurant. Imagine a darkened room with candles on the tables. What does that look like? Picture the lady playing a harp. What details help you to visualize the setting?

Analyzing the Photo As you visualized the Lakeview restaurant, did it look like this picture? Explain.

The All-American Slurp

READING WORKSHOP 1

The waiter stood looking patient. I squirmed and died at least fifty times. **9**

At long last Father gave up. "Why don't we just order four complete dinners at random?" he suggested.

"Isn't that risky?" asked Mother. "The French eat some rather peculiar things, I've heard."

"A Chinese can eat anything a Frenchman can eat," Father declared.

The soup arrived in a plate. How do you get soup up from a plate? I glanced at the other diners, but the ones at the nearby tables were not on their soup course, while the more distant ones were invisible in the darkness.

Fortunately my parents had studied books on western etiquette[7] before they came to America. "Tilt your plate," whispered my mother. "It's easier to spoon the soup up that way."

She was right. Tilting the plate did the trick. But the etiquette book didn't say anything about what you did after the soup reached your lips. As any respectable Chinese knows, the correct way to eat your soup is to slurp. This helps to cool the liquid and prevent you from burning your lips. It also shows your appreciation.

We showed our appreciation. *Shloop*, went my father. *Shloop*, went my mother. *Shloop, shloop*, went my brother, who was the hungriest.

The lady harpist stopped playing to take a rest. And in the silence, our family's **consumption** of soup suddenly seemed unnaturally loud. You know how it sounds on a rocky beach when the tide goes out and the water drains from all those little pools? They go *shloop, shloop, shloop*. That was the Lin family, eating soup.

At the next table a waiter was pouring wine. When a large *shloop* reached him, he froze. The bottle continued to pour, and red wine flooded the tabletop and into the lap of a customer. Even the customer didn't notice

---

7. **Etiquette** means the rules for manners or polite behavior, which vary in different places and cultures.

Vocabulary

consumption (kun SUMP shun) *n.* eating, drinking, or using up

Practice the Skills

9 Reviewing Skill

Connecting Have you ever felt embarrassed by something you had no control over? How does the narrator seem to feel when her parents pull out a flashlight and a dictionary to try and understand the menu?

Analyzing the Art Does this picture help you "hear" the *schloop, schloop* sound that the narrator describes? Why or why not?

anything at first, being also hypnotized by the *shloop, shloop, shloop.*

It was too much. "I need to go to the toilet," I mumbled, jumping to my feet. A waiter, sensing my urgency, quickly directed me to the ladies' room.

I splashed cold water on my burning face, and as I dried myself with a paper towel, I stared into the mirror. In this perfumed ladies' room, with its pink-and-silver wallpaper and marbled sinks, I looked completely out of place. What was I doing here? What was our family doing in the Lakeview restaurant? In America?

The door to the ladies' room opened. A woman came in and glanced curiously at me. I retreated into one of the toilet cubicles and latched the door. **10**

Time passed—maybe half an hour, maybe an hour. Then I heard the door open again, and my mother's voice. "Are you in there? You're not sick, are you?"

There was real concern in her voice. A girl can't leave her family just because they slurp their soup. Besides, the toilet cubicle had a few drawbacks as a permanent residence. "I'm all right," I said, undoing the latch.

Mother didn't tell me how the rest of the dinner went, and I didn't want to know. In the weeks following, I managed to push the whole thing into the back of my mind, where it jumped out at me only a few times a day. Even now, I turn hot all over when I think of the Lakeview restaurant.

But by the time we had been in this country for three months, our family was definitely making progress toward becoming Americanized. I remember my parents' first PTA[8] meeting. Father wore a neat suit and tie, and Mother put on her first pair of high heels. She stumbled only once. They met my homeroom teacher and beamed as she told them that I would make honor roll soon at the rate I was going. Of course Chinese etiquette forced Father to say that I was a very stupid girl and Mother to protest that the teacher was showing favoritism toward me. But I could tell they were both very proud.

---

8. **PTA** stands for Parent Teacher Association.

Practice the Skills

10 **Reviewing Skill**

Connecting Have you ever felt this embarrassed? How long did it take you to get over it? (Or are you still not over it?)

READING WORKSHOP 1

The day came when my parents announced that they wanted to give a dinner party. We had invited Chinese friends to eat with us before, but this dinner was going to be different. In addition to a Chinese-American family, we were going to invite the Gleasons.

"Gee, I can hardly wait to have dinner at your house," Meg said to me. "I just *love* Chinese food."

That was a relief. Mother was a good cook, but I wasn't sure if people who ate sour cream would also eat chicken gizzards stewed in soy sauce.

Mother decided not to take a chance with chicken gizzards. Since we had western guests, she set the table with large dinner plates, which we never used in Chinese meals. In fact we didn't use individual plates at all, but picked up food from the platters in the middle of the table and brought it directly to our rice bowls. Following the practice of Chinese-American restaurants, Mother also placed large serving spoons on the platters. **11**

The dinner started well. Mrs. Gleason exclaimed at the beautifully arranged dishes of food: the colorful candied fruit in the sweet-and-sour pork dish, the noodle-thin shreds of chicken meat stir-fried with tiny peas, and the glistening pink prawns in a ginger sauce.

At first I was too busy enjoying my food to notice how the guests were doing. But soon I remembered my duties. Sometimes guests were too polite to help themselves and you had to serve them with more food.

I glanced at Meg, to see if she needed more food, and my eyes nearly popped out at the sight of her plate. It was piled with food: the sweet-and-sour meat pushed right against the chicken shreds, and the chicken sauce ran into the prawns. She had been taking food from a second dish before she finished eating her helping from the first!

Horrified, I turned to look at Mrs. Gleason. She was dumping rice out of her bowl and putting it on her

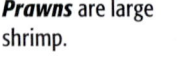

Visual Vocabulary
Prawns are large shrimp.

Practice the Skills

11 **Key Reading Skill**

Visualizing Think back to the dinner with celery at the Gleasons' house. How did you picture that dinner? Imagine the dinner with soup in the French restaurant. How did you picture that dinner? How are the details about the Chinese dinner different from the other dinners? Think about those different descriptions, and consider how visualizing helps you understand the story.

Analyzing the Photo How is this bowl of rice different from Meg's plate for the Chinese dinner? Explain your answer with details from the story.

394 UNIT 4 What Makes You Who You Are?

dinner plate. Then she ladled prawns and gravy on top of the rice and mixed everything together, the way you mix sand, gravel, and cement to make concrete.

I couldn't bear to look any longer, and I turned to Mr. Gleason. He was chasing a pea around his plate. Several times he got it to the edge, but when he tried to pick it up with his chopsticks, it rolled back toward the center of the plate again. Finally he put down his chopsticks and picked up the pea with his fingers. He really did!
A grown man!

All of us, our family and the Chinese guests, stopped eating to watch the activities of the Gleasons. I wanted to giggle. Then I caught my mother's eyes on me. She frowned and shook her head slightly, and I understood the message: the Gleasons were not used to Chinese ways, and they were just **coping** the best they could. For some reason I thought of celery strings. 🔲

When the main courses were finished, Mother brought out a platter of fruit. "I hope you weren't expecting a sweet dessert," she said. "Since the Chinese don't eat dessert, I didn't think to prepare any."

"Oh, I couldn't possibly eat dessert!" cried Mrs. Gleason. "I'm simply stuffed!"

Meg had different ideas. When the table was cleared, she announced that she and I were going for a walk. "I don't know about you, but I feel like dessert," she told me, when we were outside. "Come on, there's a Dairy Queen down the street. I could use a big chocolate milkshake!"

Although I didn't really want anything more to eat, I insisted on paying for the milkshakes. After all, I was still hostess.

Meg got her large chocolate milkshake and I had a small one. Even so, she was finishing hers while I was only half done. Toward the end she pulled hard on her straws and went *shloop, shloop*. 🔳

"Do you always slurp when you eat a milkshake?" I asked, before I could stop myself.

Meg grinned. "Sure. All Americans slurp." ○

Vocabulary

coping (KOHP ing) *v.* successfully dealing with something difficult

Analyzing the Photo Do you think that you could drink this milkshake without making a slurping noise? Explain.

Practice the Skills

12 **Literary Element**

Stereotyping Based on this dinner, what kind of stereotype could the Lin family form of Americans? Could they think all Americans are crude and greedy? Would that be accurate and fair?

13 **BIG Question**

How do you think the narrator's family and culture are a part of what makes her who she is? Write your answer on the "All-American Slurp" page of Foldable 4. Your response will help you complete the Unit Challenge later.

The All-American Slurp **395**

READING WORKSHOP 1 • Visualizing

After You Read | The All-American Slurp

Answering the BIG Question

1. What are your thoughts about what makes us who we are after reading "The All-American Slurp"?

2. **Recall** What "mistakes" does the Lin family make at the Gleasons' dinner party?
   TIP Right There

3. **Recall** How does the narrator get her mother to buy her a pair of jeans?
   TIP Right There

Critical Thinking

4. **Infer** Why does the narrator run and hide in the elegant restaurant?
   TIP Author and Me

5. **Evaluate** Why do you think it was easier for the narrator to pick up American customs than for her parents?
   TIP Author and Me

6. **Synthesize** By the end of the story, how had the narrator and her family changed or become more comfortable with their American surroundings?
   TIP Think and Search

Write About Your Reading

Write to Learn Choose one of the following activities:

- Imagine that you are a member of the Lin family and are just getting used to life in America. Write a postcard to a friend in China, describing one way in which Chinese and American customs seem very different.
- Write a letter to the narrator, comparing some of your experiences with hers.
- Draw a cartoon strip that shows what happens at a dinner with the Lins and the Gleasons. Be sure to write captions for each picture (a sentence that tells what is going on in the picture) or some speech bubbles.

Objectives (pp. 396–397)
Reading Visualize • Make connections from text to self
Literature Identify stereotyping
Vocabulary Use context clues: definition
Writing Respond to literature
Grammar Use end punctuation correctly

Skills Review

Key Reading Skill: Visualizing

7. Did visualizing parts of the story help you to understand what was happening and enjoy the story? Explain.

8. Imagine that you had to draw a scene from the story. What scene would it be? Describe the details from the story that help you to picture the scene.

Literary Element: Stereotyping

9. What did the Lin family and the Gleason family do that might keep them from forming stereotypes?

Reviewing Skills: Connecting

10. How did your own experiences or previous reading help you connect to the story? Use examples from the story to explain how you connected.

Vocabulary Check

Write the correct vocabulary word for each sentence.

coping   lavishly   consumption
disgraced   spectacle

11. The chef ___ praised the wonderful meal.
12. Owen's behavior caused him to make a ___ of himself.
13. Owen's family was embarrassed because he ___ them.
14. ___ with a difficult problem is hard.
15. My ___ of cookies doubled when I learned to bake them myself.

Web Activities For eFlashcards, Selection Quick Checks, and other Web activities, go to www.glencoe.com.

English Language Coach: Using Context Clues

16. Which words in the following sentence restate the meaning of the underlined word?

    Eating buffet style was <u>alien</u>, or strange and unfamiliar, to the Lin family.

Grammar Link: End Punctuation

Different types of sentences have different purposes. The punctuation at the end of a sentence must match the purpose of the sentence.

- A **declarative** sentence simply makes a statement. It always ends with a period.
  Example: *She saw the bus go by.*
- An **interrogative** sentence asks a question. It always ends with a question mark.
  Example: *Are you ready to go?*
- An **exclamatory** sentence expresses a strong feeling. It ends with an exclamation point.
  Example: *I can't believe it!*
- An **imperative** sentence gives a command. It may end with a period or, if the command is forceful, an exclamation point.
  Examples: *Please hand me a glass. Don't drop it!*

Remember: The purpose of the sentence determines the end punctuation.

Grammar Practice

Add correct end punctuation to these sentences.

17. That makes me furious
18. We went to visit friends
19. Do you like dumplings
20. Celery is a vegetable
21. Stop slurping right this minute

Writing Application Look back at the writing activity you did in this part of the Workshop. Make sure you have used the right end punctuation for every sentence.

The All-American Slurp 397

WRITING WORKSHOP PART 1

Poetry
Prewriting and Drafting

ASSIGNMENT Write a poem

Purpose: To write a poem about what makes you who you are

Audience: You, your teacher, classmates, family, and friends

Writing Rubric

As you work through this writing assignment, you should

- think about what makes you who you are
- use poetic forms such as lines and stanzas
- choose words appropriate to your purpose and audience

See page 438 in Part 2 for a model of a poem.

Objectives (pp. 398–401)
Writing Use the writing process: prewrite, draft • Write a poem • Use literary elements: conventions of poetry, word choice
Grammar Identify complete sentences

Writing a poem will help you think about the Unit 4 Big Question: What makes you who you are?

Prewriting
Get Ready to Write

Writing a poem is like writing a song. Poets use rhythm and often use rhyme. They also use a lot fewer words than writers of fiction and nonfiction. Most importantly, poets use word images to describe emotions. In this Writing Workshop, you will learn how to express yourself using these poetic devices.

Gather Ideas

In your Learner's Notebook, write a short paragraph describing one of your personality traits.

> My name is Max, and I like to talk. Sometimes, talking gets me in trouble with my teacher or parents. The reason I talk so much is that I like to make people laugh. My mom says that I should be a comedian because I'm always making up jokes and cheering people up when they're feeling down.

Now, write a short paragraph about an activity that you enjoy (for example, soccer, reading, drawing, karate).

> I really like gymnastics. I practice at the gym three days a week after school. My coach is really cool, and right now we are working on back handsprings. I think gymnastics is a great sport for both boys and girls because it makes your body strong and flexible.

WRITING WORKSHOP PART 1

Choose a Topic

Pick a characteristic about yourself, or an activity that is important to you, as the topic of your poem. On a fresh sheet of paper in your Learner's Notebook, write your name and topic on the first line. Make a list of words and phrases that come to mind when you think about that topic.

Writing Models For models and other writing activities, go to www.glencoe.com.

```
Max Jones    Talkative       Stephanie Carter    Gymnastics
Laughter                     Balance Beam
Voice                        Competition
My mother                    Sprained ankle
After school detention       Back handspring
```

Drafting

Start Writing!

Pick an item from the list you made in your Learner's Notebook. On a single line of paper, write your feelings about this item. This can be the first line of your poem. Keep writing, using the ideas from your list.

Get It on Paper

Poems are written in single lines of text. Many poems are divided into groups of lines called stanzas. Read the poem below. Notice that the verse is divided into four different stanzas. The bird's *key* is the highness or lowness of the notes in his song.

A Minor Bird
by Robert Frost

I have wished a bird would fly away,
And not sing by my house all day;

Have clapped my hands at him from the door
When it seemed as if I could bear no more.

The fault must partly have been in me.
The bird was not to blame for his key.

And of course there must be something wrong
In wanting to silence any song.

In your own poem, skip a line and start a new stanza when you begin a new idea or extend an idea further.

> **Writing Tip**
>
> Writing poetry is like drawing a picture with words. Describe little details to make your picture interesting. For example, instead of writing *My cat is soft,* write the details that make your cat *soft: My cat looks like a dust mop and feels like a down pillow.*

> **Writing Tip**
>
> Poetry doesn't require complete sentences or perfect punctuation. Don't worry about these things as you write your draft. Just get your main idea and feelings down on paper. You can experiment with punctuation and grammar later in the workshop.

WRITING WORKSHOP PART 1

Applying Good Writing Traits

Word Choice

So many words and so little time! The English language has hundreds of thousands of words. How do you decide which ones to use?

What Is Word Choice?

Word choice is choosing words that make your writing clear, interesting, and easy to understand.

Why Is Word Choice Important?

Words that are thoughtfully chosen make readers remember your writing long after they have finished reading. Imagine that you spent hours cleaning your room. You dusted, vacuumed, and even cleaned under your bed! You call your parents to show off your hard work, and all they say is, "Good job." Is *good* the word that you were hoping for? Probably not. *Terrific, amazing,* or *incredible* all would have been better words for that situation. People who read your poetry want the same thing—descriptive words that are carefully chosen.

How Do I Use Word Choice in My Writing?

- Use lively verbs to show action. Try to replace boring verbs such as *do* and *make* with more exciting words such as *perform* and *create*.
- Use words that match your purpose. As you write, consider who your readers are. Try to use words that you know your readers use and will understand. For example, if you are writing a letter to your grandparents, you may use different words than if you were writing a letter to a friend.

Analyzing Cartoons
The boy's dad has just used the expression "super duper." What do you think that means? Would you ever use that expression when you talk to your friends or in your writing? Why or why not?

REAL LIFE ADVENTURES © 1997 GarLanco. Reprinted with permission of UNIVERSAL SYNDICATE. All right reserved.

- Add adjectives and adverbs to your writing. Instead of writing about *the shopping mall*, write about the <u>crowded</u> shopping mall.
- Instead of saying *the dog chased the ball*, explain that *the dog <u>slowly</u> chased the <u>old, green, tennis</u> ball.*

Write to Learn Activity Write a short review of the last movie you saw. Tell why you liked it or why you didn't like it and recommend whether your readers should see it or not. As you write, use adjectives, adverbs, and words that match your purpose and audience.

Grammar Link: Complete Sentences

One thing all sentences have in common is that they must be complete.

What Is a Complete Sentence?

A complete sentence is a group of words that includes a

- subject
- verb
- complete thought

A sentence does not have to be long to be complete. These are all complete sentences:

> Cows moo.
> I am tired.
> Francine laughed.

Why Are Complete Sentences Important?

Your sentences must include a subject, a verb, and a complete thought to be understood by readers. Sentences that do not meet all three requirements are called sentence fragments. If your writing includes fragments, readers may not understand what you mean.

How Do I Write Complete Sentences?

Include a Subject
The subject of a sentence tells whom or what the sentence is about. It always includes a noun or pronoun.

My sister is thinking about moving to Greece.
Who is this sentence about? *My sister.*
My sister is the subject of this sentence.

Use a Verb
The verb part of a sentence expresses action or a state of being.
DeMarcus plans his birthday party.
What does DeMarcus do in this sentence? He *plans* his birthday party.
Plans is the verb of this sentence.
DeMarcus is twelve years old. *Is* links the subject with words that describe him.

Express a Complete Thought
Sometimes, it's not enough to just include a subject and a verb. You must not leave a reader hanging, wondering what else is supposed to be there.

Fragment: When Joey yelled.
Complete: I jumped when Joey yelled.
Complete: When Joey yelled, we came running.

Write to Learn Copy these sentences into your Learner's Notebook. Next to each, write "C" if it is a complete sentence. Write "F" if it is a sentence fragment.

1. Ryan went home.
2. Stopped to tie her shoes.
3. A dog with huge and muddy paws.
4. We saw Teresa at the game.
5. While he was playing the trumpet.
6. Slipped and fell all the way down the stairs.

Looking Ahead

Part 2 of this Writing Workshop is coming up later. Be sure to keep the writing you have done so far.

READING WORKSHOP 2

Skills Focus

You will practice using these skills when you read the following selections:
- "Life Doesn't Frighten Me," p. 406
- "Geraldine Moore the Poet," p. 412

Reading
- Responding to what you read

Literature
- Identifying rhyme, rhythm, and meter

Vocabulary
- Using context clues that involve definitions
- Understanding idioms

Writing/Grammar
- Identifying sentence framents

Skill Lesson

Responding to What You Read

Learn It!

What Is It? When you read something you enjoy, you **respond** to what you read in a personal way. Reading becomes much more meaningful when you pay attention to
- what you like
- what you find surprising
- what you find interesting
- what the writer makes you feel

Analyzing Cartoons
Baldo says that an angry response is better than no response.
Do you believe that any response is better than none?

BALDO © 2004 Baldo Partnership. Dist. BY UNIVERSAL PRESS SYNDICATE. Reprinted with permission. All rights reserved.

Objectives (pp. 402–403)
Reading Respond to literature

402 UNIT 4

READING WORKSHOP 2 • Responding

Why Is It Important? When you read actively and respond thoughtfully, you enjoy a selection more. You also learn and remember more from what you read. When you respond to a selection, you

- ask questions
- connect it to your own life
- may even argue with the author

How Do I Do It? As you read, think about how you feel about the story elements or ideas in a selection.

- What's your reaction to the characters in a story?
- What grabs your attention as you read?

Literature Online

Study Central Visit www.glencoe.com and click on Study Central to review responding to what you read.

Read the following excerpt from Shel Silverstein's poem, "Whatif."

> Whatif I get beat up?
> Whatif there's poison in my cup?
> Whatif I start to cry?
> Whatif I get sick and die?

Here is how one student responded to this poem:

> <u>I read</u> about someone wondering about being beat up or poisoned, crying, and getting sick and dying. <u>I feel</u> afraid of some of these things myself. I often worry that I might cry. <u>I wonder</u> whether any of the things in this poem happened to the speaker and what would I do if any of them happened to me.

Practice It!

Divide a page in your Learner's Notebook into three columns. Label the first one "I read . . ." Label the second one "I think/feel . . ." Label the third one, "I wonder . . ."
Use these to help you write your response to the lines above from "Whatif."

Use It!

As you read "Life Doesn't Frighten Me" and "Geraldine Moore the Poet," use the "I read" column to write down the words and phrases that trigger questions and feelings. Write your thoughts and feelings in the "I think/feel," column. List the questions that come to your mind in the "I wonder" column.

READING WORKSHOP 2 • Responding

Before You Read Life Doesn't Frighten Me

Maya Angelou

Meet the Author
Maya Angelou was born Marguerite Johnson on April 4, 1928. She became an accomplished actress, director, educator, poet, and author of twelve best-selling books. She once said, "I can be changed by what happens to me. But I refuse to be reduced by it." See page R1 of the Author Files for more on Maya Angelou.

Author Search For more about Maya Angelou, go to www.glencoe.com.

Objectives (pp. 404–407)
Reading Respond to literature • Make connections from text to self
Literature Identify poetic features: rhyme, rhythm, meter
Vocabulary Use context clues: definition, restatement

Vocabulary Preview

Write to Learn A **phobia** (FO bee uh) is a deep fear or dread of something. With a partner, use a dictionary to find out what fear, or phobia, each of these words names: *zoophobia, agoraphobia, xenophobia, arachnophobia.*

English Language Coach

Context Clues The "context" of a word is the other words and sentences around it. The context of an unfamiliar word often contains clues to its meaning. Sometimes a word's context will actually define the word. Definitions are usually introduced with clue words. For example: "The plant has begun to germinate, which means that it is starting to sprout." Maybe you don't know what "germinate" means. Then you read the clue words "which means." These words tell you that "germinate" means "to start to sprout."

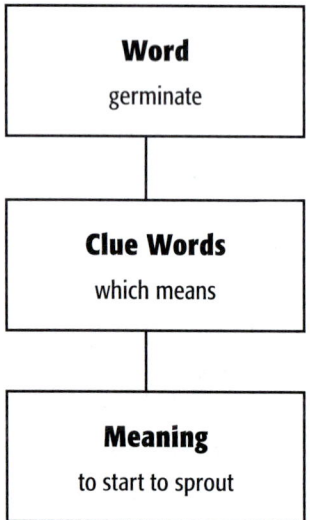

Other times, a word's context may provide another way of saying the same thing. For example, "We expected Luis to **bungle** the science experiment, but he didn't mess up a step."

On Your Own In your Learner's Notebook, write the meaning of the word *bungle* from the sentence above. List the context clues that helped you figure out the word's meaning.

404 UNIT 4 What Makes You Who You Are?

READING WORKSHOP 2 • Responding

Skills Preview

Key Reading Skill: Responding

More than most kinds of writing, poetry asks you to respond. Poems don't spell everything out; they give you hints and clues. They often offer ideas that you "get" only if you make connections to your own feelings and experiences. As you read "Life Doesn't Frighten Me," ask yourself these questions:

- What would that look like?
- What does that make me think of?
- How would that make me feel?
- Does this word have more than one meaning? Should I think of both of them?

Key Literary Element: Rhyme, Rhythm, and Meter

A **rhyme** is made up of words whose sounds match, such as *sing* and *ring* or *money* and *honey*.
- Rhyme can occur at the end of lines or within a line.
- Rhymes form patterns that connect the lines of the poem.

Rhythm is the pattern of beats made by parts that are meant to be stressed (spoken with greater force) and the parts that are meant to be softer.

In this poem, the stressed syllables are underlined. You can see that the rhythm is very regular, which is not the case in all poems.

> The <u>mon</u>sters <u>of</u> the <u>night</u>
> Will <u>soon</u> e<u>nough</u> be <u>gone</u>.
> They dis<u>appear</u> at <u>sun</u>rise
> In the <u>first</u> faint <u>light</u> of <u>dawn</u>.

Meter is a predictable rhythm.
- To find the meter of a poem, read it aloud.
- As you read, listen for the pattern of stressed and unstressed syllables.

As you read "Life Doesn't Frighten Me," look for
- rhyming words
- rhythmic beats
- a steady meter

Get Ready to Read

Connect to the Reading

What used to scare you, but no longer does? What helped you get over your fear?

Write to Learn In your Learner's Notebook, create and fill in a chart like the one below.

Overcoming Fears	
Fear	How I Overcame It

Build Background

Most people experience one or more of the following fears at some point during their childhood:

- monsters
- the dark
- deep water
- getting lost
- doctors and shots
- thunderstorms

Set Purposes for Reading

BIG Question Read the poem "Life Doesn't Frighten Me" to understand what makes the speaker the person she is.

Set Your Own Purpose What else would you like to learn from the poem that may help you answer the Big Question? Write your own purpose on the "Life Doesn't Frighten Me" page of Foldable 4.

Interactive Literary Elements Handbook
To review or learn more about the literary elements, go to www.glencoe.com.

Keep Moving

Use these skills as you read the following selection.

Life Doesn't Frighten Me 405

READING WORKSHOP 2

Life Doesn't Frighten Me

by Maya Angelou

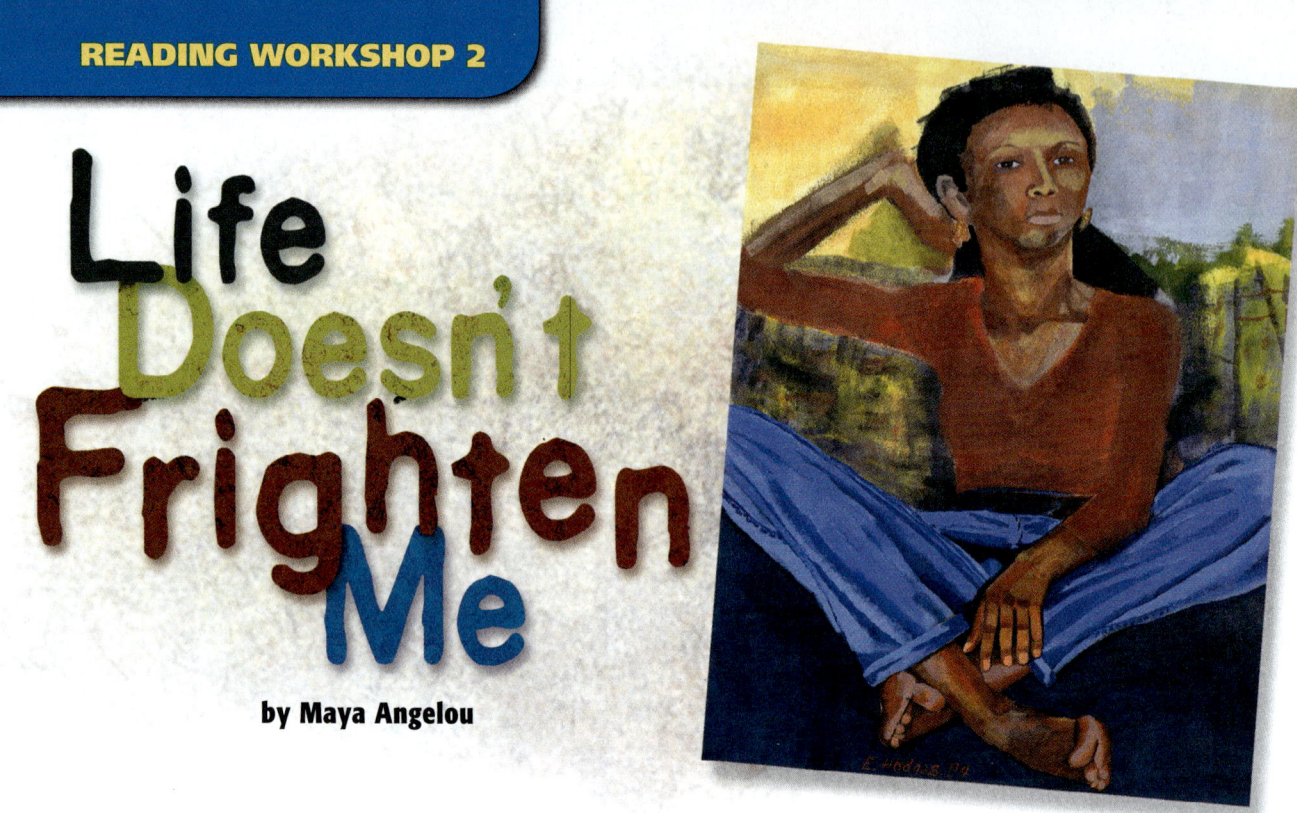

Fatima, 1994. Elizabeth Hodges. Acrylic.

Shadows on the wall
Noises down the hall
Life doesn't frighten me at all
Bad dogs barking loud
⁵ Big ghosts in a cloud
Life doesn't frighten me at all.

Mean old Mother Goose*
Lions on the loose
They don't frighten me at all
¹⁰ Dragons breathing flame 🔲1
On my counterpane*
That doesn't frighten me at all

Practice the Skills

1 Key Reading Skill

Responding Notice how the poet uses examples of things many people fear, such as loose lions, fiery dragons, and ghosts. Were you ever afraid of any of these things?

---

7 **Mother Goose** is said to be the author of many English nursery rhymes, although people are not sure where the name comes from.

11 A **counterpane** is a bedspread or quilt.

I go boo
Make them shoo
¹⁵ I make fun
Way they run
I won't cry
So they fly
I just smile
²⁰ They go wild
Life doesn't frighten me at all.

Tough guys in a fight
All alone at night
Life doesn't frighten me at all.

²⁵ Panthers in the park
Strangers in the dark **2**
No, they don't frighten me at all.

That new classroom where
Boys all pull my hair
³⁰ (**Kissy** little girls **3**
With their hair in curls)
They don't frighten me at all.

Don't show me frogs and snakes
And listen for my scream,
³⁵ If I'm afraid at all
It's only in my dreams.

I've got a magic charm
That I keep up my sleeve, **4**
I can walk the ocean floor
⁴⁰ And never have to breathe.

Life doesn't frighten me at all
Not at all
Not at all. **5**
Life doesn't frighten me at all.

Practice the Skills

2 **Key Literary Element**

Rhyme, Rhythm, and Meter What are some words in this poem that rhyme?

3 **English Language Coach**

Context Clues The word **kissy** is probably new to you. From the context, what do you think it means?

4 **Key Reading Skill**

Responding What do you think the speaker's magic charm could be? Why do you think she didn't tell you what it is?

5 **BIG Question**

Discuss with a partner what made the speaker want to look like a brave person. Write your answers on the "Life Doesn't Frighten Me" page of Foldable 4. Your response will help you complete the Unit Challenge later.

After You Read | Life Doesn't Frighten Me

Answering the BIG Question

1. How does the way you respond to scary situations make you who you are?
2. What are the first two things that the poem's speaker mentions?
   TIP Right There
3. **Recall** According to the speaker, what is the only time she is afraid?
   TIP Right There
4. **Summarize** What are three fears that the speaker mentions in the poem?
   TIP Think and Search

Critical Thinking

5. **Infer** Does life frighten the speaker at all?
   TIP Author and Me
6. **Visualize** Picture the speaker using her magic charm. What do you see as you visualize that scene? Explain.
   TIP Author and Me
7. **Respond** Do you want to be like the speaker of this poem? Why or why not?
   TIP On My Own
8. **Evaluate** Is the speaker of this poem a believable character? Explain.
   TIP On My Own

Write About Your Reading

Write a letter to the speaker in the poem.
- Tell her how you felt when you read her poem.
- Name something that you are afraid of.
- Tell her how you handle your fear.

Objectives (pp. 408–409)
Reading Respond to literature • Make connections from text to self
Literature Identify poetic features: rhyme, rhythm, meter
Vocabulary Use context clues: definition, restatement
Writing Respond to literature: personal letter
Grammar Identify sentence fragments

Skills Review

Key Reading Skill: Responding

9. Poets want readers to react to their poetry. What do you think Angelou hoped this poem would cause you to think or feel?
10. The speaker of "Life Doesn't Frighten Me" first lists harmless things that young children fear. Then she lists things that might be real fears for older kids. Do you think that her statement "Life doesn't frighten me at all" is true?

Key Literary Element: Rhyme, Rhythm, and Meter

11. Would "Life Doesn't Frighten Me" be as much fun to read if it didn't rhyme? Why or why not?
12. Do you think this poem could become a song or a rap? Why or why not?

Vocabulary Check

English Language Coach: Context Clues

For each word in dark type, write the word's meaning and the clue words you used to figure out the meaning.

13. Lily is studying **calligraphy,** which is the art of fine handwriting.
14. Norman used a **template,** or pattern, for cutting the wood to build his mother a birdhouse.
15. I wish my mother would not **admonish** me in front of my friends. Being scolded is so embarrassing.

Grammar Link: Fragments

Many times, poets do not write in complete sentences. They may think that *fragments*, incomplete sentences, sound better. Maya Angelou uses both sentences and fragments in her poem. To spot sentences, remember that

- sentences have subjects and verbs. Fragments may be missing either a subject or a verb.
- subjects can be nouns (people, places, animals, things) or pronouns (*I, we, you, he, she, it, they*). A fragment may have no subject and look like this: *Cooked her favorite meal.*
- verbs are "action words'" (describing what the subject *does*) or "being words" (describing what the subject *is, was,* or *will be*). A fragment may have no verb and look like this: *All the students in the class.*

Remember: Use complete sentences for school assignments and business writing. Use fragments only in creative writing or in conversation with family and friends.

Grammar Practice

Identify which of the following are fragments and which are complete sentences. Remember, a sentence has both a subject and a verb.

16. Mean old Mother Goose.
17. Tough guys run away when they see me coming.
18. Life doesn't frighten me at all.
19. Not at all.

Writing Application Read the letter you wrote. Make sure your sentences are complete.

Web Activities For eFlashcards, Selection Quick Checks, and other Web activities, go to www.glencoe.com.

READING WORKSHOP 2 • Responding

Before You Read: Geraldine Moore the Poet

Toni Cade Bambara

Meet the Author
Toni Cade Bambara grew up in and near New York City. She was an author, college professor, and social activist. She wrote most of her work in the 1960s and 1970s. Toni Cade added "Bambara" to her name after she found the name on a sketchbook in her great-grandmother's trunk. See page R1 of the Author Files on Toni Cade Bambara.

Author Search For more about Toni Cade Bambara, go to www.glencoe.com.

Objectives (pp. 410–417)
Reading Respond to literature • Make connections from text to self
Literature Identify point of view: third-person limited, third-person omniscient
Vocabulary Use context clues to understand idioms

Vocabulary Preview

muttered (MUT urd) *v.* spoke quietly to complain or express anger; form of the verb *mutter* **(p. 412)** *He muttered because he was annoyed.*

minded (MYN did) *v.* took charge of; form of the verb *mind* **(p. 412)** *I minded my little brother for my Mom.*

shrugged (shruhgd) *v.* raised the shoulders to show doubt, lack of interest, or uncertainty; form of the verb *shrug* **(p. 412)** *Leon shrugged because he didn't care.*

manufacturing (man yoo FAK chur ing) *v.* making out of raw materials; form of the verb *manufacture* **(p. 415)** *The factory is manufacturing steel.*

moist (moyst) *adj.* just wet enough to notice **(p. 415)** *She noticed that her hair was moist from the steam.*

expressing (eks PRES ing) *n.* the act of making feelings or opinions known **(p. 416)** *Expressing how she felt about writing was difficult for Geraldine.*

whimper (WHIM pur) *n.* a soft cry **(p. 417)** *She gave a whimper of delight when she saw the new sweater.*

English Language Coach

Context Clues Some words in English are put together into idioms, or phrases with special meaning. You often have to use context clues to understand the meaning of these idioms. Read these sentences containing idioms. See if you can use the context to figure out what the idiom means. Write the meaning in your Learner's Notebook.

Idiom	Idiom in Context
Keep your chin up	This may be the third time you've taken the driver's test, but you have to keep your chin up.
Over the top	The boy just cleaned his room. Don't you think it was over the top to celebrate the clean room with a party?
Rise and shine	Get out of bed now; it's time to rise and shine.

410 UNIT 4 What Makes You Who You Are?

READING WORKSHOP 2 • Responding

Skills Preview

Key Reading Skill: Responding

Responding to what you read may, at times, make you feel sad. Does that mean you should try not to respond? That's a difficult question, isn't it? Most of us would rather feel happy than sad. But sometimes, if we want to learn about and understand other people, we have to let ourselves feel things that may be painful. As you read "Geraldine Moore the Poet," try to imagine her life and her feelings, even if your response is to feel sad. Ask yourself some of these questions as you read.

- How would that feel?
- Would I be able to do that?
- How would I handle that?

Partner Talk Talk with a partner about reading sad stories or seeing sad movies. Do you think there's any reason to do it? Why do you think people create them?

Literary Element: Point of View

As you learned in Unit 3, when the narrator of a story is not a character in the story, the narration is called "third-person point of view." There are two main kinds of third-person point of view.

Third-person limited is called "limited" for a reason. What the narrator knows (and reveals) is limited to what one character can see, hear, or think.

Third-person omniscient is called "omniscient" because that word means "all-knowing." The narrator knows (and reveals) the knowledge and thoughts of many or all of the characters.

Interactive Literary Elements Handbook
To review or learn more about the literary elements, go to www.glencoe.com.

Get Ready to Read

Connect to the Reading

Think about how you feel when you come home from school.

- What would it be like if you didn't have a place to come home to?
- As you read this story, let yourself feel what the main character goes through.

Partner Talk Share with a partner how your home and family help to make you who you are.

- Who lives with you?
- What is your favorite thing to do at home?
- What responsibilities do you have at home?

Build Background

The number of Americans who have no place to live has risen in the last 25 years. There are many reasons why people find themselves homeless.

- It costs a great deal of money to buy or rent a home.
- Some cities do not have enough homes for people to buy or rent at prices they can afford.
- Sometimes people with low-paying jobs, or who lose their jobs, cannot get help to find a place to live.

Set Purposes for Reading

BIG Question Read "Geraldine Moore the Poet" to find out what experiences made Geraldine the person she is.

Set Your Own Purpose What else would you like to learn from the story to help you answer the Big Question? Write your own purpose on the "Geraldine Moore" page of Foldable 4.

Keep Moving

Use these skills as you read the following selection.

Geraldine Moore the Poet **411**

READING WORKSHOP 2

Geraldine Moore the Poet

by Toni Cade Bambara

Geraldine[1] paused at the corner to pull up her knee socks. The rubber bands she was using to hold them up made her legs itch. She dropped her books on the sidewalk while she gave a good scratch. But when she pulled the socks up again, two fingers poked right through the top of her left one.

"That stupid dog," she **muttered** to herself, grabbing at her books and crossing against traffic. "First he chews up my gym suit and gets me into trouble, and now my socks."

Geraldine shifted her books to the other hand and kept muttering angrily to herself about Mrs. Watson's dog, which she **minded** two days a week for a dollar. She passed the hot-dog man on the corner and waved. He **shrugged** as if to say business was very bad. **1**

Must be, she thought to herself. *Three guys before you had to pack up and forget it. Nobody's got hot-dog money around here.* **2**

Geraldine turned down her street, wondering what her sister Anita would have for her lunch. She was glad she didn't have to eat the free lunches in high school any more. She was

---

1. **Geraldine** (jehr uhl DEEN)

Vocabulary

muttered (MUT urd) *v.* spoke quietly to complain or express anger

minded (MYN did) *v.* took charge of

shrugged (shruhgd) *v.* raised the shoulders to show doubt, lack of interest, or uncertainty

Practice the Skills

1 **Key Reading Skill**

Responding What's your response to Geraldine so far? Explain.

2 **Reviewing Skill**

Drawing Conclusions Geraldine is wearing socks held up by rubber bands. For a dollar a week, she minds a dog that chews her clothes. She says that no one in her neighborhood has money to buy hot dogs. What can you conclude about Geraldine?

412 UNIT 4 What Makes You Who You Are?

sick of the funny-looking tomato soup and the dried-out cheese sandwiches and those oranges that were more green than orange.

When Geraldine's mother first took sick and went away, Geraldine had been on her own except when Miss Gladys next door came in on Thursdays and cleaned the apartment and made a meat loaf so Geraldine could have dinner. But in those days Geraldine never quite managed to get breakfast for herself. So she'd sit through social studies class, scraping her feet to cover up the noise of her stomach growling.

Now Anita,[2] Geraldine's older sister, was living at home waiting for her husband to get out of the Army. She usually had something good for lunch—chicken and dumplings if she managed to get up in time, or baked ham from the night before and sweet-potato bread. But even if there was only a hot dog and some baked beans—sometimes just a TV dinner if those soap operas[3] kept Anita glued to the TV set— anything was better than the noisy school lunchroom where monitors[4] kept pushing you into a straight line or rushing you to the tables. Anything was better than that.

Geraldine was almost home when she stopped dead. Right outside her building was a pile of furniture and some boxes. That wasn't anything new. She had seen people get put out in the street before, but this time the ironing board looked familiar. And she recognized the big, ugly sofa standing on its arm, its under-belly showing the hole where Mrs. Watson's dog had gotten to it. **3**

Miss Gladys was sitting on the stoop,[5] and she looked up and took off her glasses. "Well, Gerry," she said slowly, wiping her glasses on the hem of her dress, "looks like you'll be staying with me for a while." She looked at the men carrying out a big box with an old doll sticking up over the edge. "Anita's upstairs. Go on up and get your lunch."

The Reader #1, 1999. Diana Ong (b.1940).

Analyzing the Art Does this look to you like it could be a picture of Geraldine Moore? Why or why not?

Practice the Skills

3 **Key Reading Skill**

Responding What grabs your attention in this paragraph? Why?

---

2. ***Anita*** (uh NEE tuh)
3. ***Soap operas*** are continuing stories on daytime TV. They usually involve very dramatic situations.
4. In the passage, ***monitors*** are students who do tasks for teachers or around the school.
5. In this case, a ***stoop*** is a porch, stairway entrance, or small platform at the door of a house or apartment building.

READING WORKSHOP 2

Geraldine stepped past the old woman and almost bumped into the superintendent.[6] He took off his cap to wipe away the sweat.

"Darn shame," he said to no one in particular. "Poor people sure got a hard row to hoe." [4]

"That's the truth," said Miss Gladys, standing up with her hands on her hips to watch the men set things on the sidewalk.

Upstairs, Geraldine went into the apartment and found Anita in the kitchen.

"I dunno, Gerry," Anita said. "I just don't know what we're going to do. But everything's going to be all right soon as Ma gets well." Anita's voice cracked as she set a bowl of soup before Geraldine.

"What's this?" Geraldine said.

"It's tomato soup, Gerry."

Geraldine was about to say something. But when she looked up at her big sister, she saw how Anita's face was getting all twisted as she began to cry. [5]

That afternoon, Mr. Stern, the geometry teacher, started drawing cubes and cylinders on the board. Geraldine sat at her desk adding up a column of figures in her notebook—the rent, the light and gas bills, a new gym suit, some socks. Maybe they would move somewhere else, and she could have her own room. Geraldine turned the squares and triangles into little houses in the country.

"For your homework," Mr. Stern was saying with his back to the class, "set up your problems this way." He wrote GIVEN: in large letters, and then gave the formula[7] for the first problem. Then he wrote TO FIND: and listed three items they were to include in their answers.

Practice the Skills

[4] **English Language Coach**

Context Clues The superintendent says that "Poor people sure got a hard row to hoe." This expression is an *idiom*. Look up the word *hoe*. Look at the context of the sentence. What does the idiom tell how you about how the superintendent feels about Geraldine's situation?

[5] **Key Reading Skill**

Responding How do you feel about the girls' future after seeing how Anita acts when she talks about Ma?

Chicago, Illinois: Public Art, 1978. Franklin McMahon. Polymer painting.

Analyzing the Art What feeling do you get when you look at this painting? Is it similar to the feeling you get from reading this story? Explain.

---

6. A building **superintendent** (soo pur in TEN dint) is a person who is in charge of a building. A superintendent's job may include fixing broken things for people who live in the building, collecting rent, and cleaning.

7. A geometry **formula** (FOR myoo luh) is a rule students use to solve geometry problems.

Geraldine started to raise her hand to ask what all these squares and angles had to do with solving real problems, like the ones she had. Better not, she warned herself, and sat on her hands. *Your big mouth got you in trouble last term.*

In hygiene class,[8] Mrs. Potter kept saying that the body was a wonderful machine. Every time Geraldine looked up from her notebook, she would hear the same thing. "Right now your body is **manufacturing** all the proteins and tissues and energy you will need to get through tomorrow."

And Geraldine kept wondering, *How? How does my body know what it will need, when I don't even know what I'll need to get through tomorrow?*

As she headed down the hall to her next class, Geraldine remembered that she hadn't done the homework for English. Mrs. Scott had said to write a poem, and Geraldine had meant to do it at lunchtime. After all, there was nothing to it—a flower here, a raindrop there, moon, June, rose, nose. But the men carrying off the furniture had made her forget. 6

And now put away your books," Mrs. Scott was saying as Geraldine tried to scribble a poem quickly. "Today we can give King Arthur's knights a rest. Let's talk about poetry."

Mrs. Scott moved up and down the aisles, talking about her favorite poems and reciting a line now and then. She got very excited whenever she passed a desk and could pick up the homework from a student who had remembered to do the assignment.

"A poem is your own special way of saying what you feel and what you see," Mrs. Scott went on, her lips **moist**. It was her favorite subject.

"Some poets write about the light that . . . that . . . makes the world sunny," she said, passing Geraldine's desk. "Sometimes an idea takes the form of a picture—an image."

For almost half an hour, Mrs. Scott stood at the front of the room, reading poems and talking about the lives of the great poets. Geraldine drew more houses, and designs for curtains.

---

8. A *hygiene* (HEYE jeen) class is the same as a health class. Students learn how to get and stay healthy.

Vocabulary

manufacturing (man yoo FAK chur ing) *v.* making out of raw materials

moist (moyst) *adj.* just wet enough to notice

Practice the Skills

6 **Literary Element**

Point of View Is this story told from a **third-person limited point of view** or a **third-person omniscient point of view** (showing the thoughts of several characters)? Why do you think Bambara chose to use this point of view?

READING WORKSHOP 2

"So for those who haven't done their homework, try it now," Mrs. Scott said. "Try **expressing** what it is like to be . . . to be alive in this . . . this glorious world."

"Oh, brother," Geraldine muttered to herself as Mrs. Scott moved up and down the **aisles** again, waving her hands and leaning over the students' shoulders and saying, "That's nice," or "Keep trying." Finally she came to Geraldine's desk and stopped, looking down at her.

"I can't write a poem," Geraldine said flatly, before she even realized she was going to speak at all. She said it very loudly, and the whole class looked up.

"And why not?" Mrs. Scott asked, looking hurt.

"I can't write a poem, Mrs. Scott, because nothing lovely's been happening in my life. I haven't seen a flower since Mother's Day, and the sun don't even shine on my side of the street. No robins come sing on my window sill."

Portrait in Orange, Diana Ong

Analyzing the Art You can *respond* to art as well as to a story or poem you read. How do you respond to this picture? Explain.

Geraldine swallowed hard. She thought about saying that her father doesn't even come to visit any more, but changed her mind. "Just the rain comes," she went on, "and the bills come, and the men to move out our furniture. I'm sorry, but I can't write no pretty poem."

Teddy Johnson leaned over and was about to giggle and crack the whole class up, but Mrs. Scott looked so serious that he changed his mind.

"You have just said the most . . . the most poetic thing, Geraldine Moore," said Mrs. Scott. Her hands flew up to touch the silk scarf around her neck. "'Nothing lovely's been happening in my life.'" She repeated it so quietly that everyone had to lean forward to hear. 7

"Class," Mrs. Scott said very sadly, clearing her throat, "you have just heard the best poem you will ever hear." She went

Practice the Skills

7 **Key Reading Skill**

Responding How does Mrs. Scott react to Geraldine's outburst? How did you react?

Vocabulary

expressing (eks PRES ing) *n.* the act of making feelings or opinions known

to the board and stood there for a long time staring at the chalk in her hand.

"I'd like you to copy it down," she said. She wrote it just as Geraldine had said it, bad grammar and all.

> Nothing lovely's been happening in my life.
> I haven't seen a flower since Mother's Day,
> And the sun don't even shine on my side of the street.
> No robins come sing on my window sill.
> Just the rain comes, and the bills come,
> And the men to move out our furniture.
> I'm sorry, but I can't write no pretty poem. 8

Mrs. Scott stopped writing, but she kept her back to the class for a long time—long after Geraldine had closed her notebook.

And even when the bell rang, and everyone came over to smile at Geraldine or to tap her on the shoulder or to kid her about being the school poet, Geraldine waited for Mrs. Scott to put the chalk down and turn around. Finally Geraldine stacked up her books and started to leave. Then she thought she heard a **whimper**—the way Mrs. Watson's dog whimpered sometimes—and she saw Mrs. Scott's shoulders shake a little. 9 ○

Vocabulary

whimper (WHIM pur) *n.* a soft cry

READING WORKSHOP 2

Practice the Skills

8 BIG Question

Geraldine's poem is very different from the kind of poem Mrs. Scott asked students to write. What does Geraldine's poem say about what has made her the person she is? Explain your answer on the "Geraldine Moore" page of Foldable 4. Your response will help you complete the Unit Challenge later.

9 Key Reading Skill

Responding How do you feel about Mrs. Scott after the way she acts at the end of the story?

Geraldine Moore the Poet **417**

READING WORKSHOP 2 • Responding

After You Read — Geraldine Moore the Poet

Answering the BIG Question

1. Describe one experience in Geraldine's life that helped make her the person she was.

2. **Recall** Who is taking care of Geraldine at the time she writes her poem?
   TIP Right There

3. **Infer** From Geraldine's comments about other people who live in her neighborhood, what can you guess about them?
   TIP Think and Search

Critical Thinking

4. **Interpret** What might the author be using Geraldine's story to say about people and problems in the world in general?
   TIP Author and Me

5. **Evaluate** Geraldine is sometimes angry about what her life has become. Does she have a right to be angry? Give reasons for your answer.
   TIP Author and Me

6. **Connect** Who would you depend on if your parents or guardians could not take care of you?
   TIP On My Own

7. **Respond** What event or detail in this story grabbed your attention the most? Why?
   TIP On My Own

Write About Your Reading

Write a journal entry as if you are Geraldine and it is a year after the events in this story took place.

- What has changed in your life?
- Where are you living?
- How are your mother and your sister?
- How do you feel about the world now?

Objectives (pp. 418–419)
Reading Respond to literature
Literature Identify point of view
Vocabulary Use context clues to understand idioms
Writing Respond to literature: journal
Grammar Identify sentence fragments
• Fix sentence fragments

Skills Review

Key Reading Skill: Responding

8. Authors and poets hope that people will respond to what they read. Imagine talking with the author of "Geraldine Moore the Poet." What would you tell her about how you felt when you read her story?

Literary Element: Point of View

9. This story was written from a third-person limited point of view. Only Geraldine's thoughts were revealed. If you were to rewrite this story from another character's point of view, which character would you choose? Why?

Reviewing Skills: Drawing Conclusions

10. From what you know about Geraldine Moore, why do you think she didn't try to make up a pretty poem about flowers or raindrops?

Vocabulary Check

11. Match each word with its synonym, or word that means almost the same thing.

whine   grumbled   damp

a. muttered ___
b. moist ___
c. whimper ___

12. For each of these words, write a sentence that includes a definition or restatement.

manufacturing   shrugged   expressing

Web Activities For eFlashcards, Selection Quick Checks, and other Web activities, go to www.glencoe.com.

Grammar Link: Fixing Fragments

Do not use sentence fragments when you write for school or business. Remember, a fragment is a group of words that's missing one or more of the requirements for a sentence. Those requirements are a subject, a verb, and a complete thought.

- The blue shirt with long sleeves. (What about the shirt? This fragment needs a verb.)
- Ran like crazy toward home plate. (Who or what ran? This fragment needs a subject.)
- If Nina makes dinner. (What if she does? There's a subject and a verb, but the thought isn't complete.)

Fragments can result from ending a sentence before you've ended your thought. The whole thought may be there, but it's in two different sentence fragments instead of one complete sentence.

Incorrect: The boy next to me. Was snoring.
Correct: The boy next to me was snoring.

Sometimes only one sentence ends too soon, which also creates a fragment.

Incorrect: Mr. Reed taught English. Last year.
Correct: Mr. Reed taught English last year.

Grammar Practice

13. In the following paragraph, there are three sentences fragments. On a separate sheet of paper, fix the fragments in the way that seems best to you.

   Haley and Jeff were best friends. They were in the same grade. In school. When Haley had to move. Geoff was unhappy. Walked around the neighborhood sadly.

Writing Application Look back at the journal entry you wrote. Make sure every sentence has both a subject and a verb.

READING WORKSHOP 3

Skills Focus

You will practice using these skills when you read the following selections:
- "Same Song," p. 424
- "Flowers and Freckle Cream," p. 430

Reading
- Interpreting what you read

Literature
- Understanding sound devices: Alliteration

Vocabulary
- Using context clues that involve comparison and contrast
- Academic vocabulary: *interpret*

Writing/Grammar
- Identifying complete and simple subjects and predicates
- Identifying compound subjects and predicates

Skill Lesson

Interpreting

Learn It!

What Is It? You say hello to a friend, but she only says, "Can't talk!" How do you **interpret** this? Is she angry with you or is she just late for her next class?

You interpret other people's words and actions all the time. You decide what certain statements or behaviors mean. In reading, you often need to interpret what a story or poem or essay means. You can do this by using information the writer provides and your own experience to form an opinion about the real meaning of a writer's words. Two people might have two different interpretations about the same selection. That's okay! It's possible for more than one interpretation to be reasonable.

Analyzing Cartoons
These boys are busy interpreting certain statements. Do you think they're interpreting correctly?

Objectives (pp. 420–421)
Reading Interpret text

Academic Vocabulary

interpret (in TUR prit) *v.* to explain the meaning of; make understandable

420 UNIT 4

READING WORKSHOP 3 • Interpreting

Why Is It Important? Interpreting while you read lets you get a deeper understanding of what you are reading. It's especially important when you read poetry. That's because many poets don't come right out and declare their ideas. They often use images, sound, or something else to help get their ideas across.

How Do I Do It? Ask yourself, what is the author trying to say here? What larger idea might these events be about? What exact words did the writer use? What details stir up strong feelings in me and lead me to form opinions? Here is how one student interpreted "My Father Is a Simple Man."

Study Central Visit www.glencoe.com and click on Study Central to review interpreting.

> *He has taken me on this journey / and it's been lifelong. / He's sure I'll be healthy / so long as I eat more oranges, / and tells me the orange / has seeds and so is perpetual; / and we too will come back / like the orange trees.*

> I think the part about the seeds in the orange means that the fruit will grow into a tree and the tree will make more oranges. Kind of like the relationship the father has with his son. Maybe one day the son will grow wise like the father and tell his kids the same story about the oranges.

Practice It!

In your Learner's Notebook, practice interpreting the lines from "My Father Is a Simple Man." There are three questions you can ask yourself to help with interpretation. First answer the question, "What does the selection say?" Next, ask, "What do I know about myself and the world as it relates to this topic?" Finally, ask yourself, "What is the author really saying; is there a larger idea?"

I ask him what he thinks / about death and he says / he will gladly face it when / it comes but won't jump / out in front of a car.

Use It!

As you read "Same Song" and "Flowers and Freckle Cream," remember to use these three questions to help you interpret. Write the questions out in your Learner's Notebook ahead of time, and answer them whenever you need help interpreting.

READING WORKSHOP 3 • Interpreting

Before You Read : Same Song

Meet the Author
Pat Mora grew up in El Paso, Texas, in a bilingual home. She spends most of her time writing and traveling to schools and other events to teach young writers. See page R4 of the Author Files for more on Pat Mora.

Author Search For more about Pat Mora, go to www.glencoe.com.

Vocabulary Preview

mauve (mohv) *adj.* a light purple or violet **(p. 424)** *She likes make-up with mauve colors in it.*

peers (peerz) *v.* looks closely at something **(p. 424)** *Her daughter peers at her face in the mirror.*

biceps (BY seps) *n.* a large muscle that runs down the front of the arm from the shoulder to the elbow **(p. 425)** *Her son was doing arm-curls with heavy weights because he wanted large biceps.*

triceps (TRY seps) *n.* a large muscle at the back of the upper arm **(p. 425)** *The triceps on his arms were not as big as he wanted them to be.*

pectorals (pek TOR ulz) *n.* muscles connecting the chest walls to the bones of the upper arm and shoulder **(p. 425)** *He was trying to strengthen his pectorals, but the exercises were hard.*

Partner Talk On a separate note card, write each vocabulary word one time. Turn the note card over and write the definition and part of speech on the back. Take turns testing each other by flashing the cards.

English Language Coach

Context Clues Sometimes a word's meaning is revealed by context clues that make a comparison to something familiar.

Eating Aunt Lucy's cooking is as **perilous** as riding a bike blindfolded.

Like and *as* are often used to make comparisons, so they're useful signals. Since you know that riding a bike blindfolded would be dangerous, you can figure out that *perilous* probably means something like "dangerous."

Sometimes a word's meaning is revealed by context clues that contrast it with a familiar word or phrase.

Instead of being late for class, try to be more **punctual.**

Contrast clues are often signaled by words such as *although, but, however, in contrast to,* or *instead of.* The sentence tells you that being punctual means the opposite of being late.

On Your Own Use context clues to define each word in dark type. Then tell if the context clues provided a *comparison* or a *contrast*.

1. The mat was **resilient**, like rubber.
2. Chaz is warm and friendly, but his brother is **aloof**.

Objectives (pp. 422–425)
Reading Interpret text • Make connections from text to self
Literature Identify sound devices: alliteration
Vocabulary Use context clues: comparison, contrast

READING WORKSHOP 3 • Interpreting

Skills Preview

Key Reading Skill: Interpreting

To interpret "Same Song," think about what the speaker says about the son and daughter. Think about what each might be trying to accomplish. Also, think about your own definition of *beauty*.

Partner Talk The poet Emily Dickinson wrote, "*Beauty–be not caused–It is.*" With a partner, interpret possible meanings of that statement. Keep your interpretation in mind when you read "Same Song."

Key Literary Element: Sound Devices: Alliteration

In Reading Workshop 2, you learned about rhyme, rhythm, and meter. These are three important "sound devices," or ways to use sound effectively in writing. Another sound device is **alliteration**, which is the repetition of consonant sounds at the beginnings of words. "Peter Piper picked a peck of pickled peppers" is a famous example. Usually, though, alliteration is used for only a few words. *Seeking the man in the moon* repeats the *m* sound only once, but the alliteration is effective.

It is the *sound* not the *letter* that creates alliteration.

- *A circle of sad psychiatrists* contains three alliterative words.
- *Gigantic goats gnawed the fence* contains no alliterative words.

Alliteration is often used in poetry to call attention to certain words and to add interest to the sound of the poem. It is also used in other writing.

Write to Learn In your Learner's Notebook, write a list of five phrases that use alliteration.

Interactive Literary Elements Handbook
To review or learn more about the literary elements, go to www.glencoe.com.

Get Ready to Read

Connect to the Reading

Are you a hustle-out-the door person in the morning, taking little time to check your clothes and appearance? Or do you worry about a bad hair day? As you read "Same Song," think about how the way you *see* yourself shapes the way you experience life.

Class Discussion What do you think is more important: who you are on the inside or who you appear to be? Talk about why you think we focus so much on outward appearances. What influences how we want to appear on the outside?

Build Background

The poem you are about to read is one of Pat Mora's most popular poems. She often writes poems that celebrate her Mexican American heritage and the joy of accepting the things that make people different.

- She has often said, "I take pride in being a Hispanic writer."
- Mora says that a big reason for writing poetry "is to help people feel less lonely."
- Because she recognizes that Mexican Americans are well aware of the borders in their lives, she also likes to write about borders as places to bridge differences.

Set Purposes for Reading

BIG Question Read "Same Song" to explore whether appearances make us who we are.

Set Your Own Purpose What else would you like to learn from the reading to help you answer the Big Question? Write your purpose on the "Same Song" page of Foldable 4.

Keep Moving

Use these skills as you read the following selection.

Same Song **423**

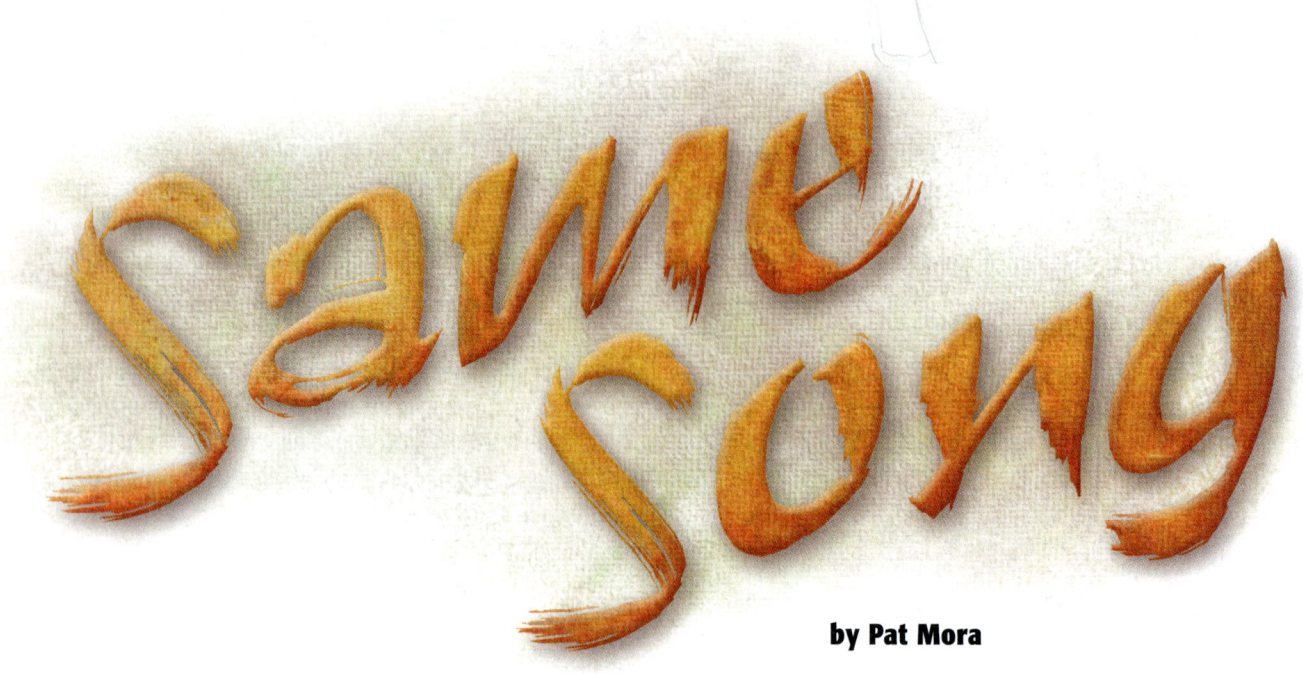

Same Song
by Pat Mora

While my sixteen-year-old son sleeps,
my twelve-year-old daughter
stumbles into the bathroom at six a.m.
plugs in the curling iron
5   squeezes into faded jeans
curls her hair carefully
strokes Aztec Blue* shadow on her eyelids
smooths Frosted **Mauve** blusher* on her cheeks
outlines her mouth in Neon Pink*
10 **peers** into the mirror, mirror on the wall
frowns at her face, her eyes, her skin,
not fair. **1**

---

7   *Aztec Blue* is just a fancy name for a shade of blue.
8   *Frosted Mauve* is a silvery or icy mauve color. *Blusher* is a kind of make-up that women use to add color to their cheeks.
9   *Neon* is a kind of light that results in very bright colors. So, *Neon Pink* is a bright pink lipstick.

Vocabulary

mauve (mohv) *adj.* a light purple or violet

peers (peerz) *v.* looks closely at something

Practice the Skills

1 **Key Literary Element**

Sound Devices: Alliteration
Reread the first three lines. What example of alliteration do you find?

424 UNIT 4   What Makes You Who You Are?

At night this daughter
stumbles off to bed at nine
[15] eyes half-shut while my son
jogs a mile in the cold dark
then lifts weights in the garage
curls and bench presses*
expanding **biceps**, **triceps**, **pectorals**,
[20] one-handed push-ups, one hundred sit-ups
peers into that mirror, mirror and frowns too. **2 3 4** ○

---

18. Curls and bench presses are two weight-lifting exercises for building muscles.

Vocabulary

biceps (BY seps) *n.* a large muscle that runs down the front of the arm from the shoulder to the elbow

triceps (TRY seps) *n.* a large muscle at the back of the upper arm

pectorals (pek TOR ulz) *n.* muscles connecting the chest walls to the bones of the upper arm and shoulder

Nancy's Sink, 2003. Pam Ingalls.

READING WORKSHOP 3

Practice the Skills

2 Key Reading Skill

Interpreting Now that you have read the entire poem, think about the first stanza. How can you use the first stanza to help you interpret the second stanza? What do you think the poet is saying about the son and daughter? What is the poet saying about our views of beauty and strength?

3 English Language Coach

Context Clues Read this interpretation: "The daughter thinks that make-up enhances her appearance, like gift wrap and ribbons do to a package." What might the word *enhances* mean?

4 BIG Question

What does this poem suggest about the importance of appearance in making us who we are? Write your answer on the "Same Song" page of Foldable 4. Your response will help you complete the Unit Challenge later.

Analyzing the Art Can you visualize the speaker's daughter putting on her make-up in front of the mirror? Can you visualize the speaker's son peering into the mirror and frowning? Explain your answers.

Same Song **425**

READING WORKSHOP 3 • Interpreting

After You Read : Same Song

Answering the BIG Question

1. How do you think the son and the daughter feel about appearances? How do you think their appearance affects who they are and what they do?

2. **Recall** What part of the son's and the daughter's appearance is most important to each?
   TIP Think and Search

3. **Summarize** What steps does the daughter take to get ready in the morning?
   TIP Think and Search

Critical Thinking

4. **Infer** What do the son and daughter have in common?
   TIP Think and Search

5. **Interpret** Why do you think the speaker starts each stanza, or section of the poem, by explaining who is sleeping, who is awake, what time it is, and what each person is doing?
   TIP Author and Me

6. **Analyze** Why do you think the author repeats the phrase "mirror, mirror"? Explain the importance of the mirror.
   TIP Author and Me

Write About Your Reading

Imagine you could write a letter to make the son and the daughter in the poem feel better about themselves. What would you tell them? What questions would you ask? Write a letter to either the boy or the girl in this poem. Think about these points as you write.

- What makes the body or face so important to the son and daughter?
- Does makeup and muscle add to who they really are?
- What might happen if all the mirrors in their home or school were covered?

Use examples from the poem in your letter. Be specific about what you have to say.

Objectives (pp. 426–427)
Reading Interpret text • Make connections from text to self
Literature Identify sound devices: alliteration
Vocabulary Use context clues: comparison, contrast
Writing Respond to literature: personal letter
Grammar Identify complete and simple subjects and predicates

Skills Review

Key Reading Skill: Interpreting

7. How do you interpret the title of the poem? Explain your answer.
8. Look at how all the lines in the poem begin. What part of speech is used most often as the first word in a line? Why do you think so many lines begin with this type of word?

Key Literary Element: Sound Devices: Alliteration

9. What example of alliteration can you find in lines 11 and 12?

Vocabulary Check

Rewrite each sentence. Write *True* or *False* after each statement.

10. If you do chin-ups, you can build up your *biceps*.
11. *Mauve* is pale green.
12. Your *triceps* are muscles in your legs.
13. *Peers* means "glances quickly."
14. Body armor that covers your chest will protect your *pectorals*.
15. **Academic Vocabulary** What does it mean to *interpret* a poem? Explain your answer.

English Language Coach Write a definition for the underlined word in each sentence below.

16. Don't excite the fans; try to subdue them instead.
17. He admonished me as if he were a parent talking to a naughty child.
18. This machine will hoist the supplies like an elevator would.

Web Activities For eFlashcards, Selection Quick Checks, and other Web activities, go to www.glencoe.com.

Grammar Link: Subjects and Predicates

Every sentence is made up of two parts: a subject and a predicate. The subject is the part that is doing or being something. The predicate is the part that tells what the subject is doing or being.

- The **complete subject** contains all the words in the subject.
- The **complete predicate** contains all the words in the predicate.

Complete Subject	Complete Predicate
Most of Kevin's friends	usually wear similar clothes.
My friendly, smart cousin	is here.
Bees	try to protect their hives.

The **simple predicate** is *just* the verb or verbs in the predicate. The **simple subject** is the word or the fewest words that can answer a "who or what?" question about the verb. (When a whole name is used, the whole name is the simple subject.) In the following sentences, the simple subject is underlined once. The simple predicate is underlined twice.

A huge, gentle <u>dog</u> with floppy ears <u>jumped</u> on me.
My team's <u>coach</u> rarely <u>sits</u> down during a game.
<u>Everyone</u> in the entire school <u>is</u> here today.

Grammar Practice

Copy each sentence. Underline the simple subject once and the simple predicate twice.

19. Good musicians play many songs by memory.
20. Some trees in the forest grow taller than others.
21. Nasty, rotten fruit of all different colors flew through the air.
22. The entire baseball team from Madison Middle School is on that bus.

Writing Application Look back at your writing assignment. Choose a sentence in which you can find the simple subject and the simple predicate. Underline the simple subject once and the simple predicate twice.

READING WORKSHOP 3 • Interpreting

Before You Read

Flowers and Freckle Cream

Meet the Author
Elizabeth Ellis learned to tell stories from her grandfather while she was growing up in the Appalachian Mountains. She has traveled all over the country and even to New Zealand, reading her stories to over 250,000 children and adults. Ellis says she loves making a living this way because she has so much fun.

Author Search For more about Elizabeth Ellis, go to www.glencoe.com.

Vocabulary Preview

inadequate (in AD ih kwit) *adj.* not good enough **(p. 432)** *My teacher said that a one-paragraph book report was inadequate.*

Write to Learn Use the vocabulary word in a sentence.

English Language Coach

Context Clues You know that you can use context clues to figure out the meaning of an unfamiliar word. The context may define it, restate it, or compare or contrast it to something that you are familiar with. Unfamiliar words are sometimes made clear by a familiar **example.** The clue words *such as, for instance,* and *for example* are often used to point out examples.

We must respond quickly to **catastrophes** such as tornadoes, floods, and large forest fires.

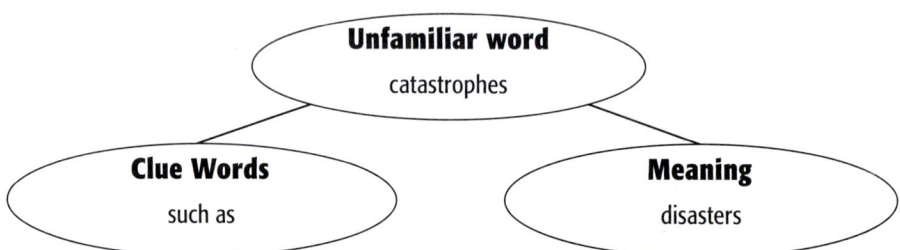

The words *such as* introduce examples of catastrophes. From the examples you can guess that *catastrophes* means "kinds of disasters."

On Your Own Use context clues to figure out the meaning of the word in dark type in the sentence below. Write the meaning of the word and the context clues that helped you figure out the word's meaning. Think about what all the animals have in common.

Domesticated animals like cows, pigs, and puppies can be found on many farms.

Objectives (pp. 428–433)
Reading Interpret text • Make connections from text to self
Literature Identify and analyze point of view
Vocabulary Use context clues: examples

READING WORKSHOP 3 • Interpreting

Skills Preview

Key Reading Skill: Interpreting
As you read, think about what you already know combined with what the author is really saying. Ask yourself these questions:
- What is the selection about?
- What do you already know about this topic?
- What is the author's larger idea?

Write to Learn In your Learner's Notebook, answer these questions as you read the story.

Literary Element: Point of View
You have already learned about first-person and third-person point of view. You also know that a story is written from a first-person point of view if the narrator is a character in the story. In such a story, the narrator refers to himself or herself as *I*.

Stories with first-person narration can be quite different from each other. Think about "Eleven" in the last unit. The narrator seemed to be eleven years old, didn't she? The author didn't use a narrator who was remembering the experience. She used a narrator who was *in* the experience—a child.

Keep these questions in mind as you read "Flowers and Freckle Cream":
* Does the narrator know more than you'd think she'd really know at that moment?
* Does the narrator ever comment on her own actions, as if from a distance?

Write to Learn Write a short paragraph using first-person point of view. Use a narrator that is *not you*. Write as if you are older or younger than you are or as if you are a very different kind of person.

Interactive Literary Elements Handbook
To review or learn more about the literary elements, go to www.glencoe.com.

Get Ready to Read

Connect to the Reading
Most people have moments when they envy someone else for their looks, their brains, or their sense of humor. "Flowers and Freckle Cream" makes you think about times when you wanted to be like someone else and—perhaps—went about it the wrong way.

Write to Learn Think about a time that you learned from a mistake. What was the mistake? How does learning from a mistake help make you who you are? Write about that mistake and how you learned from it.

Build Background
This story is about wishing you were like someone else. It's also about being able to tell about it, learn from it, and laugh about it later.
- Elizabeth Ellis is an award-winning storyteller. She travels to storytelling festivals across the country, so when she *writes* a story she makes it sound as if she is *telling* it.
- The author says she learned to tell stories from her grandfather. Notice the important role he plays in this story.
- A tiger lily is a beautiful, speckled flower.

Set Purposes for Reading
BIG Question Read the selection "Flowers and Freckle Cream" to learn about how looking back on your misfortunes and learning from them is part of what makes you who you are.

Set Your Own Purpose What else would you like to learn from the selection to help you answer the Big Question? Write your own purpose on the "Flowers and Freckle Cream" page of Foldable 4.

Keep Moving
Use these skills as you read the following selection.

Flowers and Freckle Cream **429**

READING WORKSHOP 3

Flowers and Freckle Cream

by Elizabeth Ellis

When I was a kid about twelve years old, I was already as tall as I am now, and I had a lot of freckles. I had reached the age when I had begun to really look at myself in the mirror, and I was underwhelmed.¹ Apparently my mother was too, because sometimes she'd look at me and shake her head and say, "You can't make a silk purse out of a sow's ear."² 1 2

I had a cousin whose name was Janette Elizabeth, and Janette Elizabeth looked exactly like her name sounds. She had a waist so small that men could put their hands around it . . . and they did. She had waist-length naturally curly blond hair too, but to me her unforgivable sin was that she had a flawless peaches-and-cream **complexion**. I couldn't help comparing myself with her and thinking that my life would be a lot different if I had beautiful skin too—skin that was all one color. 3

---

1. **Underwhelmed** is a joke used to mean the opposite of *overwhelmed*, so it means "not at all impressed."
2. The phrase, *a silk purse out of a sow's ear*, means that you cannot make something beautiful from something ugly.

Practice the Skills

1 Literary Element

Point of View Can you tell from this paragraph whether the narrator is a child or an adult who is remembering her childhood?

2 Reviewing Skills

Connecting A part of coming to terms with who you are is being able to accept who you are. Have you ever been embarrassed about something that you had no control over?

3 English Language Coach

Context Clues What context clue tells you what the word complexion means, and how the author defines a "flawless" *complexion*?

And then, in the back pages of Janette Elizabeth's *True Confessions* magazine, I found the answer: an advertisement for freckle-remover cream. I knew that I could afford it if I saved my money, and I did. The ad assured me that the product would arrive in a "plain brown wrapper."³ Plain brown freckle color. For three weeks I went to the mailbox every day precisely at the time the mail was delivered. I knew that if someone else in my family got the mail, I would never hear the end of it. There was no way that they would let me open the box in private. Finally, after three weeks of scheduling my entire day around the mail truck's arrival, my package came. 4

I went to my room with it, sat on the edge of my bed, and opened it. I was sure that I was looking at a miracle. But I had gotten so worked up about the magical package that I couldn't bring myself to put the cream on. What if it didn't work? What would I do then?

I fell asleep that night without even trying the stuff. And when I got up the next morning and looked at my freckles in the mirror, I said, "Elizabeth, this is silly. You have to do it now!" I smeared the cream all over my body. There wasn't

---

3. People ask for things to be delivered in a **plain brown wrapper** when they don't want anyone to know what the contents are.

Practice the Skills

4 Key Reading Skill

Interpreting Think about the name of the magazine. Why do you think she chose that name? What do you think *True Confessions* means as it relates to the story?

A tobacco farm.

Flowers and Freckle Cream **431**

READING WORKSHOP 3

as much of it as I had thought there would be, and I could see that I was going to need a part-time job to keep me in freckle remover.

Later that day I took my hoe and went with my brother and cousins to the head of the holler[4] to hoe tobacco, as we did nearly every day in the summer. Of course, when you stay out hoeing tobacco all day, you're not working in the shade. And there was something important I hadn't realized about freckle remover: if you wear it in the sun, it seems to have a reverse effect. Instead of developing a peaches-and-cream complexion, you just get more and darker freckles.

By the end of the day I looked as though I had leopard blood in my veins, although I didn't realize it yet. When I came back to the house, my family, knowing nothing about the freckle-remover cream, began to say things like, "I've never seen you with that many freckles before." When I saw myself in the mirror, I dissolved into tears and hid in the bathroom. **5**

My mother called me to the dinner table, but I ignored her. When she came to the bathroom door and demanded that I come out and eat, I burst out the door and ran by her, crying. I ran out to the well house[5] and threw myself down, and I was still sobbing when my grandfather came out to see what was wrong with me. I told him about how I'd sent for the freckle remover, and he didn't laugh—though he did suggest that one might get equally good results from burying a dead black cat when the moon was full.[6]

It was clear that Grandpa didn't understand, so I tried to explain why I didn't want to have freckles and why I felt so **inadequate** when I compared my appearance with Janette Elizabeth's. He looked at me in stunned surprise, shook his

5 Reviewing Skills

Connecting Have you ever been this disappointed? Can you remember how you felt?

---

4. The **head of the holler** is a phrase in Appalachian dialect. It is the opening of a small valley.
5. A **well house** is a shed that covers the deep hole that people used to get their fresh drinking water from.
6. **Burying a dead black cat when the moon was full** refers to a superstitious practice. The grandfather suggests that using freckle cream has about as much chance of working as a superstitious practice.

Vocabulary

inadequate (in AD ih kwit) *adj.* not good enough

head, and said, "But child, there are all kinds of flowers, and they are all beautiful." I said, "I've never seen a flower with freckles!" and ran back to my room, slamming the door.

When my mother came and knocked, I told her to go away. She started to say the kinds of things that parents say at times like that, but my grandfather said, "Nancy, leave the child alone." She was a grown-up, but he was her father. So she left me alone.

I don't know where Grandpa found it. It isn't at all common in the mountains where we lived then. But I know he put it in my room because my mother told me later. I had cried myself to sleep that night, and when I opened my swollen, sticky eyes the next morning, the first thing I saw, lying on the pillow next to my head, was a tiger lily. 6 7 ○

Practice the Skills

6 Key Reading Skill

Interpreting Consider the flower her grandfather put on her pillow. What do you think the tiger lily means to the story and to the author?

7 BIG Question

Do you think the grandfather's action at the end of the story makes Elizabeth feel differently about who she is on the outside *and* on the inside? Explain your answer on the "Flowers and Freckle Cream" page of Foldable 4. Your response will help you complete the Unit Challenge later.

Analyzing the Photo Why did the tiger lily (like the ones in this photo) in her room make the narrator feel better about her freckles?

READING WORKSHOP 3 • Interpreting

After You Read

Flowers and Freckle Cream

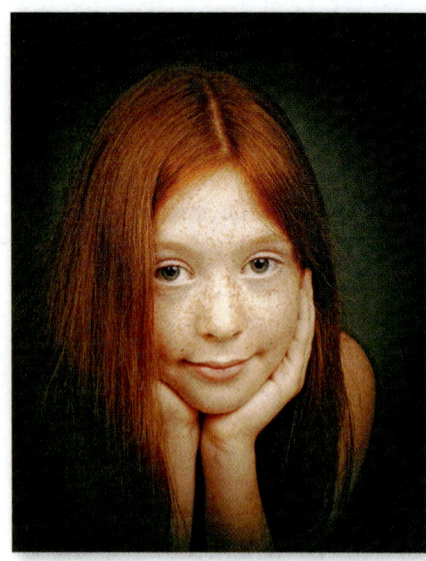

Answering the BIG Question

1. How important are the author's freckles to making her who she is?
2. **Recall** How old was the author when this story took place?
   TIP Right There
3. **Summarize** What qualities did Elizabeth's cousin have that made Elizabeth feel bad about herself?
   TIP Think and Search

Critical Thinking

4. **Infer** Where do you think the story takes place?
   TIP Author and Me
5. **Draw Conclusions** What does the narrator's grandfather know about her that she does not yet know?
   TIP On My Own
6. **Infer** When the author's mother says "You can't make a silk purse out of a sow's ear," what does this say about their relationship? Use other examples from the story to help you explain.
   TIP Author and Me

Talk About Your Reading

Beauty is Skin Deep The author measured her looks against her cousin Janette Elizabeth. How do you and the people you know measure the way you look? Sure, the way you look is a big part of what makes you who you are. But it's only *one part* of who you are. Think about your definition of *beauty*.

With a partner, or with the entire class, talk about the things that make you think someone or something is beautiful. Do your emotions affect judgments you make about beauty?

Objectives (pp. 434–435)
Reading Interpret text • Make connections from text to self
Literature Analyze point of view
Vocabulary Use context clues: examples
Grammar: Identify compound subjects and predicates

434 UNIT 4 What Makes You Who You Are?

Skills Review

Key Reading Skill: Interpreting

7. Do you think this story has a message? If not, why don't you think so? If so, what is the message?

Literary Element: Point of View

8. Imagine that the story was a series of diary entries, written as the story was taking place. Would the narrator's understanding of the situations be different?
9. Is the first-person point of view effective for this story? Why or why not?

Vocabulary Check

10. In your own words, write a definition for *inadequate* and use it in a sentence.
11. **Academic Vocabulary** Write a sentence using the word *interpret*.

English Language Coach Using the context clues in each sentence, match the underlined word in the sentences below with its synonym.

12. A carpenter needs such <u>implements</u> as a hammer and screwdriver, but an artist needs different ones, such as brushes.
13. Will your <u>vocation</u> be doctor, teacher, firefighter, auto mechanic, or something else?
14. Bill is so <u>affluent</u>. He has a swimming pool, tennis courts, and a gym in his house.

  a. occupation
  b. tools
  c. wealthy

Web Activities For eFlashcards, Selection Quick Checks, and other Web activities, go to www.glencoe.com.

Grammar Link: Compound Subjects and Predicates

As you know, every complete sentence has a subject (*who* or *what*) and a predicate (what the subject *is* or *does*). You also know that complete subjects and predicates consist of more than one word. Now, learn about compound subjects and predicates.

- A **compound subject** has two or more simple subjects that have the same predicate. The subjects are most often joined by *and* or *or*.

  The <u>girl</u> and her <u>grandfather</u> walked in the woods.

- A **compound predicate** has two or more simple predicates, or verbs, that have the same subject. The simple predicates are most often connected by *and* or *or*.

  She <u>cried</u> and <u>slammed</u> the door.

- A sentence can have both a compound subject and a compound predicate.

  The <u>boy</u> and his <u>father</u> often <u>cook</u> and <u>talk</u> in the kitchen.

Grammar Practice

Write whether each sentence has a *compound subject* or a *compound predicate* or both.

15. Daydreams and fantasies are a normal part of growing up.
16. Some people make decisions and plan their futures very early.
17. My dog and cat play and nap together.

Rewrite each sentence; add a word that completes the sentence and makes a compound subject or compound predicate. Write whether the sentence has a compound subject or a compound predicate.

18. The girls wash and ___ their hair.
19. Basil and ___ read a book for class.
20. To stay in shape we jog and ___ after school.

WRITING WORKSHOP PART 2

Poetry
Revising, Editing, Presenting

ASSIGNMENT Write a poem

Purpose: To write a poem about what makes you who you are

Audience: You, your teacher, classmates, family, and friends

Revising Rubric

Your revised poem should have

- word choice that expresses your thoughts and emotions
- figurative language, such as similes and metaphors
- sensory details
- sound patterns

Objectives (pp. 436–439)
Writing Revise writing for poetic features, including sound devices, figurative language, word choice, and sensory imagery • Edit writing for: spelling, punctuation **Listening, Speaking, and Viewing** Present poem • Use appropriate expressions and gestures • Listen for elements of poetry

In Writing Workshop Part 1, you wrote about personal traits and interests that make you who you are. You also learned that poems are usually written in lines and stanzas instead of in paragraphs. In Writing Workshop Part 2, you will learn more poetic elements such as figurative language, sensory details, and sound patterns.

Revising
Make It Better

Revising is your chance to reread your work and make any changes that you think would make your writing better.

Many poets use figurative language in their poems to help describe objects, feelings, and emotions. Figurative language consists of many different **figures of speech** such as *simile*, *metaphor*, and *personification*. These figures of speech make comparisons between things that seem unrelated. The chart below provides definitions and examples of figures of speech that you may want to use in your poem.

Figure of Speech	Definition	Example
Simile	Compares two unlike things using the words *like* or *as*.	• He rushed at me like a freight train. • Her hair was as dark as night.
Metaphor	Compares two unlike things without using the words *like* or *as*.	• His heart was a stone. • Her mind slammed shut.
Personification	Describes things as if they had human abilities, emotions, or characteristics.	• Wind kissed my hair. • The mountains stood guard over the town.

Figurative language creates images in your reader's imagination. Reread your poem and look for places where you can turn a description into a figure of speech.

436 UNIT 4 What Makes You Who You Are?

WRITING WORKSHOP PART 2

Sound Patterns

Poetry often has a rhythm, or pattern of regular beats. Poetry also may include rhyme. Rhyme is the repetition of similar sounds at the end of words, such as those in Shel Silverstein's poem "Whatif." Notice how the repetition of the word *Whatif* creates a steady rhythm in this poem.

from **Whatif**

Whatif I'm dumb in school?
Whatif they've closed the swimming pool?
Whatif I get beat up?
Whatif there's poison in my cup?
Whatif I start to cry?
Whatif I get sick and die?

Silverstein's poem has a regular pattern of rhyme. The first two lines rhyme, then the next two, and so on. A regular pattern is called a "rhyme scheme." A rhyme scheme can help a poem flow and add interest to the sound of it.

Sensory Details

Descriptions that appeal to your five senses—hearing, sight, touch, smell, and taste—are called sensory details. Writers use sensory details to describe sounds, smells, feelings, sights, or tastes so that their readers can easily imagine them. Read the lines below and write in your Learner's Notebook which one of your senses the writer is appealing to.

1. Rotten eggs stunk up the refrigerator.
2. The sweet flavor of watermelon swirled in my mouth.
3. The wind roared, and tree branches crashed to the ground.

Now, try writing your own lines in your Learner's Notebook that appeal to each of your five senses. Look over your poem to see if you can add a sensory detail to help describe sights, sounds, smells, tastes, or feelings.

Editing
Finish It Up

After you have revised your poem, edit your writing for grammar, usage, mechanics, and spelling. Use the **Editing Checklist** to help you spot your mistakes.

- ☑ The poem is written in lines and stanzas.
- ☑ Words are spelled correctly.
- ☑ Punctuation tells the reader when to pause.

> **Writing Tip**
>
> Poetic lines become more important when they are repeated. Experiment by repeating the same word or phrase in several lines of your poem.
> *My friends want to fight,*
> *But I keep walking.*
> *My family likes to argue,*
> *But I keep walking.*
> *My heart is racing,*
> *But I keep walking*
> How does repeating different lines change your poem?

> **Writing Tip**
>
> Alliteration is the repetition of a sound at the beginnings of words. Try writing a line of poetry with several words beginning with the same letter. Alliteration gives emphasis to words as their sounds are repeated. *The driver dreamt of Dublin* is an example of alliteration.

WRITING WORKSHOP PART 2

Presenting
Show It Off

- Read your poem one last time. The figurative language and sensory details should paint a picture in your head.
- On a fresh sheet of paper, draw the images that appear in your poem.
- Include the same details in your drawing that you included in your poem.
- When you finish drawing, write your poem on the back of your drawing.
- With a partner, take turns reading your poems to each other. Hold the paper so that your partner can look at your drawing as you read.
- Discuss how the words in your poem are different from or similar to what you drew.

Active Writing Model

The writer uses a simile that compares her grandpa to a hawk.

The writer creates a rhyme with the last two words in lines 2 and 4, *soar* and *eighty-four*.

The writer rhymes two words within the line to make it more interesting.

The writer uses alliteration, *brave, bold* and *bossy*, to emphasize her grandfather's strong personality.

Soft chirps is a sensory detail that describes the sound of the birds.

Writer's Model

My Grandpa
by Ayana Jackson

Just like a hawk
ready to soar,
Grandpa's real strong
though he's now eighty-four.

He's got a life
that is full of surprises.
He's ready and steady,
whatever arises!

My grandpa is brave,
and he's bossy and bold.
Will I be as daring
when I am that old?

And will I, like he,
go for walks by the lake
to hear the soft chirps
that the baby birds make?

438 UNIT 4 What Makes You Who You Are?

Listening, Speaking, and Viewing

Reading Poetry Aloud

What Is It?

Think of your favorite songs. How many of them say something about the Big Question: What Makes You Who You Are? Many times, songwriters write about their own lives—their problems, their dreams, who they are, and what makes them who they are. Poets share these same ideas in their poetry, and just like musicians, poets like to share their work with an audience.

Why Is It Important?

Most poetry has musical qualities, such as rhythm, rhyme, and interesting word choice. Just like music, these qualities are best expressed when a poem is performed aloud.

How Do I Do It?

Follow these tips for reading poetry aloud.

1. Read with emotion and understanding

Audiences want to hear readers who understand the words and messages of the poems they are reading. Before you read, ask yourself:

- Are there words I don't know or can't pronounce? (If there are, ask someone for help or check a dictionary.)

- Do I understand what the poet is saying? (If you don't, discuss it with friends, classmates, or family. Discussing poetry helps everyone understand it better.)

2. Listen for good examples

- Listen to other people read poetry—your teacher or a recording of a poet. What makes their reading good? Do they pause to give you time to understand what they read? Do they change the volume or pitch of their voices as they read?

- Organize a poetry reading with students in your class. As your classmates read their poems, watch other people in the audience. How does the reader keep the audience's attention? Write down what you notice in your Learner's Workbook.

- Practice reading your own poetry. Ask your friends and family to listen to you read and give you feedback that will help you improve reading aloud. Write their tips in your Learner's Notebook.

Writing Models For models and other writing activities, go to www.glencoe.com.

READING WORKSHOP 4

Skills Focus

You will practice these skills when you read the following selections:
- "The March of the Dead," p. 444
- "The Gene Scene," p. 452

Reading
- Monitoring comprehension

Literature
- Understanding figurative language: simile, metaphor, and personification

Vocabulary
- Reviewing context clues

Writing/Grammar
- Identifying direct and indirect objects

Objectives (pp. 440–441)
Reading Monitor comprehension

Skill Lesson

Monitoring Comprehension

Learn It!

What Is It? Have you ever read a homework assignment and then found out the next day that you couldn't answer any of the teacher's questions about it? Having done your homework doesn't help much then, does it? If this has ever happened to you, maybe you should be monitoring your comprehension.

- To *monitor* is to keep track of it or check it.
- *Comprehension* is another word for "understanding."

Analyzing Cartoons
Why do you think the cartoonist calls this "the real-life reading and comprehension test"? How should the man in the cartoon monitor his comprehension?

READING WORKSHOP 4 • **Monitoring Comprehension**

Why Is It Important? It's possible to read too quickly or not pay enough attention while reading. If that happens, it's like not having read at all. No matter what your purpose is for reading, your most important task is to understand what you have read.

How Do I Do It? Pause while you are reading and think about what you just read. Ask yourself if it makes sense to you. If it doesn't, use these tips:

- **Reread** the passage more slowly and carefully.
- **Ask yourself questions** about ideas, characters, and events.
- **Look for context clues** for words you don't understand.
- **Read on a little further,** which will sometimes clear up a confusing issue.
- **Use reference sources** such as dictionaries and encyclopedias to find information on words or topics you don't understand.

Study Central Visit www.glencoe.com and click on Study Central to review monitoring comprehension.

Here's how one student monitored her comprehension to understand a tough passage in "Geraldine Moore the Poet."

> *Nothing lovely's been happening in my life. / I haven't seen a flower since Mother's Day, / And the sun don't even shine on my side of the street. / No robins come sing on my window sill.*

> *What? I think I'll read that again. Why did Geraldine say she hasn't seen a flower since Mother's Day? I remember reading something about her mother earlier. If I go back and reread that part, it might make more sense.*

Practice It!

Practice monitoring your comprehension by reading these lines from "The March of the Dead." Write down one question you have about this section. *And then there came a shadow, swift and sudden, dark and drear; / The bells were silent, not an echo stirred. / The flags were drooping sullenly, the men forgot to cheer; / We waited, and we never spoke a word*

Use It!

Use the tips below to monitor your comprehension as you read "The March of the Dead" and "The Gene Scene."

- Read hard parts slowly, write down any words you don't understand, and use footnotes or a dictionary.
- Write down a question you have about what you've read.

READING WORKSHOP 4 • Monitoring Comprehension

Before You Read : The March of the Dead

Meet the Author
Robert Service was born in 1874 in England. As a young man he worked as a logger, dishwasher, teacher, bank clerk, ranch hand, and fruit picker before turning to writing. He explained that, in his writing, he was after "something the man in the street would take notice of and the sweet old lady would paste in her album." See page R6 of the Author Files for more on Robert Service.

Author Search For more about Robert Service, go to www.glencoe.com.

Objectives (pp. 442–447)
Reading Monitor comprehension • Make connections from text to self
Literature Identify and interpret figurative language • Identify literary elements: simile, metaphor, personification
Vocabulary Use context clues: definition, restatement, comparison, contrast, and examples

Vocabulary Preview

sullenly (SUL un lee) *adv.* gloomily and silently **(p. 445)** *The sky grew dark and the flags drooped sullenly.*

ghastly (GAST lee) *adj.* terrible, horrible **(p. 445)** *The Army of the Dead appeared frightening and ghastly as they crept out of the darkness.*

woe (woh) *n.* great sadness or suffering **(p. 445)** *The fallen soldiers had misery and woe in their eyes.*

writhing (RY thing) *adj.* twitching, twisting **(p. 446)** *Their writhing lips showed their pain as the wounded trudged through the streets.*

mirth (murth) *n.* joy, happiness **(p. 447)** *The parade of living soldiers was cause for mirth, but many were saddened by those who had fallen.*

Partner Talk Write each vocabulary word on a separate note card. Write the definition on the back. Take turns testing each other by flashing the cards.

English Language Coach

You have learned about several kinds of **context clues**.

Definition: When he got a scholarship, Bryant was <u>elated</u>–filled with joy.
• The writer gives a definition. *Elated* means "filled with joy."

Restatement: He was <u>elated</u> and this intense happiness lasted for hours.
• The writer has restated the idea. Someone who is *elated* is intensely happy.

Comparison: She was as <u>elated</u> as a fan whose team has just won the World Series.
• The writer has compared the feeling of being elated to a feeling everyone knows is a very happy one.

Contrast: Unlike his miserable friend, Norm was <u>elated</u>.
• The opposite of *elated* is "miserable," so elated must mean "very happy."

Example: There are many types of <u>precipitation</u>, including rain, sleet, hail, and snow.
• Rain, sleet, hail, and snow are examples of water that fall to earth, so that's what *precipitation* must mean.

Write to Learn Use *ravenous*, which means "extremely hungry," in a sentence using context clues. Use a type of clue mentioned above.

442 UNIT 4 What Makes You Who You Are?

READING WORKSHOP 4 • Monitoring Comprehension

Skills Preview

Key Reading Skill: Monitoring Comprehension

Use these tips to monitor your comprehension.

- Pause in your reading.
- Ask yourself what just happened.
- Try to summarize what has happened.
- Read on to see if later information helps.

Key Literary Element: Figurative Language

Someone who says, "That apple is red," just means that the apple is red. This is **literal language.** Literal language means exactly what it says. It is language without exaggeration. Language that suggests something beyond the exact meaning of the words is called **figurative language.** Someone who says, "She was so mad, she was burning up" is speaking figuratively, or using figurative language. No one was really "burning up." But it helps to create an image or feeling of just how angry the person was. Two kinds of figurative language often used to make comparisons are **similes** and **metaphors.**

- A *simile* uses the words *like* or *as* to compare two unlike things.

  Her diamond sparkled like a star.

- A *metaphor* compares two unlike things without using *like* or *as*.

  Her eyes were emeralds.

Personification is figurative language in which an animal, idea, or object is given human qualities. It is described as if it were human. In "The moon danced across the midnight sky," the moon is personified, or given a human quality—the ability to dance.

Write to Learn In your Learner's Notebook, write three sentences using figurative language.

Interactive Literary Elements Handbook
To review or learn more about the literary elements, go to www.glencoe.com.

Get Ready to Read

Connect to the Reading

"The more things change, the more they stay the same." Have you ever heard this expression? This saying applies to many things—including war. No matter how wars change, soldiers returning home from war always stir up people's feelings.

Write to Learn In your Learner's Notebook, write your feelings about war. Think about what you already know about war. Is there ever a good reason for war? Explain.

Build Background

"The March of the Dead" is a poem about a parade of British soldiers returning home from the Boer War.

- From 1899 to 1902, the British fought the Dutch for control of South Africa. The Dutch were known as the Boers, and the conflict was called the Boer War.
- The British suffered many defeats in the Boer War, and soldiers were killed on both sides.
- Robert Service, the author of the poem, saw war firsthand. He served as an ambulance driver during World War I.

Set Purposes for Reading

BIG Question Read the selection "The March of the Dead" to learn about how the wars in our time make us who we are.

Set Your Own Purpose What else would you like to learn from the reading to help you answer the Big Question? Write your purpose on "The March of the Dead" page of Foldable 4.

Keep Moving

Use these skills as you read the following selection.

The March of the Dead 443

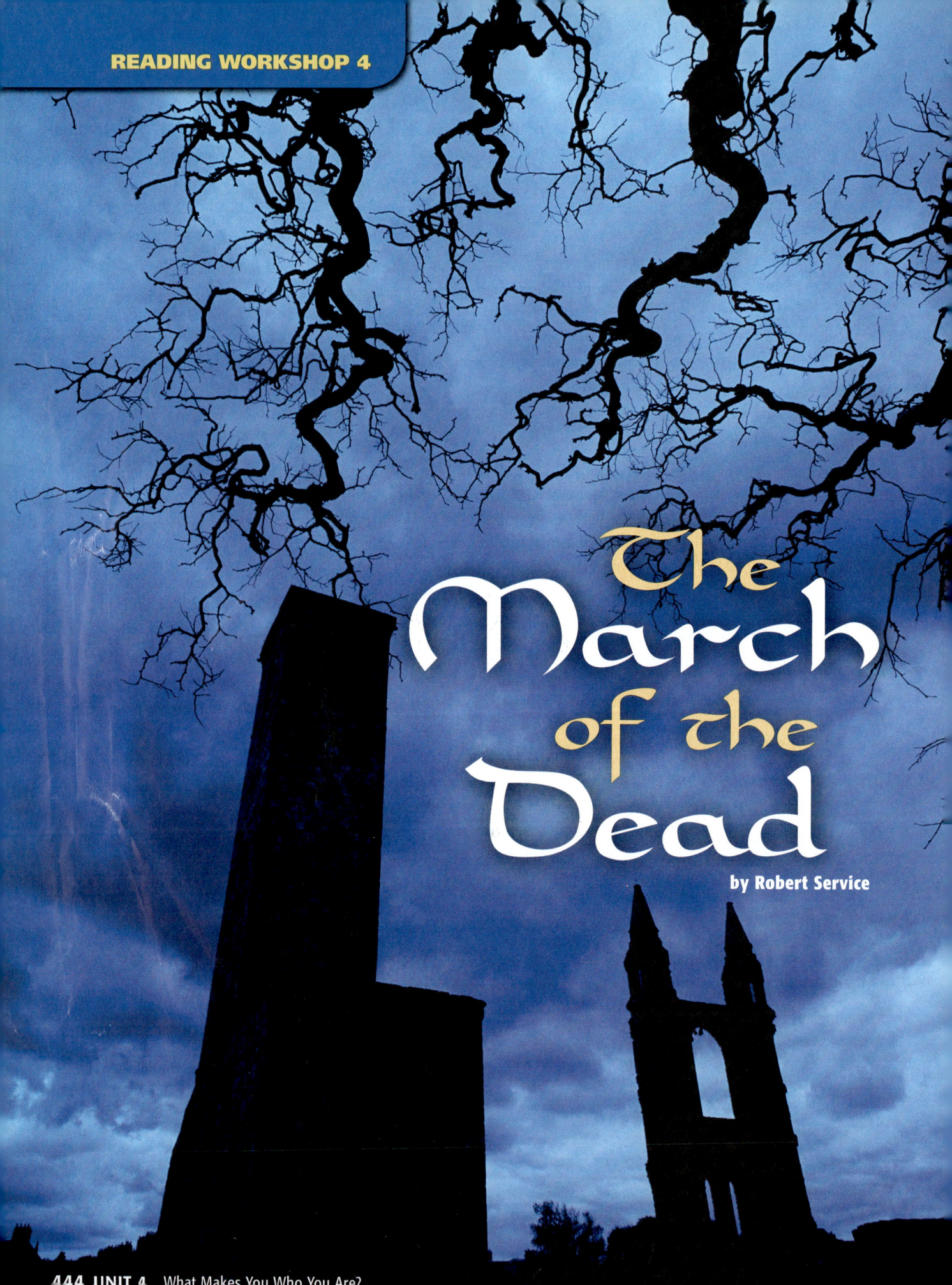

The cruel war was over—oh, the triumph was so sweet! ❶
   We watched the troops returning, through our tears;
There was triumph, triumph, triumph down the scarlet glittering street.
   And you scarce could hear the music for the cheers.
5 And you scarce could see the house-tops for the flags that flew between;
   The bells were pealing* madly to the sky;
And everyone was shouting for the Soldiers of the Queen,
   And the glory of an age was passing by. ❷

And then there came a shadow, swift and sudden, dark and drear;
10   The bells were silent, not an echo stirred.
The flags were drooping **sullenly**, the men forgot to cheer;
   We waited, and we never spoke a word.
The sky grew darker, darker, till from out the gloomy rack
   There came a voice that checked the heart with dread:
15 "Tear down, tear down your bunting now, and hang up sable black;*
   They are coming—it's the Army of the Dead."

They were coming, they were coming, gaunt* and **ghastly**, sad and slow;
   They were coming, all the crimson* wrecks of pride;
With faces seared,* and cheeks red smeared, and haunting eyes of **woe**,

Practice the Skills

❶ Key Literary Element

Figurative Language Find the example of personification in the first line. What is being personified? Think about the fact that cruelty is a human quality.

❷ Key Reading Skill

Monitoring Comprehension Each section of a poem is known as a stanza; this poem has six stanzas. Monitor your comprehension after each stanza. If you are unsure about any part, go back and reread the stanza. Look at the footnotes. Write any questions you have in your Learner's Notebook.

---

6 Here *pealing* means ringing loudly.
15 *Rack* is a mass of high clouds broken by the wind. *Checked*, as it is used here, means "stopped." *Bunting* is another word for flags and colorful banners. *Sable black* means dark cloths hung in mourning.
17 *Gaunt* means extremely thin.
18 *Crimson* is a dark red color.
19 If something is *seared*, it is burnt.

Vocabulary

sullenly (SUL un lee) *adv.* gloomily and silently

ghastly (GAST lee) *adj.* terrible, horrible

woe (woh) *n.* great sadness or suffering

The March of the Dead 445

20　　And clotted holes the khaki couldn't hide.
　　Oh, the clammy brow of anguish! the livid, foam-flecked lips!*
　　　　The reeling ranks of ruin swept along!
　　The limb that trailed, the hand that failed, the bloody finger tips!*
　　　　And oh, the dreary rhythm of their song!

25 "They left us on the veldt-side, but we felt we couldn't stop
　　　　On this, our England's crowning festal day;
　　We're the men of Magersfontein, we're the men of Spion Kop,
　　　　Colenso—we're the men who had to pay.*
　　We're the men who paid the **blood-price**. Shall the grave be all our gain?
30　　　You owe us. Long and heavy is the score. 3
　　Then cheer us for our glory now, and cheer us for our pain,
　　　　And cheer us as ye never cheered before."

　　The folks were white and stricken, and each tongue seemed weighted with lead;
　　　　Each heart was clutched in hollow hand of ice; 4
35 And every eye was staring at the horror of the dead,
　　　　The pity of the men who paid the price.
　　They were come, were come to mock us, in the first flush of our peace;
　　　　Through **writhing** lips their teeth were all agleam;
　　They were coming in their thousands—oh, would they never cease!
40　　　I closed my eyes, and then—it was a dream.

Practice the Skills

3 English Language Coach

Context Clues Reread this entire stanza. What does the author mean by the expression **blood-price** in line 29? What context clue helped you understand the meaning of *blood-price*?

4 Key Literary Element

Figurative Language What makes line 34 an example of figurative language? What does this description mean?

21　**Anguish** means great pain, and **livid** means pale.
23　**Reeling** means "staggering" or "thrown off balance." A **limb** refers to an arm or leg.
28　**Veldt** is a Dutch word for an open grazing area or field. **Festal** means festive or happy. **Magersfontein, Spion Kop,** and **Colenso** are the names of extremely bloody battles in the Boer War.

Vocabulary

writhing (RY thing) *adj.* twitching, twisting

446 UNIT 4 What Makes You Who You Are?

Analyzing the Photo What is this a photo of? What line from the poem does it illustrate?

There was triumph, triumph, triumph down the scarlet gleaming street;
    The town was mad; a man was like a boy.
A thousand flags were flaming where the sky and city meet;
    A thousand bells were thundering the joy.
45 There was music, **mirth** and sunshine; but some eyes shone with regret;
    And while we stun with cheers our homing braves,*
O God, in Thy great mercy, let us nevermore forget
    The graves they left behind, the bitter graves. 5

Practice the Skills

5 BIG Question
In what ways does this poem show how major events like war make us who we are? Write your answer on "The March of the Dead" page of Foldable 4. Your response will help you complete the Unit Challenge later.

---

46 *Homing braves* refers to the brave soldiers who are returning home.

Vocabulary

mirth (murth) *n.* joy, happiness

READING WORKSHOP 4 • Monitoring Comprehension

After You Read: The March of the Dead

Answering the BIG Question

1. Are your feelings about war part of what makes you who you are? Explain.

2. **Recall** In the first stanza of the poem, why could people scarcely hear the music or see the house-tops?
   TIP Right There

3. **Summarize** In the second stanza, how does the scene change when the Army of the Dead begins to arrive?
   TIP Think and Search

Critical Thinking

4. **Interpret a)** Why do you think the poet uses repetition in the line "There was triumph, triumph, triumph down the scarlet glittering street"? **b)** Why does he change the phrase to "gleaming street" at the end of the poem?
   TIP On My Own

5. **Infer** What does the speaker mean when he calls the soldiers "crimson wrecks of pride"?
   TIP Author and Me

6. **Analyze** Why do you think the dead feel they must march along with the living?
   TIP Author and Me

Write About Your Reading

Review Write a short review of the poem. (A review contains personal reactions as well as facts.) Your review could answer some of the following questions:
- Did it make sense?
- What did it mean to you?
- Did an image from the poem really stay in your head?
- How would you summarize the poem?
- What is the poet's message?
- Did you think it was a good poem or not? Why?

Objectives (pp. 448–449)
Reading Monitor comprehension
Literature Identify and interpret figurative language
Vocabulary Use context clues: definition, restatement, comparison, contrast, and examples
Writing Respond to literature: poetry review
Grammar Identify direct objects

448 UNIT 4   What Makes You Who You Are?

Skills Review

Key Reading Skill: Monitoring Comprehension

7. Did you understand the poem? Without looking at the poem again, describe one image you remember from the poem.

Key Literary Element: Figurative Language

8. The speaker says "and each tongue seemed weighted with lead." What does this figurative description mean?

Vocabulary Check

Write a paragraph using each vocabulary word correctly.

9. sullenly
10. ghastly
11. woe
12. writhing
13. mirth

English Language Coach Use context clues to figure out the meaning of each underlined word. Write a synonym or short definition for each.

14. Her eyesight is as <u>keen</u> as a hawk's.
15. I move quickly in the morning, but my brother is <u>sluggish</u> when he wakes up.
16. I like their <u>abode</u>. That is, I like the place where they live.

Web Activities For eFlashcards, Selection Quick Checks, and other Web activities, go to www.glencoe.com.

Grammar Link: Direct Objects

You have learned that every sentence has a subject and a predicate. In some sentences, the predicate consists of only an action verb.

*The punter **kicks**.*

Usually sentences give more information. The predicate often says who or what received the action of the verb.

*The punter **kicks** the **football**.*

In the sentence above, *football* receives the action of the verb *kicks*. It answers the question *kicked what?* In this sentence, the word *football* is called a "direct object."

- A **direct object** receives the action of a verb. It answers the question *whom?* or *what?* after an action verb.
- A verb can have more than one direct object.

  *The team carried **gloves** and **bats** into the stadium.*

- Sometimes an action verb does not have a direct object.

  The team played well.

In the sentence above, *well* does not answer the question *whom?* or *what?* after the verb *played*. It is not a direct object.

Grammar Practice

Rewrite each sentence. Draw two lines under the action verb in each sentence. If the action verb has a direct object, circle the direct object.

17. The Statue of Liberty attracts many visitors.
18. Some people ride bikes.
19. They noticed fossils in the cave walls.
20. They play football and baseball after school.

Writing Application Look back at the letter you wrote. Find three sentences with action verbs. Underline the action verbs. If they have direct objects, circle them.

READING WORKSHOP 4 • Monitoring Comprehension

Before You Read : The Gene Scene

Meet the Writer
Jordan Brown wrote this article "The Gene Scene" for *TIME* magazine.

Vocabulary Preview

generation (jen uh RAY shun) *n.* a group of persons born around the same time **(p. 452)** *Some features, like eye color, are passed on by parents to the next generation—their children.*

heredity (huh RED uh tee) *n.* the passing on of characteristics from an animal or plant to its offspring **(p. 454)** *Many of his facial features are due to heredity—he looks just like his father.*

chromosomes (KROH muh sohmz) *n.* parts of a cell in a plant or animal that carry the genes controlling features such as the color of hair and eyes **(p. 454)** *Your chromosomes are so small they are invisible to the human eye.*

Write to Learn Write a paragraph using all three vocabulary words correctly.

English Language Coach

Context Clues Getting comfortable with context clues will make reading so much easier! You will be able to read more quickly and understand more of what you read. Remember a context clue might be in a sentence before or after the difficult word. So pay close attention.

Write to Learn Copy the chart below. For each word in dark type, write the word, its meaning, and the context clues that helped you figure out the word's meaning.

1. Janet put the wet clay pot in the **kiln,** or oven, to harden.
2. The new program has been **beneficial** for the school; for example, test scores are up and absences are down.
3. Maria thought the dress was **gaudy.** The colors were loud and they clashed.
4. Robins are **migratory** birds, unlike sparrows, which live in the same place year-round.

Objectives (pp. 450–455)
Reading Monitor comprehension
• Make connections from text to self
Literature Identify literary elements: simile, metaphor
Vocabulary Use context clues

Word	Meaning	Context Clues

UNIT 4 What Makes You Who You Are?

READING WORKSHOP 4 • Monitoring Comprehension

Skills Preview

Key Reading Skill: Monitoring Comprehension

Active readers monitor their understanding as they read. They have a few good strategies for monitoring their comprehension.

- Read the passage again—one sentence at a time.
- Question important ideas, characters, and events.
- Look for context clues in the surrounding sentences.
- Use reference sources and footnotes.

Write to Learn Look at the *Build Background* section on this page. Write down one question you have about the *Build Background*.

Key Literary Element: Figurative Language

Figurative language is often used for descriptive effect. Figures of speech like **similes** and **metaphors** are a part of figurative language.

- Writers sometimes compare unlike things by using similes and metaphors.
- A simile uses the words *like* or *as* to compare two unlike things.
- A metaphor compares two unlike things without using *like* or *as*.

Write to Learn Think of two metaphors and two similes and write them in your Learner's Notebook.

Interactive Literary Elements Handbook
To review or learn more about the literary elements, go to www.glencoe.com.

Get Ready to Read

Connect to the Reading

Can you wiggle your ears or raise one eyebrow? Do you have curly hair? All of those qualities were either passed on to you or not. Think about the things that make you who you are. Chances are some of them were passed on to you from your relatives.

Self-Portrait with Genes Make a list of ten things about yourself, such as eye color, that were probably passed on to you in your genes.

Build Background

The selection you are about to read tells what makes us who we are—scientifically speaking.

- Some things, like the color of your eyes, are determined before you are born. Other qualities, like the music you listen to, have a lot to do with the person you are.
- "Nature versus nurture" is shorthand for the argument about traits you were born with (nature) versus personal experiences (nurture) in determining the way you look and act.
- Most scientists agree that both nature and nurture make you who you are.

Set Purposes for Reading

BIG Question Read "The Gene Scene" to find out how genes help to make you who you are.

Set Your Own Purpose What else would you like to learn from the reading to help you answer the Big Question? Write your purpose on the "Gene Scene" page of Foldable 4.

Keep Moving

Use these skills as you read the following selection.

The Gene Scene **451**

READING WORKSHOP 4

TIME
THE GENE SCENE

What makes you you?

By JORDAN BROWN

Genetics is the study of how special features, such as eye color, are passed on from one **generation** to another. ❶

To find out more about special features, called traits, find a friend and grab some paper and a pencil. Ask each other these questions. Then write your answers on the paper.

1. Can you curl your tongue?
You: YES   NO
Your Friend: YES   NO

2. Can you wiggle your ears?
You: YES   NO
Your Friend: YES   NO

3. Can you raise just one of your eyebrows?
You: YES   NO
Your Friend: YES   NO

4. Do you have a "hitchhiker's thumb"?[1]
You: YES   NO
Your Friend: YES   NO

1. A *hitchhiker's thumb* is a rare trait in humans where the end joint of the thumb can be bent at an angle of at least 45 degrees.

Vocabulary

generation (jen uh RAY shun) *n.* a group of persons born around the same time

❶ **Reviewing Skills**

Questioning Think about the title and the opening paragraph. Why do you think the idea of genetics might be important to the article? Does this paragraph help you understand what genetics is? What more do you want to know?

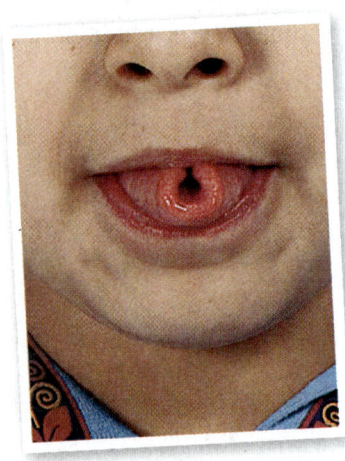

452 UNIT 4   What Makes You Who You Are?

Congratulations!

You just did a genetics investigation.

Traits are a person's special features. Some traits are more common than others. Many people can curl their tongues. But eyebrow raisers, ear-wigglers, and people with a hitchhiker's thumb are harder to find. **2**

Traits, such as the ability to roll your tongue, are passed on through genes. You get your genes from your parents. Genes are inside every living cell. They are made of a chemical called DNA.[2] Genes are tiny, but they carry tons of information. **3**

Here are some amazing things scientists have discovered so far:
- All living things have DNA. So you have something in common with zebras, trees, mushrooms, and even bacteria.
- There are about 30,000 genes in every cell of your body.
- Unless you are an identical twin, there is no one exactly like you. You are genetically unique.

Scientists are discovering many new secrets about life, such as what role genes play in determining what makes you you, whether people are healthy or sick, and how you grow. What they learn will greatly affect our future, from the medicine we take to the food we eat.

2 English Language Coach

Context Clues In this paragraph, what kind of context clue does the writer give you to help you understand the meaning of the word **traits**?

3 Key Reading Skill

Monitoring Comprehension Stop and check your reading comprehension so far. Is there anything you need to go back and reread? Any words you don't understand? Write down a question you have at this point.

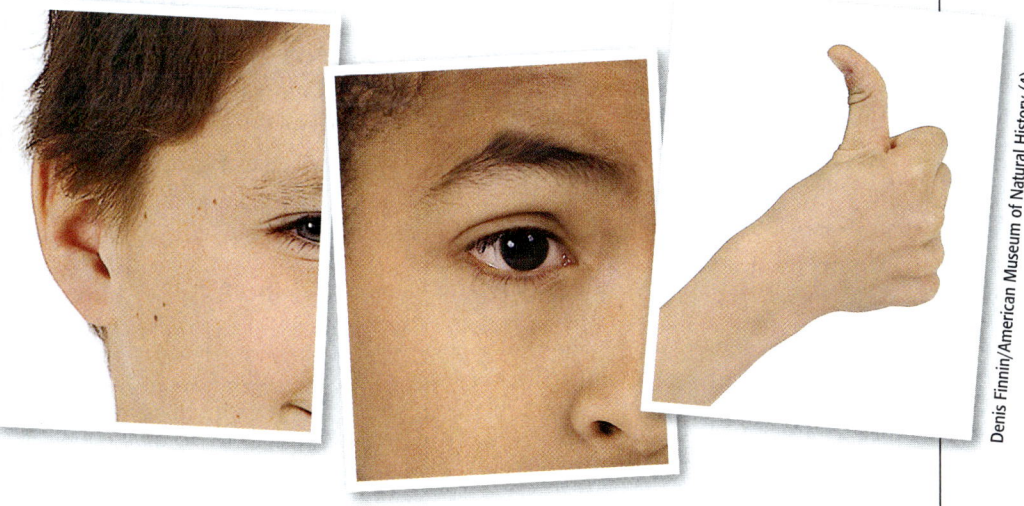

2. **DNA** is a substance that is found in the genes of cells and that stores a person's unique patterns of traits.

READING WORKSHOP 4

What Makes YOU <u>YOU</u>?
What Makes ME <u>ME</u>?

Genetics is fun!
So much to learn!
Oooh! But I have one concern.
I've searched and searched.
Where ARE my genes?
You've got to help me!
Spill the beans!

What makes you <u>you</u>?
What makes me <u>me</u>?
A lot is due to **heredity**.
Your genes control
What makes you <u>you</u>,
From the color of your hair
To the size of your shoe.

Dogs and frogs are made of cells.
Bananas have them, too!
These teeny-tiny building blocks
Even make up YOU!

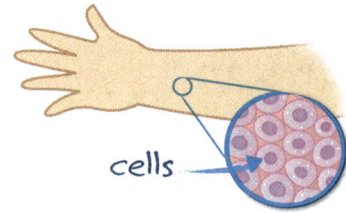

This thing here's the **nucleus**.
It's small, but even so:
It tells the cell just what to do,
It really runs the show. 4

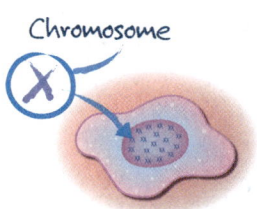

Then, there are your **chromosomes**,
They're 46 in all!
Half from mom, and half from dad,
They're really, really small.

4 English Language Coach

Context Clues In this part of the poem, what kind of context clue does the writer give you to help you understand the meaning of the word **nucleus**?

Vocabulary

heredity (huh RED uh tee) *n.* the passing on of characteristics from an animal or plant to its offspring

chromosomes (KROH muh sohmz) *n.* parts of a cell in a plant or animal that carry the genes controlling features such as the color of hair and eyes

454 UNIT 4 What Makes You Who You Are?

Your chromosomes are shaped like coils.
They always come in pairs.
They're made of stuff called DNA,
That's shaped like spiral stairs. 5

Genes are the sections of DNA,
Where many traits are placed.
Learning what each gene controls
Is the puzzle experts face.

DNA is made of four bases
We call them G, C, A, and T.
These bases are in every plant
And animal you see!
[end poem]

I GET IT NOW!
WHAT MAKES YOU <u>YOU</u>,
WHAT MAKES ME <u>ME</u>,
SHAPES EVERY LIVING THING YOU SEE.
WE'RE ALL RELATED IN A WAY
BECAUSE WE ALL HAVE DNA!

—Updated 2005, FROM *TIME FOR KIDS*, May 2001

5 Key Literary Element

Figurative Language Reread the lines "They're made of stuff called DNA / That's shaped like spiral stairs." Look at the "closer" view of DNA. It really is shaped exactly like spiral stairs, isn't it? Does this make the comparison "literal" or "figurative"?

Gregor Mendel, a scientist who lived in the 1800s, discovered the rules of genetics. By experimenting with pea plants, Mendel figured out how traits are passed from one generation to the next.

Thousands of different traits make you who you are. Some traits, such as eye color, are determined mostly or entirely by genes. These kind of traits are decided by nature.

Most traits, however, are due to a combination of nature (your genes) and nurture (everything in your life—where you live, the people you know, everything you experience). Scientists agree that both nature and nurture play important roles in making you who you are. 6

6 BIG Question

How does this article add to your understanding of what makes you who you are? Write your answer on the "Gene Scene" page of Foldable 4. Your response will help you complete the Unit Challenge later.

READING WORKSHOP 4 • Monitoring Comprehension

After You Read | The Gene Scene

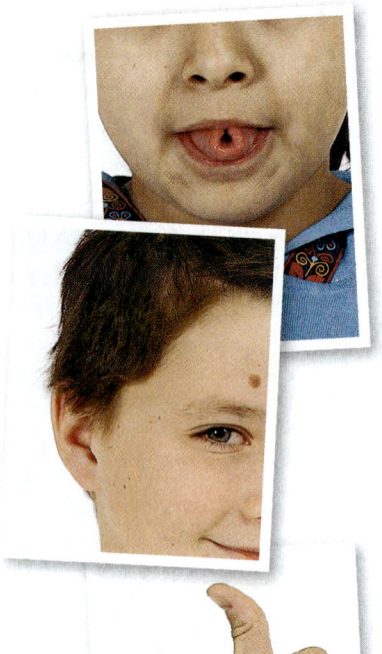

Answering the BIG Question

1. In what ways does nature determine who you are?

2. **Recall** What is the name given to the study of how special features are passed from one generation to another?
   TIP Right There

3. **Recall** According to this selection, what do you have in common with a zebra, a tree, a mushroom, and even bacteria?
   TIP Right There

Critical Thinking

4. **Infer** What do you think is the difference, genetically speaking, between identical twins and fraternal, or nonidentical, twins?
   TIP On My Own

5. **Evaluate** Why do you think the author starts his article by making you do a genetics investigation?
   TIP On My Own

6. **Analyze** What is the difference between "nature" and "nurture"?
   TIP Author and Me

Talk About Your Reading

With a partner, talk about what makes you who you are. Discuss the things that are hereditary and the things that aren't. Talk about:

- the traits that you have likely inherited from your parents (such as eye and hair color).
- the traits that you have developed, such as your style, your likes and dislikes, or your favorite hobbies or subjects in school.
- the traits that might be partly inherited but also partly developed, such as your talents and abilities.

Denis Finnin/American Museum of Natural History (4)

Objectives (pp. 456–457)
Reading Monitor comprehension • Make connections from text to self
Informational Text Identify literary elements: simile, metaphor
Vocabulary Use context clues
Grammar Identify indirect objects

Skills Review

Key Reading Skill: Monitoring Comprehension

7. How did the footnotes and vocabulary definitions help you as you monitored your comprehension?

Key Literary Element: Figurative Language

8. Think about both selections you read—a poem and an article. In which type of text do you think you'd be more likely to see similes and metaphors? Explain.

9. Rewrite the following sentences. If they are similes, turn them into metaphors. If they are metaphors, turn them into similes.
   - His feet were ice cubes.
   - Yesterday was like a nightmare.
   - Her hair was a shining helmet.

Reviewing Skills: Questioning

10. List two questions you could have asked yourself to help you think about what information was important as you read.

Vocabulary Check

Write the vocabulary word that each clue describes.

generation   heredity   chromosome

11. how traits get passed on to offspring
12. people who were born around the same time
13. the part of a cell that carries the genes

English Language Coach Use context clues to figure out the meaning of each underlined word. Write a synonym or short definition for each.

14. There was only a <u>scant</u> amount of food left, a piece of bread and one apple.
15. Hector can <u>disregard</u> the announcement, but Wally should pay attention to it.
16. That store carries <u>garments</u>, such as jeans, dresses, shirts, and coats.

Grammar Link: Indirect Objects

An **indirect object** tells *to whom* or *for whom* an action is done.

Calvin **shows** his **teammates** new shots.

The direct object in the sentence above is *shots*. The indirect object is *teammates*. *Teammates* answers the question *to whom?* after the action verb *shows*.

An indirect object appears only in a sentence that has a direct object. Two easy clues will help you find indirect objects.

- First, the indirect object always comes before a direct object.
- Second, you can add *to* or *for* before the indirect object and change its position. The sentence will still make sense, although it will no longer have an indirect object.

*The helper gives the **players** towels.*

*The helper gives the towels **to the players.***

In the first sentence, *players* is the indirect object. Notice that *players* comes before the direct object (towels). In the second, the position of *players* in the sentence is changed to follow the word *to*.

Grammar Practice

Copy each sentence. Underline each direct object once. Underline each indirect object twice.

17. The girls gave Martha her present.
18. Randy handed the lifeguard a whistle.
19. The zookeepers gave the lion his dinner.

Web Activities For eFlashcards, Selection Quick Checks, and other Web activities, go to www.glencoe.com.

COMPARING LITERATURE WORKSHOP

"maggie and milly and molly and may"
by e. e. cummings

& "Daydreamers"
by Eloise Greenfield

What You'll Learn
- How to compare two pieces of literature
- How to analyze figurative language

What You'll Read
- "maggie and milly and molly and may," p. 461
- "Daydreamers," p. 463

Point of Comparison
- Figurative language

Purpose
- To compare figurative language in two literary selections

Objectives (pp. 458–459)
Reading Compare and contrast: figurative language

Do you think comparing things is hard? It's not. Really, it's easy as pie! As a matter of fact, the sentence you just read made a comparison. It compared *making a comparison* to *eating a piece of pie*. People use comparisons all the time to make what they're saying more powerful and interesting. For example, you might say, "This test is very difficult." But that's pretty dull. Instead, you could say, "This test is a nightmare." The test isn't *really* a nightmare, but by *comparing* it to a bad dream, your point comes across more powerfully.

How to Compare Literature: Figurative Language

When you say something like "*Mason was good at basketball yesterday,*" you're using *literal* language. *Literal* language means exactly what it says.

When you say, "*Mason was a ball of fire on the court,*" though, you're using *figurative* language. *Figurative* language isn't meant to be taken as the simple, exact truth. Figurative language usually does one of these things:

- compares things that aren't really alike
- describes something as though it were something else
- exaggerates something to an impossible degree to create a more powerful image than you could with literal language

COMPARING LITERATURE WORKSHOP

Figurative language lets you be creative in describing things. In this workshop, you'll be comparing figurative language in two poems.

Get Ready to Compare

A **figure of speech** is often a comparison made using figurative language. Three of the most common types of figures of speech are *personification*, *similes*, and *metaphors*.

- **Personification** gives human characteristics to an object, animal, or idea.

    My bike hates me.

- **Similes** use the words *like* or *as* to compare two things that aren't really alike.

    She was quiet as a mouse during the lesson.

- **Metaphors** compare two unlike things without using the words *like* or *as*. A metaphor can say one thing is something else, or it can describe something as if it were something else.

    Allison was an angel while I was sick.

    (Allison is compared to an angel.)

    When Ms. Lowe called on her, Felicia's blood turned to ice water.

    (Felicia's blood is compared to ice water.)

Use Your Comparison

When you read a poem or other work of literature, take notes about the figures of speech (figurative language) that you find. A chart like this one can help you understand what the author is trying to say:

In the left circle, write down the figurative language that you found. In the center circle, write down what the author means. Then, in the right circle, write down the effect the figurative language has on the poem or the reader. Try to think of the image that it brings to mind or how it makes you feel.

In this workshop, you'll read two poems that use figurative language. For each selection, *read the poem all the way through first to get an idea of what the poem's about.* Then go back and make diagrams like the one above for each example of figurative language you find.

COMPARING LITERATURE WORKSHOP

Before You Read

maggie and milly and molly and may

Meet the Author
Edward Estlin Cummings (e. e. cummings) is famous for his experiments with poetry. Cummings rarely obeyed standard rules of grammar and capitalization in his poems. He didn't even capitalize his name when he signed his work. He felt that breaking accepted rules of grammar and usage helped him to express his ideas in a more original way. Cummings was born in 1894. He died in 1962. For more about e. e. cummings, see page R2 of the Author Files.

Author Search For more about e. e. cummings, go to www.glencoe.com.

Objectives (pp. 460–461)
Reading Compare and contrast across texts: figurative language

Vocabulary Preview

befriended (bih FREN dud) *v.* made friends with someone; form of the verb *befriend* **(p. 461)** *John befriended the boy he met in the park.*

stranded (STRAN did) *adj.* left helpless in a difficult place **(p. 461)** *When she missed the bus, the stranded girl was worried.*

rays (rayz) *n.* beams of light or energy **(p. 461)** *The sun's rays warmed my back.*

languid (LANG gwid) *adj.* slow-moving; without energy **(p. 461)** *The sound of the waves and the heat of the sun made me feel lazy and languid.*

Get Ready to Read

Connect to the Reading
Are you a worrier, a carefree type, a dreamer, or a deep thinker? Does your personality affect the way you see things and feel about them? In the poem you are about to read, four girls respond in different ways to a day at the beach. As you read "maggie and milly and molly and may," think about how who you are shapes the way you experience life.

Build Background
There is a sense of joy and fun in many of e. e. cummings's poems that makes them very popular. The poem you are about to read is one of his most widely read works.

- Cummings often wrote poems that celebrate nature and childhood.
- Sometimes, when you hold certain seashells to your ear, you can hear a noise that sounds like waves.
- Most common crabs walk sideways.
- Starfish dry out and die if they are left on the beach away from water.

Set Purposes for Reading
BIG Question Read the selection to explore how "maggie and milly and molly and may," who we are shapes the way we see the world.

Set Your Own Purpose What else would you like to learn from the poem to help you answer the Big Question? Write your own purpose on the "maggie and milly and molly and may" page of Foldable 4.

maggie and milly and molly and may

by e. e. cummings

maggie and milly and molly and may
went down to the beach(to play one day)

and maggie discovered a shell that sang 1
so sweetly she couldn't remember her troubles,and

milly **befriended** a **stranded** star
whose **rays** five **languid** fingers were;

and molly was chased by a horrible thing
which raced sideways while blowing bubbles:and

may came home with a smooth round stone
as small as a world and as large as alone.

For whatever we lose(like a you or a me)
it's always ourselves we find in the sea 2

Vocabulary

befriended (bih FREN dud) *v.* made friends with someone

stranded (STRAN did) *adj.* left helpless in a difficult place

rays (rayz) *n.* beams of light or energy

languid (LANG gwid) *adj.* slow-moving; without energy

Practice the Skills

1 Comparing Literature

Figurative Language
Cummings says that the shell "sang." Singing is normally something that people do, not objects. What kind of figurative language assigns human characteristics to objects? Why do you think cummings said the shell "sang"?

2 BIG Question
What do you think e. e. cummings means in the last two lines? Write your answer on the "maggie and milly and molly and may" page of your Foldable 4. Your response will help you complete the Unit Challenge later.

COMPARING LITERATURE WORKSHOP

Before You Read *Daydreamers*

Eloise Greenfield

Meet the Author
"I believe everyone spends time daydreaming," says Eloise Greenfield. "With writing, sometimes an idea will come, or an opening sentence, or an image, and then it may be months or years later before it really develops into a story." An award-winning author of books and poems for young people, Greenfield grew up in Washington, D.C.

Author Search For more about Eloise Greenfield, go to www.glencoe.com.

Vocabulary Preview

promenade (PROM uh nayd) *v.* to walk or stroll in a slow, relaxed manner (p. 464) *We watched the tourists promenade down the boardwalk.*

Get Ready to Read

Connect to the Reading
We've all been there. You're supposed to be concentrating on something, but instead you find yourself staring out the window, lost in a daydream. As you read this selection, connect with the daydreamers and their dreams.

Build Background
The poem you will read is about daydreaming.
- Daydreams can be a way of dealing with fears of the unknown.
- By daydreaming, people sometimes find solutions to problems or get ideas about how to do something.
- Some artists and writers are daydreamers who turned their dreams into art.
- *Hopscotch* is a children's game. To play it, children hop into squares drawn on the ground, while trying to pick up a pebble they have thrown into one of the squares.
- *Doubledutch* is a fast-paced jump-rope game in which two ropes are swung at the same time.

Set Purposes for Reading
BIG Question Read the selection "Daydreamers" to find out how daydreaming is connected to growing up and changing—becoming a person who will shape his or her own future.

Set Your Own Purpose What else would you like to learn from the story to help you answer the Big Question? Write your own purpose on the "Daydreamers" page of Foldable 4.

Objectives (pp. 462–463)
Reading Compare and contrast across texts: figurative language

462 UNIT 4 What Makes You Who You Are?

COMPARING LITERATURE WORKSHOP

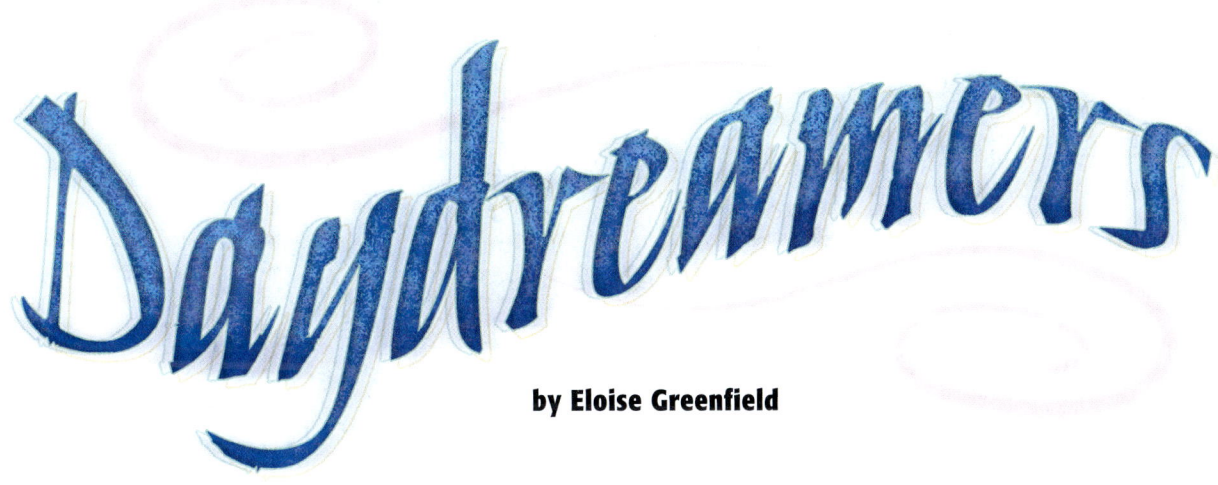

by Eloise Greenfield

Daydreamers . . .

holding their bodies still
for a time
letting the world turn around them ❶

⁵ while their dreams hopscotch,
doubledutch, dance, ❷

thoughts rollerskate,
crisscross,
bump into hopes and wishes.

¹⁰ Dreamers
thinking up new ways,
looking toward new days,

planning new tries,
asking new whys.
¹⁵ Before long,
hands will start to move again,
eyes turn outward,
bodies shift for action,
but for this moment they are still,

Practice the Skills

❶ Comparing Literature

Figurative Language What does the poet mean when she says the daydreamers let the world "turn around them"?

❷ Comparing Literature

Figurative Language While the daydreamers stand still, their dreams "hopscotch, doubledutch, dance." Is this an example of metaphor, simile, or personification? What does this suggest about the daydreams?

Daydreamers 463

COMPARING LITERATURE WORKSHOP

Lilith, 1996. Diane Griffiths. Watercolor and crayon.
Analyzing the Art Which lines from the poem would make a good caption for this painting? Explain why.

²⁰ they are
   the daydreamers,
   letting the world dizzy itself
   without them. 🔳

   Scenes passing through their minds
²⁵ make no sound
   glide from hiding places
   promenade and return
   silently

Vocabulary

promenade (PROM uh nayd) *v.* to walk or stroll in a slow, relaxed manner

🔳 **Comparing Literature**

Figurative Language Can a nonliving object become dizzy? What kind of figurative language is the poet using in the line "letting the world dizzy itself"? What do you think this means?

the children watch their memories
30 with spirit-eyes
seeing more than they saw before

feeling more
or maybe less
than they felt the time before
35 reaching with spirit-hands
to touch the dreams
drawn from their yesterdays 4
They will not be the same
after this growing time,
40 this dreaming.
In their stillness they have moved
forward

toward womanhood
toward manhood.
45 This dreaming has made them
new. 5 ○

Practice the Skills

4 Comparing Literature

Figurative Language What do you think the author means when she says children use *spirit-eyes* and *spirit-hands* to look back on their memories and touch their dreams?

5 BIG Question

What do you think the poet is saying about daydreaming and the part it plays in becoming who you are? Write your answer on the "Daydreamers" page of Foldable 4. Your response will help you complete the Unit Challenge later.

COMPARING LITERATURE WORKSHOP

After You Read

maggie and milly and molly and may & Daydreamers

Vocabulary Check

Look at the words listed below. Write the vocabulary word that each clue describes:

maggie and milly and molly and may

befriended   languid   stranded   rays

1. Someone who is lazy might look this way.
2. These are beams of light from a star.
3. When the tide goes out at the beach, some creatures find themselves in this situation.
4. Milly did this to the little animal when she helped it on the beach.

Daydreamers

Answer *true* or *false* to this statement:

5. When people *promenade*, they walk as fast as they can.

Reading/Critical Thinking

On a separate sheet of paper, answer the following questions.

maggie and milly and molly and may

6. **Recall** Which girl has a frightening experience at the beach?
   TIP Right There

7. **Compare and Contrast** How did the girls' experiences at the beach differ from one another? What does this tell you about each of the girls?
   TIP Author and Me

Objectives (pp. 466–467)
Reading Compare and contrast across texts: figurative language
Writing Write to compare and contrast literature

466 UNIT 4 What Makes You Who You Are?

COMPARING LITERATURE WORKSHOP

8. **Compare and Contrast** Do the girls' experiences at the beach support the last line of the poem, "it's always ourselves we find in the sea"?
   TIP Author and Me

Daydreamers

9. **Recall** What are the children doing while dreams go through their minds?
   TIP Right There

10. **Interpret** Why does the poet say the daydreamers "will not be the same after this growing time, this dreaming"?
    TIP Author and Me

11. **Evaluate** How well does the writer capture the thoughts and feelings of children in this poem? Why do you think this?
    TIP On My Own

Writing: Compare the Literature

Use Your Notes

12. Follow these steps to use your notes to compare the author's use of figurative language in "maggie and milly and molly and may" and "Daydreamers."

    Step 1: Look over the Figurative Language diagrams you created for both poems. Put a **P** by each example of personification, an **M** by each metaphor, and an **S** by each simile. If you found some examples of figurative language that don't seem to fit within those three categories, don't label them.

    Step 2: For each example of figurative language you found in both poems, look at the note you made in the *Effects* oval. Pick one example from each poem that you think had a strong effect.

    Step 3: With a partner, discuss the examples that the two of you selected. Do you agree about the effect that the use of figurative language has in these examples? Did either of you notice something that the other missed?

    Step 4: Look at the other examples of figurative language you identified. Think about which ones you enjoyed the most and which ones you thought were most descriptive.

Get It on Paper

Answer the following questions on a separate sheet of paper.

13. In "maggie and milly and molly and may," which example of figurative language did you enjoy the most? Explain what the effect of this example was and why you enjoyed it.

14. In "Daydreamers," which example of figurative language did you enjoy the most? Explain what the effect of this example was and why you enjoyed it.

15. Now write a paragraph that compares the two examples that you chose. For each example, write down the figure of speech you found, what it meant, and how it affected the poem or the reader. At the end of your paragraph, explain which example of figurative language you think was more effective.

BIG Question

16. After reading these poems, how do you think e. e. cummings would answer the question, "What makes you who you are?" How do you think Greenfield would answer the same question? Write your answers in your Learner's Notebook.

Comparing Literature Workshop 467

UNIT 4 WRAP-UP

Answering  What Makes You Who You Are?

You've just read about people's responses to the Big Question: What makes you who you are? Now use what you've learned to do the Unit Challenge.

The Unit Challenge

Choose Activity A or Activity B and follow the directions for that activity.

A. Play a Game: Who Am I?

Let's see if the members of your class can figure out what makes you who you are by playing this game.

1. **Get Started** Form teams of about five or six members. Each team member should get an index card. On the card, write the following:
   Likes:
   Dislikes:
   Hobbies/Interests:
   Personality:
   Something special about me:
   Each member should jot down some information about himself or herself next to each entry on the index card. Use your Foldable notes to give you some ideas. This is what makes you who you are. Here are some examples to get you started. If you have other entries you wish to use, you may use those.

2. **Put It in the Bags** Divide cards into equal batches. Each team receives a bag with the same amount of cards. Shake the bag up and begin the game.

3. **Take a Guess**
   - Decide which team goes first.
   - One member from that team takes a card from the bag and reads only the first entry aloud.
   - After the entry is read, your team will be given ten seconds to decide which person from the class the first entry describes. If you cannot agree, take a vote. If you get the person's name right, the team gets five points.
   - If you don't get the name correct, read the second entry and guess again. Each entry after the first one is worth 1 less point.
   - If all the entries on a card are read and the team has not correctly identified the person, the team loses two points. The team with the most points wins.
   - Keep playing until all teams get a turn.

Likes: watching scary movies
Dislikes: getting up early on Saturday morning
Hobbies: collecting comic books
Personality: usually in a good mood
Something special about me: can wiggle my ears

Big Question Link to Web resources to further explore the Big Question at www.glencoe.com.

UNIT 4 WRAP-UP

B. Self-Portrait Collage

It is your turn to share what you think helps to make you who you are. Use what you know about yourself to create a self-portrait collage.

1. **Get Started** Gather information about yourself. In your Learner's Notebook, list all of the things that you want to include about yourself. Here are some ideas to get you started.
   - List all your hobbies, interests, and activities.
   - Describe your likes and dislikes.
   - Include information from your Foldable notes.
   - Use this information to write a short essay about what makes you who you are.
   - Use a chart like the one below.

2. **Put It Together** Reread your essay and correct grammar or spelling errors.
   - Gather photos or drawings of you, your family, and friends. You're going to put them on a sheet of heavy paper or poster board, along with the essay that you wrote about yourself.
   - Decide how you want to arrange things before you glue them down.

3. **Show It** Present your collage to your class. Discuss the similarities and differences that you and your classmates have. Talk about what you and your classmates can do to understand and appreciate your differences.

ME		
My hobbies and interests	My likes and dislikes	Other information about me

Wrap-Up **469**

UNIT 4

Your Turn: Read and Apply Skills

Meet the Author

Lewis Carroll was the pen name of Charles Lutwidge Dodgson. Carroll was the third child of eleven brothers and sisters. Carroll taught mathematics and logic. He often used puzzles and games in his teaching. Many of his stories and poems reflect his logical mind, a joy in working through puzzling events. Carroll wrote comic fantasies and humorous verse that was often childlike. His novel *Alice's Adventures in Wonderland* was published in 1865, followed by *Through the Looking-Glass* in 1871. See page R1 of the Author Files for more about Lewis Carroll.

Author Search For more about Lewis Carroll, go to www.glencoe.com.

The Walrus and the Carpenter

by Lewis Carroll

The sun was shining on the sea,
    Shining with all his might:
He did his very best to make
    The billows* smooth and bright—
5 And this was odd, because it was
    The middle of the night.

The moon was shining sulkily,*
    Because she thought the sun
Had got no business to be there
10   After the day was done—
"It's very rude of him," she said,
    "To come and spoil the fun!"

The sea was wet as wet could be,
    The sands were dry as dry.
15 You could not see a cloud, because
    No cloud was in the sky:
No birds were flying overhead—
    There were no birds to fly.

---

4 **Billows** means big waves.
7 **Sulkily** means in a gloomy, pouting way.

The walrus and the carpenter on the shore, from *Through the Looking Glass and What Alice Found There,* by Lewis Carroll, 1872.

The Walrus and the Carpenter
20   Were walking close at hand;
They wept like anything to see
    Such quantities of sand:
"If this were only cleared away,"
    They said, "it *would* be grand!"

25 "If seven maids with seven mops
    Swept it for half a year,
Do you suppose," the Walrus said,
    "That they could get it clear?"
"I doubt it," said the Carpenter,
30   And shed a bitter tear.

"O Oysters, come and walk with us!"
    The Walrus did beseech.*
"A pleasant walk, a pleasant talk,
    Along the briny* beach:
35 We cannot do with more than four,
    To give a hand to each."

The eldest Oyster looked at him,
    But never a word he said:
The eldest Oyster winked his eye,
40   And shook his heavy head—
Meaning to say he did not choose
    To leave the oyster-bed.

But four young Oysters hurried up,
    All eager for the treat:
45 Their coats were brushed, their faces washed,
    Their shoes were clean and neat—
And this was odd, because, you know,
    They hadn't any feet.

Four other Oysters followed them,
50   And yet another four;
And thick and fast they came at last,
    And more, and more, and more—
All hopping through the frothy* waves,

32 **Beseech** means to beg or ask for in a serious way.
34 **Briny** water is salty.
53 **Frothy** water is foamy and bubbly.

The walrus and the carpenter with oysters wearing tiny shoes, from *Through the Looking Glass and What Alice Found There,* by Lewis Carroll, 1872.

And scrambling to the shore.

55 The Walrus and the Carpenter
    Walked on a mile or so,
And then they rested on a rock
    Conveniently low:
And all the little Oysters stood
60   And waited in a row.

"The time has come," the Walrus said,
    "To talk of many things:
Of shoes—and ships—and sealing-wax—
    Of cabbages—and kings—
65 And why the sea is boiling hot—
    And whether pigs have wings."

"But wait a bit," the Oysters cried,
    "Before we have our chat;
For some of us are out of breath,
70   And all of us are fat!"
"No hurry!" said the Carpenter.
    They thanked him much for that.

"A loaf of bread," the Walrus said,
    "Is what we chiefly need:
75 Pepper and vinegar besides
    Are very good indeed—
Now if you're ready, Oysters dear,
    We can begin to feed."

"But not on us!" the Oysters cried,
80   Turning a little blue.
"After such kindness, that would be
    A dismal thing to do!"
"The night is fine," the Walrus said.
    "Do you admire the view?

85 "It was so kind of you to come!
    And you are very nice!"
The Carpenter said nothing but
    "Cut us another slice:
I wish you were not quite so deaf—
90   I've had to ask you twice!"

"It seems a shame," the Walrus said,

"To play them such a trick,
    After we've brought them out so far,
        And made them trot so quick!"
95 The Carpenter said nothing but
    "The butter's spread too thick!"

"I weep for you," the Walrus said:
    "I deeply sympathize."
With sobs and tears he sorted out
100   Those of the largest size,
Holding his pocket-handkerchief
    Before his streaming eyes.

"O Oysters," said the Carpenter,
    "You've had a pleasant run!
105 Shall we be trotting home again?"
    But answer came there none—
And this was scarcely odd, because
    They'd eaten every one. ○

The walrus and the carpenter have eaten all the oysters, from *Through the Looking Glass and What Alice Found There*, by Lewis Carroll, 1872.

UNIT 4
Reading on Your Own

To read more about the Big Question, choose one of these books from your school or local library. Work on your reading skills by choosing books that are challenging to you.

Fiction

Dragon's Gate
by Laurence Yep

Fantastic characters on thrilling adventures—what more could a reader want? This tale has it all and then some! Read to find out what happens to Otter and Foxfire on "Snow Tiger," a mountain in the Sierra Nevadas, and about the many struggles they face.

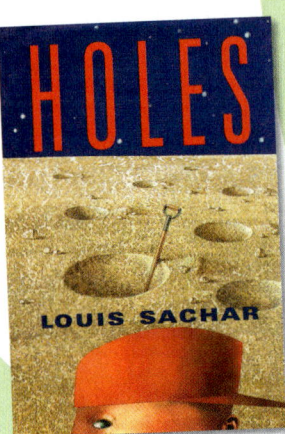

Holes
by Louis Sachar

Funny, crazy, and full of Texas-sized characters, this strange story will leave you cheering for the underdog—whose name is Stanley Yelnats. Read about Stanley's adventures at Camp Green Lake and about the unlikely friends he makes there.

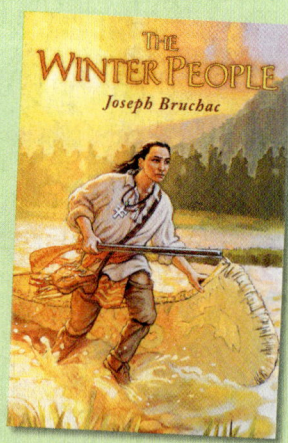

The Winter People
by Joseph Bruchac

When fourteen-year-old Saxo's village is attacked, he must track the raiders and bring his family back home. This book is a story of family, culture, courage, and survival.

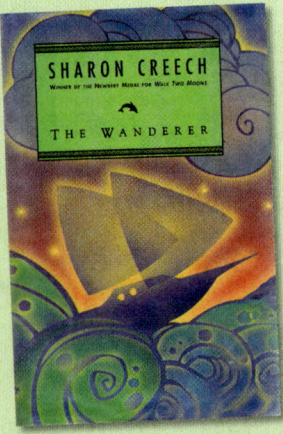

The Wanderer
by Sharon Creech

Thirteen-year-old Sophie enjoys the ride of a lifetime when she sets out on a trans-Atlantic boat ride with her family. Read this tale of globetrotting adventure to find out what Sophie learns, and where she goes, while crossing the stormy sea.

Nonfiction

But That's Another Story: Favorite Authors Introduce Popular Genres
edited by Sandy Asher

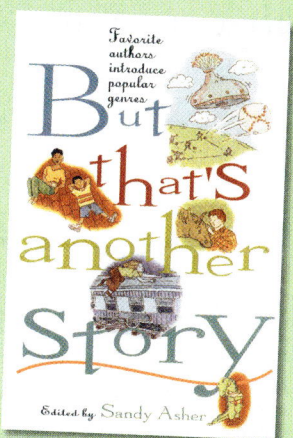

Authors of thirteen short stories discuss writing in such genres as science fiction, fantasy, horror, and realistic fiction. Learn what makes a story from the author who wrote it.

Escape to Freedom: A Play About Young Frederick Douglass
by Ossie Davis

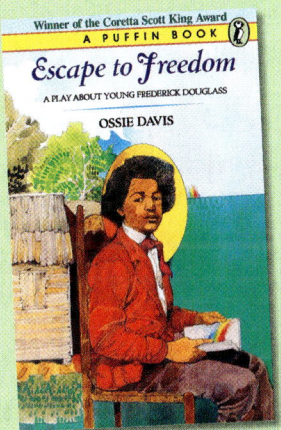

Born a slave, future statesman Douglass endures cruelty and injustice before escaping to freedom. This play brings to life the hardships and triumphs that shaped Frederick Douglass.

The Random House Book of Poetry for Children
by Jack Prelutsky

This collection of poems is divided into sections covering a wide variety of themes—such as seasons, nature, animals, children, and the city. Enjoy this collection of quick and engaging reads!

The World According to Dog: Poems and Teen Voices
by Joyce Sidman

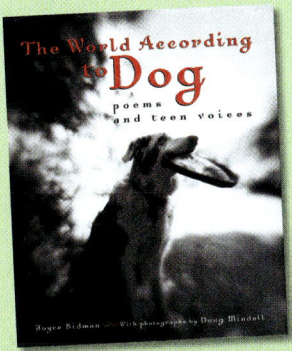

This insightful collection of essays and poems explores the bond between teens and the dogs in their lives. The selections offer a look at how dogs accept us, love us, and help make us who we are.

UNIT 4 SKILLS AND STRATEGIES ASSESSMENT

Test Practice

Part 1: Literary Elements

On a separate sheet of paper, write the numbers 1–5. Next to each number, write the letter of the right answer for that question.

Use the following poem to answer questions 1 and 2.

Afternoon on a Hill

by Edna St. Vincent Millay

I will be the gladdest thing
    Under the sun!
I will touch a hundred flowers
    And not pick one.

5 I will look at cliffs and clouds
    With quiet eyes,
Watch the wind bow down the grass,
    And the grass rise.

And when the lights begin to show
10   Up from the town,
I will mark which must be mine,
    And then start down.

1. This poem is an example of
   A. free verse.
   B. a narrative poem.
   C. a lyric poem with rhyme and rhythm.
   D. a lyric poem with rich figurative language.

2. Which one of the following lines of the poem contains alliteration?
   A. line 1   C. line 9
   B. line 3   D. line 11

Use the following sentences to answer questions 3–5.

1. Angry thunder rumbled in the sky.
2. The wind cut into me like a knife.
3. Steam rose from the still city streets.
4. My fear was a prison, and I could not break out.

3. Which sentence contains a simile?
   A. Sentence 1   C. Sentence 3
   B. Sentence 2   D. Sentence 4

4. Which sentence contains a metaphor?
   A. Sentence 1   C. Sentence 3
   B. Sentence 2   D. Sentence 4

5. Which sentence contains personification?
   A. Sentence 1   C. Sentence 3
   B. Sentence 2   D. Sentence 4

Objectives (pp. 476–477)
Literature Identify poetic features • Identify sound devices: alliteration • Identify literary elements: simile, metaphor, personification
Reading Understand purpose of monitoring comprehension • Interpret text • Respond to poetry • Visualize

SKILLS AND STRATEGIES ASSESSMENT

Part 2: Reading Skills

On a separate sheet of paper, write the numbers 1–5. Next to numbers 1–3, write the letter of the right answer for that question. Next to numbers 4 and 5, write your answers to these questions.

1. If you are having trouble understanding a poem, which part or parts are the best ones to reread?
    A. The first and last lines
    B. The parts you *do* understand
    C. The parts you find most difficult
    D. The parts with the strongest rhythm

Read the following poem and use it to answer questions 2–5.

XXXVIII

by A. E. Housman

Oh stay at home, my lad, and plough*
The land and not the sea,
And leave the soldiers at their drill
And all about the idle hill
Shepherd your sheep with me.

Oh stay with company and mirth*
And daylight and the air;
Too full already is the grave
Of fellows that were good and brave
And died because they were.

---

1. *Plough* is the British spelling of *plow*.
6. *Mirth* means "laughing gladness."

2. What is the main reason the speaker wants the listener to stay at home?
    A. The speaker needs his help with the sheep.
    B. The speaker wants him to remain safe and happy.
    C. The speaker fears that no work will get done if he leaves.
    D. The speaker knows he would do badly at another way of life.

3. All of the definitions shown below are correct meanings of *drill*. What would you interpret to be the meaning this word has in line 3?
    A. "A tool with a pointed end"
    B. "A mental exercise used to improve skill"
    C. "Military marching and practice exercises"
    D. "An approved way to accomplish something"

4. Respond briefly to this poem by telling whether you like it or not and why you feel as you do.

5. Describe one thing you visualize as you read this poem.

UNIT 4 SKILLS AND STRATEGIES ASSESSMENT

Part 3: Vocabulary Skills
On a separate sheet of paper, write the numbers 1–10. Next to each number, write the letter of the right answer for that question.

Write the letter of the word or phrase that means about the same as the underlined word.

1. a <u>perpetual</u> problem
   - A. unusual
   - B. important
   - C. everlasting
   - D. complicated

2. to be <u>stranded</u>
   - A. surprised
   - B. abandoned
   - C. wounded
   - D. overly excited

3. <u>inadequate</u> clothing
   - A. cheap
   - B. unattractive
   - C. not enough
   - D. not suitable

4. an expression of <u>woe</u>
   - A. pride
   - B. excitement
   - C. confusion
   - D. deep sadness

5. to react <u>sullenly</u>
   - A. quickly
   - B. in a gloomy way
   - C. with surprise
   - D. loudly and angrily

Use context clues to figure out the meaning of each underlined word.

6. Unlike her **voluble** friend, Chrissie rarely said a word to anyone.
   - A. rude
   - B. talkative
   - C. smart
   - D. attractive

7. The damage to the vase was **irreparable**; it simply couldn't be mended.
   - A. invisible
   - B. accidental
   - C. not fixable
   - D. done on purpose

8. Marcy **loathed** olives, and I couldn't stand them either.
   - A. hated
   - B. bought
   - C. served
   - D. greedily ate

9. One can find spiders in every **abode**, from inexpensive apartments to huge mansions.
   - A. home
   - B. classroom
   - C. jungle
   - D. container

10. Canes, crutches, and wheelchairs can improve people's **mobility**.
    - A. memory
    - B. understanding
    - C. general health
    - D. ability to move

Objectives (pp. 478–479)
Vocabulary Learn and use new vocabulary • Use context clues
Writing/Grammar Identify sentence types • Use end punctuation correctly • Identify sentence fragments • Identify sentence elements: subject, predicate, direct object

Part 4: Writing Skills

On a separate sheet of paper, write the numbers 1–7. Next to each number, write the letter of the right answer for that question.

1. Which of the following is an exclamatory sentence?
   A. The game was exciting!
   B. Does anyone know this song?
   C. "Just go away," exclaimed Bo.
   D. A patient brother and loyal friend.

2. Which of the following is an imperative sentence?
   A. I didn't mean it!
   B. Open the window.
   C. What a crazy idea.
   D. No one came to the door.

3. Which of the following is a sentence fragment?
   A. The glass is full.
   B. Was the book good?
   C. I broke the window.
   D. Running happily in the yard.

4. Which sentence below has incorrect end punctuation?
   A. That's a surprise!
   B. Did you really say that.
   C. Nobody knew he could sing.
   D. If I asked, would you help me?

5. Which sentence below has a compound predicate?
   A. I took an apple and ate it.
   B. We saw Harry and his brother.
   C. Arabian horses are small but fast.
   D. Reba and Luanne are both runners.

6. What is the complete subject of the sentence below?

   Chickens do not deserve their reputation for stupidity.
   A. Chickens
   B. Chickens do not
   C. Chickens do not deserve
   D. Chickens do not deserve their reputation

7. Which sentence below contains a direct object?
   A. You must be crazy!
   B. She pointed to the sign.
   C. Read the story more slowly.
   D. My dog smells bad when he's wet.

UNIT 5

The BIG Question

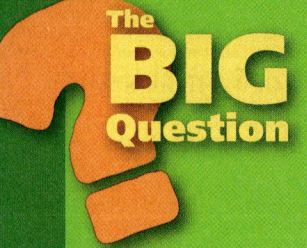

How Should You Deal with Bullies?

"Bullies are always cowards at heart . . ."

—Anna Julia Cooper,
American teacher and writer, 1858–1964

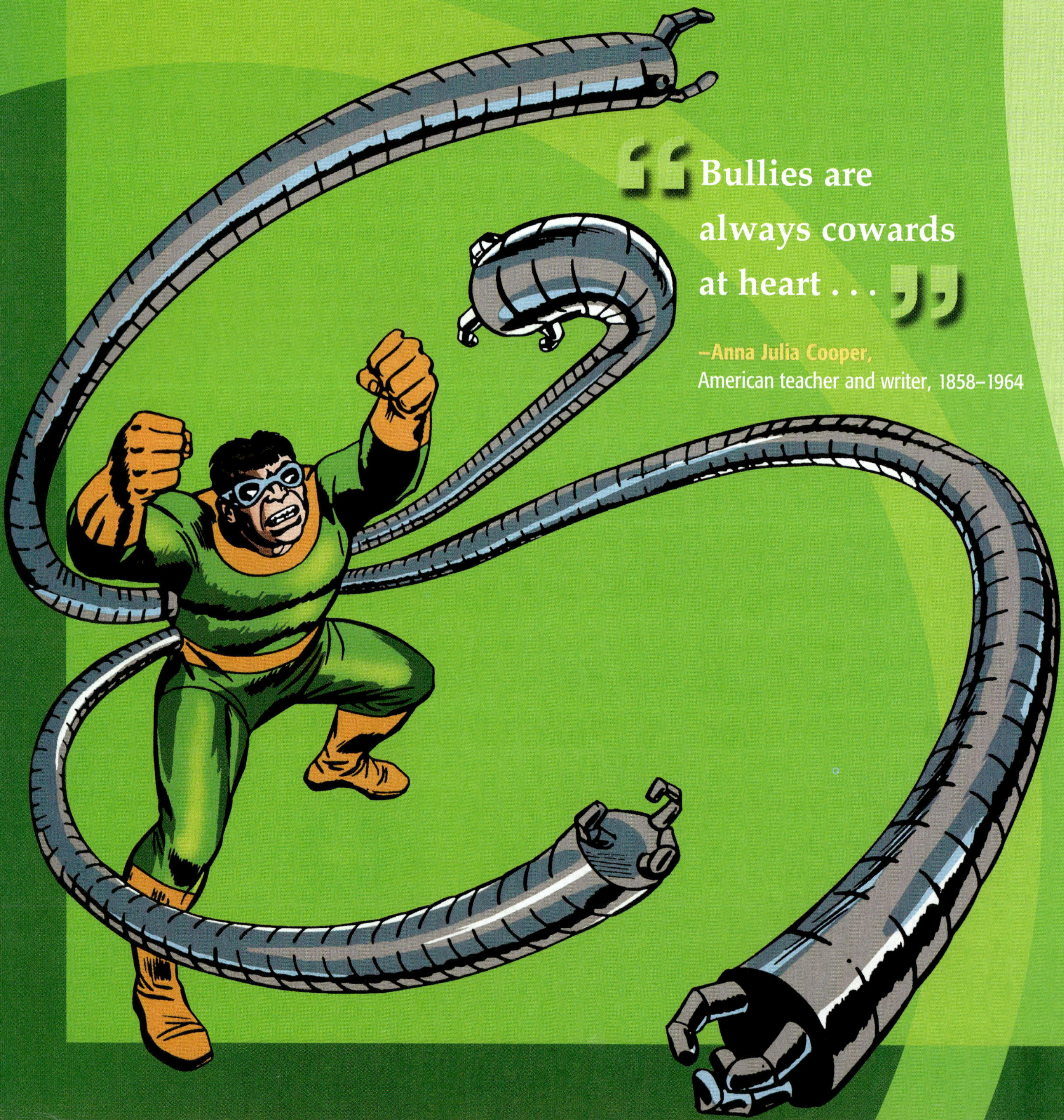

LOOKING AHEAD

The skill lessons and readings in this unit will help you develop your own answer to the Big Question.

UNIT 5 WARM-UP • Connecting to the Big Question
GENRE FOCUS: Short Story

The Fan Club 485
   by Rona Maynard

READING WORKSHOP 1 Skill Lesson: Drawing Conclusions

Street Magic 498
   by Will Eisner

What Kids Say About Bullying 510

WRITING WORKSHOP PART 1 Short Story 516

READING WORKSHOP 2 Skill Lesson: Understanding Cause and Effect

Tuesday of the Other June 524
   by Norma Fox Mazer

My Parents 540
   by Stephen Spender

READING WORKSHOP 3 Skill Lesson: Identifying Sequence

Priscilla and the Wimps 548
   by Richard Peck

Let the Bullies Beware 556
   by Ritu Upadhyay and Andrea DeSimone, from *TIME for Kids*

WRITING WORKSHOP PART 2 Short Story 562

READING WORKSHOP 4 Skill Lesson: Paraphrasing and Summarizing

Don't Let the Bedbugs Bite 570
   by Ellen Conford

The New Kid on the Block 583
   by Jack Prelutsky

READING ACROSS TEXTS WORKSHOP

Bullies in the Park 589
   by Jon Swartz, from *TIME for Kids*

The Bully Battle 593
   by Elizabeth Siris, from *TIME for Kids*

UNIT 5 WRAP-UP • Answering the Big Question

UNIT 5 WARM-UP

Connecting to The BIG Question: How Should You Deal with Bullies?

No one likes bullies. Bullies tease people and call them names. Some bullies hit, kick, or shove people. Dealing with bullies isn't easy. They can make you feel afraid or uncomfortable. In this unit, you'll read about different kinds of bullies and how kids like you handled them.

Real Kids and the Big Question

Lily is having a rough time at school. She has just moved to the neighborhood, and the classroom bully has started to pick on her. The bully likes to grab her backpack and push her around. Lily doesn't know what to do: tell the teacher, tell her parents, or fight back. What advice would you give Lily?

DENNIS is Eric's best friend. But this friendship doesn't seem to mean much to Eric. Eric does everything he can to make Dennis feel small. He makes fun of what Dennis wears and what he says. He's always telling Dennis what to do. When Eric's around other friends, he won't talk to Dennis. Dennis feels confused and hurt. What should he do?

Warm-Up Activity

Make a list of ways you think people can deal with bullies. Write a *L* next to ideas that you think would work best for Lily and a *D* next to ideas that would work best for Dennis. Compare your ideas with a partner's.

UNIT 5 WARM-UP

You and the Big Question

People deal with bullies in different ways. As you read the selections in this unit, think about how you would answer the Big Question.

Big Question Link to Web resources to further explore the Big Question at www.glencoe.com.

Plan for the Unit Challenge

At the end of the unit, you'll use notes from all your reading to complete the Unit Challenge.

You'll choose one of the following activities:

A. Brochure You'll work in a group to create a brochure about ways to deal with bullies.

B. Short Story You'll write a short story that shows how a character deals with a bully in a particular situation. To organize your story, you'll use a story map like the one below.

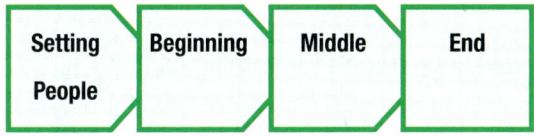

- Start thinking about which activity you'd like to do so that you can narrow your focus as you read each selection.
- In your Learner's Notebook, write your thoughts about which activity you'd like to do.
- Each time you make notes about the Big Question, think about how your ideas will help you with the Unit Challenge.

Keep Track of Your Ideas

As you read, you'll make notes about the Big Question. Later, you'll use these notes to complete the Unit Challenge. See pages R8–R9 for help with making Foldable 5. This diagram shows how it should look.

1. Use this Foldable for the selections in this unit. Label each page with a selection title. (See page 481 for titles.) You should be able to see all the titles without opening the Foldable.

2. Open each tab. Below the title, write **My Purpose for Reading.** You'll write your purpose for reading below this label.

3. A third of the way down on the page, write the label **The Big Question.** You'll write your thoughts about the Big Question below this label.

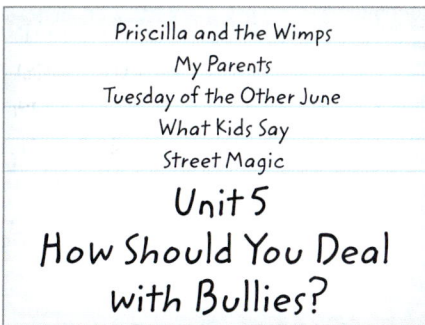

Priscilla and the Wimps
My Parents
Tuesday of the Other June
What Kids Say
Street Magic

Unit 5
How Should You Deal with Bullies?

UNIT 5 GENRE FOCUS: SHORT STORY

A **short story** is a short piece of fictional, or made-up, writing about people, places, and events. You should be able to read a short story in one sitting. A short story shares all the elements of a novel, which includes setting, characters, point of view, plot, and theme.

Why Read Short Stories?

A good short story might teach you something about yourself or others. It might take you away from everything you know. Or it might remind you of people and places you know well. When you read short stories, you'll
- travel to new lands and meet new characters
- learn how characters deal with problems similar to yours

How to Read Short Stories

Key Reading Skills

These reading skills are especially useful tools for reading and understanding short stories. You'll see these skills modeled in the Active Reading Model on pages 485–493, and you'll learn more about them later in this unit.

- ■ **Drawing conclusions** Use the information from your reading to make a general statement about people, places, events, or ideas. (See Reading Workshop 1.)
- ■ **Understanding cause and effect** Look for the causes, or the reasons actions or events happen. Also look for effects—the results of the actions or events. (See Reading Workshop 2.)
- ■ **Identifying sequence** Look for clues or signal words that reveal the order in which events in the story happened. (See Reading Workshop 3.)
- ■ **Paraphrasing and summarizing** Paraphrase what you read by retelling it in your own words. Summarize by retelling the main points and important details in a logical order and in your own words. (See Reading Workshop 4.)

Key Literary Elements

Recognizing and thinking about the following literary elements will help you understand more fully what the writer is telling you.

- ■ **Dialogue:** conversation between characters in the story (See "Street Magic.")
- ■ **Conflict:** the struggle between people, ideas, or forces in the story (See "Tuesday of the Other June.")
- ■ **Plot:** a series of related events in which a problem is explored and then solved (See "Priscilla and the Wimps.")
- ■ **Characterization:** methods a writer uses to develop the personality of a character (See "Don't Let the Bedbugs Bite.")

Skills Focus
- Key skills for reading short stories
- Key literary elements of short stories

Skills Model
You will see how to use the key reading skills and literary elements as you read
- "The Fan Club," p. 485

Objectives (pp. 484–493)
Reading Draw conclusions from text and experience • Understand cause and effect • Identify text structure: sequence • Paraphrase and summarize
Literature Identify literary elements: plot, conflict, dialogue, character

UNIT 5 GENRE FOCUS

by Rona Maynard

The notes in the side columns model how to use the skills and elements you read about on page 484.

Short Story
ACTIVE READING MODEL

It was Monday again. It was Monday and the day was damp and cold. Rain splattered the cover of *Algebra I* as Laura heaved her books higher on her arm and sighed. School was such a bore.

School. It loomed before her now, massive and dark against the sky. In a few minutes, she would have to face them again—Diane Goddard with her sleek blond hair and Terri Pierce in her candy-pink sweater. And Carol and Steve and Bill and Nancy. . . . There were so many of them, so exclusive as they stood in their tight little groups laughing and joking.

Why were they so cold and unkind? Was it because her long stringy hair hung in her eyes instead of dipping in graceful curls? Was it because she wrote poetry in algebra class and got A's in Latin without really trying? Shivering, Laura remembered how they would sit at the back of English class, passing notes and whispering. She thought of their identical brown loafers, their plastic purses, their hostile stares as they passed her in the corridors. She didn't care. They were clods, the whole lot of them. 🟣 🟢

She shoved her way through the door and there they were. They thronged[1] the hall, streamed in and out of doors, clustered under red and yellow posters advertising the latest dance. Mohair sweaters, madras shirts, pea-green raincoats. They were all alike, all the same. And in the

🟣 **Key Literary Element**
Conflict *I can see the conflict already. There's a conflict between Laura and all the cool, snooty kids in her school.*

🟢 **Key Reading Skill**
Drawing Conclusions *I can tell that Laura is not a part of their group, because she calls them "clods." I think she wishes they were nicer.*

---

1. ***Thronged*** means "crowded" or "pressed together in large numbers."

UNIT 5 GENRE FOCUS

center of the group, as usual, Diane Goddard was saying, "It'll be a riot! I just can't wait to see her face when she finds out."

Laura flushed painfully. Were they talking about her?

"What a scream! Can't wait to hear what she says!"

Silently she hurried past and submerged[2] herself in the stream of students heading for the lockers. It was then that she saw Rachel Horton—alone as always, her too-long skirt billowing[3] over the white, heavy columns of her legs, her freckled face ringed with shapeless black curls. She called herself Horton, but everyone knew her father was Jacob Hortensky, the tailor. He ran that greasy little shop where you could always smell the cooked cabbage from the back rooms where the family lived.

"Oh, Laura!" Rachel was calling her. Laura turned, startled.

"Hi, Rachel."

"Laura, did you watch *World of Nature* last night? On Channel 11?"

"No—no, I didn't." Laura hesitated. "I almost never watch that kind of program."

"Well, gee, you missed something—last night, I mean. It was a real good show. Laura, it showed this fly being born!" Rachel was smiling now; she waved her hands as she talked.

"First the feelers and then the wings. And they're sort of wet at first, the wings are. Gosh, it was a good show."

"I bet it was." Laura tried to sound interested. She turned to go, but Rachel still stood there, her mouth half open, her pale, moon-like face strangely urgent. It was as if an invisible hand tugged at Laura's sleeve. 3 4

"And Laura," Rachel continued, "that was an awful good poem you read yesterday in English."

Laura remembered how Terri and Diane had laughed and whispered. "You really think so? Well, thanks, Rachel. I mean, not too many people care about poetry."

"Yours was real nice though. I wish I could write like you. I always like those things you write."

Laura blushed. "I'm glad you do."

ACTIVE READING MODEL

3 Key Literary Element
Characterization *Interesting—a new character appears. The narrator describes Rachel as someone who is not very cool or popular.*

4 Key Literary Element
Dialogue *The way Rachel speaks shows a lot about her character.*

2. **Submerged** (sub MURJD) means "put or went under, as in water."
3. A **billowing** skirt swells out.

"Laura, can you come over sometime after school? Tomorrow maybe? It's not very far and you can stay for dinner. I told my parents all about you."

Visual Vocabulary
An ***awning*** (AW ning) is a cloth or metal cover that acts as a small roof over a door or a window.

Laura thought of the narrow, dirty street and the tattered awning in front of the tailor shop. An awful district, the kids said. But she couldn't let that matter. "Okay," she said. And then, faking enthusiasm, "I'd be glad to come." 5

She turned into the algebra room, sniffing at the smell of chalk and dusty erasers. In the back row, she saw the "in" group, laughing and joking and whispering.

"What a panic!"

"Here, you make the first one."

Diane and Terri had their heads together over a lot of little cards. You could see they were cooking up something.

Fumbling through the pages of her book, she tried to memorize the theorems⁴ she hadn't looked at the night before. The laughter at the back of the room rang in her ears. Also those smiles—those heartless smiles. . . .

A bell buzzed in the corridors; students scrambled to their places. "We will now have the national anthem," said the voice on the loudspeaker. Laura shifted her weight from one foot to the other. It was so false, so pointless. How could they sing of the land of the free, when there was still discrimination. Smothered laughter behind her. Were they all looking at her?

And then it was over. Slumping in her seat, she shuffled through last week's half-finished homework papers and scribbled flowers in the margins.

"Now this one is just a direct application of the equation." The voice was hollow, distant, an echo beyond the sound of rustling papers and hushed whispers. Laura sketched a guitar on the cover of her notebook. Someday she would live in the Village⁵ and there would be no more algebra classes and people would accept her.

5 Key Reading Skill
Understanding Cause and Effect *Maybe Laura feels sorry for Rachel and that causes her to accept Rachel's invitation.*

---

4. **Theorems** (THEER umz) are basic math rules or ideas that can be shown to be true.
5. When Laura talks about the ***Village,*** she means Greenwich Village in New York City.

UNIT 5 GENRE FOCUS

Analyzing the Photo Which characters from the story might these girls be acting like? Explain your answer with details from the story.

She turned towards the back row. Diane was passing around one of her cards. Terri leaned over, smiling. "Hey, can I do the next one?" 6

". . . by using the distributive law." Would the class never end? Math was so dull, so painfully dull. They made you multiply and cancel and factor, multiply, cancel, and factor. Just like a machine. The steel sound of the bell shattered the silence. Scraping chairs, cries of "Hey, wait!" The crowd moved into the hallway now, a thronging, jostling⁶ mass.

Alone in the tide of faces, Laura felt someone nudge her. It was Ellen. "Hey, how's that for a smart outfit?" She pointed to the other side of the hall.

The gaudy⁷ flowers of Rachel Horton's blouse stood out among the fluffy sweaters and pleated skirts. What a

ACTIVE READING MODEL

6 **Key Literary Element**
Plot Those cards they're making must be important to the story. They might have something to do with the plot. I'll keep reading to see how they figure into the story.

6. *Jostling* (JAW sling) means "pushing roughly."
7. *Gaudy* (GAW dee) means "too bright or showy."

lumpish, awkward creature Rachel was. Did she have to dress like that? Her socks had fallen untidily around her heavy ankles, and her slip showed a raggedy edge of lace. As she moved into the English room, shoelaces trailing, her books tumbled to the floor.

"Isn't that something?" Terri said. Little waves of mocking laughter swept through the crowd.

The bell rang; the laughter died away. As they hurried to their seats, Diane and Terri exchanged last-minute whispers. "Make one for Steve. He wants one too!" **7**

Then Miss Merrill pushed aside the book she was holding, folded her hands, and beamed. "All right, people, that will be enough. Now, today we have our speeches. Laura, would you begin please?"

So it was her turn. Her throat tightened as she thought of Diane and Carol and Steve grinning and waiting for her to stumble. Perhaps if she was careful they'd never know she hadn't thought out everything beforehand. Careful, careful, she thought. Look confident. **8**

"Let's try to be prompt." Miss Merrill tapped the cover of her book with her fountain pen.

Laura pushed her way to the front of the class. Before her, the room was large and still. Twenty-five round, blurred faces stared blankly. Was that Diane's laughter? She folded her hands and looked at the wall, strangely distant now, its brown paint cracked and peeling. A dusty portrait of Robert Frost, a card with the seven rules for better paragraphs, last year's calendar, and the steady, hollow ticking of the clock.

Laura cleared her throat. "Well," she began, "my speech is on civil rights." A chorus of snickers from the back of the room.

"Most people," Laura continued, "most people don't care enough about others. Here in New England, they think they're pretty far removed from discrimination and violence. Lots of people sit back and fold their hands and wait for somebody else to do the work. But I think we're all responsible for people that haven't had some of the advantages. . . ." **9**

UNIT 5 GENRE FOCUS

ACTIVE READING MODEL

7 Key Reading Skill
Understanding Cause and Effect *The bell ringing causes the students to quiet down.*

8 Key Reading Skill
Identifying Sequence *Okay, let me recall what's happened so far in the story. It's Monday, and Laura's at school. She thinks the "in" group is laughing at her. Rachel invites her for dinner. She accepts. And now she has to give a speech.*

9 Key Reading Skill
Drawing Conclusions *I think Laura is really talking about the "in" group and the advantages that they seem to have. The "in" group takes advantage of people's weaknesses and no one does anything about it.*

UNIT 5 GENRE FOCUS

Diane was giggling and gesturing[8] at Steve Becker. All she ever thought about was parties and dates—and such dates! Always the president of the student council or the captain of the football team.

"A lot of people think that race prejudice is limited to the South. But most of us are prejudiced—whether we know it or not. It's not just that we don't give other people a chance; we don't give ourselves a chance either. We form narrow opinions and then we don't see the truth. We keep right on believing that we're open-minded liberals when all we're doing is deceiving[9] ourselves." 10

How many of them cared about truth? Laura looked past the rows of blank, empty faces, past the bored stares and cynical[10] grins.

---

8. **Gesturing** (JES chur ing) is using your hands, head, or other part of the body to show your thoughts or feelings.
9. If you are **deceiving** yourself, you are accepting something as true when you know it is false.
10. **Cynical** (SIN uh kul) means "mocking" here.

ACTIVE READING MODEL

10 **Key Reading Skill**
Drawing Conclusions *Laura thinks that the "in" group doesn't give other students a chance and they form opinions about other students without knowing them.*

Analyzing the Photo Does this girl look relaxed and comfortable about giving her report in class? What advice might you give her?

490 UNIT 5 How Should You Deal with Bullies?

"But I think we should try to forget our prejudices. We must realize now that we've done too little for too long. We must accept the fact that one person's misfortune is everyone's responsibility. We must defend the natural dignity of people—a dignity that thousands are denied."

None of them knew what it was like to be unwanted, unaccepted. Did Steve know? Did Diane?

"Most of us are proud to say that we live in a free country. But is this really true? Can we call the United States a free country when millions of people face prejudice and discrimination? As long as one person is forbidden to share the basic rights we take for granted, as long as we are still the victims of irrational[11] hatreds, there can be no freedom. Only when every American learns to respect the dignity of every other American can we truly call our country free."

The class was silent. "Very nice, Laura." Things remained quiet as other students droned[12] through their speeches. Then Miss Merrill looked briskly around the room. "Now, Rachel, I believe you're next." **11**

There was a ripple of dry, humorless laughter—almost, Laura thought, like the sound of a rattlesnake. Rachel stood before the class now, her face red, her heavy arms piled with boxes.

Diane Goddard tossed back her head and winked at Steve.

"Well, well, don't we have lots of things to show," said Miss Merrill. "But aren't you going to put those boxes down, Rachel? No, no, not there!"

"Man, that kid's dumb," Steve muttered, and his voice could be clearly heard all through the room.

With a brisk rattle, Miss Merrill's pen tapped the desk for silence.

Rachel's slow smile twitched at the corners. She looked frightened. There was a crash and a clatter as the tower of boxes slid to the floor. Now everyone was giggling.

"Hurry and pick them up," said Miss Merrill sharply.

11 Key Reading Skill
Paraphrasing and Summarizing The main idea of Laura's speech is that the United States isn't really a free country because many people are treated unfairly. She says that everyone needs to care about how people are treated.

---

11. Something *irrational* (ih RA shuh nul) is not based on reason.
12. *Droned* (drohnd) means "spoke in a dull, boring way."

UNIT 5 GENRE FOCUS

ACTIVE READING MODEL

Rachel crouched on her knees and began very clumsily to gather her scattered treasures. Papers and boxes lay all about, and some of the boxes had been broken open, spilling their contents in wild confusion. No one went to help. At last she scrambled to her feet and began fumbling with her notes.

"My—my speech is on shells."

A cold and stormy silence had settled upon the room.

"Lots of people collect shells, because they're kind of pretty—sort of, and you just find them on the beach."

"Well, whaddaya know!" It was Steve's voice, softer this time, but all mock amazement. Laura jabbed her notebook with her pencil. Why were they so cruel, so thoughtless? Why did they have to laugh?

"This one," Rachel was saying as she opened one of the boxes, "it's one of the best." Off came the layers of paper and there, at last, smooth and pearly and shimmering, was the shell. Rachel turned it over lovingly in her hands. White, fluted sides, like the closecurled petals of a flower; a scrolled coral back. Laura held her breath. It was beautiful. At the back of the room snickers had begun again.

"Bet she got it at Woolworth's,"[13] somebody whispered.

"Or in a trash dump." That was Diane.

Rachel pretended not to hear, but her face was getting very red and Laura could see she was flustered. **12**

"Here's another that's kind of pretty. I found it last summer at Ogunquit."[14] In her outstretched hand there was a small, drab, brownish object. A common snail shell. "It's called a . . . It's called. . . ."

Rachel rustled through her notes. "I—I can't find it. But it was here. It was in here somewhere. I know it was." Her broad face had turned bright pink again. "Just can't find it. . . ." Miss Merrill stood up and strode toward her. "Rachel," she said sharply, "we are supposed to be prepared when we make a speech. Now, I'm sure you remember those rules on page twenty-one. I expect you to know these things. Next time you must have your material organized."

12 Key Literary Element
Dialogue The other kids are making fun of Rachel as she gives her speech. The dialogue shows that they are mean and spiteful. They enjoy making Rachel feel small and unwanted.

---

13. **Woolworth's** was a chain of stores at which people could buy things for low prices.
14. **Ogunquit** (oh GUN kwit) is a seaside town in Maine where people like to vacation.

UNIT 5 GENRE FOCUS

ACTIVE READING MODEL

The bell sounded, ending the period. Miss Merrill collected her books.

Then, suddenly, chairs were shoved aside at the back of the room and there was the sound of many voices whispering. They were standing now, whole rows of them, their faces grinning with delight. Choked giggles, shuffling feet—and then applause—wild, sarcastic, malicious[15] applause. That was when Laura saw that they were all wearing little white cards with a fat, frizzy-haired figure drawn on the front. What did it mean? She looked more closely. "HORTENSKY FAN CLUB," said the bright-red letters. **13**

So that was what the whispering had been about all morning. She'd been wrong. They weren't out to get her after all. It was only Rachel.

Diane was nudging her and holding out a card. "Hey, Laura, here's one for you to wear."

For a moment Laura stared at the card. She looked from Rachel's red, frightened face to Diane's mocking smile, and she heard the pulsing, frenzied rhythm of the claps and the stamping, faster and faster. Her hands trembled as she picked up the card and pinned it to her sweater. And as she turned, she saw Rachel's stricken look. **14**

"She's a creep, isn't she?" Diane's voice was soft and intimate.

And Laura began to clap. **15** ○

---

15. Anything that is *sarcastic* (sar KAS tik) and *malicious* (muh LISH us) is meant to hurt or make fun of someone or something.

13 Key Literary Element
Plot Now I understand what the kids were doing earlier in the story. They were planning to humiliate Rachel all along.

14 Key Literary Element
Characterization The way Laura acts here tells me a lot about her. She's not as strong as I thought. She goes against her ideas about treating people fairly when she joins the others in making fun of Rachel.

15 Key Literary Element
Conflict Laura is torn. She thinks that the group is mean, but she wants its members to like her. In the end, she gives in to the group to be accepted, even though her choice means turning against Rachel.

Think-Pair-Share Think about where and when you might use these skills outside of school: draw conclusions, understand cause and effect, identify sequence, and paraphrase and summarize. Share ideas with a partner. Then gather in a larger group to discuss how you might use these skills in everyday life.

Study Central Visit www.glencoe.com and click on Study Central to review short stories.

READING WORKSHOP 1

Skills Focus

You will practice using these skills when you read the following selections:
- "Street Magic," p. 498
- "What Kids Say About Bullying," p. 510

Reading
- Drawing conclusions

Literature
- Identifying dialogue in a short story
- Recognizing how dialogue helps develop plot, or a story's events
- Identifying author's purpose

Vocabulary
- Using base words to figure out word meanings
- Academic Vocabulary: *conclusions*

Writing/Grammar
- Identifying clauses
- Differentiating between independent clauses and dependent clauses
- Distinguishing between clauses and phrases

Objectives (pp. 494–495)
Reading Draw conclusions from text and experience

Skill Lesson

Drawing Conclusions

Learn It!

What Is It? Don't jump to conclusions! That means don't make a decision without all the facts. When you **draw conclusions**, however, you look at the facts before you make a judgment or decision. When you draw conclusions about your reading, you combine several pieces of information from the reading and your own experience. What you come up with is a conclusion about the people, events, or ideas in that selection.

- A *conclusion* is a judgment you make based on what you know.
- *Drawing conclusions* means creating bigger ideas from the information you read.

BALDO © 2004 Baldo Partnership. Distributed by UNIVERSAL PRESS SYNDICATE. Reprinted with permission. All rights reserved.

Analyzing Cartoons
What conclusion does the girl in the cartoon draw? What has she done to draw that conclusion?

Academic Vocabulary

conclusions (kun KLOO zhunz) *n.* judgments or general statements based on information, experience, and observation

READING WORKSHOP 1 • Drawing Conclusions

Why Is It Important? Drawing conclusions helps you find connections among characters, events, and ideas. It helps you see the bigger picture and understand what you read.

How Do I Do It? To draw conclusions, pay attention to details about characters, events, and ideas. Think about your own knowledge and background. Then combine the story details with your own experience to make general statements about people or events in the story.

Here's how one student used story details and her own experience to draw conclusions while reading the story "The Fan Club."

Study Central Visit www.glencoe.com and click on Study Central to review drawing conclusions.

> School. It loomed before her now, massive and dark against the sky. In a few minutes, she would have to face them again—Diane Goddard with her sleek blond hair and Terri Pierce in her candy-pink sweater. And Carol and Steve and Bill and Nancy. . . . There were so many of them, so exclusive as they stood in their tight little groups laughing and joking.

The speaker uses the words massive *and* dark *to describe her school. She talks about having to* face *a group she describes as* exclusive *and* tight. *I conclude that she feels rejected by the "cool group" and that the situation makes her dread going to school.*

Practice It!

Write a conclusion you can draw from these facts.
1. Margo returns a library book by Will Eisner.
2. Margo checks out three new books by Will Eisner.
3. Margo asks a librarian whether she can place another book by Will Eisner on hold.

Use It!

As you read "Street Magic" and "What Kids Say About Bullying," try to draw at least one conclusion about the characters, events, or ideas in each selection.

READING WORKSHOP 1 • Drawing Conclusions

Before You Read : Street Magic

Will Eisner

Meet the Author
Will Eisner was born in Brooklyn, New York, in 1917. He died in 2005. Eisner was a great storyteller. Many of his stories come from his own experiences growing up in an immigrant neighborhood. Eisner chose to tell his stories with words and pictures in comics and graphic novels. See page R2 of the Author Files for more on Will Eisner.

Author Search For more about Will Eisner, go to www.glencoe.com.

Objectives (pp. 496–505)
Reading Draw conclusions from text and experience • Make connections from text to self
Literature Identify literary elements: dialogue
Vocabulary Identify word structure: base words

Vocabulary Preview

immigrant (IM ih grunt) *n.* a person who comes to live in a country in which he or she was not born **(p. 498)** *Mr. Toledo is an immigrant from Spain.*

hostile (HOS tul) *adj.* unfriendly **(p. 498)** *For your safety, it's best to avoid hostile areas.*

outrages (OUT ray jiz) *n.* violent or cruel acts **(p. 498)** *Bullies were responsible for outrages in the neighborhood.*

authority (uh THOR ih tee) *n.* a good source of information or advice **(p. 498)** *Mersh was an authority on bullies.*

application (ap lih KAY shun) *n.* the act of putting something to use **(p. 498)** *Mersh's kid cousin watched his application of survival skills on the street.*

Write to Learn Write sentences using three of the words correctly.

English Language Coach

Base Words Sometimes you will see a word that you don't recognize. Fortunately, you may know the **base word** in that unfamiliar word. A base word serves as the main part of a word, and it can stand on its own as a complete word. It carries the word's basic meaning. If you know the base word, you can often figure out the meaning of the word you don't know. Look at the word *survival,* for example. It contains the base word *survive.* If you know that *survive* means "to continue to live," you can guess at the meaning of *survival.*

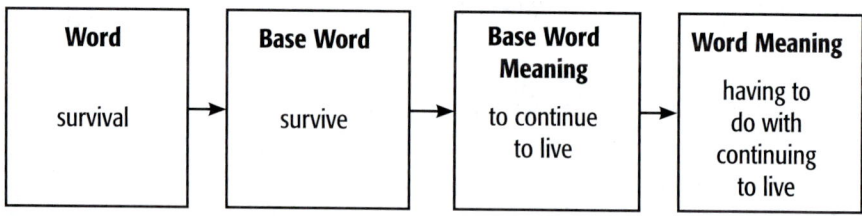

What Do You Know? Write the base words contained in the following words:

1. odorous
2. magically
3. territorial

496 UNIT 5   How Should You Deal with Bullies?

READING WORKSHOP 1 • Drawing Conclusions

Skills Preview

Key Reading Skill: Drawing Conclusions

Skillful readers are always drawing conclusions, or figuring out more than what the author says directly. As you read the next selection, follow these steps to help you draw conclusions:

- First, look at details the author gives.
- Next, combine story details with your own knowledge and experience.
- Then, come up with a general statement about a character, an event, or something else in the story.

What's the Story? Write down an example of a time you have drawn a conclusion when you did one of the following: met a new student at your school; went to the first meeting of a new club; discovered a food you had never tasted; traveled to a new city.

List the reasons that caused you to reach your conclusion.

Key Literary Element: Dialogue

Dialogue is conversation between characters in a story. Writers use dialogue to move a story's plot forward. Most of the writing in a graphic novel is dialogue. The dialogue appears in balloons above or beside the characters' heads.

As you read, use these tips to think about dialogue in the selection:

- Identify the characters who take part in dialogue.
  Which characters speak to one another?

- Think about what you learn from the dialogue. The dialogue may show something about the character's personality, for instance.
  What do the character's words tell you about him or her? Is the character funny, threatening, smart?

Write to Learn Imagine that you and a friend are together in a leaky boat in the middle of a pond. In your Learner's Notebook, write a short dialogue that might take place between you and the friend.

Get Ready to Read

Connect to the Reading

Dealing with a bully is like solving a problem. Have you ever been in a situation when you were babysitting, cooking, or doing a homework project and had a problem? What was the problem? What did you do?

Think-Pair-Share Think about a time when you saw or experienced a situation involving a bully. Share the story with a partner.

Build Background

This selection is from Will Eisner's graphic novel *Minor Miracles*.

- Eisner was one of the first people to use the term *graphic novel* for a longer story told through dialogue and drawings.
- The story he had written was serious, and he didn't want to call it a *comic book*.
- *Minor Miracles* and many of Eisner's other graphic novels tell about the tough situations many kids deal with every day in their neighborhoods.

Set Purposes for Reading

BIG Question Read the selection "Street Magic" to find out how Mersh deals with bullies in his neighborhood.

Set Your Own Purpose What else would you like to learn from the selection to help you answer the Big Question? Write your own purpose on the "Street Magic" page of Foldable 5.

Interactive Literary Elements Handbook
To review or learn more about the literary elements, go to www.glencoe.com.

Keep Moving

Use these skills as you read the following selection.

Street Magic 497

READING WORKSHOP 1

Practice the Skills

Street Magic
by Will Eisner

Immigrant families on our block believed they were in **hostile** territory. Survival skills were brought from the old country. They were kept as magic spells the family used when dealing with the **1** **predictable outrages** of neighborhood life. They were not formally taught. They were learned by emulating older and more experienced family members.

Cousin Mersh, for instance, was an **authority** on the **application** of street magic.

1 English Language Coach

Base Words What does **predictable** mean? The base word *predict* is a clue. If you know that *predict* means "to tell ahead of time," you can guess the meaning of *predictable*.

Vocabulary

immigrant (IM ih grunt) *n.* a person who comes to live in a country in which he or she was not born

hostile (HOS tul) *adj.* unfriendly

outrages (OUT ray jiz) *n.* violent or cruel acts

authority (uh THOR ih tee) *n.* a good source of information or advice

application (ap lih KAY shun) *n.* the act of putting something to use

READING WORKSHOP 1

Practice the Skills

2 Key Literary Element

Dialogue What can you tell about the men so far based on their conversation?

Street Magic **499**

READING WORKSHOP 1

Practice the Skills

3 **Key Literary Element**

Dialogue In a short story, there are usually quotation marks and words that show who is speaking, such as *said John*. Why aren't there quotation marks in this story? How can you tell who is speaking?

500 UNIT 5 How Should You Deal with Bullies?

READING WORKSHOP 1

Practice the Skills

4 **BIG Question**

How does Mersh respond to the bullies' warning that they don't want him and his cousin on their block? (Hint: What doesn't Mersh do?) Write your answer on the "Street Magic" page of Foldable 5. Your response will help you answer the Unit Challenge later.

Street Magic 501

READING WORKSHOP 1

Practice the Skills

5 **Key Reading Skill**

Drawing Conclusions
Can you draw any conclusions about what the bullies might be expecting? What facts have you learned so far? What do you know about bullies?

UNIT 5 How Should You Deal with Bullies?

READING WORKSHOP 1

Practice the Skills

6 **Key Reading Skill**

Drawing Conclusions Look closely at the drawings and think about what you've learned about these bullies. What do you think their attitude is toward Mersh?

Street Magic 503

READING WORKSHOP 1

Practice the Skills

7 **Key Literary Element**

Dialogue The bully says "Er...guilty." How does this piece of dialogue help you learn more about the bully and how he feels now?

8 **Key Reading Skill**

Drawing Conclusions At the beginning of the story, you learn that Mersh is an authority on using street magic. Now you have seen how he responds to the bullies. What conclusions can you draw about Mersh? How did he become an authority?

504 UNIT 5   How Should You Deal with Bullies?

READING WORKSHOP 1

Practice the Skills

9 Key Literary Element

Dialogue What do you learn from the dialogue between Mersh and his cousin?

10 BIG Question

How does Mersh deal with the bullies in this story? Write your answer on the "Street Magic" page of Foldable 5. Your response will help you answer the Unit Challenge later.

Street Magic **505**

READING WORKSHOP 1 • Drawing Conclusions

After You Read

Street Magic

Answering the BIG Question

1. What ideas for dealing with bullies did this selection give you?

2. **Recall** What is Cousin Mersh's special area of knowledge or experience?
   TIP Right There

3. **Recall** What instructions does Mersh give his young cousin while they are out walking?
   TIP Right There

Critical Thinking

4. **Evaluate** Do the bullies treat Mersh "fair and square"? Explain.
   TIP Author and Me

5. **Interpret** Why does the author call the immigrants' survival skills magic spells or street magic?
   TIP Author and Me

6. **Apply** Which of Mersh's ways of dealing with bullies do you think would work best for you?
   TIP On My Own

Write About Your Reading

Pretend you are Mersh. Make a list for the young kids in your neighborhood about ways to deal with the local bullies. To get started with your list, think about

- the advice that Mersh gives his cousin as they enter the "enemy block."
- Mersh's body language as the bullies approach him and talk to him.
- what Mersh says (or doesn't say) to the bullies.
- how Mersh outsmarts the bullies.
- the advice that Mersh gives his cousin as they walk away from the bullies.

Objectives (pp. 506–507)
Reading Draw conclusions from text and experience • Make connections from text to self
Literature Identify literary elements: dialogue
Vocabulary Identify word structure: base words
Writing Respond to literature: list
Grammar Identify sentence elements: independent and dependent clauses

506 UNIT 5   How Should You Deal with Bullies?

READING WORKSHOP 1 • Drawing Conclusions

Skills Review

Key Reading Skill: Drawing Conclusions

When you draw a conclusion about something in a story, you combine story details with your own knowledge and experience to make a general statement.

7. How do the bullies feel about Mersh's response to their trick? How can you tell?
8. After reading this story, what conclusion can you draw about what bullies are like? Support your conclusion with details from the story.

Key Literary Element: Dialogue

9. Which characters use the most dialogue in this story?
10. What does Mersh's lack of dialogue tell you about him as a character?
11. What can you tell about Mersh's cousin from what he says?

Vocabulary Check

Match each vocabulary word with the clue that best describes the word.

| immigrant | outrages | hostile |
| authority | application | |

12. actions meant to hurt someone
13. a person born in Germany who lives in Canada
14. rude and unkind
15. the use of something for a certain purpose
16. an expert
17. **Academic Vocabulary** If you saw people outside wearing heavy jackets and ski hats, what *conclusion* might you draw?
18. **English Language Coach** Rewrite the words listed below and underline the base words in them.

| formation | formal | formula |
| personify | personal | personality |

Grammar Link: Clauses

- A clause (klawz) is a group of words that has a subject and a verb.
- An independent clause expresses a complete thought and can stand alone as a simple sentence.
- A dependent clause expresses an incomplete thought and cannot stand alone as a sentence. A dependent clause doesn't make sense by itself and needs an independent clause to complete its meaning.

Independent clause
The bullies made a plan.

Dependent clause
when they saw Mersh

Independent and dependent clause
The bullies made a plan when they saw Mersh.

Grammar Practice

Decide whether each clause below is dependent or independent. Write D for dependent and I for independent.

19. when they were on an enemy block.
20. because Mersh had a lot of experience on the street.
21. the bullies spoke rudely to Mersh.
22. if the paper had nothing written on it.
23. Mersh swallowed the paper.

Writing Application Look back at the list you wrote. Find or add a sentence that has both an independent clause and a dependent clause. Underline the independent clause once and the dependent clause twice.

Web Activities For eFlashcards, Selection Quick Checks, and other Web activities, go to www.glencoe.com.

Street Magic **507**

READING WORKSHOP 1 • Drawing Conclusions

Before You Read: What Kids Say About Bullying

Vocabulary Preview

subjected (sub JEK tid) *v.* caused to experience; form of the verb *subject* **(p. 511)** *Bullies sometimes subjected others to violence.*

discipline (DIS uh plin) *v.* to punish **(p. 512)** *If no one will discipline bullies, they will keep hurting others.*

surveyed (sur VAYD) *adj.* polled; questioned **(p. 512)** *The kids surveyed said they were scared of bullies.*

Sentence Revision Find the sentences in which the vocabulary words appear in the selection. Then rewrite the sentences, replacing the vocabulary words with a synonym or phrase that has the same meaning. Underline the new words in the sentences.

English Language Coach

Base Words What can you do to unlock the meaning of new words? Be on the lookout for base words. Here's an example. *Operator* includes the base word *operate*. If you know that *operate* is a verb meaning "to perform a task or function," you can guess that the noun *operator* means "one who performs a task or function."

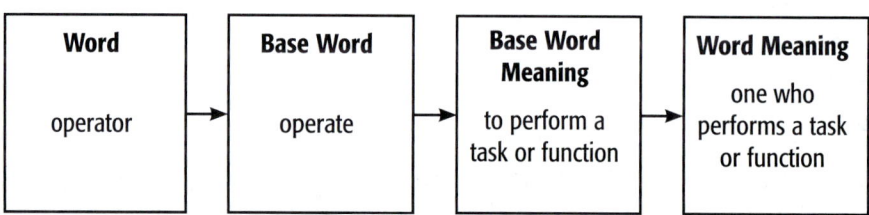

Match Up Use what you know about base words to match each word on the left to its meaning.

1. topical
2. repeatedly
3. problematic
4. victimization

a. difficult to solve or deal with
b. having to do with a particular subject
c. the act of injuring or cheating someone
d. over and over again

- More than 250,000 people a day visit KidsHealth on the Web. It's a great place to learn about health issues affecting children and teens.
- Doctors have approved every piece of information on the site, and it's all up-to-date and easy to understand.
- KidsHealth is divided into separate areas for kids, teens, and parents.
- In addition to articles such as "What Kids Say About Bullying," the kids' area has games and animations.

Objectives (pp. 508–513)
Reading Draw conclusions from text and experience • Make connections from text to self
Literature Identify literary elements: author's purpose
Vocabulary Identify word structure: base words

READING WORKSHOP 1 • Drawing Conclusions

Skills Preview

Key Reading Skill: Drawing Conclusions

You can draw conclusions while reading any kind of text. The following selection is an example of informational text. As you read, you'll use the information from the selection and your own reasoning to form opinions and draw conclusions.

Quickwrite In your Learner's Notebook, explain why you think some people bully others. With your teacher, make a list of the top three reasons given by the students in your class.

Literary Element: Author's Purpose

What's an author's purpose for writing informational text? One purpose is to inform readers about a topic, of course! To find the topic of this selection, just take a look at its title. This selection is about what kids know and think about bullies.

Use these tips to help you think about the author's purpose in writing "What Kids Say About Bullying."

- Look for clues to the author's purpose.

  Does the author state his or her purpose in a sentence or paragraph, or do you have to draw conclusions from what and how he or she writes?

- Identify the audience of the selection.

  Who is the author speaking to? How can you tell this is the audience of the selection?

- Notice the text structure, or pattern of organization.

  How is the text organized? Why has the author organized the text this way?

Write to Learn Write a few sentences about the last thing you read outside of school. Was it an advertisement, an article, a Web site? Think about what the author's purpose might have been for writing about the topic. Was it to inform, persuade, or entertain you?

Get Ready to Read

Connect to the Reading

What kinds of experiences with bullies have you had? Have any of your friends or family members been bullied? Have you ever bullied others? Explain.

Class Poll Take a poll to see how many people in your class have ever been bullied. Write yes or no on a piece of paper, fold it up, and give it to your teacher to count and announce the result.

Build Background

This selection shows that the best way to find out about kids and bullying is to ask kids themselves.

- KidsPoll gathered information about bullying from kids between the ages of 9 and 13.
- The group of kids included an almost equal number of boys and girls.
- About 86 percent of the kids said that they'd seen someone else being bullied.
- Kids said they bully others to be popular, to get their way, or just to push others around.

Set Purposes for Reading

BIG Question Read the selection "What Kids Say About Bullying" to learn about good and bad ways to deal with bullies.

Set Your Own Purpose What else would you like to learn from the selection to help you answer the Big Question? Write your own purpose on the "What Kids Say" page of Foldable 5.

Interactive Literary Elements Handbook
To review or learn more about the literary elements, go to www.glencoe.com.

Keep Moving

Use these skills as you read the following selection.

What Kids Say About Bullying **509**

READING WORKSHOP 1

INFORMATIONAL TEXT
WEB SITE
KidsHealth.org

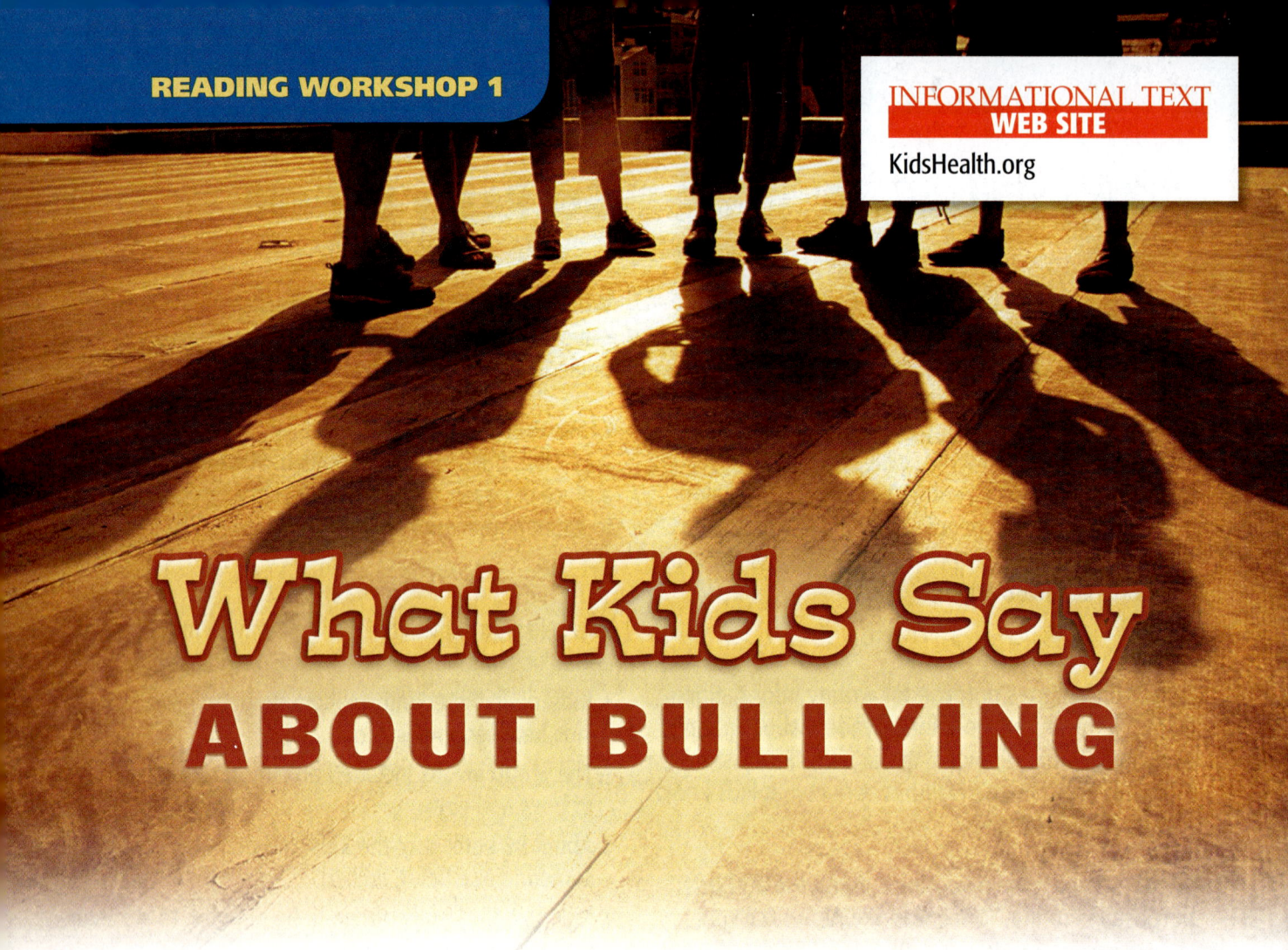

What Kids Say About Bullying

If you have been bullied, you know how bad it feels. But you might not know how many other kids have felt exactly the same way. We were wondering what kids thought about this tough topic so we asked 1,229 boys and girls to answer some questions about bullying. Nearly **half** of them said they had been bullied before. Some said it was happening every day. Others said it only happened once in a while. Here's how the group answered:

How often have you been bullied?
   every day (8%)[1]
   every week, but not every day (7%)
   once in a while, but not every week (33%)
   never (52%) **1**

---

1. The symbol % stands for "percent." See page 513 for more information about percents.

Practice the Skills

1 **Key Reading Skill**

Drawing Conclusions Look at the results of the question that asks how often students have been bullied. What conclusion can you draw from this information about how big a problem bullying is?

The KidsPoll[2] also asked how many of these kids were bullies themselves. Most of them (58%) said they never bullied others, but the rest said that they did.

22% said they bullied others once in a while
5% said they bullied others every week
15% said they bullied others every day

As you have probably guessed, some kids said they were both bullies and the victims of bullies. Why is that? D'Arcy Lyness, a child psychologist,[3] explains it this way:

"Some kids learn to bully because they have been **subjected** to mean, unfair treatment themselves—by others or by their families. That's sad, but it's no excuse," Dr. Lyness says. "Everyone can choose to act in new and better ways. It's never too late."

Most kids know what bullying is. It's when a person is repeatedly mean and hurtful toward someone else, often when that person has trouble defending himself or herself. The bully gets satisfaction (feels good) when he or she gets a **reaction** out of the person being bullied. Like if a bully tells a kid, "You're ugly!" and the kid cries and runs away, that's satisfaction for the bully. 2 3

It can be hard for kids to know what to do if a bully bothers them. About half of the kids said they fight back. There are a lot of problems with this solution. First, one or both of the kids could get hurt. Unlike on TV, where actors are just pretending to fight, when kids punch, kick, and push each other, they can get real injuries, like bruises and cuts and broken bones.

Fighting is also against the rules (both in and out of school), so the two kids could get in trouble even if the bully started the whole thing by bullying. Another reason not to fight is that doesn't really solve the problem. The bully still gets the satisfaction of seeing the picked-on kid get really upset.

---

2. **KidsPoll** gets information about what kids think about a topic by asking certain questions.
3. A **child psychologist** (sy KAWL uh jist) is someone who studies how children think and behave.

Vocabulary

subjected (sub JEK tid) *v.* caused to experience

Practice the Skills

2 English Language Coach

Base Words The base word of *reaction* is *act*. How does the meaning of the base word help you understand what a *reaction* is? Use a dictionary if you need help.

3 Key Reading Skill

Drawing Conclusions Why do some people get satisfaction from bullying others? Combine what you've read so far with your own experiences to draw a conclusion.

READING WORKSHOP 1

But the good news is that more than half of the kids said they did something other than fight. Here's what they said they do:

talk to an adult (25%)
just walk away and do nothing (20%)
try to talk to the bully (8%)

There are two keys to solving bullying, Dr. Lyness says. They are:

1. Kids should tell adults when bullying is happening to them, a friend, or a classmate.
2. Adults should take action to prevent bullying and discipline kids who are bullies.

Grown-ups are important because they can **discipline** kids who are bullies, help kids who have been bullied to build their confidence and strength, and help kids who witness bullying to use their power to change things for the better.

Without cooperation between kids and grown-ups, bullying can be a big problem that doesn't get better. And when no one does anything, the bullied kid can feel worse and worse. In fact, 14% of the kids **surveyed** said being bullied can make them afraid to go to school. 4

So what do kids do when they see someone being bullied? Well, too many of them do nothing (16%) or join in (20%). But the rest of the kids are on the right track. They said they would say or do something to try and stop it (41%) or tell someone who could help (23%).

When kids tell an adult about a bully, it's a way of saying that bullying is **not** cool. Most kids (72%) already know this and said bullies are usually sort of un-cool or very un-cool. But 28% of kids said bullies are either sort of cool or very cool. Don't let bullies get this idea at your school, Dr. Lyness says.

"Kids can support each other by letting a bully know that treating others this way isn't cool or popular," she says.

Practice the Skills

4 BIG Question

What can adults do to help kids deal with bullies? Write your answer on the "What Kids Say" page of Foldable 5. Your response will help you answer the Unit Challenge later.

Vocabulary

discipline (DIS uh plin) *v.* to punish
surveyed (sur VAYD) *adj.* polled; questioned

READING WORKSHOP 1

What's a percentage?

The results of a poll like this one are usually expressed in percentages. A **percentage** is another way of expressing a fraction, **or a part of a whole,** like one slice of a pizza. In this case, the "whole" is all 1,229 kids who participated in the KidsPoll. If 25% (one-fourth) of them said the answer was "talk to an adult" that means about 308 kids answered that way. If 33% (one-third) said "they were bullied once in a while," about 406 kids chose that answer. For each question, all the **percentages** should add up to 100% to reflect the answers from the entire group of 1,229 kids. 5 ○

Practice the Skills

5 Literary Element

Author's Purpose The author of this article wants to inform readers about bullying. What else do you think the author wants to do?

The bully in this photo may have himself been a victim of bullying.

Why is talking with an adult important?

What Kids Say About Bullying **513**

READING WORKSHOP 1 • Drawing Conclusions

After You Read

What Kids Say About Bullying

Answering the BIG Question

1. Did this selection change your ideas about how to deal with bullies? Explain.
2. **Recall** What is bullying?
   TIP Right There
3. **Recall** Besides fighting, name three other ways that kids deal with bullies.
   TIP Right There
4. **Recall** According to Dr. Lyness, what are the two keys to solving the problem of bullying?
   TIP Right There

Critical Thinking

5. **Synthesize** Why do you think fighting is the way many kids deal with bullies?
   TIP Author and Me
6. **Draw Conclusions** How does letting bullies know that they are not cool help stop them from bullying?
   TIP Author and Me
7. **Evaluate** Which way of dealing with bullies do you think works best? Why?
   TIP On My Own

Write About Your Reading

Suppose that you are going to interview one of the kids who took part in the poll. It could be one of the bullies or one of the students who was bullied. Write a list of five questions to ask him or her about bullying. Your questions might start with the words *who, what, where, when, how,* or *why.*

Objectives (pp. 514–515)
Reading Draw conclusions from text and experience
Literature Identify literary elements: dialogue
Vocabulary Identify word structure: base words
Writing Prepare an interview
Grammar Identify sentence elements: clauses, phrases

READING WORKSHOP 1 • Drawing Conclusions

Skills Review

Key Reading Skill: Drawing Conclusions

8. In your Learner's Notebook, write a paragraph about what you've learned from this selection. Start it with one conclusion that you have drawn about bullying. Support your conclusion with information from the text.

Literary Element: Author's Purpose

9. Which sentence or sentences in the selection hint that the author's purpose is to inform?
10. Who is the article's audience? How do you know?
11. How does using a survey serve the author's purpose?

Vocabulary Check

Choose the best word from the list to complete each sentence below. Rewrite each sentence with the correct word.

subjected   discipline   surveyed

12. The boys ___ were of different ages, so the researchers got mixed results.
13. Would a bully have ___ his friend to mean treatment?
14. Only an adult can ___ a bully.
15. **Academic Vocabulary** What *conclusion* have psychologists drawn about why some kids bully other kids?
16. **English Language Coach** Use what you know about the base word in *disciplinary* to explain the word's meaning in this sentence: *Disciplinary actions help stop kids from bullying others.*

Grammar Link: Clauses and Phrases

You have already learned what a **clause** is. It is a group of words that has a subject and a verb. A **phrase**

- does **not** contain both a subject and a verb
- does the job of a single part of speech

Look at this sentence:
The kid in the red baseball cap waited at the corner.

The basic sentence is *The kid waited.* All of the other words in the sentence work to describe or add information to the basic sentence.

The kid **in the red baseball cap** (The phrase in bold does the job of an adjective, describing the kid.)
waited **at the corner** (The phrase in bold does the job of an adverb, describing how the kid waited.)

Phrases can also act as nouns. To identify a phrase, look at the group of words. If it does the job of an adjective, adverb, or noun and it doesn't have a subject *and* a verb, then it is a phrase.

Grammar Practice

Decide whether each group of words below is a clause or phrase. Write a **C** or a **P** next to each.

17. While I was going
18. to the store
19. Benito ran home
20. to do his homework

Writing Application Circle three phrases you used in the writing assignment. Underline the subjects and verbs in three clauses you used.

Web Activities For eFlashcards, Selection Quick Checks, and other Web activities, go to www.glencoe.com.

What Kids Say About Bullying **515**

WRITING WORKSHOP PART 1

Short Story
Prewriting and Drafting

ASSIGNMENT Write a fictional short story about a bully

Purpose To tell a story about dealing with bullies

Audience You, your teacher, and possibly some classmates

Writing Rubric

As you work through this assignment, you should

- make a story guide
- organize a plot
- establish a setting
- create characters and conflict
- correctly use dependent and independent clauses

See page 564 in Part 2 for a model of a short story.

Objectives (pp. 516–519)
Writing Use the writing process: prewrite, draft • Use story elements: plot, setting, main character, conflict
Grammar Use sentence elements: independent and dependent clauses

In this Workshop, you will write a short story about a bully. As you write, you will think about the Unit 5 Big Question: How Should You Deal with Bullies?

A short story is a piece of short fiction. This means that the characters and events in the story are not real. Sometimes fiction writers get their ideas from real life, but they also use their imaginations to come up with the following story elements.

Main Character is the person that the story is about.
Setting is where the story takes place.
Conflict is a problem that the main character must overcome.
Plot is the series of events that happen throughout the story.

Prewriting
Get Ready to Write

Your short story should be about someone who deals with a bully. Follow the directions below to make a short story writing plan. This plan will help you organize your ideas. It will also help you start writing.

Gather Ideas

Character In your Learner's Notebook, write the name of your main character. List some traits or descriptions of your character such as:

- age
- grade
- hobbies
- physical description
- personality
- hopes and fears

Theo
- 11 years old
- 6th grade
- Listening to music
- Brown hair, wears glasses, shortest kid in his class
- Quiet, shy, and smart
- Wants to play the saxophone in a real band

WRITING WORKSHOP PART 1

Setting Decide on a location where your story will take place. Here are some examples of setting:

- house
- neighborhood park
- classroom
- airport
- shopping mall
- community center

Conflict Remember that your story must be about someone who is being bullied. Ask yourself:

- How would a bully treat my main character?
- How could my main character deal with a bully?

Writing Models For models and other writing activities, go to www.glencoe.com.

Applying Good Writing Traits

Organization

Most short stories are made up of five parts called *exposition, rising action, climax, falling action,* and *resolution.* Put together, these parts make a story's **plot**. A **conflict,** or struggle between people, ideas, or forces, is what drives the plot.

What Is Organization?

Organization is the arrangement of events and ideas in a story.

Why Is Organization Important in My Writing?

Organization helps you write your story in an order that will make sense to your readers.

How Do I Organize My Writing?

Use the five stages of plot to organize your story:

Exposition is the beginning of the story. The writer describes the main character and setting and tells the reader about the situation causing the conflict.

Theo Thomas is an eleven year old boy who attends La Hoya Middle School in Coral Springs, Florida. Theo is learning how to play the saxophone and dreams of becoming a professional jazz player. Lately, he has been picked on by a bully named Eric.

Rising Action is a series of two or three events that relate to the conflict and lead to the climax. It is usually the longest part of the story.

1st Event

Theo's MP3 player is stolen at the bus stop by a bigger student named Eric.

2nd Event

The next day at the bus stop, Eric takes Theo's lunch money.

3rd Event

Theo goes to the bus stop. He has his saxophone with him because he has a lesson at school that day.

Climax

Theo refuses to give Eric his saxophone.

Falling Action is what happens to the main character after the conflict is resolved.

Eric leaves Theo alone and goes to talk with some his friends.

Resolution is the end of the story.

Eric doesn't bother Theo at the bus stop any more.

Write to Learn Activity In your Learner's Notebook, write down the five parts of plot and ideas you have for each part in your own story.

WRITING WORKSHOP PART 1

Make a Plan

After you decide on a main character, setting, and conflict, there are a few more details you should plan before you start writing.

Secondary Characters are other characters that appear in your story. These characters may be friends, family, or the source of the conflict.

Point of View describes the way a narrator "sees" or remembers the events. You may decide to write in first-person point of view, in which case the narrator is a character. Or, you may choose to have a narrator that is not a character. This is called third-person point of view.

To organize your ideas, make a Story Plan like the one below. Fill out the plan and use it to help you write your draft.

Writing Tip
If you are having trouble planning your story, talk to a friend. Ask which ideas sound most like a story your friend would want to read.

Writing Tip
Remember that stories written in the first-person point of view are narrated by a character in the story, usually the main character. "I plugged my nose as I toured the farm," is an example of first-person narration.

Writing Tip
Stories that are written in the third-person point of view are narrated by an outside speaker, who tells the events of the story. "Mark plugged his nose as he toured the farm," is an example of third-person narration.

STORY PLAN

Main Character: Theo
Point of View: Third person
Secondary Characters: Eric
Setting: The bus stop
Conflict: Theo keeps getting his belongings stolen at the bus stop by a bully named Eric.

Rising Action
Event 1: Eric takes Theo's walkman.
Event 2: Eric takes Theo's lunch money.
Event 3: Eric tries to take Theo's saxophone.
Climax: Theo refuses to give Eric his saxophone.

Resolution: Eric stops bullying Theo at the bus stop.

Drafting
Start Writing!

Now that you have your story plan filled out, it's time to start writing your draft! Begin by introducing your main character and the setting, then go from there—follow your story plan if you don't know what to write next.

Grammar Link

Independent and Dependent Clauses

What Are They?

An **independent clause** is a group of words that states a complete thought. This group of words contains a subject and predicate. Independent clauses can stand alone as a sentence, or they can be part of a longer sentence.

Independent Clause: Holly was hungry.

Independent Clause: Holly was hungry after basketball practice.

Independent Clauses: Holly was hungry, so **she ate an orange.**

A **dependent clause** is a group of words that has a subject and a predicate, but it cannot stand alone as a sentence. A dependent clause is introduced by one of the words from the chart below.

after	even though	when
although	if	whenever
as	since	where
as if	than	whereas
as though	though	whatever
because	unless	whether
before	until	while

She returned the book **although she hadn't finished it (dependent clause).**

- To tell the difference between an independent clause and a dependent clause, ask yourself whether the clause makes sense by itself.

Independent clauses make sense by themselves; dependent clauses do not.

Complete sentence:
She returned the book. → independent clause

Not a complete sentence:
Although she hadn't finished it. → dependent clause

Why Are They Important?

When you add dependent clauses to independent clauses, your sentences become more interesting.

How Do I Use Them?

Remember that dependent clauses cannot stand alone—they must be linked to an independent clause. Use the words and phrases from the chart to link dependent clauses to independent clauses.

Grammar Practice

Underline the independent clauses and circle the dependent clauses in the following sentences.
1. I don't enjoy roller coasters because they make me dizzy.
2. Maria likes taking long walks before the sun rises.
3. When Ernie's flowers begin growing in July, he spends most of his time in the garden.
4. The teacher watched the children while they were at recess.
5. Since Mona finished first, she won the medal.

Writing Application Review your draft to make sure that all dependent clauses are attached to independent clauses.

Looking Ahead

Part 2 of the Writing Workshop is coming up later. Keep the writing you did here, and in Part 2 you'll learn how to turn your draft into a final product.

READING WORKSHOP 2

What You'll Read

You will practice using these skills when you read the following selections:
- "Tuesday of the Other June," p. 524
- "My Parents," p. 540

Reading
- Understanding cause and effect

Literature
- Identifying and analyzing conflict

Vocabulary
- Identifying suffixes
- Academic Vocabulary: *conflict*

Writing/Grammar
- Identifying parts of speech
- Understanding clauses as parts of speech

Objectives (pp. 520–521)
Reading Understand cause and effect

Skill Lesson

Understanding Cause and Effect

Learn It!

What Is It? Think about this sentence: *A river overflows its banks, and the nearby town floods.* What caused the town to flood? If you answer *a river overflowing its banks,* you're right!

- A **cause** is a person, condition, or event that makes something happen.
- What happens as a result of the cause is the **effect**.

In "The Fan Club," some students put on "HORTENSKY FAN CLUB" signs as Rachel Hortensky finishes her speech. This is a cause. The effect is that Rachel is laughed at by the entire class.

"I wish you hadn't named me Snowball. I'm freezing!"
© 2003 Randy Glasbergen

Analyzing Cartoons
The cat thinks that its name, "Snowball," is a **cause** for its being cold. What do you think is the real cause-and-effect relationship here?

READING WORKSHOP 2 • Understanding Cause and Effect

Why Is It Important? Seeing cause and effect relationships in stories will help you to understand why a character is in a certain situation and the events that led up to that situation. For example, Character A is afraid (cause) so she avoids the source of her fear (effect). Character B senses Character A's fear and seeks her out (cause). Eventually there will be a face-to-face meeting (effect).

Study Central Visit www.glencoe.com and click on Study Central to review understanding cause and effect.

How Do I Do It? You think about cause and effect all the time in everyday life. Why did your friend say that to you? What will happen if you don't do all your chores? Use the same skills as you read a story or poem. Two key questions to keep in mind are
- What is the cause of the action or event?
- What are the possible results, or effects, of the action or event?

Here's how one student thought about cause and effect in "The Fan Club."

> She turned into the algebra room, sniffing at the smell of chalk and dusty erasers. . . . Fumbling through the pages of her book, she tried to memorize the theorems she hadn't looked at the night before.

I bet I know why she's fumbling through her book. It's because she didn't study the night before. If she has a test or quiz, she could get a bad grade because she didn't memorize the theorems.

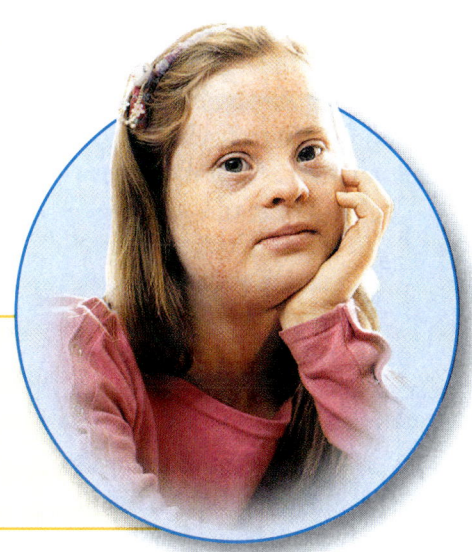

Practice It!

Think of possible causes and effects for the examples below.

Causes		Effects
You ate too much for dinner.	→	_____
_____	→	Your bike got a flat tire.
We fed the stray dog.	→	_____
_____	→	You got a good grade on the test.

Use It!

As you read "Tuesday of the Other June" and "My Parents," take notes in your Learner's Notebook about the cause and effect relationships.

READING WORKSHOP 2 • Understanding Cause and Effect

Before You Read : Tuesday of the Other June

Meet the Author
Norma Fox Mazer has written dozens of novels and short story collections for children and young adults. When talking about her books, Mazer says, "I write and my readers read to find out the answers to questions, secrets, problems, to be drawn into the deepest mystery of all—someone else's life." See page R4 of the Author Files for more on Norma Fox Mazer.

Author Search For more about Norma Fox Mazer, go to www.glencoe.com.

Objectives (pp. 522–535)
Reading Understand cause and effect • Make connections from text to self
Literature Identify literary elements: external and internal conflict
Vocabulary Identify word structure: suffixes

Vocabulary Preview

recited (rih SY tid) *v.* repeated from memory; form of the verb *recite* **(p. 525)** *June recited her mother's advice for dealing with bullies.*

rigid (RIJ id) *adj.* stiff **(p. 525)** *When June felt afraid of the dark, she would lie under the covers with her body rigid.*

bureau (BYUR oh) *n.* a low chest of drawers **(p. 529)** *June kept winter sweaters in a bureau by her bed.*

Partner Talk With a partner, take turns calling out a vocabulary word and having your partner give the definition, or call out the definition and have the partner give the word. Next, trade off using the words correctly in sentences.

English Language Coach

Suffixes A suffix is a word part added to the end of a word. Sometimes adding a suffix greatly changes the meaning of a word. For example, adding the suffix *-less* to the word *joy* makes *joyless,* which describes a person without joy. Often, though, a suffix changes the meaning just a little. Many suffixes just change words from one part of speech to another.

Suffixes	Words	Meanings
-er means "one who," "that which," or "more"	runner	one who runs
	toaster	that which makes toast
	weaker	more weak
-or means "one who"	actor	one who acts
	conductor	one who conducts
-ful means "full of"	graceful	full of grace
	youthful	full of youth
-less means "without"	hairless	without hair
	spineless	without a spine
-able means "can be" or "having quality of"	believable	can be believed
	washable	can be washed
	valuable	having value

Partner Talk With a partner, take turns identifying the part of speech of each example word above with and without its suffix.

522 UNIT 5 How Should You Deal with Bullies?

READING WORKSHOP 2 • Understanding Cause and Effect

Skills Preview

Key Reading Skill: Understanding Cause and Effect

In "Tuesday of the Other June," Norma Fox Mazer uses **cause** and **effect** by describing how characters deal with situations and how they cope with the effects of those events. The way characters relate to each other has a lot to do with the outcome of each new situation. As you read, ask yourself these questions:

- Why do the characters behave the way they do?
- What are the effects of their actions?

Write to Learn Write down a possible cause and effect for *each* of these situations: 1. Someone picks on you at school; 2. You move and have to go to a new school.

Key Literary Element: Conflict

Conflict is an important part of a story. Conflicts often create the events that characters must deal with.

When characters have **external conflicts**, they struggle with something outside themselves, such as another character, nature, the community, or even fate.

When characters have **internal conflicts**, they struggle against something inside themselves. Characters might have internal conflicts about how they act or feel.

As you read, use these tips to understand the conflicts in "Tuesday of the Other June":

- Look for external conflicts between characters.
  How does the "Other June" treat the narrator?
- Look for the characters' internal conflicts.
  What actions or feelings does the narrator struggle with in her mind?

Write to Learn Copy the questions above in your Learner's Notebook and answer them as you read.

Academic Vocabulary

conflict (KAHN flikt) *n.* a struggle between opposing forces

Get Ready to Read

Connect to the Reading

Have you ever had a problem with a bully that you just couldn't get rid of? Maybe you saw the bully just about everywhere, and even the advice of a parent or teacher just didn't work. How did you deal with the bully?

Write to Learn Write about what you should do if the advice that a parent, teacher, or friend gives you about dealing with a bully just doesn't work. Think about reasons the advice might not work. What should you do? Who could you go to?

Build Background

You will see the names April, May, and June in the story. Our months get their names from the calendar used by the ancient Romans.

Set Purposes for Reading

BIG Question Read "Tuesday of the Other June" to find out how the narrator deals with a bully who won't go away.

Set Your Own Purpose What would you like to learn from the story to help you answer the Big Question? Write your own purpose on the "Tuesday of the Other June" page of Foldable 5.

Interactive Literary Elements Handbook
To review or learn more about the literary elements, go to www.glencoe.com.

Keep Moving

Use these skills as you read the following selection.

Tuesday of the Other June **523**

READING WORKSHOP 2

Tuesday of the Other June

by Norma Fox Mazer

"Be good, be good, be good, be good, my Junie," my mother sang as she combed my hair; a song, a story, a croon, a plea. "It's just you and me, two women alone in the world, June darling of my heart; we have enough troubles getting by, we surely don't need a single one more, so you keep your sweet self out of fighting and all that bad stuff. People can be little-hearted, but turn the other cheek, smile at the world, and the world'll surely smile back." **1**

We stood in front of the mirror as she combed my hair, combed and brushed and smoothed. Her head came just above mine; she said when I grew another inch, she'd stand on a stool to brush my hair. "I'm not giving up this pleasure!" And she laughed her long honey laugh.

Practice the Skills

1 **Key Reading Skill**

Understanding Cause and Effect June's mother says that they have troubles just getting by and they don't need any more. What might be one effect of having so many troubles? Think about what June's mother asks her not to do.

READING WORKSHOP 2

My mother was April, my grandmother had been May, I was June. "And someday," said my mother, "you'll have a daughter of your own. What will you name her?"

"January!" I'd yell when I was little. "February! No, November!" My mother laughed her honey laugh. She had little emerald[1] eyes that warmed me like the sun.

Every day when I went to school, she went to work. "Sometimes I stop what I'm doing," she said, "lay down my tools, and stop everything, because all I can think about is you. Wondering what you're doing and if you need me. Now, Junie, if anyone ever bothers you—"

"—I walk away, run away, come on home as fast as my feet will take me," I recited.

"Yes. You come to me. You just bring me your trouble, because I'm here on this earth to love you and take care of you."

I was safe with her. Still, sometimes I woke up at night and heard footsteps slowly creeping up the stairs. It wasn't my mother, she was asleep in the bed across the room, so it was robbers, thieves, and murderers, creeping slowly . . . slowly . . . slowly toward my bed.

I stuffed my hand into my mouth. If I screamed and woke her, she'd be tired at work tomorrow. The robbers and thieves filled the warm darkness and slipped across the floor more quietly than cats. Rigid under the covers, I stared at the shifting dark and bit my knuckles and never knew when I fell asleep again. 2

In the morning we sang in the kitchen. "Bill Grogan's goat! Was feelin' fine! Ate three red shirts, right off the line!" I made sandwiches for our lunches, she made pancakes for breakfast, but all she ate was one pancake and a cup of coffee. "Gotta fly, can't be late."

Practice the Skills

2 **Key Reading Skill**

Understanding Cause and Effect June stuffs her hand into her mouth instead of screaming. She says she does this so she won't wake her mother. If June's mother were awakened in the middle of the night, what would be the effect the next day?

"Be good, be good, be good, be good, my Junie," my mother sang . . .

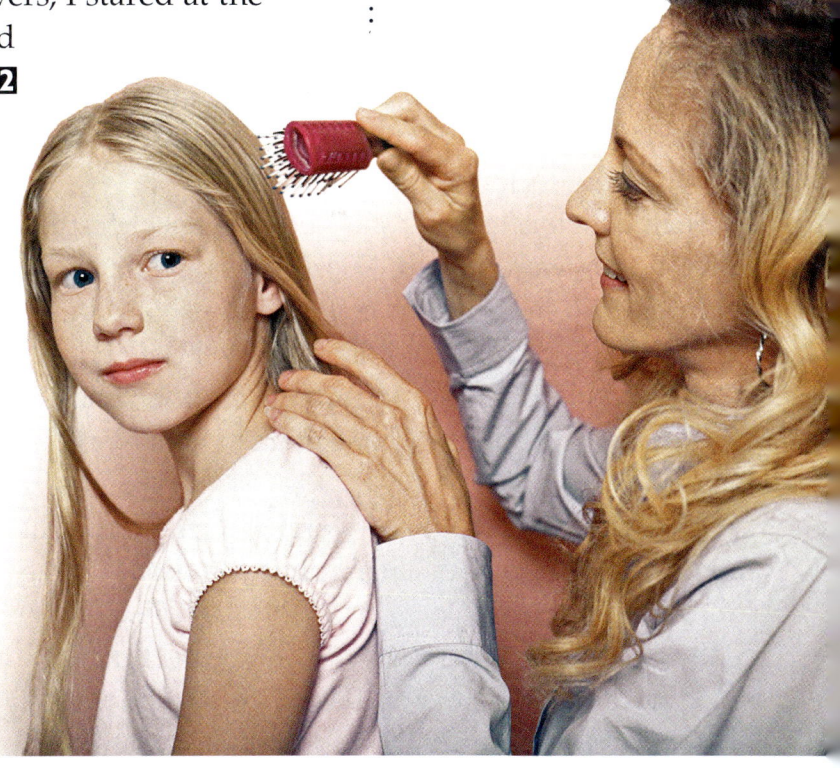

---

1. **Emerald** is a deep green color.

Vocabulary

recited (rih SY tid) v. repeated from memory
rigid (RIJ id) adj. stiff

READING WORKSHOP 2

Analyzing the Photo
Look closely at this girl's face. What do you think she is feeling? Explain.

I wanted to be rich and take care of her. She worked too hard; her pretty hair had gray in it that she joked about. "Someday," I said, "I'll buy you a real house, and you'll never work in a pot factory again."

"Such delicious plans," she said. She checked the windows to see if they were locked. "Do you have your key?"

I lifted it from the chain around my neck.

"And you'll come right home from school and—"

"—I won't light fires or let strangers into the house, and I won't tell anyone on the phone that I'm here alone," I finished for her. 3

"I know, I'm just your old worrywart mother." She kissed me twice, once on each cheek. "But you are my June, my only June, the only June."

She was wrong; there was another June. I met her when we stood next to each other at the edge of the pool the first day of swimming class in the Community Center.

Practice the Skills

3 **Key Reading Skill**

Understanding Cause and Effect June's mother makes sure the windows are locked and makes sure June will come right home after school. What effect does she want to happen?

READING WORKSHOP 2

"What's your name?" She had a deep growly voice.
"June. What's yours?"
She stared at me. "June."
"We have the same name."
"No we don't. June is my name, and I don't give you permission to use it. Your name is Fish Eyes." She pinched me hard. "Got it, Fish Eyes?"

The next Tuesday, the Other June again stood next to me at the edge of the pool. "What's your name?"
"June."
"Wrong. Your—name—is—Fish—Eyes."
"June."
"Fish Eyes, you are really stupid." She shoved me into the pool.

The swimming **teacher** looked up, frowning, from her chart. "No one in the water yet." 4

Practice the Skills

4 **English Language Coach**
Suffixes The suffix *-er* is added to *teach* to make the word **teacher.** How does the suffix change the meaning of *teach*?

Later, in the locker room, I dressed quickly and wrapped my wet suit in the towel. The Other June pulled on her jeans. "You guys see that bathing suit Fish Eyes was wearing? Her mother found it in a trash can."

"She did not!"

The Other June grabbed my fingers and twisted. "Where'd she find your bathing suit?"

"She bought it, let me go."

"Poor little stupid Fish Eyes is crying. Oh, boo hoo hoo, poor little Fish Eyes."

After that, everyone called me Fish Eyes. And every Tuesday, wherever I was, there was also the Other June—at the edge of the pool, in the pool, in the locker room. In the water, she swam alongside me, blowing and huffing, knocking into me. In the locker room, she stepped on my feet, pinched my arms, hid my blouse, and knotted my braids together. She had large square teeth; she was shorter than I was, but heavier, with bigger bones and square hands. If I met her outside on the street, carrying her bathing suit and towel, she'd walk toward me, smiling a square, friendly smile. "Oh well, if it isn't Fish Eyes." Then she'd punch me, blam! her whole solid weight hitting me. 5

I didn't know what to do about her. She was training me like a dog. After a few weeks of this, she only had to look at me, only had to growl, "I'm going to get you, Fish Eyes," for my heart to slink like a whipped dog down into my stomach. My arms were covered with bruises. When my mother noticed, I made up a story about tripping on the sidewalk.

My weeks were no longer Tuesday, Wednesday, Thursday, and so on. Tuesday was Awfulday. Wednesday was Badday. (The Tuesday bad feelings were still there.) Thursday was Betterday, and Friday was Safeday. Saturday was Goodday, but Sunday was Toosoonday, and Monday—Monday was nothing but the day before Awfulday. 6

I tried to slow down time. Especially on the weekends, I stayed close by my mother, doing everything with her, shopping, cooking, cleaning, going to the Laundromat. "Aw, sweetie, go play with your friends."

"No, I'd rather be with you." I wouldn't look at the clock or listen to the radio (they were always telling you the date and the time). I did special magic things to keep the day from

Practice the Skills

5 Key Literary Element

Conflict Remember that an external conflict is a struggle against something outside of oneself. What external conflict does June deal with?

6 Key Reading Skill

Understanding Cause and Effect The narrator says that she has renamed the days of the week. This is an effect. What do you think causes her to rename the days?

going away, rapping my knuckles six times on the bathroom door six times a day and never, ever touching the chipped place on my **bureau**. But always I woke up to the day before Tuesday, and always, no matter how many times I circled the worn spot in the living-room rug or counted twenty-five cracks in the ceiling, Monday disappeared and once again it was Tuesday.

The Other June got bored with calling me Fish Eyes. Buffalo Brain came next, but as soon as everyone knew that, she renamed me Turkey Nose.

Now at night it wasn't robbers creeping up the stairs, but the Other June, coming to torment me. When I finally fell asleep, I dreamed of kicking her, punching, biting, pinching. In the morning I remembered my dreams and felt brave and strong. And then I remembered all the things my mother had taught me and told me.

Be good, be good, be good; it's just us two women alone in the world. . . . Oh, but if it weren't, if my father wasn't long gone, if we'd had someone else to fall back on, if my mother's mother and daddy weren't dead all these years, if my father's daddy wanted to know us instead of being glad to forget us—oh, then I would have punched the Other June with a frisky heart, I would have grabbed her arm at poolside and bitten her like the dog she had made of me. **7**

One night, when my mother came home from work, she said, "Junie, listen to this. We're moving!"

Alaska, I thought. Florida. Arizona. Someplace far away and wonderful, someplace without the Other June.

"Wait till you hear this deal. We are going to be caretakers, trouble-shooters for an eight-family apartment building. Fifty-six Blue Hill Street. Not janitors; we don't do any of the heavy work. April and June, Trouble-shooters, Incorporated. If a tenant has a complaint or a problem, she comes to us and we either take care of it or call the janitor for service. And for that little bit of work, we get to live rent free!" She swept me around in a dance. "Okay? You like it? I do!"

Vocabulary

bureau (BYUR oh) *n.* a low chest of drawers

Practice the Skills

7 Reviewing Skills

Inferring It's just June and her mother; her grandparents are not a part of her life and her father is "long gone." How do you think this makes June feel? How do you think it affects her view of the world?

READING WORKSHOP 2

So. Not anywhere else, really. All the same, maybe too far to go to swimming class? "Can we move right away? Today?"

"Gimme a break, sweetie. We've got to pack, do a thousand things. I've got to line up someone with a truck to help us. Six weeks, Saturday the fifteenth." She circled it on the calendar. It was the Saturday after the last day of swimming class.

Soon, we had boxes lying everywhere, filled with clothes and towels and glasses wrapped in newspaper. Bit by bit, we cleared the rooms, leaving only what we needed right now. The dining-room table staggered on a bunched-up rug, our bureaus inched toward the front door like patient cows. On the calendar in the kitchen, my mother marked off the days until we moved, but the only days I thought about were Tuesdays—Awfuldays. Nothing else was real except the too fast passing of time, moving toward each Tuesday . . . away from Tuesday . . . toward Tuesday . . .

And it seemed to me that this would go on forever, that Tuesdays would come forever and I would be forever trapped by the side of the pool, the Other June whispering Buffalo Brain Fish Eyes Turkey Nose into my ear, while she ground her elbow into my side and smiled her square smile at the swimming teacher. 8

And then it ended. It was the last day of swimming class. The last Tuesday. We had all passed our tests, and, as if in celebration, the Other June only pinched me twice. "And now," our swimming teacher said, "all of you are ready for the Advanced Class, which starts in just one month. I have a sign-up slip here. Please put your name down before you leave." Everyone but me crowded around. I went to the locker room and pulled on my clothes as fast as possible. The Other June burst through the door just as I was leaving. "Goodbye," I yelled, "good riddance to bad trash!" Before she could pinch me again, I ran past her and then ran all the way home, singing, "Goodbye . . . goodbye . . . goodbye, good riddance to bad trash!" 9

Later, my mother carefully untied the blue ribbon around my swimming class diploma.² "Look at this! Well, isn't this wonderful! You are on your way, you might turn into an Olympic swimmer, you never know what life will bring."

---

2. A *diploma* is a document that shows the completion of a course of study.

Practice the Skills

8 Key Reading Skill

Understanding Cause and Effect Think about how June is feeling. What is the main cause of her feelings?

9 Key Reading Skill

Understanding Cause and Effect June's decision to not sign up for swimming lessons is an effect. What causes June to decide she does not want to sign up for more swimming lessons?

"I don't want to take more lessons."

"Oh, sweetie, it's great to be a good swimmer." But then, looking into my face, she said, "No, no, no, don't worry, you don't have to."

The next morning, I woke up hungry for the first time in weeks. No more swimming class. No more Baddays and Awfuldays. No more Tuesdays of the Other June. In the kitchen, I made hot cocoa to go with my mother's corn muffins. "It's Wednesday, Mom," I said, stirring the cocoa. "My favorite day."

"Since when?"

"Since this morning." I turned on the radio so I could hear the announcer tell the time, the temperature, and the day.

Thursday for breakfast I made cinnamon toast, Friday my mother made pancakes, and on Saturday, before we moved, we ate the last slices of bread and cleaned out the peanut butter jar.

"Some breakfast," Tilly said. "Hello, you must be June." She shook my hand. She was a friend of my mother's from work; she wore big hoop earrings, sandals, and a skirt as dazzling as a rainbow. She came in a truck with John to help us move our things. **10**

10 Key Reading Skill

Understanding Cause and Effect Moving can have many different effects. June thinks the effects will be good. What are some negative effects of moving to another place?

John shouted cheerfully at me, "So you're moving." An enormous man with a face covered with little brown bumps. Was he afraid his voice wouldn't travel the distance from his mouth to my ear? "You looking at my moles?" he shouted, and he heaved our big green flowered chair down the stairs. "Don't worry, they don't bite. Ha, ha, ha!" Behind him came my mother and Tilly balancing a bureau between them, and behind them I carried a lamp and the round, flowered Mexican tray that was my mother's favorite. She had found it at a garage sale and said it was as close to foreign travel as we would ever get.

The night before, we had loaded our car, stuffing in bags and boxes until there was barely room for the two of us. But it was only when we were in the car, when we drove past Abdo's Grocery, where they always gave us credit, when I turned for a last look at our street—it was only then that I understood we

READING WORKSHOP 2

were truly going to live somewhere else, in another apartment, in another place mysteriously called Blue Hill Street.

Tilly's truck followed our car.

"Oh, I'm so excited," my mother said. She laughed. "You'd think we were going across the country."

Our old car wheezed up a long, steep hill. Blue Hill Street. I looked from one side to the other, trying to see everything.

My mother drove over the crest of the hill. "And now—ta da!—our new home!"

"Which house? Which one?" I looked out the window and what I saw was the Other June. She was sprawled on the stoop of a pink house, lounging back on her elbows, legs outspread, her jaws working on a wad of gum. I slid down into the seat, but it was too late. I was sure she had seen me.

My mother turned into a driveway next to a big white building with a tiny porch. She leaned on the steering wheel. "See that window there, that's our living-room window . . . and that one over there, that's your bedroom . . ."

We went into the house, down a dim, cool hall. In our new apartment, the wooden floors clicked under our shoes, and my mother showed me everything. Her voice echoed in the empty rooms. I followed her around in a daze. Had I imagined seeing the Other June? Maybe I'd seen another girl who looked like her. A double. That could happen.

"Ho yo, where do you want this chair?" John appeared in the doorway. We brought in boxes and bags and beds and stopped only to eat pizza and drink orange juice from the carton.

"June's so quiet, do you think she'll adjust all right?" I heard Tilly say to my mother.

"Oh, definitely. She'll make a wonderful **adjustment**. She's just getting used to things."

But I thought that if the Other June lived on the same street as I did, I would never get used to things. 11 12

That night I slept in my own bed, with my own pillow and blanket, but with floors that creaked in strange voices and walls with cracks I didn't recognize. I didn't feel either happy or unhappy. It was as if I were waiting for something.

Practice the Skills

11 Key Reading Skill

Understanding Cause and Effect June has been looking forward to moving, but now something has changed her mind. What causes her to change her mind? What effect does it have on her?

12 English Language Coach

Suffixes June's mother adds the suffix -ment to the verb *adjust* in order to form the noun **adjustment**. When you attach -ment to a verb, you make a noun. Think of two other examples of words formed by adding -ment to a verb. Write them in your Learner's Notebook.

532 UNIT 5 How Should You Deal with Bullies?

READING WORKSHOP 2

Monday, when the principal of Blue Hill Street School left me in Mr. Morrisey's classroom, I knew what I'd been waiting for. In that room full of strange kids, there was one person I knew. She smiled her square smile, raised her hand, and said, "She can sit next to me, Mr. Morrisey."

"Very nice of you, June M. OK, June T., take your seat. I'll try not to get you two Junes mixed up."

I sat down next to her. She pinched my arm. "Good riddance to bad trash," she mocked.

I was back in the Tuesday swimming class, only now it was worse, because every day would be Awfulday. The pinching had already started. Soon, I knew, on the playground and in the halls, kids would pass me, grinning. "Hiya, Fish Eyes."

The Other June followed me around during recess that day, droning in my ear, "You are my slave, you must do everything I say, I am your master, say it, say, 'Yes, master, you are my master.'"

I pressed my lips together, clapped my hands over my ears, but without hope. Wasn't it only a matter of time before I said the hateful words?

"How was school?" my mother said that night.

"OK."

She put a pile of towels in a bureau drawer. "Try not to be sad about missing your old friends, sweetie; there'll be new ones."

The next morning, the Other June was waiting for me when I left the house. "Did your mother get you that blouse in the garbage dump?" She butted me, shoving me against a tree. "Don't you speak anymore, Fish Eyes?" Grabbing my chin in her hands, she pried open my mouth. "Oh, ha ha, I thought you lost your tongue." **13**

We went on to school. I sank down into my seat, my head on my arms. "June T., are you all right?" Mr. Morrisey asked. I nodded. My head was almost too heavy to lift.

The Other June went to the pencil sharpener. Round and round she whirled the handle. Walking back, looking at me, she held the three sharp pencils like three little knives.

Practice the Skills

13 BIG Question

The conflict between June and the "Other June" gets worse every day. Do you think June should confront her bully now? Or should she wait? Write your answer on your Foldable.

Tuesday of the Other June 533

READING WORKSHOP 2

Analyzing the Photo Which character in the story might this man look like? How do you know?

Someone knocked on the door. Mr. Morrisey went out into the hall. Paper planes burst into the air, flying from desk to desk. Someone turned on a transistor radio. And the Other June, coming closer, smiled and licked her lips like a cat sleepily preparing to gulp down a mouse.

I remembered my dream of kicking her, punching, biting her like a dog.

Then my mother spoke quickly in my ear: Turn the other cheek, my Junie; smile at the world, and the world'll surely smile back.

But I had turned the other cheek and it was slapped. I had smiled and the world hadn't smiled back. I couldn't run home as fast as my feet would take me. I had to stay in school—and in school there was the Other June. Every morning, there would be the Other June, and every afternoon, and every day, all day, there would be the Other June. 🔳

Practice the Skills

14 **Key Literary Element**

Conflict This paragraph lists many conflicts. What is the main reason for all of them? Is the main reason an internal conflict, an external conflict, or both?

READING WORKSHOP 2

She frisked down the aisle, stabbing the pencils in the air toward me. A boy stood up on his desk and bowed. "My fans," he said, "I greet you." My arm twitched and throbbed, as if the Other June's pencils had already poked through the skin. She came closer, smiling her Tuesday smile.

"No," I whispered, "no." The word took wings and flew me to my feet, in front of the Other June. "Noooooo." It flew out of my mouth into her surprised face.

The boy on the desk turned toward us. "You said something, my devoted fans?"

"No," I said to the Other June. "Oh, no! No. No. No. No more." I pushed away the hand that held the pencils.

The Other June's eyes opened, popped wide like the eyes of somebody in a cartoon. It made me laugh. The boy on the desk laughed, and then the other kids were laughing, too.

"No," I said again, because it felt so good to say it. "No, no, no, no." I leaned toward the Other June, put my finger against her chest. Her cheeks turned red, she squawked something—it sounded like "Eeeraaghyou!"—and she stepped back. She stepped away from me.

The door banged, the airplanes disappeared, and Mr. Morrisey walked to his desk. "OK. OK. Let's get back to work. Kevin Clark, how about it?" Kevin jumped off the desk, and Mr. Morrisey picked up a piece of chalk. "All right, class—" He stopped and looked at me and the Other June. "You two Junes, what's going on there?"

I tried it again. My finger against her chest. Then the words. "No—more." And she stepped back another step. I sat down at my desk.

"June M.," Mr. Morrisey said.

She turned around, staring at him with that big-eyed cartoon look. After a moment she sat down at her desk with a loud slapping sound.

Even Mr. Morrisey laughed.

And sitting at my desk, twirling my braids, I knew this was the last Tuesday of the Other June. 15 ○

Practice the Skills

15 BIG Question

How has June T. changed the way she deals with June M.'s bullying? How does June M. react? Write your answers in the "Tuesday of the Other June" page of Foldable 5. Your response will help you with the Unit Challenge later.

Tuesday of the Other June 535

READING WORKSHOP 2 • Understanding Cause and Effect

After You Read | Tuesday of the Other June

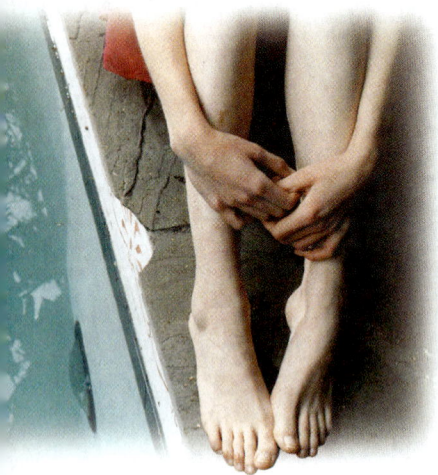

Answering the BIG Question

1. What are your thoughts about dealing with bullies after reading "Tuesday of the Other June"? Explain.
2. **Recall** Where does the narrator first meet the "Other June"?
   TIP Right There
3. **Summarize** Why do June and her mother move to Blue Hill Street?
   TIP Think and Search

Critical Thinking

4. **Infer** Why does June M. volunteer to let June T. sit next to her in Mr. Morrisey's class?
   TIP Author and Me
5. **Analyze** June M. doesn't say anything when June T. tells her "No more" at the end of the story. Why doesn't June M. respond?
   TIP On My Own
6. **Evaluate** What kind of relationship does June have with her mother? Use details from the story to help you explain your answer.
   TIP Author and Me

Write About Your Reading

"Tuesday of the Other June" describes the conflict between the two Junes from June T.'s point of view. But you don't find out much about why the "Other June" acts the way she does. Use the questions below to help you write a diary entry from the point of view of the "Other June."

- How do you feel about June T.? What events made you feel this way?
- How have you acted toward June T.? How do you feel about your actions?
- Is June T. the only person you have treated this way? If not, who else have you bullied, and why?
- How do you feel now that June T. has stood up to you?

Objectives (pp. 536–537)
Reading Understand cause and effect • Make connections from text to self
Literature Identify literary elements: external and internal conflict
Vocabulary Identify word structure: suffixes
Writing Respond to literature: diary
Grammar Identify parts of speech: nouns, verbs, adjective, adverbs

Skills Review

Key Reading Skill: Understanding Cause and Effect

7. What are the effects of June M.'s bullying? Explain.

Key Literary Element: Conflict

8. How does June T. first try to deal with the bullying? How successful is she?
9. How does June T. finally resolve her conflict with the "Other June"?
10. June T. experiences an internal conflict about disobeying her mother. Does she disobey her mother at the end of the story? Explain.

Reviewing Skills: Inferring

11. Why doesn't June tell her mother about being bullied?

Vocabulary Check

Choose the best word from the list to complete each sentence below. Rewrite each sentence with the correct word in place.

> recited   rigid   bureau

12. He memorized the poem and ___ it to the teacher for a grade.
13. Oscar kept all of his winter sweaters in the ___ next to his bed.
14. As the lightning crackled, David's body became ___ with fear.
15. **Academic Vocabulary** Suppose you saw this headline: "Conflict at Westbridge High School." What do you expect the story will be about?
16. **English Language Coach** Add the suffix *-er* to the word *dance*. How does the suffix change the meaning of the word?

Grammar Link: Parts of Speech

A word's part of speech is determined by how the word is used in a sentence. Here are four parts of speech:

- **Nouns** are words that name a person, place, thing, or idea. Some examples are *hat, actor, country, sandwich,* and *peace.*
- **Verbs** are words that express action or a state of being. They are necessary to make a statement. Some action verbs are *run, persuade,* and *laugh.* Some verbs that express a state of being are *be, become,* and *appear.*
- **Adjectives** are words that describe nouns or pronouns. Some examples are *blue, flat,* and *three.*
- **Adverbs** describe verbs, adjectives, or other adverbs. Adverbs often end in *-ly.* Some examples are *quietly, sadly,* and *heavily.* Other examples are *very* and *only.*

Grammar Practice

Rewrite each sentence. Label the parts of speech of the underlined words.

17. Our old <u>car</u> <u>wheezed</u> up a long, <u>steep</u> hill.
18. The <u>singers</u> and dancers <u>moved</u> across the stage <u>gracefully</u>.
19. Madison <u>pounced</u> on the last cookie <u>hungrily</u>.
20. <u>Tito</u> made <u>extra</u> money by walking dogs and <u>eagerly</u> offering to mow lawns.

Writing Application Look back at the diary entry you wrote for the "Other June." Add two adjectives and two adverbs to help with details and descriptions.

Web Activities For eFlashcards, Selection Quick Checks, and other Web activities, go to www.glencoe.com.

READING WORKSHOP 2 • Understanding Cause and Effect

Before You Read : My Parents

Meet the Author
English writer Sir Stephen Spender was the son of a novelist and journalist. He was a poet, a literary critic, and an editor. Spender spoke about the value of friendship: "The friends of my lifetime whom I have most admired and loved, the books and paintings I love . . . exemplify for me what I most profoundly believe." See page R6 of the Author Files for more on Stephen Spender.

Author Search For more about Sir Stephen Spender, go to www.glencoe.com.

Vocabulary Preview

coarse (kors) *adj.* rough; lacking good manners **(p. 541)** *The boys behaved in a rude, coarse way in the restaurant.*

lisp (lisp) *n.* a speech problem affecting the *s* and *z* sounds **(p. 541)** *Other kids copied Javier's lisp, which made him afraid to speak.*

lithe (lyth) *adj.* flexible and moving easily **(p. 541)** *The bullies were lithe and quick as they sprang from behind the hedges.*

Partner Talk With a partner, copy the words onto one set of index cards and the definitions onto another set. Mix the cards up and place them face down on a desk or table. Take turns turning the cards over two at a time. When you match a word and its definition, you may take the pair. Write sentences with the words you have matched.

English Language Coach

Suffixes Learning the meanings and uses of suffixes can help you build your vocabulary. Sometimes you can add many suffixes to a word. Each one gives the word a slightly different meaning.

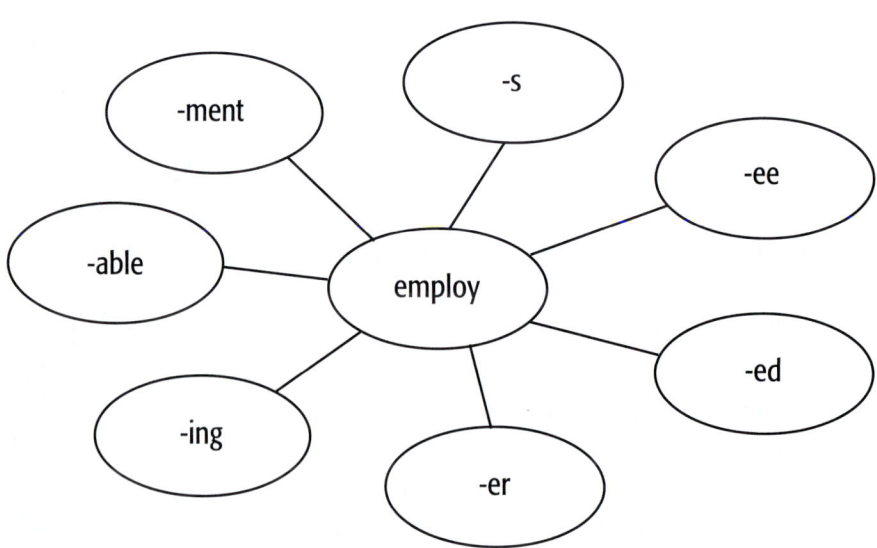

Write to Learn Write sentences using the word *employ* with each of the suffixes shown. If you are not sure what the word means when you add one of the suffixes, use a dictionary to look up the meaning. Be sure to include a sentence for the word *employ*.

Objectives (pp. 538–541)
Reading Understand cause and effect • Make connections from text to self
Literature Identify literary elements: conflict
Vocabulary Identify word structure: suffixes

538 UNIT 5   How Should You Deal with Bullies?

READING WORKSHOP 2 • Understanding Cause and Effect

Skills Preview

Key Reading Skill: Understanding Cause and Effect

Poems don't always show cause and effect as clearly as stories do. When you read a poem like "My Parents," ask yourself questions that help you to think about cause and effect:

- What sorts of activities do the speaker's parents keep him or her from? Why?
- What does the speaker do instead?
- How does this affect the speaker?

Write to Learn In your Learner's Notebook, answer the above questions as you read "My Parents."

Key Literary Element: Conflict

External and internal conflicts can make a story or poem more interesting. A writer can follow the course of a conflict from beginning to end. But sometimes the writer may give just a snapshot of a conflict and let you decide what came before or what will come later. When you think about conflict in a poem, keep in mind that:

- Authors don't always give you all the background information.

  Do you know the backgrounds of the speaker of the poem and the other children? Can you infer them?

- A conflict is not always cleared up by the end of a story or poem.

  Is the conflict between the speaker and the other boys cleared up at the end?

Partner Talk With a partner, talk about the conflicts below. First, decide if they are internal or external. Next, discuss what you should do in each of these situations.

- You're riding your bike home from school, the tire goes flat, and you get caught in a rain storm.
- Your parents told you to be home by 8:00 P.M., but your friends want you to stay out later.

Get Ready to Read

Connect to the Reading

Have you ever wanted to belong to a group of people who treated you badly? Have you ever done something to earn their respect or approval to fit in?

Write to Learn In your Learner's Notebook, quick-write about a time you did something to fit in. If you've never done something to fit in, write about someone you know who tried to fit in.

Build Background

Have you ever been told, "Sticks and stones will break your bones, but names will never hurt you." Often, we think of bullies as kids who hit or push other kids, but sometimes teasing can be just as bad.

- Often, kids who are bullied will feel bad about themselves.
- Sometimes, those kids are less likely to stand up for themselves if bullied again.

Set Purposes for Reading

BIG Question Read "My Parents" to see how one young person responds to bullying.

Set Your Own Purpose What else would you like to learn from the poem to help you answer the Big Question? Write your own purpose on the "My Parents" page of Foldable 5.

Interactive Literary Elements Handbook
To review or learn more about the literary elements, go to www.glencoe.com.

Keep Moving

Use these skills as you read the following selection.

My Parents 539

READING WORKSHOP 2

My Parents

by Stephen Spender

READING WORKSHOP 2

Patrick Garland and Alexandra Bastedo, 1998. Stephen Finer. Oil on canvas, Private Collection.

My parents kept me from **children** who were rough
Who threw words like stones and wore torn clothes
Their thighs showed through rags they ran in the street
And climbed cliffs and stripped by the country streams. **1**

5 I feared more than tigers their muscles like iron
Their jerking hands and their knees tight on my arms
I feared the salt **coarse** pointing of those boys
Who copied my **lisp** behind me on the road. **2**

They were **lithe** they sprang out behind hedges
10 Like dogs to bark at my world. They threw mud
While I looked the other way, pretending to smile.
I longed to forgive them but they never smiled. **3 4** ○

Vocabulary

coarse (kors) *adj.* rough; lacking good manners

lisp (lisp) *n.* a speech problem affecting the *s* and *z* sounds

lithe (lyth) *adj.* flexible and moving easily

Practice the Skills

1 English Language Coach

Suffixes The suffix *-ren* has been added to the word *child* to make **children.** The suffix makes the word plural, more than one child. Which of these three suffixes, *-or, -less,* or *-ness,* could also be added to the word *child*? How does the suffix change the meaning of the word?

2 Key Literary Element

Conflict The external conflict in "My Parents" is between the speaker and the other boys. Read the second stanza. What are two examples that give details of this conflict?

3 Key Reading Skill

Understanding Cause and Effect Sometimes causes and effects aren't always directly stated, especially in a poem. What causes the speaker to look "the other way, pretending to smile"? What is the effect of this behavior?

4 BIG Question

How does the speaker deal with bullies? Write your answer on the "My Parents" page of Foldable 5. Your answer will help you complete the Unit Challenge later.

READING WORKSHOP 2 • Understanding Cause and Effect

After You Read My Parents

Answering the BIG Question

1. How do you think the speaker in the poem would answer the Big Question? Explain your answer.
2. **Recall** To what animal does the speaker compare the boys?
   TIP Right There
3. **Recall** What characteristic of the speaker do the other boys copy?
   TIP Right There

Critical Thinking

4. **Infer** The speaker says that he feels the knees of the other boys "tight on my arms." What are the boys doing when he feels this?
   TIP Author and Me
5. **Interpret** Why do you think the speaker wants to forgive the boys for their cruel actions toward him?
   TIP Author and Me
6. **Synthesize** Do you think it's a good idea for parents to protect their children as the speaker's parents did? Explain.
   TIP On My Own

Talk About Your Reading

Imagine someone from a planet where there was no violence came to Earth and saw the events in the poem taking place. They have never seen anything like this before. Explain to them what is happening and why. Keep the poem in mind; be sure to use examples from the poem as you explain. Break into three groups and take these steps to get started:

- First, think about what kinds of questions someone who had *never* seen violence would ask. Write down at least three questions.
- Think about what you know from the poem and your own life to help answer those questions.
- Think about cause and effect, conflict, and the Big Question to help with your discussion.

Objectives (pp. 542–543)
Reading Understand cause and effect • Make connections from text to self
Literature Identify literary elements: conflict
Vocabulary Identify word structure: suffixes
Grammar Use sentence elements: independent and dependent clauses

Skills Review

Key Reading Skill: Understanding Cause and Effect

7. What do the bullies do that causes the speaker to fear them?

Key Literary Element: Conflict

8. What are some of the reasons for the external conflict in the poem?
9. Do you think the speaker of the poem might have an internal conflict? Why or why not?

Vocabulary Check

10. Write a paragraph in which you use each vocabulary word correctly.

    coarse
    lisp
    lithe

11. **Academic Vocabulary** Write a sentence about why *conflict* is important in a story.
12. **English Language Coach** Add each of the suffixes below to the word *move*. Then explain how adding each suffix changes the meaning of the word.

    -er
    -ment
    -able

Grammar Link: Clauses

As you have learned, a **clause** is a group of words that has a subject and a verb or verb phrase known as a predicate. There are two types of clauses: **independent** and **dependent**. An independent clause has a subject and a predicate and can stand alone as a sentence. A dependent clause has a subject and a predicate, but it cannot stand alone as a sentence.

independent	dependent
She became a vegetarian	because she loves animals.

Dependent clauses do the job of different parts of speech. A dependent clause can do the job of a noun, an adjective, or an adverb.

- **Noun clauses** act like nouns. They name persons, places, ideas, or things. Noun clauses often begin with *whoever* or *whatever*.

  Whoever saw the car wreck reported it to the police.

- **Adjective clauses** describe nouns. You can spot an adjective clause by looking for words such as *who, whom, which,* or *that*.

  The boys **who found the lost dog** received a reward.

- **Adverb clauses** tell *how, when, where, why,* or *under what conditions* the action occurs. Words such as *after, when, where,* or *because* often start adverb clauses.

  I was bored **because I broke my leg** and couldn't go out.

Grammar Practice

Each of the sentences below contains a noun clause, an adjective clause, or an adverb clause. Identify the clauses and their parts of speech.

13. I went swimming with my friends after they played soccer.
14. She will buy whatever is on sale.
15. My cat sprang out from the blankets that covered our sofa.
16. Whoever played the drum solo was extremely good.
17. I was tired because I didn't sleep last night.

Web Activities For eFlashcards, Selection Quick Checks, and other Web activities, go to www.glencoe.com.

READING WORKSHOP 3

Skills Focus

You will practice using these skills when you read the following selections:
- "Priscilla and the Wimps," p. 548
- "Let the Bullies Beware," p. 556

Reading
- Identifying and understanding sequence

Literature
- Explaining and analyzing plot structure, including rising action, climax, and resolution

Vocabulary
- Understanding word structure: prefixes
- Academic Vocabulary: *sequence*

Writing/Grammar
- Using commas in a series
- Using commas with direct address

Skill Lesson

Identifying Sequence

Learn It!

What Is It? **Sequence** is the order in which thoughts or events are arranged. Here are three common forms of sequence:

- Authors often present events in a story in **chronological,** or time, order.
- An author may present ideas in **spatial order**—or the order things are arranged in a certain space, such as a room or a playground.
- An author may present a range of ideas in their **order of importance,** either from most important to least important or from least to most.

"First my ball rolled under the sofa, then my water dish was too warm, then the squeaker broke on my squeaky rubber pork chop. I've had a horrible day and I'm completely stressed out!!!"

© 1997 Randy Glasbergen

Analyzing Cartoons
The dog lists the events of his day in chronological, or time, order. What order would you use to tell the sequence of events for a bad day in your life? Explain why.

Objectives (pp. 544–545)
Reading Identify text structure: sequence

Academic Vocabulary

sequence (SEE kwens) *n.* the order of ideas or events; the arrangement of things in time, space, or importance

READING WORKSHOP 3 • Identifying Sequence

Why Is It Important? Understanding the sequence of a selection helps you follow the writer's thinking. You'll understand and remember events and ideas better when you know the sequence the writer is using.

How Do I Do It? As you read, look at the order in which events occur or ideas are organized.

- If the author is telling a story, keep track of when events happen.
- Look for signal words that might point to either time order, spatial order, or order of importance. To learn when things happen, look for words like *first, then,* and *later.*
- Look for text features such as headings, sidebars, and lists that may give clues about the order of ideas.

Here's how one student noticed signal words to determine sequence in "The Fan Club."

Study Central Visit www.glencoe.com and click on Study Central to review identifying sequence.

> They were standing **now**, whole rows of them, their faces grinning with delight. Choked giggles, shuffling feet—and **then** applause—wild, sarcastic, malicious applause. **That was when** Laura saw that they were all wearing little white cards with a fat, frizzy-haired figure drawn on the front.

I see some signal words in this paragraph. It's easy to follow the events that the writer tells about. The students stood up. Laura heard giggling, shuffling, and then applause. That was when she realized what the kids were wearing.

Practice It!

Copy the sentences below on a sheet of paper. Fill in the blanks with words that show sequence.

(1) The ___ thing I do when I wake up is put on my slippers. (2) ___ I feed the dog and make oatmeal for breakfast. (3) ___, I get dressed, brush my teeth, and run to catch the bus.

Use It!

In your Learner's Notebook, take notes about the sequence of events and ideas in "Priscilla and the Wimps" and "Let the Bullies Beware."

READING WORKSHOP 3 • Identifying Sequence

Before You Read: Priscilla and the Wimps

Richard Peck

Meet the Author
"Priscilla and the Wimps" is Richard Peck's first short story. In the 1970s, an editor asked him to write a very short story about life in a junior high school. Peck had only thirty-six hours to write it. "But," says Peck, "I liked those characters so much, I wrote a novel for them called *Secrets of the Shopping Mall*. So now I very much believe in writing a short story first, to get me started in a certain direction." See page R5 of the Author Files for more on Richard Peck.

Author Search For more about Peck, go to www.glencoe.com.

Objectives (pp. 546–551)
Reading Identify text structure: sequence • Make connections from text to self
Literature Identify literary elements: plot
Vocabulary Identify word structure: prefixes

Vocabulary Preview

slithered (SLIH thurd) *v.* moved along with a sliding or gliding motion, as a snake; form of the verb *slither* **(p. 549)** *The students slithered like snakes down the hall.*

swaggers (SWAG urz) *v.* walks in a bold or proud way; from of the verb *swagger* **(p. 550)** *Full of confidence, Monk swaggers over to Priscilla.*

wittiness (WIT tee nes) *n.* ability to be smart and funny **(p. 550)** *He showed his wittiness when he described the scene to everyone.*

immense (ih MENS) *adj.* of great size; huge **(p. 551)** *Priscilla's hands and forearms seemed immense.*

stragglers (STRAG lurz) *n.* people who lag behind the main group **(p. 551)** *The last of the stragglers disappeared into their classroom.*

fate (fayt) *n.* a power that people believe determines events before they happen **(p. 551)** *It seemed like it was Priscilla's fate to become a legend in the school.*

Write to Learn Write a description of a day at school. Correctly use at least four vocabulary words. Share your story with the class.

English Language Coach

Prefixes A **prefix** is a word part added to the beginning of a word to form a new word. Look what happens when you add a prefix to the word *friendly*—it forms a new word that means its opposite.

$$\text{un- (not)} + \text{friendly} = \boxed{\text{unfriendly}}$$

Like *un-*, many other prefixes also reverse the meaning of a base word.
il-, in-, im- ("not")   *dis-* ("not," or "do the opposite of")
mis- ("bad" or "wrong")   *non-* ("not" or "without")
de- ("remove from" or "reduce")

Write to Learn In your Learner's Notebook, rewrite each sentence, adding one of the prefixes above to each word in dark type.
1. The student's argument was ___**logical.**
2. The warm sun made the snow ___**appear.**
3. If your homework is ___**complete,** you will get a zero.
4. When Julio visits his Grandma, he never ___**behaves.**

546 UNIT 5   How Should You Deal with Bullies?

READING WORKSHOP 3 • Identifying Sequence

Skills Preview

Key Reading Skill: Identifying Sequence

Remember that sequence is the order in which a writer presents ideas or events. As you read "Priscilla and the Wimps," look for clues that tell you about sequence.

- In a work of fiction, events usually happen in chronological, or time, order. Do events in "Priscilla and The Wimps" follow one another in chronological order? Do you see words such as *first, next, then, later,* and *eventually*?

Draw to Learn In your Learner's Notebook, make a cartoon strip with five boxes. As you read, draw a simple picture of an event from "Priscilla and the Wimps" in each box. Make sure that the events are in chronological order.

Key Literary Element: Plot

The **plot** of a story is all the events that happen. The plot is organized around the story's main conflict. A **conflict** is the struggle between opposing forces. Most plots develop in the following stages.

- The plot of the story starts with the **exposition,** which introduces the characters, setting, and conflict of the story.
- The **rising action** is all of the events that lead to the **climax.**
- The **climax** is the point of most of the action, emotion, and suspense of the story.
- The **falling action** shows what happens to the characters after the climax.
- The **resolution** shows how the conflict is resolved or the problem solved. It is the final outcome of the story.

Interactive Literary Elements Handbook
To review or learn more about the literary elements, go to www.glencoe.com.

Get Ready to Read

Connect to the Reading

Why do people bully others? Why do some people get picked on more than others? What can you do if you are bullied? As you read "Priscilla and the Wimps," think about what bullying is and why it happens.

Mini-Questionnaire Agree or disagree with these statements. Discuss your answers with a partner.

___ Bullies make life miserable for many students.
___ Most people I know have the same feelings about bullies as I do.
___ I am sure that I could handle a bully.
___ Adults can help bullies and their victims.
___ At least one person thinks I'm a bully.

Build Background

A bully is someone who tries to tease or hurt someone. Bullies may pick on people to prove how powerful they are. Some do it because they feel that they are not as good as other people. Some do it for attention. Other bullies act tough so people will not bother them.

- Bullying may be obvious, such as pushing or hitting.
- Bullying can also be sneaky, such as spreading rumors or making cruel jokes.
- Some bullies say they are "just teasing" to try to excuse what they are doing.

Set Purposes for Reading

BIG Question Read "Priscilla and the Wimps" to find out how a fictional character deals with a bully.

Set Your Own Purpose What else would you like to learn from the story to help you answer the Big Question? Write your own purpose on the "Priscilla and the Wimps" page of Foldable 5.

Keep Moving

Use these skills as you read the following selection.

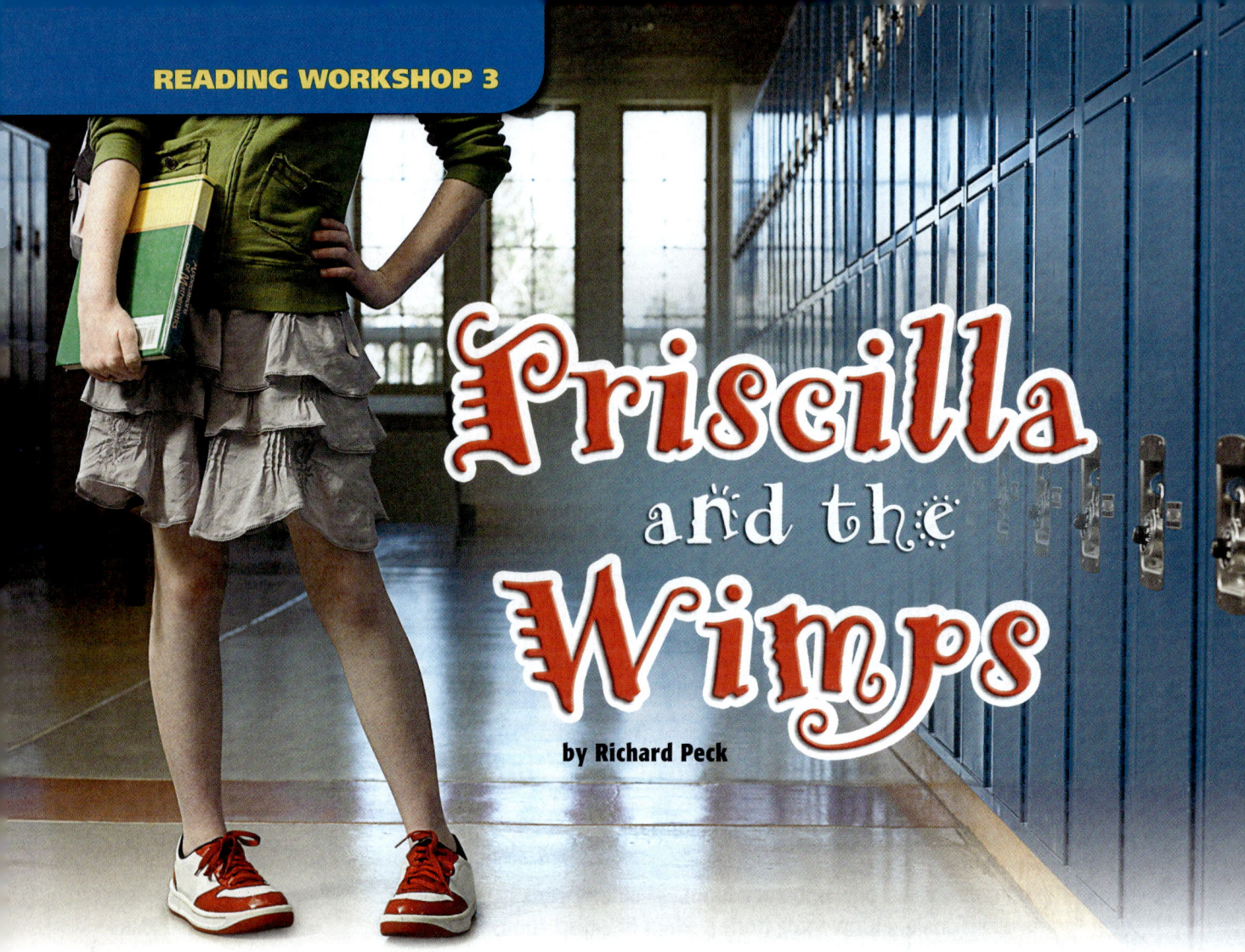

READING WORKSHOP 3

Priscilla and the Wimps
by Richard Peck

Listen, there was a time when you couldn't even go to the *rest room* around this school without a pass. And I'm not talking about those little pink tickets made out by some teacher. I'm talking about a pass that could cost anywhere up to a buck, sold by Monk Klutter.

Not that mighty Monk ever touched money, not in public. The gang he ran, which ran the school for him, was his collection agency.[1] They were Klutter's Kobras, a name spelled out in nailheads on six well-known black plastic windbreakers. 1

Monk's threads were more . . . subtle.[2] A pile-lined suede battle jacket with lizard-skin flaps over tailored Levis and a pair of ostrich-skin boots, brassed-toed and suitable for kicking people around. One of his Kobras did nothing all day but walk a half step behind Monk, carrying a fitted bag with

Practice the Skills

1 Key Literary Element

Plot The exposition sets the stage for the action and conflict. It also gives information about characters and setting. What do you learn about Monk Klutter in the first two paragraphs?

---

1. A **collection agency** is a company that tries to force people to pay their debts.
2. **Threads** is a slang word for **clothes**. **Subtle** means "not very noticeable." In this case, the use of *subtle* is sarcastic because Monk's clothes are very noticeable.

548 UNIT 5 How Should You Deal with Bullies?

Monk's gym shoes, a roll of restroom passes, a cashbox, and a switchblade that Monk gave himself manicures with at lunch over at the Kobras' table.

Speaking of lunch, there were a few cases of advanced **malnutrition** among the newer kids. The ones who were a little slow in handing over a cut of their lunch money and were therefore barred from the cafeteria. Monk ran a tight ship.[3] 2 3

I admit it. I'm five foot five, and when the Kobras slithered by, with or without Monk, I shrank. And I admit this, too: I paid up on a regular basis. And I might add: so would you.

This school was old Monk's Garden of Eden. **Unfortunately** for him, there was a serpent[4] in it. The reason Monk didn't recognize trouble when it was staring him in the face is that the serpent in the Kobras' Eden was a girl. 4

Practically every guy in school could show you his scars. Fang marks from Kobras, you might say. And they were all highly visible in the shower room: lumps, lacerations,[5] blue bruises, you name it. But girls usually got off with a warning.

Except there was this one girl named Priscilla Roseberry. Picture a girl named Priscilla Roseberry, and you'll be light years off. Priscilla was, hands down, the largest student in our particular institution of learning. I'm not talking fat. I'm talking big. Even beautiful, in a bionic[6] way. Priscilla wasn't inclined toward organized crime. Otherwise, she could have put together a gang that would turn Klutter's Kobras into garter snakes.

Priscilla was basically a loner except she had one friend. A little guy named Melvin Detweiler. You talk about The Odd Couple. Melvin's one of the smallest guys above midget status ever seen. A really nice guy, but, you know—little. They even had lockers next to each other, in the same bank as mine. I

Practice the Skills

2 English Language Coach

Prefixes The prefix *mal-* means "bad," and it reverses the meaning of the base word. What does **malnutrition** mean?

3 BIG Question

What characteristics of a bully do you see in this description of Monk in the first four paragraphs? Write your answer on your Foldable.

4 English Language Coach

Prefixes The prefix *un-* means "not, opposite of," or "lacking." What does **unfortunately** mean in this sentence? What other words can you think of with this prefix?

---

3. Running a **tight ship** means being strict.
4. In the Bible story, Adam and Eve live happily in the **Garden of Eden** until a **serpent** causes them to be sent away.
5. **Lacerations** are cuts or wounds.
6. **Bionic** refers to characters in science fiction stories who have artificial body parts that make them unusually fast and strong.

Vocabulary

slithered (SLIH thurd) *v.* moved along with a sliding or gliding motion, as a snake

don't know what they had going. I'm not saying this was a romance. After all, people deserve their privacy.

Priscilla was sort of above everything, if you'll pardon a pun.⁷ And very calm, as only the very big can be. If there was anybody who didn't notice Klutter's Kobras, it was Priscilla. **5**

Until one winter day after school when we were all grabbing our coats out of our lockers. And hurrying, since Klutter's Kobras made sweeps of the halls for after-school shakedowns.⁸

Anyway, up to Melvin's locker **swaggers** one of the Kobras. Never mind his name. Gang members don't need names. They've got group identity. He reaches down and grabs little Melvin by the neck and slams his head against his locker door. The sound of skull against steel rippled all the way down the locker row, speeding the crowds on their way.

"Okay, let's see your pass," snarls the Kobra.

"A pass for what this time?" Melvin asks, probably still dazed.

"Let's call it a pass for very short people," says the Kobra, "a dwarf tax." He wheezes a little Kobra chuckle at his own **wittiness**. And already he's reaching for Melvin's wallet with the hand that isn't circling Melvin's windpipe. All this time, of course, Melvin and the Kobra are standing in Priscilla's big shadow. **6 7**

She's taking her time shoving her books into her locker and pulling on a very large-size coat. Then, quicker than the eye, she brings the side of her enormous hand down in a chop that breaks the Kobra's hold on Melvin's throat. You could hear a pin drop in that hallway. Nobody'd ever laid a finger on a Kobra, let alone a hand the size of Priscilla's.

Then Priscilla, who hardly ever says anything to anybody except to Melvin, says to the Kobra, "Who's your leader, wimp?"

This practically blows the Kobra away. First he's chopped by a girl, and now she's acting like she doesn't know Monk Klutter, the Head Honcho of the World. He's so amazed, he tells her. "Monk Klutter." **8**

---

7. A **pun** is a joke in which a phrase has two meanings. Priscilla is "above everything" in two ways.
8. **Shakedowns** are threats that are used to demand money from victims.

Vocabulary

swaggers (SWAG urz) *v.* walks in a bold or proud way

wittiness (WIT tee nes) *n.* ability to be smart and funny

Practice the Skills

5 🌿 BIG Question

What does it mean when the narrator says, "Priscilla was sort of above everything"? Why might this be important to the story? Write your answers on your Foldable.

6 Key Reading Skill

Identifying Sequence The Kobra walks up to Melvin's locker. What is the next thing that happens? Then what does the Kobra say after that? List two more events that happen next.

7 Key Literary Element

Plot The writer has introduced the setting and characters. Now he begins the rising action. The rising action is the series of plot events that build toward the climax. Which event starts the rising action?

8 Key Reading Skill

Identifying Sequence The narrator tells this story in chronological order. Each event follows another event in time order. Scan this page and write down any signal words you see.

"Never heard of him," Priscilla mentions. "Send him to see me." The Kobra just backs away from her like the whole situation is too big for him, which it is.

Pretty soon Monk himself slides up. He jerks his head once, and his Kobras slither off down the hall. He's going to handle this interesting case personally. "Who is it around here doesn't know Monk Klutter?"

He's standing inches from Priscilla, but since he'd have to look up at her, he doesn't. "Never heard of him," says Priscilla.

Monk's not happy with this answer, but by now he's spotted Melvin, who's grown smaller in spite of himself. Monk breaks his own rule by reaching for Melvin with his own hands. "Kid," he says, "you're going to have to educate your girl friend."

His hands never quite make it to Melvin. In a move of pure poetry Priscilla has Monk in a hammerlock. His neck's popping like gunfire, and his head's bowed under the **immense** weight of her forearm. His suede jacket's peeling back, showing pile.

Visual Vocabulary
In wrestling, a **hammerlock** is a hold in which one person twists the opponent's arm behind the opponent's back.

Priscilla's behind him in another easy motion. And with a single mighty thrust forward, frog-marches⁹ Monk into her own locker. It's incredible. His ostrich-skin boots click once in the air. And suddenly he's gone, neatly wedged into the locker, a perfect fit. Priscilla bangs the door shut, twirls the lock, and strolls out of school. Melvin goes with her, of course, trotting along below her shoulder. The last **stragglers** leave quietly. 9

Well, this is where **fate**, an even bigger force than Priscilla, steps in. It snows all that night, a blizzard. The whole town ices up. And school closes for a week. 10 11 ○

---

9. When Priscilla *frog-marches* Monk, she holds him from behind and forces him to walk in front of her.

Vocabulary

immense (ih MENS) *adj.* of great size; huge

stragglers (STRAG lurz) *n.* people who lag behind the main group

fate (fayt) *n.* a power that people believe determines events before they happen

---

Practice the Skills

9 Key Literary Element

Plot The climax is the high point of interest or suspense in a story. What is the climax of "Priscilla and the Wimps"? Why do you think so?

10 Key Literary Element

Plot The resolution of a story is the final outcome. What is the resolution of "Priscilla and the Wimps"?

11 BIG Question

Do you think Priscilla chose the best way to deal with a bully? Support your opinion with details from the text. Write your conclusions on the "Priscilla and the Wimps" page of Foldable 5. Your response will help you complete the Unit Challenge later.

Priscilla and the Wimps 551

READING WORKSHOP 3 • Identifying Sequence

After You Read — Priscilla and the Wimps

Answering the BIG Question

1. How does the ending of the story compare with real-life situations involving bullies?
2. **Recall** What is the name of Monk's gang?
   TIP Right There
3. **Recall** What is the first technique Priscilla uses to handle Monk?
   TIP Right There

Critical Thinking

4. **Evaluate** Do you think Priscilla's methods of dealing with Monk are effective? Explain.
   TIP Author and Me
5. **Synthesize** Create another ending for the story in which there's no snowstorm.
   TIP On My Own
6. **Connect** What have you learned from the story that will help you deal with bullies?
   TIP Author and Me

Write About Your Reading

Make your own cartoon strip about a bully. Include a few lines of dialogue in caption bubbles. The plot should include rising action, climax, and resolution. Label at least three of the boxes to show the rising action, climax, and resolution.

Objectives (pp. 552–553)
Reading Identify text structure: sequence
Literature Identify literary elements: plot
Vocabulary Identify word structure: prefixes
Writing Respond to literature: cartoon
Grammar Use punctuation correctly: commas in a series

Skills Review

Key Reading Skill: Identifying Sequence

7. List five examples of time order signal words.
8. Write a paragraph that tells the sequence of events from the time Priscilla meets Monk until she leaves school. Use at least four signal words.

Key Literary Element: Plot

9. What is a story's exposition?
10. How are climax and conflict related to each other?
11. Is the conflict solved in the resolution of "Priscilla and the Wimps"? Why or why not?

Vocabulary Check

Answer the questions about the following vocabulary words. If you answer a question with *no,* write the correct definition of the word.

12. Does *slithered* mean "expressed emotion in an exaggerated way"?
13. Are *stragglers* people who lag behind the rest of the group?
14. Do some bold and confident people *swagger*?
15. Would you need a microscope to find something *immense*?
16. **Academic Vocabulary** Give examples of two different kinds of sequence.

English Language Coach Below are more common prefixes. Rewrite each sentence below, adding a prefix to each word in dark type. Use context clues to choose the correct prefix.

   re- ("back" or "again")   *sub-* ("below")
   post- ("after")   *pre-* ("before")

17. I watched the ___ **game** show after the football game ended.
18. The community decided to ___ **build** after the hurricane.
19. People wear seat belts as a ___ **caution** against accidents.
20. The ___ **marine** went deep into the ocean.

Grammar Link: Commas in a Series

Commas help make writing easier to read. Without commas, much of what is written would be confusing and difficult to understand. One of the most common uses for commas is to separate items in a series.

- Use commas to separate three or more words, phrases, or clauses in a series.

    Jen, Mel, Jo, and Lucy like to water ski.

    My mom always wants to know where I'm going, how I'm getting there, and when I'll be home.

- Do not use a comma before the first item in a series or after the last item in a series.

    Wrong: We bought, shorts, tank tops, flip-flops, and suntan lotion at the store.

    Wrong: We bought shorts, tank tops, flip-flops, and suntan lotion, at the store.

- If *and* or *or* is used between words, phrases, or clauses, do not use commas.

    Our breakfast included eggs and bacon and orange juice.

    Do you know who she is or where she moved from or what class she's in?

Grammar Practice

Copy the sentences below and insert commas where they are needed.
21. Priscilla was tall calm strong and loyal.
22. Monk slides up jerks his head and asks a question.
23. Priscilla bangs the door shut twirls the lock and strolls out of school.

Writing Application Look back at your cartoon. Check to be sure that you used commas correctly in any series.

Web Activities For eFlashcards, Selection Quick Checks, and other Web activities, go to www.glencoe.com.

READING WORKSHOP 3 • Identifying Sequence

Before You Read : Let the Bullies Beware

Meet the Authors
Ritu Upadhyay (oo POD e eye) wanted to be a journalist ever since she was the editor of her elementary school newspaper. She especially likes to write personality profiles for *TIME for Kids*. Andrea DeSimone writes for *Teen People* in addition to *TIME for Kids*.

Vocabulary Preview

uproar (UP ror) *n.* noisy excitement and confusion **(p. 556)** *The surprise appearance of the movie star created an uproar in the restaurant.*

policies (POL uh seez) *n.* plans or rules **(p. 557)** *Many schools have introduced anti-violence policies.*

verbal (VUR bul) *adj.* expressed in spoken words **(p. 558)** *You can brainstorm clever verbal responses to bullies' comments.*

Write to Learn Make a poster with advice about how to deal with bullies. Use at least two of the vocabulary words in your suggestions. Display the posters in the classroom.

English Language Coach

Prefixes are word parts that are added to the beginning of a word to create a new word. The prefix *under-* means "below" or "too little." So if you add *under-* to the word *fed,* you get *underfed* which means "fed too little." Another prefix is *over-*, which means "too much." Something that is *overpriced* is "priced too much," or "too expensive."

under- (below, too little) + cooked = undercooked

over- (too much) + confident = overconfident

On Your Own Read these sentences. Complete each word with the correct prefix.

under-   over-

1. The sewer pipes lay deep ___ground.
2. We think that movie actors are ___paid.
3. Hugh will weed the garden before it gets ___grown.
4. The restaurant is ___staffed, so the service is slow.

Find six words that use the prefixes *under-* or *over-*. Write these words in your Learner's Notebook.

Objectives (pp. 554–559)
Reading Identify text structure: sequence • Make connections from text to self
Informational Text Use text features: title, subheads
Vocabulary Identify word structure: prefixes

READING WORKSHOP 3 • Identifying Sequence

Skills Preview

Key Reading Skill: Identifying Sequence

Sequence is the order in which events occur or ideas are presented.

Common forms of sequence are:
- chronological order or time order—the order in which events happen
- order of importance—from the most to the least important
- spatial order—the order in which things are arranged. For example, you would use spatial order to describe where things in your school are located or what your bedroom looks like.

Write to Learn As you read "Let the Bullies Beware," write the three most important things you learned about dealing with bullies. Write them in order of importance—from the most to the least important. Write your list in your Learner's Notebook.

Text Element: Titles and Subheads

Titles and subheads tell or hint at what a selection is about. The title is at the very beginning of a selection. Subheads are located throughout a selection, and they are usually in bigger, darker type than regular text. These tips will help you use titles and subheads.

- Read the title of the article. Think about what it means.
  What hints does the title give you about what's in the article?
- Look at the subheads used to organize the text.
  What do the subheads tell you about the main ideas of the article?

Interactive Literary Elements Handbook
To review or learn more about the literary elements, go to www.glencoe.com.

Get Ready to Read

Connect to the Reading

What does it feel like to be bullied? Can bullies be stopped, or can they only be punished? What's the best way to handle bullying?

Partner Talk With a partner, act out a short talk-radio show discussion. One person should be the host who asks the questions. The other person should be the guest who is being interviewed on the subject of bullying. After two minutes, switch roles.

Build Background

Experts disagree about the need for anti-bullying laws. Some say bullying is a problem that should be handled by schools. Others say that laws would protect victims better. Here are some facts about bullying.

- Bullying generally takes place among kids in fourth through seventh grades.
- Anti-bullying programs run by schools reduce bullying behaviors by up to 50 percent.
- A study done by the FBI says that bullies are more likely to commit crimes as adults.

Set Purposes for Reading

BIG Question Read "Let the Bullies Beware" to find out how experts think kids should deal with bullies.

Set Your Own Purpose What else would you like to learn from the article to help you answer the Big Question? Write your own purpose on the "Let the Bullies Beware" page of Foldable 5.

Keep Moving

Use these skills as you read the following selection.

Let the Bullies Beware **555**

READING WORKSHOP 3

TIME
Let the Bullies BEWARE [1]

Many schools are starting programs to help keep kids safe.

By RITU UPADHYAY and ANDREA DESIMONE

The school yard of Shawnee Elementary School in Grand Tower, Illinois, is usually in an **uproar** with kids playing. But every now and then some serious words can be heard: "I don't like it when you do that. Please stop."

Children in every grade at Shawnee Elementary were taught this response as part of an **anti-bullying** program that was introduced in the school. Principal Shelly Clover says students are using what they learned in the program all the time now. "It's nice to hear them taking care of things without an argument or fight." [2]

Five million elementary- and middle-school students in the United States are bullied each year. In some cases, bullying leads to a situation in which the kids who have been bullied become bullies themselves. Researchers[1] at the National Threat Center found that in more than 2/3 of 37 violent acts in schools, the kids who were the attackers had felt "bullied or threatened, attacked or injured" by other kids.

---

1. **Researchers** are people who study a topic and then give a report about their information.

Vocabulary

uproar (UP ror) *n.* noisy excitement and confusion

---

[1] **Text Element**

Titles and Subheads
Remember that a title is the name of a selection. After reading the title, what do you think this selection will be about?

[2] **English Language Coach**

Prefixes Sometimes the prefix *anti-* has a hyphen (-) to connect it to a base word. The prefix *anti-* means "against" or "opposite." What does **anti-bullying** mean?

READING WORKSHOP 3

A class at Mountain Oak Charter School in Arizona is challenged to stop bullying.

School officials, parents, and lawmakers are looking for ways to stop such acts and make schools safer. Many schools around the country have adopted anti-bullying **policies** to help stop school violence.

States Stopping the Bullies 3

"Bullying isn't new, but it's causing children to take actions that we never dreamed of," says Colorado State Representative Don Lee. He worked to pass the Colorado Bullying Prevention Law. That state law, passed in 2001, says that all schools in Colorado must have an anti-bullying policy. Some states, including Georgia, Vermont, and New Hampshire, already have such plans.

Vocabulary
policies (POL uh seez) *n.* plans or rules

3 Text Element
Titles and Subheads
What information would you expect to find under this subhead? Explain why.

Let the Bullies Beware 557

READING WORKSHOP 3

Schools across the United States are seeing the benefits of bullying-prevention plans. At Central York Middle School in York, Pennsylvania, 700 students signed anti-teasing promises in 2001. The promises seemed to work. That year the number of fights at Central York dropped to 4 from 17 the year before.

In some schools, classroom time is set aside to teach kids how to prevent and stop bullying. At McNair Elementary School in Hazelwood, Missouri, kids learn step-by-step **verbal** responses to bullying. At first they may respond by saying, "I'm going to ask you to stop," and finally by stating, "I'm going to get help."

Penfield Tate, a former Colorado senator, hopes that anti-bullying programs will stop violence by opening the lines of communication between kids. "Students don't feel comfortable talking to adults," he says. "School programs will help them open up." 4

TFK Poll
Here's how kids answered a poll about bullying.

Has a bully ever picked on you in school?

Yes, I've been picked on	41%
No, I haven't been picked on	32%
No, I usually do the bullying	27%

Total responses: 4,019

4 BIG Question

How do the programs and policies described in this selection help kids deal with bullies? Give examples from the text. Write your answer on the "Let the Bullies Beware" page of Foldable 5.

Vocabulary

verbal (VUR bul) *adj.* expressed in spoken words

As part of an anti-bullying program, students role-play bullies and victims in class.

558 UNIT 5   How Should You Deal with Bullies?

Bully Busters

Tips to help you deal with mean kids

Believe you're bully-proof. Keep bullies away by acting confident, says Carol Watkins, M.D., a psychiatrist[2] who gives talks and workshops on bullying. Stand up straight when walking through the halls, and look everyone in the eye when you talk to them.

Stay with your friends. There's safety in numbers, Watkins says, so surround yourself with friends—especially when entering places like the lunchroom or school yard where bullies hang out.

Speak up. Ignoring bullies doesn't always work. Watkins suggests that you respond to teasing with a funny comeback.[3] If that doesn't stop the teasing, just be honest and say, "What you're doing is wrong; stop it!"

Learn self-defense. Take up martial arts[4] to build your confidence and make yourself feel safer. If bullies turn violent, you will know how to stop them with very little physical contact.

Get help. Tell your parents and/or teachers about any bullying that goes on, Watkins says. Even if you think you can handle some teasing, you should never have to feel scared. Once bullies realize that bullying can bring them serious punishment—like suspension or worse—they will probably decide that bothering you is just not worth it. 5 6

—Updated 2005, from *TIME FOR KIDS*, March 31, 2001, and *TEEN PEOPLE*, June/July 2004

---

5 BIG Question

Do you think these are helpful tips for someone who has to deal with a bully? Why or why not? Write your answers on the "Let the Bullies Beware" page of Foldable 5. Your response will help you complete the Unit Challenge later.

6 Key Reading Skill

Identifying Sequence Reread the text box titled "Bully Busters." The writers have organized the information in a sequence of tips. What tip do the writers list last? Why do you think they made it the last tip?

---

2. A **psychiatrist** (sy KY uh trist) is a medical doctor who treats people with emotional problems and mental illness.
3. A **comeback** is a quick and witty reply.
4. **Martial** (MAR shul) **arts** are methods of self-defense, such as judo and karate, that originated in Asia.

READING WORKSHOP 3 • Identifying Sequence

After You Read | Let the Bullies Beware

Answering the BIG Question

1. Why do experts say that anti-bullying programs are very important?
2. **Recall** What are states doing to prevent bullying?
   TIP Right There

3. **Recall** What are two ways that experts suggest for handling bullies?
   TIP Right There

4. **Recall** What are two verbal responses to bullying that students learn?
   TIP Right There

Critical Thinking

5. **Interpret** Why do you think the authors included the TFK poll results?
   TIP Author and Me

6. **Analyze** How do the authors try to convince you that anti-bullying programs work?
   TIP Author and Me

7. **Evaluate** Which do you think is the best piece of advice in the list of tips? Explain.
   TIP Author and Me

8. **Synthesize** Think about what you've read in this selection. Then review the unit opener quotation about bullies on page 480. Now make up a statement of your own about how to deal with bullies.
   TIP On My Own

Write About Your Reading

Write a letter to an advice column, describing a problem with a bully. Exchange letters with a partner. Write a response to your partner's letter as if you were the author of the advice column. You can use facts from the selection as well as your own opinions.

Objectives (pp. 560–561)
Reading Identify text structure: sequence • Make connections from text to self
Informational Text Use text features: title, subheads
Vocabulary Identify word structure: prefixes
Writing Respond to literature: letter
Grammar Use punctuation correctly: commas with direct address

560 UNIT 5 How Should You Deal with Bullies?

Skills Review

Key Reading Skill: Identifying Sequence

9. Name and describe two forms of sequence that writers use to organize information.

Text Element: Titles and Subheads

10. After reading the title, what did you predict the selection would be about? Were you correct?
11. Write a new title for this selection. Think about the information in the article, as well as words that will capture readers' attention.

Vocabulary Check

Write the word that best answers each question.

uproar   policies   verbal

12. If you answer a question by speaking, what kind of response are you giving?
13. If you don't obey these at school, you are likely to get in trouble.
14. If it is very loud and you can't understand what is going on, you might be in the middle of this.
15. **Academic Vocabulary** In this workshop, you learned three common types of sequence. Which type of sequence do you see most often in what you read every day? Give an example.
    - chronological order
    - spatial order
    - order of importance
16. **English Language Coach** Define each word below using the definition of its prefix.
    - *co-* ("with" or "together")
    - *inter-* ("existing between")
    - *trans-* ("across")
    - *super-* ("more than")

    cooperate   transatlantic

    superhero   intercompany

Grammar Link: Commas with Direct Address

You've used commas to separate items in a series. A comma is also used to separate the name of someone who is being talked to directly. This is called **direct address.** Look at the examples below.

Allison, please sit down.

Pardon me, Mr. Razer, when did you hurt your hand?

Can you see who's at the door, Derek?

Be careful to look at sentences closely, though. Commas are only used when someone is actually being addressed or spoken to, **not** when someone is being talked about.

Wrong: Latifah, is going to the store.
(Latifah is the subject of the sentence. She is not being addressed or spoken to.)

Right: Latifah, are you going to the store?
(Latifah is being directly addressed.)

Grammar Practice

Rewrite the following sentences, adding commas where needed.

17. Allen you have to read this article from *TIME* magazine about bullies.
18. Tanya was told that students should seek help when needed Mike.
19. Excuse me Jonathan there's a bully standing next to you.

Writing Application Review your advice column letters. Use at least one example of direct address.

Web Activities For eFlashcards, Selection Quick Checks, and other Web activities, go to www.glencoe.com.

WRITING WORKSHOP PART 2

Short Story
Revising, Editing, Presenting

ASSIGNMENT Write a fictional short story about a bully

Purpose: To tell a story about dealing with bullies

Audience: You, your teacher, and possibly some classmates

Revising Rubric

Your short story should have
- clear organization
- a developed plot line
- specific details that describe characters and setting
- descriptive dialogue

Objectives (pp. 562–565)
Writing Revise your writing for key elements, dialogue, and word choice
Grammar Use appropriate punctuation
Listening, Speaking, and Viewing Present short story • Use appropriate expressions and gestures • Maintain effective eye contact and posture

In Writing Workshop Part 1, you used a story plan to write the first draft of your short story. You decided on characters, a setting, conflict, and plot. Great job! In Writing Workshop Part 2, you will learn skills to make your work even better.

Revising
Make It Better

The first part of the revising process is to reread the draft you wrote. As you read, underline, circle, or cross out the parts of the story you want to change. Remember, your short story should have the following elements:
- a well-developed main character
- a clearly described setting
- a conflict that involves a bully
- a plot that includes exposition, rising action, climax, falling action, and resolution

If your story is missing any of these elements, now is the time to write them down and add them to the appropriate place in your draft.

Dialogue

Put the finishing touches on your story by adding dialogue. Dialogue is spoken conversations between characters in a written work. Dialogue is a helpful writing tool because readers "hear" how characters express themselves. You can tell a lot about a character by the way he or she speaks. Read the dialogue below to learn more about the characters Theo and Eric.

"Hey, shrimp, what're you grooving to on those headphones?" asked Eric.

"It's, um, it's jazz music," Theo said quietly.

"Jazz music? What kind of dork listens to jazz music?" Eric said.

"Well, I think it's all right," said Theo.

"Let me see that MP3 player—now," demanded Eric.

"Um, okay," said Theo.

This conversation tells the reader a lot about these two characters. Who is the bully? Who is being bullied? What words do the characters use that show their personalities?

WRITING WORKSHOP PART 2

Try It!

Find a scene in your draft where two characters are speaking to each other. Write a dialogue between the two characters.
- Write dialogue the way you think your characters would talk.
- Keep each character's piece of dialogue short.
- Use dialogue to help describe the setting. For example, if a character says, "It's freezing out here!" that means the weather is cold outside.

Writing Models For models and other writing activities, go to www.glencoe.com.

Dialogue is punctuated in a certain way to tell readers that the characters are speaking. Follow the rules below to punctuate dialogue.

Place quotation marks before and after the spoken words.
"Hey, shrimp, what're you grooving to on those headphones?"

Periods and commas always go inside the quotation marks.
"Jazz music isn't so bad. In fact, I think it's pretty cool," said Theo.
Theo said, "Jazz music is really cool."

When an exclamation point or question mark punctuates the dialogue, it goes inside the quotation marks.
"That saxophone sounds amazing!" said Theo.

Editing
Finish It Up

When you finish revising, check for errors in grammar, spelling, and punctuation. Use the Editing Checklist to help you spot your mistakes.

Editing Checklist
- ☑ Spelling and capitalization are correct.
- ☑ All sentences have appropriate end punctuation.
- ☑ All dependent clauses are linked to independent clauses.
- ☑ Dialogue is correctly punctuated.

> **Writing Tip**
>
> Use precise verbs to describe dialogue. Instead of *said*, use *announced, observed, admitted, begged, explained, exclaimed, hinted, barked,* or *cried*.

Presenting
Show It Off

By now you have made a lot of changes to your story and it might look messy. Using your best handwriting, copy the final version of your story onto a fresh sheet of paper. Or use a computer to type and print a final copy. Finally, read your story aloud to a partner or group of classmates.

> **Writing Tip**
>
> Improve your handwriting by using two hands! Use one hand to hold the pencil and use your other hand to hold your paper steady on a flat surface.

WRITING WORKSHOP PART 2

Active Writer's Model

Writer's Model

The writer introduces the main character and describes the setting. This is the exposition of the story.

This scene is part of the rising action. All of the events that lead up to the climax of the story are part of the rising action.

Descriptive dialogue helps the reader learn more about the characters and their personalities.

This sentence begins with a dependent clause linked to an independent clause. *After his lesson was over* cannot stand alone as a sentence.

> Bus Stop Blues
> By Samuel Lewis
>
> Theo Thomas ran a comb through his hair one last time and left the house. He was too tense to enjoy the Coral Springs, Florida, sunshine or notice the white seagulls flying through the blue sky. Theo was lost in thought. What would Eric do to him at the bus stop today? Slug him? Toss his sixth-grade science fair handbook into a mud puddle?
>
> Eric wasn't at the bus stop when Theo got there. So Theo put on his MP3 player and let his ears feast on a banquet of jazz. He'd have to try playing some of those cool sounds on his saxophone.
>
> Suddenly, the jazz was gone. Eric was towering over Theo, holding Theo's MP3 player over his head. Give it back! Theo wanted to yell. But the words wouldn't come out.
>
> The La Hoya Middle School bus screeched up to the curb. Theo considered telling the bus driver what had happened. No, he valued his life. Besides, he'd heard MP3 players weren't good for your hearing.
>
> The next morning at the bus stop, Eric swaggered up to Theo and slapped him on the back. "Hey, Four Eyes, let me have some money," he said.
>
> "I-I don't have any," Theo stammered.
>
> "Sure you do. I see you buying lunch every day."
>
> Theo wanted to say, You can't have my money. But he noticed that Eric's fists were clenched, so he handed over his lunch money.
>
> He'd just have to skip lunch. Well, it was no big deal. Theo hated sitting by himself in the cafeteria, so he decided to spend lunch practicing his saxophone.
>
> A couple of days later, Theo was standing at the bus stop, holding his saxophone. After his lesson was over, he was going to ask his music teacher, Ms. Robinson, if she thought he was good enough to play in a real band someday, and what he needed to do to become a professional jazz player.
>
> Suddenly, Eric strode up to him, saying, "Come on, let me have a look at your saxophone," in a fake-friendly voice.

564 UNIT 5 How Should You Deal with Bullies?

WRITING WORKSHOP PART 2

Active Writing Model

> This was too much. Taking Theo's saxophone wasn't like taking his lunch money, or even his MP3 player. His saxophone was his life. "You can't have my saxophone!" Theo yelled. "Leave me alone!"
>
> "Temper, temper, temper," Eric teased. But he walked away to hang out with some other eighth-grade guys.
>
> After that day, Eric never bothered Theo at the bus stop again.

This is the climax of the story because Theo faces his fears and finally stands up to Eric, the bully.

This sentence is the resolution of the story. It brings the story to an end.

Listening, Speaking, and Viewing

Reading Aloud

Reading text aloud lets you share your story, or someone else's, with an audience.

What Is Reading Aloud?

When you read aloud, you use your speaking voice to say the words that you or someone else wrote.

Why Is Reading Aloud Important?

When you read your writing aloud, you
- read the words more carefully.
- notice mistakes that you might not catch during revision.
- find parts of the story you'd like to change.
- get to share your work with family and friends.

How Do I Do It?

First decide what to read. Choose a passage from the short story you wrote in the Writing Workshop or a passage from one of the stories in this unit. Then, follow these steps.

1. Copy or type the passage onto a fresh sheet of paper.
    - Make sure you are able to read your handwriting or see the typed words clearly.
2. Hold the paper in front of you and practice reading the passage.
    - In your head, imagine what is taking place and the mood of the characters or narrator.
    - Try to express these emotions in your voice.
3. Pause every time you see a
    - comma
    - dash
    - period
4. Change the sound of your voice to match the way characters speak by
    - creating different voices for each character.
    - raising your voice when characters ask questions.
    - sounding excited when you read a sentence that ends with an exclamation point!

Try It!

After you have practiced reading aloud to yourself several times, divide into small groups. Take turns reading your passages aloud to each other. Before you start to read, do the following:
- Stand up straight and tall
- Take a deep breath
- Look at your audience

Class Reading

Choose one passage from your group to read aloud to the whole class. Divide the passage into parts and have each member of your group read a different part. Or, you may have one group member read the part of the narrator and other group members read the parts of different characters. Practice reading aloud as a group before you read to the class.

READING WORKSHOP 4

Skills Focus

You will practice using these skills when you read the following selections:
- "Don't Let the Bedbugs Bite," p. 570
- "The New Kid on the Block," p. 583

Reading
- Paraphrasing and summarizing

Literature
- Understanding characterization

Vocabulary
- Understanding word structure: roots
- Academic vocabulary: *summary*

Writing/Grammar
- Using commas with introductory words

Objectives (pp. 566–567)
Reading Paraphrase and summarize

Skill Lesson

Paraphrasing and Summarizing

Learn It!

What Are They? Paraphrasing and summarizing are ways of retelling the author's ideas in your own words.

- **Paraphrasing** means restating someone else's ideas in your own words. You might paraphrase a sentence, or you might paraphrase a longer selection in your own words.

- **Summarizing** means briefly retelling the important events and ideas of a selection in your own words. When you summarize, you ask yourself, "What's important?" A good summary includes all the main ideas and the most important details. A summary should always be shorter than the original selection.

BALDO © 2005 Baldo Partnership. Distributed by UNIVERSAL PRESS SYNDICATE. Reprinted with permission. All rights reserved.

Analyzing Cartoons
What is the boy's summary of his chances of getting an "A" in English class? What makes his summary funny?

Academic Vocabulary

summary (SUM ur ee) *n.* a brief statement of the main points of a piece of writing

READING WORKSHOP 4 • Paraphrasing and Summarizing

Why Are They Important? You use paraphrasing and summarizing to test whether you understand what you have read. Both skills teach you to rethink what you've read and to separate main ideas from details. Paraphrasing and summarizing help you remember and organize information, as well as explain a series of events.

How Do I Do Them? To paraphrase, restate the author's ideas in your own words. To summarize, ask yourself: What was that story about? Answer the questions *who, what, when, where, why,* and *how.* Use your own words. Decide what is most important. Then write the information in a logical order. Here's how one student summarized a paragraph of "What Kids Say About Bullying."

Study Central Visit www.glencoe.com and click on Study Central to review paraphrasing and summarizing.

> It can be hard for kids to know what to do if a bully bothers them. About half of the kids said they fight back. There are a lot of problems with this solution. First, one or both of the kids could get hurt. Unlike on TV, where actors are just pretending to fight, when kids punch, kick, and push each other, they can get real injuries, like bruises and cuts and broken bones.

Now that I've read, I need to ask myself, "What is the most important idea?" The paragraph is about kids who fight back against bullies. When I think about the details that support that idea, I have to keep in mind that kids can get hurt. Here is my summary:

Half of the kids will fight back against a bully who bothers them. But those kids—or the bully—might get hurt.

Practice It!

Think about one of your favorite movies. How would you describe it to someone who has not seen it? In your Learner's Notebook, write a summary of the movie. Remember to include only the most important details.

Use It!

As you read "Don't Let the Bedbugs Bite" and "The New Kid on the Block," practice paraphrasing and summarizing the authors' ideas.

READING WORKSHOP 4 • Paraphrasing and Summarizing

Before You Read: Don't Let the Bedbugs Bite

Meet the Author
Ellen Conford began writing in third grade. She says, "I write the kinds of books for children and teenagers that I liked to read at their age, books meant purely to entertain, to amuse, to divert."

Author Search For more about Ellen Conford, go to www.glencoe.com.

Objectives (pp. 568–579)
Reading Paraphrase and summarize • Make connections from text to self
Literature Identify literary elements: characterization
Vocabulary Identify word structure: roots

Vocabulary Preview

contemplate (KON tem playt) *v.* to have in mind as a possibility **(p. 571)** *Sally had to contemplate having a new sister.*

sordid (SOR did) *adj.* mean, rude **(p. 571)** *The teachers didn't want their students to spread sordid gossip.*

parody (PAIR uh dee) *n.* a piece of writing or musical work that imitates another by making fun of it **(p. 571)** *The marriage of two teachers from the same school seemed like a strange parody.*

potential (puh TEN shul) *adj.* capable of being **(p. 572)** *Sally looked for potential husbands for her mother.*

aggression (uh GRESH un) *n.* angry and unfriendly action or behavior **(p. 573)** *Tina showed aggression when she bullied many students.*

Partner Talk On a separate note card, write each vocabulary word one time. Turn the note card over and write the definition and part of speech on the back. Take turns testing each other by flashing the cards. Take it a step further and say each word in a sentence when you give the definition.

English Language Coach

Roots The main part of a word is called its **root**. When a root is a complete word, it may be called a **base word**. But most roots are not whole words—they are parts of words.

Finding the root of an unfamiliar word can often help you understand what the word means. To find the root of a word, take away any prefixes or suffixes. Look at the roots, meanings, and example words below.

ROOT	MEANING	EXAMPLES
port	carry	**port**able, im**port**
div	divide	**div**ision, **div**orce
dict	speak	pre**dict**, **dict**ate

Write to Learn Use the list of roots above (and the prefixes and suffixes you've learned) to figure out the meaning of the underlined word.

1. The stream was <u>diverted</u> from its path.
2. Look up the word in a <u>dictionary</u>.
3. They had to <u>transport</u> the food across the country in trucks.

568 UNIT 5 How Should You Deal with Bullies?

READING WORKSHOP 4 • Paraphrasing and Summarizing

Skills Preview

Key Reading Skill: Paraphrasing and Summarizing

As you read, think about the story and remember that paraphrasing and summarizing can help you

- organize main ideas and details
- explain a sequence of events
- remember what you have read

Write to Learn In your Learner's Notebook, list three times you need to paraphrase or summarize. Think about all your classes and after-school activities.

Key Literary Element: Characterization

Characterization is the way a writer develops the personality of a character. A writer bring a characters to life

- through the character's own words or actions
- by revealing the character's thoughts and feelings
- by revealing what others think about the character
- by stating directly what the character is like

As you read the story, think about the methods the author uses to make the characters in the story seem real. Ask:

- *What does the author want you to think about the character, based on his or her appearance?*
- *What does the character's speech and behavior show about the kind of person he or she is?*
- *What do the actions of others let you know about the character?*

Write to Learn Copy the list of questions above. Pick one character from the story, and, as you read, answer the questions with that character in mind.

Literature Online
Interactive Literary Elements Handbook
To review or learn more about the literary elements, go to www.glencoe.com.

Get Ready to Read

Connect to the Reading

Have you ever thought you knew all about someone and then discovered something new? Have you ever thought you wouldn't like someone and then made friends with him or her later?

Write to Learn Why might a bully tease and torment others? Why might someone want to scare other people? Copy the graphic organizer below. On the left side write the answers to these two questions *before* you read the story. *After* you've finished reading, answer the questions again on the right. Compare how your answers changed.

Before Reading	After Reading
1.	1.
2.	2.

Build Background

In this story, Sally is upset about living with someone who has bullied her. If her mother marries the bully's father, Sally will have a bully for a stepsister.

- A *stepfather* is a man who has married a person's mother after the death or divorce of the natural father. Don would become Sally's stepfather.
- A *stepmother* is a woman who has married a person's father after the death or divorce of the natural mother. Sally's mother would become Tina's stepmother.

Set Purposes for Reading

BIG Question Read "Don't Let the Bedbugs Bite" to see how getting to know a bully can surprise you.

Set Your Own Purpose What else would you like to learn from the story to help you answer the Big Question? Write your own purpose on the "Don't Let the Bedbugs Bite" page of your Foldable 5.

Keep Moving

Use these skills as you read the following selection.

Don't Let the Bedbugs Bite **569**

READING WORKSHOP 4

Don't Let the Bedbugs Bite

by Ellen Conford

READING WORKSHOP 4

I admit that when my mother told me she was going to marry Tina Grossman's father, I did not take the news very well.

"You can't do this to me!"

"I'm not doing anything to you, Sally," my mother said. "I'm marrying a very nice man whom I love very much."

"And making Gruesome Grossman my sister! You know how many times she beat me up!"

"She never beat you up."

"Well, she threatened to. Twice a week. For three years."

"Sally, that was in fifth grade."

"And sixth grade," I said, "and seventh grade."

"She had problems," my mother admitted. "How would you feel if your mother left you to run off with a vacuum-cleaner salesman?"

"No worse than I feel now," I retorted. "At least I wouldn't have to worry about my stepsister murdering me in my sleep." **1**

Gruesome Grossman, my stepsister. The thought was too horrible to **contemplate**. Sure, I knew my mother had been going out with Tina's father for a year. But they'd been trying to keep it a secret because they both teach at Locksley Hall High. My school.

My mother had sworn me to secrecy, and even though I was dying to tell my friends that she was dating their German teacher, I didn't. Even when my best friend, Selena, got a massive crush on him and wrote him thirty-seven love notes that she (fortunately) never mailed. **2**

They didn't want to be teased and spied on. They didn't want to be the object of **sordid** teenage gossip and evil rumors. I could understand that. After all, I'm a teenager. I love sordid gossip and evil rumors.

But marriage? They were two middle-aged teachers with practically grown daughters. Why did they have to get married? Why couldn't they just go right on sneaking around, without forcing their children into this bizarre **parody** of a family?

Practice the Skills

1 Key Literary Element

Characterization A character's personality is sometimes shown through his or her words or actions. What does the conversation between Sally and her mother reveal about Sally? Does it reveal anything about Tina?

2 Key Reading Skill

Paraphrasing and Summarizing Remember that paraphrasing means restating someone else's ideas in your own words. Practice paraphrasing this paragraph.

Vocabulary

contemplate (KON tem playt) *v.* to have in mind as a possibility

sordid (SOR did) *adj.* mean, rude

parody (PAIR uh dee) *n.* a piece of writing or musical work that imitates another by making fun of it

Don't Let the Bedbugs Bite **571**

READING WORKSHOP 4

I dropped into the nearest chair and glared at my mother. "Does Tina know about the impending nuptials?"[1] I said "nuptials" with such disgust that my mother winced.

"No. Remember, she was in my history class when I started seeing Don. And then, when I had to flunk her, we thought . . ."

"See! Even her father's afraid of her. And she must *hate* you. Can't you tell this is never going to work?"

"It will work," my mother said firmly, "if we work at making it work."

I scowled at her. "Nobody could work that hard."

It's not that I resented my mother remarrying. I wasn't jealous about "sharing" her with someone else. In fact, for years after my father died, I tried to fix her up with men so I could have a daddy again.

The man who came to service the oil burner, the shoe salesman who fitted me at Wee Walk Inn, even the UPS driver who occasionally delivered a package to our house—I considered all of them **potential** father material.

Of course, I was eight years old at the time, and kept seeing all these old movies on TV where a little kid brings two people together who never realize they love each other until they both realize they love *her*.

But the little kid never ended up with a stepsister. Let alone a stepsister like Tina Grossman. **3**

It was about this time that Tina—the Terror of Tyler Elementary School—began terrorizing me. Oh, she picked on other kids, too. I wasn't the only one who was afraid of her. But maybe I was the one who was most afraid of her. So naturally I was the kid she most enjoyed bullying.

Analyzing the Photo Look at the expression on the young girl's face. Do you think Sally has a similar expression on her face as she argues with her mother?

Practice the Skills

3 **Key Literary Element**

Characterization What have you learned about Sally's mother? Do you have an idea about what she is like? How does the author show you her personality?

---

1. ***Impending nuptials*** means that the wedding will take place very soon. ***Nuptials*** are the celebrations and ceremony that is part of marriage.

Vocabulary

potential (puh TEN shul) *adj.* capable of being

READING WORKSHOP 4

I handed over lunch money, granola bars, homework, snap bracelets—even pencils with my name printed on them that my grandmother had given me for Christmas.

All she had to do was stand over me with her fists on her hips and say, "Gimme that!" At first I'd say no. Then she'd say, "Gimme that or I'll break your arm."

I generally decided that I needed my arm more than the lunch money, granola bar, or whatever it was she was trying to extort from me that day.

Maybe that's why I longed for a father so much. Maybe I thought he'd protect me from Tina. But I'd gotten over it. And eventually, Tina got tired of terrorizing me, and channeled her **aggression** into school sports, where she became the captain of the softball team, the volleyball team, and the basketball team. Possibly by threatening to break all the other players' arms if they didn't elect her captain. 4

Well, I was finally getting a father. Who was just as afraid of Tina as everyone else.

"When's the wedding?" I asked sourly. "And is there time to enroll me in boarding school before then?"

"July," my mother said.

"*July?*" I groaned. "That's only two months away. It's hardly enough time to write my will."

"I know it seems soon," my mother said. "That's why Don and I thought you girls ought to get better acquainted before then."

"We could hardly be worse acquainted," I said before I realized what she was getting at.

"So Saturday we're all going into the city together," she went on. "We have marvelous plans. First we'll go to a Yankee[2] game."

"I hate baseball," I said.

"Then on to a nice restaurant for dinner," she continued.

"I'm on a diet."

"And after dinner we have tickets for *Oui,*[3] *Oui, Odette.*"

---

2. **Yankee** refers to the New York Yankees baseball team.
3. **Oui** (wee) is the French word for *yes*.

Practice the Skills

4 Key Literary Element

Characterization Think about what you already know about Tina's mother leaving the family and how that may have affected Tina. Why might she have "aggression"? How could sports have helped her? What does this paragraph tell you about both Tina and Sally?

Vocabulary

aggression (uh GRESH un) *n.* angry and unfriendly action or behavior

READING WORKSHOP 4

That shut me up. Momentarily. *Oui, Oui, Odette* was the hottest musical on Broadway.[4]

"And then Tina will come back here to sleep over." She said it rapidly, as if hoping she could slip it by me. Unfortunately, I heard it.

"It will be a wonderful day," she promised.

"It will be a day that will live in infamy,"[5] I replied.

When Mr. Grossman came to pick us up Saturday morning, Tina was sullen and withdrawn. Obviously her father had told her about the wedding plans. Obviously she was as thrilled as I was about the **prospect** of joining our families. 🔳5

She was wearing a white sleeveless T-shirt that displayed her overdeveloped biceps, and a denim skirt. For Tina this was practically formal wear. I couldn't remember ever seeing her in a skirt before.

She'd even tried to tame her long, frizzy black hair with gel or something. It wasn't as wild as it usually looked. 🔳6

Tina and I immediately positioned ourselves as far apart as possible in the backseat of her father's car. She stared out the left window, silent. I stared out the right window. Silent.

My mother and Tina's father tried to get a conversation going.

"Beautiful weather for the ball game, isn't it?" he said.

"If you like baseball," I said.

"Tina loves baseball, don't you, Tina?" my mother said. "Your dad says you're a real Yankee fan."

"Yeah," said Tina.

Things went on like this until I actually began to feel a little guilty about not trying to be nice. I liked Mr. Grossman—whom I'd been calling Don for three months. I supposed it wasn't entirely his fault that Tina was such a creep.

So as we approached the Midtown Tunnel I admired the city skyline. "There's the Chrysler Building," I said. Its golden roof and spire gleamed in the sun. "Isn't it beautiful?" Just trying to be pleasant.

"Yeah," said Tina.

"It's my favorite building in New York," I said. "What's your favorite building?"

---

4. **Broadway** in New York City is both the longest street in the world and the center of the theater district.
5. **Infamy** means "famous in a bad way."

Practice the Skills

5 English Language Coach

Roots The word **prospect** can be broken up into the prefix *pro-*, which here means "forward," and the root *spect*, which means "look." What do you think the word *prospect* means? What other words can you form with the root *spect*?

6 Reviewing Skills

Visualizing Read the descriptions of Tina in these two paragraphs. How do they help you to visualize what she looks like? What three details stand out the most in helping you picture her?

574 UNIT 5 How Should You Deal with Bullies?

Finally she turned away from the window. She looked at me as if she thought I was nuts. "Favorite *building*?" She curled her lip in contempt.

I heard a sigh from the driver's seat.

We drove the rest of the way to Yankee Stadium without anybody trying to be nice to anybody else.

But once in our seats, Tina began to show signs of life. Too much life, if you ask me. She cheered or groaned with every pitch. She leaped up at every crack of the bat. She screamed extremely foul things to the umpires, to the Red Sox,[6] to the hot-dog vendor who blocked her view, and to the Yankee batter who failed to hit with three men on base in the bottom of the last inning. 7

I was practically deaf by the time the game ended, and secretly thrilled that the Yankees had lost. Anything that made Tina so miserable made me happy.

Tina sulked all the way through dinner. We ate at a very classy, very expensive restaurant called Chez Philippe.[7] I loved my lobster bisque, my rack of lamb, and the three pastries I selected from the extravagant[8] dessert cart.

Our parents were really blowing a bundle on this stepsister-bonding business.

Tina had a hamburger. And ice cream.

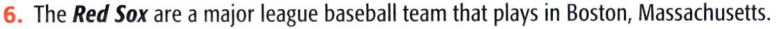

6. The **Red Sox** are a major league baseball team that plays in Boston, Massachusetts.
7. **Chez Philippe** (shay fih LEEP) means "at the house of Philippe" or "at Philippe's" in French.
8. A **bisque** (bihsk) is a thick soup, and **extravagant** means fancy.

Practice the Skills

7 Key Reading Skill

Paraphrasing and Summarizing
The main idea of a paragraph can usually be found in either the first or the last sentence. What is the main idea of this paragraph? Summarize the paragraph in your own words.

Analyzing the Photo Based on what you've read, what baseball park is this? What details in the photo support your answer?

READING WORKSHOP 4

The only way the two of us would ever bond would be if someone Krazy-Glued our shoulders together.

I think we were all pretty tired when we headed for the theater. The strain of trying to act like one big happy family was wearing us down.

Although Tina couldn't have been particularly worn down, since she wasn't trying at all.

And much as I wanted to see *Oui, Oui, Odette,* I knew that the minute it ended, I'd have to go home with Tina. A grim, ugly prospect that took the edge off my anticipation of the show.

But once *Oui, Oui, Odette* started, I forgot everything—my wicked stepsister-to-be, Don, the boring ball game, all the French pastry I was digesting. The show was a takeoff on 1930s musicals. There was terrific tap-dancing, bouncy songs, and great costumes. I was so immersed in the whole experience that I didn't even move from my seat during intermission. I just waited impatiently for the next act to start, not wanting to break the mood the play had created.

At the curtain calls, I applauded so long and so hard that my hands began to sting. I glanced over at Tina. To my surprise, she was clapping as enthusiastically as I was.

"Wasn't that a great show?" I said as we walked to the parking garage.

"Yeah," Tina agreed. "It was." I was surprised that she added two more words than was absolutely necessary to reply.

I began to hum the tune to "Tap, *Tout le Monde,* Tap," the show's big production number.[9] I was even more surprised when Tina started humming along with me. **8**

But once in the car, she **reverted** to type. She sat all the way over on the other side of the seat again, and leaned her head against the window. **9**

Don and my mother kept up an enthusiastic stream of chatter about what a wonderful day it had been.

I still had to get through the night.

I tried to tell myself that it was, after all, only one night—eight hours. We were both tired and would probably go right to sleep.

But of course, it wasn't only one night. It was the first night of the rest of my life. Or at least until I went to college. And

---

9. In French, **Tout la monde** means "all the world." The French use it to mean "everyone." A **production number** is a song and dance performed by many members of the cast.

Practice the Skills

8 **Key Literary Element**

Characterization This is not the first time that Sally has been "surprised" by Tina. Maybe she doesn't know Tina as well as she thinks she does. What does this tell you about Sally? Think about her past interactions with Tina. Why might she have a hard time seeing the good things in Tina?

9 **English Language Coach**

Roots You know that the prefix *re-* means "back" or "again." The root *vert* means "turn." What do you think the word **reverted** means?

although it seemed unlikely now that she would murder me in my sleep, what about having to deal with her the rest of the time? What about breakfasts and dinners and summers and trips and—*everything?*

I felt a very unpleasant tightness in my stomach—and it wasn't because of the three desserts.

There was a soft rumble from Tina's direction. I looked over at her. She was slumped against the window, snoring. Even sound asleep she looked tough.

When we got back to our house, Don declared that the day had been a rousing success.

"You girls ought to get right to bed," my mother urged. "Sally will show you where everything is, Tina."

Don hugged Tina and said he'd be back to pick her up in the morning. Tina got her sleeping bag and followed me up the stairs.

I felt like I was walking the Last Mile.

"The bathroom's there." I pointed. "You can use it first. My room's there." **10**

Practice the Skills

10 **Key Literary Element**

Characterization Earlier, Sally said that the day with Tina "will live in infamy." Now she talks about going upstairs as "walking the Last Mile." The "Last Mile" refers to the walk a prisoner takes to be executed. What do these two statements from Sally tell you about her character?

On Broadway you can see some of the most popular theatrical shows America has to offer. Broadway is bustling with activity; its dazzling lights have earned it the nickname, "The Great White Way."

READING WORKSHOP 4

"I don't see why we have to sleep in the same room," she said. Except for *Oui, Oui, Odette,* it was the only thing we agreed on all day. "I can put my sleeping bag anywhere."

"I don't see why, either," I said. "It's not like we're going to magically become friends overnight." Or ever. I was too tired to worry about insulting her. And she was probably too tired to punch me.

I got into my pajamas while she used the bathroom. She came back into my room wearing a green football jersey nightshirt, and unrolled her sleeping bag near my closet.

I spent a long time in the bathroom. I washed my face for five minutes and brushed my teeth till my gums nearly bled, hoping she'd be asleep by the time I got back to my room. **11**

But she wasn't. She was lying in her sleeping bag, arms behind her head, staring at the ceiling.

"Well, good night," I said.

I climbed into bed and switched off the lamp on my night table. I punched my pillow a few times, pulled the sheet halfway up over my head, and scrunched around under the covers until I was comfortable. Or as comfortable as I could get with Gruesome Grossman sharing my room.

"Uh—Sally?"

I was startled. It was the first time she'd called me by name all day.

I pulled the sheet down from my nose. "What is it?"

"Sometimes I don't sleep too well away from home." Her voice was soft, tentative—almost childlike.

I didn't know what to say. I didn't know what she was getting at. Was there something I was supposed to do to help her sleep? And why did she sound so meek?

"I sometimes have trouble sleeping in a strange bed, too," I said. "Not that you're in a bed, but—"

"Your room is so dark," she said.

"It's nighttime," I reminded her. "It's supposed to be dark."

"My room isn't this dark."

"What, you sleep with a nightlight or something?" I blurted it out without realizing how insulting it sounded.

There was a long silence. Long enough for me to figure out that I'd stumbled onto the truth. Gruesome Grossman slept with a nightlight. Gruesome Grossman was afraid of the dark. **12**

Practice the Skills

11 **Key Reading Skill**

Paraphrasing and Summarizing Why does Sally spend so much time in the bathroom? Paraphrase what Sally is doing in this paragraph. Remember to retell what is happening in your own words.

12 **Key Literary Element**

Characterization A character's personality is often revealed through what he or she says and the *way* he or she speaks. What have you just learned about Tina? Has Tina changed, or has Sally's way of seeing her changed? Explain.

578 UNIT 5 How Should You Deal with Bullies?

READING WORKSHOP 4

The shock was enough to get the adrenaline[10] pumping through my system. Suddenly I wasn't sleepy anymore. I sat up and flicked on the lamp.

Tina was hunched up like a snail in her sleeping bag. I looked at her for a long time before speaking.

"I didn't think," I said finally, "that you were afraid of *anything*."

"I'm not afraid," she snapped. "I just don't like it too dark."

"Listen, everyone's afraid of *something*," I said. I nearly added, "I'm afraid of you." But I didn't.

"I'm not afraid of the dark," she insisted. She sounded like herself again. Gruesome Grossman, spoiling for a fight, ready to deck anyone who disagreed with her.

"Okay, okay," I said. Not because I was afraid she'd deck me. But because I knew she must be feeling pretty embarrassed about this. And I found, to my surprise, that I had no desire to make her feel worse.

"Do you want me to leave the lamp on?" I asked.

She hesitated again. "But then you won't be able to sleep."

"Well," I agreed, "I do like it pretty dark." I thought for a moment. "I have an idea. There's a bulb in my closet."

I got out of bed and opened the closet door. The light came on. I closed the door halfway and got back into bed. I turned off the lamp.

"How's that?" I asked.

A narrow shaft of light illuminated the area around Tina's sleeping bag. If I turned toward the window and pulled the covers up to my nose again, it would hardly bother me.

Visual Vocabulary
A *bedbug* is a small, wingless, bloodsucking insect. A bedbug's bite is red and itchy, like a mosquito's bite.

"That's good," Tina said. She sounded relieved, as if she'd made it through a horror movie without having a heart attack.

"Thanks," she added.

"No problem," I said. "Good night."

She yawned deeply. "Good night," she said. "Sleep tight. Don't let the bedbugs bite." 13 ○

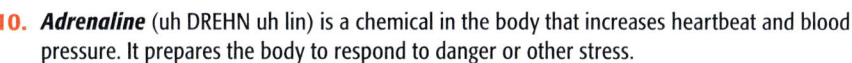

10. **Adrenaline** (uh DREHN uh lin) is a chemical in the body that increases heartbeat and blood pressure. It prepares the body to respond to danger or other stress.

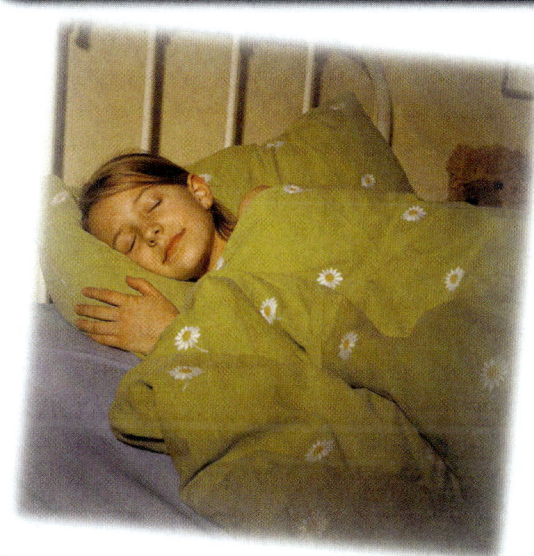

Analyzing the Photo Do you think this girl looks like Sally *before* or *after* she learns that Tina is afraid of the dark? Explain.

Practice the Skills

13 BIG Question

What do you think Sally has learned about dealing with bullies? Do you think Sally has to worry about Tina bullying her in the future? Why or why not? Write your answer on the "Don't Let the Bedbugs Bite" page of Foldable 5. Your response will help you with the Unit Challenge later.

READING WORKSHOP 4 • Paraphrasing and Summarizing

After You Read

Don't Let the Bedbugs Bite

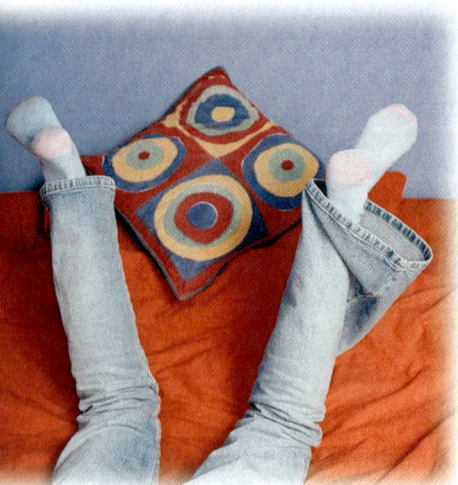

Answering the BIG Question

1. What have you learned about bullies in this story that will change the way you deal with them? Give examples from the story to support your thoughts.
2. **Recall** When did Tina bully Sally?
   TIP Right There
3. **Summarize** What reasons does Sally have for being afraid of Tina?
   TIP Author and Me
4. **Summarize** How do Sally's mother and Tina's dad try to bring their daughters together?
   TIP Think and Search

Critical Thinking

5. **Compare** How does Sally's attitude toward Tina change during the story?
   TIP Author and Me
6. **Synthesize** What effect do you think nicknames, such as "Gruesome Grossman" and "Tina, the Terror of Tyler Elementary School," have on bullies like Tina?
   TIP On My Own

Talk About Your Reading

Mohandas Gandhi led the struggle for India's freedom from British rule. He believed in nonviolent forms of dealing with an enemy. He once said, "An eye for an eye makes the whole world blind." With a partner, or in a group, talk about how the quote relates to the story. Some questions to discuss might be:

- What does the quote mean? Take turns paraphrasing the quote in your own words. How does the story relate to the quote?
- How did Tina treat Sally in elementary school, and how did Sally respond? What were the effects of this? What would you have done?
- Knowing their history, do you think it would have been easy for Sally to ignore Tina instead of getting to know her? What would you have done if you were Sally? How does this relate to the quote?

Objectives (pp. 580–581)
Reading Paraphrase and summarize • Make connections from text to self
Literature Identify literary elements: characterization
Vocabulary Identify word structure: roots
Grammar Use punctuation correctly: commas with introductory words

Skills Review

Key Reading Skill: Paraphrasing and Summarizing

7. Paraphrase this sentence: "Our parents were really blowing a bundle on this stepsister-bonding business."
8. Summarize Tina's reactions to the activities on the day in New York City.

Key Literary Element: Characterization

9. Sally's mom and Tina's dad are a big part of the story. What kind of people do they seem to be? How do you learn about them in the story?
10. Do Tina and Sally seem like people you know? Explain whether you found the two characters realistic, and why or why not.

Reviewing Skills: Visualizing

11. Which of the two characters can you picture more clearly in your head, Tina or Sally? Describe that character, using details from the story.

Vocabulary Check

Match the vocabulary words with the clues below.

parody   potential
contemplate   aggression   sordid

12. ___ mean and bad
13. ___ angry behavior
14. ___ something that copies and makes fun of something else
15. ___ to keep in mind
16. ___ capable of being
17. **Academic Vocabulary** How can writing a *summary* help you find the main idea when you read?
18. **English Language Coach** The root *tract* means "to pull or drag." In your Learner's Notebook, write at least two words that come from this root. Use a dictionary if needed.

Grammar Link: Commas with Introductory Words and Phrases

A comma can act the same way that a pause does when you are speaking, especially when you are using introductory words. An introductory word or phrase is at the beginning of a sentence and *introduces* an idea. Use a comma to show a pause after an introductory word or phrase.

- Use a comma after words such as *yes, no,* and *well* at the beginning of a sentence.

  <u>Yes,</u> I really enjoyed this short story.

  <u>No,</u> I hadn't read it before.

- Use a comma after one or more prepositional phrases at the beginning of a sentence.

  <u>At our first chess tournament this year</u>, I won first place.

  <u>By the end of the first paragraph,</u> I knew I liked the book.

- If the prepositional phrase is very short, you don't have to add a comma.

  <u>For many years</u> the Lakota hunted buffalo.

  (A comma could be used, but it is not needed.)

Grammar Practice

Insert commas where they are needed.

19. By the way this story comes from the book *I Love You, I Hate You, Get Lost.*
20. Well no one ever recommended those books to me.
21. No I didn't read that book.
22. On the second shelf in the last row you will find more books by that author.

Web Activities For eFlashcards, Selection Quick Checks, and other Web activities, go to www.glencoe.com.

READING WORKSHOP 4 • Paraphrasing and Summarizing

Before You Read : The New Kid on the Block

Meet the Author
Jack Prelutsky has tried many occupations—singer, actor, photographer, carpenter, cab driver, artist. He wrote his first poems to go with some paintings he had done. Since then he has published several books of poetry for young people. "Poetry is as delightful and surprising as being tickled or catching a snowflake on a mitten," he claims.

Author Search For more about Jack Prelutsky, go to www.glencoe.com.

Skills Preview

Key Reading Skill: Paraphrasing and Summarizing
When you read "The New Kid on the Block," think about the whole poem to help you paraphrase and summarize.

Key Literary Element: Characterization
Characterization is the way a writer brings a character to life. A writer may describe a character's actions or share what others think about the character to make the character seem real. Sometimes the writer will reveal a character's feelings or give you a glimpse of how he or she interacts with other characters.

- Look at the descriptions of the "new kid's" actions.
- How does the speaker describe the way the "new kid" looks?
- Does the speaker reveal how other kids feel about the "new kid"?
- How does the speaker feel about the "new kid"?

Get Ready to Read

Connect to the Reading
When you hear the word *bully*, what kind of person pops into your head?

Set Purposes for Reading
BIG Question Read "The New Kid on the Block" to find out how the speaker deals with a "new kid" who turns out to be a bully.

Set Your Own Purpose What else would like to learn from the poem to help you answer the Big Question? Write your own purpose on the "New Kid on the Block" page of Foldable 5.

Interactive Literary Elements Handbook
To review or learn more about the literary elements, go to www.glencoe.com.

Objectives (pp. 582–583)
Reading Paraphrase and summarize
• Make connections from text to self
Literature Identify literary elements: characterization

Keep Moving
Use these skills as you read the following selection.

582 UNIT 5 How Should You Deal with Bullies?

The New Kid on the Block

by Jack Prelutsky

There's a new kid on the block,
and boy, that kid is tough,
that new kid punches hard,
that new kid plays real rough,
⁵ that new kid's big and strong,
with muscles everywhere,
that new kid tweaked my arm,
that new kid pulled my hair. **1 2**

That new kid likes to fight,
¹⁰ and picks on all the guys,
that new kid scares me some,
(that new kid's twice my size),
that new kid stomped my toes,
that new kid swiped my ball,
¹⁵ that new kid's really bad,
I don't care for her at all. **3** ○

Practice the Skills

1 Key Reading Skill

Paraphrasing and Summarizing
How would you summarize the first stanza of this poem? What is its main idea?

2 Key Literary Element

Characterization The new kid pulls the speaker's hair, plays rough, and punches hard. What do these actions tell you about the new kid? What other descriptions help you imagine what the new kid is like?

3 BIG Question

How do you think the speaker of the poem feels about bullies? Write your answers in the "New Kid on the Block" page of Foldable 5. These notes will help you with the Unit Challenge.

After You Read: The New Kid on the Block

Answering the BIG Question

1. What advice would you give to the speaker of the poem?
2. **Recall** List three ways that the new kid bullies the speaker.
   TIP Right There
3. **Recall** Does the new kid only bully the speaker, or other children as well?
   TIP Right There

Critical Thinking

4. **Interpret** Why do you think the writer chose to call the poem "The New Kid on the Block" instead of "The New Girl on the Block"? Explain.
   TIP Author and Me
5. **Evaluate** Were you surprised by the ending of the poem? Why or why not?
   TIP Author and Me
6. **Analyze** Would *you* want to be friends with the new kid? Explain.
   TIP Author and Me

Write About Your Reading

Use the RAFT system to write about "The New Kid on the Block." A RAFT assignment provides four details:

- **R** is for your role as a writer—who or what you must pretend to be as you write.
- **A** stands for your audience—the person or group who will read what you write.
- **F** means format—the form for your writing, such as a letter or a speech.
- **T** means topic—what your writing should be about.

Role: Write as the new kid.
Audience: Write to the speaker of the poem.
Format: A letter
Topic: Explain to the speaker why you are bullying him or her.

Objectives (pp. 584–585)
Reading Paraphrase and summarize
Literature Identify elements of poetry: characterization
Writing Use the RAFT system: respond to literature
Grammar Use punctuation correctly: commas with sentence interrupters

Skills Review

Key Reading Skill: Paraphrasing and Summarizing

7. Write a summary of the poem. Remember to use your own words and to only include the main idea and the important details.

Key Literary Element: Characterization

8. Use what you learned about characterization to describe what you think about the speaker of the poem.

9. Complete a web diagram like this one to tell everything the speaker reveals about the new kid on the block.

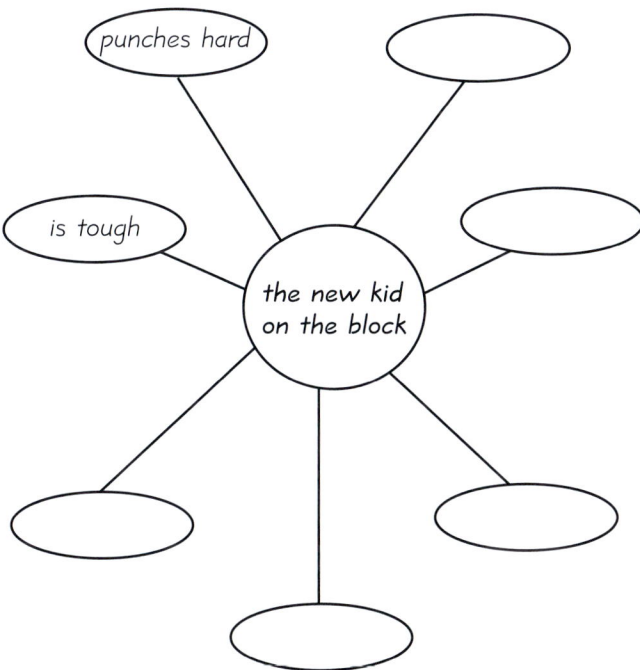

Vocabulary Check

10. **Academic Vocabulary** Suppose a friend asked you to give a *summary* of a movie you just watched. What would you tell him or her?

Grammar Link: Commas with Sentence Interrupters

Sometimes a group of words interrupts the flow of thought in a sentence. Use commas to separate these words from the rest of the sentence. Look at the examples below.

My dad, by the way, was born in Brooklyn, New York.
Nikki's poems, in my opinion, are terrific.
Ed, my neighbor, was teased by a bully.
Mr. Harris, our fifth grade teacher, helped him deal with the bully.

Grammar Practice

Insert commas where they are needed.

11. The story for example has an unexpected ending.
12. My teacher unlike my parents takes the train to work.
13. Snowy weather as you can imagine is more likely in New York than in Florida.
14. These poems as I was saying are fun to read aloud.

Writing Application

Look back at your letter. Add three sentences that use commas and sentence interrupters correctly.

Web Activities For eFlashcards, Selection Quick Checks, and other Web activities, go to www.glencoe.com.

READING ACROSS TEXTS WORKSHOP

BULLIES in the PARK
by Jon Swartz

The Bully Battle
by Elizabeth Siris

Skills Focus
You will use these skills as you read and compare the following selections:
- "Bullies in the Park," p. 589
- "The Bully Battle," p. 593

Reading
- Make connections across texts
- Compare and contrast information in different texts
- Analyze problem/solution text structure

Have you ever listened to two or three people arguing about a problem? In most cases, each person has a different idea of what is causing the problem in the first place. And they all have different solutions.

To make sense of the problem, and to find a solution that works for you, you have to act like a detective. You need to sort out the facts from the opinions, and think about how each person's personal beliefs might slant what they are telling you. You also have to consider how strong their arguments are and whether their arguments support what they are saying. Then you form your own idea of what is causing the problem and how it can be solved.

How to Read Across Texts

Comparing two informational articles about a topic is a little like listening to two people argue. You have to think like a detective to figure out what you believe and who you agree with. For both authors, you need to think about

- what problem they discuss
- what they think is causing the problem
- what solution they suggest
- what arguments they use to support their solutions
- how much you believe them

Objectives (pp. 586–587)
Reading Analyze text • Identify problems and solutions • Compare and contrast: informational articles

READING ACROSS TEXTS WORKSHOP

Get Ready to Compare

When you read two articles about similar problems, compare what the authors say, how they say it, and what solutions they offer. Sometimes two authors will agree completely. Often, though, writers will approach a problem from different angles. For example, one of these articles is about kids. The other is about elephants. What do they have in common? Both articles are also about bullies.

To help you compare the articles, ask questions like these as you read:

- What problem or issue is the author writing about?
- Does the author offer a solution? If so, what is it?
- What facts does the author give to support the cause of the problem or the best solution?
- What personal opinions or testimonials (experts' opinions) does the author use to support his or her argument?
- What is the author's purpose? What is he or she trying to convince you to do or believe?

Use Your Comparison

Before you begin to read these selections, copy this chart into your Learner's Notebook. Be sure to leave enough room to write comments in the empty boxes. Then, while you're reading, fill the chart in with comments and examples from your reading. Try to fill in as many boxes as you can for each selection.

	"Bullies in the Park"	"The Bully Battle"
Problem		
Solution		
Cause of Problem		
Facts		
Opinions		
Author's Purpose		

After you've finished, your chart will help you to compare the two articles and answer the Big Question.

READING ACROSS TEXTS WORKSHOP

Before You Read : Bullies in the Park

Animals of Africa
The animals of Africa face many problems. One of these problems is the loss of the land they live on. Only a small part of Africa is protected for game reserves and national parks. Because some African countries have large elephant populations, rangers sometimes have to reduce the herd sizes to keep the remaining elephants healthy.

Vocabulary Preview

endangered (en DAYN jurd) *adj.* in risk or danger of dying out completely **(p. 589)** *A lot of endangered animals have been hunted for many years.*

immune (ih MYOON) *adj.* not influenced or affected by **(p. 591)** *Even animals aren't immune to bullies.*

stress (stres) *n.* a harmful feeling of fear, worry, or strain **(p. 591)** *The young elephants felt the stress of living without parents.*

Get Ready to Read

Connect to the Reading
Have you ever solved one problem only to create another bigger problem? What did you do to solve the second problem? Were you able to figure out a way to solve both problems?

Build Background

- African elephants are the largest land animals on Earth. Adults can reach a height of thirteen feet at the shoulder and a weight of 13,000 pounds.
- Young elephants are cared for by their mothers and aunts.
- When young male elephants are about fourteen years old, they leave the family to live by themselves or with groups of other males.
- When raising their young, elephant mothers stroke their babies lovingly. They also slap them with their trunks when they misbehave.

This African elephant is ready for a battle with a rhino.

Set Purposes for Reading
BIG Question Read to find out how animals can be bullies, too.

Set Your Own Purpose What else would you like to learn from the article to help you answer the Big Question? Write your own purpose in the "Bullies in the Park" page of Foldable 5.

Objectives (pp. 588–591)
Reading Analyze text • Identify problems and solutions • Compare and contrast: informational articles

588 UNIT 5 How Should You Deal with Bullies?

READING ACROSS TEXTS WORKSHOP

INFORMATIONAL TEXT
MAGAZINE

TIME For Kids

BULLIES in the PARK

Africa's orphan elephants turn against the rhinos.

By JON SWARTZ

The trouble started about three years ago. Nearly every month, rangers in Pilanesberg National Park in northwestern South Africa would find an **endangered** white rhinoceros that had been killed. Then the same thing started happening at Hluhluwe-Umfolozi (Slush-loo-ey Oom-fall-o-zee) Park, in southeastern South Africa. 1

Rhinos are sometimes hunted for their valuable horns. But no one had touched the horns of these animals. Their wounds hadn't come from guns.

The rangers who solved the crime were surprised to learn what was to blame. Young male elephants, which usually leave rhinos alone, had attacked and killed them.

Practice the Skills

1 Reading Across Texts

Identifying Problem and Solution The writer begins this article almost like a mystery story. Why do you think the writer chose to start this way?

Vocabulary

endangered (en DAYN jurd) *adj.* in risk or danger of dying out completely

Bullies in the Park 589

READING ACROSS TEXTS WORKSHOP

Angry Orphans

Why would elephants murder rhinos? Experts guess the young elephants behaved badly because they had grown up without the attention of caring adults. 🔲

Several years ago, the population of elephants in South Africa's Kruger National Park was growing too large. Rangers tried to control the growth by slaughtering older elephants and then moving the young elephants to other parks and reserves. Since 1978, almost 1,500 orphans—600 of them males, or bulls—have been moved to unfamiliar locations, where they grew up without older elephants around them.

Moving the orphans helped preserve an endangered species. But it changed the elephants' social order.

"The whole thing has much to do with the setup of elephant society," says South African zoologist[1] Marian Garai. Elephants normally live in tight-knit groups. Older males keep young bulls in line. But no such role models

---

1. A *zoologist* is a scientist who studies animals.

Practice the Skills

🔲 **Reading Across Texts**

Identifying Problem and Solution People don't usually say an animal "murders" another animal. Why do you think the writer uses this word here? Do you think the writer thinks this problem is similar to a human problem? What does this tell you about the writer's purpose?

Even elephants need role models. Older bull elephants show the younger ones how to behave.

were provided for the orphans from Kruger. Garai believes this upset the young elephants and led them to lash out at rhinos. **3**

"Elephants are complex and intelligent creatures," explains Garai. "They aren't **immune** to **stress**."

What can be done? Some rangers believe the elephant bullies need foster parents. When two adult female circus elephants were returned to Pilanesberg in 1979, soon after the first orphans arrived, the nervous youngsters quickly settled down.

Now officials hope a similar plan will work for the rhino-bashing bulls. Two years ago, Kruger Park began to move entire families of elephants to new homes instead of killing the elders and hauling away their young. Early next year, a few 40-year-old male elephants will be moved to Pilanesberg.

Preserving families may be the key to raising well-behaved elephants. Meanwhile, South Africa's white rhinos had better watch out. **4 5** ○

—From *TIME FOR KIDS*

Vocabulary

immune (ih MYOON) *adj.* not influenced or affected by

stress (stres) *n.* a harmful feeling of fear, worry, or strain

Young orphan bull elephants are a danger to rhinos.

Practice the Skills

3 Reading Across Texts

Identifying Problem and Solution The zoologist says the elephants attacked the rhinos because they didn't have good role models. Is her statement a fact or an opinion? Do you believe the zoologist? Why or why not?

4 Reading Across Texts

Identifying Problem and Solution What problem is the article about? Do you think the writer has provided the facts and expert opinions about what is causing the problem? What solution is being tried? Do you think the solution is a good one? Why or why not? Add your answers to your chart.

5 BIG Question

How did this article help you understand why some people (or animals) become bullies? Record your answer on the "Bullies in the Park" page of Foldable 5. Your response will help you with the Unit Challenge.

Bullies in the Park **591**

READING ACROSS TEXTS WORKSHOP

Before You Read : The Bully Battle

Meet the Author
When Elizabeth Siris was about eight years old, she started a neighborhood newspaper with her brother and two friends. Although her newspaper didn't last, her desire to be a writer did. She has written and edited articles for a variety of magazines and webzines including *inTime, TIME For Kids, Sports Illustrated for Women,* and *Parenting Magazine.*

Vocabulary Preview

ringleaders (RING leed urz) *n.* individuals who lead groups of people, especially those who cause trouble **(p. 594)** *She is one of the ringleaders of the kids who started a fight after school.*

promote (pruh MOT) *v.* to help something grow or prosper **(p. 595)** *Several students gave speeches to promote the program.*

civility (sih VIL uh tee) *n.* polite behavior **(p. 595)** *People should treat each other with courtesy and civility.*

English Language Coach
You've learned that **prefixes** are syllables attached to the beginning of a root or base word. Prefixes change the meaning of a word. Some prefixes show *judgment.* In other words, they show if you are *for* or *against* something.

The prefix *anti-* means "against" or "not in favor of."
Example: An *anti*crime group would fight against crime.

You'll find these words in "The Bully Battle." Write them in your Learner's Notebook and try to write a definition of each before you read the article.
anti-bullying   antiviolence

Get Ready to Read

Connect to the Reading
Think of a time when you bullied someone else, were bullied yourself, or saw someone being bullied. How did you feel?

Set Purposes for Reading
BIG Question Read to learn how schools are dealing with bullies.

Set Your Own Purpose What else would you like to learn from the article to help you answer the Big Question? Write your own purpose on the "Bully Battle" page of Foldable 5.

Objectives (pp. 592–595)
Reading Analyze text • Identify problems and solutions • Compare and contrast: informational articles

READING ACROSS TEXTS WORKSHOP

INFORMATIONAL TEXT
MAGAZINE
TIME FOR KIDS

The Bully Battle

Are nasty, mean kids making your life miserable? Take action!

By ELIZABETH SIRIS

Christian Champ, 10, a fifth grader in Prescott, Arizona, got his first taste of bullying in kindergarten when a second grader pushed him off a swing. Since then, Christian has learned how to deal with bullies—people who tease, hurt, or threaten others. In fourth grade, when a bully cursed at him, tried to hit him, and started swinging a shoe, Christian followed his father's advice. "First I ignored the bully," he explains. "Then I told the teacher." 🔳

People don't like to be pushed or teased for getting good or bad grades or be made fun of for how they look. Sadly, about 1 in 7 schoolchildren is a bully or a victim of one. Five million elementary and middle school students in the U.S. are bullied each year, according to the National Association of School Psychologists. Each day, bullies' teasing leads some 160,000 fearful kids to skip school.

Practice the Skills

🔳 **Reading Across Texts**

Identifying Problem and Solution In this paragraph, the writer says, "Christian has learned how to deal with bullies." What does this tell you about the writer's purpose for this article? Fill in your chart.

READING ACROSS TEXTS WORKSHOP

The Big, Bad Bully

A recent study of bullies found that most often the popular kids, the ones liked by both kids and teachers, are doing the teasing. "Most bullies are the kids that other students look up to, the ones everybody wants to hang out with," says Dorothy Espelage, an assistant professor of psychology who co-authored[1] the study. **2**

Psychologist William Pollack agrees that too often a bully's behavior is encouraged and not stopped. Some bullies become popular **ringleaders** with other kids, but not all bullies are the cool kids, he says. Some are troubled students who may have been bullied themselves.

Taking the Bully by the Horns

Schools across the U.S. are fighting back against bullying. During one week in April, 36 states observed Safe Communities = Safe Schools Awareness Week. From October 15 to 21, about 300 communities held **anti-bullying** and **antiviolence** activities[2] for kids. The week was coordinated by Safe Schools, Safe Students, an Arizona-based group founded by Rod Beaumont. **3**

---

1. Something that is *co-authored* is written by two or more people working together.
2. *Anti-bullying and antiviolence activities* give people a chance to speak out against those who tease or bully others.

Vocabulary

ringleaders (RING leed urz) *n.* individuals who lead groups of people, especially those who cause trouble

Practice the Skills

2 Reading Across Texts

Identifying Problem and Solution According to the article, who are most bullies? Does the writer state this as a fact or opinion? What evidence does the writer give to back up her statement about who the bullies are?

3 English Language Coach

Prefixes Look at the words **anti-bullying** and **antiviolence**. You wrote these words in your Learner's Notebook and tried to define them. Did you get the definitions right? If not, correct your definitions.

Analyzing the Photo Who do you think the bullies might be in this photo? Who is the victim? Support your opinion with details from the photo.

594 UNIT 5 How Should You Deal with Bullies?

READING ACROSS TEXTS WORKSHOP

He says the purpose of the awareness week is to make people realize that bullying and other types of school violence are not something that can just be ignored.

The organization arranges bullying-prevention workshops.[3] Many of them are led by a huge, leather-wearing, tattoo-covered man called the Scary Guy. He challenges kids not to use mean words and not to push or shove others for at least seven days. "I was a bully my whole life," the Scary Guy admits, "but now I'm not." 4

The workshops teach kids that words can hurt just as much as physical violence. Rebecca Sassoon of New York City, knows this well. When Rebecca was 7 years old, she was bullied by three boys in her class for being too smart. "I got things right on tests, and they didn't, so they teased me," she recalls. "I used to go home after school and cry."

Because bullying can start early, teachers in Massachusetts use bullying-prevention lessons with kids as young as age 5.

Suffern Middle School, about 40 miles north of New York City, is among many schools that have anti-bullying programs all year long. To kick off the program in September, the school held an assembly led by Show of Love, a group that teaches about respect. One week later, teachers, students, and parents discussed how to **promote** politeness and **civility** throughout the year. 5

Bullies seem to have been around since school was invented! Can these new bully-busting programs really stop them? There may be hope. Spencer, a 10-year-old from Colorado, says bullies can change. "I teased people all the time when I was in second grade," he says, "but by third grade I got my act together. I didn't like making other people feel bad."

Some kids, like Jenna Gray of Prescott, Arizona, have their doubts. "Sometimes, the peer pressure can get to you," sighs Jenna, who has been both a bully and a victim. "It's hard to get away from it." 6 ○

—From *TIME FOR KIDS*

---

3. ***Bullying-prevention workshops*** teach student groups how to stop bullies and how to avoid being a bully.

Vocabulary

promote (pruh MOT) *v.* to help something grow or prosper

civility (sih VIL uh tee) *n.* polite behavior

Practice the Skills

4 **BIG Question**
The Scary Guy tells kids not to use mean words for at least seven days. Is that a good idea? Why or why not? Write your answer on the "Bully Battle" page of Foldable 5.

5 **Reading Across Texts**
Identifying Problem and Solution What problem is the article about? What is the cause of the problem? What solution is being tried? Do you think the solution is a good one? Why or why not?

6 **BIG Question**
Do you think programs like the ones described in this article can help to deal with the bully problem? Write your answer on the "Bully Battle" page of Foldable 5. Your response will help you complete the Unit Challenge later.

The Bully Battle **595**

READING ACROSS TEXTS WORKSHOP

After You Read

BULLIES in the PARK & The Bully Battle

Vocabulary Check

On a separate piece of paper, write each of the six vocabulary words listed below. Then write the correct definition (a – f) after each vocabulary word.

BULLIES in the PARK

1. endangered
2. immune
3. stress

    a. not influenced or affected by
    b. in risk or danger of dying out completely
    c. a harmful feeling of fear, worry, or strain

The Bully Battle

4. ringleaders   5. promote   6. civility

    d. to help something grow or prosper
    e. individuals who lead groups of people, especially those who cause trouble
    f. polite behavior

English Language Coach

7. Write one sentence for each of the following words. Each sentence should tell something about one of the selections you just read.

    anti-bullying   antiviolence

8. Now add the prefix *anti-* to each of the following words. Write each new word in a sentence.

| burglary | cruelty | litter | slavery |
| cancer | glare | noise | stress |

Objectives (pp. 596–597)
Reading Analyze text • Identify problems and solutions • Compare and contrast: informational articles
Vocabulary Identify word structure: prefixes
Writing Write to compare and contrast: problems and solutions

Reading/Critical Thinking

On a separate sheet of paper, answer the following questions.

BULLIES in the PARK

9. **Infer** How might rangers have prevented the conflict between the elephants and the rhinos?

    TIP Author and Me

10. **Synthesize** Based on the information in this article, describe one reason why human children might become bullies.

    TIP Author and Me

The Bully Battle

11. **Evaluate** Most of the quotations—things that people say—are from kids who were bullied. Should you believe what they are saying? Explain.

    TIP On My Own

12. **Evaluate** Do you think the "bully-busting" programs can really help stop bullying? Explain.

    TIP Author and Me

Writing: Reading Across Texts

13. Follow these steps to compare how the authors discussed the problems and solutions in "Bullies in the Park" and "The Bully Battle."

    Step 1: On the chart you completed, look at the problem you wrote down for each article. Write a sentence that explains how the problems are similar.

    Step 2: Look at what you wrote in the row that listed the cause of the problem. Did the authors have the same cause or causes of the problem?

    Step 3: Is the solution presented in each selection similar or different?

    Step 4: On your chart, look at the rows that list the facts and opinions that you found in the two selections. Think about whether one author supported his or her argument better than the other.

    Step 5: On your chart, look at the author's purpose for each article. Think about how the authors' purposes are similar and how they're different.

Get It on Paper

To compare how the authors discussed problems and solutions in "Bullies in the Park" and "The Bully Battle," answer these questions on a separate sheet of paper.

14. How is the problem described in "Bullies in the Park" similar to the one described in "The Bully Battle"? Did the authors deal with the cause of the problem in the same away? Give examples.

15. In "Bullies in the Park," does the author use facts to support the solution that the article describes? Does the author use opinions and testimonials to support the solution? Give examples to support your answers.

16. In "The Bully Battle," does the author use facts, opinions, or testimonials to support the solution that the article describes? Give examples.

17. Do you think the author of "Bullies in the Park" is trying to tell us something about why human children might become bullies? Explain.

18. What do you think the author of "The Bully Battle" is trying to convince us to do?

19. Do you think one article presents a better argument than the other? Explain.

BIG Question

20. Both "Bullies in the Park" and "The Bully Battle" discuss possible solutions to the problems they present. Which solution do you think is more likely to work? Explain why you picked that solution.

UNIT 5 WRAP-UP

Answering The BIG Question: How Should You Deal with Bullies?

You've just read different selections, and you thought about how to deal with bullies. Now use what you've learned to do the Unit Challenge.

The Unit Challenge

Choose Activity A or Activity B and follow the directions for that activity.

A. Group Activity: Brochure

You and three to five other students will create a brochure that explains how to deal with bullies.

1. **Discuss the Assignment** As a group, brainstorm ways to handle bullies. Look at the notes that you made on your Foldable. Think about what you learned from the selections. Also share ideas from your own experience. Choose a member of the group to write your ideas in a list.

2. **Make Choices** Brochures are short and to the point. They provide the basic information about a subject that people need. Choose two or three ideas from your list to present in your brochure.

3. **Plan Your Brochure** Think about brochures that you have seen. Maybe they're health-related or community-related. Or maybe they're advertising brochures. A brochure should have a strong, clear message and attract readers' attention. To do these things, a brochure often contains bright colors, bulleted lists, and pictures.
   - How will you organize your brochure?
   - What facts or tips will you include?
   - What pictures or graphics will you use?

4. **Create the Brochure** Work with other members of your group to plan your brochure. Take a sheet of paper and fold it into three vertical panels. Decide where you will put the information you want to include and where you will place any pictures or graphics. After you've made these decisions, put them into action and make your brochure. Divide your work among group members. Be sure to use bright colors and different text sizes to grab readers' attention.

5. **Present the Brochure** Present your brochure to the class. Then invite members of the audience to share what they learned from your brochure.

B. Solo Activity: Short Story

Write a short story—this time, from the point of view of a bully. Use "I" to refer to the bully.

1. **Choose Your Topic** In your Learner's Notebook, list any experiences you've had with bullies. Also skim your Foldable notes for any situations involving bullies that sound as though they really could happen. Add those situations to your list. Then choose the experience or situation that you think would make the best topic for your short story.

2. **Map Out the Story** Your story will have a beginning, a middle, and an ending. In your Learner's Notebook, copy the story map below. Then fill it in with details from the experience or situation you chose.

3. **Draft Your Short Story** Using your story map, make a rough draft of your short story.
   - Introduce the characters and setting.
   - Show the conflict between a character and the bully.
   - Tell how the character handles the bully.
   - Show how the bully reacts.

4. **Review Your Draft** Make sure the story you're telling is clear.
   - Are the setting and characters clearly described?
   - Do the dialogue and description explain the conflict with the bully?
   - Do you explain how the character resolves the conflict?

5. **Write Your Final Copy** Write your finished draft in your Learner's Notebook. Give your story a catchy title.

6. **Share Your Short Story** Read your short story to the class. Ask your classmates what they learned from your story about how to deal with bullies.

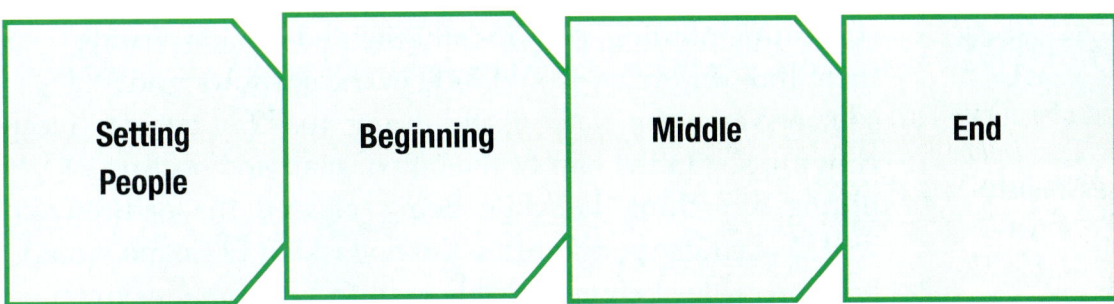

UNIT 5

Your Turn: Read and Apply Skills

Meet the Author

Charles J. Finger was born in Willesden, England, on December 25, 1867. His parents eventually moved to the United States, but Finger joined the crew of a ship that sailed to Chile. He worked at various odd jobs, including tour guide and sheepherder until 1895. He came to the United States that year and began writing newspaper articles. He settled in Texas and New Mexico and began writing stories for young adults. He wrote 36 books in the last 20 years of his life. "El Enano" is part of a book titled *Tales from Silver Lands*, which received a Newbery Medal in 1925.

Author Search For more about Charles J. Finger, go to www.glencoe.com.

EL ENANO

by Charles J. Finger

Everyone disliked El Enano who lived in the forest, because he always lay hidden in dark places, and when woodmen passed he jumped out on them and beat them and took their dinners from them. He was a squat[1] creature, yellow of skin and snag-toothed and his legs were crooked, his arms were crooked, and his face was crooked. There were times when he went about on all fours and then he looked like a great spider, for he had scraggy[2] whiskers that hung to the ground and looked like legs. At other times he had the mood to make himself very small like a little child, and then he was most horrible to see, for his skin was wrinkled and his whiskers hung about him like a ragged garment.

Yet all of that the people might have forgiven and he might have been put up with, were it not for some worse tricks. What was most disliked was his trick of walking softly about a house in the night-time while the people were inside, suspecting nothing, perhaps singing and talking. Seeing them thus, El Enano would hide in the shadows until someone went for water to the spring, then out he would leap, clinging fast to the hair of the boy or man and beating, hitting, scratching the while. Being released, the tortured one would of course run to reach the house, but El Enano would hop on one leg behind, terribly fast, and catch his victim again just as a hand was almost laid on the door latch. Nor could an alarm be raised, because El Enano cast a spell of silence, so that, try as one would, neither word nor shout would come.

1. A ***squat*** creature is short and solid.
2. ***Scraggy*** whiskers are ragged and uneven.

Then there was his other evil trick of hiding close to the ground and reaching out a long and elastic arm to catch boy or girl by the ankle. But that was not worse than his habit of making a noise like hail or rain, hearing which the people in the house would get up to close a window, and there, looking at them from the dark but quite close to their faces, would be the grinning Enano holding in his hands his whiskers that looked like a frightening curtain, his eyes red and shining like rubies. That was very unpleasant indeed, especially when a person was alone in the house. Nor was it much better when he left the window, for he would hop and skip about the house yard for hours, screaming and howling and throwing sticks and stones. So, wherever he was there was chill horror.

One day, a good old woman who lived alone went with her basket to gather berries. El Enano saw her and at once made himself into a little creature no larger than a baby and stretched himself on a bed of bright moss between two trees leafless and ugly. He pretended to be asleep, though he whimpered[3] a little as a child does when it has a bad dream.

The good old woman was short-sighted but her ears were quick, and hearing the soft whimper she found the creature and took it in her arms. To do that bent her sadly, for Enano when small was the same weight as when his full size.

"Oh, poor thing," she said. "Someone has lost a baby. Or perhaps some wild creature has carried the tender thing from its home. So, lest it perish I will take care of it, though to be sure, a heavier baby I never held."

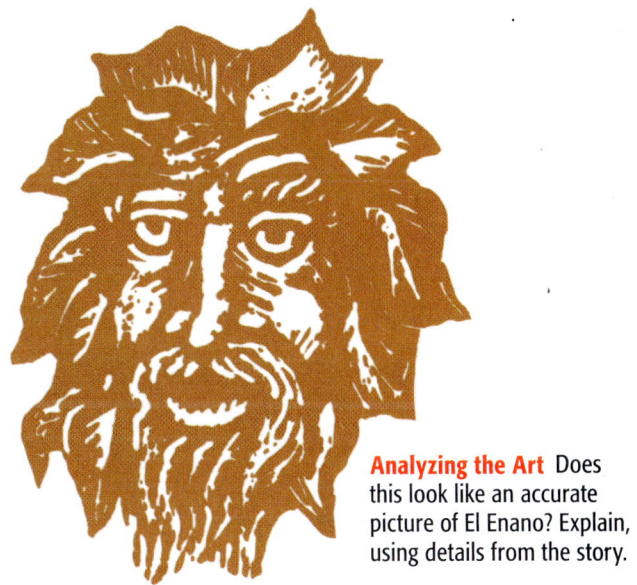

Analyzing the Art Does this look like an accurate picture of El Enano? Explain, using details from the story.

The dame[4] had no children of her own and, though poor, was both willing and glad to share what she had with any needy creature. Gently she took it home and having put dry sticks on the fire she made a bed of light twigs which she covered with a mat of feathers. Then she bustled about, getting bread and milk for supper for the little one, feeling happy at heart because she had rescued the unhappy creature from the dismal[5] forest.

At first she was glad to see the appetite of the homeless thing, for it soon finished the bread and milk and cried for more.

"Bless me! It must be half starved," she said. "It may have my supper." So she took the food she had set out for herself and El Enano swallowed it as quickly as he had swallowed the first bowl. Yet still he cried for more. Off then to the neighbors she went, borrowing milk from this one, bread from that, rice from another, until half the children of the village had to go on short commons that night. The creature

---

3. A *whimper* (WIM pur) is a weak, quiet cry.
4. *Dame* is an old word for "woman."
5. *Dismal* (DIZ mul) means "gloomy."

YOUR TURN: READ AND APPLY SKILLS

A Lonely Life, c. 1873. Hugh Cameron. National Gallery of Scotland, Edinburgh.

Analyzing the Art Study the woman in this painting. What qualities does she seem to have in common with the "good old woman" in this story? Support your answer with details from the story.

devoured⁶ all that was brought and still yelled for more and the noise it made was ear-splitting. But as it ate and felt the warmth, it grew and grew.

"Santa Maria!" said the dame. "What wonderful thing is this? Already it is no longer a baby, but a grown child. Almost it might be called ugly, but that, I suppose, is because it was motherless and lost. It is all very sad." Then, because she had thought it ugly she did the more for it, being sorry for her thoughts, though she could not help nor hinder them. As for the creature itself, having eaten all in the house, it gave a grunt or two, turned heavily on its side and went to sleep, snoring terribly.

Next morning matters were worse, for El Enano was stretched out on the floor before the fire, his full size, and seeing the dame he called for food, making so great a noise that the very windows shook and his cries were heard all over the village. So to still him, and there being nothing to eat in the house, the good old woman went out and told her tale to the neighbors, asking their help and advice, and to her house they all went flocking to look at the strange creature. One man, a stout-hearted⁷ fellow, told El Enano that it was high time for him to be going, hearing which, the ugly thing shrieked with wicked laughter.

---

6. **Devoured** (dih VOWRD) means "ate up greedily."

7. A **stout-hearted** (stowt HART id) person is courageous.

602 UNIT 5 How Should You Deal with Bullies?

"Well, bring me food," it said, looking at the man with red eyes. "Bring me food, I say, and when I have eaten enough I may leave you. But bring me no child's food, but rather food for six and twenty men. Bring an armadillo roasted and a pig and a large goose and many eggs and the milk of twenty cows. Nor be slow about it, for I must amuse myself while I wait and it may well be that you will not care for the manner of my amusement."

Indeed, there was small likelihood of any one there doing that, for his amusement was in breaking things about the house, the tables and benches, the pots and the ollas,[8] and when he had made sad havoc[9] of the woman's house he started on the house next door, smashing doors and windows, tearing up flowers by the roots, chasing the milk goats and the chickens, and setting dogs to fight. Nor did he cease in his mischief until the meal was set out for him, when he leaped upon it and crammed it down his throat with fearful haste, leaving neither bone nor crumb.

The people of the village stood watching, whispering one to another behind their hands, how they were shocked at all that sight, and when at last the meal was finished, the stout-hearted man who had spoken before stepped forward. "Now sir!" said he to El Enano, "seeing that you have eaten enough and more than enough, you will keep your word, going about your business and leaving this poor woman and us in peace. Will you?"

"No, *No* NO!" roared El Enano, each No being louder than the one before it.

"But you promised," said the man.

What the creature said when answering that made nearly everyone there faint with horror. It said:

"What I promised was that I would leave when I had eaten enough. I did not—"

The bold man interrupted then, saying, "Well, you have eaten enough."

"Ah yes, for one meal," answered the cruel Enano. "But I meant that I would leave when I have eaten enough for always. There is to-morrow and to-morrow night. There is the day after that and the next day and the next day. There are to be weeks of eating and months of eating and years of eating. You are stupid people if you think that I shall ever have eaten enough. So I shall not leave. No. *No*. NO!"

Having said that, the creature laughed in great glee and began to throw such things as he could reach against the walls, and so, many good things were shattered.

Now for three days that kind of thing went on, at the end of which time the men of the place were at their wits' ends to know what to do, for almost everything eatable in the village had gone down the creature's throat. Sad at heart, seeing what had come to pass, the good old woman went out and sat down to weep by the side of a quiet pool, for it seemed to her to be a hard thing that what she had done in kindness had ended thus, and that the house she had built and loved and kept clean and sweet should be so sadly wrecked and ruined. Her thoughts were broken by the sound of a voice, and turning she saw a silver-gray fox sitting on a rock and looking at her.

---

8. **Ollas** (OY lus) are large containers used for storage, cooking, or holding water.
9. **Havoc** (HA vik) is widespread destruction.

YOUR TURN: READ AND APPLY SKILLS

Still Life with Plums, Figs, and Bread, 18th century. Luis Melendez. Oil on canvas.

Analyzing the Art Do you think that this food would be enough to make El Enano go away? Why or why not?

"It is well enough to have a good cry," he said, "but it is better to be gay[10] and have a good laugh."

"Ah! Good evening, Señor Zorro," answered the dame, drying her tears. "But who can be gay when a horrible creature is eating everything? Who can be otherwise than sad, seeing the trouble brought on friends?" The last she added, being one of those who are always saddened by the cheerlessness of others.

"You need not tell me," said the fox. "I know everything that has passed," and he put his head a little sideways like a wise young dog and seemed to smile.

"But what is there to do?" asked the dame. "I am in serious case indeed. This alocado[11] says that he will make no stir until he has had enough to eat for all his life, and certainly he makes no stir to go away."

"The trouble is that you give him enough and not too much," said the fox.

"Too much, you say? We have given him too much already, seeing that we have given him all that we have," said the old dame a little angrily.

"Well, what you must do is to give him something that he does not like. Then he will go away," said the fox.

---

10. ***"It is better to be gay"*** means "it is better to be happy."

11. ***Alocado*** means "thoughtless or crazy" in Spanish.

"Easier said than done," answered the old woman with spirit. "Did we but give him something of which he liked not the taste, then he would eat ten times more to take the bad taste away. Señor Zorro, with all your cleverness, you are but a poor adviser."

After that the fox thought a long while before saying anything, then coming close to the old woman and looking up into her face he said:

"Make your mind easy. He shall have enough to eat this very night and all that you have to do is to see that your neighbors do as I say, nor be full of doubt should I do anything that seems to be contrary."

So the good woman promised to warn her neighbors, knowing well the wisdom of the fox, and together they went to her house, where they found El Enano stretched out on the floor, looking like a great pig, and every minute he gave a great roar. The neighbors were both angry and afraid, for the creature had been very destructive that day. Indeed, he had taken delight in stripping the thatched roofs and had desisted[12] only when the men of the place had promised to double the amount of his meal.

Not five minutes had the fox and the dame been in the house when the men of the place came in with things—with berries and armadillos, eggs and partridges, turkeys and bread and much fish from the lake. At once they set about cooking, while the women commenced[13] to brew a great bowl of knot-grass tea. Soon the food was cooked and El Enano fell to as greedily as ever.

The fox looked at Enano for a while, then said:

"You have a fine appetite, my friend. What will there be for the men and the women and the children and for me to eat?"

"You may have what I leave, and eat it when I end," said El Enano.

"Let us hope then that our appetites will be light," said the fox.

A little later the fox began to act horribly, jumping about the room and whining, and calling the people lazy and inhospitable.[14]

---

14. An *inhospitable* (in haw SPIH tuh bul) person is unfriendly and not generous.

Analyzing the Photo Does the picture of a fox help you visualize the events on this page? Explain your answer.

---

12. If something has ***desisted***, it has stopped.
13. ***Commenced*** (kuh MENST) means "started or began."

YOUR TURN: READ AND APPLY SKILLS

Analyzing the Photo How does this photo show what happens in the story? How is it different than what happens in the story?

"Think you," he said, "that this is the way to treat a visitor? A pretty thing indeed to serve one and let the other go hungry. Do I get nothing at all to eat? Quick. Bring me potatoes and roast them, or it will be bad for all of you. The mischief I do shall be ten times worse than any done already."

Knowing that some plan was afoot the people ran out of the house and soon came back with potatoes, and the fox showed them how he wanted them roasted on the hearth. So they were placed in the ashes and covered with hot coals and when they were well done the fox told everyone to take a potato, saying that El Enano, who was crunching the bones of the animals he had eaten, would not like them. But all the while the men were eating, the fox ran from one to another whispering things but quite loud enough for Enano to hear. "Hush!" said he. "Say nothing. El Enano must not know how good they are and when he asks for some, tell him that they are all gone."

"Yes. Yes," said the people, keeping in with the plan. "Do not let Enano know."

By this time El Enano was suspicious and looked from one man to another. "Give me all the potatoes," he said.

"They are all eaten except mine," said the fox, "but you may taste that." So saying he

606 UNIT 5 How Should You Deal with Bullies?

thrust the roasted potato into the hands of Enano and the creature crammed it down its throat at once.

"Ha! It is good," he roared. "Give me more. More. MORE."

"We have no more," said the fox very loud, then, quite softly to those who stood near him, he added, "Say nothing about the potatoes on the hearth,"[15] but loudly enough for El Enano to hear, though quite well he knew that there were none.

"Ah! I heard you," roared El Enano. "There are potatoes on the hearth. Give them to me."

"We must let him have them," said the fox, raking the red-hot coals to the front.

"Out of the way," cried El Enano, reaching over the fox and scooping up a double handful of hot coals, believing them to be potatoes. Red hot as they were he swallowed them and in another moment was rolling on the floor, howling with pain as the fire blazed in his stomach. Up he leaped again and dashed out of the house to fling himself by the side of the little river. The water was cool to his face and he drank deep, but the water in his stomach turned to steam, so that he swelled and swelled, and presently there was a loud explosion that shook the very hills, and El Enano burst into a thousand pieces.

---

15. A **hearth** (harth) is a brick, stone, or cement area that is the floor of a fireplace.

Analyzing the Photos Study the photos on pages 606 and 607. El Enano ate hot coals because he thought they were potatoes. Does that part of the story seem believable to you? Why or why not?

UNIT 5
Reading on Your Own

To read more about the Big Question, choose one of these books from your school or local library. Work on your reading skills by choosing books that are challenging to you.

Fiction

The Thanksgiving Visitor
by Truman Capote

Buddy recalls a Thanksgiving in 1932 when he was a second grader in rural Alabama. His best friend was an aging spinster named Miss Sook. Read to discover what happens when Miss Sook invites Buddy's bully, Odd Henderson, to Thanksgiving dinner.

Blubber
by Judy Blume

Jill goes along with her classmates when they tease Linda. But Jill never expects that they might make fun of her next.

Stepping on the Cracks
by Mary Downing Hahn

While her brother is fighting Hitler overseas, eleven-year-old Margaret faces her own enemy at home. Margaret and her friend discover secrets about the bully, Gordy. Will they use this information to make Gordy treat them better, or will they have a change of heart? You'll have to read to find out!

The Bully of Barkham Street
by Mary Stolz

Martin's only friend is his dog, Rufus. Read to find out what happens when the eleven-year-old bully of Barkham Street begins to realize that it's time for him to make a change.

Nonfiction

Homesick
by Jean Fritz

Jean Fritz is a member of an American family living in China, where Fritz attends a British elementary school. Fritz is uncomfortable singing the British national anthem, and she soon runs into trouble with her teacher and a bullying classmate.

Bullies Are a Pain in the Brain
by Trevor Romain

This book discusses different kinds of bullying behavior and presents positive ways to deal with bullies. Use its resources—like lists of helpful books, Web sites, and organizations—to help you understand and deal with the bullies you know.

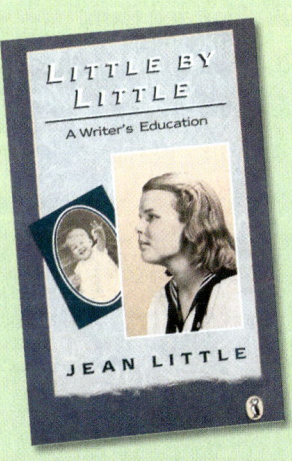

Little by Little
by Jean Little

Writer Jean Little recalls her childhood experience of entering a new class in Guelph, Ontario. Because she was visually impaired, her classmates teased her and chased her home after school. While Little's mother comforts her, she cannot solve the problem. Little discovers a place to belong when an older child takes her to the public library.

How to Handle Bullies, Teasers, and Other Meanies: A Book That Takes the Nuisance Out of Name Calling and Other Nonsense
by Kate Cohen-Posey

Sticks and stones can break your bones, but words can never hurt you. Only…they can. Sound familiar? If so, check out this guide to dealing with the verbal bully. Take the bite out of a bully's bark when you use these helpful tips.

UNIT 5 SKILLS AND STRATEGIES ASSESSMENT

Test Practice

Part 1: Literary Elements

On a separate sheet of paper, write the numbers 1–4. Next to each, write the letter of the correct answer for that question.

1. Think about the stories in this unit and other stories you have read. Which of the following stages of a plot is usually the longest and contains the most detail?
   A. exposition
   B. rising action
   C. climax
   D. falling action

Read the following passage and use it to answer questions 2–4.

   "It's time for you to give up," laughed Carly as the handle of Max's shovel broke in his hands.
   "No," replied Max, wiping the sweat from his forehead, "it's time for me to find another shovel."
   "The ground is as hard as a rock," said Carly, sympathetically. "Wouldn't you rather go swimming with me?"
   "Of course," said Max. "But then Dad would have to finish all the digging himself. No, I'm going to get this done, no matter how difficult it is."
   "Okay," sighed Carly. "Find a shovel for me, too."

2. What can you tell about Max from his dialogue?
   A. He's strong.
   B. He's determined.
   C. He's kindhearted.
   D. He's afraid of his father.

3. What can you tell about Carly from her dialogue?
   A. She's brave.
   B. She's helpful.
   C. She's confident.
   D. She's full of energy.

4. The main conflict in this passage is between
   A. Max and Carly.
   B. Max and his father.
   C. Max and the ground.
   D. Max's desire to dig and his desire to swim.

Objectives (pp. 610–611)
Reading Draw conclusions from text and experience • Paraphrase and summarize • Understand cause and effect • Identify text structure: sequence
Literature Identify literary elements: plot, conflict, dialogue, characterization

SKILLS AND STRATEGIES ASSESSMENT UNIT 5

Part 2: Reading Skills

On a separate sheet of paper, write the numbers 1–4. Next to numbers 1–3, write the letter of the correct answer for that question. Next to number 4, write your answer for that question.

[1]Wendy didn't want to go to school. [2]There were many reasons, all of which swirled inside her head as soon as the alarm awakened her. [3]She didn't want to carry her heavy backpack. [4]Worse, the seven-block walk would be cold. [5]There was going to be a spelling quiz she didn't feel ready for. [6]But the worst thing, the thing that made her heart pound and her breath come fast in shaky gasps, was that Tamara would be waiting for her. [7]Just like all of last week and the week before, Tamara would be in the hallway or out on the playground, waiting. [8]Wendy didn't think she could face one more day of trying to be brave.

---

1. This sequence of this paragraph is arranged according to
    A. time order.
    B. spatial order.
    C. order of importance.
    D. both time and space.

2. Based on the information in this paragraph, you can conclude that
    A. Wendy is smaller than Tamara.
    B. Wendy often stays home from school.
    C. Tamara is a new student at Wendy's school.
    D. Tamara has been frightening Wendy for some time.

3. Which sentence in the paragraph states the effect of all the other sentences?
    A. sentence 1
    B. sentence 2
    C. sentence 6
    D. sentence 8

4. Write a one- or two-sentence summary of the paragraph.

UNIT 5 SKILLS AND STRATEGIES ASSESSMENT

Part 3: Vocabulary Skills

On a separate sheet of paper, write the numbers 1–10. Next to each number, write the letter of the correct answer for that question.

Write the letter of the word or phrase that means about the same as the underlined word.

1. such <u>hostile</u> remarks
   - A. funny
   - B. confusing
   - C. unfriendly
   - D. welcoming

2. some <u>immense</u> animals
   - A. huge
   - B. wild
   - C. strange
   - D. dangerous

3. to <u>contemplate</u> an action
   - A. think about
   - B. recommend
   - C. disapprove of
   - D. successfully complete

4. with a <u>lithe</u> movement
   - A. sudden
   - B. flexible
   - C. sneaky
   - D. threatening

5. a <u>rigid</u> stem
   - A. thin
   - B. strong
   - C. broken
   - D. unbending

Choose the correct answer for each question.

6. Which of the following words has both a prefix and a suffix?
   - A. unselfish
   - B. friendliness
   - C. disrespect
   - D. handlebars

7. What is the base word in *dishonesty*?
   - A. dish
   - B. honest
   - C. honesty
   - D. dishonest

8. In which word are the letters *mis-* a prefix?
   - A. misty
   - B. mister
   - C. missing
   - D. misspell

9. Considering what you know about prefixes and base words, what does *disallow* mean?
   - A. permit
   - B. change
   - C. forbid
   - D. not pay for

10. Considering what you know about prefixes and base words, what does *overstate* mean?
    - A. deny
    - B. exaggerate
    - C. say again
    - D. apologize

Objectives (pp. 612–613)
Vocabulary Identify word structure
Grammar Identify sentence elements
• Use punctuation correctly

SKILLS AND STRATEGIES ASSESSMENT

Part 4: Writing Skills

On a separate sheet of paper, write the numbers 1–7. Next to each number, write the letter of the correct answer for that question.

---

1. Which of the following is a phrase?
   A. if you understand
   B. shady places in the yard
   C. when my neighbors get home
   D. after the crowd leaves the stadium

2. An adjective clause is one that
   A. can be substituted for a noun or pronoun.
   B. modifies, or tells more about, an adjective.
   C. explains what an adjective in a sentence means.
   D. functions (works) in a sentence like an adjective does.

3. Which of the following is an independent clause?
   A. flowers are blooming
   B. the fish that live in the lake
   C. before they finished the book
   D. children who never want to nap

4. Which sentence is punctuated correctly?
   A. We bought apples carrots crackers and juice.
   B. We bought, apples carrots crackers, and juice.
   C. We bought apples, carrots, crackers, and juice.
   D. We bought, apples, carrots, crackers, and juice.

5. Where should a comma be inserted in the sentence below?

   If you want me to I'll go along.
   A. after *you*
   B. after *me*
   C. after *to*
   D. after *go*

6. Which of the following sentences is punctuated correctly?
   A. No I don't think so.
   B. Yes, I plan to be there.
   C. Please Mom, let me stay home.
   D. Well give me some help, Cherise.

7. Which of the following sentences is punctuated correctly?
   A. Rafael, unlike Billy cleaned his room.
   B. Don't point, at the tourists, like that.
   C. The bleachers as I said earlier, were full.
   D. I will, if you don't mind, have another helping.

UNIT 6

The BIG Question: What Makes a Hero?

" My heroes are and were my parents. I can't see having anyone else as my heroes. "

—Michael Jordan
Probably the greatest basketball player ever, five-time Most Valuable Player; led the Chicago Bulls to six championships

LOOKING AHEAD

The skill lessons and readings in this unit will help you develop your own answer to the Big Question.

UNIT 6 WARM-UP • Connecting to the Big Question
GENRE FOCUS: FOLKTALE, FANTASY, AND MYTH

Persephone 619
  by Alice Low

READING WORKSHOP 1 — Skill Lesson: Activating Prior Knowledge

Hurricane Heroes 628
  by Thomas Fields-Meyer, Steve Helling, and Lori Rozsa, from *People*

All Stories Are Anansi's 636
  by Harold Courlander

WRITING WORKSHOP PART 1 — Fable 642

READING WORKSHOP 2 — Skill Lesson: Clarifying

The Twelve Labors of Hercules 650
  by Walker Brents

Pecos Bill 660
  by Mary Pope Osborne

READING WORKSHOP 3 — Skill Lesson: Comparing and Contrasting

Dragon, Dragon 674
  by John Gardner

The King of Mazy May 688
  by Jack London

WRITING WORKSHOP PART 2 — Fable 702

READING WORKSHOP 4 — Skill Lesson: Predicting

Aunt Millicent 710
  by Mary Steele

A Mason-Dixon Memory 734
  by Clifton Davis

COMPARING LITERATURE WORKSHOP

The Toad and the Donkey 748
  by Toni Cade Bambara

Doc Rabbit, Bruh Fox, and Tar Baby 751
  by Virginia Hamilton

UNIT 6 WRAP-UP • Answering the Big Question

UNIT 6 WARM-UP

Connecting to The BIG Question

What Makes a Hero?

In real life, heroes are people admired for great qualities or achievements. Who are *your* heroes? What do your choices suggest about the qualities and achievements you admire? In literature, *hero* has a slightly different meaning. In this unit, you'll read about some literary heroes and some real-life heroes. As you read, think about whether these heroes have qualities you admire.

Real Kids and the Big Question

JESSICA has always admired her cousin Luke. Luke is a wheelchair athlete who plays basketball. He is also an honor student. Whenever Jessica is feeling down about school, Luke always reminds her to keep a positive attitude. Luke helps Jessica with her Spanish class and acts as her big brother. If you asked Jessica what makes a hero, what do you think she might say? Why?

SHEA's father always takes time to help Shea with his homework. He drives him to baseball practice. They spend time together just talking. Shea's father tries to teach Shea those things that he feels are important in life. Shea looks up to his father. If you asked Shea what makes a hero, what do think he might say? Why?

Warm-Up Activity

In your Learner's Notebook, write the names of two people you admire and why you admire them.

You and the Big Question

Reading about heroes in different times and places may help you decide how you would answer the Big Question.

Big Question Link to Web resources to further explore the Big Question at www.glencoe.com.

Plan for the Unit Challenge

At the end of the unit, you'll use notes from all your reading to complete the Unit Challenge.

You'll choose one of the following activities:

A. Wall of Heroes You and your classmates will interview people in your school about their heroes. You will create a Wall of Heroes in your classroom that has the pictures and stories of the heroes in your community.

B. A Hero for Today Choose one of the heroes in the stories you read, and write a story about what this hero would do today if he or she were a hero in your community.

- Start thinking about which activity you'd like to do so you can focus your thinking as you go through the unit.
- If you choose the first activity, decide who you will interview and the questions you will ask them about their heroes.
- If you choose the second activity, take notes as you read the selections so you can decide which hero you'd like to use as your "Hero for Today."

Keep Track of Your Ideas

As you read, you'll make notes about the Big Question. Later, you'll use these notes to complete the Unit Challenge. See pages R8–R9 for help with making Foldable 6. This diagram shows how it should look.

1. Make one Foldable page for each selection. At the end of the unit, you'll staple the pages together into one Foldable.
2. Label the front of the fold-over page with the selection title. (See page 615 for titles.)
3. Open the Foldable. Label the top of the inside page **My Purpose for Reading.** You will write your purpose for reading the selection below this label.
4. Halfway down the inside page, write the label **The Big Question.** You'll write your thoughts about the Big Question below this label.

UNIT 6 GENRE FOCUS: FOLKTALE, FANTASY, AND MYTH

A **folktale** is a story that has been told by generations of storytellers before being written down. The story may be just fun, or it may teach a lesson about life. In this unit, you will also read fantasies and myths. A **fantasy** creates a new world very different from the world we live in today. A **myth** is usually about gods, goddesses, and large questions such as the origin of the earth, the sea, and the seasons.

Why Read Folktale, Fantasy, and Myth?

Folktales, fantasies, and myths take you to places, times, and people you never before imagined. They make you think about what's important to you and to all human beings. And they're fun to read!

How to Read Folktale, Fantasy, and Myth

Key Reading Skills

These skills are especially useful tools for reading folktales, fantasies, and myths. You'll learn more about these skills later in the unit.

- ■ **Activating prior knowledge** Before you read, recall what you already know about the characters, topic, or the setting you'll read about. (See Reading Workshop 1.)
- ■ **Clarifying** As you read, ask yourself questions about the plot, characters, setting, and point of view of the story to make sure you understand it. (See Reading Workshop 2.)
- ■ **Comparing and contrasting** As you read, compare and contrast within the story. Also compare and contrast different stories or styles to each other. (See Reading Workshop 3.)
- ■ **Predicting** Make guesses about the characters and events in the story as you learn more about them. (See Reading Workshop 4.)

Key Literary Elements

Recognizing and thinking about the following literary elements will help you understand more fully what the writer is telling you.

- ■ **Hero:** a literary work's main character, usually one with admirable qualities. A hero can be either male or female, but a female hero is sometimes called a *heroine* (HAIR oh un). (See "Hurricane Heroes.")
- ■ **Cultural context:** shared qualities and beliefs of people living in a particular time and place (See "The Twelve Labors of Hercules.")
- ■ **Theme:** the main idea of a story (See "Dragon, Dragon.")
- ■ **Setting:** the time and place of a story (See "Aunt Millicent.")

Skills Focus
- Key skills for reading folktales, fantasies, and myths
- Key literary elements of folktales, fantasies, and myths

Skills Model
You will see how to use the key reading skills and literary elements as you read
- "Persephone," p. 619

Objectives (pp. 618–623)
Reading • Activate prior knowledge • Clarify meaning • Compare and contrast • Make predictions
Literature Read folktales, fantasies, and myths • Identify key literary elements: hero, cultural context, theme, and setting

UNIT 6 GENRE FOCUS

#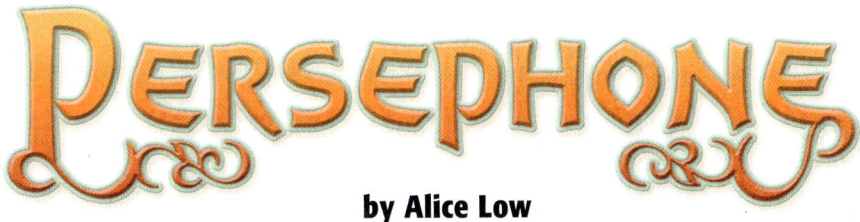
Persephone
by Alice Low

Myth
ACTIVE READING MODEL

1 Key Reading Skill
Activating Prior Knowledge *I know that things happen in myths that can't happen in real life. Gods and goddesses in myths had power over people's lives.*

2 Key Reading Skill
Clarifying *I have a feeling this story will mention several things that I don't understand very well. I'll take notes in my Learner's Notebook so I can find out about them and remember them. First, I'll write down Mount Olympus.*

Persephone[1] was a high-spirited, sunny girl who loved springtime and flowers and running outdoors with her friends. She was the daughter of Demeter,[2] goddess of the harvest, and she and her mother spent more time on earth than on Mount Olympus.[3]

One bright day on earth Persephone was picking lilies and violets with her friends. She could not gather enough of them, though her basket was overflowing. **1 2**

"Persephone, it is time to go home," called her friends.

"Just one minute longer," she called back. "I see the sweetest flower of all—a narcissus, I think. I must have one." She wandered into a far corner of the meadow, and just as she was about to pick the narcissus, she heard a deafening noise. Suddenly the earth split open at her feet. Out dashed a golden chariot pulled by black horses and driven by a stern-faced man in black armor.

Persephone dropped her basket and started to run, but the driver grabbed her by the wrist. He pulled her into

Four Seasons – Spring, (detail), 1896. Alphonse Mucha.
Analyzing the Art Do you think the young woman in this painting is a lot like Persephone? Why or why not?

---

1. **Persephone** (pur SEF uh nee)
2. **Demeter** (dih MEE tur)
3. **Mount Olympus** (oh LIM pus) is a tall mountain in Greece. People in ancient Greece believed the main gods and goddesses lived on top of this mountain.

619

Pluto and Proserpine, 1914. Henry Bryson Burroughs. Oil on canvas, 24 x 36¼ in. National Academy Museum, New York.
Analyzing the Art Pluto and Proserpine are other names for Hades and Persephone.

his chariot, which descended back into the earth as quickly as it had risen. Then the earth closed up after it.

Persephone screamed and wept, but her friends could not hear her. Though they searched for her everywhere, all they found was her basket, with a few crushed flowers lying next to it.

Down into the earth the chariot sped, through dark caverns and underground tunnels, while Persephone cried, "Who are you? Where are you taking me?"

"I am Hades,⁴ king of the underworld, and I am taking you there to be my bride."

"Take me back to my mother," screamed Persephone. "Take me back."

"Never!" said Hades. "For I have fallen in love with you. Your sunny face and golden hair will light up my dark palace." 3

The chariot flew over the river Styx⁵ where Charon,⁶ the boatman, was ferrying ghostly souls across the water. "Now we are at the gate to my kingdom," said Hades, as they landed next to the huge three-headed dog who guarded it.

---

4. In Greek mythology, the god **Hades** (HAY deez) ruled the **underworld**, a place under the earth where the dead lived.
5. **Styx** (stiks)
6. **Charon** (KAR un)

ACTIVE READING MODEL

3 **Key Reading Skill**
Comparing and Contrasting
So far, I know that Persephone is a high-spirited and sunny girl. How is she different from Hades? Let's see, it says that Hades is stern-faced and wears black armor. How are they alike? Well, one is a goddess and the other is a god.

Persephone shivered, and Hades said, "Oh, that is Cerberus.[7] He guards the gate so that no live mortals enter and no souls of the dead escape. Nobody escapes from the underworld."

Persephone became speechless. Never escape from this terrible place full of pale, shadowy ghosts, wandering through stony fields full of pale, ghostly flowers!

Beautiful Persephone, who loved sunshine, became Hades' queen and sat on a cold throne in his cold palace. Hades gave her a gold crown and bright jewels, but her heart was like ice and she neither talked nor ate nor drank.

Persephone's mother, Demeter, knew that something terrible had happened to her daughter. She alone had heard Persephone's screams, which had echoed through the mountains and over the sea.

Demeter left Olympus, disguised as an old woman, and wandered the earth for nine days and nine nights, searching for her daughter. She called to the mountains and rivers and sea, "Persephone, where are you? Come back. Come back." But there was never an answer. She did not weep, for goddesses do not cry, but her heart was heavy. She could not eat or drink or rest, so deep was her grief. 4 5

Finally she reached a placed called Eleusis, not far from the spot where Persephone had disappeared. There a prince named Triptolemus[8] recognized her and told her this story: "Over a week ago, my brother was taking care of the royal pigs. He heard a thundering noise, and the earth opened up. Out rushed a chariot, driven by a grim-faced man. He grabbed a beautiful young girl and down into the earth they went. They were swallowed up, along with the pigs."

"That man must have been Hades," cried Demeter. "I fear that he has kidnapped my daughter."

Demeter hurried to the sun, Helios,[9] who sees everything. And the sun confirmed Demeter's fears.

---

7. **Cerberus** (SUR buh rus)
8. **Triptolemus** (TRIP tuh lee mus)
9. **Helios** (HEE lee us)

UNIT 6 GENRE FOCUS

ACTIVE READING MODEL

4 Key Literary Element
Setting *The settings so far have been earth, the underworld, and Mount Olympus. There hasn't been much description of what Olympus is like, but the underworld seems really scary and creepy.*

5 Key Reading Skill
Comparing and Contrasting *Persephone and her mother react in similar ways when Persephone is first captured. Persephone is quiet and her heart is like ice. She doesn't eat or drink. Her mother Demeter can't eat or drink, and she becomes stony. But Persephone is helpless while Demeter has the power to help her daughter.*

Demeter cried, "Persephone, my gay lovely daughter, is imprisoned in the underworld, never again to see the light of day or the flowers of spring."

Then Demeter became stony and angry, and she caused the earth to suffer with her. The earth became cold and barren. Trees did not bear fruit, the grass withered and did not grow again, and the cattle died from hunger. A few men succeeded in plowing the hard earth and sowing seeds, but no shoots sprouted from them. It was a cruel year for mankind. If Demeter continued to withhold her blessings from the earth, people would perish from hunger.

Zeus begged Demeter to let the earth bear fruit again, but Demeter said, "The earth will never be green again. Not unless my daughter returns!"

Then Zeus knew that he must take action to save people from starvation. "I will see that Persephone returns," he told Demeter, "but only on one condition. She must not have eaten any of the food of the dead."

Zeus sent Hermes, messenger of the gods, down to the underworld to ask Hades for Persephone's release. When Persephone saw that Hermes had come to her home, she became lively and smiled and talked for the first time that year.

To her delight, Hades did not protest but said, "Go, my child. Although I love you, I cannot keep you here against Zeus's will. But you must eat a little something before you leave, to give you strength for your journey." Then he gave Persephone several seeds from a red pomegranate, which was the fruit eaten by the dead. He knew that if she ate even one, she would have to return to him. 6

Persephone ate four seeds quickly. Then she climbed into the golden chariot and waved good-by. Hermes drove her to earth, to the temple where Demeter waited, and mother and daughter hugged and laughed and said they would never be parted again. Then Demeter remembered Zeus's warning and said,

The Return of Persephone, 1891. Frederic Leighton. Oil on canvas. Leeds Museums and Galleries, U.K.

Analyzing the Art This painting shows the return of Persephone to her mother. Who is each person in this painting? How do you know?

ACTIVE READING MODEL

6 **Key Reading Skill**
Predicting Uh-oh. I think Zeus will make her go back to Hades because he said she can't eat any food of the dead.

"I hope you did not eat anything while you were in the underworld."

"I was too sad to eat," said Persephone. "I didn't eat or drink all year."

"Not anything at all?" said Demeter.

"Oh, just a few little pomegranate seeds before I left," said Persephone. Why do you ask?"

"Because, my dearest," cried Demeter, "if you have eaten any of the food of the dead, you must return to Hades."

Zeus heard the loud wails of Demeter and her daughter, and he decided to compromise. Persephone must spend just four months of each year in the underworld, one for each of the seeds she had eaten. The rest of the year she could be with her mother on earth. 7

That is why every year, for four months, the earth becomes cold and barren. Persephone is in the dark underworld and Demeter is overcome with grief. 8

And every year, when Persephone returns to earth, she brings spring with her. The earth is filled with flowers and fruits and grasses. And summer and fall, the seasons of growth and harvest, follow in their natural order. Every year Demeter and the whole earth rejoice that Persephone has returned. 9

ACTIVE READING MODEL

7 Key Literary Element
Hero *By the literary definition, Persephone is the hero of this story because she's the main character. But Demeter acts more like a real-life hero because she does all she can to save her daughter.*

8 Key Literary Element
Theme *I think the theme of the myth is that the gods control everything and even the other gods have to obey Zeus.*

9 Key Literary Element
Cultural Context *People in ancient Greece believed that gods and goddesses controlled everything, including the seasons.*

Write to Learn Answer these questions in your Learner's Notebook.
1. Most ancient Greeks believed that their myths were true. Why do you think they believed the myth of Persephone?
2. What myths do people today believe in? What myths do you believe in?

 **Study Central** Visit www.glencoe.com and click on Study Central to review folktale, fantasy, myth.

READING WORKSHOP 1

Skills Focus

You will practice using these skills when you read the following selections:
- "Hurricane Heroes," p. 628
- "All Stories Are Anansi's," p. 636

Reading
- Activating prior knowledge

Literature
- Distinguishing real-life heroes from literary heroes
- Understanding the heroes of folktales

Vocabulary
- Understanding compound and blended words

Writing/Grammar
- Capitalizing sentences
- Identifying simple sentences

Objectives (pp. 624–625)
Reading Activate prior knowledge

Skill Lesson
Activating Prior Knowledge

Learn It!

What Is It? Activating prior knowledge means using what you already know to understand what you are reading. This could be information you have already read or knowledge from your own experiences. Activating prior knowledge makes it easier to understand something new. For example, if you used what you already knew about Greek myths, it would be easier to understand "Persephone."

- To activate something is to make it active, to get it going so it can be useful.
- Prior knowledge is knowledge you already have—facts and experiences you remember or information you know.
- Activating prior knowledge is using what you know, or what you've already read to help clarify your understanding.

CALVIN AND HOBBES © 1995 Watterson. Dist. By UNIVERSAL PRESS SYNDICATE. Reprinted with permission. All rights reserved.

Analyzing Cartoons
Calvin didn't activate his prior knowledge in this cartoon. What should he have remembered about snowballs?

READING WORKSHOP 1 • Activating Prior Knowledge

Why Is It Important? Activating prior knowledge helps you understand what you read. It can help you guess about the meanings of related things. And it can help you predict what might happen.

How Do I Do It? Before you read, skim the text to see what it might be about. Then think about what you already know about that topic. Here's how one student used her prior knowledge of myths to understand the first paragraph of "Persephone."

Literature Online

Study Central Visit www.glencoe.com and click on Study Central to review activating prior knowledge.

> Persephone was a high-spirited, sunny girl who loved springtime and flowers and running outdoors with her friends. She was the daughter of Demeter, goddess of the harvest, and she and her mother spent more time on earth than on Mount Olympus.

I know myths usually have gods and goddesses. Since Persephone is the daughter of a goddess, this is probably a myth. I know that gods and goddesses in myths have supernatural powers. It sounds like Mount Olympus isn't on earth, so I bet that's where the gods and goddesses live.

Practice It!

Below are some topics and genres related to the selections in this unit. What do you already know about each topic or genre? In your Learner's Notebook, write two things you know about each subject.

- folktales
- myths
- hurricanes
- heroes

Use It!

As you read from "Hurricane Heroes" and "All Stories Are Anansi's," remember what you wrote in your Learner's Notebook about hurricanes and folktales. Use this knowledge to help you understand what you read.

READING WORKSHOP 1 • Activating Prior Knowledge

Before You Read : Hurricane Heroes

Meet the Authors
This selection is about actual events and was written by three authors: Thomas Fields-Meyer, Steve Helling, and Lori Rozsa. Each author reports on current events for news sources such as *People* magazine and the *Miami Herald*.

Author Search For more about the writers, go to www.glencoe.com.

Vocabulary Preview

makeshift (MAYK shift) *adj.* suitable as a temporary substitute **(p. 628)** *After a hurricane, makeshift hospitals need to be set up.*

anesthetist (uh NES thuh tist) *n.* the person who gives drugs to put a patient to sleep before surgery **(p. 629)** *It is important to have an anesthetist on an emergency medical team.*

Write to Learn Make a one-panel illustration for each word that shows the word's meaning. Add a caption explaining the illustration. Use the actual word in the caption.

English Language Coach

Compound Words Many words have interesting histories. Some come from the names of people or places. *Teddy bear,* a small stuffed bear, is named for President Teddy Roosevelt. *Hamburger,* a patty of ground meat, comes from Hamburg, Germany. Other words like *mailbox* and *riverbank* come from joining two existing words. *Mailbox* and *riverbank* are compound words. **Compound words** are made up of two or more words. One way that words enter the English language is by combining words to make new words.

You can often figure out the meaning of these compound words by thinking about the meanings of the words that make it up. For example, *mailbox* is a compound word made up of *mail* and *box*. It means "a box in which mail is deposited."

Compound words are hyphenated (like *well-known*), open (like *hot dog*), or closed (like *eggshell*). There's only one simple, clear rule to help you know which way to write a compound: Check a dictionary.

Partner Talk With a partner, talk about the individual words that form the compound words below. Then match each compound word with its definition below.

1. cry + baby
2. book + case
3. heart + ache

a. sorrow or grief
b. a person who often complains
c. shelves for books

Objectives (pp. 626–631)
Reading Activate prior knowledge • Make connections from text to self
Literature Identify literary elements: hero
Vocabulary Explore word origins: compound words

626 UNIT 6 What Makes a Hero?

READING WORKSHOP 1 • Activating Prior Knowledge

Skills Preview

Key Reading Skill: Activating Prior Knowledge

Before you read, think about the terrible hurricanes that have hit the U.S. and other places around the world. What do you remember from watching TV, reading, or hearing about hurricanes?

Class Talk With your class, discuss the responses to hurricanes that you remember.

Key Literary Element: Hero

There are three main definitions of the word **hero**.

- **Literary Hero** As you learned in the Genre Focus, the word *hero* has a specific meaning in literature. The hero of a story is the main character, who may or may not have admirable qualities. The most important character in the Genre Focus story is Persephone, and that makes her the hero. Once, most people would have called her the *heroine,* which was the term used for female main characters.

- **Mythic Hero** In mythology, the word *hero* can have another meaning. A *mythic hero* is usually a man who is superhuman and may even be half-god, half-human. This kind of hero has amazing courage and strength and the myths are about his adventures.

- **Real-Life Hero** The last definition of the word *hero* is the one we're all most familiar with: a person who acts bravely for the good of others, often putting his or her own life at risk.

Partner Talk Next you'll read about real-life heroes. With a partner, talk about what makes a real-life hero different from a literary or mythic hero.

Interactive Literary Elements Handbook
To review or learn more about the literary elements, go to www.glencoe.com.

Get Ready to Read

Connect to the Reading

Have you ever survived a difficult experience or a life-threatening situation? What was it? How did you get through? Imagine what it's like to survive something like a hurricane. What would it take for you to risk your life for someone else?

Write to Learn What kind of situation would it take for you to risk your life to try to save someone else's? In your Learner's Notebook, write for five minutes about the kind of situation that might cause you to take action.

Build Background

Hurricanes are large, severe storms with heavy rains and strong winds. You are about to read an article about a series of hurricanes that occurred in 2004 and did a great deal of damage to the southern part of the United States.

- Many hurricanes form over the Atlantic Ocean in the summer and then move west toward the U.S.
- Hurricanes are given names to help identify them and track their movements.
- The center of a hurricane is called "the eye." An eye is roughly circular, and the weather tends to be calm inside the eye.

Set Purposes for Reading

BIG Question Read "Hurricane Heroes" to find out how average people can become heroes when faced with an emergency.

Set Your Own Purpose What else would you like to learn about "Hurricane Heroes"? Write your own purpose on the "Hurricane Heroes" page of Foldable 6.

Keep Moving →

Use these skills as you read the following selection.

Hurricane Heroes **627**

READING WORKSHOP 1

HURRICANE HEROES

As storms slammed the South in 2004, some brave folks risked their lives to help others.

By THOMAS FIELDS-MEYER, STEVE HELLING, and LORI ROZSA

Charley, Frances, Ivan, Jeanne: four hurricanes in six weeks; more than 150 deaths and $44 billion in damage. Faced with wrecked bridges, shattered condos, floods, and mudslides, millions of people in Florida, Georgia, and Alabama had to decide when to flee, what to save, or whom to help. Meet three people who made it through and helped many others along the way. **1**

A Medical Marathon[1]

Ron Wegner treated wounds—some invisible

Wegner, 57, commander of Florida's 35-member Disaster Medical Assistance Team, spent several weeks living in Charley's and Ivan's disaster zones. He put in 20-hour shifts and helped treat everything from broken bones to heart attacks. Still, he says his most memorable patient was an 83-year-old woman. She came into the **makeshift** emergency

1 **Key Reading Skill**

Activating Prior Knowledge
Think about what you read in Build Background about hurricanes; add what you know about past hurricanes, like Hurricane Katrina. Activate that knowledge to help answer this question: Why does this paragraph begin with four names?

[1]. Originally, a *marathon* was a 26-mile foot race. Now the word is also used to refer to anything that lasts a long time and is difficult to bear.

Vocabulary

makeshift (MAYK shift) *adj.* suitable as a temporary substitute

628 UNIT 6 What Makes a Hero?

unit in the parking lot of a damaged Pensacola hospital where Wegner was stationed after Ivan. She showed him a bruise on her hand. "She admitted she hadn't really been injured, but her house was destroyed and she was alone, and she wanted to talk to somebody. So for 25 minutes I held her hand and we talked," he says. "Really, her problem was just as important as a chain-saw accident."

Wegner is an **anesthetist** who lives in Tampa. Like all of the disaster volunteers, Wegner was paid by the federal government what he would usually have earned in his regular job. Wegner is the nerve center of the medical team. "He's the ringmaster of the circus," says Butch Kinerney, a **spokesperson** for the Federal Emergency Management Agency.² In the first three days after Ivan, Wegner's team treated 460 people. Though he misses his girlfriend and 25-year-old daughter, there were no complaints from Wegner. "We've got our comfortable lives to go back to," he says. "A lot of these people have nothing." 2 3 4

"You see so many people just wandering about stunned," says Ron Wegner (in Gulf Breeze, Florida).

He Came, He Saw, He Sawed
Jim Williams went out on many limbs

Driving to work the morning after Hurricane Charley ripped through Sanford, Florida, mail carrier Williams was so stunned by the number of fallen trees he saw that he had to pull over. The area "was just devastated," says Williams, 45, who grew up in the quiet community 25 miles north of Orlando. "I sat in my truck and cried."

2. The **Federal Emergency Management Agency** responds to natural and manmade disasters. It's often referred to by its initials, FEMA (FEE muh). The agency has helped many thousands of people recover from disasters; however, it was severely criticized for its slow, inadequate response after Hurricane Katrina hit Gulf Coast states in 2005.

Vocabulary

anesthetist (uh NES thuh tist) *n.* the person who gives drugs to put a patient to sleep before surgery

2 English Language Coach

Compound Words
Spokesperson is a compound word. It means "one who speaks on behalf of others."

3 Key Literary Element

Hero What differences do you notice between Wegner and a typical literary hero? Use evidence from this article to support your answer.

4 Key Reading Skill

Activating Prior Knowledge
What do you think a "nerve center" is? Nerves send messages back and forth to the brain. What do you already know about a center? Combine those things with what you've already read to think about what a nerve center does.

READING WORKSHOP 1

Then he took action. Returning home, Williams grabbed his chain saw and headed to the home of a friend's parents, where two huge oak trees had fallen. He sawed the rest of the day to clear the couple's driveway. Every day for the next three weeks, Williams delivered the mail through the cleanup from Charley and Frances. But he also spent hours after work using his chain saw wherever he could help—particularly outside the homes of retired people along his 18-mile mail route.

Williams spent nearly five hours clearing a 40-foot oak from atop the home of Ginny Taffer, 79, and husband Gene, 83. "He was my angel," says Ginny. What motivates Williams? He says that when his son James, 10 (with wife Gail, 47; he also has a daughter Leah, 16), was ill with lymphoma[3] at 6, he made a pledge to help people. Besides, he adds, "I was raised right and taught to do the right thing."

"I did what I could to help," says Jim Williams, who refused payment but did accept one offering: a pecan pie.

5 | **Key Reading Skill**

Hero Do you think Williams is a hero? Why or why not? Use details from this article to support your answers.

Trapped in a Collapsing Hotel

Melissa Baldwin fought her fears and saved her guests

On August 13, 2004, the fierce winds of Charley ripped the roof off of a wing of the Best Western Waterfront in Punta Gorda, Florida. Fearing for her life, Melissa Baldwin, assistant manager of the motel, phoned her fiancé, Ted Barkenquast, from the front lobby. "Tell Mom and Dad I love them," she yelled as windows shattered around her. Then the phone went dead. Recalls Barkenquast: "All I could do was think the worst."

But the storm brought out the best in Baldwin, 33, who suffers from epileptic seizures[4] that can be brought on by

---

3. **Lymphoma** is a kind of tumor.
4. **Epilepsy** is a nervous-system disorder that causes attacks called **seizures**. A seizure may include loss of consciousness and violent shaking of the body.

stress. "I figured if I was going to go down, I'd go down saving lives," she says. She raced upstairs to the fifth floor. Then working her way down, she moved 56 guests and employees to a windowless second-floor hall. Baldwin also ran outside and gathered people from a building next door. "It sounded like a freight train was going through the building. The wind was screaming, and people were screaming," she recalls. "I honestly thought, *So this is how I'm going to die.*"

Unable to move an elderly man in room 112, she helped him into a **bathtub** and cushioned his body with pillows. When one woman resisted, "I said, 'I'm not overreacting. Just trust me,'" says Baldwin. The hurricane pounded the hotel so hard that walls collapsed and **air-conditioning** units were ripped away from the building. When the winds died down after midnight, Baldwin handed a list of the 56 guests—all breathing and unharmed—to a rescue worker. The worker marveled, "I can't believe you're all alive." 6 7

Says Baldwin's coworker Lee Phillips, "Melissa was so comforting to the guests. If there were 15 of me, I don't think I could have been as comforting. She didn't crack." Baldwin is just happy everyone scraped through. "I don't know if I'll ever get over it," she says. "But the hurricane helped show me how strong I really am." 8

—Updated 2005, from *PEOPLE*, October 4, 2004

"I didn't have time to be scared," says Melissa Baldwin (at the hurricane-devastated Best Western).

6 Key Literary Element

Hero Is Baldwin a hero? Why or why not? Use details from this article to support your answers.

7 English Language Coach

Compound Words **Bathtub** is always a closed compound. **Air-conditioning** is hyphenated when it's an adjective, but it can be either open or hyphenated when it's a noun.

8 BIG Question

Does this article change your idea about how a hero can find his or her strength? Write your answer on the "Hurricane Heroes" page of Foldable 6. Your response will help you complete the Unit Challenge later.

READING WORKSHOP 1 • Activating Prior Knowledge

After You Read | Hurricane Heroes

Answering the BIG Question

1. How might extreme events make heroes out of ordinary people?
2. **Recall** Name one real-life hero that you just read about, and give the name of the hurricane that he or she responded to.
   TIP Think and Search
3. **Summarize** What did Jim Williams do after the hurricane?
   TIP Think and Search

Critical Thinking

4. **Synthesize** Do you think the people in the article would have behaved similarly had these events unfolded before their eyes in another community? For example, if they were on vacation in another country and a hurricane struck, would they have reacted the same way? Explain.
   TIP On My Own
5. **Evaluate** Did the authors present facts, opinions, or both? Did the authors persuade you that the people in the article are real-life heroes? Explain.
   TIP Author and Me
6. **Analyze** Do you think the people described in this story always had heroic qualities or do you think they found special strength and courage when faced with an emergency? Explain.
   TIP On My Own

Talk About Your Reading

With a partner, talk about events or situations that would bring out the real-life hero in you. Would it be a natural disaster, or do you think you would be the kind of hero to stand up for a good cause? Consider the situations in "Hurricane Heroes." Think about what you already know about heroes. Use these questions to get started.

- Do you think you would be more likely to take action in an emergency, or would you be more likely to champion a cause?
- What kind of emergencies need heroes? What kind of causes need champions?
- In what ways can you start taking action to become a real-life hero right now?

Objectives (pp. 632–633)
Reading Activate prior knowledge • Make connections from text to self
Literature Identify literary elements: hero
Vocabulary Explore word origins

Skills Review

Key Reading Skill: Activating Prior Knowledge

7. Did you activate knowledge about hurricanes beyond the facts presented in Build Background? If you hadn't known anything about hurricanes, would you still have been able to understand this article? Explain your answers.

8. Besides what you knew about hurricanes, did other prior knowledge help you to understand the article? For example, did knowing what a circus ringmaster (page 629) does help you see what Jim Wegner did on his medical team? Find two examples of words or ideas that made you activate prior knowledge to understand things in the article.

Key Literary Element: Hero

9. This article describes three different people that the writers consider heroes. Describe what made them heroes. Use details from the article.
10. Which person do you admire the most? Why?
11. Describe how this article might be different if it were a myth about hurricanes and the heroes were magical.

Vocabulary Check

Choose the best word from the list to complete each sentence below. Rewrite each sentence, with the correct word in place.

anesthetist   makeshift

12. Trailers are sometimes used as ___ housing after a hurricane.
13. The work of the ___ is to stop the feeling of pain.

English Language Coach Combine each word in the first column with a word in the second column. Each new word should be a compound word.

14. grand   port
15. news   board
16. down   father
17. card   paper
18. air   town

Grammar Link: Capitalization of Sentences

It's important to capitalize the first letter of each word at the beginning of a sentence so readers can tell where one sentence ends and the next sentence starts. All complete sentences start with a capital letter.

Grammar Practice

Copy these sentences, capitalizing the first word of every sentence.

19. my sister studies hard. she wants to go to college one day.
20. few people have a chance to be heroes. everyone can practice being kind.
21. hurricanes can be horrible. their effects can last for years.
22. our neighbor coaches soccer in his spare time. many of the kids see him as a hero.

Writing Application Write a short summary of the discussion you had with your partner for Talk About Your Reading on page 632. Be sure to capitalize the first letter of each word that begins a sentence.

Web Activities For eFlashcards, Selection Quick Checks, and other Web activities, go to www.glencoe.com.

READING WORKSHOP 1 • Activating Prior Knowledge

Before You Read : All Stories Are Anansi's

Meet the Author
Like all folktales, this story was passed around by word of mouth long before it was written. This version is a retelling by Harold Courlander. Courlander has always had a special interest in using narration to improve cross-cultural communication. See page R2 of the Author Files for more on Harold Courlander.

Author Search For more about Harold Courlander, go to www.glencoe.com.

Vocabulary Preview

yearned (yurnd) *v.* had a strong desire; form of the verb *yearn* (p. 636) *Anansi yearned to own all the stories in the world.*

dispute (dis PYOOT) *n.* a difference of opinion; argument or quarrel (p. 637) *Anansi had a dispute with his wife; they disagreed about the strength of the python.*

accustomed (uh KUS tumd) *adj.* used to; familiar with (p. 638) *The leopard didn't expect a trap because he was accustomed to walking in that area.*

merely (MEER lee) *adv.* just; only (p. 639) *Anansi wasn't merely confident, he was also very clever.*

acknowledge (ak NOL ij) *v.* to recognize the truth of something (p. 639) *According to this folktale, we must acknowledge that all stories belong to Anansi.*

Write to Learn Write a paragraph about something you want to do, using at least three of the vocabulary words above.

English Language Coach

Borrowed Words English has always been a mix of languages, especially Anglo-Saxon, Latin, and Greek. Modern English continues to change by adding new words from languages around the world. Such words are called **borrowed words.** The word *safari,* for example, came from Africa. *Coffee* came from Arabia, and *ketchup* from China! As you can see, many borrowed words are so familiar that we would never imagine they came from other languages.

Partner Talk Many of the foods we eat came from other countries and so did their names. *Pizza* is Italian, and *chili* is Mexican. With a partner, list as many borrowed food names as you can.

Objectives (pp. 634–639)
Reading Activate prior knowledge
• Make connections from text to self
Literature Identify literary elements: hero
Vocabulary Explore word origins: borrowed words

634 UNIT 6 What Makes a Hero?

READING WORKSHOP 1 • Activating Prior Knowledge

Skills Preview

Key Reading Skill: Activating Prior Knowledge

Before you read the story, think about what you know about

- folktale heroes
- folktales about animals
- animals that live in Africa

Class Talk Think of other folktales that you have read. Have someone write the names of folktales on the board as class members think of them. Take turns naming the hero in each folktale. Then name a heroic action or characteristic of the hero.

Key Literary Element: Hero

Heroes in myths are often brave and strong and may even have supernatural powers. However, many cultures have folktales about a different kind of hero—a trickster. A trickster may be physically weak, but is able to use humor and cunning to get what he or she wants. As you read this story, use these tips to decide whether you admire the trickster hero, Anansi:

- Decide if he's physically strong compared to other characters. Decide if he's smart compared to other characters.
- Think about what he wants and how he gets it.
- Decide how the humor in the story affects the way you view Anansi.

Partner Talk With a partner, make a list of other trickster characters you know about. To help you remember more characters, look up the word *trickster* in an encyclopedia or on the Internet.

Get Ready to Read

Connect to the Reading

Think of a time when you were tricked by someone or when you played a trick on someone else. As you read, pay attention to how Anansi uses trickery to become a hero.

Build Background

Anansi is a favorite character in many African and Caribbean folktales. A spider-man, he is shown as either a spider or as a man with spider characteristics. Anansi is a trickster who tries to make everything turn out the best way possible—for himself. His tricks are surprising, clever, and fun to read about.

- The trickster is usually a smaller, weaker character, who must use his or her brains to outsmart a larger and more powerful opponent.
- Clever tricksters get themselves out of trouble, but in many stories they get right back into it.
- Tricksters who try to take advantage of others and change the rules to favor themselves often end up caught in their own mischief.

Set Purposes for Reading

BIG Question Read "All Stories Are Anansi's" to find out if Anansi, the trickster, has the qualities of a real-life hero.

Set Your Own Purpose What else would you like to learn from "All Stories Are Anansi's"? Write your own purpose on the "All Stories Are Anansi's" page of Foldable 6.

Interactive Literary Elements Handbook
To review or learn more about the literary elements, go to www.glencoe.com.

Keep Moving
Use these skills as you read the following selection.

READING WORKSHOP 1

All Stories Are ANANSI'S

by Harold Courlander

Mask (Okorashi Oma). African Nigeria. Wood and pigment, 10½ x 6¾ x 4 in. Harn Museum of Art. University of Florida

IN THE BEGINNING, ALL TALES AND STORIES BELONGED TO Nyame,[1] the Sky God. But Kwaku Anansi, the spider, **yearned** to be the owner of all the stories known in the world, and he went to Nyame and offered to buy them. **1**

The Sky God said: "I am willing to sell the stories, but the price is high. Many people have come to me offering to buy, but the price was too high for them. Rich and powerful families have not been able to pay. Do you think you can do it?"

Anansi replied to the Sky God: "I can do it. What is the price?"

"My price is three things," the Sky God said. "I must first have Mmoboro, the hornets. I must then have Onini, the great **python**. I must then have Osebo, the leopard. For these things I will sell you the right to tell all stories." **2**

Anansi said: "I will bring them."

---

1. **Nyame** is pronounced (en YAH may).

Vocabulary

yearned (yurnd) *v.* had a strong desire

Practice the Skills

1 ### Key Reading Skill
Activating Prior Knowledge
What do you know about the importance of stories? Why would Anansi want to own all of the stories? What do you know about folktales that will help you understand this trickster tale? Think about what you learned in the Build Background.

2 ### English Language Coach
Borrowed Words The snake that we call the **python** got its name from a monstrous snake in mythology. Its Greek name was *Pythōn*.

636 UNIT 6 What Makes a Hero?

READING WORKSHOP 1

Visual Vocabulary
A *calabash* (KAL uh bash) is a kind of gourd, or hard-shelled fruit.

He went home and made his plans. He first cut a gourd from a vine and made a small hole in it. He took a large calabash and filled it with water. He went to the tree where the hornets lived. He poured some of the water over himself, so that he was dripping. He threw some water over the hornets, so that they too were dripping. Then he put the calabash on his head, as though to protect himself from a storm, and called out to the hornets: "Are you foolish people? Why do you stay in the rain that is falling?"

The hornets answered: "Where shall we go?"

"Go here, in this dry gourd," Anansi told them.

The hornets thanked him and flew into the gourd through the small hole. When the last of them had entered, Anansi plugged the hole with a ball of grass, saying: "Oh, yes, but you are really foolish people!"

He took his gourd full of hornets to Nyame, the Sky God. The Sky God accepted them. He said: "There are two more things."

Anansi returned to the forest and cut a long bamboo pole and some strong vines. Then he walked toward the house of Onini, the python, talking to himself. He said: "My wife is stupid. I say he is longer and stronger. My wife says he is shorter and weaker. I give him more respect. She gives him less respect. Is she right or am I right? I am right, he is longer. I am right, he is stronger."

When Onini, the python, heard Anansi talking to himself, he said: "Why are you arguing this way with yourself?"

The spider replied: "Ah, I have had a **dispute** with my wife. She says you are shorter and weaker than this bamboo pole. I say you are longer and stronger." 🔳

Onini said: "It's useless and silly to argue when you can find out the truth. Bring the pole and we will measure."

Untitled, 1990. Twins Seven-Seven. African ink on plywood with plywood collage. The Pigozzi Collection, Geneva.

🔳 **English Language Coach**

Borrowed Words The word **bamboo** comes from an unusual source—Malay. That's one of the languages used by people in Southeast Asia. They spell it *bambu*.

Vocabulary

dispute (dis PYOOT) *n.* a difference of opinion; argument or quarrel

All Stories Are Anansi's **637**

READING WORKSHOP 1

So Anansi laid the pole on the ground, and the python came and stretched himself out beside it.

"You seem a little short," Anansi said.

The python stretched further.

"A little more," Anansi said.

"I can stretch no more," Onini said.

"When you stretch at one end, you get shorter at the other end," Anansi said. "Let me tie you at the front so you don't slip."

He tied Onini's head to the pole. Then he went to the other end and tied the tail to the pole. He wrapped the vine all around Onini, until the python couldn't move.

"Onini," Anansi said, "it turns out that my wife was right and I was wrong. You are shorter than the pole and weaker. My opinion wasn't as good as my wife's. But you were even more foolish than I, and you are now my prisoner."

Anansi carried the python to Nyame, the Sky God, who said: "There is one thing more."

Osebo, the leopard, was next. Anansi went into the forest and dug a deep pit where the leopard was **accustomed** to walk. He covered it with small branches and leaves and put dust on it, so that it was impossible to tell where the pit was. Anansi went away and hid. When Osebo came prowling in the black of night, he stepped into the trap Anansi had prepared and fell to the bottom. Anansi heard the sound of the leopard falling, and he said: "Ah, Osebo, you are half-foolish!"

When morning came, Anansi went to the pit and saw the leopard there.

"Osebo," he asked, "what are you doing in this hole?"

"I have fallen into a trap," Osebo said. "Help me out."

"I would gladly help you," Anansi said. "But I'm sure that if I bring you out, I will have no thanks for it. You will get hungry, and later on you will be wanting to eat me and my children." 4

Relief from one of the chapels off the Hypostyle Hall, Great Temple of Seti (13th century B.C.), Abydos. Temple of Seti I, Abydos, Egypt.

4 Key Literary Element

Hero How does Anansi's behavior with the hornets and the python show that he is a trickster hero?

Vocabulary

accustomed (uh KUS tumd) *adj.* used to; familiar with

"I swear it won't happen!" Osebo said.

"Very well. Since you swear it, I will take you out," Anansi said.

He bent a tall green tree toward the ground, so that its top was over the pit, and he tied it that way. Then he tied a rope to the top of the tree and dropped the other end of it into the pit.

"Tie this to your tail," he said.

Osebo tied the rope to his tail.

"Is it well tied?" Anansi asked.

"Yes, it is well tied," the leopard said.

"In that case," Anansi said, "you are not **merely** half-foolish, you are all-foolish."

And he took his knife and cut the other rope, the one that held the tree bowed to the ground. The tree straightened up with a snap, pulling Osebo out of the hole. He hung in the air head downward, twisting and turning. And while he hung this way, Anansi killed him with his weapons. **5 6**

Then he took the body of the leopard and carried it to Nyame, the Sky God, saying: "Here is the third thing. Now I have paid the price."

Nyame said to him: "Kwaku Anansi, great warriors and chiefs have tried, but they have been unable to do it. You have done it. Therefore, I will give you the stories. From this day onward, all stories belong to you. Whenever a man tells a story, he must **acknowledge** that it is Anansi's tale."

In this way Anansi, the spider, became the owner of all stories that are told. To Anansi all these tales belong. **7** ○

Practice the Skills

5 Reviewing Skills

Identifying Problem and Solution After Anansi caught the leopard in a pit, he had to solve the problem of how to get him out of the pit. What was his solution?

6 Key Literary Element

Hero In what way or ways is Anansi a typical literary hero?

7 BIG Question

Does Anansi have qualities you admire in real-life heroes? On the "Anansi" page of Foldable 6, write a short paragraph to support your answer. Use examples from the story. Your response will help you complete the Unit Challenge later.

Vocabulary

merely (MEER lee) *adv.* just; only

acknowledge (ak NOL ij) *v.* to recognize the truth of something

READING WORKSHOP 1 • **Activating Prior Knowledge**

After You Read : All Stories Are Anansi's

Answering the BIG Question

1. Do you think Anansi acts heroically?
2. **Recall** How did Anansi get the python to agree to be tied to a pole?
   TIP Right There
3. **Summarize** Summarize the three things Anansi had to do to pay for all the stories in the world.
   TIP Think and Search

Critical Thinking

4. **Identify** Name one way in which this folktale resembles a myth.
   TIP On My Own
5. **Infer** Anansi says he can pay Nyame's price before he knows what it is. What does that say about him?
   TIP Author and Me
6. **Analyze** Do you think the teller of this folktale expects the listener to believe that it really happened? Why or why not?
   TIP Author and Me
7. **Evaluate** Why do you think someone would want to own all the stories in the world?
   TIP On My Own

Write About Your Reading

Write a dialogue between Anansi and you. Anansi wants to take all of your stories about your life. You have to decide if you want to keep your stories or not.

- Start by having Anansi explain why he wants your stories. What will they give him? What is unique about your stories?
- Decide if you want to keep the stories about your life or if you will let them go so you can create new ones. Tell Anansi what you want to do. If you want to keep your stories, explain why. If you are willing to let him take your stories, tell him your price.
- Use words like "he said," "I asked," "he shouted," or "I whispered" to show who's talking and the emotions behind the words.

Objectives (pp. 640–641)
Reading Activate prior knowledge
• Make connections from text to self
Literature Identify literary elements: hero
Vocabulary Explore word origins: borrowed words
Writing Dialogue
Grammar Identify sentence types: simple; compound subject, compound predicate

Skills Review

Key Reading Skill: Activating Prior Knowledge

8. In your Learner's Notebook, describe something you knew about folktales, trickster heroes, or Anansi before you read this story. Tell how the knowledge helped you understand or enjoy the story.

Key Literary Element: Hero

9. Name one thing that makes Anansi a literary hero.
10. Name one thing that makes Anansi a trickster hero.
11. Name one way in which Anansi is similar to a mythic hero.

Reviewing Skills: Identifying Problem and Solution

12. Anansi must convince the hornets that it is raining in order to get them to fly into his gourd. How does he solve that problem?

Vocabulary Check

Write your own fill-in-the-blank sentence for each vocabulary word below. Make sure you include enough clues for a classmate to fill in the correct word to complete the sentence. Exchange papers with a partner and fill in the blanks in each other's sentences.

13. yearned
14. dispute
15. accustomed
16. merely
17. acknowledge
18. **English Language Coach** Besides *pizza* and *chili,* list three foods Americans "borrowed" from other countries.

Grammar Link: Simple Sentences

A **simple sentence** has one complete subject and one complete predicate.

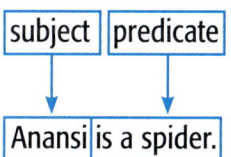

However, a simple sentence can have a compound subject, a compound predicate, or both.

Compound subject:
Lisa and Mike went to the store.

Compound predicate:
Many students read and enjoy novels.

Compound subject and predicate:
Lisa and Mike read and enjoy novels.

Grammar Practice

Decide whether each group of words below is a simple sentence. If it isn't a simple sentence, rewrite it in your Learner's Notebook as a complete simple sentence, adding the missing subject or predicate part.

19. Anansi was smart and cunning.   Yes   No
20. Anansi all the stories.   Yes   No
21. Anansi and Nyame made a deal.   Yes   No

Writing Application Read the dialogue you wrote and underline the simple sentences. Sometimes it's okay to have sentence fragments in dialogue because people don't always talk in complete sentences.

Web Activities For eFlashcards, Selection Quick Checks, and other Web activities, go to www.glencoe.com.

WRITING WORKSHOP PART 1

Fable
Prewriting and Drafting

ASSIGNMENT Write a fable

Purpose: To write a fable that teaches a moral

Audience: You, your teacher, and your classmates

Writing Rubric

As you work through this part of the workshop, you will
- describe a setting
- create characters
- develop a plot
- write dialogue
- develop voice

See page 703 in Part 2 for a model of a fable.

Objectives (642–645)
Writing Use the writing process: prewrite, draft • Write a fable • Use literary elements: setting, plot, dialogue, characterization, voice
Grammar Use compound and complex sentences

A fable is a folktale that's meant to teach a lesson about right and wrong. That lesson is called a *moral.* In "All Stories Are Anansi's," the moral is that brains are stronger than brawn (physical strength). Anansi is a small spider, but his cleverness tricks two larger animals and a swarm of hornets. In this workshop, you'll write your own fable.

Prewriting
Get Ready to Write

Before you start to write, you'll have to decide what moral you want your fable to teach. Think about phrases, sayings, or bits of wisdom that you have heard your parents or other family members say. Here are some suggestions:
- Honesty is the best policy.
- Big presents come in small packages.
- Slow and steady wins the race.

Write your moral in your Learner's Notebook.

Don't judge a book by its cover.

Create Your Characters

Characters in fables are often animals that behave like humans but still have animal qualities. Think about who your main and secondary characters will be. Write about them in your Learner's Notebook.

My main character is a beautiful peacock named Peter. He has long, beautiful feathers that magically change colors. My secondary character is a pig named Polly.

Create Your Setting and Plot

Fables often take place in the countryside. In your Learner's Notebook, write down where *your* fable will take place.

A forest

WRITING WORKSHOP PART 1

Your fable should include a conflict, three main events, and a solution that tells the reader the moral of your story. In your Learner's Notebook write three main events.

> Peter and his friends are mean to Polly because Polly is not as beautiful as the peacocks. Polly makes herself look more attractive, but Peter and his friends laugh at Polly's efforts. Peter's feathers begin to fall out and his friends desert him.

> **Writing Tip**
>
> The conflict in a fable is often connected to a contest, a race, or a challenge. Whatever you choose for a conflict, remember that it must make sense with the moral of your fable.

Drafting
Start Writing

Tell Your Tale

This is the fun part—getting your fable on paper. Here are some tips to think about as you write:

- Start your story by describing the setting and the main character.

> Peter lived in the forest with the rest of his peacock friends. Peter was the most handsome peacock in the whole forest because his feathers magically changed from one magnificent color to another.

- Follow the order of your outline to write the rest of the fable.

> One day, Polly the pig walked by the pond where Peter and his friends were brushing their feathers . . .

> **Writing Tip**
>
> The setting of a fable is usually not described in detail. This allows readers to use their imaginations.

> **Writing Tip**
>
> **Dialogue** Think about your character's voices. Who do they talk like? Your school principal? Your best friend? Do they use slang or big words? Pick a voice for each character and keep it the same throughout the fable.

Keep Going

- Don't worry about run-on sentences, spelling mistakes, or punctuation. You'll fix these things later in Writing Workshop Part 2.
- Write for ten minutes before taking a break.
- If you get stuck, look at the guide you made in your Learner's Notebook. That will tell you what to write next.

WRITING WORKSHOP PART 1

Applying Good Writing Traits

Voice

People who know you well can probably identify you when you talk, even if they can't see you. You have a certain sound. You have a certain style of speaking. You choose certain words to express your thoughts and personality. All of these things are part of your *voice*.

What Is Voice?

Like your speaking voice, your writing voice reflects your thoughts and personality. Of course, readers don't hear you the way they do when you speak. However, they can "hear" you through the words you choose and how you put them together.

In some kinds of writing, like research reports and essays, your voice needs to be formal and proper. In creative writing, like a fable, you can be freer and less formal. You don't have to worry as much about grammar. You *do,* however, want your audience to be able to understand the story, so you can't ignore *all* the rules of grammar, spelling, punctuation, and capitalization.

Why Is Voice Important in My Writing?

- Writing in your own voice makes it easier to express your ideas, thoughts, and feelings.
- When you write in your own voice, your readers can tell that you care about the topic.
- Writing in your own voice makes your writing more interesting to read.
- Your writing voice is your "personality" on paper. When you write in your own voice, readers get to know the real you.

Analyzing Cartoons
What does the boy mean when he says "I've gotta be me . . ."? Is he trying to find his *voice*? Explain.

How Do I Do It?

To write in your voice try these suggestions:
- Write the kind of words that you use when talking.
- Write sentences the way you would say them.
- Share your thoughts and opinions about the topic.
- Make sure your writing sounds like you!

Write to Learn Activity In your Learner's Notebook, write a short paragraph about the folktale "All Stories Are Anansi's." Use your own voice to answer these questions in your paragraph:
- How did Anansi buy the stories from the Sky God?
- Do you think the way Anansi captured the other animals was fair? Why or why not?
- Would you want to be friends with a character like Anansi?

When you are finished, trade paragraphs with a partner. Underline words or phrases that you can tell are written in your partner's voice.

Grammar Link: Compound and Complex Sentences

Sentences are made up of independent clauses (which can stand alone as sentences) and dependent clauses (which cannot stand alone).

What Are Compound and Complex Sentences?

A **compound sentence** is made up of two or more independent clauses. (An **independent clause** can stand alone as a complete sentence.)

The clauses in a compound sentence can be joined together by a comma and a coordinating conjunction, such as *and*, *but*, or *or*.

Deeana likes to sing, and Johnny plays piano.
   independent   *independent*

A **complex sentence** has one main clause and one or more dependent clauses. (A **dependent clause** has a subject and a predicate, but it doesn't express a complete thought. It can't stand alone as a sentence.)

When Jai moved to Iowa, he made many friends.
     dependent   *independent*

Why Are Compound and Complex Sentences Important?

The best writing is made up of sentences that flow smoothly from one to another. Read your own writing aloud sometime. Does it have a smooth flow and rhythm? Or is it choppy and made up of lots of short sentences?

When you use compound and complex sentences along with simple sentences, your sentences will vary in length and structure. That helps them have a rhythm and a smooth flow.

How Do I Use Compound and Complex Sentences?

1. Use compound sentences to combine two sentences that are equally important.

   The bear was big.
   The turtle was slow.
   The bear was big, and the turtle was slow.

2. Use complex sentences to combine an important idea (independent clause) and a less important idea (dependent clause).

   Main Idea: The rabbit will win the race.
   Less Important Idea: The rabbit might trip and lose the race.
   Complex Sentence: The rabbit will win the race, unless he trips.

Practice It

The following paragraph uses only simple sentences. On a separate sheet of paper, rewrite the paragraph, changing simple sentences to compound or complex.

Last summer I went to the lake. I went swimming every day. My brother went swimming too. One day I caught a big fish. We built a fire. We cooked the fish. We slept in a cabin. We got up early every morning. We could catch a lot of fish early in the morning.

Looking Ahead

Continue writing the first draft of your fable. In Writing Workshop Part 2 you will revise and edit your draft.

READING WORKSHOP 2

Skills Focus

You will practice using these skills when you read the following selections:
- "The Twelve Labors of Hercules," p. 650
- "Pecos Bill," p. 660

Reading
- Clarifying meaning while reading

Literature
- Recognizing the cultural contexts of Greek mythology
- Recognizing the cultural contexts of the Wild West

Vocabulary
- Recognizing borrowed words

Writing/Grammar
- Correcting run-on sentences

Objectives (pp. 646–647)
Reading Clarify ideas and text

Skill Lesson
Clarifying

Learn It!

What Is It? Have you ever read something and then realized you didn't understand it very well? If you didn't monitor your comprehension and kept reading, you probably understood less and less. By the time you finished, you may have felt clueless.

Clarifying means clearing up whatever you don't understand. As you're reading, stop when something confuses you. Take the time to find out what's going on.

Analyzing the Art
Why is a magnifying glass often a symbol for clarifying, or trying to understand something more clearly?

READING WORKSHOP 2 • Clarifying

Why Is It Important? Clarifying what you don't understand pays off! It helps you understand and enjoy the text you're reading. It also gives you more information to use in your life.

How Do I Do It? When you realize you don't understand something while you're reading, try these techniques:

- Read confusing parts slowly and carefully.
- Look up unfamiliar words.
- Use resources like dictionaries, encyclopedias, the Internet, and your teacher to figure out the things you don't understand.
- With your new information, reread the confusing parts of the text.

Here's how Dan clarified as he read about the Greeks:

Study Central Visit www.glencoe.com and click on Study Central to review clarifying.

> "When the great city of Troy was taken, all the chiefs who had fought against it set sail for their homes. But there was wrath in heaven against them, for indeed they had borne themselves haughtily and cruelly in the day of their victory. Therefore they did not all find a safe and happy return."

> I don't get the second sentence. I need to look up <u>wrath</u>. Wrath means anger. "Wrath in heaven" must mean the gods were "angry." I also need to look up <u>haughtily</u>. Haughtily means "too proudly." The gods were angry when the Greeks behaved badly in their victory. Now I get why the Greeks didn't have a safe return!

Practice It!

Choose a paragraph in one of your textbooks. Make a list of any words or ideas that need clarification. Decide which sources to use to clarify what you don't understand.

Use It!

As you read about Hercules and Pecos Bill, write a list in your Learner's Notebook of things you don't understand. Clarify as you read to get the most out of each selection.

READING WORKSHOP 2 • Clarifying

Before You Read: The Twelve Labors of Hercules

Vocabulary Preview

consciousness (KON shus nus) *n.* thoughts; awareness; the mind **(p. 650)** *The gods and goddesses had the power to control the consciousness of humans.*

delusion (dih LOO zhun) *n.* a false belief **(p. 650)** *Hercules had the delusion that he was at war and had to kill his enemies.*

remorse (rih MORS) *n.* a feeling of guilt and regret **(p. 651)** *Hercules felt remorse for killing his nephews and nieces.*

diverted (dih VUR tud) *v.* turned from one course to another; form of the verb *divert* **(p. 652)** *Hercules diverted two rivers to wash through an area that needed to be cleaned.*

grotesque (groh TESK) *adj.* very strange and unexpected in appearance **(p. 653)** *The slimy three-headed monster was grotesque.*

devoured (dih VOW urd) *v.* ate greedily; form of the verb *devour* **(p. 653)** *The birds killed their prey before they devoured it.*

foliage (FOH lee ij) *n.* plant and tree leaves **(p. 653)** *The foliage in the marsh was so thick that Hercules couldn't cut through it.*

iridescent (ir ih DES unt) *adj.* showing shimmering colors that look like a rainbow **(p. 654)** *The colors in the iridescent glass were beautiful.*

Partner Talk Play six rounds of "Twenty Questions" using the vocabulary words. One partner chooses one of the words. The other partner may ask up to twenty yes-or-no questions to guess the word.

English Language Coach

Words Borrowed from Names Some names become words. That's what happened with several names in the next selection. Atlas belonged to a family of giants called the Titans. They were so powerful that they rebelled against the gods and, for a time, ruled the earth. To punish Atlas for rebelling, the gods forced him to support the sky on his shoulders. From the names Atlas and Titan, we got these words:

- **atlas** (AT lus) *n.* a book of maps
- **titan** (TY tun) *n.* one who has great size or power
- **titanic** (ty TAN ik) *adj.* having great size or power

Write to Learn Look up *Helios* in a dictionary or encyclopedia. In your Learner's Notebook, note who he is in Greek mythology and find one English word that came from his name.

Walker Brents

Meet the Author
This myth about Hercules is a retelling by Walker Brents, a poet and storyteller. Born in 1958, Brents has loved myths since his father read to him about the Greek gods when he was five years old. Brents says, "The feeling the myths gave me was mysterious and yet somehow strangely familiar."

Author Search For more about Brents, go to www.glencoe.com.

Objectives (pp. 648–655)
Reading Clarify ideas and text • Make connections from text to self
Literature Identify key literary elements: cultural context
Vocabulary Explore word origins: words from names

READING WORKSHOP 2 • Clarifying

Skills Preview

Key Reading Skill: Clarifying
While you read about Hercules, use your Learner's Notebook to write down anything you don't understand in this myth. Include words you don't know.

Write to Learn Write this sentence from "The Twelve Labors of Hercules" in your Learner's Notebook: "Terrible remorse drove him to the oracle of the god Apollo at Delphi, and he asked the priestesses there what he could do to expiate his terrible deed." Circle every word or phrase that you don't understand.

Key Literary Element: Cultural Context
The **cultural context** is the culture that a story comes from when it was first told or written. The culture includes the time and place as well as the beliefs and practices of the people living in that time and place.

Hercules is part of Greek mythology, which was the religion of ancient Greece. In these myths, twelve gods and goddesses, living on Mount Olympus, interacted with humans and had power over all of Nature and human lives. As you read about Hercules, use these questions to help you think about the cultural context:

- Who are the gods and goddesses in this story? How do they hurt or help Hercules?
- In what ways are they powerful? In what ways are their powers limited?
- In what ways was Hercules like a god and in what ways was he human?

Class Talk The ancient Greek stories taught that there was a god or goddess for almost every element of nature (such as the sky, sea, earth, and the weather) and every major human activity (such as home, marriage, the hunt, and war). Discuss with your classmates why you think the Greeks might have written these stories.

Get Ready to Read

Connect to the Reading
Do you ever watch action or horror movies? Well, the myth of Hercules has the same sorts of things those movies do: an impossible mission, scary creatures, and bloody battles.

Build Background
The myth of Hercules includes references to these characters of Greek mythology:

- The **Oracle at Delphi** was a shrine to Apollo, the god of the sun. Apollo spoke through the priestesses who lived at Delphi. If asked, they could tell people's future.
- The **Amazons** were a tribe of warrior women.
- **Atlas** led the Titans, a race of giants, in a war against the gods of Mount Olympus. Zeus punished him by making him carry the sky on his shoulders.

Set Purposes for Reading

Read "The Twelve Labors of Hercules" to learn what made Hercules such an important hero to the ancient Greeks.

Set Your Own Purpose What else would you like to learn from this story about Hercules and his labors? Write your own purpose on "The Twelve Labors of Hercules" page of Foldable 6.

Interactive Literary Elements Handbook
To review or learn more about the literary elements, go to www.glencoe.com.

Keep Moving
Use these skills as you read the following selection.

The Twelve Labors of Hercules **649**

The TWELVE LABORS of HERCULES

by Walker Brents

The goddess Hera[1] hated Hercules from the moment of his birth. In his infancy she sent two giant serpents to kill him as he slept, but **Hercules** strangled them instead. His parents rushed into the room to find the baby shaking the dead bodies of the snakes as if they were rattles. This was an early indication of his great strength, but this strength was not always used well. **1**

Once Hera sent madness and insanity into the **consciousness** of Hercules. His thoughts became scrambled. Under the **delusion** that he was at war, he mistook his nephews and nieces for enemies, and killed them. When the madness passed and he saw what he had done he was

---

1. *Hera* (HAIR uh) is the Queen of the Greek deities (gods and goddesses). She is the goddess of marriage and birth. Zeus (zoos) is her husband.

Vocabulary

consciousness (KON shus nus) *n.* thoughts; awareness; the mind

delusion (dih LOO zhun) *n.* a false belief

Practice the Skills

1 English Language Coach

Words from Names The name **Hercules** became the English word *herculean* (hur kyuh LEE un). It can mean either "having great strength" or "having great difficulty."

overwhelmed with grief and guilt. Terrible **remorse** drove him to the oracle of the god Apollo at Delphi, and he asked the priestesses there what he could do to expiate² his terrible deed. They told him, "Go to King Eurystheus,³ and undertake the labors he will put upon you." 2 3

Hercules went to Tiryns, the land ruled by King Eurystheus. He stood before the throne. Eurystheus said to him, "Go to Nemea, where a fierce lion terrorizes the people. No weapon can pierce through its terrible skin. Kill this lion, remove its skin, carry it here and show it to me." Eurystheus was shrewd, calculating, cunning, and cowardly. Each task he was to set before Hercules was designed to be impossible, but the determination of Hercules was to overcome the impossible. He followed the lion's tracks to a deep dark cave hidden in a hillside. He saw the bones strewn at the cave's entrance, and entered in. In such a darkness he could not see his hand before his face, the dank⁴ air was filled with the smell of blood. The lion had just killed, and had carried its prey to this place which was its very den. Hercules leapt upon the lion and wrestled with it. His tremendous club and sharp knife were of no use, for the lion's hide was too thick. Hercules grasped the lion's neck with his hands and held it against the cave wall until the lion's thrashings ceased and it was dead. Then he dragged the lion into the light of day, skinning it with one of its own claws. He draped the skin over his shoulders, its head over his head like a helmet, and hurried back to the palace of King Eurystheus, who saw him approach from a distance and was so frightened at the sight that he hid in a giant olive jar. He sent his servants to Hercules to tell him of the next task. "Go to the swamp of Lerna and defeat the hydra, who lives at the confluence of the three springs."

Visual Vocabulary
A **hydra** (HY druh) is a serpent monster with nine heads that can regrow.

2. To *expiate* (EX pee ate) is to try and make up for having done something bad.
3. *Eurystheus* (yoo RIS thee us)
4. Air that is *dank* is damp and uncomfortable.

Vocabulary

remorse (rih MORS), *n.* a feeling of guilt and regret

Practice the Skills

2 Key Reading Skill

Clarifying The twelve great labors of Hercules are amazing and exciting, but they might be hard to keep track of! Clarify by writing in your Learner's Notebook each time Hercules begins a new task.

3 Key Literary Element

Cultural Context The goddess Hera made Hercules crazy. Because of this, he killed his relatives. Even though he didn't know what he was doing, Hercules wants to make up for the terrible crime. What does this say about what the ancient Greeks thought of personal responsibility?

READING WORKSHOP 2

Hercules and one of his surviving nephews, Iolaus, found the monster in the depths of the swamp, at the confluence of three springs. Hercules shot his arrows at the monster so as to anger it enough to attack and come close enough for him to fight it with his oaken club. The monster had nine heads and came toward them screaming with rage, belching great gouts of poison bloody mud. Hercules began to knock off the creature's heads, but saw that three heads grew back from where one was knocked off! Iolaus lit the branch of a tree with fire, and held his torch against the neck-stubs where Hercules knocked the heads off. The burnt blood prevented the heads from growing back. With this the tide of the battle turned. The creature was weakening. Finally, Hercules tore off the central head, the primary one. He carried it away and buried it in the ground with a great rock over it, so that it could not rejoin the body and come alive again. Then Hercules dipped his arrow points in the poison blood of the hydra, which lay in pools all around, so as to make them deadly. 4

Other labors followed, and they took Hercules far and wide. In the forest of Ceryneia he chased a deer with golden antlers for an entire year, caught it and carried it alive to King Eurystheus, then returned to Ceryneia and let the deer go. Earlier, he had gone to the land of King Augeias, who kept a stable filled with thousands upon thousands of cattle, which had never been cleaned. Eurystheus, gleefully imagining Hercules carrying baskets and baskets of dung, had ordered him to clean those stables. But Hercules **diverted** the course of two rivers and sent them through the stables so that they were entirely cleaned in one day. 5

On Mount Erymanthus there lived a great boar. Searching amid the lower slopes of this mountain Hercules met an old friend of his, Pholos the centaur, who lived in a village of centaurs. Hercules shared a meal with his friend, but accidentally spilled a drop or two of wine upon the ground. The

Visual Vocabulary
A *centaur* (SEN tawr) is a creature that is half man and half horse.

Practice the Skills

4 Key Reading Skill

Clarifying One way to clarify a difficult sentence is to break it into parts. For example, look at the last sentence in this paragraph. It might be easier to understand if you turn it into three simple sentences: "Hercules dipped his arrows in the poison blood of hydra. The poison blood lay in pools all around. The poison blood made the arrows deadly."

5 Key Literary Element

Cultural Context Hercules was a hero to the Greeks. What does that tell you about the Greeks? What qualities did they admire? Write your answer in your Learner's Notebook.

Vocabulary

diverted (dih VUR tud) *v.* turned from one course to another

652 UNIT 6   What Makes a Hero?

smell of the wine drove the centaurs insane, and they attacked Hercules, who responded with a volley of arrows tipped with the hydra's poison blood. Many were killed. Pholos was burying their bodies when an arrow came loose from one of them, fell down and pierced the flesh near his hoof. The poison entered his veins and killed him. By this time, Hercules was on the upper part of the mountain hunting for the boar, but when he heard of his friend's death he returned to the centaur village and in great sadness helped with the funeral. But he had made enemies with some of the centaurs, and one of them, Nessus, swore revenge. Hercules returned to the hunt for the boar and chased it into deep snowdrifts, where he caught it. After that he went to the land of Thrace and fought against Diomedes, killing him and his man-eating horses. **6**

Another labor brought Hercules to the marshes of Stymphalus. Somewhere in these vast marshes there lived **grotesque** vicious birds that shot their feathers like arrows into people. Then they tore the people into pieces and carried their chunks of flesh away into the marshes where they **devoured** them. No one could get to the place from which they came. Hercules came very close to their lair, but not close enough. The **foliage** was so thick not even he could hack through it with his sword, so that his forward motion was stopped, and he sat upon the ground in despair. Here an ally came to him, the goddess Athena. She helped him. She caused a set of brazen cymbals to appear upon the ground next to his feet, and spoke these words into his consciousness:

Wild Boar, 1999. Mark Adlington. Graphite, conte, and charcoal on paper. Private collection.

6 **Key Reading Skill**

Clarifying How many tasks has Hercules completed? Is fighting the centaurs one of the tasks he was sent to accomplish?

Vocabulary

grotesque (groh TESK) *adj.* very strange and unexpected in appearance

devoured (dih VOW urd) *v.* ate greedily

foliage (FOH lee ij) *n.* plant and tree leaves

READING WORKSHOP 2

"Strike the cymbals together. The sound of their brassy clashing will startle the birds from their branches and nests. They will fly into the air and become targets for your arrows." Hercules followed her instructions. As fast as the birds flew up his arrows pierced them. Most were killed and those who lived flew away and never returned.

He came to Themiscyra, where the river Thermodon flowed into the sea, in a place of many cliffs and rocky hiding places. This was the land of the Amazons, woman-warriors, whose queen, Hippolyte, had a sword-belt made of bronze and **iridescent** glass, given to her by the god of war, Ares. Hercules was to take this belt from her. Expecting a battle, he was surprised when Hippolyte gave it to him freely, but outside their meeting place, the goddess Hera filled the minds of the Amazons with rumors of war, so that as Hercules left he was suddenly attacked by battalions of Amazons. Once more his poison arrows did their deadly work, and, with the belt, he made his escape.

In Crete, he carried away the bull Poseidon gave to King Minos. On the island of Erytheia, he killed Geyron, a giant man-monster with one head and three bodies, and his two-headed dog, Orthrus. He took the herd of cattle they guarded—cattle whose hides were red as the rays of the setting sun. **Helios** the sun-god caused a floating golden cup to appear in the sea, and Hercules drove the bull of Crete and the red cattle onto this cup and floated back to Tiryns. **7**

"Your next to last task requires that you find the garden beyond the world. There, in the Garden of the Hesperides, grow the golden apples upon the branches of a tree guarded by the serpent that never sleeps. Bring back those apples." Hercules had no sooner heard these orders than he was off.

Garden of the Hesperides, 1869–73. Sir Edward Burne-Jones. Tempera, gouache, and oil on card and canvas. Hamburger Kunsthalle, Hamburg, Germany.

Practice the Skills

7 **English Language Coach**

Words from Names The name **Helios** gave us *helium* (the lighter-than-air gas used in balloons) and *heliotrope* (a plant whose flowers turn toward the sun).

Vocabulary

iridescent (ir ih DES unt) *adj.* showing shimmering colors that look like a rainbow

654 UNIT 6 What Makes a Hero?

At the world's edge he met Atlas, the giant who holds up the sky. "The three sisters who live there are my own daughters. Let me bring back the apples. I am the only one they will let have them. But you must hold up the sky while I am gone." So Atlas said as he waited for Hercules to climb atop the high mountain preparatory to taking upon himself the burden of the sky. Once the load was transferred, Hercules stood with the sky upon his back, watching Atlas stride away, already waist-deep in the ocean that encircles the world. Some few moments, hours, days, or months later Atlas returned, holding a branch with three golden apples. "Let me take the apples back to Eurystheus. You go on holding up the sky, for I am tired of it." Atlas was getting ready to go when Hercules said, "Friend, let me do just one thing before you're off. That lion's skin lying there—I carry it with me wherever I go. It would make a good pad to cushion my shoulders against this mighty burden. Kindly take up the sky again for a moment as I gather it up. Then you can return the load to me." Atlas agreed to do so, but once the sky was returned to his keeping Hercules took the branch and walked away, ignoring Atlas's angry cries for him to return. 8

The final labor required Hercules to go down to the world of the dead and bring back Cerberus, the fierce three-headed dog. The gods Hermes[5] and Athena[6] met him at the river between the two worlds and helped him. He carried Cerberus back to Tiryns and showed it to King Eurystheus. The three heads barked at him and bared their teeth, and Eurystheus died of fright. 9

Heracles leading Cerberus to Eurystheus. Black figure hydria. 530–525 BCE, Roman. Louvre, Paris, France.

Practice the Skills

8 English Language Coach

Words from Names The name **Atlas** also gave us another proper name—*Atlantic* Ocean.

9 BIG Question

Does Hercules have the qualities of a real-life hero? Find a partner and discuss. Write your conclusions on the "Twelve Labors of Hercules" page of Foldable 6. Your response will help you complete the Unit Challenge later.

---

5. **Hermes** (HUR meez) is the messenger god.
6. **Athena** (uh THEE nuh) is the goddess of wisdom.

After You Read: The Twelve Labors of Hercules

Answering the BIG Question

1. Why do you think Hercules has been such a popular hero since ancient times?
2. **Demonstrate** Give two examples that show that King Eurystheus was a coward.
   Tip Author and Me

Critical Thinking

3. **Analyze** Hercules had the traits of a hero, but he wasn't perfect. Give at least two examples from the story that show the human side of Hercules.
   Tip Author and Me

4. **Infer** Why did Hercules undertake the twelve labors?
   Tip Author and Me

5. **Compare** Name one major similarity and one major difference between Hercules and Anansi.
   Tip Author and Me

6. **Assess** What powers did the gods and goddesses in this story have? How do you know that there were limits to their powers?
   Tip Author and Me

Write About Your Reading

Pretend that you are writing a movie script for a modern version of this myth. In your version, Hercules is a hero enlisted by the President of the United States to solve twelve problems. Plan and organize the plot for your script.

- List the twelve problems you want Hercules to solve.
- List the difficulties he will encounter.
- List the skills he will use to solve each problem.

Objectives (pp. 656–657)
Reading Clarify ideas and text
Literature Identify key literary elements: cultural context
Vocabulary Explore word origins: words from names
Writing Plan and organize a movie script
Grammar Write compound sentences

Skills Review

Key Reading Skill: Clarifying

7. Look at the list of tasks you wrote in your Learner's Notebook. Do you have twelve listed? If not, go back and find the tasks you're missing.

Key Literary Element: Cultural Context

8. What beliefs of ancient Greeks do you see in this myth?
9. What weaknesses in the gods and goddesses do you see in this myth?
10. Why do you think the Greeks created imperfect heroes?

Vocabulary Check

Choose the *best* word from the list to complete each sentence below. Rewrite each sentence with the correct word in place.

consciousness   foliage   delusion   remorse

11. When Hercules thought that he was at war and had to kill his enemies, he was under a ___.
12. The gods sometimes interfered with humans by getting into their ___.
13. The ___ was so thick around the birds that even Hercules couldn't cut through it.
14. When Hercules killed his relatives, he was overcome with ___.

English Language Coach

15. If you are given a *herculean* task to do, is it an easy one or a difficult one?
16. What does *heliocentric* mean? (Hint: Our solar system is this.)

Grammar Link: Combine Sentences

Too many short sentences can make writing sound choppy or boring. One way to make your writing more interesting is to combine sentences that have closely related ideas into one longer sentence.

One way to combine sentences is to use coordinating conjunctions like *and, but, so,* and *or.* Place a comma before the conjunction.

> Hercules was strong. He liked challenges.
> Hercules was strong, and he liked challenges.

Grammar Practice

Combine each pair of sentences below using *and, but, so,* and *or*. Place a comma before the conjuction.

17. Hercules was courageous. He was smart.
18. Hera wanted to hurt Hercules. She made him temporarily insane.
19. Hercules killed Pholos. It was an accident.
20. Sam has three sisters. Matt has only one.
21. The hurricane season has begun. Fewer people are visiting Florida.
22. I might have spaghetti for dinner. My mom might order pizza.

Web Activities For eFlashcards, Selection Quick Checks, and other Web activities, go to www.glencoe.com.

READING WORKSHOP 2 • Clarifying

Before You Read: Pecos Bill

Meet the Author

Mary Pope Osborne has written more than fifty books. She is best known for her Magic Tree House books. Born in Oklahoma in 1949, Osborne feels lucky to have explored exciting topics through her books. As she puts it, "I've taken journeys to the times of dinosaurs, knights, mummies, pirates, and ninjas." See page R5 of the Author Files for more on Mary Pope Osborne.

Author Search For more about Mary Pope Osborne, go to www.glencoe.com.

Vocabulary Preview

desolate (DES uh lut) *adj.* deserted or uninhabited **(p. 660)** *Much of the land was desolate at that time.*

spunk (spunk) *n.* courage, spirit, and determination **(p. 663)** *Cowboys needed a lot of spunk to survive in the Wild West.*

drought (drowt) *n.* a long period of very dry weather **(p. 664)** *Because of the drought, there was no water to drink.*

barren (BAIR un) *adj.* having little or no plant life; empty **(p. 666)** *The land was so barren that the cattle had no grass to eat.*

Write to Learn For each vocabulary word, write a sentence using it correctly.

English Language Coach

Borrowed Words The English language has borrowed words for just about everything—clothing, colors, weather, animals, cars, and sports. *Tulip* and *peach* are Persian. *Tea* and *typhoon* are Chinese. *Banana* and *okra* come from Africa.

Partner Talk With a partner, match the lists of words below with the languages they were borrowed from. Use a dictionary, an encyclopedia, or the Internet to help you.

1. tornado, coyote, rodeo
2. karate, tycoon, haiku
3. balcony, macaroni
4. chimpanzee, zebra, jumbo
5. jungle, shampoo, bandana
6. boomerang, kangaroo, koala

a. Italian
b. Spanish
c. Japanese
d. languages of Australia and New Zealand
e. languages of India
c. languages of Africa

Then, with your partner, look up each of the following words in a dictionary to learn what language it was borrowed from.

1. barbecue
2. hurricane
3. spaghetti
4. canoe
5. yak
6. bungalow

Objectives (pp. 658–659)
Reading Clarify ideas and text
Literature Identify key literary elements: cultural context
Vocabulary Explore word origins: borrowed words

658 UNIT 6 What Makes a Hero?

READING WORKSHOP 2 • Clarifying

Skills Preview

Key Reading Skill: Clarifying
While you read about Pecos Bill, write down anything you don't understand. Also write down any words you don't know. Look up the answers in a dictionary, an encyclopedia, or on the Internet.

Partner Talk On the left are some words used in movies and books about the Wild West. With a partner, see how many you can match with words that have the same meaning in Standard American English.

Wild West Slang	Standard American English
1. howdy	a. get
2. pardner	b. jail
3. yonder	c. over there
4. chow	d. hello
5. fetch	e. food
6. pokey	f. partner

Key Literary Element: Cultural Context
The cultural context of a story has a lot to do with who tells the story. Each time and place in history has a different culture filled with people who have different beliefs and practices. Each person might tell the same story from a different cultural context. For example, "Pecos Bill" is a story about the American West. A story about the West could be told by

- a Native American
- a cowboy
- a Chinese immigrant

Depending on who is telling the story, the cultural context may change and a very different story will be told about the same time and place in history.

Interactive Literary Elements Handbook
To review or learn more about the literary elements, go to www.glencoe.com.

Get Ready to Read

Connect to the Reading
This folktale is about a hero who is "larger than life." You've probably read about larger-than-life heroes—comic-book superheroes, for example.

Class Talk Discuss who are today's most popular larger-than-life heroes.

Build Background
Folktales about the American West started being created almost as soon as the first European settlers arrived there. Books, stories, movies, and TV shows have all added to this folklore over the years. These tales often exaggerate the danger, excitement, and wildness of the area, which is why it became known as the Wild West.

The folktale you are about to read is a "tall tale." In a tall tale, things are exaggerated to be bigger and more amazing than they could possibly be in real life. A character in a tall tale might, for example, bite a nail in two or tame a tornado!

Set Purposes for Reading
BIG Question As you read, think about why settlers in the American West created heroes such as Pecos Bill.

Set Your Own Purpose What else would you like to learn about heroes in folktales? Write your own purpose on the "Pecos Bill" page of Foldable 6.

Keep Moving
Use these skills as you read the following selection.

Pecos Bill **659**

READING WORKSHOP 2

Pecos Bill

by Mary Pope Osborne

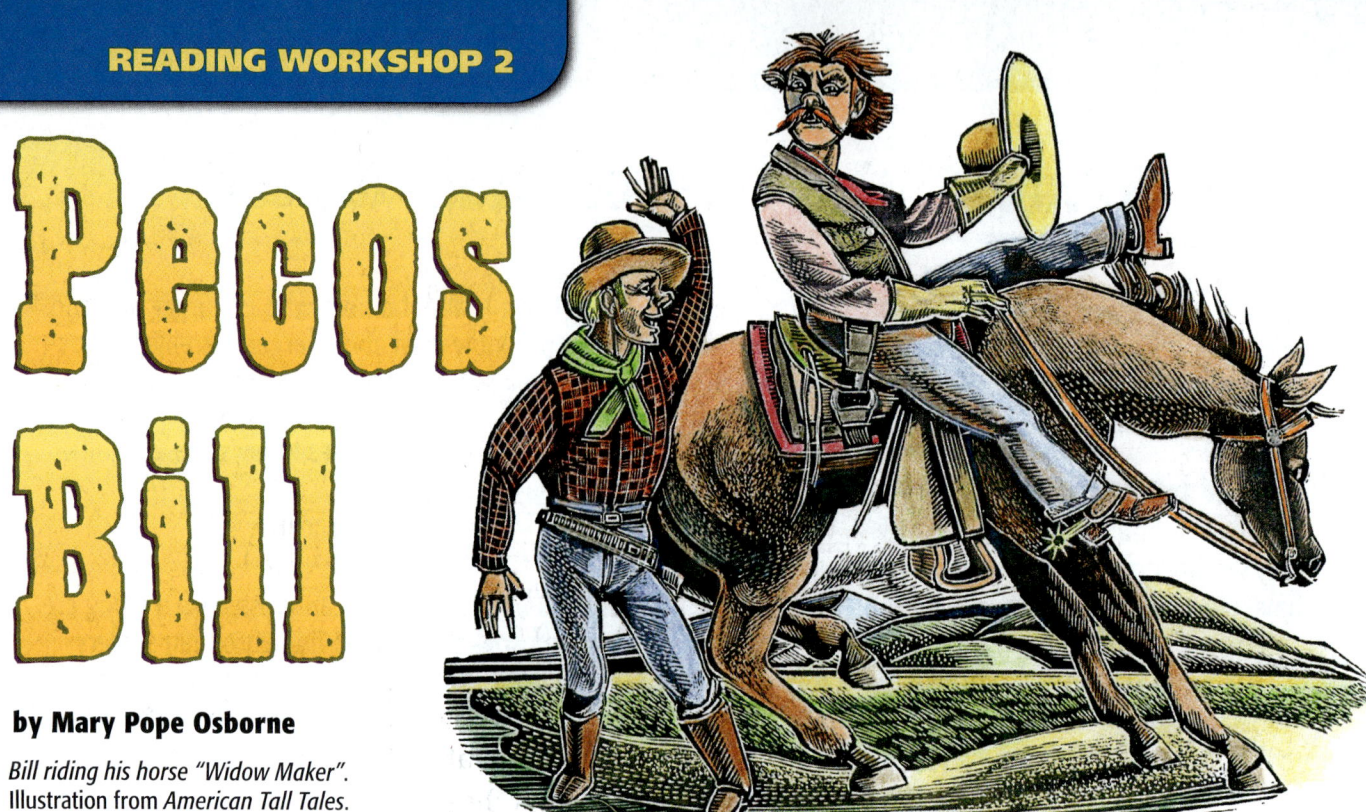

Bill riding his horse "Widow Maker".
Illustration from *American Tall Tales*.

Ask any <u>coyote</u> near the Pecos River in western Texas who was the best cowboy who ever lived, and he'll throw back his head and howl, "Ah-hooo!" If you didn't know already, that's coyote language for *Pecos Bill*. **1**

When Pecos Bill was a little baby, he was as tough as a pine knot. He teethed on horseshoes instead of teething rings and played with grizzly bears instead of teddy bears. He could have grown up just fine in the untamed land of eastern Texas. But one day his pappy[1] ran in from the fields, hollering, "Pack up, Ma! Neighbors movin' in fifty miles away! It's gettin' too crowded!" **2**

Before sundown Bill's folks loaded their fifteen kids and all their belongings into their covered wagon and started west.

As they clattered across the <mark>desolate</mark> land of western Texas, the crushing heat nearly drove them all crazy. Baby Bill got so hot and cross that he began to wallop his big brothers. Pretty soon all fifteen kids were going at one another tooth and nail. Before they turned each other into catfish bait, Bill fell out of the wagon and landed *kerplop* on the sun-scorched desert.

---

1. The word *pappy* is a changed form of papa, so it refers to a person's father.

Vocabulary

<mark>desolate</mark> (DES uh lut) *adj.* deserted or uninhabited

Practice the Skills

1 **English Language Coach**

Borrowed Words What language was **coyote** borrowed from? Write your answer in your Learner's Notebook.

2 **Key Literary Element**

Cultural Context Think of the culture of American settlers in the Wild West. How does the description of Bill show what is important to that culture?

The others were so busy fighting that they didn't even notice the baby was missing until it was too late to do anything about it.

Well, tough little Bill just sat there in the dirt, watching his family rattle off in a cloud of dust, until an old coyote walked over and sniffed him. 3

"Goo-goo!" Bill said.

Now it's an amazing coincidence, but "Goo-goo" happens to mean something similar to "Glad to meet you" in coyote language. Naturally the old coyote figured he'd come across one of his own kind. He gave Bill a big lick and picked him up by the scruff of the neck and carried him home to his den.

Bill soon discovered the coyote's kinfolk[2] were about the wildest, roughest bunch you could imagine. Before he knew it, he was roaming the prairies with the pack. He howled at the moon, sniffed the brush, and chased lizards across the sand. He was having such a good time, scuttling about naked and dirty on all fours, that he completely forgot what it was like to be a human.

Pecos Bill's coyote days came to an end about seventeen years later. One evening as he was sniffing the sagebrush, a cowpoke came loping by on a big horse. "Hey, you!" he shouted. "What in the world are you?"

Bill sat on his haunches[3] and stared at the feller.[4]

"What *are* you?" asked the cowpoke[5] again.

"Varmint,"[6] said Bill hoarsely, for he hadn't used his human voice in seventeen years.

"No, you ain't!"

"Yeah, I am. I got fleas, don't I?"

"Well, that don't mean nothing. A lot of Texans got fleas. The thing varmints got that you ain't got is a tail."

"Oh, yes, I do have a tail," said Pecos Bill.

"Lemme see it then," said the cowpoke.

Bill turned around to look at his rear end, and for the first time in his life he realized he didn't have a tail.

"Dang," he said. "But if I'm not a varmint, what am I?"

Practice the Skills

3 **Key Reading Skill**

Clarifying Be sure to read the footnotes for the meanings of words you don't understand and then reread the sentence or paragraph. That way, you won't miss any of the humor.

---

2. **Kinfolk** is another word for relatives.
3. To sit on your **haunches** is to squat.
4. **Feller** means a boy or man.
5. **Cowpoke** is cowboy slang for a cowboy.
6. A **varmint** is a pesky, annoying animal or person.

READING WORKSHOP 2

Pecos Bill and the Hell's Gate Gang. Illustration from *American Tall Tales.*

Analyzing the Art Pecos Bill stories are filled with exaggerated adventures and impossible happenings. What animal is Bill riding? What animals are on his shoulder and arm? How do the other cowboys seem to be reacting? Read on to learn what this picture is all about.

"You're a cowboy! So start acting like one!"

Bill just growled at the feller like any coyote worth his salt would. But deep down in his heart of hearts he knew the cowpoke was right. For the last seventeen years he'd had a sneaking suspicion that he was different from that pack of coyotes. For one thing, none of them seemed to smell quite as bad as he did.

So with a heavy heart he said good-bye to his four-legged friends and took off with the cowpoke for the nearest ranch.

Acting like a human wasn't all that easy for Pecos Bill. Even though he soon started dressing right, he never bothered to shave or comb his hair. He'd just throw some water on his face in the morning and go around the rest of the day looking like a wet dog. Ignorant cowpokes claimed Bill wasn't too smart. Some of the meaner ones liked to joke that he wore a ten-dollar hat on a five-cent head. 4

The truth was Pecos Bill would soon prove to be one of the greatest cowboys who ever lived. He just needed to find the kind of folks who'd appreciate him. One night when he was licking his dinner plate, his ears perked up. A couple of ranch hands were going on about a gang of wild cowboys.

Practice the Skills

4 Key Reading Skill

Clarifying What does "he wore a ten-dollar hat on a five-cent head" mean?

"Yep. Those fellas are more animal than human," one **ranch** hand was saying. [5]

"Yep. Them's the toughest bunch I ever come across. Heck, they're so tough, they can kick fire out of flint rock with their bare toes!"

"Yep. 'N' they like to bite nails in half for fun!"

"Who are these fellers?" asked Bill.

"The Hell's Gate Gang," said the ranch hand. "The mangiest,[7] meanest, most low-down bunch of low-life varmints that ever grew hair."

"Sounds like my kind of folks," said Bill, and before anyone could holler whoa, he jumped on his horse and took off for Hell's Gate Canyon.

Bill hadn't gone far when disaster struck. His horse stepped in a hole and broke its ankle.

"Dang!" said Bill as he stumbled up from the spill. He draped the lame critter around his neck and hurried on.

After he'd walked about a hundred more miles, Bill heard some mean rattling. Then a fifty-foot rattlesnake reared up its ugly head and stuck out its long, forked tongue, ready to fight.

"Knock it off, you scaly-hided fool. I'm in a hurry," Bill said.

The snake didn't give a spit for Bill's plans. He just rattled on.

Before the cussed[8] varmint could strike, Bill had no choice but to knock him cross-eyed. "Hey, feller," he said, holding up the dazed snake. "I like your **spunk**. Come go with us." Then he wrapped the rattler around his arm and continued on his way.

After Bill had hiked another hundred miles with his horse around his neck and his snake around his arm, he heard a terrible growl. A huge mountain lion was crouching on a cliff, getting ready to leap on top of him.

---

7. The word *mangiest* comes from *mange,* a skin disease of animals that causes loss of hair in spots. So "the mangiest" means "the most shabby or worn out in appearance."
8. The word *cussed* (KUS ud) means stubborn and difficult to deal with.

Practice the Skills

[5] **English Language Coach**

Borrowed Words The word *ranch* was borrowed from the Spanish word *rancho.* Do you know what a *ranch hand* is? If not, look up *hand* in a dictionary and find a meaning that makes helps you define *ranch hand.*

Vocabulary

spunk (spunk) *n.* courage, spirit, and determination

"Don't jump, you mangy bobtailed fleabag!" Bill said.

Well, call any mountain lion a mangy bobtailed fleabag, and he'll jump on your back for sure. After this one leaped onto Bill, so much fur began to fly that it darkened the sky. Bill wrestled that mountain lion into a headlock, then squeezed him so tight that the big cat had to cry uncle. 6

When the embarrassed old critter started to slink off, Bill felt sorry for him. "Aw, c'mon, you big silly," he said. "You're more like me than most humans I meet."

He saddled up the cat, jumped on his back, and the four of them headed for the canyon, with the mountain lion screeching, the horse neighing, the rattler rattling, and Pecos Bill hollering a wild war whoop.

When the Hell's Gate Gang heard those noises coming from the prairie, they nearly fainted. They dropped their dinner plates, and their faces turned as white as bleached desert bones. Their knees knocked and their six-guns shook.

"Hey, there!" Bill said as he sidled up to their campfire, grinning. "Who's the boss around here?"

A nine-foot feller with ten pistols at his sides stepped forward and in a shaky voice said, "Stranger, I was. But from now on, it'll be you."

"Well, thanky, pardner," said Bill. "Get on with your dinner, boys. Don't let me interrupt."

Once Bill settled down with the Hell's Gate Gang, his true genius revealed itself. With his gang's help, he put together the biggest ranch in the southwest. He used New Mexico as a **corral** and Arizona as a pasture. 7

He invented tarantulas and scorpions as practical jokes. He also invented roping. Some say his rope was exactly as long as the equator; others argue it was two feet shorter.

Things were going fine for Bill until Texas began to suffer the worst **drought** in its history. It was so dry that all the rivers turned as powdery as biscuit flour.

Practice the Skills

6 Key Literary Element

Cultural Context Is this story beginning to remind you of the Hercules myth you read? How are the stories similar so far? How do their cultural contexts make them different?

7 English Language Coach

Borrowed Words What language does **corral** come from? Look it up.

Visual Vocabulary
A *tarantula* is a large, hairy spider. Its sting can be painful, but it is not usually dangerous to humans.

Vocabulary

drought (drowt) *n.* a long period of very dry weather

The parched[9] grass was catching fire everywhere. For a while Bill and his gang managed to lasso water from the Rio Grande.[10] When that river dried up, they lassoed water from the Gulf of Mexico.

No matter what he did, though, Bill couldn't get enough water to stay ahead of the drought. All his horses and cows were starting to dry up and blow away like balls of tumbleweed. It was horrible.

Just when the end seemed near, the sky turned a deep shade of purple. From the distant mountains came a terrible roar. The cattle began to **stampede,** and a huge black funnel of a cyclone appeared, heading straight for Bill's ranch.

The rest of the Hell's Gate Gang shouted, "Help!" and ran.

But Pecos Bill wasn't scared in the least. "Yahoo!" he hollered, and he swung his **lariat** and lassoed that cyclone around its neck.

Bill held on tight as he got sucked up into the middle of the swirling cloud. He grabbed the cyclone by the ears and pulled himself onto her back. Then he let out a whoop and headed that twister across Texas.

The mighty cyclone bucked, arched, and screamed like a wild **bronco.** But Pecos Bill just held on with his legs and used his strong hands to wring the rain out of her wind. He wrung out rain that flooded Texas, New Mexico, and Arizona, until finally he slid off the shriveled-up funnel and fell into California. The earth sank about two hundred feet below sea level in the spot where Bill landed, creating the area known today as Death Valley. 8

"There. That little waterin' should hold things for a while," he said, brushing himself off.

After his cyclone ride, no horse was too wild for Pecos Bill. He soon found a young colt that was as tough as a tiger and as crazy as a streak of lightning. He named the colt Widow Maker and raised him on barbed wire[11] and dynamite. Whenever the two rode together, they back-flipped and somersaulted all over Texas, loving every minute of it. 9

---

9. Something that is **parched** is dried out.
10. The **Rio Grande** is a large river that forms part of the border between Texas and Mexico. The words mean "large river" in Spanish.
11. **Barbed wire** has sharp points. On the plains, fences were made from barbed wire to keep cattle in and cattle thieves out.

Practice the Skills

8 English Language Coach

Borrowed Words The words **lariat** and **bronco** come from the same language. What is that language? What does each word mean?

9 Key Reading Skill

Clarifying Why does Pecos Bill name his horse Widow Maker? What do you think the name means?

READING WORKSHOP 2

One day when Bill and Widow Maker were bouncing around the Pecos River, they came across an awesome sight: a wild-looking, red-haired woman riding on the back of the biggest catfish Bill had ever seen. The woman looked like she was having a ball, screeching, "Ride 'em, cowgirl!" as the catfish whipped her around in the air.

"What's your name?" Bill shouted.

"Slue-foot Sue! What's it to you?" she said. Then she war-whooped away over the windy water.

Thereafter all Pecos Bill could think of was Slue-foot Sue. He spent more and more time away from the Hell's Gate Gang as he wandered the **barren** cattle-lands, looking for her. When he finally found her lonely little cabin, he was so love-struck he reverted[12] to some of his old coyote ways. He sat on his haunches in the moonlight and began a-howling and ah-hooing.

Well, the good news was that Sue had a bit of coyote in her too, so she completely understood Bill's language. She stuck her head out her window and ah-hooed back to him that she loved him, too. Consequently Bill and Sue decided to get married. **10**

On the day of the wedding Sue wore a beautiful white dress with a steel-spring bustle,[13] and Bill appeared in an elegant buckskin suit.

But after a lovely ceremony, a terrible catastrophe occurred. Slue-foot Sue got it into her head that she just had to have a ride on Bill's wild bronco, Widow Maker.

"You can't do that, honey," Bill said. "He won't let any human toss a leg over him but me."

"Don't worry," said Sue. "You know I can ride anything on four legs, not to mention what flies or swims."

Bill tried his best to talk Sue out of it, but she wouldn't listen. She was dying to buck on the back of that bronco. Wearing her white wedding dress with the bustle, she jumped on Widow Maker and kicked him with her spurs.

---

12. The word *reverted* here means "returned to an earlier behavior."

13. A *bustle* is a pad or frame once worn by women under their skirts.

Vocabulary

barren (BAIR un) *adj.* having little or no plant life; empty

Practice the Skills

10 **Key Reading Skill**

Clarifying Have you understood the last two paragraphs? Were any parts confusing? Were any words unfamiliar? Reread the two paragraphs carefully. Look up any words you don't know. Then, in your own words, tell what happens in the paragraphs.

Well, that bronco didn't need any thorns in his side to start bucking to beat the band. He bounded up in the air with such amazing force that suddenly Sue was flying high into the Texas sky. She flew over plains and mesas, over canyons, deserts, and prairies. She flew so high that she looped over the new moon and fell back to earth.

But when Sue landed on her steel-spring bustle, she rebounded right back into the heavens! As she bounced back and forth between heaven and earth, Bill whirled his lariat above his head, then lassoed her. But instead of bringing Sue back down to earth, he got yanked into the night sky alongside her!

Together Pecos Bill and Slue-foot Sue bounced off the earth and went flying to the moon. And at that point Bill must have gotten some sort of foothold in a moon crater—because neither he nor Sue returned to earth. Not ever.

Folks figure those two must have dug their boot heels into some moon cheese and raised a pack of wild coyotes just like themselves. Texans'll tell you that every time you hear thunder rolling over the desolate land near the Pecos River, it's just Bill's family having a good laugh upstairs. When you hear a strange ah-hooing in the dark night, don't be fooled—that's the sound of Bill howling *on* the moon instead of *at* it. And when lights flash across the midnight sky, you can bet it's Bill and Sue riding the backs of some white-hot shooting stars. 11 ○

Practice the Skills

11 BIG Question
Was Pecos Bill a hero? On the "Pecos Bill" page of Foldable 6, write at least two reasons to support your answer. Your response will help you complete the Unit Challenge later.

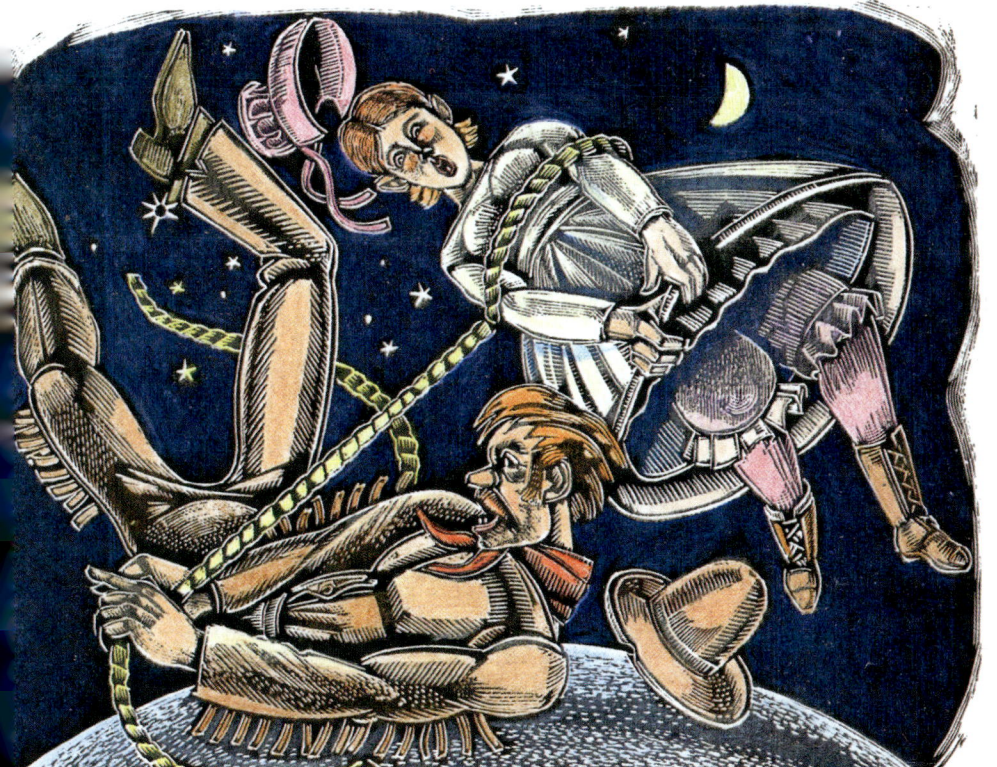

Pecos Bill and Slue-foot Sue bouncing over the moon. Illustration from *American Tall Tales.*
Analyzing the Art Which sentence from the story tells what's happening in this picture?

READING WORKSHOP 2 • Clarifying

After You Read : Pecos Bill

Answering the BIG Question

1. Do you think Pecos Bill, as a hero, is more like Anansi or Hercules? Compare his qualities with those of Anansi and Hercules.

2. **Recall** When Pecos Bill met the Hell's Gate Gang, how many animals did he have with him and what were they?
   TIP Right There

3. **Recall** How did Pecos Bill start out in life? What event caused his life to be different from that of his brothers and sisters?
   TIP Right There

4. **Identify** After Pecos Bill defeats the Hell's Gate Gang, there are two more small plots, or subplots, to the story. In the first subplot, he faces a new problem. In the second subplot, he has a new goal. Identify these two subplots.
   TIP Think and Search

Critical Thinking

5. **Analyze** What do you think is the biggest exaggeration in this story?
   TIP Author and Me

6. **Evaluate** What personality traits of Pecos Bill do you admire?
   TIP On Your Own

Talk About Your Reading

Work with a partner to create a tall tale about an imaginary hero in your school. First think of a problem that needs to be solved. Then create a hero with exaggerated traits who will tackle the problem. How can you make your school, the problem, and your hero larger than life?

Parts of my tall tale	Exaggerated descriptions
my school	
the problem	
the hero	

Objectives (pp. 668–669)
Reading Clarify ideas and text
Literature Identify key literary elements: cultural context
Vocabulary Explore word origins: borrowed words
Grammar Write complex sentences

Skills Review

Key Reading Skill: Clarifying

7. In your Learner's Notebook, read the list of things you needed to clarify in this folktale. If you haven't looked them all up, do it now.

8. Give one example of how the skill of clarifying helped you understand this story. Write your answer in your Learner's Notebook.

Key Literary Element: Cultural Context

9. Think about the character of Pecos Bill. What do his special qualities tell you about the culture of the American West?

10. Is Pecos Bill mean or violent? Why or why not? What does that tell you about the culture in the American West?

11. How does Pecos Bill interact with nature? What does that tell you about the culture of the American West?

Vocabulary Check

Write your own fill-in-the-blank sentences for the vocabulary words below. Include enough context clues for a classmate to complete each sentence correctly. Then exchange papers and fill in your classmate's exercise.

12. drought
13. spunk
14. desolate
15. barren
16. **English Language Coach** Many of the words in this story were borrowed from Spanish. What does this tell you about the American West and who lived there?

Grammar Link: Combining Sentence Clauses

A **complex sentence** has one independent clause and one or more dependent clauses. A complex sentence can sometimes make your meaning more clear than two or more simple sentences. When you write two or more sentences that are closely related in meaning, try combining them to form a complex sentence.

A **dependent clause** has a subject and a predicate, but it does not express a complete thought. A dependent clause is always used with an independent clause.

Realizing that he was not a coyote,	→	Pecos Bill went to live with people.
dependent clause		*independent clause*

Before the cussed varmint could strike,	→	Bill had no choice but to knock him cross-eyed.
dependent clause		*independent clause*

Grammar Practice

Write each sentence. Underline each dependent clause.

17. When Pecos Bill got thirsty, he squeezed a cloud to drink.

18. Pecos Bill became the leader of the Hell's Gate Gang because he was so tough.

19. Slue-foot Sue rode a huge catfish on the Pecos River, which ran through the Wild West.

Web Activities For eFlashcards, Selection Quick Checks, and other Web activities, go to www.glencoe.com.

READING WORKSHOP 3

Skills Focus

You will practice using these skills when you read the following selections:
- "Dragon, Dragon," p. 674
- "The King of Mazy May," p. 688

Reading
- Comparing and contrasting

Literature
- Recognizing and analyzing theme

Vocabulary
- Understanding word sources and histories

Writing/Grammar
- Using commas in compound and complex sentences

Skill Lesson

Comparing and Contrasting

Learn It!

What Is It? **Comparing and contrasting** means looking for similarities and differences. We do this all the time. You compare your teachers to one another and your classmates to one another, don't you? You also compare foods, the weather, cars, TV shows, and music.

Sometimes an author wants you to compare and contrast two or more characters, settings, or ideas to help you understand or feel parts of a story. For example, if one character is a coward, you may have a better appreciation of how brave another character is.

"No dolphin ever spent $2,000 just to play silly games on a computer that will be obsolete in six months. That *proves* we're smarter than humans!"
© 1995 Randy Glasbergen.

Analyzing Cartoons
The dolphins contrast themselves to humans. Why is their comparison funny?

Objectives (pp. 670–671)
Reading Compare and contrast

READING WORKSHOP 3 • Comparing and Contrasting

Why Is It Important? When you pay attention to similarities and differences, you understand things better. For example, if you are a football player and you want to understand soccer, it helps to find out how it's both similar to and different from the game of football.

How Do I Do It? As you read, be alert for things to compare. You will read a folktale about three brothers seeking their fortune. Compare and contrast everything the brothers do and say. Sometimes it's a good idea to compare and contrast something you read about to something or someone you already know—like yourself!

Here's how one student compared two characters in "Persephone."

> Persephone was a high-spirited, sunny girl who loved springtime and flowers and running outdoors with her friends . . . Suddenly the earth split open at her feet. Out dashed a golden chariot pulled by black horses and driven by a stern-faced man in black armor.

Persephone's bright and loves running in the sunlight. The man is wearing black armor and his chariot is pulled from underground by black horses. She's happy, and he's stern. I have a feeling that these differences between the characters are going to be an important part of the story.

Literature Online

Study Central Visit www.glencoe.com and click on Study Central to review comparing and contrasting.

Practice It!

Make a list of similarities between four of the characters you've read about in Unit 6: Persephone, Hades, Pecos Bill, and Hercules. Then make a list of their differences. You can compare and contrast their strengths, weaknesses, physical traits, character traits, their actions, or ideas about why they are heroes.

Use It!

As you read "Dragon, Dragon," compare and contrast the three brothers to each other. When you begin "The King of Mazy May," notice how the author compares and contrasts the main character to other boys.

READING WORKSHOP 3 • Comparing and Contrasting

Before You Read: Dragon, Dragon

Meet the Author

John Gardner wrote novels, short stories and other selections for young readers, books on how to write, and more. Gardner was also a teacher and studied classic literature. Gardner wanted his books to deliver a moral message. "True art is moral," he said. "It seeks to improve life." See page R3 of the Author Files for more on John Gardner.

Author Search For more about John Gardner, go to www.glencoe.com.

Objectives (pp. 672–683)
Reading Compare and contrast • Make connections from text to self
Literature Identify key literary elements: theme
Vocabulary Explore word histories

Vocabulary Preview

plagued (playgd) *v.* was greatly troubled or distressed; form of the verb *plague* **(p. 675)** *The kingdom was plagued by a dragon.*

ravaged (RAV ijd) *v.* destroyed violently; ruined; form of the verb *ravage* **(p. 675)** *The dragon ravaged villages and farms.*

tyrant (TY runt) *n.* a cruel, unjust ruler **(p. 676)** *The king was no tyrant; he loved his people and treated them well.*

quest (kwest) *n.* a search for a particular object or goal **(p. 679)** *The cobbler's son went on a quest to kill the dragon.*

meekly (MEEK lee) *adv.* in a timid and mild manner; gently **(p. 769)** *After hearing the dragon's roar, the boy responded meekly.*

lunged (lunjd) *v.* made a sudden forward movement; charged; form of the verb *lunge* **(p. 679)** *The dragon lunged before the boy had time to think or run.*

Write to Learn In your Learner's Notebook, write at least one synonym for each vocabulary word.

English Language Coach

Word Histories So far in this book, you've learned that many English words are based on words from other languages. You've learned to recognize roots, base words, prefixes, and suffixes. You've learned about compound words, borrowed words, and words from names. All these things are part of etymology (et uh MOL uh jee), the study of words and their histories.

People who study words enjoy discovering interesting and unusual word origins. For example, in "Dragon, Dragon," the king's magician says a *spell*. This word first meant simply "a talk" or "to talk." In the 1500s, when many people believed in magic, an additional meaning came into use—"words thought to have magical power."

Write to Learn *Abracadabra* is a well-known "magic" word (and a fun one to spell out too). What language did it come from? Write your guess in your Learner's Notebook, and then look it up.

READING WORKSHOP 3 • Comparing and Contrasting

Skills Preview

Key Reading Skill: Comparing and Contrasting

To compare and contrast means to look for similarities and differences between characters, settings, events, and ideas. To compare characters, look for the words the author uses to describe them. Notice the similarities and differences in different *kinds* of characters. For example, do all the female characters act in one way? Do all the elderly characters do the same thing? You can also compare and contrast details and ideas in the story.

Partner Talk With a partner, choose two stories you've read in this unit. Make a list of the differences between the stories in genre, setting, and heroes. Then list their similarities.

Key Literary Element: Theme

The theme is the main idea or meaning behind a story. It may be the moral of the story or simply an idea to think about, such as:

- Hard work pays off, or
- How can a member of society still be an individual?

It can be difficult to find the theme of a story. Often the author doesn't state it directly, so you must figure it out for yourself.

Write to Learn Think of a theme you might like to express in a short story. Write your theme in your Learner's Notebook.

Get Ready to Read

Connect to the Reading

What do you think it would be like to live in the time of castles, kings, queens, knights, wizards, and dragons? What fairy-tale character would you like to be? Why?

Class Talk Brainstorm a list of characters that often appear in fairy tales. Then brainstorm a list of events that usually happen. Write these lists on the board.

Build Background

This story seems to be a typical fairy tale or folktale at first. There are all the usual characters doing the usual things. But you'll notice one difference very soon—the humor. Here are some places to look for humor:

- the dragon—the ways it troubles the kingdom
- the queen—what she's turned into and how she's taken care of
- the cobbler—the advice he gives his sons

Read carefully to be sure you understand all of the jokes.

Set Purposes for Reading

 Read "Dragon, Dragon" to meet a different sort of hero.

Set Your Own Purpose What else would you like to learn from the story to help you answer the Big Question? Write your own purpose on the "Dragon, Dragon" page of Foldable 6.

Literature Online

Interactive Literary Elements Handbook
To review or learn more about the literary elements, go to www.glencoe.com.

Keep Moving

Use these skills as you read the following selection.

READING WORKSHOP 3

There was once a king whose kingdom was plagued by a dragon. The king did not know which way to turn. The king's knights were all cowards who hid under their beds whenever the dragon came in sight, so they were of no use to the king at all. And the king's **wizard**[1] could not help either because, being old, he had forgotten his magic spells. Nor could the wizard look up the spells that had slipped his mind, for he had unfortunately misplaced his wizard's book many years before. The king was at his wit's end. 🔢 2️⃣

Every time there was a full moon the dragon came out of his lair and **ravaged** the countryside. He frightened maidens and stopped up chimneys and broke store windows and set people's clocks back and made dogs bark until no one could hear himself think.

He tipped over fences and robbed graves and put frogs in people's drinking water and tore the last chapters out of novels and changed house numbers around so that people crawled into bed with their neighbors' wives.

He stole spark plugs out of people's cars and put firecrackers in people's cigars and stole the clappers from all the church bells and sprung every bear trap for miles around so the bears could wander wherever they pleased.

And to top it all off, he changed around all the roads in the kingdom so that people could not get anywhere except by starting out in the wrong direction. 3️⃣

"That," said the king in a fury, "is enough!" And he called a meeting of everyone in the kingdom.

Now it happened that there lived in the kingdom a wise old cobbler[2] who had a wife and three sons. The cobbler and his family came to the king's meeting and stood way in back by the door, for the cobbler had a feeling that since he was nobody important there had probably been some mistake, and no doubt the king had intended the meeting for everyone in the kingdom except his family and him.

---

1. A **wizard** is a magician or sorcerer.
2. A **cobbler** is a person who makes or mends shoes.

Vocabulary

plagued (playgd) *v.* was greatly troubled or distressed

ravaged (RAV ijd) *v.* destroyed violently; ruined

Practice the Skills

1 Key Reading Skill

Comparing and Contrasting
So far, does this fairy tale seem like most others you know? As you read, compare and contrast how this tale is the same as and different from what you might expect.

2 English Language Coach

Word Histories Wizard comes from a Middle English word (*wys*), meaning "wise." Another word near the end of this paragraph also comes from *wys*. Can you find it?

3 Key Reading Skill

Comparing and Contrasting
Think of a monster from a movie and compare and contrast it to this dragon. First describe two or more qualities or actions that are similar about the two beasts. Then describe two or more qualities or actions that are different between the two beasts.

Dragon, Dragon **675**

READING WORKSHOP 3

"Ladies and gentlemen," said the king when everyone was present. "I've put up with that dragon as long as I can. He has got to be stopped."

All the people whispered amongst themselves, and the king smiled, pleased with the impression he had made.

But the wise cobbler said gloomily, "It's all very well to talk about it—but how are you going to do it?"

And now all the people smiled and winked as if to say, "Well, King, he's got you there!"

The king frowned.

"It's not that His Majesty hasn't tried," the queen spoke up loyally.

"Yes," said the king, "I've told my knights again and again that they ought to slay that dragon. But I can't *force* them to go. I'm not a tyrant." 4

"Why doesn't the wizard say a magic spell?" asked the cobbler.

"He's done the best he can," said the king.

Vocabulary

tyrant (TY runt) *n.* a cruel, unjust ruler

Practice the Skills

4 BIG Question
At this point in the story, who do you think will be a hero—the king, the wizard, one of the knights, or the cobbler? Explain your answer.

Analyzing the Art Make a list of words that you would use to describe the dragon in this illustration.

676 UNIT 6 What Makes a Hero?

The wizard blushed and everyone looked embarrassed. "I used to do all sorts of spells and chants when I was younger," the wizard explained. "But I've lost my spell book, and I begin to fear I'm losing my memory too. For instance, I've been trying for days to recall one spell I used to do. I forget, just now, what the **deuce** it was for. It went something like— 5

*Bimble
Wimble
Cha, Cha*
CHOOMPF!

Suddenly, to everyone's surprise, the queen turned into a rosebush.

"Oh dear," said the wizard.

"Now you've done it," groaned the king.

"Poor Mother," said the princess.

"I don't know what can have happened," the wizard said nervously, "but don't worry, I'll have her changed back in a jiffy." He shut his eyes and racked his brain for a spell that would change her back.

But the king said quickly, "You'd better leave well enough alone. If you change her into a rattlesnake we'll have to chop off her head."

Meanwhile the cobbler stood with his hands in his pockets, sighing at the waste of time. "About the dragon . . ." he began.

"Oh yes," said the king. "I'll tell you what I'll do. I'll give the princess' hand in marriage to anyone who can make the dragon stop."

"It's not enough," said the cobbler. "She's a nice enough girl, you understand. But how would an ordinary person support her? Also, what about those of us that are already married?" 6

"In that case," said the king, "I'll offer the princess' hand or half the kingdom or both—whichever is most convenient."

The cobbler scratched his chin and considered it. "It's not enough," he said at last. "It's a good enough kingdom, you understand, but it's too much responsibility."

Practice the Skills

5 English Language Coach

Word Histories The Latin word for "two" came into French and English as **deuce** (doos). It normally refers to two of something. However, in the expression "what the deuce," *deuce* is a polite substitution for the word *devil*.

6 Key Reading Skill

Comparing and Contrasting At this point in the story, how would you describe the cobbler's behavior? How is the cobbler different from the king? How is he different from the wizard?

Dragon, Dragon **677**

READING WORKSHOP 3

"Take it or leave it," the king said.

"I'll leave it," said the cobbler. And he shrugged and went home.

But the cobbler's **eldest** son thought the bargain was a good one, for the princess was very beautiful and he liked the idea of having half the kingdom to run as he pleased. So he said to the king, "I'll accept those terms, Your Majesty. By tomorrow morning the dragon will be slain." 7

"Bless you!" cried the king.

"Hooray, hooray, hooray!" cried all the people, throwing their hats in the air.

The cobbler's eldest son beamed with pride, and the second eldest son looked at him enviously. The youngest son said timidly, "Excuse me, Your Majesty, but don't you think the queen looks a little unwell? If I were you I think I'd water her."

"Good heavens," cried the king, glancing at the queen who had been changed into a rosebush, "I'm glad you mentioned it!"

Now the cobbler's eldest son was very clever and was known far and wide for how quickly he could multiply fractions in his head. He was perfectly sure he could slay the dragon by somehow or other playing a trick on him, and he didn't feel that he needed his wise old father's advice. But he thought it was only polite to ask, and so he went to his father, who was working as usual at his cobbler's bench, and said, "Well, Father, I'm off to slay the dragon. Have you any advice to give me?"

The cobbler thought a moment and replied, "When and if you come to the dragon's lair, recite the following poem.

Dragon, dragon, how do you do?
I've come from the king to murder you.

Say it very loudly and firmly and the dragon will fall, God willing, at your feet."

"How curious!" said the eldest son. And he thought to himself, "The old man is not as wise as I thought. If I say something like that to the dragon, he will eat me up in an instant. The way to kill a dragon is to outfox[3] him." And

---

Practice the Skills

7 English Language Coach

Word Histories In Old English, *eld* meant "old." The word changed over time to *old*, but the original word left us the words *elder*, *elderly*, and **eldest**.

---

3. To *outfox* means to outsmart.

keeping his opinion to himself, the eldest son set forth on his **quest**.

When he came at last to the dragon's lair, which was a cave, the eldest son slyly disguised himself as a peddler and knocked on the door and called out, "Hello there!"

"There's nobody home!" roared a voice.

The voice was as loud as an earthquake, and the eldest son's knees knocked together in terror.

"I don't come to trouble you," the eldest son said **meekly**. "I merely thought you might be interested in looking at some of our brushes. Or if you'd prefer," he added quickly, "I could leave our catalog with you and I could drop by again, say, early next week."

"I don't want any brushes," the voice roared, "and I especially don't want any brushes next week."

"Oh," said the eldest son. By now his knees were knocking together so badly that he had to sit down.

Suddenly a great shadow fell over him, and the eldest son looked up. It was the dragon. The eldest son drew his sword, but the dragon **lunged** and swallowed him in a single gulp, sword and all, and the eldest son found himself in the dark of the dragon's belly. "What a fool I was not to listen to my wise old father!" thought the eldest son. And he began to weep bitterly.

"Well," sighed the king the next morning, "I see the dragon has not been slain yet."

"I'm just as glad, personally," said the princess, sprinkling the queen. "I would have had to marry that eldest son, and he had warts." 8

Now the cobbler's middle son decided it was his turn to try. The middle son was very strong and was known far and wide for being able to lift up the corner of a church. He felt perfectly sure he could slay the dragon by simply laying into him, but he thought it would be only polite to ask his father's advice. So he went to his father and said to him, "Well,

Practice the Skills

8 Key Literary Element

Theme What could the main idea or the meaning behind the story be? Do you expect there to be a moral or an important idea to think about? Write down one or more possible themes in your Learner's Notebook.

Vocabulary

quest (kwest) *n.* a search for a particular object or goal

meekly (MEEK lee) *adv.* in a timid and mild manner; gently

lunged (lunjd) *v.* made a sudden forward movement; charged

READING WORKSHOP 3

Father, I'm off to slay the dragon. Have you any advice for me?"

The cobbler told the middle son exactly what he'd told the eldest.

"When and if you come to the dragon's lair, recite the following poem.

Dragon, dragon, how do you do?
I've come from the king to murder you.

Say it very loudly and firmly, and the dragon will fall, God willing, at your feet."

"What an odd thing to say," thought the middle son. "The old man is not as wise as I thought. You have to take these dragons by surprise." But he kept his opinion to himself and set forth.

When he came in sight of the dragon's lair, the middle son spurred his horse to a gallop and thundered into the entrance swinging his sword with all his might.

But the dragon had seen him while he was still a long way off, and being very clever, the dragon had crawled up on top of the door so that when the son came charging in he went under the dragon and on to the back of the cave and slammed into the wall. Then the dragon chuckled and got down off the door, taking his time, and strolled back to where the man and the horse lay unconscious from the terrific blow. Opening his mouth as if for a yawn, the dragon swallowed the middle son in a single gulp and put the horse in the freezer to eat another day.

"What a fool I was not to listen to my wise old father," thought the middle son when he came to in the dragon's belly. And he too began to weep bitterly. 9

That night there was a full moon, and the dragon ravaged the countryside so terribly that several families moved to another kingdom.

"Well," sighed the king in the morning, "still no luck in this dragon business, I see."

"I'm just as glad, myself," said the princess, moving her mother, pot and all, to the window where the sun could get at her. "The cobbler's middle son was a kind of humpback."

Practice the Skills

9 **Key Reading Skill**

Comparing and Contrasting
Name at least three ways the eldest two brothers are alike and at least three ways their characters and actions are different.

680 UNIT 6 What Makes a Hero?

Now the cobbler's youngest son saw that his turn had come. He was very upset and nervous, and he wished he had never been born. He was not clever, like his eldest brother, and he was not strong, like his second-eldest brother. He was a decent, honest boy who always minded his elders. **10**

He borrowed a suit of armor from a friend of his who was a knight, and when the youngest son put the armor on it was so heavy he could hardly walk. From another knight he borrowed a sword, and that was so heavy that the only way the youngest son could get it to the dragon's lair was to drag it along behind his horse like a plow.

When everything was in readiness, the youngest son went for a last conversation with his father.

"Father, have you any advice to give me?" he asked.

"Only this," said the cobbler. "When and if you come to the dragon's lair, recite the following poem.

Dragon, dragon, how do you do?
I've come from the king to murder you.

Say it very loudly and firmly, and the dragon will fall, God willing, at your feet."

"Are you certain?" asked the youngest son uneasily.

"As certain as one can ever be in these matters," said the wise old cobbler.

And so the youngest son set forth on his quest. He traveled over hill and dale and at last came to the dragon's cave. The dragon, who had seen the cobbler's youngest son while he

The cobbler's youngest son came to the dragon's cave with heavy armor and a huge sword.

Practice the Skills

10 **Key Reading Skill**

Comparing and Contrasting
How is the youngest son different from his two brothers?

Dragon, Dragon **681**

was still a long way off, was seated up above the door, inside the cave, waiting and smiling to himself. But minutes passed and no one came thundering in. The dragon frowned, puzzled, and was tempted to peek out. However, reflecting that patience seldom goes unrewarded, the dragon kept his head up out of sight and went on waiting. At last, when he could stand it no longer, the dragon craned his neck and looked. There at the entrance of the cave stood a trembling young man in a suit of armor twice his size, struggling with a sword so heavy he could lift only one end of it at a time.

At sight of the dragon, the cobbler's youngest son began to tremble so violently that his armor rattled like a house caving in. He heaved[4] with all his might at the sword and got the handle up level with his chest, but even now the point was down in the dirt. As loudly and firmly as he could manage, the youngest son cried—

Dragon, dragon, how do you do?
I've come from the king to murder you.

"What?" cried the dragon, flabbergasted.[5] "You? *You?* Murder *Me???*" All at once he began to laugh, pointing at the little cobbler's son. *"He he he ho ha!"* he roared, shaking all over, and tears filled his eyes. *"He he he ho ho ho ha ha!"* laughed the dragon. He was laughing so hard he had to hang onto his sides, and he fell off the door and landed on his back, still laughing, kicking his legs helplessly, rolling from side to side, laughing and laughing and laughing.

The cobbler's son was annoyed. "I *do* come from the king to murder you," he said. "A person doesn't like to be laughed at for a thing like that."

"He he he!" wailed the dragon, almost sobbing, gasping for breath. "Of course not, poor dear boy! But really, *he he,* the *idea* of it, *ha ha ha!* And that simply ri*d*iculous *poem!"* Tears streamed from the dragon's eyes and he lay on his back perfectly helpless with laughter. **11**

"It's a good poem," said the cobbler's youngest son loyally. "My father made it up." And growing angrier he shouted,

---

4. Here **heaved** means "lifted an object with force."
5. To be **flabbergasted** is to be astonished.

Practice the Skills

11 Key Reading Skill

Comparing and Contrasting
List some ways the cobbler's youngest son and the dragon are different from each other.

"I want you to stop that laughing, or I'll—I'll—" But the dragon could not stop for the life of him. And suddenly, in a terrific rage, the cobbler's son began flopping the sword end over end in the direction of the dragon. Sweat ran off the youngest son's forehead, but he labored on, blistering mad, and at last, with one supreme heave, he had the sword standing on its handle a foot from the dragon's throat. Of its own weight the sword fell, slicing the dragon's head off.

"*He he ho huk,*" went the dragon—and then he lay dead. **12**

The two older brothers crawled out and thanked their younger brother for saving their lives. "We have learned our lesson," they said.

Then the three brothers gathered all the treasures from the dragon's cave and tied them to the back end of the youngest brother's horse, and tied the dragon's head on behind the treasures, and started home.

"I'm glad I listened to my father," the youngest son thought. "Now I'll be the richest man in the kingdom." **13**

There were hand-carved picture frames and silver spoons and boxes of jewels and chests of money and silver compasses and maps telling where there were more treasures buried when these ran out. There was also a curious old book with a picture of an owl on the cover, and inside, poems and odd sentences and recipes that seemed to make no sense.

When they reached the king's castle the people all leaped for joy to see that the dragon was dead, and the princess ran out and kissed the youngest brother on the forehead, for secretly she had hoped it would be him.

"Well," said the king, "which half of the kingdom do you want?"

"My wizard's book!" exclaimed the wizard. "He's found my wizard's book!" He opened the book and ran his finger under the words and then said in a loud voice, "Glmuzk, shkzmlp, blam!"

Instantly the queen stood before them in her natural shape, except she was soaking wet from being sprinkled too often. She glared at the king.

"Oh dear," said the king, hurrying toward the door. **14** ○

READING WORKSHOP 3

Practice the Skills

12 Reviewing Skill

Understanding Cause and Effect Name two different causes that led to the death of the dragon.

13 BIG Question

Do you think that the youngest son is the hero of the story? Why or why not? Write your answers on the "Dragon, Dragon" page of Foldable 6. Your response will help you complete the Unit Challenge later.

14 Key Literary Element

Theme Spend a minute or two thinking about the whole story. Then write a sentence or a phrase in your Learner's Notebook stating the story's theme.

Dragon, Dragon **683**

READING WORKSHOP 3 • Comparing and Contrasting

After You Read Dragon, Dragon

Answering the BIG Question

1. What ideas does this tale offer about what makes a hero—or what does *not* make a hero? Explain your answer, using information from the story.
2. **Recall** What trait was the eldest son known for and what example showed that trait? What trait was the middle son known for and what example showed *his* trait?
   TIP Right There
3. **Summarize** Briefly describe the damage the dragon caused throughout the kingdom.
   TIP Author and Me

Critical Thinking

4. **Contrast** In what way is the ending of this tale different from the typical ending of a fairy tale or folktale? Give an example of a typical ending to help support your answer.
   TIP Author and Me
5. **Infer** The author describes the wizard's book as having an owl on the cover. What do you think the owl stands for? The inside of the book contains "poems and odd sentences and recipes that seemed to make no sense." What do you think the author is implying with this description?
   TIP Author and Me

Write About Your Reading

Most of the characters in fairy tales play traditional roles. The men are strong and hunt and kill monsters. The women stay home waiting to be rescued and get married. Poor people work for rich people and risk their lives to save others. And all monsters are bad.

Imagine what this fairy tale would be like if the characters played different roles. In your Learner's Notebook, write about how you would change the characters and events in this fairy tale and why you would make those changes.

Objectives (pp. 684–685)
Reading Compare and contrast
Literature Identify key literary elements: theme
Vocabulary Explore word histories
Writing Respond to literature
Grammar Use punctuation: commas in compound sentences

684 UNIT 6 What Makes a Hero?

Skills Review

Key Reading Skill: Comparing and Contrasting

6. What did you learn about the brothers by comparing and contrasting them? How did this help you to understand and enjoy the fairy tale?
7. How is this tale similar to a typical fairy tale? How is it different? Do the similarities and differences make the story funnier? Why or why not?

Key Literary Element: Theme

8. Why do you think stories have themes? What purpose do they serve?
9. Does the author directly state the tale's theme or let readers figure it out? Explain your answer.
10. If you wrote a story about your life, what would be the theme?

Reviewing Skills: Understanding Cause and Effect

11. What did the wizard do to cause the queen to turn into a rosebush?
12. What did the youngest son do to make the dragon laugh?

Vocabulary Check

Rewrite each sentence, filling in the blank with the correct word from the list.

quest   tyrant   plagued   lunged

13. The king claimed that he was not a ___.
14. The kingdom was ___ with problems caused by a dragon.
15. The three brothers all went on a ___ to slay the dragon.
16. The dragon ___ at the eldest son and swallowed him in a gulp.

17. **English Language Coach** Remember that *wizard* came from *wys* ("wise"). Which of the following words does *not* come from *wys*?

   wish   wit   witch

Grammar Link: Commas in Compound Sentences

A **compound sentence** contains two or more simple sentences. When you combine the simple sentences with a coordinating conjunction like *and* or *but*, you must place a comma before the conjunction.

The people all leaped for joy to see that the dragon was dead. The princess ran out and kissed the youngest brother.

The people all leaped for joy to see that the dragon was dead, and the princess ran out and kissed the youngest brother.

Grammar Practice

Copy each sentence below, adding a comma where it belongs.

18. The wizard didn't know what happened but he said he'd change the queen back into a woman.
19. The dragon robbed graves and he put frogs in people's drinking water.
20. The eldest son didn't think he needed his father's advice but he thought it was only polite to ask.

Writing Application Read the ideas you wrote in your Learner's Notebook about making changes to "Dragon, Dragon." Make sure you have commas before coordinating conjunctions in your compound sentences.

Web Activities For eFlashcards, Selection Quick Checks, and other Web activities, go to www.glencoe.com.

READING WORKSHOP 3 • Comparing and Contrasting

Before You Read : The King of Mazy May

Meet the Author

Jack London is considered one of the greatest adventure writers of all time. He drew on his life as a pirate, sailor, and Alaskan gold prospector for locations, events, and characters in his novels and stories. "The proper function of man is to live, not exist," he once declared. See page R4 of the Author Files for more on Jack London.

Author Search For more about Jack London, go to www.glencoe.com.

Vocabulary Preview

endured (en DURD) *v.* held up under pain or hardship; form of the verb *endure* **(p. 689)** *Walt and his father endured many troubles.*

industrious (in DUS tree us) *adj.* hard-working **(p. 690)** *Finding and mining gold required people who were industrious.*

prospectors (PRAH spek turz) *n.* people who explore an area for mineral or oil deposits **(p. 690)** *Prospectors discovered gold in the Yukon and Klondike territories.*

perilously (PAIR uh lus lee) *adv.* dangerously; at risk of injury **(p. 694)** *The sled went perilously near the edge of the cliff.*

floundering (FLOUN dur ing) *v.* struggling to move or gain balance; form of the verb *flounder* **(p. 696)** *The dogs were floundering in the deep snow.*

Partner Talk With your partner, use each vocabulary word in a different question about life in the Klondike territory of northwestern Canada in the 1890s.

English Language Coach

Word Histories It isn't surprising that cowboys invented the word *stampede* to describe cattle running wild. Mexican cowboys brought *estampida* to the United States in the 1820s. American cowboys knew a good word when they heard it, and they just changed the pronunciation and spelling a little.

Old German
stampfon *v.* to beat or pound, especially with the feet

Spanish — *English*

estampar *v.* | **stamp, stomp** *v.*

Mexican Spanish
estampida *n.* a sudden rush of animals — **stampede** *n.* a sudden rush of animals or people

Partner Talk What do you suppose a stampede was called before the word *stampede* existed? With a partner, invent a new word that has the same meaning. You can use *stamp* or *stomp* as part of your word or, if you prefer, think up a whole new word.

Objectives (p. 686–699)
Reading Compare and contrast • Make connections from text to self
Literature Identify key literary elements: theme
Vocabulary Explore word histories

READING WORKSHOP 3 • Comparing and Contrasting

Skills Preview

Key Reading Skill: Comparing and Contrasting

Sometimes when people read, they compare and contrast what they read with what they know. They think about how characters are like themselves or other people in their lives. Or they compare and contrast the events in the text with events they have lived or read about. This kind of comparing and contrasting can help bring a text alive with meaning.

Write to Learn Draw a two-column chart in your Learner's Notebook. Label one column *Similarities* and one column *Differences*. While you read, fill in the chart by comparing and contrasting yourself with the King of Mazy May.

Key Literary Element: Theme

The theme of a story is the central idea the author wants you to understand or think about. It's what makes a story mean something to you. Sometimes it's a challenge to find the theme, but the challenge makes it more worthwhile.

Use these tips to find the theme:

- Stories usually have a conflict between two characters or forces.

  What people or forces are in conflict in "The King of Mazy May"?

- Often the good character or the good force wins the conflict.

  Who wins the conflict in this story? How does he win the conflict?

- The ending of the conflict shows readers what the theme of the story is.

  What do you think the author wants you to learn from this story?

Partner Talk With a partner, select one of the stories that you read in this unit. Work together to apply the above tips and find the theme.

Get Ready to Read

Connect to the Reading

The boy in "The King of Mazy May" knows what to do when he sees an injustice. Have you ever stood up for someone who was being treated badly?

Class Talk Have a discussion about movies, books, and stories you know that involve injustice. What was the injustice? Did someone do something to make things right? What risks were involved? Do you know anyone personally who's stood up for something that was right?

Build Background

In 1896 gold was discovered in the Klondike of Canada. Thousands set out to strike it rich. Perhaps they'd have stayed home if they'd known the following:

- They'd risk their lives to carry tons of needed equipment across steep, frozen mountain passes.
- Local people had already claimed most of the gold.
- The gold that remained was ten feet below permanently frozen ground.

Most fortune-seekers found only hardship—if they were lucky enough to survive!

Set Purposes for Reading

BIG Question The hero of this story is only fourteen. How could a boy that age be a hero? Read "The King of Mazy May" to find out.

Set Your Own Purpose What else would you like to learn from the story to help you answer the Big Question? Write your own purpose on the "King of Mazy May" page of Foldable 6.

Keep Moving

Use these skills as you read the following selection.

The King of Mazy May **687**

READING WORKSHOP 3

The King of Mazy May

by Jack London

Walt Masters is not a very large boy, but there is manliness in his make-up, and he himself, although he does not know a great deal that most boys know, knows much that other boys do not know. **1**

He has never seen a train of cars or an elevator in his life, and for that matter, he has never once looked upon a cornfield, a plow, a cow, or even a chicken. He has never had a pair of shoes on his feet, or gone to a picnic or a party, or talked to a girl. But he has seen the sun at midnight, watched the ice-jams on one of the mightiest of rivers, and played beneath the northern lights,[1] the one white child in thousands of square miles of frozen wilderness.

1. The **northern lights** are beautiful streams and arches of moving colored light. They're seen at times in the night sky over northern regions of Earth. The light comes from atoms speeding through Earth's magnetic field. When such lights appear in the southern hemisphere, they're called the "southern lights."

Practice the Skills

1 **Key Reading Skill**

Comparing and Contrasting
How does the author use comparing and contrasting to help you get to know the character of Walt?

READING WORKSHOP 3

Visual Vocabulary
Moccasins are soft leather shoes with the sole and sides made of one piece.

Walt has walked all the fourteen years of his life in sun-tanned, moose-hide moccasins, and he can go to the Indian camps and "talk big" with the men, and trade calico[2] and beads with them for their precious furs. He can make bread without baking-powder, yeast or hops, shoot a moose at three hundred yards, and drive the wild wolf-dogs fifty miles a day on the packed trail.

Last of all, he has a good heart, and is not afraid of the darkness and loneliness, of man or beast or thing. His father is a good man, strong and brave, and Walt is growing up like him. 2

Walt was born a thousand miles or so down the Yukon, in a trading-post below the Ramparts. After his mother died, his father and he came on up the river, step by step, from camp to camp, till now they are settled down on the Mazy May Creek in the Klondike[3] country. Last year they and several others had spent much toil and time on the Mazy May, and **endured** great hardships; the creek, in turn, was just beginning to show up its richness and to reward them for their heavy labor. But with the news of their discoveries, strange men began to come and go through the short days and long nights, and many unjust things they did to the men who had worked so long upon the creek.

2. *Calico* is a type of cotton cloth with a pattern on it. The word comes from Calicut, the town in India where the cloth was made.
3. The *Yukon* River flows from Canada's Yukon Territory through Alaska to the Bering Sea. It was a major route to the Klondike during the gold rush of 1897–1898. The *Klondike* is the name of both a river and a gold-mining region in the Yukon Territory of Canada near the Alaskan border.

Vocabulary

endured (en DURD) *v.* held up under pain or hardship

Practice the Skills

2 **Key Reading Skill**
Comparing and Contrasting
In the table you prepared in your Learner's Notebook, use the information in the first four paragraphs to fill in differences and similarities between yourself and Walt Masters.

Klondike Gold Rush, Summer 1898, Julius Price in the *Illustrated London News* 20 August 1898.

Analyzing the Art Which characters mentioned on this page might this art show? Explain your answer.

The King of Mazy May **689**

READING WORKSHOP 3

Si Hartman had gone away on a moose-hunt, to return and find new stakes driven and his claim jumped.[4] George Lukens and his brother had lost their claims in a like manner, having delayed too long on the way to Dawson to record them. In short, it was an old story, and quite a number of the earnest, **industrious prospectors** had suffered similar losses.

But Walt Masters's father had recorded his claim at the start, so Walt had nothing to fear, now that his father had gone on a short trip up the White River prospecting for quartz. Walt was well able to stay by himself in the cabin, cook his three meals a day, and look after things. Not only did he look after his father's claim, but he had agreed to keep an eye on the adjoining[5] one of Loren Hall, who had started for Dawson to record it. **3**

Loren Hall was an old man, and he had no dogs, so he had to travel very slowly. After he had been gone some time, word came up the river that he had broken through the ice at Rosebud Creek, and frozen his feet so badly that he would not be able to travel for a couple of weeks. Then Walt Masters received the news that old Loren was nearly all right again, and about to move on afoot for Dawson, as fast as a weakened man could.

Walt was worried, however; the claim was liable to be jumped at any moment because of this delay, and a fresh stampede[6] had started in on the Mazy May. He did not like the looks of the newcomers, and one day, when five of them came by with crack[7] dog-teams and the lightest of camping

Shooting the white-horse rapids en route to the Klondike gold fields, 1898. Hand-colored halftone.

3 **Key Literary Element**

Theme Do you see the beginning of a conflict here? Who do you think the "good" character will be? Write your thoughts in your Learner's Notebook.

---

4. A *claim* was a piece of land that a prospector claimed to be his or her own. The prospector drove wooden **stakes** into the ground to mark its boundaries, and then recorded the claim with the gold commissioner in the city of **Dawson**. Someone who *jumped a claim* took over and recorded a claim for land that had been staked out, but not yet recorded, by someone else.
5. *Adjoining* means "located next to."
6. Usually a *stampede* is a sudden rush of animals. In this story, the word refers to the rush of people searching for gold in the Klondike.
7. Here *crack* means "excellent, first-rate."

Vocabulary

industrious (in DUS tree us) *adj.* hard-working

prospectors (PRAH spek turz) *n.* people who explore an area for mineral or oil deposits

690 UNIT 6 What Makes a Hero?

The result of the year's "wash up": A sketch in the Bank of British North America, Dawson City, 1898. Jules M. Price. Illustration from *From Euston to Klondike*.

Analyzing the Art: What do you think the man is weighing? How important is the measurement?

outfits, he could see that they were prepared to make speed, and resolved to keep an eye on them. So he locked up the cabin and followed them, being at the same time careful to remain hidden. 4

He had not watched them long before he was sure that they were professional stampeders, bent[8] on jumping all the claims in sight. Walt crept along the snow at the rim of the creek and saw them change many stakes, destroy old ones, and set up new ones.

In the afternoon, with Walt always trailing on their heels, they came back down the creek, unharnessed their dogs, and went into camp within two claims of his cabin. When he saw them make preparations to cook, he hurried home to get something to eat himself, and then hurried back. He crept so

---

8. Here **bent** means "determined" or "intending."

Practice the Skills

4 **Key Reading Skill**

Comparing and Contrasting
Walt is given a lot of freedom but also many responsibilities. Compare and contrast this with the freedom and responsibilities in your own life.

close that he could hear them talking quite plainly, and by pushing the underbrush aside he could catch occasional glimpses of them. They had finished eating and were smoking around the fire.

"The creek is all right, boys," a large, black-bearded man, evidently the leader said, "and I think the best thing we can do is to pull out tonight. The dogs can follow the trail; besides, it's going to be moonlight. What say you?"

"But it's going to be beastly cold," objected one of the party. "It's forty below zero now."

"An' sure, can't ye keep warm by jumpin' off the sleds an' runnin' after the dogs?" cried an Irishman. "An' who wouldn't? The creek as rich as a United States mint! Faith, it's an ilegant chanst[9] to be gettin' a run fer yer money! An' if ye don't run, it's mebbe you'll not get the money at all, at all."

"That's it," said the leader. "If we can get to Dawson and record, we're rich men; and there is no telling who's been sneaking along in our tracks, watching us, and perhaps now off to give the alarm. The thing for us to do is to rest the dogs a bit, and then hit the trail as hard as we can. What do you say?"

Evidently the men had agreed with their leader, for Walt Masters could hear nothing but the rattle of the tin dishes which were being washed. Peering out cautiously, he could see the leader studying a piece of paper. Walt knew what it was at a glance—a list of all the unrecorded claims on Mazy May. Any man could get these lists by applying to the gold commissioner at Dawson. 5

Klondike Gold Rush, 1904, artist unknown.

5 Reviewing Skills

Understanding Cause and Effect Walt followed the claim-jumpers. What was the effect of his actions?

---

9. **Ilegant chanst** is the character's way of saying "elegant chance," meaning "excellent opportunity."

"Thirty-two," the leader said, lifting his face to the men. "Thirty-two isn't recorded, and this is thirty-three. Come on; let's take a look at it. I saw somebody had been working on it when we came up this morning."

Three of the men went with him, leaving one man to remain in camp. Walt crept carefully after them till they came to Loren Hall's shaft. One of the men went down and built a fire on the bottom to thaw out the frozen gravel, while the others built another fire on the dump and melted water in a couple of gold-pans. This they poured into a piece of canvas stretched between two logs, used by Loren Hall in which to wash his gold.

In a short time a couple of buckets of dirt were sent up by the man in the shaft, and Walt could see the others grouped anxiously about their leader as he proceeded to wash it. When this was finished, they stared at the broad streak of black sand and yellow gold-grains on the bottom of the pan, and one of them called excitedly for the man who had remained in camp to come. Loren Hall had struck it rich, and his claim was not yet recorded. It was plain that they were going to jump it.

Walt lay in the snow, thinking rapidly. He was only a boy, but in the face of the threatened injustice against old lame Loren Hall he felt that he must do something. He waited and watched, with his mind made up, till he saw the men begin to square up new stakes. Then he crawled away till out of hearing, and broke into a run for the camp of the stampeders. Walt's father had taken their own dogs with him prospecting, and the boy knew how impossible it was him to undertake the seventy miles to Dawson without the aid of dogs. **6**

Gaining the camp, he picked out, with an experienced eye, the easiest running sled and started to harness up the stampeders' dogs. There were three teams of six each, and from these he chose ten of the best. Realizing how necessary it was to have a good head-dog, he strove to discover a leader amongst them; but he had little time in which to do it, for he could hear the voices of the returning men. By the time the team was in shape and everything ready, the claim-jumpers came into sight in an open place not more than a hundred yards from the trail, which ran down the bed of the creek. They cried out to him, but he gave no heed, grabbing up one

Practice the Skills

6 **Key Reading Skill**

Comparing and Contrasting Add entries to your table to contrast how Walt travels to where he needs to go and how you get around.

of their fur sleeping-robes which lay loosely in the snow, and leaping upon the sled.

"**Mush!** Hi! **Mush on!**" he cried to the animals, snapping the keen-lashed whip among them. 7

The dogs sprang against the yoke-straps,[10] and the sled jerked under way so suddenly as to almost throw him off. Then it curved into the creek, poising **perilously** on one runner. He was almost breathless with suspense, when it finally righted with a bound and sprang ahead again. The creek bank was high and he could not see, although he could hear the cries of the men and knew they were running to cut him off. He did not dare to think what would happen if they caught him; he only clung to the sled, his heart beating wildly, and watched the snow-rim of the bank above him.

Suddenly, over this snow-rim came the flying body of the Irishman, who had leaped straight for the sled in a desperate attempt to capture it; but he was an instant too late. Striking on the very rear of it, he was thrown from his feet, backward, into the snow. Yet, with the quickness of a cat, he had clutched the end of the sled with one hand, turned over, and was dragging behind on his breast, swearing at the boy and threatening all kinds of terrible things if he did not stop the dogs; but Walt cracked him sharply across the knuckles with the butt of the dog-whip till he let go.

It was eight miles from Walt's claim to the Yukon—eight very crooked miles, for the creek wound back and forth like a snake, "tying knots in itself," as George Lukens said. And because it was so crooked, the dogs could not get up their best speed, while the sled ground heavily on its side against the curves, now to the right, now to the left.

Travelers who had come up and down the Mazy May on foot, with packs on their backs, had declined to go around all the bends, and instead had made short cuts across the narrow necks of creek bottom. Two of his pursuers had gone back to

Practice the Skills

7 English Language Coach

Word Histories The word **mush** as a command to dogs was first recorded in 1862. In French, *marche* means "go" or "march." French-Canadian dog-sledders got their dogs to move by shouting "*Marchon!*" (mar SHAWN), meaning "Let's go!" English-speaking dogsledders mispronounced the command, saying "Mush on!"

---

10. A **yoke-strap** is part of the dog's harness.

Vocabulary

perilously (PAIR uh lus lee) *adv.* dangerously; at risk of injury

harness the remaining dogs, but the others took advantage of these short cuts, running on foot, and before he knew it they had almost overtaken him.

"Halt!" they cried after him. "Stop, or we'll shoot!"

But Walt only yelled the harder at the dogs, and dashed round the bend with a couple of revolver bullets singing after him. At the next bend they had drawn up closer still, and the bullets struck uncomfortably near to him; but at this point the Mazy May straightened out and ran for half a mile as the crow flies. Here the dogs stretched out in their long wolf-swing, and the stampeders, quickly winded, slowed down and waited for their own sled to come up. 8

Looking over his shoulder, Walt reasoned that they had not given up the chase for good, and that they would soon be after him again. So he wrapped the fur robe about him to shut out the stinging air, and lay flat on the empty sled, encouraging the dogs, as he well knew how.

At last, twisting abruptly between two river islands, he came upon the mighty Yukon sweeping grandly to the north. He could not see from bank to bank, and in the quick-falling twilight it loomed[11] a great white sea of frozen stillness. There was not a sound, save the breathing of the dogs, and the churn of the steel-shod sled.

No snow had fallen for several weeks, and the traffic had packed the main-river trail till it was hard and glassy as glare ice. Over this the sled flew along, and the dogs kept the trail fairly well, although Walt quickly discovered that he had made a mistake in choosing the leader. As they were driven in single file, without reins, he had to guide them by his voice, and it was evident the head-dog had never learned the meaning of "gee" and "haw."[12] He hugged the inside of the curves too closely, often forcing his comrades behind him into the soft snow, while several times he thus capsized the sled.

11. Something that *loomed*, came into view in a way that seemed large and threatening.
12. These are commands used to direct the dogs. *Gee* means "to the right" and *haw* means "to the left."

Ad for the S. S. City of Columbia to Klondike Country.

Practice the Skills

8 **BIG Question**

Do you think Walt has the qualities of a real-life hero? Support your answer with details from the story.

READING WORKSHOP 3

On the Klondike. 1890s. Roper.
Analyzing the Art Compare the men in this painting with the stampeders.

There was no wind, but the speed at which he traveled created a bitter blast, and with the thermometer down to forty below, this bit through fur and flesh to the very bones. Aware that if he remained constantly upon the sled he would freeze to death, and knowing the practice of Arctic travelers, Walt shortened up one of the lashing-thongs, and whenever he felt chilled, seized hold of it, jumped off, and ran behind till warmth was restored. Then he would climb on and rest till the process had to be repeated. 9

Looking back he could see the sled of his pursuers, drawn by eight dogs, rising and falling over the ice hummocks[13] like a boat in a seaway. The Irishman and the black-bearded leader were with it, taking turns in running and riding.

Night fell, and in the blackness of the first hour or so, Walt toiled desperately with his dogs. On account of the poor lead-dog, they were constantly **floundering** off the beaten track

---

13. **Hummocks** are ridges or hills on the ice.

Vocabulary

floundering (FLOUN dur ing) *v.* struggling to move or gain balance

Practice the Skills

9 | **Key Reading Skill**

Comparing and Contrasting
Add a final row to your table comparing the weather where Walt lived and the weather where you live.

696 UNIT 6 What Makes a Hero?

READING WORKSHOP 3

into the soft snow, and the sled was as often riding on its side or top as it was in the proper way. This work and strain tried his strength sorely. Had he not been in such haste he could have avoided much of it, but he feared the stampeders would creep up in the darkness and overtake him. However, he could hear them occasionally yelling to their dogs, and knew from the sounds that they were coming up very slowly.

When the moon rose he was off Sixty Mile, and Dawson was only fifty miles away. He was almost exhausted, and breathed a sigh of relief as he climbed on the sled again. Looking back, he saw his enemies had crawled up within four hundred yards. At this space they remained, a black speck of motion on the white river-breast. Strive as they would, they could not shorten this distance, and strive as he would he could not increase it.

He had now discovered the proper lead-dog, and he knew he could easily run away from them if he could only change the bad leader for the good one. But this was impossible, for a moment's delay, at the speed they were running, would bring the men behind upon him.

When he got off the mouth of Rosebud Creek, just as he was topping a rise, the ping of a bullet on the ice beside him, and the report[14] of a gun, told him that they were this time shooting at him with a rifle. And from then on, as he cleared the summit of each ice-jam, he stretched flat on the leaping sled till the rifle-shot from the rear warned him that he was safe till the next ice-jam.

Now it is very hard to lie on a moving sled, jumping and plunging and yawing[15] like a boat before the wind, and to shoot through the deceiving moonlight at an object four hundred yards away on another moving sled performing equally wild antics.[16] So it is not to be wondered at that the black-bearded leader did not hit him. **10**

After several hours of this, during which, perhaps, a score[17] of bullets had struck about him, their ammunition began to give out and their fire slackened. They took greater care, and

---

14. A gun's **report** is the sound it makes when fired.
15. When a sled is **yawing**, it is turning from side to side and going off the course.
16. **Antics** are odd, silly, or comical actions.
17. A **score** is twenty.

Practice the Skills

10 Reviewing Skills

Understanding Cause and Effect The claim-jumper could not hit Walt no matter how many times he shot at the boy. What was the cause of this effect?

The King of Mazy May

by Edward Roper in *The Illustrated London News* 30 October 1897.

only whipped a shot at him at the most favorable opportunities. He was also beginning to leave them behind, the distance slowly increasing to six hundred yards.

Lifting clear on the crest of a great jam off Indian River, Walt Masters met his first accident. A bullet sang past his ears, and struck the bad lead-dog.

The poor brute plunged in a heap, with the rest of the team on top of him.

Like a flash, Walt was by the leader. Cutting the traces with his hunting knife, he dragged the dying animal to one side and straightened out the team.

He glanced back. The other sled was coming up like an express-train. With half the dogs still over their traces, he cried, "Mush on!" and leaped upon the sled just as the pursuing team dashed abreast of him.

The Irishman was just preparing to spring for him,—they were so sure they had him that they did not shoot,—when Walt turned fiercely upon them with his whip.

He struck at their faces, and men must save their faces with their hands. So there was no shooting just then. Before they could recover from the hot rain of blows, Walt reached out from his sled, catching their wheel-dog[18] by the fore legs in mid-spring, and throwing him heavily. This brought the whole team into a snarl, capsizing the sled and tangling his enemies up beautifully.

Away Walt flew, the runners of his sled fairly screaming as they bounded over the frozen surface. And what had seemed an accident proved to be a blessing in disguise. The proper lead-dog was now to the fore, and he stretched low to the trail and whined with joy as he jerked his comrades along.

By the time he reached Ainslie's Creek, seventeen miles from Dawson, Walt had left his pursuers, a tiny speck, far behind. At Monte Cristo Island he could no longer see them. And at Swede Creek, just as daylight was silvering the pines, he ran plump into the camp of old Loren Hall.

Almost as quick as it takes to tell it, Loren had his sleeping-furs rolled up, and had joined Walt on the sled. They permitted the dogs to travel more slowly, as there was no sign of the chase in the rear, and just as they pulled up at the gold commissioner's office in Dawson, Walt, who had kept his eyes open to the last, fell asleep.

And because of what Walt Masters did on this night, the men of the Yukon have become very proud of him, and always speak of him now as the King of Mazy May.

Practice the Skills

12 BIG Question

What qualities make Walt a hero to the people of the Mazy May Creek? How do you think he developed those qualities at such a young age? On the "King of Mazy May" page of your Foldable, write a short paragraph to support your answers. Your response will help you complete the Unit Challenge later.

13 Key Literary Element

Theme What is the theme of this story? Write a statement of the theme in your Learner's Notebook using one or two sentences.

---

18. The **wheel-dog** is the dog nearest the front end of the sled. The term was borrowed from horse teams in which the wheel horse is the horse nearest the front wheels of a wagon or carriage.

READING WORKSHOP 3 • Comparing and Contrasting

After You Read — The King of Mazy May

Answering the BIG Question

1. Walt's life and property were not in danger, yet he stole the stampeders' dogs and sled. Can someone steal and still be a hero? Explain.

2. **Recall** What evidence did Walt have that the newcomers were going to "jump" Loren Hall's claim?
   TIP Right There

3. **Support** Give an example of a time when Walt used his brains rather than his physical strength and endurance to help him come out ahead in the race.
   TIP Author and Me

Critical Thinking

4. **Interpret** At the end of the story, the men of the Yukon call Walt "the King of Mazy May." What might the word "king" suggest about the way Walt will be treated after this incident?
   TIP On My Own

5. **Explain** Jack London once declared, "The proper function of man is to live, not exist." Explain how Walt carried out the author's idea of the "proper function" even before he became a man.
   TIP Author and Me

6. **Infer** Walt saw the leader of the newcomers studying a piece of paper and "knew at a glance" what it was. Why did Walt think he knew what the paper was? Do you think Walt was right to be so sure?
   TIP Author and Me

Write About Your Reading

Imagine that it's 1898, and you've gone to the Klondike to search for gold. You're about to write a letter to a family member back home.

- Decide who you are. You can be any kind of character you want. Use a "voice" that sounds natural for that character.
- Plan what you'll write. To make your letter believable, you'll need plenty of details. What's the weather like? What hardships did you suffer to get here? What are you going through now? What adventures have you had?
- Now write your letter.

Objectives (700–701)
Reading Compare and contrast • Make connections from text to self
Literature Identify key literary elements: theme
Vocabulary Explore word histories
Writing Respond to literature: personal letter
Grammar Use punctuation: commas in complex sentences

READING WORKSHOP 3 • Comparing and Contrasting

Skills Review

Key Reading Skill: Comparing and Contrasting

7. While you read, you used a chart to compare and contrast your life to Walt's. Write three or four sentences to summarize the major similarities and differences.

Key Literary Element: Theme

8. Can you connect the theme of this story to your life? Explain why or why not.
9. Did thinking about the story's theme make the story more meaningful to you? Why or why not?

Reviewing Skills: Understanding Cause and Effect

10. What do you think caused the Gold Rush in the United States and Canada?

Vocabulary Check

Rewrite each sentence, filling in the blank with the correct word from the list.

industrious   floundering
perilously   prospectors   endured

11. All of the ___ wanted to find lots of gold.
12. It was not easy to find gold, and miners had to be ___ to succeed.
13. The dogs were ___ without a good leader.
14. The bullets came ___ close to hitting Walt.
15. Walt ___ in spite of all the difficulties.
16. **English Language Coach** What is the most common meaning of the word *stampede*? What does *stampede* mean in this story?

Grammar Link: Commas in Complex Sentences

A **complex sentence** has one independent clause and one or more dependent clauses. An independent clause has a subject and a predicate and can stand alone as a sentence. A dependent clause has a subject and a predicate but cannot stand alone.

A dependent clause that comes *before* an independent clause *should be* followed by a comma.

- **Since the dragon moved to the kingdom,** he has lived on the outside of town.

A dependent clause that comes *after* an independent clause should *not* be followed by a comma if the dependent clause is necessary to understand the independent clause.

- Everyone says **that the dragon eats the people who live in the town**.

If the dependent clause is not necessary to understand the independent clause, it should be set apart with commas.

- The dragon, **who lived on the outside of town,** scared the people in the kingdom.

Grammar Practice

Put commas in the complex sentences below to separate the dependent clauses from the independent clauses.

17. When you work hard you deserve what you get.
18. Susan the captain of the cheerleading team had the highest score on the math test.
19. Although the city fixed all the roads they still hadn't repaired the sidewalks.

Writing Application Read the letter you wrote about your trip to the Klondike. Make sure you used commas to set apart any dependent clauses in your complex sentences.

Web Activities For eFlashcards, Selection Quick Checks, and other Web activities, go to www.glencoe.com.

The King of Mazy May

WRITING WORKSHOP PART 2

Fable
Revising, Editing, and Presenting

ASSIGNMENT Write a fable

Purpose: To write a fable that teaches a moral

Audience: You, your teacher, and your classmates

Revising Rubric

Your revised folktale should have

- well-developed characters
- a conflict
- three main events
- a moral
- dialogue
- correct spelling and grammar

Objectives (pp. 702–705)
Writing Revise writing for key elements, style, voice, and dialogue
Grammar Write compound and complex sentences
Listening, Speaking, and Viewing Present fable • Use appropriate expressions and gestures • Maintain effective eye contact and posture • Ask for feedback

You started planning your fable and writing your first draft in Part 1 of this Writing Workshop. If you didn't finish your first draft, do that now. Use the story guide you created earlier to finish writing your draft.

Revising
Make It Better

Read your draft and answer the following questions:
- Does the story have a moral?
- Is there a main character?
- Does the story include three main events and a conflict?

How Do I Create Characters?

You are special and different from anyone else. Each character you create should be special and different too. Write such characters by giving them their own personalities.

The easiest way to express a character's personality is through dialogue. The way a character speaks and responds to other characters tells the reader about his or her personality. Read this example from "The Tortoise and the Hare."

> A conceited Hare boasted about her speed to everyone who would listen. "Not even the North Wind is as fast as I am!" she declared. "No animal in the forest can beat me in a race!"

What can you tell about the Hare's personality by the way she talks?

Try It

Add dialogue to your story to express your characters' personalities. Start a new line of text every time a different character speaks.

> "Without my feathers, I don't have any friends!" cried Peter.
> "Sure you do. I'm still your friend," said Polly.
> "You really want to be my friend even though I don't have any feathers?" asked Peter.
> "Of course I do!"

WRITING WORKSHOP PART 2

Editing
Finish It Up

Use the editing checklist to find and correct errors in your fable.
- ☑ Sentences are complete.
- ☑ Compound and complex sentences are correctly punctuated.
- ☑ Dialogue includes quotation marks and correct punctuation.
- ☑ Spelling is correct.

Writing Tip

Read your dialogue aloud to make sure your characters have their own ways of speaking.

Presenting
Show It Off

Print out your final draft or use your best handwriting to copy it onto a fresh sheet of paper.

Writer's Model

Fair-Feathered Friends
By Laticia Arnold

　　Peter the Peacock lived in the forest with his peacock friends. Peter was the most handsome peacock in the forest because his feathers magically changed from one magnificent color to another.
　　One day, Polly the Pig walked by the pond where Peter and his friends were brushing their feathers. "Stay away from me," warned Peter. "You'll get mud on my feathers."
　　"Get lost, you ugly pig!" said Peter's friend Pierre.
　　"You don't belong with us," said Peter. "You're fat and filthy and you don't even have any feathers!" While Peter spoke, his own feathers changed from light purple to dark red, and the other peacocks cheered.

Active Writing Model

- The writer introduces the main character and setting in the first paragraph.

- The writer does a good job of creating Peter; the way he speaks shows the reader that Peter is proud and thoughtless and says mean things.

WRITING WORKSHOP PART 2

Active Writing Model

Writer's Model

Polly slunk away, hid under a tree, and cried. When she had no more tears to shed, she decided to improve her appearance. She washed herself in a pond on the other side of the forest. After she finished her bath, she rolled around in the grass to cover her body with daisies, violets, and bright green leaves. Then she admired her reflection in the pond and said, "How beautiful I look!" She hurried back to the pond, certain that now the peacocks would be her friends.

Polly couldn't have been more wrong. The peacocks took one look at her and burst out laughing. "She thinks that trash from the forest floor is as beautiful as our feathers!" jeered Peter.

"And she's got grass and soil stains on her back," another peacock said.

"Will you be my friend?" Polly asked Peter. "Your feathers change colors, so it won't matter if I stain them a little."

"Me be friends with you?" Peter laughed. "Why should I spend time with a fat, ugly, old pig when I have the loveliest feathers in the forest?" Peter puffed up his feathers so hard that two of them fell out.

For the next few days, Peter's feathers continued to fall out. As he lost his feathers, he also lost his friends.

"You look like a plucked chicken!" the other peacocks told him. "You don't belong with us anymore."

Peter slunk away, hid under a tree, and cried. Polly came along and asked, "What's wrong?"

"Without my feathers, I don't have any friends," Peter sobbed.

"Sure you do. I still want to be your friend," said Polly.

"You still want to be my friend even though I don't have any feathers?" asked Peter.

"Of course I do!"

"You forgive me for being mean to you?"

"I'm sure you'll be nicer now that you know how it feels to be hurt."

Annotations:

- This is a complex sentence that begins with a dependent clause, so the word *bath* is followed by a comma.

- The writer uses dialogue to express the characters' personalities.

- The conflict is between appearance and behavior. Here, Peter faces the same problem Polly faced earlier.

WRITING WORKSHOP PART 2

Active Writing Model

> Polly taught Peter how to have fun splashing in the pond, rolling in the grass, and decorating himself with flowers and leaves. Before long, his feathers grew back. They even changed colors.
>
> But Peter didn't change his colors toward Polly. When Peter's peacock friends wanted him back, he said, "I'm sticking with Polly. She stuck by me when I lost my good looks. I don't need fair-feathered friends!"
>
> Moral: Don't judge others based on appearances.

This is the resolution of the conflict.

The fable ends with the moral. Peter learns that a beautiful appearance doesn't guarantee true friendship.

Listening, Speaking, and Viewing

Storytelling

Whenever you get together with your friends, stories are told—about sport events, dances, trips, or what happened in yesterday's math class. Stories are an easy way to share information about events at school and in your community.

What Is Storytelling?

Storytelling is a very old art form. Before people invented newspapers, television, or the Internet, storytelling was the only way to share information. History, legends, and myths were passed from generation to generation by professional storytellers who memorized important information and turned it into stories.

Why Is Storytelling Important?

Storytelling is fun and entertaining. It is also a good way to share a lesson or a moral. Before writing was invented, folktales were shared through storytelling. The tales were often rhymed or put to music to make them even more enjoyable.

How Do I Do It?

The main purpose of telling a story is to make the story as memorable as possible for the audience. In this workshop you will tell your fable to your classmates. The following tips will help you prepare to tell your fable:

1. Read your fable silently to yourself.
2. Read your fable aloud to a partner.
3. Start at the beginning of your fable; underline all of the important events that lead to the conclusion.
4. Consider the characters in your fable. What do their voices sound like? Use different voices when different characters speak.
5. Practice telling your fable aloud. Memorize it.
6. Keep your eyes on the audience instead of your script.

Gather Round Tell your fable to a small group of listeners. Make your fable as entertaining as possible by changing your voice for different characters, moving your body, or using props.

READING WORKSHOP 4

Skills Focus

You will practice using these skills when you read the following selections:
- "Aunt Millicent," p. 710
- "A Mason-Dixon Memory," p. 734

Reading
- Predicting

Literature
- Analyzing the setting

Vocabulary
- Understanding English word histories

Writing/Grammar
- Identifying and correcting run-on sentences

Skill Lesson

Predicting

Learn It!

What Is It? Have you ever said to yourself while watching a movie, "I know what's going to happen!"? If so, you were making a prediction. You thought about what was going on in the movie, you picked up clues, and then you made an educated guess about what would happen. Whether they turn out to be right or wrong, it's always fun to make predictions.

The skill of predicting is just as useful, satisfying, and fun when you read as when you watch a movie.

Why Is It Important? Predicting gives you another good reason to read. You want to find out if your prediction matches the events, don't you? If your prediction doesn't look like it's working out, don't worry, you can always make new predictions as the text changes. As you read, adjust or change your prediction if it doesn't fit what you learn.

© Patrick McDonnell. Reprinted with permission of King Features Syndicate.

Analyzing Cartoons
Based on this cartoon, how would you rate these two "mutts" on their skill of making predictions?

Objectives (pp. 706–707)
Reading Make predictions

READING WORKSHOP 4 • Predicting

How Do I Do It? Combine what you already know about an author or subject with what you learn as you read to guess what will happen next. Do these things as you read:

- Pay attention to details. Be on the hunt for clues.
- Stop occasionally and think about what you know.
- Ask yourself questions about what might happen.
- As the story unfolds, adjust your predictions and make new ones.

Study Central Visit www.glencoe.com and click on Study Central to review predicting.

Here's how one student made a prediction while reading "The King of Mazy May."

> Looking back he could see the sled of his pursuers, drawn by eight dogs, rising and falling over the ice hummocks like a boat in a seaway. The Irishman and the black-bearded leader were with it, taking turns in running and riding.
>
> Night fell, and in the blackness of the first hour or so, Walt toiled desperately with his dogs . . .

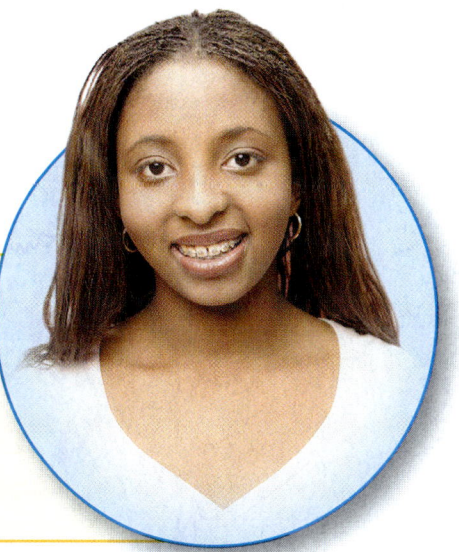

I don't know if Walt is going to escape, I think he will get away because of the title of the story. Also, since the story's about Walt I think he is going to be the King of Mazy May. They can't catch up with him now! He can only be the King if he escapes. I'll have to keep reading to see if I'm right.

Practice It!

Below are two events in "Aunt Millicent." Write at least one prediction for each situation. You might have more than one prediction; if you think of other predictions write them down too.

- The teacher assigns a report about an aunt or uncle, but Jamie doesn't have any aunts or uncles.
- Angelica has nineteen aunts and uncles and can't decide which one to write her report about.

Use It!

As you read "Aunt Millicent," remember the predictions you made. If you make other predictions, add them to your notes.

READING WORKSHOP 4 • Predicting

Before You Read : Aunt Millicent

Meet the Author
Mary Steele is one of Australia's best-loved writers for children. She writes in a humorous, light-hearted, and optimistic way. She says, "I believe that most children are born with a natural tendency toward fun and laughter."

Author Search For more about Mary Steele, go to www.glencoe.com.

Vocabulary Preview

tedious (TEE dee us) *adj.* boring; tiresome **(p. 711)** *The teacher found Angelica's bragging tedious.*

drab (drab) *adj.* lacking brightness; dull **(p. 714)** *Most people felt drab in comparison to Jamie's exciting aunt.*

expedition (ek spuh DISH un) *n.* a journey taken for a special purpose, such as exploration **(p. 716)** *Aunt Millicent was on an expedition to map the Cameroons.*

exotic (eg ZOT ik) *adj.* excitingly different; unusual; foreign **(p. 720)** *Jamie's mother brought home exotic hunting spears from Kenya.*

encounter (en KOUN tur) *n.* an unexpected or unpleasant meeting **(p. 723)** *Dr. Nutbeam did not enjoy his encounter with Mrs. Tonks.*

hoax (hohks) *n.* an act meant to fool or trick **(p. 727)** *Some people might say that Aunt Millicent was part of a hoax.*

Partner Talk Write each vocabulary word on a separate note card. Turn the note card over and write the word's definition and part of speech on the back. Take turns testing a partner by flashing each other the cards. Say each word in a sentence when you give the definition.

English Language Coach

Word Histories Another way that words come into English is, well, sort of mysterious. Some words just don't have clear histories. Take *hoax*, for example. The experts say that *hoax* is "probably" a shortened version of *hocus pocus.* Look that up, and you see that it is (again) "probably" a form of a Latin phrase.

Write to Learn The three words listed below are also related to *hocus pocus.* Copy each word into your Learner's Notebook, and tell what you know it means or might mean. Then look up the words in a good dictionary and copy one meaning for each word.

hokey

hokeypokey

hokum

Objectives (pp. 708–729)
Reading Make predictions • Make connections from text to self
Literature Identify key literary elements: setting
Vocabulary Explore word histories

READING WORKSHOP 4 • Predicting

Skills Preview

Key Reading Skill: Predicting

When you make predictions, you use your prior knowledge and the information you gather from reading to guess what will happen next. As you gather more information you might want to change your predictions. Sometimes you'll find that your guesses are right. A couple of things to ask yourself as you predict are:

- *What* will happen next?
- *Why* do I think that will happen next?

Write to Learn Read the first five paragraphs of "Aunt Millicent" and write a prediction.

Key Literary Element: Setting

Setting is the time and place in which a story's events occur. Sometimes authors give the time and place at the beginning of the story. The author may tell the setting later or gradually reveal it with clues. In "Aunt Millicent," you won't learn about the setting right away, but it is revealed eventually.

There can be more than one setting; for example, Aunt Millicent's travels call to mind other, more mysterious places. Remember the following as you think about the setting:

- You might not learn about the setting right away.
  When is the setting revealed?
- A story can have more than one setting. If the story moves to another place or time, that's a new setting.
  Do you notice more than one setting? If so, what events occur in each setting? Is there a reason events occur in different settings?
- Descriptions of characters and places, the way characters speak, and the time in which the story occurs can help show the setting.
  What details help you picture the setting?

What's *Your* Setting? Write a few sentences to describe one important setting in your life.

Get Ready to Read

Connect to the Reading

Think about what it would be like to travel all over the world and live the life of an explorer. Where would you go? What places have you always wanted to visit?

Write to Learn Make a list of the top three places you would travel to if you could go anywhere. Pick one of those places and write a paragraph explaining why you picked that place above all the others on your list.

Build Background

Jamie's exciting Aunt Millicent is rumored to be in Cameroon at one point and climbing a peak in the Peruvian Andes at another. That's the life of an explorer!

- Cameroon, officially called Republic of Cameroon, is in West Africa.
- Lima is the capital of Peru; the Andes Mountains run through Peru along the western part of South America.

Set Purposes for Reading

BIG Question Read "Aunt Millicent" to learn about a family's new—and suprising—hero.

Set Your Own Purpose What else would you like to learn from the story to help you answer the Big Question? Write your purpose on the "Aunt Millicent" page of Foldable 6.

Interactive Literary Elements Handbook
To review or learn more about the literary elements, go to www.glencoe.com.

Keep Moving

Use these skills as you read the following selection.

Aunt Millicent

by Mary Steele

"I," said Angelica Tonks, grandly, "have eight uncles and eleven aunts."

Angelica Tonks had more of most things than anyone else. She held the class record for pairs of fashion sneakers and Derwent pencil sets, and her pocket-money supply was endless. Now, it seemed, she also had the largest uncle-and-aunt collection in town. Her classmates squirmed and made faces at each other. *Awful* Angelica Tonks.

Mr. Wilfred Starling dusted the chalk from his bony hands and sighed. "Well, Angelica, aren't you a lucky one to have nineteen uncles and aunts. You'll just have to choose the most interesting one to write about, won't you?"

"But they're *all* interesting," objected Angelica. "The Tonks family is a wonderfully interesting family, you know. It will be terribly hard to choose just one." 1

There were more squirms. The class was fed up with the wonderfully interesting Tonks family. In fact, Mr. Wilfred Starling nearly screamed. He just managed to swallow his exasperation, which sank down to form a hard bubble in his stomach. Straightening his thin shoulders, he said, "Right, everyone, copy down this week's homework assignment from

Practice the Skills

1 Key Reading Skill

Predicting What do you know about Angelica Tonks at this point? Do you predict that she will be a character that you like? Why or why not?

the board. And remember, Angelica, a pen-portrait[1] of just *one* aunt or uncle is all I want. Just *one.*" *Please not a whole gallery of* tedious *and terrible Tonkses, he thought to himself.*

The class began to write. Jamie Nutbeam, sitting behind Angelica, leaned forward and hissed, "If the rest of your family is so *wonderfully interesting*, they must be a big improvement on you, Honky![2] And, anyway, I bet the aunt I write about will beat any of yours!"

"I bet she won't," Angelica hissed back. "She'll be so *boring*. What's her name, this boring aunt?"

Jamie finished copying and put down his pen. "Aunt Millicent, and she's pretty special."

"Millicent!" scoffed Angelica. "What a name! No one's called Millicent these days!"

"QUIET, you two!" barked Mr. Starling, massaging his stomach, "and start tidying up, everyone—it's time for the bell." *Oh bliss*, he thought.

As the classroom emptied, Jamie lingered behind.

"What is it, Jamie?" asked Mr. Starling wearily, piling his books and papers together and trying not to burp.

"Well, the trouble is I haven't any aunts or uncles to do a portrait of," said Jamie, turning rather red, "so is it all right if I make one up? An aunt?"

"Oh, I see! Well, in that case . . . yes, perfectly all right," replied Mr. Starling. He gazed rather sadly out the window. "The most interesting characters in the world are usually the made-up ones, you know, Jamie. Think of Sherlock Holmes and Alice and Dr. Who and Indiana Jones . . ."

Jamie interrupted. "Does anyone need to know I've made her up? This aunt?"

"Well, *I* won't say anything," promised Mr. Starling. "It's for you to make her seem real so we all believe in her. You go home and see what you can dream up." 🞂

---

1. The **pen-portrait** is an assignment to write a descriptive report about someone or something.
2. Adding this nickname to Angelica's last name makes her **Honky Tonks,** and honky-tonks just happens to be a term for cheap, noisy nightclubs.

Vocabulary

tedious (TEE dee us) *adj.* boring; tiresome

Practice the Skills

🞂 **Key Literary Element**

Setting What would you say is the main setting of the story so far? What clues tell you that? Has the author described it in great detail?

READING WORKSHOP 4

"She has a name already," Jamie called back as he left the room. "She's Aunt Millicent."

Aunt Millicent Nutbeam! The hard bubble in Mr. Starling's stomach began to melt away. 3

That evening, Jamie Nutbeam said to his family at large, "Did you know that awful Angelica Tonks has eight uncles and eleven aunts?"

"Well, everybody knows that they're a big family," replied his mother. "Prolific,³ I'd call it," grunted Jamie's father from behind his newspaper.

"Yes, dear—prolific. Now, Mrs. Tonks was a Miss Blizzard," continued Mrs. Nutbeam, "and there are lots of Blizzards around here as well as Tonkses, all related, no doubt. But fancy⁴ nineteen! Who told you there were nineteen, Jamie?"

"She did—old Honky Tonks herself. She told the whole class *and* Mr. Starling—boasting away as usual. She's a *pill*." Jamie was jotting things on paper as he talked. "We have to write a pen-portrait of an aunt or uncle for homework, and Honky can't decide which one to do because they're all so *wonderfully interesting*, she says. Urk!" He paused and then added, "I'm doing Aunt Millicent."

Jamie's father peered over the top of his newspaper. "Aunt who?"

"Who's Aunt Millicent?" demanded Jamie's sister, Nerissa.

"You haven't got an Aunt Millicent," said his mother. "You haven't any aunts at all, or uncles, for that matter."

"I *know* I haven't," Jamie snapped. "It's *hopeless* belonging to a **nuclear** family!⁵ It's unfair—I mean, awful Honky has nineteen aunts and uncles and Nerissa and I haven't got any, not one." Jamie ground the pencil between his teeth. 4

"You won't have any teeth either, if you munch pencils like that," remarked his father, who was a dentist.

Jamie glowered, spitting out wet splinters.

"Anyway, he's right," announced Nerissa. "It would be

---

3. Here **prolific** refers to having many children.
4. Here **fancy** means "imagine," said with surprise.
5. Parents and their children make up a **nuclear family.** Angelica has an extended family, which includes aunts, uncles, cousins, and other close relatives.

Practice the Skills

3 **Key Reading Skills**

Predicting What do you predict will happen next, and why? What details have already happened to make you think that? Write your prediction in your Learner's Notebook.

4 **English Language Coach**

Word Histories The word **nuclear** was first used in English in 1833, but it wasn't used to refer to a family until 1949! It comes from the Latin *nucleus*, meaning "inner part." An atom's nucleus is its center, and the nucleus of a family is the parents and their children.

712 UNIT 6 What Makes a Hero?

great to have even one aunt or uncle. Then we might have some cousins, too. Everyone else has cousins. Angelica Tonks probably has about a hundred-and-twenty-seven."

"Well, I'm sorry," sighed Mrs. Nutbeam, "but your father and I are both 'onlys' and there's nothing we can do about that, is there? Not a thing! Now, what's all this about an Aunt Millicent?"

"Oh, it's okay," grumbled her son. "Mr. Starling said to write about *an* aunt or uncle, not exactly *my* aunt or uncle. He says I can invent one."

"Will you explain that she's not real?" asked Nerissa, doubtfully.

"Mr. Starling says I don't have to, and he's not going to tell. He says I have to make people believe that she *is* real. Anyway, I don't want Honky Tonks to know that she's made up, because Aunt Millicent is going to be amazing—much better than any of those boring Tonkses. It's time Honky was taken down a peg or two."[6] **5**

Dr. Nutbeam quite understood how Jamie felt. From time to time Angelica Tonks visited his dentist's chair. She would brag about her "perfect" teeth if there was nothing to be fixed, but if she needed a filling her shrieks of "agony" would upset everyone in the waiting room and Mrs. Tonks would call Dr. Nutbeam a *brute*. He was often tempted to give Angelica a general anesthetic and post her home in a large jiffy bag.

Now he folded his newspaper; Jamie's project sounded rather fun. "Right, Jamie," he said, "tell us about Aunt Millicent and let us get some facts straight. Is she my sister, or Mum's? We must get that settled to start with."

"I can't decide," frowned Jamie. "What do you think?" **6**

"She'd better be your sister, dear," said Mrs. Nutbeam calmly to her husband. "I grew up here and everyone knows I was an only child, but you came from another town. You're more mysterious."

Dr. Nutbeam looked pleased. "Mm . . . mm. That's nice . . . having a sister, I mean. Is she younger than me?"

"No, older," said Jamie.

---

6. The expression **taken down a peg** means "made less proud and more humble."

Practice the Skills

5 **Reviewing Skills**

Responding It might seem surprising that Mr. Starling agrees to let Jamie invent an aunt. How does that make you feel about Mr. Starling? Do you like him? Explain. How do you feel about Jamie, and what do you think of his plan?

6 **Key Reading Skill**

Predicting Now Jamie's entire family is interested in his project. The project even sounds "rather fun" to his father. What do you think will happen? What clues affect your decision?

"Where does she live?" asked Nerissa. "Has she a family of her own? Lots of cousins for us?"

"No way—she hasn't time for all that sort of thing. And she doesn't live anywhere in particular."

Mrs. Nutbeam looked puzzled. "What *do* you mean, dear? What does Auntie Millicent do, exactly?"

"She's an explorer," said Jamie, proudly. "She works for foreign governments, and she's terribly busy—flat out."

There was something of a pause. Then Dr. Nutbeam said, "Ah," and stroked his bald patch. "That explains why we haven't seen her for so long."

"What does she explore?" demanded Nerissa. "Is there anything left in the world to look for?"

Jamie was beginning to feel a bit rushed. "Well, I'm not sure yet, but foreign governments need people like her to search for water in deserts and rich mineral deposits and endangered species and things . . . you know." **7**

> **7 Key Reading Skill**
> **Predicting** Do you predict that Jamie will fool everyone at school into believing that Aunt Millicent is a real person? Explain.

Visual Vocabulary
A *machete* (muh SHET ee) is a wide, heavy knife that can be used as a weapon and a tool.

Nerissa lay on the floor with her eyes closed and began to imagine her new aunt slashing a path through tangled jungle vines, searching for a rare species of dark blue frog. The mosquitoes were savage. The leeches were huge and bloated. Aunt Millicent's machete was razor sharp . . .

"This is all very unexpected," murmured Mrs. Nutbeam, "to have a sister-in-law who is an explorer, I mean. I wonder how you get started in that sort of career?" Her own job as an assistant in an antique and curio shop⁷ suddenly seemed rather drab.

Dr. Nutbeam was staring at the wall. In his mind's eye he clearly saw his sister on a swaying rope suspension bridge above a terrifying ravine.⁸ She was leading a band of native bearers to the other side. How much more adventurous, he

---

7. A *curio shop* sells rare or unusual objects.
8. In this case, the **suspension bridge** hangs from ropes attached to posts at each end of the *ravine*, which is a narrow steep-sided valley.

Vocabulary

drab (drab) *adj.* lacking brightness; dull

thought, than drilling little holes in people's teeth. He wrenched his gaze back to Jamie and asked, "Do we know what Millie is actually exploring at present?" 8

Jamie munched his pencil for a moment and then said, "She's in Africa, somewhere near the middle, but I'm not sure where, exactly."

"In the middle of Africa, is she?" echoed Dr. Nutbeam. "Mm . . . then it wouldn't surprise me if she were in the Cameroons. There's a lot of dense forest in the Cameroons, you know."

"I thought Cameroons were things to eat," frowned Nerissa. "Sort of coconut biscuits."

"No, no, dear, those are macaroons," said her mother.

"They're bad for your teeth, too," remarked her father, absently, "like eating pencils."

Jamie fetched the atlas and found a map of Africa. His father stood behind him, peering at it. "There it is, in the middle on the left-hand side, just under the bump."

"It's called Cameroon here," Jamie said. "Just one of them."

"Well, there's East Cameroon and West Cameroon, see," pointed his father, "and sometimes you lump them together and call them Cameroons. Look—here's the equator just to the south, so it must be pretty hot and steamy at sea-level."

"Poor Millicent," sighed Mrs. Nutbeam. "I do hope her feet don't swell in the heat, with all that walking."

Jamie examined the map closely. "That's peculiar—the north border of the Cameroons seems to be floating in a big lake . . . um, Lake Chad[9] . . . it looks all swampy, with funny

Aunt Millicent might have sent back a picture like this one from her travels in Africa.

8 **Key Literary Element**

Setting A few different settings have just been described, including Nerissa's image of the jungle and Dr. Nutbeam's image of the suspension bridge. How are these settings different from the story's "real" setting?

---

9. Lake Chad, in the nation of Chad, is on the northeastern border of Cameroon.

dotted lines and things. I bet that bit needs exploring. They've probably lost their border in the mud and Aunt Millicent could be on an **expedition** to find it." 9

"Is she all by herself?" asked Nerissa. "I'd be scared in a place like that."

"Of course she's not by herself," snorted Jamie. "She works for a foreign government, don't forget, and she'd have a whole support team of porters and cooks and scientists and things."

"She must be an expert at something herself, don't you think?" suggested Mrs. Nutbeam. "I would imagine that she's a surveyor."¹⁰

"Yes, she'd use one of those instruments you look through, on legs," added Nerissa.

"You mean a theodolite, dimwit," answered her brother.

"She'd certainly need one of those, if she's measuring angles and distances and drawing maps," agreed Dr. Nutbeam. "My word, what a clever old sister I have!"

"I wonder if she was good at geography at school?" said Nerissa.

"Well, you'll be able to ask Grandma tomorrow. She's coming for her winter visit, remember?"

"Oh help! What'll Grandma *say*?" gasped Jamie. "Do you think she'll mind? I mean—we've invented a daughter for her without asking!"

"I shouldn't think she'd mind," said his mother. "We'll break the news to her carefully and see how she takes it."

Grandma Nutbeam, as it turned out, was delighted.

"How exciting!" she exclaimed. "I always wanted a daughter, and it's been very lonely since Grandpa died. Now I'll have a new interest! Just show me on the map where Millicent is at the moment, please dear."

Visual Vocabulary
A **theodolite** (thee OH duh lite) is used by surveyors to measure angles.

Practice the Skills

9 Key Literary Element

Setting Jamie has thought of a setting for his story about Aunt Millicent. He has put her in a *time* and *place*. Pay close attention to how the settings help to make Aunt Millicent both real and mysterious.

---

10. A *surveyor* is a person who measures angles and distances of land to determine its boundaries, area, or elevations.

Vocabulary

expedition (ek spuh DISH un) *n.* a journey taken for a special purpose, such as exploration

716 UNIT 6 What Makes a Hero?

Jamie pointed to the dotted lines in swampy Lake Chad near the top end of the Cameroons, and Grandma stared in astonishment. 10

"Gracious heaven! What an extraordinary place to go to, the silly girl! I hope she's remembered her quinine[11] tablets. Millicent was never very good at looking after herself, you know. Let me see—I think I'll get some wool tomorrow and knit her some good stout hiking socks."

Jamie blinked. "There's no need to do that, Grandma. She's not really real, you know."

"Well, she'll be more real to me if I make her some socks," Grandma declared.

"Wouldn't they be rather hot in the Cameroons?" objected Nerissa. "It's awfully near the equator, don't forget."

"Woollen socks are best in any climate," said Grandma firmly. "They breathe."

"Now, Mother," interrupted Dr. Nutbeam, "you can tell us what Millicent was like as a girl. I can't remember her very well, as she was so much older than me, but I have a feeling that she ran away from home a lot."

Grandma pondered a moment. "Now that you mention it, she did. She did indeed. I thought we'd have to chain her up sometimes! We lived near the edge of town, you'll remember, and Millie would look out towards the paddocks[12] and hills and say that she wanted to know what was over the horizon, or where the birds were flying to, or where the clouds came from behind the hills. We never knew where she'd be off to next—but she certainly ended up in the right job! I'm so glad she became an explorer. If I were a bit younger and had better feet, I might even go and join

Practice the Skills

10 Key Reading Skill

Predicting What do you think Aunt Millicent will be like? Will she be kind, brave, stubborn, angry, mean, or something else entirely?

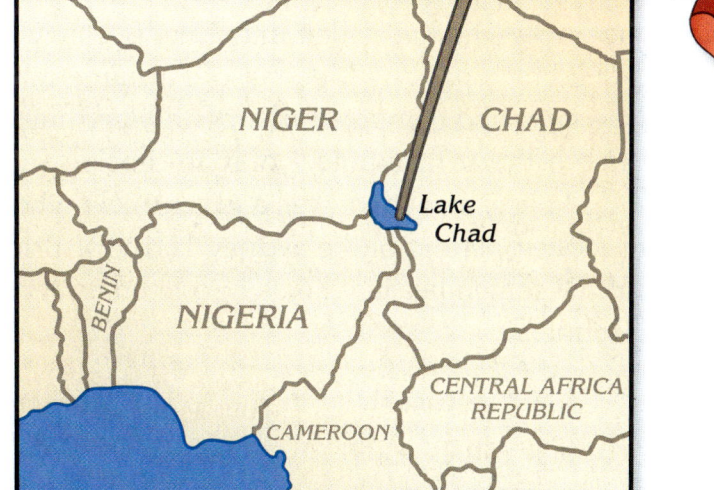

---

11. **Quinine** (QWY nine) is a drug made from the bark of a tree, used to treat malaria and other diseases.
12. **Paddocks** are small, fenced fields in which animals can graze and exercise.

her. It would be most interesting to see the Cameroons. It's full of monkeys, I believe."

"Was Aunt Millicent good at geography at school?" Nerissa remembered to ask.

"Let me think—yes, she must have been because one year she won a prize for it, and the prize was a book called *Lives of the Great Explorers*."

"Well, there you are," remarked Mrs. Nutbeam. "That's probably how it all started."

Next day, Grandma Nutbeam began to knit a pair of explorer's socks. She decided on khaki with dark blue stripes round the top.

Angelica Tonks had found it so difficult to select one of the nineteen aunts and uncles, that her pen-portrait was left until the very last minute and then scrawled out in a great hurry. She had finally chosen Aunt Daisy Blizzard, Mrs. Tonks's eldest sister. **11**

Mr. Wilfred Starling asked Angelica to read her portrait to the class first, to get it over with. As he had expected and as Jamie Nutbeam had hoped, Angelica's aunt sounded anything but wonderfully interesting. She had always lived in the same street, her favorite color was deep purple and she grew African violets on the bathroom shelf, but that was about all.

Many of the other portraits weren't much better, although there was one uncle who had fallen into Lake Burley Griffin and been rescued by a passing Member of Parliament.[13] Someone else's aunt had competed in a penny-farthing bicycle race in Northern Tasmania,[14] only to capsize and sprain both her knees; and there was a great-uncle who had been present at the opening of the Sydney Harbour Bridge in 1932, but couldn't remember it at all as he'd been asleep in his pram[15] at the time.

Practice the Skills

11 **Key Reading Skill**

Predicting What do you think will happen when the students present their pen-portraits?

---

13. **Lake Burley Griffin** is a man-made lake near the **Parliament** buildings in Canberra, the capital of Australia.
14. **Tasmania** is an island off the southeastern coast of Australia. The **penny-farthing** is a type of bicycle that has a very large front wheel and a very small back wheel.
15. **Sydney Harbour Bridge** is in the city of Sydney in southern Australia. A **pram** is what Australians call a baby carriage.

Mr. Starling saved Jamie's portrait until last, hoping for the best. Jamie cleared his throat nervously and began:

"I have never met Aunt Millicent and no one in my family knows her very well, as she hasn't been in Australia for a long time. This is because Aunt Millicent is an explorer . . ."

Mr. Wilfred Starling had been hoping for a bright spot in his day, and Aunt Millicent Nutbeam was it. He smiled happily when Jamie explained how Millicent had gained her early training as an explorer by regularly running away from home. He sighed with pleasure as Jamie described the swampy region of Lake Chad, where Millicent was searching through the mud and papyrus[16] for the northern border of the Cameroons. He positively beamed when he heard that Grandma Nutbeam was knitting explorer's socks for her daughter.

The rest of the class sat spellbound as Jamie read on, except for Angelica Tonks, whose scowl grew darker by the minute. Jamie had barely finished his portrait when her hand was waving furiously.

Mr. Starling's beam faded. "What is it, Angelica?"

"I don't believe it. Women don't go exploring! I think Jamie's made it all up! He's a cheat!"

Mr. Starling's stomach lurched, but before he had time to say anything the other girls in the class rose up in a passion and rounded on Angelica.

"Who *says* women don't go exploring?"

"Women can do anything they want to these days, Angelica Tonks! Don't you know that?"

"*I'd* really like to be an explorer or something—maybe a test-pilot."

"Well, *I'd* like to be a diver and explore the ocean floor and have a good look at the Titanic."[17]

"What does your aunt wear when she's at work?"

"What color are her new socks?"

The boys began to join in.

"Can your aunt really use a machete?" [12]

"How many languages can she speak?"

Practice the Skills

12 **English Language Coach**

Word Histories Like *hoax*, **machete** is a word whose origin is not certain. American natives had invented the knife long before Europeans came to the New World. Spanish explorers probably adapted their noun *macho* ("big hammer"). Though we usually think of a machete as a cutting tool, its wide, flat side is good for pounding.

---

16. Surrounded by swamps, Lake Chad is the sort of place where **papyrus,** a tall grassy plant, grows well.
17. The **Titanic** was an ocean liner that sank in the North Atlantic in 1912 after hitting an iceberg.

"Does she always carry a gun? I bet she's a crack shot!"

"How does a theodolite work?"

The clamor[18] was so great that hardly anyone heard the bell. Angelica Tonks heard it and vanished in a sulk. Mr. Starling heard it and happily gathered up his books. He gave Jamie a secret wink as he left the room. **13**

The end of the assignment was not the end of Aunt Millicent. At school, the careers teacher ran some special sessions on "Challenging Occupations for Women" after he had been stormed by the girls from Jamie's class for information about becoming test-pilots, mobile-crane drivers, buffalo hunters and ocean-floor mappers. The science teacher was asked to explain the workings of a theodolite to the class.

At home, Aunt Millicent settled happily into the Nutbeam family, who all followed her adventures with great interest. Dr. Nutbeam brought home library books about the Cameroons and Central Africa. Jamie roared his way through one called *The Bafut Beagles*. Mrs. Nutbeam rummaged through an old storeroom at the curio shop and began to collect **exotic** objects. She brought home a brace[19] of hunting spears from Kenya, which she hung on the family-room wall.

Visual Vocabulary
A *mongoose* is a small mammal native to parts of Asia, Africa, and Europe. It has a pointy face and shaggy fur and is two to three feet long.

"Just the sort of **souvenir** Millicent could have sent us," she explained. "See—those marks on the blades are very probably dried bloodstains." **14**

Another time she unwrapped a stuffed mongoose, announcing that Auntie had sent this from India on one of her earlier trips.

Jamie and Nerissa stroked it. "What a funny animal," said Nerissa. "Like a weasel."

Practice the Skills

13 Key Reading Skill

Predicting Aunt Millicent is very popular with all of the students, and even Mr. Starling is pleased with her. Angelica, on the other hand, thinks that Jamie "made it all up." Now that Aunt Millicent is such a hit, what do you think will happen to her? What clues help with your prediction?

14 English Language Coach

Word Histories The word **souvenir** comes from the Latin word *subvenire*. *Sub* means "up," and *venire* means "to come." So *subvenire* meant "to come up" or "to come to mind." In English, the word became *souvenir*, or something that reminds us of where we've been.

---

18. A *clamor* is a loud noise.
19. Here a *brace* is a pair.

Vocabulary

exotic (eg ZOT ik) *adj.* excitingly different; unusual; foreign

Grandma was knitting her way down the second sock leg. "That funny animal is a very brave creature," she admonished,[20] tapping the mongoose with her knitting needle. "I'll always remember Kipling's story of Rikki-Tikki-Tavi and how he fought that dreadful king cobra. Brrr!"

"Who won?" asked Jamie.

"You could read it yourself and find out, young man," said Grandma, starting to knit a new row. "I expect Millicent has met a few cobras in her time."

Nerissa had splendid dreams nearly every night. Aunt Millicent strode through most of them, wielding her machete or shouldering her theodolite. Sometimes Nerissa found herself wading through swirling rivers or swinging on jungle vines like a gibbon. Jamie was often there, too, or some of her school friends, or Grandma followed by a mongoose on a lead.[21] Once, Mrs. Nutbeam speared a giant toad, which exploded and woke Nerissa up. In another dream, Nerissa's father was polishing the fangs of a grinning crocodile, which lay back in the dentist's chair with its long tail tucked neatly under the sterilizer. It looked slightly like Mrs. Tonks.

Visual Vocabulary
A *gibbon* is a type of small ape.

Mrs. Nutbeam brought home still more **curios**: a bamboo flute and a small tom-tom which Jamie and Nerissa soon learnt to play. Mysterious drumbeats and thin flutey tunes drifted along the street from the Nutbeams' house. School friends came to beat the tom-tom and to stroke the mongoose and to see how the explorer's socks were growing. 15

"Will you be sending them off soon, to the Cameroons?" they asked Grandma, who was turning the heel of the second sock.

"I think I'll make another pair, perhaps even three pairs," replied Grandma. "I might just as well send a large parcel as a small one."

Visual Vocabulary
The *bamboo flute* is a woodwind instrument. It has an airy sound and is usually hand carved. A *tom-tom* is a long narrow drum that is typically beaten with the hands.

---

20. *Admonished* means "scolded mildly."
21. The mongoose is on a leash, or *lead*.

Practice the Skills

15 English Language Coach

Word Histories *Curios* are objects that are considered rare or strange. *Curio* is a shortened form of *curiosity*.

"Yes, and then Aunt Millie will have spare pairs of socks she can wash," said Nerissa. "Socks must get very smelly near the equator."

Word of Millicent Nutbeam, intrepid[22] explorer, began to spread through the town. Children told their families about the spears, the tom-tom, the mongoose and the khaki socks. Not every small town could claim to be connected to a famous international explorer—it was exciting news. 16

Angelica Tonks, however, told her mother that she didn't believe Jamie's aunt was an explorer at all. "I bet he just invented that to make his aunt seem more interesting than all the rest," she scoffed.

Mrs. Tonks sniffed a good deal and then decided it was time to have a dental check-up. "I'll get to the bottom of that Millicent Nutbeam, you mark my words," she told Angelica, as she telephoned Dr. Nutbeam's surgery[23] for an appointment.

Well, well—good morning Mrs. Tonks," said Dr. Nutbeam, a few days later. "We haven't seen you for a while! Just lie right back in the chair please, and relax!"

Mrs. Tonks lay back, but she didn't relax one bit. Her eyes were sharp and suspicious. "Good morning, Dr. Nutbeam. How is the family?" she enquired. "And how is your sister?"

Dr. Nutbeam pulled on his rubber gloves. "My sister? Which one? . . . Er, probe, please nurse."

Before he could say "Open wide," Mrs. Tonks snapped, "Your sister the so-called explorer. Huh! The one in the Cameroons."

"Ah, *that* sister. You mean Millicent . . . now, just open wider and turn this way a little. Yes, our Millie, she does work so hard . . . oops, there's a beaut cavity! A real crater!" He crammed six plugs of cotton wool around

Practice the Skills

16 BIG Question
How and why has Aunt Millicent become a hero for the town? Does a hero have to be real? Think about how the girls in Jamie's class view her. Think about how the town views her.

Here's another picture that Aunt Millicent might have sent from her travels in Africa.

---

22. Someone who is **intrepid** is very brave.
23. In Australia a doctor's or dentist's office is called a **surgery**.

Mrs. Tonks's gums. "My word, what a lot of saliva! We'll have some suction please nurse, and just wipe that dribble from the patient's chin." He continued to poke and scrape Mrs. Tonks's molars, none too gently. "Ah, here's another trouble spot. Mm . . . have you ever been to the Cameroons, Mrs. Tonks?"

Mrs. Tonks's eyes glared. She tried to shake her head, but could only gurgle, "Arggg . . ." **17**

"No, I didn't think you had. Such a fascinating place!" Dr. Nutbeam turned on the squealing high-speed drill and bored into her decaying tooth, spraying water all over her chin.

When he had told his family about this **encounter** with Mrs. Tonks, his wife complained, "It's all very well for you. You can just cram people's mouths full of wadding and metal contraptions and suction tubes if they start asking awkward questions, but what am I supposed to do?"

The truth was that increasing numbers of townsfolk were calling at the antique shop where Mrs. Nutbeam worked. They were eager to know more about Millicent Nutbeam and her adventurous life. They felt proud of her.

"It's getting quite tricky," Mrs. Nutbeam explained. "People are asking to see photos of Millicent and wanting us to talk at the elderly citizens' club about her. This aunt is becoming an embarrassment. I wish people weren't so curious. Sometimes I don't know what to say!"

Grandma found herself on slippery ground, too, when she met the postman at the gate.

"Morning," he said, sorting through his mailbag. "You must be Jamie's grandmother, then."

"Yes, I am," Grandma replied, rather surprised.

"Mother of the explorer, eh?"

"Gracious!" exclaimed Grandma. "Fancy you knowing about that!"

"Oh, my girl Julie has told us all about it. She's in Jamie's class at school. Funny thing—Julie's gone round the twist since she heard about all that exploring business. Says she

Practice the Skills

17 **Key Literary Element**

Setting So far the story has more than one setting. What is the setting for this encounter? Can you think of two other settings you have noticed besides this one? What clues give the setting away? Think about Dr. Nutbeam's job.

Vocabulary

encounter (en KOUN tur) *n.* an unexpected or unpleasant meeting

READING WORKSHOP 4

wants to buy a camel and ride it round Australia, and one of her friends is going to apply for a job on an oil rig. I ask you!"

"Well, that's nice," said Grandma, soothingly. "Girls are so enterprising[24] these days."

"Huh! Mad, I call it." The postman held out a bundle of letters. "Here you are. Now, that's *another* funny thing—the Nutbeams don't get much foreign mail, come to think of it. You'd think the explorer would write to them more often, her being in the traveling line."

Grandma breathed deeply. "Oh, it's not easy, you know, writing letters when you're exploring. For one thing, there's never a decent light in the tent at night—and besides, there's hardly ever a post office to hand when you need it. She glanced through the letters. "Goodness! There's one from South America . . . Peru." [18]

"That's what made me wonder. Is it from her?" asked the postman, eagerly.

"Her? Ah . . . Millicent. I don't know. It's for Dr. Nutbeam, my son, and it's typed. Anyway, as far as we know, Millicent is still in the Cameroons, although we've not had word for some time."

"She could have moved on, couldn't she?" suggested the postman, "Peru, eh?

Oh well, I'd better move on, too. G'day to you!"

Practice the Skills

[18] Key Reading Skill

Predicting Who do you think wrote the letter from Peru?

---

24. Someone who is **enterprising** is ready and willing to undertake new projects.

724 UNIT 6 What Makes a Hero?

READING WORKSHOP 4

At school, Julie the postman's daughter said to Jamie, "Why has your auntie gone to South America? What's she exploring now?"

"Who said she's gone to South America?" demanded Jamie. He felt he was losing control of Aunt Millicent.

"My dad said there was a letter from her in Peru," replied Julie.

"Well, no one told *me*," growled Jamie.

At home he announced, "Julie is telling everybody that our Aunt Millicent is in Peru! What's she talking about? What's happening?"

Grandma stopped knitting. "Julie. Is that the name of the postman's girl?"

"Yes—her dad said there was a letter for us from Auntie in Peru, or somewhere mad."

"Oh, I remember—he asked me about it," said Grandma.

"Well . . . what did you *say*?" wailed Jamie.

"I just said I didn't know who the letter was from and that I thought Millicent was still in the Cameroons, but that we hadn't heard for a while where she was. That's all."

"The letter from Peru," chuckled Dr. Nutbeam, "is about the World Dental Conference on plaque, which is being held next year in Lima.²⁵ It has nothing to do with Millicent."

"Well of *course* it hasn't," spluttered Jamie. "She doesn't exist!"

"But Jamie, in a funny sort of way she *does* exist," said Mrs. Nutbeam.

His father grinned. "My sister is quite a girl! She's begun to live a life of her own!"

"That's the trouble," said Jamie. "She seems to be doing things we don't know about." 19

Practice the Skills

19 Key Reading Skill

Predicting Did you predict earlier that the Nutbeams would fool the town into thinking that Aunt Millicent was a real person? Is your prediction the same now? Explain.

Analyzing the Photos Describe what you see in these pictures from the Andes.

---

25. This kind of **plaque** (plak) is film that forms on teeth if not removed by cleaning. The conference is in **Lima** (LEE muh), the capital of Peru.

Aunt Millicent **725**

READING WORKSHOP 4

While they were talking, the telephone rang. Dr. Nutbeam was no longer grinning when he came back from answering it. "That was Frank Figgis from the local paper."

"Frank, the editor?" asked Mrs. Nutbeam. "What did he want?"

"He wants to do a full-page feature on our Millicent," groaned her husband. "He's heard that she's about to set out on a climbing expedition in the Andes! Up some peak that has never yet been conquered!"

"What nonsense!" snapped Grandma. "She's too old for that sort of thing."

"It's just a rumor!" shouted Jamie. "Who said she's going to the Andes? *I* didn't say she was going there. She's still in the Cameroons!"

"Calm down, dear," said his mother, "and let's hear what Dad said to Frank Figgis."

Dr. Nutbeam was rubbing his head. "I stalled for time—I said we'd not heard she was in the Andes, but that we'd make enquiries[26] and let him know. Whatever happens, Millicent mustn't get into print. We'll all be up on a charge of false pretenses[27] or something!"

Jamie snorted. "Well, if she's climbing an Ande, it might be best if she fell off and was never seen again."

Nerissa shrieked, "*No!* She mustn't—she's our only aunt and we've only just got her!"

Mrs. Nutbeam sighed. "Listen, Jamie, perhaps the time has come to own up[28] that Aunt Millicent is not real."

"We can't do that!" wailed Jamie. "Everyone would think we're loony . . . and that Grandma's absolutely bonkers, knitting socks for an aunt who isn't there. And what about the mongoose? Anyway, I *can't* let Honky Tonks find out now—she'd never stop crowing and she'd be more awful than ever." **20**

Jamie decided to lay the whole problem of Aunt Millicent Nutbeam before Mr. Starling, right up to her unexpected expedition to the Andes and Mr. Figgis's plan to write a full-page feature about her for the local paper. He finished by saying, "I think I might have to kill her off."

20 Key Reading Skill

Predicting What do you think will happen to Aunt Millicent?

---

26. To **make enquiries** is to ask questions.
27. The term **false pretenses** refers to acts of lying or misleading.
28. The expression **own up** means to "confess fully."

READING WORKSHOP 4

"That'd be a shame," sighed Mr. Starling. "She's quite a lady, your aunt!"

"It would be pretty easy to get rid of her," Jamie went on. "In her sort of job she could sink into a quicksand, or be trampled by a herd of elephants, or something."

Mr. Starling shook his head violently. "No, no—it would only make things worse if she died a bloodcurdling death like that. No one would be likely to forget her if she was squashed flat by a stampeding elephant. She'd become more interesting than ever!"

"Well, she could die of something boring, like pneumonia," said Jamie. "Or . . . will I have to own up that she isn't real?"

"Do you want to own up?"

"Not really. I'd feel stupid, and I specially don't want Angelica Tonks to know I invented an aunt."

Mr. Starling quite understood. "I see! Anyway, a lot of people would be sad to discover that Millicent Nutbeam was a **hoax**. The girls in your class, for example—she means a lot to them."

"What'll I do then?"

"If you want people to lose interest in her, you'll just have to make her less interesting. I think she should retire from exploring, for a start."

"Aw, gee!" Jamie felt very disappointed. "I suppose so. I'll see what they think at home." **21**

"**W**hat he means," said Dr. Nutbeam, when Jamie had repeated Mr. Starling's advice, "is that it's time my dear sister Millicent settled down."

"I quite agree with that," remarked Grandma, who was up to the sixth sock foot. "She's not as young as she was, and it's high time she had some normal home life. I think she should get married, even though she's getting on a bit. Perhaps to a widower."

"That sounds terribly boring," yawned Nerissa.

"Well, that's what we need," said Jamie, "something terribly boring to make people lose interest."

Practice the Skills

21 **Key Reading Skill**

Predicting Now that rumors about Aunt Millicent are out of control, Jamie doesn't know what to do with her. She has taken on a life of her own! What do you think will become of Aunt Millicent?

Vocabulary

hoax (hohks) *n.* an act meant to fool or trick

Aunt Millicent **727**

Grandma sniffed. "In my day it would have been called a happy ending."

"Well, I suppose it's a happier ending than being squashed by an elephant," conceded Jamie.

"How about marrying her to a retired accountant who used to work for a cardboard box company?" suggested his father. "That sounds pretty dull."

"Good heavens, it's all rather sudden!" said Mrs. Nutbeam. "Last time we heard of her she was climbing the Andes!"

"No, she wasn't." At last Jamie felt he had hold of Aunt Millicent again. "That South American stuff was just a rumor. The postman started it because of the letter from Peru, and then the story just grew!"

Dr. Nutbeam nodded. "Stories seem to have a habit of doing that, and so do rumors! But we can easily squash this one about the Andes. I'll just explain about the World Dental Conference on plaque. I even have the letter to prove it."

Dr. Nutbeam called Frank Figgis on the phone. He explained about the letter from Peru and about the ridiculous rumor which the postman had started. "In your profession Frank," he added sternly, "you should be much more careful than to listen to baseless rumor.[29] It could get you into all sorts of trouble! In any case, Millicent is giving up exploring to marry a retired accountant. She's had enough."

Frank Figgis was fast losing interest. "I see—well, sometime when she's in Australia we could do an interview about her former life . . . maybe."

"Maybe, although she has no immediate plans to return here. I believe she and her husband are going to settle down in England—somewhere on the seafront, like Bognor." 22

Jamie passed on the same information to his classmates. The girls were shocked.

"She's what?"

"Getting married to an *accountant?*"

"She can't be!"

"How boring for her!"

22 Key Literary Element

Setting Compared to other places mentioned in the story, what do you imagine Bognor, England, would be like? What was the most detailed setting in the entire story? How did that affect the story?

---

29. A ***baseless rumor*** is a rumor that cannot be supported by facts.

READING WORKSHOP 4

"Where in the world is Bognor? Is there really such a place?"

Angelica Tonks smiled like a smug pussycat. "See! Your Aunt Millicent is just like any other old aunt, after all!"

Jamie caught Mr. Starling's eye. It winked.

Aunt Millicent Nutbeam retired, not to Bognor but to live quietly with her family. Nerissa still had wonderful dreams. Dr. Nutbeam still brought home books about far-off places. The blood-stained spears remained on the wall and the mongoose on the shelf. Jamie and Nerissa still played the tom-tom and the bamboo flute.

Grandma Nutbeam's holiday came to an end and she packed up to return home. She left a parcel for Jamie. When he opened it, he found three pairs of khaki socks with dark blue stripes, and a card which said:

Dear Jamie,

Aunt Millicent won't have any use for these now that she has settled down, so you might as well have them for school camps. Isn't it lucky that they are just your size!

With love from Grandma **23**

Practice the Skills

23 BIG Question
Who do you think is most like a real-life hero in this story? Explain. Write your conclusions on the "Aunt Millicent" page of Foldable 6. Your responses to all of the Big Question sidenotes will help you complete the Unit Challenge later.

Aunt Millicent **729**

After You Read: Aunt Millicent

Answering the BIG Question

1. Does Aunt Millicent have qualities of a real-life hero? Explain.
2. **Recall** Why wasn't Angelica's pen-portrait as good as she said it would be?
   TIP Right There

Critical Thinking

3. **Analyze** What lasting effect has the story of Aunt Millicent had on the Nutbeam family? What lasting effect has the story had on the students at the school? Give evidence from the story to support your answer.
   TIP Author and Me
4. **Evaluate** Does marrying an accountant and retiring sound like something Aunt Millicent would really do? Explain.
   TIP On My Own
5. **Synthesize** Imagine that Jamie created an Uncle Milton rather than Aunt Millicent. Do you think the story would have been as meaningful to Jamie's classmates? Why or why not?
   TIP On My Own
6. **Interpret** At the end of the story, Grandma sends Jamie three pairs of socks with a card that says, "Isn't it lucky that they are just your size." What do you think that message means?
   TIP On My Own

Talk About Your Reading

With a partner, or in a small group, think up an imaginary person with an interesting life. Decide on the age, gender, appearance, and past history of your imaginary person. Then introduce your imaginary person to the class, telling a bit about him or her. Think about these questions to get started, but don't stop there. Let the person take on a life of his or her own, like Jamie's Aunt Millicent.

- How would you describe this person?
- What job qualities, hobbies, or traits does this person have that make him or her interesting?
- What adventures has this person had?
- Where does this person live?

Objectives (pp. 730–731)
Reading Make predictions
Literature Identify key literary elements: setting
Vocabulary Explore word histories
Grammar Identify run-ons

Skills Review

Key Reading Skill: Predicting

7. At what point in the story did you have to change one of your predictions? Explain why you changed it and what your new prediction was.

Key Literary Element: Setting

8. Describe the main setting of this story in one or two sentences. Pick another setting and describe it in one or two sentences.
9. How did Jamie's use of setting help to make Aunt Millicent's travels seem real to other characters in the story?

Reviewing Skills: Responding

10. Would you want a relative like Aunt Millicent? Why or why not?

Vocabulary Check

Rewrite this postcard from an explorer and put the vocabulary words in the correct spaces.

**tedious   drab   expedition   exotic
encounter   hoax**

Life seemed 11. ___ after our exciting 12. ___ to an island that wasn't on the map. We had hoped for an 13. ___ with an 14. ___ bird believed to be extinct. Rumor had it that the bird could still be found on the island. We never saw the bird, so the tales could have been a 15. ___, but who knows! Its feathers are 16. ___ in color and it blends in with tree bark (making it hard to spot).

17. **English Language Coach** Why are word histories important?

Web Activities For eFlashcards, Selection Quick Checks, and other Web activities, go to www.glencoe.com.

Grammar Link: Recognizing Run-on Sentences

Remember, an independent clause has a subject and a predicate. It can stand alone as a complete sentence. Sometimes, though, a writer puts together two independent clauses, or sentences, without the correct punctuation.

A **run-on sentence** is two or more sentences incorrectly written as one sentence.

> **Example:** *Tonight we are going to a skating competition I hope it is like the Olympics.*

Now study these three ways to correct a run-on sentence.

A. Separate the two independent clauses with a period. Begin the second sentence with a capital letter.

> **Example:** Tonight we are going to a skating competition. I hope it is like the Olympics.

B. Place a comma and a coordinating conjunction between two independent clauses.

> **Example:** Tonight we are going to a skating competition, and I hope it is like the Olympics.

C. Place a semicolon between to two independent clauses.

> **Example:** Tonight we are going to a skating competition; I hope it is like the Olympics.

Grammar Practice

On a separate sheet of paper, write a correct version of each run-on sentence.

18. Yori took an aspirin there was only one left.
19. Of all the birds at the pet store, we liked the parrots best.
20. Look at all the people at the parade I wonder where we can sit.
21. The actors are sewing their own costumes it is quite a challenge.

READING WORKSHOP 4 • Predicting

Before You Read: A Mason-Dixon Memory

Meet the Author
Clifton Davis is an actor, singer, and songwriter. One of his songs, "Never Can Say Goodbye," sold two million records. He has acted in several movies, Broadway plays, and TV shows. Davis told his "Mason-Dixon Memory" story to Mel White, who wrote it in Davis's voice.

Author Search For more about Clifton Davis, go to www.glencoe.com.

Vocabulary Preview

civic (SIV ik) *adj.* having to do with a city or the duties of a citizen **(p. 734)** *Civic leaders from around the country came to hear Dondré Green speak.*

predominantly (prih DOM uh nunt lee) *adv.* mainly; mostly **(p. 734)** *Dondré attended a predominantly white school in Louisiana.*

resolve (rih ZOLV) *v.* to make a firm decision **(p. 737)** *The boys could give up, or they could resolve to stand up for Dondré.*

ominous (OM ih nus) *adj.* threatening **(p. 738)** *The woman explained the Mason-Dixon line in ominous tones.*

bigotry (BIG uh tree) *n.* unfair and unreasonable opinions or treatment of a person or group **(p. 740)** *Dondré learned that love can overcome hatred and bigotry.*

Vocabulary Concentration With a partner, copy the words onto one set of note cards and the definitions onto another set. Mix the cards up and place them face down on a desk or table. Take turns turning the cards over two at a time. When you match a word and its definition take the pair; use the word in a sentence once you make a match.

English Language Coach

Word Histories Sometimes it's difficult to figure out how a modern word came from a very different older word. For example, look at these words from the selection you're about to read:

- **banquet** (BANK wut) *n.* a large meal celebrating a special event [Middle French, from Old Italian *banchetto,* from *banca* "bench"]
- **chaperone** (SHAP uh rohn) *n.* a person who goes with and is responsible for a group of young people [French *chaperon,* from earlier French *chape,* from Latin *cappa* "head covering; cloak"]

Class Discussion Using your imagination and logic, discuss how
- *banquet* could come from a word meaning "bench."
- *chaperone* could come from a word meaning "head covering; cloak."

Objectives (pp. 732–741)
Reading Make predictions • Make connections from text to self
Literature Identify key literary elements: setting
Vocabulary Explore word histories

732 UNIT 6 What Makes a Hero?

READING WORKSHOP 4 • Predicting

Skills Preview

Key Reading Skill: Predicting

"A Mason-Dixon Memory" is told in three parts. There are many places you could pause and make a prediction. Whenever you notice a break in the story, ask yourself what you think will happen in the next part. As you read, adjust or change your predictions if you notice the story isn't turning out as you first predicted.

Partner Talk With a partner, discuss the passage below and make predictions about what you think might happen next.

> *Although most of his friends and classmates were white, Dondré's race was never an issue. Then, on April 17, 1991, Dondré's black skin provoked an incident that made nationwide news.*

Key Literary Element: Setting

The setting often helps to create an atmosphere, or mood. Knowing the setting will help you to understand a story by "placing" the events—connecting them to other things you know about that time and place. "A Mason-Dixon Memory" brings together two incidents that happened in different places and times. The two settings are thirty-two years and almost a thousand miles apart.

As you think about the setting notice

- the different times and places in the story

  Do the differences in time and place affect each situation?

- descriptions of places and the way characters speak

  What details help you picture the setting?

Partner Talk After you read the selection, discuss the questions above with a partner.

Interactive Literary Elements Handbook
To review or learn more about the literary elements, go to www.glencoe.com.

Get Ready to Read

Connect to the Reading

What would you do if someone you know was experiencing discrimination? What if you had to make the decision to defend them or do nothing?

Write to Learn Write about a time you made the right decision while others pressured you to do something that would affect another person in a negative way. Answer these questions as you write:

- What was the situation (bullying, discriminating, lying) and what decision did you make?
- How did you know what the *right* decision was?
- Why did you decide as you did?

Build Background

In the story you are about to read, the Mason-Dixon line is described as "a kind of invisible border between the North and the South."

- Originally, the Mason-Dixon line was the boundary between Maryland and Pennsylvania.
- It was a 233-mile-long invisible line determined by Charles Mason and Jeremiah Dixon in 1765–68 to settle a land dispute between the Penn family of Pennsylvania and the Calvert family of Maryland.
- By 1820 the Mason-Dixon line was used to show the dividing line between the slave states to the south and the free states to the north.

Set Purposes for Reading

BIG Question Read to find out how real boys fought against racism and became heroes.

Set Your Own Purpose What else would you like to learn from the story to help you answer the Big Question? Write your own purpose on the "A Mason-Dixon Memory" page of Foldable 6.

Keep Moving

Use these skills as you read the following selection.

A Mason-Dixon Memory 733

READING WORKSHOP 4

A MASON-DIXON Memory

by Clifton Davis

Dondré Green glanced uneasily at the **civic** leaders and sports figures filling the hotel ballroom in Cleveland. They had come from across the nation to attend a fund-raiser for the National Minority College Golf Scholarship Foundation. I was the banquet's featured entertainer. Dondre, an 18-year-old high school senior from Monroe, Louisiana, was the evening's honored guest.

"Nervous?" I asked the handsome young man in his starched white shirt and rented tuxedo.

"A little," he whispered, grinning.

One month earlier, Dondré had been just one more black student attending a **predominately** white school. Although most of his friends and classmates were white, Dondre's race was never an issue. Then, on April 17, 1991, Dondré's black skin provoked[1] an incident that made nationwide news. 1

---

1. *Provoked* means "caused to feel or act."

Vocabulary

civic (SIV ik) *adj.* having to do with a city or the duties of a citizen

predominantly (prih DOM uh nunt lee) *adv.* mainly; mostly

Practice the Skills

1 **Key Literary Element**

Setting In what time and place does the story begin? Although the author hasn't mentioned the exact year, does it seem to be taking place recently or long ago? Explain.

734   UNIT 6   What Makes a Hero?

"Ladies and gentlemen," the emcee said, "our special guest, Dondré Green."

As the audience stood applauding, Dondré walked to the microphone and began his story. "I love golf," he said quietly. "For the past two years, I've been a member of the St. Frederick High School golf team. And though I was the only black member, I've always felt at home playing at mostly white country clubs across Louisiana."

The audience leaned forward; even the waiters and busboys stopped to listen. As I listened, a memory buried in my heart since childhood fought its way to life.

"Our team had driven from Monroe," Dondré continued. "When we arrived at the Caldwell Parish Country Club in Columbia, we walked to the putting green."

Dondré and his teammates were too absorbed to notice the conversation between a man and St. Frederick athletic director James Murphy. After disappearing into the clubhouse, Murphy returned to his players. **2**

"I want to see the seniors," he said. "On the double!" His face seemed strained as he gathered the four students, including Dondré.

"I don't know how to tell you this," he said, "but the Caldwell Parish Country Club is reserved for whites only." Murphy paused and looked at Dondré. His teammates glanced at each other in disbelief.

"I want you seniors to decide what our response should be," Murphy continued. "If we leave, we forfeit this tournament. If we stay, Dondré can't play."

As I listened, my own childhood memory from 32 years ago broke free. **3**

Dondré Green (top row, 2nd from left) poses for the yearbook with his golf team.

Practice the Skills

2 **Key Reading Skill**

Predicting What do you think Coach Murphy is going to talk to his players about? How do you know?

3 **Key Reading Skill**

Predicting Now that you've come to the first break, think about what you know. The narrator has begun to tell you a story about someone else, Dondré Green. What do you think the narrator will tell you about in the next section? Find two clues that lead you to your prediction.

READING WORKSHOP 4

In 1959 I was thirteen years old, a poor black kid living with my mother and stepfather in a small black ghetto on Long Island, New York. My mother worked nights in a hospital, and my stepfather drove a coal truck. Needless to say, our standard of living was somewhat short of the American dream. 4

Nevertheless, when my eighth-grade teacher announced a graduation trip to Washington, D.C., it never crossed my mind that I would be left behind. Besides a complete tour of the nation's capital, we would visit Glen Echo Amusement Park in Maryland. In my imagination, Glen Echo was Disneyland, Knott's Berry Farm, and Magic Mountain rolled into one.

My heart beating wildly, I raced home to deliver the mimeographed[3] letter describing the journey. But when my mother saw how much the trip cost, she just shook her head. We couldn't afford it.

After feeling sad for ten seconds, I decided to try to fund the trip myself. For the next eight weeks, I sold candy bars door-to-door, delivered newspapers, and mowed lawns. Three days before the deadline, I'd made just barely enough. I was going!

The day of the trip, trembling with excitement, I climbed onto the train. I was the only nonwhite in our section.

Our hotel was not far from the White House. My roommate was Frank Miller, the son of a businessman. Leaning together out of our window and dropping water balloons on tourists quickly cemented our new friendship.

The White House

Practice the Skills

4 Key Literary Element

Setting The author introduces a new setting in this paragraph. Use at least three details from the paragraph to describe the setting.

---

3. If a letter was *mimeographed,* many copies were made.

READING WORKSHOP 4

The Lincoln Memorial in Washington, D.C., is a tribute to the 16th President of the United States, Abraham Lincoln. It is a symbol of freedom and the sacrifices of the Civil War.

Every morning, almost a hundred of us loaded noisily onto our bus for another adventure. We sang our **school** fight song dozens of times–en route[4] to Arlington National Cemetery and even on an afternoon cruise down the Potomac River. 5

We visited the Lincoln Memorial twice, once in daylight, the second time at dusk. My classmates and I fell silent as we walked in the shadows of those thirty–six marble columns, one for every state in the Union that Lincoln labored to preserve. I stood next to Frank at the base of the nineteen-foot seated statue. Spotlights made the white Georgian marble seem to glow. Together, we read those famous words from Lincoln's speech at Gettysburg, remembering the most bloody battle in the War Between the States: ". . . we here highly **resolve** that these dead shall not have died in vain — that this nation, under God, shall have a new birth of freedom . . ."

As Frank motioned me into place to take my picture, I took one last look at Lincoln's face. He seemed alive and so terribly sad.

5 English Language Coach

Word Histories Some word histories reveal how people's thinking changes over time. **School** came from the Latin word *schola* and meant "school." But the original Greek word meant "spare time." Thousands of years ago in Greece, only rich people had time to study at what we now call school.

4. **En route** (awn ROOT) means "on the way."

Vocabulary

resolve (rih ZOLV) *v.* to make a firm decision

A Mason-Dixon Memory

READING WORKSHOP 4

The next morning, I understood a little better why he wasn't smiling. "Clifton," a chaperone said, "could I see you for a moment?"

The other guys at my table, especially Frank, turned pale. We had been joking about the previous night's direct water-balloon hit on a fat lady and her poodle. It was a stupid, dangerous act, but luckily nobody got hurt. We were celebrating our escape from punishment when the chaperone asked to see me.

"Clifton," she began, "do you know about the Mason-Dixon line?"

"No," I said, wondering what this had to do with drenching fat ladies.

"Before the Civil War," she explained, "the Mason-Dixon line was originally the boundary between Maryland and Pennsylvania — the dividing line between the slave and free states." Having escaped one disaster, I could feel another brewing. I noticed that her eyes were damp and her hands were shaking.

"Today," she continued, "the Mason-Dixon line is a kind of invisible border between the North and the South. When you cross that invisible line out of Washington, D.C., into Maryland, things change."

There was an **ominous** drift to this conversation, but I wasn't following it. Why did she look and sound so nervous?

"Glen Echo Amusement Park is in Maryland," she said at last, "and the management doesn't allow Negroes inside." She stared at me in silence. **6 7**

I was still grinning and nodding when the meaning finally sank in.

"You mean I can't go to the park," I stuttered, "because I'm a Negro?"

She nodded slowly. "I'm sorry, Clifton," she said, taking my hand.

"You'll have to stay in the hotel tonight. Why don't you and I watch a movie on television?"

I walked to the elevators feeling confusion, disbelief, anger,

Practice the Skills

6 Key Reading Skill

Predicting Did you predict what the chaperone would say? Were you right? Sometimes an author will lead you to make a certain prediction, but what you thought would happen turns out to be wrong. Why would an author do this?

7 Key Literary Element

Setting The chaperone talks about a difference in the settings between North and South. How is the Mason-Dixon line an important part of the setting, even though it is an "invisible border"? Think about what you learned in the Build Background, and add that to what the chaperone tells Clifton.

Vocabulary

ominous (OM ih nus) *adj.* threatening

and a deep sadness. "What happened, Clifton?" Frank said when I got back to the room. "Did the fat lady tell on us?"

Without saying a word, I walked over to my bed, lay down, and began to cry. Frank was stunned into silence. Junior-high boys didn't cry, at least not in front of each other.

It wasn't just missing the class adventure that made me feel so sad. For the first time in my life, I was learning what it felt like to be a "nigger." Of course there was discrimination in the North, but the color of my skin had never officially kept me out of a coffee shop, a church — or an amusement park.

"Clifton," Frank whispered, "what is the matter?"

"They won't let me go to Glen Echo Park tonight," I sobbed.

"Because of the water balloon?" he asked.

"No," I answered, "because I'm a Negro."

"Well, that's a relief!" Frank said, and then he laughed, obviously relieved to have escaped punishment for our caper with the balloons. "I thought it was serious!"

Wiping away the tears with my sleeve, I stared at him. "It *is* serious. They don't let Negroes into the park. I can't go with you!" I shouted. "That's pretty damn serious to me."

I was about to wipe the silly grin off Frank's face with a blow to his jaw when I heard him say, "Then I won't go either."

For an instant we just froze. Then Frank grinned. I will never forget that moment. Frank was just a kid. He wanted to go to that amusement park as much as I did, but there was something even more important than the class night out. Still, he didn't explain or expand. 8

The next thing I knew, the room was filled with kids listening to Frank. "They don't allow Negroes in the park," he said, "so I'm staying with Clifton."

Practice the Skills

8 Reviewing Skills

Interpreting The author points out that Frank didn't "explain or expand" about why he decided to stay behind. He also mentions that it was because "there was something more important than the class night out." What is the author *really* saying? What do you already know that can help you interpret those sentences?

A Mason-Dixon Memory **739**

READING WORKSHOP 4

"Me, too," a second boy said.

"Those jerks," a third muttered. "I'm with you, Clifton." My heart raced. Suddenly, I was not alone. A pint-size revolution had been born. The "water-balloon brigade,"[5] eleven white boys from Long Island, had made its decision: "We won't go." And as I sat on my bed in the center of it all, I felt grateful. But, above all, I was filled with pride. 9

Dondré Green's story brought that childhood memory back to life. His golfing teammates, like my childhood friends, faced an important decision. If they stood by their friend it would cost them dearly. But when it came time to decide, no one hesitated.

"Let's get out of here," one of them whispered.

"They just turned and walked toward the van," Dondré told us. "They didn't debate it. And the younger players joined us without looking back."

Dondré was astounded by the response of his friends — and the people of Louisiana. The whole state was outraged and tried to make it right. The Louisiana House of Representatives proclaimed a Dondré Green Day and passed legislation permitting lawsuits for damages, attorneys' fees and court costs against any private facility that invites a team, then bars any member because of race.

As Dondré concluded, his eyes glistened with tears. "I love my coach and my teammates for sticking by me," he said. "It goes to show that there are always good people who will not give in to **bigotry**. The kind of love they showed me that day will conquer hatred every time."

My friends, too, had shown that kind of love. As we sat in the hotel, a chaperone came in waving an envelope. "Boys!" he shouted. "I've just bought thirteen tickets to the Senators-Tigers game. Anybody want to go?"

Practice the Skills

9 Key Reading Skill

Predicting A break in the text is a good time to predict. What do you think will happen next? Keep in mind that there are really two stories: Clifton's and Dondré Green's. Have you heard the rest of Dondré's story yet? How do you think it will relate to Clifton's story?

---

5. A ***brigade*** (brih GAYD) is a group of people organized for a specific purpose.

Vocabulary

bigotry (BIG uh tree) *n.* unfair and unreasonable opinions or treatment of a person or group

The room erupted⁶ in cheers. Not one of us had ever been to a professional baseball game in a real baseball park.

On the way to the stadium, we grew silent as our driver paused before the Lincoln Memorial. For one long moment, I stared through the marble pillars at Mr. Lincoln, bathed in that warm, yellow light. There was still no smile and no sign of hope in his sad and tired eyes.

". . . We here highly resolve . . . that this nation, under God, shall have a new birth of freedom . . ." **10**

In his words and in his life, Lincoln made it clear, that freedom is not free. Every time the color of a person's skin keeps him out of an amusement park or off a country-club fairway, the war for freedom begins again. Sometimes the battle is fought with fists and guns, but more often the most effective weapon is a simple act of love and courage.

Whenever I hear those words from Lincoln's speech at Gettysburg, I remember my eleven white friends, and I feel hope once again. I like to imagine that when we paused that night at the foot of his great monument, Mr. Lincoln smiled at last.

As Dondré said, "The kind of love they showed me that day will conquer hatred every time." **11** ○

---

6. *Erupted* means exploded or burst forth.

Practice the Skills

10 **Key Literary Element**

Setting Thinking of all the different settings in this story, why do you suppose the author chose to end at the Lincoln Memorial? What happened when he was there earlier? How did he feel? How does a return to this setting add to the story's meaning?

11 **BIG Question**

How many heroes did you read about in "A Mason-Dixon Memory?" On the "Mason-Dixon Memory" page of Foldable 6, list and write about the heroes in this selection. Explain what each one of them did to become a hero. Your response will help you complete the Unit Challenge later.

A Mason-Dixon Memory 741

READING WORKSHOP 4 • Predicting

After You Read | A Mason-Dixon Memory

Answering the BIG Question

1. The author states that "freedom is not free." In what ways did the heroes in this story have to pay for freedom?

2. **Summarize** In what ways did Dondré's experience prompt the state of Louisiana to make changes? Give two examples of those changes.
   TIP Think and Search

3. **Recall** Where did the author, Clifton Davis, have his experience with racism? Name the state and place.
   TIP Right There

Critical Thinking

4. **Evaluate** Were the heroes in the story born heroes or just ordinary people who did the right thing? Support your answer by explaining your definition of a hero.
   TIP On My Own

5. **Draw Conclusions** In both cases, do you think the other boys would have defended Dondré or the narrator if they had not known them? Explain.
   TIP Author and Me

6. **Analyze** What is the Mason-Dixon line a symbol of in this story?
   TIP Author and Me

Write About Your Reading

Answer the questions to trace the similarities and differences between the two experiences—Dondré's and Clifton's. Use your answers to write a paragraph that compares and contrasts the two experiences.

- In what year did each experience take place?
- How old was the narrator? Dondré?
- In what state did the narrator grow up? Dondré?
- Where did they experience racism? Write the state and setting.
- Who stood up for the narrator? Dondré?
- List the heroes in each case. Why are they heroes?

Objectives (pp. 742–743)
Reading Make predictions • Make connections from text to self
Literature Identify key literary elements: setting
Vocabulary Explore word histories
Writing Write a paragraph: compare and contrast
Grammar Correct run-ons

742 UNIT 6   What Makes a Hero?

Skills Review

Key Reading Skill: Predicting

7. Did anything happen in this story that you did not predict? Explain.
8. How did predicting help you to understand the story better?

Key Literary Element: Setting

9. How were the settings important to both Dondré's and the narrator's experiences?
10. What does the title of the story have to do with setting?
11. How does the difference in time play a part in the outcomes of both experiences?

Reviewing Skills: Interpreting

12. What does the Lincoln Memorial mean to the author? What does it come to stand for by the end of the story? Explain.

Vocabulary Check

Choose the best word from the list to complete each sentence below. Rewrite each sentence with the correct word in place.

ominous bigotry civic resolve predominantly

13. The goldfish were ___ orange, but a few were white.
14. To have a world free of ___ you must learn to understand people who are different from you.
15. You should write your ___ leaders if you want to influence their decisions.
16. Every New Year's Eve, we ___ to watch less television.
17. We came in after the sky turned to a scary, ___ gray and the thunder began to boom.
18. **English Language Coach** In a sentence or two, tell how the modern meaning of the noun *banquet* relates to the Old Italian word that meant "bench."

Grammar Link: Correcting Run-on Sentences

A **run-on sentence** is two or more sentences incorrectly written as one sentence.

Example: *Jordon won the race the crowd cheered.*

Correct a run-on sentence by

- writing separate sentences
  Jordon won the race. The crowd cheered.
- combining the sentences with a semicolon (;)
  Jordon won the race; the crowd cheered.
- combining the sentences with a comma and *and, or,* or *but.*
  Jordon won the race, and the crowd cheered.

Grammar Practice

Rewrite this paragraph, correcting the run-on sentences.

    If you're looking for something to do with your free time, start a collection. Collecting is fun, collecting can be profitable. The items you collect can increase in value over the years, stamps, and coins are a good example. Some people collect baseball cards, some people collect the autographs of famous people, did you know there are even some people who collect shopping bags from different stores?

Writing Application Read the comparison and contrast you wrote about Dondré and the narrator's experiences. Correct any run-on sentences in your paragraph.

Web Activities For eFlashcards, Selection Quick Checks, and other Web activities, go to www.glencoe.com.

COMPARING LITERATURE WORKSHOP

The Toad and the Donkey
by Toni Cade Bambara

& Doc Rabbit, Bruh Fox, and Tar Baby
by Virginia Hamilton

Skills Focus

You will use these skills as you read and compare the following selections:

- "The Toad and the Donkey," p. 748
- "Doc Rabbit, Bruh Fox, and Tar Baby," p. 757

Reading

- Making connections across texts
- Comparing and contrasting myths, fables, and their heroes

Literature

- Recognizing and analyzing heroes

A real-life hero overcomes hardship or danger to do something generous for someone else. So are all heroes equal? No. You learned in this unit that a hero in literature can be very different from a real-life hero. In fact, one kind of literary hero—the trickster—often does not seem like a hero at all.

How to Compare Literature: Heroes

Trickster tales are found all around the world. In fact, they're especially common on cartoon shows you might have watched. Bugs Bunny, for example, is a trickster hero. In a trickster tale, the *trickster hero* uses clever tricks to defeat an opponent who's usually bigger, stronger, or faster than he is.

Some trickster heroes have good reasons for playing tricks. Other tricksters might just want to cheat someone or steal something. When you compare trickster tales, think about who the trickster hero is and why he's tricking his opponent.

Objectives (pp. 744–745)
Reading Compare and contrast heroes

COMPARING LITERATURE WORKSHOP

Get Ready to Compare

In a trickster tale, the trickster's opponent usually has some weakness that allows him or her to be tricked. The opponent may not be as smart as the trickster, or he may be greedy or self-centered. The trickster then takes advantage of this weakness to defeat his opponent. To understand the trickster tales "The Toad and the Donkey" and "Doc Rabbit, Bruh Fox, and Tar Baby," keep track of the tricks that are played in a chart like the one below. For each trick:

- describe the trick
- identify the trickster and opponent
- briefly describe the strengths and weaknesses of the trickster and opponent.

You'll find that in some tales several tricks are played. And more than one character in a single tale might be a trickster!

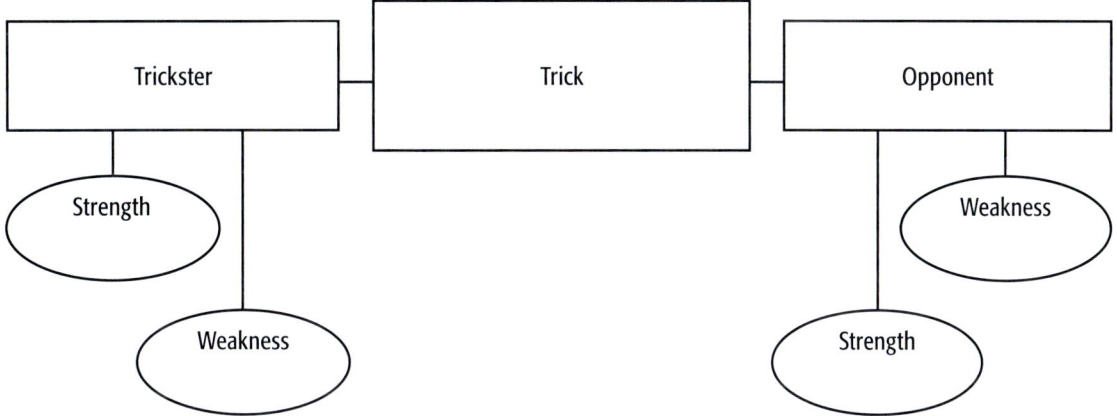

Here's a hint to help you with your charts: in "The Toad and the Donkey," only one trick is played, though it is repeated several times. You only have to make one chart for that selection. In "Doc Rabbit, Bruh Fox, and Tar Baby," though, several tricks are played, so you'll need several charts.

Use Your Comparison

After you have filled out your *Tricks* charts, think about why the trickster played the tricks in both selections. Did the trickster have a good reason for playing the trick or was he just taking advantage of the other character?

COMPARING LITERATURE WORKSHOP

Before You Read : The Toad and the Donkey

Meet the Author
Toni Cade added "Bambara" to her name after she found the name on a sketchbook in her great-grandmother's trunk. Born in the Harlem community of New York, she became a college professor, a writer, and an activist for African American women.

Bambara was born in 1939 and died in 1995. This story was published in 1971. See page R1 of the Author Files for more about Toni Cade Bambara.

Author Search For more about Toni Cade Bambara, go to www.glencoe.com.

Objectives (pp. 746–749)
Reading Compare and contrast heroes

Vocabulary Preview

reputation (rep yuh TAY shun) *n.* what other people think of someone (**p. 748**) *The donkey had a reputation for being a very fast runner.*

milepost (MYL pohst) *n.* one of a number of posts placed one mile apart (**p. 748**) *Toad's relatives hid in wait at each milepost.*

well (wel) *n.* a hole dug in the ground to get water (**p. 749**) *Donkey paused at the well for a drink.*

slashed (slasht) *v.* hit sharply enough to cause a cut; form of the verb *slash* (**p. 749**) *He slashed his back with his own tail.*

horsewhip (HORS whip) *n.* a whip or stick used to make a horse go faster (**p. 749**) *He used his tail like a horsewhip.*

Get Ready to Read

Connect to the Reading
Think about a time when you got mad at someone who bragged too much. Did you want to teach that person a lesson? How do you think you would have felt if someone had fooled that person by playing a trick on him or her?

Build Background
Trickster tales were common among enslaved African Americans during the 1800s. Many trickster tales have been handed down and rewritten by famous writers.

- In this tale Brother Spider proposes that Toad and Donkey race.
- In Africa the spider Anansi is an important figure in trickster tales and mythology.
- Donkeys have a reputation for being slow and stubborn.

One of the most popular types of folktales in cultures around the world is the trickster tale. In a trickster tale, the trickster hero is usually a smaller weaker character, while the opponent is larger and more powerful. But the opponent has some weakness or flaw that allows him to be tricked. The trickster takes advantage of the opponent's weakness to defeat him.

746 UNIT 6 What Makes a Hero?

COMPARING LITERATURE WORKSHOP

What Are Trickster Tales?

In many Native American, African American, and African folktales, the trickster is a rabbit. The rabbit seems small and helpless, but it wins by being quick and smart. In other cultures, foxes, turtles, spiders, ravens, badgers, and many other animals are the heroes of trickster tales.

Clever tricksters use their wits to get themselves out of trouble or to win a contest. But in many stories, the trickster gets right back into trouble. Tricksters who try to take advantage of others or cheat their opponents often get caught up in their own mischief. Sometimes they even become the victims of other tricksters.

Same Story, Different Culture

Some folktales are told in slightly different versions in different cultures. In *The People Could Fly: American Black Folktales,* Virginia Hamilton writes, "There are some three hundred versions of the Tar Baby tale. . . . In the Bahamas the elephant creates the tar baby; in Brazil an old woman or man traps a monkey in a sticky wax (doll). There is a version from India, and there are African versions among the Ewes and Yorubas [people of Western Africa], all showing the great . . . universality of this tale."

Set Purposes for Reading

BIG Question Read to find out if anyone in this tale has the qualities of a real-life hero.

Set Your Own Purpose What other purpose might you have for reading this tale? Write your own purpose on the "Toad and the Donkey" page of Foldable 6.

COMPARING LITERATURE WORKSHOP

The Toad and the Donkey

by Toni Cade Bambara

One day Brother Spider didn't have nothing better to do so he asked ole Toad and ole Donkey to have a race across the island.

The donkey said, "What? You want me, the fastest dude around here, to race that little old hop frog. I've got a **reputation**, you know." **1**

And the toad said, "Never mind all that, Big Mouth—let's race." **2**

The donkey thought to himself, this is ridiculous. But since Brother Spider always had good prizes (Brother Spider was a terrific thief), he agreed.

"O.K.," said Spider. "The only rule is that Brother Donkey has to howl every mile so we can know where you all are."

Toad says, "Fine with me. Let's set the race for Saturday."

"Oh no," says Donkey, for he suspected something trickified. "Tomorrow morning."

So Toad went home for dinner and put it to the family like so: "Listen here, we spread out along the path in the bushes, then at every **milepost** when Mr. Donkey howls out, one of you steps out and howls too." So they each packed a little breakfast of gungo peas and sweet potato bread and bakes all wrapped up in tanya leaves and took up their positions along the road.

Practice the Skills

1 **Comparing Literature**

Heroes What do you think Donkey's *strength* will be in this tale? Who do you think the trickster will be in this tale?

2 **Comparing Literature**

Heroes How does Toad feel about what Donkey has just said? What do you think Donkey's weakness will be?

Vocabulary

reputation (rep yuh TAY shun) *n.* what other people think of someone

milepost (MYL pohst) *n.* one of a number of posts placed one mile apart

So the race began. And Spider lit a cigar and lay back.

Brother Donkey took off at a light trot, his tail stuck up in the air to match his nose, stopping every now and then to stick his face through somebody's fence to munch on some grass. And when he got to the first milepost, he sang out, "La, la, la. Here I am. Where are you? Ha ha." **3**

And way in front of him Uncle Julius Toad sang back, "Up here. La, la, la," and licked his fingers.

Which really surprised Donkey. So he cut out the grass eating and got a move on. But then he passed a **well** and decided he had time for a drink, for how much hopping can a toad do. And at the next post he sang out, "Tra, la, la. Here I am. Where are you?"

And way up ahead Aunt Minnie Toad sang back, "Up here. Ha, ha."

By the fifth post, Donkey started getting a little worried so he **slashed** himself with his tail like a **horsewhip** and started galloping. But Cousins Emery, Walter and Cecil Toad were on the case. And it's the same story each time. "Tra la la, I'm up the road ahead of you, Donkey."

And Donkey began to get sad in his mind when he realized he was not going to beat Toad. And he decided before he even got to the finish line that he would never race again. And donkeys have been kind of stubborn about running ever since. **4 5** ○

Illustration for *Public and Private Animals*. 1877. by J Granville.

Practice the Skills

3 **Comparing Literature**

Heroes Does Donkey seem to be taking the race seriously? How does Donkey's attitude help to excuse Toad for playing a trick on him?

4 **Comparing Literature**

Heroes In some trickster tales, like myths, the trickster hero's actions explain why something happens in nature. What does this tale explain about donkeys?

5 **BIG Question**

Toad was a trickster hero in this tale. If something like this happened in real life, would you call him a hero?

Vocabulary

well (wel) *n.* a hole dug in the ground to get water

slashed (slasht) *v.* hit sharply enough to cause a cut

horsewhip (HORS wip) *n.* a whip or stick used to make a horse go faster

COMPARING LITERATURE WORKSHOP

Before You Read

Doc Rabbit, Bruh Fox, and Tar Baby

Virginia Hamilton

Meet the Author
"I grew up within the warmth of loving aunts and uncles, all reluctant farmers but great story-tellers," says Virginia Hamilton. She is proud to be descended from Levi Perry, who escaped from slavery and settled in Ohio.

Virginia Hamilton was born in 1936. This story was published in 1985.

Author Search For more about Virginia Hamilton, go to www.glencoe.com.

Vocabulary Preview

crock (krok) *n.* a large clay or ceramic pot **(p. 751)** *The boys kept their apple cider in a crock.*

toiled (toyld) *v.* worked hard; form of the verb *toil* **(p. 752)** *Raphael toiled all day weeding the garden.*

scurried (SKUR eed) *v.* ran quickly; form of the verb *scurry* **(p. 752)** *The mouse scurried across the floor to escape.*

Get Ready to Read

Connect to the Reading
Have you ever enjoyed a television program, movie, or story in which the characters kept playing tricks on each other? Which character did you like the best? Who did you want to "win"?

Build Background
This is one of many different stories from around the world that feature a rabbit or hare as a trickster.

- A hare is a larger relative of a rabbit, although people often use the words "hare" and "rabbit" to mean the same thing. A hare can grow to be the size of a large cat.
- There are many different trickster tales about a rabbit and a tar baby.
- Tar is the thick, sticky black substance that is often used to pave blacktop roads.

Set Purposes for Reading
BIG Question Read to find out whether any of the characters in this tale are like real-life heroes.

Set Your Own Purpose What else would you like to learn from this tale? Write your own purpose on the "Doc Rabbit, Bruh Fox, and Tar Baby" page of Foldable 6.

Objectives (pp. 750–755)
Reading Compare and contrast heroes
Literature Recognize and analyze heroes

COMPARING LITERATURE WORKSHOP

Doc Rabbit, Bruh Fox, and Tar Baby

by Virginia Hamilton

Heard tell about Doctor Rabbit and Brother Fox. They were buildin a house. And they kept a **crock** of cream in the bubbly brook down below the house they were buildin. Every once in a while, Doc Rabbit got thirsty. And he hollered aside so Bruh Fox wouldn't know who it was, "Whooo-hooo, whooo-hooo, whooo-hooo," like that. Scared Bruh Fox to death. **1**

"Who is it there?" Bruh Fox say.

"Sounds like somebody callin bad," said Doc Rabbit.

"Well, can you tell what they want?" Bruh Fox say.

"Can't tell nothin and I'm not lookin to see," said Doc.

"Oh, but yer the doctor. Yer the doctor, you'd better go see," says Bruh Fox. **2**

So Doc Rabbit went off down to the bubbly brook where the water ribbled, keepin the cream cold. He drank a long drink of sweet cream. Then he went back to help Bruh Fox with the house.

"Who was it callin?" asks Bruh Fox.

"Just started callin me, was all it was," said Doc Rabbit.

So Doc Rabbit got down to work. But the sun was hot and he came thirsty again. He went about callin out the side of his mouth:

"Whoo-ahhh, whooo-ahhh, whoo-ahhh!"

Practice the Skills

1 Comparing Literature

Heroes Who do you think is going to be the trickster? What do you think Bruh Fox's weakness is?

2 Comparing Literature

Heroes Why do you think Doc Rabbit tells Bruh Fox that he doesn't want to go see who is calling?

Vocabulary

crock (krok) *n.* a large clay or ceramic pot

"Who is callin so scared?" says Bruh Fox, trembly all over.

"Somebody callin me for help, I expect," Doc Rabbit said. "But I am sure not goin this time, me."

"You have to go. You have to, yer the only doctor. Go ahead on, you," Bruh Fox say.

Big Doc Rabbit went down to the brook again. The water was so cool and ribbly and it kept the crock of cream so fresh and cold. Doc Rabbit drank about half of the cream this time. Then he went back up to help Brother Fox with the hard labor of raisin the roof.

Bruh Fox says, "What was the name of the one callin you this time?"

"Name of about half done callin," mumbled Doc Rabbit. "Whew! This work is hard labor."

The rabbit **toiled** and sweated until his fur was wringin wet. He took off his fur coat, too. He wrung it dry and put it back on. But that didn't even cool him any. He says over his shoulder, says, "Whooo-wheee, whooo-wheee!" like that. 3

The fox says, lookin all around, "Somebody else callin you, Rabbit."

"I sure am not goin this time," Doc Rabbit said. "I'll just stay right here this time."

"You go on," says Bruh Fox. "Go ahead on, folks needin you today."

So Doc Rabbit **scurried** down to the ribblin brook. It was nice by the water. He sat himself down, took up the crock of cream. He drank it all down. Then he ran off.

Fox feel a suspicion. He went down there, saw the cream was all gone. He filled up the crock with some lemon and sugar water he had. He knew Rabbit was after anything cold and sweet.

"Who are you, I say" Harrison Candy. Engraving.

Practice the Skills

3 🥕**BIG Question**

How do you feel about the trick Doc Rabbit is playing on Bruh Fox? If something like this happened in real life, would you call Doc Rabbit a hero?

Vocabulary

toiled (toyld) *v.* worked hard
scurried (SKUR eed) *v.* ran quickly

"Think I'll catch me a doctor and a hare together," Fox says to himself. **4**

Next, he made a little baby out of the tar there. The baby lookin just like a baby rabbit. He named it Tar Baby and sat it right there on the waterside. Bruh Fox went back up the hill and he worked on his house. He thought he might keep the house to himself. Doc Rabbit was bein bad so and not workin at all. **5**

Doc Rabbit came back for a drink. He spied the new crock full. And he spied Tar Baby just sittin, gazin out on the water.

"What you doin here, baby rabbit?" Rabbit asked Tar Baby.

Tar Baby wouldn't say. Too stuck up.

"You better speak to me," Doc Rabbit said, "or I'll have to hurt you."

But the Tar Baby wasn't gone speak to a stranger.

So Doc Rabbit kicked Tar Baby with his left hind foot. Foot got stuck, it did.

"Whoa, turn me loose!" the rabbit cried. "Turn me loose!" **6**

Tar Baby stayed still. Gazin at the water. Lookin out over the ribbly water.

So Doc Rabbit kicked hard with his right hind foot. "Oh, oh, I'm stuck again. You'd better let me loose, baby," Doc Rabbit said. "I got another good foot to hit you with."

Tar Baby said nothin. Gazin at the water. Lookin far on by the waterside.

Doc Rabbit kicked Tar Baby with another foot, and that foot got stuck way deep. "Better turn me loose," Rabbit hollered, gettin scared now. Shakin now. Says, "I got one foot left and here it comes!" **7**

He kicked that tar baby with the one foot left, and that got stuck just like the other three.

"Well, well, well," said Doc Rabbit, shakin his head and lookin at Tar Baby.

Tar Baby gazin on the water. Watchin out for the pretty birds.

"Well, I still got my head," Doc Rabbit said. "I'm mad, now! I'm agone use my head, too."

He used his head on the little tar baby. Butted his head in the tar baby's stomach as hard as he could. Doc Rabbit's head got stuck clear up to his eyes. His big rabbit ears went whole in the tar of Tar Baby.

COMPARING LITERATURE WORKSHOP

Practice the Skills

4 Comparing Literature

Heroes Who do you think is going to be the trickster now? What weakness of Doc Rabbit does Bruh Fox take advantage of?

5 Comparing Literature

Heroes Do you think Bruh Fox was right in feeling that he should keep the house for himself? Explain.

6 Comparing Literature

Heroes How did Bruh Fox know that Doc Rabbit would kick or hit Tar Baby? What strength does Bruh Fox have now?

7 Comparing Literature

Heroes Doc Rabbit keeps kicking Tar Baby, even though he keeps getting more and more stuck. What is Doc Rabbit's weakness in this part of the story?

Doc Rabbit, Bruh Fox, and Tar Baby 753

COMPARING LITERATURE WORKSHOP

Brer Rabbit stuck on the Tar Baby. Engraving.
Analyzing the Art Who seems to be having the last laugh? What might Doc Rabbit do next?

That was the way Bruh Fox found him. Doc Rabbit was stuck in Tar Baby. Bruh Fox got him loose.

"What must I do with you?" Bruh Fox said. He led Rabbit along to the house they were buildin. "You the one drank up my crock of cream. I didn't get one taste. Have a mind to burn you in a fire, too."

"Oh, I like fires," Doc Rabbit said. "Do go on burn me up, Bruh Fox, for it's my pleasure to have my coat on fire."

"Well, then, I won't burn you," said the fox. "Burnin up is too good for you." 8

"Huh," grunted Doc Rabbit. He said no more. Bruh Fox had him in his mouth, a-danglin down his back. Then he laid the rabbit under his paws so he could speak.

"Well, I think I'll throw you in that thorny briar patch," Bruh Fox said. "How do you like that?"

Practice the Skills

8 Comparing Literature

Heroes Why does Doc Rabbit tell Bruh Fox to burn him in the fire? Who is being the trickster now?

754 UNIT 6 What Makes A Hero?

COMPARING LITERATURE WORKSHOP

Hare, William De Morgan (1839–1917) Watercolor on paper. Private collection.

"Oh, mercy, don't do that!" cried Doc Rabbit. "Whatever you do with me, don't dare throw me in those thorny briars!"

"That's what I'll do, then," Bruh Fox said.

And that's what Brother Fox did. He sure did. Took Doc Rabbit by the short hair and threw him—*Whippit! Whappit!*—right in the briar patch.

"Hot lettuce pie! This is where I want to be," Doc Rabbit hollered for happiness. He was square in the middle of the briar patch. "Here is where my mama and papa had me born and raised. Safe at last!" 9

"Didn't know rabbits have they homes in the briars," Bruh Fox said, scratching his tail.

He knows it now. 10 ○

Practice the Skills

9 Comparing Literature

Heroes What is the final trick played in this tale? Who is the trickster?

10 BIG Question

Which character in this tale would you rather have as a friend? Would either of these characters be a hero in real life? Explain your answer on the "Doc Rabbit, Bruh Fox, and Tar Baby" page of Foldable 6. Your response will help you complete the Unit Challenge later.

COMPARING LITERATURE WORKSHOP

After You Read

The Toad and the Donkey & Doc Rabbit, Bruh Fox, and Tar Baby

Vocabulary Check

Copy each sentence, filling in the blank with the best word from the list.

The Toad and the Donkey

reputation   milepost   well   slashed   horsewhip

1. Angelina went to the ___ to get some water.
2. The toad had a ___ for being a trickster.
3. The cowboy used a ___ to make his horse go faster.
4. The thorny weeds ___ at his ankles.
5. Tony could tell by the ___ how far he had traveled.

Doc Rabbit, Bruh Fox, and Tar Baby

crock   toiled   scurried

6. Jasmine ___ all day to get the house cleaned up.
7. People sometimes used to keep milk in a ___ .
8. When we heard the thunder, we ___ home.

Objectives (pp. 756–757)
Reading Compare and contrast: heroes
Writing Create a chart: compare and contrast

Reading/Critical Thinking

On a sheet of paper, answer the following questions.

The Toad and the Donkey

9. **Recall** Why does Donkey agree to race against Toad?
   TIP Right There

10. **Evaluate** Was Toad justified in tricking Donkey? Explain.
    TIP On My Own

Doc Rabbit, Bruh Fox, and Tar Baby

11. **Recall** What does Bruh Fox do right after he creates the tar baby?
    TIP Right There

12. **Evaluate** Who do you think would be a better friend—Doc Rabbit or Bruh Fox? Explain why you picked that character.
    TIP On My Own

Writing: Compare the Literature

Use Your Notes

13. Follow these steps to compare the trickster heroes.

Step 1: Look over the charts you made. For each trick that you listed, think about the weakness in the trickster's opponent that allowed the trickster to fool him. Then look at the strengths you listed for each trickster on your charts.

Step 2: Now think about why the trickster played each trick. Did the trickster's opponent deserve to be tricked?

Step 3: Which two tricksters do you think were most alike? Write a short paragraph that explains why you feel those two tricksters were most alike. Consider their strengths, weaknesses, the kind of tricks they played, and why they played the trick.

Get It on Paper

To compare the trickster heroes in "The Toad and the Donkey" and "Doc Rabbit, Bruh Fox, and Tar Baby," answer the following questions on a separate sheet of paper.

14. Which trickster do you think is the cleverest? Explain why you chose this answer.

15. Which opponent do you think most deserves to be fooled by the trickster? Explain your answer.

16. Which opponent do you think least deserves to be fooled by the trickster? Explain.

BIG Question

17. Would you consider any of these tricksters real heroes, not just literary heroes? Explain why or why not.

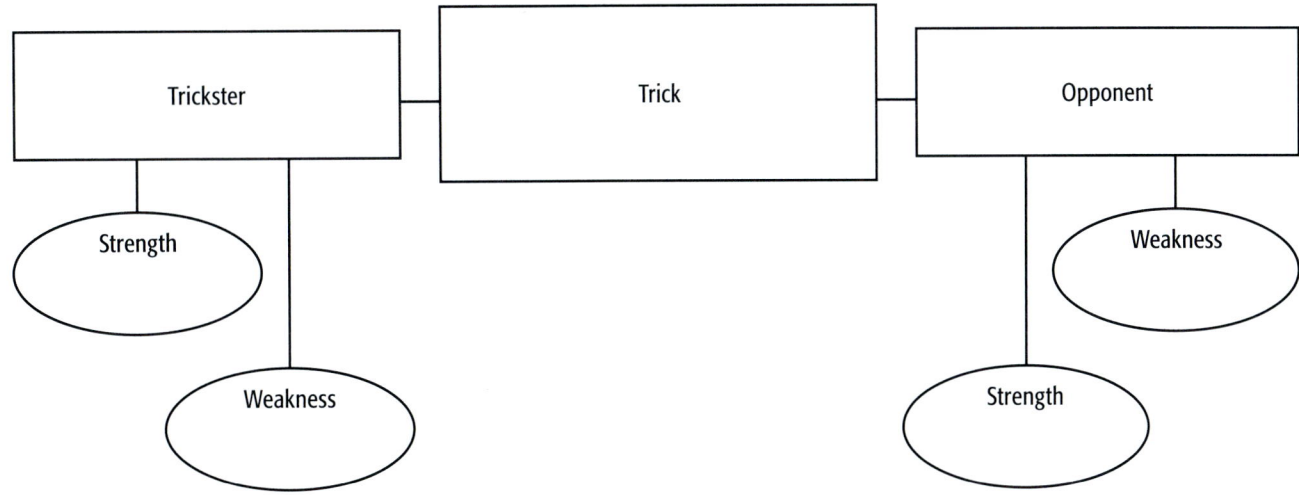

UNIT 6 WRAP-UP

Answering The BIG Question: What Makes a Hero?

You've learned about many different types of heroes—heroes of folktale, fantasy, and myth as well as heroes in real life. Now apply what you've learned to do the Unit Challenge.

The Unit Challenge

Choose Activity A or Activity B and follow the directions for that activity.

A. Group Activity: A Wall of Heroes

With three other students, imagine that you have been hired by your school to discover the local heroes in your community. Your school has asked you to interview people about their heroes and create a wall so that everyone can learn about them.

1. **Design Interviews** Make a list of three or four people in your class that you want to interview about their heroes. Decide if you will interview each person together or if each member of your group will interview one person. Using the notes from your Foldables, write three or four questions you will ask each person about their heroes. What do you want to know about the heroes?

2. **Interviews** Once you have a list of people to interview and a list of questions, it's time to do the interviews. Find a quiet place in the classroom and start your interviews. Ask your questions slowly and give people time to talk while you listen. Write down their answers. Ask people if they have pictures of their heroes they would like to put on the wall.

3. **Put the Results Together** After your interviews, put together a list of local heroes. Write a paragraph describing each hero and attach a picture of the hero to each paragraph if you have one.

4. **Create a Wall of Heroes** Find a place in your classroom like a wall or a bulletin board to put up the paragraphs and pictures about local heroes. Design your wall so people can learn about the heroes and their accomplishments. Use markers, paints, and colored paper to make the wall look good. Invite people from your school to come and look at the Wall of Heroes.

Fruits of Expression mural inspired by American Bill of Rights, Albuquerque, New Mexico.

B. Solo Activity: A Hero for Today

The world can always use another hero. You've just read about many heroes from the past and some heroes from the present. What kind of hero do you think the world needs today?

1. **Choose a Hero** Look over your notes on the heroes you read about in this unit. Which one do you like the best? What skills did he or she use? Choose a hero for today.

2. **Bring Your Hero Alive** Think of the problems of today. Which ones would you like to solve? How could a hero help do this? Write a list of traits you want to give to your hero to help solve problems of today. Your hero can have all the traits you read about, but he or she may need new ones for today's problems. Use a web like the one below to think of powers and skills that would help your hero solve the problem you chose.

3. **Write a Story** Write a story about how your hero helps solve the type of problems people face today. What adventures does he or she have? What powers does your hero use? How does your hero make the world a better place? Draw a picture of your hero to go with your story.

4. **Tell Your Story** Once you finish writing your story, it's time to tell it to the class. Use your best storytelling skills and bring your hero alive for your classmates by telling them about the adventures of your hero and why your hero is a hero for today.

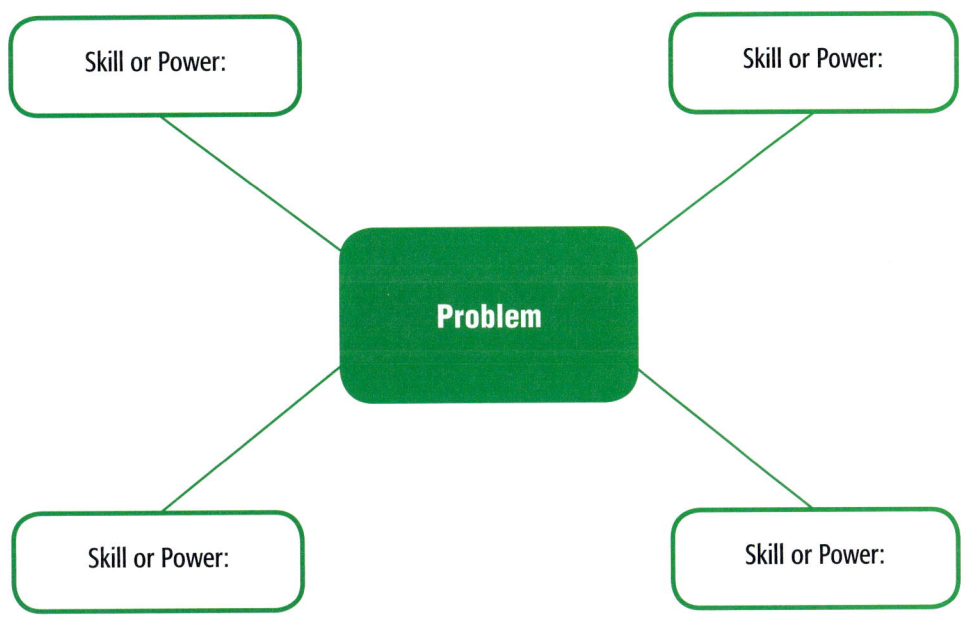

UNIT 6
Your Turn: Read and Apply Skills

Meet the Author
Alma Luz Villanueva is a poet and novelist. She uses themes from her Mexican American and Yaqui Indian heritage, such as the Native American sense of oneness with nature. She says that the inspiration for her writing is mysterious because "when we touch the most personal, the most hidden within ourselves, we touch the universal." See page R7 of the Author Files for more about Alma Luz Villanueva.

Author Search For more about Alma Luz Villanueva, go to www.glencoe.com.

The Sand Castle

by Alma Luz Villanueva

"HAVE YOU DRESSED YET?" their grandmother called. "Once a month in the sun and they must almost be forced," she muttered. "Well, poor things, they've forgotten the warmth of the sun on their little bodies, what it is to play in the sea, yes. . . ." Mrs. Pavloff reached for her protective sun goggles that covered most of her face.

It screened all ultraviolet light[1] from the once life-giving sun; now, it, the sun, scorched the Earth, killing whatever it touched. The sea, the continents, had changed. The weather, as they'd called it in the last century, was entirely predictable now: warming.

Mrs. Pavloff slipped on the thick, metallic gloves, listening to her grandchildren squabble and she heard her mother's voice calling her, "Masha, put your bathing suit under your clothes. It's so much easier that way without having to go to the bathhouse first. Hurry! Father's waiting!" She remembered the ride to the sea, the silence when the first shimmers of water became visible. Her father had always been first into the chilly water. "Good for the health!" he'd yell as he dove into it, swimming as far as he could, then

---
1. The sun's ***ultraviolet light*** is invisible, and it can be harmful.

760 UNIT 6 What Makes a Hero?

back. Then he'd lie exhausted on the sand, stretched to the sun. Such happiness to be warmed by the sun.

Then the picnic. She could hear her mother's voice, "Stay to your knees, Masha! Only to your knees!" To herself: "She'd be a mermaid if I didn't watch," and she'd laugh. Masha would lie belly down, facing the sea and let the last of the waves roll over her. She hadn't even been aware of the sun, only that she'd been warm or, if a cloud covered it, cold. It was always there, the sun: its light, its warmth. But the sea—they traveled to it. So, she'd given all of her attention to the beautiful sea.

She saw her father kneeling next to her, building the sand castle they always built when they went to the sea. Her job was to find seashells, bird feathers, and strips of seaweed to decorate it. How proud she'd felt as she placed her seashells where she chose, where they seemed most beautiful. Only then was the sand castle complete. She heard her father's voice, "The Princess's castle is ready, now, for her Prince! Come and look, Anna! What do you think?" She saw herself beaming with pride, and she heard her mother's laugh. "Fit for a queen, I'd say! Can I live in your castle, too, Masha? Please, Princess Masha?"

Analyzing the Art Does this sand castle look like the one Masha and her father built? Why or why not?

YOUR TURN: READ AND APPLY SKILLS

"Of course, Mother! You can live with me always. . . . " She remembered her mother's laughing face, her auburn hair lit up by the sun, making her look bright and beautiful.

The sun, the sun, the sun. The scientists were saying that with the remedies they were employing now and the remedies begun twenty years ago—they'd stopped all nuclear testing and all manufacturing of ozone-depleting[2] chemicals was banned[3] worldwide—the scientists were saying that the sun, the global problem, would begin to get better. Perhaps for her grandchildren's children. Perhaps they would feel the sun on their unprotected bodies. Perhaps they would feel the delicious warmth of the sun.

All vehicles were solar powered. The populations took buses when they needed transportation and people emerged mainly at night. So, most human activity was conducted after the sun was gone from the sky. Those who emerged during the day wore protective clothing. Everything was built to screen the sun's light. Sometimes she missed the natural light of her childhood streaming through the windows so intensely the urge to just run outside would overtake her. She missed the birds, the wild birds.

But today they were going out, outside in the daytime, when the sun was still in the sky. Masha knew they were squabbling because they hated to dress up to go outside. The clothing, the gloves, the goggles, were uncomfortable and cumbersome.[4] She sighed, tears coming to her eyes. Well, they're coming, Masha decided. They can remove their goggles and gloves on the bus.

The sea was closer now and the bus ride was comfortable within the temperature controlled interior. Those with memories of the sea signed up, bringing grandchildren, children, friends, or just went alone. Masha had taken her grandchildren before, but they'd sat on the sand, listlessly,[5] sifting it through their gloved hands with bored little faces. She'd tried to interest them in the sea with stories of her father swimming in it as far as he could. But they couldn't touch it, so it, the sea, didn't seem real to them. What was it: a mass of undrinkable, hostile water. Hostile like the sun. They'd taken no delight, no pleasure, in their journey to the sea.

But today, yes, today we will build a sand castle. Masha smiled at her secret. She'd packed everything late last night to surprise them at the sea.

Why haven't I thought of it before? Masha asked herself, and then she remembered the dream, months ago, of building a sand castle with her father at the sea. It made her want to weep because she'd forgotten. She'd actually forgotten one of the most joyful times of her girlhood. When the sea was still alive with life.

Today we will build a sand castle.

---

2. **Ozone-depleting chemicals** reduce (or "deplete") the ozone layer. This upper layer of the atmosphere protects life on earth by blocking certain kinds of harmful radiation.

3. **Banned** means "forbidden" or "outlawed."

4. Something that is **cumbersome** is hard to handle or carry because of size or weight.

5. **Listlessly** means "with little energy, interest, or concern."

Beach Scene. Charles-Garabed Atamian (1913–1942). Private collection.

They trudged[6] on the thick, dense sand toward the hiss of pale blue. Only the older people picked up their step, excited by the smell of salt in the air. Masha's grandchildren knew they'd be here for two hours and then trudge all the way back to the bus. The darkened goggles made the sunlight bearable. They hated this forlorn place where the sun had obviously drained the life out of everything. They were too young to express it, but they felt it as they walked, with bored effort, beside their grandmother.

"We're going to build a sand castle today—what do you think of that?" Masha beamed, squinting to see their faces.

"What's a sand castle?" the boy mumbled.

"You'll see, I'll show you. . . ."

"Is it fun, Grandmama?" the girl smiled, taking her grandmother's hand.

"Yes, it's so much fun. I've brought different sized containers to mold the sand, and, oh, you'll see!"

The boy gave an awkward skip and nearly shouted, "Show us, Grandmama, show us what you mean!"

---

6. Trudged means "walked steadily but with great effort."

YOUR TURN: READ AND APPLY SKILLS

Masha laughed, sounding almost like a girl. "We're almost there, yes, we're almost there!"

The first circle of sandy shapes was complete, and the children were so excited by what they were building they forgot about their protective gloves.

"Now, we'll put a pile of wet sand in the middle and build it up with our hands and then we'll do another circle, yes, children?"

The children rushed back and forth from the tide line carrying the dark, wet sand. They only had an hour left. Their eyes, beneath the goggles, darted with excitement.

"Just don't get your gloves in the water, a little wet sand won't hurt, don't worry, children. When I was a girl there were so many birds at the sea we'd scare them off because they'd try to steal our food. Seagulls, they were, big white birds that liked to scream at the sea, they sounded like eagles to me. . . ."

"You used to eat at the sea, Grandmama?" the girl asked incredulously.[7]

"We used to call them picnics. . . ."

"What are eagles, Grandmama?" the boy wanted to know, shaping the dark sand with his gloved hands.

"They used to be one of the largest, most beautiful wild birds in the world. My grandfather pointed them out to me once. . . ." Until that moment, she'd forgotten that memory of nearly sixty years ago. They'd gone on a train, then a bus, to the village where he'd been born. She remembered her grandfather looking up toward a shrill, piercing cry that seemed to come from the sky. She'd seen the tears in

---

7. **Incredulously** (in KREJ uh lus lee) means "having a hard time believing."

her grandfather's eyes and on his cheeks. He'd pointed up to a large, dark flying-thing in the summer blue sky: "That's an eagle, my girl, the spirit of the people."

Sadness overtook Masha, but she refused to acknowledge its presence. The sand castle, Masha told herself sternly—the sand castle is what is important now. "I've brought a wonderful surprise, something to decorate the sand castle with when we're through building it."

"Show us, Grandmama, please?"

"Yes, please, please show us now!"

Masha sighed with a terrible, sudden happiness as she brought out the plastic bag. Quickly, she removed each precious shell from its protective cotton: eight perfect shells from all over the world.

"But Grandmama, theses are your special shells! You said the sea doesn't make them anymore. . . ."

"It will, Anna, it will." Masha hugged her granddaughter and made her voice brighten with laughter. "Today we will decorate our sand castle with the most beautiful shells in the world, yes!"

UNIT 6
Reading on Your Own

To read more about the Big Question, choose one of these books from your school or local library. Work on your reading skills by choosing books that are challenging to you.

Fiction

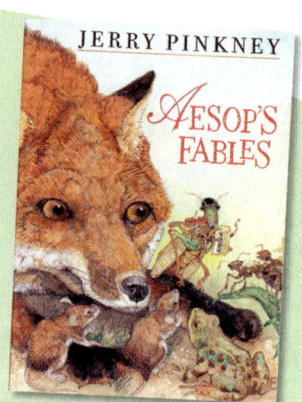

Aesop's Fables
Aesop, adapted by Jerry Pinkney

This collection includes brief retellings of more than sixty of Aesop's fables. Read this entertaining batch of retellings to find human flaws in animal forms and to learn the source of sayings like, "Don't count your chickens before they hatch."

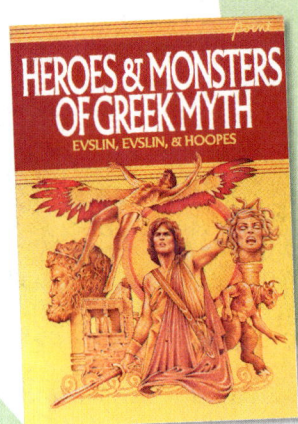

Heroes & Monsters of Greek Myth
by Bernard Evslin

Want to know how Perseus slays the Medusa, or how the Minotaur devours its victims? Ever wonder how the very-married Zeus juggles so many girlfriends? If so, check out this classic collection of great Greek myths.

Anansi the Spider: A Tale from the Ashanti
by Gerald McDermott

Anansi the Spider, the wise and mischievous hero of traditional folktales of Ghana, got into all sorts of trouble but was saved by his six sons. Read to find out how Anansi decides which son to reward with a very special gift.

The Call of the Wild
by Jack London

This classic book relates the adventures of a dog named Buck. When Buck is kidnapped from his comfortable California home—and forced to work as a sled dog in the Yukon gold rush of the late 1800s—he doesn't know what lies ahead. Follow Buck as he fights to survive out in the big, wide world.

Nonfiction

Old Hickory: Andrew Jackson and the American People
by Albert Marrin

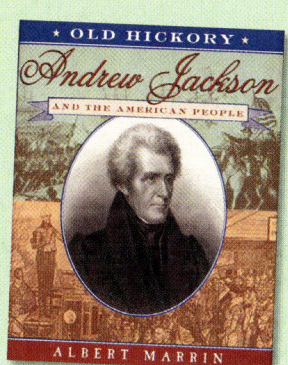

Andrew Jackson lacked formal schooling, but that didn't stand between him and success. Known for his fierce intelligence and stubborn disposition, Jackson excelled as a solider, a lawyer, a judge, and a president. Read to learn more about the man history calls "Old Hickory."

The Civil Rights Movement for Kids
by Mary Turck

This is a complete history of the civil rights movement in the United States in the twentieth century. Read to learn what it was like to live under discrimination laws and how the struggle for freedom and equality changed the country.

50 American Heroes Every Kid Should Meet
by Dennis Denenberg and Lorraine Roscoe

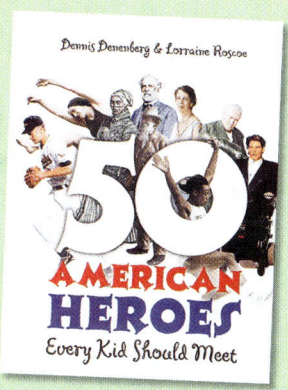

This book contains short biographies of famous people from various eras and fields of accomplishment. Read to learn about such heroes as Susan B. Anthony, Frederick Douglass, Cesar Chavez, Dolores Huerta, Bill Cosby, John Glenn, and Harriet Tubman.

Martin Luther King, Jr.
by Amy Pastan

This biography tells the story of the man who was at the forefront of the fight for racial justice in the United States during the 1950s and 1960s. Read to understand the nonviolent methods that Dr. King used to fight oppression and inequality.

UNIT 6 SKILLS AND STRATEGIES ASSESSMENT

Test Practice

Part 1: Literary Elements

On a separate sheet of paper, write the numbers 1–4. Next to each, write the letter of the correct answer for that question.

Read the following passage and use it to answer questions 1 and 2.

When Hank rode into town, the streets were empty, but a group of men had gathered outside the sheriff's office. Hank tied his horse to a hitching post and stepped up onto the wooden sidewalk.

"Howdy," he said, nodding at the men, none of whom wore the star-shaped badge he was looking for. "Is the sheriff inside?"

"We don't have a sheriff these days," replied one man. "Vic Morrison ran him right out of town."

Hank hooked his thumbs in his belt and looked out at the deserted street. "Is Morrison still around?"

"Sure is," said the tallest of the group. "He's over at the café with some of his men. They've pretty much taken over the town. With no sheriff, the law-abiding folks around here don't have much of a chance."

"We'll see about that," said Hank softly. He took off his hat, smoothed his hair, and replaced the hat firmly. "We'll just see."

---

1. Which of the following is a clue to what the setting of this story is?
   A. "The streets were empty . . ."
   B. "Hank tied his horse to a hitching post . . ."
   C. "Hank hooked his thumbs in his belt . . ."
   D. "He took off his hat, smoothed his hair . . ."

2. If Hank turns out to be the hero of this story, that will be because he
   A. is a stranger in town.
   B. is friendly and polite.
   C. has confidence in himself.
   D. demonstrates strength and bravery.

3. The theme of this story is **most** likely to have something to do with the importance of
   A. love.   C. courage.
   B. patience.   D. hard work.

4. It be most important for you to learn about the cultural context of
   A. a short story written in the 1960s.
   B. a poem written last year by someone you know.
   C. a news article about jazz, written ten years ago.
   D. a Native American myth from hundreds of years ago.

Objectives (pp. 768–769)
Reading Activate prior knowledge • Make predictions • Compare and contrast
Literature Identify key literary elements: setting, hero, cultural context, theme

SKILLS AND STRATEGIES ASSESSMENT

Part 2: Reading Skills

On a separate sheet of paper, write the numbers 1–4. Next to each number, write the letter of the correct answer for that question.

Story 1: A crow who was dying of thirst saw a pitcher and flew to it, hoping to get a drink. He found only a few inches of water at the bottom. Because the pitcher was tall and narrow, the crow could not get to the water. He was desperate, but nothing he tried was successful. Finally, he collected stones and dropped them, one by one, into the pitcher. This caused the water to rise until it was at a height he could reach, thus saving his life.

Story 2: A fox saw a crow steal a bit of cheese and settle in a tree with the cheese in his beak. The fox walked up to the tree and said, "How handsome you look, Crow! Your feathers are so glossy and your eyes so bright. If your voice were also beautiful, you would surely be considered the King of Birds." Then the crow opened his beak to let out his best "Caw, caw, caw," which is as close as any crow can come to singing. The cheese dropped to the ground, and the fox quickly snapped it up.

1. Imagine that while you were reading Story 2, you didn't understand why the crow tried to sing. In this case, it would be most helpful to activate your prior knowledge about
   A. how animals react to cheese.
   B. common reactions to flattery.
   C. what a beautiful bird song sounds like.
   D. what glossy feathers and bright eyes look like.

2. In which story does the crow get what he wants?
   A. Story 1
   B. Story 2
   C. Both stories
   D. Neither story

3. In which story does an animal behave cleverly?
   A. Story 1
   B. Story 2
   C. Both stories
   D. Neither story

4. Imagine that Story 2 went on to say: "A few weeks later, the crow met the same fox again. But, this time, the crow was ready for him." What would be *most* likely to happen next?
   A. The fox would trick the crow again.
   B. The fox would be unable to trick the crow.
   C. The fox would give some cheese to the crow.
   D. The fox and the crow would become friends.

UNIT 6 SKILLS AND STRATEGIES ASSESSMENT

Part 3: Vocabulary Skills

On a separate sheet of paper, write the numbers 1–9. Next to each number, write the letter of the correct answer for that question.

For questions 1–5, write the letter of the word or phrase that means about the same as the underlined word.

1. to <u>acknowledge</u> a fact
   - A. hide
   - B. admit
   - C. understand
   - D. worry about

2. the <u>ominous</u> sounds
   - A. loud
   - B. funny
   - C. interesting
   - D. threatening

3. to be a <u>tyrant</u>
   - A. hero
   - B. winner
   - C. cruel ruler
   - D. spoiled child

4. such <u>tedious</u> work
   - A. boring
   - B. important
   - C. difficult
   - D. dangerous

5. to express <u>remorse</u>
   - A. excitement
   - B. deep anger
   - C. guilty regret
   - D. determination

Choose the correct answer for each question.

6. What do the following words have in common?

   banana   macaroni   karate   rodeo

   - A. They come from names.
   - B. They are very new words.
   - C. They are borrowed words.
   - D. They can be used as nouns or verbs.

7. Which of the following words is a compound word?
   - A. shoelace
   - B. preschool
   - C. moustache
   - D. subscription

8. What is the "etymology" of a word?
   - A. its history
   - B. its spelling
   - C. its pronunciation
   - D. its part of speech

9. Which of the following is <u>most</u> likely a true statement about the word *e-mail*?
   - A. It comes from a person's name.
   - B. It is a recent addition to the language.
   - C. It was borrowed from another language.
   - D. It came into the language during the Civil War.

Objectives (pp. 770–771)
Vocabulary Explore word histories • Identify word origins • Identify borrowed words
Grammar Identify sentence types • Use correct punctuation
Writing Use key elements: voice

SKILLS AND STRATEGIES ASSESSMENT **UNIT 6**

Part 4: Writing Skills

On a separate sheet of paper, write the numbers 1–7. Next to each number, write the letter of the correct answer for that question.

1. Which of the following is a simple sentence?
    A. A long walk on the beach.
    B. Rabbits ate all the petunias.
    C. Max got there early, but Lucy was late.
    D. When Jessie and Max arrive with food.

2. Which of the following is a compound sentence?
    A. Delia and Jeremy argued for hours.
    B. When I was younger, I didn't like swimming.
    C. They were late, and the train left without them.
    D. I threw a stick for my dog to catch and bring back.

3. Which of the following is a complex sentence?
    A. Tigers live in India, not Africa.
    B. If you feel sick, you should stay home.
    C. She dropped off the book and came home.
    D. Rita hit a fly ball, and Rafael scored from third.

4. Which sentence is punctuated correctly?
    A. We had sandwiches, and some fruit.
    B. If there's enough food, I'd like another helping.
    C. I don't enjoy being outdoors, when it's really cold.
    D. Nobody knew what to do, before the ambulance arrived.

5. Which sentence is punctuated correctly?
    A. That's the man, that I saw before.
    B. If Sam helps me I'll get my work done faster.
    C. When people tell lies, life can be very confusing!
    D. The movie had already started, when we got there.

6. Which of the following is a run-on sentence?
    A. Cheri walks to school so does Marcella.
    B. Nobody is sure about what the answer is.
    C. I wish I knew what to do, but I'm just not sure.
    D. Don't be rude, but do try to keep the conversation short.

7. What does it mean to describe a piece of writing as having "a clear voice"?
    A. A reader can tell what the writer is like.
    B. A reader can easily understand the writing.
    C. The writer has included a great deal of dialogue.
    D. The writer has used correct spelling and punctuation.

Skills and Strategies Assessment **771**

UNIT 7

The BIG Question
What Can We Learn from Our Mistakes?

"Anyone who has never made a mistake has never tried anything new."

—Albert Einstein
1921 Nobel Prize winner in physics, known for his Theory of Relativity

LOOKING AHEAD

The skill lessons and readings in this unit will help you develop your own answer to the Big Question.

UNIT 7 WARM-UP • Connecting to the Big Question
GENRE FOCUS: Historical Fiction and Nonfiction

The Great Radio Scare 777

READING WORKSHOP 1   Skill Lesson: Synthesizing

The Gold Cadillac 786
    by Mildred D. Taylor

Nadia the Willful 806
    by Sue Alexander

WRITING WORKSHOP PART 1   Personal Narrative 814

READING WORKSHOP 2   Skill Lesson: Identifying Main Idea and Supporting Details

The Bracelet 822
    by Yoshiko Uchida

Too Soon a Woman 832
    by Dorothy M. Johnson

READING WORKSHOP 3   Skill Lesson: Evaluating

President Cleveland, Where Are You? 844
    by Robert Cormier

Nobody's Perfect 860
    by David Fischer from *Sports Illustrated for Kids*

WRITING WORKSHOP PART 2   Personal Narrative 866

READING WORKSHOP 4   Skill Lesson: Inferring

The Shutout 874
    by Patrica C. McKissack and Fredrick McKissack, Jr.

The Talking Skull 884
    by Donna L. Washington

READING ACROSS TEXTS WORKSHOP

from *The Great Fire* 897
    by Jim Murphy

Letters About the Fire 905
    by Justin and Fannie Belle Becker

UNIT 7 WRAP-UP • Answering the Big Question

UNIT 7 WARM-UP

Connecting to The BIG Question

What Can We Learn from Our Mistakes?

Everyone makes mistakes. And that's a good thing. Why? Making mistakes is part of being human. Mistakes teach you a lot about yourself and others. Mistakes help you grow and change. In this unit, you'll read about mistakes different people made and what they learned from them.

Real Kids and the Big Question

RAMÓN and Jaime were friends. Ramón knew what people were saying about Jaime wasn't true, but Ramón told the story to some other kids anyway. He wanted the other kids to notice him. He wasn't thinking of Jaime. What's worse, Jaime heard that Ramón was helping to spread the story. Jaime told Ramón they weren't friends anymore. What do you think Ramón will learn from his mistake?

CAROLYN didn't even think of calling home. When the other girls said they were going to Katara's and asked her to come along, she just went. Most afternoons Carolyn went straight home. When Carolyn didn't come home, her mother began to worry. She had no idea where Carolyn was. What will Carolyn learn from her mistake?

Warm-Up Activity
With a small group, act out two short skits that show what Ramón and Carolyn should have done in each situation.

UNIT 7 WARM-UP

You and the Big Question

You can turn a mistake into a learning experience. As you read the selections in this unit, think about how you would answer the Big Question.

Big Question Link to Web resources to further explore the Big Question at www.glencoe.com.

Plan for the Unit Challenge

At the end of the unit, you'll use notes from all your reading to complete the Unit Challenge.

You'll choose one of the following activities:

A. Chart You'll work in a group to create a chart about making mistakes and learning from them.

B. Bumper Sticker You'll create slogans for several bumper stickers about learning from mistakes. A slogan (SLOH gun) is a phrase or saying that expresses an idea.

- Start thinking about the activity you'd like to do. Make the activity the focus of your thinking as you work through the unit.
- In your Learner's Notebook, quickwrite about why you chose the activity. Tell how it will help you answer the Big Question and learn from your mistakes.
- When you take notes about the Big Question, think about how those ideas will help you complete the Unit Challenge activity.

Keep Track of Your Ideas

As you read, you'll make notes about the Big Question. Later, you'll use these notes to complete the Unit Challenge. See pages R8–R9 for help with making each Unit 7 Foldable. This diagram shows how each should look.

1. Make one Foldable for each workshop. Keep all of your Foldables for the unit in your Foldables folder.
2. On the bottom fold of your Foldable, write the workshop number and the Big Question.
3. Write the titles of the selections in the workshop on the front of the flaps—one title on each flap. (See page 773 for the titles.)
4. Open the flaps. At the very top of each flap, write **My Purpose for Reading**. Below each crease, write **The Big Question**.

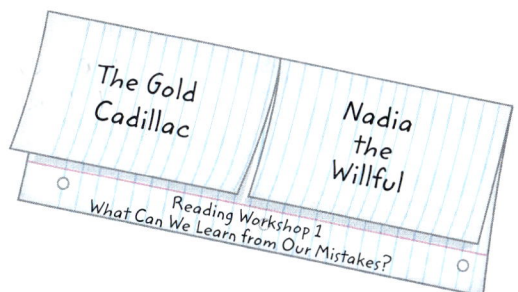

UNIT 7 GENRE FOCUS: HISTORICAL FICTION AND NONFICTION

In **historical fiction** the characters, plot, and setting are fictional, or imaginary, but the time period is true. **Historical nonfiction** is writing that tells about real people, real places, and real events in the past. Biographies, autobiographies, essays, letters, and documents are some examples of historical nonfiction.

Why Read Historical Fiction and Nonfiction?

Historical writing takes readers to different places and times in history. It introduces readers to people and ways of life from the past. You'll read historical fiction and nonfiction to
- gain an understanding of past events
- learn how people lived, how they dressed, and how they spoke

How to Read Historical Fiction and Nonfiction

Key Reading Skills

These key reading skills are especially useful tools for reading and understanding historical fiction and nonfiction. You'll learn more about these skills later in the unit.

- **Synthesizing** As you read, bring together information and ideas from the text to make new ideas of your own. (See Reading Workshop 1.)
- **Identifying main idea and supporting details** Find the most important idea in a paragraph or in a selection. Look for examples, reasons, or details that explain it. (See Reading Workshop 2.)
- **Evaluating** Make judgments and form opinions as you read. Decide whether characters are interesting, events are believable, or information is one-sided, for example. (See Reading Workshop 3.)
- **Inferring** Use clues from the text to figure out what the author isn't directly telling you.

Key Literary Elements

Recognizing and thinking about the following literary elements will help you understand more fully what the author is telling you.

- **Symbol:** any object, person, place, or experience that stands for something else (See "The Gold Cadillac.")
- **Narrator:** the person who tells a story or relates an experience (See "The Bracelet.")
- **Description:** a detailed explanation of a person, a place, a thing, or an event (See "President Cleveland, Where Are You?")
- **Sequence of events/Time order:** the order in which events take place, the steps in a process, or the order of importance (See "The Shutout.")

Skills Focus
- Key skills for reading historical fiction and nonfiction
- Key literary elements of historical fiction and nonfiction

Skills Model
You will see how to use the key reading skills and literary elements as you read
- "The Great Radio Scare," p. 777

Objectives (pp. 776–781)
Reading Synthesize information • Identify main ideas and supporting details • Evaluate text • Make inferences
Literature Identify literary devices: symbolism • Identify literary elements: narrator, description • Identify text structure: sequence, time order

UNIT 7 GENRE FOCUS

The Great Radio Scare

U.S. Terrorized by Radio's 'Men From Mars'

NEW YORK, Oct 30, 1938 (AP)—Hysteria[1] among radio listeners throughout the nation and actual panicky evacuations from sections of the metropolitan area resulted from a too-realistic radio broadcast tonight describing a fictitious and devastating visitation of strange men from Mars.

Excited and weeping persons all over the country swamped newspaper and police switchboards with the question:

"It is true?"

FALLING METEORS

It was purely a figment of H.G. Wells's imagination[2] with some extra flourishes of radio dramatization by Orson Welles. It was broadcast by the Columbia Broadcasting System.

The broadcast was an adaptation of Wells's "War of the Worlds" in which meteors[3] and gas from Mars menace the Earth. 1 2

New York police were unable to contact the CBS studios by telephone so swamped was its switchboard and a radio car was sent there for information.

A woman ran into a church in Indianapolis screaming: "New York destroyed. It's the end of the world. You might as well go home to die. I just heard it on the radio." Services were dismissed immediately.

---

1. **Hysteria** is behavior that shows uncontrolled panic or fear.
2. When you say that something is a **figment of someone's imagination,** you mean that that person made it up.
3. A **meteor** (MEE tee ur) is a piece of rocky material from space that falls to Earth at a high speed. It becomes very hot and glows as it enters Earth's atmosphere.

The notes in the side columns model how to use the skills and elements you read about on page 776.

Historical Fiction and Nonfiction

ACTIVE READING MODEL

1 Key Reading Skill
Synthesizing *The broadcast happened in the 1930s. That was a long time ago. I know from science class that we have sent machines to Mars since then. People must not have known much about Mars back then.*

2 Key Literary Element
Symbol *Meteors and gas from Mars may have been symbols of the end of the world to some people. Maybe that's why they were so scared.*

Actor Orson Welles broadcast *War of the Worlds* on his radio show, *The Mercury Theater on the Air*

Five boys at Brevard (N.C.) college fainted and panic gripped the campus for a half hour with many students fighting for telephones to inform their parents to come and get them.

PLEA FOR REASSURANCE

At Fayette, N.C., people with relatives in the section of New Jersey where the mythical visitation had its locale,[4] went to a newspaper office in tears, seeking information.

Many New Yorkers seized personal effects and raced out of their apartments, some jumping into their automobiles and heading for the wide open spaces.

A message from Providence, R.I., said:

"Weeping and hysterical women swamped the switchboard of the Providence Journal for details of the massacre[5] and destruction at New York and officials of the electric company received scores of calls urging them to turn off all lights so that the city would be safe from the enemy."

At Concrete, Wash., women fainted and men prepared to take their families into the mountains for safe-keeping when electric power failed during the radio dramatization.

At a highly effective dramatic high in the radio program when all sorts of monsters were flocking down on New Jersey from the planet Mars, lights went out in most of the homes of the town of 1000. For a time the village verged on[6] mass hysteria. 🔳

Because of the power failure, many persons actually thought the invasion had reached Washington State.

Elsewhere in the Northwest calls poured into newspaper and press association offices by the thousands.

The Boston Globe told of one woman who "claimed she could 'see the fire' and said she and many others in her neighborhood were 'getting out of here.'"

In this picture, Orson Welles and others are getting ready for the *War of the Worlds* broadcast.

ACTIVE READING MODEL

🔳 **Key Reading Skill**
Identifying Main Idea and Supporting Details *This section gives examples of what people did when they heard the broadcast. Those details tell me that the main idea of the section is that people all across the country were scared and wanted to know what was happening.*

---

4. A ***locale*** (loh KAL) is the place of an event.
5. A ***massacre*** (MAS uh kur) is a bloody killing of many people or animals.
6. ***Verged*** (vurjd) ***on*** means "was close to or on the border of."

PHONE BOARDS DELUGED

Minneapolis and St. Paul police switchboards were deluged[7] with calls from frightened people.

In Atlanta there was worry in some quarters[8] that "the end of the world" had arrived.

It finally got so bad in New Jersey that the State police put reassuring messages on the state teletype[9] instructing their officers what it was all about.

And all this despite the fact that the radio play was interrupted four times by the announcement: "This is purely a fictional play."

The Times-Dispatch of Richmond, Va., reported some of their telephone calls came from people who said they were "praying." [4]

The Kansas City bureau of the Associated Press received queries[10] on the "meteors" from Los Angeles, Salt Lake City, Beaumont, Texas, and St. Joseph, Mo.

One telephone informant said he had loaded all his children into his car, had filled it with gasoline and was going somewhere.

"Where is safe?" he wanted to know.

Residents of Jersey City, N.J., telephoned their police frantically, asking where they could get gas masks. In both Jersey City and Newark hundreds of citizens ran out into the streets. . . .

In Birmingham, Ala., people gathered in groups and prayed, and Memphis had its full quota[11] of weeping women calling in to learn the facts. [5]

SYSTEM'S STATEMENT

In later broadcasts tonight the Columbia system announced:

"For the listeners who tuned to Orson Welles's Mercury Theater of the Air, broadcast from 8 to 9 p.m. Eastern standard time, tonight and did not realize that the program was merely a radio adaptation of H.G. Wells's famous novel

UNIT 7 GENRE FOCUS

ACTIVE READING MODEL

[4] **Key Reading Skill**
Evaluating *Wait a minute! The radio play was interrupted four times by an announcement that it was all made up. People couldn't have been paying much attention. I'm sure that I would have noticed and understood what was going on.*

[5] **Key Literary Element**
Narrator *This is a newspaper article. The author of the article is the person telling the story to the reader.*

---

7. **Deluged** (DEL yoojd) is another way of saying overwhelmed or swamped.
8. Here, **quarters** means "areas."
9. A **teletype** was a machine used to send and receive messages from far away before the Internet and e-mail existed.
10. **Queries** (KWEER eez) are questions.
11. A **quota** (KWOH tuh) is the part of a total amount that is expected from a group.

Genre Focus: Historical Fiction and Nonfiction   779

'The War of the Worlds,' we are repeating the fact, made four times on the program that the entire content of the play was entirely fictitious."

The Columbia System also issued a formal statement which said in part:

"Naturally it was neither Columbia nor the Mercury Theater's intent to mislead anyone, and when it became evident that part of the audience has been disturbed by the performance five announcements were made over the network later in the evening to reassure those listeners." . . . 6

The program which brought such unexpected developments opened with a regular announcement that another of the Mercury Theater of the Air's radio dramatizations—H.G. Wells's novel—was about to be presented.

The drama began with dance music, which was interrupted after a few seconds with a breath-taking announcement in news broadcast tempo.

"We interrupt our program of dance music to bring you a special bulletin from the Intercontinental Radio News," it said. "Twenty minutes before 8, Professor Farrell of the Mt. Jennings Observatory, Chicago, Ill., reports observing several explosions of incandescent[12] gas occurring at regular intervals on the planet Mars."

An object was reported "moving toward the Earth with enormous velocity,[13] like a jet of blue gas shot from a gun.

"We return you now to our New York studios," the drama continued.

After a few more bars of music, the scene shifted to an observatory at Princeton, N.J., for an interview with an astronomer about the phenomenon[14] just reported.

Illustration of a Man Encountering a Martian by Alvim Correa, 1906

Analyzing the Art Study this illustration from the H.G. Wells novel *War of the Worlds*. Based on the selection you are reading, what do you think is happening here? Explain.

ACTIVE READING MODEL

6 **Key Reading Skill**
Inferring Even though the author doesn't say it, I think the company does not want people to blame them.

---

12. *Incandescent* (in kun DES unt) means "glowing with great heat."
13. *Velocity* (vuh LOS uh tee) is speed or rate of motion.
14. A *phenomenon* (fuh NOM uh nun) is an unusual event.

After some routine astronomical questions, the "announcer" in the drama asked the scientist about the possibility of life on Mars. The actor replied the chances were a thousand to one against it, noting that Mars was 40,000,000 miles away.

INTENSE SHOCK

. . . The scene shifted back to the New York studios; whereupon there was an announcement that a meteorite had struck at "Grovers Mill, New Jersey," and that a mobile broadcasting unit was being rushed there for a description.

There was 30 seconds more of music, and the broadcast from the supposed scene started. The announcer described huge men, like octopuses, emerging from the meteorite. Just as they were starting to wield[15] a death-dealing "heat ray," his description broke off. **7**

The program returned to New York "because of circumstances beyond our control" and a few seconds later there came a "telephone bulletin" from the scene reporting that the bodies of more than 40 people had been found there. This program ended a few seconds later. **8**

---

15. To *wield* (weeld) means to hold or use a weapon or tool.

Illustration of a Martian Fighting Machine Attacking Humans by Alvim Correa, 1906.
Analyzing the Art What do you think is happening in *this* picture from the H.G. Wells novel?

Partner Talk You read how the *War of the Worlds* radio program created a great scare. With a partner, talk about what you might have done if you thought Martians had really come to this planet.

ACTIVE READING MODEL

7 Key Literary Element
Description The announcer described giant men that looked like octopuses coming out of the meteorite. That description must have terrified the people who were listening.

8 Key Literary Element
Sequence of Events/Time Order Let's see. What was the order of the program? It began with dance music that was interrupted by a special bulletin. After that, there was more music. Then more announcements interrupted the music until the program finally ended.

Study Central Visit www.glencoe.com and click on Study Central to review historical fiction and nonfiction.

READING WORKSHOP 1

Skills Focus

You will practice using these skills when you read the following selections:
- "The Gold Cadillac," p. 786
- "Nadia the Willful," p. 806

Reading
- Synthesizing

Literature
- Identifying symbols and analyzing their use in texts
- Explaining and analyzing plot sequence (exposition, rising action, climax, falling action, resolution)

Vocabulary
- Using base words and roots to understand word meanings
- Academic Vocabulary: *synthesize*

Writing/Grammar
- Identifying verbs

Objectives (pp. 782–783)
Reading Synthesize information

Skill Lesson
Synthesizing

Learn It!

What Is It? When you **synthesize**, you combine ideas to come up with something new. It may be a new understanding of an important idea or a new way of presenting information.

The ideas you bring together may come from different places. Many readers take ideas from their reading and combine them with what they already know to come to new understandings. For example, you might combine information from an article like "What Kids Say About Bullying" with your own experiences in order to come up with a plan for dealing with bullies.

CALVIN AND HOBBES © 1995 Watterson. Dist. By UNIVERSAL PRESS SYNDICATE. Reprinted with permission. All rights reserved.

Analyzing Cartoons
Calvin has read the library book. He has thought about a lot of the ideas in the book. What new idea does he come up with?

Academic Vocabulary

synthesize (SIN thuh syz) *v.* to bring together to create something new

782 UNIT 7

READING WORKSHOP 1 • Synthesizing

Why Is It Important? Synthesizing helps you move to a higher level of thinking. You go beyond remembering what you've learned from someone else to creating something new of your own. You might create your own ending to a story. You might develop your own position on an issue. You might think of a new way you can use information or a new idea.

How Do I Do It? Start by thinking about the ideas or events in a selection. Then, take a step beyond what you've learned. Ask yourself:

- Do I see something more than the main ideas here? Do I imagine the events developing in a different way?
- What can I create with what I know? How can I use this information?

Here's what Michelle thought about while reading "Aunt Millicent." She combined ideas from the story with her own experience.

Literature Online

Study Central Visit www.glencoe.com and click on Study Central to review synthesizing.

> Mrs. Nutbeam sighed. "Listen, Jamie, perhaps the time has come to own up that Aunt Millicent is not real."
>
> "We can't do that!" wailed Jamie. "Everyone would think we're looney . . . and that Grandma's absolutely bonkers, knitting socks for an aunt who isn't there."

I thought about Jamie's problem. He had a lot of fun making up stories about an imaginary Aunt Millicent, but the situation got out of hand when the whole town got involved. I also thought about "The Great Radio Scare," the account of another made-up story that caused problems when people believed it was real. After thinking about these stories and my own experiences, I decided that I don't want to ever let a story or joke go too far.

Practice It!
In your Learner's Notebook, write a paragraph about what you learned from "Aunt Millicent" and "The Great Radio Scare" that you can use in your everyday life.

Use It!
As you read "The Gold Cadillac" and "Nadia the Willful," look for ideas from the selections to combine with your own thoughts to create and reach new understandings.

READING WORKSHOP 1 • Synthesizing

Before You Read : The Gold Cadillac

Mildred D. Taylor

Meet the Author

Mildred D. Taylor was born in Mississippi in 1943. When she was very young, her family moved to Ohio, where she went to public school and to college. Taylor grew up to become a well-known writer. She won the Newbery Medal for *Roll of Thunder, Hear My Cry.* See page R6 of the Author Files for more on Mildred D. Taylor.

Author Search For more about Mildred D. Taylor, go to www.glencoe.com.

Objectives (pp. 784–801)
Reading Synthesize information
• Make connections from text to self
Literature Identify literary devices: symbolism
Vocabulary Identify word structure: roots and bases

Vocabulary Preview

features (FEE churz) *n.* parts or qualities **(p. 787)** *The dashboard in the new car had many special features.*

practical (PRAK tih kul) *adj.* having or showing good sense about everyday activities **(p. 787)** *The mother was practical, so she wanted to save money.*

caravan (KAIR uh van) *n.* a group of people or vehicles traveling together **(p. 791)** *The relatives got into their cars and set out for Mississippi in a caravan.*

Choose a Synonym Choose the best example for the word in **dark** type. Write your answer in your Learner's Notebook.

1. Which of the following is an example of a **caravan**?
   a. wagon train   b. foot race   c. cruise ship
2. Which of the following is an example of a car's **features**?
   a. road   b. driver   c. air bags
3. Which of the following is a **practical** place to save money?
   a. mall   b. museum   c. bank

English Language Coach

Base Words and Roots You run across a word you don't know, but you don't have a dictionary handy. And there aren't enough context clues to help you with the word's meaning. You're not clueless! Many words themselves contain clues to their meanings. A familiar base word or root can give information about the meaning of a word.

Take the word *drowsiness,* for example. *Drowsiness* contains the base word *drowsy.* If you know that *drowsy* means "sleepy," you might guess that *drowsiness* means "a sleepy feeling."

Word	Base Word	Meaning
drowsiness →	drowsy = sleepy →	a sleepy feeling

Take a Guess Find the base word you see in each word, and then use it to guess the word's meaning.

1. heroism
2. unnatural
3. irregularity

784 UNIT 7 What Can We Learn from Our Mistakes?

READING WORKSHOP 1 • Synthesizing

Skills Preview

Key Reading Skill: Synthesizing
"That's it! Now I get it!" It's like a light bulb goes on in your head. Suddenly everything comes together, and you understand. You're synthesizing. Here's how it happens.
- You identify the most important ideas.
- You see connections among the ideas.
- You come up with new ideas or understandings of your own.

Think-Pair-Share "Aha!" moments often happen while you're reading. Think of a time when you got a new idea from something you read. Share the experience with a partner.

Key Literary Element: Symbol
A **symbol** is an object, person, place, or experience that stands for something else. Symbols usually represent something abstract—that is, an idea or thought. For example, a dove is a symbol for peace. Writers use symbols in stories to add meaning. In "The Gold Cadillac," cars have special meanings.

Write to Learn Write the following questions in your Learner's Notebook. As you read, use them to think about the meaning of symbols in the selection.
- What does the gold Cadillac stand for?
- What do the Mercury cars represent?

Interactive Literary Elements Handbook
To review or learn more about the literary elements, go to www.glencoe.com.

Get Ready to Read

Connect to the Reading
When people go through something together, they often grow closer to one another. Think of an experience, such as a trip, school project, party, or crisis, that you've shared with your family or another group. Did the experience help you become closer? Explain.

Write to Learn In your Learner's Notebook, write a short description of your experience and how it helped you become closer to members of your family or another group.

Build Background
This story takes place in 1950. At that time, segregation was allowed in many Southern states.
- Segregation is the separation of groups of people according to some characteristic, such as race.
- In some cities, schools, hospitals, hotels, trains, buses, restaurants, and theaters were segregated.
- Some drinking fountains were labeled "White Only" or "Colored." Some city parks had signs reading "Whites Only."

Mildred Taylor's family moved north from Mississippi when she was just a baby. Every year they visited their relatives in the South. The family had to pack food for the trip, because as African Americans, they were not welcome in many Southern restaurants in those days.

Set Purposes for Reading
BIG Question Read the selection "The Gold Cadillac" to find out how a father and his family learn from their mistakes about what's really important.

Set Your Own Purpose What else would you like to learn from the selection to help you answer the Big Question? Write your own purpose on the "Gold Cadillac" part of the Workshop 1 Foldable.

Keep Moving
Use these skills as you read the following selection.

The Gold Cadillac 785

READING WORKSHOP 1

The Gold Cadillac

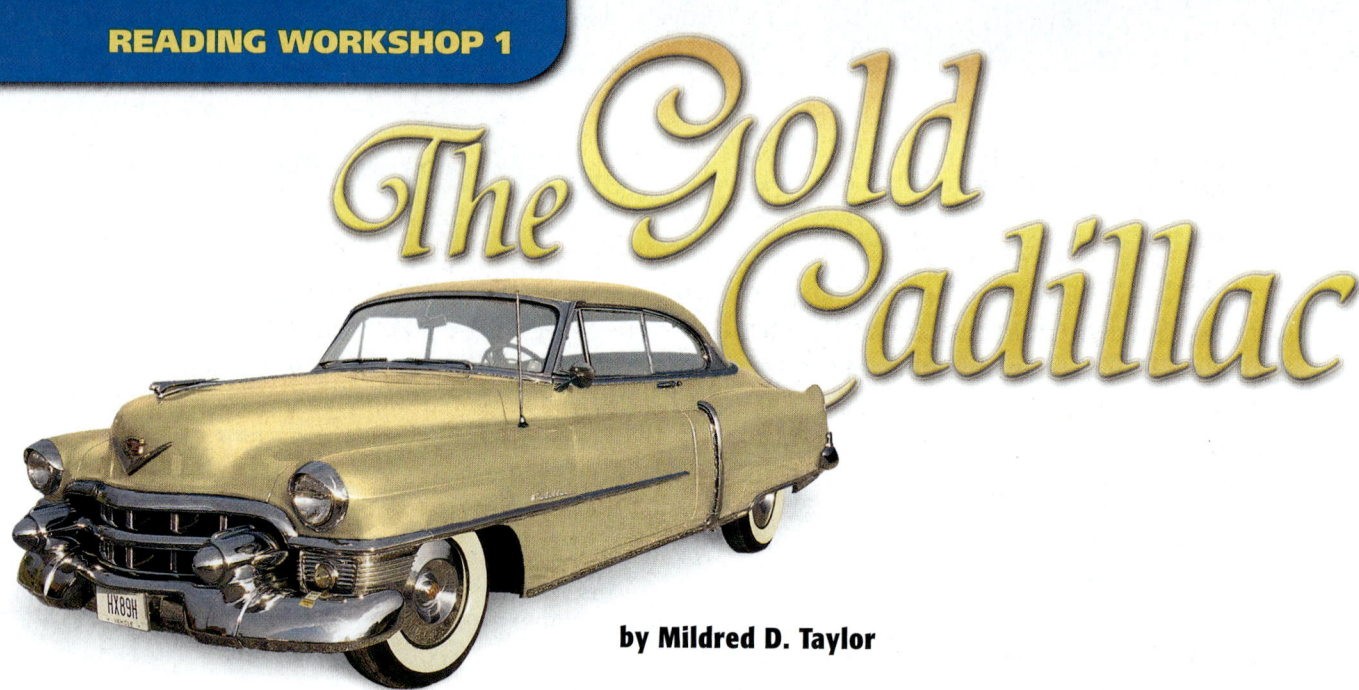

by Mildred D. Taylor

My sister and I were playing out on the front lawn when the gold Cadillac rolled up and my father stepped from behind the wheel. We ran to him, our eyes filled with wonder. "Daddy, whose Cadillac?" I asked.

And Wilma demanded, "Where's our Mercury?"

My father grinned. "Go get your mother and I'll tell you all about it."

"Is it ours?" I cried. "Daddy, is it ours?"

"Get your mother!" he laughed. "And tell her to hurry!" Wilma and I ran off to obey as Mr. Pondexter next door came from his house to see what this new Cadillac was all about. We threw open the front door, ran through the downstairs front parlor[1] and straight through the house to the kitchen where my mother was cooking and one of my aunts was helping her. "Come on, Mother-Dear!" we cried together. "Daddy say come on out and see this new car!"

"What?" said my mother, her face showing her surprise. "What're you talking about?"

"A Cadillac!" I cried. 1

"He said hurry up!" relayed Wilma.

And then we took off again, up the back stairs to the second floor of the duplex.[2] Running down the hall, we

---

1. A *parlor* (PAR lur) is a room used for entertaining guests.
2. *Duplex* (DOO pleks) means "double." A duplex apartment building has rooms on two floors, and a duplex house has two separate living spaces for two families.

Practice the Skills

1 Key Reading Skill

Synthesizing Why is the Cadillac so important? Think about what you've read and combine it with your knowledge of vocabulary and punctuation. Why did the sisters' eyes *fill with wonder*? Why did the author use an exclamation point after "A Cadillac"? Now, can you understand what a Cadillac means to them?

banged on all the apartment doors. My uncles and their wives stepped to the doors. It was good it was a Saturday morning. Everybody was home.

"We got us a Cadillac! We got us a Cadillac!" Wilma and I proclaimed in unison.[3] We had decided that the Cadillac had to be ours if our father was driving it and holding on to the keys. "Come on see!" Then we raced on, through the upstairs sunroom, down the front steps, through the downstairs sunroom, and out to the Cadillac. Mr. Pondexter was still there. Mr. LeRoy and Mr. Courtland from down the street were there too and all were admiring the Cadillac as my father stood proudly by, pointing out the various **features**.

"Brand-new 1950 Coupe deVille!"[4] I heard one of the men saying.

"Just off the showroom floor!" my father said. "I just couldn't resist it."

My sister and I eased up[5] to the car and peeked in. It was all gold inside. Gold leather seats. Gold carpeting. Gold dashboard. It was like no car we had owned before. It looked like a car for rich folks.

"Daddy, are we rich?" I asked. My father laughed. 2

"Daddy, it's ours, isn't it?" asked Wilma, who was older and more **practical** than I. She didn't intend to give her heart too quickly to something that wasn't hers.

"You like it?"

"Oh, Daddy, yes!"

He looked at me. "What 'bout you, 'lois?"[6]

"Yes, sir!"

My father laughed again. "Then I expect I can't much disappoint my girls, can I? It's ours all right!"

Wilma and I hugged our father with our joy. My uncles came from the house and my aunts, carrying their babies,

---

3. **Proclaimed** means "announced publicly", and **in unison** means "speaking the same words at the same time."
4. **Coupe deVille** (koop duh VIL) is a style of car.
5. When you **ease up to** something, you move slowly or carefully toward it.
6. Daddy is referring to Eloise by her nickname, 'lois.

Vocabulary

features (FEE churz) *n.* parts or qualities

practical (PRAK tih kul) *adj.* having or showing good sense about everyday activities

---

READING WORKSHOP 1

Practice the Skills

2 Key Literary Element

Symbol Symbols take many forms. They can be objects, people, places, or experiences. In this story, the gold Cadillac symbolizes, or stands for, different things to different people in the story. What do you think the Cadillac symbolizes to 'lois?

The Gold Cadillac 787

READING WORKSHOP 1

came out too. Everybody surrounded the car and owwed and ahhed. Nobody could believe it.

Then my mother came out.

Everybody stood back grinning as she approached the car. There was no smile on her face. We all waited for her to speak. She stared at the car, then looked at my father, standing there as proud as he could be. Finally she said, "You didn't buy this car, did you, Wilbert?" 3

"Gotta admit I did. Couldn't resist it."

"But . . . but what about our Mercury? It was perfectly good!"

"Don't you like the Cadillac, Dee?"

"That Mercury wasn't even a year old!"

My father nodded. "And I'm sure whoever buys it is going to get themselves a good car. But we've got ourselves a better one. Now stop frowning, honey, and let's take ourselves a ride in our brand-new Cadillac!"

My mother shook her head. "I've got food on the stove," she said and turning away walked back to the house.

There was an awkward silence and then my father said, "You know Dee never did much like surprises. Guess this here Cadillac was a bit too much for her. I best go smooth things out with her."

Everybody watched as he went after my mother. But when he came back, he was alone.

"Well, what she say?" asked one of my uncles.

My father shrugged and smiled. "Told me I bought this Cadillac alone, I could just ride in it alone."

Another uncle laughed. "Uh-oh! Guess she told you!"

"Oh, she'll come around," said one of my aunts. "Any woman would be proud to ride in this car."

"That's what I'm banking on,"7 said my father as he went around to the street side of the car and opened the door. "All right! Who's for a ride?"

"We are!" Wilma and I cried.

All three of my uncles and one of my aunts, still holding her baby, and Mr. Pondexter climbed in with us and we took off for the first ride in the gold Cadillac. It was a glorious ride and we drove all through the city of Toledo.8 We rode past

Practice the Skills

3 **Key Literary Element**

Symbol Remember that the way characters feel about an object can hint at what it symbolizes for them. The writer uses the words *proudly* and *proud* to describe how 'lois's father acts as he shows off the gold Cadillac. What do you think the Cadillac symbolizes to him?

---

7. If someone is **banking on** something, he or she is depending on it.
8. **Toledo** (tuh LEE doh) is a city in northwestern Ohio, near the state's border with Michigan. **Detroit** (dih TROYT) is north of Toledo, in Michigan.

READING WORKSHOP 1

Dolly and Rach, 1930. John Wesley Hardrick. Oil on board, 38 x 33 in. Collection of Georgia A. Hardrick Rhea.

Analyzing the Painting In what ways does the relationship between the girls in the painting reflect the relationship between Wilma and 'lois?

the church and past the school. We rode through Ottawa Hills where the rich folks lived and on into Walbridge Park and past the zoo, then along the Maumee River. But none us had had enough of the car so my father put the car on the road and we drove all the way to Detroit. We had plenty of family there and everybody was just as pleased as could be about the Cadillac. My father told our Detroit relatives that he was in the doghouse[9] with my mother about buying the Cadillac. My uncles told them she wouldn't ride in the car. All the Detroit family thought that was funny and everybody, including my father, laughed about it and said my mother would come around.[10] 4

Practice the Skills

4 **Key Literary Element**

Symbol From reading the footnote, you know that *in the doghouse* means "being in trouble." Why do you think being sent to a doghouse symbolizes being in trouble?

---

9. When you're *in the doghouse,* you're in trouble with someone.
10. *Come around* is a way of saying "give in to a point of view or action."

The Gold Cadillac **789**

READING WORKSHOP 1

It was early evening by the time we got back home, and I could see from my mother's face she had not come around. She was angry now not only about the car, but that we had been gone so long. I didn't understand that, since my father had called her as soon as we reached Detroit to let her know where we were. I had heard him myself. I didn't understand either why she did not like that fine Cadillac and thought she was being terribly **disagreeable** with my father. That night as she tucked Wilma and me in bed I told her that too. 5

"Is this your business?" she asked.

"Well, I just think you ought to be nice to Daddy. I think you ought to ride in that car with him! It'd sure make him happy."

"I think you ought to go to sleep," she said and turned out the light.

Later I heard her arguing with my father. "We're supposed to be saving for a house!" she said.

"We've already got a house!" said my father.

"But you said you wanted a house in a better neighborhood. I thought that's what we both said!"

"I haven't changed my mind."

"Well, you have a mighty funny way of saving for it, then. Your brothers are saving for houses of their own and you don't see them out buying new cars every year!"

"We'll still get the house, Dee. That's a promise!"

"Not with new Cadillacs we won't!" said my mother and then she said a very loud good night and all was quiet. 6 7

The next day was Sunday and everybody figured that my mother would be sure to give in and ride in the Cadillac. After all, the family always went to church together on Sunday. But she didn't give in. What was worse she wouldn't let Wilma and me ride in the Cadillac either. She took us each by the hand, walked past the Cadillac where my father stood waiting and headed on toward the church, three blocks away. I was really mad at her now. I had been looking forward to driving up to the church in that gold Cadillac and having everybody see.

On most Sunday afternoons during the summertime, my mother, my father, Wilma, and I would go for a ride. Sometimes we just rode around the city and visited friends

Practice the Skills

5 English Language Coach

Base Words and Roots Look at the word **disagreeable**. You probably know the meaning of the base word *agree*. The prefix *dis-* means "not" or "the opposite of." Take a guess about what *disagreeable* means.

6 Key Reading Skill

Synthesizing You have now read why the mother doesn't like the Cadillac. Combine it with your own experience or with other things you have read about wanting a better life for yourself or your family. Has your understanding of the mother changed? Why or why not?

7 Key Literary Element

Symbol The gold Cadillac symbolizes one thing for the father and something very different for the mother. What does the new car represent for the mother? What statement explains the symbolism, or meaning, of the gold Cadillac for the mother?

and family. Sometimes we made short trips over to Chicago or Peoria or Detroit to see relatives there or to Cleveland where we had relatives too, but we could also see the Cleveland Indians play. Sometimes we joined our aunts and uncles and drove in a **caravan** out to the park or to the beach. At the park or the beach Wilma and I would run and play. My mother and my aunts would spread a picnic and my father and my uncles would shine their cars.

But on this Sunday afternoon my mother refused to ride anywhere. She told Wilma and me that we could go. So we left her alone in the big, empty house, and the family cars, led by the gold Cadillac, headed for the park. For a while I played and had a good time, but then I stopped playing and went to sit with my father. Despite his laughter he seemed sad to me. I think he was missing my mother as much as I was. 8

Vocabulary

caravan (KAIR uh van) *n.* a group of people or vehicles traveling together

Practice the Skills

8 BIG Question
The gold Cadillac continues to create problems in 'lois's family. How has it changed the family's Sunday afternoons? What signs are there that 'lois's father has begun to think that buying the gold Cadillac was a mistake? Write your answers on your Foldable. Your response will help you complete the Unit Challenge later.

Toledo, Ohio, in the 1950s

The Gold Cadillac 791

READING WORKSHOP 1

Springtime (Portrait of Ella Mae Moore), 1933. John Wesley Hardrick. Oil on board, 48 x 32 in. Private Collection.

Analyzing the Painting Does this woman remind you of 'lois's mother? Why or why not?

That evening my father took my mother to dinner down at the corner café. They walked. Wilma and I stayed at the house chasing fireflies in the backyard. My aunts and uncles sat in the yard and on the porch, talking and laughing about the day and watching us. It was a soft summer's evening, the kind that came every day and was expected. The smell of charcoal and of barbecue drifting from up the block, the sound of laughter and music and talk drifting from yard to yard were all a part of it. Soon one of my uncles joined Wilma and me in our chase of fireflies and when my mother and father came home we were at it still. My mother and father watched us for awhile, while everybody else watched them to see if my father would take out the Cadillac and if my mother would slide in beside him to take a ride. But it soon became evident that the dinner had not changed my mother's mind. She still refused to ride in the Cadillac. I just couldn't understand her objection to it.

Though my mother didn't like the Cadillac, everybody else in the neighborhood certainly did. That meant quite a few folks too, since we lived on a very busy block. On one corner was a grocery store, a cleaner's, and a gas station. Across the street was a beauty shop and a fish market, and down the street was a bar, another grocery store, the Dixie Theater, the café, and a drugstore. There were always people strolling to or from one of these places and because our house was right in the middle of the block just about everybody had to pass our house and the gold Cadillac. Sometimes people took in[11] the Cadillac as they walked, their heads turning for a longer look as they passed. Then there were people who just outright[12] stopped and took a good look before continuing on their way. I was proud to say that car belonged to my family. I felt mighty important as people called to me as I ran down the street. "'Ey, 'lois! How's that Cadillac, girl? Riding fine?" I told my mother how much everybody liked that car. She was not impressed and made no comment.

Since just about everybody on the block knew everybody else, most folks knew that my mother wouldn't ride in the Cadillac. Because of that, my father took a lot of good-natured kidding from the men. My mother got kidded too as the women said if she didn't ride in that car, maybe some other woman would. And everybody laughed about it and began to bet on who would give in first, my mother or my father. But then my father said he was going to drive the car south into Mississippi to visit my grandparents and everybody stopped laughing.

My uncles stopped.
So did my aunts.
Everybody. **9**

---

11. **Took in** is another way of saying "became aware of" or "noticed."
12. **Outright** means "suddenly" or "completely."

Practice the Skills

9 Reviewing Skills

Activating Prior Knowledge
Think about what you learned in the Build Background section. Why do you think everyone stops laughing when the father says that he is driving the Cadillac to Mississippi?

READING WORKSHOP 1

"Look here, Wilbert," said one of my uncles, "it's too dangerous. It's like putting a loaded gun to your head."[13]

"I paid good money for that car," said my father. "That gives me a right to drive it where I please. Even down to Mississippi."

My uncles argued with him and tried to talk him out of driving the car south. So did my aunts and so did the neighbors, Mr. LeRoy, Mr. Courtland, and Mr. Pondexter. They said it was a dangerous thing, a mighty dangerous thing, for a black man to drive an expensive car into the rural[14] South.

"Not much those folks hate more'n to see a northern Negro coming down there in a fine car," said Mr. Pondexter. "They see those Ohio license plates, they'll figure you coming down uppity, trying to lord[15] your fine car over them!"

I listened, but I didn't understand. I didn't understand why they didn't want my father to drive that car south. It was his.

"Listen to Pondexter, Wilbert!" cried another uncle. "We might've fought a war to free people overseas, but we're not free here! Man, those white folks down south'll lynch[16] you soon's look at you. You know that!"

Wilma and I looked at each other. Neither one of us knew what *lynch* meant, but the word sent a shiver through us. We held each other's hand.

My father was silent, then he said: "All my life I've had to be **heedful** of what white folks thought. Well, I'm tired of that. I worked hard for everything I got. Got it honest, too. Now I got that Cadillac because I liked it and because it meant something to me that somebody like me from Mississippi could go and buy it. It's my car, I paid for it, and I'm driving it south." [10] [11]

My mother, who had said nothing through all this, now stood. "Then the girls and I'll be going too," she said.

---

13. *It's like putting a loaded gun to your head* is a way of saying that you risk being killed.
14. **Rural** (RER ul) means "in the country, away from cities or towns."
15. When someone **lords** something over someone else, he or she behaves in a grand, overly proud way.
16. **Lynch** (linch) means "to murder, usually by hanging, through the action of a mob." Someone who is lynched does not get a lawful trial and often is put to death because of racial hatred.

Practice the Skills

[10] **English Language Coach**

Base Words and Roots What does **heedful** mean? You can figure that out if you know that *heed* means "pay attention." Now explain what 'lois's father means when he says that all his life he's had to be heedful of what white people thought.

[11] **Key Literary Element**

Symbol Has the information on this page changed what you think the Cadillac symbolizes for the father? Explain.

"No!" said my father.

My mother only looked at him and went off to the kitchen. **12**

My father shook his head. It seemed he didn't want us to go. My uncles looked at each other, then at my father. "You set on doing this, we'll all go," they said. "That way we can watch out for each other." My father took a moment and nodded. Then my aunts got up and went off to their kitchens too.

All the next day my aunts and my mother cooked and the house was filled with delicious smells. They fried chicken and baked hams and cakes and sweet potato pies and mixed potato salad. They filled jugs with water and punch and coffee. Then they packed everything in huge picnic baskets along with bread and boiled eggs, oranges and apples, plates and napkins, spoons and forks and cups. They placed all that food on the back seats of the cars. It was like a grand, grand picnic we were going on, and Wilma and I were mighty excited. We could hardly wait to start.

My father, my mother, Wilma, and I got into the Cadillac. My uncles, my aunts, my cousins got into the Ford, the Buick, and the Chevrolet, and we rolled off in our caravan headed south. Though my mother was finally riding in the Cadillac, she had no praise for it. In fact, she said nothing about it at all. She still seemed upset and since she still seemed to feel the same about the car, I wondered why she had insisted upon making this trip with my father.

We left the city of Toledo behind, drove through Bowling Green and down through the Ohio countryside of farms and small towns, through Dayton and Cincinnati, and across the Ohio River into Kentucky. On the other side of the river my father stopped the car and looked back at Wilma and me and said, "Now from here on, whenever we stop and there're white people around, I don't want either one of you to say a word. *Not one word!* Your mother and I'll do all the talking. That understood?"

"Yes, sir," Wilma and I both said, though we didn't truly understand why.

My father nodded, looked at my mother and started the car again. We rolled on, down Highway 25 and through the bluegrass hills of Kentucky. Soon we began to see signs.

Practice the Skills

12 **Reviewing Skills**

Interpreting The mother has been unwilling to ride in the Cadillac, but now she decides that she and the girls will go on the trip to Mississippi. Up to this point, the father has wanted them all to ride in the car, but now he says, "No." What reasons do you think they might have for changing their minds?

READING WORKSHOP 1

Signs that read: WHITE ONLY, COLORED NOT ALLOWED. Hours later, we left the Bluegrass State and crossed into Tennessee. Now we saw even more of the signs saying: WHITE ONLY, COLORED NOT ALLOWED. We saw the signs above water fountains and in restaurant windows. We saw them in ice cream parlors and at hamburger stands. We saw them in front of hotels and motels, and on the restroom doors of filling stations. I didn't like the signs. I felt as if I were in a foreign land.

I couldn't understand why the signs were there and I asked my father what the signs meant. He said they meant we couldn't drink from the water fountains. He said they meant we couldn't stop to sleep in the motels. He said they meant we couldn't stop to eat in the restaurants. I looked at the grand picnic basket I had been enjoying so much. Now I understood why my mother had packed it. Suddenly the picnic did not seem so grand. **13**

Finally we reached Memphis. We got there at a bad time. Traffic was heavy and we got separated from the rest of the family. We tried to find them but it was no use. We had to go on alone. We reached the Mississippi state line and soon after we heard a police siren. A police car came up behind us. My father slowed the Cadillac, then stopped. Two white policemen got out of their car. They eyeballed[17] the Cadillac and told my father to get out.

---

17. When you **eyeball** something, you look at it closely in order to evaluate it.

Practice the Skills

13 **Key Reading Skill**

Synthesizing Think about the preparations 'lois's family made for their trip south. Combine that information with what 'lois and her sister see as they travel into the South. What new understanding do you and 'lois have of the grand picnic basket the family packed?

Analyzing the Photo What did 'lois do when she saw signs like the ones in this photo? How did she feel?

796 UNIT 7 What Can We Learn from Our Mistakes?

"Whose car is this, boy?"[18] they asked.

I saw anger in my father's eyes. "It's mine," he said.

"You're a liar," said one of the policemen. "You stole this car."

"Turn around, put your hands on top of that car and spread eagle,"[19] said the other policeman.

My father did as he was told. They searched him and I didn't understand why. I didn't understand either why they had called my father a liar and didn't believe that the Cadillac was his. I wanted to ask but I remembered my father's warning not to say a word and I obeyed that warning. **14**

The policemen told my father to get in the back of the police car. My father did. One policeman got back into the police car. The other policeman slid behind the wheel of our Cadillac. The police car started off. The Cadillac followed. Wilma and I looked at each other and at our mother. We didn't know what to think. We were scared.

The Cadillac followed the police car into a small town and stopped in front of the police station. The policeman stepped out of our Cadillac and took the keys. The other policeman took my father into the police station.

"Mother-Dear!" Wilma and I cried. "What're they going to do to our daddy? They going to hurt him?"

"He'll be all right," said my mother. "He'll be all right." But she didn't sound so sure of that. She seemed worried.

We waited. More than three hours we waited. Finally my father came out of the police station. We had lots of questions to ask him. He said the police had given him a ticket for speeding and locked him up. But then the judge had come. My father had paid the ticket and they had let him go. **15**

He started the Cadillac and drove slowly out of the town, below the speed limit. The police car followed us. People standing on steps and sitting on porches and in front of stores stared at us as we passed. Finally we were out of the town. The police car still followed. Dusk was falling. The night grew black and finally the police car turned around and left us.

---

18. The policeman calls 'lois's father **boy** to put him down.

19. To stand **spread eagle** is to stand with arms and legs spread wide. In this position, a person cannot surprise a police officer by pulling out a hidden weapon.

Practice the Skills

14 **Key Reading Skill**

Synthesizing Sometimes grown-up black men were called "boy" by white people. Use all the information you have learned in the story to answer these questions: Why would calling a grown man "boy" be insulting? Why might some white people have used this term? Why might the policeman have used it with the father?

15 **Key Reading Skill**

Synthesizing In your Learner's Notebook, write a description of what the father might have been thinking while he was locked up. Keep in mind everything you've learned about the South and the treatment that the father received from the policemen.

The Gold Cadillac

READING WORKSHOP 1

We drove and drove. But my father was tired now and my grandparents' farm was still far away. My father said he had to get some sleep and since my mother didn't drive, he pulled into a grove of trees at the side of the road and stopped.

"I'll keep watch," said my mother.

"Wake me if you see anybody," said my father.

"Just rest," said my mother.

So my father slept. But that bothered me. I needed him awake. I was afraid of the dark and of the woods and of whatever lurked there. My father was the one who kept us safe, he and my uncles. But already the police had taken my father away from us once today and my uncles were lost.

"Go to sleep, baby," said my mother. "Go to sleep."

But I was afraid to sleep until my father woke. I had to help my mother keep watch. I figured I had to help protect us too, in case the police came back and tried to take my father away again. There was a long, sharp knife in the picnic basket and I took hold of it, clutching it tightly in my hand. Ready to strike, I sat there in the back of the car, eyes wide, searching the **blackness** outside the Cadillac. Wilma, for a while, searched the night too, then she fell asleep. I didn't want to sleep, but soon I found I couldn't help myself as an unwelcome drowsiness came over me. I had an **uneasy** sleep and when I woke it was dawn and my father was gently shaking me. I woke with a start[20] and my hand went up, but the knife wasn't there. My mother had it. **16**

My father took my hand. "Why were you holding the knife, 'lois?" he asked.

I looked at him and at my mother. "I—I was scared," I said.

My father was thoughtful. "No need to be scared now, sugar," he said. "Daddy's here and so is Mother-Dear." Then after a glance at my mother, he got out of the car, walked to the road, looked down it one way, then the other. When he came back and started the motor, he turned the Cadillac north, not south.

"What're you doing?" asked my mother.

"Heading back to Memphis," said my father. "Cousin Halton's there. We'll leave the Cadillac and get his car. Driving this car any farther south with you and the girls in the car, it's just not worth the risk."

---

20. **With a start** is another way of saying "with a sudden movement that can't be controlled."

Practice the Skills

16 **English Language Coach**

Base Words and Roots Look at the underlined words in this paragraph. Write down the base words and their definitions. Then explain how the prefix and the suffix change the meaning of each base word.

And so that's what we did. Instead of driving through Mississippi in golden splendor,[21] we traveled its streets and roads and highways in Cousin Halton's solid, yet not so splendid, four-year-old Chevy. When we reached my grandparents' farm, my uncles and aunts were already there. Everybody was glad to see us. They had been worried. They asked about the Cadillac. My father told them what had happened, and they nodded and said he had done the best thing.

We stayed one week in Mississippi. During that week I often saw my father, looking deep in thought, walk off alone across the family land. I saw my mother watching him. One day I ran after my father, took his hand, and walked the land with him. I asked him all the questions that were on my mind. I asked him why the policemen had treated him the way they had and why people didn't want us to eat in the restaurants or drink from the water fountains or sleep in the hotels. I told him I just didn't understand all that.

21. *Splendor* (SPLEN dur) is great brightness or beauty.

Analyzing the Photo Use this photo to help you visualize the family's land in Mississippi. If you had serious things to think about, would this be a good place to walk and think? Explain.

My father looked at me and said that it all was a difficult thing to understand and he didn't really understand it himself. He said it all had to do with the fact that black people had once been forced to be slaves. He said it had to do with our skins being colored. He said it had to do with stupidity and ignorance. He said it had to do with the law, the law that said we could be treated like this here in the South. And for that matter, he added, any other place in these United States where folks thought the same as so many folks did here in the South. But he also said, "I'm hoping one day though we can drive that long road down here and there won't be any signs. I'm hoping one day the police won't stop us just because of the color of our skins and we're riding in a gold Cadillac with northern plates." **17**

When the week ended, we said a sad good-bye to my grandparents and all the Mississippi family and headed in a caravan back toward Memphis. In Memphis we returned Cousin Halton's car and got our Cadillac. Once we were home my father put the Cadillac in the garage and didn't drive it. I didn't hear my mother say any more about the Cadillac. I didn't hear my father speak of it either.

Some days passed and then on a bright Saturday afternoon while Wilma and I were playing in the backyard, I saw my father go into the garage. He opened the garage doors wide so the sunshine streamed in, and began to shine the Cadillac. I saw my mother at the kitchen window staring out across the yard at my father. For a long time, she stood there watching my father shine his car. Then she came out and crossed the yard to the garage and I heard her say, "Wilbert, you keep the car."

He looked at her as if he had not heard.

"You keep it," she repeated and turned and walked back to the house.

My father watched her until the back door had shut behind her. Then he went on shining the car and soon began to sing. About an hour later he got into the car and drove away. That evening when he came back he was walking. The Cadillac was nowhere in sight.

"Daddy, where's our new Cadillac?" I demanded to know. So did Wilma.

He smiled and put his hand on my head. "Sold it," he said as my mother came into the room.

"But how come?" I asked. "We poor now?"

Practice the Skills

17 **Reviewing Skills**

Drawing Conclusions What general statement can you make about African Americans in the United States in the 1950s, given what 'lois's father says in this paragraph?

"No, sugar. We've got more money towards our new house now and we're all together. I figure that makes us about the richest folks in the world." He smiled at my mother and she smiled too and came into his arms.

After that we drove around in an old 1930s Model A Ford my father had. He said he'd factory ordered us another Mercury, this time with my mother's approval. Despite that, most folks on the block figured we had fallen on²² hard times after such a splashy showing of good times and some folks even laughed at us as the Ford rattled around the city. I must admit that at first I was pretty much embarrassed to be riding around in that old Ford after the splendor of the Cadillac. But my father said to hold my head high. We and the family knew the truth. As fine as the Cadillac had been, he said, it had pulled us apart for awhile. Now, as ragged and noisy as that old Ford was, we all rode in it together and we were a family again. So I held my head high. 18

Still though, I thought often of that Cadillac. We had had the Cadillac only a little more than a month, but I wouldn't soon forget its splendor or how I'd felt riding around inside it. I wouldn't soon forget either the ride we had taken south in it. I wouldn't soon forget the signs, the policemen, or my fear. I would remember that ride and the gold Cadillac all my life. ○

---

22. *Fallen on* means "met with."

Practice the Skills

18 BIG Question

At the end of the story, does 'lois's mother think that she has made a mistake about the Cadillac? Does 'lois's father think that he made a mistake? Write your answers on your Foldable. Your response will help you complete the Unit Challenge later.

African American family, Detroit, Michigan, 1942.

READING WORKSHOP 1 • Synthesizing

After You Read — The Gold Cadillac

Answering the BIG Question

1. Why does 'lois's mother change her mind about the Cadillac? What does she learn through the family's experience with the Cadillac?

2. **Recall** Why is 'lois's mother angry about the gold Cadillac?
   TIP Think and Search

3. **Recall** What do 'lois's uncles, aunts, and neighbors think about driving the Cadillac to the South?
   TIP Think and Search

4. **Summarize** What happens when the family takes the Cadillac to Mississippi?
   TIP Think and Search

Critical Thinking

5. **Infer** When does 'lois's mother decide to ride in the car after all? Why does she make this decision?
   TIP Author and Me

6. **Infer** Why do you think 'lois's father sells the Cadillac?
   TIP Author and Me

7. **Interpret** How do you think the trip to Mississippi changes 'lois? How does it change her father?
   TIP Author and Me

8. **Evaluate** Would you have sold the Cadillac? Why or why not?
   TIP On My Own

Write About Your Reading

The girls' parents have different feelings about the Cadillac. Write two paragraphs, one for each parent, describing their different views of the car. Include the following in each paragraph:

- Tell how the parent feels about the car at the beginning of the story.
- Describe how the parent shows his or her feelings about the car.
- Explain how and why the parent's view changes after the trip to Mississippi.

Objectives (pp. 802–803)
Reading Synthesize information
Literature Identify literary devices: symbolism
Vocabulary Identify word structure: roots and bases
Writing Compare and contrast
Grammar Identify parts of speech: verbs

Skills Review

Key Reading Skill: Synthesizing

9. When you synthesize, you combine ideas to create something new. What new understanding did you gain about why people might take risks? Explain.

Key Literary Element: Symbol

10. Before the trip to Mississippi, 'lois's father says: "I got that Cadillac because I liked it and because it meant something to me that somebody like me from Mississippi could go and buy it. It's my car, I paid for it, and I'm driving it south." What does this say about what the car symbolizes for him?

11. At the beginning of the story, do you think 'lois's mother understands what the car symbolizes to 'lois's father? Explain.

12. Remember that the Cadillac is gold. What does this add to its symbolism? Explain.

Reviewing Skills: Drawing Conclusions

13. After reading this story, what conclusions can you draw about life in the South for African Americans in the 1950s?

Vocabulary Check

Write the vocabulary word that each clue describes.

features   practical   caravan

14. Driving in one might keep you from getting lost.
15. A new computer has many of these.
16. It means "realistic and sensible."
17. **Academic Vocabulary** Write a sentence using the word *synthesize* correctly.
18. **English Language Coach** The word *unison* contains the root *uni*. The root means *one* or *single*. Use the root to explain the meaning of *unison*. Use a dictionary if you need help.

Grammar Link: Finding the Verb

- Every sentence has a subject and a verb.
- Some verbs show action, or what the subject *does*.
   Their father *stepped* out of the new car.
   Wilma and 'lois *ran* to him.
- Other verbs tell what the subject *is* or *is like*.
   The new car *was* a gold Cadillac.
   The girls' mother *seemed* angry.
- The verb often directly follows the subject.
   The old Ford *rattled*.

Grammar Practice

Copy the sentences below. Circle the verb in each sentence.

19. Wilma and 'lois rode in the Cadillac with their father.
20. The girls went for a ride with their father.
21. Their other car was less than a year old.
22. At two o'clock, the caravan of cars rolled across the Ohio River.
23. The whole family drove south.
24. Two policemen stopped them in Mississippi.
25. Their mother looked worried.
26. People who were not white were not allowed in hotels in Mississippi.

Writing Application List the verbs in the paragraphs you wrote. Put a checkmark next to the verbs that directly follow their subjects.

Web Activities For eFlashcards, Selection Quick Checks, and other Web activities, go to www.glencoe.com.

READING WORKSHOP 1 • Synthesizing

Before You Read: Nadia the Willful

Meet the Author

Sue Alexander based the story "Nadia the Willful" on a problem in her own life. When her own brother died, her father did not want anyone to talk about him. Alexander says, "I knew my father was wrong, but I didn't know how to tell him so. So I did what I've always done when I've had a problem—I wrote a story." Alexander said she chose a different setting and characters for the story to make telling it less painful.

Author Search For more information about Sue Alexander, go to www.glencoe.com.

Objectives (pp. 804–811)
Reading Synthesize information
• Make connections from text to self
Literature Identify literary elements: plot
Vocabulary Identify word structure: roots and bases

Vocabulary Preview

utter (UT ur) *v.* to speak or say aloud **(p. 807)** *No one was allowed to utter Hamed's name.*

cease (sees) *v.* to stop **(p. 809)** *Nadia would not stop saying Hamed's name even after her mother told her to cease.*

banished (BAN isht) *v.* sent away, forced to be separate from a place or group **(p. 810)** *Tarik banished whoever said his son's name.*

pondered (PON durd) *v.* thought about **(p. 811)** *Nadia pondered what to say to her father.*

Choose a Synonym For each word in the **bold** type, choose the word that has nearly the same meaning.
utter   talk   total   sing   write
cease   buy   begin   fold   halt
banished welcomed   expend   separated   questioned
pondered stomped   ignored   considered   took

English Language Coach

Base Words and Roots Sometimes the best clue to a word's meaning is in the word itself. Look closely at a new word, and you might see a familiar base word. Or you might find a root whose meaning you know. A *root* is a **word part** that forms the base of a word. A *base word* is a **whole word** that is part of a larger word.

Table It Copy the table below into your Learner's Notebook. Put each word listed below next to its root and root meaning or next to its base word. The first two are done for you.

survive   illogical
telescope   replace
interrupt   nonexistent
variety   misbehave
spectator   distrust

Root	Base
viv = *live* survive	logic illogical
var = *different*	trust
spec = *to look at*	exist
rupt = *break*	behave
tele = *distant*	place

READING WORKSHOP 1 • Synthesizing

Skills Preview

Key Reading Skill: Synthesizing
When you synthesize information, you use many of the skills you have already learned. You connect, use your prior knowledge, clarify, and draw conclusions. The result is a new understanding about what you read and about life. It might sound hard, but don't worry! If you are an active reader and thinker, then you synthesize all the time when you read.

Literary Element: Plot
Plot is a story's events. Most plots center on a conflict, or problem, for one or more of the characters. Most plots also develop in five stages: exposition, rising action, climax, falling action, and resolution. The diagram shows the five stages in the plot, or story line.

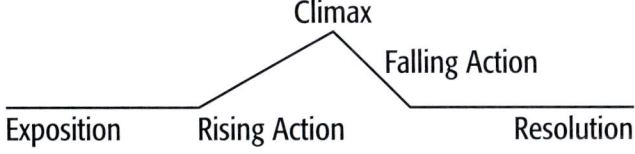

Use these tips to understand and identify the stages in the plot.

- The exposition introduces the characters, setting, and conflict of the story.
  Who are the main characters? Where and when does the story take place? What is the conflict?

- The rising action adds complications to the conflict.
  How does the conflict develop?

- The climax is the point of greatest interest or suspense.
  What is the highest point of the story?

- The falling action is the logical result of the climax.
  What happens after the climax?

- The resolution presents the final outcome.
  How is the conflict resolved? How does the story end?

What's the Plot? Copy the diagram into your Learner's Notebook. Use two side-by-side pages to make it as large as possible. Write your answers to the questions about stages in the plot on the diagram as you read.

Get Ready to Read

Connect to the Reading
People—even friends and family members—disagree at times. Have you ever had a conflict with a friend or family member? What was it about? How did it end?

Write to Learn In your Learner's Notebook, write about a time you came into conflict with someone else. Describe what you both said and how the conflict was resolved.

Build Background
Sue Alexander chose the Bedouin and the desert to be the characters and setting for this story.

- The Bedouin are people of the Middle East. They speak Arabic.
- The Bedouins used to be nomads, which means they moved from place to place in the deserts of Saudi Arabia, Iraq, Syria, Jordan, and Sudan. They traveled by camel and were sheep and goat herders. Today, most Bedouins live in settlements.

Set Purposes for Reading
BIG Question Read the selection "Nadia the Willful" to learn what a father and his family learned from a mistake.

Set Your Own Purpose What else would you like to learn from the selection to help you answer the Big Question? Write your own purpose on the "Nadia the Willful" part of the Workshop 1 Foldable.

Interactive Literary Elements Handbook
To review or learn more about the literary elements, go to www.glencoe.com.

Keep Moving
Use these skills as you read the following selection.

Nadia the Willful **805**

READING WORKSHOP 1

Nadia the Willful

by Sue Alexander

In the land of the drifting sands where the Bedouin move their tents to follow the fertile grasses, there lived a girl whose stubbornness and flashing temper caused her to be known throughout the desert as Nadia the **Willful**. ❶

Nadia's father, the sheik[1] Tarik, whose kindness and graciousness caused his name to be praised in every tent, did not know what to do with his willful daughter.

Only Hamed, the eldest of Nadia's six brothers and Tarik's favorite son, could calm Nadia's temper when it flashed. "Oh, angry one," he would say, "shall we see how long you can stay that way?" And he would laugh and tease and pull at her dark hair until she laughed back. Then she would follow Hamed wherever he led. ❷

One day before dawn, Hamed mounted his father's great white stallion and rode to the west to seek new grazing ground for the sheep. Nadia stood with her father at the edge of the oasis and watched him go.

Hamed did not return.

Nadia rode behind her father as he traveled across the desert from oasis to oasis, seeking Hamed.

---

1. The head of a family and of tribes and other groups among the Bedouin is called a *sheik* (sheek).

Practice the Skills

❶ English Language Coach

Base Words and Roots *Willful* is going to be an important word in the story. It contains the base word *will*, which means "determination" or "firmness of purpose." Think about what it means to say that someone is "full" of will. Then use your own words to tell what *willful* means.

❷ Literary Element

Plot The exposition, or first stage in the plot, gives the reader important background information. It tells the setting and main characters. Add the setting and character information to the exposition part of your plot chart.

Shepherds told them of seeing a great white stallion fleeing before the pillars of wind that stirred the sand. And they said that the horse carried no rider.

Passing merchants, their camels laden[2] with spices and sweets for the bazaar,[3] told of the emptiness of the desert they had crossed.

Tribesmen, strangers, everyone whom Tarik asked, sighed and gazed into the desert, saying, "Such is the will of Allah." 3

At last Tarik knew in his heart that his favorite son, Hamed, had been claimed, as other Bedouin before him, by the drifting sands. And he told Nadia what he knew—that Hamed was dead.

Nadia screamed and wept and stamped the sand, crying, "Not even Allah[4] will take Hamed from me!" until her father could bear no more and sternly bade her to silence.[5]

Nadia's grief knew no bounds.[6] She walked blindly through the oasis, neither seeing nor hearing those who would console[7] her. And Tarik was silent. For days he sat inside his tent, speaking not at all and barely tasting the meals set before him.

Then, on the seventh day, Tarik came out of his tent. He called all his people to him, and when they were assembled, he spoke. "From this day forward," he said, "let no one **utter** Hamed's name. Punishment shall be swift for those who would remind me of what I have lost."

Hamed's mother wept at the decree.[8] The people of the clan[9] looked at one another uneasily. All could see the hardness that had settled on the sheik's face and the coldness in his eyes, and so they said nothing. But they obeyed. 4

---

2. *Laden* (LAY dun) means "loaded down."
3. A *bazaar* (buh ZAR) is an outdoor market of small shops.
4. *Allah* (AW luh) is the name for God in the Islamic religion.
5. *Bade her to silence* is another way of saying "ordered her to keep quiet."
6. The expression *knew no bounds* means "had no limits."
7. *Console* (kun SOHL) means "to comfort."
8. A *decree* (dih KREE) is an official order or decision.
9. A *clan* is a group of related families.

Vocabulary

utter (UT ur) *v.* to speak or say aloud

Practice the Skills

3 Key Reading Skill

Synthesizing Try connecting the pieces of information in the story to explain what you think happened to Hamed.

4 Key Literary Element

Plot The exposition part of the plot is finished, a conflict has been introduced, and the rising action has begun. What event do you think started the rising action? What do you think will be the main conflict in the story? Add these notes to the rising action part of your plot chart.

READING WORKSHOP 1

Nadia, too, did as her father decreed, though each day held something to remind her of Hamed. As she passed her brothers at play, she remembered games Hamed had taught her. As she walked by the women weaving patches for the tents and heard them talking and laughing, she remembered tales Hamed had told her and how they had made her laugh. And as she watched the shepherds with their flock, she remembered the little black lamb Hamed had loved.

Each memory brought Hamed's name to Nadia's lips, but she stilled the sound. And each time that she did so, her unhappiness grew until, finally, she could no longer contain it. She wept and raged at anyone and anything that crossed her path. Soon everyone at the oasis fled at her approach. And she was more lonely than she had ever been before.

One day, as Nadia passed the place where her brothers were playing, she stopped to watch them. They were playing one of the games that Hamed had taught her. But they were playing it wrong.

Without thinking, Nadia called out to them. "That is not the way! Hamed said that first you jump this way and then you jump back!"

Her brothers stopped their game and looked around in fear. Had Tarik heard Nadia say Hamed's name? But the sheik was nowhere to be seen. 5

Practice the Skills

5 Literary Element

Plot During the *rising action*, new complications are added to the plot. What new complication has just happened?

Bedouins live in the deserts of the Middle East and North Africa.

"Teach us, Nadia, as our brother taught you," said her smallest brother.

And so she did. Then she told them of other games and how Hamed had taught her to play them. And as she spoke of Hamed, she felt an easing of the hurt within her. **6**

So she went on speaking of him.

She went to where the women sat at their loom and spoke of Hamed. She told them tales that Hamed had told her. And she told how he had made her laugh as he was telling them.

At first the women were afraid to listen to the willful girl and covered their ears, but after a time, they listened and laughed with her.

"Remember your father's promise of punishment!" Nadia's mother warned when she heard Nadia speaking of Hamed. "**Cease**, I implore you!" **7**

Nadia knew that her mother had reason to be afraid, for Tarik, in his grief and bitterness, had grown quick-tempered and sharp of tongue. But she did not know how to tell her mother that speaking of Hamed eased the pain she felt, and so she said only, "I will speak of my brother! I will!" And she ran away from the sound of her mother's voice.

She went to where the **shepherds** tended the flock and spoke of Hamed. The shepherds ran from her in fear and hid behind the sheep. But Nadia went on speaking. She told of Hamed's love for the little black lamb and how he had taught it to leap at his whistle. Soon the shepherds left off their hiding and came to listen. Then they told their own stories of Hamed and the little black lamb. **8**

The more Nadia spoke of Hamed, the clearer his face became in her mind. She could see his smile and the light in his eyes. She could hear his voice. And the clearer Hamed's voice and face became, the less Nadia hurt inside and the less her temper flashed. At last, she was filled with peace.

But her mother was still afraid for her willful daughter. Again and again she sought to quiet Nadia so that Tarik's bitterness

Vocabulary

cease (sees) *v.* to stop

Practice the Skills

6 **Key Reading Skill**

Synthesizing Nadia was in great pain when she could not talk about Hamed. She feels better when she does talk about him. Combine this information with anything else you have read or know from your own experience. Why does Nadia need to talk about Hamed?

7 **BIG Question**

Do you think Nadia's father made a mistake in not allowing anyone to talk about Hamed? Why or why not? Write your response on your Foldable. Your response will help you complete the Unit Challenge later.

8 **English Language Coach**

Base Words and Roots What is a **shepherd**? The word *shepherd* comes from a root word that means *sheep,* and from the base word *herd,* which means *gather.* Use that information to figure out the meaning of the word.

would not be turned against her. And again and again Nadia tossed her head and went on speaking of Hamed.

Soon, all who listened could see Hamed's face clearly before them.

One day, the youngest shepherd came to Nadia's tent, calling, "Come, Nadia! See Hamed's black lamb; it has grown so big and strong!"

But it was not Nadia who came out of the tent.

It was Tarik.

On the sheik's face was a look more fierce than that of a desert hawk, and when he spoke, his words were as sharp as a scimitar.

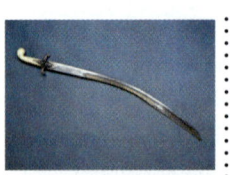

Visual Vocabulary
A *scimitar* (SIM uh tur) is a curved sword.

"I have forbidden my son's name to be said. And I promised punishment to whoever disobeyed my command. So shall it be. Before the sun sets and the moon casts its first shadow on the sand, you will be gone from this oasis—never to return."

"No!" cried Nadia, hearing her father's words.

"I have spoken!" roared the sheik. "It shall be done!"

Trembling, the shepherd went to gather his possessions.

And the rest of the clan looked at one another uneasily and muttered among themselves.

In the hours that followed, fear of being **banished** to the desert made everyone turn away from Nadia as she tried to tell them of Hamed and the things he had done and said.

And the less she was listened to, the less she was able to recall Hamed's face and voice. And the less she recalled, the more her temper raged within her, destroying the peace she had found. **9**

By evening, she could stand it no longer. She went to where her father sat, staring into the desert, and stood before him.

"You will not rob me of my brother Hamed!" she cried, stamping her foot. "I will not let you!"

Tarik looked at her, his eyes colder than the desert night. **10**

Vocabulary
banished (BAN isht) *v.* sent away, forced to be separate from a place or group

Practice the Skills

9 **Literary Element**

Plot Suspense builds as the conflict in the story continues to develop. How does the conflict become more complicated after the young shepherd is banished?

10 **Key Literary Element**

Plot The climax is the point of highest conflict in the story. Describe the climax of this story.

But before he could utter a word, Nadia spoke again. "Can you recall Hamed's face? Can you still hear his voice?"

Tarik started in surprise, and his answer seemed to come unbidden[10] to his lips. "No, I cannot! Day after day I have sat in this spot where I last saw Hamed, trying to remember the look, the sound, the happiness that was my beloved son—but I cannot."

And he wept.

Nadia's tone became gentle. "There is a way, honored father," she said. "Listen."

And she began to speak of Hamed. She told of walks she and Hamed had taken and of talks they had had. She told how he had taught her games, told her tales, and calmed her when she was angry. She told many things that she remembered, some happy and some sad.

And when she was done with the telling, she said gently, "Can you not recall him now, Father? Can you not see his face? Can you not hear his voice?"

Tarik nodded through his tears, and for the first time since Hamed had been gone, he smiled.

"Now you see," Nadia said, her tone more gentle than the softest of the desert breezes, "there is a way that Hamed can be with us still."

The sheik **pondered** what Nadia had said. After a long time, he spoke, and the sharpness was gone from his voice.

"Tell my people to come before me, Nadia," he said. "I have something to say to them."

When all were assembled, Tarik said, "From this day forward, let my daughter Nadia be known not as willful but as wise. And let her name be praised in every tent, for she has given me back my beloved son." **11**

And so it was. The shepherd returned to his flock, kindness and graciousness returned to the oasis, and Nadia's name was praised in every tent. And Hamed lived again—in the hearts of all who remembered him. **12**

---

10. *Unbidden* means "without being asked."

Vocabulary

pondered (PON durd) *v.* thought about

Practice the Skills

11 Literary Element

Plot The falling action is what happens after the climax. The resolution is the final outcome. In this story, what are the falling action and the resolution? Add these details to your plot chart.

12 BIG Question

What does Nadia's father learn from his mistake? Write your answer on your Foldable. Your response will help you complete the Unit Challenge later.

Bedouin clothing protects wearers from intense sunlight and heat.

Nadia the Willful 811

READING WORKSHOP 1 • Synthesizing

After You Read | Nadia the Willful

Answering the BIG Question

1. What new ideas did this selection give you about learning from mistakes?

2. **Recall** Why were Nadia and Hamed so close?
   TIP Right There

3. **Summarize** How does Nadia feel when she can't speak of Hamed after he is gone? How does she feel when she does speak of him?
   TIP Think and Search

Critical Thinking

4. **Visualize** Can you picture a scene in the desert from this story? What details help you visualize it?
   TIP Author and Me

5. **Respond** How did you feel toward Tarik when he said that Hamed's name could not be uttered?
   TIP Author and Me

6. **Compare and Contrast** How are Tarik and Nadia alike? How do they differ?
   TIP Author and Me

7. **Infer** Why do people break Tarik's rule against talking about Hamed?
   TIP Author and Me

8. **Evaluate** What is the best way to deal with losing someone you love?
   TIP On My Own

Talk About Your Reading

In the story, Nadia talks about Hamed to various people. One person Nadia doesn't talk to is her mother. With a partner, role play a dialogue between Nadia and her mother. Have Nadia describe how talking about Hamed helps her deal with her loss. Have Nadia's mother tell her how she feels.

Objectives (pp. 812–813)
Reading Synthesize information
Literature Identify literary elements: plot
Vocabulary Identify word structure: roots and bases
Grammar Identify parts of speech: verbs

Skills Review

Key Reading Skill: Synthesizing

9. Answer the following questions:
   - What is the most important event or idea to understand in this selection?
   - How does it relate to your own life?

Literary Element: Plot

10. The falling action shows what happens to characters after the climax. What happens as a result of the climax in this story?
11. How is the conflict between Nadia and her father resolved?

Vocabulary Check

Choose the correct word to fill the blank in each sentence.

12. It was forbidden to ___ Hamed's name.
    utter
    cease
13. When Nadia spoke of Hamed, her mother told her to ___.
    utter
    cease
14. Anyone who mentioned Hamid would be ___.
    banished
    pondered
15. Tarik ___ Nadia's words.
    banished
    pondered

16. **Academic Vocabulary** In which of the following sentences is the word *synthesize* used correctly?
    - When I write an essay, I *synthesize* all that I read on the subject and draw my own conclusions.
    - When I go shopping, I *synthesize* all the groceries into the shopping cart.

17. **English Language Coach** *Willpower* and *willingness* both contain the base word *will*. Use the words *willpower* and *willingness* correctly in sentences.

Grammar Link: Finding the Verb

- Words sometimes come between the subject and the verb.

  Subject   Verb
  Nadia's *memories* of Hamed *were* strong.
  The *merchants* in the bazaar *knew* nothing.

- The verb sometimes comes before its subject.
  There *was* a girl with a flashing temper.
  Out of the tent *came* Tarik.
  Try to recall Hamed's face.

- Sometimes the verb or verb phrase stands alone. The word *you* is understood to be the subject.
  (You) *Tell* us about Hamed.
  (You) *Do* not *say* his name.

Grammar Practice

Copy the sentences below. Circle the verb or verb phrase in each sentence.

18. Across the sands galloped a white stallion.
19. Here is the sheik.
20. Speak of Hamed.
21. Do you miss him?

Web Activities For eFlashcards, Selection Quick Checks, and other Web activities, go to www.glencoe.com.

WRITING WORKSHOP PART 1

Personal Narrative
Prewriting and Drafting

ASSIGNMENT Write a personal narrative

Purpose: Write a narrative about a time you made a mistake

Audience: You, your teacher, and classmates

Writing Rubric

As you work through this assignment, you should

- share a personal experience
- include important details
- write an essay that has a beginning, middle, and end
- use chronological time order
- use correct subject-verb agreement

See page 868 in Part 2 for a model of a personal narrative.

Objectives (pp. 814–817)
Writing Use the writing process: personal narrative, prewrite, draft • Use text structure: chronological order • Use elements of writing: voice
Grammar Use correct subject and verb agreement

In this Writing Workshop, you will write a personal narrative to help you answer the Unit 7 Big Question: What can we learn from our mistakes?

What Is It?

A personal narrative is a true story about a memorable event in your life. The event may be really big (traveling to a foreign country, meeting the president) or fairly ordinary (dinner at your grandparents' house, going to the mall). The most important thing about this personal narrative is that the writer (you) learned a lesson worth sharing.

Your assignment is to write a personal narrative about a time you made a mistake.

Prewriting
Get Ready to Write

Everybody makes mistakes now and then. Mistakes are important because they teach lessons that you can't learn in a book or a classroom. When you make a mistake, it is up to you to fix it, or else you have to live with the consequences.

Gather Ideas

Have you ever said something that you wish you could take back?
Have you ever made a decision that turned out to be a bad one?
Have you ever accidentally hurt someone's feelings?
Have you ever done something wrong that wasn't on purpose?

If you answered yes to any of these questions, then you have a topic for your personal narrative. In small groups, discuss the mistake that you are going to write about. Tell your group members:

- The mistake you made
- Who was involved
- The result of your mistake
- What you learned from your mistake

Tell your group members what you like about their stories. Tell them what parts you think they can leave out. Ask your group if your story is interesting and what details they want to hear more about. Write down the suggestions and points of your story that interested your group members. Make sure you include these points when you start your draft.

814 UNIT 7 What Can We Learn from Our Mistakes?

WRITING WORKSHOP PART 1

Make a Plan

Your narrative should be written in chronological order. That means you should write the events in the order they happened. Before you start writing, make a time line that includes the important events that led to your mistake and the events that resulted from the mistake. You can use the time line to help you write your draft.

Writing Models For models and other writing activities, go to www.glencoe.com.

> **Writing Tip**
>
> **Prewriting** When you make your time line, only include the events that are important to the story you are telling.

Drafting
Start Writing!

Your narrative should be divided into three sections: beginning, middle, and end.

Beginning The beginning of your narrative should describe the setting and introduce the people involved in your story.

It was my eleventh birthday, and I was sitting at the dining room table with all my friends. Well, actually, I was sitting there with all my friends and Jerry. Last June, Jerry showed he <u>wasn't</u> my friend when he had our whole class over to his swimming pool in the middle of the school day. He knew I couldn't swim . . .

Middle The middle of your narrative is when the main action happens.

Al started laughing about Jerry's silly new haircut. This was my party, and I knew that if I joined in, everybody else would too. So I shouted out, "Who cut your hair, Jerry, your baby sister?"

End The ending of your narrative brings the story to a close. You tell how the experience was resolved and what you learned from it.

Jerry said he was sorry and that he had forgotten that I couldn't swim. Then we both went back to my party. Next time one of my friends upsets me, I'll tell him why I'm angry instead of trying to get even.

> **Writing Tip**
>
> **Drafting** Start new paragraphs by skipping a line and indenting a space before you write more. Start a new paragraph when you get to the middle and end of your story or when a new character speaks.

WRITING WORKSHOP PART 1

Applying Good Writing Traits

Voice

Reading a personal narrative or autobiography is a good way to find out what a person is like. You can discover a writer's personality from the way he or she "talks" on paper.

What Is Voice?

Just as each person has his or her own unique speaking voice, a writer has a particular writing voice. It is a voice that clearly shows a writer's personality. The writer's personality comes through in word choices, tone, and sentence patterns he or she uses. Here's how two different people might write about the same subject.

Trees and Cans

Yowza!! Who would have thought the same stuff that we drink our sodas out of might change the game of baseball? But it's true! Aluminum bats send the old hardball at least twelve feet farther than the old wooden ones. Look out, outfield!

Ash versus Aluminum

The game of baseball is about to change. It looks as though the day of aluminum has arrived. Bats of that metal send the ball twelve feet farther than their more natural ancestors. All those who want the day of the Louisville Slugger to remain, say your prayers. There is little hope left for you now.

Why Is Voice Important in My Writing?

- Writing in your own voice helps you express your real thoughts, ideas, and feelings.
- Writing in your own voice is easier than trying to sound like someone else.
- Reading something written in your voice is more interesting to your audience. It shows there's a real person behind the writing.

How Do I Do It?

- Write words that you might use when you're talking.
- Don't try to write like someone else. Find your own voice.
- Think about what you're trying to say. Say it aloud. Then write it down.
- Let your feelings guide what you're trying to say about your topic.

Write to Learn Pick a subject that you feel strongly about and write a paragraph about it. Let your words flow. Don't worry about making mistakes; you can fix those later. With a partner, read aloud what you wrote and feel the rhythm of your words as you read. This is your voice. Your writing should show the "real" you. Then rewrite or change any words or sentences so that your voice is heard in your writing.

WRITING WORKSHOP PART 1

Grammar Link

Subject-Verb Agreement

What Are Subjects and Verbs?

The **subject** is the part of a sentence that is doing something or about which something is said. The **verb** is the part of a sentence that tells what the subject is doing.

- The subject and verb must agree in person and number.

  With a singular subject (**fire**), use the singular form of the verb (**burns**). With a plural, or more than one, subject (**fires**), use the plural form of the verb (**burn**).

  A **fire burns** in Chicago.
  Fire is the singular subject, so the singular form of the verb *burn* is used.

  Fires burn in different parts of the city.
  The word *fires* is the plural subject. Since there is more than one fire, the plural form of the verb *burn* is used.

Why Is Subject and Verb Agreement Important?

When the subject and verb of a sentence do not agree in person and number, a major rule of English grammar is broken. This confuses readers and distracts them from what they are reading.

How Do I Make Subjects and Verbs Agree?

- Find the subject and verb in a sentence.
  Joshua *eats* pizza for dinner.
- Make sure that the verb agrees with the subject in person and number.
  Joshua (singular) *eats* (singular) pizza for dinner.
  Joshua and Sadie (plural) *eat* (plural) pizza for dinner.

Grammar Practice

For each sentence, underline the subject. Circle the correct form of the verb so that the subject and verb agree.

1. Mr. Gray (write, writes) to Mr. Holden.
2. His arguments (is, are) persuasive.
3. The journalist (has, have) done his research.
4. He (hope, hopes) the Council will be persuaded.
5. The Council members must (build, builds) a bridge between Chicago's past and future.

Writing Application Review your draft. Make sure that all your subjects and verbs agree.

Looking Ahead

Part 2 of this Writing Workshop is coming up later. Save the writing you did so far, you'll need it to complete your final draft.

READING WORKSHOP 2

Skills Focus

You will practice using these skills when you read the following selections:
- "The Bracelet," p. 822
- "Too Soon a Woman," p. 832

Reading
- Identifying main idea and supporting details

Literature
- Explaining how the narrator affects a story

Vocabulary
- Understanding word structure: Latin roots

Writing/Grammar
- Identifying subject-verb agreement

Skill Lesson

Identifying Main Idea and Supporting Details

Learn It!

What Is It? The most important idea in a selection, passage, or paragraph is the **main idea.** The examples or details that support the main idea are called **supporting details.**

- Sometimes an author states the main idea. Other times, readers must figure out the main idea.
- The main idea often will be the first sentence of a paragraph. But a main idea may be anywhere, even in the last sentence.
- You can find main ideas and supporting details in almost any paragraph. However, a selection may also have one central main idea.

© Patrick McDonnell. Reprinted with permission of King Features Syndicate.

Analyzing Cartoons
What main idea is the cat trying to express? What details support that main idea?

Objectives (pp. 818–819)
Reading Identify main ideas and supporting details

818 UNIT 7

READING WORKSHOP 2 • Identifying Main Idea and Supporting Details

Why Is It Important? Finding main ideas and details helps you understand what the author is writing about and why it is important. Details will also help you form your own opinions and decide whether you agree with the author.

Study Central Visit www.glencoe.com and click on Study Central to review identifying main idea and supporting details.

How Do I Do It? Consider what you know about the author and the topic. Notice how the author organizes ideas. Then look for the one idea that all of the sentences in the paragraph, or all of the paragraphs in a selection, are about. To find the main idea, ask yourself:

- What is each sentence about?
- Is there one sentence that explains the whole passage or is more important than the others?
- If the main idea is not directly stated, what main idea do the supporting details point out?

Here's how one student found the main idea and supporting details in a paragraph from "Nadia the Willful."

> Nadia, too, did as her father decreed, though each day held something to remind her of Hamed. As she passed her brothers at play, she remembered games Hamed had taught her. As she walked by the women weaving patches for the tents and heard them talking and laughing, she remembered tales Hamed had told her and how they had made her laugh.

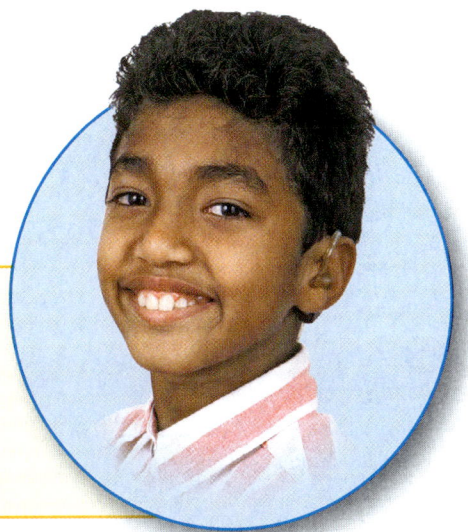

This paragraph is about things that remind Nadia of Hamed. The first sentence says that Nadia saw things that made her think about Hamed. That must be the main idea. The other sentences give details of what she saw and how they remind her of him.

Practice It!

Choose a paragraph from "The Gold Cadillac" on p. 786. Find and write the main idea. List at least two supporting details.

Use It!

Copy the questions from "How Do I Do It?" Answer the questions at the end of the selections you read to help you figure out what the main idea and supporting details are.

READING WORKSHOP 2 • **Identifying Main Idea and Supporting Details**

Before You Read : The Bracelet

Yoshiko Uchida

Meet the Author
Yoshiko Uchida was born in Alameda, California. Her parents came from Japan. She says of her writing, "I feel it's so important for Japanese American . . . children to be aware of their history and culture. . . . At the same time, I write for *all* children, and I try to write about values and feelings that are universal." See page R7 of the Author Files for more on Yoshiko Uchida.

Author Search For more about Yoshiko Uchida, go to www.glencoe.com.

Objectives (pp. 820–827)
Reading Identify main ideas and supporting details • Make connections from text to self
Literature Identify literary elements: narrator
Vocabulary Identify word structure: Latin roots

Vocabulary Preview

evacuated (ih VAK yoo ay tid) *v.* removed; moved out of; form of the verb *evacuate* **(p. 822)** *The government evacuated Japanese Americans from their homes on the West Coast.*

forsaken (for SAY kun) *adj.* abandoned **(p. 824)** *The town looked run down and forsaken.*

looming (LOO ming) *adj.* appearing in the distance **(p. 826)** *The girls saw the camp looming ahead as they drove down the highway.*

Write to Learn Answer each question about the vocabulary words.
1. What does a building look like after it has been **evacuated**?
2. What happens when a town looks **forsaken**?
3. What do mountains **looming** in the distance look like?

English Language Coach

Latin Roots A root carries the basic meaning of a word. Most roots are not complete words on their own—they need other word parts to form complete words. Many words in English come from Latin roots. One Latin root is *ject*, which means "to throw." Look at the following English words formed from the root *ject*.

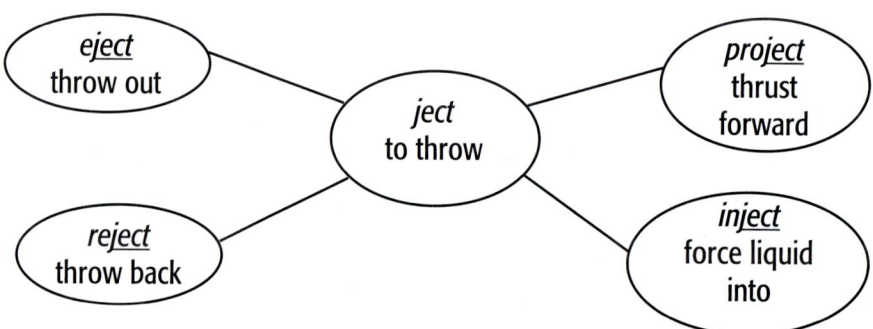

On Your Own List two examples each of words that use the following roots. Give a brief definition for each word, showing how it is related to the meaning of the root. Use a dictionary if you need help.
1. *port,* meaning "to carry"
2. *dict,* meaning "to say"

820 UNIT 7 What Can We Learn from Our Mistakes?

READING WORKSHOP 2 • Identifying Main Idea and Supporting Details

Skills Preview

Key Reading Skill: Identifying Main Idea and Supporting Details

The main idea is the most important idea in a paragraph or a selection. Other sentences in the paragraph or selection add information to or support the main idea.

Often a writer will directly state the main idea. Sometimes, though, a writer will not state the main idea, and it's up to you (the reader) to figure it out. To find the main idea, ask yourself: "What is the one idea that all of the sentences in the paragraph are about? What is the one idea that all of the paragraphs in the selection are about?"

Write to Learn Turn to the first page of "The Bracelet." Read the first five paragraphs. In one sentence, write the main idea. Next, list three supporting details.

Key Literary Element: Narrator

A **narrator** is the person or "voice" that tells a story. When a story uses words like *I* and *my,* the story is told from the **first-person point of view.** Readers see and experience what happens in the story through that first-person **narrator.**

As you read, ask yourself these questions to help you think about the narrator:

- *Who is telling the story?*
- *How would this story change if it were told from a different point of view?*
- *How does knowing the narrator's thoughts and feelings affect you as you read the story?*

Interactive Literary Elements Handbook
To review or learn more about the literary elements, go to www.glencoe.com.

Get Ready to Read

Connect to the Reading

Suppose that you have brown hair, and a new law states that all brown-haired people must go to special jails. How would you feel if this happened to you? How would you feel if your hair were a different color? As you read "The Bracelet," think about what it was like for the characters who were forced to leave home for reasons that made no sense to them.

Partner Talk With your partner, discuss your answers to the questions above.

Build Background

During World War II the United States was at war with Japan. "The Bracelet" is an account of how Japanese people living on the West Coast at that time were sent to live in internment camps, or relocation centers.

- Some U.S. leaders feared that Japanese Americans might spy on or damage military bases.
- In 1942 President Franklin D. Roosevelt gave the U.S. War Department the authority to take Japanese Americans from their homes and send them to internment (in TURN ment) camps. An *internment camp* is a place where people are forced to stay.
- About 110,000 Japanese Americans were forced to live in internment camps. Two-thirds of them were U.S. citizens.
- Years later, in 1988, the U.S. Congress apologized to all the Japanese Americans who had been interned in these camps.

Set Purposes for Reading

BIG Question As you read "The Bracelet," think about what we can learn from mistakes.

Set Your Own Purpose What else would you like to learn from the story to help you answer the Big Question? Write your own purpose on "The Bracelet" part of the Workshop 2 Foldable.

Keep Moving

Use these skills as you read the following selection.

The Bracelet 821

READING WORKSHOP 2

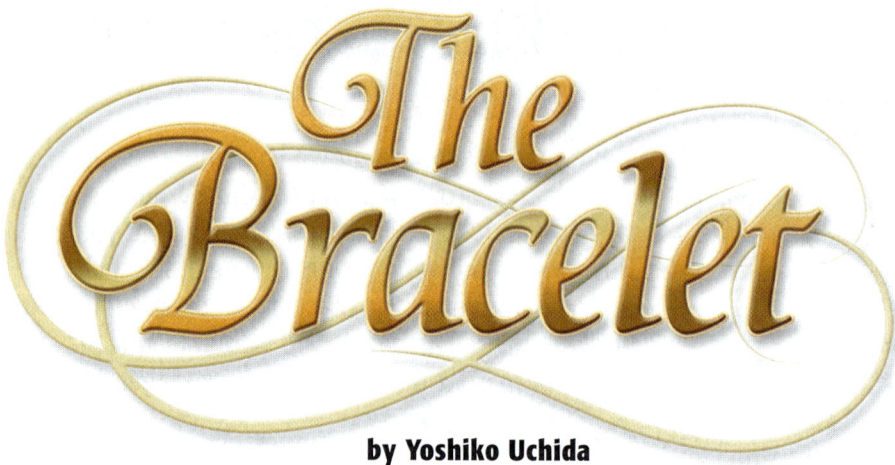

The Bracelet

by Yoshiko Uchida

"Mama, is it time to go?"

I hadn't planned to cry, but the tears came suddenly, and I wiped them away with the back of my hand. I didn't want my older sister to see me crying.

"It's almost time, Ruri," my mother said gently. Her face was filled with a kind of sadness I had never seen before.

I looked around at my empty room. The clothes that Mama always told me to hang up in the closet, the junk piled on my dresser, the old rag doll I could never bear to part with—they were all gone. There was nothing left in my room, and there was nothing left in the rest of the house. The rugs and furniture were gone, the pictures and drapes were down, and the closets and cupboards were empty. The house was like a gift box after the nice thing inside was gone: just a lot of nothingness. **1**

It was almost time to leave our home, but we weren't moving to a nicer house or to a new town. It was April 12, 1942. The United States and Japan were at war, and every Japanese person on the West Coast was being **evacuated** by the government to a concentration camp.[1] Mama, my sister Keiko, and I were being sent from our home, and out of Berkeley, and eventually out of California.

The doorbell rang, and I ran to answer it before my sister could. I thought maybe by some miracle a messenger from the government might be standing there, tall and proper and

---

1. A **concentration camp** is a place where political prisoners and prisoners of war are confined.

Practice the Skills

1 **Key Literary Element**

Narrator The narrator is the person who "speaks," or tells the story. This narrator has a certain point of view. What is the narrator's point of view? How do you know?

Vocabulary

evacuated (ih VAK yoo ay tid) *v.* removed; moved out of

buttoned into a uniform, come to tell us it was all a terrible mistake, that we wouldn't have to leave after all. Or maybe the messenger would have a **telegram** from Papa, who was interned[2] in a prisoner-of-war camp in Montana because he had worked for a Japanese business firm. **2 3**

The FBI had come to pick up Papa and hundreds of other Japanese community leaders on the very day that Japanese planes had bombed Pearl Harbor.[3] The government thought they were dangerous enemy aliens.[4] If it weren't so sad, it would have been funny. Papa could no more be dangerous than the mayor of our city, and he was every bit as loyal to the United States. He had lived here since 1917.

When I opened the door, it wasn't a messenger from anywhere. It was my best friend, Laurie Madison, from next door. She was holding a package wrapped up like a birthday present, but she wasn't wearing her party dress, and her face drooped like a wilted tulip.

"Hi," she said. "I came to say goodbye."

She thrust the present at me and told me it was something to take to camp. "It's a bracelet," she said before I could open the package. "Put it on so you won't have to pack it." She knew I didn't have one inch of space left in my suitcase. We had been instructed to take only what we could carry into camp, and Mama had told us that we could each take only two suitcases.

"Then how are we ever going to pack the dishes and blankets and sheets they've told us to bring with us?" Keiko worried.

"I don't really know," Mama said, and she simply began packing those big impossible things into an enormous duffel bag—along with umbrellas, boots, a kettle, hot plate, and flashlight.

"Who's going to carry that huge sack?" I asked.

But Mama didn't worry about things like that. "Someone will help us," she said. "Don't worry." So I didn't.

Laurie wanted me to open her package and put on the bracelet before she left. It was a thin gold chain with a heart dangling on it. She helped me put it on, and I told her I'd never take it off, ever. **4**

---

2. Someone who is **interned** is detained, confined, or imprisoned.
3. The Japanese bombed the U.S. naval base at **Pearl Harbor,** Hawaii, on December 7, 1941. This attack brought the United States into World War II.
4. **Aliens** are people who are not citizens of the country in which they live.

Practice the Skills

2 English Language Coach

Latin Roots Telegram is formed by combining the Latin root *gram*, which means "write," with *tele*, which means "far off." How are these meanings combined in the meaning of *telegram*?

3 Key Literary Element

Narrator How does the narrator's point-of-view make you feel about what is happening?

4 Key Reading Skill

Identifying Main Idea and Supporting Details What is the main idea of this paragraph? What details support that main idea?

"Well, goodbye, then," Laurie said awkwardly. "Come home soon."

"I will," I said, although I didn't know if I would ever get back to Berkeley again.

I watched Laurie go down the block, her long blond pigtails bouncing as she walked. I wondered who would be sitting in my desk at Lincoln Junior High now that I was gone. Laurie kept turning and waving, even walking backward for a while, until she got to the corner. I didn't want to watch anymore, and I slammed the door shut. 5

The next time the doorbell rang, it was Mrs. Simpson, our other neighbor. She was going to drive us to the Congregational Church, which was the Civil Control Station where all the Japanese of Berkeley were supposed to report.

It was time to go. "Come on, Ruri. Get your things," my sister called to me.

It was a warm day, but I put on a sweater and my coat so I wouldn't have to carry them, and I picked up my two suitcases. Each one had a tag with my name and our family number on it. Every Japanese family had to register and get a number. We were Family Number 13453.

Mama was taking one last look around our house. She was going from room to room, as though she were trying to take a mental picture of the house she had lived in for fifteen years, so she would never forget it.

I saw her take a long last look at the garden that Papa loved. The irises beside the fish pond were just beginning to bloom. If Papa had been home, he would have cut the first iris blossom and brought it inside to Mama. "This one is for you," he would have said. And Mama would have smiled and said, "Thank you, Papa San"5 and put it in her favorite cut-glass vase.

But the garden looked shabby and **forsaken** now that Papa was gone and Mama was too busy to take care of it. It looked the way I felt, sort of empty and lonely and abandoned.

Practice the Skills

5 **Key Literary Element**

Narrator Think about the narrator's descriptions of Laurie. The narrator's point of view does not allow you to read Laurie's mind, but you still get a feel for her thoughts and feelings. How do you think Laurie feels? How can you tell?

---

5. *San* is a term of respect added to Japanese names.

Vocabulary

forsaken (for SAY kun) *adj.* abandoned

READING WORKSHOP 2

When Mrs. Simpson took us to the Civil Control Station, I felt even worse. I was scared, and for a minute I thought I was going to lose my breakfast right in front of everybody. There must have been over a thousand Japanese people gathered at the church. Some were old and some were young. Some were talking and laughing, and some were crying. I guess everybody else was scared too. No one knew exactly what was going to happen to us. We just knew we were being taken to the Tanforan Racetracks,[6] which the army had turned into a camp for the Japanese. There were fourteen other camps like ours along the West Coast. **6**

What scared me most were the soldiers standing at the doorway of the church hall. They were carrying guns with mounted bayonets.[7] I wondered if they thought we would try to run away and whether they'd shoot us or come after us with their bayonets if we did.

A long line of buses waited to take us to camp. There were trucks, too, for our baggage. And Mama was right; some men were there to help us load our duffel bag. When it was time to board the buses, I sat with Keiko, and Mama sat behind us. The bus went down Grove Street and passed the small Japanese food store where Mama used to order her bean-curd cakes and pickled radish. The windows were all boarded up, but there was a sign still hanging on the door that read, "We are loyal Americans." **7**

---

6. **Tanforan Racetrack** was a famous racetrack near San Francisco. It opened in 1899 and burned down in 1964. People came to Tanforan to see horse races and car races.
7. **Bayonets** are long knives on the end of rifles.

Practice the Skills

6 Reviewing Skills

Clarifying Think about the things you might need to clarify in this paragraph: How can you find out what the Civil Control Station is? What is happening at the Tanforan Racetracks? If you're not sure about the answers, go back and read or look at the footnotes.

7 Key Reading Skill

Identifying Main Idea and Supporting Details Is the description of the Japanese food store a main idea or a minor detail? Explain.

Irises (detail), Edo Period. Ogata Korin. Colour on gilded paper, 150.9 x 338 cm. Nezu Museum, Tokyo, Japan.

The Bracelet 825

READING WORKSHOP 2

The crazy thing about the whole evacuation was that we were all loyal Americans. Most of us were citizens because we had been born here. But our parents, who had come from Japan, couldn't become citizens because there was a law that prevented any Asian from becoming a citizen. Now everybody with a Japanese face was being shipped off to concentration camps.

"It's stupid," Keiko muttered as we saw the racetrack **looming** up beside the highway. "If there were any Japanese spies around, they'd have gone back to Japan long ago."

"I'll say," I agreed. My sister was in high school and she ought to know, I thought.

When the bus turned onto Tanforan, there were more and more armed guards at the gate, and I saw barbed wire strung around the entire grounds. I felt as though I were going into a prison, but I hadn't done anything wrong.

We streamed off the buses and poured into a huge room, where doctors looked down our throats and peeled back our eyelids to see if we had any diseases. Then we were given our housing assignments. The man in charge gave Mama a slip of paper. We were in Barrack 16, Apartment 40.

"Mama!" I said. "We're going to live in an apartment!" The only apartment I had ever seen was the one my piano teacher lived in. It was in an enormous building in San Francisco, with an **elevator** and thick-carpeted hallways. I thought how wonderful it would be to have our own elevator. A house was all right, but an apartment seemed elegant and special. 8 9

We walked down the racetrack, looking for Barrack 16. Mr. Noma, a friend of Papa's, helped us carry our bags. I was so busy looking around I slipped and almost fell on the muddy track. Army barracks had been built everywhere, all around the racetrack and even in the center oval.

Mr. Noma pointed beyond the track toward the horse stables. "I think your barrack is out there."

He was right. We came to a long stable that had once housed the horses of Tanforan, and we climbed up the wide ramp. Each stall had a number painted on it, and when we got to 40, Mr. Noma pushed open the door.

"Well, here it is," he said, "Apartment 40."

Practice the Skills

8 English Language Coach

Latin Roots The word **elevator** comes from the Latin root *levare*, meaning "to raise." Think about how the root's meaning relates to an *elevator*.

9 Key Literary Element

Narrator When the narrator is a character in the story, readers see the action through that character's eyes. Do you think Ruri is right that her new home will be elegant and special? Explain.

Analyzing the Photo Based on what you've read, what do you think is happening in this photo?

Vocabulary

looming (LOO ming) *adj.* appearing in the distance

826 UNIT 7 What Can We Learn from Our Mistakes?

The stall was narrow and empty and dark. There were two small windows on each side of the door. Three folded army cots were on the dust-covered floor, and one light-bulb dangled from the ceiling. That was all. This was our apartment, and it still smelled of horses.

Mama looked at my sister and then at me. "It won't be so bad when we fix it up," she began. "I'll ask Mrs. Simpson to send me some material for curtains. I could make some cushions too, and . . . well . . ." She stopped. She couldn't think of anything more to say.

Mr. Noma said he'd go get some mattresses for us. "I'd better hurry before they're all gone." He rushed off. I think he wanted to leave so that he wouldn't have to see Mama cry. But he needn't have run off, because Mama didn't cry. She just went out to borrow a broom and began sweeping out the dust and dirt. "Will you girls set up the cots?" she asked.

It was only after we'd put up the last cot that I noticed my bracelet was gone. "I've lost Laurie's bracelet!" I screamed. "My bracelet's gone!"

We looked all over the stall and even down the ramp. I wanted to run back down the track and go over every inch of ground we'd walked on, but it was getting dark and Mama wouldn't let me.

I thought of what I'd promised Laurie. I wasn't ever going to take the bracelet off, not even when I went to take a shower. And now I had lost it on my very first day in camp. I wanted to cry. **10**

I kept looking for it all the time we were in Tanforan. I didn't stop looking until the day we were sent to another camp, called Topaz, in the middle of a desert in Utah. And then I gave up.

But Mama told me never mind. She said I didn't need a bracelet to remember Laurie, just as I didn't need anything to remember Pap or our home in Berkeley or all the people and things we loved and had left behind.

"Those are things we can carry in our hearts and take with us no matter where we are sent," she said.

And I guess she was right. I've never forgotten Laurie, even now. **11** ○

Analyzing the Photo How does this picture help you understand the author's description of Tanforan? Explain, using details from the text.

Practice the Skills

10 **Key Reading Skill**

Identifying Main Idea and Supporting Details What did the bracelet mean to Ruri when Laurie gave it to her? What details support your answer? How is the loss of the bracelet important in the story?

11 **BIG Question**

Does Ruri think that losing the bracelet means losing her friend? What does her mother's advice teach Ruri? Write your answers on your Foldable. Your response will help you complete the Unit Challenge later.

READING WORKSHOP 2 • Identifying Main Idea and Supporting Details

After You Read : The Bracelet

Answering the BIG Question

1. Name one mistake in "The Bracelet" that the world can learn from. Explain your answer.
2. **Summarize** Why was Ruri's father not with the family?
   TIP Think and Search
3. **Recall** What makes Ruri want to cry the first day she is in her new "apartment" at Tanforan?
   TIP Right There

Critical Thinking

4. **Interpret** Why do you think the people in the story went to the camps without a fight?
   TIP Author and Me
5. **Interpret** Why is the bracelet so important to Ruri?
   TIP Think and Search
6. **Evaluate** Do you agree or disagree with Ruri's mother that Ruri doesn't need the bracelet to help her remember Laurie? Explain.
   TIP On Your Own

Talk About Your Reading

This story takes place in 1942 when Franklin D. Roosevelt was president of the United States. What if Ruri had the chance to talk to President Roosevelt and share her story about the internment camp? With a partner, take turns role-playing Ruri's argument. Try to imagine how it would feel to lose your freedom. Use these questions to get started.

If you could talk to the president about the internment camps, what would you say to persuade him to shut down the camps?

- Think about ways the situation affected your community, your family, and your life; what should you tell him?
- How did you feel about leaving the life you knew?
- What examples from the story will you use to support your point-of-view?

Objectives (pp. 828–829)
Reading Identify main ideas and supporting details • Make connections from text to self
Literature Identify literary elements: narrator
Vocabulary Identify word structure: Latin roots
Grammar Identify parts of speech: subjects and verbs

828 UNIT 7   What Can We Learn from Our Mistakes?

Skills Review

Key Reading Skill: Identifying Main Idea and Supporting Details

7. What is the main idea in "The Bracelet?"

Key Literary Element: Narrator

8. **a)** Describe Ruri as a narrator. **b)** Is she believable? Explain. **c)** Can you relate to her? Explain.
9. How did the narrator's descriptions cause you to feel or respond to events in the story? What part of those descriptions made the biggest impression on you?

Reviewing Skills: Clarifying

10. Name a part of the story that you clarified. How did you do it?

Vocabulary Check

Write *True* or *False* for each sentence. If the answer is *false*, rewrite the statement to make it *true*. Be sure to use the vocabulary word.

11. If you have **evacuated**, you have stayed in place.
12. If you followed through with something, you have **forsaken** your goals.
13. A storm **looming** in the distance might mean a dark sky on the horizon.
14. **English Language Coach** The Latin root *vers* means "turn." How does this root relate to the words below? Write a definition for each word, showing how it is related to the meaning of the root. Use a dictionary if you need help.

    universe
    version
    conversation

Grammar Link: Subjects Separated from Verbs

When a prepositional phrase comes between a subject and the verb, the verb must agree with the subject, not the object of the preposition.

- Mentally remove the word or phrase from the sentence. Read the sentence without the prepositional phrase.

    Thousands of Italian Americans were arrested.

    Think: *Thousands were arrested.*

- Make sure that the verb agrees with the subject, not the noun closest to the verb.

    Incorrect: *A park on the islands contain a volcano.*

    The subject is *park*. *Islands* is the object of the preposition *on*.

    Correct: *A park on the islands contains a volcano.*

Grammar Practice

For each of the following sentences, write the verb that agrees with the subject.

15. Relocation camps in Arizona (was/were) in terrible condition.
16. The duffel bag with a kettle, a hot plate, and boots (was/were) heavy.
17. A friend of her parents (helps/help) them move into the horse stall.
18. The guard next to the towers (look/looks) angry
19. The flowers in the garden (is/are) blooming.
20. The stable with the cots (is/are) where we will live.

Web Activities For eFlashcards, Selection Quick Checks, and other Web activities, go to www.glencoe.com.

READING WORKSHOP 2 • Identifying Main Idea and Support Details

Before You Read : Too Soon a Woman

Dorothy M. Johnson

Meet the Author
Dorothy M. Johnson moved to Montana from Iowa when she was a child. The beautiful scenery and the exciting history of the Old West inspired her stories for both children and adults. An honorary member of the Blackfoot tribe, Johnson wrote vividly about Native Americans, cowboys, and outlaws.

Author Search For more information about Dorothy M. Johnson, go to www.glencoe.com.

Vocabulary Preview

skimpy (SKIM pee) *adj.* lacking in quantity; barely or not quite enough **(p. 832)** *The family's load was skimpy because they were almost out of food.*

hospitality (hos pih TAL uh tee) *n.* friendly treatment of guests **(p. 833)** *They showed hospitality toward the strangers and gave them food.*

grudging (GRUJ ing) *adj.* given resentfully or without wanting to **(p. 833)** *The father finally gives Mary a grudging nod hello.*

sedately (sih DAYT lee) *adv.* in a quiet, calm manner **(p. 837)** *Mary sedately accepted the father's thanks.*

Partner Talk Discuss the pronunciation and definition of each vocabulary word with a partner. Then use each word in a sentence to be sure you understand its definition.

English Language Coach

Latin Roots Look at this family of words based on the Latin root *flect* or *flex*, which means "to bend."

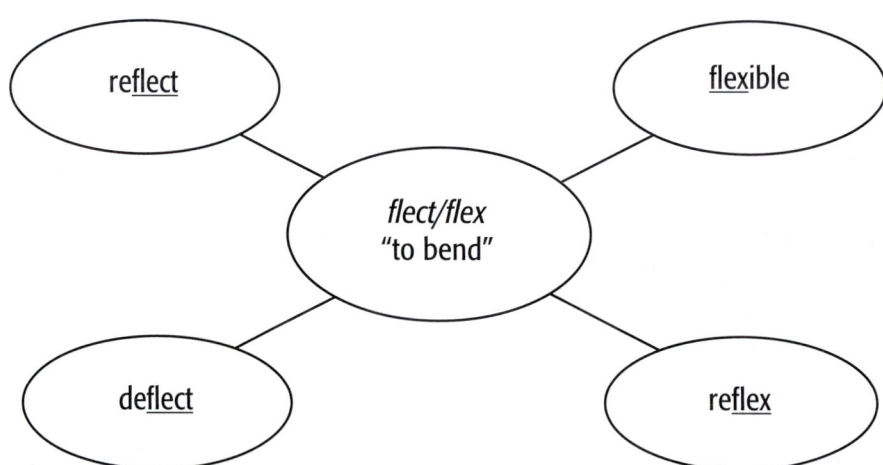

On Your Own Copy the words in the circles in your Learner's Notebook. Think about how the root relates to each word and write the meaning of each word. Use a dictionary if you need help.

Objectives (pp. 830–837)
Reading Identify main ideas and supporting details • Make connections from text to self
Literature Identify literary elements: narrator
Vocabulary Identify word structure: Latin roots

READING WORKSHOP 2 • Identifying Main Idea and Supporting Details

Skills Preview

Key Reading Skill: Identifying Main Idea and Supporting Details

Use these questions to help you find the **main idea** and **supporting details** in "Too Soon a Woman."

- What **main idea** do you get from each section of this story?
- What **details** support each main idea?
- What overall main idea do you get from the whole story?
- What are two details that support that main idea?

Write to Learn In your Learner's Notebook, draw a box, leaving room to write the main idea in it. Draw smaller boxes under the main idea box to be filled with supporting details. As you read "Too Soon a Woman," fill in this diagram with possible main ideas and supporting details.

Key Literary Element: Narrator

The narrator is the one telling the story. The narrator explains what happens from his or her point of view. Here are three points of view.

- **First-person:** The narrator is a character in the story.
- **Third-person:** The narrator is outside the story.
- **Omniscient:** The narrator is not in the story but knows all of the characters' thoughts and actions.

As you read, use these tips to help you learn about the story through the narrator.

- Identify the narrator.

  Does a character tell the story? If so, who is it?

- Think about why the author chose this character to tell the story.

  How would the story change if it were told from another point of view?

- Consider what the narrator tells you about events and other characters.

  How does knowing the narrator's thoughts and feelings affect you as you read the story?

Get Ready to Read

Connect to the Reading

What if you were starving in a life-and-death situation? You might eat things you wouldn't usually consider eating. Bugs? Strange plants? What risks would you be willing to take to survive?

Write to Learn In your Learner's Notebook, write what you would do to survive if you were starving in the wilderness.

Build Background

During the 1800s many families moved west. These trips were never easy, and settlers could expect to face many trials along the way.

- Pioneers, or settlers, traveled west on overland routes such as the Oregon Trail.
- Pioneers began traveling the Oregon Trail in the 1840s.
- Beginning in 1843, and for the next twenty-five years, more than half a million people traveled the Oregon Trail to the West Coast.

Set Purposes for Reading

BIG Question Read "Too Soon a Woman" to find out why it may never be too late to learn from your mistake in time to correct it.

Set Your Own Purpose What else would you like to learn from the short story to help you answer the Big Question? Write your own purpose on the "Too Soon a Woman" part of the Workshop 2 Foldable.

Interactive Literary Elements Handbook
To review or learn more about the literary elements, go to www.glencoe.com.

Keep Moving

Use these skills as you read the following selection.

Too Soon a Woman

by Dorothy M. Johnson

We left the home place behind, mile by slow mile, heading for the mountains, across the prairie where the wind blew forever.

At first there were four of us with the one-horse wagon and its **skimpy** load. Pa and I walked, because I was a big boy of eleven. My two little sisters romped and trotted until they got tired and had to be boosted up into the wagon bed. **1**

That was no covered Conestoga,[1] like Pa's folks came west in, but just an old farm wagon, drawn by one weary horse, creaking and rumbling westward to the mountains, toward the little woods town where Pa thought he had an old uncle who owned a little two-bit[2] sawmill.

Two weeks we had been moving when we picked up Mary, who had run away from somewhere that she wouldn't tell. Pa didn't want her along, but she stood up to him with no fear in her voice.

"I'd rather go with a family and look after the kids," she said, "but I ain't going back. If you won't take me, I'll travel with any wagon that will."

Pa scowled at her, and her wide blue eyes stared back.

"How old are you?" he demanded.

"Eighteen," she said. "There's teamsters[3] come this way sometimes. I'd rather go with you folks. But I won't go back."

"We're prid'near out of grub," my father told her. "We're clean out of money. I got all I can handle without taking

Practice the Skills

1 **Key Literary Element**

Narrator The narrator is the one who tells the story. A narrator may or may not be a character in the story. What do you know about the narrator so far? From what point of view is this story told?

---

1. A **Conestoga** (kahn ih STOW gah) is a covered wagon with a canvas top and large, wood wheels.
2. The expression **two-bit** means "practically worthless."
3. **Teamsters** are people who drove teams, or groups, of horses or oxen.

Vocabulary

skimpy (SKIM pee) *adj.* lacking in quantity; barely or not quite enough

anybody else." He turned away as if he hated the sight of her. "You'll have to walk," he said.

So she went along with us and looked after the little girls, but Pa wouldn't talk to her. **2**

On the prairie, the wind blew. But in the mountains, there was rain. When we stopped at little timber claims along the way, the homesteaders[4] said it had rained all summer. Crops among the blackened stumps were rotted and spoiled. There was no cheer anywhere and little **hospitality**. The people we talked to were past worrying. They were scared and desperate. **3** **4**

So was Pa. He traveled twice as far each day as the wagon. He ranged through the woods with his rifle, but he never saw game. He had been depending on venison,[5] but we never got any except as a **grudging** gift from the homesteaders.

He brought in a porcupine once; that was fat meat and good. Mary roasted it in chunks over the fire, half crying with the smoke. Pa and I rigged up the tarp sheet for a shelter to keep the rain from putting the fire clean out.

The porcupine was long gone, except for some of the tried-out[6] fat that Mary had saved, when we came to an old, empty cabin. Pa said we'd have to stop. The horse was wore out, couldn't pull anymore up those grades on the deep-rutted roads in the mountains.

At the cabin, at least there was shelter.

We had a few potatoes left and some corn meal. There was a creek that probably had fish in it, if a person could catch them. Pa tried it for half a day before he gave up. To this day I don't care for fishing. I remember my father's sunken eyes in his gaunt, grim face.

He took Mary and me outside the cabin to talk. Rain dripped on us from branches overhead.

---

4. **Homesteaders** are people who claimed and settled land.
5. **Venison** is deer meat.
6. **Tried-out** refers to the melted and hardened fat from the roasted porcupine.

Vocabulary

hospitality (hos pih TAL uh tee) *n.* friendly treatment of guests

grudging (GRUJ ing) *adj.* given resentfully or without wanting to

---

READING WORKSHOP 2

Practice the Skills

2 **Reviewing Skills**

Interpreting When you interpret, you use your own understanding of the world and what you've read in the text to decide what the events or ideas in a selection mean. Why do you think Pa decided to let Mary go with the family?

3 **Key Reading Skill**

Identifying Main Idea and Supporting Details What is the main idea of this paragraph? Is the main idea directly stated or do you have to think about it? Find two details that support the main idea.

4 **English Language Coach**

Latin Roots The word **hospitality** comes from the Latin root *hospes,* meaning "guest." The word *hospice* (a lodge for travelers) and the word *hospital* both have the same root. What might those words have in common with *hospitality*?

Too Soon a Woman 833

"I think I know where we are," he said. "I calculate[7] to get to old John's and back in about four days. There'll be grub in the town, and they'll let me have some whether old John's still there or not."

He looked at me. "You do like she tells you," he warned. It was the first time he had admitted Mary was on earth since we picked her up two weeks before.

"You're my pardner," he said to me, "but it might be she's got more brains. You mind what she says." 5

He burst out with bitterness, "There ain't anything good left in the world, or people to care if you live or die. But I'll get grub in the town and come back with it." 6

He took a deep breath and added, "If you get too all-fired hungry, butcher the horse. It'll be better than starvin'."

He kissed the little girls good-bye and plodded off through the woods with one blanket and the rifle.

The cabin was moldy and had no floor. We kept a fire going under a hole in the roof, so it was full of blinding smoke, but we had to keep the fire so as to dry out the wood.

The third night, we lost the horse. A bear scared him. We heard the racket, and Mary and I ran out, but we couldn't see anything in the pitch dark.

In gray daylight I went looking for him, and I must have walked fifteen miles. It seemed like I had to have that horse at the cabin when Pa came or he'd whip me. I got plumb[8] lost two or three times and thought maybe I was going to die there alone and nobody would ever know it, but I found the way back to the clearing.

That was the fourth day, and Pa didn't come. That was the day we ate up the last of the grub.

The fifth day, Mary went looking for the horse. My sisters whimpered, huddled in a quilt by the fire, because they were scared and hungry.

I never did get dried out, always having to bring in more damp wood and going out to yell to see if Mary would hear me and not get lost. But I couldn't cry like the little girls did, because I was a big boy, eleven years old.

It was near dark when there was an answer to my yelling, and Mary came into the clearing.

---

7. To **calculate** means to "figure out" or "estimate."
8. **Plumb** means "completely."

Practice the Skills

5 Key Literary Element

Narrator Think about what Pa tells Mary and the narrator. Think about the way the narrator shares conversations and events. What do you learn about the other characters through the narrator? How would the story be different if Pa or Mary were telling the story?

6 Reviewing Skills

Interpreting Think about what Pa means when he says, "There ain't anything good left in the world, or people to care if you live or die." Why do you think he says this? How do you feel about this statement?

Mary didn't have the horse—we never saw hide nor hair of that old horse again—but she was carrying something big and white that looked like a pumpkin with no color to it.

She didn't say anything, just looked around and saw Pa wasn't there yet, at the end of the fifth day.

"What's that thing?" my sister Elizabeth demanded.

"Mushroom," Mary answered. "I bet it hefts[9] ten pounds."

"What are you going to do with it now?" I sneered. "Play football here?"

"Eat it—maybe," she said, putting it in a corner. Her wet hair hung over her shoulders. She huddled by the fire.

My sister Sarah began to whimper again. "I'm hungry!" she kept saying.

"Mushrooms ain't good eating," I said. "They can kill you."

"Maybe," Mary answered. "Maybe they can. I don't set up to know all about everything, like some people."

"What's that mark on your shoulder?" I asked her. "You tore your dress on the brush."

"What do you think it is?" she said, her head bowed in the smoke.

"Looks like scars," I guessed.

" 'Tis scars. They whipped me. Now mind your own business. I want to think." **7**

Elizabeth whimpered, "Why don't Pa come back?"

"He's coming," Mary promised. "Can't come in the dark. Your pa'll take care of you soon's he can."

She got up and rummaged around in the grub box.

"Nothing there but empty dishes," I growled. "If there was anything, we'd know it."

Mary stood up. She was holding the can with the porcupine grease.

"I'm going to have something to eat," she said coolly. "You kids can't have any yet. And I don't want any squalling,[10] mind."

Analyzing the Art Describe what you see in this picture. Do you think this cabin is similar to the one the family is in? Explain.

Practice the Skills

7 🎯 **BIG Question**

Do you think that making the trip was a mistake for Mary? What must her choices have been? Keep in mind that she said she was "whipped." At this point does the trip seem like a mistake for the entire family? Write your answer on your Foldable.

---

9. In this sentence, something that **hefts** ten pounds weighs ten pounds. *Hefts* actually means "lifts up."
10. **Squalling** is the screaming cries of complaint Mary expects from the hungry little girls.

It was a cruel thing, what she did then. She sliced that big, solid mushroom and heated grease in a pan.

The smell of it brought the little girls out of their quilt, but she told them to go back in so fierce a voice that they obeyed. They cried to break your heart.

I didn't cry. I watched, hating her.

I endured the smell of the mushroom frying as long as I could. Then I said, "Give me some."

"Tomorrow," Mary answered. "Tomorrow, maybe. But not tonight." She turned to me with a sharp command: "Don't bother me! Just leave me be."

She knelt there by the fire and finished frying the slice of mushroom.

If I'd had Pa's rifle, I'd have been willing to kill her right then and there.

She didn't eat right away. She looked at the brown, fried slice for a while and said, "By tomorrow morning, I guess you can tell whether you want any."

The little girls stared at her as she ate. Sarah was chewing an old leather glove. 8

When Mary crawled into the quilts with them, they moved away as far as they could get.

I was so scared that my stomach heaved, empty as it was.

Mary didn't stay in the quilts long. She took a drink out of the water bucket and sat down by the fire and looked through the smoke at me.

She said in a low voice, "I don't know how it will be if it's poison. Just do the best you can with the girls. Because your pa will come back, you know. . . . You better go to bed, I'm going to sit up."

And so would you sit up. If it might be your last night on earth and the pain of death might seize you at any moment, you would sit up by the smoky fire, wide-awake, remembering whatever you had to remember, savoring life.

Practice the Skills

8 **Key Literary Element**

Narrator Think about the different points of view a narrator might have. Which type of narrator would know Mary's thoughts as she eats the mushroom? Explain.

READING WORKSHOP 2

We sat in silence after the girls had gone to sleep. Once I asked, "How long does it take?"

"I never heard," she answered. "Don't think about it."

I slept after a while, with my chin on my chest. Maybe Peter dozed that way at Gethsemane[11] as the Lord knelt praying.

Mary's moving around brought me wide-awake. The black of night was fading.

"I guess it's all right," Mary said. "I'd be able to tell by now, wouldn't I?"

I answered gruffly, "I don't know."

Mary stood in the doorway for a while, looking out at the dripping world as if she found it beautiful. Then she fried slices of the mushroom while the little girls danced with anxiety.

We feasted, we three, my sisters and I, until Mary ruled, "That'll hold you," and would not cook any more. She didn't touch any of the mushroom herself.

That was a strange day in the moldy cabin. Mary laughed and was gay; she told stories, and we played "Who's Got the Thimble?" with a pine cone.

In the afternoon we heard a shout, and my sisters screamed, and I ran ahead of them across the clearing.

The rain had stopped. My father came plunging out of the woods leading a packhorse—and well I remember the treasures of food in that pack.

He glanced at us anxiously as he tore at the ropes that bound the pack.

"Where's the other one?" he demanded.

Mary came out of the cabin then, walking **sedately**. As she came toward us, the sun began to shine.

My stepmother was a wonderful woman. 9

---

11. The New Testament of the Christian Bible says that Jesus, knowing his death was near, went to the Garden of **Gethsemane** (geth SE muh nee) to pray. Although **Peter** and the other disciples had come to pray with him, they all fell asleep.

Vocabulary

sedately (sih DAYT lee) *adv.* in a quiet, calm manner

Practice the Skills

9 BIG Question

The characters have learned from the challenges in this story. Choose one character, and explain what he or she has learned. Write your answer on your Foldable. Your response will help you complete the Unit Challenge later.

Too Soon a Woman **837**

READING WORKSHOP 2 • Identifying Main Idea and Supporting Details

After You Read : Too Soon a Woman

Answering the BIG Question

1. Who makes a mistake in "Too Soon a Woman"? Support your opinion with details from the story.
2. **Recall** What is the biggest problem that the family and Mary have to solve?
   TIP Think and Search
3. **Recall** What do you find out about Mary from the last sentence of the story?
   TIP Right There

Critical Thinking

4. **Infer** What can you infer about the mother of the family?
   TIP Author and Me
5. **Draw Conclusions** Why does Mary refuse to share the mushroom at first?
   TIP Author and Me
6. **Analyze** Why do think the author chose "Too Soon a Woman" for the title?
   TIP Author and Me

Write About Your Reading

Write a journal entry about the trip from Pa or Mary's point of view. In addition to telling about the experience, explain your feelings at the end of the story. Answer these questions as you write your entry:

- How did you feel throughout the ordeal?
- Why might you have made some of the decisions you made, and did you learn from any mistakes?
- What would you do differently? Why?

Objectives (pp. 838–839)
Reading Identify main ideas and supporting details • Make connections from text to self
Literature Identify literary elements: narrator
Vocabulary Identify word structure: Latin roots
Writing Respond to literature: journal entry
Grammar Use correct subject and verb agreement: compound subjects

838 UNIT 7   What Can We Learn from Our Mistakes?

Skills Review

Key Reading Skill: Identifying Main Idea and Supporting Details

7. Does the title of the story support the main idea, or is it the main idea? Explain, and give examples from the story.

Key Literary Element: Narrator

8. List three things you learn about the narrator from what he says about himself.
9. What else might readers learn from this story if it were told by an omniscient narrator?

Reviewing Skills: Interpreting

10. Interpret the title of the story. What does it mean? Give examples from the story to support your interpretation.

Vocabulary Check

In each blank, write the vocabulary word that has the opposite meaning of the underlined word.

skimpy   hospitality   grudging   sedately

11. We expected <u>stinginess</u>, but everyone showed their ___.
12. Some people react ___ to good news, while others jump up and down <u>excitedly</u>.
13. The portions that were served weren't <u>generous</u> at all; they were actually ___.
14. People want <u>willing</u> help when someone volunteers for a task, not ___ participation.
15. **English Language Coach** The Latin root *terra* means "land." How does this root relate to the words below? Write a definition for each word, showing how it is related to the meaning of the root. Use a dictionary if you need help.

    territory
    terrain
    terrestrial

Grammar Link: Agreement with Compounds

- A **compound subject** contains two or more subjects that have the same verb. Compound subjects may require a plural or singular verb, depending on how the subjects are joined.
- When *and* joins compound subjects, use the plural form of the verb.

  A <u>horse</u> and a <u>mule</u> <u>cross</u> the path in front of us.
  Horse and *mule* are the subjects; *cross* is the verb.

- When *or* or *nor* joins compound subjects, the verb should agree with the subject that is closest to the verb.

  Two <u>cars</u> or a <u>van</u> is needed.
  The verb *is* agrees with *van*, which is the subject closest to it.

Grammar Practice

Rewrite each sentence using the correct verb. Underline the compound subject in each sentence.

16. The bears and the raccoons (raid, raids) our campsite.
17. A boat or a canoe (work, works) well enough.
18. The experienced campers or the ranger (lead, leads) the hikes.
19. Neither the trees nor the building (block, blocks) our view.

Writing Application Look back at the journal entry you wrote. Make sure that your subjects and verbs agree in sentences with compound subjects.

Web Activities For eFlashcards, Selection Quick Checks, and other Web activities, go to www.glencoe.com.

READING WORKSHOP 3

Skills Focus

You will practice using these skills when you read the following selections:
- "President Cleveland, Where Are You?," p. 844
- "Nobody's Perfect," p. 860

Reading
- Evaluating

Literature
- Describing characters, images, and ideas

Vocabulary
- Understanding word meanings, using Greek roots
- Academic Vocabulary: *evaluate*

Writing/Grammar
- Identifying subjects and verbs
- Using correct subject-verb agreement

Objectives (pp. 840–841)
Reading Evaluate text

Skill Lesson

Evaluating

Learn It!

What Is It? When you **evaluate**, you make a judgment or form an opinion. If you've attended a movie, play, or concert, you've probably heard people comment on the performance. They're evaluating what they saw when they say, "The story was silly, but the special effects were awesome!"

- When you evaluate something, you make judgments about its strengths and weaknesses.
- An evaluation has to be supported with facts and examples to be convincing.
- As you read, you might evaluate a character, an author's style, or the value of the information in the text.

At the Slinky Quality Control Center.
© 1998 John McPherson/Dist. by Universal Press Syndicate

Analyzing Cartoons
The workers in this cartoon are trying to evaluate, or make a judgment about, the slinky's quality. When you evaluate something, you form an opinion about it. What judgments do you make when you read? What kinds of things influence your opinions?

Academic Vocabulary

evaluate (ih VAL yoo ayt) *v.* to find value; to judge or determine worth

READING WORKSHOP 3 • **Evaluating**

Why Is It Important? **Evaluating** helps you become a smart reader. For example, when you judge whether an author is qualified to write about a topic or whether the author's points make sense, you can avoid being misled by what you read. It will also help you decide what you like or don't like, and why.

Study Central Visit www.glencoe.com and click on Study Central to review evaluating.

How Do I Do It? As you read, ask yourself these questions:
- Do I understand this? Has the author been clear?
- Is this believable? Am I convinced?
- Is this information presented completely and accurately?
- What are the strengths and weaknesses?

Here's how one student evaluated a short passage from "The Gold Cadillac."

> The next day was Sunday and everybody figured that my mother would be sure to give in and ride in the Cadillac. . . . But she didn't give in. What was worse she wouldn't let Wilma and me ride in the Cadillac either. She took us each by the hand, walked past the Cadillac where my father stood waiting and headed on toward the church, three blocks away.

I think the mother is a really stubborn person. But at least she stands up for herself. She's a strong person, too. And she doesn't yell or scream at the dad. So it seems like she's not really a mean person either.

Practice It!

You can do more than just evaluate characters when you read. Use the tips from **How Do I Do It?** to evaluate the following description from "The Gold Cadillac." What do you think of this description? Did the author do a good job describing the Cadillac?

My sister and I eased up to the car and peeked in. It was all gold inside. Gold leather seats. Gold carpeting. Gold dashboard. It was like no car we had owned before. It looked like a car for rich folks.

Use It!

In your Learner's Notebook, write questions you can ask yourself to evaluate fiction. Consider questions about plot, conflict, and theme.

READING WORKSHOP 3 • Evaluating

Before You Read: President Cleveland, Where Are You?

Meet the Author
Like the main character in this story, Robert Cormier (kor MEER) was a boy during the 1930s. Cormier started writing in the seventh grade. But he was never published until his college art teacher sent one of his stories to a magazine. The $75 he was paid for that story started his professional career. See page R2 of the Author Files for more on Robert Cormier.

Author Search For more information about Robert Cormier, go to www.glencoe.com.

Objectives (pp. 842–855)
Reading Evaluate text • Make connections from text to self
Literature Identify literary elements: description, sensory details
Vocabulary Identify word structure: Greek roots

Vocabulary Preview

splurge (splurj) *v.* to spend more money than usual **(p. 847)** *It was only occasionally that the boys could splurge on extra cards.*

obsessed (ub SEST) *adj.* concentrating completely **(p. 850)** *The boys were obsessed with collecting the president cards.*

dismal (DIZ mul) *adj.* gloomy; miserable; cheerless **(p. 850)** *Life seemed dismal to the boys when cowboy cards were gone.*

dominant (DOM ih nunt) *adj.* having the greatest power or force; controlling **(p. 852)** *Card collecting was the dominant activity that summer.*

dejection (dih JEK shun) *n.* sadness; low spirits **(p. 853)** *Armand's face showed dejection, not hope, as he sat on the steps.*

blissfully (BLIS fuh lee) *adv.* in an extremely happy way; joyfully **(p. 854)** *Jerry went off blissfully to find the Grover Cleveland card.*

Write to Learn Write a brief paragraph about something you collect or would like to collect, such as trading cards or coins. Use at least three of the vocabulary words in your paragraph.

English Language Coach

Greek Roots The **root** of a word is its main part. Knowing the meaning of a word's root can help you figure out the meaning of the whole word. English contains many Greek roots, prefixes, and suffixes. Some of these word parts are called "combining forms" because they are so often used with other Greek parts. For example, any word with the root *meter* (which means "measure") has something to do with measurement. A *thermometer* measures your body temperature, for example.

This chart shows some common Greek roots or combining forms.

Root	Meaning	Example
bio	life	biography
geo	earth	geography
meter	measure	centimeter
graph	write/record	graphic
log/logy	word/study/speak	dialogue, biology

Partner Talk With a partner discuss what you think **geology** means. When you have decided upon a definition, check the meaning in a dictionary. Then write the word's meaning in your Learner's Notebook.

842 UNIT 7 What Can We Learn from Our Mistakes?

READING WORKSHOP 3 • Evaluating

Skills Preview

Key Reading Skill: Evaluating

As you read, think about the story and what makes it interesting. These questions will help you to evaluate what you read. Don't forget to support your opinions.

- What makes the plot believable or unbelievable?
- How does the setting add to the story?
- Which characters do you like or dislike?

Write to Learn In your Learner's Notebook, write an evaluation of a movie you've seen recently. You might evaluate the plot, setting, characters, or theme. Or you might evaluate how well the actors played the parts. You might even evaluate how well the camera person shot the movie. It's up to you! Whichever elements you choose to evaluate, be sure to back up your judgments with details from the movie.

Key Literary Element: Description

Descriptive writing brings experiences and events to life. Good descriptive writing helps readers see, hear, smell, taste, and feel details from the story. As you read, pay attention to the kinds of descriptive details the writer provides.

- Sensory details: *Which senses does the writer appeal to? What colors, shapes, sizes, and textures can you picture or feel?*
- Word choice: *What nouns, verbs, adjectives, and adverbs are especially lively?*
- Comparisons: *Which comparisons does the author make? Are the comparisons new and fresh, or have you heard them many times before?*

Interactive Literary Elements Handbook
To review or learn more about the literary elements, go to www.glencoe.com.

Get Ready to Read

Connect to the Reading

Have you ever tried to collect something such as model cars, dolls, or some other toy? What was the hardest part of completing your collection? In this story, you'll read about Jerry. He makes a choice to collect trading cards.

Partner Talk Think of a mistake you've made in the past that involved a family member or close friend. Share your experience with your partner.

Build Background

- This story takes place during the Great Depression, which began in late 1929 and lasted through the 1930s. It was a time of hardship for many people. Banks closed and so did many other businesses. Thousands of people lost their savings. Millions of people lost their jobs.

Set Purposes for Reading

BIG Question Read the selection to find out if someone learns from a mistake.

Set Your Own Purpose What would you like to learn from the selection to help you answer the Big Question? Write your own purpose on the "President Cleveland" part of the Workshop 3 Foldable.

Keep Moving

Use these skills as you read the following selection.

President Cleveland, Where Are You? **843**

READING WORKSHOP 3

PRESIDENT CLEVELAND, Where Are You?
by Robert Cormier

That was the autumn of the cowboy cards—Buck Jones and Tom Tyler and Hoot Gibson and especially Ken Maynard.[1] The cards were available in those five-cent packages of gum: pink sticks, three together, covered with a sweet white powder. You couldn't blow bubbles with that particular gum, but it couldn't have mattered less. The cowboy cards were important—the pictures of those rock-faced men with eyes of blue steel. **1**

On those wind-swept, leaf-tumbling afternoons we gathered after school on the sidewalk in front of Lemire's Drugstore, across from St. Jude's Parochial School,[2] and we swapped and bargained and matched for the cards. Because a Ken Maynard serial[3] was playing at the Globe every Saturday afternoon, he was the most popular cowboy of all, and one of his cards was worth at least ten of any other kind.

Rollie Tremaine had a treasure of thirty or so, and he guarded them jealously. He'd match you for the other cards, but he risked his Ken Maynards only when the other kids threatened to leave him out of the competition altogether.

You could almost hate Rollie Tremaine. In the first place, he was the only son of Auguste Tremaine, who operated the Uptown Dry Goods Store, and he did not live in a tenement[4] but in a big white birthday cake of a house on Laurel Street.

Practice the Skills

1 **Key Literary Element**

Description Good descriptive writing helps you experience details from the story. What details are used to describe the gum? What details are used to describe the cowboys?

---

1. **Buck Jones, Tom Tyler, Hoot Gibson, and Ken Maynard** were all popular stars of cowboy movies in the 1930s.
2. A **parochial** (puh ROH kee ul) **school** is run by a church or another religious organization rather than by a city or state government.
3. In the 1930s, moviegoers watched **serials,** long stories that were shown in individual episodes.
4. Here, **tenement** means "apartment building."

He was too fat to be effective in the football games between the Frenchtown Tigers and the North Side Knights, and he made us constantly aware of the jingle of coins in his pockets. He was able to stroll into Lemire's and casually select a quarter's worth of cowboy cards while the rest of us watched, aching with envy.

Once in a while I earned a nickel or dime by running errands or washing windows for blind old Mrs. Belander, or by finding pieces of copper, brass, and other valuable metals at the dump and selling them to the junkman. The coins clutched in my hand, I would race to Lemire's to buy a cowboy card or two, hoping that Ken Maynard would stare boldly out at me as I opened the pack. At one time, before a disastrous matching session with Roger Lussier (my best friend, except where the cards were involved), I owned five Ken Maynards and considered myself a millionaire, of sorts.

One week I was particularly lucky; I had spent two afternoons washing floors for Mrs. Belander and received a quarter. Because my father had worked a full week at the shop, where a rush order for fancy combs had been received, he allotted my brothers and sisters and me an extra dime along with the usual ten cents for the Saturday-afternoon movie. Setting aside the movie fare, I found myself with a bonus of thirty-five cents, and I then planned to put Rollie Tremaine to shame the following Monday afternoon. **2**

Monday was the best day to buy the cards because the candy man stopped at Lemire's every Monday morning to deliver the new assortments. There was nothing more exciting in the world than a fresh batch of card boxes. I rushed home from school that day and hurriedly changed my clothes, eager to set off for the store. As I burst through the doorway, letting the screen door slam behind me, my brother Armand blocked my way.

He was fourteen, three years older than I, and a freshman at Monument High School. He had recently become a stranger to me in many ways—indifferent to such matters as cowboy cards and the Frenchtown Tigers—and he carried himself with a mysterious dignity that was fractured now and then when his voice began shooting off in all directions like some kind of vocal fireworks.

Practice the Skills

2 **Key Reading Skill**

Evaluating You can evaluate or judge characters by what they say and do. What kind of person do you think the narrator is, based on what he says about earning money and buying cards?

Collector's cards of Presidents Benjamin Harrison and Warren Harding.

President Cleveland, Where Are You? **845**

"Wait a minute, Jerry," he said. "I want to talk to you." He motioned me out of earshot of my mother, who was busy supervising the usual after-school skirmish[5] in the kitchen.

I sighed with impatience. In recent months Armand had become a figure of authority, siding with my father and mother occasionally. As the oldest son he sometimes took advantage of his age and experience to issue rules and regulations. 3

"How much money have you got?" he whispered.

"You in some kind of trouble?" I asked, excitement rising in me as I remembered the blackmail plot of a movie at the Globe a month before.

He shook his head in annoyance. "Look," he said, "it's Pa's birthday tomorrow. I think we ought to chip in and buy him something . . ."

I reached into my pocket and caressed the coins. "Here," I said carefully, pulling out a nickel. "If we all give a nickel we should have enough to buy him something pretty nice."

He regarded me with contempt. "Rita already gave me fifteen cents, and I'm throwing in a quarter. Albert handed over a dime—all that's left of his birthday money. Is that all you can do—a nickel?"

"Aw, come on," I protested. "I haven't got a single Ken Maynard left, and I was going to buy some cards this afternoon."

"Ken Maynard!" he snorted. "Who's more important—him or your father?"

His question was unfair because he knew that there was no possible choice—"my father" had to be the only answer. My father was a huge man who believed in the things of the spirit, although my mother often maintained that the spirits[6] he believed in came in bottles. He had worked at the Monument Comb Shop since the age of fourteen; his booming laugh—or grumble—greeted us each night when he returned from the factory. A steady worker when the shop had enough work, he quickened with gaiety on Friday nights and weekends, a bottle of beer at his elbow, and he was fond of making long speeches about the good things in life. In the middle of the Depression, for instance, he paid cash for a

Practice the Skills

3 **Key Literary Element**

Description How does the author bring Armand to life? Are any of the author's word choices especially interesting or lively? Does he use comparisons (figurative language)?

---

5. A *skirmish* is a brief or minor disagreement.
6. Spiritual matters are often called **things of the spirit**, but bottled *spirits* are alcoholic beverages.

READING WORKSHOP 3

Analyzing the Photo What attitudes toward winning do you see on these boys' faces?

piano, of all things, and insisted that my twin sisters, Yolande and Yvette, take lessons once a week.

I took a dime from my pocket and handed it to Armand.

"Thanks, Jerry," he said. "I hate to take your last cent."

"That's all right," I replied, turning away and consoling myself with the thought that twenty cents was better than nothing at all.

When I arrived at Lemire's I sensed disaster in the air. Roger Lussier was kicking disconsolately[7] at a tin can in the gutter, and Rollie Tremaine sat sullenly on the steps in front of the store.

"Save your money," Roger said. He had known about my plans to **splurge** on the cards.

"What's the matter?" I asked.

"There's no more cowboy cards," Rollie Tremaine said. "The company's not making any more."

"They're going to have President cards," Roger said, his face twisting with disgust. He pointed to the store window. "Look!" 4

---

7. **Disconsolately** means "hopelessly unhappy" or "cheerless."

Vocabulary

splurge (splurj) *v.* to spend more money than usual

Practice the Skills

4 **Key Literary Element**

Description The details in the description of the boys' actions and facial expressions tell how the boys felt. Point out one detail that shows how the boys felt.

President Cleveland, Where Are You? **847**

READING WORKSHOP 3

A placard in the window announced: "Attention, Boys. Watch for the New Series. Presidents of the United States. Free in Each 5-Cent Package of Caramel Chew."

"President cards?" I asked, dismayed.

I read on: "Collect a Complete Set and Receive an Official Imitation Major League Baseball Glove, Embossed with Lefty Grove's Autograph."**8**

Glove or no glove, who could become excited about Presidents, of all things?

Rollie Tremaine stared at the sign. "Benjamin Harrison, for crying out loud," he said. "Why would I want Benjamin Harrison when I've got twenty-two Ken Maynards?"

I felt the warmth of guilt creep over me. I jingled the coins in my pocket, but the sound was hollow. No more Ken Maynards to buy.

"I'm going to buy a Mr. Goodbar," Rollie Tremaine decided.

I was without appetite, indifferent even to a Baby Ruth, which was my favorite. I thought of how I had betrayed Armand and, worst of all, my father. **5**

"I'll see you after supper," I called over my shoulder to Roger as I hurried away toward home. I took the shortcut behind the church, although it involved leaping over a tall wooden fence, and I zigzagged recklessly through Mr. Thibodeau's garden, trying to outrace my guilt. I pounded up the steps and into the house, only to learn that Armand had already taken Yolande and Yvette uptown to shop for the birthday present.

I pedaled my bike furiously through the streets, ignoring the indignant**9** horns of automobiles as I sliced through the traffic. Finally I saw Armand and my sisters emerge from the Monument Men's Shop. My heart sank when I spied the long, slim package that Armand was holding. **6**

"Did you buy the present yet?" I asked, although I knew it was too late.

---

8. Robert Grove (1900–1970) was an outstanding pitcher for the Philadelphia Athletics and the Boston Red Sox between 1925 and 1941. A machine carved his **embossed** autograph by making shallow cuts in the glove's leather.

9. If the car horns sound **indignant,** the drivers are beeping because they're angry and annoyed.

Practice the Skills

5 **BIG Question**

Jerry thinks that he betrayed his father and Armand. What was Jerry's mistake? Write your answer on your Foldable.

6 **Key Literary Element**

Description The author uses vivid verbs and adverbs to describe how Jerry raced through the town. On a piece of paper, write three verbs and two adverbs that tell about his journey.

Analyzing the Photo How are these young people like Jerry and his friends at Lemire's Drugstore?

848 UNIT 7 What Can We Learn from Our Mistakes?

"Just now. A blue tie," Armand said. "What's the matter?"

"Nothing," I replied, my chest hurting.

He looked at me for a long moment. At first his eyes were hard, but then they softened. He smiled at me, almost sadly, and touched my arm. I turned away from him because I felt naked and exposed.

"It's all right," he said gently. "Maybe you've learned something." The words were gentle, but they held a curious dignity, the dignity remaining even when his voice suddenly cracked on the last syllable.

I wondered what was happening to me, because I did not know whether to laugh or cry. **7**

Sister Angela was amazed when, a week before Christmas vacation, everybody in the class submitted a history essay worthy of a high mark—in some cases as high as A-minus. (Sister Angela did not believe that anyone in the world ever deserved an A.) She never learned—or at least she never let on that she knew—we all had become experts on the Presidents because of the cards we purchased at Lemire's. Each card contained a picture of a President, and on the reverse side, a summary of his career. We looked at those cards so often that the **biographies** imprinted themselves on our minds without effort. Even our street-corner conversations were filled with such information as the fact that James Madison was called "The Father of the Constitution," or that John Adams had intended to become a minister. **8**

The President cards were a roaring success and the cowboy cards were quickly forgotten. In the first place we did not receive gum with the cards, but a kind of chewy caramel. The caramel could be tucked into a corner of your mouth, bulging your cheek in much the same manner as wads of tobacco bulged the mouths of baseball stars. In the second place the competition for collecting the cards was fierce and frustrating—fierce because everyone was intent on being the first to send away for a baseball glove and frustrating because although there were only thirty-two Presidents, including Franklin Delano Roosevelt, the variety at Lemire's was at a minimum. When the deliveryman left the boxes of cards at the store each Monday, we often discovered that one entire box was devoted to a single President—two weeks in a row

Practice the Skills

7 **BIG Question**
What lesson does Armand think Jerry may have learned? Write your answer on your Foldable.

8 **English Language Coach**
Greek Roots The word **biographies** comes from two Greek roots, *bio* meaning "life" and *graph* meaning "write" or "describe." Define *biography* using the meanings of these Greek roots.

READING WORKSHOP 3

the boxes contained nothing but Abraham Lincoln. One week Roger Lussier and I were the heroes of Frenchtown. We journeyed on our bicycles to the North Side, engaged three boys in a matching bout and returned with five new Presidents, including Chester Alan Arthur, who up to that time had been missing.

Perhaps to sharpen our desire, the card company sent a sample glove to Mr. Lemire, and it dangled, orange and sleek, in the window. I was half sick with longing, thinking of my old glove at home, which I had inherited from Armand. But Rollie Tremaine's desire for the glove outdistanced my own. He even got Mr. Lemire to agree to give the glove in the window to the first person to get a complete set of cards, so that precious time wouldn't be wasted waiting for the postman.

We were delighted at Rollie Tremaine's frustration, especially since he was only a substitute player for the Tigers. Once after spending fifty cents on cards—all of which turned out to be Calvin Coolidge—he threw them to the ground, pulled some dollar bills out of his pocket and said, "The heck with it. I'm going to buy a glove!"

"Not that glove," Roger Lussier said. "Not a glove with Lefty Grove's autograph. Look what it says at the bottom of the sign."

We all looked, although we knew the words by heart: "This Glove Is Not For Sale Anywhere."

Rollie Tremaine scrambled to pick up the cards from the sidewalk, pouting more than ever. After that he was quietly **obsessed** with the Presidents, hugging the cards close to his chest and refusing to tell us how many more he needed to complete his set. 9

I too was obsessed with the cards, because they had become things of comfort in a world that had suddenly grown **dismal**. After Christmas a layoff at the shop had thrown my father out of work. He received no paycheck for four weeks, and the only income we had was from Armand's after school job at the Blue and White Grocery Store—a job he lost finally when business dwindled as the layoff continued.

Vocabulary

obsessed (ub SEST) *adj.* concentrating completely

dismal (DIZ mul) *adj.* gloomy; miserable; cheerless

Practice the Skills

9 Key Reading Skill

Evaluating Think about the description of Rollie Tremaine at the beginning of the story. Add that information to the description of Rollie on this page. What do you think of Rollie? Evaluate him as a person. What are his strengths and weaknesses? Use details from the selection in your answer.

850 UNIT 7 What Can We Learn from Our Mistakes?

Although we had enough food and clothing—my father's credit had always been good, a matter of pride with him—the inactivity made my father restless and irritable. He did not drink any beer at all, and laughed loudly, but not convincingly, after gulping down a glass of water and saying, "Lent[10] came early this year." The twins fell sick and went to the hospital to have their tonsils removed. My father was confident that he would return to work eventually and pay off his debts, but he seemed to age before our eyes. **10**

When orders again were received at the comb shop and he returned to work, another disaster occurred, although I was the only one aware of it. Armand fell in love.

I discovered his situation by accident, when I happened to pick up a piece of paper that had fallen to the floor in the bedroom he and I shared. I frowned at the paper, puzzled.

"Dear Sally, When I look into your eyes the world stands still . . ."

The letter was snatched from my hands before I finished reading it.

"What's the big idea, snooping around?" Armand asked, his face crimson. "Can't a guy have any privacy?"

He had never mentioned privacy before. "It was on the floor," I said. "I didn't know it was a letter. Who's Sally?"

He flung himself across the bed. "You tell anybody and I'll muckalize[11] you," he threatened. "Sally Knowlton."

Nobody in Frenchtown had a name like Knowlton.

"A girl from the North Side?" I asked, incredulous.[12]

He rolled over and faced me, anger in his eyes, and a kind of despair too. **11**

"What's the matter with that? Think she's too good for me?" he asked. "I'm warning you, Jerry, if you tell anybody . . ."

"Don't worry," I said. Love had no particular place in my life; it seemed an unnecessary waste of time. And a girl from the North Side was so remote that for all practical purposes she did not exist. But I was curious. "What are you writing her a letter for? Did she leave town, or something?"

Practice the Skills

10 Key Reading Skill

Evaluating Evaluating how a character is described is different than evaluating the character as a person. Look back at the description of Jerry's father on page 846. Combine it with the description of him on this page. Is he a believable character? Is the author making him come alive for you? Use details from the story to explain your answers.

11 Key Literary Element

Description What vivid words does the author use to describe Armand's reaction to Jerry reading the letter?

---

10. **Lent** is the forty-day period before Easter. During Lent some Christians show sorrow for their sins by giving up something they enjoy.
11. **Muckalize** is a made-up word. Muck is dirty, sticky, slimy mud, or anything that's messy and disgusting. The suffix *-ize* means "cause to be or become."
12. To be **incredulous** (in KREH joo lus) is to be unwilling or unable to believe something.

President Cleveland, Where Are You? **851**

READING WORKSHOP 3

"She hasn't left town," he answered. "I wasn't going to send it. I just felt like writing to her."

I was glad that I had never become involved with love—love that brought desperation[13] to your eyes, that caused you to write letters you did not plan to send. Shrugging with indifference, I began to search in the closet for the old baseball glove. I found it on the shelf, under some old sneakers. The webbing was torn and the padding gone. I thought of the sting I would feel when a sharp grounder slapped into the glove, and I winced.

"You tell anybody about me and Sally and I'll—"

"I know. You'll muckalize me."

I did not divulge[14] his secret and often shared his **agony**, particularly when he sat at the supper table and left my mother's special butterscotch pie untouched. I had never realized before how terrible love could be. But my compassion was short-lived because I had other things to worry about: report cards due at Eastertime; the loss of income from old Mrs. Belander, who had gone to live with a daughter in Boston; and, of course, the Presidents. **12**

Because a stalemate[15] had been reached, the President cards were the **dominant** force in our lives—mine, Roger Lussier's and Rollie Tremaine's. For three weeks, as the baseball season approached, each of us had a complete set—complete except for one President, Grover Cleveland. Each time a box of cards arrived at the store we hurriedly bought them (as hurriedly

Analyzing the Photo What does this photograph tell you about the 1930s?

Practice the Skills

12 **English Language Coach**

Greek Roots The word **agony** comes from the Greek root *agon*, which means "struggle" or "anguish." Can you see how *agony* came to mean "great suffering of the mind or body"?

---

13. **Desperation** means "distress caused by great need or loss of hope."
14. To **divulge** a secret is to reveal it or make it known.
15. A **stalemate** refers to a situation in which no further action is possible.

Vocabulary

dominant (DOM ih nunt) *adj.* having the greatest power or force; controlling

852 UNIT 7 What Can We Learn from Our Mistakes?

as our funds allowed) and tore off the wrappers, only to be confronted by James Monroe or Martin Van Buren or someone else. But never Grover Cleveland, never the man who had been the twenty-second and the twenty-fourth President of the United States. We argued about Grover Cleveland. Should he be placed between Chester Alan Arthur and Benjamin Harrison as the twenty-second President or did he belong between Benjamin Harrison and William McKinley as the twenty-fourth President? Was the card company playing fair? Roger Lussier brought up a horrifying possibility—did we need *two* Grover Clevelands to complete the set?

Indignant, we stormed Lemire's and protested to the harassed[16] storeowner, who had long since vowed never to stock a new series. Muttering angrily, he searched his bills and receipts for a list of rules.

"All right," he announced. "Says here you only need one Grover Cleveland to finish the set. Now get out, all of you, unless you've got money to spend."

Visual Vocabulary
A *piazza* (pee AHT zuh) is a large covered porch.

Outside the store, Rollie Tremaine picked up an empty tobacco tin and scaled it across the street. "Boy," he said. "I'd give five dollars for a Grover Cleveland." 13

When I returned home I found Armand sitting on the piazza steps, his chin in his hands. His mood of **dejection** mirrored my own, and I sat down beside him. We did not say anything for a while.

"Want to throw the ball around?" I asked.

He sighed, not bothering to answer.

"You sick?" I asked.

He stood up and hitched up his trousers, pulled at his ear and finally told me what the matter was—there was a big dance next week at the high school, the Spring Promenade,[17] and Sally had asked him to be her escort.

I shook my head at the folly of love. "Well, what's so bad about that?"

---

16. Someone who is **harassed** (huh RAST) is repeatedly bothered or annoyed by someone else.
17. A formal dance or ball was once called a **promenade**. Today, the term is shortened to *prom*.

Vocabulary

dejection (dih JEK shun) *n.* sadness; low spirits

Practice the Skills

13 **Key Reading Skill**

Evaluating What do you think about this part of the story? What do you think about the boys collecting president cards? Is it believable? Has the author described it well? Explain your answer using details from the story.

President Cleveland, Where Are You? **853**

READING WORKSHOP 3

Visual Vocabulary
A *corsage* (kor SAZH) is a flower or small bunch of flowers worn by a woman, usually at the shoulder or on the waist.

"How can I take Sally to a fancy dance?" he asked desperately. "I'd have to buy her a corsage . . . And my shoes are practically falling apart. Pa's got too many worries now to buy me new shoes or give me money for flowers for a girl."

I nodded in sympathy. "Yeah," I said. "Look at me. Baseball time is almost here, and all I've got is that old glove. And no Grover Cleveland card yet . . ." 🔲

"Grover Cleveland?" he asked. "They've got some of those up on the North Side. Some kid was telling me there's a store that's got them. He says they're looking for Warren G. Harding."

"Holy Smoke!" I said. "I've got an extra Warren G. Harding!" Pure joy sang in my veins. I ran to my bicycle, swung into the seat—and found that the front tire was flat.

"I'll help you fix it," Armand said.

Within half an hour I was at the North Side Drugstore, where several boys were matching cards on the sidewalk. Silently but **blissfully** I shouted: President Grover Cleveland, here I come!

After Armand had left for the dance, all dressed up as if it were Sunday, the small green box containing the corsage under his arm, I sat on the railing of the piazza, letting my feet dangle. The neighborhood was quiet because the Frenchtown Tigers were at Daggett's Field, practicing for the first baseball game of the season.

I thought of Armand and the ridiculous expression on his face when he'd stood before the mirror in the bedroom. I'd avoided looking at his new black shoes. "Love," I muttered.

Spring had arrived in a sudden stampede of apple blossoms and fragrant breezes. Windows had been thrown open and dust mops had banged on the sills all day long as the women busied themselves with housecleaning. I was puzzled by my lethargy.¹⁸ Wasn't spring supposed to make everything bright and gay?

Practice the Skills

🔲 **English Language Coach**

Greek Roots The Greek root *path* means "disease" or "feeling." Find a word on in this paragraph that contains *path* and means "the ability to feel and understand other people's sorrow."

---

18. **Lethargy** (LETH er jee) is a feeling or condition of laziness or drowsiness.

Vocabulary

blissfully (BLIS fuh lee) *adv.* in an extremely happy way; joyfully

I turned at the sound of footsteps on the stairs. Roger Lussier greeted me with a sour face.

"I thought you were practicing with the Tigers," I said.

"Rollie Tremaine," he said. "I just couldn't stand him." He slammed his fist against the railing. "Jeez, why did he have to be the one to get a Grover Cleveland? You should see him showing off. He won't let anybody even touch that glove . . ."

I felt like Benedict Arnold[19] and knew that I had to confess what I had done.

"Roger," I said, "I got a Grover Cleveland card up on the North Side. I sold it to Rollie Tremaine for five dollars."

"Are you crazy?" he asked.

"I needed that five dollars. It was an—an emergency."

"Boy!" he said, looking down at the ground and shaking his head. "What did you have to do a thing like that for?"

I watched him as he turned away and began walking down the stairs.

"Hey, Roger!" I called.

He squinted up at me as if I were a stranger, someone he'd never seen before.

"What?" he asked, his voice flat.

"I had to do it," I said. "Honest." **15**

He didn't answer. He headed toward the fence, searching for the board we had loosened to give us a secret passage.

I thought of my father and Armand and Rollie Tremaine and Grover Cleveland and wished that I could go away someplace far away. But there was no place to go.

Roger found the loose slat in the fence and slipped through. I felt betrayed: weren't you supposed to feel good when you did something fine and noble?

A moment later two hands gripped the top of the fence and Roger's face appeared. "Was it a real emergency?" he yelled.

"A real one!" I called. "Something important!"

His face dropped from sight and his voice reached me across the yard: "All right."

"See you tomorrow!" I yelled.

I swung my legs over the railing again. The gathering dusk began to soften the sharp edges of the fence, the rooftops, the distant church steeple. I sat there a long time, waiting for the good feeling to come. **16**

---

19. Benedict Arnold was an American general who became a traitor during the Revolutionary War.

READING WORKSHOP 3

Practice the Skills

15 **BIG Question**

Does Jerry make a mistake by selling the card to Rollie Tremaine? Explain. Write your answer on your Foldable. Your response will help you complete the Unit Challenge later.

16 **Key Reading Skill**

Evaluating How would you evaluate Jerry's actions? Do you think he did a good thing? Explain.

President Cleveland, Where Are You? **855**

READING WORKSHOP 3 • Evaluating

After You Read

President Cleveland, Where Are You?

Answering the BIG Question

1. What mistake does Jerry make early in the story? Does he correct this mistake? Explain.
2. **Connect** From this story, what have you learned about making and correcting mistakes?
   TIP Author and Me

3. **Recall** How does Jerry get the Grover Cleveland card?
   TIP Right There

Critical Thinking

4. **Infer** Why don't the boys like Rollie Tremaine?
   TIP Think and Search

5. **Draw Conclusions** How does Armand get the shoes and corsage?
   TIP Author and Me

6. **Interpret** At the beginning of the story, why do the boys enjoy collecting cards?
   TIP Author and Me

7. **Interpret** Why doesn't Jerry feel good at the end of the story?
   TIP Author and Me

8. **Draw Conclusions** What values does Jerry learn from Armand throughout the story?
   TIP Author and Me

Write About Your Reading

Write an e-mail to a friend. In your e-mail, tell your friend what you thought about "President Cleveland, Where Are You?" Evaluate the characters and the plot, and explain how well the author entertained you through his story. End your e-mail by telling your friend why he or she should or should not read the story.

Objectives (pp. 856–857)
Reading Evaluate text • Make connections from text to self
Literature Identify literary elements: description, sensory details
Vocabulary Identify word structure: Greek roots
Writing Respond to literature: personal e-mail
Grammar Use correct subject and verb agreement: *here* and *there*

856 UNIT 7 What Can We Learn from Our Mistakes?

Skills Review

Key Reading Skill: Evaluating

9. Does the setting (the Depression) make the story better? Does it not affect the story? Or does it hurt the story? Explain your answer.

10. A great piece of literature has a timeless message that remains true for many generations of readers. Do you consider "President Cleveland, Where Are You?" a great short story? Explain.

Key Literary Element: Description

11. Does the author devote more description to setting or to characterization? Explain your answer using details from the story.

Vocabulary Check

Rewrite the following sentences, inserting the correct vocabulary word in each.

obsessed   splurge   dismal   dominant

12. After winning the lottery, Gladys plans to ___ on vacations and cars.
13. That black Labrador puppy is the strongest and most ___ in the litter.
14. November is a ___ month, filled with gray skies, dead leaves, and cold winds.
15. Many young children are ___ with dinosaurs when they are young.
16. **Academic Vocabulary** How does evaluating make you more aware as a reader?
17. **English Language Coach** The Greek root *phon* or *phone* means "sound." It is often used at the end of a word. How many words can you think of that end in the word *phone*? (Hint: Some are musical instruments.) How do their definitions relate to sound?

Grammar Link: Subject-Verb Agreement with *Here* and *There* Sentence Beginnings

Some sentences begin with *here* or *there*. But *here* or *there* is never the subject of the sentence. Follow these tips for identifying the subject and verb in sentences beginning with *here* or *there*.

- In sentences that begin with *here* or *there,* the verb will appear before the subject. Example: There **were** too many **people** in line. The *verb* **were** comes before the *subject* **people.**
- In sentences that begin with *here* or *there,* choose the verb that agrees with the subject. Example: Here **is** a great **poem**. The *verb* **is** agrees with the *subject* **poem.**

Grammar Practice

Choose the verb that agrees with the subject.

18. Here (comes, come) my very favorite car.
19. There (seem, seems) to be several spelling mistakes in this paragraph.
20. Here (lie, lies) the greatest baseball player who ever lived.
21. There (is, are) only twelve letters in the Hawaiian alphabet.

Writing Application Look back at your e-mail from the **Write About Your Reading** exercise. Check to be sure that your subjects and verbs agree in sentences that begin with *here* or *there*.

Web Activities For eFlashcards, Selection Quick Checks, and other Web activities, go to www.glencoe.com.

READING WORKSHOP 3 • Evaluating

Before You Read : Nobody's Perfect

Meet the Author
David Fischer is a feature writer for a magazine. His goal is to entertain and to inform. Feature articles deal with interesting subjects that grab a reader's attention.

Author Search For more about David Fischer, go to www.glencoe.com.

Vocabulary Preview

competing (kum PEET ing) *v.* taking part in a contest; form of the verb *compete* **(p. 860)** *The runner was competing in the race.*

barrier (BAIR ee ur) *n.* something that prevents passage; an obstacle **(p. 862)** *The skater accidentally flew over the barrier.*

fumbled (FUM buld) *v.* lost one's grasp on something; form of the verb *fumble* **(p. 862)** *The football player fumbled the ball.*

referee (ref uh REE) *n.* a sports official who makes sure rules are followed in a game **(p. 862)** *The referee called the player out.*

Partner Activity With a partner, write a sports article about a recent game or competitive event. Use the vocabulary words above to write your article.

English Language Coach

Greek Roots You learned that the **root** of a word is its main part. Knowing the meaning of a word's root can help you figure out the meaning of the whole word. The English language borrowed many roots, prefixes, and suffixes from Greek. These word parts are called "combining forms" because they are often used with other Greek parts. The word part *mono* means "one" or "alone." A *monologue* is a long speech given by one person. Here are some other examples of Greek roots.

Root	Meaning	Example
auto	self	automatic, automobile
cycle	circle, ring	recycle
gram	write/draw	diagram, telegram
graph	write	autograph
mono	one/alone/single	monogram, monorail
scope	see	telescope
tele	far	telegraph, telephone

On Your Own Make flash cards for Greek roots. Use the list above to help you. On the front of the card, write the Greek root. On the back of the card, write the root's meaning and three words that contain the root. Review your flash cards with a partner.

Objectives (pp. 858–863)
Reading Evaluate text • Make connections from text to self
Informational text Identify literary elements: description, sensory details
Vocabulary Identify word structure: Greek roots

READING WORKSHOP 3 • Evaluating

Skills Preview

Key Reading Skill: Evaluating

Good readers do more than just understand what they read. They also evaluate the writer's ideas. When you evaluate, you judge the value of what you have read. In the last selection, you evaluated a fictional, or made up, story. In the next selection, you will be evaluating a news article that is nonfiction. Evaluating nonfiction is a lot like evaluating fiction, but you ask some different questions.

- Does the author make his or her purpose clear?
- Does the information make sense?
- Does the author present information in such a way that allows me to form my own opinion?
- Does the author present facts or only opinions?
- Does the author's style match the article's subject?

Write to Learn Write the questions listed above in your Learner's Notebook. Use them as a checklist. Answer the questions as you read the selection.

Key Literary Element: Description

Writers use descriptions to engage readers in the text. Descriptions help you understand a text better. An effective description presents a clear picture to the reader. As you read the article, ask yourself these questions:

- What words does the writer use to describe the athletes and their mistakes?
- How do the words make the article more exciting or humorous?

Interactive Literary Elements Handbook
To review or learn more about the literary elements, go to www.glencoe.com.

Get Ready to Read

Connect to the Reading

Everyone makes mistakes. It's how people react to their mistakes that really matters. How do you react when you make a mistake?

Partner Talk With a classmate, discuss a mistake that you have made. Explain what happened and how you reacted. Then, discuss what you learned from the mistake and how you've avoided similar blunders since then.

Build Background

Everyone makes mistakes—even professional athletes. It's bad enough to do something embarrassing in front of your friends or teammates, but imagine making a big mistake in front of millions of people watching TV. This selection is about famous athletes who made mistakes and learned from them. Some of the athletes you'll read about are

- Brett Favre, a record-holding NFL football player who started a foundation that provides aid to disadvantaged and disabled children.
- Kevin Garnett, who achieved the honor of being the NBA's Most Valuable Player in his ninth NBA season.
- Midori Ito, an Olympic silver medalist who has been ice skating since she was four years old.

Set Purposes for Reading

BIG Question As you read "Nobody's Perfect," think about why athletes have to bounce back from their mistakes.

Set Your Own Purpose What else would you like to learn from the article to help you answer the Big Question? Write your own purpose on the "Nobody's Perfect" part of the Workshop 3 Foldable.

Keep Moving

Use these skills as you read the following selection.

Nobody's Perfect **859**

READING WORKSHOP 3

TIME
Nobody's Perfect

Making a mistake is not the end of the world. It can be pretty funny!

By **DAVID FISCHER**

Everyone makes mistakes, even great **athletes**. In sports, mistakes are called bloopers. The best way to get over a mistake is to figure out what you did wrong, correct it, and then laugh about it. Here are some of our favorite bloopers. **1**

It's Not Over?

Suzy Favor Hamilton is one of the best distance runners in the United States, but in 1994 she lost a race because she lost count.

Suzy was **competing** in the mile event at a track meet in Fairfax, Virginia. The runners had to complete eight laps. Near the end of lap 7, Suzy sprinted into the lead. As soon as she crossed the finish line, she stopped running. Suzy thought that the race was over and that she had won! As she watched the other racers run past, she realized her mistake.

"I wanted to tell everybody to stop so that I could jump back in the race," says Hamilton.

> Suzy Hamilton stopped running one lap before the race was over.

1 English Language Coach

Greek Roots The word **athlete** comes from the Greek root *athlon*, meaning "contest." In your own words, explain how the root helps to show the meaning of *athlete*.

Keith Locke

Vocabulary

competing (kum PEET ing) *v.* taking part in a contest

860 UNIT 7 What Can We Learn from Our Mistakes?

Somebody Get Brett!

Quarterback Brett Favre[1] of the Green Bay Packers is cool under pressure. He proved how cool he can be when he led the Packers to victory in Super Bowl XXXI in 1997. But Brett wasn't always so calm.

In 1992, Brett was the Packers' second-string[2] quarterback. In the third game of the season, he went into action against the Cincinnati Bengals. In the fourth quarter, Green Bay trailed Cincinnati by 13 points. But in the last eight minutes of the game, Brett led Green Bay to two touchdowns.

After the second touchdown, he ran off the field. He started jumping and screaming. Brett was so busy celebrating that he forgot an important part of his job. To win the game, Green Bay needed to kick the extra point. Brett was supposed to be on the field, holding the ball for the kick! **2**

Green Bay kicker Chris Jacke ran to the sideline and dragged Brett back onto the field. Chris then kicked the extra point, and the Packers won the game, 24–23.

Where's My Jersey?

Basketball forward Kevin Garnett of the Minnesota Timberwolves joined the NBA in 1995. He was 19 years old and straight out of high school.

During a game in the early days of his career, Kevin found that he had left something important behind in the locker room. Near the end of the first quarter, Minnesota's coach told Kevin to enter the game. Kevin ran to the scorer's table and pulled off his warm-up top. Then he looked down. Surprise! He was wearing only a T-shirt from practice. Kevin had to race back to the locker room to get the official game jersey that was part of his uniform.

Even though he's older now, Kevin sometimes still acts like a kid. **3**

Keith Locke

Hey, Brett: Get in the game!

2 Key Literary Element

Description Look at the verbs the author uses in this paragraph to describe what happened. Does he use active verbs that bring the scene to life, or not? Write your answers in your Learner's Notebook and include examples from the selection.

3 Key Reading Skill

Evaluating What do you think of this part of the article? Has the author given you the facts you need to understand his point? Does the author prove his last statement? Explain.

---

1. *Favre* (farv)
2. A player who is **second-string** substitutes for a starting player.

READING WORKSHOP 3

Look Out Below!

Midori Ito[3] of Japan is one of the best jumpers in figure skating. But during the 1991 World Championships, Midori jumped right out of the skating rink!

During the short program of the women's singles event, Midori was performing a jump. She started the jump too close to the edge of the rink. She flew over a 12-inch wooden barrier at the edge of the ice and landed on a cameraman!

Midori got up, hopped back over the **barrier**, and completed her routine. She finished in fourth place. **4**

4 Key Literary Element

Description What words help you visualize what happened to Midori Ito?

Which Way Do I Go?

Jim Marshall was a star defensive end for the Minnesota Vikings from 1960 to 1979. He is best remembered for getting lost on the football field.

It happened in a 1964 game when the Vikings were playing the San Francisco 49ers. In the third quarter, a 49er running back **fumbled** the football. Jim scooped up the loose ball and ran 66 yards to the end zone.

Jim was pumped.[4] He thought he had scored a touchdown. "A 49ers player ran up and gave me a hug," says Jim. "That's when I knew something was wrong." He had run to the wrong end zone!

The **referee** ruled that Jim had scored a safety (2 points) for San Francisco. Even so, the Vikings won the game, 27–22. "I still feel embarrassed about that play," says Jim. "But I don't see any reason to hide. I know I was hustling. If people want to laugh, I'll go along with it." **5**

5 Key Reading Skill

Evaluating The writer says that Jim Marshall is best remembered for getting lost on the football field. Does the writer prove this? Explain.

Out By a Foot

Third baseman Dani Tyler of the United States women's softball team learned a lesson at the 1996 Summer Olympics: Always watch your step.

---

3. **Midori Ito** (meh DOOR ee   EE toh)
4. **Pumped** is a shortened slang expression for **pumped up**, which means filled with excitement, strength, and energy.

Vocabulary

barrier (BAIR ee ur) *n.* something that prevents passage; an obstacle

fumbled (FUM buld) *v.* lost one's grasp on something

referee (ref uh REE) *n.* a sports official who makes sure rules are followed in a game

862   UNIT 7   What Can We Learn from Our Mistakes?

In the fifth inning of a scoreless game against Australia, Dani hit a home run. When she reached home plate, she leaped to high-five[5] a teammate and jumped right over the plate! The umpire called her out because she never touched home. The United States lost the game in extra innings. It was the U.S. team's second international loss in 10 years.

After the game, Dani said, "From now on, I'm going to paint a big X on home plate and step on it with both feet." The United States went on to win the gold medal. **6**

Wrong Target

At the 2004 Summer Olympic Games in Athens, Greece, Matthew Emmons of the United States was in first place before his final shot in the 50-meter rifle three-position[6] competition.

Matthew was one easy shot away from his second gold medal of the Olympics. All he needed to do was hit the target. So how did Matthew end up in eighth place? He shot at an Austrian competitor's target in the next lane. This Austrian competitor ended up winning the bronze medal.[7] **7**

—Updated 2005, from *Sports Illustrated for Kids*, April 1997

---

5. A **high-five** is a gesture of greeting or victory in which two people slap each other's upraised hands.
6. A **three-position competition** includes firing from a standing position, a seated position, and a prone (lying on the stomach) position.
7. A **bronze medal** is awarded to an athlete for winning third place.

6 Key Literary Element

Description How does the description of the event help you visualize what's happening? Write your answer in your Learner's Notebook. Remember to select examples from the text to support your answer.

7 BIG Question

What do you think the athletes mentioned in this article would say about what a person can learn from his or her mistakes? Record your answer on your Foldable. This response will help you complete the Unit Challenge.

Dani danced over the plate.

Keith Locke

READING WORKSHOP 3 • Evaluating

After You Read — Nobody's Perfect

Keith Locke

Answering the BIG Question

1. After reading this article, what are your thoughts about what you can learn from your mistakes?

2. **Recall** What did Midori Ito do after she fell over the barrier of the rink?
   TIP Right There

3. **Recall** What did Kevin Garnett do when he realized that he had forgotten his jersey?
   TIP Right There

4. **Summarize** What happened to Dani Tyler at the softball game?
   TIP Right There

Critical Thinking

5. **Draw Conclusions** What do you think Suzy Favor Hamilton learned from her mistake?
   TIP Author and Me

6. **Draw Conclusions** Overall, what do you think caused most of the mistakes described in the article?
   TIP Author and Me

7. **Evaluate** The deck at the beginning of the article says that mistakes can be funny. Do you think the writer proved this point?
   TIP Author and Me

8. **Draw Conclusions** What is the best way to get over a mistake?
   TIP On My Own

Write About Your Reading

Write an interview between a news reporter and one of the athletes in the article. First, come up with questions that a reporter would ask about the mistakes the athlete made. Then, imagine that you are the athlete and write responses to the questions. When you are done, proofread your interview to correct any errors in grammar, punctuation, and spelling.

Objectives (pp. 864–865)
Reading Evaluate text • Make connections from text to self
Informational text Identify literary elements: description, sensory details
Vocabulary Identify word structure: Greek roots
Writing Respond to literature: interview
Grammar Use correct subject-verb agreement: inverted sentences

Skills Review

Key Reading Skill: Evaluating

9. Does the writer present the information in a way that allows you to understand and enjoy the article? Explain.
10. What was the writer's purpose? Was he successful in achieving that purpose? Why or why not?

Key Literary Element: Description

11. Reread the third paragraph under the subhead "Somebody Get Brett!" To what senses does the writer appeal in this paragraph?
12. Of all the events described in the story, which do you think was the most interesting and vivid? Why?

Vocabulary Check

Match each definition with the correct vocabulary word.

13. competing ___
14. barrier ___
15. fumbled ___
16. referee ___

a. something that prevents passage; an obstacle
b. a sports official who makes sure rules are followed in a game
c. taking part in a contest
d. lost one's grasp on something

17. **Academic Vocabulary** In which of the following sentences is the word *evaluate* used correctly?

> The judges will **evaluate** the dancers' performances before they announce the winner.
>
> Marco will **evaluate** the clock when he arrives late for class.

18. **English Language Coach** The words *democracy, demography,* and *pandemic* all share the same Greek root. What is that root, what does it mean, and how does it relate to the definitions of the three words? Use a dictionary.

Grammar Link: Subject-Verb Agreement in Inverted Sentences

In most sentences, the subject comes before the verb.

Example: Subject   Verb
Langston Hughes   wrote stories about living in Harlem.

Other kinds of sentences, such as questions, begin with part or all of the predicate. This type of sentence is an inverted sentence. The subject comes after the verb.

Example: Verb   Subject   Predicate
Are   you   still reading that short story?

The best way to find the subject and verb is to rephrase the sentence so that the subject comes before the verb.

Example 1: Where (is/are) the instructions for the game? (Rephrased: The instructions for the game are where? *Instructions* is the subject. *Are* is the verb.)

Example 2: Under the shelves (was/were) a frightened mouse. (Rephrased: A frightened mouse was under the shelves. *Mouse* is the subject. *Was* is the verb.)

Choose the verb that agrees with the subject.

19. On his feet (was/were) brand new shoes.
20. When (are/is) your parents coming?
21. (Doesn't/Don't) Amy know the way to the mall?
22. In the back of the closet (was/were) Alan's birthday presents.

Writing Application Look back at your interview from **Write About Your Reading.** Check to be sure that your subjects and verbs agree, particularly those in inverted sentences.

Web Activities For eFlashcards, Selection Quick Checks, and other Web activities, go to www.glencoe.com.

WRITING WORKSHOP PART 2

Personal Narrative
Revising, Editing, and Presenting

ASSIGNMENT Write a personal narrative

Purpose: Write a narrative about a time you made a mistake

Audience: You, your teacher, and classmates

Revising Rubric

As you revise your draft, you should

- write in your own voice
- use a tone appropriate to purpose and audience
- revise your draft for word choice
- use suggestions from other students to improve your narrative

Objectives (pp. 866–869)
Writing Use the writing process: personal narrative • Use literary elements: voice • Revise a draft to include: main ideas and supporting details, description • Edit writing for: grammar, spelling, punctuation • Present writing
Listening, Speaking, and Viewing Present a news report • Listen actively

---

In Writing Workshop Part 1, you drafted a personal narrative about a mistake you once made. In this workshop, you will share your work with classmates to improve your writing.

Revising
Make It Better

Sharing your writing with other people may seem scary, but it is actually a great way to find the parts of your work that need to be revised. Sometimes writers get so involved in the piece they are working on that they forget about the audience who will someday read their work.

Start by trading drafts with a partner. As you read your partner's work, underline the parts of the draft that you find confusing. Circle the parts that you especially like. Then answer the Writing Response Sheet questions on a blank piece of paper.

Writing Response Sheet

Writer's Name:
Reader's Name:
What mistake was this narrative about?
What did the writer learn from his or her mistake?
Did the narrative have a beginning, a middle, and an end?
What words, descriptions, or sentences did you most enjoy?
What part(s) did you find confusing? Why?
What suggestions do you have for the writer?

Return the completed Writing Response Sheet to your partner along with the marked up draft. With your partner, talk about the strengths and weaknesses of each other's writing. Here are some example topics to get your discussion started:

- It isn't clear to me why this event is a mistake.
- The image of "broken piñatas" really struck my mind.
- I'd like to know more about what you learned from this experience.

Make Adjustments

Focus on revising the parts of your narrative that your partner found most confusing. You may need to:

- Add details and description to make your writing more interesting.

    When I got home, *a half-eaten birthday cake, broken piñatas, and melted ice cream* were all that remained of my sister's birthday party.

- Delete repeated information.

    I felt so guilty for skipping the party. I didn't want to face my family ~~because I felt so guilty~~.

Raise Your Voice

Check your narrative style by reviewing voice and word choice. A personal narrative is about something that happened to *you;* make your writing sound as much like *you* as possible. Ask yourself:

- ☑ Does the narrative voice sound like me?
- ☑ Do I use these words and expressions when I talk?
- ☑ Have I used words that reflect my emotions about the topic?

Editing — Finish It Up

After you revise your personal narrative, edit your work by following the checklist below.

Proofreading Checklist

- ☑ Thoughts and feelings are clearly expressed.
- ☑ Subjects and verbs agree in person and number.
- ☑ Sentences have proper end punctuation.
- ☑ Names and places are capitalized.
- ☑ All words are spelled correctly.

Presenting — Show It Off

Copy your narrative neatly and read it aloud to your classmates. Be sure to read your narrative slowly enough that people can understand you.

Writing Models For models and other writing activities, go to www.glencoe.com.

Writing Tip

Writing Tip Make certain that your narrative includes your thoughts and opinions about the topic you chose.

Writing Tip

Writing Tip Check your narrative for mistakes in verb forms. Remember, most past tense verbs end in *-ed*. Past tense forms of irregular verbs, though, do not end in *-ed*.

WRITING WORKSHOP PART 2

Active Writing Model

Writer's Model

Getting Even Doesn't Feel So Good
By Wallace Schultz

- This is the beginning of the story.

Last June my best friend Jerry showed he wasn't my friend when he had our whole class over for a swimming party on his birthday. I sat alone, watching everybody else swimming and having a great time.

- The writer uses time references to indicate that events happen in chronological order.

Two weeks ago, Jerry had the nerve to ask my mom if he was invited to my birthday party. My mom told him yes! She knew what happened at Jerry's party, but she thought it was my own fault. She said that I could have played in the water even if I couldn't swim. That really made me angry! I didn't want Jerry at my party, enjoying my birthday cake, after what he'd done to me!

- The writer's voice is expressive as though he were telling the story instead of writing it.

- This is the middle of the story.

The day of my party arrived. Everyone from class was there, and I was determined to get even with Jerry. My friend Al started laughing about how silly Jerry's new haircut was. This was my party, and I knew if I joined in, everybody else would too. So I shouted out, "Who cut your hair, Jerry, your baby sister?" Everyone started laughing. It felt good to see Jerry turn red in the face. Now he knew how I'd felt at his pool party.

- Specific details help the reader understand what the characters experienced.

- This paragraph ends the story.

But it didn't feel good to see Jerry get up, grab his present, and run out of the house. My mom gave me a stern look and told me I'd better go find him. I found Jerry sitting on the porch steps. I apologized for making fun of him. I told him I'd wanted to get even for having a party with nothing to do but swim. Jerry said he was sorry and that he had forgotten that I couldn't swim. Then we both went back to my party. Next time instead of being a jerk when my friend upsets me, I'll tell him why I'm angry instead of trying to get even.

- The writer tells what he learned from his mistake.

868 UNIT 7 What Can We Learn from Our Mistakes?

Listening, Speaking, and Viewing

News Report

Many of the reading selections in this unit are about topics and events that happened in the past. When you read about the past, you read about events that have already happened. One of the first sources to report events that have already happened is nightly news broadcasts.

What Is It?

A news broadcast is a program on television or radio that reports the most important news stories from that day. Each story is told by a reporter or a news anchor. A reporter is someone who goes out and researches a story. A news anchor reads the news from the radio or television station.

Why Is It Important?

People depend on news broadcasts to learn about events that happen in their neighborhood, in other parts of the country, and around the world.

How Do I Do It?

The most important rule in news reporting is to write only the facts. This means that everything you include in your report must be true and have really happened. The best way to report a news story is to find out the 5 W's of the story; *who, what, when, where,* and *why.*

- Choose a historical event that interests you or a historical topic that you have read about in this unit. Examples from the unit include desegregation, internment camps, the great radio scare, and westward migration.
- Answer the 5 W's about your topic. You may have to use the Internet, encyclopedias, or textbooks to find your answers.
- Make a chart like the one below to organize your research.

Japanese Internment

Who	Japanese Americans
What	Much of the Japanese population in the United States was forced to leave their homes and live together in large camps.
When	beginning in 1942
Where	in the western part of the United States
Why	because the United States and Japan were fighting against each other during World War II

- Once you have researched your topic and identified the 5 W's, turn your notes into a short paragraph about your topic. Remember to include only facts, not your own opinions, about the topic.

Speak to Learn Imagine you are a news reporter assigned to broadcast a story about your topic. Use the information you collected to present a short news report about your chosen historical event. Practice reading your paragraph aloud. Speak slowly and clearly, making certain that your broadcast includes the 5 W's. Practice reporting your story to a partner before sharing it with the class.

READING WORKSHOP 4

Skills Focus

You will practice using these skills when you read the following selections:
- "The Shutout," p. 874
- "The Talking Skull," p. 884

Reading
- Making inferences

Literature
- Identifying, analyzing, and evaluating sequence of events/time order

Vocabulary
- Using Anglo-Saxon roots to determine the meanings of unfamiliar words

Writing/Grammar
- Determining subject-verb agreement for special noun subjects

Skill Lesson

Inferring

Learn It!

What Is It? You already learned about making inferences in Unit 3, but let's go back over the basics. You **infer** when you figure out information the author doesn't give you directly. You "read between the lines." **Inferring** uses many of the skills you have learned in the previous units, such as activating your prior knowledge, connecting, asking questions, and predicting. Reading would not be much fun if the author didn't give you a chance to infer!

Analyzing Cartoons
What can you infer from this cartoon? Does the boy like to do homework?

© 2002 Bill Amend/Distributed by Universal Press Syndicate

Objectives (pp. 870–871)
Reading Make inferences

READING WORKSHOP 4 • Inferring

Why Is It Important? If you infer as you read, reading is more fun, and you understand more of what you read. It helps you understand characters, identify main ideas and themes, and connect to what you are reading.

How Do I Do It? As you read, follow these steps:
- Ask "I wonder" questions as you read.
- Look at the text for important clues.
- Think about what you already know that connects to information in the text.
- See if you can now answer your "I wonder" questions.

Here is how one student made an inference while reading "The Gold Cadillac."

Study Central Visit www.glencoe.com and click on Study Central to review inferring.

> The policeman told my father to get in the back of the police car. My father did. One policeman got back into the police car. The other policeman slid behind the wheel of our Cadillac. The police car started off. The Cadillac followed. Wilma and I looked at each other and at our mother. We didn't know what to think. We were scared.

Wait a minute. I can't quite picture this scene. Who is driving the Cadillac? The text tells me that the policeman slid behind the wheel of the Cadillac. I know that whoever is driving is behind the wheel. Even though the author doesn't come right out and say it, I know that the policeman must be driving the Cadillac. Now the picture is clearer.

Practice It!
In your Learner's Notebook, copy the steps listed in "How Do I Do It?"

Use It!
As you read the selections, ask and try to answer your "I Wonder" questions.

READING WORKSHOP 4 • Inferring

Before You Read : The Shutout

Meet the Authors

The McKissacks are a husband-and-wife writing team. Since 1984, they have written more than 100 books. Fred does the research, and Patricia does the writing. Fred McKissack says, "One of the reasons we write for children is to introduce them to African and African American history and historical figures and to get them to internalize the information not just academically, but also emotionally. We want them to feel the tremendous amount of hurt and sadness that racism and discrimination cause all people, regardless of race."

Author Search For more about the McKissacks, go to www.glencoe.com.

Objectives (pp. 872–879)
Reading Make inferences • Make connections from text to self
Literature Identify text structure: sequence, time order
Vocabulary Explore word origins: Anglo-Saxon

Vocabulary Preview

rivaling (RY vul ing) *v.* being equal to or matching; form of the verb *rival* **(p. 875)** *Baseball is rivaling basketball in popularity.*

privileged (PRIH vih lijd) *adj.* having or enjoying one or more advantages **(p. 878)** *Horse racing was a sport enjoyed only by privileged people.*

composed (kum POHZD) *v.* formed by putting together; form of the verb *compose* **(p. 878)** *The Negro Leagues were composed of the best players.*

documentation (dok yuh men TAY shun) *n.* something recorded that serves as proof **(p. 879)** *Players needed documentation to be included in the Hall of Fame.*

Write to Learn In your Learner's Notebook, write a sentence for each vocabulary word that fits its meaning.

English Language Coach

Anglo-Saxon Origins Anglo-Saxon is the name of a language also known as Old English. It developed when the Angles and the Saxons conquered England in the fifth century.

Many English base words and roots come from Anglo-Saxon, or Old English. Most of the basic, simple words that we use generally come from Old English. Look at the words *silly* and *ridiculous*. Which word do you think comes from Old English? That's right, *silly* comes from Old English. *Ridiculous* comes from Latin.

Guess the Roots Guess which word in each pair is the one that came from Old English. Then check your guesses in a dictionary. (The history of a word is given inside [] marks at the beginning of the dictionary entry. "OE" means "Old English.")

1. forward/advance
2. like/admire
3. fear/panic
4. revolve/spin

READING WORKSHOP 4 • Inferring

Skills Preview

Key Reading Skill: Inferring

Before you read, look at the steps for inferring you wrote in your Learner's Notebook.

Remember that inferring is not making wild guesses! Your answer to your "I wonder" questions must be backed up by clues from the text.

Key Literary Element: Sequence of Events/Time Order

Sequence of events is the order in which events take place. Often the sequence of events organizes a written work. But sometimes writers will go back and forth in time. To understand the sequence of events, it is important to keep track of when things happen.

As you read, use these tips to understand the order in which things happen.
- Pay attention to dates and times.
- Make a list of important dates and events.

Date	Event
1820	Baseball was played in Mr. Mumford's pasture.
1834	Carver wrote about American version of rounders.

Write to Learn Use a chart like the one above to help you organize dates and events as you read "The Shutout." Label the left-hand column *Date*. Label the other column *Event*.

- Read a few paragraphs at a time before filling in the chart because events may not be mentioned in chronological order.
- Enter your notes in pencil. As you read, you may find information that needs to be inserted before something you have already written.
- In the *Date* column, it may not always be possible to list an exact year; for example, you may have to list a period of time such as *Before the Civil War*.

Get Ready to Read

Connect to the Reading

Have you ever been excluded, or kept out, of a team, a club, or a group of friends? Why were you excluded? How did being excluded make you feel? How did you react? How was the problem solved?

Write to Learn In your Learner's Notebook, write about this experience. If you wish, volunteer to read your entry aloud to the class.

Build Background

The title "The Shutout" is a pun—a play on words in which a double meaning is given to the same word. In baseball, the word *shutout* means "a game in which one team doesn't score any runs." Shut out also means "to exclude" or "to not allow to join or participate." In this article, it refers to African American players' being kept from joining all-white baseball teams.

Set Purposes for Reading

BIG Question Read "The Shutout" to find out what kinds of mistakes were made as the game of baseball developed and what lessons were learned from them.

Set Your Own Purpose What else would you like to learn from the selection to help you answer the Big Question? Write your own purpose for reading this selection on "The Shutout" part of the Workshop 4 Foldable.

Interactive Literary Elements Handbook
To review or learn more about the literary elements, go to www.glencoe.com.

Keep Moving

Use the skills above as you read the following selection.

The Shutout 873

READING WORKSHOP 4

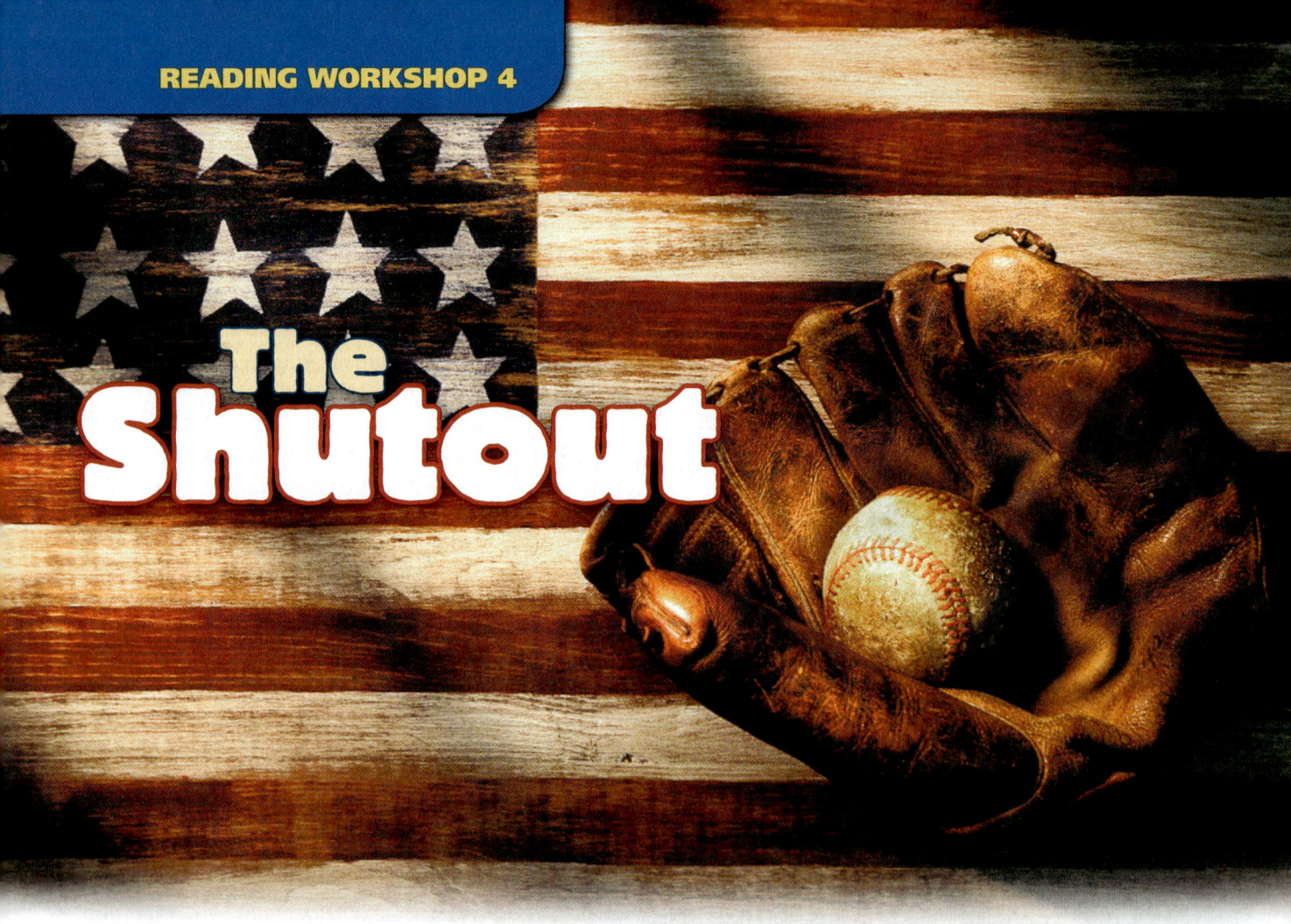

The Shutout

by Patricia C. McKissack and Frederick McKissack, Jr.

The history of baseball is difficult to trace because it is embroidered with wonderful anecdotes[1] that are fun but not necessarily supported by fact. There are a lot of myths that persist about baseball—the games, the players, the owners, and the fans—in spite of contemporary research that disproves most of them. For example, the story that West Point cadet[2] Abner Doubleday "invented" baseball in 1839 while at Cooperstown, New York, continues to be widely accepted, even though, according to his diaries, Doubleday never visited Cooperstown. A number of records and documents show that people were playing stick-and-ball games long before the 1839 date. 🔲

---

1. **Anecdotes** (AN ik dohts) are short, entertaining tales.
2. **West Point** in New York is the location of the United States Military Academy. A **cadet** (kuh DET) is a student at the academy.

Practice the Skills

1 **Key Reading Skill**

Inferring You have to make an inference to understand what the authors are saying in this paragraph. Ask yourself this question: "I wonder, did Abner Doubleday invent baseball?" Look for clues in the paragraph.

Albigence Waldo, a surgeon with George Washington's troops at Valley Forge,[3] wrote in his diary that soldiers were "batting balls and running bases" in their free time. Samuel Hopkins Adams (1871–1958), an American historical novelist, stated that his grandfather "played baseball on Mr. Mumford's pasture" in the 1820's.

Although baseball is a uniquely American sport, it was not invented by a single person. Probably the **game** evolved[4] from a variety of stick-and-ball games that were played in Europe, Asia, Africa, and the Americas for centuries and brought to the colonies by the most diverse[5] group of people ever to populate a continent. More specifically, some historians believe baseball is an outgrowth of its first cousin, *rounders,* an English game. Robin Carver wrote in his *Book of Sports* (1834) that "an American version of rounders called *goal ball* was **rivaling** cricket[6] in popularity." ▣2

It is generally accepted that by 1845, baseball, as it is recognized today, was becoming popular, especially in New York. In that year a group of baseball enthusiasts organized the New York Knickerbocker Club. They tried to standardize the game by establishing guidelines for "proper play." ▣3

The Knickerbockers' rules set the playing field—a diamond-shaped infield with four bases (first, second, third, and home) placed ninety feet apart. At that time, the pitching distance was forty-five feet from home base and the "pitch" was thrown underhanded. The three-strikes-out rule, the three-out inning, and the ways in which a player could be called out were also specified. However, the nine-man team and nine-inning game were not established until later. Over the years, the Knickerbockers' basic rules of play haven't changed much.

---

3. **Valley Forge,** Pennsylvania, was the site of the 1777–1778 winter quarters of George Washington and his Continental Army during the Revolutionary War.
4. Something that has **evolved** (ih VOLVD) has developed slowly.
5. A **diverse** (dih VURS) group is made up of members from different races or backgrounds.
6. **Cricket** (KRIK uht) is an English ball game played by two sides of 11 players each on a field with two wickets, or sets of stumps, set 66 feet apart. The ball is bowled at the wickets, each of which is defended by a batsman.

Vocabulary

rivaling (RY vul ing) *v.* being equal to or matching

Practice the Skills

▣2 **English Language Coach**

Anglo-Saxon Origins Look up the word **game** in a dictionary. What is the Old English word for *game*?

▣3 **Key Literary Element**

Sequence of Events/Time Order What date did the writers include in this paragraph? Why? What else happened that year? Record the date and the two events on your chart.

READING WORKSHOP 4

In 1857–1858, the newly organized National Association of Base Ball Players was formed, and baseball became a business. Twenty-five clubs—mostly from eastern states—formed the Association for the purpose of setting rules and guidelines for club and team competition. The Association defined a professional player as a person who played for money, place, or emolument (profit)." The Association also authorized an admission fee for one of the first "all-star" games between Brooklyn and New York. Fifteen hundred people paid fifty cents to see that game. Baseball was on its way to becoming the nation's number-one sport. 5

Grand match for the championship at the Elysian Fields, Hoboken, New Jersey. Currier and Ives, 1865

Analyzing the Art Study this picture of a baseball game of the late 1800s. Based on the picture, in what ways was baseball different than it is today? In what ways was it similar to baseball today?

Practice the Skills

5 **Key Literary Element**

Sequence of Events/Time Order What year did baseball become a business? Record this on your chart. What year is the date of one of the earliest mentions of baseball? (Make sure this date is on your chart.)

READING WORKSHOP 4

Monte Irvin, Willie Mays, and Henry Thompson played in the 1951 World Series for the New York Giants. It was the first time in World Series history that a team had an all African American outfield.

By 1860, the same year South Carolina seceded[7] from the Union, there were about sixty teams in the Association. For obvious reasons none of them were from the South. Baseball's development was slow during the Civil War years, but teams continued to compete, and military records show that, sometimes between battles, Union soldiers chose up teams and played baseball games. It was during this time that records began mentioning African-American players. One war journalist noted that black players were "sought after as teammates because of their skill as ball handlers." 6 7

Information about the role of African Americans in the early stages of baseball development is slight. Several West African cultures had stick-and-ball and running games, so at least some blacks were familiar with the concept of baseball. Baseball, however, was not a popular southern sport, never

---

7. After South Carolina **seceded** (sih SEE dud) from the Union in 1860, ten other states also withdrew and formed the Confederate States of America during the Civil War (1861–1865).

Practice the Skills

6 **Key Literary Element**

Sequence of Events/Time Order Record the date 1860 on your chart. What happened in that year? Enter the event in the Event column.

7 **Key Reading Skill**

Inferring "I wonder why none of the teams were from the South?" What clue do the writers give you to answer this question? (Hint: Would two groups at war with each other play in the same association?)

The Shutout 877

equal to boxing, wrestling, footracing, or horse racing among the **privileged** landowners.

Slave **owners** preferred these individual sports because they could enter their slaves in competitions, watch the event from a safe distance, pocket the winnings, and personally never raise a sweat. There are documents to show that slave masters made a great deal of money from the athletic skills of their slaves. 8

Free blacks, on the other hand, played on and against integrated[8] teams in large eastern cities and in small midwestern hamlets.[9] It is believed that some of the emancipated[10] slaves and runaways who served in the Union Army learned how to play baseball from northern blacks and whites who had been playing together for years.

After the Civil War, returning soldiers helped to inspire a new interest in baseball all over the country. Teams sprung up in northern and Midwestern cities, and naturally African Americans were interested in joining some of these clubs. But the National Association of Base Ball Players had other ideas. They voted in December 1867 not to admit any team for membership that "may be **composed** of one or more colored persons." Their reasoning was as irrational[11] as the racism that shaped it: "If colored clubs were admitted,"

Practice the Skills

8 **English Language Coach**
Anglo-Saxon Origins Look up the word **owner** in a dictionary. What was the Old English word it came from?

A batter for the New York Black Yankees stands at home plate with Newark Eagles' catcher and the umpire waiting for a pitch.

---

8. *Integrated* (IN tuh gray tid) teams were open to both African American and white players.
9. *Hamlets* (HAM luhts) are small villages.
10. *Emancipated* (ih MAN suh pay tid) slaves had been freed from slavery.
11. Reasoning that is *irrational* (ih RASH uh nul) is unreasonable or lacking sense.

Vocabulary

privileged (PRIH vih lijd) *adj.* having or enjoying one or more advantages

composed (kum POHZD) *v.* formed by putting together

the Association stated, "there would be in all probability some division of feeling whereas, by excluding them no injury could result to anyone . . . and [we wish] to keep out of the convention the discussion of any subjects having a political bearing as this [admission of blacks on the Association teams] undoubtedly would." **9**

So, from the start, organized baseball tried to limit or exclude African-American participation. In the early days a few black ball players managed to play on integrated minor league teams. A few even made it to the majors, but by the turn of the century, black players were shut out of the major leagues until after World War II. That doesn't mean African Americans didn't play the game. They did. **10**

Black people organized their own teams, formed leagues, and competed for championships. The history of the old "Negro Leagues" and the players who barnstormed[12] on black diamonds is one of baseball's most interesting chapters, but the story is a researcher's nightmare. Black baseball was outside the mainstream of the major leagues, so team and player records weren't well kept, and for the most part, the white press ignored black clubs or portrayed them as clowns. And for a long time the Baseball Hall of Fame didn't recognize any of the Negro League players. Because of the lack of **documentation**, many people thought the Negro Leagues' stories were nothing more than myths and yarns, but that is not the case. The history of the Negro Leagues is a patchwork of human drama and comedy, filled with legendary heroes, infamous owners, triple-headers, low pay, and long bus rides home—not unlike the majors. **11** ○

---

12. Players who **barnstormed** (BARN stormd) toured rural areas, stopping briefly to take part in baseball games.

Vocabulary

documentation (dok yuh men TAY shun) *n.* something recorded that serves as proof

---

Practice the Skills

9 **Key Literary Element**

Sequence of Events/Time Order Two events in this paragraph belong on your chart. The first event does not have an exact date. How will you list it in the Date column?

10 **Key Literary Element**

Sequence of Events/Time Order After baseball became a business, what year were African American players shut out of the major leagues? Record the event and the year it happened on your chart.

11 **BIG Question**

Did anyone make a mistake in this selection? What was the mistake? Was the mistake corrected? Did anyone learn from the mistake? Write your answers on your Foldable. Your response will help you complete the Unit Challenge.

The Shutout 879

READING WORKSHOP 4 • Inferring

After You Read · The Shutout

Answering the Big Question

1. After reading this selection, what are your thoughts about learning from mistakes?
2. **Recall** Who created the playing rules for baseball?
   TIP Right There
3. **Summarize** What do historians know about the origins of the game of baseball?
   TIP Think and Search

Critical Thinking

4. **Infer** In what way did the end of the Civil War help baseball grow in popularity?
   TIP Author and Me
5. **Connect** How might you have felt as an African American baseball player who was not allowed to play in the major leagues?
   TIP On My Own
6. **Synthesize** Do you think that there is segregation in sports today? Explain.
   TIP On My Own
7. **Evaluate** The National Association of Base Ball Players argued that they were keeping African Americans out of the Association so that "no injury could result to anyone." Do you agree with that argument? Explain.
   TIP On My Own

Objectives (pp. 880–881)
Reading Make inferences
Literature Identify text structure: sequence, time order
Vocabulary Explore word origins: Anglo-Saxon
Writing Use the RAFT system: respond to literature
Grammar Use correct subject-verb agreement: special nouns

Write About Your Reading

Use the RAFT system to write about "The Shutout."
Role: A Union Army soldier
Audience: Your family
Format: A letter
Topic: The new game you just learned about (baseball)

880 UNIT 7   What Can We Learn from Our Mistakes?

Skills Review

Key Reading Skill: Inferring

8. When the authors write that slave owners could "watch the event from a safe distance, pocket the winnings, and personally never raise a sweat," what are they inferring about slave owners?

Key Literary Element: Sequence of Events/Time Order

Use your chart to answer the following questions.

9. When did Albigence Waldo see a game of "batting balls and running bases"?
10. When did Robin Carver write about *goal ball*?
11. When was the Knickerbocker Club organized?
12. When were African Americans allowed into the major leagues?

Vocabulary Check

Match the following vocabulary words with their definitions.

13. rivaling
14. documentation
15. privileged
16. composed

a. formed by putting together
b. having or enjoying one or more advantages
c. being equal to
d. something recorded that serves as proof

17. **English Language Coach** The Anglo-Saxon root and prefix *fore* has two meanings. One is "before" and the other is "in front of."

Look at the words below and define four of them using your knowledge of *fore*.

foretell	forewarn	foresee
foreleg	forehead	forefather
forecast	foremost	foreclose

Grammar Link: Subject-Verb Agreement with Special Nouns

Subject-verb agreement can be a problem when nouns such as *glasses, pants, pliers,* and *scissors* are used as the subject of a sentence.

- Even if they stand for only one item, some words that end in *s* (such as *pants*) are considered plural. Because they are plural, they need plural verbs.

    My **pants are** in the closet.

- It is a different story when *pair of* comes before those same words *(pair of pants)*. The words then take a singular verb. This is because the word *pair* becomes the subject, and *of pants* becomes a prepositional phrase. The word *pair* is singular.

    A **pair of pants is** hanging in the closet.

Watch Out! There are words that don't follow this rule. Even though *news* ends in an *s*, it is a singular noun. The same goes for the word *measles*.

Grammar Practice

On a separate sheet of paper, write the correct verb for each sentence.

18. The scissors (is, are) in the art box.
19. The pliers (is, are) in the drawer.
20. That pair of scissors (need, needs) to be sharpened.
21. The news (is, are) on at ten o'clock.
22. Where (is, are) your glasses?
23. Those pants (is, are) too tight.

Writing Application Look back at the RAFT assignment you wrote. Make sure that all of the subjects and the verbs agree.

Web Activities For eFlashcards, Selection Quick Checks, and other Web activities, go to www.glencoe.com.

READING WORKSHOP 4 • Inferring

Before You Read : The Talking Skull

Meet the Author
Donna L. Washington is a writer, storyteller, and actress. "The Talking Skull" is from Washington's book *A Pride of African Tales*.

Author Search For more about Donna L. Washington, go to www.glencoe.com.

Objectives (pp. 882–891)
Reading Make inferences • Make connections from text to self
Literature Identify text structure: sequence, time order
Vocabulary Explore word origins: Anglo-Saxon • Identify compound words

Vocabulary Preview

stammer (STAM mur) *v.* to speak with difficulty; to repeat the same sound several times when trying to say a word **(p. 886)** *Eventually, the man was able to stammer some words.*

spout (spowt) *v.* to speak rapidly; to say something in a loud, boastful manner **(p. 886)** *The man was amazed that the skull was able to spout words of wisdom.*

commotion (kuh MOH shun) *n.* noisy rushing about; confusion **(p. 889)** *There was so much commotion, the chief came to see what was going on.*

intellectual (in tuh LEK choo ul) *adj.* requiring thought and understanding **(p. 890)** *The scholar was sure the chief would understand an intellectual matter.*

Write to Learn Be creative. Write one or two paragraphs about a strange walk in the woods. Use as many vocabulary words as you can.

English Language Coach

Anglo-Saxon Origins and Compound Words Many basic English words come from Anglo-Saxon, or Old English. These basic words can often be combined to form compound words. A compound word combines two words. The meaning of a compound word combines the meanings of the individual words in some way.

Here are some compounds formed from words with Anglo-Saxon origins.

Compound Word	Definition
homemade	made in the home
rowboat	a small boat designed to be rowed
horseshoe	iron put on a horse's hoof to protect it

Write to Learn How many compound words can you create by combining the words below? What are their definitions?

day	night	time	play
home	one	every	some
body	to	thing	no

READING WORKSHOP 4 • Inferring

Skills Preview

Key Reading Skill: Inferring

Because they are not stated directly in the text, inferences can be easy to miss. Fiction writers can ask you to infer a lot more than nonfiction writers.

Use these tips to help you infer as you read:
- Monitor your comprehension. Stop when you get confused.
- Ask yourself "I wonder" questions.
- Look for clues in the text.
- Hint: Writers sometimes use punctuation, style, or word choice to give you clues about what they are inferring.
- Use your own experience and knowledge to help you figure out what the writer isn't saying directly.

Write to Learn In your Learner's Notebook, make a list of points to remember so that you can infer as you read.

Key Literary Element: Sequence of Events/Time Order

In fiction, the sequence of events is the plot, or action, of the story. In the plot, a problem is explored and then usually solved. The sequence of events can move the plot forward in two ways: by relating to past or present action or by suggesting future action.

As you read, ask yourself the following questions about each event in the plot:
- What does this event tell me about past action?
- What does this event tell me about present action?
- What does this event tell me about future action?

Write to Learn In your Learner's Notebook, write each important event in the story's plot. For each entry, write whether the event relates to a past action, a present action, or a future action.

Get Ready to Read

Connect to the Reading

Has someone you know ever made the same mistake over and over? What was the mistake? Why did the person continue to make it? Why didn't the person learn his or her lesson after making the mistake the first or second time? What finally helped the person not to make the mistake again?

Partner Talk With a partner, discuss your answers to the questions above.

Build Background

This fable is from Cameroon, a country in western Africa. Here are some facts about the people of Cameroon:
- Most of the people live in small towns or villages.
- Most of the people are farmers of cacao, coffee, tobacco, cotton, or bananas. Others are herders of cattle, goats, sheep, or pigs.
- The people belong to more than 200 ethnic groups. Each group speaks its own language.

Set Purposes for Reading

BIG Question Read the selection "The Talking Skull" to find out about learning from mistakes.

Set Your Own Purpose What else would you like to learn from the article to help you answer the Big Question? Write your own purpose on "The Talking Skull" part of the Workshop 4 Foldable.

Interactive Literary Elements Handbook
To review or learn more about the literary elements, go to www.glencoe.com.

Keep Moving

Use these skills as you read the following selection.

The Talking Skull **883**

READING WORKSHOP 4

The Talking Skull

A Fable from Cameroon from *A Pride of African Tales*

by Donna L. Washington

"The Talking Skull" is an African fable about the importance of listening and thinking before opening one's mouth.

Once a man was walking down the road toward his village. He was not paying attention to anything around him. This man considered himself a scholar[1] of life. He was always deep in thought. He liked to think about important things. He did not put his mind to ordinary problems. If it wasn't impossible, or at least very complicated, he didn't care about it at all.

This man spent all day looking out over the ocean, and he only noticed things he thought were useful. He didn't notice the beauty of the ocean. The only things he considered were sharks and **shipwrecks**. 1 He didn't notice the clear blue sky. He was

---

1. A *scholar* is a person who has knowledge in a certain area.

Practice the Skills

1 **English Language Coach**

Anglo-Saxon Origins and Compound Words What two basic words make up the compound word **shipwrecks**? What are *shipwrecks*?

READING WORKSHOP 4

thinking about all the storms that must have been churning far away. He did not notice the wonderful songs of the birds. He only thought about how many of their nests had been robbed. He didn't notice the playful animals swinging through branches or rustling in the grass. He only wondered whether or not the great cats were on the prowl. That was the kind of man he was. **2**

As he walked back toward the village that day, he happened to pass a pile of bones. They were bleached white and they gleamed in the bright sun. He stopped and stared down at them. He was the sort of man who would stop to stare down at a pile of bones. The skull on the pile was resting above all the other bones, and it seemed to be watching the man just as intently as he was watching it. **3**

The man reached out and picked up the skull. He held it one way and then another. He looked gravely into the empty eye sockets and said, "What brought you here, brother?"

"Talking," the skull replied without much interest.

The man was so shocked, he dropped the skull and jumped back. He watched the skull for a few minutes before he managed to **stammer** out, "You can talk!"

"Yes," said the skull. "Talking is very easy. All you have to do is open up your mouth and out it comes. Talking is easy. Finding something worthwhile to say is not."

The man was amazed. He had never seen a talking skull before, let alone one that could **spout** such wisdom. "I must take you to the village!" the man exclaimed.

He scooped up the skull and ran as fast as he could. The villagers saw him coming, and a great many of them ran for their homes. You see, he was the kind of man who was always getting busy people into useless conversations when there was work to be done. He never seemed to be quiet, and he never spoke about anything anyone ever wanted to hear.

Practice the Skills

2 **Key Reading Skill**

Inferring What is the author inferring about the man?

3 **Key Literary Element**

Sequence of Events/Time Order What events have taken place so far in the plot? Has anything in the story so far told you about past action?

Vocabulary

stammer (STAM mur) v. to speak with difficulty; to repeat the same sound several times when trying to say a word

spout (spowt) v. to speak rapidly; to say something in a loud, boastful manner

READING WORKSHOP 4

The Talking Skull

READING WORKSHOP 4

As he entered the village, he called out to his neighbors, "Come quickly! I have something wonderful to show you!" No one came.

The man was so excited that he did not even realize that the few people in sight were moving away from him. "Put down whatever you are doing, everyone! I have a marvelous mystery to show all of you, the likes of which you have never before seen!"

When the man said the word "mystery," you can be sure he got the attention of some of the villagers. They started poking their heads out of their houses. Women left their yams cooking, men put down their digging sticks, and children stopped their playing. They all began to gather around the man. ▮4

When he saw that he had everyone's attention, he drew out the skull. He could not have prepared himself for what happened next.

Everyone stared at the skull for a moment. Then they all started yelling.

"Mama! What is he doing?" cried a little boy.

"How dare you bring that thing here!" his mother howled, waving a spoon.

"Somebody do something!" said another, clutching her child.

"Send him away!" demanded a third mother.

The men who still had gardening tools in their hands started waving them.

"Move out of the way!" yelled a man with a digging stick.

"Somebody get the chief!" said an old man holding his grandson's hand. ▮5

There was so much **commotion,** the chief came to see what was happening.

"What is going on?" the chief roared. He was a very orderly chief, and he did not like all this yelling and brandishing[2] of gardening tools in the middle of the village.

2. *Brandishing* something means waving or shaking it in a challenging way.

Vocabulary

commotion (kuh MOH shun) *n.* noisy rushing about; confusion

Practice the Skills

▮4 **Key Reading Skill**

Inferring What is the author inferring when she says that the word *mystery* got some people's attention?

▮5 **Key Literar Element**

Sequence of Events/Time Order A new event has taken place in the plot. What is it? Has this event happened in time order? What does this event tell you about present action?

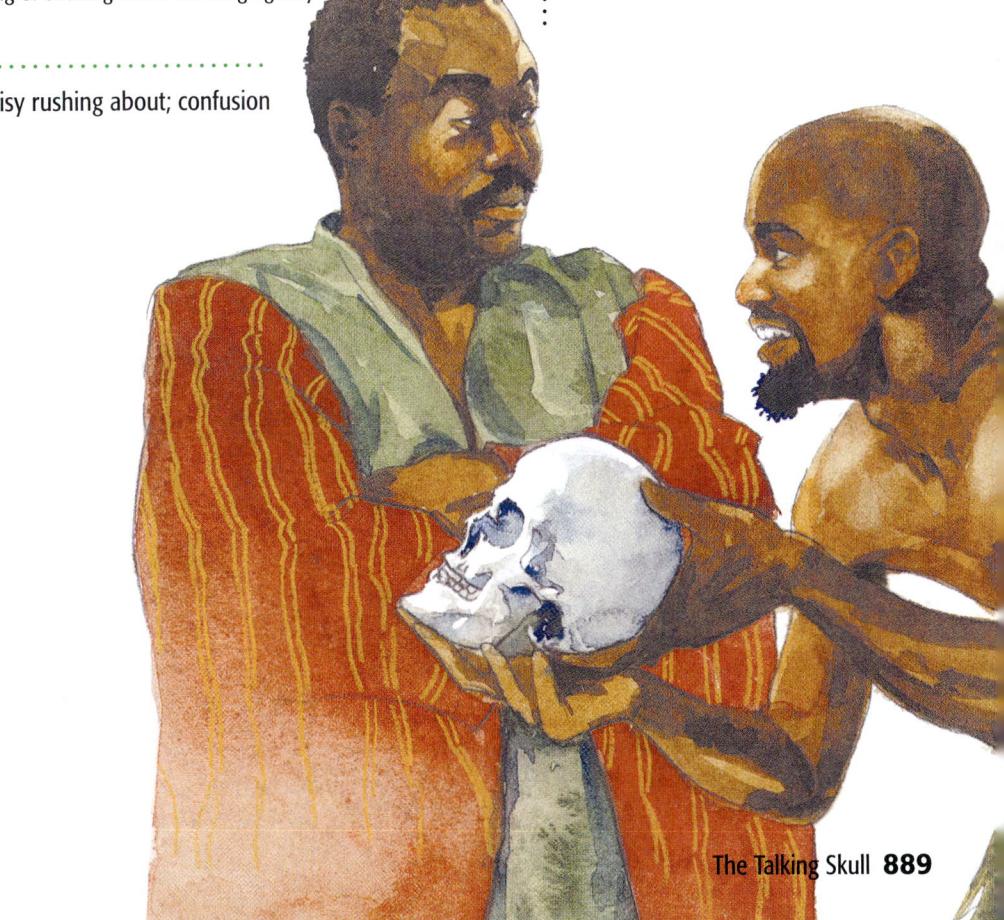

The Talking Skull

All the people were silent except for one villager. He stood up and pointed to the man with the skull.

"This man told us he had something to show us. Then he pulled out that awful skull. We thought he was trying to call the Dark Spirits to the village, and we were trying to stop him."

"Oh," said the chief, eyeing the man with the skull. "And were you going to call Dark Spirits to my village?"

"Certainly not!" the scholar declared, glad that the chief was there. He was sure the chief would understand this **intellectual** matter.

"Then what were you doing?" the chief asked with curiosity.

"Well," the man said in a pompous[3] voice, "I was on my way home from the ocean when I came across a pile of bones. On top of the heap was this skull. It spoke to me! I brought it here to share this wonder with the village." **6**

The chief did not look convinced.

"I'll show you," the man said, raising the skull so that it looked at the chief. "Say something to the chief," he commanded.

The skull said nothing. The chief frowned.

"Speak!" the man said. "I command you!"

The skull remained silent. One of the children laughed.

"Speak!" he said. "You must speak!" The man started getting nervous.

The skull said nothing. The man begged and pleaded with the skull. The skull remained silent. The people began to get angry again, and the chief got angry right along with them.

"You are always a troublemaker in my village, and now you come here with this nonsense!" The chief and the people had had enough. They took the skull from the man, found the mound of bones he had taken it from, and put it back there.

That very day the villagers held a meeting with the chief and decided to throw the man out of their village. They watched him collect his few belongings and said to him, "Since you found that skull so much company, why don't you go live with it!" **7**

---

3. A **pompous** voice is one that sounds self-important.

Vocabulary

intellectual (in tuh LEK choo ul) *adj.* requiring thought and understanding

Practice the Skills

6 Reviewing Skills

Evaluating The man says that he has brought the skull to the village because he wants to share it. Do you believe him? Explain.

7 Key Literary Element

Sequence of Events/Time Order A new event has taken place in the plot. What is it? Has this event happened in time order? What does the event tell you about future action?

The man stormed out of the village and down the road to the pile of bones. He picked up the skull. Before he could get one word out of his mouth, the skull said, "Sorry about that."

"What? Now you talk! That is not going to do me much good! Why didn't you say something back in the village?"

"I told you," the skull replied. "It is easy to talk. It is not always easy to find something **worthwhile** to say." 8

"You are absolutely unpleasant!" the man screamed. "I don't know what trouble you caused that brought you to this sorry state, but you deserve everything you got!"

"I already told you what got me into trouble," the skull replied. "Talking. Same as you." 9 ○

Practice the Skills

8 English Language Coach

Anglo-Saxon Origins and Compound Words What are the origins and meanings of the words *worth* and *while*? What does **worthwhile** mean?

9 BIG Question

What mistake do you think the skull made in the past? What lesson is he trying to teach the man? Record your response on your Foldable. Your response will help you complete the Unit Challenge later.

READING WORKSHOP 4 • Inferring

After You Read : The Talking Skull

Answering the BIG Question

1. After reading this fable, what are your thoughts about learning from your mistakes?

2. **Recall** Why do the villagers panic when they see the skull?
   TIP Right There

3. **Recall** What does the skull do when the man asks it to speak to the villagers?
   TIP Right There

Critical Thinking

4. **Evaluate** Do you think the chief is a good leader? Explain.
   TIP Author and Me

5. **Predict** What do you think will happen to the man now? Explain.
   TIP On Your Own

6. **Connect** Do you agree with the skull's opinion that talking is easy but finding something worthwhile to say is not? Explain.
   TIP On Your Own

Write About Your Reading

Use the RAFT system to write about "The Talking Skull."
Role: The talking skull
Audience: The main character
Format: A letter
Topic: Your story of how you made your mistake and what happened after you made it

Objectives (pp. 892–893)
Reading Make inferences • Make connections from text to self
Literature Identify text structure: sequence, time order
Vocabulary Explore word origins: Anglo-Saxon • Identify compound words
Writing Use the RAFT system: respond to literature
Grammar Use correct subject-verb agreement: indefinite pronouns

Skills Review

Key Reading Skill: Inferring

7. How do you think the man feels about himself? What clues in the text help you answer this question?
8. Did the skull learn from its mistake? Explain.

Key Literary Element: Sequence of Events/Time Order

Use your notes from your reading to answer the following questions.

9. What was one event in the plot that told you about past action?
10. What was one event in the plot that told you about present action?
11. What was one event in the plot that told you about future action?

Vocabulary Check

Match each vocabulary word with its definition.

12. spout
13. intellectual
14. stammer
15. commotion

a. to speak with difficulty
b. to say something in a loud, boastful manner
c. noisy rushing about; confusion
d. requiring thought

16. **English Language Coach** Use the words *ship, wreck, wind, break, worth, while,* or compound words that contain them as you write a diary entry about a trip to the beach in winter.

Web Activities For eFlashcards, Selection Quick Checks, and other Web activities, go to www.glencoe.com.

Grammar Link: Subject-Verb Agreement with Indefinite Pronouns

An indefinite pronoun is a pronoun that does not stand for a particular person, place, or thing. The chart shows which indefinite subject pronouns use singular verbs, which use plural verbs, and which use singular or plural verbs, depending on the words to which they refer.

Indefinite Pronouns – Singular Verbs
another, anybody, anyone, anything, each, either, everybody, everyone, everything, much, neither, nobody, no one, nothing, one, somebody, someone, something
Examples
Another bus was coming.   Anybody is welcome here. Either hat will be warm.   Everyone was invited.
Indefinite Pronouns – Plural Verbs
both, few, many, others, several
Examples
Many are asked to dance.   Few were chosen to sing.
Indefinite Pronouns – Singular or Plural Verbs
all, any, enough, most, some, none **Tip:** When you can count the thing to which a pronoun refers, the pronoun uses a plural verb. Otherwise it uses a singluar verb.
Examples
All of the ants were here.   All of the pie was here. Some of the pens are red.   Some of the water is red.

Grammar Practice

Complete the following sentences with the correct verb.

17. Someone (need, needs) to wash the clothes.
18. Several (come, comes) to the show every day.
19. All of the sky (is, are) blue.

Writing Application Look back at the RAFT assignment you wrote. Make sure that all of the subjects and the verbs agree. Pay close attention to subject-verb agreement with indefinite pronouns.

The Talking Skull

READING ACROSS TEXTS WORKSHOP

from The Great Fire
by Jim Murphy

Letters About the Fire
by Justin and Fannie Belle Becker

Skills Focus
You will use these skills as you read and compare the following selections:
- from *The Great Fire*, p. 897
- "Letters About the Fire," p. 905

Reading
- Making connections across texts
- Comparing/contrasting information in different texts

Literature
- Reading and understanding informative text
- Evaluating author's credibility

Do you believe everything you hear? Probably not. If two people tell you about something, their stories will hardly ever be exactly the same. You use your intelligence and experience to figure out who and what you want to believe. When you figure out who to believe and how much to believe, you're evaluating the speaker's **credibility.**

How to Read Across Texts: Author's Credibility

Credibility is believability. If you think that someone knows a topic well and you don't think he or she is lying, you consider him or her to be *credible*. If you don't think that person is biased, or influenced by someone or something, you think he or she is *credible*. You believe the speaker or writer.

You evaluate speakers' and writers' credibility everyday. When you read or hear something, you should think about
- who said or wrote it
- whether they know about the topic
- why they said or wrote what they did
- whether you believe it

Objectives (pp. 894–895)
Reading Compare and contrast: author's credibility across texts

READING ACROSS TEXTS WORKSHOP

Get Ready to Compare

When you want to learn about something, it's a good idea to get different points of view on the subject. You can do that by asking different people, or by reading articles, stories, and letters by different people. Then you decide which information and which people are most credible.

When you're reading about an event, ask yourself questions like these to determine which information is credible:

- **Knowledge** Does the author seem to know a lot about the event or one small part of the event?
- **Firsthand Experience** Did the author experience the event himself or herself (firsthand experience), or did the author get information from reading or speaking to other people?
- **Time** How long after the event did the author write the article or letter?
- **Details** Does the author give you many details? Are the details believable?
- **Purpose and Bias** What is the author's purpose for writing? Does the author seem to be trying to get you to believe his or her opinion? Does the author seem to be biased toward one opinion?
- **Fact and Opinion** Does the author present facts, opinions, or a combination of both?

Use Your Comparison

The three selections in this workshop are about the Great Chicago Fire. To help you evaluate the credibility of the authors and information in these selections, create a chart like the one pictured below in your Learner's Notebook. As you read, use the questions listed above to help you fill in this chart. You'll use the notes you enter in this chart to compare the selections later.

	from *The Great Fire*	Letter– Justin	Letter–Fannie Belle Becker
Knowledge			
Firsthand Experience			
Time			
Details			
Purpose and Bias			
Fact and Opinion			

READING ACROSS TEXTS WORKSHOP

Before You Read from *The Great Fire*

Meet the Author

Jim Murphy writes books about everything from lonely dinosaurs to weird inventions. He often writes about young people involved in historic events. According to Murphy, "... children weren't just observers of our history. They were actual participants and sometimes did amazing and heroic things."

To find out about the Great Chicago Fire, Murphy read letters and articles by people who were caught in the fire.

The Great Fire was published in 1995.

Author Search For more about Jim Murphy, go to www.glencoe.com.

Vocabulary Preview

remnants (REM nunts) *n.* what is left over; small remaining parts **(p. 897)** *Remnants of the burned house continued to glow.*

consequences (KON suh kwen suz) *n.* results of an action; outcomes **(p. 899)** *Poor communication led to tragic consequences.*

phantom (FAN tum) *adj.* looking or seeming real but is not **(p. 899)** *Firefighters wasted time looking for a phantom fire.*

vapor (VAY pur) *n.* small particles of mist, steam, or smoke that can be seen **(p. 899)** *When you breathe through your mouth in the winter, your breath turns to vapor.*

singe (sinj) *v.* to burn slightly **(p. 900)** *Flames began to singe the hair on the firefighters' heads and arms.*

velocity (vuh LOS uh tee) *n.* speed **(p. 902)** *The velocity of the wind helped spread the fire.*

Get Ready to Read

Connect to the Reading

What would you do if you saw a blazing fire in your neighborhood? Discuss your answer with a partner.

Build Background

On a fall evening in 1871, a fire broke out near the barn of Katherine O'Leary at 137 DeKoven Street in Chicago. By the time the fire was under control, a day and a half later, it had destroyed much of one of America's largest cities and left 90,000 people homeless. One-third of Chicago was destroyed in the Great Fire. The Great Chicago Fire is one of the most famous disasters in United States history.

Set Purposes for Reading

BIG Question Read to find out what mistakes allowed the Great Chicago Fire to spread so quickly.

Set Your Own Purpose What would you like to learn from *The Great Fire* that could help you to answer the Big Question? Write your own purpose on "The Great Fire" part of the Reading Across Texts Foldable.

Objectives (pp. 896–903)
Reading Compare and contrast: author's credibility across texts • Make connections from text to self

896 UNIT 7 What Can We Learn from Our Mistakes?

READING ACROSS TEXTS WORKSHOP

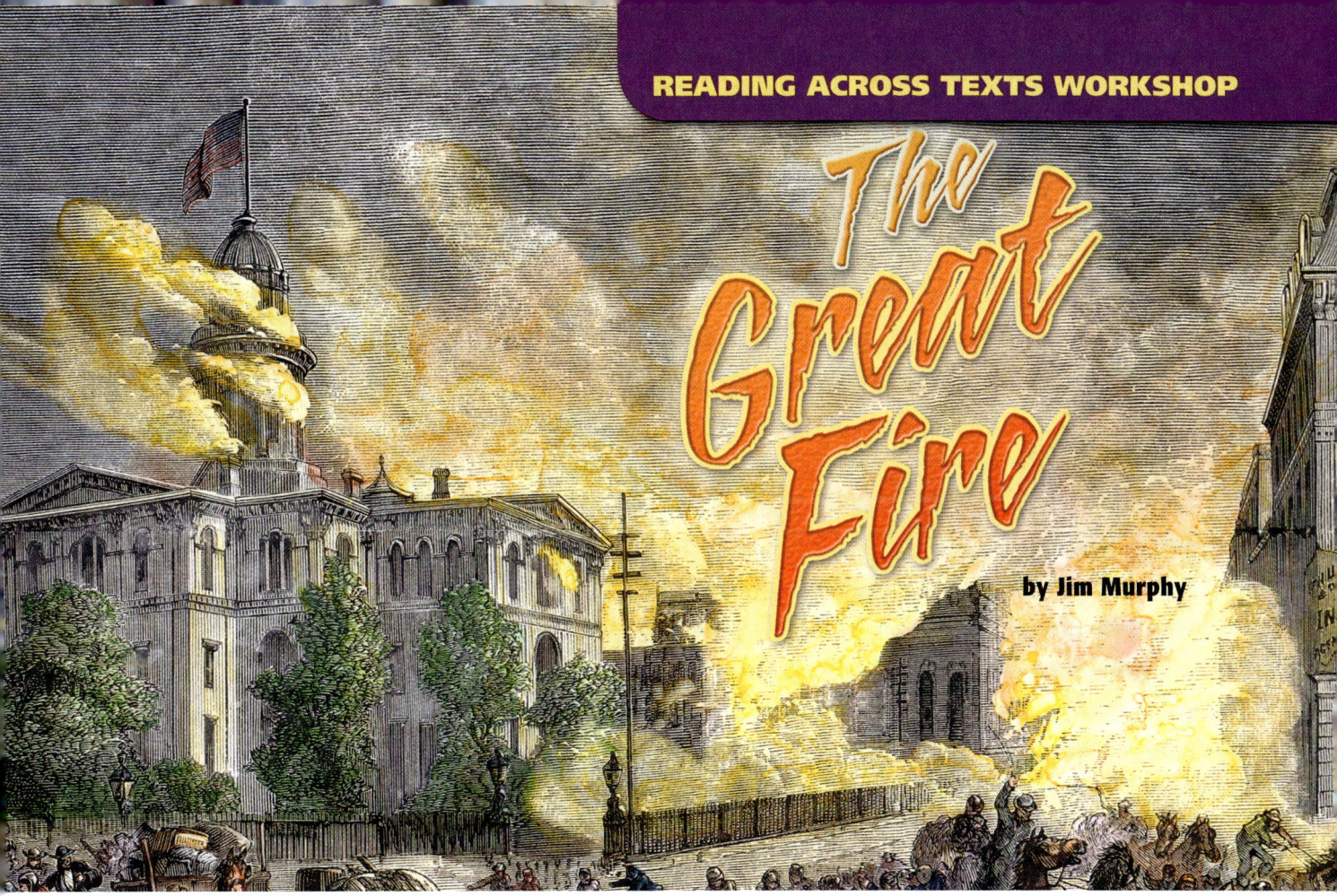

The Great Fire

by Jim Murphy

Courthouse Square becoming engulfed in flames during the Chicago Fire, 1871. Hand-colored woodcut.

The fire that swept through the heart of Chicago began on Sunday night, October 8, 1871. The Great Fire would burn for the rest of Sunday, all of Monday, and into the early hours of Tuesday with little real opposition. **1**

On duty at the Courthouse[1] that night was forty-year-old Mathias Schaffer. Schaffer was showing some visitors around the tower when one of them pointed to smoke in the distance. Schaffer glanced at the smoke, but dismissed the sighting. It was just the smoldering embers from the previous night's fire, he assured them. Nothing to worry about.

Several minutes passed before Schaffer looked up from what he was doing and saw flames leaping wildly into the black sky. The light *was* from a different fire after all; he'd been fooled because this new blaze was almost directly behind the still-flickering **remnants** of the Saturday October 7 fire.

1. The **Courthouse** was a building with a high tower that was used to watch for fires. When a fire was sighted, a watchman in the tower sent an alarm to a firehouse near the blaze.

Vocabulary

remnants (REM nunts) *n.* what is left over; small remaining parts

Practice the Skills

1 **Reading Across Texts**

Author's Credibility Reread **Meet the Author** and answer these questions: Do you think the author knows a lot about this subject? Is this firsthand experience? How much time passed between when the event happened and when the author wrote the story? Fill in your chart.

from *The Great Fire* 897

READING ACROSS TEXTS WORKSHOP

Flaming buildings and boats along the Chicago River during the Great Fire, 1871. Hand-colored woodcut.
Analyzing the Art How do you think people in Chicago felt as they saw buildings and boats aflame along the Chicago River?

He studied the flames, trying to determine their exact location. This wasn't easy because of the distance and tall buildings between him and the flames. In addition, the moonless sky was made even murkier[2] by the swirling, smoky haze. Schaffer signaled down the speaking tube[3] and had his assistant strike Box 342.[4] This sent engines rumbling through the streets—to a location almost a mile away from the O'Leary's barn. 🔲

Schaffer's first signal went out at 9:30. Several minutes later, Schaffer realized his mistake and ordered Box 319 struck. This was still seven blocks away from the O'Learys', but close enough that firefighters could see the flames and alter their course. Unfortunately, Schaffer's young assistant, William J. Brown, stubbornly refused to strike Box 319, saying he was afraid it would confuse the situation. Brown was so stubborn about his decision that even after the fire he was able to write

2. **Murky** means "hazy" or "hard to see through." It was hard for the watchman to see because the smoke from earlier fires made the sky **murkier.**
3. A **speaking tube** was a pipe made to carry a voice from one part of a building to another.
4. Watchmen at the courthouse sent alarms to local fire stations by hitting numbered boxes that were linked to the local stations. The station linked to **Box 342** was a mile from the fire.

Practice the Skills

🔲 **BIG Question**

Murphy describes the first mistake that fire officials made in responding to the fire. What was it? Start a list titled "Mistakes Made" on "The Great Fire" part of your Foldable. Write your answer as the first item on this list. Add to your list as your read further.

arrogantly⁵ in a letter that "I am still standing the watch⁶ that burned Chicago." **3**

These errors had two fatal **consequences**. The most obvious was that a number of engines and dozens of firefighters were sent on a wild-goose chase⁷ and did not get to the fire for many minutes. More critical is that it kept fire companies located near De Koven Street⁸ in their stations. Several had seen the eerie, dancing glow beyond the rooftops near them and, even without official notice from Schaffer, prepared to respond. When they heard Box 342 rung, however, they assumed the fire was out of their territory and unhitched the horses. Only two fire companies were not fooled by the misleading alarm. **4**

The clang of bells and the sound of pounding hooves could be heard above the roar of the fire. *America* arrived on the scene first, closely followed by *Little Giant*. Hoses were rolled out, attached to water outlets, and the water turned on. Unfortunately, *America* was a hose cart and could not throw water any great distance, while *Little Giant* was eleven years old (the oldest engine in service). Their limited range forced firefighters to stand very close to the flames. The newer, more powerful pumping engines were either a mile away searching for a **phantom** fire, or still in their stations. **5**

The fire had begun near the corner of De Koven and Jefferson and quickly fanned out thanks to increasingly gusty winds. One tongue traveled north up Jefferson, while the other headed east toward Lake Michigan. There was no way firefighters from two engines could contain a wind-driven fire with such a wide front. Still, they did their best.

Two men hauled the cumbersome canvas hose as close to the flames as possible and aimed a stream of water at the burning building. The water hissed and boiled when it struck the burning wood, sending up a **vapor** of white steam. The

---

5. When you act ***arrogantly***, you act like you think you're smarter or more important than other people.
6. ***Standing the watch*** means "being on guard duty."
7. A ***wild-goose chase*** is a search that has no chance of success.
8. The fire started near 137 **DeKoven** Street.

Vocabulary

consequences (KON si kwen siz) *n.* results of an action; outcomes

phantom (FAN tum) *adj.* looking or seeming real but is not

vapor (VAY pur) *n.* small particles of mist, steam, or smoke that can be seen

---

READING ACROSS TEXTS WORKSHOP

Practice the Skills

3 Reading Across Texts

Author's Credibility The author describes Brown's attitude as "stubborn" and says that Brown wrote "arrogantly" about his decision. Are the author's statements facts or opinions? Where do you think the author got this information? Fill in your chart.

4 BIG Question

What mistakes resulted from Brown's actions? Write your answer on your Foldable.

5 Reading Across Texts

Author's Credibility The main idea of this article is that the Great Chicago Fire would not have been so bad if it weren't for a series of mistakes and some bad luck. What does this tell you about the author's purpose? Is he biased? What details support the author's main idea? Continue filling in your chart.

from *The Great Fire*

READING ACROSS TEXTS WORKSHOP

firefighters held their position until the fierce heat began to **singe** the hair on their heads and arms, and their clothes began to smolder. When the pain became unbearable, they staggered back from the flames for a moment's relief, then lunged forward again.

More engines began arriving at the scene, as did the department's Chief Marshal Robert A. Williams. A common fire-fighting technique of the time was to surround a blaze with engines and use a flood of water to stop it from spreading. Williams immediately set about repositioning engines, hoping to halt the fire's advance until all the missing equipment could get to the scene.

The firefighters were already engulfed in a wave of withering heat, and the flames were reaching out toward them. "Marshal," one of the men yelled, "I don't believe we can stand it here!"

"Stand it as long as you can," Williams told them, before hurrying to another engine. Along the way he noticed that several houses were smoking and on the verge of igniting.

He came upon the driver of *America* and its foreman, John Dorsey. "Turn in a second alarm!" Williams ordered Dorsey. "This is going to spread!" A second alarm would bring in additional engines and men. **6**

Meanwhile, Chamberlin[9] had retreated several blocks in the face of the advancing flames. "I stepped in among some sheds south of Ewing Street; a fence by my side began to blaze; I beat a hasty retreat, and in five minutes the place where I had stood was all ablaze. Nothing could stop that conflagration there. It must sweep on until it reached a broad street, and then, everybody said, it would burn itself out."

The heat and dry air had left twelve-year-old Claire Innes tired and listless all day. She went to bed sometime between eight and eight-thirty only to be startled awake later when a horse-and-wagon clattered past her window at high speed. This was followed by loud voices from the street below her window.

"I was only half awake and not inclined to get up when I heard a man outside say that a fire was burning in the West

---

9. One of the first people to reach the fire was Joseph E. **Chamberlin**, a reporter for the *Chicago Evening Post*.

Vocabulary

singe (sinj) *v.* to burn slightly

Practice the Skills

6 **Reading Across Texts**
Author's Credibility Look at the quotations in this paragraph. Do you think the author knew exactly what Williams and the firefighter said in those moments? Where do you think the author got this information? Continue filling in your chart.

The Great Fire in Chicago, October 8–10, 1871. Currier & Ives. Contemporary lithograph.

Sailboats and steamboats fled to the safety of Lake Michigan, as flames destroyed the city.

READING ACROSS TEXTS WORKSHOP

Division. Father went to the door and asked about the fire and the man repeated what he had told his companions, but this time he added that the fire was a big one and that they were going to have a look at it. Father came inside and said something to Mother. . . . His voice did not sound unusual, [so] I turned over and closed my eyes again."

Claire and her family were staying in the South Division of the city, many blocks from the fire. There really was no reason for them to become alarmed. In fact, most citizens would see the glowing nighttime sky and dismiss it as nothing important. Not even the warning words in that day's *Chicago Tribune* drew much attention: "For dayspast alarm has followed alarm, but the comparatively trifling losses have familiarized us to the pealing of the Courthouse bell, and we [have] forgotten that the absence of rain for three weeks [has] left everything in so dry and inflammable a condition that a spark might set a fire which would sweep from end to end of the city." 7

But no one seemed very concerned. This was evident by what Alfred L. Sewell observed while strolling through the city at around 9:30 that night. "Many people were just returning from the Sunday evening services at the various churches when the general alarm was given, but, beyond the immediate vicinity of the beginning of the conflagration, no unusual fear or solicitude

Practice the Skills

7 Reading Across Texts

Author's Credibility The author gives us quotations from Claire Innes and the *Chicago Tribune* newspaper to support his point that people weren't worried about the fire even though they were warned. Does the author's use of quotations add to his credibility? Fill in your chart.

from *The Great Fire* 901

READING ACROSS TEXTS WORKSHOP

was felt by the citizens. The German beerhouses were filled with merry crowds, and as it was a warm evening, the streets all over the city were filled with joyful idlers and promenaders, in their Sunday apparel. A pleasanter, quieter, or a happier evening than was that one is seldom known in a great city."

And despite his own paper's editorial, not even the editor in chief of the *Chicago Tribune,* Horace White, smelled a good story in the smoke that was blowing into his neighborhood. "I had retired to rest, though not to sleep [that night], when the great bell struck the alarm; but fires had been so frequent of late, and had been so speedily extinguished, that I did not deem it worthwhile to get up and look at it, or even to count the strokes of the bell to learn where it was."

As the rest of the city went about its business, fireman Dorsey was racing through the streets to the closest signal box, which happened to be at Goll's drugstore. He opened the small door on the box and used his thumb to pull down the lever. Dorsey then headed back to the scene of the fire, not realizing that he'd made a mistake—he had forgotten to pull down the lever four times, a special signal that would have made it a true second alarm. At the Courthouse, Schaffer and Brown would hear Dorsey's alarm, but, assuming it was simply another signal telling them about the original fire, they failed to call out more engines. The fire had now been burning for over an hour, and the wind was increasing in **velocity.** 8

Despite this, Chief Marshal Williams had managed to get a thin circle of engines around the fire. He had five steamers at the scene now, plus three hose carts and a hook-and-ladder wagon, all of them pumping water into the fire at various locations. Spectators were asked to help and many responded by chopping up fences and sidewalks, hoping to deprive the fire of fuel.

Meanwhile the heat was beginning to wear down some of the firemen. Charles Anderson remembered when his friend Charles McConners came by and said, "Charley, this is hot!"

"It is, Mac," Anderson replied.

His friend disappeared for a few moments, then returned carrying a wooden door, which he positioned like a warrior's

Chicago Fire victims' camp on Lake Michigan shore near Lincoln Park, 1871. Hand-colored woodcut.

Some Chicagoans lived in tents on the shore of Lake Michigan after the Great Fire destroyed much of their city.

Practice the Skills

8 BIG Question

What mistake did Dorsey make? At the Courthouse, do you think Schaffer and Brown should have called out more engines even though they hadn't received a true second alarm signal? Explain.

Vocabulary

velocity (vuh LOS uh tee) *n.* speed

READING ACROSS TEXTS WORKSHOP

shield between Anderson and the fire.

I have it now, Anderson thought. I can stand it a considerable time.

Anderson no sooner thought this when the door caught fire and burned McConners' hand. McConners flung the door down and then Anderson's clothes began to smoke. The heat was so intense that his leather hat began to twist out of shape.

Williams came by and issued new orders. "Charley, come out as fast as possible. Wet the other side of the street or it will burn!"

With the help of onlookers, Anderson began to reposition his hose. He hadn't gotten it very far when water pressure suddenly dropped and only a trickle of liquid came from the hose. A powerful steam engine had arrived at the fire and had simply removed Anderson's hose from its water plug. This was routine procedure, done under the assumption that a steamer would always be more effective than a simple hose cart. Sadly, the steamer did not drag its hose to Anderson's position and he had to watch as four or five houses across the street caught fire.

At the same moment that Anderson's hose stopped, another steamer malfunctioned and its water also gave out. A well-aimed rap of a hammer got the engine working again, but then, at about 10:30, an old section of hose burst and the flow of water stopped again. Two valuable links in the chain of defense were gone, and there was nothing to stop the fire in these locations. **9**

Williams rushed to get the water going and to reposition his engines, but it was too late. The wind had pushed the fire past his circle, a wind that was blowing directly toward the heart of the city.

Later at the official inquiry, all of the mistakes and missed chances that occurred in the opening minutes of the fire would be discussed in great detail. As one firefighter put it, "From the beginning of that fatal fire, everything went wrong!" **10** ○

Practice the Skills

9 Reading Across Texts

Author's Credibility The author gives you a lot of details about what happened to the firefighters. Based on what you know about the author and what you have read so far, do you believe these details? Explain why or why not in your chart.

10 BIG Question

What mistakes turned the fire into a major disaster? What can you learn from those mistakes? Write your answer on your Foldable. Your response will help you complete the Unit Challenge later.

from *The Great Fire* 903

READING ACROSS TEXTS WORKSHOP

Before You Read : Letters About the Fire

Meet the Authors
A boy named Justin (we don't know his last name for sure) and a girl named Fannie Belle lived through the Great Chicago Fire of 1871. Like other people who lived through that disaster, they wrote what they saw, heard, and felt on those October days. Justin wrote his letter eleven days after the fire broke out. Fannie wrote hers about two years after the fire. These and other eyewitness accounts are kept by the Chicago Historical Society and can be found online at www.chicagohs.org/fire.

Vocabulary Preview
cinders (SIN durz) *n.* hot ashes **(p. 906)** *Cinders from the fire filled the air.*

stifled (STY fuld) *v.* choked; smothered **(p. 906)** *The heat of the fire stifled everyone's breathing.*

Get Ready to Read

Connect to the Reading
The families in these letters rescue items from the fire that are important to them. What would you rescue? What things have special memories for you?

Build Background
- By the 1870s, Chicago was already an important city. It connected businesses in the East with the farms in the West.
- Before the fire, Chicago had 57 miles of wood-paved streets and more than 500 miles of wooden sidewalks.
- Justin's house burned during the Great Chicago Fire. He and his family were in their house when it started to burn. His family and the family goat escaped without harm.
- Fannie Belle and her mother left their home as the fire approached them. Fannie Belle rescued her doll named Jennie. Fannie Belle kept Jennie as a reminder of the Great Fire.
- Hundreds of survivors of the fire wrote letters and articles about their experiences in the fire.

Set Purposes for Reading
BIG Question Read to find out how two families dealt with a dangerous situation and what mistakes they made.

Set Your Own Purpose What can you learn from these accounts of escaping the Great Chicago Fire? Write your purpose for reading on the "Letters About the Fire" part of the Reading Across Texts Foldable.

Objectives (pp. 904–907)
Reading Compare and contrast: author's credibility across texts • Make connections from text to self

READING ACROSS TEXTS WORKSHOP

Letters About the Fire

Justin

Justin sent this letter about his family fleeing to his "chum" Philip Prescott on October 19, 1871. **1**

Dear Chum,

We are burnt out of house and home and so we had to come up here.[1] I suppose you would like to hear about the fire and how we escaped from it. Half past one Monday morning we were awakened by a loud knocking at the front door we were awake in an instant and dressing ourselves we looked about and saw a perfect shower of sparks flying over our house. I got some water and went out in the yard while my brother went up on the roof we worked for one or two hours at the end of that time we had to give up. We tried to get a wagon but could not so we put two trunks on a wheelbarrow and each of us shouldered a bundle and we marched for the old skating park I leading my goat. We got along very well until the Pes[h]tigo Lumber yard[2] caught on fire then it was all we could do to breathe. Mother caught on fire once but we put it out at last we heard that there was a little shanty that hadn't burnt down so we marched there but had to leave our trunks and everything else but Charlie and father went back and got one but could not get the other as the sand was blowing in their faces and cut like glass at last a wagon drove up and we all piled in and escaped so good by **2**
yours Justin

1. **Justin** wrote his letter from Lake Forest, Illinois, a town about thirty miles north of Chicago, where his family had found shelter.
2. The **Peshtigo Lumber Yard,** a large lumberyard in Chicago, burned during the Great Fire.

Practice the Skills

1 **Reading Across Texts**

Author's Credibility Reread Meet the Authors. Do you think Justin knows a lot about this subject? Does he have firsthand experience? How much time passed between when the event happened and when he wrote the letter? Fill in your chart.

2 **Reading Across Texts**

Author's Credibility What do you think was Justin's purpose for writing this letter? Does he have bias? If so, what is it? Does the author include many details? Is the letter mostly fact or opinion? Continue filling in your chart.

READING ACROSS TEXTS WORKSHOP

Fannie Belle Becker

Fannie Belle Becker (later Fanny Dement), ten at the time of the fire, wrote "My Experience of the Chicago Fire" almost exactly two years later. 3

Analyzing the Art How does this image of the Great Chicago Fire show the confusion and fear that Fannie and her family experienced?

Saturday evening Oct the 8th 1871 there was a large Fire in Chicago it was probably the largest Fire ever in that city then it was the lumberyard burning there was a great many people out to see it. They stayed untill a late hour and so were very tired but did not get much rest for Monday morning at three o'clock I was awakened and told to Dress for the Fire was all around us and we would soon be burnt out. My ma put all her valubals[3] into her sewing machine and locked it up and threw some things in to her trunk. I carried ma's fur box (with furs in it), and, account book,[4] and a parasol,[5] and, a little lady called Jennie. And perhaps some of my little friends in Fruit-Port have made her [acquaintance] but some of you may not know who little Jennie is so I will say that she is a little China doll[6] a Christmas present when I was Five years old and I will always keep her as a Relic[7] of the Chicago Fire. We could not save the Sewing Machine but did save the trunk. We had a gentleman friend who helped us; we all went down right away but ma stayed, she said that she would stay as long as she could. So we went around the corner to monroe street and waited and when she came she brought a large hair[8] Matrass. The air was so full of **cinders** and was so hot that it almost **stifled** her. We could not get an express man to carry the things for there were none to be had. So our friend drew[9] our trunk and a trunk that belonged to a friend of his who

Practice the Skills

3 Reading Across Texts

Author's Credibility Do you think Fannie Belle Becker knows a lot about her subject? Does she have firsthand experience? How much time passed between when the event happened and when she wrote her story? Fill in your chart.

---

3. **Valubals** is an incorrect spelling of the word *valuables*.
4. An **account book** is a notebook in which records about money are kept.
5. A **parasol** (PAIR uh sawl) is a light umbrella that protects a person (usually a woman) from the sun.
6. A **China doll** is a doll with a head made of porcelain, a breakable material.
7. A **relic** is a thing from the past.
8. A **hair Matrass (mattress)** is a mattress filled with animal hair. Hair mattresses can catch fire.
9. In this letter, **drew** means "pulled."

Vocabulary

cinders (SIN durs) *n.* hot ashes

stifled (STY fuld) *v.* choked; smothered

was out of the city. He lashed the two together and lashed the Matrass on top of the trunks, and then drew them along. The trunks both has castors[10] on. When we got to the corners of Dearborn street ma told me to go Down on Jackson st. a few blocks away to the house of a friend and see if they thought the fire would come there and if not we would go there and stay. And Just as I was about to start a man who had been standing near and heard what ma said told her that he would see me safe there. Ma thanked him and said we would not trouble him but he said it was no trouble and walked along beside me. He said he would take my account book I did not like his looks and so told him that I could carry it myself, and, as we went through a crowd just then I dodged away from him and ran and I have not seen anything of him since. When I got to the house they had all their things packed and out on the side walk and, in a little while ma came and then we went back to monroe st and then as the Fire came on we went on toward Lake Michagan as we went on we came to our friends brothers house we stayed here until the fire drove us out then the heat was so intense that it drove us down to the waters Edge and then my uncle who was with us (and, had arrived Saturday) took his hat and poured water on the things to keep them from burning but thousands and thousands of dollar's worth of goods were burned right there on the waters Edge. Although our things were saved we sat there until I was almost blind with the dirt and cinders that filled the air I could not open my eyes, so that when I walked ma had to lead me. I did not have anything to eat from Sunday afternoon until Monday afternoon at about four o'clock. Then we went out to the City limits on the South side to the house of a friend I stayed there two days and then I went out in the country with my cousins, and stayed there one week and then I came to Fruit-Port [Michigan]. I shall ever remember with thankfulness my reception by my little friends in Fruit-Port. I almost went barefoot and without any good clothes. I was well treated and one of them even took off her over shoes and let me wear them that I might go out in the cold weather and play. Never while I live will I forget my friends in Fruit Port. 4 5 ○

10. **Castors** is a misspelling of the word *casters*. Casters are small wheels attached to the bottom of heavy objects. These wheels make objects easy to move by rolling.

Practice the Skills

4 Reading Across Texts

Author's Credibility What do you think was the author's purpose for writing this story? Does she have bias? Does she include details? Is the letter fact or opinion?

5 BIG Question

Did Fannie Belle or her mother make any mistakes? If so, do you think they learned from them? Write your answers on your Foldable.

Analyzing the Art List some ways that these boys from the 1800s seem different from kids today.

READING ACROSS TEXTS WORKSHOP

After You Read

from The Great Fire & Letters About the Fire

Vocabulary Check

For items 1–8, choose the best words from the lists to fill in each blank. Then write the complete sentences on a separate sheet of paper.

**consequences   phantom   remnants
singe   vapor   velocity   cinders   stifled**

1. The heat and smoke from the fire nearly ___ Fannie Belle and her mother.

2. One of the ___ of sending the wrong signal was that the firemen went to the wrong part of the city.

3. The ___ of the wind increased, causing the fire to spread.

4. The more powerful engines were on a wild-goose chase, looking for a ___ fire.

5. Fannie Belle described the burning ___ that filled the hot air.

6. The new blaze could have been started by the ___ of a fire from the previous day.

7. The water hissed when it hit the burning wood, sending up a cloud of ___.

8. The heat from the fire began to ___ the firefighters' hair.

Objectives (pp. 908–909)
Reading Compare and contrast: author's credibility across texts • Make connections from text to self
Writing Respond to informational text: author's credibility

Reading/Critical Thinking

On a separate sheet of paper, answer the following questions.

from *The Great Fire*

9. **Recall** When the fire first started, what mistakes kept fire trucks from going to the right location?

    TIP Right There

10. **Evaluate** Murphy describes events from the points of view of many people at the Great Fire. Does this technique of using several points of view make his narrative more or less believable? Explain.

    TIP Author and Me

Letters About the Fire

11. **Infer** Why do you think Justin sounds both excited and relieved?

    TIP Author and Me

12. **Draw a Conclusion** Do you think Fannie did the right thing when the man offered to carry the account book? Explain why or why not.

    TIP Author and Me

Writing: Reading Across Texts

Use Your Notes

13. Follow these steps to compare the credibility of the authors of "The Great Fire" and "Letters About the Fire."

    Step 1: Review the chart you've completed. Which author seems to know the most about how the fire started and why the firemen couldn't put it out? How does that author know those details? Do you believe the author?

    Step 2: Which author or authors depend on what other people say for their information? Which author or authors actually saw and experienced the fire?

    Step 3: Did the authors have different purposes for writing? What were they? Were any of the authors biased? If so, did that affect whether you believed them?

    Step 4: Do any of these writers present opinions as if they were facts? Explain.

    Step 5: Think about what persuades you to believe a writer. Is it the writer's knowledge, firsthand experience, supporting details, or what?

Get It on Paper

To show what you think about the credibility of these authors and selections, answer the following questions on a separate sheet of paper.

14. Which writer, do you think, had the best knowledge of how it felt to be caught in the fire *at the time that he or she wrote the selection*? Explain why you chose this writer over the other writers.

15. Which writer seemed to give you the most opinions about why and how things happened? Did that writer back up those opinions with enough details to be credible?

16. If you wanted to know exactly how the fire spread through Chicago, which writer would you ask? Explain why you chose that writer.

17. Explain why you feel Murphy's use of quotations to describe the fire scenes is or is not effective.

BIG Question

18. After reading both selections, do you believe that the mistakes made in the Great Chicago Fire could be repeated today? Explain the reasons for your answer.

UNIT 7 WRAP-UP

Answering The BIG Question: What Can We Learn from Our Mistakes?

While reading the selections, you've been thinking about what people can learn from their mistakes. Now use what you've learned to complete the Unit Challenge.

The Unit Challenge

Choose Activity A or Activity B and follow the directions for that activity.

A. Group Activity: Chart

- You know that everyone makes mistakes and that mistakes have consequences. With group of classmates make a chart of mistakes and what can be learned as a result of the mistakes.
- Your chart can help you think about your decisions and learn from your mistakes.

1. Discuss the Assignment

- Choose one group member to be the note-taker for the discussion.
- Review the notes you wrote in your Learner's Notebook and on your Foldables for the selections you read in this unit.
- Discuss the mistakes you think the characters made. Then discuss what you can learn, or what the characters learned, from their mistakes. For example, in "Nadia the Willful," Nadia's father learned that it's a mistake to not remember someone you love. He corrected his mistake by letting Nadia and the rest of the people remember what her brother meant to them.
- Think about people you know who have made mistakes. Then discuss what happened as the result of their mistakes, and what can be learned from the mistakes. Make a list of those mistakes.

2. Create a Chart Draw a chart like the one below. Use your list to fill in the Mistake column. Brainstorm with the classmates about lessons learned from the mistakes.

Now fill in the "What I Learned" column. If you can't think of something that was learned, leave it blank. You can fill it in later.

3. Present Your Chart Have a group member read the chart to the class. Discuss any mistakes that they think could be added to the chart. Add any ideas about mistakes they have. Discuss the most common mistakes that people make. What do you think can prevent these kinds of mistakes?

Mistake	What I Learned
I forgot my homework.	I should put my homework in my book bag.
I stayed out past curfew.	I should call if I'm going to be late.

B. Solo Activity: Bumper Sticker

Bumper stickers are a form of advertising. They advertise, or make public, ideas and beliefs. You'll use words and pictures to create several bumper stickers about learning from mistakes.

1. **Consider the Topic** Review your Foldable notes to recall what people in the selections learned from their mistakes. In your Learner's Notebook, make notes about what you've learned from mistakes. Describe two or three mistakes you've made, tell what you learned from them, and how they helped you grow or change.

2. **Diagram Ideas** In your Learner's Notebook, draw a web like the one below. Write the Big Question in the center box. In the outside boxes, write lessons you or characters from the selections learned from mistakes. You don't have to include a lesson for every selection or from every experience of your own. Just include those you think might suggest good slogans for bumper stickers.

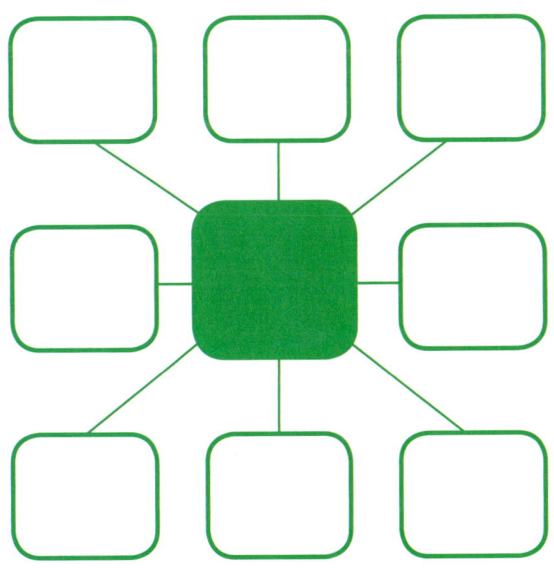

3. **Brainstorm Slogans** Which four boxes in the web do you think show the most important lessons about learning from mistakes? From each of these boxes draw a line and box. In each new box write a slogan that summarizes the idea. Here are some tips.

   - A slogan should be *concise* (kun SYS), or short. Use no more than ten or fifteen words for each slogan.
   - A slogan should be *catchy*. Choose words that will grab people's interest.
   - A slogan should be *clear*. Test out each slogan. Say it to a classmate, friend, or family member and ask him or her to explain what it means.
   - Rewrite each slogan until it's just right—that is, concise, catchy, and clear.
   - Here are some examples of slogans.

     The only really bad mistake is the one you make more than once.

     Those who don't learn from their mistakes are sure to repeat them again.

     No child is mistake proof.

     Show me a mistake, and I made it.

     For every mistake, there is a lesson to be learned.

4. **Design Bumper Stickers** Draw four rectangles in your Learner's Notebook. Write one slogan in each rectangle. Then decorate each with a border, drawings, photos, or symbols that have to do with the idea expressed in the slogan.

5. **Create a Bumper Sticker** Which of your four bumper sticker ideas do you find most inspiring? Use paper or cardboard to create that bumper sticker for yourself. Post it by your bed or desk or tape it on your notebook or backpack.

UNIT 7

Your Turn: Read and Apply Skills

Meet the Author

Stan Sakai was born in Japan and grew up in Hawaii. He lives in California with his wife and children. His character Usagi Yojimbo first appeared in comics in 1984. Stan received the National Cartoonists Society Comic Book Division Award for his work.

Author Search For more about Stan Sakai, go to www.glencoe.com.

by Stan Sakai

A LESSON IN COURTESY

YOUR TURN: READ AND APPLY SKILLS

YOUR TURN: READ AND APPLY SKILLS

YOUR TURN: READ AND APPLY SKILLS

YOUR TURN: READ AND APPLY SKILLS

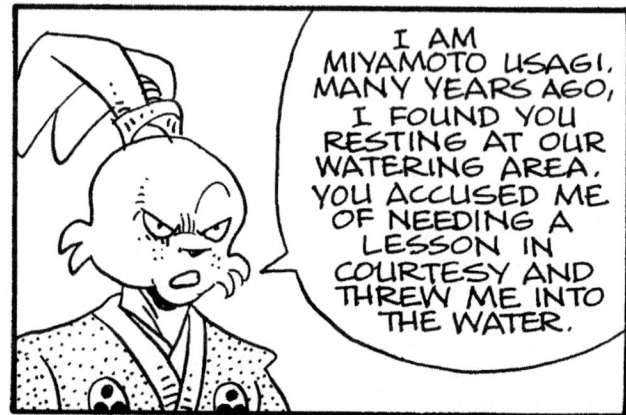

YOUR TURN: READ AND APPLY SKILLS

UNIT 7
Reading on Your Own

To read more about the Big Question, choose one of these books from your school or local library. Work on your reading skills by choosing books that are challenging to you.

Fiction

The Secret Garden
by Frances H. Burnett

Lonely and bad tempered, Mary is an orphan who lives in an empty mansion on the Yorkshire moors. She begins to change when she discovers a secret walled garden and meets a boy named Dickon. Read to find out what Mary learns from her secret garden.

Cages
by Peg Kehret

It was the most terrible day of Kit's life—the day she tried shoplifting and got caught. Sentenced to twenty hours of volunteer work at the Humane Society, Kit ends up with some time to think. Read to find out what she learns from her mistake.

Island of the Blue Dolphins
by Scott O'Dell

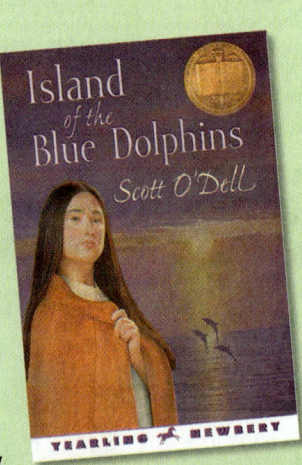

When Karana is accidentally abandoned by her people, she spends eighteen years on a lonely island by herself. Read to find out more about what she discovered on that island—strength, serenity, and an amazing will to survive.

A Christmas Carol
by Charles Dickens

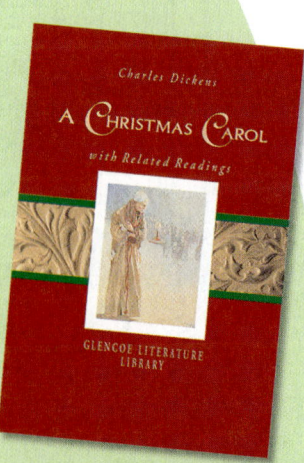

Ebenezer Scrooge is so obsessed with business and money that he has isolated himself from others. On Christmas Eve, several spirits visit Scrooge. The spirits take Scrooge to revisit scenes from his own life in an effort to reawaken the humanity within him. Read to find out what Scrooge learns from his mistakes.

Nonfiction

Malcolm X: By Any Means Necessary
by Walter Dean Myers

By age twenty, Malcolm Little was in prison. There he discovered Islam as a way to recover his dignity and set his life straight. Later, he became a revered leader of the Nation of Islam. Read to find out what Malcolm believed and how he changed the world.

The Story of Thomas Alva Edison
by Margaret Cousins

Thomas Edison made many mistakes before he invented a successful light bulb. Read to find out how his curiosity about how things work lasted a lifetime—and made the world a brighter place.

Knots in My Yo-yo String: The Autobiography of a Kid
by Jerry Spinelli

The creator of *Maniac Magee* recalls his childhood from six to sixteen like this: " ten years of . . . salamanders and snakes and candy cigarettes, coal dust on the clothesline, baseball cleats swinging from my handlebars, Ovaltine in my milk, knots in my yo-yo string." Read to find out more about Spinelli's exciting adventures.

Michelle Kwan: Heart of a Champion
by Michelle Kwan

Ever wondered what it's like to be a figure skating champion at the age of twelve? If so, check out this book. Read to find out more about Michelle Kwan's triumphs, her disasters, and her incredible love of skating.

UNIT 7 SKILLS AND STRATEGIES ASSESSMENT

Test Practice

Part 1: Literary Elements

Read the passage. On a separate sheet of paper, write the numbers 1–4. Next to numbers 1–3, write the letter of the correct answer. Next to number 4, write your answer to the question.

When my mother left North Carolina, she couldn't bring her sisters or the deep feather bed she'd slept in or the thick forests of her childhood. She couldn't bring the splashing mountain streams. So she brought what she could, a lilac bush.

On the prairie where my parents settled, a bitter wind blew endlessly. My mother built a small stone wall to protect her lilac until our small house went up and could take over that job. I remember finding her on cold, damp, spring mornings, crouched by the bush, studying its glossy green leaves. She was waiting, waiting. And soon, a softly warm afternoon would come. The first purple-blue blossoms would appear on delicate branches. For the next three weeks, a sweet and spicy fragrance filled our yard.

During this time every spring, my mother was different. Her usual happiness was deeper. Her eyes were filled with memory. She would spend too much money on a ham and bake the fluffy biscuits her own mother had taught her, years ago, to make. Over dinner, she would tell stories about relatives I had never met and descriptions of birds and forest animals I had never seen. And then the lilac's flowers would fade, and my mother would turn her attention back to our everyday life.

---

1. Which of the following sentences reveals that the narrator is using a first-person point of view?
   A. "On the prairie where my parents settled, a bitter wind blew endlessly."
   B. "So she brought what she could, a lilac bush."
   C. "And soon, a softly warm afternoon would come."
   D. "The first purple-blue blossoms would appear on delicate branches."

2. What does the lilac bush symbolize for the narrator's mother?
   A. loss, sadness, and pain
   B. the life she left behind
   C. the importance of change
   D. the hardships of everyday life

3. Which of the following events actually occurs *first*?
   A. The mother moves to the prairie.
   B. The narrator's house is built.
   C. The narrator hears stories.
   D. The mother learns to make biscuits.

4. Explain how the author's use of description in this passage can help a reader experience the story. Give at least two examples.

Objectives (pp. 922–923)
Reading Identify main ideas and supporting details • Synthesize information • Make inferences • Evaluate text
Literature Identify literary elements: point of view, narrator, symbolism, description, sensory details

SKILLS AND STRATEGIES ASSESSMENT UNIT 7

Part 2: Reading Skills

On a separate sheet of paper, write the numbers 1–4. Next to each number, write the letter of the right answer.

Read the following passages and use them to answer questions 1 and 2.

Passage 1. In December of 1777, the American army set up camp at Valley Forge, Pennsylvania, where they would remain all winter. The location kept the soldiers safe from attack. They were not safe from nature. Many of the soldiers had no shoes. Most were dressed in rags. They huddled together in small crowded wooden huts. The army's commander, George Washington, did what he could to obtain supplies. On most days, however, their only food was flat pancakes made of flour and water. Their rag-wrapped feet left blood on the snow as they marched and trained. Disease was common, frostbite more so. By spring, thousands had died.

Passage 2. It was miserably hot in New Jersey on June 28, 1778. The men tramping down the road had once been farmers and shopkeepers in America's countryside and towns. Now they were soldiers fighting to be free. Their respect for their leader, George Washington, meant they would obey any command he gave. Soon he would be giving the command to fight. The Battle of Monmouth was only hours away.

1. What is the main idea of Passage 1?
   A. The winter at Valley Forge was a very difficult one.
   B. The housing at Valley Forge was crowded and cold.
   C. The American army was led by George Washington.
   D. Those who survive hardship are stronger because of it.

2. Synthesize information in Passage 2 to decide which of the following statements is true.
   A. Farmers and shopkeepers make poor soldiers.
   B. The Battle of Monmouth took place on June 28, 1778.
   C. George Washington became the army's commander in 1778.
   D. More soldiers died in the Battle of Monmouth than in any other battle.

3. What can you infer from Passage 1?
   A. George Washington was a bad commander.
   B. The year 1777 was the coldest on record.
   C. The soldiers were not well supplied.
   D. The soldiers did not know how to march.

4. Which of the following is always involved in evaluating a story or other text?
   A. making inferences
   B. synthesizing information
   C. combining ideas to create new ones
   D. coming up with opinions about the text

UNIT 7 SKILLS AND STRATEGIES ASSESSMENT

Part 3: Vocabulary Skills

On a separate sheet of paper, write the numbers 1–10. Next to each number, write the letter of the correct answer for that question.

Write the letter of the word or phrase that means about the same as the underlined word.

1. told her to <u>cease</u>
   - A. stop
   - B. stand
   - C. watch
   - D. speak

2. a <u>forsaken</u> town
   - A. busy
   - B. abandoned
   - C. large
   - D. successful

3. their <u>dismal</u> life
   - A. active
   - B. complicated
   - C. miserable
   - D. peaceful

4. too much <u>commotion</u>
   - A. violence
   - B. difficulty
   - C. reckless speed
   - D. noise and disorder

5. a <u>grudging</u> welcome
   - A. loud
   - B. joyful
   - C. shy
   - D. unwilling

Write the letter of the best answer.

6. Use what you know about base words to complete the sentence below.

   A person who is *desirous* of water is
   - A. wet.
   - B. thirsty.
   - C. busily swimming.
   - D. afraid of drowning.

7. The Latin root *aud* means "hear," as in *audience*. What part of your body would a doctor who's an <u>audiologist</u> need to examine?
   - A. ears
   - B. eyes
   - C. nose
   - D. throat

8. The Latin root *brev* means "short," as in *abbreviation*. If someone complains about the <u>brevity</u> of a movie, that person is saying it was
   - A. boring.
   - B. too violent.
   - C. poorly acted.
   - D. not long enough.

9. The Greek root *astr* or *aster* means "star," as in *astronomy* and *astrology*. Which of the following symbols is an <u>asterisk</u>?
   - A. &
   - B. *
   - C. #
   - D. $

10. The Latin root *mono* means "one" and the Greek root *chrome* means "color." Which of the following is most likely to be <u>monochromatic</u>?
    - A. a rainbow
    - B. a snowy field
    - C. a nation's flag
    - D. a flower garden

Objectives (pp. 924–925)
Vocabulary Identify word structure: bases, roots • Identify compound words
Grammar Identify parts of speech: verbs, nouns • Use correct subject-verb agreement

924 UNIT 7 What Can We Learn from Our Mistakes?

SKILLS AND STRATEGIES ASSESSMENT **UNIT 7**

Part 4: Writing Skills

On a separate sheet of paper, write the numbers 1–8. For the first 7 questions write the letter of the correct answer for that question. Next to number 8, write your answer to that question.

---

1. What is the verb in the following sentence?

   The players on the team rarely arrived on time for the game.

   A. players   **C.** arrived
   B. rarely   **D.** on

2. What is the subject in the following sentence?

   The people in the park were walking dogs, playing catch, and having fun.

   A. The   **C.** park
   B. people   **D.** dogs

3. Which of the following sentences has a compound subject?

   A. My favorite animals are dogs.
   B. A sandwich and an apple will be enough.
   C. Did Sayid call, or was that Nathaniel?
   D. Grown-ups who are mean to kids make me mad.

4. Which forms of the verbs belong in the following sentence?

   The bikes in the garage (needs, need) new tires, but nobody (has, have) money to buy them.

   A. needs, has   **C.** needs, have
   B. need, has   **D.** need, have

5. Which forms of the verbs belong in the following sentence?

   Inside the box (was, were) a tie and a pair of pants, and the pants (was, were) just my size.

   A. was, was   **C.** were, was
   B. was, were   **D.** were, were

6. Which forms of the verbs belong in the following sentence?

   Everybody (knows, know) the best running shoes in the whole store (is, are) the ones over there.

   A. knows, is   **C.** know, is
   B. knows, are   **D.** know, are

7. Which forms of the verbs belong in the following sentence?

   How (do, does) Luke know which of the scissors (is, are) his?

   A. do, is   **C.** does, is
   B. do, are   **D.** does, are

8. What can you do to make sure your writing (especially in a personal narrative) reflects your voice?

UNIT 8

The BIG Question
What Makes a Friend?

> "The only way to have a friend is to be one."
>
> —Ralph Waldo Emerson,
> American author, poet, and philosopher

LOOKING AHEAD

The skill lessons and readings in this unit will help you develop your own answer to the Big Question.

UNIT 8 WARM-UP • Connecting to the Big Question
GENRE FOCUS: Drama
from *Novio Boy* 931
  by Gary Soto

READING WORKSHOP 1 Skill Lesson: Visualizing
The Reluctant Dragon, Scene 1 942
  by Kenneth Grahame
The Reluctant Dragon, Scene 2 954
  by Kenneth Grahame

WRITING WORKSHOP PART 1 Speech 966

READING WORKSHOP 2 Skill Lesson: Clarifying
Damon and Pythias 974
  by Fan Kissen
Charlie Johnson 988
  by Joe Smith

READING WORKSHOP 3 Skill Lesson: Skimming and Scanning
The Bully of Barksdale Street 1000
  by Eric Alter
Tales of the Tangled Tresses 1016
  by Christina Hamlett

WRITING WORKSHOP PART 2 Speech 1032

READING WORKSHOP 4 Skill Lesson: Predicting
Zlateh the Goat 1040
  by Isaac Bashevis Singer
Best of Buddies 1052
  by Kevin Gray and Cindy Dampier, from *People*

READING ACROSS TEXTS WORKSHOP
Baby Hippo Orphan Finds a Friend 1059
  by Catherine Clarke Fox, from *National Geographic Kids News*
from *The Caretaker's Diary* 1063
  by Stephen Tuei

UNIT 8 WRAP-UP • Answering the Big Question

UNIT 8 WARM-UP

Connecting to The BIG Question: What Makes a Friend?

How do you know who's a real friend—and who isn't? Sometimes it's hard to know. Of course, a friend is someone you like to hang out with, someone who makes you laugh. A friend is someone you can talk to and trust. In this unit, you'll read about different people and how they figured out who their real friends were.

Real Kids and the Big Question

REBECCA and Alexandra have been best friends since third grade. But suddenly, things are changing. Alexandra is hanging out with a new crowd, and Rebecca feels left out. On the one hand, she's jealous, but on the other hand, she doesn't really like the kids in that group. She wishes things could be the way they used to be. What would you tell Rebecca?

SAMMY is really angry. His best friend, Keith, is doing stupid stuff. Sammy tried talking to Keith, but Keith told him to mind his own business. Sammy could keep his mouth shut, but he doesn't want to abandon his friend. What do you think Sammy should do?

Warm-Up Activity
In a small group, talk about the advice you would give Rebecca and Sammy. Explain to each other why you would give that advice.

UNIT 8 WARM-UP

You and the Big Question

Reading about how other people decided who their real friends were will help you think about how you would answer the Big Question.

Plan for the Unit Challenge

At the end of the unit, you'll use notes from all your reading to complete the Unit Challenge.

Literature Online

Big Question Link to Web resources to further explore the Big Question at www.glencoe.com.

You'll choose one of the following activities:

A. The Friendship Play Work with a group to write, rehearse, and perform a play about friendship.

B. Create a Friendship Story Create your own graphic story about friendship that illustrates the dos and don'ts of being a good friend.

- Start thinking about which activity you'd like to do so that you can focus your thinking as you go through the unit.
- In your Learner's Notebook, write which activity you'd like to do.
- Each time you make notes about the Big Question, think about how your ideas will help you with the Unit Challenge activity you chose.

Keep Track of Your Ideas

As you read, you'll make notes about the Big Question. Later, you'll use these notes to complete the Unit Challenge. See pages R8–R9 for help with making Foldable 8. This diagram shows how it should look.

1. Use this Foldable for all selections in this unit.
2. On the front, write **Unit 8** and **What Makes a Friend?** Leave the other half of that folded page blank.
3. Across the top of each of the next folded pages, write a selection title. (See page 927 for titles.)
4. To the left of each crease, write **My Purpose for Reading.** Below this heading, you will write your purpose for reading each selection.
5. To the right of each crease, write **The Big Question.** Below this, you will write your thoughts about the Big Question.

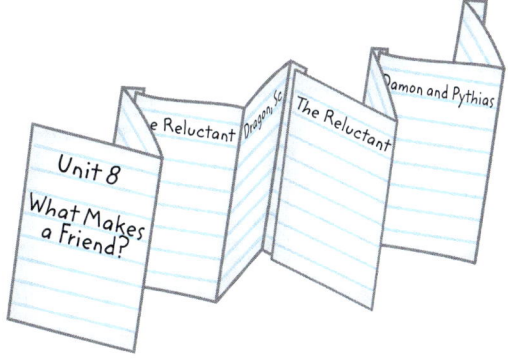

UNIT 8 GENRE FOCUS: DRAMA

Drama is a work of literature that is performed for an audience. Since ancient times, people have been acting out exciting stories of heroes and their deeds. In modern times, writers have written plays to be performed for the stage, the movies, on the radio, or on television. Elements of drama, like fiction, include character, setting, theme, and plot.

Why Read Drama?

Plays are performed in front of audiences, but they can also be read. Reading a play can be a very different experience from reading a story or a poem. You'll find out that you identify with some of the characters and their problems. You're about to read part of a play called *Novio Boy,* by Gary Soto. In this excerpt, two friends discuss a problem that is typical for boys their age.

How to Read Drama?

Key Reading Skills

These key reading skills are especially useful tools for reading and understanding drama. You'll learn more about these skills later in the unit.

- **Visualizing** is picturing a writer's ideas or descriptions in your mind's eye. (See Reading Workshop 1.)
- **Clarifying** is looking at difficult sections of text in order to clear up what is confusing. (See Reading Workshop 2.)
- **Skimming and scanning** is looking over an entire selection quickly to get a general idea of what the piece is about (skimming) and glancing quickly over a selection in order to find specific information (scanning). (See Reading Workshop 3.)
- **Predicting** is taking a reasonable guess about what will happen in a selection. (See Reading Workshop 4.)

Key Literary Elements

Recognizing and thinking about the following literary elements will help you understand what you read more fully.

- **Act and scene:** the section into which plays are divided. Each scene usually takes place in a different setting or time and may have different scenery. (See "The Reluctant Dragon, Scene 1.")
- **Characterization:** the way a writer shows the personality of a character (See "Damon and Pythias.")
- **Stage directions:** instructions that have to do with actors' movements, sound effects, and other details of a play. (See "The Bully of Barksdale Street.")
- **Sensory imagery:** language that appeals to any of the reader's five senses (See "Zlateh the Goat.")

Skills Focus
- Key skills for reading drama
- Key literary elements of drama

Skills Model
You will see how to use the key reading skills and literary elements as you read
- from *Novio Boy,* p. 931

Objectives (pp. 930–937)
Reading Read drama • Visualize • Clarify ideas and text • Skim and scan text • Make predictions
Literature Understand elements of drama: act and scene • Understand literary elements: characterization • Understand elements of drama: stage directions • Identify sensory imagery

from **NOVIO BOY**

by Gary Soto

SCENE ONE

The scene begins in a backyard where two boys, both Mexican American, are philosophizing[1] about girls. They are sloppy-looking, with holes in the knees of their pants. Stage right, two girls are silhouetted on a couch in a living room. The room is dim. Lights come up on RUDY and ALEX. RUDY paces back and forth and ALEX tries to keep up with him. RUDY throws himself down on a lawn chair. ALEX keeps pacing for a moment and then, noticing that his friend has sat down, joins him.

RUDY: What am I gonna talk about? She's older than me and good-looking.

ALEX: Just level with her. Tell her you're sorry you look like you do.

RUDY: Sorry? You mean I should be sorry that I look like Tom Cruise? (*pause*) You're cold, homes.[2] You're no help at all.

ALEX: (*giggling*) Just joking, Rudy. Listen man, you got to start simple. Break the ice. Ask her . . . what her favorite color is or something.

RUDY: Color?

ALEX: Yeah, color. Like, red or white.

Drama
ACTIVE READING MODEL

1 Key Literary Element
Act and Scene *I see that this is Scene One. I wonder if this excerpt includes other scenes.*

2 Key Reading Skill
Skimming and Scanning *Before I start reading, I'll skim the selection. I see the excerpt is dialogue between two characters, Alex and Rudy. It looks easy to read. I wonder what they're talking about.*

3 Key Literary Element
Stage Directions *I can see that these are stage directions because there's no name in front of them, and the kind of type looks different. Stage directions tell where the play takes place, who's onstage, and what they are doing.*

---

1. To **philosophize** means "to talk about life, love, and other basic questions."
2. **Cold** is slang for cold-hearted, or unfeeling. **Homes** as used here is slang for "friend."

RUDY: You mean, like, blue or yellow?

ALEX: Lavender!

RUDY: Purple!

ALEX: Forest green!

RUDY: Chevy chrome!

ALEX: That's it, man.

(*RUDY gets up and starts to pace. ALEX gets up, too.*) 4

RUDY: (*incredulous*[3]) Colors?

ALEX: Colors. I picked up this little *secreto* from Mama Rosa on the Spanish station.

RUDY: Mama Rosa! You get your advice from her?

ALEX: She's for real. She's an expert about love and things. She says you got to get your *boca*[4] rattling. One thing leads to the next, you know.

RUDY: No, I don't know.

ALEX: Listen, man. Sometimes I'm talking about nothing and the next thing I know people are listening. Like I'm the president or something.

RUDY: You're not the president.

ALEX: I know that. What I'm saying is that you got to just talk stuff—anything!

(*Pause. RUDY reflects.*)

RUDY: I just start talking?

ALEX: That's right.

RUDY: Just . . . say things?

ALEX: Colors, start with colors. Just ask, "Patricia, what's your favorite color?"

---

3. **Incredulous** means "with disbelief."
4. **Boca** means "mouth" in Spanish.

> **4 Key Reading Skill**
> **Visualizing** The stage directions help me visualize the two boys and what they are doing.

RUDY: She won't think I'm weird? 5

ALEX: No. She'll know immediately you're trying to start something, so she'll play along. She'll say something like "Green" or "Pink."

RUDY: And I'll tell her that my favorite color is dark blue.

ALEX: There you go, homes. (*pause*) So guess mine.

RUDY: Your what?

ALEX: My favorite color!

RUDY: Black and silver, like the Raiders?

ALEX: Nope.

RUDY: Blue and gold, like the Chargers?

ALEX: Nah. It's red, like my tongue.

(*ALEX wiggles tongue at RUDY.*)

RUDY: (*punching ALEX*) That's asco!

ALEX: (*chuckling*) Don't worry, homes. Just be cool.

RUDY: Cool.

ALEX: Like an iceberg.

(*The boys pace around the stage. They stop.*)

RUDY: Man, I can't believe I'm going out with a girl in the eleventh grade. And yesterday, guess what I was doing.

ALEX: Helping your dad pour cement at a job site?

(*RUDY shakes his head.*)

ALEX: Lifting weights?

RUDY: You won't laugh if I tell you?

ALEX: Laugh at my best friend?

ACTIVE READING MODEL

5 Key Literary Element
Characterization *Rudy doesn't seem very sure of himself. I bet that's why he's getting advice from his friend.*

UNIT 8 GENRE FOCUS

RUDY: (*hesitates; long pause*) I was playing G.I. Joes with my cousin Isaac. Man, it was fun. G.I. Joe was beating up Ken, and Barbie was kicking back watching the *pleitos*.[5]

(*ALEX laughs.*)

RUDY: I got another problem. I told Patricia I was taking her to grub at Steaks, Steaks, y Más Steaks.[6]

ALEX: You told her you were taking her there? What's wrong with you, homes? Those hamburgers cost twice as much as McDonald's. And you got to tip, too.

(*RUDY reflects on his error.*)

ALEX: You got enough money?

RUDY: How much do you think I'll need?

ALEX: At least fifteen bones.

RUDY: Fifteen dollars!

(*RUDY shakes his head and shrugs his shoulders. ALEX starts to go through his pockets.*)

ALEX: (*teasing*) Here, this should help.

(*RUDY takes ALEX's quarter and looks at it.*)

RUDY: (*sarcastically*) You're cool, Alex. This quarter might get me a piece of gum.

(*They sit and reflect on the dilemma.*)

ALEX: (*perks up*) Let me give you some advice. You got to talk intelligent, like you know something.

RUDY: Like I know something?

ALEX: Remember, she's two years ahead of you and in eleventh grade. You got to be *suave*, kind of like—*pues*,[7] like me. (*hooks a thumb at himself*) 6

---

5. **Pleitos** means "fights" in Spanish.
6. **Steaks, Steaks, y Más Steaks** means "Steaks, Steaks, and More Steaks."
7. **Suave** means "smooth and confident." **Pues** is a Spanish expression for "y'know."

ACTIVE READING MODEL

6 **Key Literary Element**
Characterization Alex is the cool one with all the answers. He says what he thinks. He tries to give Rudy some good advice so he won't look bad on his date. He's being a good friend.

RUDY: Help me then, Alex.

ALEX: (*thinking about it*) It so happens I got this love letter from Sylvia Hernandez. Remember her?

RUDY: No.

ALEX: Yeah, you do. She threw up *huevos con* weenies[8] in fifth grade. (*imitates someone vomiting*) It was all over the classroom and down the hall. It was like that old movie The Blob after she was all done.

RUDY: (*reflecting*) Yeah, I remember that girl now. She got some on my shoes. (*pause*) So what did the letter say?

ALEX: (*reaches into his pocket*) Got it right here. 7

(*ALEX sniffs the letter for perfume, and RUDY sniffs it as well. ALEX starts to read letter.*)

ALEX: "Alex, I think you have the coolest eyes. And the cutest nose."

RUDY: You got a fat *huango*[9] nose.

ALEX: Hey, dude, you want me to help you or not?

RUDY: I take that back. You got a real cute nose. (*pulls up his own nose into the shape of a pig's snout*)

ALEX: That's better. (*continues reading*) "I really care about you a lot, Alex. I really don't know how to say this, but here goes. I think that you like me but don't want to tell me because of what your friends might say. Forget them. They don't have to live your life. You do! Last year I fell totally in love with this guy Kendall—"

RUDY: What kind of name is Kendall?

(*ALEX gives RUDY a look.*)

ALEX: (*continues reading*) "At first Kendall was nice to me. Then he started being mean to me and talking behind my back. It hurt me when he told this girl from Selma that I

---

8. **Huevos con weenies** is eggs with hot dogs.
9. **Huango** is Spanish slang. Here it means something like "big and floppy."

UNIT 8 GENRE FOCUS

ACTIVE READING MODEL

7 Key Reading Skill
Predicting *This letter that Alex is reading to Rudy must be important, or else he wouldn't share it. Let's see if I am right.*

UNIT 8 GENRE FOCUS

was stuck-up. I guess it was to get me to stop liking him. But I didn't stop liking him for a long time. Now I like you, Alex. I dream about—"

RUDY: Man, she knows how to talk.

ALEX: ¡Cállate![10] You're interrupting the flow of my love letter. (*pause*) Here's a good part. "Alex, you're nicer than Kendall. You're cute, too. All the boys from Roosevelt are cute, but you're the cutest. Please don't be like Kendall. I will shower you with kisses forever and ever."

RUDY: (*takes the letter and examines it*) Sounds like poetry. No, like *mi abuelita's telenovelas*.[11]

ALEX: This letter should be the floor plan for your love life. You got to lay it on thick. Be romantic, ese. Suave.[12]

RUDY: (*reflecting*) Suave. (*pulls out a small notepad*) I better write some of this stuff down so I don't forget: "Be romantic." "Lay it on thick." 8

ALEX: I went on a date once.

RUDY: You're lying.

ALEX: No, I did. (*pause*) It wasn't exactly a date. Me and this girl went to the playground. 9

RUDY: Get serious.

ALEX: Yeah, I picked her up on my bike and . . . don't laugh.

RUDY: Why would I laugh at my best friend?

ALEX: I can see it. You're gonna laugh!

RUDY: No, I promise.

(*RUDY and ALEX trade glances.*)

---

10. *¡Cállate!* means "shut up" in Spanish.
11. *Mi abuelitas's telenovelas* means "my grandmother's soap operas."
12. *Ese* is Spanish slang with a meaning similar to *dude* or *man* or *homie*.

ACTIVE READING MODEL

8 Key Reading Skill

Clarifying *So I get the picture now. Alex read the letter to show Rudy techniques for breaking the ice and starting a conversation when he goes on his date. He wants Rudy to be suave.*

9 Key Reading Skill

Predicting *Now the tables are turned and Alex is going to make a confession. Just like Rudy did before. But now it's Alex who is afraid that Rudy is going to laugh. I predict he's going to reveal something about himself that shows he isn't as cool as he pretends to be.*

ALEX: She had to pedal the bike because I didn't have enough leg strength. It's hard with two people!

(*RUDY chokes, muffling his laugh.*)

ALEX: (*continuing*) It was a lot of fun. We spent a couple hours on the monkey bars. Then we played tetherball, and then a game of chess. Yeah, it was going pretty good—until Frankie Torres came by and started teasing me.

RUDY: Frankie did that?

ALEX: Yeah. Because I was all dressed up. (*laughs*) I had on this pink shirt, and a bow tie, and buckets of my dad's Aqua Velva.[13] **10**

RUDY: Dressed up at the playground?

ALEX: Yeah, plus . . .

RUDY: What?

(*ALEX kicks at the ground, embarrassed.*)

RUDY: Hey, I'm your *carnal*.[14]

ALEX: She was getting a drink of water, so I was holding her purse.

RUDY: And that's when Frankie saw you.

ALEX: (*nodding his head*) He called me a girl because I had her purse on my shoulder. (*Pause. ALEX stands up.*) That was my first date. Age nine.

(*RUDY shakes his head sympathetically. He takes the letter from ALEX and reads it silently. Lights fade.*) **11**

10 Key Literary Element
Sensory Imagery *This description appeals to the senses of sight and smell. I can see Alex in my mind, and I can almost smell him drenched in aftershave.*

11 Key Literary Element
Characterization *Even though Alex revealed an embarrassing story to Rudy, Rudy did not laugh. I can tell that these boys are very good friends.*

---

13. **Aqua Velva** is a brand of aftershave for men.
14. In Mexican slang, **"I'm your carnal"** means "I'm your brother" in the way that a friend is like a brother. It is similar to "bro" in English.

Partner Talk Discuss how the boys in the play react to each other's embarrassing stories. Do the boys have a healthy sense of humor about themselves? Explain your answers.

 **Study Central** Visit www.glencoe.com and click on Study Central to review drama.

READING WORKSHOP 1

Skills Focus

You will practice these skills when you read the following selections:
- "The Reluctant Dragon," Scene 1, p. 942
- "The Reluctant Dragon," Scene 2, p. 954

Reading
- Visualizing

Literature
- Understanding act and scene

Vocabulary
- Slang and dialect

Writing/Grammar
- Using hyphens in compound words
- Using hyphens to divide words

Skill Lesson

Visualizing

Learn It!

What Is It? You learned about **visualizing** in Unit 4, so you remember that visualizing is "seeing" what is being described in words. In *Novio Boy*, both the dialogue and the stage directions provided information you needed to visualize what was happening.

- To visualize something is to form a picture of it in your mind. The writer chooses words to help you "see" a person, place, or thing.

Why Is It Important? Visualizing helps you understand anything you read. It's especially important while reading a play. All plays except radio plays are meant to be seen. So, you need to visualize what's happening in order to understand the play.

CALVIN AND HOBBES © 1990 Watterson. Distributed By UNIVERSAL PRESS SYNDICATE. Reprinted with permission. All rights reserved.

Analyzing Cartoons
What does Calvin visualize in the third frame of this cartoon? How does what he "sees" change his mind about doing his math homework?

Objective (pp. 938–939)
Reading Visualize

READING WORKSHOP 1 • Visualizing

How Do I Do It? Understanding stage directions will help you visualize. The most important thing to know is that stage directions are written for the people in the play. So, start by imagining that you are an actor on a stage.

- *Stage left* and *stage right* are left and right for an actor on the stage who is looking at the audience. For someone in the audience looking at the stage, stage left is to the right. So, these directions are the opposite of what you might expect.
- *Upstage* is toward the back of the stage (away from the audience). *Downstage* is toward the front (close to the audience). *Center stage* is in the middle of the stage.
- *Off* means "off the stage," where the audience can't see.

Sometimes, playwrights use shorthand. So, *right, left, up, down,* and *center* all have an invisible *stage* in them.

Here is how Kezia used information from the stage directions at the beginning of *Novio Boy.*

The scene begins in a backyard where two boys, both Mexican-American, are philosophizing about girls. They are sloppy-looking, with holes in the knees of their pants. . . . RUDY *paces back and forth and* ALEX *tries to keep up with him.*

> The stage directions really help me imagine the boys—what they're wearing and doing. People often pace when they're worried, so I'll bet Rudy is worried.

Practice It!

Below is an image related to a selection in this workshop. In your Learner's Notebook, write or sketch what you "see" in your mind's eye when you think about:

- a knight fighting a bright green dragon

Use It!

As you read remember the notes or sketches you made to practice visualizing. When you find a detail that you can picture clearly, add it to your notes and sketches.

READING WORKSHOP 1 • Visualizing

Before You Read: The Reluctant Dragon Scene 1

Meet the Author
Kenneth Grahame was born in Edinburgh, Scotland, on March 8, 1859, and died in 1932. As a student he did well in school and sports, but didn't have enough money to attend college. He became a banker and, in his spare time, wrote children's stories. When his son Alastair went on a vacation he asked his father to send him bedtime stories by mail. Grahame's best-known book, "The Wind in the Willows," started out in these letters. Grahame mailed the letters to his son every day. For more about Kenneth Grahame, see page R3 of the Author Files.

Author Search For more about Kenneth Grahame, go to www.glencoe.com.

Vocabulary Preview

scourge (skurj) *n.* cause of widespread hardship or suffering **(p. 947)**
The grasshoppers were a scourge that ate most of our crops.

solemnly (SOL um lee) *adv.* seriously; without joy or humor **(p. 947)**
He spoke so solemnly that we knew he wasn't kidding.

lavishly (LAV ish lee) *adv.* plentifully; with more than is usual or needed **(p. 947)** *The table was lavishly heaped with gifts.*

elaborately (ih LAB ur it lee) *adv.* in a fancy way that involves many details or complicated parts **(p. 948)** *Their handshake was done so elaborately that I knew I couldn't copy it.*

exasperated (eg ZAS pur ay tid) *adj.* angered or greatly irritated **(p. 949)** *Ruth yelled in an exasperated way when the dog knocked over her bucket of water.*

Partner Talk On a separate note card write each vocabulary word one time. Turn the note card over and write the definition and part of speech on the back. Take turns testing each other by flashing the cards.

English Language Coach

Slang Informal language that is appropriate for casual conversation but not for formal speech or writing is **slang**. It is language in which made-up words and ordinary words are used to mean something different than in formal English. Some slang is widely understood. Some slang, however, is only understood by people within a certain social group. Each new generation creates its own original words and expressions for describing things.

Here are some examples of slang:

Slang	Slang Meaning	Example
cool	very nice, excellent	That's a cool hat you're wearing.
ride	automobile, such as a car, truck, or SUV	Wow, that's a nice ride.
chill	to relax	You need to chill.

Partner Talk Now brainstorm six other slang sayings with a partner. Make sure the slang is appropriate for use in school.

Objectives (pp. 940–951)
Reading Visualize • Make connections from text to self
Literature Understand elements of drama: act and scene
Vocabulary Identify and understand slang

READING WORKSHOP 1 • Visualizing

Skills Preview

Key Reading Skill: Visualizing

Before you read the selection, visualize
- a shepherd boy
- dragons you've seen in books or movies
- places where dragons live

Write to Learn In your Learner's Notebook, jot down a few notes about the pictures that came to mind when you thought about the topics above. After you read, check to see if what you visualized from the text matches your notes.

Key Literary Element: Act and Scene

Books (except for very short ones) are divided into sections called chapters. Plays are also divided into sections. A short play is often called a "one-act play" because it has only one main part, that is, one **act**. Longer plays may have two or even three acts.

Each act in a play is divided into scenes. A **scene** is the section of a play that presents events in a single setting. A new scene begins whenever there is a change in the place where events are taking place or in the time.

"The Reluctant Dragon" is a one-act play that has two scenes.
- Each scene takes place at a particular place and time.

  Ask yourself: When and where does this scene take place?
- Each scene adds to the plot, or storyline, of the drama.

  Ask yourself: What happens in this scene and how does it move the plot forward?

Interactive Literary Elements Handbook
To review or learn more about the literary elements, go to www.glencoe.com.

Get Ready to Read

Connect to the Reading

How would you feel if you saw something that wasn't *supposed* to exist, like a sea monster or a dragon? What if—instead of being ferocious—it turned out to be friendly?

Write to Learn Write about a fictional creature you'd like to meet. Why would you want to meet that creature? What would it look like? What questions would you ask it?

Build Background

Dragons are legendary creatures often pictured with wings and claws. Usually, dragons are shown as giant fire-breathing lizards. Dragons have symbolized different things in different cultures throughout history.
- In China, dragons are a sign of happiness and success.
- Ancient Greeks and Romans sometimes saw dragons as symbols of good related to the secrets of the earth and sometimes as symbols of evil.
- The image of a dragon was seen as a warlike sign in Norse cultures and medieval England.

Set Purposes for Reading

BIG Question Read Scene 1 of "The Reluctant Dragon" to discover how getting to know an enemy may help to teach you the true meaning of friendship.

Set Your Own Purpose What else would you like to learn from the selection to help you answer the Big Question? Write your purpose on the "Reluctant Dragon" page of Foldable 8.

Keep Moving

Use these skills as you read the following selection.

The Reluctant Dragon **941**

READING WORKSHOP 1

the Reluctant Dragon

by Kenneth Grahame
Adapted by Adele Thane

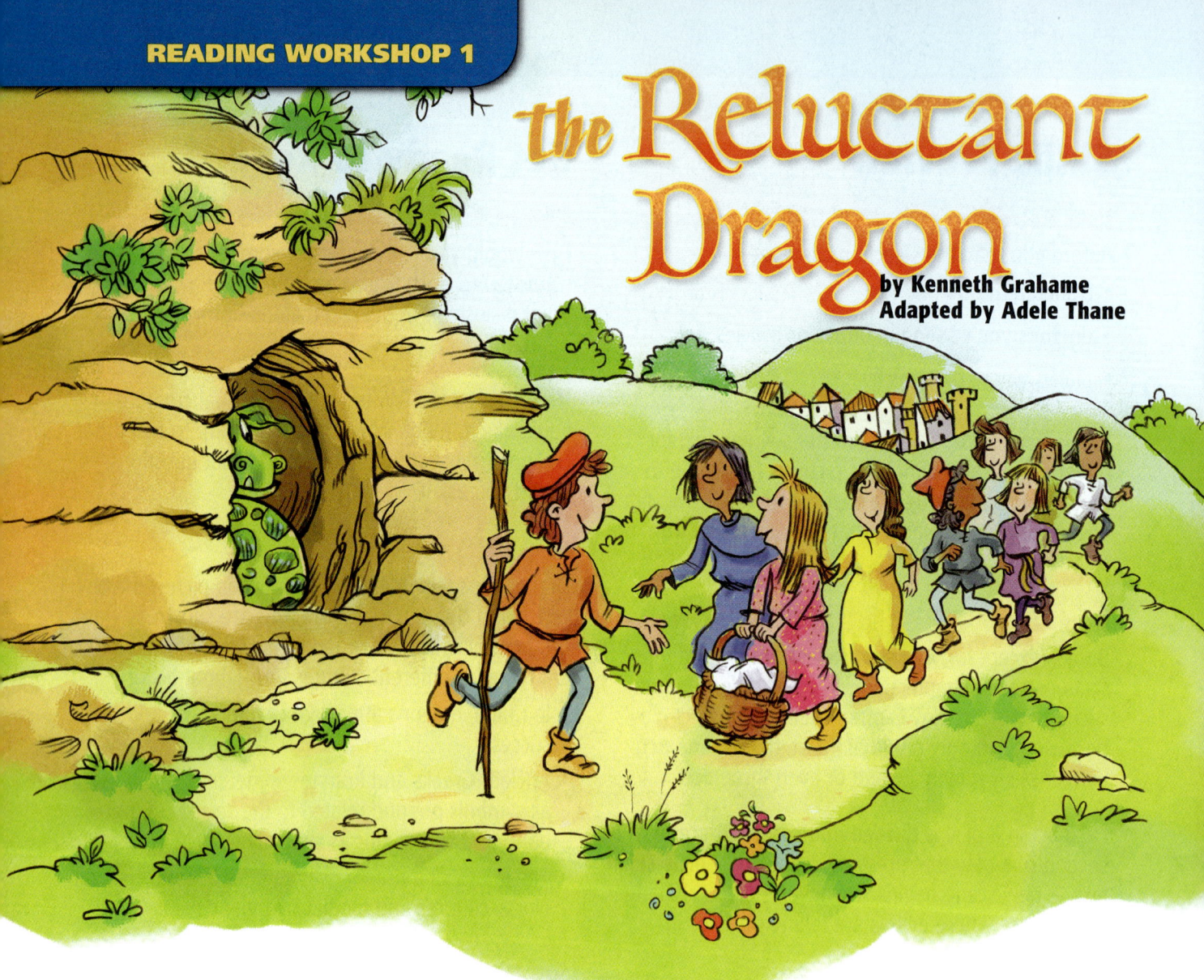

Characters
EDWARD, *a shepherd boy*
SELINA, *his sister*
HORACE, *the dragon*
ST. GEORGE
CHILDREN
VILLAGERS

SCENE 1 **1**

TIME: *Once upon a time. A summer day.*

SETTING: *A hillside in England. The green rolling countryside can be seen in the distance, with a hint of old gray cities on the horizon. The opening to Horace's cave is left; the path to the village is at right.* **2**

Practice the Skills

1 **Key Literary Element**

Act and Scene The beginning of a new scene usually includes an explanation of the time and setting. Think about how the time and setting will affect the action.

2 **Key Reading Skill**

Visualizing Can you picture the scene?

AT RISE: *Inside the cave, but visible to audience, is what appears to be a large green rock. Actually, this is* HORACE, *the dragon, curled up asleep.* EDWARD *runs in, stops, and looks around curiously.*

EDWARD: (*Shouting and beckoning off right*): Come on, hurry up! This is the place. (SELINA *and* CHILDREN *enter, carrying picnic baskets.*)

SELINA: Oh, Edward, it's a lovely place for a picnic!

1ST GIRL (*Standing on a rock at back*): Look at the view! I can see the spire of the cathedral a hundred miles away.

1ST BOY (*Standing on another rock*): There's the village. I can see my house. 3

2ND BOY (*Glancing about*): How did you know about this place, Edward?

EDWARD: I bring the sheep up here.

3RD BOY (*Peering into cave*): What's this cave?

EDWARD: Oh, just a cave.

3RD BOY: Let's explore it.

2ND GIRL: No, let's eat first. I'm starved.

3RD GIRL: So am I.

1ST BOY (*As he joins* 3RD BOY *in front of cave*): You girls unpack the baskets while we boys explore the cave.

1ST GIRL (*Coming over*): No, we want to go with you.

2ND BOY (*Catching sight of* HORACE *inside cave*): Hey! Look at that rock all covered with emeralds![1]

EDWARD: Where?

2ND BOY (*Pointing*): There.

EDWARD: That's funny. I never saw that rock before.

3RD BOY: I'll bet this cave is full of treasures. Come on!

---

1. **Emeralds** are very valuable green stones.

Practice the Skills

3 Key Reading Skill

Visualizing Reread the description of the view from the rock. Then close your eyes. Can you picture the village and the spire of the cathedral?

The Reluctant Dragon **943**

READING WORKSHOP 1

(As CHILDREN *are about to enter cave,* 2ND BOY, *who is in the lead, suddenly stops short, frightened.*)

2ND BOY: Wait!

3RD BOY: What's the matter?

2ND BOY: That rock just moved!

1ST BOY: You're crazy!

2ND BOY: I'm not! It did! (CHILDREN *stare at* HORACE *in amazement as he slowly gets to his feet, stretches, yawns, then sneezes.* CHILDREN *scream and scatter, hiding behind the rocks upstage-all except* EDWARD, *who stands at center.*)

EDWARD: Don't be afraid. It's only a dragon.

1ST GIRL: Only a *dragon!*

3RD GIRL: *Only* a dragon! (HORACE *peeks out of cave.*)

EDWARD: I've always said this cave was a dragon cave and ought to have a dragon in it.

3RD BOY: Well, it has a dragon in it, and I'm going home!

1ST BOY: Let's clear out of here! (CHILDREN *run toward exit, but* EDWARD *bars the way.*)

EDWARD: Why? He's not **ramping** or **carrying on** or doing anything wrong, is he? 4

2ND BOY: Look here, Edward, dragons may be your line, but they're not mine. Let me by! (*He pushes* EDWARD *out of the way.*)

1ST BOY: Come on, everybody, or the dragon will eat you!

3RD BOY: I'll beat you to the village and be the first to tell! (*He runs off, and the other* CHILDREN *race after him.* EDWARD *catches hold of* SELINA's *arm.*)

EDWARD: Selina, you will stay, won't you?

SELINA (*Glancing toward the cave*): I—I'll come back later—maybe. (*She hands* EDWARD *picnic basket and runs off right.* EDWARD *looks after her and sighs, then turns to* HORACE, *who has come out of cave, and is walking upright.*)

Practice the Skills

4 **English Language Coach**

Slang Carrying on is slang for making a fuss or making trouble. **Ramping** is not slang. It's an unusual word that means "to stand up on the back legs and raise the forelegs in a threatening way."

944 UNIT 8 What Makes a Friend?

READING WORKSHOP 1

EDWARD (*Cheerfully*): Hello, dragon!

HORACE (*Cowering*): Now don't you hit me, or throw stones, or squirt water at me. I won't have it! (*He sneezes.*) Atchoo!

EDWARD: I'm not going to hit you. I just want to ask you how you are, but if I'm in the way, I'll go.

HORACE (*Hastily*): No, no, don't go! I'm sorry I misjudged you. (*He bows apologetically.*) Permit me to introduce myself. My name is Horace. (*He holds out his paw, and EDWARD shakes it.*)

EDWARD: <u>Howdy do</u>, Horace. I'm Edward. Are you hungry? 5

HORACE: Terribly!

EDWARD (*In a matter-of-fact tone*): You don't eat children, do you?

HORACE (*Revolted*): Oh, no! Or grown-ups, either.

EDWARD (*Digging into picnic basket*): That's good, because there are only egg and cheese sandwiches in here. Shall we sit down?

HORACE: By all means. (*He sneezes.*) Atchoo!

EDWARD: Do you have a cold?

HORACE (*Sniffling and wiping his eyes*): No—hay fever. (*They sit on a rock and eat sandwiches as they talk.*)

EDWARD: Are you planning to stay here long?

HORACE: I think I will. It seems a nice enough place—and besides, I'm such a lazy fellow! I'm not much for moving around.

EDWARD (*Politely*): Is that so?

HORACE: All the other dragons I knew were so active and earnest—always rampaging, and chasing knights, and devouring damsels.

EDWARD: And you didn't?

Practice the Skills

5 English Language Coach

Slang When Edward says, "<u>Howdy do</u>, Horace," this is slang. He really means, *How do you do?* Can you see how Edward turned a phrase like *How do you do?* into *Howdy Do?* What kind of phrases do you shorten or change to make slang when you talk with your friends?

READING WORKSHOP 1

HORACE: No, I liked to get my meals regularly and then snooze a bit. So when it happened, I really got caught!

EDWARD: When what happened, Horace?

HORACE: The earthquake. The bottom dropped right out from under me, and I found myself miles underground, wedged in as tight as tight. After a while, I began to work my way upstairs, and I came out through this cave. (*HORACE rises and looks about with satisfaction.*) Hm-m. This is the place for me, Edward. Nice view—nice country. Quiet, too. And no ragweed.[2] (*He sneezes.*) Atchoo! Well, maybe some. 6

EDWARD (*Getting up*): What will you do up here all day long?

HORACE (*Looking away bashfully*): Uh—did you ever—just for fun—try to make up—well—poetry?

EDWARD: Of course I have, heaps of it, and some of it is quite good, too.

HORACE: Now you have culture,[3] you have! I hope my other neighbors are as cultured as you are.

---

2. A *ragweed* is a weedy herb that produces allergy-causing pollen.
3. Here *culture* means knowledge of the fine arts.

Practice the Skills

6 Key Reading Skill

Visualizing Can you visualize what Horace just described? How would a dragon like Horace get out of that kind of situation? Would his way be different from another dragon's?

Analyzing the Art Does Horace look like a fearsome, dangerous dragon? Does he look like "an enemy of the human race"? Explain your answer.

EDWARD (*Trying to break it gently*): Horace, I'm afraid there won't be any other neighbors.

HORACE: How's that?

EDWARD: Well, you are a dragon, aren't you?

HORACE (*Throwing out his chest*): Yes, and I'm mighty proud of it!

EDWARD: But being a dragon makes you an enemy of the human race.

HORACE (*Happily*): Don't have an enemy in the world! Too lazy to make them. And what if I do read other fellows my poetry? I'm always ready to listen to theirs!

EDWARD: Oh, dear, don't you understand? When the other people find you out, they'll come after you with shovels and pitchforks and all sorts of things.

HORACE (*Innocently*): Why? I'm not doing anything to them.

EDWARD: That's not the point. The way they see it, you are a scourge and a pest, and they will have to get rid of you.

HORACE (*Shaking his head solemnly*): There's not a word of truth in that. Couldn't I read them my poetry? That ought to convince them I'm harmless. Now, here's a little verse I was working on this morning. (*He removes a piece of bark from under a scale of his costume and reads from it.*) Summer.
By Horace Dragon.
Atchoo! Atchoo! The ragweed is in bloom.
Sowing far and wide allergic gloom.
How lavishly it pollinates the breeze,
And, oh! how lavishly it makes me sneeze. Atchoo!
(HORACE *pauses to blow his nose.*) Well, Edward, what do you think of it? 7

Practice the Skills

7 Key Reading Skill

Visualizing Review all the stage directions for Horace on this page. Tell how they help you visualize this conversation.

Vocabulary

scourge (skurj) *n.* cause of widespread hardship or suffering

solemnly (SOL um lee) *adv.* seriously; without joy or humor

lavishly (LAV ish lee) *adv.* plentifully; with more than is usual or needed

READING WORKSHOP 1

EDWARD (*Hesitating*): Well—it's certainly—unusual.

HORACE (*Beaming*): Yes, isn't it! (SELINA *has entered from right during these speeches.* HORACE *sees her and bows* elaborately.) Welcome, fair damsel!

EDWARD (*Pleased*): Selina! You did come back!

SELINA (*Bursting out excitedly*): Oh, Edward, the village is in an uproar!

EDWARD: I thought it would be.

HORACE: What about?

SELINA: About you, sir. They say you are a pest and a scourge and must be destroyed.

EDWARD (*To* HORACE): Didn't I tell you?

HORACE: But I haven't disturbed even a hen roost!

SELINA: That has nothing to do with it. You are a dragon, and they are afraid of you. The funny part of it is, they are proud of you, too.

HORACE: Why, my dear?

SELINA (*Smiling*): It's not every village that has a dragon of its own, you know. You are quite a feather in our cap.[4]

HORACE (*More confused than ever*): Then why do they want to destroy me?

EDWARD (*Breaking in*): Because dragons have been destroyed since the beginning of time. It's the custom.

HORACE: But I don't behave like a dragon. 8

EDWARD: It doesn't make sense, does it, Horace? But our village is famous for not making sense.

---

4. A *feather in our cap* means "a success or achievement that others will see as a credit to us."

Vocabulary

elaborately (ih LAB ur it lee) *adv.* in a fancy way that involves many details or complicated parts

Practice the Skills

8 Key Reading Skill

Visualizing What details from the play help you to imagine Horace? Even though he doesn't act like a dragon, how must the way he looks affect the way people feel? Make a list of the things people find frightening about his appearance.

SELINA: That's not all, Edward. They are going to send for St. George![5]

HORACE: St. George! (*He sneezes.*) Atchoo!

EDWARD (*Shaking* HORACE *by the tail for emphasis*): Now you will have to pull yourself together and do something!

HORACE (*Pulling his tail out of* EDWARD's *hand*): Don't be so violent, Edward! Sit down and listen to another poem.

EDWARD (**Exasperated**): That's right, take it calmly. I hope you'll be half as calm when St. George gets here. Of course you can lick him—a great big fellow like you!

HORACE: Oh, dearie me, this is too awful! I won't see him, and that's that! When he comes, you must tell him to go away at once. Say he can write if he likes, but I can't give him an interview.

EDWARD: Oh, Horace, don't be so pigheaded! You have to fight him some time or other.

HORACE: I don't see why.

EDWARD: Because he is St. George and you are a dragon.

HORACE (*Gravely*): My dear boy, please understand, once and for all, that I can't fight and I won't fight. I've never fought in my life, and I'm not going to begin now, just to give your village a Roman holiday.[6]

EDWARD (*Miserably*): But if you don't fight, St. George will cut off your head!

HORACE: Oh, I don't think so. You will be able to arrange something, Edward—you are such a good manager. I leave it entirely up to you. And now, if you will excuse me, I should get back to my writing. Thank you for the sandwiches. (*He goes into the cave.*) 9

---

5. **St. George** is a legendary figure and patron saint of England. He is often seen as an example of bravery and defender of the poor and helpless. Although he was a real person, writers and artists have shown him as a dragon-slayer.
6. By **Roman holiday**, Horace means he doesn't want to be a source of amusement.

Vocabulary

exasperated (eg ZAS pur ay tid) *adj.* angered or greatly irritated

Practice the Skills

9 Reviewing Skills

Comparing and Contrasting Think about what you know or have read about dragons. How is Horace similar to or different from those dragons?

READING WORKSHOP 1

Visual Vocabulary
Croquet is a game in which players use mallets (which resemble wooden golf clubs) to drive wooden balls through a series of small arches on a lawn.

EDWARD (*To* SELINA): Arrange something indeed! Horace treats the whole affair as if it were an invitation to play croquet! Come on, let's go home. (*He picks up picnic basket and exits right, followed by* SELINA. *After a moment,* HORACE *appears in entrance to cave, carrying a stool and several pieces of bark. He places stool just outside cave, sits down and begins to scribble on a piece of bark with a lump of charcoal. He ponders over words, rhyming them out loud, and sneezes once or twice. Presently,* SELINA *enters from right and speaks to HORACE softly.*) **10**

SELINA: Mr. Horace—

HORACE (*Looking up with a start*): Oh! My dear! (*He rises and bows.*) I didn't expect you back so soon.

SELINA (*Crossing to him*): Mr. Horace, if there's anything I can do for you—like mend things, or set the cave to rights, or cook a little something when you're writing poetry and forget about meals, I—I'd be glad to do it.

HORACE: Thank you, Selina. I'd appreciate that.

SELINA: I'll start tomorrow. Is there anything in particular you'd like?

HORACE: I wonder if you'd bring me a bit of flannel to polish my scales with. (*He sneezes.*) Atchoo!

SELINA: Bless you! I'll bring the flannel and some smelling salts[7] for that hay fever, too. Goodbye!

HORACE: Goodbye, my dear. (SELINA *skips away, singing.*) What a nice child. I'll write a sonnet[8] to her. (*He sits down again, selects a clean piece of bark, and inscribes the title with a flourish.*) To Selina. By Horace Dragon. Now, let me think—how shall I begin it? (*He speaks the lines as he slowly sets them down.*)

Practice the Skills

10 **Key Reading Skill**
Visualizing Pay close attention to the stage directions. How do they help you visualize what Horace does?

---

7. **Smelling salts** are a strong-scented mixture used for waking up someone who has fainted. They used to be used for hay fever.
8. A **sonnet** is a fourteen line rhyming poem.

READING WORKSHOP 1

Analyzing the Art What is Horace writing in this picture? How do you know?

Selina in her braids and calico
Is fairer far than any flower I know.
So sweet is she, this dainty shepherd's daughter,
I blush to say she makes my big mouth water. (HORACE *writes on the bark, then holds up his poem and regards it with delight. Suddenly he jumps to his feet with a cry of horror.*) Oh! What am I thinking of? Is it possible that I am a damsel-devouring dragon after all? Oh, dearie, dearie me! (*He reaches behind for his tail and, using it as an eraser, he frantically rubs out what he has written, as curtain falls.*) 11 ○

Practice the Skills

11 BIG Question
Would you make friends with a dragon like Edward and Selina do, or would you run away like the other children? What about Horace might make him a good friend? Write your answer on the "Reluctant Dragon, Scene 1" page of Foldable 8. Your answer will help you complete the Unit Challenge later.

The Reluctant Dragon

After You Read

The Reluctant Dragon Scene 1

Answering the BIG Question

1. Would you want to be friends with Horace? Explain your answer.

Critical Thinking

2. **Analyze** Think about Horace's personality. What makes him a *reluctant* dragon?

   TIP Author and Me

Talk About Your Reading

Scene 1 ends with Horace concerned that he might *really* be a "damsel-devouring dragon after all." What do you think? With a partner, talk about what might happen in the next scene, and why it might happen.

Skills Review

Key Reading Skill: Visualizing

3. Find all the descriptions of what Horace looks like. (Hint: They're all on the first few pages.) Now use your imagination to make a sketch of him.

Key Literary Element: Scene

4. How do details like *time* and *setting* at the beginning of a new scene help you to understand what is happening in the play?

Vocabulary Check

Rewrite the sentences using four of the words that fit best.

scourge   solemnly   lavishly   elaborately   exasperated

The invaders were a **5.** ___ throughout the kingdom. The king spent money **6.** ___ to make sure the castle was protected. However, with a sad face, he **7.** ___ announced he could not protect the people. The knights were so **8.** ___ by this that they decided to fight on their own.

9. **Academic Vocabulary** What does it mean to visualize as you read?
10. **English Language Coach** What is another slang term for *carrying on*?

Objectives (p. 952)
Reading Visualize
Literature Understand elements of drama: act and scene
Vocabulary Identify and understand slang

READING WORKSHOP 1 • Visualizing

Before You Read: The Reluctant Dragon Scene 2

Vocabulary Preview

contemplation (kon tem PLAY shun) *n.* a state of deep thought **(p. 954)** *The knight was lost in contemplation.*

crevice (KREV is) *n.* narrow opening; split or crack **(p. 954)** *His spear was wedged in the crevice of a rock.*

conceited (kun SEE tid) *adj.* having a high opinion of oneself **(p. 961)** *The dragon became proud and conceited when the crowd cheered for him.*

warily (WAIR uh lee) *adv.* cautiously **(p. 961)** *The knight warily circled the dragon.*

spar (spar) *v.* to move around as if fighting without landing a blow **(p. 961)** *A crowd gathered when the knight and the dragon began to spar.*

English Language Coach

Dialect The way a language is spoken in one area or by a group of people is called **dialect**. Some dialects might look like Standard English but use a different vocabulary or word order. At other times, written dialect can look very different. For example, "Twarn't no good a-tall" in Standard English would be: "It wasn't any good at all."

Skills Preview

Key Reading Skill: Visualizing
As you read the next scene, use what you already know about the characters to visualize them.

Key Literary Element: Act and Scene
Directions at the beginning of a new scene will help you to understand actions and learn about characters.

Get Ready to Read

Partner Talk With a partner, discuss what you think will happen between Horace and St. George.

Keep Moving
Use these skills as you read the following selection.

Objectives (pp. 953–963)
Reading Visualize
Literature Understand elements of drama: scene
Vocabulary Identify and understand dialect

The Reluctant Dragon **953**

READING WORKSHOP 1

the Reluctant Dragon

by Kenneth Grahame
Adapted by Adele Thane

SCENE 2

TIME: Three days later.

SETTING: The same as Scene 1.

AT RISE: ST. GEORGE *is standing on a rock upstage, leaning on his sword, lost in* contemplation *of distant hills. His red-plumed*[1] *helmet is resting on the rock beside him. His spear is stuck upright in a* crevice. HORACE *is nowhere to be seen. After a moment,* EDWARD *enters from right.* 🔲

EDWARD (*Politely*): St. George, sir!

ST. GEORGE (*Turning, startled*): Yes?

EDWARD: I hope I'm not intruding, sir.

ST. GEORGE: Not at all, boy. I'm just getting the lay of the land. Magnificent view up here. What can I do for you? (*He comes down from rock.*)

EDWARD: If you please, sir, I'd like to talk to you about the dragon.

ST. GEORGE (*Sighing*): Alas! Is it another tale of misery and wrong?

---

1. A **red-plumed** helmet has a cluster of red feathers on it.

Vocabulary

contemplation (kon tem PLAY shun) *n.* a state of deep thought

crevice (KREV is) *n.* narrow opening; split or crack

Practice the Skills

🔲 **Key Literary Element**

Act and Scene This is Scene 2. From details about the *time* and *setting*, what do you notice about this new scene?

EDWARD: Nothing of the sort! There's a misunderstanding somewhere, and I want to put it right. The fact is, sir, this is a *good* dragon.

ST. GEORGE (*Smiling*): Exactly. A good dragon—a worthy foe of my steel (*He lifts his sword high*), and no feeble specimen of his noxious tribe.[2]

EDWARD: He's not noxious! I tell you, he's a *good* dragon, and a friend of mine. Why, he has been so kind to my sister, she'd do anything for him.

ST. GEORGE (*Clapping EDWARD on shoulder*): I like a fellow who sticks up for his friends! What is your name, boy?

EDWARD: Edward, sir.

ST. GEORGE: Now, Edward, I'm sure the dragon has his good points, but that's not the question. He has been stealing and killing—

EDWARD (*Shocked*): Horace? Stealing and killing? (*Impatiently*) Oh, you've been listening to all those **yarns** the villagers have been telling. Why, our villagers are the biggest story-tellers in the country.

ST. GEORGE (*Amazed*): Do you mean that the dragon hasn't molested[3] anybody?

EDWARD: That's right. Horace is a real gentleman, every inch of him. All the villagers want is to see a fight.

ST. GEORGE: But what are we to do? (*Pointing to cave.*) In there is the dragon and out here am I, and we're supposed to be thirsting for each other's blood. What do you suggest? Can't you arrange things, somehow? 🔳

Analyzing the Illustration Does this picture match the way you visualize St. George? Why or why not?

---

2. **Noxious** means "harmful" and a **specimen** is an example of something. When St. George says, *"no feeble specimen of his noxious tribe,"* he means that Horace would be a worthy opponent, not a weak dragon.

3. Here, **molested** means "injured or bothered."

Practice the Skills

🔳 **English Language Coach**

Dialect *Yarn*, which means "exaggerated story," is an example of dialect in this story. It's common in old-fashioned ways of speaking. Also, in a dialect, words may be arranged differently than you'd expect. Find an example near the end of this page where that occurs.

EDWARD: That's just what Horace said! Really, the way you two seem to leave everything to me! (*Coaxing*) I suppose, sir, you couldn't be persuaded to go away quietly, could you?

ST. GEORGE (*Loftily*): Impossible! It's quite against the rules.

EDWARD: Then would you please see the dragon and talk it over?

ST. GEORGE: We-e-ell, it's irregular, but I guess it's the most sensible thing to do.

EDWARD: I'm glad you feel that way, St. George. (*He goes to entrance of cave and calls out loudly.*) Horace! I've brought a friend to see you! (*There is a sneeze inside cave, and* SELINA *comes running out, holding a bottle of smelling salts.*)

SELINA: He'll be right out.

ST. GEORGE: What ho! A damsel in distress! (*He draws his sword.*)

EDWARD: Hold on! That's my sister, Selina. She looks after him.

ST. GEORGE (*With a sheepish grin*): Oh. (*He puts his sword away.* HORACE *appears, rubbing his scales with a square of flannel. He gives the flannel to* SELINA *and extends his paw to* ST. GEORGE.)

HORACE: Pleased to make your acquaintance, sir.

EDWARD: This is St. George.

HORACE (*Frightened*): St. George?

ST. GEORGE (*Shaking* HORACE's *paw*): How do you do, Horace.

HORACE: So—so glad to meet you. (SELINA *hovers over* HORACE *during the following scene, polishing his scales and giving him smelling salts whenever he shows signs of sneezing.*) 🔳

EDWARD: We've come to talk things over quietly, Horace, so for goodness' sake, do let us have a little straight common sense.

Practice the Skills

🔳 **Key Reading Skill**

Visualizing Reread the stage directions describing Selina and Horace. How do you visualize Horace and Selina's actions?

ST. GEORGE (*Pleasantly*): Now, don't you think that the simplest plan would be just to fight it out and let the best man win?

EDWARD: Oh, yes, do, Horace! It will save such a lot of bother.

ST. GEORGE: They are betting on you down in the village, Horace, but I don't mind.

HORACE: Believe me, George, there's nobody in the world I'd sooner oblige than you and Edward, but the whole thing is nonsense. There's absolutely nothing to fight about. Anyhow, I'm not going to fight, so that settles it. 4

ST. GEORGE (*Slightly angry*): Suppose I make you fight?

HORACE: You can't. I should only go into my cave and stay there. You'd soon get sick of sitting outside and waiting for me to come out and fight.

ST. GEORGE (*As he gazes about*): But Horace, this would be a beautiful place for a fight. What a picture we would make!—I in my golden armor showing up against your big green scaly coils. 5

HORACE (*Wavering*): Now you're trying to get at me through my poetic sense,[4] but it won't work.

EDWARD: Don't you see, Horace, that there *has* to be a fight of some sort, even if it's only "pretend"?

HORACE: You mean, a mock fight?

ST. GEORGE (*Eagerly*): Yes! I'm sure we can manage it. (*He studies his sword.*) I would have to touch you somewhere, but I won't hurt you very much. How about here? (*He places the tip of his sword behind* HORACE's *knee.*)

HORACE (*Giggling*): You're tickling me, George! (*He sneezes.*) That place won't do. I'd only laugh and spoil everything. (*He sniffs the smelling salts that* SELINA *holds under his nose.*)

Practice the Skills

4 Reviewing Skills

Predicting Do you think that Horace will fight or not? Explain your prediction.

5 Key Reading Skill

Visualizing Even St. George is visualizing. Do his descriptions fit the way *you* visualize St. George and Horace?

---

4. By *poetic sense*, Horace means his appreciation of beauty. He realizes that the image of a bright green dragon fighting a knight in golden armor would be a poetic moment.

READING WORKSHOP 1

ST. GEORGE: Well, here, then. (*He flicks his sword at the nape of* HORACE's *neck.*) If I nicked you here, you'd never know I'd done it.

HORACE (*Anxiously*): Are you sure you can hit the right place?

ST. GEORGE: Now, don't you fret. Of course you will have to do your share of the fighting, too, Horace. Can you **ramp** and breathe fire? 6

HORACE (*Confidently*): Oh, I can ramp all right. I'm a little out of practice breathing fire, but I'll do my best. 7

EDWARD (*Concerned*): Look here, St. George, if there's to be a fight and Horace is to be licked, what is he going to get out of it?

HORACE: That's right, George. What will I get out of it?

ST. GEORGE: Well, you will be led in triumph down to the market place—

EDWARD: Exactly—led in triumph by you!

ST. GEORGE: Then there will be toasts and speeches, and I shall explain that Horace has converted.

EDWARD: And then?

ST. GEORGE: Why, then there will be a big banquet, and that is where Horace will come in.

HORACE: What do you mean?

ST. GEORGE: I mean, you will read some of your poetry with the dessert, and everyone will know how clever you are!

HORACE: Splendid! I might even go into society and read my poems at garden parties and teas.

ST. GEORGE (*Picking up his helmet from the rock*): There ought to be a princess chained to this rock. Edward, can't you arrange a princess?

EDWARD (*Firmly*): No, I can't arrange a princess, and anyway, here come the villagers to see the fight. (*Noise of a crowd is heard from off right.*)

Practice the Skills

6 English Language Coach

Dialect You learned what *ramping* means on page 944, so you can figure out what *ramp* means here. This is another old-fashioned word.

7 Key Reading Skill

Visualizing Is it easy to visualize Horace breathing fire? Why or why not?

ST. GEORGE: Horace, get into your cave and don't come out until I call you. (HORACE *trots into cave.*) Come, Edward, you will be my squire[5] and carry my spear. (*He loosens spear from crevice and gives it to* EDWARD; *then he strides off left of cave.*)

EDWARD (*To* SELINA, *as he follows* ST. GEORGE *off*): Act as if you'd just arrived! (SELINA *hastily tosses flannel cloth into cave and sits on a rock, assuming a casual pose.* VILLAGERS *and* CHILDREN *enter, dressed in their Sunday best, laughing and chattering gaily. They group themselves, sitting and standing, on the rocks,* CHILDREN *in the foreground and* VILLAGERS *behind.*)

1ST BOY: Who do you think will win?

2ND BOY: The dragon.

3RD BOY: St. George.

1ST BOY (*To* 2ND BOY): Hey, don't sit so close to the cave!

2ND BOY: Why not?

1ST BOY: If the dragon wins, he'll bite off your head! (BOYS *cuff at*[6] *each other. Then* VILLAGERS *on higher portions of the rocks begin to cheer and wave their handkerchiefs as they look off left.*)

VILLAGERS: St. George! Here comes St. George! (ST. GEORGE *enters, followed by* EDWARD, *who carries spear.* ST. GEORGE *takes up a position downstage in front of cave, with* EDWARD *beside him.*) 8

EDWARD (*In a low tone, to* ST. GEORGE): Do you think Horace can be depended on, sir?

ST. GEORGE: Oh, I think so.

EDWARD: He might consider the whole thing a lot of bosh[7] and change his mind.

ST. GEORGE: Haven't you more faith in your friend than that? (EDWARD *sits cross-legged, with his back to audience.*

---

5. Here, **squire** means someone who carries a knight's shield, armor, or weapon.
6. To **cuff at** each other is to slap at each other with open hands.
7. **Bosh** means nonsense.

Practice the Skills

8 Key Reading Skill

Visualizing How do you visualize the villagers? Think about the villagers you have already met, like Edward and Selina. What details in the script help you to picture the villagers in your imagination?

READING WORKSHOP 1

ST. GEORGE *faces opening of cave, and talks loudly to* HORACE.) Dragon, come forth! (*Inside cave, there is low muttering, mingled with snorts and sneezes, which rises to a bellowing roar. Then a cloud of smoke rolls out of the cave, and* HORACE *prances magnificently forth, lashing his long tail from side to side.*)

VILLAGERS: Ooh! Ooh!

EDWARD (*Applauding wildly*): Bully for you, Horace! I didn't think you had it in you! (ST. GEORGE *draws his sword and charges at* HORACE, *who rears back with a loud roar.*) 9

VILLAGERS: Missed! (ST. GEORGE *retreats and swings his sword high in the air, then charges again.* HORACE *sits down and roars viciously.*)

EDWARD (*Shouting, as he stands up and waves the spear*): End of Round One! (SELINA *runs to his side and whispers to him uneasily.*)

SELINA: I hope St. George won't get excited and hurt Horace.

Practice the Skills

9 **English Language Coach**

Dialect To understand dialect in what you read, it is extremely helpful to use your context clues skills. Look at what Edward is doing and what he says after he says, "Bully for you, Horace!" What do you think "Bully for you" means?

Analyzing the Art Study this picture. Do Horace and St. George seem to be putting on a good show? Do you think the villagers are enjoying the battle? Support your answers with details from the picture.

960 UNIT 8 What Makes a Friend?

EDWARD: I don't think he will. What a regular play-actor that Horace is! (ST. GEORGE *looks toward them as he wipes his brow. He smiles and nods and holds up three fingers.*) That means he will finish off Horace in Round Three. Whatever is that old fool of a dragon up to now? (HORACE *is giving a ramping performance for* VILLAGERS. *He swaggers around and around in a wide circle.* EDWARD *raps on ground with the spear.*) Time! (HORACE *begins to leap from side to side with ungainly bounds, whooping like an Indian.* ST. GEORGE *dances about, thrusting his sword at* HORACE, *but is unable to make contact.* VILLAGERS *cheer.* HORACE *struts to and fro, his tail in the air.* ST. GEORGE *comes toward* EDWARD *and* SELINA, *tightening his armor.*) It's a grand fight, St. George. Can't you let it last a bit longer?

ST. GEORGE: No, I'd better not. Horace is getting **conceited** now that they've started to cheer him. He'll forget all about the agreement and play the fool. There's no telling how far he might go. I'll just finish him off this round.

SELINA: Oh, *do* be careful, sir—of Horace, I mean.

ST. GEORGE (*Kindly*): Now don't you worry. I've marked the exact spot. (ST. GEORGE *turns upstage and cautiously approaches* HORACE, *who crouches, flicking his tail so that it cracks like a whip.* ST. GEORGE *circles* **warily** *around him.* HORACE *paces guardedly around the same circle, occasionally feinting*[8] *with his head. They* **spar** *for an opening, while the spectators maintain a breathless silence. Then suddenly there is a lightning movement of* ST. GEORGE's *arm, a whirl and a confusion of scales, claws, tail and flying bits of turf.* VILLAGERS *cheer as* ST. GEORGE *stands astride* HORACE. ST. GEORGE *holds his sword over* HORACE, *menacingly.* EDWARD *and* SELINA *run to* ST. GEORGE.) **10**

EDWARD: Oh, sir, he isn't really hurt, is he? (HORACE *lifts his head slightly, looks at* EDWARD, *then collapses again.*)

---

8. By **feinting** Horace is making a false move, or "faking out" his opponent.

Vocabulary

conceited (kun SEE tid) *adj.* having a high opinion of oneself
warily (WAIR uh lee) *adv.* cautiously
spar (spar) *v.* to move around as if fighting without landing a blow

Practice the Skills

10 **Key Reading Skill**

Visualizing How do you visualize the fight between Horace and St. George? Imagine Horace cracking his tail *"like a whip,"* as the two pace in a circle. Imagine St. George's *"lightning movement,"* and a whirl of *"scales, claws, tail and . . . flying bits of turf."* What other details from the play help you to visualize the fight?

READING WORKSHOP 1

1ST VILLAGER (*An old man in the crowd*): Aren't you goin' to cut 'is 'ead off, master? **11**

ST. GEORGE (*Affably*): Not today, grandfather. I'll give him a good talking-to, and you'll find he will be a very different dragon.

VILLAGERS: Three cheers for St. George! Three cheers for the dragon! (*While the crowd is cheering,* ST. GEORGE *pretends to scold* HORACE, *wagging his finger at him with a stern expression.* VILLAGERS *start to form for the march to the village, and* ST. GEORGE *raises his hand to get their attention.*)

ST. GEORGE: Just a moment! I have something to say to all of you. The dragon has been thinking things over, and he says he's not going to rampage any more. He would like to settle down here and write poetry. So you must make friends with him and admit him into society.⁹ (VILLAGERS *cheer again.*)

HORACE (*To* ST. GEORGE): I couldn't have done it better myself. Jolly fight, wasn't it? I didn't sneeze once. (*He sneezes, and* SELINA *whips out the smelling salts.*) Thank you, my dear.

ST. GEORGE: Well, shall we start down to the village?

HORACE: Wait! My poems!

SELINA: I'll get them for you! (*She rushes into the cave;* CHILDREN *and* VILLAGERS *joyfully march offstage and down through the audience, singing to the tune of "The Campbells Are Coming."*¹⁰)

Practice the Skills

11 **English Language Coach**

Dialect A new dialect has just been introduced—one that is very common in London, England. (It's called "cockney.") How does the old man pronounce *his* and *head*?

---

9. To **admit him into society** means "let him be a part of the community."
10. **"The Campbells Are Coming"** is a traditional Scottish bagpipe tune.

READING WORKSHOP 1

ALL (*Singing*):
St. George caught a dragon,
　Hooray! Hooray!
A strange sort of dragon,
　Hooray! Hooray!
He sits in his cave
　Writing poems all day!
A strange sort of dragon,
　Hooray! Hooray!

(EDWARD, ST. GEORGE, SELINA, *and* HORACE, *with his poems tucked under his scales, bring up the rear,* HORACE *singing loudest of all, as curtain falls.*)

THE END 12 ○

Practice the Skills

12 BIG Question
Even though dragons and people are supposed to be enemies, Edward and Selina befriend Horace. What does this tell you about friendship? Write your answer on the "Reluctant Dragon, Scene 2" page of Foldable 8. Your answer will help you complete the Unit Challenge later.

Analyzing the Art Review the end of the play, beginning with Selina's final line. Then answer the question: What is happening in this picture? Support your answer with details from the play and from the picture.

The Reluctant Dragon **963**

READING WORKSHOP 1 • Visualizing

After You Read

The Reluctant Dragon Scene 2

Answering the BIG Question

1. If you could pick one of the characters as a friend, whom would you pick and why do you think the character would make a good friend? Support your answer with details from the story.

2. **Recall** How does Horace first react when he meets St. George?
   TIP Right There

3. **Summarize** How did Edward and St. George persuade Horace to fight?
   TIP Think and Search

Critical Thinking

4. **Infer** What is Horace's attitude toward the fight with St. George while the battle is going on? How can you tell?
   TIP Author and Me

5. **Analyze** What is the message about friendship in "The Reluctant Dragon"?
   TIP Author and Me

6. **Synthesize** Do you think the rest of the village will make friends with Horace "and admit him into society" as St. George instructs? Support your answer with details from the story.
   TIP On Your Own

Write About Your Reading

Part of making a great play is designing the costumes. What kind of costumes would you design for Horace and St. George?

- Skim through the play and make a list of any details you find that will help you to visualize the way Horace and St. George look.
- Using those descriptions, draw the costumes.
- Write a paragraph about why you designed the costumes as you did. Be sure to include the details from the play that you put on your list.

Objectives (pp. 964–965)
Reading Visualize
Literature Understand elements of drama: scene
Vocabulary Understand dialect
Writing Design and write about costumes
Grammar Use punctuation correctly: hyphens

964 UNIT 8 What Makes a Friend?

Skills Review

Key Reading Skill: Visualizing

7. Was it easier for you to visualize the scenery, the characters, or the action? Explain.
8. Make a sketch of the stage, showing the cave, the path to the village, and whatever else you want to add.
9. The author writes, "ST. GEORGE *takes up a position downstage in front of the cave, with* EDWARD *beside him*." Where are Edward and St. George? Add them to your sketch.

Key Literary Element: Act and Scene

10. Why do you think it's important to change scenes in a play?

Reviewing Skills: Predicting

11. What part of the play turned out differently from one of your predictions? What did *you* predict would happen instead of what did happen?

Vocabulary Check

Answer each statement *true* or *false*. If the statement is false, rewrite it to make it true.

12. A person in the act of **contemplation** is sleeping.
13. A surface with a **crevice** is perfectly smooth.
14. A **conceited** person doesn't have much confidence.
15. A spy would never behave **warily**.
16. If you **spar** with a friend you don't actually touch him or her.
17. **English Language Coach** Rewrite, "Ain't you fightin' dat dragon?" in Standard English.

Grammar Link: Hyphens

- A **hyphen** (-) is a punctuation mark that's used to show that words or parts of words belong together.
  He is a well-known artist. (The hyphen shows that *well* and *known* go together as a compound adjective.)
- Use a hyphen in compound numbers.
  My coat cost sixty-five dollars.
- Use a hyphen or hyphens in certain compound words. Use a dictionary if you aren't sure how to write a compound word.
  bull's-eye   brother-in-law   wide-awake
- Use a hyphen to show the division of a word at the end of a line. Always divide the word between syllables.
  Last term my social studies grade was a disappoint-ment.

Grammar Practice

Match up the words from Column A and Column B to form compound words. Then write each compound word in your Learner's Notebook. Add a hyphen if you think it is needed. Then check your answers in a dictionary to see if you have used hyphens correctly.

	Column A	Column B
18.	narrow	size
19.	life	spoken
20.	soft	minded

Writing Application Circle any hyphens you used in the Write About Your Reading activity you completed. Fix any mistakes you made.

Web Activities For eFlashcards, Selection Quick Checks, and other Web activities, go to www.glencoe.com.

WRITING WORKSHOP PART 1

Speech
Prewriting and Drafting

ASSIGNMENT Write a speech and present it in front of an audience

Purpose: To write a speech about a friend and why your friendship is special

Audience: You, your teacher, and classmates

Writing Rubric

As you work through this writing assignment, you should

- describe an important friendship
- gather interesting details
- organize your speech into three main parts: the beginning, the middle, and the end
- include visual aids

See page 1034 in Part 2 for a model of a speech.

Objectives (pp. 966–969)
Writing Use the writing process: prewrite, draft • Write a speech • Use text structure: beginning, middle, end • Write with fluency and clarity • Practice presentation
Grammar Use punctuation correctly: apostrophes

A speech is great way to share what you know and what you believe in. There are three types of speeches. They are explained below:

Speech	Purpose
Informative	Share information and your knowledge about a topic to educate the audience
Persuasive	Persuade the audience to agree with your views and opinions about a topic
Demonstrative	Show the audience how to do something or how something works

Prewriting
Get Ready to Write

Making friends isn't always easy. Keeping those friends takes work, too. In this workshop, you will write an informative speech about an important friend in your life and what makes your friendship work.

Choose a Topic

Think about the friendships you have read about in this unit. In *Novio Boy*, Rudy and Alex share secrets and advice. Who is one friend you talk to when you have a problem? This person will be the topic of your speech.

Gather Ideas

Now that you have chosen a topic, follow the steps below to gather ideas.

1. Freewrite about your friend for five minutes. Write descriptions, experiences, feelings, or memories about that person.
2. Talk to other people who know your friend. What do they have to say? Write their responses in your Learner's Notebook.
3. Choose the main reason why this person is your friend. Write that reason as a phrase or sentence.

Christine is my friend because we both like karate.

Drafting
Start Writing!

A speech has three main parts: a beginning, middle, and end. Speeches are different from most writing because they are heard by an audience, not read. As you begin to write, remember that your audience will be listening to what you write. To make your speech interesting:

- include descriptions that help the audience picture in their minds what you are saying.
- write in a way that will sound natural when you speak.

Get It on Paper

Use these tips as you write each part of your draft.

Strong Beginning

The introduction of your speech must grab your listeners' attention. Here are some suggestions for a great opening.

- Ask a question: *How many of your friends do you fight with just for fun?*
- Share a surprising story: *Even though Christine is my best friend, we fight nearly every day. Luckily, the fights take place at Kick Start, a martial arts studio in Mayfield.*
- Read a quote: *"Christine is full of promise and strength," says May Lee, one of Christine's karate instructors at Kick Start.*
- Report a fact: *Christine was the first student in the class to pass the examination on her first try.*

Informative Middle

Now that you have your audience's attention, get to the main point of your speech.

- Describe your friend, using interesting descriptions.
- Explain how you keep your friendship strong.
- Use quotes from other people to support your claims about your friend.

Powerful Ending

Your ending should retell the main reason for your speech and bring your speech to a natural sounding close. Here are some suggestions for ending.

- Share a joke or short story about your friendship.
- Use a quote about the importance of friendship.
- Repeat a part of the introduction.

Writing Models For models and other writing activities, go to www.glencoe.com.

> **Writing Tip**
>
> **Beginning** Get your audience's attention by asking them to imagine a scenario or incident that relates to your speech.
> *Imagine it's your first day at a new school . . .*
> *Try to imagine your best friend in a karate tournament.*

> **Writing Tip**
>
> **Middle** Organize the body of your speech by using the cause-and-effect structure. Describe a quality about your friend. Then tell what effect that quality has on your friendship.

> **Writing Tip**
>
> **End** If your speech topic is complex, allow audience members to ask questions at the end of the speech.

WRITING WORKSHOP PART 1

Applying Good Writing Traits

Heart of the City © 1998 Mark Tatulli. Distributed by Universal Press Syndicate.

Analyzing Cartoons List three details from the cartoon that show how important *presentation* is to the girl—even at lunch.

Presentation

The way you present, or share, your speech is just as important as the words you wrote. If your presentation is sloppy, your audience will not be interested in what you have to say.

What Is Presentation?

Presentation is a combination of the spoken message, voice, gesture, and overall appearance.

Why Is Presentation Important?

- A thoughtful presentation makes your speech easy to understand and is more likely to interest your audience.
- The audience will take your speech more seriously if you have a polished presentation.

How Do I Do It?

Each person who presents a speech is different. Most likely, everyone in your class will have a different presentation style. The most important part of presenting a speech is that you be yourself. Your personality makes you special, so let it shine!

1. Do not start your speech until everyone in the audience is focused on you, the speaker. If you don't have the full attention of your audience from the start, your speech will likely be forgotten or ignored.
2. Make sure that all audience members can see you and your visual aids clearly.
3. Stand up straight and tall. Good posture tells your audience that you are comfortable and confident.
4. Speak loudly enough to be heard in the back of the room. If audience members can't hear you, they will lose interest in your speech.
5. Relax! Audiences respond better to a speaker who is relaxed and conversational, not one who is stiff and formal.

Write to Learn Enhance your presentation by adding graphics. Find photos, maps, or illustrations that relate to your speech. Use a projector or computer, or make multiple copies to display the graphic.

Grammar Link

Apostrophes

Apostrophes are small marks of punctuation (') that have several different uses. This Grammar Link will show when to use apostrophes.

What Are Apostrophes?

Apostrophes are used to show possession and to form contractions.

Why Are Apostrophes Important?

An apostrophe is a big tool in a little package. This small mark of punctuation (') can combine words and replace letters.

How Do I Use Apostrophes?

1. Use an apostrophe to show that letters have been left out of a word or phrase. This is called a contraction.
- **can't** (the *n* and *o* of *cannot* is replaced by an apostrophe)
- **We're** (an apostrophe replaces the *a* of the phrase *we are*)
2. Use an apostrophe followed by the letter *s* to form the possessive of a singular noun.
- Chad**'s** bike is green with black stripes.
- The band**'s** song hit the top of the charts.
3. To show the possessive form of a plural noun, just add an apostrophe after the *s*.
- My parents**'** car is blue.
- The two schools**'** principals discussed the game.

Watch Out!

Not all plural nouns end in *s* (*women, children, mice*). Use an apostrophe and an *s* to form the possessive of a plural noun that does not end in *s*.
- *women's, children's, mice's*

Grammar Practice

Try rewriting each sentence below to include an apostrophe.

1. She is going to Florida for vacation.
2. These chips do not taste good.
3. It is going to rain.

Each sentence below has a misplaced apostrophe. Rewrite the sentence putting the apostrophe in the right place.

1. Leroys' kick is strong.
2. All of my sibling's eyes are green.
3. The cars' engine is hot.

Looking Ahead

Keep all of the writing you've done so far. You will finish your speech in Writing Workshop Part 2.

READING WORKSHOP 2

Skills Focus

You will practice these skills when you read the following selections:
- "Damon and Pythias," p. 974
- "Charlie Johnson," p. 988

Reading
- Clarifying

Literature
- Understanding characterization

Vocabulary
- Understanding idioms
- Academic Vocabulary: *clarify*

Writing/Grammar
- Using semicolons to separate independent clauses
- Using semicolons with conjunctive adverbs

Objectives (pp. 970–971)
Reading Clarify ideas and text

Skill Lesson

Clarifying

Learn It!

What Is It? Clarifying is one way to understand the hardest parts of a text. When you pause in your reading to really think about and clear up a confusing section, you are clarifying. To **clarify**, stop reading to make sure you understand what you've read. Read slowly, reread, and ask questions. Good readers clarify information as they read.

Analyzing Cartoons
The characters in the cartoon ask a question to *clarify* the cat's complaint. What is the question they ask? What is the cat's answer?

Mutts © 2005 Patrick McDonnell. Distributed by King Features.

Academic Vocabulary

clarify (KLAR uh fy) *v.* to make clear

READING WORKSHOP 2 • Clarifying

Why Is It Important? In a text, the information you *have read* is as important as the information you *will read.* Authors often build ideas one on another. It's important to clear up confusing passages as you go so you will understand main ideas and the information that comes later.

How Do I Do It? If something you are reading becomes unclear, slow down. Go back and read that section again. Look up words you don't know, and read any footnotes. Ask questions about what you don't understand. Sometimes you may want to read on to see if further information helps. Start with these questions as you clarify:

- Do characters in the play or story make their thoughts and ideas clear?
- Do examples and descriptions make sense?
- Do I understand the main points the author is trying to make?

Study Central Visit www.glencoe.com and click on Study Central to review clarifying.

Here's how a student clarified some lines from "The Reluctant Dragon."

St. George: Exactly. A good dragon—a worthy foe of my steel (*He lifts his sword high*), and no feeble specimen of his noxious tribe.

> That was so confusing I slowed down and read it twice. I understood that his *steel* was his sword, but at first I forgot to look at the footnote. When I did, I understood most of it, but I need to look up the word foe.

Practice It!

With a partner, practice clarifying this poem by Horace Dragon.

Atchoo! Atchoo! The ragweed is in bloom,
Sowing far and wide allergic gloom.
How lavishly it pollinates the breeze,
And, oh! how lavishly it makes me sneeze! Atchoo!

Use It!

Copy this list of questions in your Learner's Notebook. As you read, write answers to the questions to help you clarify.
- Are thoughts and ideas clear?
- Do examples and descriptions make sense?
- Can I state the main points in my own words?

READING WORKSHOP 2 • Clarifying

Before You Read : Damon and Pythias

Meet the Author
Fan Kissen was born in 1893 and died in 1978. Kissen spent most of her writing career turning folktales and legends into plays for young people. The plays were first performed on radio on Kissen's series, *Tales from the Four Winds.* Before writing radio plays, Kissen taught elementary school in New York City.

Author Search For more about Fan Kissen, go to www.glencoe.com.

Vocabulary Preview

proclaimed (pruh KLAYMD) *v.* declared publicly, announced; form of the verb *proclaim* **(p. 975)** *The king proclaimed that no one could speak against him.*

champion (CHAM pyun) *n.* one who fights for or speaks for another person; one who defends a cause; hero **(p. 976)** *The poor citizens needed a champion to stand up for them.*

Write to Learn Below each vocabulary word in dark type, there are four words. Three of them are synonyms. One is not. Which one is not?

proclaimed

told   asked   stated   declared

champion

assistant   defender   hero   protector

English Language Coach

Idiom An **idiom** (ID ee um) is an expression that has a different idea than the literal (actual and ordinary) meaning of the words. Different languages and regions sometimes have their own idioms. Some idioms can be found in a dictionary, but many cannot. Luckily, you can figure out the meanings of many of them. Look at these examples:

Idiom	Meaning
Zip your lip	Be quiet
Turn a blind eye	Ignore it
Call it a day	Quit working for the day
Spitting image	Exact likeness

Partner Talk Copy the graphic organizer below into your Learner's Notebook. Read each idiom and talk with a partner about what it means. If it's unfamiliar, try to figure it out. Write the meaning in the right column of the graphic organizer.

Idiom	Meaning
Keep an eye on your little brother.	
Let's *step on it* so we're not late.	
It's late; I need to *hit the sack*.	
I would never *bad-mouth* a friend.	

Objectives (pp. 972–983)
Reading Clarify ideas and text • Make connections from text to self
Literature Understand literary elements: characterization
Vocabulary Identify and understand idioms

972 UNIT 8   What Makes a Friend?

READING WORKSHOP 2 • Clarifying

Skills Preview

Key Reading Skill: Clarifying

If you read something that doesn't make sense, take a minute and clarify. To clarify hard sections in "Damon and Pythias," look for footnotes; make sure you understand the words. Slow down and read the confusing sections again. Ask these questions:

- Are the characters' thoughts and ideas clear?
- Do examples and descriptions make sense?
- Do I understand the main points the author is trying to make, and can I state them in my own words?

If you are unsure about the answers, clarify.

Write to Learn Before you read, look over the passage and list words you aren't sure you know. Try to write definitions for the words on your list. (Hint: Do you recognize parts of these words? Are any words similar to ones you know?) After you read, use a dictionary to check your definitions.

Key Literary Element: Characterization

Characterization is the way an author presents details that give you clues to a character's personality. Writers develop a character

- by describing what the character looks like
- by revealing the character's thoughts, feelings, words, and actions
- by revealing what other characters think or say about the character and how they behave toward him or her
- by stating directly what a character is like

Write to Learn Write a few lines presenting details about a character. Your character can be from real life, a TV show, a movie, or from something you've read.

Interactive Literary Elements Handbook
To review or learn more about the literary elements, go to www.glencoe.com.

Get Ready to Read

Connect to the Reading

In these scenes you'll read about two friends, Damon and Pythias, who are legendary for their loyalty to each other. As you read the story, think about your friends and what you would have done in Damon's place.

Partner Talk With a partner, talk about a time when a friend stood up for you or you showed loyalty to one of your friends. Discuss what happened and how it affected the friendship.

Build Background

Two thousand years ago, a Roman statesman and author named Cicero wrote about the ancient Greek story of Damon and Pythias.

- According to Cicero, Damon and Pythias lived in the fourth century B.C.
- Cicero identified the tyrant in this story as Dionysius, King of Syracuse.
- There are many versions of the Damon and Pythias story.
- The play you are about to read was first published in 1964.
- This play is a radio play. That means it was not written to be *seen*; it was written to be *heard*. Keep that in mind as you read.

Set Purposes for Reading

BIG Question Read "Damon and Pythias" and think about what makes a friend.

Set Your Own Purpose What else would you like to learn from the selection to help you answer the Big Question? Write your purpose on the "Damon and Pythias" page of Foldable 8.

Keep Moving

Use these skills as you read the following selection.

Damon and Pythias **973**

READING WORKSHOP 2

Damon and Pythias

by Fan Kissen

Cast
DAMON
FIRST ROBBER
FIRST VOICE
PYTHIAS
SECOND ROBBER
SECOND VOICE
KING
MOTHER
THIRD VOICE
SOLDIER
NARRATOR

[*Sound: Iron door opens and shuts. Key in lock.*]
[*Music: Up full and out.*]

NARRATOR. Long, long ago there lived on the island of Sicily two young men named Damon and Pythias. They were known far and wide for the strong friendship each had for the other. Their names have come down to our own times to mean true friendship. You may hear it said of two persons:

FIRST VOICE. Those two? Why, they're like Damon and Pythias!

NARRATOR. The king of that country was a cruel tyrant. He made cruel laws, and he showed no

mercy toward anyone who broke his laws. Now, you might very well wonder:

SECOND VOICE. Why didn't the people rebel? ❶

NARRATOR. Well, the people didn't dare rebel because they feared the king's great and powerful army. No one dared say a word against the king or his laws—except Damon and Pythias speaking against a new law the king had **proclaimed**.

SOLDIER. Ho, there! Who are you that dares to speak so about our king?

PYTHIAS. [*Unafraid.*] I am called Pythias.

Vocabulary

proclaimed (pruh KLAYMD) *v.* declared publicly, announced

Practice the Skills

❶ **Key Reading Skill**

Clarifying Remember, this is a radio play. Many of the "stage directions" are sounds. Imagine hearing the sound of an iron door locking. What do you imagine when you hear that? Now, think about the Voices. Why do you think they are named that?

This ancient Greek-Roman theater is on the island of Sicily—the same island where "Damon and Pythias" takes place.

SOLDIER. Don't you know it is a crime to speak against the king or his laws? You are under arrest! Come and tell this opinion of yours to the king's face!

[*Music: A few short bars in and out.*]

NARRATOR. When Pythias was brought before the king, he showed no fear. He stood straight and quiet before the throne.

KING. [*Hard, cruel.*] So, Pythias! They tell me you do not approve of the laws I make.

PYTHIAS. I am not alone, your Majesty, in thinking your laws are cruel. But you rule the people with such an iron hand that they dare not complain. ❷

Street Musicians, before A.D. 79. Dioscurides of Samos. Mosaic from the Villa of Cicero, Pompeii. Musea Archeologico Nazionale, Naples, Italy.

Analyzing the Art List some ways that these street musicians are different from street musicians today.

KING. [*Angry.*] But you have the daring to complain for them! Have they appointed you their **champion**?

PYTHIAS. No, your Majesty. I speak for myself alone. I have no wish to make trouble for anyone. But I am not afraid to tell you that the people are suffering under your rule. They want to have a voice in making the laws for themselves. You do not allow them to speak up for themselves.

KING. In other words, you are calling me a tyrant! Well, you shall learn for yourself how a tyrant treats a rebel! Soldier! Throw this man into prison!

Practice the Skills

❷ **English Language Coach**

Idiom Pythias tells the king that he rules with "an iron hand." What does Pythias mean? What are some characteristics of iron? How are those characteristics like the way the king rules?

Vocabulary

champion (CHAM pyun) *n.* one who fights for or speaks for another person; one who defends a cause; hero

SOLDIER. At once, your Majesty! Don't try to resist, Pythias!

PYTHIAS. I know better than to try to resist a soldier of the king! and for how long am I to remain in prison, your Majesty, merely for speaking out for the people?

KING. [*Cruel.*] Not for very long, Pythias. Two weeks from today at noon, you shall be put to death in the public square as an example to anyone else who may dare to question my laws or acts. Off to prison with him, soldier! 3

[*Music: In briefly and out.*] 4

NARRATOR. When Damon heard that his friend Pythias had been thrown into prison, and about the severe punishment that was to follow, he was heartbroken. He rushed to the prison and persuaded the guard to let him speak to his friend.

DAMON. Oh, Pythias! How terrible to find you here! I wish I could do something to save you!

PYTHIAS. Nothing can save me, Damon, my dear friend. I am prepared to die. But there is one thought that troubles me greatly.

DAMON. What is it? I will do anything to help you.

PYTHIAS. I'm worried about what will happen to my mother and my sister when I'm gone.

DAMON. I'll take care of them, Pythias, as if they were my own mother and sister.

PYTHIAS. Thank you, Damon. I have money to leave them. But there are other things I must arrange. If only I could go see them before I die! But they live two days' journey from here, you know.

DAMON. I'll go to the king and beg him to give you your freedom for a few days. You'll give your word to return at the end of that time. Everyone in Sicily knows you for a man who has never broken his word.

Practice the Skills

3 Key Literary Element

Characterization What can you tell about Pythias from his behavior when he challenges the king?

4 Key Reading Skill

Clarifying Plays are usually divided into acts and scenes, which often are signaled by a stage curtain opening and closing. A radio play does not have the same cues. What signals a change of setting here?

PYTHIAS. Do you believe for one moment that the king would let me leave this prison, no matter how good my word may have been all my life?

DAMON. I'll tell him that I shall take your place in the prison cell. I'll tell him that if you do not return by the appointed day, he may kill *me* in your place!

PYTHIAS. No, no, Damon! You must not do such a foolish thing! I cannot—I will not—let you do this! Damon! Damon! Don't go! [*To himself.*] Damon, my friend! You may find yourself in a cell beside me! 5

[*Music: In briefly and out.*]

DAMON. [*Begging.*] Your Majesty! I beg of you! Let Pythias go home for a few days to bid farewell to his mother and sister. He gives his word that he will return at your appointed time. Everyone knows that his word can be trusted.

KING. In ordinary business affairs—perhaps. But he is now a man under sentence of death. To free him even for a few days would strain his honesty—*any* man's honesty—too far. Pythias would never return here! I consider him a traitor, but I'm certain he's no fool.

DAMON. Your Majesty! I will take his place in the prison until he comes back. If he does not return, then you may take *my* life in his place.

KING. [*Astonished.*] What did you say, Damon?

DAMON. I'm so certain of Pythias that I am offering to die in his place if he fails to return on time.

KING. I can't believe you mean it!

DAMON. I do mean it, your Majesty.

KING. You make me very curious, Damon, so curious that I'm willing to put you and Pythias to the test. This exchange of prisoners will be made. But Pythias must be back two weeks from today, at noon.

DAMON. Thank you, your Majesty!

Practice the Skills

5 Key Reading Skill

Clarifying Question anything that might not seem to make sense. Why does Pythias speak to himself here?

KING. The order with my official seal shall go by your own hand,[1] Damon. But I warn you, if your friend does not return on time, you shall surely die in his place! I shall show no mercy.

[*Music: In briefly and out.*]

NARRATOR. Pythias did not like the king's bargain with Damon. He did not like to leave his friend in prison with the chance that he might lose his life if something went wrong. But at last Damon persuaded him to leave and Pythias set out for his home. More than a week went by. The day set for the death sentence drew near. Pythias did not return. Everyone in the city knew of the condition on which the king had permitted Pythias to go home. Everywhere people met, the talk was sure to turn to the two friends.

FIRST VOICE. Do you suppose Pythias will come back?

SECOND VOICE. Why should he stick his head under the king's ax once he has escaped?

THIRD VOICE. Still would an honorable man like Pythias let such a good friend die for him?

FIRST VOICE. There's no telling what a man will do when it's a question of his own life against another's. 6

SECOND VOICE. But if Pythias doesn't come back before the time is up, he will be killing his friend.

Practice the Skills

6 English Language Coach
Idiom Do you know what the idiom "there's no telling" means? Can you figure it out from the context?

Tragic and Comic Masks (detail). before A.D. 79. Mosaics from the House of the Faun, Pompeii. Museo Archeologico Nazionale, Naples, Italy.

---

1. In asking Damon to carry the order in his **own hand,** the king means that Damon should carry the order himself.

READING WORKSHOP 2

THIRD VOICE. Well, there's still a few days' time. I, for one, am certain that Pythias *will* return in time.

SECOND VOICE. And *I am* just as certain that he will *not*. Friendship is friendship, but a man's own life is something stronger, *I say!* 7

NARRATOR. Two days before the time was up, the king himself visited Damon in his prison cell.

[*Sound: Iron door unlocked and opened.*]

KING. [*Mocking.*] You see now, Damon, that you were a fool to make this bargain. Your friend has tricked you! He will not come back here to be killed! He has deserted you.

DAMON. [*Calm and firm.*] I have faith in my friend. I know he will return.

KING. [*Mocking.*] We shall see! 8

[*Sound: Iron door shut and locked.*]

NARRATOR. Meanwhile, when Pythias reached the home of his family, he arranged his business affairs so that his mother and sister would be able to live comfortably for the rest of their years. Then he said a last farewell to them before starting back to the city.

MOTHER. [*In tears.*] Pythias, it will take you two days to get back. Stay another day, I beg you!

PYTHIAS. I dare not stay longer, Mother. Remember, Damon is locked up in my prison cell while I'm gone. Please don't weep for me. My death may help bring better days for all our people. 9

NARRATOR. So Pythias began his journey in plenty of time. But bad luck struck him on the very first day. At twilight, as he walked along a lonely stretch of woodland, a rough voice called:

FIRST ROBBER. Not so fast there, young man! Stop!

PYTHIAS. [*Startled.*] Oh! What is it? What do you want?

Practice the Skills

7 **BIG Question**
How do the Voices help you think about friendship? Write your answer on the "Damon and Pythias" page of Foldable 8.

8 **Key Literary Element**
Characterization What kind of person is the king? In what ways has the author let you know what he is like?

9 **Key Literary Element**
Characterization Review what Pythias has just said. Based on his words, what kind of person is he? Do you think he really means what he says? Explain.

980 UNIT 8 What Makes a Friend?

READING WORKSHOP 2

SECOND ROBBER. Your money bags.

PYTHIAS. My money bags? I have only this small bag of coins. I shall need them for some favors, perhaps, before I die.

FIRST ROBBER. What do you mean, before you die? We don't mean to kill you, only take your money.

PYTHIAS. I'll give you my money, only don't delay me any longer. I am to die by the king's order three days from now. If I don't return on time, my friend must die in my place.

FIRST ROBBER. A likely story! What man would be fool enough to go back to prison ready to die?

SECOND ROBBER. And what man would be fool enough to die *for* you?

FIRST ROBBER. We'll take your money, all right. And we'll tie you up while we get away.

PYTHIAS. [*Begging.*] No! No! I must get back to free my friend! [*Fade.*] I must go back!

NARRATOR. But the two robbers took Pythias's money, tied him to a tree, and went off as fast as they could. Pythias struggled to free himself. He cried out for a long time. But no one traveled through that lonesome woodland after dark. The sun had been up for many hours before he finally managed to free himself from the ropes that had tied him to the tree. He lay on the ground, hardly able to breathe. 🔟

[*Music: In briefly and out.*]

NARRATOR. After a while Pythias got to his feet. Weak and dizzy from hunger and thirst and his struggle to free himself, he set off again. Day and night he traveled without stopping, desperately trying to reach the city in time to save Damon's life.

[*Music: Up and out.*]

NARRATOR. On the last day, half an hour before noon, Damon's hands were tied behind his back, and he was taken into the public square. The people muttered angrily as

Practice the Skills

🔟 **Key Literary Element**

Characterization Think about the conversation between the robbers. What can you learn about them from their discussion?

Damon was led in by the jailer. Then the king entered and seated himself on a high platform.

[*Sound: Crowd voices in and hold under single voices.*] **11**

SOLDIER. [*Loud.*] Long live the king!

FIRST VOICE. [*Low.*] The longer he lives, the more miserable our lives will be!

Visual Vocabulary
The **noon mark** appears on a sundial, a device that indicates the time of day by the position and length of a shadow cast on a surface marked with numerals.

KING. [*Loud, mocking.*] Well, Damon, your lifetime is nearly up. Where is your good friend Pythias now?

DAMON. [*Firm.*] I have faith in my friend. If he has not returned, I'm certain it is through no fault of his own.

KING. [*Mocking.*] The sun is almost overhead. The shadow is almost at the noon mark. And still your friend has not returned to give back your life!

DAMON. [*Quiet.*] I am ready and happy to die in his place.

KING. [*Harsh.*] And you shall, Damon! Jailer, lead the prisoner to the—

[*Sound: Crowd voices up to a roar, then under.*]

FIRST VOICE. [*Over noise.*] Look! It's Pythias!

SECOND VOICE. [*Over noise.*] Pythias has come back!

PYTHIAS. [*Breathless.*] Let me through! Damon!

DAMON. Pythias!

PYTHIAS. Thank the gods I'm not too late!

DAMON. [*Quiet, sincere.*] I would have died for you gladly, my friend.

CROWD VOICES. [*Loud, demanding.*] Set them free! Set them both free!

11 Key Reading Skill

Clarifying Do you understand this stage direction? (Think about the meanings of *in* and *hold*.) It means that crowd noises come into the scene and remain there under the sounds of Damon's discussion with the king. How does that sound help create the scene?

KING. [*Loud.*] People of the city! [*Crowd voices out.*] Never in all my life have I seen such faith and friendship, such loyalty between men. There are many among you who call me harsh and cruel. But I cannot kill *any* man who proves such strong and true friendship for another. Damon and Pythias, I set you both free. [*Roar of approval from crowd*.] I am king. I command a great army. I have stores of gold and precious jewels. But I would give all my money and power for one friend like Damon or Pythias. **12**

[*Sound: Roar of approval from crowd up briefly and out.*]
[*Music: Up and out.*] ○

Practice the Skills

12 🌰 **BIG Question**

Do you agree with what the king says about friendship? Explain your answer and write it on the "Damon and Pythias" page of Foldable 8. Your response will help you complete the Unit Challenge later.

Tragic and Comic Masks (detail). before A.D. 79. Mosaics from the House of the Faun, Pompeii. Museo Archeologico Nazionale, Naples, Italy.

READING WORKSHOP 2 • Clarifying

After You Read : Damon and Pythias

Answering the BIG Question

1. **Why** did Damon and Pythias become known for their friendship? How does their story help you answer the question "What makes a friend?"
2. **Recall** How much time did Pythias have to return to the prison before Damon would be put to death in his place?
   TIP Right There
3. **Summarize** Why didn't the robbers believe Pythias?
   TIP Think and Search

Critical Thinking

4. **Interpret** Why did the First Voice say that the longer the king lived, the more miserable his people's lives would be?
   TIP On My Own
5. **Visualize** Try to picture Damon standing tall and brave in a dark, damp, stone prison cell. Write down the scene you picture.
   TIP On My Own
6. **Evaluate** Was Damon foolish to risk his life on the faithfulness of his friend Pythias?
   TIP On My Own

Talk About Your Reading

With a partner, debate this issue:
Would the king really give up all of his power and money for one friend like Damon or Pythias?
Consider these questions:
- If the king doesn't mean what he said, why did he release Damon and Pythias?
- If the king does mean what he said, why does he treat people so cruelly?

Objectives (pp. 984–985)
Reading Clarify ideas and text • Make connections from text to self
Literature Understand literary elements: characterization
Vocabulary Identify and understand idioms
Grammar Use punctuation correctly: semicolons with independent clauses

984 UNIT 8 What Makes a Friend?

Skills Review

Key Reading Skill: Clarifying

7. After Pythias asks the king how long he will have to remain in prison, the king says, "Not for very long, Pythias." What does he mean by this?
8. On page 981, the author includes the stage direction "[*Fade.*]" in the middle of Pythias's line. What do you think this means? What might Pythias's voice sound like after this direction? What effect was the author trying to create?

Key Literary Element: Characterization

9. How would you describe the character of Pythias? Use examples from the play.
10. How would you describe the king? Use examples from the play.

Vocabulary Check

Below each vocabulary word in dark type, there are three words. Which one is a synonym of the vocabulary word?

11. **proclaimed**

    silenced   announced   denied

12. **champion**

    defender   coward   opponent

13. **Academic Vocabulary** When you *clarify* a section of text, what are you doing?

In the sentences below, the idioms are underlined. Copy each idiom and write down what it means. If you don't know, make a reasonable guess.

14. That's my book; <u>hand it over</u>.
15. The future is <u>in your hands</u>.
16. Could you <u>give me a hand</u> with this box?
17. The band was great, so let's <u>give them a hand</u>.

Web Activities For eFlashcards, Selection Quick Checks, and other Web activities, go to www.glencoe.com.

Grammar Link: Semicolons with Independent Clauses

A semicolon is used in only a few situations. One of those uses is to join two independent clauses when they are not joined with a conjunction. (You learned about independent clauses in Unit 5.)

Once in a while, you might write two sentences that are very closely related to each other. A period between them provides a strong separation. If you want to let one thought flow right into the next, you could use a semicolon instead of a period. That emphasizes how closely related the statements are.

Example: Simon couldn't stand his cousin; he disliked every single thing she did.

The two clauses must be closely related. If they are not, do not join them!

Correct: Americans eat far too much junk food; they should eat almost none at all.

Incorrect: Josie really likes dogs; she is eleven years old.

Grammar Practice

Read each sentence and determine if the semicolons are used correctly. On a separate sheet of paper, write a "C" if the sentence correct and an "I" if it is incorrect.

18. The main characters of the play are Damon, Pythias, and the king; some theaters have over two hundred seats.
19. Pythias arranged his business affairs to provide for his mother and sister; they would be able to live comfortably for the rest of their lives.
20. The king said he would give up all of his money and power for a true friend like Damon or Pythias; they lived on the island of Sicily.

READING WORKSHOP 2 • Clarifying

Before You Read : Charlie Johnson

Meet the Author
Joe Smith's story, "Charlie Johnson," was published in *Cricket* magazine in December 1998. *Cricket* has been in publication for over thirty years. During that time, it has won virtually every award given to kids' literary magazines.

Author Search For more about Joe Smith, go to www.glencoe.com.

Vocabulary Preview

hick (hik) *adj.* small, rural, unexciting **(p. 988)** *Ben moved from the city of Boston to a place he thought of as a hick town.*

obituaries (oh BIH choo air eez) *n.* notices of deaths, usually in newspapers **(p. 992)** *Ben found out about the man's death when he read the obituaries in the local newspaper.*

Partner Talk With a partner, make a list of the things you might find—or *not* find—in a **hick** town. Then make a list of the kinds of information you might find in **obituaries.**

English Language Coach

Idioms Some phrases have a literal meaning and an idiomatic meaning. Your mother might really *put her foot down*—on the floor, the ground, or the gas pedal. However, if you say that your mother *put her foot down* about the mess in your room, you are using the phrase as an idiom. It means "to tell someone in a strong way that something must be done or must not be done." This is why you might hear someone say something like "He was *literally* all tied up." This makes it clear that the person was actually restrained by a rope rather than simply being very busy with something.

Other idioms make no sense at all with their literal meaning. It never actually *rains cats and dogs* (rains hard). No one is ever actually *on cloud nine* (very happy).

Even if an idiom is unfamiliar, you can often figure out what it means if you think about the literal meaning and use context clues.

Write to Learn The idioms in the sentences below are underlined. Combine your prior knowledge, literal meanings, and context clues to figure out what they mean. Write each idiom and your definition in your Learner's Notebook.

- After I realized my mistake, I had to go back to square one.
- Brad had the latest news, and Jacinta was all ears.
- My boss hates to fire people, so she makes her assistant do her dirty work for her.
- Rafi was feeling under the weather today, so he didn't come to school.
- When Amy saw someone bullying a smaller child, it made her blood boil.

Objectives (pp. 986–993)
Reading Clarify ideas and text • Make connections from text to self
Literature Understand literary elements: characterization
Vocabulary Identify and understand idioms

986 UNIT 8 What Makes a Friend?

Skills Preview

Key Reading Skill: Clarifying

If you become confused while reading a piece of nonfiction, you might go to another source of information for help. You might use an encyclopedia or the Internet to help you clarify. When you're reading fiction, you *usually* use another source only to find word definitions. There are, however, other steps to take that are just as useful with fiction as with nonfiction.

- Reread the confusing part more slowly.
- Read on further to see if later information helps.
- Ask yourself questions about what you don't understand.

Partner Talk With a partner, look through a magazine, newspaper, library book, or one of your textbooks. Find a section that you don't fully understand. It can be a sentence, paragraph, idea, or instruction. Work together to make a plan for clarifying that section. First, write down the steps you took to clarify. Next, discuss the meaning of the section.

Key Literary Element: Characterization

Characterization, revealing the personality of a character, is a big part of most stories. Characters are usually developed by their words, their actions, and the way others relate and respond to them. Think about these questions as you read:

- What do the characters' words and actions tell you about their personalities?
- What information about the characters does the narrator reveal?
- What do the characters think of each other?

Interactive Literary Elements Handbook
To review or learn more about the literary elements, go to www.glencoe.com.

Get Ready to Read

Connect to the Reading

In the story "Charlie Johnson," you will read about a friendship between a teenage boy and an elderly man. Do you have any friends who are much older than you? What are the benefits to you of a friendship with an older person?

Write to Learn If you could have a friendship with any adult in the world, who would you choose? Why would you choose that person? Write a short note to that person explaining why you would like to have him or her as a friend.

Build Background

Charlie Johnson is a Christmas tree farmer. Growing trees is a full-time, year-round job. Of course the busiest time of year for Christmas tree farmers is in November and December when trees are cut down and sold. However, during the rest of the year they must

- plant new seedlings—very young trees
- protect the trees from insects, disease, and bad weather
- constantly remove weeds and other plants that could crowd out the trees
- prune the trees to give them their traditional shape

Set Purposes for Reading

BIG Question As you read this story, notice what Ben Evans says, does, and thinks about his friendship with Charlie Johnson.

Set Your Own Purpose What would you like to learn from the selection to help you answer the Big Question? Write your purpose on the "Charlie Johnson" page of Foldable 8.

Keep Moving

Use these skills as you read the following selection.

READING WORKSHOP 2

Charlie Johnson

by Joe Smith

It was almost four months since we had moved from Boston to this stupid little hick town, and the aura¹ of being the new kid was wearing thin. I had to do something soon to make my reputation. **1**

Dave Johnson was the perfect target. He was a big dumb farmer whose place was just down the road from our house. The kids said that he had a temper to match his size, and they were all scared stiff of him. I figured that if I pulled one over on Johnson, I'd really be somebody. **2**

I put my plan into effect one December afternoon after school. Mom and Dad weren't home, as usual, so I grabbed a saw out of the cellar and headed down the path behind our house. A short distance through the woods there was a stone wall, then a field full of Christmas trees. Johnson's Christmas trees.

It was almost too easy. I jumped over the wall into the rows of trees and chose a likely victim. As I sawed, I thought about what I was going to tell the kids at school the next day. But as

1. An *aura* is a quality that seems to surround a person or thing.

Vocabulary

hick (hik) *adj.* small, rural, unexciting

Practice the Skills

1 English Language Coach

Idioms When the narrator says the aura of being the new kid is "wearing thin," he does not mean that something is literally wearing out. He means that he is getting tired of being seen that way. Look for another idiom in the last sentence of the following paragraph.

2 Key Literary Element

Characterization Consider the narrator's plan to make a reputation for himself. What does it tell you about his character?

soon as I had the tree cut, a shadow fell over me. I looked up to find the giant farmer standing there. Without a word he hauled me off to his truck and drove me to the farm. "Wait here," he grunted, then disappeared into the barn.

A moment later a figure emerged, but it wasn't the big farmer. It was an old man, wearing a red-checkered coat and big boots.

He shuffled up to my side of the truck and stared at me with watery eyes that were almost hidden by bushy eyebrows. Then he smiled.

"So you're the tree rustler," he said in a gravelly voice. "Come out here where I can get a good look at you."

I glanced nervously toward the barn, and the man chuckled. "I see you've met my son. Don't worry about him. He gets upset easy, but he'll calm down."

"Why, you're barely thirteen or fourteen," he said as he looked me up and down. "The way Dave was talking, I thought we had a hardened criminal on our hands!"

Then he shoved a huge hand toward me. "My name's Charlie Johnson," he said. "You must be the Evans kid that just moved in down the road."

"Yeah, Ben Evans," I said. His grip was surprisingly strong.

"Well, listen, Ben. We're kind of busy right now. Maybe you could lend me a hand for a few minutes."

I had been ready for a lecture, even for some yelling and screaming, but this caught me off balance. **3**

I followed the old man around to the back of the truck and accepted the trees he handed to me. Then I followed him to the row of empty stands, where we leaned each of the trees in place.

He talked as we worked. I had never met him before, but somehow he seemed to know all about me, my parents, and my friends.

We soon had the stands full of trees. He grabbed one and shoved it toward me.

"Throw it on the back of the truck and get in. I'll give you a ride home. I figure I almost worked the price of that tree out of you by now."

I had to laugh. Until that moment I hadn't realized what the old man was doing.

Practice the Skills

3 English Language Coach

Idioms What do you think Ben means when he says that Charlie's response "caught me off balance"?

"Almost, but not quite," he continued. "If you come back about the middle of April when the new trees come in, I'll get another hour of work out of you, and then we'll call it even. How does that sound?"

What could I say? I agreed, and he drove me home.

"What are you going to tell your parents about the tree?" he asked as we pulled into the driveway.

"I doubt they'll even care. I barely see them anyway," I said as I hopped out and grabbed the tree. He frowned when I said that, but he gave me a big smile and a wave as he drove away.

My parents didn't ask, but I told everyone at school that I stole the tree, figuring I might as well get something out of the mess. I think some of the kids even believed me. 4

Winter passed slowly. I had forgotten all about the old man and his trees. He hadn't forgotten about me, though. One spring day I came home to find him sitting in his truck in my driveway.

Practice the Skills

4 **Key Reading Skill**

Clarifying Ben says he told everyone he stole the tree so he'd "get something out of the mess." What do you think he hopes to get?

Field of Dreams, Cindy Coakley
Analyzing the Art Do you think Charlie Johnson's truck looked like this one? Explain your answer.

READING WORKSHOP 2

He brought me to the barn, where there were several long boxes full of seedlings. He showed me the different kinds of trees, and I helped to count and separate them.

When we were done, Charlie told me that if I came back Saturday, he'd pay me to help him plant the trees. I'd never planted a tree in my life and I had better things to do with my Saturday, but a little money would sure impress the other kids, so I said yes.

I showed up early on Saturday. He took me out to the field and showed me what to do. It was hard going, but Charlie kept up a steady stream of talk the whole time.

He had come here when he was younger, too. "Bought this farm and thought I was gonna show the locals how it should be done," he said.

But the '38 hurricane came and blew down his barn and most of the trees on the property. "I would've packed it in right there, but the whole town came together and helped me rebuild the barn and get started again. I wasn't such a hotshot after that." He started planting trees to replace what was lost and he'd been at it ever since. 5

By the end of the day, I was sore all over. The worst part of it was that Charlie had planted twice as many trees as I had and was as fit at the end as when we started.

I spent a lot of time at the farm that summer and earned a bit of money, too. Most times I'd see the younger Johnson, but he'd just scowl and turn away when he saw me. Charlie kept me busy, shearing the trees or mowing the grass between the rows.

I kind of felt sorry for the old man. His son took care of the milk cows and the hayfields, so it seemed as if all he had left were his trees. And the way he bent my ear, I figured I must be the only one he had to talk to.

I didn't mind listening, though. I guess I even learned something, and it was funny how he always knew what I'd been up to. I figured that perhaps I was such a celebrity the whole town was talking about me. 6

That Christmas I bought a tree with my own money. Charlie just laughed, winked, and pocketed the bills. It felt good.

It was a pretty bad winter, and I didn't get over to see him for a couple of months. Then, one gray March morning, my

Practice the Skills

5 English Language Coach

Idioms Charlie says, "I would've packed it in right there . . ." What does he mean?

6 Key Literary Element

Characterization Sometimes we learn about a character from what he or she says or thinks. What do you learn about Ben from what he reveals about himself?

Charlie Johnson **991**

father shoved the morning paper under my nose. There was Charlie's picture on the page. It was a few moments before I figured out that I was looking at the **obituaries**.

The funeral was a couple of days later. Since I knew he didn't have too many friends, I decided to go so at least someone was there.

The service was held in the church at the center of town. As I walked down the main street I was surprised to see so many cars go by. As I got closer I could see parked cars lining both sides of the street and a policeman directing traffic, but it wasn't until I saw the line before the church door that I realized they were all going the same place I was.

Somewhat in shock, I joined the crowd. When I finally made it inside, all the seats were taken, and I had to stand up against the wall behind the last pew.

I listened as, one after another, people got up to speak. They talked about all Charlie had done for the town and the people in it, how he was always ready to help, but most of all, they talked about how he was their friend. **7**

The minister said a few more words, then the people started rising and filing out of the church. I slipped out and stood looking at the crowd as it grew on the lawn. About an hour before, I was a big shot, going to an old man's funeral out of pity; now I was just a jerk. Embarrassed by my own stupidity, I turned and hurried home. **8**

It was in early April that I found my feet leading me back to the farm. Dave Johnson was in the empty farm stand. He looked up as I approached, that old familiar scowl on his face. "What do you want?" he snarled.

"I thought I could help. With the trees."

Analyzing the Art Does this picture help you understand how Ben felt at Charlie Johnson's funeral service? Explain.

Practice the Skills

7 **Key Literary Element**

Characterization Sometimes we learn about a character from what others say or do. What does the information about the people at Charlie's funeral reveal about him?

8 **Key Reading Skill**

Clarifying Ben felt stupid when he saw a crowd of people at Charlie's funeral. Do you understand why Ben had not known that Charlie had many other friends? If not, go back and reread.

Vocabulary

obituaries (oh BIH choo air eez) *n.* notices of deaths, usually in newspapers

He looked annoyed. "Come with me," he said.

He led me into the barn. Three big boxes full of seedlings were on the floor. "It's kind of funny you should show up; they just came this morning." Then he turned and sat on one of them and looked at me.

"I never understood why my father wanted to bother with you," he said, "but I guess he saw something there that I couldn't see. You'd come strutting around here like you were doing him a favor, and I felt like thrashing you. He'd just laugh, though, and he'd say, 'Don't worry, he'll be all right.' I thought he was nuts."

I could have told him to stick it. Maybe a little while ago I would have, but now all I could say was "I'm sorry."

His face softened at that, and I think for a moment he was at a loss for words. "You didn't have to come here," he finally said, "but you did. Maybe Charlie was right after all." 9 10

Then he put out his hand, and in the darkness of the barn, I shook it, not because I had anything to prove or because I wanted to impress anyone, but because I just wanted to be his friend. 11

Practice the Skills

9 Key Literary Element

Characterization Now you see a different side of Dave Johnson's character. Do you think this is the *real* Dave?

10 Key Reading Skill

Clarifying What was Charlie right about? Think about the entire story. Can you clarify the author's main idea about friendship?

11 BIG Question

Why do you think Dave is willing to reach out to Ben? Why do you think Ben wants to become friends with Dave? Write your answers on the "Charlie Johnson" page of Foldable 8. Your response will help you complete the Unit Challenge later.

Analyzing the Photo
Do you think Ben might see a tree decorated like this one on the Johnsons' land? Why or why not?

READING WORKSHOP 2 • Clarifying

After You Read — Charlie Johnson

Answering the BIG Question

1. How is Charlie a good friend to Ben?
2. **Recall** Name three jobs Ben did for Charlie.
   TIP Think and Search

3. **Summarize** In the end, what changes Dave's opinion of Ben?
   TIP Think and Search

Critical Thinking

4. **Evaluate** Is Ben a good friend to Charlie?
   TIP Author and Me

5. **Analyze** How does Ben's friendship with Charlie change his character?
   TIP Author and Me

6. **Infer** When Ben tried to steal the tree, why do you think Charlie made him work on the farm instead of calling the police or Ben's parents?
   TIP On My Own

Write About Your Reading

Which character in "Charlie Johnson" would you the most want to be friends with—Charlie, Dave, or Ben? Why? Write a letter to that character introducing yourself and explaining why you would like to become friends.

- Describe your personality and interests.
- State what interests you about Charlie, Dave, or Ben.
- If there is something you have in common, mention it.
- End with a statement about the kind of friendship you hope will develop.

Objectives (pp. 994–995)
Reading Clarify ideas and text • Make connections from text to self
Literature Understand literary elements: characterization
Vocabulary Identify and understand idioms
Writing Respond to literature: letter
Grammar Use punctuation correctly: semicolons with conjunctive adverbs

994 UNIT 8   What Makes a Friend?

Skills Review

Key Reading Skill: Clarifying

7. Why did Dave always scowl (frown in an unfriendly way) at Ben?
8. Did Charlie talk to Ben because he was lonely or for some other reason? Explain.

Key Literary Element: Characterization

9. Did you learn more about Charlie from Charlie's own words and actions or through the way other characters reacted to him? Give examples to support your answer.
10. Do the characters in "Charlie Johnson" seem true to life? Why or why not? Support your answer with examples of their behavior or conversation.
11. Which character do you think the author characterized as changing the most, Ben or Dave? Explain your answer.

Vocabulary Check

12. What information would you find by reading the **obituaries** in a newspaper?
13. Would most people consider Chicago to be a **hick** town?
14. **Academic Vocabulary** List three ways to *clarify* a text.
15. **English Language Coach:** Charlie and Ben use two very similar idioms to describe themselves. Charlie says he was a *hotshot* when he was younger. Ben thought he was a *big shot* before he went to Charlie's funeral. What do those two idioms mean?

Web Activities For eFlashcards, Selection Quick Checks, and other Web activities, go to www.glencoe.com.

Grammar Link: Semicolons with Conjunctive Adverbs

You've learned about using a semicolon to connect two related independent clauses if the clauses are not connected by a conjunction.

Correct: Erika plays the drums; she is really good.
Incorrect: Erika plays the drums; and she is really good.

Here is another common use for semicolons. There are certain words that aren't conjunctions but that do connect parts of a sentence. They include *however* and *therefore*. These special words, called "conjunctive adverbs," require a semicolon before them and a comma after them.

- The cat was small; however, he was brave.
- I overslept; therefore, I missed the bus.

Grammar Practice

Read each sentence and decide if it is correct or incorrect. On a separate sheet of paper, write a "C" if the sentence is correct and an "I" if it is incorrect. (Think about both uses of semicolons taught in this workshop.)

16. Ben was new in town; therefore, he didn't know many people.
17. Dave Johnson had a temper; he grew Christmas trees.
18. Ben made a plan; he intended to steal a tree.
19. At first, Dave scared Ben, however, he didn't hurt him.
20. Ben didn't want to work on Saturdays; but he wanted to earn some money.
21. Charlie Johnson's barn was destroyed; however, the town helped him rebuild it.
22. Charlie was respected in the town; many people admired his hard work and helpfulness.

Writing Application Review your Write About Your Reading activity. Check to see if you have two closely related sentences that can be connected using a semicolon.

READING WORKSHOP 3

Skills Focus

You will practice these skills when you read the following selections:
- "The Bully of Barksdale Street," p. 1000
- "Tales of the Tangled Tresses," p. 1016

Reading
- Skimming and scanning

Literature
- Understanding stage directions in a play

Vocabulary
- Understanding jargon and clipped words

Writing/Grammar
- Using a colon to introduce a list
- Using a colon in a time notation and after a salutation

Skill Lesson

Skimming and Scanning

Learn It!

What Is It? Skimming and scanning are reading strategies that you can use to get the general idea of a text or to answer specific questions you might have.

- **Skimming** is reading rapidly through a piece of writing. You skim a text to get a general idea of what it is about or to refresh your memory of it.
- **Scanning** is running your eyes quickly over a piece of writing. You scan to look at section headings, words in boldfaced type, and key words or phrases to find specific information.

CALVIN AND HOBBES © 1987 Watterson. Distributed By UNIVERSAL PRESS SYNDICATE. Reprinted with permission. All rights reserved.

Analyzing Cartoons
Would you ever skim or scan the way that Calvin does? Why or why not?

Objectives (pp. 996–997)
Reading Skim and scan text

READING WORKSHOP 3 • Skimming and Scanning

Why Is It Important? Skimming a piece of writing gives you an idea of what to expect when you read it carefully later. If the piece of writing isn't what you are looking for, you don't need to read all of it. Scanning helps you find information quickly. Instead of reading an entire piece of writing, you can scan it for the particular fact or idea that you need.

How Do I Do It? To skim a piece of writing, read its title and then look quickly through the whole piece. Read headings, captions, and maybe the beginning of several paragraphs to get the main idea. For a play, read the first page to find out where and when the play takes place and who the main characters are. Then read a few lines from each page to get a general idea of what's happening.

To scan a piece of writing, move your eyes quickly over the lines until they fall on headings, words in boldfaced type, or key words or phrases that are about the information you are looking for. Here is what one student said as he skimmed and scanned "Damon and Pythias."

Study Central Visit www.glencoe.com and click on Study Central to review skimming and scanning

> When I skimmed the play, I found out it takes place long ago in Sicily. The main characters are friends named Damon and Pythias. The play has a king, soldiers, a narrator, and "Voices."
>
> I never heard of "Voices" in a play, so I scanned to find out what kind of things they said. Sometimes they seemed like part of the audience, and sometimes they seemed like regular characters in the play.

Practice It!

When you're getting ready to read a play, you might skim over it to get an idea of what it's like. You can also scan for anything that you're curious about. In your Learner's Notebook, jot down these four questions:

1. What does the play seem to be about?
2. Does the play seem to be serious or funny?
3. Have I ever heard of any of the characters in the play before?

Use It!

Before you read this play, skim over it to answer the first two questions you wrote down. Then scan the play until you find the answer to question 3. Write all your answers in your Learner's notebook.

READING WORKSHOP 3 • Skimming and Scanning

Before You Read: The Bully of Barksdale Street

Eric Alter

Meet the Author
Eric Alter has written more than 40 plays and screenplays for a wide variety of audiences. He also directs plays and writes novels.

Author Search For more about Eric Alter, go to www.glencoe.com.

Objectives (pp. 998–1011)
Reading Skim and scan text • Make connections from text to self
Literature Understand elements of drama: stage directions
Vocabulary Identify clipped words

Vocabulary Preview

tribute (TRIB yoot) *n.* something done to show respect **(p. 1000)** *In his speech, Joe made a tribute to his best friend.*

backdrop (BAK drop) *n.* a curtain or temporary wall that covers the back of a stage **(p. 1000)** *We painted a picture of a desert on the backdrop.*

fencing (FEN sing) *n.* the sport of fighting with swords **(p. 1003)** *The swords used in fencing have a dull protective tip on the end so people won't get hurt.*

rambling (RAM bling) *v.* talking in a disorganized manner **(p. 1005)** *I had trouble understanding Jason because he was rambling so much.*

pummel (PUM ul) *v.* to hit or beat someone **(p. 1006)** *The bully tried to pummel Antoine, but he failed.*

mocking (MOK ing) *v.* making fun of someone by imitating the person in a ridiculous manner **(p. 1007)** *When Jennifer started mocking John, he got very angry.*

menacingly (MEN uh sing lee) *adv.* in a threatening manner **(p. 1007)** *The dark clouds hung menacingly over the city.*

English Language Coach

Clipped Words A **clipped word** is a word that has been shortened. In a clipped word, the beginning, the end, or both the beginning and the end of the word have been cut off. People use clipped words every day. Look at these examples, and think about clipped words you use.

Clipped Word	Full Word
bike	bicycle
flu	influenza
fridge	refrigerator
ump	umpire

Write to Learn In your Learner's Notebook, write the clipped word you would use instead of each of the following words: *teenager, telephone, mathematics, photograph, referee.*

998 UNIT 8 What Makes a Friend?

READING WORKSHOP 3 • Skimming and Scanning

Skills Preview

Key Reading Skill: Skimming and Scanning

Before you read the selection, skim it to get a general idea of what it is about and how it is structured. Then scan the selection quickly to find out the answers to the questions below. Write the answers in your Learner's Notebook.

- Where does the play take place?
- Which characters are talking when the play begins?
- Who is the character who appears later in the play?

Key Literary Element: Stage Directions

Stage directions are written in italics and are often enclosed in brackets or parentheses. They are a playwright's instructions to the actors, the director, and the stage crew. When a play is performed, the stage directions are not spoken. Instead, the actors or others involved with the play *do* what the stage directions indicate.

In Reading Workshop 1, you learned some of the terms playwrights use to refer to parts of the stage and actors' movements on the stage. Now, look for stage directions that have to do with:

- scenery and props—objects and furniture onstage
- lighting—which parts of the stage are lit
- movement of actors onstage
- action by an actor—anything that an actor does
- emotions that the actor should show
- how the actor should say the lines
- music and sound effects

Interactive Literary Elements Handbook
To review or learn more about the literary elements, go to www.glencoe.com.

Get Ready to Read

Connect to the Reading

Have you ever needed someone's help when you had a serious problem? Were you able to get help from a friend? Do you think a person has a right to ask his or her friend to do something difficult in order to help solve a problem?

Group Talk If your friend has a problem, is it your problem too? In a small group, talk about this question.

Build Background

Millions of people around the world collect some type of item. Some people collect things because they believe the items will increase in value as time passes. Other people collect things simply because they like them.

Collecting baseball cards has been a popular hobby in the United States for more than 75 years. Some baseball cards from the early days of professional baseball are worth more than $100,000. The value of a baseball card depends on several things:

- the condition of the card
- how rare the card is
- the company that made the card
- the year that the card was issued
- how popular the player is or was

Set Purposes for Reading

BIG Question Read "The Bully of Barksdale Street" to find out how one boy helped his friend out of a difficult situation.

Set Your Own Purpose What else would you like to learn from the selection that will help you answer the Big Question? Write your own purpose for reading this selection on the "Bully of Barksdale Street" page of Foldable 8.

Keep Moving

Use these skills as you read the following selection.

The Bully of Barksdale Street 999

READING WORKSHOP 3

The Bully of Barksdale Street

by Eric Alter

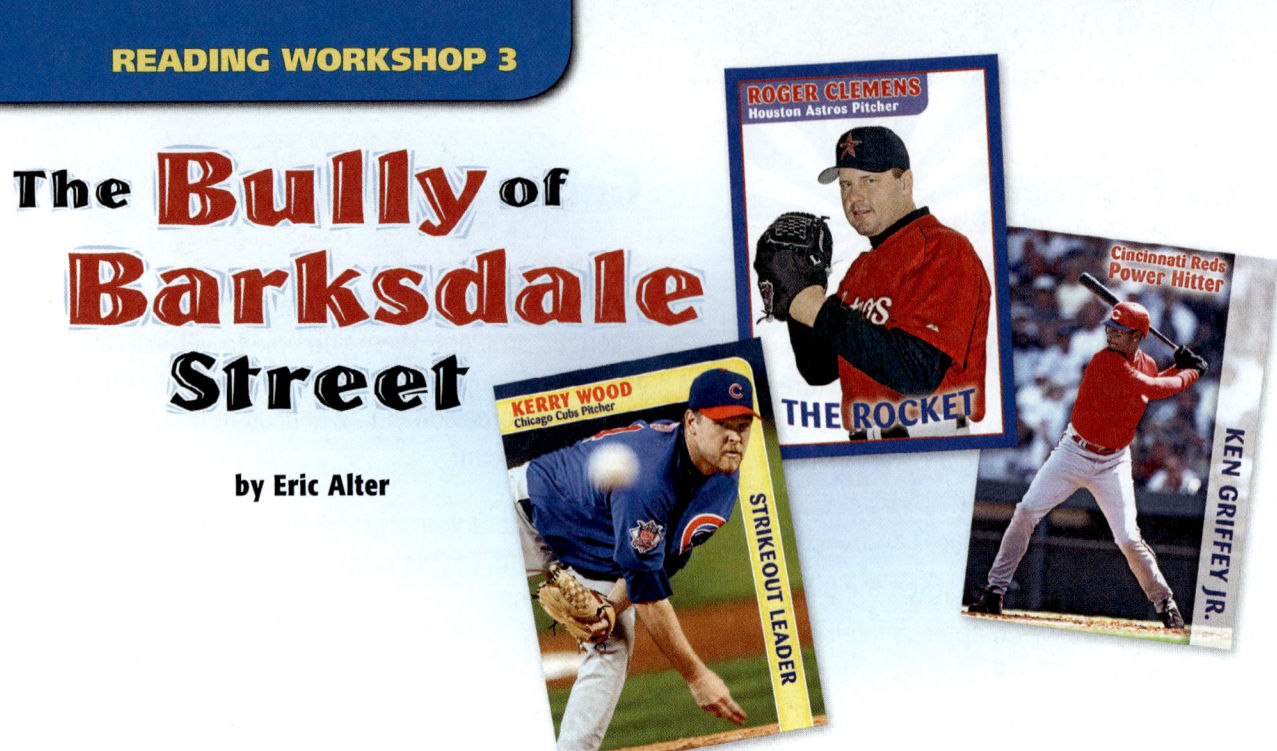

Josh outsmarts the neighborhood tough guy—a **tribute** to best friends and baseball-card collectors everywhere. . . .

Characters
BILLY WINSTON, 11
JOSH, 11
BLANE

TIME: *The present.*

SETTING: *A street in a typical American suburb.* **Backdrop** *may show houses if desired. There is a street sign up left that reads,* BARKSDALE STREET. **1**

AT RISE: *Standing underneath the street sign is* BILLY WINSTON. *He wears backpack, holds baseball cards, and looks around nervously. After a moment, he waves to* JOSH, *who enters.* JOSH *also wears backpack.* **2**

JOSH: Hey!

BILLY: Hey!

Vocabulary

tribute (TRIB yoot) *n.* something done to show respect

backdrop (BAK drop) *n.* a curtain or temporary wall that covers the back of a stage

Practice the Skills

1 **Key Literary Element**

Stage Directions Remember that *left* and *right* are from the actor's point of view, and *up* is short for *upstage* which means "toward the back of the stage area, away from the audience." What do you think "up left" means?

2 **Key Literary Element**

Stage Directions "AT RISE" means when the play begins. Where do you think that term came from? (Think about curtains and lights.)

1000 UNIT 8 What Makes a Friend?

READING WORKSHOP 3

JOSH: You got some new ones, huh?

BILLY (*Looking at his cards*): Yep.

JOSH: Sweet! ▣

BILLY: Thanks for meeting me over here.

JOSH: No problem.

BILLY: Your mom is so nice.

JOSH: How do you know?

BILLY: When I called you last night, she was really nice. Nobody else's mom asks me how I'm doing when I call.

JOSH: Yeah. She's cool. Lets me stay up late, too. (*After a pause*) Hey, get this—I made the baseball team at my school.

BILLY (*Impressed*): No way!

JOSH: Yeah! (*They high-five one another.*)

BILLY: Maybe I could come and watch some games.

Practice the Skills

3 **Key Reading Skill**

Skimming and Scanning
Scan the stage directions for the next two pages to find where Billy "holds up a card proudly." What card does he hold up?

The Bully of Barksdale Street **1001**

READING WORKSHOP 3

JOSH: I dunno . . . it's far.

BILLY: Yeah. (*After a pause*) I really wish I could go to your school.

JOSH: Yeah, me, too.

BILLY: I don't like school.

JOSH: How come?

BILLY: Just because.

JOSH: You'd like my school. We get to eat lunch outside when it's nice.

BILLY: No way!

JOSH: Yeah. But we start school earlier.

BILLY: Yeah, that's not a good thing.

JOSH: You wanna come over?

BILLY: I can't. I only have like fifteen minutes. I have to go to the hardware store with my dad. He's working on some project for the house this weekend, and he wants me to help.

JOSH: Cool!

BILLY: Not really.

JOSH: Yeah, well, just remember . . . you have a dad.

BILLY: Yeah. Sorry. You know I didn't mean—

JOSH: I know. It's O.K. (*After a pause*) So, what have you got?

BILLY (*Holding a card up proudly*): The Topps Ken Griffey[1]—in mint condition,[2] of course.

JOSH: No way! Lemme see. (JOSH *begins examining the card carefully.*)

BILLY: What have you got to trade? (JOSH *pulls out a huge wad of cards from backpack.*) **4**

---

1. **Ken Griffey** is a famous baseball player.
2. **Mint condition** means that something looks like it is brand new.

Practice the Skills

4 **Key Literary Element**

Stage Directions List three things you learn from the stage directions on this page.

JOSH: I got a Kerry Wood . . .

BILLY: Fleer or Topps?[3]

JOSH: Fleer, of course.

BILLY: No way! Lemme see. (*Now* BILLY *examines the card carefully.*)

JOSH: Trade?

BILLY (*Smiling*)**:** Trade! (*They high-five one another.*)

JOSH: O.K. . . . let's see what else I've got.

BILLY: O.K. (JOSH *begins pulling out cards from everywhere. Some fall on the ground.*) 5

JOSH: They don't let us have baseball cards in school, so I had to sneak them in. I kept a few of them in the back of my math book.

BILLY: Wow. Private school is strict.

JOSH: Not really . . . we can chew gum during lunch.

BILLY: Wow. Is there anything you can't do during lunch?

JOSH: Yeah. (*Smiles*) Trade baseball cards. Do you know how much my collection would grow if I could trade?

BILLY: Yeah. So . . . you guys have gym three times a week? 6

JOSH: We have it twice a week.

BILLY: We're playing softball now.

JOSH: We're doing **fencing**.

BILLY: Fencing?

JOSH: Yeah, you know . . . swords and stuff.

BILLY: Wow. Man, you private school kids are smart.

---

3. **Kerry Wood** is a famous baseball player. **Topps** and **Fleer** are brands of baseball cards.

Vocabulary

fencing (FEN sing) *n.* the sport of fighting with swords

Practice the Skills

5 Key Literary Element

Stage Directions Using these stage directions, how could the actor who plays Josh make this a funny moment in the play?

6 English Language Coach

Clipped Words There is a clipped word in this line. In your Learner's Notebook write the clipped word and the whole word that it comes from.

READING WORKSHOP 3

JOSH (*Laughing*): What else you got?

BILLY (*Shrugging*): Um . . . not much.

JOSH: What do you mean?

BILLY: Well, I uh . . . kinda lost some.

JOSH: Lost some? What do you mean?

BILLY: Nothing. I just . . . well . . . (*Shrugs*) lost some of 'em.

JOSH: Baseball cards are like—candy. You don't lose them!

BILLY: Yeah . . . well, I did.

JOSH: How many did you lose? (BILLY *doesn't answer.*) You still have my Sammy Sosa[4] you promised me, right?

BILLY: Um . . . well . . . 7

JOSH: Billy! You promised me. I had to trade some serious players for that!

BILLY: I know, I know. I'm sorry, Josh.

JOSH: Well, what about Clemens? I know you have Roger Clemens,[5] right?

BILLY (*Shaking his head quickly no*): Lost it.

JOSH: Where?!

BILLY: On my way home from school.

JOSH: Are you kidding me?

BILLY: No.

JOSH: How long ago?

BILLY: Last week sometime.

JOSH: Well, let's go and see if we can find them! Maybe no one picked them up yet. It hasn't rained in a week. They could be—

BILLY (*Interrupting*): Nah . . . they're probably just gone.

---

4. ***Sammy Sosa*** is a famous baseball player.
5. ***Roger Clemens*** is a famous baseball player.

Practice the Skills

7 Key Literary Element

Stage Directions In your Learner's Notebook, write stage directions for this short line so that the audience can see how Billy feels. Write one stage direction that tells how the lines should be delivered (tone of voice, emotion) and one stage direction that tells what Billy should be doing while he says his line.

JOSH: I don't understand. . . . (*Suddenly* BILLY *notices someone behind* JOSH. *He squints to make the person out while* JOSH *just keeps* rambling *on.*) Roger Clemens . . . (*Shakes head*) Man, how does someone lose Roger Clemens?

BILLY: Oh, no. Not here.

JOSH: What?

BILLY: No!

JOSH: What's the matter?

BILLY (*Quickly*): Look . . . I lied, O.K.?

JOSH: About what? You still have Roger Clemens?

BILLY: No, I lied about losing them. I didn't exactly lose them.

JOSH: What's wrong with you? What? (JOSH *begins to look behind him.*)

BILLY: No, don't look behind you!

JOSH: Why? What's going on?

BILLY: O.K., I gotta go. (*Bends down and begins packing up his books*)

JOSH: Billy, what's wrong?

BILLY: I didn't lose them. This kid, Blane Davenport . . . he took them.

JOSH: Huh?

BILLY: Look, this kid's been bothering me, and he's about— please don't turn around . . . he's about a hundred yards from us. He never comes this way! I thought I'd be safe.

JOSH: Wait a sec . . . this kid Blane has been bothering you? 8

BILLY: Yeah. I try and race home every day, but he always catches up with me.

Practice the Skills

8 English Language Coach

Clipped Words What is the clipped word in this line? Write it and the word it comes from in your Learner's Notebook.

Vocabulary

rambling (RAM bling) *v.* talking in a disorganized manner

The Bully of Barksdale Street

READING WORKSHOP 3

JOSH: What grade is he in?

BILLY: Seventh. He's huge.

JOSH: And lemme guess . . . he likes baseball cards?

BILLY: If I give him cards, he doesn't rearrange my face. It's a nice agreement. I gotta run. . . .

JOSH: Wait a second. Just wait a second.

BILLY: I really don't want to stick around. . . .

JOSH: How far is he?

BILLY: Thirty yards.

JOSH: Stand up. 9

BILLY (*Confused*): What are you—

JOSH: Stand up! I want you to do exactly what I tell you to do.

BILLY: What're you talking about? He'll **pummel** us both!

JOSH: Just do what I tell you to do, O.K.?

Vocabulary

pummel (PUM ul) *v.* to hit or beat someone

Practice the Skills

9 **BIG Question**
Billy "lost" the baseball cards that Josh was expecting. Is Josh mad at Billy for not having the cards? What does Josh's reaction tell you about their friendship?

BILLY: No, I don't want—(BLANE DAVENPORT *enters.*)

JOSH (*Firmly*): Billy, just do what I tell you to do . . . understand?

BLANE (*Calling out*): Hey, Winston!

JOSH (*After a pause, in a loud voice, to* BILLY): I said . . . I want to see all your cards!

BILLY: Huh?

JOSH (*Whispering*): Do what I say. (*After a pause, again in a loud voice*) I said I want to see your cards! Now! Open your bag and let me see!

BLANE (*Calling out,* **mocking**): Oh, Winston! (*Crosses to join* JOSH *and* BILLY)

JOSH (*To* BILLY; *loudly*): Forget about him. Do what I tell you. (BILLY *grabs some cards and hands them to* JOSH.) This is it? This is all you've got?

BLANE: Hey, what's—(JOSH *turns to face* BLANE; *gives him an up-and-down stare.*) **10**

JOSH (*To* BLANE): Hey, pal, beat it, would ya? I'm working over here. (*After a pause; to* BILLY) I asked you a question! I said is this all you have?!

BLANE: Hey—

JOSH (*Slowly turning to* BLANE): Hey, maybe you didn't hear me. I said I'm working over here.

BLANE (*Puzzled*): What do you mean?

JOSH: I mean I'm taking this kid's baseball cards. It's what I do around here. I take all the cards that I want.

BLANE (*Laughing*): Are you kidding me? You? How about I take your cards and his cards. (*He looks down* **menacingly** *at* JOSH. JOSH *doesn't flinch.*)

Vocabulary

mocking (MOK ing) *v.* making fun of someone by imitating the person in a ridiculous manner

menacingly (MEN uh sing lee) *adv.* in a threatening manner

Practice the Skills

10 **Key Literary Element**

Stage Directions Josh gives Blane an "up-and-down stare." What do you think that kind of stare means?

READING WORKSHOP 3

BILLY: I could just give both you guys my cards—

JOSH (*Breaking from* BLANE's *stare*): I said be quiet. I will deal with you in a minute. (*Goes back to staring at* BLANE) You could try—and I do mean try. But you see, you're wearing white. **11**

BLANE: Yeah, so?

JOSH: You ever see blood get on a white shirt?

BLANE: Huh?

JOSH: Doesn't come out. Trust me. Three days ago, I knocked a kid's front teeth out, blood got all on my good white shirt—had to throw it out. (*After a long pause*) But if you'd like to give it a go, we could. (*Quick pause*) But lemme just warn you . . . well, I am supposed to warn you—that's what my karate instructor tells me. He says with my talent and speed, I should warn someone before I fight him . . . and if I do, and they choose to continue to fight me, the police won't press charges.

BLANE: Huh?

JOSH: Enough of this talk. (*After a beat, turns to* BILLY, *then checks his watch*) This is only gonna take about two minutes, and when I'm done, I'm gonna deal with you. So don't run off, or else I'm gonna have to chase you down. (*Turns to* BLANE) You ready?

BLANE: What was that you said about karate?

JOSH: What about it? Been doing it since I was five. Black belt. Why?

BLANE: Well, I . . . uh . . .

JOSH: You—uh—nothing. You mean you never heard of me?

BLANE (*Shaking his head*): No. You don't go to our school.

JOSH: 'Course I don't. I go to reform school. They wouldn't let me in that public school.

BLANE: How come?

Practice the Skills

11 **BIG Question**
Why does Josh tell Billy to be quiet? Is Josh really being rude to Billy?

JOSH: How come? (*Snorts in laughter*) 'Cause in fourth grade I was shaking down kids for lunch money every day. One of the kids happened to be the nephew of the principal. Bad scene. **12**

BLANE: Wow.

JOSH: This is my area. I deal with all the kids from South Orange Middle School.

BLANE: Yeah, but—

JOSH: That is . . . until this kid here tells me he doesn't have the Roger Clemens that I want, or the Sammy Sosa, and a bunch of other cards, and that gets me mad. (*After a pause*) Wait a second . . . are you really telling me you never heard of me?

BLANE (*After a long pause*): Not really. (JOSH *begins looking around; the street sign catches his attention.*)

JOSH: I'm the bully of Barksdale Street.

BLANE (*Slowly nodding*): Yeah. (*Smiling*) Oh, yeah . . . I think I have heard of you.

JOSH: You think?

BLANE (*Nodding*): I remember it now.

JOSH (*Slowly nodding*): You're interfering with my territory, Blane.

BLANE: How'd you know my name?

JOSH: You don't think I do my homework? Billy here tells me you've been shaking him down for the past few weeks.

BLANE: Yeah, but I—

JOSH (*Smiling calmly*): Look, I can somewhat appreciate what you do. (*Looks at* BILLY, *then winks at him*) I mean, he's a weakling, but he's my weakling, you understand?

BLANE: I . . . uh . . . guess.

Practice the Skills

12 **English Language Coach**

Clipped Words There's a clipped word in this speech. Find the clipped word, and write it and the word it comes from in your Learner's Notebook.

JOSH: You see, Blane, I don't think it's such a good idea for you to be bullying people. Not around here, anyway . . . not anyone at South Orange Middle School. That's my neck of the woods. (*Loudly*) Understand?!

BLANE (*Slowly nodding*): Uh-huh.

JOSH: Now, before you go, I want you to understand: I don't want Billy touched. That's my job. Get it?

BLANE: Uh-huh.

JOSH: Good. And before I let you go . . . I think there's something you have that belongs to me.

BLANE: Huh?

JOSH: Roger Clemens, Sammy Sosa, and a bunch of other cards you took from my kid over here.

BLANE (*Stalling*): I—uh—I don't have them on me.

JOSH: Oh, boy.

BLANE (*Quickly*): But I can get them to you. I'll give them to Billy first thing tomorrow. Then he can give them to you. (*After a pause*) You'd make sure he gets them, right, Billy?

BILLY (*To* JOSH): You're gonna want all the cards, right? (*Winks at* JOSH)

JOSH: Yeah, Blane . . . all of 'em. (*After a beat*) So, we have an understanding, right? **13**

BLANE: Yeah, we do.

JOSH: Good. Now, if you'll excuse me, I've got some pummeling of my own to do.

BLANE: Oh, yeah . . . sure.

JOSH: In other words . . . BEAT IT.

BLANE: Good luck, Billy. (BLANE *runs off.*)

JOSH (*Calling out*): Don't forget the cards!

BILLY (*Shaking his head*): That was amazing.

Practice the Skills

13 Key Literary Element

Stage Directions A *beat* is a pause. Why do you think the playwright indicated a "beat" here?

JOSH: Is he gone?

BILLY: Long gone. (JOSH *lets out the longest sigh*.) Josh, I don't know what to say. That was . . . incredible!

JOSH (*Relieved*): Whew . . . he bought it.

BILLY: I am amazed! How did you—

JOSH (*Shrugging*): Bullies . . . they're not used to anyone standing up to them. That's why they're bullies. They pick on people smaller, people they think won't give them any problems. (*After a pause*) But the moment you stand up to one, that can all change.

BILLY (*Smiling*): The Bully of Barksdale Street?

JOSH: Has a nice ring to it, huh? (*They laugh.*)

BILLY: I don't know how to say thanks.

JOSH: Don't worry about it . . . you'd do the same for me.

BILLY: What would you have done if it didn't work?

JOSH: Run. Fast. Very fast.

BILLY: Yeah.

JOSH: He could only get one of us then, right? (*Laughing*)

BILLY (*Laughing*): Man . . . you're smart, Josh . . . really smart. (*They high-five one another as curtain falls.*) 14

THE END

Practice the Skills

14 **BIG Question**
How would you describe the friendship between Josh and Billy? What makes them such good friends? Write your answers on the "Bully of Barksdale Street" page of Foldable 8. Your response will help you complete the Unit Challenge later.

READING WORKSHOP 3 • Skimming and Scanning

After You Read

The Bully of Barksdale Street

Answering the BIG Question

1. In your opinion, what kind of help should you be able to expect from a friend when you are in trouble? Explain your answer by drawing on events from the selection.

2. **Recall** Which of the boys made the baseball team at school?
   TIP Right There

3. **Summarize** In your own words, summarize how Josh helps Billy get his baseball cards back.
   TIP Think and Search

Critical Thinking

4. **Interpret** Why did Billy wish that he could go to Josh's school at the beginning of the story? Do you think he would still like to go to Josh's school at the end of the story? Refer to specific places in the text that support your answer.
   TIP Author and Me

5. **Evaluate** Do you think that the trick Josh plays on Blane is a realistic solution to Billy's problem? Explain the reasons for your answer.
   TIP Author and Me

6. **Synthesize** At the end of the play, what do you think Billy has learned about dealing with bullies? If another bully tried to take away his baseball cards, do you think he would do anything differently? Explain your answer.
   TIP Author and Me

Write About Your Reading

Use the RAFT system to write about "The Bully of Barksdale Street."

Role: Josh
Audience: Middle school students who are having trouble with bullies
Format: Letter to be published in the school newspaper
Topic: How to deal with a bully

Write a letter to the editor that could be published in a school newspaper, telling students how they can deal with a bully.

Objectives (pp. 1012–1013)
Reading Skim and scan text • Make connections from text to self
Literature Understand elements of drama: stage directions
Vocabulary Identify clipped words
Writing Use the RAFT system: letter to the editor
Grammar Use punctuation correctly: colons in time notations, in salutations

Skills Review

Key Reading Skill: Skimming and Scanning

7. After you have read a text, if there's a particular fact from the text that you can't remember, would you skim the text or scan the text to find the answer?

Key Literary Element: Stage Directions

8. What is the setting for "The Bully of Barksdale Street"?
9. Besides describing the setting, list at least three things that stage directions can do.

Vocabulary Check

For each sentence, choose the word in boldface type that best fits in the blank.

**pummel   tribute   fencing   menacingly
rambling   mocking   backdrop**

10. In Elise's speech, she was ___ so much that we couldn't tell what she was trying to say.
11. The honors ceremony was a ___ to the students who had worked so hard.
12. The ___ hangs at the back of the stage.
13. Craig was ___ the girls when he talked with an exaggerated version of their accent.
14. Jeremy was afraid the bully would ___ him.
15. Ike looked ___ at his enemy before he attacked.
16. Lauren doesn't like swords, so I don't think she would like ___ .
17. **English Language Coach** In your Learner's Notebook, write the clipped word that would come from each of these words: gasoline, hamburger, airplane.

Grammar Link: Using Colons in Time Notations and After Salutations

- Use a colon to separate the hour and the minutes when you write the time of day.

  Mr. Jordon announced that Violet Haskins would arrive at the gymnasium at exactly 12:14 P.M.

- Also use a colon after the salutation, or greeting, of a business letter.

  Dear Mr. Spencer:

Grammar Practice

Add a colon wherever one is necessary.

18. Dear Mr. Greenberg
19. The parade will start at exactly 11 00 A.M.
20. At about 11 30 A.M. the parade will turn right on Valen Street.

Writing Application Review the Write About Your Reading activity. Make sure that you used colons correctly after the salutation of the letter and in any time notations.

Web Activities For eFlashcards, Selection Quick Checks, and other Web activities, go to www.glencoe.com.

READING WORKSHOP 3 • Skimming and Scanning

Before You Read

Tales of the Tangled Tresses

Christina Hamlett

Meet the Author
A former actress and theater director, Christina Hamlett has written more than 20 books and 110 plays and musicals. One of her books is designed to help teenagers write their own plays. Hamlett has also written hundreds of articles on topics ranging from the performing arts to travel. She lives in California.

Author Search For more about Christina Hamlett, go to www.glencoe.com.

Objectives (pp. 1014–1029)
Reading Skim and scan text • Make connections from text to self
Literature Understand elements of drama: stage directions
Vocabulary Identify jargon

Vocabulary Preview

tresses (TRES uz) *n.* long hair **(p. 1016)** *She combed her lovely dark tresses.*

frills (frilz) *n.* things that are added on for decoration but are not really necessary **(p. 1016)** *Jack bought a basic CD player with no frills or added features.*

brunette (broo NET) *n.* a person with black or brown hair **(p. 1020)** *The brunette next to Ahmed dropped her soda.*

widower (WID oh ur) *n.* a man whose wife has died **(p. 1021)** *My uncle has been a widower for four years.*

fiasco (fee AS koh) *n.* something that has failed completely, possibly in a ridiculous way **(p. 1022)** *When Edith tried to paint her room, it turned into a real fiasco.*

Write to Learn Using at least three of the vocabulary words, write a one-paragraph story about getting a haircut. Find a partner and read each other's stories.

English Language Coach

Jargon There is a special kind of slang called **jargon.** (It's also called "lingo.") Jargon is easily understood by members of a group but often unknown to other people. The group may be people who do the same kind of work or who share a particular interest.

In almost any job, there are words or terms that are known to people who do that kind of work. Doctors, computer programmers, cooks, and hairdressers have their own jargon. Activities other than work also have their own jargon. In baseball jargon, a *can of corn* is a fly ball that's easy to catch. In rock-and-roll jargon, an *axe* is a guitar.

As you read, look for examples of jargon. Use context clues to figure out what the term might mean. If context doesn't provide a good idea, look in a dictionary. Like any slang, if jargon is used for long enough, it becomes part of the language and enters the dictionary.

Group Talk In a small group, try to list several examples of jargon that your parents, grandparents, or some other people in your class might not understand. Then write down who might use those terms and the meaning of each term. Compare your lists with other groups.

READING WORKSHOP 3 • Skimming and Scanning

Skills Preview

Key Reading Skill: Skimming and Scanning

When you skim and scan a piece of literature, you can get an idea of when and where it takes place, whether it is realistic or not, and whether it is serious or funny.

Write to Learn Before you read "Tales of the Tangled Tresses" carefully, skim and scan it to find out the answers to the questions from page 997 that you wrote in your Learner's Notebook. Answer them.

Key Literary Element: Stage Directions

Stage directions tell the actors what to do while the play is going on. For example, if a stage direction says *[picks up telephone],* then the actor pauses and picks up the telephone.

Stage directions also tell the director of the play when to use sound, lighting, and other special effects on stage. For example, a stage direction might say *[The painting on the wall suddenly crashes to the floor].*

Stage directions are

- printed in *italics* and are often set in *brackets* **[ ]** or *parentheses.*
- not spoken aloud when the play is performed

Literature Online

Interactive Literary Elements Handbook
To review or learn more about the literary elements, go to www.glencoe.com.

Get Ready to Read

Connect to the Reading

Does anyone you know go to a particular store, shop, or restaurant to find out the neighborhood news or hang out with friends? As you read this play, imagine what you would think if you were sitting in the Fabulous Frills Salon while all these unusual people came in and told their stories.

Partner Talk With your partner, discuss places in your neighborhood where people go to hang out with friends.

Build Background

A beauty salon is a shop where people can have their hair cut, colored, and styled and makeup applied. Many people make close friendships with the people they meet at beauty salons or barber shops.

In this play, some of the characters who are mentioned are from famous myths.

- In ancient Greek mythology, King Menelaus's wife, Helen, was kidnapped by a man named Paris and taken off to the city of Troy. The Trojan War was fought to get Helen back from Troy.
- Midas was a king who wished that everything he touched would turn to gold. His wish was granted.
- Medusa had snakes on her head instead of hair. Anyone who looked at her turned to stone.

Set Purposes for Reading

BIG Question Read "Tales of the Tangled Tresses" to see how two friends who work together deal with some unusual customers.

Set Your Own Purpose What else would you like to learn from the selection that might help you answer the Big Question? Write your own purpose for reading on the "Tales of the Tangled Tresses" page of Foldable 8.

Keep Moving
Use these skills as you read the following selection.

Tales of the Tangled Tresses **1015**

READING WORKSHOP 3

Tales of the Tangled Tresses

by Christina Hamlett

Fairy tale characters get major makeovers at Fabulous Frills Salon. . . .

Characters
OLIVIA, owner of the Fabulous Frills Salon
HILDA, her assistant
GOLDILOCKS
RAPUNZEL
CINDERELLA
BRIAR ROSE
ALICE

SCENE 1

[TIME: The present.]

[SETTING: Reception area of Fabulous **Frills** Salon; color scheme is pink and white. Receptionist table with a phone on it is down left. Three archways leading to "styling booths" are upstage. Main entrance to salon is right. Photos of different hairstyles adorn walls, and wig heads, hair spray cans, magazines, etc., round out the salon décor.] **2**

Vocabulary

tresses (TRES uz) *n.* long hair

frills (frilz) *n.* things that are added on for decoration but are not really necessary

Practice the Skills

1 **Key Literary Skill**

Skimming and Scanning
Skim the play before you read it to answer these two questions.

- Where and when does the play take place?
- Is the play real-life or fantasy?

2 **Key Literary Element**

Stage Directions Notice that the scene begins with stage directions that tell the reader where and when the action is taking place. Can you picture this scene in your head? Review the definitions on page 939. Then, in your Learner's Notebook, make a rough drawing of what you think the set would look like.

1016 UNIT 8 What Makes a Friend?

AT RISE: *OLIVIA is sitting at table doing her nails. HILDA enters from one of the arches and crosses to her. Both women have extreme hairstyles.*

HILDA (*Sighing heavily*): This has to be the slowest day we've ever had!

OLIVIA: You can say that again. I'm almost tempted to close up shop and call it a day.

HILDA: That's pretty bad, considering it's not even lunchtime yet.

OLIVIA: Well, we've styled and restyled each other's hair so much already that—(*Phone rings.*)

HILDA: Hey! Things could be looking up!

OLIVIA (*Answering phone*): Fabulous Frills Salon. Olivia speaking. . . . This afternoon? (*Smiles at HILDA*) Yes, I'm pretty sure we can fit you in. (*Reaches for the calendar*) Name, please? . . . Helen. . . . Yes, two-o'clock would be fine. . . . A special occasion? (*Nods*) Your face is going to launch a thousand ships so you want to look your best for the press? Well, don't worry, Helen. My assistant Hilda will send you out in style. See you at two. (*Hangs up*) **3**

HILDA: A new client? Where's she from?

OLIVIA: She says she's from Sparta[1] and her last name is Menelaus.

HILDA: Wow! You think she's any relation to the king?

OLIVIA: It sure wouldn't hurt our business if she was. Can you imagine the publicity that would generate? Anyway, she says she wants to look special for Paris.

HILDA: Sounds like there's going to be a big tip in it if she's pleased.

OLIVIA: In your capable hands, Hilda, how could she be anything else?

---

1. **Sparta** was a city in ancient Greece. The caller, **Helen,** is Helen of Troy.

Practice the Skills

3 **Key Literary Element**

Stage Directions Look over the stage directions during this speech. Can you visualize what Olivia is doing as she's talking on the phone? Why do you think Olivia smiles at Hilda?

READING WORKSHOP 3

HILDA: Well, as you always say, don't count your curlers until they're in! (*A breathless GOLDILOCKS suddenly rushes in, looking behind her as if she's being pursued.*)

OLIVIA: Can I help you?

GOLDILOCKS: Is this the Fabulous Frills Salon?

HILDA: At your service. I'm Hilda and this is my boss, Olivia.

GOLDILOCKS: And is it true what your sign says: "Curl Up to a New You"?

OLIVIA (*Pleased*): I thought of that slogan[2] myself.

HILDA: What can we do for you, Miss . . . ?

GOLDILOCKS: Locks. Goldi Locks. And what you can do is get me out of a lot of hot water!

OLIVIA: What seems to be the problem?

GOLDILOCKS: Well, it all started with these three bears—

OLIVIA and HILDA (*In unison; startled*): Bears?! 4

GOLDILOCKS: Yeah, there's a father bear, a mother bear, and a little kid bear who's really a whiner.

OLIVIA: And you say you know these bears personally, dear?

GOLDILOCKS: Oh, I've seen 'em wandering around the neighborhood, but we've never been formally introduced. Anyway, it seems they've got a warrant out for my arrest.

HILDA: Why would a bunch of bears want to arrest someone they don't even know?

---

2. A *slogan* is a short, catchy phrase that is used to advertise a product or store.

Practice the Skills

4 **BIG Question**
Do you have a friend so close that you finish each other's sentences or say the same things at the same time? Do you think Olivia and Hilda have this kind of friendship?

"Goldilocks" is the next customer at Fabulous Frills.
Analyzing the Art What is Goldilocks doing in this picture? Whose house is she in? How do you know?

GOLDILOCKS: Listen, it's nothing serious, really. I wandered into their house by mistake and they got in a big huff about it. I tried to explain, but would they listen? Of course not! In fact, they were downright grizzly about it.

OLIVIA: I don't think I like the sound of this. 5

HILDA: Why didn't you just tell them you were in the wrong house? That kind of thing could happen to anyone.

OLIVIA: Especially if it was late at night and out in those confusing suburbs.

GOLDILOCKS: Actually it was the middle of the morning and—(*She hesitates.*)

HILDA: And what?

GOLDILOCKS: And I kinda sorta broke some furniture while I was there. Oh, and they'd left their breakfast out and I was sorta hungry so I helped myself.

OLIVIA: Didn't you have breakfast at home before you went out?

HILDA: It is the most important meal of the day.

GOLDILOCKS (*With a shrug*): I was in a hurry. What can I say? Anyway, I really need your help.

HILDA: Doing what?

GOLDILOCKS (*Pointing to her head*): Well, you see this hair?

OLIVIA: It's very pretty.

HILDA: Quite lovely, yes.

GOLDILOCKS: It's also a dead giveaway to the police.

OLIVIA and HILDA (*In unison*): The police?

GOLDILOCKS: Based on what those stupid bears told 'em, they've got an APB out on a girl with golden locks. Until I can get a good attorney to defend me, I need a disguise. 6

Practice the Skills

5 Key Literary Element

Stage Directions How does Olivia react to Goldilocks's story here? What could Olivia do onstage that would make her reaction even clearer to the audience? In your Learner's Notebook, write at least one stage direction that tells Olivia what to do while she's listening to Goldilocks. Use the author's stage directions as a model for your writing.

6 English Language Coach

Jargon An APB is an All Points Bulletin. It is a message that police stations send out to local police officers to let them know to look for someone

READING WORKSHOP 3

HILDA: What sort of disguise?

OLIVIA: We're hairdressers, dear, not wizards.

HILDA: Although we have been known to work magic with split ends and cowlicks.

GOLDILOCKS: I was thinking of something **brunette**. Maybe super-straight with feathered bangs. 7

OLIVIA: Well . . .

HILDA: She really does seem like a nice girl, Olivia.

OLIVIA: But what about the bears? Breaking and entering is a crime, you know.

HILDA: Yes, but you know how grumpy bears can be when they get up on the wrong side of the bed. She said herself that they wouldn't even let her apologize.

GOLDILOCKS: Will you do it, please? (*Looks at her watch*) They could be here any second!

OLIVIA: Oh, all right. (*To HILDA*) Take her back to Gladys.

HILDA: Will do.

OLIVIA (*To GOLDILOCKS*): You'll be a different person in no time flat!

GOLDILOCKS (*Thankfully*): Thanks! You won't regret it! (*Phone rings.*)

OLIVIA (*Answering phone*): Good morning, Fabulous Frills Salon. (*Responds in amazement*) What? Could you say that again, please? . . . No, I have to admit I've never heard anything like that before. How exactly did it happen? . . . (*HILDA returns.*) I'm at a loss on what to tell you to do, sir. Are you sure it turned completely gold and not just dishwater blond? . . . Even the hairbrush? Well, you might try a good conditioner first and, if that doesn't work, we can schedule an emergency appointment for you. . . . O.K., good luck. (*Hangs up, shaking head*)

Practice the Skills

7 **English Language Coach**

Jargon Some words and phrases that are familiar to everyone started out as jargon. What word in this line was probably first used by hairdressers?

Vocabulary

brunette (broo NET) *n.* a person with black or brown hair

HILDA: What was that all about?

OLIVIA: Remember the Midas family? They moved here a year or so ago?

HILDA: A widower, wasn't he? With a little girl, I seem to recall.

OLIVIA: The apple of his eye. Yes, that's the one. Well, apparently he's come down with this very peculiar condition.

HILDA: What kind of condition?

OLIVIA: Whenever he touches things, they turn to gold.

HILDA: Hm-m . . . that could come in pretty handy between paydays.

OLIVIA: Not if it happens to everything. This morning, for instance, he offered to brush his daughter's hair, and as soon as he touched it—zap! Fourteen carat and the brush along with it!

HILDA: That's the weirdest thing I've ever heard in my life!

RAPUNZEL (*Offstage*): Yoo-hoo! Are you open? 8

HILDA (*Waving a welcome*): Sure! Come on in! (*RAPUNZEL enters with hair so long that it drags on the floor.*)

RAPUNZEL: Thank goodness! (*She trips over her tresses.*) I've been tripping all over the street looking for a good salon.

OLIVIA (*In disbelief*): My goodness, Hilda, just look at her hair!

HILDA: It's absolutely gorgeous!

OLIVIA: Have you ever seen hair that long?

Practice the Skills

8 Key Literary Element

Stage Directions The stage direction (*Offstage*) means that the audience can't see the actor when he or she is delivering the lines. Usually the actor stands to the side of the set behind the curtain and yells or speaks loudly so that the audience can hear him or her.

Grimm's Fairy Tales Book Illustration with Rapunzel in Her Tower, 19th Century

Analyzing the Art Do you think that Rapunzel should get her hair cut at Fabulous Frills? Why or why not?

Vocabulary

widower (WID oh ur) *n.* a man whose wife has died

RAPUNZEL: That's exactly why I'm here. I want you to cut it.

OLIVIA and HILDA (*In unison*): Cut it?!

HILDA: Are you sure that's what you want, dear?

OLIVIA: We have clients who would give their eye teeth to be able to grow tresses that tremendous! 9

RAPUNZEL: Yeah, well, they'd shear their chignons, too, if they knew how much trouble this hair is worth.

HILDA: Like what?

RAPUNZEL: Like having a witch keep me locked up in a huge tower with no elevator or stairs.

OLIVIA: But if it doesn't have an elevator or stairs, how does a person—

RAPUNZEL (*Pointing to her hair*): Three guesses and the first two don't count.

OLIVIA: By climbing up your hair?

RAPUNZEL: Bingo.

HILDA (*Rubbing her head in sympathy*): Ouch! That's gotta hurt.

RAPUNZEL: Talk about a major headache, too.

OLIVIA: Not to mention a follicle[4] **fiasco**.

RAPUNZEL: It's also inconvenient. I mean, there I am, just doing my nails or watching the soaps, and I have to listen to "Rapunzel, Rapunzel, let down your hair" day in and day out. I'm sick of it.

HILDA: You're really sure you want to do this?

---

4. A **follicle** is the root of a hair.

Practice the Skills

9 BIG Question

When Rapunzel wants to cut her hair, Hilda and Olivia try to talk her out of it. Do they do that because cutting her hair will be too difficult, or because they're trying to stop her from doing something she might regret later? When should a person try to stop a friend from doing something he or she might regret?

Vocabulary

fiasco (fee AS koh) *n.* something that has failed completely, possibly in a ridiculous way

READING WORKSHOP 3

OLIVIA: It could take quite awhile to grow it back that long again.

HILDA: Not to mention how long it will take to sweep out the salon afterwards.

OLIVIA: Are you positive you've given this enough thought?

RAPUNZEL: Absolutely! And besides the sign out front says your prices are a steal.

OLIVIA (*Contemplating RAPUNZEL's features*): Something short and perky, maybe?

HILDA: She'd look awfully cute in a "Winona," don't you think? 10

OLIVIA (To HILDA): Take her back to Loretta. She loves to chop locks.

RAPUNZEL: That's great she can take me on short notice. If she does a good job, I'll be grateful all the way to my roots! (*She and HILDA exit upstage. Phone rings. OLIVIA answers it.*)

OLIVIA: Good morning, Fabulous Frills Salon. . . . Uh-huh. . . . Uh-huh. . . . Uh-huh. Yes, that sounds horribly messy. . . . Well, of course, I'd be startled if that happened, too. (*HILDA returns as she's talking.*) This was a big spider, you say? . . . Oh dear! Well, you might try a good shampoo and give us a call if it doesn't come out. . . . Certainly, any time. (*She hangs up.*)

HILDA: Who was that?

OLIVIA: One of Esther's regulars—that Muffet girl who's into health foods?

HILDA: I remember that stuff she was eating under the dryer last week. Curds and whey—ick!⁵ 11

OLIVIA: Well, it seems that she was eating a big bowl of it outside and a spider came along and scared her so much that she jumped and the entire bowl of it ended up on her head.

HILDA: Serves her right for eating it in the first place.

Practice the Skills

10 English Language Coach

Jargon Barbers and hair stylists often invent names for new hairstyles. In this hair salon, "Winona" is jargon for a particular style of haircut.

11 Key Literary Element

Stage Directions Write a stage direction that tells Hilda how she should react to curds and whey.

---

5. Cottage cheese is a common form of **curds and whey.** The curds are the solid clumps, while the whey is the liquid.

Tales of the Tangled Tresses **1023**

READING WORKSHOP 3

(CINDERELLA limps in, wearing ragged clothes and one shoe which appears to be made of glass.)

CINDERELLA: Excuse me, but do you take walk-ins? 12

OLIVIA: It looks more like "limp-ins" to me. What happened to you?

HILDA: Why are you walking around with only one shoe?

OLIVIA: And a glass shoe at that!

CINDERELLA: It's a long story. I really don't want to bother you.

HILDA: Take your time, sweetie. That's what hairdressers are here for.

CINDERELLA: Well, it all began after I got to the dance club last night. I wasn't really supposed to go at all, you see. My stepmother and stepsisters had this long list of horrible chores for me to do instead. Anyway, I managed to sneak out of the house with the help of my fairy godmother and I met this wonderful guy who turned out to be a prince.

OLIVIA: How romantic!

HILDA: And was it love at first sight?

CINDERELLA: Well, I think it could have been if I hadn't kept watching the clock.

HILDA: Why were you watching the clock?

CINDERELLA: Because if I didn't get out by midnight, I'd be stuck with a bunch of mice and a double-parked pumpkin and I'd have no way to get home. Anyway, I want to look really fantastic this afternoon because this guy is going to be paying me a visit.

HILDA: How nice!

CINDERELLA: Yes, especially if it fits.

OLIVIA (*Puzzled*): If what fits?

Practice the Skills

12 English Language Coach

Jargon "Walk-in" is a term commonly used in hair salons, doctors' offices, and other businesses that people go to. It refers to a person who comes in without an appointment.

Cinderella, ca. 1905, Hans Printz (1865–1925)

CINDERELLA: The shoe he found in the parking lot—the mate to this one. If it does, I can leave this life of drudgery and despair behind and waltz off in grand style.

OLIVIA (*Checking the calendar*): Francine just happens to have an opening. Hilda will show you the way.

CINDERELLA: Thanks, guys! By the way, if the shoe fits, I'll see that you get an invitation to the wedding. 13

HILDA (*As she walks her back*): So this friend of yours—the prince?—does he happen to have a brother? (*BRIAR ROSE enters wearing a long princess-style dress covered with cobwebs. Her hair is a tangled mess with curls tied in different color ribbons.*) 14

BRIAR ROSE: Hi there. 15

OLIVIA (*Gasping*): Oh, no! (*Calling out*) Hilda, come quick! You have to see this! (*HILDA rushes back.*)

HILDA: What's wrong? (*She sees BRIAR ROSE and gasps in shock.*) Oh, my! I haven't seen hair like that since—goodness, but I can't even remember!

OLIVIA: You're here for an appointment . . . I hope?

BRIAR ROSE: Do you have one available on short notice?

HILDA: Forgive us for appearing rude, but where have you been for the last hundred years?

BRIAR ROSE: Actually, I've been asleep.

HILDA (*Suddenly remembering*): So you must be that girl I read about in the Gazette, the one named—

OLIVIA: Sleeping Beauty, isn't it?

BRIAR ROSE: That's me.

HILDA: Well, I'm as much in favor of a good nap as the next person, but honestly—a hundred years?! Isn't that a little excessive?

BRIAR ROSE: Unfortunately, I didn't have much say-so about it. You see, I pricked my finger on a magic spinning wheel and fell into a really deep sleep. The next thing I knew,

Practice the Skills

13 **Key Reading Skill**

Skimming and Scanning Before you read about Briar Rose, scan the names of the characters who speak in the remainder of the play. What other new characters will come into the salon before the end of the play?

14 **Key Literary Element**

Stage Directions Read the stage directions that describe what Briar Rose is wearing and how she looks. Can you guess who she is?

15 **Key Reading Skill**

Skimming and Scanning Scan the next page to see where Alice appears. What does she look like? What does she ask?

this strange man I had never seen before was giving me a kiss and I woke up.

HILDA: That explains the hairstyle.

BRIAR ROSE: Does it also explain why he fainted?

OLIVIA: Well, it is rather alarming, dear. No one has worn that style for decades. Or, in your case, centuries. Not to worry, though. Hilda's going to take you back to Martha. She's a whiz with the latest styles. (*She and HILDA exit upstage just as a frantic ALICE enters. Her long blond hair is quite disheveled and, in fact, has a bunch of leaves and a couple of playing cards in it.*)

ALICE: Am I late?

OLIVIA: Late for what?

ALICE: For a very important date.

OLIVIA (*Reaching in confusion for the calendar*): Did you have an appointment?

ALICE: Oh dear, I just can't seem to recall. My life has been rather turbulent lately. And it's all because of that silly hare.

OLIVIA: Whose hair?

ALICE: Hare as in rabbit. The one with the waistcoat and pocketwatch that I followed down the rabbit hole? It was infinitely more interesting, you see, than being read to by my sister from a book without any pictures. Books without pictures are so boring! 16

OLIVIA: I suppose. But what about the rabbit?

ALICE: Well, he led me on a wild goose chase. Or rather, a wild rabbit chase all over the countryside. That's the last time I'll ever do that, that's for sure!

OLIVIA: Excuse me, but your hair—

Sleeping Beauty, Roland Risse (b. 1835)

Practice the Skills

16 **Key Literary Element**

Stage Directions Write a stage direction giving Alice an action to do while she says this line.

ALICE: It's a mess, isn't it? Tell me about it! The way my afternoon went yesterday, I'm lucky I still have a head on my shoulders. It was bad enough eating those mushrooms and playing Trivial Pursuit about ravens and writing desks at the tea party, but when the Red Queen started shouting, "Off with her head!"—well, I had quite a busy day, as you can imagine. 17

OLIVIA: Then you've come to the right place for relaxation. Can I set you up with an appointment?

ALICE: Sure, that would be—(*Something offstage suddenly catches her eye.*) Oh! There he goes again!

OLIVIA (Puzzled): Who?

ALICE: That stupid rabbit. (*As she runs out*) He's got a lot of explaining to do! (*Phone rings. OLIVIA answers it.*) 18

OLIVIA: Fabulous Frills Salon. . . . What's that you say? . . . (*HILDA returns.*) . . . No, I'm afraid none of us here have any experience with managing snakes.

Practice the Skills

17 Key Literary Element

Stage Directions Pick two sentences in the speech that could use stage directions. Then, in your Learner's Notebook, write each of those sentences followed by a stage direction that you create for Alice.

18 Reviewing Skills

Evaluating You've probably seen a movie or cartoon of "Alice in Wonderland" or read the story. How does this Alice compare to the one you're familiar with? Does this Alice act the way you would expect? Explain your answer.

Alice in Wonderland is the next customer in the "Fabulous Frills Salon."

Tales of the Tangled Tresses

READING WORKSHOP 3

HILDA (*Puzzled*): Snakes?

OLIVIA (*Into phone*): Well, I'd recommend you look in the phone book under snake charmers. Maybe you can find someone to get them to settle down and behave themselves. (*Hangs up*)

HILDA: What was that all about?

OLIVIA: Mrs. Medusa. She said she woke up this morning with a head full of snakes.

HILDA (*Laughing*): More "coils" than she knew what to do with?

OLIVIA: She said her neighbors were so scared at the sight of her that they all turned to stone.

HILDA: Well, that's just "asping" for trouble.

OLIVIA: Not to mention "adderly"[6] ridiculous! (*They chuckle as GOLDILOCKS emerges from upstage wearing a wig of long, straight, black hair.*) **19**

GOLDILOCKS: You guys are just fantastic! Look at this! I love it! (*She starts to exit.*)

HILDA: Going so soon?

GOLDILOCKS: The porridge has probably cooled down by now. And in all that excitement of being chased by bears, I totally forgot about lunch! (*She exits. RAPUNZEL comes out next, sporting a sleek, modern style.*)

RAPUNZEL: Wow! I feel 50 pounds lighter already! Not to mention how much I'm going to save on shampoo.

HILDA: Can I offer you some coffee before you leave? You don't have to rush off so soon.

RAPUNZEL: Thanks, but no. I've got a date with this dreamy guy I met the other day while I was hanging my hair out the window to dry. Bye! (*She exits. CINDERELLA emerges next. She has her hair piled on top of her head in a very elegant style. In fact, she looks like she's ready to go to a ball.*) **20**

---

6. **Asps** and **adders** are types of poisonous snakes.

Practice the Skills

19 Reviewing Skills

Evaluating Several times during this play, Olivia has spoken to people (like Little Miss Muffet) on the phone. Although we never actually see or hear those people, we learn their stories through Olivia's half of the phone conversation. Do you like the way the author uses the telephone to introduce additional characters' stories? Why do you think the author doesn't have those characters come into the salon?

20 Key Reading Skill

Skimming and Scanning Will Briar Rose be happy with her haircut? Skim the next page to find out.

CINDERELLA: My fairy godmother was right. You two really do work miracles around here! (*She proceeds to exit, with both women calling after her.*)

OLIVIA: Don't forget about that wedding invitation!

HILDA: Don't forget to ask the prince if he has a brother! (*The last one to come out now is BRIAR ROSE, whose hairstyle is multi-color, spikey and really huge.*)

BRIAR ROSE: Well! What do you think of the new and improved me?

OLIVIA: Briar Rose! For a second I didn't even recognize you!

BRIAR ROSE: Pretty chic, huh?

OLIVIA: Think you'll become one of our regulars?

BRIAR ROSE: Sure, why not!

HILDA: Just don't wait another hundred years! (*Laughing, BRIAR ROSE exits.*)

OLIVIA: I can't believe they all left so fast.

HILDA: I guess they were just in a hurry to turn people's heads.

OLIVIA (*Contemplating the empty salon*): It sure got quiet all of a sudden.

HILDA: Maybe that's why they say what they do.

OLIVIA: And what's that?

HILDA: Hair today and gone tomorrow! (*They laugh; quick curtain*) **21**

THE END ○

Practice the Skills

21 **BIG Question**
Think about how Olivia and Hilda talk to each other and how they work together. Do you think they're close friends? Give two or three examples from the play to explain your answer. Write your answer on the "Tales of the Tangled Tresses" page of Foldable 8. Your response will help you complete the Unit Challenge later.

READING WORKSHOP 3 • Skimming and Scanning

After You Read

Tales of the Tangled Tresses

Answering the BIG Question

1. Hilda and Olivia work together every day in a small shop. What do you think two people have to do to build and keep a friendship when they're working closely together?

2. **Recall** Name two of the people who called Olivia on the telephone.
   TIP Right There

3. **Summarize** Summarize what Goldilocks wanted Hilda and Olivia to do and why she wanted them to do it.
   TIP Right There

Critical Thinking

4. **Evaluate** Do you think Hilda and Olivia should have helped Goldilocks to change her appearance? Give reasons to back up your answer.
   TIP On Your Own

5. **Infer** Why does Hilda say to Cinderella, "So this friend of yours—does he happen to have a brother?"
   TIP Author and Me

6. **Evaluate** Do Hilda and Olivia treat their customers better, as well as, or worse than most shopkeepers, barbers, and hairdressers? Explain your answer.
   TIP Author and Me

Write About Your Reading

Imagine that your favorite superhero or a character from a movie walks into the Fabulous Frills Salon with a big problem that only Hilda and Olivia can solve. Write some additional lines of dialogue for "Tales of the Tangled Tresses" that tell what happens.

For your dialogue:

- Make sure you identify who is speaking at the beginning of each speech.
- Make sure to have the characters explain the problem and how to solve it.
- Include at least one stage direction.

Objectives (pp. 1030–1031)
Reading Skim and scan text
Literature Understand elements of drama: stage directions
Vocabulary Identify jargon
Writing Write dialogue
Grammar Use punctuation correctly: colons with a list

Skills Review

Key Reading Skill: Skimming and Scanning

7. If you were asked to find and highlight all of the stage directions in this play, how would scanning help you?

Key Literary Element: Stage Directions

8. How does a playwright indicate which parts of a play are the stage directions?
9. Why are stage directions included in a play?

Vocabulary Check

For each sentence, choose the word that best fits in the blank.

tresses   frills   brunette   widower   fiasco

10. The ___ asked the hairdressers if they could lighten her hair enough to make it blond.
11. Joel's attempt to cut Martin's hair with nail scissors turned into a real ___.
12. Her long ___ were so beautiful that nobody could understand why she wanted to cut them.
13. He was a ___ for seven years before he decided to marry again.
14. My uncle saved a lot of money by buying a car that had now power windows or other ___.

English Language Coach Answer the questions below. Use a dictionary if necessary. (Some of the terms will be there.)

15. With what activity or profession is this jargon associated?

air ball   fake   pick   box out

16. With what activity or profession is this jargon associated?

virus   boot   laptop   crash

Grammar Link: Using a Colon to Introduce a List

A punctuation mark called a colon (:) is sometimes used to introduce a list of items that ends a sentence.

- Use a word or a phrase such as *these, the following,* or *as follows* somewhere in the sentence to introduce the list.

  The following five people came into the Fabulous Frills Salon: Goldilocks, Rapunzel, Cinderella, Briar Rose, and Alice.

- Do not use a colon immediately after a verb or preposition. Either leave the colon out or reword the sentence.

  Hilda enjoyed talking **to** *Alice, Rapunzel, and Briar Rose.*

  Goldilocks **made** *Papa Bear, Mama Bear, and Baby Bear very angry.*

Grammar Practice

Write each of the following sentences in your Learner's Notebook. Place a colon in a sentence if you think it is needed. Remove a colon from a sentence if it is used incorrectly. Write *correct* if the sentence does not need to be changed.

17. Please obey the following rules stay with your group, follow your guide, and take notes.
18. We saw the machines that manufactured: barbers' chairs, barber poles, and hair-cutting tools.
19. For his birthday, Jesse received these gifts: a football, a backpack, three books, and a shirt.
20. The shelves were full of: scissors, brushes, combs, and hair spray.

Web Activities For eFlashcards, Selection Quick Checks, and other Web activities, go to www.glencoe.com.

WRITING WORKSHOP PART 2

Speech
Revising, Editing, and Presenting

ASSIGNMENT Write a speech and present it in front of an audience

Purpose: To write a speech about a friend and why your friendship is special

Audience: You, your teacher, and classmates

Revising Rubric

Your revised speech should have

- clear description
- relevant stories or anecdotes
- three main parts: the beginning, the middle, and the end
- a presentation outline or note cards
- visual aids

Objectives (pp. 1032–1035)
Writing Revise for key elements, style, and word choice • Use transitions
Listening, Speaking, and Viewing Give a speech • Use visuals in presentation • Use appropriate expressions and gestures • Utilize note cards

In Writing Workshop Part 1, you drafted a speech about an important friendship. Now you will revise your work and prepare to present your speech in front of an audience.

Revising
Make It Better

Reread your draft. Keep in mind that everything you wrote you will have to say in front of an audience. You may need to rewrite some parts of your speech to make it easier for you to present and your audience to understand.

Try It Out

Quietly read your speech aloud. Underline sentences that you have difficulty reading. These are the parts you need to focus on revising. Consider the following tips:

- Use words and phrases that you feel comfortable saying.
- Delete extra sentences that do not apply to the topic of your speech.
- Use transition phrases when you move to a new thought. For example, "*Another* reason Christine is a good friend . . ."

Add a Visual

Visual aids are useful tools when giving a speech because they focus the audience's attention. Choose your visuals carefully. Too many visuals may confuse your audience or cause the audience to ignore your actual speech. Some visuals that can support your speech are

- photographs
- posters
- slides
- artwork
- handouts
- short videos

If you use a visual, it should support and add to your speech. Read over your draft. Try to think of pictures or objects that would help the audience visualize the things you describe in your speech.

WRITING WORKSHOP PART 2

Editing
Finish It Up

Read your speech again and use the Editing Checklist to help you spot errors. Use the proofreading symbols on page R19 to mark your corrections.

Editing Checklist
- ☑ Verbs and subjects agree and all verb tenses are correct.
- ☑ Pronouns refer clearly to their antecedents and agree with them in person, number, and gender.
- ☑ Punctuation is correct. (Especially apostrophes.)
- ☑ Capitalization and spelling are correct.

Presenting
Show It Off

Instead of turning a final draft in to your teacher, you will present your speech in front of an audience. Unless you choose to memorize your speech, you will probably need your written work in front of you when you present your speech. From the choices below, pick the format you feel most comfortable using. Rewrite your speech in the format you choose.

1. Full Text
Type, or neatly write, your entire speech on fresh paper. This format allows you to say everything that you planned to say because your whole speech will be right in front of you.

2. Partial Text
Type, or neatly write, the introduction and conclusion of your speech and type, or neatly write, only notes for the middle part. The notes should remind you of key points you want to cover. Using notes instead of a full text allows you more eye contact with the audience.

3. Note Cards
This format involves using index cards for notes. They are small and easy to organize and hold during a speech. You can easily write only the main points on the cards. Using only note cards allows for a great deal of eye contact with the audience. It also, often, results in a natural-sounding speech.

Writing Models For models and other writing activities, go to www.glencoe.com.

> **Writing Tip**
> **Presenting** The main advantage of using the full text is that all of your words are right in front of you. But don't read your speech word-for-word and forget about the audience! Practice pausing and making eye contact with audience members every few sentences.

> **Writing Tip**
> **Presenting** Number your note cards in the order they will be presented. If you happen to drop the cards during your speech, the numbers will help you to quickly put them back in order.

WRITING WORKSHOP PART 2

Writer's Model

The surprising opening sentence grabs the audience's attention.

> Even though Christine is my best friend, we fight nearly every day. Luckily, most of our fights take place at Kick Start, a martial arts studio in Mayfield. We've been taking karate lessons there since we were seven.

The writer includes outside opinions to strengthen her main idea.

The writer supports a main idea with an anecdote.

> Miko Sadako, one of our instructors at Kick Start, is always saying Christine is a fair fighter because she follows all the rules. Christine is a fair fighter in our friendship too. Even though she's a little taller and stronger than I am, she always flips a coin to see who throws the first punch when we practice together. We have most of our Friday night karate practice sleepovers at my house because I have my own room, and Christine has to share a room with her little sister. But she invites me to sleep over at her house whenever her sister goes to a slumber party.

The beginning phrase of this sentence, *I also*, creates a smooth transition from one topic to another.

> I also have loads of fun chatting with Christine on the phone every night. I can talk to her about anything because I know that if she disagrees with me, she'll explain her point of view without putting me down. If I do something that upsets Christine, she doesn't act cold or insult me or try to get even. Instead, she tells me exactly why she's angry and listens to what I have to say in my defense.

> Last year, when I hurt my right wrist in a tournament, Christine showed me she was always there for me, even when I wished she'd go away. I didn't want to do anything except sit around watching TV and feeling sorry for myself. But Christine came over every day and made sure I got my homework done. As soon as I was strong enough, she made me practice karate, too, using just my legs and left arm.

The writer includes one more example of Christine's fairness.

> She didn't take any advantage of the fact that I could strike and block with only one arm. And when I got overconfident and wanted to try blocking with my right arm too soon, she told me I'd better wait until my doctor said I was ready.

The writer ends the speech with a strong sentence that restates her purpose for speaking.

> When things go wrong, and when they go right, I can always count on Christine to be a fair fighter and a true friend.

Listening, Speaking, and Viewing

Oral Presentation

The final step of writing a speech is presenting it before an audience.

What Is an Oral Presentation?

An oral presentation is a speech, or report, that is usually presented by a single speaker. The speaker's main tool for sharing information is the spoken word.

Why Is It Important?

- Oral presentations allow speakers to share important information with many people, all at the same time.
- Oral presentations are a great way for listeners to learn about a new topic without having to do any research.

How Do I Give an Oral Presentation?

Once you write your speech, practice it as much as possible.

- Read the speech to yourself several times.
- Practice in front of a mirror. Pause between sentences and check for unnatural facial expressions or gestures.
- Record yourself reading the speech. As you listen to yourself, notice the parts where you sound awkward or dull. Work on these spots.
- Rehearse in front of your family and friends.

Before the Presentation

You've prepared and practiced; now you just need to relax. Take deep breaths and think about all the hard work you have put into your presentation. After all your hard work, you know more about your topic than anyone else in the room. Take deep breaths and remain confident!

Scan the Audience

Before you begin, take a moment to look at the audience. You created your presentation just for them. Keeping this in mind will help you stay confident.

During the Presentation

- Pause a moment after making an important point. This allows the audience to think about what you've said.
- Look around the room as you speak, and try to make eye contact with members of the audience.
- Speak loud enough to be heard in the last row of the audience.
- After you finish your prepared speech, thank the audience for their attention. You may also choose to ask the audience if there are any questions about the presentation.

Listen and Speak to Learn Use the guidelines above to present the speech you wrote in this workshop. As you listen to others' speeches, take notes about what makes a good friend.

READING WORKSHOP 4

Skills Focus

You will practice using these skills when you read the following selections:
- "Zlateh the Goat" p. 1040
- "Best of Buddies" p. 1052

Reading
- Predicting what will happen in a selection

Literature
- Understanding sensory imagery
- Understanding problem and solution

Vocabulary
- Understanding figurative meanings of words
- Identifying and understanding idioms

Writing/Grammar
- Using quotation marks

Objectives (pp. 1036–1037)
Reading Make predictions

Skill Lesson

Predicting

Learn It!

What Is It? As you learned in Unit 2, whenever you make a guess about what someone you know (or a character in a story or TV show or movie) will do next, you are **predicting**. When you predict, you make a good guess about what will happen next. Your guess is called a prediction.

- Predicting is a useful reading skill that helps you understand ideas as you read.
- When you predict, you think about what you already know about the topic, author, or characters. Then you use that information to help you guess what will happen later.

Analyzing Cartoons
What prediction does the boy's mom make? Do you think her prediction will be correct? Explain your answer.

BALDO © Baldo Partnership. Distributed By UNIVERSAL PRESS SYNDICATE. Reprinted with permission. All rights reserved.

READING WORKSHOP 4 • Predicting

Why Is It Important? Predicting helps you remember important ideas. Predicting also gives you a reason to read, and it makes reading more interesting.

How Do I Do It? As you read, use what you already know about the author or story to guess what you will learn or what might happen next. Make guesses about story events, characters, and outcomes. Make guesses before and during your reading. Don't worry about whether your original guess is accurate. In fact, many authors will lead you into making the wrong prediction on purpose! They do this because they want the story to contain a series of surprises. This makes the story more interesting and fun to read. So as you read, just change your predictions if they don't match the events. Here's one student's prediction after reading part of "The Bully of Barksdale Street." Is her prediction correct? Was yours when you read it?

Literature Online

Study Central Visit www.glencoe.com and click on Study Central to review predicting.

JOSH: How far is he?

BILLY: Thirty yards.

JOSH: Stand up.

BILLY (*Confused*): What are you—

JOSH: Stand up. I want you to do exactly what I tell you to do.

I think Josh has got a plan to distract the bully. Then he and Billy will be able to run away.

Practice It!

Read the paragraph below and make a prediction. What do you think will happen next? Write your prediction in your Learner's Notebook.

"Get in there, Chacha! You know you can make the team. I'll try out, too, but you know I don't have a shot. We've been playin' ball together for nine years, and I gotta tell you *this is your chance.* Someday I'll be sayin', 'I knew him when!'"

Use It!

As you read "Best of Buddies" and "Zlateh the Goat," predict what will happen next in the story. Record your predictions in your Learner's Notebook. Use the suggestions under **How Do I Do It?** to help you. After you have read the story, review your notes and see if your predictions were correct.

READING WORKSHOP 4 • Predicting

Before You Read: Zlateh the Goat

Meet the Author
Isaac Bashevis Singer was born in Poland in 1904. As a boy, he visited his grandfather's *shtetl,* or rural Jewish village. Village life later inspired much of his writing. Singer left Poland for New York City in 1935. There he began a long career as a journalist and writer.

Author Search For more about Isaac Bashevis Singer, go to www.glencoe.com

Objectives (pp. 1038–1047)
Reading Make predictions • Make connections from text to self
Literature Identify literary elements: sensory imagery • Understand problem and solution
Vocabulary Understand figurative meanings of words

Vocabulary Preview

dense (dens) *adj.* thick **(p. 1041)** *The snow was so dense that Aaron couldn't see where he was going.*

penetrated (PEN uh tray tid) *v.* passed into or through; form of the verb *penetrate* **(p. 1041)** *The icy cold wind penetrated Aaron's jacket.*

astray (uh STRAY) *adv.* off the right path or route **(p. 1043)** *Aaron realized that they'd gone astray when his boots touched the soft, plowed field.*

eddies (ED eez) *n.* circling currents of air, water, or snow **(p. 1043)** *The wind caused snow eddies in the fields where Aaron and Zlateh walked.*

contented (kun TEN tid) *adj.* happy, pleased, or satisfied with one's situation **(p. 1044)** *Zlateh was contented when she had hay to eat.*

chaos (KAY ahs) *n.* total confusion **(p. 1044)** *The blowing snow had created chaos outside the haystack.*

Partner Talk With a partner, take turns calling out a vocabulary word and having your partner give the definition.

English Language Coach

Literal and Figurative Meanings
You have already learned about figurative language, such as metaphors and similes. Single words can also have both **literal** and **figurative** meanings. If a figurative meaning is used often enough, it becomes part of the dictionary definition of a word.

Days of hard rain **flooded** the town. (Here, *flooded* means "covered with water.")

The new style of pants **flooded** the stores. (Here, *flooded* means "plentifully filled," like a flood of water would fill an area.)

If a word is used in a way that is unfamiliar to you, it often helps to think of its familiar meaning. That can be a clue to a figurative meaning.

Group Discussion With your group, discuss the meaning of each underlined word below. Remember, think about the word's most literal meaning and go from there.

1. Latreece tries to mirror Simone's behavior.
2. Their bad acting butchered the play.
3. Success on the track team helped Seth bloom in other areas.
4. Barry spent the whole day spreading the poisonous gossip.

1038 UNIT 8 What Makes a Friend?

READING WORKSHOP 4 • Predicting

Skills Preview

Key Reading Skill: Predicting

When you make a prediction, you use story clues and the knowledge you already have to guess what might happen next. As you read "Zlateh the Goat," pay attention to what the characters say and do. Use that information to help you make predictions. Record your predictions in your Learner's Notebook.

- What do you think will happen next?
- What will happen to Aaron and Zlateh?
- How do you think the story will end?
- After you have finished reading the story, go back and see if your predictions were correct.

Key Literary Element: Sensory Imagery

Sensory imagery is language that appeals to any of the reader's five senses. Authors use sensory imagery to bring a scene in a story to life. Good sensory imagery can help you see, hear, smell, feel, and even taste what is being described.

As you read, keep in mind your five senses. Pay attention to descriptions that help you understand

- how something *looks*
- how something *sounds*
- how something *smells*
- how something *feels*
- how something *tastes*

Example: The wind whipped Lara's hair across her face, and salty seawater stung her eyes. She gasped and flung out a hand to grip the railing of the wildly rocking boat.

This description provides a pretty good idea of what the scene looks like and what Lara is feeling.

Interactive Literary Elements Handbook
To review or learn more about literary elements, go to www.glencoe.com.

Get Ready to Read

Connect to the Reading

Have you ever felt alone and scared? Would it have helped if you'd had a friend to talk to? Read about how an unusual friendship helps Aaron through a bad time.

Partner Talk Share with a partner how an animal or favorite pet befriended you in a time of need.

Build Background

Hanukkah (or Chanukah) is an eight-day Jewish holiday that celebrates an event that took place thousands of years ago.

- Greeks had captured Palestine, where many Jews lived. They didn't let the Jewish people practice their religion. Instead the Greeks used the temple for worshipping Greek gods and goddesses.
- The Jews overthrew the Greeks and became independent once again. To rededicate their temple, they burned a *menorah*, or holder of oil-filled candles.
- They had enough oil for only one night, yet the candles burned for eight nights, long enough for them to prepare more oil.
- Today, the lighting of the candles is an important part of Hanukkah.

Set Purposes for Reading

BIG Question Read "Zlateh the Goat" to find out what makes a friend for Aaron and Zlateh.

Set Your Own Purpose What else would you like to learn from the story to help you answer the Big Question? Write your answer on the "Zlateh the Goat" page of Foldable 8.

Keep Moving

Use these skills as you read the following selection.

Zlateh the Goat **1039**

Zlateh the Goat

by Isaac Bashevis Singer
Translated by the author and Elizabeth Shuh

At Hanukkah time the road from the village to the town is usually covered with snow, but this year the winter had been a mild one. Hanukkah had almost come, yet little snow had fallen. The sun shone most of the time. The peasants complained that because of the dry weather there would be a poor harvest of winter grain. New grass sprouted, and the peasants[1] sent their cattle out to pasture.

For Reuven the furrier[2] it was a bad year, and after long hesitation he decided to sell Zlateh the goat. She was old and gave little milk. Feivel the town butcher had offered eight gulden[3] for her. Such a sum would buy Hanukkah candles, potatoes and oil for pancakes, gifts for the children, and other holiday necessaries for the house. Reuven told his oldest boy Aaron to take the goat to town. **1**

Aaron understood what taking the goat to Feivel meant, but had to obey his father. Leah, his mother, wiped the tears from her eyes when she heard the news. Aaron's younger sisters, Anna and Miriam, cried loudly. Aaron put on his quilted jacket and a cap with earmuffs, bound a rope around Zlateh's neck, and took along two slices of bread with cheese to eat on the road. Aaron was supposed to deliver the goat by evening, spend the night at the butcher's, and return the next day with the money. **2**

---

1. **Peasants** were poor farmers.
2. A **furrier** is someone who makes or sells fur clothing.
3. **Gulden** (GOOL den) is the name of gold or silver coins once used in many European countries.

Practice the Skills

1 **Key Reading Skill**
Predicting What do you think Feivel will do with Zlateh?

2 **BIG Question**
The author provides clues about how the family feels about Zlateh. In your Foldable, write how each family member reacts to Zlateh's leaving.

While the family said goodbye to the goat, and Aaron placed the rope around her neck, Zlateh stood as patiently and good-naturedly as ever. She licked Reuven's hand. She shook her small white beard. Zlateh trusted human beings. She knew that they always fed her and never did her any harm.

When Aaron brought her out on the road to town, she seemed somewhat astonished. She'd never been led in that direction before. She looked back at him questioningly, as if to say, "Where are you taking me?" But after a while she seemed to come to the conclusion that a goat shouldn't ask questions. Still, the road was different. They passed new fields, pastures, and huts with thatched[4] roofs. Here and there a dog barked and came running after them, but Aaron chased it away with his stick.

The sun was shining when Aaron left the village. Suddenly the weather changed. A large black cloud with a bluish center appeared in the east and spread itself rapidly over the sky. A cold wind blew in with it. The crows flew low, croaking. At first it looked as if it would rain, but instead it began to hail as in summer. It was early in the day, but it became dark as dusk. After a while the hail turned to snow.

In his twelve years Aaron had seen all kinds of weather, but he had never experienced a snow like this one. It was so **dense** it shut out the light of the day. In a short time their path was completely covered. The wind became as cold as ice. The road to town was narrow and winding. Aaron no longer knew where he was. He could not see through the snow. The cold soon **penetrated** his quilted jacket. 3

4. A *thatched* roof is made of thick grass or straw.

Vocabulary

dense (dens) *adj.* thick

penetrated (PEN uh tray tid) *v.* passed into or through

When the family said goodbye to the goat, and Aaron placed the rope around her neck, Zlateh stood as patiently and good-naturedly as ever.

Practice the Skills

3 **Key Literary Element**

Sensory Imagery In the last two paragraphs, which of your senses have been used? Do you *feel* the cold? Do you *hear* the crows? Do you *see* the clouds and snow?

READING WORKSHOP 4

Practice the Skills

When Aaron saw the huge haystack, he realized that he and Zlateh were saved from the blizzard. 4

4 **Key Reading Skill**

Predicting Do you think the huge haystack will save Aaron and Zlateh from the blizzard? Why or why not?

1042 UNIT 8 What Makes a Friend?

At first Zlateh didn't seem to mind the change in weather. She, too, was twelve years old and knew what winter meant. But when her legs sank deeper and deeper into the snow, she began to turn her head and look at Aaron in wonderment. Her mild eyes seemed to ask, "Why are we out in such a storm?" Aaron hoped that a peasant would come along with his cart, but no one passed by.

The snow grew thicker, falling to the ground in large, whirling flakes. Beneath it Aaron's boots touched the softness of a plowed field. He realized that he was no longer on the road. He had gone **astray**. He could no longer figure out which was east or west, which way was the village, the town. The wind whistled, howled, whirled the snow about in **eddies**. It looked as if white imps[5] were playing tag on the fields. A white dust rose above the ground. Zlateh stopped. She could walk no longer. Stubbornly she **anchored** her cleft hooves[6] in the earth and bleated as if pleading to be taken home. Icicles hung from her white beard, and her horns were glazed with frost. **5**

Aaron did not want to admit the danger, but he knew just the same that if they did not find shelter they would freeze to death. This was no ordinary storm. It was a mighty blizzard. The snowfall had reached his knees. His hands were numb, and he could no longer feel his toes. He choked when he breathed. His nose felt like wood, and he rubbed it with snow. Zlateh's bleating began to sound like crying. Those humans in whom she had so much confidence had dragged her into a trap. Aaron began to pray to God for himself and for the innocent animal.

Suddenly he made out the shape of a hill. He wondered what it could be. Who had piled snow into such a huge heap? He moved toward it, dragging Zlateh after him. When he came near it, he realized that it was a large haystack which the snow had blanketed. **6**

---

5. Here, **imps** are playful, fairylike spirits.
6. A **cleft** is a space or opening. Goats, sheep, cattle, and pigs all have **cleft** (split) hooves.

Vocabulary

astray (uh STRAY) *adv.* off the right path or route

eddies (ED eez) *n.* circling currents of air, water, or snow

READING WORKSHOP 4

Practice the Skills

5 **English Language Coach**

Literal and Figurative Meanings An *anchor* is a heavy metal object. Sailors throw it off a boat with a rope. Its weight keeps the boat in place. But what does the word **anchored** mean in this story? How does Zlateh *anchor* her hooves into the earth? Use the literal meaning of *anchor* as a clue.

6 **English Language Coach**

Literal and Figurative Meanings What does the word *blanket* mean to you? Is there a real blanket in this passage? How did the snow blanket the haystack?

READING WORKSHOP 4

Aaron realized immediately that they were saved. With great effort he dug his way through the snow. He was a village boy and knew what to do. When he reached the hay, he hollowed out a nest for himself and the goat. No matter how cold it may be outside, in the hay it is always warm. And hay was food for Zlateh. The moment she smelled it she became **contented** and began to eat. Outside, the snow continued to fall. It quickly covered the passageway Aaron had dug. But a boy and an animal need to breathe, and there was hardly any air in their hideout. Aaron bored a kind of a window through the hay and snow and carefully kept the passage clear.

Zlateh, having eaten her fill, sat down on her hind legs and seemed to have regained her confidence in man. Aaron ate his two slices of bread and cheese, but after the difficult journey he was still hungry. He looked at Zlateh and noticed her udders were full. He lay down next to her, placing himself so that when he milked her he could squirt the milk into his mouth. It was rich and sweet. Zlateh was not accustomed to being milked that way, but she did not resist. On the contrary, she seemed eager to reward Aaron for bringing her to a shelter whose very walls, floor, and ceiling were made of food.

Through the window Aaron could catch a glimpse of the **chaos** outside. The wind carried before it whole drifts of snow. It was completely dark, and he did not know whether night had already come or whether it was the darkness of the storm. Thank God that in the hay it was not cold. The dried hay, grass, and field flowers exuded[7] the warmth of the summer sun. Zlateh ate frequently; she nibbled from above, below, from the left and right. Her body gave forth an animal warmth, and Aaron cuddled up to her. He had always loved Zlateh, but now she was like a sister. He was alone, cut off from his family, and wanted to talk. He began to talk to Zlateh. "Zlateh, what do you think about what has happened to us?" he asked. 7

---

7. **Exuded** (ig ZOOD id) means gave off or oozed forth.

Vocabulary

contented (kun TEN tid) *adj.* happy, pleased, or satisfied with one's situation

chaos (KAY ahs) *n.* total confusion

Practice the Skills

7 Key Literary Element

Sensory Imagery In the last two paragraphs, the author has provided descriptions that appeal to all five senses. In your Learner's Notebook, write down the five senses and give an example of sensory imagery from the text for each.

1044 UNIT 8 What Makes a Friend?

READING WORKSHOP 4

"Maaaa," Zlateh answered.

"If we hadn't found this stack of hay, we would both be frozen stiff by now," Aaron said.

"Maaaa," was the goat's reply.

"If the snow keeps on falling like this, we may have to stay here for days," Aaron explained.

"Maaaa," Zlateh bleated.

"What does 'maaaa' mean?" Aaron asked. "You'd better speak up clearly."

"Maaaa, maaaa," Zlateh tried.

"Well, let it be 'maaaa' then," Aaron said patiently. "You can't speak, but I know you understand. I need you and you need me. Isn't that right?"

"Maaaa."

Aaron became sleepy. He made a pillow out of some hay, leaned his head on it, and dozed off. Zlateh, too, fell asleep.

When Aaron opened his eyes, he didn't know whether it was morning or night. The snow had blocked up his window. He tried to clear it, but when he had bored through to the length of his arm, he still hadn't reached the outside. Luckily he had his stick with him and was able to break through to the open air. It was still dark outside. The snow continued to fall and the wind wailed, first with one voice and then with many. Sometimes it had the sound of devilish laughter. Zlateh, too, awoke, and when Aaron greeted her, she answered, "Maaaa." Yes, Zlateh's language consisted of only one word, but it meant many things. Now she was saying, "We must accept all that God gives us—heat, cold, hunger, satisfaction, light, and darkness."

Aaron had awakened hungry. He had eaten up his food, but Zlateh had plenty of milk.

For three days Aaron and Zlateh stayed in the haystack. Aaron had always loved Zlateh, but in these three days he loved her more and more. She fed him with her milk and helped him keep warm. She comforted him with her patience. He told her many stories, and she always cocked her ears and listened. When he patted her, she licked his hand and his face. Then she said, "Maaaa," and he knew it meant, I love you, too. **8**

The snow fell for three days, though after the first day it was not as thick and the wind quieted down. Sometimes

Practice the Skills

8 **Key Reading Skill**

Predicting Reread this paragraph. What can you predict about the goat's fate?

Zlateh the Goat **1045**

Aaron felt that there could never have been a summer, that the snow had always fallen, ever since he could remember. He, Aaron, never had a father or mother or sisters. He was a snow child, born of the snow, and so was Zlateh. It was so quiet in the hay that his ears rang in the stillness. Aaron and Zlateh slept all night and a good part of the day. As for Aaron's dreams, they were all about warm weather. He dreamed of green fields, trees covered with blossoms, clear brooks, and singing birds. By the third night the snow had stopped, but Aaron did not dare to find his way home in the darkness. The sky became clear and the moon shone, casting silvery nets on the snow. Aaron dug his way out and looked at the world. It was all white, quiet, dreaming dreams of heavenly splendor. The stars were large and close. The moon swam in the sky as in a sea.

On the morning of the fourth day Aaron heard the ringing of sleigh bells. The haystack was not far from the road. The peasant who drove the sleigh pointed out the way to him—not to the town and Feivel the butcher, but home to the village. Aaron had decided in the haystack that he would never part with Zlateh. 9

Aaron's family and their neighbors had searched for the boy and the goat but had found no trace of them during the storm. They feared they were lost. Aaron's mother and sisters cried for him; his father remained silent and gloomy. Suddenly one of the neighbors came running to their house with the news that Aaron and Zlateh were coming up the road.

For three days Aaron and Zlateh stayed in the haystack.

Practice the Skills

9 **Key Reading Skill**

Predicting How do you think Aaron's father will react when he finds out about Aaron's decision to never leave Zlateh?

There was great joy in the family. Aaron told them how he had found the stack of hay and how Zlateh had fed him with her milk. Aaron's sisters kissed and hugged Zlateh and gave her a special treat of chopped carrots and potato peels, which Zlateh gobbled up hungrily.

Visual Vocabulary
Similar to spinning a top, the *dreidel* is a toy used in a game played during Hanukkah.

Nobody ever again thought of selling Zlateh, and now that the cold weather had finally set in, the villagers needed the services of Reuven the furrier once more. When Hanukkah came, Aaron's mother was able to fry pancakes every evening, and Zlateh got her portion, too. Even though Zlateh had her own pen, she often came to the kitchen, knocking on the door with her horns to indicate that she was ready to visit, and she was always admitted. In the evening Aaron, Miriam, and Anna played dreidel. Zlateh sat near the stove watching the children and the flickering of the Hanukkah candles.

Once in a while Aaron would ask her, "Zlateh, do you remember the three days we spent together?"

And Zlateh would scratch her neck with a horn, shake her white bearded head, and come out with the single sound which expressed all her thoughts, and all her love. **10**

10 BIG Question
In the last paragraphs of the story, what do you learn about what makes a friend? Write your answer on the "Zlateh the Goat" page of Foldable 8. Your answer will help you complete the Unit Challenge later.

After You Read : Zlateh the Goat

Answering the BIG Question

1. What qualities of friendship are present in Aaron and Zlateh's relationship?
2. **Recall** How do Aaron's mother and sister react when his father tells him to take the goat to Feivel?
   TIP Right There
3. **Summarize** What happens to Aaron and Zlateh on their way to town?
   TIP Think and Search

Critical Thinking

4. **Compare** When he hears that he must take Zlateh to Feivel, how does Aaron's reaction differ from that of his sisters and mother? Why do you think he reacts this way?
   TIP Think and Search
5. **Analyze** Do you think Zlateh is really thinking or saying all the things the author says she is? Why or why not?
   TIP Author and Me
6. **Evaluate** In the beginning of the story, the family needs to sell Zlateh for money. In the end, do you think the family's decision to keep Zlateh instead is a wise one? Why or why not?
   TIP On My Own
7. **Connect** Which person or animal can you count on as a friend if you need help?
   TIP On My Own

Write About Your Reading

Pretend that you are Aaron. A week after your return, your father has decided, once again, to sell Zlateh to Feivel the butcher. Write a letter to your father asking him to keep Zlateh. Explain why the goat should not be sold. Use events from the story to help support your argument.

When you have finished, proofread your letter. Try to examine your writing as though you were reading it for the first time. Check for errors in spelling, grammar, and punctuation.

Objectives (pp. 1048–1049)
Reading Make predictions • Make connections from text to self
Literature Understand sensory imagery
Vocabulary Understand figurative meanings of words
Writing Respond to literature: letter
Grammar Use punctuation correctly: quotation marks

Skills Review

Key Reading Skill: Predicting

8. What change in the setting helps the reader to predict that Aaron and Zlateh will find themselves in trouble?

Key Literary Element: Sensory Imagery

9. What sensory imagery in the story affected you the most? Explain your answer.

10. To which sense does this description appeal?

"His hands were numb, and he could no longer feel his toes. He choked when he breathed. His nose felt like wood, and he rubbed it with snow."

Vocabulary Check

Choose the best answer for each question.

11. A **contented** person would be most likely to
   a. whine.   **b.** smile.   **c.** yell.

12. To keep from going **astray**, people use
   a. maps.   **b.** diets.   **c.** medicine.

13. There is most likely to be **chaos** during a
   a. play.   **b.** riot.   **c.** funeral.

14. Water moves in **eddies** when it is
   a. falling as rain.
   b. shooting up in fountains.
   c. being drained out of tubs and sinks.

English Language Coach

In each sentence below, decide whether the underlined word is used figuratively or literally.

15. a. The <u>dense</u> cloud of smoke drove the firefighters out of the building.
   b. Habib is so <u>dense</u> that he can't even answer a simple question.

16. a. His words <u>penetrated</u> me deeply.
   b. The smell <u>penetrated</u> the room.

Grammar Link: Quotation Marks

When an author provides the exact words of a speaker, he or she is using a **quotation.** Quotations are easy to spot because **quotation marks** appear at the beginning and end of the speaker's statement.

There are rules for quotations—for both punctuation and capitalization. The following tips will be helpful as you write quotations.

- Use quotation marks before and after the speaker's exact words. Example: "I feel fine," said Joshua.
- When the quotation is a complete sentence, always capitalize the first letter of the first word. Example: "**H**e's my friend," she said.
- If a quoted sentence is interrupted to identify the speaker, do *not* capitalize the first word of the second part of the sentence. Example: "She was," explained Kathy, "**a** great teacher."

Grammar Practice

Read each pair of sentences. Write the letter of the one that uses quotation marks correctly and has correct punctuation and capitalization.

17. a. Aaron would ask her, Zlateh, do you remember the three days we spent together?"
   b. Aaron would ask her, "Zlateh, do you remember the three days we spent together?"

18. a. "Take Zlateh to Feivel the butcher," said Reuven.
   b. "take Zlateh to Feivel the butcher," said Reuven.

19. a. "If we hadn't found this stack of hay," Aaron said, "We would be frozen stiff by now."
   b. "If we hadn't found this stack of hay," Aaron said, "we would be frozen stiff by now."

Writing Application Look back at your Write About Your Reading assignment for this selection. Add two quotations to your letter. Follow the rules above to help you.

Zlateh the Goat **1049**

READING WORKSHOP 4 • Predicting

Before You Read : Best of Buddies

Author Search For information about Kevin Gray and Cindy Dampier, go to www.glencoe.com.

Vocabulary Preview

integrate (IN tuh grayt) *v.* to bring together or make something part of a whole **(p. 1052)** *Anthony was able to integrate his friend into his life.*

routine (roo TEEN) *n.* a regular way of doing something **(p. 1052)** *Shriver hoped that people could add new friends without a big change in their routine.*

professional (proh FESH uh nul) *adj.* relating to a lifelong occupation or career **(p. 1053)** *Shriver's organization trains people for professional jobs.*

develop (dih VEL up) *v.* to get or bring about little by little over a period of time **(p. 1053)** *People need to develop skills before they can get good jobs.*

isolated (EYE suh lay tid) *v.* to be set or kept away from others **(p. 1053)** *Mentally challenged people are often isolated.*

addresses (uh DRES uz) *v.* deals with or pays attention to; form of the verb *address* **(p. 1053)** *Shriver has made sure that his organization addresses many needs of people with mental disabilities.*

Partner Talk With a partner, take turns calling out a vocabulary word and having your partner give the definition.

English Language Coach

Idioms When people talk with each other, they often use **idioms.** An idiom is a phrase that has a special meaning that is different from the actual meaning of the phrase. For example, if something is very easy, we often say it's "a piece of cake." Of course, the task itself is not really a slice of cake. The saying is just used to express that something is simple to do. Take a look at the following idiom and its actual meanings.

Idiom	Actual meaning	Special meaning of idiom
spill the beans	to drop beans on the floor	to reveal a secret

Group Talk With a small group, think of three more idioms. Discuss what each idiom means. Record the idiom, the actual meaning, and the special meaning of each idiom in your Learner's Notebook.

Objectives (pp. 1050–1053)
Reading Make predictions • Make connections from text to self
Informational text Identify problem and solution
Vocabulary Identify and understand idioms

READING WORKSHOP 4 • Predicting

Skills Preview

Key Reading Skill: Predicting

As you read "Best of Buddies," look for clues that will help you predict, or figure out, what may happen next. As you gather more information you might want to change your predictions, and that's a big part of predicting. As you read, ask yourself:

- *What* will I learn from this article?
- *What* will happen next?
- *Why* do I think that will happen next?

Write to Learn Use your Learner's Notebook to record your predictions.

Literary Element: Problem and Solution

Many informational texts are about **problems and solutions**. It is important to be able to recognize them when you read. In order to do so, ask yourself the following questions:

Find the Problem
- Is something going wrong?
- Is something bad happening?
- Is there a conflict?

Find the Solution
- Who cares about the problem?
- Are they taking action?
- What action are they taking?
- Is it working?

Get Ready to Read

Connect to the Reading

How do you choose a friend? Have any of your friendships started with an offer of help? Read about someone who values friendships so much that he started an entire organization to arrange them!

Think-Pair-Share With a partner, make a list of qualities you look for in a friend. Then answer the following question: How can you tell if a person is a true friend? Discuss your answer with your partner.

Build Background

The Americans with Disabilities Act of 1990 (ADA) made it illegal for employers to discriminate against people with mental disabilities.

- According to the ADA, a mental disability is one that keeps someone from taking part in one or more of the main activities of life.
- Some learning disabilities—for example, those that keep someone from being able to read and understand—are also covered by the ADA.

Set Purposes for Reading

BIG Question Read "Best of Buddies." When you are finished, use the selection to help you think about what makes a friend.

Set Your Own Purpose What else would you like to learn from the selection to help you answer the Big Question? Write your own purpose on the "Best of Buddies" page of Foldable 8.

Interactive Literary Elements Handbook To review or learn more about literary elements, go to www.glencoe.com.

Keep Moving

Use these skills as you read the following selections.

READING WORKSHOP 4

TIME

Best of BUDDIES

Anthony Shriver's program for the mentally disabled encourages people to stop staring and start sharing.

By KEVIN GRAY and CINDY DAMPIER

Shriver teams up with buddy Jorge Mentado (left).

Anthony Kennedy Shriver[1] is thinking about the day in 1994 when he and Jorge Mentado,[2] 39, went shopping together. Shriver and Mentado, who is mentally challenged, are good friends. "You'd think World War III[3] had broken out," says Shriver, with a chuckle. "Jorge is very hard to understand. He had on big boots with the laces untied. In [one shop], he'd say hello to every pretty girl and talk to the salespeople. One woman came in with a little dog, and Jorge started petting it. It was like a movie. People need to see that sort of thing."

Shriver is founder and president of Best Buddies. The main goal of Best Buddies is to better the lives of people with mental disabilities. The program helps them to make new friends and to find jobs. Another goal "is to make it so people won't stare," says Shriver. "So, when you go downtown or into a church, they're used to having people with mental disabilities in there." **1**

Shriver came up with the idea in 1987 while he was a student at Georgetown University. "I saw a lot of my buddies not doing a whole heck of a lot in the community," he says. "I figured it wouldn't take a huge effort for them to **integrate** someone into their daily **routine**." Fifty volunteers came to Shriver's first Best

1 **Literary Element**

Problem and Solution What is one problem identified so far in this article? What is the solution?

---

1. **Shriver** (SHREYE vur)
2. **Jorge Mentado** (HOHR hay mayn TAH doh)
3. **World War III** is a name people use for the next global war. World Wars I and II took place in the twentieth century.

Vocabulary

integrate (IN tuh grayt) *v.* to bring together or make something part of a whole

routine (roo TEEN) *n.* a regular way of doing something

Buddies meeting. He paired them with people from group homes[4] and special schools. After Shriver graduated, interest in the project continued. He received calls from students who wanted to start branches of Best Buddies at other colleges.

"I thought I'd just take a couple of months to get this going at a couple of other colleges. I never stopped," recalls Shriver. **2**

Since then, Best Buddies has grown to include more than 6,500 "buddies." Today, Best Buddies International Inc. has branches in all 50 states and in more than 12 countries. There are even branches in middle schools and high schools and in corporations and churches. Best Buddies Jobs trains the mentally challenged so they can get **professional** jobs, not just jobs bagging groceries. Shriver believes everyone has a special talent. "It's up to us," he says, "to create opportunities for these individuals to **develop** and share their skills."

Best Buddies helps people to realize what they have in common, instead of focusing on differences. In schools, students are paired with kids in special education. These friends meet weekly to have lunch, shop, go to an event, or just hang out and talk. **3**

Judy Hales of Miami, whose mentally challenged son David, 12, has a buddy, calls the program a roaring success. "The first time David went out," she says, "our family all said, 'Where's David?' because he never got to go out without one of us." George Zitnay, an expert on mental disabilities, says getting people like David into the community is a great idea. "People with mental disabilities have been **isolated** for too long," says Zitnay. "Best Buddies **addresses** the need for valued friendship."

Shriver's hope is that one day Best Buddies will no longer be needed. "Hopefully, people will just start having these friendships naturally," he says. Until then, Best Buddies will continue educating students, employers, and communities about the needs and abilities of people with mental disabilities. **4**

—Updated 2005, from *PEOPLE*, February 27, 1995

---

4. **Group homes** give mentally disabled people an opportunity to live away from family and still be within a group setting. Many times, group homes help people learn life skills, such as cooking and cleaning.

Vocabulary

professional (proh FESH uh nul) *adj.* relating to a lifelong occupation or career

develop (dih VEL up) *v.* to get or bring about little by little over a period of time

isolated (EYE suh lay tid) *v.* to be set or kept away from others

addresses (uh DRES uz) *v.* deals with or pays attention to

READING WORKSHOP 4

2 Key Reading Skill

Predicting Do you think the Best Buddies program will start branches in places other than colleges? Explain why. Write your prediction and your explanation in your Learner's Notebook.

3 English Language Coach

Idioms People in the Best Buddies program sometimes "hang out." What is the actual meaning of *hang out*? What is the special meaning of the idiom? Record your answer in your Learner's Notebook.

4 BIG Question

What can people learn about being a friend from the Best Buddies program? Write your answer on the "Best of Buddies" page of Foldable 8. Your answer willl help you complete the Unit Challenge later.

READING WORKSHOP 4 • Predicting

After You Read : Best of Buddies

Answering the BIG Question

1. Who does Anthony Kennedy Shriver consider a good friend? What makes this person a good friend?
2. **Recall** When did Shriver start Best Buddies?
   TIP Right There
3. **Summarize** What does Best Buddies do?
   TIP Think and Search

Critical Thinking

4. **Infer** How might Shriver's friendship with Mentado make him feel? How might the friendship make Mentado feel?
   TIP Think and Search
5. **Draw Conclusions** What can you tell about Shriver from his words?
   TIP Think and Search
6. **Evaluate** Is the Best Buddies program a good idea? Support your opinion with details from the article.
   TIP Author and Me

Talk About Your Reading

Discuss the article with a partner. Share your thoughts about Best Buddies and Shriver's efforts. What do you think about the program? What are some of the advantages of being a "buddy?" Tell why you think you and your partner should or should not participate in the program. Use a chart like the one below to help organize your thoughts.

Best Buddies	
What I think about the program	
Advantages of being a "buddy"	
Why we should (or shouldn't) participate in Best Buddies	

Objectives (pp. 1054–1055)
Reading Make predictions • Make connections from text to self
Informational text Identify problem and solution
Vocabulary Identify and understand idioms
Grammar Use punctuation correctly: quotation marks

READING WORKSHOP 4 • Predicting

Skills Review

Key Reading Skill: Predicting

Authors give clues to help readers guess what will happen next in a selection. Answer the following to see how Kevin Gray and Cindy Dampier provided information to help you make predictions.

7. Which words help you predict that Shriver's friends will get involved?
8. In paragraph 3, what information helps you predict the growth of Best Buddies International Inc.?

Literary Element: Problem and Solution

9. Summarize the problem introduced in this article.
10. Summarize Shriver's solution.

Vocabulary Check

11. Which word means *to get or bring about little by little*?
    integrate   routine   develop
12. Which word means *to bring together or make something part of a whole*?
    develop   integrate   isolated
13. Which word completes this sentence? *Going to the gym every day is a part of my dad's daily ___.*
    professional   routine   addresses
14. Answer *true* or *false* to this statement: To **isolate** a person is to keep the person far away from others.
15. **English Language Coach** Using idioms can be fun. What are some other reasons why people use idioms?

Grammar Link: Quotation Marks

Quotation marks are used around a speaker's exact words. These tips will help you use them correctly.

- Use quotation marks before and after a direct quotation. Example: "I'm hungry," said Ed.
- Use quotation marks only if the speaker's exact words are used. Example: Ed said he was hungry.
- If the speaker is identified at the beginning, put a comma after the identification. Put a period at the very end, inside the end quotation mark. Example: Lena said, "I'm not going."
- If the speaker is identified at the end, put a comma after what was said and put the period after the identification. Example: "Sure," replied Tom.
- When a quoted sentence is interrupted to identify the speaker, place quotation marks around both parts. Place a comma directly after the last word in the first part. Also place a comma at the end of the interruption. Example: "Well," said Murray, "I don't think that's a good idea."
- When a quotation ends with a question mark or exclamation point, place the question mark or exclamation point inside the end quotation mark. Examples: "What do you want for breakfast?" asked Dad. "Pancakes!" replied Susan.

Grammar Practice

Rewrite each of the following sentences. Add quotation marks and the correct punctuation.

16. Tito shouted Look out
17. I don't think said Ana that we should go.
18. Is that your bike asked Wesley.

Web Activities For eFlashcards, Selection Quick Checks, and other Web activities, go to www.glencoe.com.

Best of Buddies **1055**

READING ACROSS TEXTS WORKSHOP

Baby Hippo Orphan Finds a Friend
by Catherine Clarke Fox

& from The Caretaker's DIARY
by Stephen Tuei

Skill Focus
You will use these skills as you read and compare the following selections:
- "Baby Hippo Orphan Finds a Friend," p. 1059
- from *The Caretaker's Diary,* p. 1063

Reading
- Making connections across texts
- Comparing/contrasting information in different texts
- Analyzing multiple points of view of a real-world situation

Literature
- Reading and understanding informative text
- Reading primary source documents

Objectives (pp. 1056–1057)
Reading Compare and contrast: primary and secondary sources

Suppose you wanted to find out whether your favorite team won a championship game. Would you check the news or would you try to find one of the player's diaries? Well, if you're like most people, you'd probably check the news. But what if you wanted to know how it felt to be part of the team? You'd get a clearer picture by reading the journal or diary of one of the team members.

How to Read Across Texts

A **primary source** is a piece of writing by a person who took part in an event or witnessed it. Letters, diaries, speeches, interviews, and autobiographies are all primary sources. Primary sources are most often written from the first-person point of view.

A **secondary source** is written after the events it describes. History books, biographies, and many magazine articles are secondary sources. The writer may *use* primary sources (such as interviews) to get information, but the writer didn't take part in the events being described. He or she didn't experience the events or witness them. Secondary sources are most often written from the third-person point of view.

In this workshop, you'll read a diary (primary source) and a Web site article (secondary source) about an unlikely friendship. As you read, think about what information you get from each selection and how it fits together to give you a complete picture.

READING ACROSS TEXTS WORKSHOP

Get Ready to Compare

Diaries, letters, and other primary sources are often written from the first-person point of view. They include words like "I and "we" because the writers are talking about their own experiences and feelings. A diary tells you what a person did and experienced and how he or she felt.

Secondary sources are generally written from the third-person point of view. They include words like "he," "she," and "they" instead of "I" or "we" because the writers didn't experience the events. Secondary sources gather information from primary sources and then summarize the most important points.

Sometimes it's interesting to read both a primary source and a secondary source to find out about a topic. From the primary source, you can find out how it felt to be a person involved in a news story. You can also get a detailed personal description of what happened. From the secondary source, you can find out background information, and sometimes you can get information that was collected from a lot of different people.

As you read each of these selections, use a chart like the one below to keep track of the types of information you get from each source. In the left column, list each major event in the selection. Next, list a few facts the writer gives (if any). Does the writer include his or her feelings and opinions about the event? If so, fill those in under "Feelings and Opinions." Does the writer include details? Give a few examples of those details. (Remember, details can be facts, feelings, or opinions, so you can repeat those on your chart.)

Selection: *(put the title here)*
Point of View: *(put the point of view here)*

Events and Facts	Feelings & Opinions	Details

Use Your Comparison

After you have read the selections and completed your charts, look back over them to see what types of information came from each type of selection.

READING ACROSS TEXTS WORKSHOP

Before You Read

Baby Hippo Orphan Finds a Friend

Meet the Author
"Writing is like getting paid to learn about the world. The sky's the limit," says author Catherine Clarke Fox. Fox launched her career in publishing when she joined the staff of *National Geographic* magazine. Since then, she's written for newspapers, magazines, webzines, atlases, and encyclopedias. The mother of an eleven-year-old son and a fourteen-year-old daughter, Fox balances her love of gardening, cycling, hiking, and fishing with her passion for writing.

Author Search For more about Catherine Clarke Fox, go to www.glencoe.com.

Objectives (pp. 1058–1061)
Reading Compare and contrast: primary and secondary sources

Vocabulary Preview

tsunami (tsoo NAH mee) *n.* a huge ocean wave that is caused by an underwater earthquake, volcano, or landslide **(p. 1060)** *The tsunami caused flooding and destruction in Asia and East Africa.*

surf (surf) *n.* breaking waves and foam near the shore of an ocean, lake, or river **(p. 1060)** *Trees and litter floated in the surf by the beach.*

sanctuary (SANK choo wair ee) *n.* a safe and protected place **(p. 1060)** *Since the park is a sanctuary for animals, it forbids hunting.*

tortoise (TOR tus) *n.* a large turtle that lives on land **(p. 1060)** *A tortoise can live to be more than 100 years old.*

Get Ready to Read

Connect to the Reading
Have you ever seen two different kinds of pets become friends? Does it surprise you that animals of two different kinds can become friends and help each other? What do you think can cause two animals of different species to become friends?

Build Background
On December 26, 2004, an undersea earthquake caused an enormous tsunami to strike parts of Asia and Africa. The earthquake and tsunami killed more than 250,000 people and countless animals. Many people and animals were left homeless.

- Hippopotamuses are social animals by nature and like to stay with their mothers for the first four years of their lives.
- Tortoises can live to be well over 100 years old.
- Mombasa, Kenya, is a large city on the coast of the Indian Ocean. Almost 2,000 years old, it is Kenya's only large port.

Set Purposes for Reading
BIG Question Read "Baby Hippo Orphan Finds a Friend" to find out about an unusual friendship between a hippopotamus and a tortoise.

Set Your Own Purpose What else would you like to find out about the unusual friendship between these two animals? Write your own purpose on the "Baby Hippo" page of Foldable 8.

1058 UNIT 8 What Makes a Friend?

Baby Hippo Orphan Finds a Friend

by Catherine Clarke Fox

READING ACROSS TEXTS WORKSHOP

INFORMATIONAL TEXT
WEB SITE

nationalgeographic.com

Have you noticed that sometimes the most unlikely pairs form the best friendships? Late last December [2004], flood waters in the East African country of Kenya swept a herd of hippopotamuses down the Sabaki River[1] and into the Indian Ocean (see map). After a few days, most of them struggled to shore and returned inland. 🔟

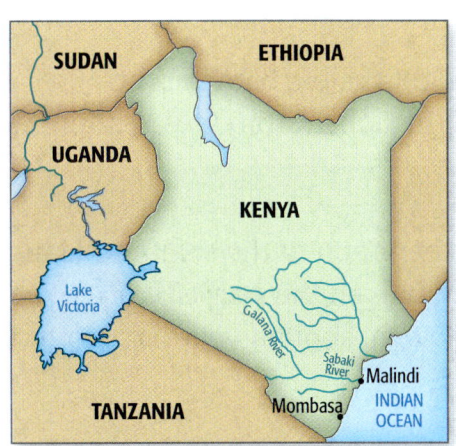

Analyzing the Map Find the place where the Sabaki River meets the Indian Ocean. What city name do you see there?

Practice the Skills

🔟 **Reading Across Texts**

Primary and Secondary Sources What events and facts does the writer provide? (Graphics, such as maps, count!) Fill these in on your chart.

---

1. The **Sabaki River** is the second largest river in Kenya.

READING ACROSS TEXTS WORKSHOP

Hippos live in and around fresh water.

Then, right after the Asian **tsunami** hit on December 26, local people spotted a baby hippo in the rough **surf**, apparently left behind by the herd. They were worried. 2

Hippos live around fresh water, and the people figured the salt water wasn't good for the little fellow. Besides, he had no mother to look out for him.

After hours of effort, they caught the big baby (about 600 pounds, or 270 kilograms). They named him Owen after one of his rescuers. 3

Wildlife officials took Owen the hippo to the safety of Haller Park, a **sanctuary** for wild animals in the port city of Mombasa. To their surprise, Owen, about a year old, trotted right up to a giant gray **tortoise**. 3

Vocabulary

tsunami (tsoo NAH mee) *n.* a huge ocean wave that is caused by an underwater earthquake, volcano, or landslide

surf (surf) *n.* breaking waves and foam near the shore of an ocean, lake, or river

sanctuary (SANK choo wair ee) *n.* a safe and protected place

tortoise (TOR tus) *n.* a large turtle that lives on land

Practice the Skills

2 Reading Across Texts

Primary and Secondary Sources How can you tell that the writer did not participate in the events she is describing? (That means the article must be a secondary source.) This clue also tells you the point of view of the article. Fill in the "Point of View" above your chart.

3 Reading Across Texts

Primary and Secondary Sources What new event(s) have occurred? What facts, feelings, opinions, and details (if any) has the writer included? Use your answers to fill in your chart.

READING ACROSS TEXTS WORKSHOP

Tortoises are among the longest-living creatures on Earth. This one's name is Mzee, which means "old man" in the Swahili language. He is more than a hundred years old.

"Mzee hissed, lifted himself up off the ground, and tried to run," reported Paula Kahumbu, an ecologist in charge of Haller Park. (Ecologists study how living things relate to their surroundings.) "But by the next morning, they were together!"

They have been together ever since, even staying close and touching when they sleep.

Owen could weigh more than 6,000 pounds (2,700 kilograms) when he is grown—heavier than a minivan. Eventually he will be introduced to Cleo, an adult hippo, so he can be with his own kind.

But Kahumbu said Owen and Mzee will still spend time together if they wish. To find out what happens next, check out the caretaker's diary at the Lafarge Eco Systems Web site. 4 5 ○

Analyzing the Photo Would you say that Owen and Mzee seem to be friends in this picture? Explain your answer.

Practice the Skills

4 Reading Across Texts

Primary and Secondary Sources Add to your chart all the events included in the last few paragraphs. Add any facts, opinions, or details the author includes.

5 BIG Question

Why do you think Owen befriended Mzee so quickly? What makes Owen and Mzee such good friends? Write your answer on the "Baby Hippo" page of Foldable 8. Your response will help you complete the Unit Challenge later.

Baby Hippo Orphan Finds a Friend

READING ACROSS TEXTS WORKSHOP

Before You Read

from The Caretaker's DIARY

Meet the Author
As caretaker of animals at Haller Park in Kenya, Stephen Tuei makes sure that all animals are fed and cared for properly. He has raised and bottle-fed many different kinds of animals from infancy, including antelopes and hippopotamuses. His day begins by 7:00 A.M., when he takes the antelope out to grazing areas and continues past 8:00 P.M., when he feeds the owls and other night-loving animals. Tuei is often accompanied on his rounds by his eleven-year-old son Kibet.

Author Search For more about Stephen Tuei, go to www.glencoe.com.

Objectives (pp. 1062–1069)
Reading Compare and contrast: primary and secondary sources
Writing Compare and contrast: sources of information

Vocabulary Preview

convoy (KON voy) *n.* a group of cars, trucks, or other vehicles traveling together **(p. 1063)** *I saw a convoy of trucks traveling down the road.*

subdued (sub DOOD) *adj.* quiet, weak, under control **(p. 1064)** *The cat looked subdued after it came back into the house.*

traumatized (TROM uh tyzd) *adj.* upset or injured as a result of a frightening event **(p. 1064)** *Fireworks made the puppy feel traumatized.*

enclosure (en KLOH zhur) *n.* a fenced-in or walled-in place **(p. 1065)** *We built an enclosure in the yard for the dogs.*

hissed (hisd) *v.* made a sound like air escaping from a balloon; form of the verb *hiss* **(p. 1066)** *Her cat hissed when the dog walked by.*

Get Ready to Read

Connect to the Reading
Have you ever become friends with someone who is very different from you? What caused you to become friends?

Build Background
- This selection includes parts of a diary that has been kept since Owen and Mzee were first brought together.
- The diary was originally published on a Web site. New entries were put on the Web site as they were written. Thousands of people have read the diary since it was first published.
- There have been many instances of unusual animal friendships. In 2002, a lioness in Samburu National Park in Africa tried to adopt and care for several baby antelopes. Lions normally hunt antelope for food.

Set Purposes for Reading
BIG Question Read from "The Caretaker's Diary" to find out how the friendship between Owen and Mzee developed and changed.

Set Your Own Purpose What else would you like to find about the friendship of these unlikely buddies? Write your own purpose on the "Caretaker's Diary" page of Foldable 8.

READING ACROSS TEXTS WORKSHOP

INFORMATIONAL TEXT
WEB SITE

lafargeecosystems.com

from The Caretaker's DIARY

by Stephen Tuei

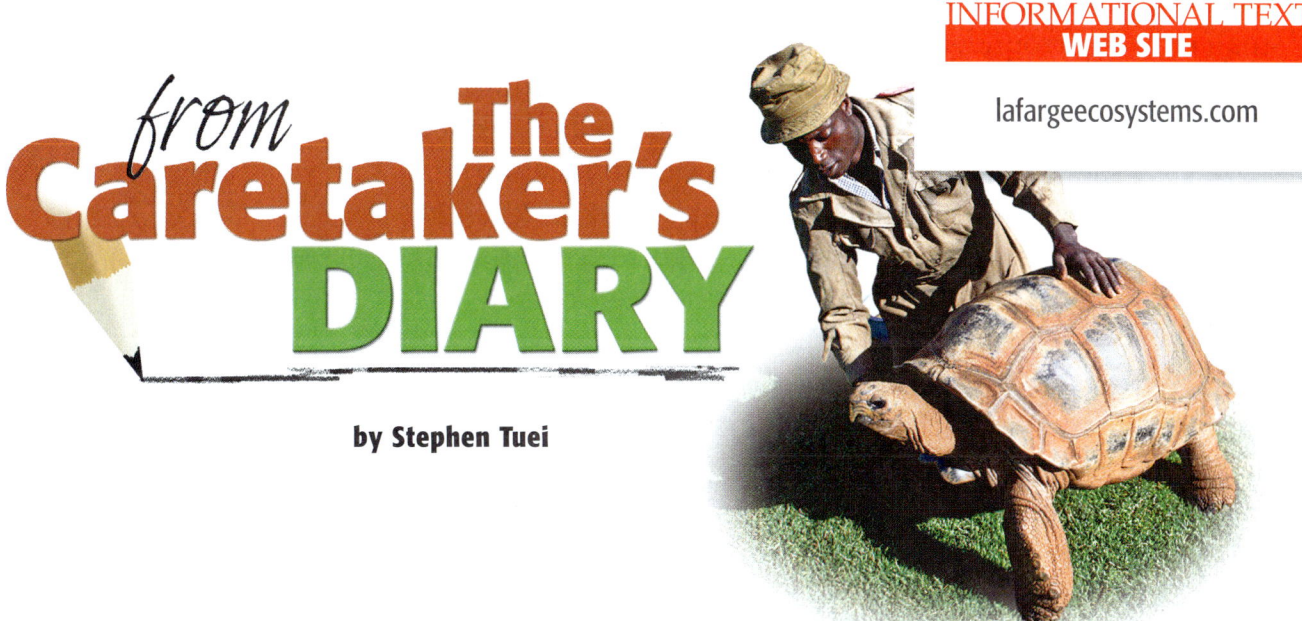

27th December, 2004

Today is a day that I will never forget. I was at the hospital getting treatment when my phone rang. Only my boss Sabine Baer would call me during the holiday. I knew it must be important.

"Stephen, we have to rescue a baby hippo, can you come?"

I didn't hesitate "Yes" I said. "It will take me twenty minutes to get to the office from the hospital." **1**

"But you have malaria,[1] perhaps you should rest?"

"No, the malaria has gone." It was a half lie, my head was sore but I would not give up on a baby hippo for anything. **2**

I rode my motorbike back as fast as I possibly could safely. Paula, the General Manager, she was waiting with two other people who would also help with bringing the baby back. Sabine would work as fast as possible with another team to prepare the baby's home.

We contacted Dr. Kashmiri, a local wildlife veterinarian who joined us and we drove in **convoy**. It took us two long hours to drive to Malindi, a small coastal town north of Mombasa.

---

1. **Malaria** is a serious disease caused by the bite by an infected mosquito.

Vocabulary

convoy (KON voy) *n.* a group of cars, trucks, or other vehicles traveling together

Practice the Skills

1 **Reading Across Texts**

Primary and Secondary Sources What clues indicate that this is a diary? Write the point of view above your chart.

2 **BIG Question**

Most people believe that a good friend is someone you can rely on when you need help. What does the caretaker say that shows that he is a good friend to animals? Write your answer on your Foldable.

READING ACROSS TEXTS WORKSHOP

We drove straight to the Malindi Marine Park[2] where a small crowd surrounded a green pickup truck. Inside lay something tightly wrapped in fishing nets. The crowd had been here for hours and seemed relieved that we had arrived.

We introduced ourselves and got to work. Dr. Kashmiri examined the hippo which looked very **subdued**, quiet and tired. He had small wounds all over his legs, his color was a dull dark gray, and he lay silently. His head was covered and my job was to keep him constantly wet to keep his body cool.[3] We decided on a plan to unwrap him from the fishing net, and all hands were at work trying to get him out of the tangle. Suddenly he stood up and some people backed off in fear, then Kashmiri gave the order to remove the net quickly. Everyone was busy but the tangle was a mess. It seemed impossible and the hippo was getting upset, standing up and lying down every few minutes.

Then the worst thing happened, the blanket fell off his face and for the first time he saw all of us around him. That must have given him a huge shock. There were cameras flashing everywhere and the excited voices of the helpers probably scared him even more. He started trying desperately to jump out of the truck while snapping at everyone around.

Most people fled, but Dr. Kashmiri and I have handled many wild animals before. We held onto him as others struggled to put the blanket over his eyes again. It was a scary few minutes—if he had jumped out of the car he would have suffered serious injuries. **3**

After that the unwrapping became much easier, and before long the net was returned to its owner and the hippo was safely tied to prevent him from biting or seeing anyone. He was moved by many hands to Paula's car which was quickly closed. We did not waste time saying goodbye, we knew the hippo was **traumatized** and needed to get to a safe place

---

2. **Malindi Marine Park** is a park on the north coast of Kenya where people observe wildlife and plants and go swimming, diving, and snorkeling.
3. Scientists covered the head of the baby hippo to keep him from being frightened by the crowd surrounding him.

Vocabulary

subdued (sub DOOD) *adj.* quiet, weak, under control
traumatized (TROM uh tyzd) *adj.* upset or injured as a result of a frightening event

---

Practice the Skills

3 **Reading Across Texts**

Primary and Secondary Sources Does this selection provide more information about the rescue of the hippo than the first one did? What facts, feelings, opinions, and details are included in this diary? Put this information in your chart.

quickly. But before we left, we asked the crowd what name they wanted to give him. At first the name Mark rang out. Mark Easterbrook is an honorary game warden[4] who lives in Malindi and who helped coordinate the rescue. But Mark would not take the honor, he suggested Owen, and a young French man looked up in surprise. "What?" "Yes," Mark said, "You are the person with the greatest courage for the final rugby[5] tackle that brought Owen down." The crowd agreed and laughed as they practiced the name "Owen the hippo." 4

We drove back to Mombasa at a slow pace, baby Owen just slept. We stopped twice and I poured cold water over him.

By the time we arrived in Haller Park,[6] it was getting dark. A small team of our staff led by Sabine were here to meet us and help. Their expressions of joy were unmistakable.

It didn't take long for us to get Owen out of the vehicle, and he seemed more than eager to get away from us. It took ten of us to lift him out of the car, then I helped Dr. Kashmiri remove all the ties and let him go. Owen hardly glanced at us then trotted off away into the **enclosure** that Sabine and her

---

4. A *game warden* is a person in charge of managing animals and wildlife.
5. *Rugby* is a game similar to football that is popular in Europe, Africa, and India.
6. *Haller Park* is an environmental park in Mombasa.

Vocabulary

enclosure (en KLOH zhur) *n.* a fenced-in or walled-in place

READING ACROSS TEXTS WORKSHOP

Practice the Skills

4 BIG Question
Mark Easterbrook—the honorary game warden—could have had the baby hippo named after him. But he suggested that it be named after the man who tackled the hippo. What does this tell you about Mark Easterbrook? Do you think he might make a good friend? Why? Write your answers on your Foldable.

Analyzing the Photo What seems to be happening in this picture? Explain your answer.

READING ACROSS TEXTS WORKSHOP

team had prepared. They had piled up lots of freshly cut grass and even brought bottles of milk in case he needed it. We stood and watched him as the light faded. He didn't explore his new home, but went straight up to one of our oldest giant tortoises named Mzee and stood with him.

To be honest, Mzee does not appreciate his new roommate and at first **hissed** angrily at Owen, then lifted himself up and tried to run. Imagine a 100 year old giant tortoise trying to run! It was not hard for Owen to keep up.

Once darkness had fallen everyone left, except Sabine and I. I am responsible for making sure that Owen is alright all night long. It was such an exciting day, I am exhausted, but I am so happy, all of this and I've got malaria too. 5

2nd January, 2005

Today I noticed that Mzee is beginning to show some interest in Owen. He does not seem to mind Owen following him. In the heat of the day Owen was sleeping beside him, some part of his body always touches Mzee, just like a human child reaching out for some security.

Owen has started following Mzee to the pond to swim, and then back out again to the food, and the most extraordinary thing happened today. I noticed Owen copying Mzee in eating dairy cubes (concentrated food that we give the other hippos) and drinking water. I wonder if my eyes are deceiving me, but Owen seemed to be copying Mzee. 6

5th January, 2005

Owen is much stronger now and his attachment to Mzee is greater now than ever. Most of the time they are just together, but now Owen is trying to get Mzee to

Practice the Skills

5 **Reading Across Texts**

Primary and Secondary Sources What major event(s) has the author described in the last two pages? Were they included in the previous selection? Add the major event(s) to your chart and fill in the other columns.

6 **BIG Question**

Mzee didn't seem to like Owen at first. But now he seems to be more interested in Owen. Why do you think he changed his mind? Write your answer on your Foldable.

Vocabulary

hissed (hisd) v. made a sound like air escaping from a balloon

1066 UNIT 8 What Makes a Friend?

respond. This evening he licked Mzee on the face several times and I am sure that Mzee liked it! But as affectionate as Owen is I have to remember that he is still a hippo and hippos are territorial and strong. Especially males. Today he charged me and I discovered just how fast he really is! I had to dash behind a big old fig tree. I'm nearby all the time but Owen does not take his eyes off me. Does he think I am going to hurt Mzee? **7**

11th January, 2005

The story of Owen's amazing relationship with Mzee has gone all around the world. Everyone is interested and fascinated in this strange behavior and I have to admit, in all my 20 years of working with wild animals, I have never seen anything like it.

I suppose it is unique because the story has had such an impact all over the world—we have appeared on CNN, German TV, and people have contacted us from so many countries including Australia, India, France, USA, Germany, and South Africa. We actually captured a scene where Mzee put his head into Owen's mouth as if they are playing. I really wish I could understand what these two are saying to each other. **8**

15th January, 2005

It has been almost three weeks since we rescued Owen and he is doing so much better. He has regained his beautiful pink color, and is looking really fat and healthy. The media are still really excited about his relationship with Mzee.

30th January, 2005

During the day, when Mzee the tortoise is feeding on the grass, Owen follows him around and they feed together.

Practice the Skills

7 **BIG Question**
Sometimes two people just seem to like each other the first time they meet. But sometimes, one person has to "win" the other person's friendship. What is Owen doing to win Mzee's friendship? Have you ever seen or been involved in a relationship in which one person had to win the other person's friendship? Explain on your Foldable.

8 **Reading Across Texts**
Primary and Secondary Sources The author is giving you some details of life with Owen. Add any important events and information to your chart.

READING ACROSS TEXTS WORKSHOP

Owen also spends a lot of time trying to cool himself in the small pond while Mzee walks around often away from Owen. Even though they are inseparable, they are giving each other some space. 9

7th February, 2005

Owen spent most of his time resting in the water with the tortoises. There are two tortoises in the enclosure, he shares his attention between the two. Owen's now changed his feeding habits as after feeding, he has started to feed on carrots and he also wanders freely around the enclosure, feeding on fallen leaves, fallen branches from trees around.

From about 6:45 P.M., he loves walking around alone at night. Visitors now enjoy watching him during his and Mzee's feeding time (which is daily at 4:30 P.M.). I think he has settled very, very well into his new home and he is finally at ease.

22nd April, 2005

Sometimes I think that Owen and Mzee are communicating, they often look as if they are deep in conversation. When they move Mzee sometimes waits for Owen to get up before he moves on. Owen always looks for Mzee before he goes exploring. At one point Owen looked as if he was helping Mzee to climb over a fallen log by nudging the back of his shell when he seemed stuck with all four legs off the ground! The bond between them is stronger than ever. Owen can sometimes be seen licking Mzee's wrinkled face and neck as the old tortoise stretches his neck out, or nudging Mzee's shell with his fat foot when he wants to go for a walk.

Practice the Skills

9 BIG Question
What do you think the author means when he says, "They are giving each other some space"? Do you think that friends need to "give each other some space"? Why or why not? Write your answer on your Foldable.

Analyzing the Photo From viewing this photo, what can you say about the friendship between Owen and Mzee? Explain your answer.

He still sleeps with his head nestled comfortably on Mzee's enormous scaly arm. Mzee reciprocates[7] and has been filmed putting his head trustingly into Owen's mouth during a yawn.

When they fell asleep Mzee looked as if he was watching over Owen and only put his head down after Owen had closed his eyes. **10**

10th November, 2005

When Owen wants to go somewhere, he bites Mzee's foot. That's what happened when I brought their dinner today. Mzee wasn't interested, he had filled up on leaves. But Owen wanted the carrots and dairy cubes but didn't want to go to the feeding site alone. He could hear me whistling to call him and got up first but Mzee was busy eating leaves. He nudged Mzee and then mouthed his foot and kept doing it until Mzee moved to the food. Every now and again Mzee grumbled but he didn't sound too angry. When the crowds have left Haller Park and Mzee is settled Owen gets to lie down against him. He looks like he is in Hippo heaven.

28th November, 2005

It is so enjoyable updating this diary because I enjoy reading all your comments. I must thank you all for caring so much about Owen and Mzee. I hope you will come and visit Owen and Mzee here in Mombasa. They have pleased thousands of visitors already this year. Please keep checking the Diary and let us know what you would like to read about. **11**

Practice the Skills

10 BIG Question
How do Owen and Mzee help and take care of each other? How do human friends help and take care of each other? Write your answers on the "Caretaker's Diary" page of Foldable 8. Your response will help you complete the Unit Challenge later.

11 Reading Across Texts
Primary and Secondary Sources Look over the last few paragraphs and add to your Comparison Chart any facts or events that you think are important.

---

7. When someone *reciprocates,* he or she gives something back of equal value to what he or she received.

READING ACROSS TEXTS WORKSHOP

After You Read

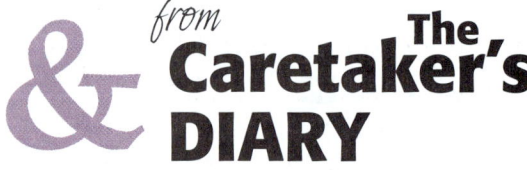

Baby Hippo Orphan *Finds a Friend* & *from* The Caretaker's DIARY

Vocabulary Check

On a separate sheet of paper, write the numbers 1–4. Next to each number, write *T* or *F* to show whether the statement is true or false. Then write your answer to item 5.

Baby Hippo Orphan *Finds a Friend*

tsunami
surf
sanctuary
tortoise

1. A tsunami can cause flooding and destruction.
2. A tortoise usually has fur and loves to run quickly.
3. A wildlife sanctuary is a place where animals are safe from hunters.
4. The ocean's surf is found between deep water and dry land.
5. Now, on your sheet of paper, write a paragraph that uses all four of the vocabulary words correctly.

from The Caretaker's DIARY

For items 6–10, choose the letter of the definition that best matches each word. Write your answers on a separate sheet of paper.

6. ___ convoy
7. ___ subdued
8. ___ traumatized
9. ___ enclosure
10. ___ hissed

a. very upset
b. made a sound like air escaping
c. fenced-off place
d. quiet and weak
e. a group of cars traveling together

Objectives (pp. 1070–1071)
Reading Compare and contrast: primary and secondary sources
Writing Compare and contrast: sources of information

READING ACROSS TEXTS WORKSHOP

Reading/Critical Thinking

On a separate sheet of paper, answer the following questions.

Baby Hippo Orphan Finds a Friend

11. **Recall** How did the baby hippo end up in the Indian Ocean?
    TIP Right There

12. **Draw Conclusions** As an ecologist, why would Paula Kahumbu not expect the tortoise to become a friend of Owen's?
    TIP Author and Me

from The Caretaker's DIARY

13. **Interpret** At the beginning of the journal, how do you think the caretaker felt when he learned he was needed to rescue a baby hippopotamus?
    TIP Author and Me

14. **Analyze** Why do you think Owen first selected Mzee as his friend?
    TIP Author and Me

15. **Analyze** Why do you think so many people came to see Owen and Mzee in the park?
    TIP On My Own

Writing: Reading Across Texts

Use Your Notes

16. Follow these steps to find out what types of information come from primary sources and secondary sources.

    Step 1: Look over the charts you made for these two selections. As you compare the charts, remember that "The Caretaker's Diary" was much longer than "Baby Hippo Orphan Finds a Friend," so you will probably have more entries on that chart.

    Step 2: Look over your charts carefully. What is the point of view in each selection? Which chart has more feelings and opinions? Which chart has more details?

    Step 3: Think about the facts, details, feelings, and opinions in each selection.

Get It on Paper

To compare the secondary source article and the primary source, answer the following questions on a separate sheet of paper.

17. Which selection gives you a shorter overview of what happened? Explain your answer.

18. Which selection gives you more details about how the friendship between Owen and Mzee developed?

19. Which selection gives you a better idea of what it would be like to work with Owen and Mzee? Explain why you chose that selection.

20. If you wanted to get general information about a topic quickly, would you go to a primary source or a secondary source? Explain your choice.

21. If you wanted to find out what a particular kind of job was like, would you go to a news article about that job or the diary of someone who held that job? Explain your choice.

BIG Question

22. These selections are about how two very different animals became close friends. How can people make friends with others who are very different from themselves?

UNIT 8 WRAP-UP

Answering The BIG Question: What Makes a Friend?

You've just read about people who faced the Big Question: What makes a friend? Now use what you've learned to do the Unit Challenge.

The Unit Challenge

Choose Activity A or Activity B and follow the directions for that activity.

A. Group Activity: The Friendship Play

A play has many different elements, including acts and scenes, dialogue, characterization, and stage directions. Now get ready to write your own play.

1. **Think About Your Scene** Divide into groups of four or five. Each group will write a scene based on the Big Question: What makes a friend? As a group, use the notes you each made in your Foldables to help you decide how you want your scene to answer the Big Question.

2. **Script Development** To write your script:
   - Decide what problem (or conflict) the scene is about. Then decide on the solution.
   - Choose one student to play the Narrator. Discuss what you think the Narrator should say to introduce the scene.
   - Discuss the types of characters you want in the scene.
   - Start by role-playing. As you role-play, make up what characters will say and do. Have one or two group members take notes.
   - Choose group members to create the setting, props, and costumes, as needed.

3. **Theater Artists at Work** When you have all the elements of the scene worked out, do the following:
   - Writers: Create the final draft of the script and give everyone a copy. Remember to include stage directions that tell when and where the scene is set.
   - Set designers: Create the scenery and props.
   - Actors: Practice your lines.

4. **Dress Rehearsal** Now it's time to rehearse:
   - Set up the scenery, put the props in place, have actors get into costumes (if necessary), and rehearse the scene.
   - If actors have trouble remembering the lines, allow them to make up their own lines.
   - Be sure to work toward having a scene that is lively and explores the Big Question in some way. The Narrator can comment on the action or address the Big Question directly.

5. **Perform and Present** Each group should perform its scene for the class.

B. Solo Activity: Create a Friendship Comic Book

Today, the comic book (or graphic novel) is considered an art form. It's a visual way to explore important themes. You'll create a comic book that answers the Big Question: What makes a friend?

1. **Create a Storyboard** Review your Foldable notes.
   - Think about a situation that shows what you think makes a friend. Use that situation as the story for your comic book.
   - Create your storyboards—rough sketches and descriptions of what you think each page of your comic book will look like.

2. **Design Your Panels, Plan Your Story**
   - Begin to sketch the different scenes, write dialogue, and write descriptions that go with your sketches. Plan as you go. Make more storyboards if necessary.
   - In a comic book, as in a play, there is often a Narrator. Who will be the Narrator in your comic? It might be one of the characters. It could be you, commenting on the action. Either way, the Narrator should introduce and directly address the Big Question: What makes a friend?

3. **Pen and Ink**
   In the comic book industry, the author "pens" the story and the illustrator "inks" the pictures. In this case, you do both.
   - Add the dialogue to your panels.
   - Add color to your story.
   - Don't forget the cover and title.

4. **Publish**
   Present your book to the class. Leave it on permanent display somewhere in the classroom where your classmates can read it.

UNIT 8

Your Turn: Read and Apply Skills

Meet the Author
Robert Frost was born in 1874 and died in 1963. A farmer for part of his life, he often wrote about our relationship to nature. He used the harsh New England countryside as a backdrop for his thoughts and observations. In 1961, he read a poem for the inauguration of President John F. Kennedy. After Frost's death, President Kennedy remembered the poet in this way: "Our national strength matters; but the spirit which informs and controls our strength matters just as much. This was the special significance of Robert Frost." See page R3 of the Author Files for more on Robert Frost.

Author Search For more about Robert Frost, go to www.glencoe.com.

by Robert Frost

When a friend calls to me from the road
And slows his horse to a meaning walk,[1]
I don't stand still and look around
On all the hills I haven't hoed,
5   And shout from where I am, What is it?

---

1. Here, the ***meaning walk*** is a "meaningful or purposeful pace," with the friend slowing down to show that he wishes to talk with the speaker of the poem.

YOUR TURN: READ AND APPLY SKILLS

No, not as there is a time to talk.
I thrust my hoe in the mellow ground,
Blade-end up and five feet tall,
And plod:[2] I go up to the stone wall
10 For a friendly visit.

---

2. To *plod* is to walk along slowly and heavily.

UNIT 8
Reading on Your Own

To read more about the Big Question, choose one of these books from your school or local library. Work on your reading skills by choosing books that are challenging to you.

Fiction

Things Not Seen
by Andrew Clements

Bobby's new friend, Alicia, is blind, but that doesn't stop her from helping Bobby solve a problem. When Bobby wakes up invisible one morning, he relies on Alicia—and her special sight—to help him tackle his biggest challenge ever.

Bronx Masquerade
by Nikki Grimes

The students at a Bronx high school gain a new respect for their own inner lives—and for the lives of their classmates—when they begin to read their own poems aloud. Read to find out how language and performance changed these students' lives.

The Princess Diaries
by Meg Cabot

Mia is fourteen and lives in New York when she discovers that her father is the Prince of Genovia. With the help of a good friend and a caring grandmother, Mia survives (and thrives!) during this unexpected life change.

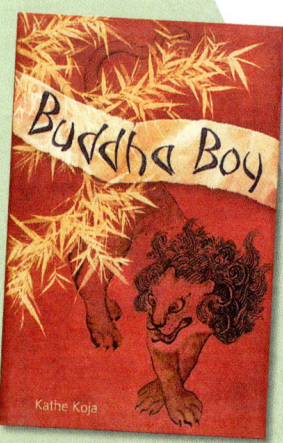

Buddha Boy
By Kathe Koja

Justin is just trying to get through high school unnoticed when he meets Jinsen, an artistic and soft-spoken Buddhist whose religious devotion sets him apart from his schoolmates. Read to find out what Justin learns from his unlikely friendship with the young man the others call "Buddha Boy."

Nonfiction

The Story of My Life
by Helen Keller

Everything changed for Helen Keller when she met Anne Sullivan. Deaf, blind, and unable to speak, Keller was virtually cut off from the world. Then Anne broke through and helped Helen unlock her powers of communication. Read to learn more about the lifelong friendship these women shared.

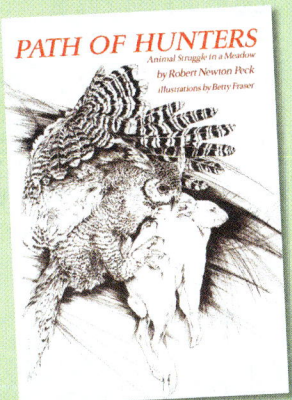

Path of Hunters
by Robert Newton Peck

Robert Newton Peck grew up on a farm in Vermont where he learned to respect even the smallest of animals. Check out this book to learn more about nature and the survival of meadow animals.

Through a Window
by Jane Goodall

Ever wonder how chimpanzees talk to each other, or what they do all day? This book answers those questions and many more. Read to meet chimps Gigi, Goblin, and Passion and to find out why protecting them—and their environment—is more important now than ever.

Living Up the Street
by Gary Soto

This powerful collection of coming-of-age stories peels back the curtain of time on Gary Soto's childhood. Read to learn more about his growing-up experiences on the industrial side of Fresno, California.

UNIT 8 SKILLS AND STRATEGIES ASSESSMENT

Test Practice

Part 1: Literary Elements

Read the following play excerpt and use it to answer the questions. On a separate sheet of paper, write the numbers 1–4. Next to numbers 1–3, write the letter of the correct answer. Next to number 4, write your answer to the question.

Act One
Scene One

The lights come up on the tidy bedroom of Lily, *who is working at a computer. The walls are covered with posters of women's basketball. A wastebasket has a hoop (with net) above it. Another teenage girl,* Sasha, *enters hurriedly.*

Sasha. (*Frantic*) Lily, you've got to help me!

Lily. (*Reading from a spiral notebook as she types*) George Washington lived on a plantation named Mount Vernon . . .

Sasha. Lily! Listen to me!

Lily. (*Tearing herself away from the screen*) What? I'm in the middle of—

Sasha. Let it wait, Lily! I'm in terrible trouble! Can't you help your own sister when she's in terrible trouble?

Lily. Again? Oh, Sasha, you're always in trouble, and it's always terrible trouble, and you always get into it without my help. And then I have to drop what I'm doing and rescue you. Why should I keep getting you out of trouble I didn't get you into?

---

1. Sasha's character is revealed **mainly** by
   A. stage directions.
   B. what she does.
   C. what she says about herself.
   D. what Lily says about her.

2. Which of the following do the stage directions reveal?
   A. what Lily is writing
   B. Sasha's attitude toward Lily
   C. what the relationship is between Lily and Sasha
   D. some clues about Lily's personality and interests

3. To which sense does the description of the set appeal?
   A. sight   B. hearing
   C. smell   D. taste

4. When in the play does this scene occur?

Objectives (pp. 1078–1079)
Reading Skim and scan text • Visualize • Make predictions • Clarify text and ideas
Literature Understand literary elements: characterization • Understand elements of drama: act and scene, stage directions • Identify sensory imagery

SKILLS AND STRATEGIES ASSESSMENT UNIT 8

Part 2: Reading Skills

On a separate sheet of paper, write the numbers 1–4. Next to each number, write the letter of the correct answer. Read the following play excerpt and use it to answer the questions.

Scene Two

The lights come up on a backyard. A five-foot, solid fence extends across the back of the stage. Lily *and* Sasha *are gazing over the fence.*

Lily. Good grief! What did you do? It used to be so beautiful! How'd you get it home?

Sasha. Oh, it drives all right. It just looks sort of . . . bad.

Lily. Sort of? This morning, that was a shiny, racy, dazzling little sports car . . . and now it's a crumpled, smashed, twisted *mess.* Dad's going to have a fit!

Sasha. But see, that's why I need your help! OK, I did kind of mess up the car. And Dad will be unhappy. But think how much more unhappy he'd be if he knew his own daughter did it. Think how much better it would be for him if he thought a stranger took it and crashed it and . . . left it somewhere.

Lily. (*Backing away from Sasha*) Stop right there! I do not like the direction you're headed.

---

1. Imagine that a reader is confused about what Lily is referring to as *it* in her first few lines. What would be the best way to clarify the situation?
   A. Reread Lily's first few lines.
   B. Look up words in a dictionary.
   C. Ask questions of another reader.
   D. Read on to see if further information helps.

2. What is the most likely reason that this section of the play has details about the car's appearance?
   A. to show that Lily is an expert on cars
   B. to help the audience or reader visualize the car
   C. to make the reader feel sorry for Sasha
   D. to show how Sasha looks at the problem

3. If the rest of this scene were printed here, which of the following could you tell if you **only** scanned it?
   A. whether Lily agrees to help Sasha
   B. exactly what Sasha's plan involves
   C. if any new characters are in the scene
   D. how Sasha got into a wreck involving the car

4. Which of the following is the most logical prediction of what will happen next?
   A. Lily and Sasha will argue.
   B. Lily will take the blame for Sasha.
   C. Sasha will decide the problem isn't serious.
   D. The car will get fixed before the father comes home.

UNIT 8 SKILLS AND STRATEGIES ASSESSMENT

Part 3: Vocabulary

On a separate sheet of paper, write the numbers 1–10. Next to each number, write the letter of the correct answer for that question.

Write the letter of the word or phrase that means about the same as the underlined word.

1. to move <u>warily</u>
   A. quickly
   B. very carefully
   C. unexpectedly
   D. in a clumsy way

2. to be a <u>fiasco</u>
   A. problem
   B. total flop
   C. courage
   D. amusing event

3. <u>penetrated</u> her coat
   A. ruined
   B. went through
   C. decorated
   D. made a mess of

4. to be <u>conceited</u>
   A. hidden
   B. worried
   C. stuck up
   D. dishonest

5. to <u>integrate</u> them
   A. notice
   B. choose
   C. favor
   D. combine

Write the letter of the best answer.

6. Which sentence contains slang?
   A. That was a good game.
   B. That boy's sure got game.
   C. Do you want to play a game?
   D. I don't know the rules of the game.

7. What does the underlined idiom mean in the sentence below?
   I don't have time to hear all the details, so <u>cut to the chase</u>.
   A. Go away.
   B. Tell me later.
   C. Come with me.
   D. Get to the point.

8. Use logic to choose the word that the clipped word *ad* comes from.
   A. advice
   B. admission
   C. adjustment
   D. advertisement

9. In which sentence is the word *swims* used figuratively?
   A. Jose swims every day.
   B. The trout swims upstream.
   C. The moon swims in the inky sky.
   D. The otter swims playfully in the lake.

10. Use what you know about *mob* to figure out what *mob* means in the sentence below?
    Let's <u>mob</u> to the party, okay?
    A. hurry
    B. be late
    C. go as a group
    D. take a short cut

Objectives (pp. 1080–1081)
Vocabulary Identify slang, idioms, clipped words, figurative meanings of words
Grammar Use punctuation correctly: hyphens, apostrophes, semicolons, colons, quotation marks

Part 4: Writing Skills

On a separate sheet of paper, write the numbers 1–7. Next to each number, write the letter of the correct answer for that question.

1. Which phrase uses an apostrophe correctly?
   A. a horses' head
   B. the childrens' bikes
   C. both teachers' ideas
   D. my grandparents's house

2. Which of the following could be divided with a hypen if it appeared at the end of a line?
   A. mouse
   B. branch
   C. maybe
   D. straight

3. Which of the following sentences uses apostrophes correctly?
   A. Im sure thats something we shouldn't do.
   B. I'm sure that's something we should'nt do.
   C. I'm sure thats something we shouldn't do.
   D. I'm sure that's something we shouldn't do.

4. Which of the following sentences is written correctly?
   A. I wish I had pets I really like them.
   B. I wish I had pets; I really like them.
   C. I wish I had pets, I really like them.
   D. I wish I had pets; because I really like them.

5. Which of the following is written correctly?
   A. The time is now 4:30.
   B. I want: a big house and a car.
   C. So I said: "Give me that, now!"
   D. I think we deserve: a second chance.

6. What sentence is written correctly?
   A. "Don't be so sure Pete said, angrily."
   B. "If you help," said Teresa, "we'll soon be done."
   C. "I wonder," said Barbra, "About what you mean."
   D. "Really"? asked Paul. "Are you serious about that?"

7. Which correction should be made to the sentence below?
   Kelly said "that she liked your gift."
   A. Capitalize *that*.
   B. Remove the quotation marks.
   C. Start the quotation before *said*.
   D. Add a comma after *said*.

REFERENCE SECTION

- **Author Files** R1
- **Foldables** R8
- **Literary Terms Handbook** R10
- **Writing Handbook** R17
  - The Writing Process R17
  - Writing Modes R20
  - Research Report Writing R21
  - Business Writing R25
  - Using a Computer for Writing R27
- **Language Handbook** R28
  - Troubleshooter R28
  - Troublesome Words R33
  - Mechanics R36
  - Spelling R43
- **Listening, Speaking, and Viewing Handbook** R45
- **Study and Test-Taking Skills Handbook** R49
- **Glossary/Glosario** R54

Index of Skills R70

Index of Authors and Titles R79

Index of Art and Artists R81

Acknowledgments R83

AUTHOR FILES

Maya Angelou (1928–)
- was originally named Marguerite; Maya is the name her brother called her as a child
- at the age of three, was sent to live with her grandmother who ran the only black-owned general store in the town of Stamps, Arkansas
- has been a professor at Wake Forest University for more than twenty years
- speaks French, Spanish, Italian, Arabic, and Fanti (a language of southern Ghana) fluently

Avi (1937–)
- his grandmother, an aunt, and his parents were writers; two uncles were painters and another a composer
- late in his school career, it was discovered that he has dysgraphia, an impairment that causes him to reverse letters or misspell words
- his twin sister gave him the name "Avi" when they were both about a year old

Quote: *"Everybody has ideas. The vital question is, what do you do with them?"*

Toni Cade Bambara (1939–1995)
- studied acting and mime in Italy and France
- worked as an investigator for the New York State Department of Welfare for two years
- was encouraged by her mother to be creative
- contributed to several films as a writer and commentator

Quote: *"She gave me permission to wonder, to dawdle, to daydream."*

Ray Bradbury (1920–)
- does not like technology even though he writes about it; he doesn't drive a car, use a computer, or fly in airplanes
- feels that much of his work is too fantastic to be considered science fiction, which he said he felt had to be based on possibilities for the future
- has written more than 30 books and 600 short stories

Quote: *"The great fun in my life has been getting up every morning and rushing to the typewriter…"*

Gwendolyn Brooks (1917–2000)
- was born in Topeka, Kansas, but lived most of her life in Chicago
- was the first black writer to win the Pulitzer Prize (1950) and the first black woman appointed poetry consultant to the Library of Congress
- followed Carl Sandburg as Poet Laureate of Illinois in 1968; served until her death in 2000

Quote: *"I am interested in telling my particular truth as I have seen it."*

Lewis Carroll (1832–1898)
- Charles Lutwidge Dodson, the third of eleven children, took the pen name Lewis Carroll in his twenties
- wanted to be a clergyman like his father, but a severe stutter prevented him from most public speaking
- in addition to the children's books for which he is best known, he published more than ten books on mathematics

AUTHOR FILES

Sandra Cisneros (1954–)
- was the only girl in a family of seven children
- was in the news in Texas for two years because of the color of her house
- has been a National Endowment for the Arts fellow and was awarded the American Book Award from the Before Columbus Foundation

Quote: *"I feel like a cartographer. I'm determined to fill a literary void."*

Judith Ortiz Cofer (1952–)
- grew up speaking Spanish at home but learned English well enough to become a writer and college professor
- lives in Georgia on a farm that has been in her husband's family for generations
- believes that immigrants do not have to choose one identity over another and says she uses her art "as a bridge between [her] cultures…traveling back and forth without fear and confusion"

Robert Cormier (1925–2000)
- in eighth grade, saw through his classroom window that his house was on fire; was not allowed to check on his family until he had recited the rosary
- his book for young adults, *The Chocolate War*, was banned in many cities

Quote: *"I was a skinny kid living in a ghetto-type neighborhood wanting the world to know that I existed."*

Harold Courlander (1908–1996)
- was a farmer, a historian, an editor, a press officer, and a writer
- won a copyright infringement suit against *Roots* author Alex Haley
- worked "in the field" studying and recording the folktales of people in Haiti, Cuba, Ethiopia, Nigeria, Ghana, the Pacific Islands, and the American Southwest

E. E. Cummings (1894–1962)
- joined the ambulance service in World War I because he believed that violence was wrong
- published over forty texts, including books of poetry, artwork, and plays
- once characterized himself as "an author of pictures"
- changed modern poetry by bending or breaking rules of grammar, punctuation, and even the placement of words on a page

Will Eisner (1917–2005)
- is credited with a leading role in creating the graphic novel form
- helped the careers of many other famous comic artists, such as Jack Kirby and Bob Kane
- used his drawing abilities in the service of his country when he was drafted into the Army
- co-founded the famous Eisner-Iger studio

Robert Frost (1874–1963)
- lived during times of great change; was born less than ten years after the Civil War and died less than ten years before a man walked on the moon
- decided to be a poet when he was sixteen
- married Elinor White and had six children; Elinor and four of the children died during his lifetime
- was very shy but developed a style of quoting poetry that made him one of the most popular performers in America and overseas

John Gardner (1933–1982)
- when he was eleven, a tractor he was riding ran over his seven-year-old brother
- wrote thirty-five books in twenty-five years
- died in a motorcycle accident
- was the son of an English-teacher mother and a preacher/ dairy farmer father

Quote: *"True art is moral; it seeks to improve life, not debase it."*

Nikki Giovanni (1943–)
- her real first name is Yolande, the same as her mother's
- during the 1960s she was known as the "Princess of Black Poetry"
- named "Woman of the Year" three times by well-known publications
- appeared on *The Tonight Show* in 1972

Quote: *"Everything will change. The only question is growing up or decaying."*

Kenneth Grahame (1859–1932)
- became the Secretary of the Bank of England
- was born blind in one eye, with a severe squint in the other
- created his most famous character, Toad, to amuse and educate his young son Alastair
- he and his two siblings were brought up by elderly relatives, after the illness of their father and death of their mother
- his cousin, Sir Anthony Hope Hawkins, wrote *The Prisoner of Zenda*

Jim Haskins (1941–2005)
- in college, was arrested for marching on Montgomery, Alabama, as part of the Civil Rights movement
- started his writing career by keeping a diary of his thoughts when he was teaching public school in Harlem
- wrote the book *The Cotton Club,* which was made into a movie
- published more than 100 books
- read the encyclopedia as a child, because he could not use the segregated town library

Kristin Hunter (1931–)
- her novel *The Landlord* was made into a movie
- was awarded both the 1968 Council on Interracial Books for Children Award and the 1971 Lewis Carroll Shelf Award
- landed her first writing job as a teenager; for six years, as a high school and college student, wrote a column for a newspaper

Quote: *"Every one of us is a wonder. Every one of us has a story."*

AUTHOR FILES

Francisco Jiménez (1943–)
- is a former illegal immigrant migrant worker; went on to earn advanced college degrees
- has taught in universities in the United States and in Mexico
- won awards for his children's books, his nonfiction, and his teaching
- his collection of autobiographical short stories has been translated into Spanish, Chinese, Japanese, and Korean

Bill Littlefield (1948–)
- in addition to writing books and essays, frequently contributes to newspapers
- has been a National Public Radio commentator since 1984
- has won six Associated Press Awards
- taught writing courses at the Harvard University Summer School and the John F. Kennedy School Summer Program for Masters Candidates

Jack London (1876–1919)
- was a coal shoveler, a sailor, a hobo, and a convict all before he entered high school; he then went to the Yukon in search of gold
- wrote nearly two dozen novels, as well as hundreds of short stories
- was raised by his "Aunt Jennie" after mental illness made his mother too weak to care for him
- in 1894, marched on Washington, D.C., to protest mass unemployment
- ran for mayor of Oakland, California, in 1901

Norma Fox Mazer (1931–)
- to support their family, she and her husband wrote fiction for the women's romance and confession market
- as a teenager, her nickname was "the Cold One"
- has published 31 books
- decided to become a writer when she was thirteen

Quote: "I write and my readers read to find out the answers to questions, secrets, problems, to be drawn into the deepest mystery of all—someone else's life."

Patricia C. & Frederick McKissack, Jr. (1944–), (1939–)
- husband and wife team have worked together on more than fifty books
- best known for their biographies of important African Americans, written for younger readers
- were jointly awarded the Coretta Scott King Award twice

Quote: on marching in the Civil Rights Movement, "In a sense we marched from the Old South to a new America."

Pat Mora (1942–)
- has written picture books, a biography, a board book, a counting book, and two retellings of Mayan folktales
- her grandparents left Mexico during the revolution to escape the violent raids of Pancho Villa
- winner of more than twenty major awards

Quote: "Writing is a way of finding out how I feel about anything and everything."

Lensey Namioka (1929–)
- says she is the only person in the world named Lensey; her father made up the name
- is the daughter of a linguist (an expert in languages) and a doctor/writer
- was encouraged by her parents to love music, which became a subject for many of her books
- is from China and her husband is from Japan, so she is interested in writing about both places
- has been writing books for more than thirty years and has won numerous awards

Mary Pope Osborne (1949–)
- lived in a cave in Crete for six weeks
- grew up in a military family and had lived on two continents and more than six army posts before she was fifteen
- loves the theater and has worked as a drama teacher
- survived an earthquake in northern Afghanistan and a riot in Kabul

Quote: *"Our imaginations plus our reading and writing skills … take us wherever we want to go."*

Richard Peck (1934–)
- his book *Amanda/Miranda* was a bestseller and has been translated into nine languages
- three of his young adult novels have been made into TV movies
- started writing books for young people after being a high school teacher

Quote: *"You and I, we people of the word, spend our lives hollering across the famous generation gap, hoping to hear an answering echo."*

Cynthia Rylant (1954–)
- wrote her first children's book in one hour; drew on her own life as a child in the Appalachian Mountains for that book and many others
- has written novels, stories, and poems for young children, teenagers, and young adults
- has written more than 60 books and won the Newbery Medal in 1993

Quote: *"I love being a writer because I want to leave something here on earth to make it better, prettier, stronger."*

Stan Sakai (1953–)
- grew up reading the work of Stan Ditko, and Marvel and DC comics
- is the Chief Executive Officer of *Usagi Studios*, which has one employee–himself
- was born in Kyoto; moved with his family to Hawaii at the age of two
- winner of the Eisner Award several times
- does his own historical research for his comic set in Japan's past

Luis Omar Salinas (1937–)
- orphaned at the age of four; lived with his aunt and uncle and considered them his parents
- particularly enjoys reaching audiences by reading his poetry aloud
- attended Fresno State University and also became a creative writing instructor there

Quote: *"Sometimes life is harsh, and the poet has to find a way to escape."*

AUTHOR FILES

Robert Service (1874–1958)
- lived and traveled in many different countries
- was an instant success after his first book was published
- worked during World War I as a correspondent and an ambulance driver
- had several of his books made into movies
- has three schools named after him in Alaska and Canada and was honored on a Canadian stamp
- was the most popular poet in America but called himself "only a 'rhymer' and an 'inkslinger'"

Shel Silverstein (1930–1999)
- played guitar, piano, saxophone, and trombone
- was first published in *Playboy* magazine
- wrote and recorded "A Boy Named Sue," a song made famous by Johnny Cash
- worked as a writer, cartoonist, lyricist, musician, composer, and even an actor
- his first book for children was made into an animated movie

Isaac Bashevis Singer (1904–1991)
- won the 1978 Nobel Prize in Literature
- wrote almost all his works in Yiddish and sometimes re-wrote them in English
- son of a Hassidic rabbi; both his grandfathers were also rabbis
- published hundreds of short stories, volumes of autobiography, a dozen novels, and even more children's books

Quote: "A writer has to write in his own language or not at all."

Gary Soto (1952–)
- is a third-generation Mexican American
- has edited story collections and written poetry, essays, novels, young adult and children's books, and made movies
- taught English and Chicano Studies at the University of California, Berkeley
- enjoys theater, tennis, basketball, traveling, and working in the garden

Quote: "I discovered that reading builds a life inside the mind."

Stephen Spender (1909–1995)
- primarily known as one of the "Oxford poets;" his name was frequently linked with W. H. Auden
- served on the UN Economic and Scientific Committee (UNESCO)
- in 1993, filed a lawsuit claiming that the novel *While England Sleeps* was taken from his own autobiography
- received the knighthood in 1983
- much of his early poetry was political and social protest

Mildred D. Taylor (1943–)
- as part of the Peace Corps in Ethiopia, she taught English and history for two years
- helped create a Black Studies program at the University of Colorado
- was born in Mississippi; her family moved to newly-integrated Toledo, Ohio, when she was only three months old
- won the Coretta Scott King Award for three of her books

Yoshiko Uchida (1921–1992)
- graduated from high school in just two and a half years
- during World War II, lived in a Japanese-American internment camp for about a year
- received a Ford Foundation fellowship in 1952
- is known primarily for her children's books; has also written fiction and nonfiction for adults

Quote: "I write to celebrate our common humanity, for the basic elements of humanity are present in all our strivings."

Alma Luiz Villanueva (1944–)
- lived in the Mission district of San Francisco until she was eleven years old
- served on the National Endowment for the Arts fiction panel
- was raised by her Yaqui Indian grandmother and Mexican-American aunt
- began publishing poetry in her early thirties

Quote: "Poetry for me is the source, the mother tongue, the sun, moon, and stars."

Judith Viorst (1931–)
- her first break as a writer came when she was hired to write a book for NASA
- her credits include a magazine column, nonfiction works, collections of poetry, and picture books
- she and her husband, writer and political analyst Milton Viorst, have three sons
- her most famous children's book is *Alexander and the Terrible, Horrible, No Good, Very Bad Day*

Mary Whitebird
- is the pen name of a writer/filmmaker who is neither an Indian nor a woman
- once received a letter from a Cherokee reader who said about Whitebird's work, "Only an Indian could have written this."
- another correspondent wrote: "It's obvious that, as a woman, you are concerned with feminist issues."

Jane Yolen (1939–)
- is the daughter of two authors; her father also popularized kite flying, and her mother created crossword puzzles for magazines
- studied music and ballet
- has written more than 250 books, which have been translated into 22 languages
- ran a workshop for new authors for twenty years

Quote: "My advice for young people interested in writing: read and write. Read and read and read."

Paul Zindel (1936–2003)
- had a troubled childhood—said in an interview, "I felt worthless as a kid, and dared to speak and act my feelings only in fantasy and secret"
- wrote stories that involve the gap between teens and the adults who don't understand them
- wrote a memoir, *The Pigman and Me,* and the novel *The Pigman*

Quote: "I know it's a continuing battle to get through the years between twelve and twenty ... so I write always from their point of view."

FOLDABLES™

by Dinah Zike, M.Ed., Creator of Foldables™

Reading and Thinking with Foldables™

As you read the selections in each unit, the following Foldables will help you keep track of your ideas about the Big Questions. Follow these directions to make your Foldable, and then use the directions in the Unit Warm Up for labeling your unit Foldable.

Foldable 1 and Foldable 5—For Units 1 and 5

Step 1 Stack three sheets of paper with their top edges about a half-inch apart. These top edges will be tabs, so be sure to keep them straight.

Step 2 Fold up the bottom edges of the papers to form six tabs. Align the edges so that all of the layers or tabs are the same distance apart. Crease the bottom tightly.

Step 3 Follow steps 1 and 2 again to make a second set of tabbed pages. Then place the two sets of tabbed pages back-to-back and staple them together at the bottom.

Step 4 On the top page of one side of the tabbed pages, write the unit number and the big question. Then, working your way up, label the tabs in order with the titles of the reading selections in the Reading Workshops and the Comparing Literature or Reading Across Texts Workshop. Use both tabbed sides.

Step 5 Below each title, write **My Purpose for Reading.** A third of the way down from that, write the label **The Big Question.**

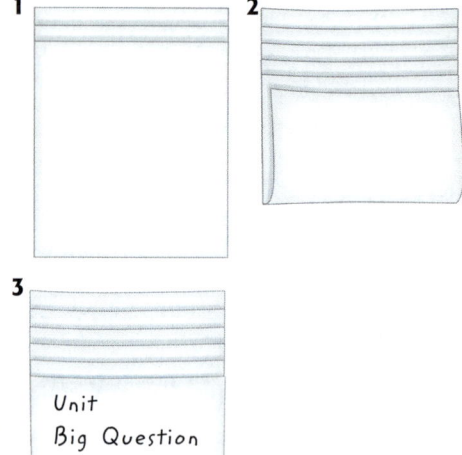

Foldable 2 and Foldable 7—For Units 2 and 7

Step 1 Fold a sheet of paper in half so that one side is one inch longer than the other side. Fold the one-inch tab over the short side to form a fold. On the fold, write the workshop number and the Big Question for that unit.

Step 2 Cut the front flap in half toward the top crease to create two flaps. Write the title of the first selection in Reading Workshop 1 on the left flap and the title of the second selection on the right flap.

Step 3 Open the flaps. At the very top of each flap, write **My Purpose for Reading.** Below each crease, write **The Big Question.**

Step 4 Repeat these steps for each remaining Reading Workshop and the

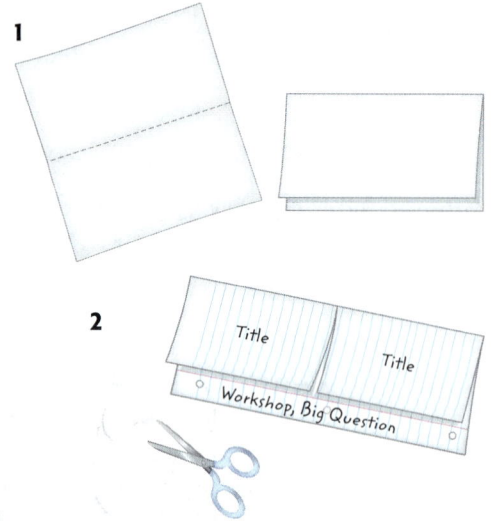

Continued on page R9

Continued from page R8

Reading Across Texts or Comparing Literature Workshop.

Step 5 Fold a 11 x 14 sheet of paper in half. Open the paper and fold up one of the long sides two inches to form a pocket. Glue the outer edges of the pocket. Refold the paper so that the pockets are on the inside. Keep your Foldables for the unit inside.

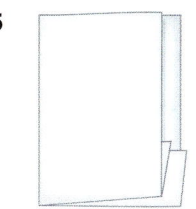

Foldable 3 and Foldable 6—For Units 3 and 6

Step 1 Fold ten sheets of paper in half.

Step 2 On the top flap of each folded paper, make a cut one inch from the side (top flap only)

Step 3 Stack the folded papers on top of one another. Staple the ten sections together. Write the unit number and Big Question on the stapled edge.

Step 4 On the top flap, write the first selection title from Reading Workshop 1. Open the flap. Near the top of the page, write **My Purpose for Reading.** Below the crease, write **The Big Question.**

Step 5 Repeat these steps for each remaining selection in the Reading Workshops and the Comparing Literature Workshop.

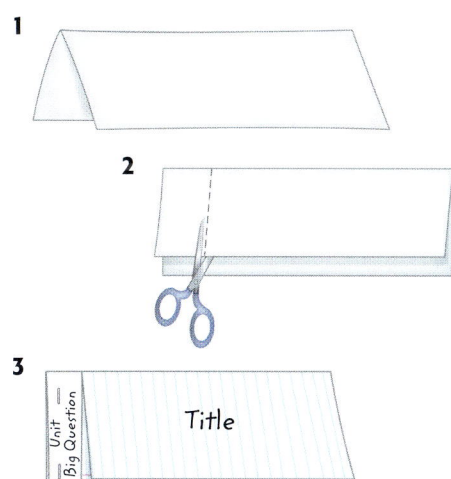

Foldable 4 and Foldable 8—For Units 4 and 8

Step 1 Fold six sheets of paper in half and cut the sheets in half along the fold line.

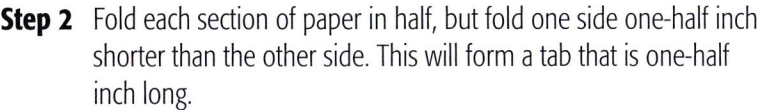

Step 2 Fold each section of paper in half, but fold one side one-half inch shorter than the other side. This will form a tab that is one-half inch long.

Step 3 Fold each tab over the shorter side and then fold it back the opposite way.

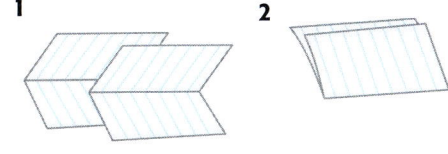

Step 4 Glue the straight edge of one section into the tab valley of another section. Glue all the sections together to form an accordion.

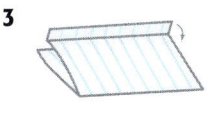

Step 5 On the front cover, write the unit number and the Big Question. Turn the page. Across the top, write the selection title. To the left of the crease, write **My Purpose for Reading.** To the right of the crease, write **The Big Question.** Repeat until you have all the titles from the Reading Workshops and the Comparing Literature or Reading Across Texts Workshop in your Foldable.

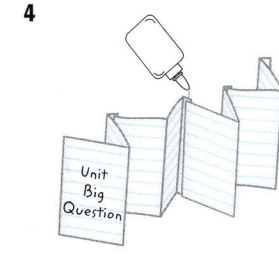

LITERARY TERMS HANDBOOK

A

Act A major unit of a drama. A play may be subdivided into several acts. Many modern plays have two or three acts. A short play can be composed of one or more scenes but only one act.
See also SCENE.

Alliteration The repetition of consonant sounds, usually at the beginnings of words or syllables. Alliteration gives emphasis to words. For example,

Over the cobbles he clattered and clashed

Allusion A reference in a work of literature to a well-known character, place, or situation in history, politics, or science or from another work of literature, music, or art.

Analogy A comparison between two things, based on one or more elements that they share. Analogies can help the reader visualize an idea. In informational text, analogies are often used to explain something unfamiliar in terms of something known. For example, a science book might compare the flow of electricity to water moving through a hose. In literature, most analogies are expressed in metaphors or similes.
See also METAPHOR, SIMILE.

Anecdote A brief, entertaining story based on a single interesting or humorous incident or event. Anecdotes are frequently biographical and reveal some aspect of a person's character.

Antagonist A person or force that opposes the protagonist, or central character, in a story or a drama. The reader is generally meant not to sympathize with the antagonist.
See also CONFLICT, PROTAGONIST.

Anthropomorphism Representing animals as if they had human emotions and intelligence. Fables and fairy tales often contain anthropomorphism.

Aside In a play, a comment made by a character that is heard by the audience but not by the other characters onstage. The speaker turns to one side, or "aside," away from the other characters onstage. Asides are common in older plays—you will find many in Shakespeare's plays—but are infrequent in modern drama.

Assonance The repetition of vowel sounds, especially in a line of poetry.
See also RHYME, SOUND DEVICES.

Author's purpose The intention of the writer. For example, the purpose of a story may be to entertain, to describe, to explain, to persuade, or a combination of these purposes.

Autobiography The story of a person's life written by that person. *I know Why the Caged Bird Sings* by Maya Angelou, is an example of autobiography.
See also BIOGRAPHY, MEMOIR.

B

Ballad A short musical narrative song or poem. Folk ballads, which usually tell of an exciting or dramatic episode, were passed on by word of mouth for generations before being written down. Literary ballads are written in imitation of folk ballads.
See also NARRATIVE POETRY.

Biography The account of a person's life written by someone other than the subject. Biographies can be short or book-length.
See also AUTOBIOGRAPHY, MEMOIR.

C

Character A person in a literary work. (If a character is an animal, it displays human traits.) Characters who show varied and sometimes contradictory traits are called **round.** Characters who reveal only one personality trait are called **flat.** A **stereotype** is a flat character of a familiar and often-repeated type. A **dynamic** character changes during the story. A **static** character remains primarily the same throughout the story.

Characterization The methods a writer uses to develop the personality of the character. In **direct characterization,** the writer makes direct statements about a character's personality. In **indirect characterization,** the writer reveals a character's personality through the character's words and actions and through what other characters think and say about the character.

Climax The point of greatest emotional intensity, interest, or suspense in a narrative. Usually the climax comes at the turning point in a story or drama, the point at which the resolution of the conflict becomes clear. The climax in "Icarus and Daedelus" occurs when Icarus forgets his father's warning and flies too high.

Comedy A type of drama that is humorous and has a happy ending. A heroic comedy focuses on the exploits of a larger-than-life hero. In American popular culture, comedy can take the form of a scripted performance involving one or more performers—either as a skit that is part of a variety show, as in vaudeville, or as a stand-up monologue.

See also HUMOR.

Conflict The central struggle between opposing forces in a story or drama. An **external conflict** exists when a character struggles against some outside force, such as nature, society, fate, or another person. An **internal conflict** exists within the mind of a character who is torn between opposing feelings or goals.

See also ANTAGONIST, PLOT, PROTAGONIST.

Consonance A pleasing combination of sounds, especially in poetry. Consonance usually refers to the repetition of consonant sounds in stressed syllables.

See also SOUND DEVICES.

Couplet Two successive lines of verse that form a unit and usually rhyme.

D

Description Writing that seeks to convey the impression of a setting, a person, an animal, an object, or an event by appealing to the senses. Almost all writing, fiction and nonfiction, contains elements of description.

Details Particular features of things used to make descriptions more accurate and vivid. Authors use details to help readers imagine the characters, scenes, and actions they describe.

Dialect A variation of language spoken by a particular group, often within a particular region. Dialects differ from standard language because they may contain different pronunciations, forms, and meanings.

Dialogue Conversation between characters in a literary work.

See also MONOLOGUE.

Drama A story intended to be performed by actors on a stage or before movie or TV cameras. Most dramas before the modern period can be divided into two basic types: tragedy and comedy. The script of a drama includes dialogue (the words the actors speak) and stage directions (descriptions of the action and scenery).

See also COMEDY, TRAGEDY.

E

Elegy A mournful or melancholy poem that honors someone who is dead. Some elegies are written in rhyming couplets that follow a strict metric pattern.

Epic A long narrative poem, written in a dignified style, that celebrates the adventures and achievements of one or more heroic figures of legend, history, or religion.

See also NARRATIVE POETRY.

Essay A short piece of nonfiction writing on a single topic. The purpose of the essay is to communicate an idea or opinion. A **formal essay** is serious and impersonal. An **informal essay** entertains while it informs, usually in a light conversational style.

Exposition The part of the plot of a short story, novel, novella, or play in which the characters, setting, and situation are introduced.

Extended metaphor An implied comparison that continues through an entire poem.

See also METAPHOR.

F

Fable A short, simple tale that teaches a moral. The characters in a fable are often animals who speak and act like people. The moral, or lesson, of the fable is usually stated outright.

Literary Terms Handbook **R11**

Falling action In a play or story, the action that follows the climax.
See also PLOT.

Fantasy A form of literature that explores unreal worlds of the past, the present, or the future.

Fiction A prose narrative in which situations and characters are invented by the writer. Some aspects of a fictional work may be based on fact or experience. Fiction includes short stories, novellas, and novels.
See also NOVEL, NOVELLA, SHORT STORY.

Figurative language Language used for descriptive effect, often to imply ideas indirectly. Expressions of figurative language are not literally true but express some truth beyond the literal level. Although it appears in all kinds of writing, figurative language is especially prominent in poetry.
See also ANALOGY, FIGURE OF SPEECH, METAPHOR, PERSONIFICATION, SIMILE, SYMBOL.

Figure of speech Figurative language of a specific kind, such as **analogy, metaphor, simile,** or **personification.**

First-person narrative. See POINT OF VIEW.

Flashback An interruption in a chronological narrative that tells about something that happened before that point in the story or before the story began. A flashback gives readers information that helps to explain the main events of the story.

Folklore The traditional beliefs, customs, stories, songs, and dances of the ordinary people (the "folk") of a culture. Folklore is passed on by word of mouth and performance rather than in writing.
See also FOLKTALE, LEGEND, MYTH, ORAL TRADITION.

Folktale A traditional story passed down orally long before being written down. Generally the author of a folktale is anonymous. Folktales include animal stories, trickster stories, fairy tales, myths, legends, and tall tales.
See also LEGEND, MYTH, ORAL TRADITION, TALL TALE.

Foreshadowing The use of clues by an author to prepare readers for events that will happen in a story.

Free verse Poetry that has no fixed pattern of meter, rhyme, line length, or stanza arrangement.
See also RHYTHM.

G

Genre A literary or artistic category. The main literary genres are prose, poetry, and drama. Each of these is divided into smaller genres. For example: **Prose** includes fiction (such as novels, novellas, short stories, and folktales) and nonfiction (such as biography, autobiography, and essays). **Poetry** includes lyric poetry, dramatic poetry, and narrative poetry. **Drama** includes tragedy, comedy, historical drama, melodrama, and farce.

H

Haiku Originally a Japanese form of poetry that has three lines and seventeen syllables. The first and third lines have five syllables each; the middle line has seven syllables.

Hero A literary work's main character, usually one with admirable qualities. Although the word *hero* is applied only to males in traditional usage (the female form is *heroine*), the term now applies to both sexes.
See also LEGEND, MYTH, PROTAGONIST, TALL TALE.

Historical fiction A novel, novella, play, short story, or narrative poem that sets fictional characters against a historical backdrop and contains many details about the period in which it is set.
See also GENRE.

Humor The quality of a literary work that makes the characters and their situations seem funny, amusing, or ludicrous. Humorous writing can be as effective in nonfiction as in fiction.
See also COMEDY.

I

Idiom A figure of speech that belongs to a particular language, people, or region and whose meaning cannot be obtained, and might even appear ridiculous, by joining the meanings of the words composing it. You would be using an idiom if you said you *caught* a cold.

Imagery Language that emphasizes sensory impressions to help the reader of a literary work see, hear, feel, smell, and taste the scenes described in the work.
See also FIGURATIVE LANGUAGE.

Informational text One kind of nonfiction. This kind of writing conveys facts and information without introducing personal opinion.

Irony A form of expression in which the intended meaning of the words used is the opposite of their literal meaning. *Verbal irony* occurs when a person says one thing and means another—for example, saying "Nice guy!" about someone you dislike. *Situational irony* occurs when the outcome of a situation is the opposite of what was expected.

J

Journal An account of day-to-day events or a record of experiences, ideas, or thoughts. A journal may also be called a diary.

L

Legend A traditional story, based on history or an actual hero, that is passed down orally. A legend is usually exaggerated and gains elements of fantasy over the years. Stories about Daniel Boone and Davy Crockett are American legends.

Limerick A light humorous poem with a regular metrical scheme and a rhyme scheme of *aabba*.
See also HUMOR, RHYME SCHEME.

Local color The fictional portrayal of a region's features or peculiarities and its inhabitants' distinctive ways of talking and behaving, usually as a way of adding a realistic flavor to a story.

Lyric The words of a song, usually with a regular rhyme scheme.
See also RHYME SCHEME.

Lyric poetry Poems, usually short, that express strong personal feelings about a subject or an event.

M

Main idea The most important idea expressed in a paragraph or an essay. It may or may not be directly stated.

Memoir A biographical or autobiographical narrative emphasizing the narrator's personal experience during a period or at an event.
See also AUTOBIOGRAPHY, BIOGRAPHY.

Metaphor A figure of speech that compares or equates seemingly unlike things. In contrast to a simile, a metaphor implies the comparison instead of stating it directly; hence, there is no use of connectives such as *like* or *as*.
See also FIGURE OF SPEECH, IMAGERY, SIMILE.

Meter A regular pattern of stressed and unstressed syllables that gives a line of poetry a predictable rhythm.
See also RHYTHM.

Monologue A long speech by a single character in a play or a solo performance.

Mood The emotional quality or atmosphere of a story or poem.
See also SETTING.

Myth A traditional story of unknown authorship, often involving goddesses, gods, and heroes, that attempts to explain a natural phenomenon, a historic event, or the origin of a belief or custom.

N

Narration Writing or speech that tells a story. Narration is used in prose fiction and narrative poetry. Narration can also be an important element in biographies, autobiographies, and essays.

Narrative poetry Verse that tells a story.

Narrator The person who tells a story. In some cases the narrator is a character in the story.
See also POINT OF VIEW.

Nonfiction Factual prose writing. Nonfiction deals with real people and experiences. Among the categories of nonfiction are biographies, autobiographies, and essays.

Literary Terms Handbook

See also AUTOBIOGRAPHY, BIOGRAPHY, ESSAY, FICTION.

Novel A book-length fictional prose narrative. The novel has more scope than a short story in its presentation of plot, character, setting, and theme. Because novels are not subject to any limits in their presentation of these elements, they encompass a wide range of narratives.

See also FICTION.

Novella A work of fiction shorter than a novel but longer than a short story. A novella usually has more characters, settings, and events and a more complex plot than a short story.

O

Ode A lyric poem, usually rhymed, often in the form of an address and usually dignified or lofty in subject.

See also LYRIC POETRY.

Onomatopoeia The use of a word or a phrase that actually imitates or suggests the sound of what it describes.

See also SOUND DEVICES.

Oral tradition Stories, knowledge, customs, and beliefs passed by word of mouth from one generation to the next.

See also FOLKLORE, FOLKTALE, LEGEND, MYTH.

P

Parallelism The use of a series of words, phrases, or sentences that have similar grammatical form. Parallelism emphasizes the items that are arranged in the similar structures.

See also REPETITION.

Personification A figure of speech in which an animal, object, or idea is given human form or characteristics.

See also FIGURATIVE LANGUAGE, FIGURE OF SPEECH, METAPHOR.

Plot The sequence of events in a story, novel, or play. The plot begins with **exposition,** which introduces the story's characters, setting, and situation. The plot catches the reader's attention with a **narrative hook.** The **rising action** adds complications to the story's conflict, or problem, leading to the **climax,** or point of highest emotional pitch. The **falling action** is the logical result of the climax, and the **resolution** presents the final outcome.

Plot twist An unexpected turn of events in a plot. A surprise ending is an example of a plot twist.

Poetry A form of literary expression that differs from prose in emphasizing the line as the unit of composition. Many other traditional characteristics of poetry—emotional, imaginative language; use of metaphor and simile; division into stanzas; rhyme; regular pattern of stress, or meter—apply to some poems.

Point of view The relationship of the narrator, or storyteller, to the story. In a story with **first-person point of view,** the story is told by one of the characters, referred to as "I." The reader generally sees everything through that character's eyes. In a story with a **limited third-person point of view,** the narrator reveals the thoughts of only one character, but refers to that character as "he" or "she." In a story with an **omniscient point of view,** the narrator reveals the thoughts of several characters.

Props Theater slang (a shortened form of *properties*) for objects and elements of the scenery of a stage play or movie set.

Propaganda Speech, writing, or other attempts to influence ideas or opinions, often through the use of stereotypes, faulty generalizations, logical fallacies, and/or emotional language.

Prose Writing that is similar to everyday speech and language, as opposed to poetry. Its form is based on sentences and paragraphs without the patterns of rhyme, controlled line length, or meter found in much poetry. Fiction and nonfiction are the major categories of prose. Most modern drama is also written in prose.

See also DRAMA, ESSAY, FICTION, NONFICTION.

Protagonist The central character in a story, drama, or dramatic poem. Usually the action revolves around the protagonist, who is involved in the main conflict.

See ANTAGONIST, CONFLICT.

Pun A humorous play on two or more meanings of the same word or on two words with the same sound. Today puns often appear in advertising headlines and slogans—for example, "Our hotel rooms give you suite feelings."

See also HUMOR.

R

Refrain A line or lines repeated regularly, usually in a poem or song.

Repetition The recurrence of sounds, words, phrases, lines, or stanzas in a speech or piece of writing. Repetition increases the feeling of unity in a work. When a line or stanza is repeated in a poem or song, it is called a refrain.

See also PARALLELISM, REFRAIN.

Resolution The part of a plot that concludes the falling action by revealing or suggesting the outcome of the conflict.

Rhyme The repetition of sounds at the ends of words that appear close to each other in a poem. **End rhyme** occurs at the ends of lines. **Internal rhyme** occurs within a single line. **Slant rhyme** occurs when words include sounds that are similar but not identical. Slant rhyme usually involves some variation of **consonance** (the repetition of consonant sounds) or **assonance** (the repetition of vowel sounds).

Rhyme scheme The pattern of rhyme formed by the end rhyme in a poem. The rhyme scheme is designated by the assignment of a different letter of the alphabet to each new rhyme. For example, one common rhyme scheme is *ababcb*.

Rhythm The pattern created by the arrangement of stressed and unstressed syllables, especially in poetry. Rhythm gives poetry a musical quality that helps convey its meaning. Rhythm can be regular (with a predictable pattern or meter) or irregular, (as in free verse).

See also METER.

Rising action The part of a plot that adds complications to the problems in the story and increases reader interest.

See also FALLING ACTION, PLOT.

S

Scene A subdivision of an act in a play. Each scene takes place in a specific setting and time. An act may have one or more scenes.

See also ACT.

Science fiction Fiction dealing with the impact of real science or imaginary superscience on human or alien societies of the past, present, or future. Although science fiction is mainly a product of the twentieth century, nineteenth-century authors such as Mary Shelley, Jules Verne, and Robert Louis Stevenson were pioneers of the genre.

Screenplay The script of a film, usually containing detailed instructions about camera shots and angles in addition to dialogue and stage directions. A screenplay for an original television show is called a teleplay.

See also DRAMA.

Sensory imagery Language that appeals to a reader's five senses: hearing, sight, touch, taste, and smell.

See also VISUAL IMAGERY.

Sequence of events The order in which the events in a story take place.

Setting The time and place in which the events of a short story, novel, novella, or play occur. The setting often helps create the atmosphere or mood of the story.

Short story A brief fictional narrative in prose. Elements of the short story include **plot, character, setting, point of view, theme,** and sometimes symbol and irony.

Simile A figure of speech using *like* or *as* to compare seemingly unlike things.

Sonnet A poem containing fourteen lines, usually written in iambic pentameter. Sonnets have strict patterns of rhyme and usually deal with a single theme, idea, or sentiment.

Sound devices Techniques used to create a sense of rhythm or to emphasize particular sounds in writing. For example, sound can be controlled through the use of **onomatopoeia, alliteration, consonance, assonance,** and **rhyme.**

See also RHYTHM.

LITERARY TERMS HANDBOOK

Speaker The voice of a poem—sometimes that of the poet, sometimes that of a fictional person or even a thing. The speaker's words communicate a particular tone or attitude toward the subject of the poem.

Stage directions Instructions written by the dramatist to describe the appearance and actions of characters, as well as sets, costumes, and lighting.

Stanza A group of lines forming a unit in a poem. Stanzas are, in effect, the paragraphs of a poem.

Stereotype A character who is not developed as an individual but as a collection of traits and mannerisms supposedly shared by all members of a group.

Style The author's choice and arrangement of words and sentences in a literary work. Style can reveal an author's purpose in writing and attitude toward his or her subject and audience.

Suspense A feeling of curiosity, uncertainty, or even dread about what is going to happen next. Writers increase the level of suspense in a story by giving readers clues to what may happen.

See also FORESHADOWING, RISING ACTION.

Symbol Any object, person, place, or experience that means more than what it is. **Symbolism** is the use of images to represent internal realities.

T

Tall tale A wildly imaginative story, usually passed down orally, about the fantastic adventures or amazing feats of folk heroes in realistic local settings.

See also FOLKLORE, ORAL TRADITION.

Teleplay A play written or adapted for television.

Theme The main idea of a story, poem, novel, or play, usually expressed as a general statement. Some works have a **stated theme,** which is expressed directly. More frequently works have an **implied theme,** which is revealed gradually through other elements such as plot, character, setting, point of view, symbol, and irony.

Third-person narrative. See POINT OF VIEW.

Title The name of a literary work.

Tone The attitude of the narrator toward the subject, ideas, theme, or characters. A factual article would most likely have an objective tone, while an editorial on the same topic could be argumentative or satiric.

Tragedy A play in which the main character suffers a downfall. That character often is a person of dignified or heroic stature. The downfall may result from outside forces or from a weakness within the character, which is known as a tragic flaw.

V

Visual imagery Details that appeal to the sense of sight.

Voice An author's distinctive style or the particular speech patterns of a character in a story.

See also STYLE, TONE.

WRITING HANDBOOK

The Writing Process

The writing process consists of five stages: prewriting, drafting, revising, editing/proofreading, and publishing/presenting. By following the stages in order, you can turn your ideas into polished pieces of writing. Most writers take their writing through all five stages, and repeat stages when necessary.

The Writing Process

Prewriting

Prewriting is the process of gathering and organizing your ideas. It begins whenever you start to consider what you will write about or what will interest your readers. Try keeping a small notebook with you for several days and using it to jot down possible topics. Consult the chart below for tips on using the prewriting techniques known as listing, questioning, and clustering.

Listing, Questioning, and Clustering

LISTING List as many ideas as you can—whatever comes into your head on a particular subject. This is called brainstorming. Then go back over the list and circle the ideas you like best. Eventually you'll hit on an idea you can use.

QUESTIONING If your audience is your classmates, ask yourself questions such as the following:
- *What do my friends like to learn about?*
- *What do my friends like to read about?*
- *What have I done that my friends might like to hear about?*

CLUSTERING Write your topic in the middle of a piece of paper. Organize related ideas around the topic in a cluster of circles, with lines showing how the ideas are related. Clustering can help you decide which part of a topic to write about.

When you have selected your topic, organize your ideas around the topic. Identify your main ideas and supporting ideas. Each main idea needs examples or facts to support it. Then write a plan for what you want to say. The plan might be an organized list or outline. It does not have to use complete sentences.

Drafting

Drafting is the stage that turns your list into sentences and paragraphs. Use your prewriting notes to remember what you want to say. Begin by writing an introduction that gets the reader's attention. Move ahead through the topic, paragraph by paragraph. Let your words flow. This is the time to express yourself or try out a new idea. Don't worry about mistakes in spelling and grammar; you can correct them later. If you get stuck, try one of the tricks below.

Tips for drafting
- Work on the easiest part first. You don't have to begin at the beginning.
- Make a diagram, sketch, or drawing of the topic.
- Focus on just one sentence or paragraph at a time.
- Freewrite your thoughts and images. You can organize them later.
- Pretend that you are writing to a friend.
- Ask more questions about your topic.
- Speak your ideas into a tape recorder.
- Take a break. Take a walk or listen to music. Return to your writing later.

Revising

The goal of revising is to make your writing clearer and more interesting. When you revise, look at the whole piece of writing. Ask whether the parts go together smoothly and whether anything should be added or

Writing Handbook R17

deleted. You may decide to organize the draft in a different way. Some writers make several revisions before they are satisfied. Ask yourself these questions:

- ☑ Did I stick to my topic?
- ☑ Did I accomplish my purpose?
- ☑ Did I keep my audience in mind?
- ☑ Does my main idea come across clearly?
- ☑ Do all the details support the main idea?
- ☑ Did I give enough information? too much?
- ☑ Did I use transition words such as *first, then* and *next* to make my sentences flow smoothly?

Tips for revising

- Step back. If you have the time, set your draft aside for a while. When you look at it again, you may see it from a new point of view. You may notice that some information is missing or that part of the paper is disorganized.
- Read your paper aloud. Listen carefully as you read your paper aloud. How does it sound?
- Have a writing conference with a peer reviewer, one of your friends or classmates. A second opinion helps. Your reader can offer a fresh point of view.

Peer review

You can direct peer responses in one or more of the following ways.

- Ask readers to tell you what they have read in their own words. If you do not hear your ideas restated, revise your writing for clarity.
- Ask readers to tell you the part they liked best and why. You may want to expand those parts.
- Repeat what the readers have told you in your own words. Ask the readers if you have understood their suggestions.
- Discuss your writing with your readers. Listen to their suggestions carefully.

As you confer, make notes of your reviewers' comments. Then revise your draft, using your own judgment and including what is helpful from your reviewers' comments.

Editing/Proofreading

When you are satisfied with the changes you've made, edit your revised draft. Replace dull, vague words with lively verbs and precise adjectives. Vary the length of your sentences. Take time to correct errors in spelling, grammar, capitalization, and punctuation. Refer to the Proofreading Checklist on page R19 and on the inside back cover of this book.

Editing for style

Use the following checklist:

- ☑ Have I avoided clichés?
- ☑ Have I avoided wordiness?
- ☑ Is the tone of my writing appropriate to my purpose?
- ☑ Have I made clear connections between ideas?
- ☑ Do my sentences and paragraphs flow smoothly?

Publishing/Presenting

Now your writing is ready for an audience. Make a clean, neat copy, and add your name and date. Check that the paper has a title. If you wish, enclose the paper in a folder or binder to give it a professional look. Hand it in to your teacher, or share it in one of the ways described below. When the paper is returned, keep it in your writing portfolio.

Ideas for presenting

- **Illustrations** A photograph, diagram, or drawing can convey helpful information.
- **Oral presentation** Almost any writing can be shared aloud. Try including music, slides, or a group oral reading.
- **Class book** A collection of class writing is a nice contribution to the school library.
- **Newspaper** Some schools have a school newspaper. Local newspapers often publish student writing, especially if it is about local people and events.
- **Literary magazine** Magazines such as *Cricket* and *MidLink* publish student writing. Some schools have a literary magazine that publishes student writing once or twice a year.
- **Bulletin board** A rotating display of student writing is an effective way to see what your classmates have written. Illustrations and photographs add interest.

Some writing, such as journal writing, is private and not intended for an audience. However, even if you don't share your paper, don't throw it away. It might contain ideas that you can use later.

Proofreading Help

Use this proofreading checklist to help you check for errors in your writing, and use the proofreading symbols in the chart below to mark places that need corrections.

- ☑ Have I avoided run-on sentences and sentence fragments and punctuated sentences correctly?
- ☑ Have I used every word correctly, including plurals, possessives, and frequently confused words?
- ☑ Do verbs and subjects agree? Are verb tenses correct?
- ☑ Do pronouns refer clearly to their antecedents and agree with them in person, number, and gender?
- ☑ Have I used adverb and adjective forms and modifying phrases correctly?
- ☑ Have I spelled every word correctly, and checked the unfamiliar ones in a dictionary?

Proofreading Symbols

Symbol	Example	Meaning
⊙	Lieut. Brown	Insert a period.
∧	No one came to the party.	Insert a letter or a word.
≡	I enjoyed paris.	Capitalize a letter.
/	The Class ran a bake sale.	Make a capital letter lowercase.
⌒	The campers are home sick.	Close up a space.
⊘	They visited N.Y.	Spell out.
∧ ∧	Sue please come I need your help.	Insert a comma or a semicolon.
∼	He enjoyed feild day.	Transpose the position of letters or words.
#	alltogether	Insert a space.
ꝺ	We went to to Boston.	Delete letters or words.
∨∨ ∨	She asked Whos coming?	Insert quotation marks or an apostrophe.
/=/	mid January	Insert a hyphen.
¶	"Where?" asked Karl. "Over there," said Ray.	Begin a new paragraph.

Writing Handbook

Writing Modes

There are four main types, or modes, of writing—expository, descriptive, narrative, and persuasive. Each mode has its own purpose and characteristics.

Expository Writing

Expository writing communicates knowledge. It provides and explains information; it may also give general directions or step-by-step instructions for an activity.

Use this checklist as you write.

- ☑ Is the opening paragraph interesting?
- ☑ Are my explanations accurate and complete? Is information clear and easy to read?
- ☑ Is information presented in a logical order?
- ☑ Does each paragraph have a main idea? Does all the information support the main idea?
- ☑ Does my essay have an introduction, a body, and a conclusion?
- ☑ Have I defined any unfamiliar terms?
- ☑ Are my comparisons clear and logical?

Kinds of expository writing

Expository writing covers a wide range of styles. The chart below describes some of the possibilities.

Descriptive Writing

Descriptive writing can make a person, place, or thing come to life. The scene described may be as unfamiliar and far away as the bottom of the sea or as familiar and close as the gym locker room. By presenting details that awaken the reader's senses, descriptive writing can help your readers see the world more clearly.

Use this checklist to help you revise your description.

- ☑ Does my introduction identify the person or place that will be described?
- ☑ Are my details vivid? Are nouns and adjectives precise?
- ☑ Do all the details contribute to the same impression?
- ☑ Is it clear why this place or person is special?
- ☑ Are transitions clear? Do the paragraphs follow a logical order?
- ☑ Does each paragraph contain a main idea?
- ☑ Have I communicated a definite impression or mood?

Kinds of Expository Writing	Examples
Instructional writing	Explain how to train for a cross-country race, how to arrange a surprise party, or how to avoid cleaning up your room.
Compare-and-contrast essay	Compare two athletes or two sports, two fictional characters, two books or movies, two places, or two kinds of vacations.
Step-by-step directions	Give directions for building a model plane, making apple pie, or drawing on a computer screen.
Information and explanation	Explain what causes sunspots, how plants grow in the desert, or why camels have a hump.
Report or essay	Write a book report, a report on the Buddhist religion, or a report on a new wildlife center.

Narrative Writing

Narrative writing tells a story, either real or fictional. It answers the question *What happened?*

A well-written narrative holds the reader's attention by presenting interesting characters in a carefully ordered series of events.

This checklist will help you improve your narrative.
- ☑ Does my first sentence get the reader's attention?
- ☑ Are the characters and setting introduced with enough detail?
- ☑ Do the characters speak and behave realistically?
- ☑ Are the events narrated in an order clear enough for the reader to follow?
- ☑ Are there places where dialogue should be added?
- ☑ Is my ending satisfying to the reader?

Persuasive Writing

Persuasive writing presents an opinion. Its goal is to make readers feel or think a certain way about a situation or an idea. The writer includes facts and opinions often designed to urge readers to take action. Good persuasive writing can sometimes be hard to resist.

As you revise your persuasive writing, use this checklist as a guide.
- ☑ Is my main idea expressed in a clear statement?
- ☑ Have I presented good reasons to support my point of view?
- ☑ Have I supported my reasons with facts and opinions?
- ☑ Have I taken account of the opposing points of view?
- ☑ Have I addressed the interests of my audience?
- ☑ Have I ended with a strong closing statement?

Research Report Writing

When you write a research report, you explore a topic by gathering factual information from several different resources. Through your research, you develop a point of view or draw a conclusion. This point of view or conclusion becomes the main idea, or thesis, of your report.

Select a Topic

Because a research report usually takes time to prepare and write, your choice of topic is especially important. Follow these guidelines.
- Brainstorm a list of questions about a subject you would like to explore. Choose one that is neither too narrow nor too broad for the length of paper you will write. Use that question as your topic.
- Select a topic that genuinely interests you.
- Be sure you can find information on your topic from several different sources.

Do Research

Start by looking up your topic in an encyclopedia to find general information. Then find specific information in books, magazines, and newspapers, on CD-ROMs and the Internet, and from personal interviews when this seems appropriate. Use the computerized or card catalog in the library to locate books on your topic. Then search for up-to-date information in periodicals (magazines) or newspapers and from electronic sources, such as CD-ROMs or the Internet. If you need help in finding or using any of these resources, ask the librarian.

As you gather information, make sure each source you use relates closely to your topic. Also be sure that your source is reliable. Be extra careful if you are using information from the Internet. If you are not sure about the reliability of a source, consult the librarian or your teacher.

Writing Handbook

Make Source Cards

In a research report, you must document the source of your information. To keep track of your sources, write the author, title, publication information, and location of each source on a separate index card. Give each source card a number and write it in the upper right-hand corner. These cards will be useful for preparing a bibliography.

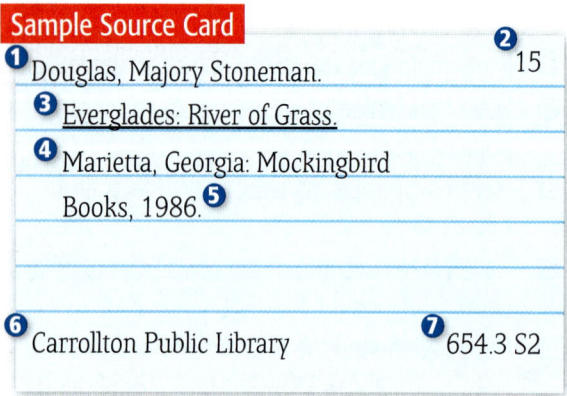

Sample Source Card
① Douglas, Majory Stoneman. ② 15
③ *Everglades: River of Grass.*
④ Marietta, Georgia: Mockingbird Books, 1986. ⑤

⑥ Carrollton Public Library   ⑦ 654.3 S2

① Author
② Source number
③ Title
④ City of publication/Publisher
⑤ Date of publication
⑥ Location of source
⑦ Library call number

Take Notes

As you read, you encounter many new facts and ideas. Taking notes will help you keep track of information and focus on the topic. Here are some helpful suggestions:

- Use a new card for each important piece of information. Separate cards will help you to organize your notes.
- At the top of each card, write a key word or phrase that tells you about the information. Also, write the number of the source you used.
- Write only details and ideas that relate to your topic.
- Summarize information in your own words.
- Write down a phrase or a quote only when the words are especially interesting or come from an important source. Enclose all quotes in quotation marks to make clear that the ideas belong to someone else.

This sample note card shows information to include.

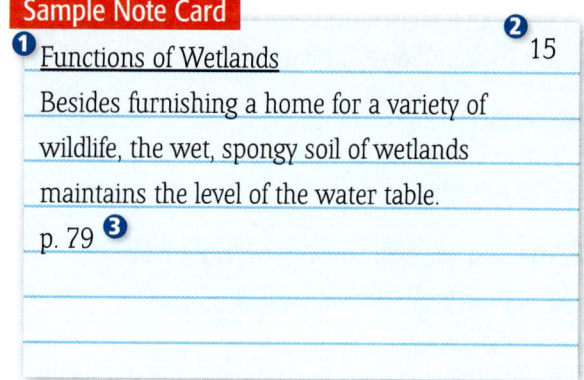

Sample Note Card
① Functions of Wetlands   ② 15
Besides furnishing a home for a variety of wildlife, the wet, spongy soil of wetlands maintains the level of the water table.
p. 79 ③

① Write a key word or phrase that tells you what the information is about.
② Write the source number from your source card.
③ Write the number of the page or pages on which you found the information.

Develop Your Thesis

As you begin researching and learning about your topic, think about the overall point you want to make. Write one sentence, your *thesis statement,* that says exactly what you plan to report on.

Sample Thesis Statement

Everglades National Park is a beautiful but endangered animal habitat.

Keep your thesis in mind as you continue to do research and think about your topic. The thesis will help you determine what information is important. However, be prepared to change your thesis if the information you find does not support it.

Write an Outline

When you finish taking notes, organize the information in an outline. Write down the main ideas that you want to cover. Write your thesis statement at the beginning of your outline. Then list the supporting details. Follow an outline form like the one on the next page.

❶ Everglades National Park is a beautiful but endangered animal habitat.
   I. Special aspects of the Everglades
      A. Characteristics of wetlands
   ❷ B. Endangered birds and animals
   II. Pressures on the Everglades
      A. Florida agriculture
      B. Carelessness of visitors
   III. How to protect the Everglades
      A. Change agricultural practices
      B. Educate park visitors
         1. Mandatory video on safety for
         ❸ individuals and environment
         2. Instructional reminders posted throughout the park

❶ The thesis statement identifies your topic and the overall point you will make.

❷ If you have subtopics under a main topic, there must be at least two. They must relate directly to your main topic.

❸ If you wish to divide a subtopic, you must have at least two divisions. Each must relate to the subtopic above it.

Document Your Information

You must document, or credit, the sources of all the information you use in your report. There are two common ways to document information.

Footnotes

To document with footnotes, place a number at the end of the information you are documenting. Number your notes consecutively, beginning with number 1. These numbers should be slightly raised and should come after any punctuation. The documentation information itself goes at the bottom of the page, with a matching number.

In-text number for note:
The Declaration of Independence was read in public for the first time on July 6, 1776.[3]
Footnote at bottom of page:
   [3] John Smith, The Declaration of Independence (New York: DI, 2001) 221.

Parenthetical Documentation

In this method, you give the source for your information in parentheses at the end of the sentence where the information appears. You do not need to give all the details of the source. Just provide enough information for your readers to identify it. Here are the basic rules to follow.

- Usually it is enough to give the author's last name and the number of the page where you found the information.

  The declaration was first read in public by militia colonel John Nixon (Smith 222).

- If you mention the author's name in the sentence, you do not need to repeat it in the parentheses.

  According to Smith, the reading was greeted with wild applause (224).

- If your source does not identify a particular author, as in a newspaper or encyclopedia article, give the first word or two of the title of the piece.

  The anniversary of the reading was commemorated by a parade and fireworks ("Reading Celebrated").

Full information on your sources goes in a list at the end of your paper.

Bibliography or Works Cited

At the end of your paper, list all the sources of information that you used in preparing your report. Arrange them alphabetically by the author's last name (or by the first word in the title if no author is mentioned) as shown below. Title this list *Works Cited*. (Use the term *bibliography* if all your sources are printed media, such as books, magazines, or newspapers.)

Writing Handbook   **R23**

Works Cited

[2] Bertram, Jeffrey. "African Bees: Fact or Myth?" *Orlando Sentinel* 18 Aug. 1999: D2.

[3] Gore, Rick. "Neanderthals." National Geographic. January 1996: 2–35. [8]

[4] Gould, Stephen J. The Panda's Thumb. New York: W. W. Norton & Co., 1982.

[5] "Governor Chiles Vetoes Anti-Everglades Bills–5/13/98." [9] Friends of the Everglades. May 1998. 26 Aug 1998 <http://www.everglades.org/pressrel_may28.htm>.

[6] "Neanderthal man." The Columbia Encyclopedia. 5th Edition. New York: Columbia University Press, 1993.

[7] Pabst, Laura (Curator of Natural History Museum), Interview. March 11, 1998.

[1] Indent all but the first line of each item.
[2] Newspaper article
[3] Magazine article
[4] Book with one author
[5] On-line article
[6] Encyclopedia
[7] Interview
[8] Include page numbers for a magazine article but not for a book, unless the book is a collection of essays by different authors.
[9] Include database (underlined), publication medium (online), computer service, and date of access.

Business Writing

Two standard formats for business letters are block style and modified block style. In block style all the parts of the letter begin at the left-hand margin.

Business Letter

The following business letter uses modified block style

❶ 10 Pullman Lane
Cromwell, CT 06416
January 16, 2006

❷ Mr. Philip Fornaro
Principal
Cromwell School
179 West Maple St.
Cromwell, CT 06416

❸ Dear Mr. Fornaro:

❹ My friends and I in the seventh grade at Brimmer Middle School feel that there is not enough to do in Cromwell during the winter vacation week. Some students can afford to go away for vacation. Many families, however, cannot afford to go away, or the parents have to work.

❺ I would like to suggest that you keep the Brimmer Middle School gym open during the vacation week. If the gym were open, the basketball teams could practice. The fencing club could meet. We could meet our friends there instead of going to the mall.

❻ Thanks for listening to my request. I hope you will think it over.

❼ Sincerely,
Kim Goodwin
Kim Goodwin

❶ In the heading, write your address and the date on separate lines.

❷ In the inside address, write the name and address of the person to whom you are sending the letter.

❸ Use a colon after the greeting.

❹ In your introduction, say who you are and why you are writing.

❺ In the body of your letter, provide details concerning your request.

❻ Conclude by restating your purpose and thanking the person you are writing to.

❼ In the closing, use *Sincerely, Sincerely yours,* or *Yours truly* followed by a comma. Include both your signature and your printed or typed name.

General guidelines

Follow these guidelines when writing a business letter.

- Use correct business-letter form. Whether you write by hand, or use a computer, use 8 1/2-by-11-inch white or off-white paper. Be sure your letter is neat and clean.
- Use Standard English. Check your spelling carefully.
- Be polite, even if you are making a complaint or expressing a negative opinion.
- Be brief and to the point. State your reason for writing within the first two or three sentences.
- Include all necessary information.
- If you are making a request, be specific. Make sure what you are asking is reasonable. Express your appreciation at the end of the letter.
- Be considerate. Request only information you cannot get another way.
- When expressing an opinion or a complaint, state your reasons clearly and logically. Avoid emotional language.
- When requesting an interview, make it easy for the interviewee to meet with you. Suggest a few dates.

Writing Handbook **R25**

Writing a Memo

A memo, or memorandum, is a brief, efficient way of communicating information to another person or group of people. It begins with a header that provides basic information. A memo does not have a formal closing.

> TO: *Brimmer Banner* newspaper staff
> FROM: Terry Glinski
> SUBJECT: Winter issue
> DATE: January 18, 2006
>
> Articles for the winter issue of the *Brimmer Banner* are due by February 1. Please see Terry about your assignment as soon as possible! The following articles or features have not yet been assigned:
>
> Cafeteria Mess: Who Is Responsible?
> Teacher Profile: Mr. Jinks, Ms. Magee
> Sports roundup

Using a Computer for Writing

Using a computer offers advantages at every stage of the writing process.

Prewriting

A computer can help you gather and organize ideas and information.

Brainstorming
While brainstorming for topics or details, you can dim the computer screen and do "invisible writing." Some writers find that this technique allows their ideas to flow more freely.

Researching
Use the Internet or a CD-ROM encyclopedia to find not only text and pictures, but also sound, animated cartoons or graphics, and live-action video clips.

Outlining
Some word-processing programs offer an outlining feature that automatically indents headings and uses different type styles for main headings and subheadings.

Drafting/Revising

Most word-processing programs make it easy to do the following.
- *insert* new text at any point in your document
- *delete* or *copy* text
- *move* text from one position to another
- *undo* a change you just made
- *save* each draft or revision of your document
- *print* copies of your work-in-progress for others to read

Editing/Proofreading

You can edit and proofread directly on the computer, or you can mark your changes on a printout, or hard copy, and then input the changes on screen. The following word-processing features are helpful.

- **Grammar checker** The computer finds possible errors in grammar and suggests revisions.
- **Spelling checker** The computer finds misspellings and suggests corrections.
- **Thesaurus** If you want to replace an inappropriate or overused word, you can highlight the word and the computer will suggest synonyms.
- **Search and replace** If you want to change or correct something that occurs several times in your document, the computer can quickly make the change throughout the document.

> **TIP**
> The grammar checker, spelling checker, and thesaurus cannot replace your own careful reading and judgment. Because English grammar is so complex, the suggestions that the grammar checker makes may not be appropriate. Also, the spelling checker will not tell you that you have typed *brake* when you meant *break*, for example, because both are valid words. The thesaurus may offer you several synonyms for a word, but you need to consider the connotations of each before deciding which, if any, fits your context.

Presenting

The computer allows you to enhance the readability, attractiveness, and visual interest of your document in many ways.

Formatting your text
The computer gives you a variety of options for the layout and appearance of your text. You can easily add or change the following elements.
- margin width
- number of columns
- type size and style
- page numbering
- header or footer (information such as a title that appears at the top or bottom of every page)

Visual aids
Some word-processing programs have graphic functions that allow you to create graphs, charts, and diagrams. Collections of *clip art,* pictures you can copy and paste into your document, are also available.

LANGUAGE HANDBOOK

Troubleshooter

Use the Troubleshooter to recognize and correct common writing errors.

Sentence Fragment

A sentence fragment does not express a complete thought. It may lack a subject or verb or both.

- **Problem: Fragment that lacks a subject**

    The lion paced the floor of the cage. Looked hungry. *frag*

    Solution: Add a subject to the fragment to make a complete sentence.

    The lion paced the floor of the cage. He looked hungry.

- **Problem: Fragment that lacks a predicate**

    I'm painting my room. The walls yellow. *frag*

    Solution: Add a predicate to make the sentence complete.

    I'm painting my room. The walls are going to be yellow.

- **Problem: Fragment that lacks both a subject and a predicate**

    We walked around the reservoir. Near the parkway. *frag*

    Solution: Combine the fragment with another sentence.

    We walked around the reservoir near the parkway.

 TIP

You can use fragments when talking with friends or writing personal letters. Some writers use fragments to produce a special effect. Use complete sentences, however, for school or business writing.

Run-on Sentence

A run-on sentence is two or more sentences written incorrectly as one sentence.

- **Problem: Two main clauses separated only by a comma**

    Roller coasters make me dizzy, I don't enjoy them. *run-on*

    Solution A: Replace the comma with a period or other end mark. Start the second sentence with a capital letter.

    Roller coasters make me dizzy. I don't enjoy them.

    Solution B: Replace the comma with a semicolon.

    Roller coasters make me dizzy; I don't enjoy them.

- **Problem: Two main clauses with no punctuation between them**

    Acid rain is a worldwide problem there are no solutions in sight. *run-on*

    Solution A: Separate the main clauses with a period or other end mark. Begin the second sentence with a capital letter.

    Acid rain is a worldwide problem. There are no solutions in sight.

    Solution B: Add a comma and a coordinating conjunction between the main clauses.

    Acid rain is a worldwide problem, but there are no solutions in sight.

- **Problem: Two main clauses with no comma before the coordinating conjunction**

    Our chorus has been practicing all month but we still need another rehearsal. *run-on*

R28 Language Handbook

Solution: Add a comma before the coordinating conjunction.

Our chorus has been practicing all month, but we still need another rehearsal.

Lack of Subject-Verb Agreement

A singular subject calls for a singular form of the verb. A plural subject calls for a plural form of the verb.

- **Problem: A subject that is separated from the verb by an intervening prepositional phrase**

  The two policemen at the construction site looks bored. *agr*

  The members of my baby-sitting club is saving money. *agr*

  Solution: Make sure that the verb agrees with the subject of the sentence, not with the object of the preposition. The object of a preposition is never the subject.

  The two policemen at the construction site look bored.

  The members of my baby-sitting club are saving money.

  TIP

  When subject and verb are separated by a prepositional phrase, check for agreement by reading the sentence without the prepositional phrase.

- **Problem: A sentence that begins with *here* or *there***

  Here come the last bus to Pelham Heights. *agr*

  There is my aunt and uncle. *agr*

  Solution: In sentences that begin with *here* or *there*, look for the subject after the verb. Make sure that the verb agrees with the subject.

  Here comes the last bus to Pelham Heights.

  There are my aunt and uncle.

- **Problem: An indefinite pronoun as the subject**

  Each of the candidates are qualified. *agr*

  All of the problems on the test was hard. *agr*

  Solution: Some indefinite pronouns are singular; some are plural; and some can be either singular or plural, depending on the noun they refer to. Determine whether the indefinite pronoun is singular or plural, and make sure the verb agrees with it.

  Each of the candidates is qualified.

  All of the problems on the test were hard.

- **Problem: A compound subject that is joined by *and***

  Fishing tackle and a life jacket was stowed in the boat. *agr*

  Peanut butter and jelly are delicious. *agr*

  Solution A: If the compound subjects refer to different people or things, use a plural verb.

  Fishing tackle and a life jacket were stowed in the boat.

  Solution B: If the parts of a compound subject name one unit or if they refer to the same person or thing, use a singular verb.

  Peanut butter and jelly is delicious.

- **Problem: A compound subject that is joined by *or* or *nor***

  Either my aunt or my parents plans to attend parents' night. *agr*

  Neither onions nor pepper improve the taste of this meatloaf. *agr*

  Solution: Make the verb agree with the subject that is closer to it.

  Either my aunt or my parents plan to attend parents' night.

  Neither onions nor pepper improves the taste of this meatloaf.

Language Handbook

Incorrect Verb Tense or Form

Verbs have different tenses to show when the action takes place.

- **Problem: An incorrect or missing verb ending**

    The Parks Department install a new water fountain last week. *tense*

    They have also plant flowers in all the flower beds. *tense*

    Solution: To form the past tense and the part participle, add -ed to a regular verb.

    The Parks Department installed a new water fountain last week.

    They have also planted flowers in all the flower beds.

- **Problem: An improperly formed irregular verb**

    Wendell has standed in line for two hours. *tense*

    I catched the fly ball and throwed it to first base. *tense*

    Solution: Irregular verbs vary in their past and past participle forms. Look up the ones you are not sure of.

    Wendell has stood in line for two hours.

    I caught the fly ball and threw it to first base.

- **Problem: Confusion between the past form and the past participle**

    The cast for *The Music Man* has began rehearsals. *tense*

    Solution: Use the past participle form of an irregular verb, not its past form, when you use the auxiliary verb *have*.

    The cast for *The Music Man* has begun rehearsals.

- **Problem: Improper use of the past participle**

    Our seventh grade drawn a mural for the wall of the cafeteria. *tense*

    Solution: Add the auxiliary verb *have* to the past participle of an irregular verb to form a complete verb.

    Our seventh grade has drawn a mural for the wall of the cafeteria.

TIP

Because irregular verbs vary, it is useful to memorize the verbs that you use most often.

Incorrect Use of Pronouns

The noun that a pronoun refers to is called its antecedent. A pronoun must refer to its **antecedent** clearly. Subject pronouns refer to subjects in a sentence. Object pronouns refer to objects in a sentence.

- **Problem: A pronoun that could refer to more than one antecedent**

    Gary and Mike are coming, but he doesn't know the other kids. *ant*

    Solution: Substitute a noun for the pronoun to make your sentence clearer.

    Gary and Mike are coming, but Gary doesn't know the other kids.

- **Problem: Personal pronouns as subjects**

    Him and John were freezing after skating for three hours. *pro*

    Lori and me decided not to audition for the musical. *pro*

    Solution: Use a subject pronoun as the subject part of a sentence.

    He and John were freezing after skating for three hours.

    Lori and I decided not to audition for the musical.

- **Problem: Personal pronouns as objects**

    Ms. Wang asked Reggie and I to enter the science fair *pro*

    Ms. Wang helped he and I with the project. *pro*

    Solution: Use an object pronoun as the object of a verb or a preposition.

    Ms. Wang asked Reggie and me to enter the science fair.

    Ms. Wang helped him and me with the project.

Incorrect Use of Adjectives

Some adjectives have irregular forms: comparative forms for comparing two things and superlative forms for comparing more than two things.

Problem: Incorrect use of *good, better, best*

Their team is **more good** at softball than ours.

They have **more better** equipment too.

Solution: The comparative and superlative forms of *good* are *better* and *best*. Do not use *more* or *most* before irregular forms of comparative and superlative adjectives.

Their team is better at softball than ours.

They have better equipment too.

Problem: Incorrect use of *bad, worse, worst*

The flooding on East Street was the **baddest** I've seen.

Mike's basement was in **badder** shape than his garage.

Solution: The comparative and superlative forms of *bad* are *worse* and *worst*. Do not use *more* or *most* or the endings *-er* or *-est* with *bad*.

The flooding on East Street was the worst I've seen.

Mike's basement was in worse shape than his garage.

Problem: Incorrect use of comparative and superlative adjectives

The Appalachian Mountains are **more older** than the Rockies.

Mount Washington is the **most highest** of the Appalachians.

Solution: Do not use both *-er* and *more* or *-est* and *most* at the same time.

The Appalachian Mountains are older than the Rockies.

Mount Washington is the highest of the Appalachians.

Incorrect Use of Commas

Commas signal a pause between parts of a sentence and help to clarify meaning.

Problem: Missing commas in a series of three or more items

Sergio put mustard catsup and bean sprouts on his hot dog.

Solution: If there are three or more items in a series, use a comma after each one, including the item preceding the conjunction.

Sergio put mustard, catsup, and bean sprouts on his hot dog.

Problem: Missing commas with direct quotations

"A little cold water" the swim coach said "won't hurt you."

Solution: The first part of an interrupted quotation ends with a comma followed by quotation marks. The interrupting words are also followed by a comma.

"A little cold water," the swim coach said, "won't hurt you."

Problem: Missing commas with nonessential appositives

My sneakers a new pair are covered with mud.

Solution: Determine whether the appositive is important to the meaning of the sentence. If it is not essential, set off the appositive with commas.

My sneakers, a new pair, are covered with mud.

LANGUAGE HANDBOOK

Incorrect Use of Apostrophes

An apostrophe shows possession. It can also indicate missing letters in a contraction.

Problem: Singular possessive nouns

A parrots toes are used for gripping. *poss*
The bus color was bright yellow. *poss*

Solution: Use an apostrophe and an *s* to form the possessive of a singular noun, even one that ends in *s*.

A parrot's toes are used for gripping.
The bus's color was bright yellow.

Problem: Plural possessive nouns ending in -s

The visitors center closes at five o'clock. *poss*
The guide put several tourists luggage in one compartment. *poss*

Solution: Use an apostrophe alone to form the possessive of a plural noun that ends in *s*.

The visitors' center closes at five o'clock.
The guide put several tourists' luggage in one compartment.

Problem: Plural possessive nouns not ending in -s

The peoples applause gave courage to the young gymnast. *poss*

Solution: Use an apostrophe and an *s* to form the possessive of a plural noun that does not end in *s*.

The people's applause gave courage to the young gymnast.

Problem: Possessive personal pronouns

Jenny found the locker that was her's; she waited while her friends found their's. *poss*

Solution: Do not use apostrophes with possessive personal pronouns.

Jenny found the locker that was hers; she waited while her friends found theirs.

Incorrect Capitalization

Proper nouns, proper adjectives, and the first words of sentences always begin with a capital letter.

Problem: Words referring to ethnic groups, nationalities, and languages

Many canadians in the province of quebec speak french. *cap*

Solution: Capitalize proper nouns and adjectives that refer to ethnic groups, nationalities, and languages.

Many Canadians in the province of Quebec speak French.

Problem: Words that refer to a family member

Yesterday aunt Doreen asked me to baby-sit. *cap*
Don't forget to give dad a call. *cap*

Solution: Capitalize words that are used as part of or in place of a family member's name.

Yesterday Aunt Doreen asked me to baby-sit.
Don't forget to give Dad a call.

> **TIP**
> Do not capitalize a word that identifies a family member when it is preceded by a possessive adjective: *My father bought a new car.*

Problem: The first word of a direct quotation

The judge declared, "the court is now in session." *cap*

Solution: Capitalize the first word in a direct quotation.

The judge declared, "The court is now in session."

> **TIP**
> If you have difficulty with a rule of usage, try rewriting the rule in your own words. Check with your teacher to be sure you understand the rule.

Troublesome Words

This section will help you choose between words and expressions that are often confusing or misused.

accept, except
Accept means "to receive." *Except* means "other than."

> Phillip walked proudly to the stage to accept the award.
>
> Everything fits in my suitcase except my sleeping bag.

affect, effect
Affect is a verb meaning "to cause a change in" or "to influence." *Effect* as a verb means "to bring about or accomplish." As a noun, *effect* means "result."

> Bad weather will affect our plans for the weekend.
>
> The new medicine effected an improvement in the patient's condition.
>
> The gloomy weather had a bad effect on my mood.

ain't
Ain't is never used in formal speaking or writing unless you are quoting the exact words of a character or a real person. Instead of using *ain't*, say or write *am not, is not, are not;* or use contractions such as *I'm not, she isn't.*

> The pizza is not going to arrive for another half hour.
>
> The pizza isn't going to arrive for another half hour.

a lot
The expression *a lot* means "much" or "many" and should always be written as two words. Some authorities discourage its use in formal writing.

> A lot of my friends are learning Spanish.
>
> Many of my friends are learning Spanish.

all ready, already
All ready, written as two words, is a phrase that means "completely ready." *Already,* written as one word, is an adverb that means "before" or "by this time."

> By the time the fireworks display was all ready, we had already arrived.

all right, alright
The expression *all right* should be written as two words. Some dictionaries do list the single word *alright* but usually not as a preferred spelling.

> Tom hurt his ankle, but he will be all right.

all together, altogether
All together means "in a group." *Altogether* means "completely."

> The Minutemen stood all together at the end of Lexington Green.
>
> The rebel farmers were not altogether sure that they could fight the British soldiers.

among, between
Use *among* for three or more people, things, or groups. Use *between* for two people, things, or groups.

> Mr. Kendall divided the jobs for the car wash among the team members.
>
> Our soccer field lies between the gym and Main Street.

amount, number
Use *amount* with nouns that cannot be counted. Use *number* with nouns that can be counted.

> This recipe calls for an unusual amount of pepper.
>
> A record number of students attended last Saturday's book fair.

bad, badly
Bad is an adjective; it modifies a noun.
Badly is an adverb; it modifies a verb, an adjective, or another adverb.

> The badly burnt cookies left a bad smell in the kitchen.
>
> Joseph badly wants to be on the track team.

Language Handbook

beside, besides
Beside means "next to." *Besides* means "in addition to."

> The zebra is grazing beside a wildebeest.
>
> Besides the zoo, I like to visit the aquarium.

bring, take
Bring means "to carry from a distant place to a closer one." *Take* means "to carry from a nearby place to a more distant one."

> Please bring a bag lunch and subway money to school tomorrow.
>
> Don't forget to take your art projects home this afternoon.

can, may
Can implies the ability to do something. *May* implies permission to do something.

> You may take a later bus home if you can remember which bus to get on.

> **TIP**
> Although *can* is sometimes used in place of *may* in informal speech, a distinction should be made when speaking and writing formally.

choose, chose
Choose means "to select." *Chose,* the past tense of *choose,* means "selected."

> Dad helped me choose a birthday card for my grandmother.
>
> Dad chose a card with a funny joke inside.

doesn't, don't
The subject of the contraction **doesn't** *(does not)* is the third-person singular (*he* or *she*). The subject of the contraction **don't** *(do not)* is *I, you, we,* or *they.*

> Tanya doesn't have any tickets for the concert.
>
> We don't need tickets if we stand in the back row.

farther, further
Farther refers to physical distance. *Further* refers to time or degree.

> Our new apartment is farther away from the school.
>
> I will not continue this argument further.

fewer, less
Fewer is used to refer to things or qualities that can be counted. *Less* is used to refer to things or qualities that cannot be counted. In addition, *less* is used with figures that are regarded as single amounts.

> Fewer people were waiting in line after lunch.
>
> There is less fat in this kind of peanut butter.
>
> Try to spend less than ten dollars on a present. [The money is treated as a single sum, not as individual dollars.]

good, well
Good is often used as an adjective meaning "pleasing" or "able." *Well* may be used as an adverb of manner telling how ably something is done or as an adjective meaning "in good health."

> That is a good haircut.
>
> Marco writes well.
>
> Because Ms. Rodriguez had a headache, she was not well enough to correct our tests.

in, into
In means "inside." *Into* indicates a movement from outside toward the inside.

> Refreshments will be sold in the lobby of the auditorium.
>
> The doors opened, and the eager crowd rushed into the auditorium.

it's, its
Use an apostrophe to form the contraction of *it is.* The possessive of the personal pronoun *it* does not take an apostrophe.

> It's hard to keep up with computer technology.
>
> The computer industry seems to change its products daily.

lay, lie
Lay means "to place." *Lie* means "to recline."

    I will lay my beach towel here on the warm sand.

    Help! I don't want to lie next to a hill of red ants!

learn, teach
Learn means "to gain knowledge." *Teach* means "to give knowledge."

    I don't learn very quickly.

    My uncle is teaching me how to juggle.

leave, let
Leave means "to go away." *Let* means "to allow." With the word *alone,* you may use either *let* or *leave.*

    Huang has to leave at eight o'clock.

    Mr. Davio lets the band practice in his basement.

    Leave me alone. Let me alone.

like, as
Use *like,* a preposition, to introduce a prepositional phrase. Use *as,* a subordinating conjunction, to introduce a subordinate clause. Many authorities believe that *like* should not be used before a clause in formal English.

    Andy sometimes acts like a clown.

    The detective looked carefully at the empty suitcase as she examined the room.

> **TIP**
>
> *As* can be a preposition in cases like the following: *Jack went to the costume party as a giant pumpkin.*

loose, lose
Loose means "not firmly attached." *Lose* means "to misplace" or "to fail to win."

    If you keep wiggling that loose tooth, you might lose it.

raise, rise
Raise means to "cause to move up." *Rise* means "to move upward."

    Farmers in this part of Florida raise sugarcane.

    The hot air balloon began to rise slowly in the morning sky.

set, sit
Set means "to place" or "to put." *Sit* means "to place oneself in a seated position."

    I set the tips of my running shoes against the starting line.

    After running the fifty-yard dash, I had to sit down and catch my breath.

than, then
Than introduces the second part of a comparison. *Then* means "at that time" or "after that."

    I'd rather go to Disney World in the winter than in the summer.

    The park is too crowded and hot then.

their, they're
Their is the possessive form of *they. They're* is the contraction of *they are.*

    They're visiting Plymouth Plantation during their vacation.

to, too, two
To means "in the direction of." *Too* means "also" or "to an excessive degree." *Two* is the number after one.

    I bought two tickets to the concert.

    The music was too loud.

    It's my favorite group too.

who, whom
Who is a subject pronoun. *Whom* is an object pronoun.

    Who has finished the test already?

    Mr. Russo is the man to whom we owe our thanks.

who's, whose
Who's is the contraction of *who is. Whose* is the possessive form of *who.*

    Who's going to wake me up in the morning?

    The policeman discovered whose car alarm was making so much noise.

Mechanics

This section will help you use correct capitalization, punctuation, and abbreviations in your writing.

Capitalization

Capitalizing Sentences, Quotations, and Salutations

Rule: A capital letter appears at the beginning of a sentence.

Example: Another gust of wind shook the house.

Rule: A capital letter marks the beginning of a direct quotation that is a complete sentence.

Example: Sabrina said, "The lights might go out."

Rule: When a quoted sentence is interrupted by explanatory words, such as she said, do not begin the second part of the sentence with a capital letter.

Example: "There's a rainbow," exclaimed Jeffrey, "over the whole beach."

Rule: When the second part of a quotation is a new sentence, put a period after the explanatory words; begin the new part with a capital letter.

Example: "Please come inside," Justin said. "Wipe your feet."

Rule: Do not capitalize an indirect quotation.

Example: Jo said that the storm was getting worse.

Rule: Capitalize the first word in the salutation and closing of a letter. Capitalize the title and name of the person addressed.

Example: Dear Dr. Menino
Dear Editor
Sincerely

Capitalizing Names and Titles of People

Rule: Capitalize the names of people and the initials that stand for their names.

Example: Malcolm X   J. F. K.
Robert E. Lee   Queen Elizabeth I

Rule: Capitalize a title or an abbreviation of a title when it comes before a person's name or when it is used in direct address.

Example: Dr. Salinas
"Your patient, Doctor, is waiting."

Rule: Do not capitalize a title that follows or is a substitute for a person's name.

Example: Marcia Salinas is a good doctor.
He asked to speak to the doctor.

Rule: Capitalize the names and abbreviations of academic degrees that follow a person's name. Capitalize Jr. and Sr.

Example: Marcia Salinas, M.D.
Raoul Tobias, Attorney
Donald Bruns Sr.
Ann Lee, Ph.D.

Rule: Capitalize words that show family relationships when used as titles or as substitutes for a person's name.

Example: We saw Uncle Carlos.
She read a book about Mother Teresa.

Rule: Do not capitalize words that show family relationships when they follow a possessive noun or pronoun.

Example: Your brother will give us a ride.
I forgot my mother's phone number.

Rule: Always capitalize the pronoun I.

Example: After I clean my room, I'm going swimming.

Capitalizing Names of Places

Do not capitalize articles and prepositions in proper nouns: *the* Rock *of* Gibraltar, *the* Statue *of* Liberty.

Rule: Capitalize the names of cities, counties, states, countries, and continents.

Example: St. Louis, Missouri
Marin County
Australia
South America

Rule: Capitalize the names of bodies of water and other geographical features.

Example: the Great Lakes   Cape Cod
the Dust Bowl

Rule: Capitalize the names of sections of a country and regions of the world.

Example: East Asia
New England
the Pacific Rim
the Midwest

Rule: Capitalize compass points when they refer to a specific section of a country.

Example: the Northwest   the South

Rule: Do not capitalize compass points when they indicate direction.

Example: Canada is north of the United States.

Rule: Do not capitalize adjectives indicating direction.

Example: western Utah

Rule: Capitalize the names of streets and highways.

Example: Dorchester Avenue   Route 22

Rule: Capitalize the names of buildings, bridges, monuments, and other structures.

Example: World Trade Center
Chesapeake Bay Bridge

Capitalizing Other Proper Nouns and Adjectives

Rule: Capitalize the names of clubs, organizations, businesses, institutions, and political parties.

Example: Houston Oilers
the Food and Drug Administration
Boys and Girls Club

Rule: Capitalize brand names but not the nouns following them.

Example: Zippo brand energy bar

Rule: Capitalize the names of days of the week, months, and holidays.

Example: Saturday   June
Thanksgiving Day

Rule: Do not capitalize the names of seasons.

Example: winter, spring, summer, fall

Rule: Capitalize the first word, the last word, and all important words in the title of a book, play, short story, poem, essay, article, film, television series, song, magazine, newspaper, and chapter of a book.

Example: *Not Without Laughter*
World Book Encyclopedia
"Jingle Bells"
Star Wars
Chapter 12

Rule: Capitalize the names of ethnic groups, nationalities, and languages.

Example: Latino   Japanese
European   Spanish

Rule: Capitalize proper adjectives that are formed from the names of ethnic groups and nationalities.

Example: Shetland pony
Jewish holiday

Punctuation

Using the Period and Other End Marks

Rule: Use a period at the end of a declarative sentence.

My great-grandfather fought in the Mexican Revolution.

Rule: Use a period at the end of an imperative sentence that does not express strong feeling.

Please set the table.

Rule: Use a question mark at the end of an interrogative sentence.

How did your sneakers get so muddy?

Rule: Use an exclamation point at the end of an exclamatory sentence or a strong imperative.

How exciting the play was!

Watch out!

Using Commas

Rule: Use commas to separate three or more items in a series.

The canary eats bird seed, fruit, and suet.

Rule: Use commas to show a pause after an introductory word and to set off names used in direct address.

Yes, I offered to take care of her canary this weekend.

Please, Stella, can I borrow your nail polish?

Rule: Use a comma after two or more introductory prepositional phrases or when the comma is needed to make the meaning clear. A comma is not needed after a single short prepositional phrase, but it is acceptable to use one.

From the back of the balcony, we had a lousy view of the stage.

After the movie we walked home. (no comma needed)

Rule: Use a comma after an introductory participle and an introductory participial phrase.

Whistling and moaning, the wind shook the little house.

Rule: Use commas to set off words that interrupt the flow of thought in a sentence.

Tomorrow, I think, our projects are due.

Rule: Use a comma after conjunctive adverbs such as *however, moreover, furthermore, nevertheless,* and *therefore*.

The skating rink is crowded on Saturday; however, it's the only time I can go.

Rule: Use commas to set off an appositive if it is not essential to the meaning of a sentence.

Ben Wagner, a resident of Pittsfield, won the first round in the golf tournament.

Rule: Use a comma before a conjunction (*and, or, but, nor, so, yet*) that joins main clauses.

We can buy our tickets now, or we can take a chance on buying them just before the show.

Rule: Use a comma after an introductory adverb clause.

Because I stayed up so late, I'm sleepy this morning.

Rule: In most cases, do not use a comma with an adverb clause that comes at the end of a sentence.

The picnic will be canceled unless the weather clears.

Rule: Use a comma or a pair of commas to set off an adjective clause that is not essential to the meaning of a sentence.

Tracy, who just moved here from Florida, has never seen snow before.

Rule: Do not use a comma or pair of commas to set off an essential clause from the rest of the sentence.

Anyone who signs up this month will get a discount.

Rule: Use commas before and after the year when it is used with both the month and the day. If only the month and the year are given, do not use a comma.

On January 2, 1985, my parents moved to Dallas, Texas.

I was born in May 1985.

Rule: Use commas before and after the name of a state or a country when it is used with the name of a city. Do not use a comma after the state if it is used with a ZIP code.

> The area code for Concord, New Hampshire, is 603.
>
> Please forward my mail to 6 Madison Lane, Topsham, ME 04086

Rule: Use commas or a pair of commas to set off an abbreviated title or degree following a person's name.

> The infirmary was founded by Elizabeth Blackwell, M.D., the first woman in the United States to earn a medical degree.

Rule: Use a comma or commas to set off *too* when *too* means "also."

> We, too, bought groceries, from the new online supermarket.

Rule: Use a comma or commas to set off a direct quotation.

> "My nose," exclaimed Pinocchio, "is growing longer!"

Rule: Use a comma after the salutation of a friendly letter and after the closing of both a friendly letter and a business letter.

> Dear Gary,
>
> Sincerely,
>
> Best regards,

Rule: Use a comma when necessary to prevent misreading of a sentence.

> In math, solutions always elude me.

Using Semicolons and Colons

Rule: Use a semicolon to join the parts of a compound sentence when a coordinating conjunction, such as *and, or, nor,* or *but,* is not used.

> Don't be late for the dress rehearsal; it begins at 7 o'clock sharp.

Rule: Use a semicolon to join parts of a compound sentence when the main clauses are long and are subdivided by commas. Use a semicolon even if these clauses are already joined by a coordinating conjunction.

> In the gray light of early morning, on a remote airstrip in the desert, two pilots prepared to fly on a dangerous mission; but accompanying them were a television camera crew, three newspaper reporters, and a congressman from their home state of Nebraska.

Rule: Use a semicolon to separate main clauses joined by a conjunctive adverb. Be sure to use a comma after the conjunctive adverb.

> We've been climbing all morning; therefore, we need a rest.

Rule: Use a colon to introduce a list of items that ends a sentence. Use words such as *these, the following,* or *as follows* to signal that a list is coming.

> Remember to bring the following items: a backpack, a bag lunch, sunscreen, and insect repellent.

Rule: Do not use a colon to introduce a list preceded by a verb or preposition.

> Remember to bring a backpack, a bag lunch, sunscreen, and insect repellent. (No colon is used after *bring*.)

Rule: Use a colon to separate the hour and the minutes when you write the time of day.

> My Spanish class starts at 9:15.

Rule: Use a colon after the salutation of a business letter.

> Dear Dr. Coulombe:
> Director of the Personnel Dept.:

Using Quotation Marks and Italics

Rule: Use quotation marks before and after a direct quotation.

> "Curiouser and curiouser," said Alice.

Rule: Use quotation marks with both parts of a divided quotation.

> "This gymnastics trick," explained Amanda, "took me three months to learn."

Rule: Use a comma or commas to separate a phrase such as *she said* from the quotation itself. Place the comma that precedes the phrase inside the closing quotation marks.

"I will be late," said the cable technician, "for my appointment."

Rule: Place a period that ends a quotation inside the closing quotation marks.

Scott said, "Thanks for letting me borrow your camping tent."

Rule: Place a question mark or an exclamation point inside the quotation marks when it is part of the quotation.

"Why is the door of your snake's cage open?" asked my mother.

Rule: Place a question mark or an exclamation point outside the quotation marks when it is part of the entire sentence.

How I love "The Pit and the Pendulum"!

Rule: Use quotation marks for the title of a short story, essay, poem, song, magazine or newspaper article, or book chapter.

short story: "The Necklace"
poem: "The Fish"
article: "Fifty Things to Make from Bottlecaps"

Rule: Use italics or underlining for the title of a book, play, film, television series, magazine, newspaper, or work of art.

book: *To Kill a Mockingbird*
magazine: *The New Republic*
painting: *Sunflowers*

Rule: Use italics or underlining for the names of ships, trains, airplanes, and spacecraft.

ship: *Mayflower*
airplane: *Air Force One*

Using Apostrophes

Rule: Use an apostrophe and an *s* (*'s*) to form the possessive of a singular noun.

my brother's rock collection
Chris's hat

Rule: Use an apostrophe and an *s* (*'s*) to form the possessive of a plural noun that does not end in *s*.

the geese's feathers
the oxen's domestication

> **TIP**
>
> If a thing is owned jointly by two or more individuals, only the last name should show possession: *Mom and Dad's car*. If the ownership is not joint, each name should show possession: *Mom and Dad's parents are coming for Thanksgiving.*

Rule: Use an apostrophe alone to form the possessive of a plural noun that ends in *s*.

the animals' habitat
the instruments' sound

Rule: Use an apostrophe and an *s* (*'s*) to form the possessive of an indefinite pronoun.

everyone's homework
someone's homework

Rule: Do not use an apostrophe in a possessive pronoun.

The dog knocked over its dish.
Yours is the best entry in the contest.
One of these drawings must be hers.

Rule: Use an apostrophe to replace letters that have been omitted in a contraction.

it + is = it's
can + not = can't
I + have = I've

Rule: Use an apostrophe to form the plural of a letter, a figure, or a word that is used as itself.

Write three 7's.
The word is spelled with two m's.
The sentence contains three and's.

Rule: Use an apostrophe to show missing numbers in a year.

the class of '02

Using Hyphens, Dashes, and Parentheses

Rule: Use a hyphen to show the division of a word at the end of a line. Always divide the word between its syllables.

> With the new recycling pro-
> gram, more residents are recycling
> their trash.

TIP
One-letter divisions (for example, *e-lectric*) are not permissible. Avoid dividing personal names, if possible.

Rule: Use a hyphen in a number written as a compound word.

> He sold forty-six ice creams in one hour.

Rule: Use a hyphen in a fraction.

> We won the vote by a two-thirds majority.
> Two-thirds of the votes have been counted.

Rule: Use a hyphen or hyphens in certain compound nouns.

> great-grandmother
> merry-go-round

Rule: Hyphenate a compound modifier only when it precedes the word it modifies.

> A well-known musician visited our school.
> The story was well written.

Rule: Use a hyphen after the prefixes *all-, ex-,* and *self-* when they are joined to any noun or adjective.

> all-star
> ex-president
> self-conscious

Rule: Use a hyphen to separate any prefix from a word that begins with a capital letter.

> un-American
> mid-January

Rule: Use a dash or dashes to show a sudden break or change in thought or speech.

> Daniel—he's kind of a pest—is my youngest cousin.

Rule: Use parentheses to set off words that define or helpfully explain a word in the sentence.

> The transverse flute (*transverse* means "sideways") is a wind instrument.

Abbreviations

Rule: Abbreviate the titles *Mr., Mrs., Ms.,* and *Dr.* before a person's name. Also abbreviate any professional or academic degree that follows a name. The titles *Jr.* and *Sr.* are *not* preceded by a comma.

> Dr. Stanley Livingston (doctor)
> Luisa Mendez, M.A. (Master of Arts)
> Martin Luther King Jr.

Rule: Use capital letters and no periods with abbreviations that are pronounced letter by letter or as words. Exceptions are *U.S.* and *Washington, D.C.,* which do use periods.

NAACP	National Association for the Advancement of Colored People
UFO	unidentified flying object
MADD	Mothers Against Driving Drunk

Rule: With exact times use A.M. (*ante meridiem,* "before noon") and P.M. (*post meridiem,* "after noon"). For years use B.C. (before Christ) and, sometimes, A.D. (*anno Domini,* "in the year of the lord," after Christ).

> 8:15 A.M.   6:55 P.M.
> 5000 B.C.   A.D. 235

Rule: Abbreviate days and months only in charts and lists.

> School will be closed on
> Mon., Sept. 3
> Wed., Nov. 11
> Thurs., Nov. 27

Rule: In scientific writing abbreviate units of measure. Use periods with English units but not with metric units.

inch(es)	in.	yard(s)	yd.
meter(s)	m	milliliter(s)	ml

Rule: On envelopes only, abbreviate street names and state names. In general text, spell out street names and state names.

Ms. Karen Holmes
347 Grandville St.
Tilton, NH 03276
Karen lives on Grandville Street in Tilton, New Hampshire.

Writing Numbers

Rule: In charts and tables, always write numbers as numerals. Other rules apply to numbers not in charts or tables.

Student Test Scores

Student	Test 1	Test 2	Test 3
Lai, W.	82	89	94
Ostos, A.	78	90	86

Rule: Spell out a number that is expressed in one or two words.

We carried enough supplies for twenty-three days.

Rule: Use a numeral for a number of more than two words.

The tallest mountain in Mexico rises 17,520 feet.

Rule: Spell out a number that begins a sentence, or reword the sentence so that it does not begin with a number.

One hundred forty-three days later the baby elephant was born.
The baby elephant was born 143 days later.

Rule: Write a very large number as a numeral followed by the word *million* or *billion*.

There are 15 million people living in or near Mexico City.

Rule: Related numbers should be written in the same way. If one number must be written as a numeral, use numerals for all the numbers.

There are 365 days in the year, but only 52 weekends.

Rule: Spell out an ordinal number (*first, second*).

Welcome to our fifteenth annual convention.

Rule: Use words to express the time of day unless you are writing the exact time or using the abbreviation A.M. or P.M.

My guitar lesson is at five o'clock. It ends by 5:45 P.M.

Rule: Use numerals to express dates, house and street numbers, apartment and room numbers, telephone numbers, page numbers, amounts of money of more than two words, and percentages. Write out the word *percent*.

August 5, 1999
9 Davio Dr.
Apartment 9F
24 percent

Spelling

The following rules, examples, and exceptions can help you master the spelling of many words.

Spelling *ie* and *ei*

Put *i* before *e* except when both letters follow *c* or when both letters are pronounced together as an **a** sound.

believe   sieve   weight
receive   relieve   neighborhood

It is helpful to memorize exceptions to this rule. Exceptions include the following words: *species, science, weird, either, seize, leisure,* and *protein*.

Spelling unstressed vowels

Notice the vowel sound in the second syllable of the word *won-d_r-ful*. This is the unstressed vowel sound; dictionary respellings use the schwa symbol (ə) to indicate it. Because any of several vowels can be used to spell this sound, you might find yourself uncertain about which vowel to use. To spell words with unstressed vowels, try thinking of a related word in which the syllable containing the vowel sound is stressed.

Unknown Spelling	Related Word	Word Spelled Correctly
wond_rful	wonder	wonderful
fort_fications	fortify	fortifications
res_dent	reside	resident

Suffixes and the silent *e*

For most words with silent *e*, keep the *e* when adding a suffix. When you add the suffix *-ly* to a word that ends in *l* plus silent *e*, drop the *-le*. Also drop the silent *e* when you add a suffix beginning with a vowel or a *y*.

wise + ly = wisely
peaceful + ly = peacefully
skate + ing = skating
gentle + ly = gently

There are exceptions to the rule, including the following:

awe + ful = awful
judge + ment = judgment

true + ly = truly
noise + y = noisy
dye + ing = dyeing
mile + age = mileage

Suffixes and the final *y*

When you are adding a suffix to words ending with a vowel + *y*, keep the *y*. For words ending with a consonant + *y*, change the *y* to *i* unless the suffix begins with *i*. To avoid having two *i*'s together, keep the *y*.

enjoy + ment = enjoyment
merry + ment = merriment
display + ed = displayed
lazy + ness = laziness
play + ful = playful
worry + ing = worrying

Note: For some words, there are alternate spellings:

sly + er = slyer or slier
shy + est = shyest or shiest

Adding prefixes

When you add a prefix to a word, do not change the spelling of the word.

un + done = undone
re + schedule = reschedule
il + legible = illegible
semi + sweet = semisweet

Doubling the final consonant

Double the final consonant when a word ends with a single consonant following one vowel and the word is one syllable, or when the last syllable of the word is accented both before and after adding the suffix.

sit + ing = sitting
rub + ing = rubbing
commit + ed = committed
confer + ed = conferred

Language Handbook **R43**

Do not double the final consonant if the suffix begins with a consonant, if the accent is not on the last syllable, or if the accent moves when the suffix is added.

cancel + ing = canceling
commit + ment = commitment
travel + ed = traveled
defer + ence = deference

Do not double the final consonant if the word ends in two consonants or if the suffix begins with a consonant.

climb + er = climber
nervous + ness = nervousness

import + ance = importance
star + dom = stardom

When adding -ly to a word that ends in ll, drop one l.

hill + ly = hilly   full + ly = fully

Forming compound words

When forming compound words, keep the original spelling of both words.

home + work = homework
scare + crow = scarecrow
pea + nut = peanut

Forming Plurals

General Rules for Plurals		
If the noun ends in	**Rule**	**Example**
s, ch, sh, x, or z	add -es	loss→losses, latch→latches, box→boxes, bush→bushes, quiz→quizzes
a consonant + y	change y to i and add -es	ferry→ferries, baby→babies, worry→worries
a vowel + y	add -s	chimney→chimneys, monkey→monkeys, toy→toys
a vowel + o	add -s	cameo→cameos, radio→radios, rodeo→rodeos
a consonant + o	add -es but sometimes add -s	potato→potatoes, echo→echoes photo→photos, solo→solos
f or ff	add -s but sometimes change f to v and add -es	proof→proofs, bluff→bluffs sheaf→sheaves, thief→thieves, hoof→hooves
lf	change f to v and add -es	calf→calves, half→halves, loaf→loaves
fe	change f to v and add -s	knife→knives, life→lives

Special Rules for Plurals	
Rule	**Example**
To form the plural of most proper names and one-word compound nouns, follow the general rules for plurals.	Jones→Joneses, Thomas→Thomases, Hatch→Hatches
To form the plural of hyphenated compound nouns or compound nouns of more than one word, make the most important word plural.	credit card→credit cards mother-in-law→mothers-in-law district attorney→district attorneys
Some nouns have irregular plural forms and do not follow any rules.	man→men, foot→feet, tooth→teeth
Some nouns have the same singular and plural forms	deer→deer, species→species, sheep→sheep

LISTENING, SPEAKING, AND VIEWING HANDBOOK

Listening Effectively

A large part of the school day is spent either listening or speaking to others. By becoming a better listener and speaker, you will know more about what is expected of you, and understand more about your audience.

Listening to instructions in class

Some of the most important listening in the school day involves listening to instructions. Use the following tips to help you.

- First, make sure you understand what you are listening for. Are you receiving instructions for homework or for a test? What you listen for depends upon the type of instructions being given.
- Think about what you are hearing, and keep your eyes on the speaker. This will help you stay focused on the important points.
- Listen for keywords, or word clues. Examples of word clues are phrases such as *above all, most important,* or *the three basic parts.* These clues help you identify important points that you should remember.
- Take notes on what you hear. Write down only the most important parts of the instructions.
- If you don't understand something, ask questions. Then if you're still unsure about the instructions, repeat them aloud to your teacher to receive correction on any key points that you may have missed.

Interpreting nonverbal clues

Understanding nonverbal clues is part of effective listening. Nonverbal clues are everything you notice about a speaker *except* what the speaker says. As you listen, ask yourself these questions:

- Where and how is the speaker standing?
- Are some words spoken more loudly than others?
- Does the speaker make eye contact?
- Does he or she smile or look angry?
- What message is sent by the speaker's gestures and facial expression?

PRACTICE

Work with a partner to practice listening to instructions. Each of you should find a set of directions for using a simple device–for example, a mechanical tool, a telephone answering machine, or a VCR. Study the instructions carefully. If you can bring the device to class, ask your partner to try to use it by following your step-by-step instructions. If you cannot have the device in class, ask your partner to explain the directions back to you. Then change roles and listen as your partner gives you a set of directions.

Speaking Effectively

- Speak slowly, clearly, and in a normal tone of voice. Raise your voice a bit, or use gestures to stress important points.
- Pause a few seconds after making an important point.
- Use words that help your audience picture what you're talking about. Visual aids such as pictures, graphs, charts, and maps can also help make your information clear.
- Stay in contact with your audience. Make sure your eyes move from person to person in the group you're addressing.

Speaking informally

Most oral communication is informal. When you speak casually with your friends, family, and neighbors, you use informal speech. Human relationships depend on this form of communication.

- Be courteous. Listen until the other person has finished speaking.
- Speak in a relaxed and spontaneous manner.
- Make eye contact with your listeners.
- Do not monopolize a conversation.
- When telling a story, show enthusiasm.
- When giving an announcement or directions, speak clearly and slowly. Check that your listeners understand the information.

Presenting an oral report

The steps in preparing an oral report are similar to the steps in the writing process. Complete each step carefully and you can be confident of presenting an effective oral report.

Steps in Preparing an Oral Report	
Prewriting	Determine your purpose and audience. Decide on a topic and narrow it.
Drafting	Make an outline. Fill in the supporting details. Write the report.
Revising and editing	Review your draft. Check the organization of ideas and details. Reword unclear statements.
Practicing	Practice the report aloud in front of a family member. Time the report. Ask for and accept advice.
Presenting	Relax in front of your audience. Make eye contact with your audience. Speak slowly and clearly.

PRACTICE

Pretend that you have been invited to give an oral report to a group of fifth graders. Your report will tell them what to expect and how to adjust to new conditions when they enter middle school. As you plan your report, keep your purpose and your audience in mind. Include lively descriptions and examples to back up your suggestions and hold your audience's attention. As you practice giving your report, be sure to give attention to your body language as well as your vocal projection. Ask a partner to listen to your report to give you feedback on how to improve your performance. Do the same for your partner after listening to his or her report.

Viewing Effectively

Critical viewing means thinking about what you see while watching a TV program, newscast, film, or video. It requires paying attention to what you hear and see and deciding whether information is true, false, or exaggerated. If the information seems to be true, try to determine whether it is based on a fact or an opinion.

Fact versus opinion

A **fact** is something that can be proved. An opinion is what someone believes is true. **Opinions** are based on feelings and experiences and cannot be proved.

Television commercials, political speeches, and even the evening news contain both facts and opinions. They use emotional words and actions to persuade the viewer to agree with a particular point of view. They may also use faulty reasoning, such as linking an effect with the wrong cause. Think through what is being said. The speaker may seem sincere, but do his or her reasons make sense? Are the reasons based on facts or on unfair generalizations?

Commercials contain both obvious and hidden messages. Just as you need to discover the author's purpose when you read a writer's words, you must be aware of the purpose of nonverbal attempts to persuade you.

What does the message sender want, and how is the sender trying to influence you?

For example, a magazine or TV ad picturing a group of happy teenagers playing volleyball on a sunny beach expresses a positive feeling. The advertiser hopes viewers will transfer that positive feeling to the product being advertised—perhaps a soft drink or a brand of beachwear. This technique, called **transfer,** is one of several propaganda techniques regularly used by advertisers to influence consumers.

Following are a few other common techniques.

Testimonial—Famous and admired people recommend or praise a product, a policy, or a course of action even though they probably have no professional knowledge or expertise to back up their opinion.

Bandwagon—People are urged to follow the crowd ("get on the bandwagon") by buying a product, voting for a candidate, or whatever else the advertiser wants them to do.

Glittering generalities—The advertiser uses positive, good-sounding words (for example, *all-American* or *medically proven*) to impress people.

PRACTICE

Think of a television commercial that you have seen often or watch a new one and take notes as you watch it. Then analyze the commercial.

- What is the purpose behind the ad?
- What is expressed in written or spoken words?
- What is expressed nonverbally (in music or sound effects as well as in pictures and actions)?
- What methods does the advertiser use to persuade viewers?
- What questions would you ask the advertiser if you could?
- How effective is the commercial? Why?

Working in Groups

Working in a group is an opportunity to learn from others. Whether you are planning a group project (such as a class trip) or solving a math problem, each person in a group brings specific strengths and interests to the task. When a task is large, such as planting a garden, a group provides the necessary energy and talent to get the job done.

Small groups vary in size according to the nature of the task. Three to five students is a good size for most small-group tasks. Your teacher may assign you to a group, or you may be asked to form your own group. Don't work with your best friend if you are likely to chat too much. Successful groups often have a mix of student abilities and interests.

Individual role assignments give everyone in a group something to do. One student, the group recorder, may take notes. Another may lead the discussion, and another report the results to the rest of the class.

Tips for working in groups

- Review the group assignment and goal. Be sure that everyone in the group understands the assignment.
- Review the amount of time allotted for the task. Decide how your group will organize its time.
- Check that all the group members understand their roles in the group.
- When a question arises, try to solve it as a group before asking a teacher for help.
- Listen to other points of view. Take turns during a discussion.
- When it is your turn to talk, address the subject and help the project move forward.

Roles for a Small Group	
Reviewer	Reads or reviews the assignment and makes sure everyone understands it
Recorder 1 (of the process)	Takes notes on the discussion
Recorder 2 (of the results)	Takes notes on the final results
Reporter	Reports results to the rest of the class
Discussion leader	Asks questions to get the discussion going; keeps the group focused
Facilitator	Helps the group resolve disagreements and reach a compromise

For a small group of three or four students, some of these roles can be combined. Your teacher may assign a role to each student in your group. Or you may be asked to choose your own role.

STUDY AND TEST-TAKING SKILLS HANDBOOK

Study Skills

Studying for school and doing your homework are like any other tasks—if you understand your assignment, set a goal, and make a plan, you'll save time and do great work. The tips that follow will teach you the skills you need to make schoolwork easier and more enjoyable.

Get Organized

- Keep an assignment notebook. Keep it up to date.
- Keep your notes for each course together in one place.
- Find a good place to study. Choose a place that has as few distractions as possible. Try to study in the same place each day.
- Try to study at the same time each day.
- Don't study one subject too long. If you haven't finished after thirty minutes, switch to another subject.
- Take notes on your reading. Keep your notes in one place.

Understand Your Purpose

The purpose is the reason you have been given a particular assignment. If you understand the purpose, you should be able to set a goal to work toward. With schoolwork, this means making sure you understand your assignment and you know how long you have to do it.

Set goals

These steps will help you set study goals for an assignment.
1. Listen as the teacher explains the assignment. Find out everything you need to do to finish the assignment.
2. Understand the quality of work your teacher expects from you. Are you supposed to turn in a finished paper or a rough draft?
3. Find out how much time you have. Ask: Is everything due on the same day, or are some parts due earlier?
4. In your assignment notebook, write down the assignment details and the dates when your work is due.

Homework Checklist

Goal: To understand and finish my homework assignment.
Plan: Follow these steps to reach my goal:
- ☑ Bring home the all the materials I need, including this textbook, and my notebook.
- ☑ Find a quiet space where I can concentrate. Also, make sure I have a table or other hard, flat surface to write on.
- ☑ Keep my notebook out and take notes as I read.
- ☑ Write down questions about the parts of the assignment that I don't understand. Ask my teacher or an adult at home to help me understand.
- ☑ Check this plan from time to time to make sure I stay on task.
- ☑ Take my completed homework back to school and hand it in.

Make a Plan

Making a plan is the best way to reach your goals. Try to make plans that include the work you have finish and the time you have until the assignment is due. Think about how you study best, when you might need help, and what gets in your way.

You can use a **task, obstacle, and solution chart** to show
1. what you need to do (task)
2. what might get in your way (obstacle)
3. how you can get around an obstacle (solution)

Karen's goal is to read a chapter of science before school tomorrow. Check out the chart she made which includes **task, obstacle, and solution.**

1. (task)	I have to…	read chapter 4 tonight
2. (obstacle)	But…	after dinner I have basketball practice
3. (solution)	So I need to…	read before practice

Try it! In your **Learner's Notebook,** make your own **task, obstacle, and solution chart** for an assignment from this book. You can use Karen's plan as a model.

Take Notes

Writing notes about what you read or what you hear in a presentation will help you remember information you're expected to learn. The Cornell Note-Taking System is a way to organize the notes you take in class or the notes you take as you read. Use this system to organize your note-taking and make sense of the notes you take.

Cornell Notes

Divide the pages that you're using for notes into two sections or columns as shown below. As you read or listen, write notes in Section B. In Section A, write the highlights (main ideas and vocabulary) from Section B.

| Section A [highlights] Use this section SECOND. Review the notes you took in Section B and write in this section:
• Vocabulary words to remember
• Main idea statements
• Questions and other hints that will help you remember the information | Section B [notes] Use this section FIRST. As you read or listen, take notes in this section:
• When you're taking notes on your reading, write down the subtitles that break the text into different section. In most cases, subtitles form an outline of the information in a chapter.
• Write down the most important information: main ideas and concepts. Don't write every word or take time to write complete sentences. (Hint: if the teacher writes something on the board, it's probably important.)
• Use abbreviations and shortened word forms to get the ideas on paper quickly. (For example, POV is a good abbreviation for Point of View.)
• Define new terms and concepts in your own words so that you'll be able to understand them later. |

Model These are some notes one student made as she read about biographies and autobiographies.

| A. biography

 autobiography

 Major elements of biography | B. Looking at the Genre: Biography
 What is it?
  real people, real life
  Autobiography is about yourself
 Why is it important?
  many reasons (interest, learn, entertain, etc.)
 What are the important elements?
  Narrator: who tells the story
  Point of view: from who's telling the story
  Setting: time and place of a story |

Try It! Divide a sheet of paper into two columns as shown above. Practice taking notes using the Cornell system as you read your homework assignment.

Test-Taking Skills

How well you perform on a test is not a matter of chance. Some specific strategies can help you answer test questions. This section of the handbook will show how to improve your test-taking skills.

Tips for preparing for tests

Here are some useful suggestions for preparing to take a test.

- Gather information about the test. When will it be given? How long will it take? Exactly what material will it cover?
- Review material from your textbook, class notes, homework, quizzes, and handouts. Review the study questions at the end of each section of a textbook. Try to define terms in boldface type.
- Make up some sample questions and answer them. As you skim selections, try to predict what may be asked.
- Draw charts and cluster or Venn diagrams to help you remember information and to picture how one piece of information relates to another.
- Give yourself plenty of time to study. Avoid cramming for a test. Several short review sessions are more effective than one long one.
- In addition to studying alone, study with a partner or small group. Quiz one another on topics you think the test will cover.

Plan your strategy

Try following these steps:

- Read all directions carefully. Understanding the directions can prevent mistakes.
- Ask for help if you have a question.
- Answer the easier items first. By skipping the hard items, you will have time to answer all the easy ones.
- In the time that is left, return to the items you skipped. Answer them as best you can. If you won't be penalized for doing so, guess at an answer.
- If possible, save some time at the end to check your answers.

Objective Tests

An objective test is a test of factual information. The questions are usually either right or wrong; there is no difference of opinion. On an objective test, you are asked to recall information, not to present your ideas. Objective test questions include true-or-false items, multiple-choice items, fill-in-the-blanks statements, short-answer items, and matching items. At the beginning of an objective test, scan the number of items. Then budget your time.

Multiple-choice items Multiple-choice questions ask you to answer a question or complete a sentence. They are the kind of question you will encounter most often on objective tests. Read all the choices before answering. Pick the best response.

> What is a peninsula?
> (a) a range of mountains
> (b) a circle around the moon
> (c) a body of land surrounded by water on three sides

Correct answer: (c)

- Read the question carefully. Be sure that you understand it.
- Read all the answers before selecting one. Reading all of the responses is especially important when one of the choices is "all of the above" or "none of the above."
- Eliminate responses that are clearly incorrect. Focus on the responses that might be correct.
- Look for absolute words, such as *never, always, all, none*. Most generalizations have exceptions. Absolute statements are often incorrect. (Note: This tip applies to true/false items also.)

Answering essay questions

Essay questions ask you to think about what you have learned and to write about it in one or more paragraphs. Some tests present a choice of essay questions. If a test has both an objective part and an essay part, answer the objective questions first, but leave yourself enough time to work on the essay.

Read the essay question carefully. What does it ask you to do? Discuss? Explain? Define? Summarize? Compare and contrast? These key words tell what kind of information you must give in your answer.

Key Verbs in Essay Questions	
Argue	Give your opinion and supporting reasons.
Compare and contrast	Discuss likenesses and differences.
Define	Give details that show exactly what something is like.
Demonstrate	Give examples to support a point.
Describe	Present a picture with words.
Discuss	Show detailed information on a particular subject.
Explain	Give reasons.
Identify	Give specific characteristics.
List (also outline, trace)	Give details, give steps in order, give a time sequence.
Summarize	Give a short overview of the most important ideas or events.

Tips for answering essay questions
You might wish to consider the following suggestions:
- Read the question or questions carefully. Determine the kind of information required by the question.
- Plan your time. Do not spend too much time on one part of the essay.
- Make a list of what you want to cover.
- If you have time, make revisions and proofreading corrections.

Taking standardized tests

Standardized tests are taken by students all over the country. Your performance on the test is compared with the performance of other students at your grade level. There are many different kinds of standardized tests. Some measure your progress in such subjects as English, math, and science, while others measure how well you think. Standardized tests can show how you learn and what you do best.

Preparing for standardized tests
There is no way to know exactly what information will be on a standardized test, or even what topics will be covered. The best preparation is to do the best you can in your daily schoolwork. However, you can learn the *kinds* of questions that will appear on a standardized test. Some general tips will also help.

Tips for taking standardized tests
You might find the following suggestions helpful.
- Get enough sleep the night before the test. Eat a healthful breakfast.
- Arrive early for the test. Try to relax.
- Listen carefully to all test directions. Ask questions if you don't understand the directions.
- Complete easy questions first. Leave harder items for the end.
- Be sure your answers are in the right place on the answer sheet.
- If points are not subtracted for wrong answers, guess at questions that you aren't sure of.

Analogies Analogy items test your understanding of the relationships between things or ideas. On standardized tests, analogies are written in an abbreviated format, as shown below.

    man : woman :: buck : doe

The symbol : means "is to"; the symbol :: means "as."

This chart shows some word relationships you might find in analogy tests.

Relationship	Definition	Example
Synonyms	Two words have a similar meaning.	huge : gigantic :: scared : afraid
Antonyms	Two words have opposite meanings.	bright : dull :: far : near
Use	Words name a user and something used.	farmer : tractor :: writer : computer
Cause-Effect	Words name a cause and its effect.	tickle : laugh :: polish : shine
Category	Words name a category and an item in it.	fish : tuna :: building : house
Description	Words name an item and a characteristic of it.	knife : sharp :: joke : funny

GLOSSARY/GLOSARIO
Academic and Selection Vocabulary

English

Español

A

abandoned (uh BAN dund) *v.* given up or left behind (p. 292)

accustomed (uh KUS tumd) *adj.* used to; familiar with (p. 638)

acknowledge (ak NOL ij) *v.* to recognize the truth of something (p. 639)

acquired (uh KWY urd) *v.* obtained, got, received (p. 349)

addresses (uh DRESS uz) *v.* deals with or pays attention to (p. 1053)

administrator (ad MIN uh stray tur) *n.* person who manages or directs (p. 21)

adopt (uh DOPT) *v.* to accept and put into effect (p. 303)

advisory (ad VY zuh ree) *adj.* having the power to give advice (p. 21)

aggression (uh GRESH un) *n.* angry and unfriendly action or behavior (p. 573)

amassed (uh MAST) *v.* piled up, collected, or gathered a great quantity of something (p. 93)

ambitions (am BISH unz) *n.* strong desires to succeed (p. 193)

anesthetist (uh NES thuh tist) *n.* the person who gives drugs to put a patient to sleep before surgery (p. 629)

application (ap lih KAY shun) *n.* the act of putting something to use (p. 498)

appointed (uh POIN tid) *v.* selected or named for an office or position (p. 180)

architect (AR kuh tekt) *n.* a person who designs buildings (p. 271)

astray (uh STRAY) *adv.* off the right path or route (p. 1043)

authority (uh THOR ih tee) *n.* a good source of information or advice (p. 498)

abandonado(a) *adj.* que se renunció a algo; que fue dejado sin amparo (p. 292)

acostumbrado(a) *adj.* habituado; usual (p. 638)

reconocer *v.* admitir o aceptar un hecho real (p. 639)

adquirió *v.* obtuvo, consiguió, compró; forma del verbo *adquirir* (p. 349)

trata *v.* que habla de algo o lo estudia; forma del verbo *tratar* (p. 1053)

administrador(a) *s.* persona que dirige o dispone (p. 21)

adoptar *v.* tomar resoluciones y hacerlas propias (p. 303)

consultivo(a) *adj.* junta establecida para ser consultada y brindar opiniones (p. 21)

agresión *s.* ataque violento (p. 573)

acumuló *v.* juntó, recolectó o amontonó en grandes cantidades; forma del verbo *acumular* (p. 93)

aspiraciones *s.* objetivos pretendidos o deseados (p. 193)

anestesista *s.* especialista en aplicar una sustancia que produce la pérdida de la sensibilidad de los pacientes durante una cirugía (p. 629)

aplicación *s.* puesta en práctica de algo con un uso determinado (p. 498)

designó *v.* que eligió o nombró a alguien para un cargo público o puesto; forma del verbo *designar* (p. 180)

arquitecto(a) *s.* persona que proyecta y construye edificios (p. 271)

extraviado(a) *adj.* que se desvió del camino o lo perdió (p. 1034)

autoridad *s.* que tiene crédito o prestigio en su conocimiento y competencia en una materia (p. 498)

B

backdrop (BAK drop) *n.* a curtain or temporary wall that covers the back of a stage (p. 1000)

banished (BAN isht) *v.* sent away; forced to be separate from a place or group (p. 810)

barren (BAIR un) *adj.* having little or no plant life; empty (p. 666)

barrier (BAIR ee ur) *n.* something that prevents passage; an obstacle (p. 862)

beckoned (BECK und) *v.* moved the head or a hand to make a sign to approach or come nearer (p. 272)

befriended (bih FREN dud) *v.* made friends with someone (p. 461)

biceps (BY seps) *n.* a large muscle that runs down the front of the arm from the shoulder to the elbow (p. 425)

bigotry (BIG uh tree) *n.* unfair and unreasonable opinions or treatment of a person or group (p. 740)

blissfully (BLIS fuh lee) *adv.* in an extremely happy way; joyfully (p. 854)

brilliant (BRIL yunt) *adj.* having or showing ability or talent (p. 43)

brunette (broo NET) *n.* a person with black or brown hair (p. 1020)

buffet (BUF it) *v.* to strike with force (p. 275)

bureau (BYUR oh) *n.* a low chest of drawers (p. 529)

telón de fondo *frase nom.* cortina que cierra la escena y forma la decoración (p. 996)

desterró *v.* abandonó un lugar o fue expulsado de la patria; forma del verbo *desterrar* (p. 810)

yermo(a) *adj.* terreno estéril o sin cultivo; despoblado (p. 666)

barrera *s.* valla o impedimento que cierra el paso; obstáculo (p. 862)

hizo una seña *frase verbal* dio indicios; realizó gestos o para dar algo a entender; forma del verbo *hacer* (p. 272)

fraternizó *v.* se hizo amigo de alguien; forma del verbo *fraternizar* (p. 461)

bíceps *s.* músculo de dos orígenes o cabezas que se extiende por el antebrazo desde el hombro hasta el codo (p. 425)

fanatismo *s.* intolerancia (p. 740)

dichosamente *adv.* con gran felicidad; con regocijo (p. 854)

brillante *adj.* admirable o sobresaliente por sus cualidades (p. 43)

morena *s.* mujer de cabello negro o castaño (p. 1020)

golpear *v.* pegar con fuerza (p. 275)

cómoda *s.* mueble con cajones que se usa para guardar ropa (p. 529)

C

calories (KAL uh reez) *n.* units used to measure the energy supplied by food (p. 22)

caravan (KAIR uh van) *n.* a group of people or vehicles traveling together (p. 791)

cavities (KAV ih teez) *n.* hollow spaces in a tooth caused by decay (p. 88)

cease (sees) *v.* to stop (p. 809)

champion (CHAM pyun) *n.* one who fights for or speaks for another person; one who defends a cause; hero (p. 974)

chaos (KAY ahs) *n.* total confusion and disorder (p. 198, 1044)

calorías *s.* unidad de medida que determina el valor energético de los alimentos (p. 22)

caravana *s.* grupo de personas o vehículos que viajan juntos (p. 791)

caries *s.* erosión del esmalte dental causada por bacterias (p. 88)

dejar (de) *v.* cesar, detenerse (p. 809)

campeón(ona) *s.* persona que defiende con esfuerzo una causa o doctrina; héroe (p. 974)

caos *s.* gran confusión y desorden (p. 198, 1044)

chromosomes (KROH muh sohmz) *n.* parts of a cell in a plant or animal that carry the genes controlling features such as the color of hair and eyes (p. 454)

cicadas (sih KAY duz) *n.* large insects also called locusts; males make a buzzing sound (p. 271)

cinders (SIN durz) *n.* hot ashes (p. 906)

civic (SIV ik) *adj.* having to do with a city or the duties of a citizen (p. 734)

civility (sih VIL uh tee) *n.* polite behavior (p. 595)

clarify (KLAIR uh fy) *v.* to make clear (p. 970)

coarse (kors) *adj.* rough; lacking good manners (p. 541)

coincidence (koh IN sih dens) *n.* a situation in which two events that seem unrelated accidentally occur at the same time (p. 341)

commotion (kuh MOH shun) *n.* noisy rushing about; confusion (p. 889)

competing (kum PEET ing) *v.* taking part in a contest (p. 860)

composed (kum POHZD) *v.* formed by putting together (p. 878)

conceited (kun SEE tid) *adj.* having a high opinion of oneself (p. 960)

conclusions (kun KLOO zhuns) *n.* judgments or general statements based on information, experience, and observation (p. 494)

condemn (kun DEM) *v.* to express a strong feeling against something (p. 264)

confiscated (KON fis kay tid) *v.* took someone's property by authority (p. 79)

conflict (KON flikt) *n.* struggle between opposing forces (p. 523)

confrontations (kON frun TAY shunz) *n.* unpleasant face-to-face meetings (p. 154)

Congress (KONG gris) *n.* the part of the United States government that makes laws (p. 180)

consciousness (KON shus ness), *n.* thoughts; awareness; the mind (p. 650)

consequences (KON suh kwen suz) *n.* results of an action; outcome (p. 899)

consumption (kun SUMP shun) *n.* the act of eating, drinking, or using up (p. 392)

contemplate (KON tem playt) *v.* to have in mind as a possibility (p. 571)

cromosomas *s.* parte del núcleo de las células de animales y plantas que transmiten información genética tal como el color del cabello y los ojos (p. 454)

cigarras *s.* insectos de cabeza y abdomen gruesos con alas transparentes; los machos hacen un zumbido estridente y monótono (p. 271)

ceniza *s.* polvo residual de una combustión (p. 906)

cívico(a) *adj.* que pertenece a la ciudad o al comportamiento de los ciudadanos (p. 734)

civilidad *s.* educación, urbanidad (p. 595)

aclarar *v.* poner en claro; explicar (p. 970)

tosco(a) *adj.* sin delicadeza; sin educación (p. 541)

coincidencia *s.* sucesos que ocurren en forma casual, en el mismo lugar y al mismo tiempo (p. 341)

conmoción *s.* tumulto; confusión (p. 889)

compitiendo *v.* luchar o rivalizar con otros para obtener un objetivo (p. 860)

compuesto(a) *v.* formado con varias cosas juntas (p. 878)

engreído(a) *adj.* persona demasiado convencida de su propio valor (p. 960)

conclusión *s.* deducción o resolución basada en la información, la experiencia y la observación (p. 494)

condenar *v.* reprobar o desaprobar algo (p. 264)

decomisó *v.* se apoderó por la fuerza de la propiedad ajena; forma del verbo *decomisar* (p. 79)

nudo *s.* enlace o complicación de la acción en una obra literaria (p. 523)

encaramientos *s.* colocarse frente a otro en una actitud violenta (p. 154)

Congreso *s.* organismo gubernamental de los Estados Unidos que elabora las leyes (p. 180)

conciencia *s.* noción del mundo y de uno mismo (p. 650)

consecuencias *s.* hechos que resultan de otros; resultado (p. 899)

consumo *s.* utilización de comestibles o elementos que se extinguen (p. 392)

contemplar *v.* considerar con atención y cuidado (p. 571)

contemplation (kon tem PLAY shun) *n.* a state of deep thought (p. 949)

contented (kun TEN tid) *adj.* happy, pleased, or satisfied with one's situation (p. 1044)

convoy (KON voy) *n.* a group of cars, trucks, or other vehicles traveling together (p. 1063)

coping (KOHP ing) *v.* successfully dealing with something difficult (p. 395)

crevice (KREV is) *n.* narrow opening; split or crack (p. 949)

crock (krok) *n.* a large clay or ceramic pot used to hold liquid (p.751)

contemplación *s.* estado de meditación profunda (p. 949)

satisfecho(a) *adj.* contento, complacido, conforme (p. 1044)

convoy *s.* grupo de vehículos o barcos que viajan juntos (p. 1063)

sobrellevando *v.* afrontar un problema o situación, forma del verbo *sobrellevar* (p. 395)

grieta *s.* abertura estrecha; hendidura (p. 949)

vasija *s.* recipiente de barro o cerámica que se usa para contener líquidos (p.751)

D

dazed (dayzd) *adj.* stunned or confused as a result of a blow or a surprise (p. 550)

decent (DEE sunt) *adj.* kind or thoughtful (p. 219)

defiance (dih FY uns) *n.* bold resistance to authority (p. 199)

dejection (dih JEK shun) *n.* sadness; low spirits (p. 853)

delusion (dih LOO zhun), *n.* a false belief (p. 650)

dense (dens) *adj.* thick (p. 1041)

desolate (DES uh lit) *adj.* deserted or uninhabited (p. 660)

develop (dih VEL up) *v.* to get or bring about little by little over a period of time (p. 1053)

devoured (dih VOWrd) *v.* ate up greedily (p. 655)

discipline (DIS uh plin) *v.* to punish (p. 512)

discipline (DIS uh plin) *n.* self-control; the obeying of rules (p. 303)

disgraced (dis GRAYSD) *v.* brought shame or dishonor upon (p. 386)

dismal (DIZ mul) *adj.* gloomy; miserable; cheerless (p. 850)

dismay (dis MAY) *n.* a sudden feeling of disappointment or unpleasant surprise (p. 341)

dispute (dis PYOOT) *n.* a difference of opinion; argument or quarrel (p. 637)

distinguish (dis TING gwish) *v.* to know the difference between, tell apart (p. 260)

distress (dis TRES) *n.* pain or suffering (p. 294)

aturdido(a) *adj.* perturbado o confundido por un golpe, un ruido o una mala noticia (p. 550)

decente *adj.* amable o respetuoso (p. 219)

desafío *s.* oposición o contradicción a la autoridad (p. 199)

abatimiento *s.* desaliento; pérdida del ánimo (p. 853)

engaño *s.* equivocación, falsa impresión (p. 650)

denso(a) *adj.* espeso (p. 1041)

desolado(a) *adj.* despoblado, desierto (p. 660)

desarrollar *v.* acrecentar, aumentar, crecer en lo físico, intelectual o moral (p. 1053)

devoraron *v.* comieron con ansia; forma del verbo *devorar* (p. 655)

sancionar *v.* castigar (p. 512)

disciplina *s.* acatamiento de una persona a las normas que desarrollan autocontrol y orden (p. 303)

avergonzó *v.* causar humillación y deshonra; forma del verbo *avergonzar* (p. 386)

deprimente *adj.* sombrío; taciturno; triste (p. 850)

consternación *s.* alteración del ánimo y pérdida de la tranquilidad (p. 341)

polémica *s.* diferencia de opinión; altercado o discusión (p. 637)

distinguir *v.* ser capaz de diferenciar (p. 260)

aflicción *s.* dolor o sufrimiento (p. 294)

diverted (dih VUR tud) *v.* turned from one course to another (p. 652)

documentation (dok yuh men TAY shun) *n.* something recorded that serves as proof (p. 879)

dominant (DOM ih nunt) *adj.* having the greatest power or force; controlling (p. 852)

drab (drab) *adj.* lacking brightness; dull (p. 714)

drone (drohn) *n.* steady, low, humming sound (p. 351)

drought (drowt) *n.* a long period of very dry weather (p. 664)

E

eddies (ED eez) *n.* circling currents of air, water, or snow (p. 1043)

elaborately (ih LAB ur it lee) *adv.* in a fancy way that involves many details or complicated parts (p. 946)

emerald (EM ur uld) *adj.* brightly or richly green (p. 161)

emerged (ih MERJD) *v.* came out (p. 198)

enclosure (en KLOH zhur) *n.* a fenced-in or walled-in place (p. 1065)

encounter (en KOWN ter) *n.* an unexpected or unpleasant meeting (p. 723)

endangered (en DAYN jurd) *adj.* at risk or in danger of dyiing out completely (p. 589)

endure (en DOOR) *v.* to put up with (p. 264)

endured (en DURD) *v.* held up under pain or hardship (p. 690)

envy (EN vee) *n.* jealousy; desire to have something that someone else has (p. 286)

evacuated (ih VAK yoo ay tid) *v.* removed; moved out of area (p. 822)

evaluate (ih VAL yoo ayt) *v.* to find value; to judge or determine worth (p. 840)

exasperated (eg ZAS pur ay tid) *v.* greatly angered or irritated (p. 947)

exotic (eg ZOT ik) *adj.* excitingly different; unusual; foreign (p. 720)

expedition (ek spuh DISH un) *n.* a journey taken for a special purpose, such as exploration (p. 716)

exploits (EK sploytz) *n.* brave acts or deeds (p. 156)

---

desvió *v.* cambió la dirección o el curso; forma del verbo *desviar* (p. 652)

documentación *s.* conjunto de registros que sirven de evidencia de algo (p. 879)

dominante *adj.* que prevalece o es superior a algo; controlador (p. 852)

soso(a) *adj.* sin gracia; apagado (p. 714)

zumbido *s.* ruido sordo y continuado (p. 351)

sequía *s.* período largo de tiempo seco (p. 664)

remolinos *s.* movimiento circular rápido del aire, agua o nieve (p. 1043)

detalladamente *adv.* minuciosamente (p. 946)

esmeralda *adj.* de color verde azulado brillante (p. 161)

aparecieron *v.* salieron; pretérito del verbo *aparecer* (p. 198)

cerca *s.* vallado o muro que protege o divide algo (p. 1057)

encuentro *s.* discusión, pelea (p. 723)

en vías de extinción *frase idiomática* en peligro de desaparecer; cuando la existencia de una especie animal o vegetal está comprometida debido a que solo queda un reducido número de miembros (p. 589)

soportar *v.* tolerar o aguantar (p. 264)

soportaron *v.* resistieron al dolor y a las dificultades; forma del verbo *soportar* (p. 690)

envidia *s.* celos; deseo de lo que no se posee o es un bien ajeno (p. 286)

evacuó *v.* desocupar o desalojar; forma del verbo *evacuar* (p. 822)

evaluar *v.* examinar detalladamente; estimar (p. 840)

(se) exasperó *v.* se irritó o se enfureció; forma del verbo *exasperar(se)* (p. 947)

exótico(a) *adj.* extraño; raro; extranjero (p. 720)

expedición *s.* viaje de exploración (p. 716)

hazañas *s.* acciones valerosas, proezas (p. 156)

expressing (eks PRES ing) *n.* the act of making feelings or opinions known (p. 416)

F

familiar (FUH mil yur) *adj.* commonly seen, heard or experienced; well-known (p. 43)

fanfare (FAN fair) *n.* a very noticeable public display (p. 381)

fate (fayt) *n.* a power that people believe determines events before they happen (p. 551)

feat (feet) *n.* an act that shows skill, strength, or courage (p. 96)

features (FEE churz) *n.* parts or qualities (p. 787)

fencing (FEN sing) *n.* the sport of fighting with swords (p. 1003)

fiasco (fee AS koh) *n.* something that has failed completely, possibly in a ridiculous way (p. 1022)

floundering (FLOUN dur ing) *v.* struggling to move or gain balance (p. 695)

foliage (FOH lee ij) *n.* plant and tree leaves (p. 653)

formal (FOR mul) *adj.* proper, following rules (p. 34)

former (FOR mur) *adj.* earlier; coming before in time (p. 88)

forsake (for SAYK) *v.* to give up someone or something (p. 265)

forsaken (for SAY kun) *adj.* given up or abandoned (p. 824)

fragments (FRAG munts) *n.* small pieces that are broken off (p. 81)

frills (frilz) *n.* things that are added on for decoration but are not really necessary (p. 1010)

fumbled (FUM buld) *v.* lost one's grasp on something (p. 862)

G

generation (jen uh RAY shun) *n.* a group of persons born around the same time (p. 452)

ghastly (GAST lee) *adj.* terrible, horrible (p. 445)

gloomy (GLOO mee) *adj.* dull, dark, and depressing (p. 226)

expresar *v.* manifestar sentimientos y opiniones (p. 416)

familiar *adj.* que resulta conocido; que se tiene por sabido (p. 43)

fanfarria *s.* música interpretada por un conjunto de instrumentos, gen. en actos públicos (p. 381)

destino *s.* fuerza que actúa inevitablemente sobre sucesos y personas (p. 551)

proeza *s.* hazaña que muestra gran fuerza y valentía (p. 96)

características *s.* cualidades propias de algo (p. 787)

esgrima *s.* deporte en el que se combate con espadas (p. 1003)

fiasco *s.* fracaso, decepción, chasco (p. 1022)

(se) resbalaban *v.* desplazarse o deslizarse involuntariamente perdiendo el equilibrio; forma del verbo *resbalar(se)* (p. 695)

follaje *s.* ramas y hojas de árboles y plantas (p. 653)

formal *adj.* conforme a las reglas o requisitos (p. 34)

antiguo(a) *adj.* que fue hace mucho tiempo (p. 88)

renunciar *v.* dejar o abandonar algo (p. 265)

abandonado(a) *adj.* descuidado o dejado (p. 824)

fragmento(s) *s.* trozo separado de un todo (p. 81)

adornos *s.* detalles agregados para embellecer algo pero que no son necesarios (p. 1010)

dejó caer *frase verbal* perdió el control de la pelota, esp. en fútbol americano (p. 862)

generación *s.* conjunto de personas nacidas alrededor de la misma fecha (p. 452)

espantoso(a) *adj.* terrible, horrible (p. 445)

sombrío(a) *adj.* lúgubre, oscuro y deprimente (p. 226)

goal (gohl) *n.* something that you aim for (p. 192)

grief (greef) *n.* unhappiness or suffering, often about the loss of something (p. 329)

grotesque (groh TESK) *adj.* very strange and unexpected (p. 653)

grudging (GRUJ ing) *adj.* resentfully or without wanting to (p. 833)

grudgingly (GRUJ ing lee) *adv.* unhappily, unwillingly (p. 293)

H

heredity (huh RED uh tee) *n.* the passing on of characteristics from an animal or plant to its offspring (p. 454)

hesitantly (HEZ uh tunt lee) *adv.* in a way that shows uncertainty or fear (p. 353)

hick (hik) *adj.* small, rural, unexciting (p. 985)

hissed (hisd) *v.* made a sound like air escaping from a balloon (p. 1058)

hoax (hohks) *n.* an act meant to fool or trick (p. 727)

horsewhip (HORS wip) *n.* a whip or stick used to make a horse go faster (p. 749)

hospitality (hos pih TAL uh tee) *n.* friendly treatment of guests (p. 833)

hostile (HOS tul) *adj.* unfriendly (p. 498)

I

immense (ih MENS) *adj.* of great size; huge (p. 551)

immigrant (IM ih grunt) *n.* a person who comes to live in a country in which he or she was not born (p. 498)

immune (ih MYOON) *adj.* not influenced or affected by (p. 591)

inadequate (ih AD ih kwit) *adj.* not good enough (p. 432)

incident (IN suh dunt) *n.* an event or situation (p. 97)

indifference (in DIF fur uns) *n.* a lack of feeling or concern (p. 200)

indignities (in DIG nuh teez) *n.* insulting treatment (p. 264)

---

meta *s.* fin u objetivo personal que se desea alcanzar (p. 192)

dolor *s.* sentimiento de gran pena o sufrimiento (p. 329)

grotesco(a) *adj.* ridículo, de mal gusto (p. 653)

hecho(a) de mala gana *frase adj.* realizado a regañadientes; sin voluntad (p. 833)

de mala gana *frase adv.* a regañadientes, sin voluntad (p. 293)

H

herencia *s.* transmisión de los caracteres genéticos de los seres vivos a su descendencia (p. 454)

con titubeos *frase adv.* que muestra indecisión o perplejidad (p. 353)

campesino(a) *adj. peyor.* pequeño, rural, apegado a costumbres lugareñas (p. 985)

silbó *v.* hacer sonidos dejando escapar el aire; pretérito del verbo *silbar*; para sonidos de animales: *bufar* o *resoplar* (p. 1058)

broma *s.* chiste o truco (p. 727)

fusta *s.* látigo o vara usada para estimular o castigar a los caballos (p. 749)

hospitalidad *s.* recibimiento acogedor que se da a invitados (p. 833)

hostil *adj.* que muestra enemistad (p. 498)

I

inmenso(a) *adj.* muy grande; enorme (p. 551)

inmigrante *s.* persona que llega a un lugar, distinto del que nació, para establecerse en él (p. 498)

inmune *adj.* que está exento de peligros o de enfermedades (p. 591)

impropio(a) *adj.* sin las cualidades convenientes (p. 432)

incidente *s.* suceso o episodio (p. 97)

indiferencia *s.* falta de sentimientos o de interés (p. 200)

indignidades *s.* humillaciones, falta de mérito (p. 264)

individuality (in duh vij oo AL uh tee) *n.* the combined qualities or characteristics that make one person or thing different from another (p. 303)

industrious (in DUS tree us) *adj.* hardworking (p. 690)

infer (in FUR) *v.* to use reason and experience to figure out what an author does not say directly (p. 298)

instinctively (in STINK tiv lee) *adv.* in a way that comes naturally, without thinking (p. 351)

integrate (IN tuh grayt) *v.* to bring together or make something part of a whole (p. 1052)

intellectual (in tuh LEK choo ul) *adj.* requiring thought and understanding (p. 890)

interpret (in TUR prit) *v.* to explain the meaning of; make understandable (p. 420)

interrogated (in TAIR uh gay tid) *v.* asked questions harshly or in great detail (p. 79)

iridescent (ir ih DES unt) *adj.* showing shimmering colors that look like a rainbow (p. 654)

isolated (EYE suh lay tid) *v.* to be set or kept away from others (p. 1053)

individualidad *s.* propiedad de alguien o algo por lo que se lo distingue de lo demás (p. 303)

laborioso(a) *adj.* muy trabajador (p. 690)

inferir *v.* deducir conclusiones de un texto usando la experiencia o el razonamiento (p. 298)

instintivamente *adv.* que proviene de un impulso natural (p. 351)

integrar *v.* incorporar o unir a un todo (p. 1052)

intelectual *adj.* relacionado con la facultad de razonar y comprender (p. 890)

interpretar *v.* explicar el significado de algo; hacer comprensible (p. 420)

interrogó *v.* hacerle preguntas a alguien para aclarar un asunto; forma del verbo *interrogar* (p. 79)

iridiscente *adj.* que muestra o destella los colores del arco iris (p. 654)

aislado(a) *v.* apartado o separado del trato con los demás (p. 1053)

K

kin (kin) *n.* family or relatives (p. 329)

familia *s.* congéneres o parientes (p. 329)

L

languid (LANG gwid) *adj.* slow-moving; without energy (p. 461)

laughingstock (LAF ing STOK) *n.* a person or thing that is made fun of (p. 89)

lavishly (LAV ish lee) *adv.* in a way that provides much more than is needed (p. 387, 946)

lisp (lisp) *n.* a speech problem affecting the *s* and *z* sounds (p. 541)

lithe (lyth) *adj.* flexible and moving easily (p. 541)

looming (LOO ming) *adj.* appearing in the distance (p. 826)

lunged (lunjd) *v.* made a sudden forward movement; charged (p. 679)

lánguido(a) *adj.* débil; falto de ánimo; sin energía (p. 461)

hazmerreír *s.* personas que por su aspecto o comportamiento sirven de diversión a los demás (p. 89)

espléndidamente *adv.* hecho con generosidad y desprendimiento (p. 387, 946)

ceceo *s.* problema de pronunciación que afecta a los sonidos *s* y *z* (p. 541)

ágil *adj.* que se mueve con agilidad y soltura (p. 541)

(se) levantaba *v.* que sobresale en altura, que se yergue y separa; forma de verbo *levantar(se)* (p. 826)

arremetió *v.* atacó con ímpetu; embistió; forma del verbo *arremeter* (p. 679)

M

makeshift (MAKE shift) *adj.* suitable as a temporary substitute (p. 628)

mane (mayn) *n.* the long, thick hair on an animal's neck or head (p. 161)

manufacturing (man yuh FAK chur ing) *v.* making out of raw materials (p. 415)

mauve (mohv) *adj.* a light purple or violet (p. 424)

meekly (MEEK lee) *adv.* in a timid and mild manner; gently (p. 679)

menacingly (MEN uh seen lee) *adv.* in a threatening manner (p. 1007)

merely (MEER lee) *adv.* just, only (p. 639)

migrant (MY grunt) *adj.* moving from place-to-place (p. 173)

milepost (MYL pohst) *n.* one of a number of signs placed one mile apart (p. 748)

minded (MYN did) *v.* took charge of (p. 412)

mirth (murth) *n.* joy, happiness (p. 447)

mocking (MOK ing) *v.* making fun of someone by imitating them in a ridiculous manner (p. 1007)

moist (moyst) *adj.* just wet enough to notice (p. 415)

monitor (MON ih tur) *v.* to check or watch (p. 36)

mope (mohp) *v.* to be gloomy or in low spirits (p. 134)

morale (muh RAL) *n.* the state of a person's mind and spirit (p. 181)

muster (MUS tur) *v.* to find and gather together; collect (p. 342)

muttered (MUT urd) *v.* spoke quietly to complain or express anger (p. 412)

N

nourished (NUR ishd) *v.* provided with food or other substances necessary for life (p. 72)

nutrition (noo TRI shun) *n.* the process by which living things use food (p. 72, 287)

O

obesity (oh BEE sih tee) *n.* condition of being extremely overweight (p. 20)

---

provisorio(a) *adj.* temporal, no permanente (p. 628)

crin *s.* conjunto de cerdas o pelos gruesos que crece en el cuello de algunos animales, por ej., el caballo (p. 161)

fabricar *v.* producir o elaborar objetos mecánicamente; forma del verbo *fabricar* (p. 415)

malva *adj.* de color violeta pálido (p. 424)

dócilmente *adv.* de modo apacible y obediente; sumisamente (p. 679)

amenazante *adv.* de modo intimidante o peligrosamente (p. 1007)

simplemente *adv.* solamente, sólo (p. 639)

itinerante *adj.* que va de un lugar a otro (p. 173)

mojón *s.* poste usado para señalar la distancia y la posición en un camino (p. 748)

cuidé *v.* se ocupó de algo; pretérito del verbo *cuidar* (p. 412)

regocijo *s.* alborozo, felicidad (p. 447)

burlarse *v.* hacer bromas o ridiculizar a alguien (p. 1007)

húmedo(a) *adj.* ligeramente mojado (p. 415)

controlar *v.* vigilar o verificar (p. 36)

andar deprimido(a) *frase verbal* que tiene el ánimo decaído o con la moral baja (p. 134)

moral *s.* estado de ánimo o de confianza en uno mismo (p. 181)

juntar *v.* reunir o agrupar; acumular (p. 342)

refunfuñó *v.* habló expresando enojo o enfado; pretérito del verbo *refunfuñar* (p. 412)

nutrido(a) *v.* que recibe las sustancias necesarias para crecer y desarrollarse (p. 72)

nutrición *s.* función por la cual los seres vivos se alimentan (p. 72, 287)

obesidad *s.* gordura en exceso (p. 20)

obituaries (oh BIH chuh wair eez) *n.* notices of deaths, usually in newspapers (p. 988)

observant (ub ZER vunt) *adj.* good at noticing details (p. 216)

obsessed (ub SEST) *adj.* concentrating completely (p. 850)

ominous (OM ih nus) *adj.* threatening (p. 738)

outrages (OUT ray jiz) *n.* violent or cruel acts (p. 498)

P

paranoid (PAIR uh noyd) *adj.* feeling like everyone is against you (p. 211)

parody (PAIR uh dee) *n.* a piece of writing or musical work that imitates another by making fun of it (p. 571)

pectorals (pek TOR ulz) *n.* muscles connecting the chest walls to the bones of the upper arm and shoulder (p. 425)

peers (peerz) *v.* looks closely at something (p. 424)

pelted (PEL tid) *v.* struck over and over again (p. 94)

penetrated (PEN uh tray tid) *v.* passed into or through (p. 1041)

perilously (PAIR uh lus lee) *adv.* dangerously, at risk of injury (p. 694)

perpetual (pur PEH choo ul) *adj.* continuing forever (p. 380)

phantom (FAN tum) *adj.* looking or seeming real although unreal (p. 899)

plagued (playgd) *v.* was greatly troubled or distressed (p. 675)

policies (POL uh seez) *n.* plans or rules (p. 557)

pondered (PON durd) *v.* thought about (p. 811)

potential (puh TEN shuhl) *adj.* capable of being or becoming something possible (p. 152, 572)

practical (PRAK tih kul) *adj.* having or showing good sense about everyday activities (p. 787)

predominantly (prih DOM ih nunt lee) *adv.* mainly; mostly (p. 734)

prejudice (PREJ uh dis) *n.* an opinion that is formed unfairly (p. 154)

obituario *s.* sección de noticias necrológicas de un periódico o revista (p. 988)

observador(a) *adj.* que advierte y nota con mucho (p. 216)

obsesivo(a) *adj.* que tiene fijación con ciertas ideas que no puede quitar de su mente (p. 850)

ominoso(a) *adj.* alarmante, de mal agüero (p. 738)

atrocidades *s.* crueldades muy grandes (p. 498)

paranoico(a) *adj.* obsesionado con una idea fija, por ej., que todos están en su contra (p. 211)

parodia *s.* imitación burlesca y exagerada de algo (p. 571)

pectorales *s.* músculos del pecho conectados a los huesos de los hombros y los antebrazos (p. 425)

(se) escruta *v.* explora y examina cuidadosa y atentamente; forma del verbo *escrutar(se)* (p. 424)

(se) acribillaban *v.* causar muchas heridas o picaduras repetidamente; forma del verbo *acribillar(se)* (p. 94)

penetró *v.* se introdujo o se infiltró; forma del verbo *penetrar* (p. 1041)

peligrosamente *adv.* que puede causar un daño o riesgo (p. 693)

perpetuo(a) *adj.* que dura para siempre (p. 380)

fantasma *adj.* sentimiento o visión de algo imaginario o irreal (p. 899)

atormentado *v.* que causa disgusto o aflicción; forma del verbo *atormentar* (p. 675)

políticas *s.* métodos y orientaciones designadas para un fin (p. 557)

caviló *v.* pensó profundamente; forma del verbo *cavilar* (p. 811)

potencial *adj.* que puede ser (p. 152, 572)

práctico(a) *adj.* que tiene buen juicio para captar la realidad y actúa de acuerdo a ella (p. 787)

predominantemente *adv.* que prevalece en cantidad numérica (p. 734)

prejuicio *s.* opinión o juicio desfavorable formado de antemano (p. 154)

pretense (PREE tens) *n.* a false show or appearance; pretending (p. 381)

prior (PRY ur) *adj.* earlier; coming before (p. 126)

privileged (PRIH vih lijd) *adj.* having or enjoying one or more advantages (p. 878)

process (PRAH ses) *n.* a series of steps to follow in making or doing something (p. 51)

proclaimed (pruh KLAYMD) *v.* declared publicly, announced (p. 973)

professional (pruh FESH uh nul) *adj.* relating to a life-long occupation or career (p. 1053)

profile (PROH fyl) *n.* a side view (p. 131)

promenade (PROM uh nayd) *v.* to walk or stroll in a slow, relaxed manner (p. 464)

prominent (PROM uh nunt) *adj.* well-known (p. 171)

promote (pruh MOT) *v.* to help grow or prosper (p. 595)

pronunciation (pro nun see AY shun) *n.* how a word is said (p. 000)

prospectors (PRAH spek turs) *n.* people who explore an area for mineral or oil deposits (p. 690)

pummel (PUM ul) *v.* to hit or beat someone (p. 1006)

apariencia *s.* falso, que parece algo que no es (p. 381)

previo(a) *adj.* anterior; que viene primero (p. 126)

privilegiado(a) *adj.* que tiene ventajas o beneficios especiales (p. 878)

proceso *s.* conjunto de pasos sucesivos en la producción de un fenómeno u operación (p. 51)

proclamó *v.* anunciar o declarar públicamente y en voz alta, forma del verbo *proclamar* (p. 973)

profesional *adj.* personas que ejercen un trabajo con relevante capacidad y aplicación (p. 1053)

perfil *s.* contorno de la vista lateral de algo (p. 131)

pasear(se) *v.* andar o desplazarse de un lugar a otro por ejercicio o distracción (p. 464)

prominente *adj.* ilustre, famoso, destacado (p. 171)

promocionar *v.* dar a conocer algo para mejorarlo en reputación y apreciación (p. 595)

pronunciación *s.* forma en que se emite y articula un sonido para hablar (p. 000)

explorador(a) *s.* persona que investiga una cosa o lugar para hacer descubrimientos (p. 690)

golpear con los puños *frase v.* pegar con los puños (p. 1006)

Q

quest (kwest) *n.* a search for a particular object or goal (p. 679)

quivers (KWIV urz) *v.* shakes or moves with a slight trembling motion (p. 161)

búsqueda *s.* indagación que se hace para conseguir algo (p. 679)

vibrar *v.* temblar o estremecerse con movimientos pequeños y rápidos (p. 161)

R

rambling (RAM bling) *v.* talking in a disorganized manner (p. 1005)

ravaged (RAV ijd) *v.* destroyed violently; ruined (p. 675)

rays (rayz) *n.* beams of light or energy (p. 461)

recited (rih SY tid) *v.* repeated from memory (p. 525)

referee (ref uh REE) *n.* a sports official who makes sure rules are followed in a game (p. 862)

relish (REL ish) *v.* to enjoy (p. 204)

divagando *v.* hablando o escribiendo separándose del tema principal; forma del verbo *divagar* (p. 1005)

devastado(a) *v.* destruido, arrasado; forma del verbo *devastar* (p. 675)

rayos *s.* haces de luz o energía (p. 461)

recitado(a) *v.* repetido de memoria y en voz alta; forma del verbo *recitar* (p. 525)

árbitro(a) *s.* persona que hace que se cumpla el reglamento en competencias deportivas (p. 862)

saborear *v.* disfrutar el sabor de algo que se come o se bebe (p. 204)

remnants (REM nuhts) *n.* what is left over; small remaining parts (p. 897)

remorse (rih MORS), *n.* feeling of guilt and regret (p. 651)

reputation (rep yuh TAY shun) *n.* what other people think about someone (p. 230, 748)

resolve (rih ZOLV) *v.* to make a firm decision (p. 738)

resourceful (rih SORS ful) *adj.* able to deal with new or difficult situations (p. 44)

retreat (rih TREET) *v.* to move backward, away from a situation (p. 225)

rigid (RIJ id) *adj.* stiff (p. 525)

ringleaders (RING leed urz) *n.* individuals who lead groups of people, expecially those who cause trouble (p. 594)

rivaling (RY vul ing) *v.* being equal to or matching (p. 875)

routine (roo TEEN) *n.* a regular way of doing something (p. 1052)

S

sanctuary (SANK choo wair ee) *n.* a safe and protective place (p. 1060)

sarcastic (sar KAS tik) *adj.* describes sharp or bitter words that are meant to hurt or make fun of someone (p. 81)

savoring (SAY vur ing) *v.* taking great delight in (p. 352)

scholar (SKOL ur) *n.* a person of great learning (p. 381)

scourge (skurj) *n.* cause of widespread hardship or suffering (p. 946)

scurried (SKUR eed) *v.* ran quickly (p. 752)

sedately (sih DAYT lee) *adv.* in a quiet, calm manner (p. 837)

self-discipline (self DIS uh plin) *n.* control over your behavior in order to improve yourself (p. 170)

seminary (SEM ih nair ee) *n.* a school for advanced education (p. 180)

sequence (SEE kwens) *n.* the order of ideas or events; the arrangement of things in time, space, or importance (p. 544)

remanente *s.* aquello que queda de algo (p. 897)

remordimiento *s.* inquietud o culpa que queda después de una mala acción (p. 651)

reputación *s.* fama o prestigio ante las personas (p. 230, 748)

resolver *v.* tomar una determinación decisiva (p. 738)

con recursos *frase prep.* que tiene los medios para conseguir lo deseado en caso de necesidad (p. 44)

retirar(se) *v.* apartarse de algo, irse (p. 225)

rígido(a) *adj.* tieso; que no se puede doblar (p. 525)

cabecilla *s.* jefe de un grupo de rebeldes (p. 594)

rivalizaba *v.* que estaba en competencia con otro (p. 875)

rutina *s.* costumbre de hacer algo repetidamente de la misma manera (p. 1052)

santuario *s.* lugar que se considera valioso por alguna razón (p. 1060)

sarcástico(a) *adj.* que expresa burlas o ironías crueles para ofender o humillar a alguien (p. 81)

saborear *v.* percibir con deleite el sabor de lo que se come o bebe (p. 352)

erudito(a) *s.* persona con conocimientos profundos adquiridos mediante el estudio (p. 381)

azote *s.* instrumento de castigo (p. 946)

se escabulló *v.* escapó a toda prisa; forma del verbo *escabullir(se)* (p. 752)

tranquilamente *adv.* de manera calmada (p. 837)

autodisciplina *s.* capacidad de control sobre uno mismo en la conducta (p. 170)

instituto educativo *frase nom.* centro de enseñanza de educación superior (p. 180)

secuencia *s.* sucesión de elementos relacionados entre sí (p. 544)

sharecropper (SHAIR krop ur) *n.* a farmer who works land owned by someone else and shares the crop or the money from its sale with the landowner (p. 347)

sheared (sheerd) *v.* cut off sharply (p. 329)

shrugged (shrugd) *v.* raised the shoulders to show doubt, lack of interest, or uncertainty (p. 412)

singe (sinj) *v.* to burn slightly (p. 900)

skimpy (SKIM pee) *adj.* lacking in quantity; barely or not quite enough (p. 832)

slashed (slasht) *v.* hit sharply enough to cause a cut (p. 749)

slithered (SLITH urd) *v.* moved along with a sliding or gliding motion, as a snake (p. 549)

slums (slumz) *n.* parts of cities where poor people live in crowded, run-down buildings (p. 173)

solemnly (SOL um lee) *adv.* seriously; without joy or humor (p. 946)

sordid (SOR did) *adj.* mean; rude of human nature (p. 571)

spar (spar) *v.* to move around as if fighting without landing a blow (p. 960)

spectacle (SPEK tik ul) *n.* something that attracts too much of the wrong kind of attention (p. 388)

splurge (splurj) *v.* to spend more money than usual (p. 847)

spout (spowt) *v.* to speak rapidly; to say something in a loud, boastful manner (p. 886)

spunk (spunk) *n.* courage, spirit, and determination (p. 663)

stammer (STAM mur) *v.* to speak with difficulty; to repeat the same sound several times when trying to say a word. (p. 886)

stifled (STY fuld) *v.* choked; smothered (p. 906)

stragglers (STRAG lurz) *n.* people who lag behind the main group (p. 551)

stranded (STRAND id) *adj.* left helpless in a difficult place (p. 329, 461)

stress (stres) *n.* a harmful feeling of fear, worry, or strain (p. 591)

subdued (sub DOOD) *adj.* quiet, weak, under control (p. 1064)

aparcero *s.* persona que trabaja unas tierras bajo contrato a cambio de dar al propietario de las tierras una parte de los beneficios que de ellas obtenga (p. 347)

(se) recortaba *v.* perfilar, forma del verbo *recortar* (p. 329)

encogió los hombros *frase v.* elevar los hombros de manera simultánea para mostrar falta de interés o conocimiento; expresión *encogerse de hombros* (p. 412)

chamuscar *v.* quemar la parte exterior o superficialmente (p. 900)

escaso(a) *adj.* limitado, corto, insuficiente (p. 832)

acuchilló *v.* hirió o cortó con un arma afilada; forma del verbo *acuchillar* (p. 749)

reptaron *v.* se arrastraron o deslizaron como una serpiente, forma del verbo *reptar* (p. 549)

barrios bajos *frase nom.* zona poblada por las clases sociales más pobres (p. 173)

solemnemente *adv.* con mucha seriedad o gravedad (p. 946)

sórdido(a) *adj.* sucio, escandaloso, indecente (p. 571)

entrenar *v.* simular una pelea sin llegar a golpear (p. 960)

espectáculo *s.* acción que causa extrañeza o escándalo (p. 388)

derrochar *v.* gastar demasiado sin pensar (p. 847)

hablar a borbotones *frase v.* expresar una idea aceleradamente, queriendo decirlo todo de una sola vez (p. 886)

arrojo *s.* osadía, coraje, atrevimiento (p. 663)

tartamudear *v.* hablar entrecortadamente y con repetición (p. 886)

sofocar *v.* ahogar; impedir la respiración (p. 906)

rezagados(as) *s.* personas que se quedan atrás separándose del resto del grupo (p. 551)

varado(a) *adj.* quedarse detenido imprevistamente en un lugar (p. 329, 461)

estrés *s.* tensión nerviosa provocada por situaciones agobiantes (p. 591)

subyugado *adj.* dominado, bajo el control de algo o alguien (p. 1064)

subjected (sub JEKT id) *v.* caused to experience (p. 511)

sullenly (SUL un lee) *adj.* gloomily and silently (p. 445)

summary (SUM uh ree) *n.* a brief statement of the main points of a piece of writing (p. 566)

surf (surf) *n.* breaking waves and foam near the shore of an ocean, lake, or river (p. 1060)

surveyed (sur VAYD *or* SUR vayd) *adj.* polled; questioned (p. 512)

swaggers (SWAG urz) *v.* walks in a bold or proud way (p. 550)

synthesize (SIN thuh syz) *v.* to bring together to create something new (p. 782)

sometido(a) *v.* dominio impuesto sobre alguien por la fuerza, forma del verbo *someter* (p. 511)

sombríamente *adj.* triste, melancólico (p. 445)

resumen *s.* reducción de un escrito a sus puntos básicos (p. 566)

oleaje *s.* sucesión de olas en el mar, lago o río (p. 1060)

encuestaron *v.* preguntaron a un número de personas sobre un tema determinado para conocer el estado de opinión general; forma del verbo *encuestar* (p. 512)

(se) pavonea *v.* hacer ostentación de algo, presumir con exageración; forma del verbo *pavonear(se)* (p. 550)

sintetizar *v.* componer algo a través de la suma de sus partes (p. 782)

T

taunt (tawnt) *v.* to try to anger someone by teasing him or her (p. 222)

tedious (TEE dee us) *adj.* boring; tiresome (p. 711)

tended (TEN did) *v.* cared for; kept in working order (p. 330)

text (tekst) *n.* the printed or written words of a page, book, or another form of communication (p. 8)

timidly (TIM ud lee) *adv.* fearfully (p. 292)

toiled (toyld) *v.* worked hard (p. 752)

tortoise (TOR tus) *n.* a large turtle that lives on land (p. 1060)

traumatized (TROM uh tyzd) *adj.* upset or injured as a result of a frightening event (p. 1064)

treacherous (TRECH ur us) *adj.* dangerous and unpredictable (p. 95)

tresses (TRES uz) *n.* long hair (p. 1016)

tribute (TRIB yoot) *n.* something done to show respect (p. 1000)

triceps (TRY seps) *n.* a large muscle at the back of the upper arm (p. 425)

tsunami (tsoo NAH mee) *n.* a huge ocean wave that is caused by an underwater earthquake, volcano, or landslide (p. 1060)

fastidiar *v.* molestar a alguien provocando su enfado o disgusto (p. 222)

tedioso(a) *adj.* aburrido, molesto (p. 711)

atendía *v.* se ocupaba o cuidaba de algo o alguien, forma del verbo *atender* (p. 330)

texto *s.* grupo de palabras que forman un documento escrito (p. 8)

tímidamente *adv.* con temor (p. 292)

(se) afanó *v.* trabajó duro, forma del verbo *afanar(se)* (p. 752)

tortuga *s.* reptil del orden de los Quelonios, los hay de tipo terrestre y de tipo marino; tienen el cuerpo cubierto por un caparazón del que salen las extremidades (p. 1060)

traumatizado(a) *adj.* que ha sufrido una impresión fuerte, negativa y duradera (p. 1064)

traicionero(a) *adj.* que es astuto e imprevisible (p. 95)

mechones *s.* porciones de pelo (p. 1016)

tributo *s.* manifestación de admiración y respeto; reconocimiento (p. 1000)

tríceps *s.* músculo de tres porciones que se extiende al antebrazo (p. 425)

tsunami *s.* ola de gran tamaño causada por un terremoto o una erupción volcánica en el fondo del mar (p. 1060)

tyrant (TY runt) *n.* a cruel, unjust ruler (p. 676)

tirano(a) *s.* gobernante cruel que abusa de su poder y que es injusto (p. 676)

U

ultimate (UL tih mut) *adj.* greatest; most important (p. 22)

principal *adj.* fundamental; más importante (p. 22)

unique (yoo NEEK) *adj.* having no like or equal (p. 287)

único(a) *adj.* solo, sin otro de su misma especie (p. 287)

unmindful (un MYND ful) *adj.* not aware (p. 204)

ignorante *adj.* que desconoce un asunto; carente de información (p. 204)

uproar (UP ror) *n.* noisy excitement and confusion (p. 556)

alboroto *s.* desorden, tumulto (p. 556)

ushers (USH urz) *n.* people who help others find their seats in a theater or stadium (p. 15)

acomodadores(as) *s.* persona que indica a los asistentes de un teatro o estadio los asientos que ocuparán (p. 15)

utter (UT ur) *v.* to speak or say aloud (p. 807)

pronunciar *v.* emitir o articular sonidos al hablar; decir en voz alta (p. 807)

V

vapor (VAY pur) *n.* small particles of mist, steam, or smoke that can be seen (p. 899)

vapor *s.* gas que se forma cuando un líquido es transformado por la acción del calor (p. 899)

velocity (vuh LOS uh tee) *n.* speed; swiftness (p. 902)

velocidad *s.* rapidez de movimiento (p. 902)

vendors (VEN durz) *n.* people who sell products or services (p. 14)

vendedores(as) *s.* personas que venden productos o servicios (p. 14)

verbal (VUR bul) *adj.* expressed in spoken words (p. 558)

verbal *adj.* que se sirve de la palabra hablada (p. 558)

vicious (VISH us) *adj.* mean and cruel (p. 216)

fiero(a) *adj.* cruel y de trato difícil (p. 216)

victory (VIK tur ee) *n.* the win in a contest or battle (p. 193)

victoria *s.* triunfo; éxito en un enfrentamiento (p. 193)

vile (vyl) *adj.* very bad; unpleasant; foul (p. 344)

repugnante *adj.* asqueroso; aversivo; horrible (p. 344)

vinyl (VY nul) *adj.* made of vinyl, which is a tough, shiny plastic (p. 130)

vinilo *adj.* resina dura plastificable (p. 130)

visualize (VIZH wul ize) *v.* to form a mental image or picture of (p. 376)

visualizar *v.* formar una imagen mental de algo (p. 376)

W

warily (WAIR uh lee) *adv.* cautiously (p. 960)

cautelosamente *adv.* con cuidado y recelo (p. 960)

well (WEL) *n.* a hole dug in the ground to get water (p. 749)

pozo *s.* hoyo profundo en la tierra que, por lo general, se hace para sacar agua (p. 749)

well-being (wel BEE ing) *n.* good physical and mental condition (p. 286)

bienestar *s.* en buen estado físico y mental (p. 286)

whimper (WIM pur) *n.* a soft cry (p. 417)

widower (WID oh ur) *n.* a man whose wife has died (p. 1021)

withdrawn (with DRAWN) *adj.* shy, reserved, or unsociable (p. 344)

wittiness (WIT tee nes) *n.* ability to be smart and funny (p. 550)

woe (woh) *n.* great sadness or suffering (p. 445)

writhing (RY thing) *adj.* twitching, twisting (p. 446)

Y

yearned (yurnd) *v.* had a strong desire (p. 636)

yearning (YUR ning) *n.* wanting something badly (p. 201)

quejido *s.* llanto suave y corto; voz lastimosa de dolor o pesar (p. 417)

viudo *s.* hombre cuya esposa ha muerto (p. 1021)

retraído(a) *adj.* tímido, reservado, apartado (p. 344)

agudeza *s.* perspicacia o viveza de ingenio; facultad mental para crear con rapidez (p. 550)

infortunio *s.* desdicha, fortuna adversa (p. 445)

retorcido(a) *adj.* doblado, contorsionado (p. 446)

anhelaba *v.* tenía un deseo vehemente por conseguir algo, forma del verbo *anhelar* (p. 636)

anhelo *s.* deseo intenso (p. 201)

INDEX OF SKILLS

References beginning with RH refer to Reading Handbook pages.

References beginning with R refer to Handbook pages.

Literary and Text Elements

Act 930, R10
Action R12
    falling 547, 805, 813
    rising 547, 805
Alliteration 423, 437, R10
Allusion R10
Analogy R10
Anecdote R10
Antagonist R10
Anthropomorphism R10
Aside R10
Assonance R10
Author's credibility 894
Author's purpose 5, 71, 77, 84, 85, 509, 515, R10
Autobiography 118, R10
Ballads R10
Bandwagon R47
Bias 256, 285
Biography 118, R10
Characters R10
    dynamic R10
    flat R10
    round R10
    static R10
Characterization 484, 569, 582, 930, 973, 987, R11
    direct 569
    indirect 569
Climax 547, 805, 813, R11
Comedy R11
Conflict 336, 484, R11
Consonance R11
Couplet R11
Cultural context 618, 649, 659
Description 776, 843, 859, R11

Details 68, 71, 75, 77, R11
Dialect R11, 953
Dialogue 484, 497, 1030, 1036, 1039, 1051, R11
Drama 930, R11
Elegy R11
Epic R11
Essays 278, 314, R11
Exposition 547, 805, R11
Extended metaphor (*See* Metaphor) R11
Fable 618, 642, 702, R11
Falling action 547, 805, 813, R12
Fantasy 618, R12
Fiction R12
    historical 776, R12
    science R15
Figurative language 374, 436, 443, 451, 458, R12
    metaphor 436, 443, 451
    personification 436, 443, 451
    simile 436, 443, 451
Figurative meanings 1038
Figures of speech (*See* Figurative language)
Flashback R12
Folklore R12
Folktales 618, R12
Foreshadowing R12
Free verse 374, R12
Genre R12
Glittering generalities R47
Graphics 5, 48, 51, 55, 57, 63, RH18
Haiku R12
Hero 618, 627, 633, 635, 744, R12
Historical fiction 776, R12
Humor R12
Hyperbole 262
Idioms 972, 986, 1050, R12
Imagery 437, R13
    sensory 437, 930
    visual RH10
Informational text R13
Irony R13
Journal R13

Legend R13
Limerick R13
Literal meanings 1038
Local color R13
Lyric R13
Lyric poetry 374, R13
Main idea 5, 68, 71, 77, 776, 818, 821, 831, R13
Memoir R13
Metaphor 436, 443, 451, R13
    extended R11
Meter 374, 405, R13
Monologue R13
Mood 256, 327, R13
Moral 642
Myth 618, R13
Narration R13
Narrative poetry 374, R13
Narrator 118, 129, 138, 385, 397, 776, 821, 831, R13
Nonfiction 776, R13
Novel R14
Novella R14
Ode R14
Onomatopoeia R14
Oral tradition R14
Organization
    cause and effect RH16
    chronological order 118, 167, 179, RH10
    compare and contrast RH16
    order of importance RH17
    problem-solution 318, 321, 327, 1057, RH17
    sequence of events/time order 484, 544, 547, 555, 776, 873, RH10, RH17, R15
    spatial order RH17
    time order/sequence 484, 544, 547, 555, 776, 873, RH10, RH17, R15
Parallelism R14
Personification 436, 443, R14
Plot R14, 484, 547, 805
    climax 547, 805
    conflict 484, 523, 539, R11

external 523
internal 523
exposition 547, 805
falling action 547, 805, R12
resolution 547, 805
rising action 547, 805, R15
Plot twist R14
Poetry 374, 379, 398, 436, R14
features 374, 379, 398, 437
free verse 374, 383
lyric 374
narrative 374
Point of view 118, 149, 160, 429, R14
first-person 149, 160, 429, 435, 821, 831
third-person 429, 831
limited 831
omniscient 831
Process 5, 51, 57
Props R14
Propaganda R14
Prose R14
Protagonist R14
Pun R14
Refrain R15
Repetition 307, R15
Resolution 547, 805, R15
Rhyme 405, R15
end 405
internal R15
slant R15
Rhyme scheme R15
Rhythm 374, 405, R15
Rising action 547, 805, R15
Scene 930, 941, R15
Science fiction R15
Screenplay R15
Semantic slanting 300
Sensory details 437
Sensory imagery 437, 930, 1039, R15
Sequence of events/time order 484, 544, 547, 555, 776, 873, RH10, RH17, R15
Setting 618, 709, 733, R15
Short story 484, 516, R15
Simile 436, 443, 451, R15
Sonnet R15
Sound devices 374, 423, 427, 437, R15
Speaker 138, R16

Stage directions 930, 999, 1015, R16
Stanza R16
Stereotype R10, R16
Style 28, 256, 263, 269, R16
Subheads 5, 33, 41, 555, RH18
Subtitles RH18
Suspense R16
Symbol 776, 785, R16
Tall tale R16
Teleplay R16
Testimonial R47
Text features 5, 11, 19, RH17
Text structure (See Organization)
Theme 618, 673, 687, R16
implied R16
stated R16
Title 5, 555, R16
Tone R16
Tragedy R16
Visual imagery R16
Voice R16

Reading and Thinking Skills

Activating prior knowledge 118, 126, 129, 138, 615, 618, 627, 633, 635, RH9
Adjusting reading rate RH6
Advertising 4
Analyzing RH14
advertisements 67
art 81, 89, 131
cartoons 48, 57, 164, 188
graphics 5, 14, 15, 48, 51, 57
Autobiography 118, R10
Ballads R10
Biography 118, R10
Brainstorming 913, R27
Cause and effect 484, 520, 539, RH16
Clarifying 256, 282, 285, 291, 618, 646, 649, 659, 930, 970, 973, 987, RH11
Comparing and contrasting 20, 84, 208, 336, 458, 587, 618, 671, 673, 687, 744, 757, 894, 1056, RH16
author's credibility 894
author's purpose 84
characters 208
conflict 336
figurative language 458

heroes 744
primary and secondary source 1056
Connecting 11, 118, 146, 149, 159, 160, 163, RH8
Context clues 32, 39, 40, 47, 50, 56, 63, 378, 384, 404, 410, 428, 442, 450, RH3
multiple meanings 32, 39, 40, 47, 50, 56, 63
Description 776, 843, 859
Distinguishing fact and opinion 256, 260, 263, 269, RH14
Drama 930, R11
Drawing conclusions 484, 494, 497, 509, RH14
Evaluating 776, 841, 843, 859, RH15
Fables 642, 702, R11
Fantasy 618, RH12
Fiction R12
historical 776, R12
science R15
Fluency RH5
Folklore R12
Folktales R12, 618
Foreshadowing R12
Free verse 374
Genre R12
Graphic aids RH18
charts 209, 296, 320, 326, RH18
character 209
comparison 209, 296, 757
pro and con 304
diagrams RH18
timelines 180
webs 284, 320, 820, RH7
flowcharts RH7
graphs RH18
maps RH18
tables RH18
timelines 180
word webs 320, 820, RH7
Graphic novels 57
Haiku R12
Historical fiction 776, R12
Important details 26, 68, 71, 77, 776, 818, 821, 831
Inferring 256, 298, 301, 307, 776, 870, 873, 883, RH13
Informational text 4

Informational media 4
   advertising 4
   Internet 4
   news articles 4, 6
   newspaper 4
   radio 4
   television 4
   Web pages 4
   Web site 4
Interpreting 374, 420, RH13
Legend R13
Limerick R13
Lyric poetry 374, R13
Main idea 5, 68, 71, 77, 776, 818, 821, 831, RH11
Memoirs R13
Minor details 26
Monitoring comprehension 374, 440, 443, 451, RH11
Moral 642
Myth 618, R13
Narrative poems 374
Nonfiction R13, 776
Novel R14
Novella R14
Oral tradition R14
Paraphrasing 484, 566, 569, RH12
Poetry 374, 398
   free verse 374
   haiku R12
   lyric 374
   narrative 374
Predicting 118, 164, 167, 179, 618, 706, 709, 733, 930, 1036, 1039, 1051, 1055, RH10
Previewing RH9
Problem and solution 256, 318, 321, 327, 1051, RH17
Process 5, 51, 57
Prose R14
Questioning 118, 188, 191, 197, RH11
Read fluently RH5
Responding to reading 374, 402, 405, 411, RH8
Review RH11
Sensory imagery 437
Scanning 5, 30, 33, 41, 930, 996, 999, 1015, RH6
Science fiction R15
Sequence/time order 484, 544, 547, 555, 776, RH10, RH17, R15
Setting a purpose for reading 5, 8, 11, 19, RH6
Short story R15, 484, 516
Skimming and scanning 5, 30, 33, 41, 930, 996, 999, 1015, RH6
Summarizing 26, 484, 566, RH12
Supporting details 26, 68, 77, 776, 818, 821, 831
Synthesizing 776, 782, 785, 805, RH15
Taking and reviewing notes RH18
Teleplay R16
Text features 5, 11, 19, RH18
   subheads 5, 11, 33, 41, 555, RH18
   subtitles 11, RH18
   titles 5, 11, 33, 41, 555, RH18
Visualizing 374, 376, 379, 385, 397, 930, 938, RH10

Grammar and Language

Abbreviations R41–R42
Adjective clauses 543
Adjectives 17, 267, 281, 289, R31
   comparative 289
   demonstrative 305
   proper R37
   superlative 289
Adverb clauses 543
Adverbs 17, 277, 281, 297
   comparative 297
   superlative 297
Agreement
   pronoun-antecedent 159
   subject-verb 817, 829, 857, 865, 881, 893, R29
Antecedents 159
Apostrophes 969, R32
   in contractions 969
   in possessive nouns 969
Appositives R31, R38
Articles 313
   definite 313
   indefinite 313
Capitalization 145, 633, R32, R36
   first words of sentences 633
   names and titles of people R36
   names of places R37
   proper nouns and adjectives 145
   of quotations 1049
   of sentences 633
Clauses 515, 519, 543
   adjective 543
   adverb 543
   dependent (subordinate) 519, 543, 669
   independent (main) 519, 543, 669, 955
   noun 543
Colons 1013, 1031
   after salutations 1013
   to introduce list 1031
   in time notations 1013
Commas 553, 561, 581, 585, 645, 657, 685, 701, R31
   in combining sentences 645, 657
   in complex sentences 645, 701
   in compound sentences 645, 685
   in series 553
   with direct address 561
   with direct quotations R31, R39
   with interruptions 585
   with introductory clauses 645, 701
   with introductory words 581
   with nonessential appositives R31, R38
Comparative adjectives 289
Comparative adverbs 297
Complex sentences 645, 701
Compound predicate 435, 641
Compound sentences 645, 685
   semicolons with 985, 995
Compound subject 435, 641
Compound words 626, 633
Conjunctions 17, 645
   coordinating 645
Contractions 969
Dashes R41
Declarative sentences 383, 397
Demonstratives 305
Direct objects 449
End punctuation 397
Exclamation point 397
Exclamatory sentences 383, 397
Fragments 409, 419, R28
Hyphens 965
Imperative sentences 383, 397
Indefinite pronouns 163, 893
Indirect objects 457
Interjections 17, 335

Interrogative sentences 383, 397
Italics R40
Nonessential appositives R31, R38
Nouns 17, 137, 145
   abstract 145
   collective 145
   common 137, 145
   plural 145
   proper 137, 145
Object pronouns 141
Objects
   direct 449
   indirect 457
Parentheses R41
Parts of speech 17, 537
   adjectives 17, 267, 281, 289, 537, R31
   adverbs 17, 277, 281, 297, 537
   conjunctions 17
   interjections 17, 335
   nouns 17, 137, 145, 537
   prepositions 17
   pronouns 17, 141, 163, 177, 183, 195, 207, 893, R30
   verbs 17, 25, 29, 39, 47, 55, 63, 75, 83, 537, 803, 813
Periods 397
   with abbreviations R41
Personal pronouns 207
Phrases 515
Possessives 969
   apostrophes 969
Predicates 427, 435, 641
   complete 427
   compound 435, 641
   simple 427, 641
Prepositional phrases R29
Prepositions 17
Pronoun case 195
   objective 195
   possessive 195
   subjective 195
Pronouns 17, 141, 163, 177, 183, 195, 207, 893, R30
   demonstrative 305
   indefinite 163, 893
   intensive 183
   object 141, 207
   personal 141, 207
   possessive 195
   reflexive 177

   subject 141, 195
Proper adjectives R39
Proper nouns 137, 145
Punctuation R38
   apostrophes 969, R32
   colons 1013, 1031
   commas 553, 561, 581, 585, 645, 657, 685, 701, R31
   dashes R41
   exclamation points 397
   hyphens 965
   italics R40
   parentheses R41
   periods 397
   question marks 397
   quotation marks 1049, 1055
   semicolons 985, 995
Question marks 397
Quotation marks 1049, 1055
Quotations 1049, 1055
   direct 1049, 1055
Run-on sentences 731, 743, R28
Semicolons 985, 995
   with long clauses 995
   with main clauses 985
Sentence fragments 409, 419, R28
Sentences 383, 397, 401, 633, 641, 657, 669, 685
   capitalization 633
   combining 645, 657
   complete 401
   complex 645, 657, 669, 701
   compound 645, 685
   declarative 383, 397
   exclamatory 383, 397
   imperative 383, 397
   interrogative 383, 397
   run-on 731, 743
   simple 641
Spelling
   adding prefixes R43
   doubling final consonant R43, R44
   forming compound words 626, R44
   forming plurals R44
   ie and *ei* R43
   suffixes and final *y* R43
   suffixes and silent *e* R43
   unstressed vowels R43
Subject pronouns 141, 195, 207
Subjects 207, 401, 427

   complete 401, 427
   compound 435
   simple 427
Subject-verb agreement 817, 829, 857, 865, 881, 893, R29
   compound subjects 435, 641
   with *here* and *there* 857
   indefinite pronouns 163, 893
   in inverted sentences 865
   special nouns 881
   subjects separated from verbs 829
Superlative adjectives 289
Superlative adverbs 297
Troublesome words R33–R35
   accept, except R33
   affect, effect R33
   ain't R33
   a lot R33
   allready, already R33
   allright, alright R33
   all together, altogether R33
   among, between R33
   amount, number R33
   bad, badly R33
   beside, besides R34
   bring, take R34
   can, may R34
   choose, chose R34
   doesn't, don't R34
   farther, further R34
   fewer, less R34
   good, well R34
   in, into R34
   it's, its R34
   lay, lie R35
   learn, teach R35
   leave, let R35
   like, as R35
   loose, lose R35
   raise, rise R35
   set, sit R35
   than, then R35
   their, they're R35
   to, too, two R35
   who, whom R35
   who's, whose R35
Verbs 17, 25, 29, 39, 47, 55, 63, 75, 83, 557, 803, 813
   action 29
   helping 39, 47

INDEX OF SKILLS

irregular 75, 83
linking 29
main 39, 47
regular 75
Verb tense 55, 75, 83, R30
future tense 75
past 83
past perfect 63
past progressive 55, 63
past tense 55, 83
present perfect 63
present progressive 47, 63
present tense 47, 55, 75, 83

Vocabulary

Anglo-Saxon origins 872, 882, RH1
Antonyms 148, 220
Base words 496, 508, 568, 784, 804, RH1
Borrowed words 634, 648, 658
Clipped words 998
Compound words 626
Connotation 290, 306, RH4
Context clues 32, 40, 50, 56, 378, 384, 404, 410, 422, 428, 442, 450, RH3
multiple meanings 32, 40, 50, 56
Denotation 290, 306, RH4
Dialect 953, R11
Dictionaries 86, RH3
Footnotes 92
Glossary RH4
Graphic aid RH18
charts 209, 296, 320, 326, RH18
word webs 320, 820, RH7
Greek Roots 842, 858, RH1
Idioms 972, 986, 1050, R12
Jargon 1014
Latin roots 820, 830, RH1
Multiple-meaning words 32, 40, 50, 56
Prefixes 166, 178, 546, 592, RH1
Root words 568, 784, 804, 858, 872, 882, RH1
Semantic slanting 284, 300, 320, 326
Slang 940
Suffixes 522, 538, RH1
Synonyms 128, 220, 320, 326
Syntax RH2
Thesaurus 18, RH4
Word choice 190, 195, 196, 320, 326

Word histories 672, 686, 708, 732
Word meanings RH4
Word parts (See Base words, Prefixes, Root words, and Suffixes)
Word references 18, 70, 76, 86, 92, RH3
Word webs 284, 320, 820, RH7

Writing

Active writing models 66, 186, 316, 438, 564, 703, 868, 1034
Audience (See RAFT)
Autobiographical narratives 142, 184
Bulletin board R18
Bumper stickers 911
Business writing R25–R26, 644
Class book R18
Clustering R17
Comic books 1073
Conventions 144
Descriptive writing R20
Details 27, 68, 184, 776, 818, 821, 831
Dialogue 484, 497, 562, R11
Drafting 26, 142, 279, 399, 518, 643, 815, 966, R17
Editing 64, 185, 315, 437, 563, 703, 867, R18
E-mail messaging 856
Essays 278, 314, R11
formal R11
informal R11
Expository writing R20
Fables 642, 702, R11
5Ws and H 869
Ideas 27
Illustrations RH18
Literary magazine R18
Making a plan 815
Memos R26
Narrative writing 142, 184, R21
Note taking (See Taking and reviewing notes)
Oral presentations 1035
Organization 28, 279, RH17, RH18
chronological order 167, 179, RH17
Outlining RH18
Parallelism R14

Paraphrase 566, 569, RH12
Personal narrative 142, 814, 866
Persuasive writing 278, 314
Plays 930, 999, 1015
Poetry 398, 436
Prewriting 26, 142, 278, 398, 516, 642, 814, 912, 966, R17, R27
Process R17
Proofread 65, 185
Propaganda R14
Prose R14
Presenting 65, 185, 315, 438, 563, R18
Publishing R18
RAFT (Role, Audience, Format, Topic) 312, 382, 584, 880, 892, 1012
Research reports R21–R24
Revise 24, 64, 184, 314, 436, 508, 562, 702, 866, 1032, R17, R18
Rubrics 64, 184, 278, 314, 436, 562, 702, 866, 1032
Sentence fluency 280
Short story 516, 562, R15
Speech 966, 1032
Structure (See Organization)
Style 28, 256, 263, 269, 277
Summarize 26, 64, 484, 566, 569, RH12
Taking and reviewing notes RH18
Traits of good writing 27, 144, 280, 400, 517, 644, 705, 816, 968
Transitions 280
Trickster tales 744, 747
Using a computer for writing R27
Visual aids 1032
Voice 702
Word choice 196, 400
Word roots 568, 784, 804, 858, 872, 882, RH1

Listening, Speaking, and Viewing Skills

Acting out skits 774
Active listening 187
Analyzing
advertisements 288
art 81, 89, 131, 133, 146, 258, 275, 963, 990, 992, 1018
cartoons 57, 126, 164, 260, 318
graphics 48

R74 Index of Skills

illustrations 68
paintings 343
photographs 13, 91, 222, 796, 799, 993
Dialect R11, 953
Distinguishing fact and opinion 256, 260, 263, 267, 269, 277, RH14, R47
Group work R48
Idioms 972, 986, 1050, R12
Imagery R12
Jargon 1014
Listening to class instructions R45
Monologue R13
News reports 869
Nonverbal clues R45
Oral presentations 317, 1035, R46
Reading aloud 439, 565
Slang 940
Speaking effectively 317, R46
Speaking informally R46
Speeches 317, 966, 1032
Storytelling 705
Testimonial R47
Transfer R47
Viewing effectively R47
Visual aids 67, 1032
Visual imagery RH10
Voice 317

Research and Study Skills

Analyzing RH14
Autobiography 118, R10
Bibliography or works cited R23, R24
Biography 118, R10
Developing a thesis R22
Dictionaries 10, RH3
Distinguishing fact and opinion 256, 260, 263, 269, RH14
Documenting information R23
Drawing conclusions 484, 494, 497, 509, RH14
Essay questions R52
Footnotes R23
Glossary RH4
Informational media 4
 advertising 4
 Internet 4
 news articles 4
 newspaper 4
 radio 4
 television 4
 Web pages 4
 Web site 4
Make a plan R49
Note taking (*See* Taking and reviewing notes)
Objective tests R51
Organizing information RH18
Outlining RH18
Parenthetical documentation R23
Primary sources 1056
Question RH11
Reference sources RH3
Researching R21
Research reports R21
Secondary sources 1056
Selecting topics R21
Setting a purpose for reading 5, 8, 11, 17, 19, 25, RH6
Set goals R49
Source cards R22
Standardized tests R52
Study skills R49
Summarizing 484, 566, 569, RH12
Taking and reviewing notes RH18
Test-taking skills 110–113, 248–251, 366–369, 476–479, 610–613, 768–771, 922–925, 1078–1081
Thesaurus 18, RH4

INDEX OF AUTHORS AND TITLES

50 Simple Things Kids Can Do to Save the Earth, from 322

A

ALEXANDER, SUE 806
All Stories Are Anansi's 636
All Summer in a Day 358
All-American Slurp, The 386
ALLEN, SARA VAN ALSTYNE 161
ALTER, ERIC 1000
And Ain't I a Woman? 257
ANGELOU, MAYA 406
Animal Attraction 6
Aunt Millicent 710
AVI 221

B

Baby Hippo Orphan Finds a Friend 1059
Ballpark Food 12
BAMBARA, TONI CADE 412, 748
BERLTOTTO, MELANIE 302
BERTRAND, AMY 20
Best of Buddies 1052
Bracelet, The 822
BRADBURY, RAY 358
BRENTS, WALKER 650
BROOKS, GWENDOLYN 72
BROWN, JORDAN 452
Bullies in the Park 589
Bully Battle, The 593
Bully of Barksdale Street, The 1000

C

Caretaker's Journal, The, from 1063
CARROLL, LEWIS 470
Charlie Johnson 988
Circuit, The 347
CISNEROS, SANDRA 308
COFER, JUDITH ORTIZ 198
Concha 93
CONFORD, ELLEN 570
CORMIER, ROBERT 844

COURLANDER, HAROLD 636
CUMMINGS, E. E. 461

D

DAHL, ROALD 1008
Damon and Pythias 974
DAMPIER, CINDY 1052
DAVIS, CLIFTON 734
Daydreamers 463
DE SIMONE, ANDREA 556
Doc Rabbit, Bruh Fox, and Tar Baby 751
Don't Let the Bedbugs Bite 570
Dragon, Dragon 674
Dressed for Success? 302
DURBIN, RICHARD 264

E

EarthWorks Group 322
EISNER, WILL 498
Eleanor Roosevelt 168
El Enano 600
Eleven 308
ELLIS, ELIZABETH 430

F

Fan Club, The 485
FIELDS-MEYER 628
FINGER, CHARLES J. 600
FISCHER, DAVID 860
Flowers and Freckle Cream 430
FOX, CATHERINE CLARKE 1059
FROST, ROBERT 1074

G

GAIMAN, NEIL 78
GARDNER, JOHN 676
Gene Scene, The 452
Gentleman of the Pool 192
Geraldine Moore the Poet 412
GIBBS, NANCY 42
GIOVANNI, NIKKI 139
Gold Cadillac, The 786
Goodness of Matt Kaizer, The 221

GRAHAME, KENNETH 942
GRAY, KEVIN 1052
Great Cow Race, The, from 58
Great Fire, The 897
Great Radio Scare, The 777
GREENFIELD, ELOISE 463
Greyling 328

H

HAMILTON, VIRGINIA 751
HAMLETT, CHRISTINA 1016
HASKINS, JIM 119
HELLING, STEVE 630
HOFFMAN, KATHRYN R. 34
How He Did It: Health Advice, Kid-to-Kid 20
HUNTER, KRISTIEN 102
Hurricane Heroes 628

I

In Eleanor Roosevelt's Time 180

J

Jacket, The 130
JACOBS, WILLIAM JAY 168
JIMÉNEZ, FRANCISCO 347
JOHNSON, DOROTHY M. 832

K

King of Mazy May, The 688
KISSEN, FAN 974

L

Lesson in Courtesy, A 916
Let the Bullies Beware 556
Letters About the Fire 905
Life Doesn't Frighten Me 406
LITTLEFIELD, BILL 150
LONDON, JACK 688
Looking for America 270
LOW, ALICE 619

M

Madame C. J. Walker 119
maggie and milly and molly and may 461
Make Your Own Kite 52
March of the Dead, The 444
Mason-Dixon Memory, A 734
MAYNARD, RONA 485
MAZER, NORMA FOX 524
MCKISSACK, FREDERICK, JR. 874
MCKISSACK, PATRICIA C. 874
Messaging Mania 34
MORA, PAT 424
MURPHY, JIM 897
My Father Is a Simple Man 380
My Parents 540

N

Nadia the Willful 806
NAMIOKA, LENSEY 386
New Kid on the Block, The 583
Nobody's Perfect 860
Novio Boy, from 931

O

OSBORNE, MARY POPE 660

P

PARK, ALICE 192
PARTRIDGE, ELIZABETH 270
PECK, RICHARD 548
Pecos Bill 660
Persephone 619
Pigman & Me, The 211
PONCE, MARY HELEN 93
PRELUTSKY, JACK 583
Preserving a Great American Symbol 264
President Cleveland, Where Are You? 844
Primary Lessons 198
Priscilla and the Wimps 548

R

Real Magic of Harry Potter, The 42
Reluctant Dragon, The 942
ROZSA, LORI 628
RYLANT, CYNTHIA 292

S

SAKAI, STAN 916
SALINAS, LUIS OMAR 380
SALINAS, MARTA 339
Same Song 424
Sand Castle, The 760
Satchel Paige 150
Scholarship Jacket, The 339
Scribe, The 102
SERVICE, ROBERT 444
Shutout, The 874
SILVERSTEIN, SHEL 375
SINGER, ISAAC BASHEVIS 1040
SIRIS, ELIZABETH 593
SMITH, JEFF 58
SMITH, JOE 988
Song for a Surf-Rider 161
SOTO, GARY 130, 931
Southpaw, The 88
SPENDER, STEPHEN 540
STEELE, MARY 710
STICH, SALLY S. 6
Stray 292
Street Magic 498
SWARTZ, JON 589

T

Tales of the Tangled Tresses 1016
Talking Skull, The 884
Ta-Na-E-Ka-Ta 238
TAYLOR, MILDRED D. 786
THANE, ADELE 942
Time to Talk, A 1074
To Young Readers 72
Toad and the Donkey, The 748
Too Soon a Woman 832
TRUTH, SOJOURNER 257
TUEI, STEPHEN 1063
Tuesday of the Other June 524
Twelve Labors of Hercules, The 650
Two Advertisements 286

U

UCHIDA, YOSHIKO 822
UPADHYAY 556

V

VILLANUEVA, ALMA LUZ 760
VIORST, JUDITH 88

W

Walrus and the Carpenter, The 470
WASHINGTON, DONNA L. 884
What Kids Say About Bullying 510
Whatif 375
WHITEBIRD, MARY 238
Why Books Are Dangerous 78
World Is Not a Pleasant Place to Be, The 139

Y

YOLEN, JANE 328

Z

ZINDEL, PAUL 211
Zlateh the Goat 1040

INDEX OF ART AND ARTISTS

A

Adlington, Mark, *Wild Boar* 653
Apple Tree, Gustav Klimt 212
Arab Scribe, Cairo, The, John Frederick Lewis 104
Atamian, Charles-Garabed, *Beach Scene* 763

B

Bazile, Castera, *Trabajadores* 348
Beach Scene, Charles-Garabed Atamian 763
Blumenschein, Ernest L., *New Mexico Peon* 343
Borders & Boundaries, Diana Ong 218
Burne-Jones, Sir Edward, *Garden of the Hesperides* 654
Burroughs, Henry Bryson, *Pluto and Proserpine* 620

C

Cady, Harrison, *"Who are you, I say?"* 752
Cameron, Hugh, *A Lonely Life* 602
Carnations and Clematis in Crystal Vase, Edouard Manet 230
Catlett, Elizabeth, *In Sojourner Truth I Fought for the Rights of Women as Well as Blacks* 258
Chicago, Illinois: Public Art, Franklin McMahon 414
Children's Games, Rufino Tamoya 96
Cinderella, Hans Printz 1024
Coakley, Cindy, *Field of Dreams* 990
Comic Mask, Unknown (Pompeii) 983
Correa, Alvim, *Man Encountering a Martian* 780
Correa, Alvim, *Martian Fighting Machine Attacking Humans* 781
Currier & Ives, *Elysian Fields, Hoboken, New Jersey* 876
Currier & Ives, *The Great Fire in Chicago, October 8-10, 1871* 901

D

D'Arcangelo, Allan, *U.S. Highway 1, Number 5* 275
De Morgan, William, *Hare* 755
Despedida, Hector Poleo 349
Dioscurides of Samos, *Street Musicians* 976
Dolly and Rach, John Wesley Hardrick 789

E

Eisner, Will, *Street Magic* 498
El Sol Asombre, Rafael Ferrer 200
Elysian Fields, Hoboken, New Jersey, Currier & Ives 876

F

Fatima, Elizabeth Hodges 406
Ferrer, Rafael, *El Sol Asombre* 200
Field of Dreams, Cindy Coakley 990
Finer, Stephen, *Patrick Garland and Alexandra Bastedo* 541
Four Seasons—Spring, Alphonse Mucha 619

G

Garden of the Hesperides, Sir Edward Burne-Jones 654
Genoves, Graciela, *La Nina del Chupetin* 95
Girl Sitting in Classroom, Alberto Ruggieri 417
Granville, J., *Public and Private Animals* 749
Great Cow Race, The, Jeff Smith 58
Great Fire in Chicago, October 8-10, 1871, The, Currier & Ives 901
Griffiths, Diane, *Lillith* 464

H

Hardrick, John Wesley, *Dolly and Rach* 789
Hardrick, John Wesley, *Springtime (Portrait of Ella Mae Moore)* 792
Hare, William De Morgan 755
Headmaster, Norman Rockwell 81
Heracles Leading Cerberus to Eurystheus, Unknown (Rome) 655
Hodges, Elizabeth, *Fatima* 406

I

In Sojourner Truth I Fought for the Rights of Women as Well as Blacks, Elizabeth Catlett 258
Ingalls, Pam, *Nancy's Sink* 425
Inness, George, *Sunrise* 363
Inness, George, *Sunset Over the Sea* 331
Irises, Ogata Korin 825

K

Klimt, Gustav, *Apple Tree* 212
Klondike Gold Rush, 1904, Price, Julius M. 689
Klondike Gold Rush, Summer 1898, Julius M. Price 692
Korin, Ogata, *Irises* 825

L

La Nina del Chupetin, Graciela Genoves 95
Lawrence, Jacob, *The Library* 73
Leighton, Frederic, *The Return of Persephone* 622
Lesson in Courtesy, A, Stan Sakai 912
Lewis, John Frederick, *The Arab Scribe, Cairo* 104
Library, The, Jacob Lawrence 73
Lillith, Diane Griffiths 464
Lonely Life, A, Hugh Cameron 602

M

Man Encountering a Martian, Alvim Correa 780

INDEX OF ART AND ARTISTS

Manet, Edouard, *Carnations and Clematis in Crystal Vase* 230
Martian Fighting Machine Attacking Humans, Alvim Correa 781
Mask, Unknown (Nigeria) 636
McMahon, Franklin, *Chicago, Illinois: Public Art* 414
Meeting on the Mound, Gary K. Stretar 89
Melendez, Luis, *Still Life with Plums, Figs, and Bread* 604
Mucha, Alphonse, *Four Seasons —Spring* 619
Munch, Edvard, *The Sick Spaniard* 233

N

Nancy's Sink, Pam Ingalls 425
New Mexico Peon, Ernest L. Blumenschein 343

O

On the Klondike, Edward Roper 696
Ong, Diana, *Borders & Boundaries* 218
Ong, Diana, *Portrait in Orange* 416
Ong, Diana, *The Reader #1* 413

P

Patrick Garland and Alexandra Bastedo, Stephen Finer 541
Pluto and Proserpine, Henry Bryson Burroughs 620
Poleo, Hector, *Despedida* 349
Portrait in Orange, Diana Ong 416
Price, Julius M., *Klondike Gold Rush, 1904* 689
Price, Julius M., *Klondike Gold Rush, Summer 1898* 692
Printz, Hans, *Cinderella* 1024
Public and Private Animals, J. Granville 749

R

Ransome, James, *The Talking Skull* 884
Reader #1, The, Diana Ong 413
Return of Persephone, The, Frederic Leighton 622
Risse, Roland, *Sleeping Beauty* 1026
Rockwell, Norman, *Headmaster* 81
Roper, Edward, *On the Klondike* 696
Ruggieri, Alberto, *Girl Sitting in Classroom* 417

S

Sakai, Stan, *A Lesson in Courtesy* 912
Sendak, Maurice, *"Zlateh the Goat"* 1040
Seven-Seven, Twins, *Untitled*
Sick Spaniard, The, Edvard Munch 233
Sleeping Beauty, Roland Risse 1026
Smith, Jeff, *The Great Cow Race* 58
Springtime (Portrait of Ella Mae Moore), John Wesley Hardrick 792
Still Life with Plums, Figs, and Bread, Luis Melendez 604
Street Magic, Will Eisner 498
Street Musicians, Dioscurides of Samos 976
Stretar, Gary K., *Meeting on the Mound* 89
Sunrise, George Inness 363
Sunset Over the Sea, George Inness 331

T

Talking Skull, The, James Ransome 884
Tamoya, Rufino, *Children's Games* 96
Tenniel, John, *The Walrus and the Carpenter* 471, 472, 473
Trabajadores, Castera Bazile 348
Tragic Mask, Unknown (Pompeii) 979

U

U.S. Highway 1, Number 5, Allan D'Arcangelo 275
Untitled, Twins Seven-Seven 637

W

Walrus and the Carpenter on Shore, The, John Tenniel 471
Walrus and the Carpenter with Oysters, The, John Tenniel 472
Walrus and the Carpenter After Eating, The, John Tenniel 473
Wild Boar, Mark Adlington 653
"Who are you, I say?" Harrison Cady 752

ACKNOWLEDGMENTS

Unit 1

"Ballpark Foods" by Consumer Reports 4 Kids. From zillions.org.

"How He Did It: Health Advice, Kid-to-Kid" by Amy Bertrand. *St. Louis Post-Dispatch*, May 2, 2005. Reprinted with permission of the St. Louis Post-Dispatch, copyright © 2005.

"Messaging Mania" by Kathryn R. Hoffman. Updated 2005, from *TIME for Kids*, May 2, 2003.

"Make Your Own Kite." From sears.com.

"To Young Readers" by Gwendolyn Brooks. Reprinted by consent of Brooks Permissions.

"Why Books Are Dangerous" by Neil Gaiman, copyright © 2005, from *Guys Write for Guys Who Read*, ed. by Jon Scieszka. Published by Viking, a division of Penguin Young Readers Group.

"The South Paw" by Judith Viorst. Copyright © 1974 by Judith Viorst. From *Free to Be . . . You and Me*. This usage granted by permission. All rights reserved.

"Concha" by Mary Helen Ponce. Reprinted by permission of the author.

"The Scribe" from *Guests in the Promised Land* by Kristin Hunter. Copyright © 1968 by Kristin E. Lattany. Reprinted by permission of Dystel & Goderich Literary Management.

Unit 2

"Madam C. J. Walker" from *One More River to Cross: The Story of Twelve Black Americans* by Jim Haskins. Copyright © 1992 by James Haskins.

"The Jacket" by Gary Soto appears in *The Effects of Knut Hamsun on a Fresno Boy: Recollections and Short Essays* by Gary Soto. Copyright © 1983, 2000 by Gary Soto. Reprinted by permission of Book Stop Literary Agency and Persea Books, Inc. (New York).

"The World Is Not a Pleasant Place to Be" from *My House* by Nikki Giovanni. Copyright © 1972 by Nikki Giovanni. Reprinted by permission of HarperCollins Publishers.

"Satchel Paige" from *Champions: Stories of Ten Remarkable Athletes* by Bill Littlefield. Copyright © 1993 by Bill Littlefield (text); copyright © 1993 by Bernie Fuchs (illustrations). By permission of Little, Brown and Co., Inc. and Mews Books.

"Song for a Surf-Rider" by Sara Van Alstyne. Copyright © 1966 by Scholastic, Inc.

"Eleanor Roosevelt" reprinted with the permission of Atheneum Books for Young Readers, an imprint of Simon & Schuster Children's Publishing Division from *Great Lives: Human Rights* by William Jay Jacobs. Copyright © 1990 William Jay Jacobs.

"Primary Lessons" is reprinted with permission from the publisher of *Silent Dancing* by Judith Ortiz Cofer (Houston: Arte Publico Press—University of Houston, copyright © 1990).

From "Pigman & Me" by Paul Zindel. Copyright © 1990 by Paul Zindel. First appeared in *The Pigman & Me*, published by HarperCollins. Reprinted by permission of Curtis Brown, Ltd.

"The Goodness of Matt Kaizer" copyright © 1994 by Avi. From his book *What Do Fish Have To Do With Anything?* (Candlewick Press). Reprinted by permission.

"Ta-Na-E-Ka-Ta," by Mary Whitebird. Copyright ©1973 by Scholastic, Inc.

Unit 3

"Perserving a Great American Symbol," by Richard Durbin.

"Looking for America" by Elizabeth Partridge, copyright © 2003, from *Open Your Eyes*, ed. by Jill Davis. Reprinted by permission of Elizabeth Partridge. All rights are reserved by the author.

"Stray" reprinted with permission of Atheneum Books for Young Readers, an imprint of Simon & Schuster Children's Publishing Division from *Every Living Thing* by Cynthia Rylant. Copyright © 1985 Cynthia Rylant.

"Eleven" from *Woman Hollering Creek*. Copyright © 1991 by Sandra Cisneros. Published by Vintage Books, a division of Random House, Inc., and originally in hardcover by Random House, Inc. Reprinted by permission of Sandra Bergholz Literary Services, New York. All rights reserved.

From *50 Simple Things Kids Can Do To Save the Earth* © 1990 EarthWorks press. Reprinted with permission of Andrews McMeel Publishing. All rights reserved.

"Greyling," copyright © 1968 by Jane Yolen. First appeared in *Greyling*, published by Penguin Putnam, Inc. Reprinted by permission of Curtis Brown Ltd.

"The Circuit" by Franciso Jimenez. Reprinted by permission of the author.

"All Summer in a Day" by Ray Bradbury. Copyright © 1954, renewed 1982 by Ray Bradbury. Reprinted by permission of Don Congdon Associates, Inc.

Unit 4

"Whatif" from *A Light in the Attic* by Shel Silverstein. Copyright © 1981 by Evil Eye Music, Inc. Used by permission of HarperCollins Publishers.

"My Father Is a Simple Man" is reprinted with permission from the publisher of *The Sadness of Days* by Luis Omar Salinas (Houston: Arte Publico Press–University of Houston, © 1987).

"The All-American Slurp" by Lensey Namioka, copyright © 1987, from *Visions*, ed. by Donald R. Gallo. Reprinted by permission of Lensey Namioka. All rights are reserved by the author.

"A Minor Bird" from *The Poetry of Robert Frost* edited by Edward Connery Lathem. Copyright © 1928, 1969 by Henry Holt and Company. Copyright © 1956 by Robert Frost. Reprinted by permission of Henry Holt and Company LLC.

"Life Doesn't Frighten Me" copyright © 1978 by Maya Angelou, from *And Still I Rise* by Maya Angelou. Used by permission of Random House, Inc.

"Geraldine Moore the Poet" by Toni Cade Bambara. Reprinted by permission of Karma Bambara.

"Same Song" is reprinted with permission from the publisher of *Borders* by Pat Mora (Houston: Arte Publico Press–University of Houston, © 1986).

"Flowers and Freckle Cream" by Elizabeth Ellis. Reprinted by permission of the author.

"maggie and milly and molly and may," copyright © 1956, 1984, 1991 by the Trustees for the E.E. Cummings Trust, from *Complete Poems: 1904–1962* by E.E. Cummings, edited by George J. Firmage. Used by permission of Liveright Publishing Corporation.

From *Daydreamers* by Eloise Greenfield, copyright © 1981 by Eloise Greenfield. Used by permission of Dial Books for Young Readers, a division of Penguin Young Readers Group, a member of Penguin Group (USA) Inc., 345 Hudson Street, New York, NY 10014. All rights reserved.

Unit 5

"The Fan Club" by Rona Maynard. Reprinted by permission of the author.

"What Kids Say About: Bullying." This information was provided by KidsHealth, one of the largest resources online for medically reviewed health information written for parents, kids and teens. For more articles like this one, visit www.KidsHealth.org or www.TeensHealth.org.

"Tuesday of the Other June" by Norma Fox Mazer. Copyright ©1986 by Norma Fox Mazer.

"My Parents" from *Collected Poems: 1928–1985* by Stephen Spender. Copyright ©1934 and renewed ©1962 by Stephen Spender.

"Priscilla and the Wimps" by Richard Peck, from *Sixteen: Short Stories* ed. by Donald R. Gallo. Copyright ©1984 by Richard Peck.

"Don't Let the Bed Bugs Bite" from *I Love You, I Hate You, Get Lost*, by Ellen Conford. Copyright ©1995 by Scholastic, Inc.

From *The New Kid on the Block* by Jack Prelutsky. Copyright © 1984 by Jack Prelutsky. Used by permission of HarperCollins Publishers.

"Bullies in the Park: Elephants vs. Rhinos" by Jon Swartz, from *Time for Kids*.

"The Bully Battle" by Elizabeth Siris, from *Time for Kids*.

"El Enano" from *Tales From Silver Lands*, by Charles J. Finger.

Unit 6

"Persephone" reprinted with the permission of Simon & Schuster Books for Young Readers, an imprint of Simon & Schuster's Children's Publishing division from *The Macmillan Book of Greek Gods and Heroes* by Alice Low. Copyright © 1985 Macmillan Publishing Company.

"All Stories Are Anansi's" from *The Hat-Shaking Dance and Other Ashanti Tales from Ghana* by Harold Courlander with Albert Kofi Prempeh, copyright © 1957, 1985 by Harold Courlander. Reprinted by permission of Michael Courlander.

From "The Twelve Labors of Hercules" by Walker Brents. Reprinted by permission of the author.

"Pecos Bill" from *American Tall Tales* by Mary Pope Osborne, copyright © 1991 by Mary Pope Osborne. Illustrations copyright © 1991 by Michael McCurdy. Used by permission of Alfred A. Knopf, an imprint of Random House Children's Books, a division of Random House, Inc. [**For electronic/digital uses:** Used by permission of Brandt & Hochman Literary Agents, Inc. Any electronic copying or distribution of this text is expressly forbidden.]

"Dragon, Dragon" from *Dragon, Dragon and Other Tales* by John Gardner. Copyright © 1975 by Boskydell Artists, Ltd. Reprinted by permission of Georges Borchardt, Inc., for the Estate of John Gardner.

"Aunt Millicent" by Mary Steele, from *Dream Time*, edited by Toss Gascoigne, Jo Goodman and Margot Tyrell. Copyright © 1989 by Mary Steele. Collection copyright © 1989 by the Children's Book Council of Australia. Reprinted by permission of Houghton Mifflin Co. All rights reserved.

"A Mason-Dixon Memory" by Clifton Davis, adapted from *Reader's Digest*, March 1993. Copyright ©1993 by Mel White.

"The Toad and the Donkey," by Toni Cade Bambara.

"Doc Rabbit, Bruh Fox and Tar Baby" from *The People Could Fly: American Black Folktales* by Virginia Hamilton, illustrated by Leo and Diane Dillon, copyright © 1985 by Virginia Hamilton. Illustrations copyright © 1985 by Leo and Diane Dillon. Used by permission of Alfred A. Knopf, an imprint of Random House Children's Books, a division of Random House, Inc.

"The Sand Castle" by Alma Luz Villanueva. Reprinted by permission of the author.

Unit 7

"US terrorized by radio's 'Men from Mars'" Reprinted with permission of the Associated Press, copyright © 1938. All rights reserved.

From *The Gold Cadillac* by Mildred D. Taylor, copyright © 1987 by Mildred D. Taylor, text. Used by permission of Dial Books for Young Readers, a division of Penguin Young Readers Group, a member of Penguin Group (USA) Inc., 345 Hudson St., New York, NY 10014. All rights reserved.

"Nadia the Willful," copyright © 1983 by Sue Alexander. First appeared in *Nadia the Willful*, published by Alfred A. Knopf. Reprinted by permission of Curtis Brown, Ltd.

"The Bracelet" by Yoshiko Uchida, from *Desert Exile*, copyright © 1982 by Yoshiko Uchida, courtesy of the Bancroft Library, University of California, Berkeley.

"Too Soon a Woman" by Dorothy M. Johnson. Copyright ©1953 and renewed ©1981 by Dorothy M. Johnson.

"President Cleveland, Where Are You?" copyright © 1965 by Robert Cormier, from *Eight Plus One: Stories* by Robert Cormier. Used by permission of Random House Children's Books, a division of Random House, Inc.

"The Shut Out" from *Black Diamond: The Story of the Negro Baseball Leagues* by Patricia C. and Frederick McKissack, Jr. Copyright © 1994 by Patricia C. and Frederick McKissack, Jr.

"The Talking Skull" from *A Pride of African Tales* by Donna Washington, illustrated by James Ransome. Text copyright © 2004 by Donna Washington. Used by permission of HarperCollins Publishers.

From "The Great Fire" by Jim Murphy. Copyright © 1995 by Jim Murphy.

"Letter About the Fire" from The Chicago Historical Society.

Unit 8

From *Novio Boy*, copyright © 1997 by Gary Soto, reprinted by permission of Harcourt, Inc.

"The Reluctant Dragon" by Kenneth Grahame as adapted by Adele Thane from March 1963 © *Plays, the Drama Magazine for Young People and Plays from Famous Stories and Fairy Tales*, copyright © 1967 and © 1997, reprinted with the permission of the publisher Plays/Sterling Partners, Inc., PO Box 600160, Newton, MA 02460.

"The Legend of Damon and Pythias" from *The Bag of Fire and Other Plays* by Fan Kissen. Copyright © 1964 by Houghton Mifflin Company, renewed © 1993 by John Kissen Heaslip. Reprinted by permission of Houghton Mifflin Company. All rights reserved.

"Charlie Johnson" by Joseph K. Smith, reprinted by permission of *Cricket* magazine, December 1998, Vol. 26, No. 4, text © 1998 by Joseph K. Smith.

"The Bully of Barksdale Street" by Eric Alter, January/February *Plays, the Drama Magazine for Young People,* copyright © January 2006, is reprinted with the permission of the publisher Plays/Sterling Partners, Inc., PO Box 600160, Newton, MA 02460.

"Tales of the Tangled Tresses" by Christina Hamlett, January/February *Plays, the Drama Magazine for Young People,* copyright © January 2006, is reprinted with the permission of the publisher Plays/Sterling Partners, Inc., PO Box 600160, Newton, MA 02460.

"Zlateh the Goat" from *Zlateh the Goat and Other Stories* by Isaac Bashevis Singer. Text copyright 1966 © by Isacc Bashevis Singer.

"Baby Hippo Orphan Finds a Friend" by Catherine Fox. *National Geographic Kids News*, March 4, 2004. Reprinted by permission of the National Geographic Society.

From "The Caretaker's Diary" by Stephen Tuei. From lafargeecosystems.com, 2005.

Photography

Cover Imtek Imagineering/Masterfile; 0 Getty Images, 2 (l)Jose Luis Pelaez/CORBIS, (r)Mary Kate Denny/PhotoEdit; 7 Edwin Fotheringham; 8 HEART OF THE CITY © 2004 Mark Tatulli. Dist. By UNIVERSAL PRESS SYNDICATE. Reprinted with permission. All rights reserved; 9 John Evans; 12 CORBIS; 13 (b)Associated Press, OLATHE DAILY NEWS, (t)Paul A. Sauders/CORBIS; 15 (l)Spot Jason Hosking/Zefa/CORBIS, (r)Icon SMI/CORBIS; 16 (l)CORBIS, (r)Images.com/CORBIS; 20 John Paterson/Getty Images; 21 Tom Stewart/CORBIS; 23 Rolf Bruderer; 24 John Paterson/Getty Images; 27 Images.com/CORBIS; 30 Randy Glasbergen; 30 Getty Images; 31 (r)John Evans, (l)PhotoObjects.net; 35 37 38 Dean MacAdam; 42 Glynis Sweeny Time for Kids; 43 (br)Gottfried Stoppel Time for Kids; 44 (tr)Murdo Macleod/CORBIS/Sygma Time for Kids; 45 (tr)Pitchal Frederic/CORBIS/Sygma Time for Kids; 46 (tl)Glynis Sweeny Time for Kids; 48 (c)CLOSE TO HOME 2005 John McPherson. Reprinted with permission of UNIVERSAL PRESS SYNDICATE. All rights reserved; 49 Getty Images; 52 54 Don Smetzer/Stone/Getty Images; 58 59 60 61 62 From BONE ®: THE GREAT COW RACE by Jeff Smith. Copyright © 2005, 1993, 1992 by Jeff Smith. Published by Graphix, an imprint of Scholastic Inc. Reprinted by permission. Scholastic; 68 Images.com/CORBIS; 69 Getty Images; 70 Bettmann/CORBIS; 73 Smithsonian American Art Museum, Washington, DC/Art Resource, NY National Museum of American Art; 74 Smithsonian American Art Museum, Washington, DC/Art Resource, NY National Museum of American Art; 76 Neville Elder/CORBIS; 78 Stockbyte/Creatas; 79 Janine Wiedel Photolibrary/Alamy; 80 Getty Images; 81 Printed by permission by the Norman Rockwell Family Agency. 1926. The Norman Rockwell Family Entities. John Rockwell; 82 Stockbyte/Creatas; 86 AP/Wide World Photos; 88 Getty Images; 89 Gary Stretar, courtesy www.skylinepictures.com. AIM Enterprises; 90 Mark C. Burnett; 91 Ken Chernus/Taxi/Getty Images; 92 Courtesy of Mary Helen Ponce; 93 Brand X Pictures/Creatas; 94 Tim Flach/Getty Images; 95 Zurbaran Galeria/SuperStock; 96 With respect to 1983.208, Rufino Tamayo (Mexican, 1899-1991), Children's Games, 1959, Oil on Canvas; 51 1/4 x 76 3/4 in., The Metropolitan Museum of Art, Gift of Mr. and Mrs. Ralph E. Colin, 1983 (1983.208) Photograph 1984; 97 Getty Images; 98 (l)Getty Images, (r)Tim Flach/Getty Images; 102 Mitch Kezar/Stone/Getty Images; 103 Marc Asnin/CORBIS; 104 The Arab Scribe, Cairo, John Frederick Lewis (1805-76)/Private Collection, Christie's Images/Bridgeman Art Library; 107 CORBIS; 108 109 Eclipse Studios; 114 Taxi/Getty Images; 116 (l)Taxi/Getty Images, (r)WireImageStock/Masterfile; 119 121 122 123 A.Lelia Bundles/Walker Family Collection; 124 (tr)Underwood & Underwood/CORBIS; 125 (bl)A. Lelia Bundles/Walker Family Collection; 126 CALVIN AND HOBBES, Watterson. Dist. By UNIVERSAL PRESS SYNDICATE. Reprinted with permission; 128 Courtesy of Gary Soto; 130–135 Chris Vallo; 138 Courtesy of Nikki Giovanni; 139 140 Images.com/CORBIS; 144 HOME by UNIVERSAL PRESS SYNDICATE. Reprinted with permission. All rights reserved.; 146 CORBIS; 148 L. Barry Hetherington; 150 Associated Press; 151 PhotoObjects.net/Jupiter Images, (b)National Baseball Hall of Fame Library, Cooperstown, NY; 153 The Granger Collection, NY; 154 Bettmann/CORBIS; 155 Bettmann/CORBIS; 157 158 AP/Wide World; 161 Peter Griffith/Masterfile; 162 Peter Griffith/Masterfile; 164 CLEATS Bill Hinds. Dist. by UNIVERSAL PRESS SYNDICATE. Reprinted with permission. All rights reserved; 168 Bettmann/CORBIS; 169 CORBIS; 170 Bettmann/CORBIS; 171 Bachrach/Keystone/Getty Images; 172 (t)Courtesy of the Franklin D. Roosevelt Presidential Library, (b)The Art Archive/Culver Pictures; 173 Thomas D. Mcavoy/Time Magazine, Copyright Time Inc./Time Life Pictures/Getty Images; 174 Topham/The Image Works; 175 Leo Rosenthal/Time Life Pictures/Getty Images; 176 180 Bettmann/CORBIS; 181 (t)CORBIS, (b)Andre Jenny/The Image Works; 182 Bettmann/CORBIS; 188 Patrick McDonnell. Reprinted with permission of King Features Syndicate.; 189 RIchard Hutchings/Photo Researchers; 192 194 Mike Blake/Reuters/NewsCom; 196 (tl)Miriam Berkley; 198 CORBIS; 199 courtesy Judith Ortiz Cofer; 200 Rafael Ferrer; 203 Charles E. Rotkin/CORBIS; 205 Ira Nowinski/CORBIS; 206 UPI/CORBIS; 210 Roger Ressmeyer/CORBIS; 211 Dirk Anschutz/The Image Bank/Getty Images; 212 Erich Lessing/Art Resource, NY; 214 Matthias Kulka/CORBIS; 216 Peter Scoones/Photo Researchers; 217 Images.com/CORBIS; 218 Purestock/SuperStock; 221 Kurt Stier/CORBIS; 222 Rubberball/SuperStock; 226 PhotoAlto/Getty Images; 229 Images.com/CORBIS; 230 Edimedia/CORBIS; 233 Scala/Art Resource, NY.; 234 Dirk Anschutz/The Image Bank/Getty Images, (b)Kurt Stier/CORBIS; 238 Frank Krahmer/Zefa/CORBIS; 240 H. Reinhard/Zefa/CORBIS; 242 Getty Images; 243 Tipp Howell/Taxi/Getty Images; 246 247 Eclipse Studios; 252 Dave Bartruff/CORBIS; 257 Hulton Archive; 258 Hampton University Museum, Hampton, VA/ Elizabeth Catlett/Licensed by VAGA, New York, NY; 259 file photo 260 POOCH CAFE 2005 Dist. by UNIVERSAL PRESS SYNDICATE. Reprinted with permission; 261 John Evans; 262 Courtesy of Richard Durban; 264 Taxi/Getty Images; 266 Taxi/Getty Images; 270 Getty Images; 271 Stone/Getty; 272 Michael Alberstat/Masterfile; 275 Digital Image The Museum of Modern Art/Licensed by SCALA / Art Resource, NY; 276 Getty Images; 283 Getty Images; 286 288 Gaslight Advertising Archives; 290 courtesy Blue Sky Press; 292 Rommel/Masterfile; 293 Pat Doyle/CORBIS; 295 Getty Images; 296 Rommel/Masterfile; 298 Calvin & Hobbes Watterson. Dist. By UNIVERSAL PRESS SYNDICATE; 299 John Evans; 303 (t)Courtesy of Long Beach Unified School District, (b)Courtesy of Allen Lichtenstein; 306 M. Toussant/Liaison/Getty Images; 308 file photo; 310 Dave Robertson/Masterfile; 311 Andrew Judd/Masterfile; 312 file photo; 318 CALVIN & HOBBES Watterson. Dist. By UNIVERSAL PRESS SYNDICATE. Reprinted with permission. All rights reserved.; 319 Rubberball/SuperStock; 323 324 Jose Luis Pelaez/CORBIS; 326 Jason Stemple; 328 The Image Bank/Getty Images; 331 Brooklyn Museum of Art/CORBIS; 332 David Job/Getty Images; 334 The Image Bank/Getty Images; 339 Masterfile; 340 Mark Burnett; 342 Walter H. Hodge/Peter Arnold, Inc.; 343 Gerald Peters Gallery, Santa Fe, NM; 345 Tom Stewart/CORBIS; 346 San Jose Mercury News photographer: Eugene Louie; 347 Ed and Chris Kumler; 348 Trabajadores, 1950. Castera Bazile. Oil on canvas, 27 x 19Z\x in. Private collection.; 349 Despedida, 1941. Hector Poleo. Oil on linen, 60 x 50 cm. Private collection.; 350 Index Stock Imagery; 354 Masterfile; 354 Eising Food Photography/Stockfood America; 358 (l)Satelight/Gamma Liaison, (r)Michael Prince/CORBIS; 359 Freeman Patterson/Masterfile; 360 Trinette Reed/CORBIS; 362 file photo; 363 Brooklyn Museum of Art/CORBIS; 370 Catherine Karnow/CORBIS; 372 (l) NOVASTOCK/PhotoEdit, (r)Stone/Getty Images; 375 Shel Silverstein; 376 (c)CALVIN AND HOBBES, Watterson. Dist. By UNIVERSAL PRESS SYNDICATE. Reprinted with permission. All rights reserved.; 377 CORBIS; 380 382 Jose Luis Pelaez/CORBIS; 384 Courtesy Lensey Namioka-photo by Don Perkins; 386 CORBIS; 388 Mary Kate Denny/Getty Images; 391 (l)JupiterImages/Comstock, (r)Dale Kennington/SuperStock; 392 Images.com/CORBIS; 394 (l)Arthur Beck/CORBIS

ACKNOWLEDGMENTS

Stock Market, (r)Getty Images; 395 Matthew Klein/CORBIS; 396 CORBIS; 400 REAL LIFE ADVENTURES 1997 GarLanco. Reprinted with permission of UNIVERSAL PRESS SYNDICATE. All rights reserved; 402 BALDO, Baldo Partnership. Dist. By UNIVERSAL PRESS SYNDICATE. Reprinted with permission. All rights reserved.; 403 Kevin Dodge/CORBIS; 404 Gregory Pace/CORBIS Sygma; 406 Elizabeth Barakah Hodges/SuperStock; 408 Elizabeth Barakah Hodges/SuperStock; 410 courtesy of Toni Cade Bambara; 413 Diana Ong/SuperStock; 414 Franklin McMahon/CORBIS; 416 Diana Ong/SuperStock; 418 Richard Hutchings/PhotoEdit; 420 BALDO, Baldo Partnership. Dist. By UNIVERSAL PRESS SYNDICATE. Reprinted with permission. All rights reserved.; 421 Spencer Grant/PhotoEdit; 425 Pam Ingalls/CORBIS; 426 Pam Ingalls/CORBIS; 430 Steven Biver/The Image Bank/Getty Images; 431 Lowell Georgia/CORBIS; 433 Masterfile; 434 Steven Biver/The Image Bank/Getty Images; 440 NON SEQUITUR 2001 Wiley Miller. Dist. By UNIVERSAL PRESS SYNDICATE. Reprinted with permission. All rights reserved.; 442 (tl)The Granger Collection, NY; 444 Jim Richardson/CORBIS; 447 Bill Heinsohn/Photographers Choice/Getty Images; 448 Jim Richardson/CORBIS; 452 453 456 Denis Finnin/American Museum of Natural History; 460 Bettmann/CORBIS; 461 Anne Ackermann/Taxi/Getty Images; 462 Steven M. Cummings; 464 The Grand Design/SuperStock; 466 Anne Ackermann/Taxi/Getty Images; 466 The Grand Design/SuperStock; 470 Bettmann/CORBIS; 471 472 473 Stock Montage/The Newbery Library; 474 Eclipse Studios; 480 Marvel/CORBIS; 482 (l)CORBIS, (r)BananaStock/Alamy; 487 Owen Franken/CORBIS; 488 (t)Image Source/Imagestate, (tl)Tony Freeman/PhotoEdit; 490 Digital Vision/Getty Images; 494 BALDO, Baldo Partnership. Dist. by UNIVERSAL PRESS SYNDICATE. Reprinted with permission. All rights reserved.; 495 Ron Chapple/Creatas; 496 (tl)Getty Images, 1661455; 498-508 Will Eisner; 510 Stockbyte; 513 (l)David Moore/Getty Images, (r)LWA-Dann Tardif/CORBIS; 514 Stockbyte; 520 Randy Glasbergen; 521 CORBIS; 524 Erica Shires/Zefa/CORBIS; 525 Fotosearch; 526 Brooke Fasani/CORBIS; 527 Guy Crittenden/ImageState; 534 Yellow Dog Productions/Getty Images; 536 Erica Shires/Zefa/CORBIS; 538 Hulton Getty Picture Collection/Tony Stone Images; 540 Patrick Garland and Alexandra Bastedo, 1998 (oil on canvas), Finer, Stephen (Contemporary Artist) / Private Collection/Bridgeman; 542 Patrick Garland and Alexandra Bastedo, 1998 (oil on canvas), Finer, Stephen (Contemporary Artist) / Private Collection./Bridgeman; 544 Randy Glasbergen; 545 ThinkStock/SuperStock; 546 courtesy Penguin Putnam; 548 Thomas Barwick/Getty Images; 551 David Madison; 552 Getty Images; 557 Jeff Topping for Time for Kids; 558 Getty Images; 560 Jeff Topping for Time for Kids; 566 BALDO 2005 Baldo Partnership. Dist. by UNIVERSAL PRESS SYNDICATE. Reprinted with permission. All rights reserved.; 567 SuperStock; 570 CORBIS; 572 Ronnie Kaufman/CORBIS; 575 Alan Schein Photography/CORBIS; 577 Shannon Stapleton/Reuters/CORBIS; 579 (r)BananaStock/Creatas, (l)Anthony Bannister/Gallo Images/CORBIS; 580 CORBIS; 583 reprinted from Harper-Collins, illustration by James Stevenson; 584 reprinted from Harper-Collins, illustration by James Stevenson; 588 Murray Patti/Animals Animals-Earth Sciences; 589 Karl Ammann/CORBIS; 590 imagebroker/Alamy; 591 Murray Patti/Animals Animals-Earth Sciences; 594 Creasource/CORBIS; 596 (tl) Karl Ammann/CORBIS; 596 Creasource/CORBIS; 600 Courtesy of the University of Arkansas Museum; 601 Fotosearch; 602 A Lonely Life, c.1873, Cameron, Hugh (1835-1918), National Gallery of Scotland, Edinburgh, Scotland, Bridgeman Art Library; 604 Archivo Iconografico, S.A./CORBIS; 605 Barbra Leigh/CORBIS; 606 Christopher Thomas/Getty Images; 607 Paul Sisul/Getty Images; 608 609 Eclipse Studios; 614 image 100/SuperStock; 616 (l)Gerard Fritz/Imagestate, (r)Getty Images; 619 Mucha Trust/ADAGP, Paris/ARS, New York; 620 Henry Bryson Burroughs/The Bridgeman Art Library; 622 Leeds Museums and Galleries (City Art Gallery) U. K./The Bridgeman Art Library; 623 Stapleton Collection/CORBIS; 624 1995 Watterson. Dist. By UNIVERSAL PRESS SYNDICATE. Reprinted with permission. All rights reserved.; 625 (cr) ThinkStock / SuperStock; 629 (tr)Karena Cawthon/Silver Image; 630 Ben Baker/Redux; 631 Ben Baker/Redux; 632 Karena Cawthon/Silver Image; 634 Michael Courlander; 636 Harn Museum of Art Collection/University of Florida, gift of Rod McGalliard-1990.14.103; 637 Ian Murphy/Getty Images; 637 Photo by Claude Postel/C.A.A.C. The Pigozzi Collection; 638 Erich Lessing/Art Resource, NY; 640 Photo by Claude Postel/C.A.A.C. The Pigozzi Collection; 646 Images.com/CORBIS; 647 CORBIS; 648 Joyce Romano; 650 Archive Timothy McCarthy/Art Resource, NY; 651 The Art Archive/Bargello Museum Florence / Dagli Orti; 652 Francesco Venturi/CORBIS; 653 Mark Adlington/The Bridgeman Art Library/Getty Images; 654 Garden of the Hesperides, 1869-73 (tempera, gouache and oil on card and canvas); 655 Réunion des Musées Nationaux / Art Resource, NY; 656 Archive Timothy McCarthy/Art Resource, NY; 660 Michael McCurdy; 662 Michael McCurdy; 664 Mary Clay/Getty Images; 667 Michael McCurdy; 668 Michael McCurdy; 670 Randy Glasbergen; 671 Stockbyte/Creatas; 672 Bettmann/CORBIS; 684 Patrick Kelley; 688 Rolf Kopfle/Bruce Coleman; 689 Werner Forman/CORBIS; 689 Mary Evans Picture Library; 690 691 North Wind Picture Archives; 692 Mary Evans Picture Library; 695 North Wind Picture Archives; 696 orth Wind Picture Archives; 698 Mary Evans Picture Library; 700 Rolf Kopfle/Bruce Coleman; 706 Patrick McDonnell. Reprinted with permission of King Features Syndicate.; 707 CORBIS; 710 Y. Arthus-Bertrand/Peter Arnold, Inc.; 714 Doug Martin; 715 Ric Ergenbright Photography; 716 Natalie Fobes/CORBIS; 720 ABI/Lonely Planet Images; 721 (l)Tom McHugh/Photo Researchers, (r)David Wall/Lonely Planet Images; 722 Frank Kroenke/Peter Arnold, Inc.; 724 Robert Frerck/Panoramic Images; 725 David L. Perry; 730 Y. Arthus-Bertrand/Peter Arnold, Inc.; 734 Lee Snider/Photo Images/CORBIS; 735 Getty Images; 736 Joseph Sohm; Visions of America/CORBIS; 737 Ron Watts/CORBIS; 739 From the files of the National Park Service; Photographer: William J. Moore; 741 Miles Ertman/Masterfile; 742 Lee Snider/Photo Images/CORBIS; 746 courtesy of Toni Cade Bambara; 748 Larry West/Getty Images; 749 Edward Pierce; 750 Virginia Hamilton/Scholastic, Inc; 752 Harrison Cady. Engraving; 754 file photo; 755 Hare (w/c on paper), Morgan, William De (1839-1917)/Private Collection, The Stapleton Collection/ Bridgeman Art Library; 756 Edward Pierce; 756 file photo; 758 Karl Lehmann/Lonely Planet; 760 Courtesy Alma Luz Villanueva; 761 David Ash/CORBIS; 763 Beach Scene by Atamian, Charles-Garabed (fl.1913-42)_Private Collection Gavin Graham Gallery, London, UK_Turkish, in copyright 764 Guy Motil/CORBIS; 765 Ron Sanford/CORBIS; 767 Eclipse Studios; 772 Mika/Zefa/CORBIS; 774 (l)Masterfile; 774 (r)Chuck Savage/CORBIS; 777 778 780 781 (br)Bettmann/CORBIS; 782 CALVIN AND HOBBES, 1995 Watterson. Dist. By UNIVERSAL PRESS SYNDICATE. Reprinted with permission. All rights 783 SuperStock; 784 Jack Ackerman; 786 Mark C. Burnett; 789 Collection of Georgia A. Hardrick Rhea; 791 Underwood & Underwood/CORBIS; 792 Springtime (Portrait of Ella Mae Moore), 1933. John Wesley Hardrick. Oil on board, 48 x 32 in. Private Collection.; 796 The Library of Congress from Photo Researchers; 799 Karen Kasmauski/CORBIS; 801 CORBIS; 802 Collection of Georgia A. Hardrick Rhea; 804 courtesy of Sue Alexander; 806 Jose Fuste Raga/CORBIS; 808 Frans Lemmens/Zefa/CORBIS; 810 Victoria and Albert Museum, London/Art Resource, NY; 811 Alamy Images; 812 Jose Fuste Raga/CORBIS; 818 Patrick McDonnell. Reprinted with permission of King Features Syndicate.; 819 Laura Dwight/PhotoEdit; 820 courtesy of McMillan; 824 PEMCO-Webster & Stevens Collection; Museum of History and Industry, Seattle/CORBIS; 825 Sakamoto Photo Research Laboratory/CORBIS; 826 Farm Security Administration-Office of War Information Photograph Collection/Library of Congress; 827 CORBIS; 828 Farm Security Administration - Office of War Information Photograph Collection/Library of Congress; 830 Mansfield Library Archives, University of Montana, Missoula; 832 Prokudin-Gorskii, Sergei Mikhailovich, 1863-1944/Library of Congress; 835 The Granger Collection, NY; 838 Prokudin-Gorskii, Sergei Mikhailovich, 1863-1944/Library of Congress; 840 1998 John McPherson/Dist. by Universal Press Syndicate; 841 Michael Newman/PhotoEdit; 842 Courtesy Robert Cormier, photo by Beth Bergman; 844 Bettmann/CORBIS; 845 From the collection of David J. and Janice L. Frent; 847 UPI/CORBIS; 848 Getty Images; 852 (tr)Minnesota Historical Society/CORBIS; 853 (cl)Creatas; 854 (tl)David Olds/Getty Images; 856 (tl)Bettmann/CORBIS; 860 Keith Locke; 861 863 864 Keith Locke; 870 Bill Amend/Dist. by Universal Press Syndicate; 871 CORBIS; 874 Alamy Images; 876 Mary Evans Picture Library/The Image Works; 877 Bettmann/CORBIS;

878 Lucien Aigner/CORBIS; 880 Alamy Images; 882 Courtesy of Donna Washington; 885 through 892 Text copyright by Donna L. Washington. Illustrations copyright by James Ransome 897 Northwind Picture Archives; 898 North Wind Picture Archives; 901 The Granger Collection, NY; 902 North Wind Picture Archives; 906 Farm Security Administration-Office of War Information Photograph Collection/Library of Congress; 907 Minnesota Historical Society/CORBIS; 908 Farm Security Administration-Office of War Information Photograph Collection/Library of Congress; 910 Northwind Picture Archives; 912-919 Usagi Yojimbo & Stan Sakai; 920, 921 Eclipse Studios; 926 Susan Findlay/Masterfile; 928 Rob Lewine/CORBIS; 928 Rolf Bruderer/CORBIS; 936 CORBIS; 937 Ben Welsh/AGE Fotostock; 938 CALVIN AND HOBBES 1990 Watterson. Dist. By UNIVERSAL PRESS SYNDICATE. Reprinted with permission. All rights reserved.; 939 Ron Chapple/Creatas; 950 CORBIS; 959 CORBIS; 968 1998 Mark Tatulli/Dist. By UNIVERSAL PRESS SYNDICATE; 970 Patrick McDonnell. Reprinted with permission of King Features Syndicate; 971 Pierre Arsenault/Masterfile; 988 Will Datene/Jupiter Images; 990 Cindy Coakley; 992 Getty Images; 993 The Image Bank/Getty Images; 994 Will Datene/Jupiter Images; 996 CALVIN AND HOBBES Watterson. Dist. By UNIVERSAL PRESS SYNDICATE. Reprinted with permission. All rights reserved.; 997 Creatas; 998 Courtesy of Eric Alter; 1000 (b)Duomo/CORBIS, (c)Marc Serota/Reuters/CORBIS, (t)Stringer/Jonathan Ernst/Reuters/CORBIS; 1014 Courtesy of Christina Hamlett; 1016 JupiterImages/www.comstock.com; 1018 Leonard de Selva/CORBIS; 1021 Blue Lantern Studio/CORBIS; 1024 SuperStock, Inc./SuperStock; 1026 Christies Images/CORBIS; 1027 Images.com/CORBIS; 1030 JupiterImages/www.comstock.com; 1036 BALDO Baldo Partnership. Dist. By UNIVERSAL PRESS SYNDICATE. Reprinted with permission. All rights reserved.; 1037 Rubberball/SuperStock; 1038 Susan Greenwood/The Liaison Agency; 1041 reprinted from Harper-Collins, illustration by Maurice Sendak; 1042 reprinted from Harper-Collins, illustration by Maurice Sendak; 1045 reprinted from Harper-Collins, illustration by Maurice Sendak; 1046 Getty Images; 1048 reprinted from Harper-Collins, illustration by Maurice Sendak; 1052 Stephen Ellison/Outline; 1054 Stephen Ellison/Outline; 1058 Lucie L. Snodgrass; 1059 (t)Sally A. Morgan; Ecoscene/CORBIS, (b)file photo; 1060 Carl & Ann Purcell/CORBIS; 1061 AFP/Getty Images; 1063 Lee Foster/Lonely Planet Images; 1065 Peter Greste/Reuters; 1066 Malie Rich-Griffith/infocusphotos.com; 1067 Getty Images; 1068 1070 AFP/Getty Images; 1074 Alamy Images.